Find Public Records Fast

The National Directory of Government Agencies That House Public Records

4th Edition

©2005 by Facts on Demand Press
206 West Julie Drive, Suite 2
Tempe, AZ 85283
(800) 929-3811
www.brbpub.com

Find Public Records Fast

The National Directory of Government Agencies That House Public Records
Fourth Edition

©2005 by Facts on Demand Press
206 West Julie Drive, Suite #2, Tempe, AZ 85283
(800) 929-3811

ISBN: 1-889150-46-0
Edited by Michael L. Sankey and Peter J. Weber.
Cover Design by Robin Fox & Associates

Cataloging-in-Publication Data:
Find public records fast : the national directory of
  governmental agencies that house public records /
[edited by Michael L. Sankey and Peter J. Weber]. -- 4th
ed.
  p. cm.
  ISBN 1-889150-46-0

  1. Courthouses--United States--States--Directories.
  2. Court records--United States--States--Directories.
  3. Public records--United States--States--Directories.
  I. Sankey, Michael L., 1949- II. Weber, Peter J. (Peter
Julius), 1952-

  KF8700.A19F56 2005   342.73'0662'025
                        QBI04-200507

Table of Contents

—Find Public Records Fast

Introduction

The access to and use of current public records is one of the fundamental pillars of our democratic society, yet the words "Public Records" often convey a complex, almost mysterious source of information that is perceived as difficult to access, hard to decipher, and likely to be of interest only to private investigators and reporters. This view could not be further from the truth.

Today there are literally thousands of public records and public information sources accessible by anyone with a computer and a modem, or a phone or fax, or with an envelope and a stamp. With this rapid growth it becomes necessary for users to understand what information is available and what information is not, to know where the information is, and how to access.

Your Access to Over 10,000 Government Agencies

The purpose of *Find Public Records Fast* is to assist the reader in knowing where categories of records can be found and how to search. The book contains many searching hints and is an excellent overall source of information that will especially help those not familiar with searching government records.

In less than 15 seconds you can find the paper or computer trails that begin or are maintained at the federal, state, county, and in certain instances, the city and town level. *Find Public Records Fast* is especially useful for these applications:

- Legal Research
- Background Investigation
- Pre-Employment and Tenant Screening

- Locating People
- Locating Assets
- Skiptracing
- Genealogy

Public records are meant to be used for the benefit of society. As a member of the public, you or someone in authority is entitled to review the public records held by government agencies. Whether you are a business owner, a reporter, an investigator, or a father trying to check on your daughter's first date, you can access public records to meet your needs. Equipped with the information contained in this book, you can find the facts to gain access to the information you need and even track your own "information trail!"

Some Suggestions on How to Use This Book

The first three chapters of *Find Public Records Fast* can be used as a "Public Record Primer." These chapters assist the reader in knowing where categories of records can be found and how to search. Here are many searching hints and is an excellent overall source of information that will especially help those not familiar with searching government records, whether online or not.

An important segment in Chapter 1 is the discussion of privacy issues including public information vs. personal information and how records enter the public domain.

The government agency chapters have been compiled into an easy to use format. The beginning of each government agency chapter has an overall discussion of the public records policies, with important characteristics and searching hints. In Chapters 5 and 6, each state sub-chapter begins with an overall summary of structure, policies, searching procedures and data on online access. This is important component of the book and we strongly recommend reviewing this content. Four chapters or sections are presented in this order:

- Chapter 4 - State Agencies
- Chapter 5 - County, City (and Parish or Borough) Recording Offices
- Chapter 6 - County (and Parish or Borough) Courts
- Chapter 7 - Federal Courts

On pages that list information, at the bottom you will find a "Key" that shows the meanings of the icons used in the text. These icons show how information may be accessed at that agency, or that court. For instance, 🖳 indicates that information is accessible by computer. ⊠ indicates that data is available by mail; ☎ by phone, etc.

Chapter 8 Searching Online for Other Federal Records contains an excellent article by Alan Schlein, author of *Find it Online!* (Facts on Demand Press). Mr. Schlein presents a unique dissertation about the best federal government Internet sites and gateways to find federal information quickly and efficiently.

If You Need More Details

For those of you who need to know more or need to have this information constantly updated, we can recommend several expanded versions of this product. For example, the following details have been fully researched and are presented for 26,000 over 25,000 government and private agencies:

- **Searching Facts:** methods of access; indexing; search requirements; if records are available online; when free public access terminals are at the counter; turnaround times, how far back (years) records are kept.
- **Privacy Facts:** restrictions the agencies impose on searchers or types of searchers; when signed releases or notarized statements are required.
- **Fees:** access fees, copy fees; certification fees; expedited fees, if credit cards accepted; what types of checks accepted; to whom to make the check payable.
- **Other Key Facts:** how to purchase databases or customized lists; if more than one agency must be visited in the county to get all records; if results can be returned by fax, etc.

The Public Records Research System (PRRS) is available as a subscription service on the Internet at www.publicrecordsources.com and is also available on CD-ROM. The print edition, *The Sourcebook to Public Record Information,* represents thousands of hours of research right up to the day of printing. For more information, visit www.brbpub.com.

Chapter 1

Essential Guidelines for Finding Public Records

Definition of Public Records

The strict definition of public records is—

> *"Those records maintained by government agencies that are open without restriction to public inspection, either by statute or by tradition."*

If access to a record that is held by a government agency is restricted in some way, then it is not a public record.

Accessibility Paradox

Adding to the mystique of government records is the accessibility paradox. For example, in some states a specific category of records is severely restricted, and therefore those records are not "public," while the very same category of records may be 100% open in other states. Among these categories are criminal histories, vehicle ownership records and workers' compensation records.

At times, you will see the following advice throughout *Find Public Records Fast*. We are not trying to fill up space. As your public record searching takes you from state-to-state, this is the one important adage to keep in mind.

> "Just because records are maintained in a certain way in your state or county, do not assume that any other county or state does things the same way you are used to."

Public vs. Private vs. Personal

Before reading further, let us define types of records held by government or by private industry. Of course, not all information about a company or individual is public. The boundaries between public and private information are not well understood, and continually undergo intense scrutiny. The following is an introduction to the subject from a viewpoint of a professional record searcher.

Public Record

Public records are records of incidents or actions filed or recorded with a government agency for the purpose of notifying others about the matter — the "public." The deed to your house recorded at the county recorder's office is a public record — it is a legal requirement that you record with the county recorder. Anyone requiring details about your property may review or copy the documents.

Public Information

Your telephone listing in the phone book is public information; that is, you freely furnished the information to ease the flow of commercial and private communications.

Personal Information

Any information about a person or business that the person or business might consider private and confidential in nature, such as your Social Security Number, is personal information. Such information will remain private to a limited extent unless it is disclosed to some outside entity that could make it public. Personal information may be found in either public records or in public information.

How Personal Information Enters the Public Domain

Many people confuse the three categories above, lump them into one and wonder how "big brother" accumulated so much information about them. Therefore, these distinctions are important. The reality is that much of this information is given willingly.

Actually, there are two ways that personal information can enter the public domain — statutory and voluntary. In a voluntary transaction, you share personal information of your own free will. In a statutory transaction, you disclose personal information because the law requires you to.

The confusion of terms used today feeds the increasing conflict between privacy advocates and commercial interests. This, in turn, is driving legislation towards more and more restrictions on the dissemination of personal information — the same personal information that, in fact, is willingly shared by most people and companies in order to participate in our market economy.

Where Public Records are Held

There are two places you can find public records—

1. at a government agency
2. within the database of a private company

Government agencies maintain records in a variety of ways. While many state agencies and highly populated county agencies are computerized, many others use microfiche, microfilm, and paper to store files and indexes. Agencies that have converted to computer will not necessarily place complete file records on their system; they are more apt to include only an index, pointer or summary data to the files.

Private enterprises develop their databases in one of two ways: they buy the records in bulk from government agencies; or they send personnel to the agencies and compile this information by using a copy machine or keying information into a laptop computer. The database is then available for internal use or for resale purposes. An example of such a company is Superior Information (800 848-0489). Superior maintains a very comprehensive database of civil judgments, tax liens, Uniform Commercial Code filings, and bankruptcy data gathered from the Mid-Atlantic States.

Common Methods Used to Access Public Records

The following is a look at the various methods available to access public records.

Visit in Person

This is easy if you live close by. Many courthouses and recorders offices have free access terminals open to the public. Certain records, such as corporate or UCC records generally found at the Secretary of State, can be viewed or pulled for free, but will incur a fee for copies. A signed release is a common requirement for accessing motor vehicle and criminal records.

Mail, Fax, or Telephone

Although some agencies permit phone or fax requests, the majority of agencies prefer mail requests. Some agencies consider fax requesting to be an expedited service that incurs higher fees. Agencies that permit telephone requests may merely answer "Yes" or "No" to questions such as "Does John Doe have a civil court case in his name?" We have indicated when telephone and fax requesting is available.

Online

The Internet may serve as a free means to certain agency records or may be the conduit to a subscription or commercial site. Also, private dial systems (non-Internet) still exist for some subscription services. Subscription online access of public records is much more prevalent at the state level compared to the county level. Keep in mind many agencies, such as DMVs, only provide access to pre-approved, high volume, ongoing accounts. Typically, this access involves fees and a specified amount of usage.

However, there is a definite trend of certain agencies posting public record data on the Internet for free. Two examples are Secretary of State offices (whose records include corporation, UCC and tax liens) and county/city tax assessor offices (whose records reveal property ownership). Usually this information is limited to name indexes and summary data, rather than document images. In addition, a growing number of state licensing boards are posting their membership lists on the net (although addresses and phone numbers of the licensed individuals typically are not listed).

Also, the Internet is a good place to find general information about government agencies. Many websites enable one to download, read and/or print current forms, policies and regulations.

The availability of online public records is not as widespread as one might think. According to our research:

- only 35% of public records can be found online;
- most of the sites merely give an index of records, and not the records themselves;
- nearly every free government public record website contains no personal identifiers beyond the name.

This topic is discussed in more detail at the end of Chapter 3.

Hire Someone Else

As mentioned previously, one method to access public records is from a vendor. These companies must comply with state and federal laws, thus if the government agency will not release a record, chances are a vendor company will not either. There are a variety of companies that can be hired to perform record searches. An excellent, quick source to find the right vendor for a particular need is www.publicrecordsources.com or *Public Records Online* by Facts on Demand Press.

Bulk or Database Purchases

Many agencies offer programs to purchase all or parts of their database for statistical or commercial purposes. The restrictions vary widely from state to state, even within the same record type or category. Typically, records are available (to those who qualify) in the following media types; CDs, FTP, magnetic tapes, cartridges, paper printouts, labels, disks, microfiche and/or microfilm.

Using the Freedom of Information Act

The Federal Freedom of Information Act has no bearing on state, county or local government agencies because these agencies are subject to that state's individual act. Further, the government agencies profiled in this book generally already have systems in place to release information and the act is not needed. However, if you are trying to obtain records from agencies beyond the scope of this book, there are many useful internet sites that will give you the information you need to complete such a request. We can recommend these sites:

> www.usdoj.gov/04foia/
> www.spj.org/foia.asp

Fees, Charges, and Usage

Public records are not necessarily free of charge, certainly not if they are maintained by private industry. Remember that public records are records of incidents or transactions. These incidents can be civil or criminal court actions, recordings, filings or occurrences such as speeding tickets or accidents. It costs money (time, salaries, supplies, etc.) to record and track these events. Common charges found at the government level include copy fees (to make copies of the document), search fees (for clerical personnel to search for the record), and certification fees (to certify a document as being accurate and coming from the particular agency). Fees can vary from $.10 per page for copies to a $52.00 search fee for government personnel to do the actual look-up. Most government agencies will allow you to walk into an office and view records at no charge, but few will release information over the phone for no fee.

If a private enterprise is in the business of maintaining a public records database, it generally does so to offer these records for resale. Typical clients include financial institutions, the legal industry, the insurance industry, and pre-employment screening firms among others. Usually, records are sold via online access or on a CD-ROM.

Also, there are a number of public record vendors (we call them search firms) companies that will do a name search — for a fee. These companies do not warehouse the records, but search on demand for a specific name.

Private companies usually offer different price levels based on volume of usage, while government agencies have one price per category, regardless of the amount of requests.

Importance of Identifiers

Every source will require certain identifiers to process a search request. For example, the agency (or vendor) may ask for the full name, Social Security Number, date of birth and last known address of the person to be checked. These "Identifiers" serve two different, though related purposes.

First, these identifiers ensure that the repository will be able to access its records to conduct a search. For example, the files may be indexed by name or Social Security Number. Thus, the office simply may not be able to process a record request if it does not have one or the other of these identifiers.

Second, the identifiers act as an important safeguard for both the requesting party and the subject of the search. There is always the chance that the "Harold Johnson" on whom a given repository has a record is not the same "Harold Johnson" on whom a check has been requested. However, the possibility of a misidentification can be decreased substantially if other identifiers can be matched on the individual.

As a general rule, information beyond the minimum should be provided whenever possible. Every available piece of information can aid their search. For example, maiden, alias or other previous names should always be included. Although no repository can be expected to give a 100% positive identification (without a fingerprint card), the more pointers matched, the smaller the chance of a mistake.

Two Rules to Always Keep in Mind

As you use this book to find government record sources, keep the following points in mind:

1. Very little government record information is truly open to the public. Even presumably harmless information is subject to restrictions somewhere in the U.S.A. Likewise, items that you believe should be highly confidential are probably considered "public information" in one or more states.

2. Just because your state or county has certain rules, regulations and practices regarding the accessibility and content of public records does not mean that any other state or county follows the same rules.

Chapter 2

Searching Hints for Record Types & Categories

The following are descriptions of the record types and categories found in this book. These types and categories can fall into our definitions of either "public records" or "restricted information" meaning that in one jurisdiction the records may be open, yet in another the same record type may be closed.

Business Records

Corporation Records (found at the state level)

Checking to see if a company is incorporated is considered a "**status check**." The information that results from a status check typically includes the date of incorporation, status, type, registered agent and, sometimes, officers or directors. This is a good way to find the start of a paper trail and/or to find affiliates of the subject of your search. Some states permit status checks over the telephone.

If available, articles of incorporation (or amendments to them) as well as copies of annual reports may also provide useful information about a business or business owner. However, corporate records may *not* be a good source for a business address because most states allow corporations to use a registered agent as their address for service of process.

Partnership Records (found at the state level)

Some state statutes require registration of certain kinds of partnerships at the state level. Sometimes, these partner names and addresses may be available from the same office that handles corporation records. Some states have a department created specifically to administer limited partnerships and the records associated with them. These filings provide a wealth of information about other partners. Such information can be used to uncover other businesses that may be registered as well.

Limited Liability Companies (found at state level)

A newer form of business entity, similar to a corporation but with the favorable tax characteristics of a partnership, is known as the Limited Liability Company (LLC). An LLC is legal in most every state. An offspring of this, which many states now permit, is the Limited Liability Partnership (LLP).

Trademark and Trade Name (found at state or county levels)

"Trade names" and "trademarks" are relative terms. A trademark may be known as a "service mark." Trade names may be referred to as "fictitious names," "assumed names," or "DBAs." States (or counties) will not let two entities register and use the same (or close to the same) name or trademark

Typically, the agency that oversees corporation records usually maintains the files for trademarks and/or trade names. Most states will allow verbal status checks of names or worded marks. Some states will administer "fictitious names" at the state level while county agencies administer "trade names," or vice versa.

Sales Tax Registrations (found at state level)

Any individual or firm that sells applicable goods or services to an end-user, is required to register with the appropriate state agency. Such registration is necessary to collect applicable sales tax on the goods and services, and to ensure remittance of those taxes to the state.

45 states collect some sort of sales tax on a variety of goods and services. Of these, 38 will at the very least confirm that a tax permit exists. Each sales tax registrant is given a special state tax permit number, which may be called by various names, including tax ID number or seller's permit number. These numbers are not to be confused with the federal employer identification number.

SEC and Other Financial Data

The Federal Securities and Exchange Commission (SEC) is the public repository for information about publicly held companies. These companies are required to share their material facts with existing and prospective stockholders. See Chapter 8 for information about the SEC database EDGAR.

Private companies, on the other hand, are not subject to public scrutiny. Their financial information is public information only to the extent that the company itself decides to disclose information.

Lien and Security Interest Records

Uniform Commercial Code
(found at state and sometimes at county or city levels)

All 50 states and the District of Columbia have passed a version of the model Uniform Commercial Code (UCC). UCC filings are used to record liens in financing transactions such as equipment loans, leases, inventory loans, and accounts receivable financing. The Code allows potential lenders to be notified that certain assets of a debtor are already used to secure a loan or lease. Therefore, examining UCC filings is an excellent way to find bank accounts, security interests, financiers, and assets.

Revised Article 9 (see Chapter 5) of the Code made significant changes to the location of filings and records. Prior to July 2001, of the 7.5 million new UCC financing statements filed annually, 2.5 million were filed at the state level; 5 million were filed at the local level. Now, less than 3% of filings are done so at the local level. Although there are significant variations among state statutes, the state level is now the best starting place to uncover liens filed against an individual or business.

Tax Liens (found at state and sometimes at county or city levels)

The federal government and every state have some sort of taxes, such as those associated with sales, income, withholding, unemployment, and/or personal property. When these taxes go unpaid, the appropriate state agency can file a lien on the real or personal property of the subject. **Normally, the state agency that maintains UCC records also maintains tax liens.**

Individuals vs. Businesses

Tax liens filed against individuals are frequently maintained at separate locations from those liens filed against businesses. For example, a large number of states require liens filed against businesses to be filed at a central state location (i.e., Secretary of State's office) and liens against individuals to be filed at the county level (i.e., Recorder, Register of Deeds, Clerk of Court, etc.).

State vs. Federal Liens

Liens on a company may not all be filed in the same location. A federal tax lien will not necessarily be filed (recorded) at the same location/jurisdiction as a lien filed by the state. This holds true for both individual liens and as well as business liens filed against personal property. Typically, state tax liens on personal property will be found where UCCs are filed. Tax liens on real property will be found where real property deeds are recorded, with few exceptions. Unsatisfied state and federal tax liens may be renewed if prescribed by individual state statutes. However, once satisfied, the time the record will remain in the repository before removal varies by jurisdiction.

Real Estate and Tax Assessor (found at county and local levels)

Traditionally, real estate records are public so that everyone can know who owns what property. Liens on real estate must be public so a buyer knows all the facts. The county (or parish) recorder's office is the record source. However, many private companies purchase entire county record databases and create their own database for commercial purposes.

This category of public record is perhaps the fastest growing in regards to being freely accessible over the Internet. We have indicated all the recorder offices that offer web name queries; many more offer location searches (using maps and parcel numbers to locate an address).

Bankruptcies (found at federal court level)

This entails case information about people and businesses that have filed for protection under the bankruptcy laws of the United States. Only federal courts handle bankruptcy cases. Many types of financial records maintained by government agencies are considered public records; bankruptcy records, unlike some other court records, are in this class of fully open court records. There are several private companies that compile databases with names and dates of these records.

Important Individual Records

Criminal Records (found at state level, county courts, and federal courts)

Every state has a central repository of major misdemeanor, felony arrest records and convictions. States submit criminal record activity to the National Crime Information Center (which is not open to the public). Not all states open their criminal records to the public. Of those states that will release records to the public, many require fingerprints or signed release forms. Information that could be disclosed on the report includes the arrest record, criminal charges, fines, sentencing and incarceration information.

In states where records are not released, the best places to search for criminal record activity is at the city or county level with the county or district court clerk. Many of these searches can be done with a phone call.

For further information regarding the use of criminal records, refer to *The Criminal Records Manual* by Derek Hinton, Facts On Demand Press.

The following excerpt, taken from Mr. Hinton's book, is an excellent overview of some "non-criminal criminal records."

From The Criminal Records Manual...
By Derek Hinton

There are several other types of public records that, while not strictly "criminal records," will disclose past criminal activity. While the information may not be particularly germane or useful for employment screening in all cases, the careful researcher may choose to search these various sources to complement their criminal record check.

Incarceration Records

Federal Incarceration Records

These are records of offenders who have been incarcerated in a federal facility after commission of a federal offense. The information is public record, and the value of this search is that you do not have to know the particular federal court that convicted the individual. The federal incarceration search is nationwide in scope.

The downside of this search is that it will not disclose minor offenses or, at least, those that did not result in incarceration.

The Federal Bureau of Prisons offers an inmate locator on its website, www.bop.gov. At this website, click "Inmate Info" at left. This Inmate Locator database also contains information about former inmates, dating back to 1982.

State Incarceration Records

Most states allow access to incarceration records. As with Federal incarceration records, state incarceration records may offer current and past information regarding an individual's incarceration history. In most states, inmates on probation are considered as current inmates. Twenty-seven states permit access to current inmate records via their website. Of these, 10-12 state websites also provide past inmate records.

Here are recommended websites that have multiple links to state inmate locators:

- www.corrections.com/links/viewlinks.asp?Cat=20

- www.crimetime.com/bbostate.htm — select state and search for "inmates"
- www.brbpub.com/pubrecsites.asp

Probation Records

Federal Probation Records

Some federal offenders are not sentenced to prison, but instead are fined and sentenced to probation. Probation means that all or part of the sentence has been reduced in return for a promise of proper conduct. These records are public, but must be obtained by contacting the Federal Chief Probation Officer in the judicial district where the individual was sentenced.

State Probation Records

Most states do not have a central state repository for the records of individuals currently serving probation. However, these records do not have the utility of other records. You will learn in the *State Profiles* in Chapter 16, [referring to Chapter 16 in the Criminal Records Manual] a number of the incarceration agency websites permit searches of inmates online and also have limited searching for former inmates on probation.

State Sexual Offender Records

In 1994, the Jacob Wetterling Crimes Against Children and Sexually Violent Offender Registration Act was enacted. The Jacob Wetterling Act required all states to establish stringent registration programs for sex offenders by September 1997, including the identification and lifetime registration of "sexual predators." The Jacob Wetterling Act is a National law that is designed to protect children and was named after Jacob Wetterling, an eleven year old boy who was kidnapped in October 1989. Jacob is still missing.

Megan's Law, the first amendment to the Jacob Wetterling Crimes Against Children and Sexually Violent Offenders Act, was passed in 1996. Megan's Law goals include:

Sex Offender Registration - Each state and the federal government are compelled to register individuals who have been convicted of sex crimes against children.

Community Notification - Each state and the federal government are compelled to make private and personal information on convicted sex offenders available to the public. Community notification is based on the presumption that it will:

- Assist law enforcement in investigations;
- Establish legal grounds to hold known offenders;
- Deter sex offenders from committing new offenses, and;
- Offer citizens information they can use to protect children from victimization.

The criteria for implementing Megan's Law are left up to the states, with the understanding that the state is to follow certain specific guidelines. Despite the guidelines, what has resulted is disparities among the states' rules, and access. For instance, many states make information on registered offenders available on the Internet or by mail, some only the severe offenders, and some states barely make the information available at all.

Approximately forty-two state agencies plus the District of Columbia post their sex offender registry via the Internet. In some cases a state agency may not post the information, although a local law enforcement agency may post for offenders within their jurisdiction only. In some cases, the state agency posts the registry and the local agencies post as well.

Here are three recommended websites that maintain multiple links to state sex offender databases:

- www.sexoffender.com
- www.parentsformeganslaw.com/html/links.lasso
- www.publicrecordsources.com

Litigation and Civil Judgments (found at county, local, and federal courts)

Actions under federal laws are found at U.S. District Courts. Actions under state laws are found within the state court system at the county level. Municipalities also have courts. Records of civil litigation case and records about judgments are often collected by commercial database vendors. For more information, please refer to the County Court Records chapter.

Motor Vehicle Records
(found at state level, but, on occasion, accessible at county level)

The retrieval industry often refers to driving records as "MVRs." Typical information on an MVR might include full name, address, Social Security Number, physical description and date of birth along with the conviction and accident history. Also, the license type, restrictions and/or endorsements can provide background data on an individual.

In recent years there have been major changes regarding the release of motor vehicle data to the public. This is a direct result of the Driver's Privacy Protection Act (DPPA). States must differentiate between **permissible users** (14 are designated in DPPA) and **casual requesters** to determine who may receive a record and/or how much personal information is reported on the record. For example, if a state DMV chooses to sell a record to a "casual requester," the record can contain personal information (address, etc.) **only with the consent** of the subject.

Pay particular attention to the restriction requirements mentioned in this category throughout this publication. For those interested in extensive, detailed information about either driver or vehicle records, refer to BRB Publications' *The MVR Book*.

Vehicle and Vessel Ownership, Registration, VINs, Titles, and Liens
(found at state and, on occasion, at county level)

State repositories of vehicle/vessel registration and ownership records hold a wide range of information. Generally, record requesters submit a name to uncover vehicle(s) owned or submit vehicle information to obtain an owner name and address. However, this category of record information is also subject to the DPPA as described above.

The original language of DPPA required the states to offer an "opt out" option to drivers and vehicle owners, if they (the states) sold marketing lists or individual records to casual requesters (those requesters not specifically mentioned in DPPA). Public Law 106-69 reversed this. Effective June 1, 2000, states automatically opted out all individuals, unless the individual specifically asked to be included. While nearly all states have this "opt in" procedure in place, very few individuals request to be placed on marketing lists and such.

Passage of Public Law 106-69 was dramatic since it essentially did away with sales of:

- marketing lists;
- records (with addresses and other personal information) to "casual" requesters;
- and record databases to information vendors and database compilers (except for vehicle recall purposes, etc.).

Accident Reports (found at state level or local level)

The State Police or Department of Public Safety usually maintains accident reports. For the purposes of this book, "accident records" are designated as those prepared by the investigating officer. Copies of a citizen's accident report are not usually available to the public. Typical information found on a state accident report includes drivers' addresses and license numbers as well as a description of the incident. Accidents investigated by local officials or minor accidents where the damage does not exceed a reporting limit (such as $1,000) are not available from state agencies. When state DMVs hold accident reports, they follow the DPPA guidelines with regards to record requests.

Occupational Licensing and Business Registration (found at state boards)

Occupational licenses and business registrations contain a plethora of information readily available from various state agencies. A common reason to call these agencies is to corroborate professional or industry credentials. Often, a telephone call to the agency may secure an address and phone number.

GED Records (found at state level)

By contacting the state offices that oversee GED Records, one can verify whether someone truly received a GED certificate for the high school education equivalency. These records are useful for pre-employment screening or background checking purposes. Most state agencies will verify over the phone the existence of a GED certificate. Many even offer copies of transcripts free-of-charge. When doing a record search, you must know the name of the student at the time of the test and a general idea of the year and test location. GED Records are not useful when trying to locate an individual.

Hunting and Fishing Licenses (found at state, county and local levels)

We have singled out one type of state license that merits a closer look. When trying to locate an individual, state hunting and fishing license information can be very informative. Currently 44 states maintain a central repository of fishing and/or hunting license records and 31 states permit access in some capacity by the public.

The trend is that many of these record repositories are becoming more computerized and are progressing from the days of storing in boxes in the basement. This movement began in 1992 when the U.S. Fish and Wildlife Service implemented a Migratory Bird Harvest Information Program that changed state hunting licensing procedures. Under this cooperative program, many states began to computerize their collection of licensees' names and addresses. The release of these records for investigative or search purposes may depend upon individual "state sunshine laws."

Workers' Compensation Records (found at state level)

Research at state workers' compensation boards is generally limited to determining if an employee has filed a claim and/or obtaining copies of the claim records themselves. With the passage of the Americans with Disabilities Act (ADA) in the early 1990s, using information from workers' compensation boards for pre-employment screening was virtually eliminated. However, **a review of workers' compensation histories may be conducted only after a conditional job offer has been made and when medical information is reviewed.** The legality of performing this review is subject to individual state statutes, which vary widely.

Voter Registration (found at state and county levels)

Voting Registration Records are a good place to find addresses and voting history, and can generally be viewed at the local level.

Every state has a central election agency or commission, and most have a central repository of voter information collected from the county level agencies. The degree or level of accessibility to these records varies widely from state to state. Over half of the states will sell portions of the registered voter database, but only 10 states permit individual searching by name. Most states only allow access for political purposes such as "Get Out the Vote" campaigns or compilation of campaign contribution lists. Nearly every state and local agency blocks the release of Social Security Numbers and telephone numbers found on these records.

Vital Records: Birth, Death, Marriage, and Divorce Records (found at state and county levels)

Copies of vital record certificates are needed for a variety of reasons — social security, jobs, passports, family history, litigation, lost heir searching, proof of identity, etc. Most states understand the urgency of these requests, and many offer an expedited service. A number of states will take requests over the phone if you use a credit card. Searchers must also be aware that in many instances certain vital records are not kept at the state level. The searcher must then turn to city and county record repositories to find the information needed.

Most states offer expedited fax and online ordering through the services of an outside vendor known as VitalChek. This state endorsed vendor maintains individual fax order telephone lines at each state office they service. They require the use of a credit card and with that an extra fee in the range of $5.50 to $10.05. Their website www.vitalchek.com is also a good place to order vital records online from many states; keep in mind that results are still mailed.

Older vital records are usually found in the state archives. There is an excellent website of extensive historical genealogy-related databases at http://ancestry.com/mainv.htm. Another source of historical vital record information is the Family History Library of the Church of Jesus Christ of Latter Day Saints (located at 35 North West Temple, Salt Lake City 84150). They have millions of microfilmed records from church and civil registers from all over the world.

Credit Information and Social Security Numbers

Social Security Numbers

The Social Security Number (SSN) is the subject of a persistent struggle between privacy rights groups and various business interests. The truth is that many individuals gave up the privacy of their number by writing it on a voter registration form, product registration form, or any of a myriad of other voluntary disclosures made over the years. It is probable that a good researcher can still legally find the SSN of anyone (along with at least an approximate birth date) with some effort. In the past, a major source of finding a SSN was in the "header" of a credit report. But not any more, see below.

Credit Information

Credit data is derived from financial transactions of people or businesses. **Private companies maintain this information; government only regulates access.** Certain credit information about individuals is restricted by law, such as the Fair Credit Reporting Act, at the federal level and by even more restrictive laws in many states. Credit information about businesses is not restricted by law and is fully open to anyone who requests (pays for) it.

A credit report essentially has two parts — the credit header and the credit history. A credit header is essentially the upper portion of a credit report containing the Social Security Number, age, phone number, last several addresses, and any AKAs. Recently, access to credit header information (see below) has been closed to most business entities.

Credit Header Ban Went Into Effect July 1st, 2001

July 1st, 2001 was an important date for skiptracers, fraud investigators, and other businesses that rely on "credit headers." This data has always been available without the consent of the individual subject. Per a federal court ruling, beginning July 1st 2001, access to credit header information was treated in the same manner as access to credit reports—there has to be permission granted by the individual.

The basis of this ban is traced to the Gramm-Leach-Bliley Act (GLB). Section 502 of this act prohibits a financial institution from disclosing nonpublic personal information about a consumer to non-affiliated third parties unless a consumer has elected not to opt out from disclosure. Trans Union and other members of the Individual References Services Group (IRSG), among others, filed suit in an effort to keep this information open for "appropriate commercial purposes." The ruling, dated April 30th, denied this argument. The sale of credit headers seemed to be on borrowed time anyway—originally, the ban was to begin November 2000. However, due to the lawsuits and action involving the FTC, a provision changed the start of the ban until July 1st, 2001.

Impact of Changes

The impact of the ruling (and an FTC opinion) was far ranging. The ruling restricted credit bureaus from selling the above-mentioned data to information vendors who compile their own proprietary databases. But there are some alternatives to those business entities that rely on this type of public record information. The data is grandfathered. Provider companies that purchased files from the credit bureaus can continue to sell the data to their customers. Although data will never be updated from the credit bureaus, the existing data can still be used without the restrictions imposed by the ruling.

The Gramm-Leach-Bliley Act did not deny access to public record sources or databases that may contain age, SSN, phone, prior addresses, and AKAs. The Act only forbade financial institutions from disclosing this data. Therefore, those businesses shut-off from credit headers had to investigate alternative sources of public records.

Additional Record Sources Worthy of Mention

Education and Employment

Information about an employee's or prospective employee's schooling, training, education, and jobs is important to any employer. Learning institutions maintain their own records of attendance, completion and degree/certification granted. Also, employers will confirm certain information about former employees. This is an example of private information that becomes public by voluntary disclosure. As part of your credit record, this information would be considered restricted. If, however, you disclose this information to Who's Who, or to a credit card company, it becomes public information.

Environment

Information about hazards to the environment is critical. There is little tradition and less law regarding how open or restricted information is at the state and local (recorder's office) levels. Most information on hazardous materials, soil composition, even OSHA inspection reports is public record. OSHA stands for Occupational Safety and Health Administration, which is part of the U.S. Department of Labor. Their website is www.osha.gov.

But many federal websites have removed information since 9-11-2001. Two examples are the U.S. Environmental Protection Agency found at www.epa.gov/records and the U.S. Geological Survey at www.usgs.gov.

Medical

Medical record Information about an individual's medical status and history are summarized in various repositories that are accessible only to authorized insurance and other private company employees. Medical information is neither public information nor a closed record. Like credit information, it is not meant to be shared with anyone unless you give authorization.

Military

Each branch maintains its own records. Much of this, such as years of service and rank, is open public record. However, some details in the file of an individual may be subject to restrictions on access — approval by the subject may be required.

Refer to Chapter 8 for more information about sources of military records.

Chapter 3

Exposing Three Myths About Public Records

1. Anyone Can Do a Background Check for an Employer

Not true.

There are federal and state laws that clearly dictate how public records can be used by employers, especially when the records are searched by others.

Perhaps the best way to fully explain this issue is to quote from Lester S. Rosen's *The Safe Hiring Manual* by Facts on Demand Press.

Why is a Basic Understanding of the FCRA So Important to Employers?

By Lester S. Rosen

When an employer uses a third party outside agency to help conduct a background check, there is a critical Federal law that the employer must be familiar with. The law is called the **Fair Credit Reporting Act (FCRA).** Even though the name of the law uses the term "Credit," the FCRA goes far beyond credit reports. The FCRA establishes specific requirements and rules for a pre-employment background report, called **Consumer Report,** which is much broader in scope than just a credit report.

A Consumer Report can include a wide variety of obtained information concerning job applicants, such as criminal and civil records, driving records, civil lawsuits, reference checks and any other information obtained by a **Consumer Reporting Agency**. Therefore, the FCRA fundamentally controls the information on applicants that is assembled, evaluated and disseminated by certain third parties and used for employment purposes.

When first passed in 1970, the FCRA was primarily meant to promote confidentiality (privacy), accuracy, and relevancy regarding information gathered about consumers. The law was extensively amended in 1996 with changes effective on September 30, 1997. That amendment substantially overhauled the use of consumer reports for employment purposes by providing greater protection to consumers. Other important amendments were made in 1998 and additional amendments were passed in 2003.

Definitions

Here are definitions of the most important terms found in the FCRA.

What is a Consumer Report?

A consumer report is a report prepared by a consumer reporting agency that consists of any written or oral or other communication of any information by a consumer reporting agency bearing on the applicant's or employee's credit worthiness, credit standing, credit capacity, character, general reputation, personal characteristics or mode of living, if this information is used or expected to be used or collected for employment purposes.

What is an Investigative Consumer Report?

An Investigate Consumer Report is a special type of consumer report when the information is gathered through personal interviews (by phone calls or in person) of neighbors, friends, or associates of the employee or applicant reported on, or from other personal acquaintances or persons who may have knowledge about information bearing on the applicant's or employee's credit worthiness, credit standing, credit capacity, character, general reputation, personal characteristics or mode of living, if this information is used or expected to be used or collected for employment purposes. The Investigative Consumer Report includes reference checks with former employers about job performance. However, a report would NOT be an Investigative Consumer Report if it was simply a verification of former employment limited to only factual matters such as the date started, date ended, salary or job title. Once a reference checker asks about eligibility for rehire and job performance, the report then becomes an Investigative Consumer Report.

What is a Consumer Reporting Agency (CRA)?

A Consumer Reporting Agency, or CRA, is any person or entity which, for monetary fees, dues or on a cooperative nonprofit basis, regularly engages in whole or in part in the practice of assembling or evaluating consumer credit information or other information on consumers for the purposes of furnishing reports to third parties. It includes private investigators that "regularly" engage in pre-employment inquires.

What is Meant by Employment Purposes?

A report is prepared for employment purposes when the report is used for the purpose of evaluating an applicant or employee for employment, reassignment or retention as an employee.

What is Meant by Adverse Action?

Adverse action in relationship to employment means a denial of employment or any other decision for employment purposes that adversely affects any current or prospective employee.

The Four Groups Affected

The FCRA addresses the rights and obligations of four groups. The descriptions below are focused on the groups as they relate to employment.

Consumer Reporting Agencies (CRA's). Again, these are third parties such as background screening firms or private investigators that provide Consumer Reports. [1]

Users of consumer information. These are primarily employers who hire CRA's to prepare Consumer Reports.

Furnishers of consumer information. Furnishers can range from credit card companies that report payment histories to the three national credit collecting agencies, to past employers or schools who answer phone calls from Consumer Reporting Agencies that are preparing background reports.

Consumers. The FCRA provides consumers (applicants) with a host of rights in the process.

Here is the bad news and the good news about the FCRA. The bad news is that the FCRA is a very complex and convoluted law that makes little sense if an employer sits down and tries to read it. The good news is there are only four basic steps an employer needs to know about the FCRA in order to begin a background-screening program through an employment screening firm. These steps are…

1. Employer Certification to the CRA
2. Authorization by the consumer and a disclosure to the consumer about the process
3. Pre and post adverse action notices
4. The effect of state laws

Here is an important fact to keep in mind—the FCRA kicks in when a pre-employment background pre-screening is conducted by the Consumer Reporting Agency. The basic purpose of the law is to regulate what third parties do. Therefore, if an employer works with professional pre-employment background firm (which is a CRA), the employer should select the firm based in part upon the background firm's knowledge of the FCRA. A competent background firm should know how to fully comply with legal requirements of the FCRA, including the preparation of the all documents and forms needed for a fully compliant screening program.

Anyone wanting to read the law can go to the website for the Federal Trade Commission (FTC), the federal agency charged with administering the law.

The text of the FCRA is available online at www.ftc.gov/os/statutes/031219fcra.pdf

The FTC's home page for the FCRA is at www.ftc.gov/os/statutes/fcrajump.htm

---

[1] Some Private Investigators have incorrectly assumed that the FCRA does not apply to them because they have a state license. Nothing can be further from the truth. Any Private Investigator who "regularly" does pre-employment screening is also a CRA, and absolutely subject to the rules and regulations of the FCRA. There is no exact definition of the term "regularly" but any investigator who does more then one background screen for employment purposes must assume that the FCRA applies.

The text below is also reprinted from *The Safe Hiring Manual*.

An Important Area NOT Covered by the FCRA

By Lester S. Rosen

What if a business needs to investigate another business before entering into an economic relationship, such as investing, joint venturing, licensing agreements, merger or acquisition, or to just check out trade credit? A business may even want to check out a competitor. The research may involve criminal or civil records, judgments, liens or bankruptcies or even a business credit report such as a Dun and Bradstreet report (www.dnb.com/us/). None of these investigations are covered by the FCRA, even if done by third party. This is because the investigation is not focused on an individual and the **FCRA only protects individuals.**

What if a business wanted information about the people behind the other business? Any business relationship ultimately depends upon the integrity of the people involved. All the agreements and lawyers in the world cannot protect you or your business if the people you are dealing with lack integrity. Even in that scenario, a firm or a third party working on their behalf may check public records and even call schools and employers as long as the purpose is NOT employment. Here are three important considerations below.

Even if the investigation is for business due diligence, under no circumstances can the business or their agent pull a personal credit report on any individual involved without consent. A personal credit report is ALWAYS covered by the FCRA, and can only be pulled for FCRA approved purposes. If the economic transaction really amounts to starting an employment relationship, such as the acquisition of a small corporation where the principal is going to go to work for the acquiring company, this could trigger the need for full FCRA compliance. There may be other laws that apply as well. In some states, the investigation can only be conducted by a licensed private investigator.

2. I Can Do a National Criminal Record Search

Not so. There is no comprehensive national computer database of criminal records available to the general public or private employers who have not been given statutory authority. Period. End of story.

Contrary to popular belief, obtaining a criminal record is not as easy as going on a computer and getting thumbs up or thumbs down. There are over 10,000 state and Federal courthouses in the United States, spread out over some 3,300 jurisdictions, each with its own database of records.

Yes, the FBI and state law enforcement have access to a national computer database called the National Crime Information Center (NCIC). However, it is absolutely illegal for most private companies to obtain criminal information from law enforcement computer databases without specific legal authorization. Government criminal checks are only available for positions such as schoolteachers or childcare workers or other positions where state or federal law specifically mandates such a check.

The text below is taken from Derek Hinton's *The Criminal Record Manual* by Facts on Demand Press. This publication is the leading authoritative book about criminal records in the U.S.

The FBI NCIC Database

By Derek Hinton

The FBI database's formal name is the ***National Crime Information Center (NCIC)*** and is an automated database of criminal justice and justice-related records maintained by the FBI. The database includes the "hot files" of wanted and missing persons, stolen vehicles and identifiable stolen property, including firearms. Two important points about the NCIC are:

1. The NCIC is not nearly as complete as portrayed in the movies. Because of the chain of events that must happen in multiple jurisdictions in order for a crime to appear in NCIC, many records of crime do not make it.

2. The information the NCIC does have is predominantly solely arrest-related. The disposition of most crimes in NCIC must be obtained by going to the adjudicating jurisdiction. This can be an important issue to employers.

Occasionally an employer happens upon a "good deal." This good deal usually consists of a friend in law enforcement that obtains criminal records from NCIC and provides them free or sells them to the employer. The problem is that this is illegal, and the Feds have been targeting and prosecuting violators.

One might ask "If there is no national government database of criminal records available to the public, surely there must be a private vendor who has assembled a national database?" Again, the answer is no. However, there are vendors who offer a "national search." Sounds like the same thing, doesn't it? Well, there is a big difference.

We again call upon Mr. Rosen and his book *The Safe Hiring Manual* to give guidance on this issue.

Take Caution When Using Private Databases

By Lester S. Rosen

Perhaps the newest tool being touted to employers is a "national database search" of criminal records. There are a number of vendors who advertise they have or have access to a "national database of criminal record information." These services typically talk about having over a 120 million records from 38 or more states. Unfortunately, the form of advertising can create an impression in the minds of employers that they are getting the real thing — a true record of the nation's criminal records. Nothing could be further from the truth.

These databases are compiled from a number of various state and county sources. There are a number of reasons that database information may not be accurate or complete. It is critical to understand that these multi-state database searches represent a **research tool only, and under no circumstances are they a substitute for a hands-on search at the county level**.

The bottom line is that just because a person's name appears in one of these databases, it does not mean the subject is a criminal. On the other hand, if a person's name does not appear, this likewise should not be taken as conclusive the person is not a criminal. An employer should not develop a false sense of security because an applicant passed a database search without understanding that there are numerous circumstances as described below that even a person with a serious criminal record may not show up.

Our discussion of these databases will focus on two areas — VALUE and LIMITATIONS.

Value

The value of using these database searches is they cover a much larger geographical area then traditional county-level searches. By casting a much wider net than a single county level search, a researcher may pick up information that would be missed. The firms that sell database information can show test names of subjects that were "cleared" by a traditional county search, but where criminal records were found using a search of their database.

In fact, it could be argued that failure to utilize such a database demonstrates a failure to exercise due diligence given the widespread availability and low price.

So overall, the best use of these databases is as a secondary research tool, or "lead generator" that tells a researcher where else to look.

Limitations

The data that is complied comes from three sources: court records, correctional records, and from a small number of counties that contribute data. The limitations of searching a private database are the inherent issues about completeness, name variations, timeliness, and legal compliance.

Completeness Issues

The various databases that vendors purchase or collect may not be the equivalent of a true all-encompassing multi-state database. First, the databases purchased for resale or accessed at a gateway may not contain complete records from all jurisdictions. For example, not all unified court systems contain records from all counties. Second, for reporting purposes, the records that are actually reported may be incomplete or lack sufficient detail about the offense or the subject. Third, some databases contain only felonies or contain only offenses where a state corrections unit was involved. Fourth, the database may not carry subsequent information or some other matter that could render the database not reportable under the FCRA, or result in some violation of state law concerning the use of criminal records.

The result is a crazy quilt patchwork of data from various sources, with widely different reliability.

Name Variation Issues

An electronic search of a vendor's database may not be able to recognize variations in a subject name, which a person may potentially notice if manually looking at the index. The applicant may have been arrested under a different first name or some variation of first and middle name. A female applicant may have a record under a previous name. Some database vendors have attempted to resolve this problem with a wild card first name search (i.e. instead of Robert, the search use Rob* so that any variations of ROB will come up). However, there are still too many different first and middle name variations. There is also the chance of name confusion for applicants who have a different naming convention where a combination of mother and father's name is used. In addition, some vendors require the use of date of birth in order to prevent too many records from being returned. If an applicant used a different date of birth with the police or courts, this can also cause errors.

Timeliness Issues

There is also the possibility the records in a vendor's database are stale to some extent. With very slim exceptions, these records are normally updated monthly, at best. Even after a vendor receives new data, there can be lag time before the new data is downloaded into the vendor database. As a result, generally the most current offenses are the ones less likely to come up in a database search.

Legal Compliance Issues

When there is a hit, an employer must be concerned about legal compliance. If the employer performs a search in-house, then that employer must have an understanding of the proper use of criminal records in that state. If the employer acts on the results at face value without any additional research, then the employer could potentially be sued by an applicant, if the record was not about that applicant.

If a screening firm locates a criminal hit, then the screening firm has an obligation under the FCRA Section 613 (a)(2) to send researchers to the court and to pull the actual court records or alternatively send a notice to the consumer.

This section requires that whenever a background-screening firm reports a matter of public record, then the background firm must—

maintain strict procedures designed to insure that whenever public record information, which is likely to have an adverse effect on a consumer's ability to obtain employment, is reported, it is complete and up to date. For purposes of this paragraph, items of public record relating to arrests, indictments, convictions, suits, tax liens, and outstanding judgments shall be considered up to date if the current public record status of the item at the time of the report is reported.

For a detailed discussion about the legal uses of a database, see an article co-authored by the author of this book and Carl Ernst (a national expert on the FCRA) called, *"National" Criminal History Databases,* at www.brbpub.com/CriminalHistoryDB.pdf.

Conclusion about Private Databases

Criminal record vendors should make clear, and employers need to understand, the exact nature and limitations of the data they are accessing. These private database searches are ancillary and can be very useful, but proceed with caution. In other words, it cannot be assumed that a search of a proprietary criminal database by itself will show that a person either is or is not a criminal, but these databases are outstanding secondary tools to do a much wider search.

3. I Can Find All the Public Records I Need Online

The Internet does not contain all the answers. In fact the availability of online public records is not nearly as widespread as one might think. According to research by BRB Publications:

- only 35% of public records can be found online;
- most of the sites merely give an index of records, and not the records themselves;
- nearly every free government public record website contains no personal identifiers beyond the name.

It is true that many local county or city recording offices or assessor offices can be very informative. These online sites show real estate ownership, document numbers or location and are extremely helpful. Also quite useful are the business records kept by the state agencies such as corporation records or Uniform Commercial Code filings.

If you are doing a "name search" using Internet public record sites, then you may very well have trouble confirming that records found truly belong to the name you are searching. The more common the name, the more important it is to confirm the identity of the subject. Free government sites no longer give Social Security Numbers, although some may cloak or mask the first five digits. Free government sites will cloak the month and day of the DOB and only release the year of birth, if at all. This is a real problem for record searchers who require a certain amount of due diligence. Adverse information may have to be checked by performing a hands-on search.

In reality, most government online sites can be used for a "lead" of where possible records may be located.

Also, many government websites offering online record access include a warning or disclosure statement that the data can have errors and/or should be used for informational purposes only. For example, a criminal record check from such as source may not in and by itself comply with the Fair Credit Reporting Act regulations involving pre-employment screening.

Commercial or Pay-For Sites are Usually Best

There are a number of government agencies that offer online access to records on a fee or subscription basis. Access to these sites generally requires prior approval by the agency. These sites generally do disclose at least partial personal identifiers, if not full access to personal identifiers. In most cases, users must demonstrate a clear legitimate business need for the information and most adhere to state or federal laws.

An import point is there are over 200 private companies offer online access to their proprietary databases (or gateways) of public record information. Keep in mind they hold many records that may not be otherwise found online via the government online sources.

An excellent source of these commercial sites (government and private sector) is found in the book *Public Record Online* by Facts on Demand Press.

Chapter 4

State Agencies

This chapter lists state agencies for over 30 categories of record types. We suggest to review Chapter 2 for an overview about each of these record types.

Important State Offices

Each state begins with four important state offices that may be helpful to your record searching needs. An added bonus is the web page for searching the state's database of unclaimed property and funds.

Governor's Office

The office of the Governor is a good place to start if you are looking for an obscure agency, phone number or address. We have found that typically the person who answers the phone will point you in the right direction if he or she cannot answer your question. This book provides address, phone, fax, and website for the Governor's office.

Attorney General's Office

This is another excellent starting point. For example, if you are looking for a non-profit organization, the Attorney General's Office may be able to help. This book provides address, phone, fax, and website.

State Archives

The state archives contain an abundance of historical documents and records, especially useful to those interested in genealogy. In this book, the archives phone number and website is provided.

State Legislation

Most state legislative bodies offer free Internet access to bill text and status, some even offer subject queries. Notwithstanding federal guidelines, the state legislatures and legislators control the policies and provisions for the release of state held information. Every year there is a multitude of bills introduced in state legislatures that would, if passed, create major changes in the access and retrieval of records and personal information. In this book, the phone number and website is provided.

About The State Agency Listings

After the preceding four state offices mentioned, the various state agency profiles are presented, starting with the state criminal records agency. Each of these state agency listings indicates contact information and record access methods, and regular business hours. If the mailing address is a post office box, then a full or abbreviated version of the physical address may be given in parenthesis.

About the State Court Administrator and Other Statewide Court Records, Criminal Records, Incarceration Records, and Sexual Predator Lists

The court administrator oversees the state court system, which is also known as the county court system. The state judicial website is a good place to find opinions from the state supreme court and for appeals court opinions. In some states, the state court administration office oversees a statewide online access system to court records. Some of these systems are commercial fee-based. Other systems offer free access, but are usually very limited in comparison. There is an entry for each statewide system.

Agencies that manage records related to crime are listed in this book. This includes agencies that manage incarceration records, a statewide criminal database, and locations of registered sex offenders. Please note that how these record types are managed and accessed can vary widely from state to state.

Listed below are some **critical components to the record access procedures** at these state agencies. Remember: *Just because records are maintained in a certain way in your state, do not assume that any other state does things the same way.*

Indexing and Storage

Record searchers are advised to examine the following—

- How many years of records are accessible
- How long before new records are available
- How records are indexed and in what format are they maintained.

Searching Requirements and Privacy

There are a myriad of possible searching requirements and privacy restrictions that could be in place. You should ask what the agencies requirements are for doing a search, such as if a signed release is needed from the subject or if a certain state form must be used.

Fee and Payments

Be aware that many fees exist including search fees, copy fees, certification fees, and expedite fees. Also ask if credit cards are accepted, if personal checks (many agencies only accept business checks) are accepted, and whom to make the check payable.

Some Records May Not Be Available

As discussed in Chapter 1, there are times when record data is truly unavailable to the public. Perhaps the state agency does not release any information period except to government personnel, or records are maintained by a state level agency and are held at the local level.

Alabama

Governor's Office   334-242-7100
   600 Dexter Ave, #N-104,   Fax 334-353-0004
   www.governor.state.al.us   8AM-5PM

Attorney General's Office
   State House, 11 S Union St, 3rd Fl   334-242-7300
   Montgomery, AL 36130   Fax 334-242-4891
   www.ago.state.al.us   8AM-5PM

State Website: www.alabama.gov

Legislative Records   www.legislature.state.al.us
   334-242-7826 (Senate)   334-242-7637 (House)
State Archives
   334-242-4435   www.archives.state.al.us
Capital: Montgomery, in Montgomery County

Search Unclaimed Property Online

www.treasury.state.al.us/website/ucpd/ucpd_searchfra
me.html or www.treasury.state.al.us/new_search.asp

Criminal Records

Alabama Bureau of Investigation, Identification Unit - Record Checks, PO Box 1511, Montgomery, AL 36102-1511 (301 S Ripley St, Montgomery, AL 36104); 334-353-4340, 8AM-5PM. www.dps.state.al.us/public/abi/ ✉ ✋

Statewide Court Records

Director of Courts, 300 Dexter Ave, Montgomery, AL 36104-3741; 334-242-0300, Fax: 334-242-2099, 8AM-5PM. www.alacourt.gov/ 💻

Sexual Offender Registry

Department of Public Safety, Sexual Offender Registry, PO Box 1511, Montgomery, AL 36102-1511 (301 S Ripley); 334-353-1172, Fax: 334-353-2563, 8AM-5PM. www.dps.state.al.us ✉ ☎ Fax ✋ 💻

Incarceration Records

Alabama Department of Corrections, Central Records Office, PO Box 301501, Montgomery, AL 36130 (relocating in August, 2004.,); 334-240-9500, 8AM-5PM. http://doc.state.al.us ✉ 💻

Uniform Commercial Code, Federal and State Tax Liens

UCC Division - SOS, UCC Records, PO Box 5616, Montgomery, AL 36103-5616 (11 South Union St, Suite 200, Montgomery, AL 36104); 334-242-5231, Fax: 334-353-8269, 8AM-5PM. www.sos.state.al.us ✉ ✋ 💻

Corporation Records, Limited Partnership Records, Limited Liability Company Records, Limited Liability Partnerships, Trade Names, Trademarks/Servicemarks

Secretary of State, Corporations Division, PO Box 5616, Montgomery, AL 36103-(11 S Union St, Ste 207,); 334-242-5324, 334-242-5325 (Trademarks), Fax: 334-240-3138, 8-5PM. www.sos.state.al.us ✉ ☎ Fax ✋ 💻

Sales Tax Registrations

Access to Records is Restricted
Alabama Department of Revenue, Sales, Use and Business Tax Division, 4303 Gordon Persons Bldg, 50 N Ripley St, Montgomery, AL 36104; 334-353-7867, Fax: 334-242-8916, 8AM-5PM. www.ador.state.al.us According to state law 40-2A-10, Code of Alabama 1975, this agency is unable to release any information about tax registrations.

Birth Certificates, Death Records, Marriage Records

Center for Health Statistics, Record Services Division, PO Box 5625, Montgomery, AL 36103-5625 (RSA Tower Suite 1150, 201 Monroe St, Montgomery, AL 36104); 334-206-5418, Fax: 334-262-9563, 8AM-5PM. http://ph.state.al.us/chs/VitalRecords/VRE CORDS.HTMl ✉ ☎ Fax ✋ 💻

Divorce Records

Center for Health Statistics, Record Services Division, PO Box 5625,

Montgomery, AL 36103-5625 (RSA Tower Suite 1150, 201 Monroe St, Montgomery, AL 36104); 334-206-5418, Fax: 334-206-2659, 8AM-5PM. http://ph.state.al.us/chs/VitalRecords/VRE CORDS.HTMl ✉ ☎ Fax ✋ 💻

Workers' Compensation Records

Dept. of Industrial Relations, Disclosure Unit-Central Cashier, 649 Monroe Street, Rm. 2684, Montgomery, AL 36131; 334-242-8981, Fax: 334-242-2304, 7-5PM. http://dir.alabama.gov/wc/ ✉ Fax ✋

Driver Records

Department of Public Safety, Driver Records-License Division, PO Box 1471, Montgomery, AL 36102-1471 (301 S Ripley Street, Montgomery, AL 36104); 334-242-4400, Fax: 334-242-4639, 8AM-5PM. www.dps.state.al.us/ ✉ ✋ 💻

Vehicle Ownership, Vehicle Identification

Motor Vehicle Division, Records & Registration Unit, PO Box 327630, Montgomery, AL 36132-7630 (50 North Ripley St, #1229, 1202 Gordon Persons Bldg, Montgomery, AL 36140); 334-242-9056 (Registration), 334-242-9102 (Title Inquiry), Fax: 334-353-8038, 8AM-5PM. www.ador.state.al.us/motorvehicle/index.html ✉

Accident Reports

Alabama Department of Public Safety, Accident Records, PO Box 1471, Montgomery, AL 36102-1471 (502 Washington Ave, Montgomery, AL 36104); 334-242-4241, 8AM-5PM. ✉ ✋

Vessel Ownership, Vessel Registration

Dept of Conservation & Natural Resources, Marine Police Div. Boat Reg. Records, PO Box 301451, Montgomery, AL 36130 (64 N Union St, Montgomery); 334-242-3673, Fax: 334-242-0336, 8AM-5PM. www.dcnr.state.al.us ✉ ☎ **Fax** ✍

Voter Registration

Access to Records is Restricted
Secretary of State-Elections Division, PO Box 5616, State Capitol E-210, Montgomery, AL 36103; 334-242-4337, Fax: 334-242-2940, 8AM-5PM. www.sos.state.al.us/election/index.cfm Individual name requests must be done at the county level, there are no restrictions.

GED Certificates

State Dept of Education, GED Testing Office, 401 Adams Ave #280, Montgomery, AL 36104; 334-353-4886, Fax: 334-353-4884, 8AM-5PM. www.acs.cc.al.us/ged/ged.aspx ✉ **Fax** ✍

Hunting License and Fishing License Information

Access to Records is Restricted
Conservation & Natural Resources Department, Department of License Section, 64 N Union Street, Room 457, Montgomery, AL 36130-1456; 334-353-5239, Fax: 334-242-0771, 8AM-5PM. No central computerized database. Records must be hand searched and are grouped by issuing agent. The agency will sell a list of lifetime license purchasers.

Alaska

Governor's Office
PO Box 110001
Juneau, AK 99811-0001
www.gov.state.ak.us

907-465-3500
Fax 907-465-3532
8AM-5PM

Attorney General's Office
Law Department
PO Box 110300
Juneau, AK 99811-0300
www.law.state.ak.us

907-465-3600
Fax 907-465-2075
8AM-4:30PM

State Website: www.state.ak.us

Legislative Records
907-465-4648 www.legis.state.ak.us

State Archives
907-465-2270 www.archives.state.ak.us

Capital: Juneau, in Juneau Borough

Search Unclaimed Property Online
www.revenue.state.ak.us/treasury/UCP/ucpsrch.asp

Criminal Records

Department of Public Safety, Records and Identification, 5700 E Tudor Rd, Anchorage, AK 99507; 907-269-5765, Fax: 907-269-5091, 8AM-4:30PM. www.dps.state.ak.us ✉ ✍

Statewide Court Records

Office of the Administrative Director, Alaska Court System, 820 W 4th Ave, Anchorage, AK 99501; 907-264-8269, Fax: 907-264-8291, 8AM-4:30PM. www.state.ak.us/courts/ 💻

Sexual Offender Registry

Department of Public Safety, Permits and Licensing-SOCR Unit, 5700 E Tudor Rd, Anchorage, AK 99507; 907-269-0396, Fax: 907-269-5091, 8AM-4:30PM. www.dps.state.ak.us/nSorcr/asp/ ✉ ✍ 💻

Incarceration Records

Alaska Department of Corrections, DOC Classification Office, 4500 Diplomacy Drive, Suite 340, Anchorage, AK 99508-

5918; 907-269-7426, Fax: 907-269-7439, 8-4:30PM.www.correct.state.ak.us ✉

Corporation Records, Trademarks/Servicemarks, Fictitious Name, Assumed Name, Limited Partnership Records, Limited Liability Company Records, Limited Liability Partnerships

Corporation Section, Department of Community & Econ Dev, PO Box 110808, Juneau, AK 99811-0808 (150 Third Street Rm 217, Juneau, AK 99801); 907-465-2530, Fax: 907-465-3257, 8AM-5PM. www.dced.state.ak.us/bsc/corps.htm ✉ ☎ **Fax** ✍ 💻

Uniform Commercial Code

UCC Central File Systems Office, State Recorder's Office, 550 West 7th Ave #1200A, Anchorage, AK 99501-3564; 907-269-8873, 907-269-8899, Fax: 907-269-8945, 8AM-3:30PM.

www.dnr.state.ak.us/ssd/ucc/index.cfm ✉ **Fax** ✍ 💻

Federal and State Tax Liens

Records not maintained by a state level agency.
All tax liens are filed at local District Recorder Offices.

Sales Tax Registrations

State does not impose sales tax.

Birth Certificates, Death Records, Marriage Certificates, Divorce Records

Department of Health & Social Services, Bureau of Vital Statistics, 5441 Commercial Blvd, Juneau, AK 99801; 907-465-3391, Fax: 907-465-3618, 8AM-4:30PM. www.hss.state.ak.us/dph/bvs/ ✉ ☎ **Fax** ✍

Key: Access state agency records by:. phone-☎ mail-✉ fax-**Fax** in person-✍ online-💻 email-**Email**

Workers' Compensation Records

Workers' Compensation, PO Box 25512, Juneau, AK 99802 (1111 W Eighth St, Room 307, Juneau, AK 99802); 907-465-2790, Fax: 907-465-2797, 8AM-4:30PM. www.labor.state.ak.us/wc/wc.htm ✉☎Fax👋

Driver Records

Division of Motor Vehicles, Driver's Records, 2760 Sherwood Lane #B, Juneau, AK 99801; 907-465-4361 (Motor Vehicle Reports Desk), 907-465-4363 (Licensing), Fax: 907-465-5509, 8AM-5PM. www.state.ak.us/dmv ✉👋💻

Vehicle Ownership, Vehicle Identification, Vessel Registration

Division of Motor Vehicles, Research, 1300 W Benson Blvd #200, Anchorage,

AK 99503-3600; 907-269-5551, 8:30AM-4:30PM. www.state.ak.us/dmv ✉👋

Accident Reports

Department of Public Safety, Driver Services, 2760 Sherwood Lane #B, Juneau, AK 99801; 907-465-4361, Fax: 907-463-5509, 8AM-5PM. www.state.ak.us/dmv ✉☎👋

Vessel Ownership

Records not maintained by a state level agency.
Alaska is not a title state. Liens are filed with Dept. of Natural Resources, Recorder's Section at 907-269-8882. Also, until Jan. 1, 2001, all boat registrations were done through the US Coast Guard (970-463-2294).

Voter Registration

Division of Elections, PO Box 110017, Juneau, AK 99811 (Court Plaza Bldg, 4th

Fl, 240 Main Street, Juneau, AK 99801); 907-465-4611, Fax: 907-465-3203, 8-5. www.elections.state.ak.us ✉☎Fax👋

GED Certificates

Department of Labor, Employment Security Division, PO Box 25509, Juneau, AK 99802 (1111 8th St #210, Juneau); 907-465-4685, Fax: 907-465-8753, 8AM-4:30. www.ajcn.state.ak.us/abe/ ✉Fax👋

Hunting License and Fishing License Information

Department of Fish & Game, Licensing Section, PO Box 25525, Juneau, AK 99802-5525 (1255 W 8th St); 907-465-2376, Fax: 907-465-2440, 8AM-5PM. www.adfg.state.ak.us/ ✉☎Fax👋

Arizona

Governor's Office
  1700 W Washington   602-542-4331
  Phoenix, AZ 85007   Fax 602-542-1381
  www.governor.state.az.us   8AM-5PM

Attorney General's Office
  1275 W Washington   602-542-5025
  Phoenix, AZ 85007   Fax 602-542-4085
  www.attorneygeneral.state.az.us 8AM-5PM

State Website: www.az.gov/webapp/portal/

Legislative Records: www.azleg.state.az.us
  602-542-3559 Senate 602-542-4221 House

State Archives
  602-542-4159 www.dlapr.lib.az.us/archives

Capital: Phoenix, in Maricopa County

Search Unclaimed Property Online
  www.missingmoney.com/main/index.cfm

Criminal Records

Department of Public Safety, Applicant Team One, PO Box 18430//Mail Code 2250, Phoenix, AZ 85005-8430 (2320 N 20th Ave, Phoenix, AZ 85005); 602-223-2223, Fax: 602-223-2972, 8AM-5PM. www.dps.state.az.us ✉

Statewide Court Records

Administrative Offices of the Courts, Arizona Supreme Court Bldg, 1501 W Washington, Phoenix, AZ 85007-3231; 602-542-9301, Fax: 602-542-9484, 8AM-5PM. www.supreme.state.az.us/ 💻

Sexual Offender Registry

Department of Public Safety, Sex Offender Compliance, PO Box 6638//Mail Code 9999, Phoenix, AZ 85005-6638 (2102 W Encanto, Phoenix, AZ 85009); 602-255-0611, Fax: 602-223-2915, 8AM-5PM. www.azsexoffender.com/ ✉💻

Incarceration Records

Arizona Department of Corrections, Records Department, 1601 W. Jefferson St., Phoenix, AZ 85007; 602-542-5586, Fax: 602-542-1638, 8AM-5PM. www.adc.state.az.us Fax💻

Corporation Records, Limited Liability Company Records

Corporation Commission, Corporation Records, 1300 W Washington, Room 101, Phoenix, AZ 85007; 602-542-3026 (Status), 602-542-3285 (Annual Reports), Fax: 602-542-3414, 8AM-5PM. www.cc.state.az.us/corp/index.htm ✉👋💻

Fictitious Name, Assumed Name

Records not maintained by a state level agency.
Records are found at the county level.

Trademarks/Servicemarks, Trade Names, Limited Partnership Records

Secretary of State, Trademarks/Tradenames/Limited Partnership Division, 1700 W Washington, 7th Fl, Phoenix, AZ 85007 (Customer Service, 14 N 18th Ave, Phoenix); 602-542-6187, Fax: 602-542-7386, 8AM-5PM. www.azsos.gov/business_services/trademarksandtradenames.htm ✉ ☎ ✋ 🖥

Uniform Commercial Code, Federal and State Tax Liens

UCC Division, Secretary of State, 1700 W Washington, 7th Fl, Phoenix, AZ 85007 (Customer Service Center, 14 North 18th Ave, Phoenix, AZ 85007); 602-542-6187, Fax: 602-542-7386, 8AM - 5PM. www.sosaz.com/business_services/ucc.htm ✉ ☎ **Fax** ✋ 🖥

Sales Tax Registrations

Revenue Department, Transaction (Sales) Tax Licenses and Registration, 1600 W Monroe, Phoenix, AZ 85007; 602-542-4565, Fax: 602-542-4772, 8AM-5PM. www.revenue.state.az.us ✉ ☎ ✋

Birth Certificates, Death Records

Department of Health Services, Vital Records Section, PO Box 3887, Phoenix, AZ 85030 (2727 W Glendale Ave, Phoenix); 602-255-3260, 602-364-1300 (Recording), Fax: 602-249-3040, 8-5PM. www.hs.state.az.us/vitalrcd/index.htm ✉ **Fax** ✋ 🖥

Marriage Certificates, Divorce Records

Records not maintained by a state level agency.
These records are not available from the state; they must be requested from the county or court of issue.

Workers' Compensation Records

State Compensation Fund, Claims Information, 3030 N 3rd St, Phoenix, AZ 85012; 602-631-2000 x4, 602-631-2869-copies, 8-5. www.statefund.com ✉ ✋

Driver Records

Motor Vehicle Division, Correspondence Unit, PO Box 2100, Mail Drop 539M, Phoenix, AZ 85001-2100 (Customer Records Services, 1801 W Jefferson, Rm 111, Phoenix, AZ 85007); 602-712-8420, 8-5. www.dot.state.az.us/MVD/mvd.htm ✉ ✋ 🖥

Vehicle Ownership, Vehicle Identification

Motor Vehicle Division - Director's Office, Record Services Section, PO Box 2100, Mail Drop 504M, Phoenix, AZ 85001-2100 (Customer Records Services, 1801 W Jefferson, Rm 111, Phoenix, AZ 85007); 602-712-8420, 8AM-5PM. www.dot.state.az.us/MVD/mvd.htm ✉ ✋ 🖥

Accident Reports

Department of Public Safety, Accident Reports, PO Box 6638, Mail Drop 1110, Phoenix, AZ 85005 (2102 W Encanto, 1st Fl, Phoenix, AZ 85005-6638); 602-223-2230, 8AM-5PM. ✉ ✋ 🖥

Vessel Ownership, Vessel Registration

Game & Fish Dept, Watercraft Department, 2221 W Greenway Rd, Phoenix, AZ 85023-4399; 602-942-3000, Fax: 602-789-3729, 8AM-5PM M-F. www.azgf.com ✉ ☎ **Fax** ✋

Voter Registration

Records not maintained by a state level agency.
Records are only maintained at the county recorder offices. Their records are permitted to be sold in bulk only for political related purposes. Go to the county level to can confirm names on a single inquiry basis.

GED Certificates

Department of Education, GED Testing, 1535 W Jefferson, Phoenix, AZ 85007; 602-254-0265, Fax: 602-258-4977, 8AM-5PM. www.ade.az.gov/adult-ed/ ✉ ✋

Hunting License and Fishing License Information

Game & Fish Department, Information & Licensing Division, 2221 W Greenway Rd, Phoenix, AZ 85023-4399; 602-942-3000, Fax: 602-789-3924, 8AM-5PM. www.azgfd.com ✉

Arkansas

Governor's Office
   State Capitol, #250
   Little Rock, AR 72201
   www.arkansas.gov/governor

             501-682-2345
      Fax 501-682-3597
         8AM-5PM

Attorney General's Office
   323 Center St #200
   Little Rock, AR 72201
   www.ag.state.ar.us

             501-682-2007
      Fax 501-682-8084
         8AM-5PM

State Website: www.state.ar.us

Legislative Records
   501-682-5070 www.arkleg.state.ar.us

State Archives
   501-682-6900 www.ark-ives.com

Capital: Little Rock, in Pulaski County

Search Unclaimed Property Online

www.state.ar.us/auditor/unclprop/

Key: Access state agency records by:. phone-☎ mail-✉ fax-**Fax** in person-✋ online-🖥 email-**Email**

Arkansas Criminal Records

Arkansas State Police, Identification Bureau, #1 State Police Plaza Dr, Little Rock, AR 72209; 501-618-8500, Fax: 501-618-8404, 7:30AM-4:30PM. www.asp.state.ar.us ⊠ ✍ 🖳

Statewide Court Records

Administrative Office of Courts, 625 Marshall Street, 1100 Justice Bldg, Little Rock, AR 72201-1078; 501-682-9400, Fax: 501-682-9410, 8AM-5PM. www.courts.state.ar.us 🖳

Sexual Offender Registry

Access to Records is Restricted
Arkansas Crime Information Center, Sexual Offender Registry, One Capitol Mall, Little Rock, AR 72201; 501-682-2222, Fax: 501-682-2269. www.acic.org/Registration/index.htm Offenders are assigned the following levels: Level 1: Low Risk; Level 2: Moderate Risk; Level 3: High Risk; Level 4: Sexually Violent Predator. Local law enforcement agencies release names of those determined most likely to re-offend. ⊠ 🖳

Incarceration Records

Department of Corrections, Records Supervisor, 7500 Corrections Circle, Pine Bluff, AR 71603; 870-267-6424, 8-4:30. www.accessarkansas.org/doc/inmate_info ⊠ 🖳

Corporation Records, Fictitious Name, Limited Liability Company Records, Limited Partnerships

Secretary of State, Business Services Div, State Capitol Bldg, Little Rock, AR 72201 (Commercial Service Division, Victory Bldg - 1401 W Capitol Ave, Little Rock, AR 72201); 501-682-3409, 888-233-0325, Fax: 501-682-3437, 8-5PM (4:30 on F). www.sos.arkansas.gov/corps/ ⊠ ☎ ✍ 🖳

Trademarks/Servicemarks

Secretary of State, Trademarks Section, State Capitol Bldg, Little Rock, AR 72201 (Business & Commercial Services Div, Victory Bldg - 1401 W Capitol Ave, Little Rock, AR 72201); 501-682-3409, 888-233-0325, Fax: 501-682-3437, 8AM-5PM

www.sos.arkansas.gov/corps/trademk/ ⊠ ☎ ✍ 🖳

Uniform Commercial Code, Federal Tax Liens

UCC Division - Commercial Srvs, Secretary of State, State Capitol Bldg, Little Rock, AR 72201 (Commercial Service Division, Victory Bldg - 1401 W Capitol Ave, Little Rock, AR 72201); 501-682-5078, Fax: 501-682-3500, 8AM-5PM. www.sos.arkansas.gov ⊠ **Fax** 🖳

State Tax Liens

Records not maintained by a state level agency.
Records are at the county level.

Sales Tax Registrations

Finance & Administration Department, Sales & Use Tax Office - Reg. Dept, PO Box 1272, Little Rock, AR 72203; 501-682-1895, Fax: 501-682-7900, 8-4:30PM. www.state.ar.us/dfa/taxes/salestax/ ⊠ ☎ **Fax** ✍

Birth Certificates, Death Records, Marriage Certificates, Divorce Records

Arkansas Department of Health, Division of Vital Records, 4815 W Markham St, Slot 44, Little Rock, AR 72205; 501-661-2174, 501-661-2336 (Message Number), 501-661-2726 (Credit Card Line), 800-637-9314 (Toll Free), Fax: 501-663-2832, 8AM-4:30PM. www.healthyarkansas.com ⊠ ☎ **Fax** ✍ 🖳

Workers' Compensation Records

Workers Compensation Department, Operations/Compliance, 324 Spring Street, PO Box 950, Little Rock, AR 72203-0950; 501-682-3930, 800-622-4472, Fax: 501-682-6761, 8AM-4:30PM www.awcc.state.ar.us ⊠ ☎ **Fax** ✍ 🖳

Driver Records

Department of Driver Services, Driving Records Division, PO Box 1272, Room 1130, Little Rock, AR 72203-1272 (1900 W 7th, #1130, Little Rock, AR 72201); 501-682-7207, 501-682-7908, Fax: 501-682-2075, 8AM-4:30PM. www.access arkansas.org/dfa/driverservices/ ⊠ ✍ 🖳

Vehicle Ownership, Vehicle Identification

Office of Motor Vehicles, MV Title Records, PO Box 1272, Room 1100, Little Rock, AR 72203 (7th & Battery Sts, Ragland Bldg, #1100, Little Rock, AR 72201); 501-682-4692, 800-662-8247, 8-4:30PM. www.accessarkansas.org/dfa/ ⊠ ☎ **Fax** ✍

Accident Reports

Arkansas State Police, Crash Records Section, 1 State Police Plaza Drive, Little Rock, AR 72209; 501-618-8130, Fax: 501-618-8131, 8AM-5PM. www.asp.state.ar.us/cr/cr.html ⊠ ☎ ✍

Vessel Ownership, Vessel Registration

Office of Motor Vehicles, Boat Registration, PO Box 1272, Little Rock, AR 72203; 501-682-4692, Fax: 501-682-1116, 8AM-4:30PM. www.arkansas.gov/dfa/motorvehicle/index.html ⊠ ☎ **Fax** ✍

Voter Registration

Access to Records is Restricted
Secretary of State, Voter Services, State Capitol, Room 026, Little Rock, AR 72201; 501-682-3526, Fax: 501-682-3548, 8AM-5PM. State will sell the voter database for voting or election purposes. All individual search requests must be at the local County Clerk's office. Requests for bulk release of records must be in writing and state "pursuant to the Freedom of Information Act." CD-rom includes name, address, DOB, district data. www.sosweb.state.ar.us/elections.html

GED Certificates

GED Testing, Dept of Workforce Education, #3 Capitol Mall, Room 305D, Little Rock, AR 72201; 501-682-1978 Fax: 501-682-1982, 8AM-4:30PM. http://dwe.arkansas.gov/ged.htm ⊠ **Fax** ✍

Hunting License and Fishing License Information

Game & Fish Commission, Attn: Records, Two Natural Resources Dr, Little Rock, AR 72205; 501-223-6300, 800-364-4263, Fax: 501-223-6425, 8AM-4:30PM. www.agfc.com ⊠ **Fax** ✍

California

Governor's Office
  State Capitol, 1st Floor   916-445-2841
  Sacramento, CA 95814   Fax 916-445-4633
  www.governor.ca.gov

Attorney General's Office
  Justice Department   916-445-9555
  PO Box 944255   Fax 916-324-5205
  Sacramento, CA 94244-2550   8AM-5PM
  http://caag.state.ca.us
  Web: www.state.ca.us/state/portal/myca_homepage.jsp

Legislative Records
  916-445-2323   www.leginfo.ca.gov
State Archives: 916-653-7715/2246
www.ss.ca.gov/archives/archives.htm
Capital: Sacramento, in Sacramento County

Search Unclaimed Property Online

https://scoweb.sco.ca.gov

Criminal Records

Access to Records is Restricted

Department of Justice, Records Search Section, PO Box 903417, Sacramento, CA 94203-4170 (4949 Broadway, Sacramento, CA 95820); 916-227-3460 (Dept of Justice), 916-227-3849 (General Information), 916-227-3812 (Sealing & Dismissal), 8-5PM. www.caag.state.ca.us SEVERE LIMITATIONS! Penal Code Sec. 11105.3 limits access to searches involving only child care, education, the handicapped and mentally impaired. The subject can obtain their own copy. Entities must be pre-appoved before records can be ordered.✉

Statewide Court Records

Administration Office of Courts, Office of Cummunications, 455 Golden Gate Ave, San Francisco, CA 94102-3660; 415-865-4200, Fax: 415-865-4205, 8AM-5PM. www.courtinfo.ca.gov 🖥

Sexual Offender Registry

Department of Justice, Sexual Offender Program, PO Box 903387, Sacramento, CA 94203-3870 (4949 Broadway, Rm H216, Sacramento, CA 95820); 900-448-3000 (Fee Search), 916-227-4199 (Tracking), Fax: 916-227-4345, 8AM-5PM. www.caag.state.ca.us ✉ ☎

Incarceration Records

California Department of Corrections, Communications Office, PO Box 942883, Sacramento, CA 94283-0001; 916-557-5933, 916-445-6713 (24 Hour Inmate Locator), 916-445-7682 (Dept. of

Corrections Main), Fax: 916-327-1988, 8AM-5PM. www.corr.ca.gov ✉ ☎ Fax

Corporation Records, Limited Liability Company Records, Limited Partnerships, Limited Liability Partnerships,

Secretary of State, Information Retrieval/Certification Unit, 1500 11th St, 3rd Fl, Sacramento, CA 95814; 916-657-5448 x1, 8AM-4:30PM. www.ss.ca.gov ✉ ☎ Fax 🖐 🖥

Assumed Name, Fictitious Name

Records not maintained by a state level agency.
Records are found at the county level.

Trademarks/Servicemarks, Limited Partnership Records

Secretary of State, Trademark Unit, PO Box 944225, Sacramento, CA 94244-2250 (1500 11th Street, Rm 345, Sacramento, CA 95814); 916-653-4984 (Trademark/Servicemarks), 916-653-3365 (Partnership Information), 8AM-5PM. www.ss.ca.gov ✉ ☎ 🖐

Uniform Commercial Code, Federal and State Tax Liens

UCC Division, Secretary of State, PO Box 942835, Sacramento, CA 94235 (1500 11th St, Room 255, Sacramento, CA 95814); 916-653-3516 x2, 8AM-5PM.

www.ss.ca.gov/business/ucc/ucc.htm ✉ 🖐 🖥

Sales Tax Registrations

Board of Equalization, Sales and Use Tax Department, PO Box 942879, Sacramento, CA 94279-0001; 916-445-6362, 800-400-7115 (In California Only), Fax: 916-324-4433, 8AM-5PM. www.boe.ca.gov ✉ ☎ Fax 🖥

Birth Certificates, Death Records, Marriage Certificates, Divorce Records

State Department of Health Svcs, Office of Vital Records - MS 5103, PO Box 997410, Sacramento, CA 95899-7410 (1501 Capitol Ave, Rm 71-1110, Sacramento); 916-445-2684 (Recording), 916-445-1719 (Attendant), 8-4:30PM. www.dhs.ca.gov/chs/default.htm ✉

Workers' Compensation Records

Division of Workers' Compensation, Headquarters, 455 Golden Gate Ave, 9th Fl, San Francisco, CA 94102; 415-703-4600, Fax: 415-703-4717, 8AM-5PM. www.dir.ca.gov/dwc/dwc_home_page.ht m ✉ Fax 🖐

Driver Records

Department of Motor Vehicles, Information Services Branch, PO Box 944247, Mail Station G199, Sacramento, CA 94244-2470 (2415 First Ave, Sacramento, CA 95818); 916-657-8098,

Key: Access state agency records by:. phone-☎   mail-✉   fax-Fax   in person-🖐   online-🖥   email-Email

916-657-5564 (Requester Accounts), 8AM-5PM. www.dmv.ca.gov ✉☎💻

Accident Reports

Department of Motor Vehicles, Accident Reports, PO Box 942884, Sacramento, CA 94284; Fax: 916-675-5651, 8-5PM (open at 9AM of F). www.dmv.ca.gov ✉

Vehicle Ownership, Vehicle Identification, Vessel Ownership, Vessel Registration

Department of Motor Vehicle, Office of Information Services, PO Box 944247, MS-G199, Sacramento, CA 94244-2470

(2415 First Ave, Sacramento); 916-657-8098, 916-657-5564 (Com'l Accounts), 916-657-6893 (Vessel Regis.), 8AM-5PM. www.dmv.ca.gov ✉💻

Voter Registration

Access to Records is Restricted
Secretary of State, Elections Division, 1500 11th Street, Sacramento, CA 95814; 916-657-2166, Fax: 916-653-3214, 8AM-5PM. Records are not open and cannot be viewed at this agency. Individual verification must be done at the local level. The state will sell CDs with all or portions of the statewide database for political or pre-approved purposes. Call for details.

GED Certificates

Dept of Education, State GED Office, 1430 N st Suite 5408, Sacramento, CA 94244; 916-445-8049, 800-331-6316, 8AM-5PM. www.cde.ca.gov/ta/tg/gd/ ✉

Hunting License and Fishing License Information

Access to Records is Restricted
Department of Fish & Game, License & Revenue Branch, 3211 "S" St, Sacramento, CA 95816; 916-227-2245, Fax: 916-227-2261, www.dfg.ca.gov Records are not available to the public.

Colorado

Governor's Office
136 State Capitol Bldg
Denver, CO 80203-1792
www.colorado.gov/governor

303-866-2471
Fax 303-866-2003
8AM-5PM

Attorney General's Office
Department of Law
1525 Sherman St, 5th Floor
Denver, CO 80203
www.ago.state.co.us

303-866-4500
Fax 303-866-5691
8AM-5PM

State Website: www.state.co.us

Legislative Records
303-866-3055 www.leg.state.co.us

State Archives
303-866-2055 http://statearchives.us/colorado.htm

Capital: Denver, in Denver County

Search Unclaimed Property Online
www.missingmoney.com/main/index.cfm

Criminal Records

Bureau of Investigation, State Repository, Identification Unit, 690 Kipling St, Suite 3000, Denver, CO 80215; 303-239-4208, Fax: 303-239-5858, 8AM-4:30PM. http://cbi.state.co.us ✉✋💻

Statewide Court Records

State Court Administrator, 1301 Pennsylvania St, Suite 300, Denver, CO 80203-2416; 303-861-1111, 800-888-0001, Fax: 303-837-2340, 8AM-5PM. www.courts.state.co.us 💻

Sexual Offender Registry

Colorado Bureau of Investigation, SOR Unit, 690 Kipling St, Suite 4000, Denver, CO 80215; 303-239-4222, Fax: 303-233-8336, 8AM-4:30PM. http://sor.state.co.us ✉✋💻

Incarceration Records

Department of Corrections, Offender Records Customer Support, 2862 S Circle Dr. #418, Colorado Springs, CO 80906; 719-226-4884, 719-226-4880 (Locator Service), Fax: 719-226-4899, 8AM-5PM. www.doc.state.co.us/index.html ✉☎Fax

Corporation Records, Trademarks/Servicemarks, Fictitious Name, Limited Liability Company Records, Assumed Name, Trade Name

Secretary of State, Business Division, 1560 Broadway, Suite 200, Denver, CO 80202; 303-894-2200 x2 (Business Entities), Fax: 303-869-4864, 7:30-5PM. www.sos.state.co.us ✉☎Fax✋💻

Uniform Commercial Code, Federal Tax Liens, State Tax Liens

Secretary of State, UCC Division, 1560 Broadway, Suite 200, Denver, CO 80202; 303-894-2200 x2, Fax: 303-869-4864, 7:30AM-5PM. www.sos.state.co.us ✉☎Fax✋💻

Sales Tax Registrations

Revenue Department, Taxpayers Services Office, 1375 Sherman St, Denver, CO 80261 (1625 Broadway, Ste 805, Denver, CO); 303-238-7378, Fax: 303-866-3211, 8AM-4:30PM. www.revenue.state.co.us ☎✋💻

Key: Access state agency records by:. phone-☎ mail-✉ fax-**Fax** in person-✋ online-💻 email-**Email**

Birth Certificates, Death Records, Marriage Certificates, Divorce Records

Department of Public Health & Environment, Vital Records Section HSVR-A1, 4300 Cherry Creek Dr S, Denver, CO 80246-1530; 303-756-4464 (recorded message), 303-692-2224 (credit card orders), 303-692-2234 (general info), Fax: 800-423-1108, 8:30AM-4:30PM. www.cdphe.state.co.us/hs/certs.asp ✉☎Fax✍🖥

Workers' Compensation Records

Division of Workers' Compensation, Customer Service, 1515 Arapahoe St, Tower 2, Ste 500, Denver, CO 80202-2117; 303-318-8700, Fax: 303-318-8710, 8-5PM. www.coworkforce.com/DWC/ ✉☎Fax✍

Driver Records

Motor Vehicle Business Group, Driver Control, Denver, CO 80261-0016 (1881 Pierce Street, Lakewood, CO 80214); 303-205-5613, Fax: 303-205-5990, 8AM-5PM. www.mv.state.co.us ✉✍🖥

Vehicle Ownership, Vehicle Identification

Motor Vehicle Business Group, Title, Registration and Emissions, Denver, CO 80261-0016 (1881 Pierce Street, Lakewood, CO 80214); 303-205-5607 (Titles), 303-205-5765 (Registration), Fax: 303-205-5990, 8AM-5PM. www.mv.state.co.us/mv.html ✉✍

Accident Reports

Motor Vehicle Business Group, Driver Control, Denver, CO 80261-0016 (1881 Pierce Street, Lakewood, CO); 303-205-5613, 8-5PM. www.mv.state.co.us ✉✍

Vessel Ownership, Vessel Registration

Colorado State Parks, Registration, 13787 S Highway 85, Littleton, CO 80125; 303-791-1920, Fax: 303-470-0782, 8-5PM. http://parks.state.co.us/boating/ ✉Fax✍

Voter Registration

Department of State, Elections Department, 1560 Broadway #200, Denver, CO 80202; 303-894-2200 x6307, Fax: 303-894-7732, 8:30AM-5PM. www.sos.state.co.us/pubs/elections/main.htm ✉Fax✍

GED Certificates

Dept of Education, GED Testing, 201 E Colfax Ave Rm 100, Denver, CO 80203; 303-866-6613, 8AM-4:55PM. www.cde.state.co.us/index_adult.htm ✉✍

Hunting License and Fishing License Information

Access to Records is Restricted
Dept. of Natural Resources, Division of Wildlife, 6060 Broadway, Denver, CO 80216; 303-297-1192, Fax: 303-294-0874, 8-5PM. www.wildlife.state.co.us The attorney general decided that no data on holders of individual hunting and fishing licenses can be given to the public. It is only available to law enforcement officials or to the licensed individual.

Connecticut

Governor's Office
  State Capitol, 210 Capitol Ave   860-566-4840
  Hartford, CT 06106   Fax 860-566-4677
  www.ct.gov/governor   8AM-5PM

Attorney General's Office
  PO Box 120   860-808-5318
  Hartford, CT 06141-0120   Fax 860-808-5387
  www.cslib.org/attygenl   8:30AM-4:30PM

  State Website: www.state.ct.us

Legislative Records
  860-757-6550 www. cga.state.ct.us/default.asp

State Archives
  860-757-6580 www.cslib.org/archives.htm

Capital: Hartford, in Hartford County

Search Unclaimed Property Online
www.state.ct.us/ott/ucplisting.htm

Criminal Records

Department of Public Safety, Bureau of Identification, PO Box 2794, Middletown, CT 06757-9294 (1111 Country Club Rd, Middleton, CT 06457); 860-685-8480, Fax: 860-685-8361, 8:30AM-4:30PM. www.state.ct.us/dps/spbi.htm ✉✍

Statewide Court Records

Chief Court Administrator, 231 Capitol Ave, Hartford, CT 06106; 860-757-2100,

860-757-2270 (External Affairs), Fax: 860-757-2215, 8AM-5PM. www.jud.state.ct.us 🖥

Sexual Offender Registry

Department of Public Safety, Sex Offender Registry Unit, PO Box 2794, Middletown, CT 06757 (1111 Country Club Rd, Middleton, CT 06457); 860-685-8060, Fax: 860-685-8349, 8:30-4:30PM. www.state.ct.us/dps/Sex_Offender_Registry.htm 🖥

Incarceration Records

Connecticut Dept. of Corrections, Public Information Office, 24 Wolcott Hill Rd, Wethersfield, CT 06109; 860-692-7780 (Locater), Fax: 860-692-7783, 8:30AM-4:30PM. www.ct.gov/doc/site/default.asp ✉☎🖥

Key: Access state agency records by:. phone-☎   mail-✉   fax-Fax   in person-✍   online-🖥   email-Email

Corporation Records, Limited Partnership Records Trademarks/Servicemarks, Limited Liability Company and Limited Liability Partnership Records, Statutory Trust Records

Secretary of State, Commercial Recording Division, 30 Trinity St, Hartford, CT 06106; 860-509-6003, Fax: 860-509-6069, 8:30AM-4PM. www.sots.state.ct.us ✉☎Fax✋🖥

Uniform Commercial Code, Federal and State Tax Liens

UCC Division, Secretary of State, PO Box 150470, Hartford, CT 06115-0470 (30 Trinity St, Hartford, CT 06106); 860-509-6002, Fax: 860-509-6069, 8:30AM-4PM. www.sots.state.ct.us ✉Fax✋🖥

Sales Tax Registrations

Dept of Revenue - Taxpayer Services Division, Sales Tax Registrations, 25 Sigourney St, Hartford, CT 06106; 860-297-4885, Fax: 860-297-5714, 8-5PM. www.ct.gov/drs/site/default.asp ✉☎Fax✋

Birth Certificates, Death Records, Marriage Certificates

Access to Records is Restricted
Department of Public Health, Vital Records Section MS# 11VRS, PO Box 340308, Hartford, CT 06134 (410 Capitol Ave, Hartford, CT 06134); 860-509-7897,

Fax: 860-509-7964, 8:30AM-4:30PM www.dph.state.ct.us/OPPE/hpvital.htm
The state is in the process of microfilming birth, death, and marriage records. You must contact the town/city clerk of occurrence to obtain copies of records. Website lists towns and phone numbers.

Divorce Records

Records not maintained by a state level agency.
The state does not maintain divorce records; records are available from the Chief Clerks of the 15 Judicial District Courts; See the County Courts Section. The State Vital Records Section (860-509-7897) will also provide contact info for the 15 courts.

Workers' Compensation Records

Workers Compensation Commission, 21 Oak Street, Hartford, CT 06106; 860-493-1500, Fax: 860-247-1361, 7:45-4:30PM. http://wcc.state.ct.us ✉☎Fax✋

Driver Records

Department of Motor Vehicles, Copy Records Unit, 60 State St., Wethersfield, CT 06161-0503; 860-263-5154, 8:30-4:30 T-F. www.ct.gov/dmv/site/default.asp ✉✋🖥

Vehicle Ownership, Vehicle Identification

Department of Motor Vehicles, Copy Record Unit, 60 State St,, Wethersfield, CT 06161; 860-263-5154, 8:AM-4:30PM

Tue-Fri. www.ct.gov/dmv/site/default.asp ✉✋🖥

Accident Reports

Department of Public Safety, Reports and Records Unit, PO Box 2794, Middletown, CT 06457-9294; 860-685-8250, 8:30AM-4:30PM. ✉☎

Vessel Ownership, Vessel Registration

Department of Motor Vehicles, Marine Vessel Section, 60 State Street, Wethersfield, CT 06161; 860-263-5151, Fax: 860-263-5555, 8-5PM T-F; til 12:30 PM Sat. www.ct.gov/dmv/cwp/view.asp?A=818&Q=245044 ✉✋

Voter Registration

Records not maintained by a state level agency.
Records are open at the town level. There are 169 towns.

GED Certificates

Department of Education, GED Records, 25 Industrial Park Rd, Middletown, CT 06457; 860-807-2110, Fax: 860-807-2112, 8AM-5PM. www.state.ct.us/sde/ ✉Fax✋

Hunting License and Fishing License Information

Department of Environmental Protection, License Division, 79 Elm St, Hartford, CT 06106; 860-424-3105, Fax: 860-424-4072, 9AM-4. www.dep.state.ct.us ✉✋

Delaware

Governor's Office
 820 N. French St   302-577-3210
 Wilmington, DE 19801   Fax 302-577-3118
 www.state.de.us/governor/index.shtml8AM-5:30PM

Attorney General's Office
 Carvel State Office Bldg   302-577-8400
 820 N French St   Fax 302-577-6630
 Wilmington, DE 19801   8:30AM-5PM
 www.state.de.us/attgen

State Website: http://delaware.gov
Legislative Records: 302-744-4114
 www.legis.state.de.us/Legislature.nsf?Open
State Archives
 302-744-5000 www.state.de.us/sos/dpa/
Capital: Dover, in Kent County

Search Unclaimed Property Online

www.missingmoney.com/main/index.cfm

Criminal Records

Delaware State Police, State Bureau of Identification, PO Box 430, Dover, DE 19903-0430 (1407 N Dupont Highway, Dover, DE 19930); 302-739-5880, 302-739-4794 (Fingerprinting/ Criminal Background phone), Fax: 302-739-5888, 8AM-4PM. www.state.de.us/dsp/ ✉ ✋

Statewide Court Records

Administrative Office of the Courts, Supreme Court of Delaware, 820 N French, 11th Fl, Wilmington, DE 19801; 302-255-0090, Fax: 302-255-2217, 8:30AM-5PM. http://courts.state.de.us 💻

Sexual Offender Registry

Delaware State Police, Sex Offender Central Registry, PO Box 430, Dover, DE 19903-0430 (1407 N Dupont Highway, Dover, DE 19901); 302-739-5882, Fax: 302-739-5888, 8AM-4PM. www.state.de.us/dsp/sexoff/ 💻

Incarceration Records

Delaware Department of Corrections, Central Records, 511 Maple Parkway, Dover, DE 19901; 302-739-5387 (Locator), Fax: 302-739-7486, 8-4PM. www.state.de.us/correct/index.htm ☎

Corporation Records, General Partnerships, Limited Partnership Records Trademarks/Servicemarks, Limited Liability Company Records, Limited Liability Partnerships

Secretary of State, Corporation Records, PO Box 898, Dover, DE 19903 (401 Federal Street #4, Dover); 302-739-3073, Fax: 302-739-3812, 8AM-4:30PM. www.state.de.us/corp ✉ ☎ Fax ✋ 💻

Uniform Commercial Code, Federal Tax Liens

UCC Division, Secretary of State, PO Box 793, Dover, DE 19903 (Townsend Bldg, 401 Federal Street #4, Dover, DE 19901); 302-739-3077, Fax: 302-739-3813, 8:30-4:30PM. www.state.de.us/corp/ucc.shtml ✉ Fax ✋

State Tax Liens

Records not maintained by a state level agency.
Records are at the county level.

Sales Tax Registrations

Finance Department - Div. Rev., Groos Receipt Tax Registration, PO Box 8750, Wilmington, DE 19899-8750 (Carvel State Office Bldg, 820 N French St, 9th Fl, Wilmington, DE 19801); 302-577-8238, Fax: 302-577-8203, 8AM-4:30PM. www.state.de.us/revenue/obt/lic_gr.htm ✉ ☎ Fax ✋

Birth Certificates, Death Records, Marriage Certificates, Divorce Records

Department of Health, Office of Vital Statistics, PO Box 637, Dover, DE 19903 (William Penn & Federal Sts, Jesse Cooper Bldg, Dover, DE 19901); 302-744-4549, Fax: 302-736-1862, 8-4:30PM www.state.de.us/dhss/dph/ss/vitalstats.html ✉ Fax ✋ 💻

This agency will verify whether a divorce occurred after 1935 but will issue no copies of the record. For records 1976 to present, go to the Family Court at the county; prior to 1976, go to the Prothonotary at the county level.

Workers' Compensation Records

Labor Department, Industrial Accident Board, 4425 N Market Street, 3rd Fl, Wilmington, DE 19802; 302-761-8200 x2, Fax: 302-761-6601, 8AM-4:30PM. www.delawareworks.com/industrialaffairs/services/workerscomp.shtml ✉

Driver Records

Division of Motor Vehicles, Driver Services, PO Box 698, Dover, DE 19903 (303 Transportation Circle, Dover, DE 19901); 302-744-2506, Fax: 302-739-2602, 8AM-4:30PM M-T-TH-F; Noon-8PM W. www.dmv.de.gov/ ✉ ✋ 💻

Vehicle Ownership, Vehicle Identification

Division of Motor Vehicles, Correspondence Section, PO Box 698, Dover, DE 19903 (303 Transportation Circle, Dover, DE 19901); 302-744-2511, 302-744-2538, Fax: 302-739-2042, 8AM-4:30PM M-T-TH-F; 12-8PM W. www.dmv.de.gov/Vehicle_Services/ve_main.html ✉ ✋ 💻

Accident Reports

Delaware State Police, Traffic Records, PO Box 430, Dover, DE 19903 (1441 N Dupont Hwy, Dover, DE 19901); 302-739-5931, Fax: 302-739-5982, 8AM-4PM. ✉ ☎

Vessel Ownership, Vessel Registration

Dept of Natural Resources & Environmental Control, Boat Registration Office, 89 Kings Highway, Dover, DE 19901; 302-739-3498, Fax: 302-739-6157, 8AM-4:30PM. www.dnrec.state.de.us/dnrec2000/Boating.asp ✉ ☎ Fax ✋

Voter Registration

Commissioner of Elections, Voter Registration Records, 111 S West St #10, Dover, DE 19904; 302-739-4277, 8AM-4:30PM. www.state.de.us/election ✉ ✋

GED Certificates

Dept. of Education, Adult Education - GED Testing, PO Box 1402, Dover, DE 19903; 302-739-3743, Fax: 302-739-1318, 8AM-4:30PM. www.doe.state.de.us ✉ Fax ✋

Hunting License and Fishing License Information

Access to Records is Restricted
Division of Fish & Wildlife, License Records, 89 Kings Hwy, Dover, DE 19901; 302-739-5296, Fax: 302-739-6157 www.dnrec.state.de.us/fw/index.htm 8AM-4:30PM. Records are not computerized, but are kept on paper and filed alphabetically. Agency will release name, address, driver license #, physical characteristics. ✉ ☎ Fax ✋

District of Columbia

Mayor's Office
1350 Pennsylvania Ave NW 202-727-2980
Washington, DC 20004 Fax 202-727-0505
http://dc.gov/mayor/index.shtm 8:30AM-5:30PM

Legislative Records
202-724-8050 www.dccouncil.washington.dc.us

District Archives
202-671-1105

District Website www.washingtondc.gov

Search Unclaimed Property Online

www.missingmoney.com/main/index.cfm

Criminal Records

Metropolitan Police Dept, Identification and Records Section, 300 Indiana Ave NW, Rm 3055, Washington, DC 20001; 202-727-4245 (Police), 202-879-1373 (Sup'r Ct), Fax: 202-638-5352, 8-5PM. www.mpdc.dc.gov/main.shtm ✉ ✋

Sexual Offender Registry

Metropolitan Police Department, Sex Offender Registry Unit, 300 Indiana Ave NW, Rm 3009, Washington, DC 20001; 202-727-4407, Fax: 202-727-9292, 8-5. www.mpdc.dc.gov/serv/sor/sor.shtm Fax ✋ 💻

Incarceration Records

District of Columbia Department of Corrections, DC Detention Facility, Office of Records, 1901 D. Street, S.E., Washington, DC 20003; 202-673-8136, 202-673-8136 option 2 (VINE Inmate info line), 202-673-8257 (Administration), 8-5PM. www.mpdc.dc.gov/main.shtm ✉

Corporation Records, Limited Partnership Records, Limited Liability Company Records

Department of Consumer & Regulatory Affairs, Corporations Division, 941 N Capitol St NE, Washington, DC 20002; 202-442-4432, Fax: 202-442-4523, 8:30AM-4PM. http://dcra.dc.gov/dcra/site/default.asp ✉ ☎ ✋

Uniform Commercial Code, Federal and State Tax Liens

UCC Recorder, District of Columbia Recorder of Deeds, 515 D Street NW, Washington, DC 20001; 202-727-0400, 202-727-5374, 8:30AM-4:30PM. www.washington.dc.us.landata.com ✉ ✋ 💻

Sales Tax Registrations

Office of Tax and Revenue, Sales Tax Certificates, 941 N. Capitol Street NE, Washington, DC 20002; 202-727-4829, Fax: 202-442-6550, 8:15AM-4:30PM. http://brc.dc.gov/tax/tax.asp ✉ ☎ Fax ✋

Birth Certificates, Death Records

Department of Health, Vital Records Division, 825 North Capitol St NE, 1st Fl, Washington, DC 20002; 202-442-9009, Fax: 202-442-4848, 8:30AM-3:30PM. http://dchealth.dc.gov/index.asp ✉ ☎ Fax ✋ 💻

Marriage Certificates

Superior Court House, Marriage Bureau, 500 Indiana Ave, NW, Room 4485, Washington, DC 20001; 202-879-4840, Fax: 202-879-1280, 9AM-4PM. ✉ ✋

Divorce Records

Superior Court House, Divorce Records, 500 Indiana Ave, NW, Room 4230, Washington, DC 20001; 202-879-1261, Fax: 202-879-1572, 8:30-5PM. ✉ Fax ✋

Workers' Compensation Records

Office of Workers' Compensation, PO Box 56098 2nd Fl, Washington, DC 20011 (77 P St, NE 2nd Fl); 202-671-1000, Fax: 202-671-1929, 8:30AM-5PM. www.does.dc.gov/main.shtm ✉ Fax ✋

Driver Records

Department of Motor Vehicles, Driver Records Division, 65 K Street NE, Rm 200A, Washington, DC 20002; 202-727-1530, 202-727-5000 (General), 8:15AM-4PM. www.dmv.dc.gov ✉ ✋ 💻

Vehicle Ownership, Vehicle Identification

Department of Motor Vehicles, Vehicle Control Division, 301 "C" St, NW, Room 1063, Washington, DC 20001; 202-727-5000, 8:15AM-4PM M-T-TH-F. www.dmv.dc.gov ✉ ✋

Accident Reports

Metro. Police Dept., Accident Report Section, 300 Indiana Ave NW, Room 3075, Washington, DC 20001; 202-727-4357, 7AM-4PM (8PM on Wed). www.dmv.washingtondc.gov ✉ ✋

Vessel Ownership, Vessel Registration

Access to Records is Restricted

Metropolitan Police Dept, Harbor Patrol, 550 Water St SW, Washington, DC 20024; 202-727-4582, Fax: 202-727-3663, http://mpdc.dc.gov/main.shtm 7AM-3PM. All vessels regardless of size must be titled and registered. Information is not open to the public. Any emergency requests must be in writing and the agency will use some discretion in release of data for lawful purposes. ✉

Voter Registration

DC Board of Elections and Ethics, Voter Registration Records, 441 4th St NW, #250 North, Washington, DC 20001; 202-727-2525, 8:30AM-4:45PM. www.dcboee.org ✉ ☎ Fax ✋

GED Certificates

GED Testing Center, State Education Agency, 4200 Connecticut Ave NW, MB1005, Washington, DC 20008; 202-274-7173, Fax: 202-274-6507, 9AM-1PM. www.dcadultliteracy.org/ ✉ ✋

Fishing License and Hunting License Information
Access to Records is Restricted

Environmental Health Regulation, Fisheries & Wildlife Division, 51 N Street NE - 5th Fl, Washington, DC 20002-3323; 202-535-2266, Fax: 202-535-1359, 8AM-5PM. http://dchealth.dc.gov/about/Index_environmental.shtm Hunting of any kind is prohibited within the District of Columbia. Fishing records are not available to the public, they are only released as a FOIA request.

Florida

Governor's Office
The Capitol – 400 S Monroe St   850-488-4441
Tallahassee, FL 32399-0001   Fax 850-487-0801
www.myflorida.com/b_eog/owa/b_eog_www.html.
main_page   8AM-5PM

Attorney General's Office
Legal Affairs Department   850-414-3300
The Capitol, PL-01   Fax 850-410-1630
Tallahassee, FL 32399-1050   8AM-5PM
http://myfloridalegal.com

State Website: www.myflorida.com
Legislative Records: 850-488-4371
www.flsenate.gov/Welcome/index.cfm
State Archives
850-245-6700; http://dlis.dos.state.fl.us/barm/
Capital: Tallahassee, in Leon County

Search Unclaimed Property Online
http://up.dbf.state.fl.us/Isearch.cfm

Criminal Records
Florida Department of Law Enforcement, User Services Bureau, PO Box 1489, Tallahassee, FL 32302 (2331 Phillip Rd, Tallahassee, FL 32308); 850-410-8109, 850-410-8107, Fax: 850-410-8201, 8AM-5PM. www.fdle.state.fl.us ✉ 🖐 🖥

Statewide Court Records
Office of the State Courts Administrator, Supreme Court Bldg, 500 S Duval, Tallahassee, FL 32399-1900; 850-922-5081, Fax: 850-488-0156, 8AM-5PM. www.flcourts.org 🖥

Sexual Offender Registry
Florida Department of Law Enforcement, Sexual Offender/Predator Unit, PO Box 1489, Tallahassee, FL 32302 (2331 Phillips Rd, Tallahassee); 888-357-7332, 850-410-8572, Fax: 850-410-8599, 8AM-5PM. http://www3.fdle.state.fl.us/sexual_predators/index.asp ✉ ☎ Fax 🖐 🖥

Incarceration Records
Florida Department of Corrections, Central Records Office, 2601 Blair Stone Rd, Tallahassee, FL 32399-2500; 850-488-2533, 850-488-1503 (Records), 850-922-0000 (Parole Commission), Fax: 850-413-8302, 8AM-5PM. www.dc.state.fl.us ✉ ☎ Fax 🖐 🖥

Corporation Records, Limited Partnership Records, Limited Liability Company Records, Trademarks/Servicemarks, Fictitious Names, Federal Tax Liens
Division of Corporations, Department of State, PO Box 6327, Tallahassee, FL 32314 (409 E Gaines St, Tallahassee, FL 32399); 800-755-5111 (phone inquiries), 850-245-6053 (copy requests), 850-245-6056 (Annual Reports), 8AM-5PM. www.sunbiz.org ✉ ☎ Fax 🖐 🖥

Uniform Commercial Code
UCC Filings, FLORIDAUCC, Inc, 2670 Executive Center Circle West, #100, Tallahassee, FL 32301; 850-222-8526, 8-5PM. www.floridaucc.com ✉ 🖐 🖥

State Tax Liens
Records not maintained by a state level agency.
These records are filed and found at the county level.

Sales Tax Registrations
Florida Department of Revenue, Sales Tax Registration Records, 168 Blountstown Highway #C, Tallahassee, FL 32304-3702; 850-488-9925, Fax: 850-922-5936, 8AM-5PM. www.state.fl.us/dor ✉ Fax 🖐

Birth Certificates, Death Records, Marriage Certificates, Divorce Records
Department of Health, Office of Vital Statistics, PO Box 210, Jacksonville, FL 32231-0042 (1217 Pearl St, Jacksonville, FL 32202); 904-359-6900 x9000, 877-550-7330 (order line), 877-550-7428 (fax order line), Fax: 904-359-6993, 8AM-5PM. www.doh.state.fl.us ✉ ☎ Fax 🖐

Workers' Compensation Records
Workers Compensation Division, Information Management Unit, 200 E Gaines St, Tallahassee, FL 32399-4226; 850-488-3030, Fax: 850-414-7341, 7:30-5PM. www.fldfs.com/wc/ ✉ Fax 🖐

Driver Records
Division of Drivers Licenses, Bureau of Records, PO Box 5775, Tallahassee, FL 32314-5775 (2900 Apalachee Pky, MS90, Neil Kirkman Bldg, Tallahassee, FL 32399); 850-488-0250, 850-922-9000, Fax: 850-487-7080, 8AM-5PM. www.hsmv.state.fl.us ✉ 🖐 🖥

Vehicle Ownership, Vehicle Identification

Division of Motor Vehicles, Information Research Unit, Neil Kirkman Bldg, A-126, Tallahassee, FL 32399; 850-488-5665, 850-921-6122, Fax: 850-488-8983, 8-4:30. www.hsmv.state.fl.us ✉ ✋ 💻

Accident Reports

DHSMV- MS-28, Crash Records-Room A-325, 2900 Apalachee Prky, Tallahassee, FL 32399-0537; 850-488-5017, 850-488-1009 (Older Homicide Records (5 yrs)), Fax: 850-922-0488, 8AM-4:45PM. www.hsmv.state.fl.us ✉ ✋

Vessel Ownership, Vessel Registration

Dept of Highway Safety, Vessel Records, Bureau of Titles & Registrations, 2900 Apalachee Parkway, MS 68, Tallahassee, FL 32399; 850-922-9000, Fax: 850-921-1935, 8-5. www.hsmv.state.fl.us ✉ ✋

Voter Registration

Access to Records is Restricted

Dept of State - Division of Elections, 500 South Bronough St, RA Gray Building, Room 316, Tallahassee, FL 32399-0250; 850-245-6200, Fax: 850-245-6217, 8AM-5PM. http://election.dos.state.fl.us All individual searching must be done at the county level. However, the state maintains a central voter file for data and statistical purposes.

GED Certificates

GED Transcripts/Certificates, 325 W Gaines St Rm 634, Tallahassee, FL 32399; 850-245-0449, Fax: 850-245-0990, 8AM-5PM. www.firn.edu/doe/workforce/ged_dipl.htm ✉ ☎ Fax ✋

Hunting License and Fishing License Information

Fish & Wildlife Cons. Comm, Licensing & Permit Board, 2590 Executive Center Circle, #200, Tallahassee, FL 32301; 850-488-3641, Fax: 850-414-8212, 8AM-5PM. www.floridaconservation.org ✉ ✋

Georgia

Governor's Office
203 State Capitol
Atlanta, GA 30334
www.ganet.org/governor/index_flash.html

404-656-1776
Fax 404-657-7332
8AM-4:30PM

Attorney General's Office
40 Capitol Square SW
Atlanta, GA 30334-1300
www.law.state.ga.us

404-656-3300
Fax 404-651-9148
8AM-5PM

State Website: www.georgia.com/home.asp

Legislative Records
404-656-2370 www.legis.state.ga.us

State Archives
404-656-2393 www.sos.state.ga.us/archives/

Capital: Atlanta, in Fulton County

Search Unclaimed Property Online
www.state.ga.us/dor/ptd/ucp

Criminal Records

Georgia Bureau of Investigation, Attn: GCIC, PO Box 370748, Decatur, GA 30037-0748 (3121 Panthersville Rd); 404-244-2639, Fax: 404-244-2878, 8AM-4PM. www.ganet.org/gbi ✉ ✋ 💻

Statewide Court Records

Administrative Office of the Courts, 244 Washington St SW, #300, Atlanta, GA 30334-5900; 404-656-5171, Fax: 404-651-6449, 8:30-5. www.georgiacourts.org 💻

Sexual Offender Registry

Georgia Bureau of Investigations, GCIC - Sexual Offender Registry, PO Box 370748, Decatur, GA 30037-0748 (3121 Panthersville Rd, Decatur, GA 30034); 404-244-2835, Fax: 404-212-3028, 8AM-4PM. www.ganet.org/gbi/disclaim.html ✉ ✋ 💻

Incarceration Records

Georiga Department of Corrections, Inmate Records Office, Eastern Tower, 2 Martin Luther King, Jr. Drive, S.E., Atlanta, GA 30334-4900; 404-656-4593, Fax: 404-463-6232, 8AM-4:30PM. www.dcor.state.ga.us ✉ ☎ Fax ✋ 💻

Corporation Records, Limited Partnership Records, Limited Liability Partnerships, Limited Liability Company Records

Sec of State - Corporation Division, Record Searches, 315 W Tower, #2 ML King Drive, Atlanta, GA 30334-1530; 404-656-2817, 8AM-5PM. www.sos.state.ga.us/corporations ✉ ☎ ✋ 💻

Trademarks/Servicemarks

Secretary of State, Trademark Division, 2 Martin Luther King, Room 315, W Tower, Atlanta, GA 30334; 404-656-2861, Fax: 404-657-6380, 8AM-5PM. www.sos.state.ga.us/corporations/trademarks.htm ✉ ✋ 💻

Uniform Commercial Code

Superior Court Clerks' Cooperative Authority, 1875 Century Blvd, #100, Atlanta, GA 30345; 404-327-9058, Fax: 404-327-7877, 8:30AM-5PM. www.gsccca.org ✉ Fax ✋ 💻

Federal and State Tax Liens

Records not maintained by a state level agency.

All tax liens are filed at the county level.

Sales Tax Registrations

Sales & Use Tax Division, Registration Information, PO 49512, Atlanta, GA 30359-1512; 404-417-4490 (Registration), 404-417-6601 (General Info), Fax: 404-651-9490, 8AM-4:30PM. http://www2.state.ga.us/departments/dor

Birth Certificates, Death Records, Marriage Certificates, Divorce Records

Department of Human Resources, Vital Records Unit, 2600 Skyland Dr NE, Atlanta, GA 30319; 404-679-4701, 877-572-6343 (credit card line), Fax: 404-679-4730, 8AM-4PM. http://health.state.ga.us/programs/vitalrecords/index.asp ☒☎Fax✋

Workers' Compensation Records

State Board of Workers Compensation, 270 Peachtree St, NW, Atlanta, GA 30303-1299; 404-656-3875, 8AM-4:30PM. www.sbwc.georgia.gov/ ☒

Driver Records

Department of Motor Vehicle Safety, Driver's Services Section, MVR Unit, PO Box 80447, Conyers, GA 30013 (2206 East View Parkway, Conyers, GA 30013); 678-413-8441, 8AM-3:30PM. www.dmvs.ga.gov ☒✋🖳

Vehicle Ownership, Vehicle Identification

Department of Motor Vehicle Safety, Motor Vehicle Services - Research, PO Box 740381, Atlanta, GA 30374-0381; 404-362-6500, Fax: 404-362-2729, 8AM-4:30PM. www.dmvs.ga.gov ☒✋🖳

Accident Reports

Department of Motor Vehicle Safety, Accident Reporting Section, PO Box 80447, Conyers, GA 30013; 678-413-8647, Fax: 678-413-8584, 8AM-4:30PM. ☒☎✋

Vessel Ownership, Vessel Registration

Georgia Dept of Natural Resources, Boat Registration Office, PO Box 105310, Atlanta, Georgia 30348-5310; 770-414-3337, Fax: 770-414-3344, 8AM-4:30PM. www.gadnr.org/ ☒☎Fax✋

Voter Registration

Secretary of State, Elections Division, 2 Martin Luther King Dr SE, Suite 1104, Atlanta, GA 30334; 404-656-2871, Fax: 404-651-9531, 8AM-5PM. www.sos.state.ga.us/elections ☒Fax🖳

GED Certificates

GED Testing Service, 1800 Century Pl #555, Atlanta, GA 30345; 404-679-1644, 8:30AM-4:30PM www.dtae.org ☒✋

Hunting License and Fishing License Information

Access to Records is Restricted
Department of Natural Resources, Hunting & Fishing Licenses, 2189 Northlake Pkwy, Bldg 10, #108, Tucker, GA 30084; 770-918-6400, Fax: 770-414-3344, 8-4:30. www.georgiawildlife.com The request must be in writing and cite that under the Georgia Open Records Act you request that a search be done. The database may not be current for non-resident licenses and license purchases made via the website.

Hawaii

Governor's Office
State Capitol — 808-586-0034
415 S Beretania St — Fax 808-586-0006
Honolulu, HI 96813 — 7:45AM-5PM
http://gov.state.hi.us

Attorney General's Office
425 Queen St — 808-586-1500
Honolulu, HI 96813 — Fax 808-586-1239
www.state.hi.us/ag — 7:45AM-4:30PM

State Website: www.state.hi.us

Legislative Records
808-587-0700 www.capitol.hawaii.gov

State Archives
808-586-0329 www.state.hi.us/dags/archives

Capital: Honolulu, in Honolulu County

Search Unclaimed Property Online
www.ehawaiigov.org/cgi-bin/bf/ucp/exe/hiucp.cgi

Criminal Records

Hawaii Criminal Justice Data Center, Liane Moriyama, Administrator, 465 S King St, Room 101, Honolulu, HI 96813; 808-587-3106, 8AM-4PM. www.state.hi.us/hcjdc/ ☒✋

Statewide Court Records

Administrative Director of Courts, 417 S. King St, Honolulu, HI 96813; 808-539-4900, 808-539-4909 (Public Affairs Ofc.) Fax: 808-539-4855, 7:45AM-4:30PM. www.courts.state.hi.us/index.jsp 🖳

Sexual Offender Registry

Access to Records is Restricted
Hawaii Criminal Justice Data Center, Sexual Offender Registry, 465 S King St, Room 101, Honolulu, HI 96813; 808-587-3106, 8AM-4PM. www.state.hi.us/hcjdc/ Database not available for name searches. Court will decide if an offender's data is necessary to protect the public.

Key: Access state agency records by:. phone-☎ mail-☒ fax-Fax in person-✋ online-🖳 email-Email

Incarceration Records

Hawaii Department of Public Safety, Hawaii Criminal Justice Data Center, 465 South King Street, Room 101, Honolulu, HI 96813; 808-587-3100, 7:45AM-4:30PM. www.hawaii.gov/hcjdc/ ✉

Corporation Records, Trade Name, Limited Partnership Records, Assumed Name, Trademarks/Servicemarks, Limited Liability Company Records, Limited Liability Partnerships

Business Registration Division, PO Box 40, Honolulu, HI 96810 (1010 Richard St, 1st Fl, Honolulu, HI 96813); 808-586-2727, Fax: 808-586-2733, 7:45AM-4:30PM. www.businessregistrations.com ✉☎Fax✋💻

Uniform Commercial Code, Federal and State Tax Liens, Real Estate Recordings

UCC Division, Bureau of Conveyances, PO Box 2867, Honolulu, HI 96803 (Dept. of Land & Natural Resources, 1151 Punchbowl St, Honolulu); 808-587-0154, Fax: 808-587-4380, 7:45AM-4:30PM. www.state.hi.us/dlnr/bc/bc.html ✉✋💻

Sales Tax Registrations

State does not impose sales tax.

Birth Certificates, Death Records, Marriage Certificates, Divorce Records

State Department of Health, Vital Records Section, PO Box 3378, Honolulu, HI 96801 (1250 Punchbowl St, Room 103, Honolulu); 808-586-4533, 7:45AM-2:30PM. www.hawaii.gov/doh ✉✋💻

Workers' Compensation Records

Labor & Industrial Relations, Disability Compensation Div., 830 Punchbowl St, Room 209, Honolulu, HI 96813; 808-586-9174, Fax: 808-586-9219, 7:45-4:30PM. www.state.hi.us/hrd/workcmp.html ✉Fax✋

Driver Records

Traffic Violations Bureau, Abstract Section, 1111 Alakea St, 2nd Fl, Honolulu, HI 96813; 808-538-5530, 808-961-7470 (Hawaii Court), 808-244-2800 (Maui Court), 808-246-3330 (Kauai Ct), Fax: 808-538-5520, 7:45AM-9PM. www.hawaii.gov/dot/highways/ ✉✋

Vehicle Ownership, Vehicle Identification

Access to Records is Restricted

Accident Reports

Records not maintained by a state agency. Records are maintained at the county level at the police departments and are only available to those involved.

Vessel Ownership, Vessel Registration

Land & Natural Resources, Division of Boating & Recreation, 333 Queen St Rm 300, Honolulu, HI 96813; 808-587-1970, Fax: 808-587-1977, 7:45AM-4:30PM. www.hawaii.gov/dlnr/dbor/dbor.html ✉Fax✋

Voter Registration

Records not maintained by a state level agency.
Voter information is maintained by the County Clerks. City and County of Honolulu 808-523-4293; County of Hawaii 808-961-8277; County of Maui 808-270-7749; Kauai 808-241-6350.

GED Certificates

Department of Education, GED Records, 634 Pensacola, #222, Honolulu, HI 96814; 808-594-0170, Fax: 808-594-0181, 8AM-4PM. ✉Fax✋

Hunting License and Fishing License Information

Access to Records is Restricted
Land & Natural Resources Department, 1151 Punchbowl St, Kalanimokui Bldg, Honolulu, HI 96813; 808-587-0100 (Fishing), 808-587-0166 (Hunting), 7:45AM-4:30PM. www.state.hi.us/dlnr Fishing information is kept by the Aquatic Resources Division; Hunting information by the Division of Forestry & Wildlife. 808-587-0115 is fax for Fishing; 808-587-0160 is fax for Hunting. Limited record data is released to the public. Generally, data is only released to law enforcement.

Idaho

Governor's Office
PO Box 83720
Boise, ID 83720-0034
http://www2.state.id.us/gov/index.htm

208-334-2100
Fax 208-334-2175
8AM-6PM

Attorney General's Office
PO Box 83720
Boise, ID 83720-0010
http://www2.state.id.us/ag

208-334-2400
Fax 208-334-2530
8AM-5PM

Legislative Records: 208-334-2475
http://www2.state.id.us/legislat/legislat.html

State Website: www.state.id.us

State Archives
208-334-3356 http://idahohistory.net

Capital: Boise, in Ada County

Time Zone: MST*

* Idaho's ten northwestern-most counties are PST: They are: Benewah, Bonner, Boundary, Clearwater, Idaho, Kootenai, Latah, Lewis, Nez Perce, Shoshone.

Search Unclaimed Property Online

http://tax.idaho.gov/ucp_search_idaho.htm

Key: Access state agency records by:. phone-☎ mail-✉ fax-Fax in person-✋ online-💻 email-Email

Idaho Criminal Records

State Repository, Bureau of Criminal Identification, PO Box 700, Meridian, ID 83680-0700 (700 S Stratford Dr, Meridian); 208-884-7130, Fax: 208-884-7193, 8-4PM. www.isp.state.id.us ✉ ✋

Statewide Court Records

Administrative Director of the Courts, PO Box 83720, Boise, ID 83720-0101 (451 W State St, Boise, ID 83720); 208-334-2246, Fax: 208-334-2146, 9AM-5PM. www.isc.idaho.gov/ 💻

Sexual Offender Registry

State Repository, Central Sexual Offender Registry, PO Box 700, Meridian, ID 83680-0700 (700 S Stratford Dr, Meridian, ID 83642); 208-884-7305, Fax: 208-884-7193, 8AM-5PM. www.isp.state.id.us ✉ ✋ 💻

Incarceration Records

Dept. of Corrections, Records Bureau, 1299 N. Orchard Street, #110, Boise, ID 83706; 208-658-2000, Fax 208-327-7444, 8AM-5PM. www.corrections.state.id.us ✉ ☎ Fax ✋ 💻

Corporation Records, Limited Partnerships, Trademarks/Servicemarks, Limited Liability Companys, Limited Liability Partnerships, Assumed Names

Secretary of State, Corporation Division, PO Box 83720, Boise, ID 83720-0080 (700 W Jefferson, Boise, ID 83720); 208-334-2301, Fax: 208-334-2080, 8-5PM. www.idsos.state.id.us ✉ ☎ Fax ✋ 💻

Uniform Commercial Code, Federal and State Tax Liens

UCC Division, Secretary of State, PO Box 83720, Boise, ID 83720-0080 (700 W Jefferson, Boise, ID 83720); 208-334-

3191, Fax: 208-334-2847, 8AM-5PM. www.idsos.state.id.us ✉ ☎ Fax ✋ 💻

Sales Tax Registrations

Revenue Operations Division, Records Management, PO Box 36, Boise, ID 83722 (800 Park, Boise, ID 83722); 208-334-7660, 208-334-7792 (records mgmt.) Fax: 208-334-7650, 8AM-5:00PM. http://tax.idaho.gov/SalesUseTaxRate.htm ✉ ☎ Fax ✋ 💻

Birth Certificates, Marriage Certificates, Divorce Records

Vital Records, PO Box 83720, Boise, ID 83720-0036 (450 W State St, 1st Fl); 208-334-5988, Fax: 208-389-9096, 8-5PM. www.healthandwelfare.idaho.gov ✉ Fax

Death Records

Vital Records, PO Box 83720, Boise, ID 83720-0036 (450 W State St, 1st Fl); 208-334-5988, Fax: 208-389-9096, 8AM-5PM. www.healthandwelfare.idaho.gov/ Death index of records older than 50 available at http://abish.byui.edu/specialCollections/fhc/Death/searchForm.cfm. ✉ Fax 💻

Workers' Compensation Records

Industrial Commission of Idaho, Attn: Records Management, PO Box 83720, Boise, ID 83720-0041; 208-334-6000, Fax: 208-334-2321, 8AM-5PM. http://www2.state.id.us/iic ✉ Fax ✋

Driver Records

Idaho Transportation Department, Driver's Services, PO Box 34, Boise, ID 83731-0034 (3311 W State, Boise, ID 83703); 208-334-8736, Fax: 208-334-8739, 8:30AM-5PM. www.itd.idaho.gov/dmv/ ✉ Fax ✋ 💻

Vehicle Ownership, Vehicle Identification, Vessel Ownership

Idaho Transportation Department, Vehicle Services, PO Box 34, Boise, ID 83731-0034 (3311 W State St); 208-334-8773, 208-334-8663, Fax: 208-334-8542, 8:30AM-5PM. www.itd.idaho.gov/dmv/ ✉ Fax ✋ 💻

Accident Reports

Idaho Transportation Department, Office of Highway Safety-Accident Records, PO Box 7129, Boise, ID 83707-1129 (3311 W State St, Boise, ID 83707); 208-334-8100, Fax: 208-334-4430, 8AM-12:00PM; 1PM-5PM. ✉ ☎ Fax ✋

Vessel Registration

Idaho Parks & Recreation, PO Box 83720, Boise, ID 83720-0065 (5657 Warm Springs, Boise, ID 83712); 208-334-4197, Fax: 208-334-2639, 8AM-5PM. www.idahoparks.org ✉ ☎ Fax ✋

Voter Registration

Records not maintained by a state level agency.
Records are maintained by County Clerks. The counties will generally release name, address, and voting precinct on individual request. Lists may be purchased but not for commercial purposes.

GED Certificates

Department of Education, GED Testing, PO Box 83720, Boise, ID 83720-0027; 208-332-6980, Fax: 208-334-4664, 8AM-5PM. www.sde.state.id.us ✉ ☎ Fax ✋

Hunting License and Fishing License Information

ID Department of Fish & Game, Licenses Division, PO Box 25, Boise, ID 83707-0025 (1075 Park Blvd, Boise); 208-334-3717 (License Dept.), 208-334-3736 (Enforcement Ofc.), Fax: 208-334-2148, 8AM-5PM. http://fishandgame.idaho.gov/ ✉ ☎ ✋

Key: Access state agency records by:.   phone-☎   mail-✉   fax-Fax   in person-✋   online-💻   email-**Email**

Illinois

Governor's Office
222 S College, 1st Fl
Springfield, IL 62706
www.illinois.gov/gov/

217-782-0244
Fax 217-524-4049
8:30AM-5PM

Attorney General's Office
500 S 2nd St
Springfield, IL 62706
www.ag.state.il.us

217-782-1090
Fax 217-524-4701
8:45AM-4:45PM

State Website: http://www100.state.il.us

Legislative Records: 217-782-3944;
House (or Senate) Bills Division, 217-782-7017
www.legis.state.il.us

State Archives: 217-782-4682
www.sos.state.il.us/departments/archives/archives.html

Capital: Springfield, Sangamon County

Search Unclaimed Property Online

www.cashdash.net

Criminal Records

Illinois State Police, Bureau of Identification, 260 N Chicago St, Joliet, IL 60432-4075; 815-740-5216 x5184, Fax: 815-740-5215, 8AM-4PM M-F. www.isp.state.il.us ✉ ✋ 💻

Statewide Court Records

Administrative Office of Courts, 222 N. LaSalle - 13th Fl, Chicago, IL 60601; 312-793-3250, Fax: 312-793-1335, 8AM-5PM. www.state.il.us/court/ 💻

Sexual Offender Registry

Illinois State Police, SOR Unit, 400 Iles Park Place, #140, Springfield, IL 62703-2978; 217-785-0653, 8AM-4PM M-F. www.isp.state.il.us/sor/frames.htm 💻

Incarceration Records

Illinois Department of Corrections, Public Information Office, PO Box 19277, Springfield, IL 62794-9277 (1301 Concordia Court,, Springfield, IL 62794); 217-522-2666 x2008, Fax: 217-522-3568, 8:30-5PM www.idoc.state.il.us ✉ ☎ 💻

Corporation Records, Limited Partnership Records, Trade Names, Assumed Name, Limited Liability Company Records

Department of Business Services, Corporate Department, 330 Howlett Bldg, 3rd Fl, Copy Section, Springfield, IL 62756 (501 S 2nd St, Springfield, IL 62756); 217-782-7880, 217-782-9521 (Name Availability), 217-524-5248 (Expedited Srv), Fax: 217-782-4528, 8-4:30PM. www.ilsos.net/ ✉ ☎ ✋ 💻

Uniform Commercial Code, Federal Tax Liens

Secretary of State, UCC Division, 2nd & Edwards St, Howlett Bldg, #350 West, Springfield, IL 62756; 217-782-7518, 8AM-4:30PM.
www.cyberdriveillinois.com ✉ ✋

State Tax Liens

Records not maintained by a state level agency.
All state tax liens are filed at the county.

Sales Tax Registrations

Revenue Department, Taxpayer Services, PO Box 19041, Springfield, IL 62794-9041 (101 W Jefferson, Springfield, IL 62702); 800-732-8866, 217-782-7897, Fax: 217-782-4217, 8AM-5PM. www.iltax.com/Businesses/ ✉ ☎ ✋

Birth Certificates, Death Records

IL Department of Public Health, Division of Vital Records, 605 W Jefferson St, Springfield, IL 62702-5097; 217-782-6554, 217-782-6553 (Instructions), Fax: 217-523-2648, 8:30AM-5PM. www.idph.state.il.us/vitalrecords/index.htm ✉ ☎ Fax ✋ 💻

Marriage Certificates, Divorce Records

Records not maintained by a state level agency.
State will verify marriage or divorce from 1962-present, but will not issue certificate. Find records of marriage and divorce at the county of issue. Search free statewide Marriage Index for 1763-1900 of State

Archives at www.cyberdriveillinois.com/departments/archives/marriage.html. 💻

Workers' Compensation Records

Industrial Commission, 100 W Randolph, 8th Fl, Chicago, IL 60601; 312-814-6611, 8:30AM-5PM. www.state.il.us/agency/iic ✉ ☎ ✋ 💻

Driver Records

Abstract Information Unit, Drivers Services Department, 2701 S Dirksen Prky, Springfield, IL 62723; 217-782-2720, 8AM-4:30PM. www.sos.state.il.us ✉ ✋ 💻

Vehicle Ownership, Vehicle Identification

Vehicle Services Department, Vehicle Record Inquiry, 501 S 2nd Street #408, Springfield, IL 62756; 217-782-6992, Fax: 217-524-0122, 8AM-4:30PM. www.sos.state.il.us ✉ ✋ 💻

Accident Reports (Crash Reports)

Illinois State Police, Patrol Records Unit, 500 Iles Park Place, Ste 200, Springfield, IL 62703-2982; 217-785-0614, Fax: 217-785-2325, 8AM-5PM. www.isp.state.il.us ✉ ☎ ✋ 💻

Vessel Ownership, Vessel Registration

Department of Natural Resources, 1natural Resources Way, Springfield, IL 62702; 800-382-1696, 217-557-0180, Fax: 217-782-5016, 8AM-5PM. http://dnr.state.il.us ✉ ☎

Voter Registration

Access to Records is Restricted
Board of Elections, 1020 S Spring, Springfield, IL 62704; 217-782-4141, Fax: 217-782-5959, 8AM-4:30PM. www.elections.state.il.us The data is not considered public record at the state level and is only available in bulk format to political committees and government agencies. County Clerks control the information at the local level.

GED Certificates

Access to Records is Restricted
State Board of Education, GED Testing, 100 N 1st St S-230, Springfield, IL 62777; 217-782-2948 (Main Number), Fax: 217-524-8750, 8:AM-4:30PM. All GED data is kept at the county level. You must contact the county where the test was taken. If you need assistance determining which county, contact the State Board of Education at the number listed here.

Hunting License and Fishing License Information

Access to Records is Restricted
IL Dept of Natural Resources, License Section, PO Box 19459, Springfield, IL 62794; 217-782-2965, Fax: 217-782-5016, 8:30AM-5PM. http://dnr.state.il.us At this time, records are not available. The vendors hold license records for years prior to 2002. Search Vendor at http://dnr.state.il.us/admin/systems/vendor.htm.

Indiana

Governor's Office
206 State House
Indianapolis, IN 46204-2797
www.in.gov/gov

317-232-4567
Fax 317-232-3443
8AM-5PM

Attorney General's Office
402 W Washington
Indianapolis, IN 46204
www.in.gov/attorneygeneral

317-232-6201
8:30AM-5PM

State Website: www.state.in.us

Legislative Records
317-232-9856 www.in.gov/legislative

State Archives
317-591-5222 www.in.gov/icpr

Capital: Indianapolis, in Marion County

Time Zone: EST*

* Indiana's eleven northwestern-most counties are CST: They are: Gibson, Jasper, Laporte, Lake, Newton, Porter, Posey, Spencer, Starke, Vanderburgh, Warrick.

Search Unclaimed Property Online

www.IN.gov/apps/ag/ucp/ucp

Criminal Records

Indiana State Police, Central Records, IGCN - 100 N Senate Ave, Rm N302, Indianapolis, IN 46204-2259; 317-232-8266, Fax: 317-233-8813, 8AM-4PM. www.IN.gov/isp/ ✉ ✋ 🖥

Statewide Court Records

State Court Administrator, 200 W Washington St, #1080, Indianapolis, IN 46204; 317-232-2542, Fax: 317-233-6586, 8:30AM-4:30PM. www.in.gov/judiciary/ 🖥

Sexual Offender Registry

Sex and Violent Offender Directory Manager, Indiana Criminal Justice Institute, One North Capitol, Suite 1000, Indianapolis, IN 46204; 317-232-1233, Fax: 317-232-4979. https://secure.in.gov/serv/cji_sor ✉ ☎ ✋ 🖥

Incarceration Records

Department of Corrections, IGCS, Supervisor of Records, Room E-334, 302 W Washington St, Indianapolis IN 46204; 317-232-5765, Fax: 317-232-5728, 8AM-4:30PM. www.in.gov/indcorrection ✉ ☎ Fax 🖥

Corporation Records, Limited Partnerships, Fictitious Name, Assumed Name, Limited Liability Company Records, Limited Liability Partnerships

Corporation Division, Secretary of State, 302 W Washington St, Room E018, Indianapolis, IN 46204; 317-232-6576, Fax: 317-233-3387, 8AM-5:30PM M-F. www.IN.gov/sos/ ✉ ☎ ✋ 🖥

Trademarks/Servicemarks

Secretary of State, Trademark Division, 302 W Washington St, IGC-South, Room E018, Indianapolis, IN 46204; 317-232-6540, Fax: 317-233-3675, 8:AM-4:30PM. www.in.gov/sos/business/trademarks.html ✉ ☎ Fax ✋

Uniform Commercial Code

UCC Division, Secretary of State, 302 W Washington St, #E-018, Indianapolis, IN 46204; 317-233-3984, Fax: 317-233-3387, www.in.gov/sos/business/ucc.html 8AM-5:30PM. ✉ ✋ 🖥

Federal and State Tax Liens

Records not maintained by a state agency. Tax liens found at county level.

Sales Tax Registrations

Dept of Revenue, Sales Tax Registrations, PO Box 7218, Indianapolis, IN 46207; 317-233-4015, Fax: 317-232-2103, 8:15-4:45PM. www.in.gov/dor/ ✉ ☎

Birth Certificates, Death Records

State Department of Health, Vital Records Office, PO Box 7125, Indianapolis, IN 46206 (2 N Meridian); 317-233-2700, Fax: 317-233-7210, 8:15AM-4:45PM. www.in.gov/isdh/index.htm ✉ Fax ✋ 🖥

Key: Access state agency records by:. phone-☎ mail-✉ fax-Fax in person-✋ online-🖥 email-Email

Marriage Certificates, Divorce Records

Records not maintained by a state level agency.

Marriage and divorce records are found at county of issue. The index may also be found at the Indiana State Library.

Workers' Compensation Records

Workers Compensation Board, 402 W Washington St, Room W196, Indianapolis, IN 46204-2753; 317-232-3808, Fax: 317-233-5493, 8AM-4:30PM. www.in.gov/workcomp/index.html ✉

Driver Records

BMV-Driving Records, 100 N Senate Ave, Indiana Government Center North, Room N405, Indianapolis, IN 46204; 317-232-6000 ext. 2, 8:15AM-4:30PM. www.IN.gov/bmv/ ✉ 🖐 💻

Vehicle Ownership, Vehicle Identification, Vessel Ownership, Vessel Registration

Bureau of Motor Vehicles, Records, 100 N Senate Ave, Room N404, Indianapolis, IN 46204; 317-233-2513 (Titles), 317-233-6000 (Registration), 8:15AM-4:45PM. www.in.gov/bmv/ ✉ 🖐 💻

Accident Reports

State Police Department, Vehicle Crash Records Sections, Room N301, Indiana Government Center, Indianapolis, IN 46204; 317-232-8286, Fax: 317-232-0652, 8AM-4PM. ✉ ☎ 🖐

Voter Registration

Access to Records is Restricted

Election Division, 302 Washington, Room E-204, Indianapolis, IN 46204-2767; 317-232-3939, Fax: 317-233-6793, 8AM-4:30PM. www.IN.gov/sos/elections/ This agency will not sell records for commercial or investigative reasons, but will sell bulk data for political purposes. Circuit Court has records locally.

GED Certificates

Division of Adult Education, GED Testing, State House Rm 229, Indianapolis, IN 46204-2798; 317-232-0522, Fax: 317-233-0859, 8AM-4:30PM. www.doe.state.in.us/adulted/ ✉**Fax**

Hunting License and Fishing License Information

Records not maintained by a state level agency.

There is not a true statewide centralized database. Llicenses purchased online are warehoused by www.accessIndiana.com. Vendors throughout the state keep all hard copies of their records.

Iowa

Governor's Office
State Capitol Bldg
Des Moines, IA 50319
www.governor.state.ia.us/
515-281-5211
Fax 515-281-6611
8AM-4:30PM

Attorney General's Office
Hoover Bldg, 1305 E Walnut St
Des Moines, IA 50319
www.state.ia.us/government/ag
515-281-5164
Fax 515-281-4209
8AM-4:30PM

State Website: www.iowa.gov/state/main/index.html

Legislative Records
515-281-5129 www.legis.state.ia.us
State Archives
515-281-5111 www.iowahistory.org
Capital: Des Moines, in Polk County

Search Unclaimed Property Online
http://greatiowatreasurehunt.com/dsp_search.cfm

Criminal Records

Division of Criminal Investigations, Bureau of Identification, Wallace State Office Bldg, 502 E. 9th, Des Moines, IA 50319; 515-281-4776, Fax: 515-242-6876, 8AM-4:30PM. www.state.ia.us/government/dps/dci/crimhist.htm ✉**Fax**🖐

Statewide Court Records

State Court Administrator, Judicial Branch Bldg, 111 East Court Ave, Des Moines, IA 50319; 515-281-5241, Fax: 515-242-0014, 8AM-4:30PM. www.judicial.state.ia.us/courtadmin 💻

Sexual Offender Registry

Division of Criminal Investigations, SOR Unit, Wallace State Office Bldg, Des Moines, IA 50319; 515-281-8716, Fax: 515-242-6297, 8AM-4:30PM. www.iowasexoffenders.com/ ✉ 💻

Incarceration Records

Iowa Department of Corrections, 420 Watson Powell Jr. Way,, Des Moines, IA 50309-1639; 515-242-5710, Faxes: 515-281-4062 and 515-281-7345, 8AM-4:30PM. www.doc.state.ia.us ✉ ☎ 💻

State Tax Liens

Records not maintained by a state level agency. Records are found at the county recorder's offices.

Corporation Records, Limited Liability Company Records, Fictitious Name, Limited Partner Records, Trademarks/Servicemarks

Secretary of State - Corporation Division, 321 E 12th Street, 1st Fl, Lucas Bldg, Des Moines, IA 50319; 515-281-5204, Fax: 515-242-5953, 8AM-4:30PM. www.sos.state.ia.us ✉ ☎ **Fax** 🖐 💻

Uniform Commercial Code, Federal Tax Liens

UCC Division, Secretary of State, 1st Fl, Lucas Bldg, Des Moines, IA 50319; 515-281-5204, 515-242-5953 (Other Fax Line), Fax: 515-242-6556, 8AM-4:30PM. www.sos.state.ia.us ✉ ☎ Fax ✍ 🖥

Sales Tax Registrations

Department of Revenue, Taxpayer Services Division, Hoover State Office Bldg, Des Moines, IA 50306-0465; 515-281-3114, Fax: 515-242-6487, 8AM-4PM. www.state.ia.us/tax ✉ ☎ Fax

Birth Certificates, Death Records, Marriage Certificates

Iowa Department of Public Health, Bureau of Vital Records, 321 E 12th St, Lucas Bldg, Des Moines, IA 50319-0075; 515-281-4944, 515-281-5871 (recording), 7-4:45PM. www.idph.state.ia.us ✉ ☎ ✍

Divorce Records

Records not maintained by a state level agency. Divorce records are found at the county court issuing the decree.

Workers' Compensation Records

Iowa Workforce Development, Division of Workers' Compensation, 1000 E Grand Ave, Des Moines, IA 50319; 515-281-5387, Fax: 515-281-6501, 8AM-4:30PM. www.iowaworkforce.org/wc ✉ Fax ✍

Driver Records

Department of Transportation, Driver Service Records Section, PO Box 9204, Des Moines, IA 50306-9204 (Park Fair Mall, 100 Euclid, Des Moines, IA 50306); 515-244-9124, 800-532-1121 (Iowa only), Fax: 515-237-3152, 8AM-4:30PM. www.dot.state.ia.us/mvd ✉ Fax ✍ 🖥

Vehicle Ownership, Vehicle Identification

Department of Transportation, Office of Vehicle Services, PO Box 9278, Des Moines, IA 50306-9278 (Park Fair Mall, 100 Euclid); 515-237-3148, 515-237-3049, Fax: 515-237-3181, 8AM-4:30PM. www.dot.state.ia.us/mvd/ ✉ Fax ✍ 🖥

Accident Reports

Department of Transportation, Office of Driver Services, Park Fair Mall, 100 Euclid, Des Moines, IA 50306; 515-244-9124, 800-532-1121, Fax: 515-239-1837, 8AM-4:30PM. www.dot.state.ia.us/mvd/ods/index.htm ✉ Fax ✍

Vessel Ownership, Vessel Registration

Records not maintained by a state level agency.
Vessels are registered at the county level.

Voter Registration

Secretary of State, Voter Registration Division, Lucas State Office Building, 1st Fl, Des Moines, IA 50319; 515-281-5781, Fax: 515-242-5953, 8AM-4:30PM. www.sos.state.ia.us ☎ Fax ✍

GED Certificates

Department of Education, GED Records, Grimes State Office Building, Des Moines, IA 50319-0146; 515-281-7308, 515-281-3636, Fax: 515-281-6544, 8AM-5PM. ✉ ☎ Fax ✍

Hunting License and Fishing License Information

Department of Natural Resources, Wallace Building, 502 E 9th Street, Des Moines, IA 50319-0034; 515-281-8688, Fax: 515-281-6794, 8AM-4PM. www.state.ia.us ✉ ☎ Fax ✍

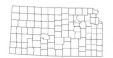

Kansas

Governor's Office
   State Capitol Bldg, Room 212S   785-296-3232
   Topeka, KS 66612-1590   Fax 785-296-7973
   www.ksgovernor.org/   8AM-5PM

Attorney General's Office
   Memorial Hall, 120 SW 10th Ave   785-296-2215
   Topeka, KS 66612-1597   Fax 785-296-6296
   www.accesskansas.org/ksag/   8AM-5PM

Legislative Records: 785-296-2149
   www.kslegislature.org

State Website: www.accesskansas.org

State Archives: 785-272-8681   www.kshs.org

Capital: Topeka, in Shawnee County

Time Zone: CST*
   * Kansas' five western-most counties are MST: They are: Greeley, Hamilton, Kearny, Sherman, Wallace,

Search Unclaimed Property Online

www.kansascash.com/cgi-win/lookup_1.kst

Criminal Records

Kansas Bureau of Investigation, Criminal Records Division, 1620 SW Tyler, Crim. History Record Sec., Topeka, KS 66612-1837; 785-296-8200, Fax: 785-368-7162, www.accesskansas.org/kbi/ ✉ Fax 🖥

Statewide Court Records

Judicial Administrator, Kansas Judicial Center, 301 SW 10th St,, Topeka, KS 66612-1507; 785-296-4873, Fax: 785-296-7076, www.kscourts.org ☎ 🖥

Sexual Offender Registry

Kansas Bureau of Investigation, Sexual Offender Registry, 1620 SW Tyler, Topeka, KS 66612-1837; 785-296-8200, Fax: 785-296-6781, 8AM-5PM. www.accesskansas.org/kbi/ro.shtml ✉ Fax ✍ 🖥

Key: Access state agency records by:. phone-☎   mail-✉   fax-Fax   in person-✍   online-🖥   email-Email

Incarceration Records

Kansas Department of Corrections, Public Information Officer, 900 SW Jackson, 4th Fl, Topeka, KS 66612-1284; 785-296-3310, Fax: 785-296-7023, 8AM-5PM. http://docnet.dc.state.ks.us ✉ ☎Fax🖳

Corporation Records, Limited Partnerships, Limited Liability Companys

Secretary of State, Memorial Hall, 1st Fl, 120 SW 10th Ave, Topeka, KS 66612-1594; 785-296-4564, Fax: 785-296-4570, 8AM-5PM. www.kssos.org/main.html ✉ ☎Fax🖐🖳

Trademarks/Servicemarks

Secretary of State, Trademarks/ Servicemarks Division, 120 SW 10th Ave, Rm 100, Topeka, KS 66612-1240; 785-296-4564, Fax: 785-296-4570, 8AM-5PM. www.kssos.org ✉ ☎Fax🖐

Uniform Commercial Code, Federal and State Tax Liens

Secretary of State - UCC Searches, Memorial Hall, 1st Fl, 120 SW 10th Ave, Topeka, KS 66612; 785-296-4564, Fax: 785-296-3659, www.kssos.org/business/business_ucc.html ✉ ☎Fax🖐🖳

Sales Tax Registrations

Access to Records is Restricted

Department of Revenue, Record requests, Docking State Office Bldg, 915 SW Harrison, Topeka, KS 66625-3570; 785-296-3081, Fax: 785-296-7928, 7AM-5PM. www.ksrevenue.org/ Sales tax registration information is considered confidential and not public record.

Birth Certificates, Marriage Certificates, Divorce & Death Records

Dept. of Health & Environment, Office of Vital Statistics, 1000 SW Jackson, #120, Topeka, KS 66612-2221; 785-296-1400, 785-296-3253 (Phone Credit Card Orders), Fax: 785-357-4332, 8AM-5PM. www.kdhe.state.ks.us/vital ✉ ☎Fax🖐

Workers' Compensation Records

Human Resources Department, Workers Compensation Division, 800 SW Jackson, Suite 600, Topeka, KS 66612-1227; 785-296-6762, Fax: 785-296-3430, 8-5PM. www.dol.ks.gov/index.html ✉ ☎Fax🖐

Driver Records, Accident Reports

Department of Revenue, Driver Control Bureau, PO Box 12021, Topeka, KS 66612-2021 (Docking State Office Bldg, 915 Harrison, Rm 100, Topeka); 785-296-3671, Fax: 785-296-6851, 8AM-4:45PM. www.ksrevenue.org/vehicle.htm ✉ 🖐🖳

Vehicle Ownership, Vehicle Identification

Division of Vehicles, Title and Registration Bureau, 915 Harrison, Rm 155, Topeka, KS 66626-0001; 785-296-3621, Fax: 785-296-3852, 8AM-4:45PM. www.ksrevenue.org/vehicle.htm ✉ 🖐🖳

Vessel Ownership, Vessel Registration

Department of Wildlife & Parks, Boat Registration, 512 SE 25th Ave, Pratt, KS 67124-8174; 620-672-5911, Fax: 620-672-3013, 8AM-5PM M-F. www.kdwp.state.ks.us ✉Fax🖐

Voter Registration

Access to Records is Restricted

Secretary of State - Elections Division, Memorial Hall, 1st Fl, 120 SW 10th Ave, Topeka, KS 66612-1594; 785-296-4564, Fax: 785-291-3051, 8AM-5PM. www.kssos.org Individual records must be searched at the county level.

GED Certificates

Board of Regents, GED Records, 1000 SW Jackson St #520, Topeka, KS 66612-1368; 785-296-3191, Fax: 785-296-0983, 8-4:30PM. www.kansasregents.org ✉

Hunting License and Fishing License Information

Dept of Wildlife & Parks, Licensing and Permits, 512 SE 25th Ave, Pratt, KS 67124; 620-672-5911, Fax 620-672-3013, 8AM-5PM. www.kdwp.state.ks.us ✉🖐

Kentucky

Governor's Office
700 Capitol Ave, Room 100   502-564-2611
Frankfort, KY 40601   Fax 502-564-2517
http://gov.state.ky.us   7:30AM-5PM

Attorney General's Office
700 Capitol Ave, Ste. 118   502-696-5300
Frankfort, KY 40601   Fax 502-564-2894
www..law.state.ky.us   8AM-5PM

State Website: www.kentucky.gov

Legislative Records
502-372-7181 www.lrc.state.ky.us

Archives: 502-564-8300   www.kdla.ky.gov/index.htm

Capital: Frankfort, in Franklin County

Time Zone: EST*

* Kentucky's forty western-most counties are CST: They are: Adair, Allen, Ballard, Barren, Breckinridge, Butler, Caldwell, Calloway, Carlisle, Christian, Clinton, Crittenden, Cumberland, Daviess, Edmonson, Fulton, Graves, Grayson, Hancock, Hart, Henderson, Hickman, Hopkins, Livingstone, Logan, Marshall, McCracken, McLean, Metcalfe, Monroe, Muhlenberg, Ohio, Russell, Simpson, Todd, Trigg, Union, Warren, Wayne, Webster.

Search KY Unclaimed Property Online

www.missingmoney.com/main/index.cfm

Key: Access state agency records by:. phone-☎   mail-✉   fax-Fax   in person-🖐   online-🖳   email-Email

Kentucky Criminal Records

Kentucky State Police, Criminal Identification and Records Branch, 1250 Louisville Rd, Frankfort, KY 40601; 502-227-8713, Fax: 502-226-7422, 8-4PM. www.kentuckystatepolice.org ✉ ✋

Statewide Court Records

Administrative Office of Courts, Pre-trail Services Records Division, 100 Mill Creek Park, Frankfort, KY 40601; 502-573-1682, 800-928-6381, Fax: 502-573-1669, 7:30-5. www.kycourts.net ✉ ✋ 💻

Sexual Offender Registry

Kentucky State Police, Criminal Identification and Records Branch, 1250 Louisville Rd, Frankfort, KY 40601; 502-227-8718, 866-564-5652 (Alert Line), Fax: 502-226-7419, 8AM-4PM. www.kentuckystatepolice.org/sor.htm ☎☎💻

Incarceration Records

Kentucky Department of Corrections, Offender Information Services, PO Box 2400, Frankfort, KY 40602-2400 (275 E. Main, Room 619, Frankfort, KY 40602); 502-564-2433, 800-511-1670 (Victim Notification Line), Fax: 502-564-1471, 8AM-4:30PM. www.corrections.ky.gov ✉Fax💻

Corporation Records, Limited Partnerships, Assumed Name, Limited Liability Company Records

Secretary of State, Corporate Records, PO Box 718, Frankfort, KY 40602-0718 (700 Capitol Ave, Room 156, Frankfort, KY 40601); 502-564-7330, Fax: 502-564-4075, 8AM-4PM. www.sos.state.ky.us ✉☎Fax✋💻

Trademarks/Servicemarks

Secretary of State, Trademarks Section, 700 Capitol Ave, Suite 152, Frankfort, KY 40601; 502-564-2848 x442, Fax: 502-564-1484, 8AM-4:30PM. www.sos.state.ky.us ✉☎Fax✋💻

Uniform Commercial Code

UCC Division, Secretary of State, PO Box 1470, Frankfort, KY 40602 (363C Versailles Rd, Mare Manor, Frankfort); 502-573-0265, Fax: 502-573-0259, 8AM-4:30PM. www.kysos.com ✉✋💻

Federal and State Tax Liens

Records not maintained by a state level agency.

All tax liens are at the county level.

Sales Tax Registrations

Revenue Cabinet, Tax Compliance Department, Sales Tax Section, Station 53, PO Box 181, Frankfort, KY 40602-0181 (200 Fair Oaks, Bldg 2, Frankfort); 502-564-5170, Fax: 502-564-2041, 8AM-4:30PM. http://revenue.ky.gov ✉✋

Birth Certificates, Death Records, Marriage Certificates, Divorce Records

Department for Public Health, Vital Statistics, 275 E Main St - IE-A, Frankfort, KY 40621-0001; 502-564-4212, Fax: 502-227-0032, 8AM-4PM. http://chs.ky.gov/publichealth/vital.htm ✉☎Fax✋💻

Workers' Compensation Records

Kentucky Office of Workers' Claims, Prevention Park, 657 To Be Announced Ave, Frankfort, KY 40601; 502-564-5550, Fax: 502-564-5732, 8AM-4:30PM. http://labor.ky.gov/dwc ✉Fax✋

Driver Records

Division of Driver Licensing, KY Transportation Cabinet, 200 Mero Street, Frankfort, KY 40622; 502-564-6800 x2250, Fax: 502-564-5787, 8-4:30PM. www.kytc.state.ky.us/drlic/ ✉✋💻

Vehicle Ownership, Vehicle Identification

Department of Motor Vehicles, Division of Motor Vehicle Licensing, PO Box 2014, Frankfort, KY 40622; 502-564-4076 (Title History), 502-564-3298 (Other Requests), 502-564-2737 (Questions), Fax: 502-564-1686, 8AM-4:30PM. www.kytc.state.ky.us ✉✋💻

Accident Reports

State Police, Criminal Ident. & Records Branch, 1250 Louisville Rd, Frankfort, KY 40601; 502-226-2169, Fax: 502-226-7418, www.kentuckystatepolice.org 8AM-4:30PM. ✉Fax✋

Vessel Ownership, Vessel Registration

Division of Motor Vehicle Licensing, Vessel Titles and Registration, State Office Building, 3rd Fl, Frankfort, KY 40622; 502-564-2737 (Registration), 8AM-5PM. www.kytc.state.ky.us ✉✋

Voter Registration

State Board of Elections, 140 Walnut, Frankfort, KY 40601; 502-573-7100, Fax: 502-573-4369, 8AM-4:30PM. www.kysos.com/index/main/elecdiv.asp ✉Fax✋

GED Certificates

Dept for Adult Education and Literacy, GED Program, Capitol Plaza Tower, 500 Mero St, 3rd Fl, Frankfort, KY 40601; 502-573-5114 x2, Fax: 502-573-5436. http://adulted.state.ky.us ✉✋

Hunting License and Fishing License Information

Fish & Wildlife Resources Department, Division of Administrative Services, 1 Game Farm Rd, Arnold Mitchell Bldg, Frankfort, KY 40601; 502-564-4224, Fax: 502-564-6508, 8AM-4:30PM. www.kdfwr.state.ky.us ✉Fax✋

Louisiana

Governor's Office
  PO Box 94004   225-342-0991
  Baton Rouge, LA 70804-9004   Fax 225-342-7099
  www.gov.state.la.us   8AM-5PM

Attorney General's Office
  LA Department of Justice   225-342-7013
  PO Box 94005   Fax 225-342- 8703
  Baton Rouge, LA 70804-9005   8:30AM-5PM
  www.ag.state.la.us

State Website: www.state.la.us

Legislative Records
  225-342-2456 www.legis.state.la.us
State Archives: 225-922-1000
  www.sec.state.la.us/archives/archives/archives-
  index.htm
Capital: Baton Rouge, in East Baton Rouge Parish

  Search Unclaimed Property Online

  www.treasury.state.la.us/ucpm/index.htm

Criminal Records

Access to Records is Restricted
State Police, Bureau of Criminal Identification, 7979 Independence Blvd, Baton Rouge, LA 70806-6409; 225-925-6095, Fax: 225-925-7005, 8AM-4:30PM. www.lsp.org Records are RESTRICTED and are not available to the public in general. Records are available for employment or licensing purposes as state law dictates. Authorized forms are available from this department. ✉**Fax** 🤚

Statewide Court Records

Judicial Administrator, Judicial Council of the Supreme Court, 400 Royal Street, Suite 1190, New Orleans, LA 70130-8101; 504-310-2550, Fax: 504-310-2587, 9AM-5PM. www.lasc.org ✉ 🖥

Sexual Offender Registry

State Police, Sex Offender and Child Predator Registry, PO Box 66614, Box A-6, Baton Rouge, LA 70896; 225-925-6100, 800-858-0551, Fax: 225-925-7005, 8-4:30PM. www.lasocpr.lsp.org/socpr/ ✉☎**Fax**🤚🖥

Incarceration Records

Department of Public Safety and Corrections, P.O. Box 94304, Attn: Office of Adult Services, Baton Rouge, LA 70804-9304; 225-342-6642, 225-342-9711 (Locator), Fax: 225-342-3349, 8AM-4:30PM. www.corrections.state.la.us ✉☎**Fax**🖥

Corporation Records, Limited Partnership Records, Limited Liability Company Records, Trademarks/Servicemarks

Commercial Division, Corporation Department, PO Box 94125, Baton Rouge, LA 70804-9125 (8549 United Plaze Blvd, Baton Rouge); 225-925-4704, Fax: 225-925-4726, 8AM-4:30PM. www.sos.louisiana.gov ✉☎**Fax**🤚🖥

Uniform Commercial Code

Secretary of State, UCC Records, PO Box 94125, Baton Rouge, LA 70804; 800-256-3758, Fax: 225-342-7011, 8AM-4:30PM. www.sec.state.la.us/comm/ucc/ucc-index.htm 🖥

Federal and State Tax Liens

Records not maintained by a state level agency.
Records are filed with the Clerk of Court at the parish level.

Sales Tax Registrations

Access to Records is Restricted
Revenue Department, Taxpayer Services Division, PO Box 201, Baton Rouge, LA 70821-0201 (617 N 3rd St, Baton Rouge, LA 70802); 225-219-7356, Fax: 225-219-2210, 8AM-4:30PM. www.rev.state.la.us This agency will confirm is an entity has a sales tax permit. It will only provide registration information to the registrant itself. ✉☎🤚

Birth Certificates, Death Records

Vital Records Registry, Office of Public Health, PO Box 60630, New Orleans, LA 70160 (325 Loyola Ave Room 102, New Orleans); 504-568-5152, 504-568-8353, 800-454-9570, Fax: 866-761-1855, 8-4. www.oph.dhh.state.la.us/recordsstatistics/vitalrecords/ ✉**Fax**🤚🖥

Marriage Certificates, Divorce Records

Records not maintained by a state level agency.
Only Orleans Parish marriage records are available from 1948 on at the VR Registry. Other marriage & all divorce records are found at parish of event. Marriage Records older than 50 years are open to the public.

Workers' Compensation Records

Department of Labor, Office of Workers' Compensation, PO Box 94040, Baton Rouge, LA 70804-9040 (LA Department of Labor, Office of Workers' Compensation, Baton Rouge, LA 70802); 800-201-3457, Fax: 225-342-7582, 8AM-5PM. www.laworks.net ✉☎**Fax**🤚

Driver Records

Dept of Public Safety and Corrections, Office of Motor Vehicles, PO Box 64886, Baton Rouge, LA 70896 (109 S Foster Dr, Baton Rouge); 877-368-5463, 225-925-6388, Fax: 225-925-6915, 8AM-4:30PM. www.expresslane.org ✉☎**Fax**🤚🖥

Vehicle Ownership, Vehicle Identification

Department of Public Safety & Corrections, Office of Motor Vehicles, PO Box 64886, Baton Rouge, LA 70896 (7979 Independence Blvd, Baton Rouge, LA 70806); 225-925-4955, 877-368-5463, Fax: 225-925-4256, 8AM-4PM. www.dps.state.la.us/omv/home.html ✉

Accident Reports

Louisiana State Police, Traffic Records Unit - A27, PO Box 66614, Baton Rouge, LA 70896 (7919 Independence Blvd, Baton Rouge, LA 70806); 225-925-6157, Fax: 225-925-4922, 8AM-4PM. www.lsp.org/safety_crash.html ✉☎✋

Vessel Ownership, Vessel Registration

Department of Wildlife & Fisheries, Vessel Records, PO Box 14796, Baton Rouge, LA 70898 (2000 Quail Dr, Baton Rouge); 225-765-2898, Fax: 225-763-5421, 8:15AM-4:15PM. www.wlf.state.la.us/apps/netgear/page3.asp ✉

Voter Registration

Secretary of State, Elections Division, PO Box 94125, Baton Rouge, LA 70804-9125; 225-922-0900, Fax: 225-219-9608, 8AM-5PM. www.sos.louisiana.gov/elections/elections-index.htm

GED Certificates

Div of Family, Career, and Technical Education, PO Box 94064, Baton Rouge, LA 70804-9064; 225-342-0444 (Main Number), Fax: 225-219-4439, 8AM - 4:30PM. ✉**Fax**✋

Hunting License and Fishing License Information

Access to Records is Restricted
Wildlife & Fisheries Department, License Division, PO Box 98000, Baton Rouge, LA 70898-9000 (2000 Quail Dr, Baton Rouge); 225-765-2881, Fax: 225-765-3150, 8:-4:30PM. www.wlf.state.la.us/

Maine

Governor's Office
   1 State House Station, Room 236   207-287-3531
   Augusta, ME 04333-0001   Fax 207-287-1034
   www.state.me.us/governor   7:30AM-5:30PM

Attorney General's Office
   6 State House Station   207-626-8800
   Augusta, ME 04333   Fax 207-626-8828
   www.state.me.us/ag   8AM-5PM

State Website: www.state.me.us

Legislative Records
   207-287-1692 http://janus.state.me.us/legis

State Archives
   207-287-5795 www.state.me.us/sos/arc

Capital: Augusta, in Kennebec County

   Search Unclaimed Property Online
   http://thor.dafs.state.me.us/pls/treasurer/tredev.unclaimed_property.search_form

Criminal Records

Maine State Police, State Bureau of Identification, 500 Civic Center Dr, Augusta, ME 04333; 207-624-7240, Fax: 207-287-3421, 8AM-5PM. www.informe.org/PCR/ ✉**Fax**✋🖥

Statewide Court Records

State Court Administrator, PO Box 4820, Portland, ME 04112; 207-822-0792, Fax: 207-822-0781, 8AM-4PM. www.courts.state.me.us 🖥

Sexual Offender Registry

State Bureau of Investigation, 36 Hospital St., Attn: SOR, Augusta, ME 04333; 207-624-7009, Fax: 207-624-7088, 8-5PM. www.state.me.us/dps/ ✉☎**Fax**✋🖥

Incarceration Records

Maine Department of Corrections, Inmate Records, 111 State House Station, Augusta, ME 04333; 207-287-2711, 207-287-4381 (Probation info), 800-968-6909 (Victim Svcs/Inmate info), Fax: 207-287-4370, www.state.me.us/corrections 8AM-4:30PM. ✉☎**Fax**🖥

Corporation Records, Limited Partnerships, Trademarks/Servicemarks, Assumed Name, Limited Liability Company Records, Limited Liability Partnerships

Secretary of State, Reports & Information Division, 101 State House Station, Augusta, ME 04333-0101; 207-624-7752, 207-624-7736(main #), Fax207-287-5874,

8AM-5PM. www.state.me.us/sos/cec/corp ✉☎**Fax**✋🖥

Uniform Commercial Code, Federal and State Tax Liens

Secretary of State, UCC Records Section, 101 State House Station, Augusta, ME 04333-0101 (Burton McCross State Office Bldg, 109 Sewell St, 4th Fl, Augusta, ME 04333); 207-624-7760, Fax: 207-287-5874, 8AM-5PM. www.maine.gov/sos/cec/corp/ucc.htm ✉☎**Fax**✋🖥

Sales Tax Registrations

Maine Revenue Services, Sales, Fuel & Special Tax Division, 24 State House Station, Augusta, ME 04333; 207-624-9693, Fax: 207-287-6628, 8AM-4PM. www.maine.gov/revenue ✉☎**Fax**✋

Birth Certificates, Death Records, Marriage Certificates, Divorce Records

Dept. of Human Svcs, Vital Records, 221 State St, Station 11, Augusta, ME 04333-0011; 207-287-3181, 877-523-2659 (VitalChek), Fax: 207-287-1093, 8-5PM. www.state.me.us/dhs/vitalrecords.htm ✉☎✍🖥

Workers' Compensation Records

Workers Compensation Board, 27 State House Station, Augusta, ME 04333-0027; 207-287-7071, Fax: 207-287-5895, 7:30AM-5PM. www.state.me.us/ ✉✍

Driver Records

BMV - Driver License Services, 101 Hospital Street, 29 State House Station, Augusta, ME 04333-0029; 207-624-9000 x52116, Fax: 207-624-9090, 8AM-5PM. www.state.me.us/sos/bmv ✉Fax✍🖥

Vehicle Ownership, Vehicle Identification

Department of Motor Vehicles, Registration Section, 29 State House Station, Augusta, ME 04333-0029; 207-624-9000 x52149, Fax: 207-624-9204, 8AM-5PM www.state.me.us/sos/bmv/ ✉☎Fax✍🖥

Accident Reports

Maine State Police, Traffic Division, Station 20, Augusta, ME 04333-0020 (397 Water St, Gardiner, ME 04345); 207-624-8944, Fax: 207-624-8945, 8AM-5PM. www.state.me.us/dps/msp ✉✍

Vessel Ownership, Vessel Registration

Dept of Inland Fisheries & Wildlife, Vessel Records, 41 State House Station, 284 State St, Augusta, ME 04333-0041; 207-287-5231, Fax: 207-287-8094, 8AM-5PM. www.state.me.us/ifw ✉☎Fax✍

Voter Registration

Records not maintained by a state level agency.
The data is considered public record in Maine, but can only be accessed at the municipality level.

GED Certificates

Dept of Education, Attn: GED, 23 State House Station, Augusta, ME 04333; 207-624-6752, Fax: 207-624-6731, 8AM-5PM. http://janus.state.me.us/education ✉☎Fax✍🖥

Hunting License and Fishing License Information

Inland Fisheries & Wildlife Department, Licensing Division, 284 State St, Augusta, ME 04333; 207-287-5209, Fax: 207-287-8094, 8AM-5PM. www.state.me.us/ifw ✉☎✍

Maryland

Governor's Office
State House, 100 State Circle
Annapolis, MD 21401   410-974-3901
www.gov.state.md.us   Fax 410-974-3275
                             9AM-5PM

Attorney General's Office
200 St Paul Place   410-576-6300
Baltimore, MD 21202   Fax 410-576-6404
www.oag.state.md.us   8AM-5PM

State Website: www.maryland.gov

Legislative Records
410-946-5400 http://mlis.state.md.us

State Archives
410-260-6400 www.mdarchives.state.md.us

Capital: Annapolis, in Anne Arundel County

Search Unclaimed Property Online
https://interactive.marylandtaxes.com/unclaim/default.asp

Criminal Records

Criminal Justice Information System, Public Safety & Correctional Records, PO Box 5743, Pikeville, MD 21282-5743 (6776 Reisterstown Rd, Rm 200, Pikeville, MD 21208); 410-764-4501, 888-795-0011, Fax: 410-653-6320, 7:30-5PM. www.dpscs.state.md.us ✉✍

Statewide Court Records

Administrative Office of the Courts, 580 Taylor Ave, Annapolis, MD 21401; 410-260-1400, Fax: 410-974-2169, 8AM-5PM. www.courts.state.md.us 🖥

Sexual Offender Registry

Criminal Justice Information System, PO Box 5743, SOR Unit, Pikeville, MD 21282-5743 (6776 Reisterstown Rd, Baltimore, MD); 410-585-3649, 866-368-8657, Fax: 410-653-5690, 7:30AM-5PM. www.dpscs.state.md.us/sor/ ✉🖥

Incarceration Records

Dept of Public Safety and Correctional Services, Division of Corrections, 6776 Reisterstown Road, Suite 310, Baltimore, MD 21215-2342; 410-585-3351, Fax: 410-764-4182, 8AM-4:30PM. www.dpscs.state.md.us/doc ✉☎Fax🖥

Corporation Records, Limited Partnerships, Trade Names, Limited Liability Company Records, Fictitious Name, Limited Liability Partnerships

Department of Assessments and Taxation, Corporations Division, 301 W Preston St, Room 801, Baltimore, MD 21201; 410-767-1340, 410-767-1330 (Charter Info), Fax: 410-333-7097, 8AM-4:30PM. www.dat.state.md.us/ ✉☎Fax✍🖥

Key: Access state agency records by:. phone-☎ mail-✉ fax-Fax in person-✍ online-🖥 email-Email

Trademarks/Servicemarks

Secretary of State, Trademarks Division, State House, Annapolis, MD 21401; 410-974-5521, 410-974-5479, Fax: 410-974-5527, 9AM-5PM.   www.sos.state.md.us ✉☎Fax✋🖥

Uniform Commercial Code

UCC Division - Taxpayer's Svcs., Dept. of Assessments & Taxation, 301 W Preston St, Baltimore, MD 21201; 410-767-1340 x2, Fax: 410-333-7097, 8AM-4:30PM. http://sdatcert3.resiusa.org/ucc-charter/ ✉✋🖥

Federal and State Tax Liens

Records not maintained by a state agency. Tax liens filed at county level.

Sales Tax Registrations

Taxpayer Services, Revenue Administration Division, 301 W Preston St #206, Baltimore, MD 21201; 410-767-1313, Fax: 410-767-1571, 8AM-5PM. www.comp.state.md.us ✉☎Fax🖥

Birth or Marriage Certificate, Death and Divorce Records

Department of Health, Division of Vital Records, PO Box 68760, Baltimore, MD 21215-0020 (6550 Reisterstown Plaza, Baltimore); 410-764-3038, 410-764-3170 (Order), 410-318-6119 (Recording), Fax:

410-358-7381, 8AM-4PM M-F; www.dhmh.state.md.us ✉☎Fax✋🖥

Workers' Compensation Records

Workers Compensation Commission, 10 E Baltimore St, Baltimore, MD 21202; 410-864-5100, 410-864-5120 (IT Dept.), 8AM-4:30PM. www.charm.net/~wcc ✉☎✋🖥

Driver Records

MVA, Driver Records Unit, 6601 Ritchie Hwy, NE, Glen Burnie, MD 21062; 410-787-7758, Fax: 410-424-3678, 8:15AM-4:30PM. www.mva.state.md.us ✉✋🖥

Vehicle Ownership, Vehicle Identification

Dept. of Motor Vehicles, Vehicle Regis. Division, Room 204, 6601 Ritchie Hwy, NE, Glen Burnie, MD 21062; 410-768-7250, Fax: 410-768-7653, 8:15AM-4:30PM. www.mva.state.md.us ✉✋🖥

Accident Reports

Maryland State Police, Central Records Division, 1711 Belmont Ave, Baltimore, MD 21244; 410-298-3390, Fax: 410-298-3198, 8AM-5PM. ✉✋

Vessel Ownership, Vessel Registration

Dept of Natural Resources, Licensing & Registration Service, 580 Taylor Ave C-1, Annapolis, MD 21401; 410-260-3220, 8:30-4:30. www.dnr.state.md.us ✉✋

Voter Registration

Access to Records is Restricted

State Board of Elections, PO Box 6486, Annapolis, MD 21401-0486 (151 West Street, #200); 410-269-2840, 800-222-8683, Fax: 410-974-2019, 8-5PM. www.elections.state.md.us Agency may sell voter registration lists in bulk media for all jurisdictions to MD registered voter only. If voter history is requested, then list must be purchased from local jurisdiction. Commercial use of list is banned.✉

GED Certificates

State Department of Education, GED Office, 200 W Baltimore St, Baltimore, MD 21201; 410-767-0538, Fax: 410-333-8435, 8:30AM-5PM. www.research.umbc.edu/~ira/GED1.html ✉Fax✋

Hunting License and Fishing License Information

Department of Natural Resources, Licensing & Registration Service, 580 Taylor Ave, Annapolis, MD 21401; 410-260-3220, Fax: 410-260-8239, 8:30AM-4:30PM. www.dnr.state.md.us ✉✋

Massachusetts

Governor's Office	
State House, Room 360	617-727-6250
Boston, MA 02133	Fax 617-727-9725
www.mass.gov/gov	8AM-6PM

Attorney General's Office	
One Ashburton Place, Room 2010	617-727-2200
Boston, MA 02108-1698	Fax 617-727-5768
www.ago.state.ma.us	9AM-5PM

State Website: www.mass.gov/portal/index.jsp

Legislative Records
617-722-2860 www.mass.gov/legis/

State Archives
617-727-2816 www.sec.state.ma.us/arc/

Capital: Boston, in Suffolk County

Search Unclaimed Property Online
http://abpweb.tre.state.ma.us/abp/frmNewSrch.aspx

Criminal Records

Criminal History Systems Board, 200 Arlington Street, #2200, Chelsea, MA

02150; 617-660-4600, Fax: 617-660-4613, 9-5PM. www.mass.gov/chsb/ ✉

Statewide Court Records

Chief Justice for Administration & Management, 2 Center Plaza, Room 540, Boston, MA 02108; 617-742-8575, Fax:

Key: Access state agency records by:. phone-☎   mail-✉   fax-**Fax**   in person-✋   online-🖥   email-**Email**

617-742-0968, 8:30AM-5PM. www.ma
ss.gov/courts/admin/index.html 🖥

Sexual Offender Registry

Sex Offender Registry Board, PO Box
4547, Salem, MA 01970; 978-740-6400,
Fax: 978-740-6464, 8:45AM-5PM.
www.mass.gov/sorb/ ✉🖥

Incarceration Records

Massachusetts Executive Office of Public
Safety, Criminal History Systems Board,
200 Arlington #2200, Chelsea, MA
02150; 617-660-4600, 877-421-8463
(Locator), 617-660-4690 (Criminal
Histories Systems Board), 8AM-5PM.
www.mass.gov/doc/ ✉☎🖥

Corporation Records, Trademarks/Servicemarks, Limited Liability Partnerships, Limited Partnerships, Limited Liability Companys

Secretary of the Commonwealth, Corp.
Division, One Ashburton Pl, 17th Fl,
Boston, MA 02108; 617-727-9640
(Corporations), 617-727-2850 (Records),
617-727-8329 (Trademarks), 617-727-
9440 (forms request), Fax: 617-742-4538,
www.sec.state.ma.us/cor/coridx.htm
8:45AM-5PM. ✉☎👋🖥

Uniform Commercial Code, State Tax Liens

UCC Division, Secretary of the
Commonwealth, One Ashburton Pl, Room
1711, Boston, MA 02108; 617-727-2860,
900-555-4500 (Computer Prints), 900-
555-4600 (Copies), 8:45AM-5PM.
http://corp.sec.state.ma.us/portal/UCC/UC
CMain.htm ✉👋🖥

Sales Tax Registrations

Revenue Department - Customer Serv.
Bur, Sales Tax Registrations, PO Box
7010, Boston, MA 02204 (200 Arlington

Street, 4th Fl, Chelsea, MA 02150); 617-
887-6367, 8AM-5PM.
www.dor.state.ma.us ✉☎Fax👋

Birth Certificates, Death Records, Marriage Certificates

Registry of Vital Records and Statistics,
150 Mt Vernon St, 1st FL, Dorchester,
MA 02125; 617-740-2600, 617-740-2606,
Fax: 617-825-7755, 8:45AM-4:45PM.
www.mass.gov/dph/bhsre/rvr/vrcopies.ht
m ✉☎Fax👋🖥

Divorce Records

Access to Records is Restricted

Registry of Vital Records and Statistics,
150 Mt Vernon St, 1st FL, Dorchester,
MA 02125; 617-740-2600, 617-740-2606
www.mass.gov/dph/bhsre/rvr/vrcopies.ht
m Divorce records are found at county of
issue. However, this agency maintains an
index from 1952 to present. The state will
do a search for free by mail only to
determine the county. ✉

Workers' Compensation Records

Keeper of Records, Department of
Industrial Accidents, 600 Washington St,
7th Fl, Boston, MA 02111; 617-727-4900
x301,209, Fax: 617-727-4440, 8AM-4PM.
www.mass.gov/dia ✉👋

Driver Records-Registry

Registry of Motor Vehicles, Driver
Control Unit, Box 199150, Boston, MA
02119-1950; 617-351-9213 (Registry),
Fax: 617-351-9219, 8-4:30PM M-T-W-F;
8-7 TH. www.mass.gov/rmv/ ✉☎👋

Driver Records-Insurance

Merit Rating Board, Attn: Driving
Records, PO Box 199100, Boston, MA
02119-9100; 617-351-4400, Fax: 617-
351-9660, 8:45AM-5:00PM.
www.mass.gov/rmv/ ✉👋🖥

Vehicle Ownership, Vehicle Identification

Registry of Motor Vehicles, Document
Control, PO Box 199100, Boston, MA
02119-9100; 617-351-9458, Fax: 617-
351-9524, 8AM-4:30PM.
www.mass.gov/rmv/ ✉Fax👋🖥

Accident Reports

Crash Records, Registry of Motor
Vehicles, PO Box 199100, Roxbury, MA
02119-9100; 617-351-9434, Fax: 617-
351-9401, 8:45AM-5PM.
www.mass.gov/rmv/forms/21278.htm ✉

Vessel Ownership, Vessel Registration

Environmental Police, Registration and
Titling Bureau, 251 Causeway Street,
#101, Boston, MA 02114; 617-626-1610,
Fax: 617-626-1630, 8:45AM-5PM.
www.mass.gov/dfwele/dle/dle_toc.htm
✉☎Fax

Voter Registration

**Records not maintained by a state
level agency.**
Records are maintained at the local city
and town level. In general, they are open
to the public.

GED Certificates

Massachusetts Dept of Education, GED
Processing, 350 Main St, Malden, MA
02148; 781-338-6636, 781-338-3391,
Fax: 781-338-3391, 9AM-5PM.
www.doe.mass.edu/ged ✉Fax

Hunting License and Fishing License Information

Division of Fisheries & Wildlife, 251
Causeway St #400, Boston, MA 02114-
2104; 617-626-1590, Fax: 617-626-1517,
9-5PM. www.mass.gov/dfwele/ ✉👋

Michigan

Governor's Office
PO Box 30013
Lansing, MI 48909
www.michigan.gov/gov

517-373-7858
Fax 517-335-6863
8AM-5PM

Attorney General's Office
PO Box 30212
Lansing, MI 48909
www.michigan.gov/ag/

517-373-1110
Fax 517-373-3042
8AM-5PM

State Website: www.michigan.gov

Legislative Records
517-373-0169 www.michiganlegislature.org

State Archives
517-373-1408   www.sos.state.mi.us/history/archive

Capital: Lansing, in Ingham County

Time Zone: EST*

* Four northwestern Michigan counties are CST. They are: Dickinson, Gogebic, Iron, Menominee.

Search Unclaimed Property Online

www.michigan.gov/treasury/0,1607,7-121-1748_1876_1912-7924--,00.html

Criminal Records

Michigan State Police, Criminal History Section, Criminal Justice Information Ctr, 7150 Harris Dr, Lansing, MI 48913; 517-322-1956, Fax: 517-322-0635, 8AM-5PM. www.michigan.gov/msp ⊠ 🖳

Statewide Court Records

State Court Administrator, PO Box 30048, Lansing, MI 48909 (925 W Ottawa St); 517-373-2222, Fax: 517-373-2112, 8:30-5PM. http://courts.michigan.gov 🖳

Sexual Offender Registry

Michigan State Police, SOR Unit, 7150 Harris Dr, Lansing, MI 48913; 517-322-5098, Fax: 517-322-4957, 8AM-5PM. www.mipsor.state.mi.us/ 🖳

Incarceration Records

Michigan Department of Corrections, Central Records Office, PO Box 30003, Lansing, MI 48909 (206 E. Michigan Ave., Lansing, MI 48909); 517-373-0284, Fax: 517-373-2628, 8AM-4:30PM. www.michigan.gov/corrections ⊠ ☎Fax🖳

Corporation Records, Limited Liability Company Records, Limited Partnership Records, Assumed Name

Department of Consumer & Industry Svcs, bureau of Commercial Services, PO Box 30054, Lansing, MI 48909-7554 (7150 Harris Dr, Lansing); 517-241-6470,

Fax: 517-241-0538, 8AM-N, 1-5PM. http://michigan.gov/cis/0,1607,7-154-10557_12901---,00.html ⊠ ☎Fax🖐🖳

Trademarks/Servicemarks

Bureua of Commercial Services, Trademarks & Service Marks, PO Box 30054, Lansing, MI 48909-7554 (7150 Harris Dr, Lansing, MI 48909); 517-241-6470, 8AM-5PM (closed at noon for 1 hr). www.michigan.gov/cis/0,1607,7-154-10557_21107---,00.html ⊠ ☎Fax🖐🖳

Uniform Commercial Code, Federal and State Tax Liens

MI Department of State, UCC Section, PO Box 30197, Lansing, MI 48909-7697 (7064 Crowner Dr, Dimondale, MI 48821); 517-322-1144, Fax: 517-322-5434, 8AM-5PM. www.michigan.gov/sos ⊠ ☎Fax🖐🖳

Sales Tax Registrations

Access to Records is Restricted
Michigan Dept of Treasury, Sales, Use, Withholding Tax Division,, Lansing, MI 48922; 517-636-4660, 517-636-4491, Fax: 517-335-1135, 8AM-4:45PM. www.michigan.gov/treasury The agency will only verify or confirm data, no searches provided. ⊠ ☎

Workers' Compensation Records

Department of Labor & Economic Dev., Workers' Compensation Agency, 7150 Harris Dr, Lansing, MI 48909; 888-396-

5041, Fax: 517-322-1808, 8AM-5PM. www.michigan.gov/wca ⊠ 🖳

Birth Certificates, Death Records, Marriage Certificates, Divorce Records

Department of Health, Vital Records Requests, PO Box 30721, Lansing, MI 48909 (3423 N Martin Luther King, Jr Blvd, Lansing, MI 48906); 517-335-8656 (Instructions), 517-335-8666 (Request Unit), Fax: 517-321-5884, 8AM-5PM. www.michigan.gov/mdch ⊠ 🖐🖳

Driver Records

Department of State Police, Record Look-up Unit, 7064 Crowner Dr, Lansing, MI 48918; 517-322-1624 (Look-up Unit), Fax: 517-322-1181, 8AM-4:45PM. www.michigan.gov/sos ⊠ ☎Fax🖐🖳

Vehicle Ownership, Vehicle Identification, Vessel Ownership, Vessel Registration

Department of State Police, Record Look-up Unit, 7064 Crowner Dr, Lansing, MI 48918; 517-322-1624, Fax: 517-322-1181, 8-4:45PM. www.michigan.gov/sos ⊠ ☎Fax🖐🖳

Accident Reports

Department of State Police, Criminal Justice Information Center, 7150 Harris Dr, Lansing, MI 48913; 517-322-5509 (FOIA), Fax: 517-323-5350, 8AM-5PM.

Key: Access state agency records by:. phone-☎   mail-⊠   fax-Fax   in person-🖐   online-🖳   email-Email

www.michigan.gov/msp/0,1607,7-123--28578--,00.html ✉Fax🖐🖥

Voter Registration

Bureau of Elections, Election Liaison Division, 430 W Allegan St, 1st Fl, Lansing, MI 48918; 517-373-2540, Fax: 517-373-0941, 8AM-5PM. www.michigan.gov/sos/1,1607,7-127-1633---,00.html ✉Fax

GED Certificates

Department of Labor & Econ Growth, Adult Education - GED Testing, 201 N Washington Square, 3rd Fl, Lansing, MI 48913; 517-373-1692, Fax: 517-335-3461, www.michigan.gov/adulteducation 7AM-5PM. ✉☎Fax🖐🖥

Hunting License and Fishing License Information

Access to Records is Restricted
Dept of Natural Resources, Customer Systems, PO Box 30181, Lansing, MI 48909 (530 W Allegan St, Lansing, MI 48933); 517-373-1204, Fax: 517-335-6813, 8AM-5PM. Hunting and fishing license data is no longer released.

Minnesota

Governor's Office
130 State Cap. Bldg, 75 Constitution Ave 651-296-3391
St Paul, MN 55155   Fax 651-296-2089
www.governor.state.mn.us   7:30AM-5PM

Attorney General's Office
1400 NCL Tower   651-296-3353
445 Minnesota St   Fax 651-297-4193
St Paul, MN 55101   www.ag.state.mn.us

State Website: www.state.mn.us

Legislative Records
651-296-2887 www.leg.state.mn.us

State Archives
651-296-6126 www.mnhs.org

Capital: St. Paul, in Ramsey County

Search Unclaimed Property Online

www.state.mn.us/cgi-bin/portal/mn/jsp/content.do?id=-536881373&agency=Commerce

Criminal Records

Bureau of Criminal Apprehension, Criminal Justice Information Systems, 1430 Maryland Ave E, St Paul, MN 55106; 651-793-2400, Fax 651-793-2401, 8:15-4. www.bca.state.mn.us/ ✉🖐

Statewide Court Records

State Court Administrator, 135 Minnesota Judicial Center, 2 Rev ML King Blvd, St Paul, MN 55155; 651-296-2474, Fax: 651-297-5636, 8AM-4:30PM. www.courts.state.mn.us/home/ 🖥

Sexual Offender Registry

Bureau of Criminal Apprehension, Minnesota Predatory Offender Program, 1430 Maryland Ave E, St Paul, MN 55106; 651-793-7070, 888-234-1248, Fax: 651-793-7071, 8AM-4:30PM. www.dps.state.mn.us/bca/ 🖥

Incarceration Records

Minnesota Department of Corrections, Records Management Unit, 450 Energy Park Drive, Suite 200, St. Paul, MN 55108; 651-642-0200, Fax: 651-643-3588, 8AM-5PM. www.corr.state.mn.us ✉☎Fax🖥

Corporation Records, Limited Liability Company Records, Assumed Name, Trademarks/Servicemarks, Limited Partnerships

Business Records Services, Secretary of State, 180 State Office Bldg, 100 Martin Luther King Blvd, St Paul, MN 55155-1299; 651-296-2803 (Information), Fax: 651-297-7067, 8AM-4:30PM. www.sos.state.mn.us ✉☎Fax🖐🖥

Uniform Commercial Code, Federal and State Tax Liens

UCC Division, Secretary of State, 180 State Office Bldg, St Paul, MN 55155-1299; 651-296-2803, Fax: 651-215-1009, 8-4:30. www.sos.state.mn.us ✉Fax🖐🖥

Sales Tax Registrations

Minnesota Revenue Dept, Tax OPS Division, 600 N Robert Street MS:4410, St Paul, MN 55146-4410; 651-282-5225, Fax: 651-556-3124, 9AM-4PM. www.taxes.state.mn.us ✉☎Fax🖐🖥

Birth Certificates, Death Records

Minnesota Department of Health, Vital Records, PO Box 9441, Minneapolis, MN 55440-9441 (717 Delaware St SE, Minneapolis, MN 55414); 612-676-5120, Fax: 612-331-5776, 8AM-4:30PM. www.health.state.mn.us ✉Fax🖐

Marriage Certificates, Divorce Records

Records not maintained by a state level agency.
Marriage and divorce records are found at the county level. The Section of Vital Records has an index and they will direct you to the proper county (Marriage since 1958, Divorce since 1970). Call the Section of Vital Records at 612-676-5120.

Workers' Compensation Records

Labor & Industry Department Workers Compensation Division - File Review, 443 Lafayette Rd, St Paul, MN 55155; 651-284-5435, Fax: 651-284-5731, www.doli.state.mn.us/workcomp.html 8AM-4:30PM. ✉☎Fax🖐

Driver Records

Driver & Vehicle Services, Records Section, 445 Minnesota St, #180, St Paul, MN 55101; 651-296-6911, 8AM-4:30PM. www.dps.state.mn.us/dvs/index.html

Vehicle Ownership, Vehicle Identification

Driver & Vehicle Services, Vehicle Record Requests, 445 Minnesota St, #180, St Paul, MN 55101; 651-296-6911 (General Information), 8AM-4:30PM. www.dps.state.mn.us/dvs/index.html

Accident Reports

Driver & Vehicle Services, Accident Records, 445 Minnesota St, Suite 181, St Paul, MN 55101-5181; 651-296-2060,

Fax: 651-282-2360, 8AM-4:30PM. www.mndriveinfo.org ✉Fax✋

Vessel Ownership, Vessel Registration

Department of Natural Resources, License Bureau, 500 Lafayette Rd, St Paul, MN 55155-4026; 651-296-2316, 800-285-2000, Fax: 651-297-8851, 8AM-4:30PM. www.dnr.state.mn.us ✉☎Fax✋

Voter Registration

Access to Records is Restricted
Secretary of State-Election Division, 180 State Office Bldg, 100 Dr Martin L King Blvd, St Paul, MN 55155; 651-215-1440, 877-600-8683, Fax: 651-296-9073, 8AM-4:30PM. www.sos.state.mn.us/election/ Records are sold by the state only for political, election, or law enforcement purposes and only to MN registered

voters. Some counties will honor record requests. ✉Fax

GED Certificates

Department of Children, Families & Learning, GED Testing, 1500 Highway 36 West, Roseville, MN 55113-4266; 651-582-8446, 651-582-8445 (Instructions), Fax: 651-582-8458, 7AM-3:30PM. http://education.state.mn.us/html/intro_adult_ged.htm ✉☎Fax

Hunting License and Fishing License Information

ELS Licensing, DNR License Bureau, 500 Lafayette Rd, St Paul, MN 55155. 651-297-1230, 888-646-6367, Fax: 651-297-8851, 8-4:30PM. www.dnr.state.mn.us ✉☎Fax✋

Mississippi

Governor's Office
PO Box 139
Jackson, MS 39201
www.governor.state.ms.us

601-359-3100
Fax 601-359-3741
8AM-5PM

Attorney General's Office
PO Box 220
Jackson, MS 39205
www.ago.state.ms.us

601-359-3680
Fax 601-359-3796
8AM-5PM

State Website: www.ms.gov

Legislative Records www.ls.state.ms.us
601-359-3229 (Senate) 601-359-3358 (House)

State Archives
601-359-6850 www.mdah.state.ms.us

Capital: Jackson, in Hinds County

Search Unclaimed Property Online
www.missingmoney.com/main/index.cfm

Criminal Records

Access to Records is Restricted
Criminal Information Center, Dept. of Public Safety, PO Box 958, Jackson, MS 39205; 601-933-2600. No access to the central state repository of criminal records except for pre-approved entities with purposes provided for by state statute such as health care, banking/finance, military, childcare and schools. Obtain information at the county level.

Statewide Court Records

Administrative Office of Courts, PO Box 117, Jackson, MS 39205 (450 High St); 601-354-7406, Fax: 601-354-7459, 8AM-5PM. www.mssc.state.ms.us Fax🖥

Sexual Offender Registry

Dept. of Public Safety, Sexual Offender Registry, PO Box 958, Jackson, MS 39205; www.sor.mdps.state.ms.us/ 601-368-1740. ✉☎🖥

Incarceration Records

Mississippi Department of Corrections, Records Department, PO Box 880, Parchman, MS 38738; 601-359-5608, 8-5PM. www.mdoc.state.ms.us ✉☎🖥

Uniform Commercial Code, Federal and State Tax Liens

Secretary of State, Business Services - UCC, PO Box 136, Jackson, MS 39205-0136 (700 N Jackson St, Jackson, MS 39202); 601-359-1633, 800-256-3494,

Fax: 601-359-1607, 8AM-5PM. www.sos.state.ms.us ✉☎✋🖥

Corporation Records, Limited Partnership Records, Limited Liability Company Records, Trademarks/Servicemarks

Corporation Commission, Business Services, PO Box 136, Jackson, MS 39205-0136; 601-359-1633, 800-256-3494, Fax: 601-359-1607, 8AM-5PM. www.sos.state.ms.us ✉☎Fax✋🖥

Sales Tax Registrations

Office of Revenue, Sales and Use Tax Bureau, PO Box 1033, Jackson, MS 39215-1033 (1577 Springridge Rd,

Raymond, MS 39154); 601-923-7000, 8AM-5PM. www.mstc.state.ms.us ✉☎Fax✍💻

Birth Certificates, Death Records, Marriage Certificates, Divorce Records

State Department of Health, Vital Statistics & Records, PO Box 1700, Jackson, MS 39215-1700 (571 Stadium Dr, Jackson); 601-576-7960, 601-576-7988, Fax: 601-576-7505, 7:30AM-5PM www.msdh.state.ms.us/phs/index.htm ✉☎Fax✍

Workers' Compensation Records

Workers Compensation Commission, PO Box 5300, Jackson, MS 39296-5300 (1428 Lakeland Dr, Jackson); 601-987-4200, 8AM-5PM. www.mwcc.state.ms.us ✉✍💻

Driver Records

Department of Public Safety, Driver Records, PO Box 958, Jackson, MS 39205

(1900 E Woodrow Wilson, Jackson, MS 39216); 601-987-1274, 8AM-5PM. www.dps.state.ms.us ✉✍💻

Vehicle Ownership, Vehicle Identification

Mississippi State Tax Commission, Registration Department, PO Box 1140, Jackson, MS 39215 (1577 Springridge Rd, Raymond, MS 39154); 601-923-7100 (Registration), 601-923-7200 (Titles), Fax: 601-923-7134, 8-5PM. www.mstc.state.ms.us/mvl/main.htm ✉✍

Accident Reports

Safety Responsibility, Accident Records, PO Box 958, Jackson, MS 39205 (1900 E Woodrow Wilson, Jackson, MS 39216); 601-987-1254, Fax: 601-987-1261, 8AM-5PM. www.dps.state.ms.us ✉

Vessel Ownership, Vessel Registration

Dept of Wildlife, Fisheries, & Parks, Boating Registration, PO Box 451, Jackson, MS 39205; 601-432-2067, 601-

432-2066, Fax: 601-432-2071, 8AM-5PM. www.mdwfp.com ✉☎Fax✍

Voter Registration

Secretary of State, Elections Division, PO Box 136, Jackson, MS 39205-0136; 800-829-6786, 601-359-1350, Fax: 601-359-5019, 8AM-5PM. www.sos.state.ms.us/elections/elections.asp ✉

GED Certificates

State Board for Community & Jr Colleges, GED Office, 3825 Ridgewood Rd, Jackson, MS 39211; 601-432-6338, Fax: 601-432-6890, 8AM-5PM. www.sbcjc.cc.ms.us ✉✍

Hunting License and Fishing License Information

Department of Wildlife, Fisheries & Parks, PO Box 451, Jackson, MS 39205; 601-432-2055 (License Div.), 601-432-2041 (Data Processing Div), Fax: 601-432-2071, 8AM-5PM. www.mdwfp.com ✉☎Fax✍

Missouri

Governor's Office
PO Box 720
Jefferson City, MO 65102-0720
www.gov.state.mo.us

573-751-3222
Fax 573-751-1495
8AM-5PM

Attorney General's Office
PO Box 899
Jefferson City, MO 65102
www.ago.state.mo.us

573-751-3321
Fax 573-751-0774
8AM-5PM

State Website: www.state.mo.us

Legislative Records
573-751-4633 www.moga.state.mo.us

State Archives
573-751-3280 www.sos.mo.gov/archives/

Capital: Jefferson City, in Cole County

Search Unclaimed Property Online
www.missingmoney.com/main/index.cfm

Criminal Records

Missouri State Highway Patrol, Criminal Record & Identification Division, 1510 E Elm St, Jefferson City, MO 65102; 573-526-6153, Fax: 573-751-9382, 8AM-5PM. www.mshp.dps.missouri.gov ✉✍

Statewide Court Records

Court Administrator, 2112 Industrial Drive - PO Box 104480, Jefferson City, MO 65110; 573-751-4377, Fax: 573-751-5540, 8-5PM. www.osca.state.mo.us 💻

Sexual Offender Registry

Missouri State Highway Patrol, Sexual Offender Registry, PO Box 9500, Jefferson City, MO 65102-0568 (1510 E Elm St, Jefferson City, MO 65102); 573-526-6153, Fax: 573-751-9382, 8AM-5PM. www.mshp.dps.missouri.gov/ 💻

Incarceration Records

Missouri Department of Corrections, Probation and Parole, 1511 Christy Dr., Jefferson City, MO 65101; 573-751-8488, Fax: 573-751-8501, 8AM-5PM.

www.corrections.state.mo.us/ ✉☎Fax💻

Corporation Records, Fictitious Name, Limited Partnership Records, Assumed Name, Trademarks/Servicemarks, Limited Liability Company Records

Secretary of State, Corporation Services, PO Box 778, Jefferson City, MO 65102

(600 W Main, Jefferson City, MO 65101); 573-751-4153, 866-223-6535, Fax: 573-751-5841, 8AM-5PM. www.sos.mo.gov ✉☎Fax✋🖥

Uniform Commercial Code

UCC Division, Attn: Records, PO Box 1159, Jefferson City, MO 65102 (600 W Main St, Rm 302, Jefferson City, MO 65101); 866-223-6565, 8AM-5PM. www.sos.state.mo.us/ucc/ ✉☎✋🖥

Federal and State Tax Liens

Records not maintained by a state level agency.
All tax liens are filed at the county level.

Sales Tax Registrations

Access to Records is Restricted
Department of Revenue, Business Tax, PO Box 3300, Jefferson City, MO 65105-3300; 573-751-5860, 573-751-2836, Fax: 573-522-1722, 7:45AM-4:45PM. www.dor.mo.gov/tax/ This agency will neither confirm nor supply any information. Confidential information is only released to owners or corporate officers registered with the Department. They suggest requesters to check at the city level.

Birth Certificates, Death Records

Department of Health, Bureau of Vital Records, PO Box 570, Jefferson City, MO 65102-0570 (930 Wildwood, Jefferson City, MO 65109); 573-751-6387, 573-751-6400 (message number), 866-550-1851 (orders), Fax: 573-526-3846, 8-5 www.health.state.mo.us ✉☎Fax✋🖥

Marriage Certificates, Divorce Records

Records not maintained by a state level agency.
Actual marriage and divorce records are found at county of issue. For marriage, contact the county Record of Deeds. For divorce decrees, visit the Clerk of the county where issued.

Workers' Compensation Records

Labor & Industrial Relations Department, Workers Compensation Division, PO Box 58, Jefferson City, MO 65102-0058 (3315 W Truman Blvd, Jefferson City); 573-751-4231 x5, Fax: 573-751-2012, 8AM-4:30PM. www.dolir.mo.gov ✉Fax✋

Driver Records

Department of Revenue, Driver and Vehicle Services Bureau, PO Box 200, Jefferson City, MO 65105-0200 (Harry S Truman Bldg, 301 W High St, Room 470, Jefferson City, MO 65105); 573-751-4300, Fax: 573-526-7367, 7:45-4:45PM. www.dor.state.mo.us/mvdl/drivers ✉☎Fax✋🖥

Vehicle Ownership, Vehicle Identification, Vessel Ownership, Vessel Registration

Dept. of Revenue, Driver and Vehicle Services Bureau, PO Box 100, Jefferson City, MO 65105-0100 (Harry S Truman Bldg, 301 W High St); 573-526-3669, 573-751-4509, Fax: 573-751-7060, www.dor.state.mo.us/mvdl/default.htm 7:45AM-4:45PM. ✉☎Fax✋

Accident Reports

Missouri Highway Patrol, Traffic Division, PO Box 568, Jefferson City, MO 65102-0568 (1510 E Elm St, Jefferson City, MO 65101); 573-526-6113, Fax: 573-751-9921, 8AM-5PM. www.mshp.dps.mo.gov ✉✋

Voter Registration

Access to Records is Restricted
Secretary of State, Division of Elections, PO Box 1767, Jefferson City, MO 65102; 573-751-2301, Fax: 573-526-3242, 8AM-5PM. www.sos.mo.gov/section4.asp For individual look-ups, the agency recommends searching at the county level by the County Clerks. ✉✋

GED Certificates

GED Office, PO Box 480, Jefferson City, MO 65102; 573-751-3504, 8AM-4:30PM. http://dese.mo.gov/divcareered/ ✉✋

Hunting License and Fishing License Information

Conservation Department, Business & Support Services, PO Box 180, Jefferson City, MO 65102-0180 (2901 W Truman Blvd, Jefferson City, MO 65109); 573-751-4115, Fax: 573-751-4467, 8AM-5PM. www.mdc.missouri.gov/ ✉Fax

Montana

Governor's Office
PO Box 200801, State Capitol   406-444-3111
Helena, MT 59620-0801   Fax 406-444-5529
www.discoveringmontana.com/gov2/css/default.asp

Attorney General's Office
PO Box 201401   406-444-2026
Helena, MT 59620   Fax 406-444-3549
www.doj.state.mt.us/   8AM-5PM

Website: www.discoveringmontana.com/default.asp

Legislative Records
    406-444-3064   www.leg.state.mt.us
State Archives
    406-444-2694   www.his.state.mt.us
Capital: Helena, in Lewis and Clark County

Search Unclaimed Property Online
www.missingmoney.com/main/index.cfm

Key: Access state agency records by:. phone-☎ mail-✉ fax-Fax in person-✋ online-🖥 email-Email

Montana Criminal Records

Department of Justice, Criminal Records, PO Box 201403, Helena, MT 59620-1403 (303 N Roberts, 4th Fl, Helena, MT 59620); 406-444-3625, Fax: 406-444-0689, 8-5PM. www.doj.state.mt.us ✉✋

Statewide Court Records

Court Administrator, PO Box 203002, Helena, MT 59620-3002 (215 N Sanders, Justice Bldg Rm 315, Helena, MT 59620); 406-444-2621, Fax: 406-444-0834, 8AM-5PM. www.lawlibrary.state.mt.us 💻

Sexual Offender Registry

Dept. of Justice, Sexual and Violent Offender Registry, PO Box 201417, Helena, MT 59620; 406-444-9479, Fax: 406-444-2759, 8-5PM. http://svor2.doj.state.mt.us:8010/index.htm ✉☎Fax✋💻

Incarceration Records

Montana Department of Corrections, Directors Office, PO Box 201301, Helena, MT 59620-1301 (1539 11th Ave, Helena, MT 59620); 406-444-3930, 406-444-7461 (Info. Officer), Fax: 406-444-4920, 8:30-4:30PM. www.cor.state.mt.us/ ✉☎💻

Corporation Records, Limited Liability Company Records, Fictitious Name, Limited Partnerships, Assumed Name, Trademarks/Servicemarks

Business Services Bureau, Secretary of State, PO Box 202801, Helena, MT 59620-2801 (1236 East 6th Ave, Helena); 406-444-3665, Fax: 406-444-3976, 8AM-5PM. http://sos.state.mt.us/css/index.asp ✉☎Fax✋💻

Uniform Commercial Code, Federal Tax Liens

Business Services Bureau, Secretary of State, Rm 260, PO Box 202801, Helena, MT 59620-2801 (1236 East 6th Ave, Helena); 406-444-1212, Fax: 406-444-3976, http://sos.state.mt.us/css/index.asp 8AM-5PM. ✉Fax✋💻

State Tax Liens

Records not maintained by a state level agency.
Records are at the county level.

Sales Tax Registrations

State does not impose sales tax.

Birth Certificates, Death Records

Montana Department of Health, Vital Records, PO Box 4210, Helena, MT 59604 (111 N Sanders, Rm 209, Helena); 406-444-4228 (Recording), 406-444-2685, Fax: 406-444-1803, 8AM-5PM. http://vhsp.dphhs.state.mt.us/dph_l2.htm ✉Fax✋💻

Marriage Certificates, Divorce Records

Records not maintained by a state level agency.
Marriage and divorce records are found at county of issue. This agency is required by law to maintain an index of these records. The index is from 1943 to present. The State can direct you to the correct county for a fee.

Workers' Compensation Records

Montana State Fund, PO Box 4759, Helena, MT 59604-4759 (5 S. Last Chance Gulch, Helena, MT 59601); 406-444-6500, Fax: 406-444-7796, 8-5PM. www.montanastatefund.com ✉Fax

Driver Records

Motor Vehicle Division, Driver's Services, PO Box 201430, Helena, MT 59620-1430 (Records Unit, 303 N Roberts, Room 260, Helena); 406-444-3292, Fax: 406-444-7623, 8AM-5PM. www.doj.state.mt.us/driving/default.asp ✉✋💻

Vehicle Ownership, Vehicle Identification, Vessel Ownership, Vessel Registration

Department of Justice, Title and Registration Bureau, 1032 Buckskin Drive, Deer Lodge, MT 59722; 406-846-6000, Fax: 406-846-6039, 8AM-5PM. www.doj.state.mt.us/driving/vehicletitleregistration.asp ✉✋💻

Accident Reports

Montana Highway Patrol, Crash Records, 2550 Prospect Ave, Helena, MT 59620-1419; 406-444-3278, Fax: 406-444-4169, www.doj.state.mt.us/department/highwaypatroldivision.asp 8AM-5PM. ✉☎✋

Voter Registration

Secretary of State, Elections Bureau, PO Box 202801, Helena, MT 59620-2801; 406-444-5376, Fax: 406-444-2023, 8-5. http://sos.state.mt.us ✉☎Fax✋💻

GED Certificates

Office of Public Instruction, GED Program, PO Box 202501, Helena, MT 59620; 406-444-4438, Fax 406-444-1373, 7-4. www.opi.state.mt.us/GED/Index.html ✉✋

Hunting License and Fishing License Information

Fish, Wildlife & Parks Department, Licensing, PO Box 200701, Helena, MT 59620-0701 (1420 E 6th Ave, Helena); 406-444-2950, Fax: 406-444-8403, 8AM-5PM. http://fwp.state.mt.us ✉☎✋

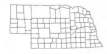 # Nebraska

Governor's Office
PO Box 94848   402-471-2244
Lincoln, NE 68509-4848   Fax 402-471-6031
http://gov.nol.org   8AM-5PM

Attorney General's Office
2115 State Capitol   402-471-2682
Lincoln, NE 68509   Fax 402-471-3297
www.ago.state.ne.us/   8AM-5PM

State Website: www.state.ne.us

Legislative Records
402-471-2271   http://court.nol.org/AOC

State Archives
402-471-4771   www.nebraskahistory.org

Capital: Lincoln, in Lancaster County

Time Zone: CST*

* Nebraska's nineteen western-most counties are MST: They
are: Arthur, Banner, Box Butte, Chase, Cherry, Cheyenne,
Dawes, Deuel, Dundy, Garden, Grant, Hooker, Keith, Kimball,
Morrill, Perkins, Scotts. Bluff, Sheridan, Sioux.

> ### Search Unclaimed Property Online
> www.treasurer.state.ne.us/ie/uphome2.asp

Criminal Records

Nebraska State Patrol, CID, PO Box 94907, Lincoln, NE 68509-4907 (1500 Nebraska Highway 2, Lincoln, NE 68502); 402-479-4924, 402-471-4545, Fax: 402-479-4002, 8AM-4PM. www.nsp.state.ne.us/ ✉ ✋

Statewide Court Records

Court Administrator, PO Box 98910, Lincoln, NE 68509-8910; 402-471-3730, Fax: 402-471-2197, 8AM-4:30PM. http://court.nol.org/AOC/index.html 💻

Sexual Offender Registry

State Patrol, Sexual Offender Registry, PO Box 94907, Lincoln, NE 68509-4907 (1500 Nebraska Highway 2, Lincoln); 402-471-8647, Fax: 402-471-8496, 8AM-4PM. www.nsp.state.ne.us/sor/ ✉ ☎ 💻

Incarceration Records

Nebraska Department of Correctional Services, Central Records Office, PO Box 94661, Lincoln, NE 68509-4661; 402-479-5765, Fax 402-479-5913, 8AM-5PM. www.corrections.state.ne.us ✉ ☎Fax💻

Corporation Records, Limited Liability Company Records, Limited Partnerships, Trade Names, Trademarks/Servicemarks

Secretary of State, Corp Commission, 1301 State Capitol Bldg, Lincoln, NE 68509; 402-471-4079, Fax 402-471-3666,
www.sos.state.ne.us/htm/corpmenu.htm 8AM-5PM. ✉ ☎Fax✋💻

Uniform Commercial Code, Federal and State Tax Liens

UCC Division, Secretary of State, Rm 1301, PO Box 95104, Lincoln, NE 68509-5104 (1301 State Capitol Bldg, Lincoln); 402-471-4080, Fax 402-471-4429, 7:30-5. www.sos.state.ne.us/htm/UCCmenu.htm ✉Fax✋💻

Sales Tax Registrations

Revenue Department, Taxpayer Assistance, PO Box 94818, Lincoln, NE 68509-4818 (301 Centennial Mall South) 402-471-5729, Fax 402-471-5990 8-5PM. www.revenue.state.ne.us/salestax.htm ✉☎✋💻

Birth Certificates, Death Records, Marriage Certificates, Divorce Records

Health & Human Services System, Vital Statistics Section, PO Box 95065, Lincoln, NE 68509-5065 (301 Centennial Mall S, 3rd Fl, Lincoln, NE 68509); 402-471-2871, 402-471-6440, 8AM-5PM. www.hhs.state.ne.us/ced/nevrinfo.htm ✉ ☎ in person

Workers' Compensation Records

Workers' Compensation Court, PO Box 98908, Lincoln, NE 68509-8908 (State Capitol, 13th Fl, Lincoln, NE 68509);
402-471-6468, 800-599-5155 (In-state), Fax: 402-471-2700, 8AM-5PM. www.nol.org/workcomp ✉Fax✋💻

Driver Records

Department of Motor Vehicles, Driver & Vehicle Records Division, PO Box 94789, Lincoln, NE 68509-4789 (301 Centennial Mall, S, Lincoln, NE 68509); 402-471-3918, Fax: 402-471-8694, 8AM-5PM. www.dmv.state.ne.us ✉ ✋💻

Vehicle Ownership, Vehicle Identification, Vessel Ownership

Department of Motor Vehicles, Driver & Vehicle Records Division, PO Box 94789, Lincoln, NE 68509-4789 (301 Centennial Mall, S, Lincoln, NE 68509); 402-471-3918, Fax: 402-471-8694, 8AM-5PM. www.dmv.state.ne.us ✉ ✋💻

Accident Reports

Department of Roads, Accident Records Bureau, Box 94669, Lincoln, NE 68509 (1500 Nebraska Highway 2, Lincoln, NE 68502); 402-479-4645, Fax: 402-479-3637, 7AM-5PM. www.dor.state.ne.us ✉☎Fax✋

Vessel Registration

Records not maintained by a state level agency.
All boats must be registered. Records are found at county recorder offices.

Voter Registration
Secretary of State, Elections Division-Records, PO Box 94608, Lincoln, NE 68509; 402-471-2554 x2, Fax: 402-471-3237, 8AM-5PM. www.sos.state.ne.us/Elections/election.htm ✉ ☎

GED Certificates
NE Dept of Education, Adult Education, PO Box 94987, Lincoln, NE 68509 (301 Centennial Mall S,); 402-471-2475, Fax: 402-471-8127, 8AM-5PM. www.nde.state.ne.us/ADED/home.htm ✉ **Fax**✋

Hunting License and Fishing License Information
Game & Parks Commission, PO Box 30370, Lincoln, NE 68503 (2200 N 33rd St, Lincoln, NE 68503); 402-471-5455, Fax: 402-471-6586, 8AM-5PM. www.ngpc.state.ne.us/homepage.html ✉ ☎ ✋

Nevada

Governor's Office
Capitol Building   775-684-5670
Carson City, NV 89701   Fax 775-684-5683
http://gov.state.nv.us   8AM-5PM

Attorney General's Office
100 N Carson St   775-684-1100
Carson City, NV 89701   Fax 775-684-1108
http://ag.state.nv.us   8AM-5PM

State Website: www.nv.gov

Legislative Records   www.leg.state.nv.us
775-684-6800; 775-684-6827 (Bill Status)
State Archives
775-684-3360   http://dmla.clan.lib.nv.us/docs/nsla

Capital: Carson City, in Carson City County

> Search Unclaimed Property Online
> http://nevadatreasurer.com/unclaimed/search.asp

Criminal Records
DPS, Nevada Highway Patrol, Record & ID Services, 808 W Nye Lane, Carson City, NV 89703; 775-687-1600, Fax: 775-687-1843, 8AM-5PM. www.nvrepository.state.nv.us ✉ ✋

Statewide Court Records
Supreme Court of Nevada, Administrative Office of the Courts, 201 S Carson St, #250, Carson City, NV 89701-4702; 775-684-1700, Fax: 775-684-1723, 8-5PM. www.nvsupremecourt.us/aoc/aoc.html 💻

Sexual Offender Registry
Records and Identification Bureau, Sex Offender Registry, 808 W Nye Lane, Carson City, NV 89703; 775-687-1600 x253, Fax: 775-687-1844, 8AM-5PM. www.nvsexoffenders.gov ✉ ☎ **Fax**✋ 💻

Incarceration Records
Nevada Department of Corrections, Attn: Records, PO Box 7011, Carson City, NV 89702 (5500 Snyder Ave, Bldg 89, Carson City, NV 89701); 775-887-3285, Fax: 775-687-6715, 8AM-5PM. www.doc.nv.gov ✉ ☎ 💻

Sales Tax Registrations
State does not impose sales tax.

Corporation Records, Limited Partnerships, Limited Liability Company Records,
Secretary of State, Records, 202 N Carson City, Carson City, NV 89701-4707; 775-684-5708 (Expedite), 775-684-5645 (Fax Expedite), 702-486-2880 (Las Vegas Ofc.:), 702-486-2888 (Las Vegas Ofc fax:), Fax: 775-684-5725, 8AM-5PM. www.sos.state.nv.us ✉ ☎ ✋ 💻

Assumed Name, Fictitious Name
Records not maintained by a state agency. Records at the county level.

Trademarks/Servicemarks
Secretary of State, Corporate Expedite Office, 555 E. Washington Ave, #4000, Las Vegas, NV 89101, 702-486-2880, Fax: 702-486-2888, 8AM-5PM. http://secretaryofstate.biz/comm_rec/trademk/index.htm ✉ ☎ ✋

Uniform Commercial Code, Federal and State Tax Liens
UCC Division, Secretary of State, 200 N Carson St, Carson City, NV 89701-4069; 775-684-7708, Fax: 775-684-5630, 8AM-5PM. www.sos.state.nv.us ✉ **Fax**✋ 💻

Birth Certificates, Death Records
Nevada Department of Health, Office of Vital Statistics, 505 E King St, Rm 102, Carson City, NV 89701; 775-684-4242, 775-684-4280 (message phone), Fax 775-684-4156, 8-4. http://health2k.state.nv.us/ ✉ ☎ **Fax**✋ 💻

Marriage Certificates, Divorce Records
Access to Records is Restricted
Nevada Department of Health, Office of Vital Statistics, 505 E King St, Rm 102, Carson City, NV 89701-4749; 775-684-4481. http://health2k.state.nv.us/ Marriage and Divorce records are found at county of issue. However, the Vital Statistics Office (see above) has an index and will relate the county and date of the event. Call 775-684-4242. Request form is available at the webpage.

Workers' Compensation Records
Employers Insurance Co of NV, Workers Compensation Insurance, 2550 Paseo Verde Parkway, Henderson, NV 89074-7117; 888-682-6671, Fax: 702-671-7175, 8AM-5PM. www.eicn.com ✉ **Fax**✋

Driver Records

Department of Motor Vehicles, Records Section, 555 Wright Way, Carson City, NV 89711-0250; 775-684-4590, 800-992-7945 (In-state), Fax: 775-684-4899, 8AM-5PM. www.dmvstat.com ✉ ☎ 💻

Vehicle Ownership, Vehicle Identification

Department of Motor Vehicles, Motor Vehicle Record Section, 555 Wright Way, Carson City, NV 89711-0250; 775-684-4590, Fax: 775-684-4740, 8AM-5PM. www.dmvnv.com ✉ ☎

Accident Reports

Department of Public Safety, Nevada Highway Patrol, 555 Wright Way, Carson City, NV 89711; 775-684-4488, Fax: 775-684-4879, http://nhp.nv.gov/index.htm 8AM-5PM. ✉ Fax 🖐

Vessel Ownership, Vessel Registration

Department of Wildlife Headquarters, Boat Registration, 1100 Valley Rd, Reno, NV 89512-2815; 775-688-1983, Fax: 775-688-1509, 8-5PM www.ndow.org ✉ 🖐

Voter Registration

Records not maintained by a state level agency. Records are open to the public at the county level. The state has plans in the near future to create a statewide database.

GED Certificates

Department of Education, State GED Administrator, 700 E 5th Street, Carson City, NV 89701; 775-687-9104, Fax: 775-687-9114, www.literacynet.org/nvadulted/ 8AM-5PM. ✉ Fax 🖐

Hunting License and Fishing License Information

Department of Wildlife, Licensing Office, 4600 Kietzke LN, D135, Reno, NV 89502; 775-688-1507, Fax: 775-688-1509, 8AM-5PM. www.ndow.org ✉

New Hampshire

Governor's Office
State House   603-271-2121
107 N Main St, Rm 204   Fax 603-271-5686
Concord, NH 03301-4990   8AM-5PM
www.state.nh.us/governor/index.html

Attorney General's Office
33 Capitol St   603-271-3658
Concord, NH 03301-6397   Fax 603-271-2110
http://doj.nh.gov   8AM-5PM

State Website: www.state.nh.us
Legislative Records
603-271-2239   http://gencourt.state.nh.us/ie
State Archives
603-271-2236   www.sos.nh.gov/archives/
Capital: Concord, in Merrimack County

Search Unclaimed Property Online

www.missingmoney.com/main/index.cfm

Criminal Records

State Police Headquarters, Criminal Records, James H. Hayes Bldg,, 33 Hazen Dr, Concord, NH 03305; 603-271-2538, Fax: 603-271-2339, 8:15AM-4:15PM. www.state.nh.us/safety/nhsp/cr.html ✉ 🖐

Statewide Court Records

Administrative Office of Courts, 2 Noble Dr, Supreme Ct Bldg, Concord, NH 03301; 603-271-2521, Fax: 603-271-3977, 8-5PM. www.courts.state.nh.us/ 💻

Sexual Offender Registry

State Police Headquarters, Special Investigations Unit-SOR, James H. Hayes Bldg, 33 Hazen Dr, Concord, NH 03305; 603-271-2538, Fax: 603-271-6479,
www.state.nh.us/safety/nhsp/cr.html
8:15AM-4:15PM. ✉ 🖐 💻

Incarceration Records

New Hampshire Department of Corrections, Offender Records Office, PO Box 14, Concord, NH 03302; 603-271-1825, Fax: 603-271-1867, 8AM-4PM. www.nh.gov/doc/ ✉ ☎ Fax 🖐

Uniform Commercial Code, Federal and State Tax Liens

UCC Division, Secretary of State, 25 Capitol St, State House Annex, 3rd Fl, Concord, NH 03301; 603-271-3276, 9-3:30PM www.sos.nh.gov/ucc//index.htm ✉ 🖐 💻

Sales Tax Registrations

State does not impose sales tax.

Corporation Records, Limited Partnership Records, Limited Liability Company Records, Trademarks/Servicemarks, Trade Names, Limited Liability Partnerships, Not For Profit Entities

Secretary of State, Corporation Division, State House, Room 204, Concord, NH 03301; 603-271-3246, 603-271-3244, Fax: 603-271-3247, 8AM-4:30PM. www.sos.nh.gov/corporate ✉ ☎ Fax 🖐 💻

Key: Access state agency records by:. phone-☎ mail-✉ fax-Fax in person-🖐 online-💻 email-Email

Birth Certificates, Death Records, Marriage Certificates, Divorce Records

Office of Community and Public Health, Bureau of Vital Records, 6 Hazen Dr, Concord, NH 03301; 603-271-4650, 603-271-4654 (Recording), 800-852-3345 x4651 (In-state), Fax: 603-223-6614, 8:30AM-4PM. www.sos.nh.gov/vitalrecords/index.html ✉☎Fax✋🖥

Workers' Compensation Records

Labor Dept., Workers Compensation Division, 95 Pleasant St, Concord, NH 03301; 603-271-3174, Fax: 603-271-6149, 8AM-4:30PM. ✉Fax

Driver Records

Department of Motor Vehicles, Driving Records, 33 Hazen Dr, Concord, NH 03305; 603-271-2322, 8:15AM-4:15PM. www.nh.gov/safety/dmv/ ✉✋🖥

Vehicle Identification

Department of Safety, Bureau of Titles, 33 Hazen Dr, Concord, NH 03305; 603-271-3111-title bureau, Fax 603-271-0369 http://nh.gov/safety/dmv/registration/index.html 8:15AM-4:15PM. ✉✋

Vessel Registration

Department of Safety, Bureau of Registration, Boat Desk, 33 Hazen Dr, Concord, NH 03305; 603-271-2333, 603-271-3242 (Liens), Fax: 603-271-1061, 8:15AM-4:15PM. ✉✋

Accident Reports

Department of Safety, Crash Section, 23 Hazen Dr, Concord, NH 03305; 603-271-2128, 8:15AM-4:15PM. ✉✋

Voter Registration

Records not maintained by a state level agency. All records are kept by Town Clerks. Records are open.

GED Certificates

Adult Education - Dept of Education, GED Testing, 21 S Fruit Street #20, Concord, NH 03301; 603-271-6699, Fax: 603-271-3454, 8AM-4:30PM. www.ed.state.nh.us/GEDhome.htm ✉Fax

Hunting License and Fishing License Information

Fish & Game Dept., Licensing Dept., Eleven Hazen Dr, Concord, NH 03301; 603-271-3421, Fax: 603-271-5829, 8AM-4:30PM. www.wildlife.state.nh.us ✉✋

New Jersey

Governor's Office
PO Box 001, 125 W State St — 609-292-6000
Trenton, NJ 08625-0001 — Fax 609-292-3454
www.state.nj.us/governor — 8:30AM-4:30PM

Attorney General's Office
Law & Public Safety Department — 609-292-8740
PO Box 080, 25 Market St — Fax 609-292-3508
Trenton, NJ 08625-0080 — 8:30AM-5PM
www.state.nj.us/lps

State Website: www.state.nj.us

Legislative Records
609-292-4840 www.njleg.state.nj.us

State Archives
609-292-6260 www.state.nj.us/state/darm/index.html

Capital: Trenton, in Mercer County

Search Unclaimed Property Online

http://webdb.state.nj.us/treasury/taxation/unclaimsrch.htm

Criminal Records

Division of State Police, Records and Identification Section, PO Box 7068, West Trenton, NJ 08628-0068; 609-882-2000 x2878, Fax: 609-530-5780, 9AM-5PM. www.njsp.org ✉✋

Statewide Court Records

Administrative Office of Courts, RJH Justice Complex, 7th Fl, PO Box 037, Trenton, NJ 08625; 609-984-0275, Fax: 609-984-6968, 8:30AM-4:30PM. www.judiciary.state.nj.us/admin.htm 🖥

Sexual Offender Registry

Division of State Police, Sexual Offender Registry, PO Box 7068, West Trenton, NJ 08628-0068; 609-882-2000 x2886, Fax: 609-538-0544, 9-5PM. www.njsp.org/ 🖥

Incarceration Records

New Jersey Department of Corrections, Central Administrative Offices, PO Box 863, Trenton, NJ 08625-0863; 609-777-5753, Fax: 609-777-8367, 8AM-5PM. www.state.nj.us/corrections/index.html ✉☎Fax🖥

Corporation Records, Limited Liability Company Records, Fictitious Name, Limited Partnerships

Division of Revenue, Records Unit, PO 450, Trenton, NJ 08625 (225 W State St, 3rd Fl, Trenton, NJ 08608); 609-292-9292, Fax: 609-984-6855, 8:30-4:30PM. www.state.nj.us/treasury/revenue/certcomm.htm ✉☎Fax✋🖥

Trademarks/Servicemarks

Dept. of Treasury, Trademark Division, PO Box 453, Trenton, NJ 08625-0453 (225 W State St, 3rd Fl, Trenton, NJ

08608); 609-292-9292, Fax: 609-984-6681, www.state.nj.us/treasury/revenue/ 8:30AM-5PM. ✉ ✋ 🖥

Uniform Commercial Code

UCC Section, Certification and Status Unit, PO 303, Trenton, NJ 08625 (225 West State St); 609-292-9292, 8AM-5PM. www.state.nj.us/njbgs ✉ **Fax** ✋ 🖥

Federal and State Tax Liens

Records not maintained by a state level agency. Federal tax liens are filed with the county clerk or register of deeds. All state "docket judgment" liens are filed at the Superior Court in Trenton. "Certificates of Debt" are filed at the respective county superior court.

Sales Tax Registrations

Access to Records is Restricted
Dept. of Revenue, Sales tax Licensing, PO Box 252, Trenton, NJ 08646-0252; 609-292-1730, Fax: 609-292-4291, 8:30-4:30. www.state.nj.us/treasury/taxation Sales tax information is considered confidential. Order forms and information about publications are available on this agency's website. ✉ ☎ **Fax** ✋

Birth Certificates, Death Records, Marriage Certificates

Department of Health, Bureau of Vital Statistics, PO Box 370, Trenton, NJ 08625-0370 (S Warren St, Room 504, Health & Agriculture Building, Trenton, NJ 08625); 609-292-4087, 877-622-7549 (credit card requests), Fax 609-392-4292,

www.state.nj.us/health/vital/vital.htm 9AM-5PM. ✉ ☎ **Fax** ✋ 🖥

Divorce Records

Clerk of Superior Court, Records Center, PO Box 967, Trenton, NJ 08625-0967 (Corner of Jerser & Tremont Streets, Building #2, Trenton, NJ 08625); 609-777-0092, Fax: 609-777-0094, 8:30-4PM. www.judiciary.state.nj.us ✉ **Fax** ✋ 🖥

Workers' Compensation Records

Labor Department, Division of Workers Compensation, PO Box 381, Trenton, NJ 08625-0381 (Labor Building, 6th Fl, John Fitch Plaza, Trenton, NJ 08625); 609-292-6026, 609-292-2515 (General Hotline), Fax: 609-984-2515, 8:30AM-4:30PM. www.nj.gov/labor/wc/wcindex.html ✉ ✋ 🖥

Driver Records

Motor Vehicle Services, Driver History Abstract Unit, PO Box 142, Trenton, NJ 08666; 609-292-6500 (Forms request), 609-292-7500 (Suspensions), 8AM-4:30PM. www.state.nj.us/mvc/ ✉ ✋ 🖥

Vehicle Ownership, Vehicle Identification, Vessel Ownership, Vessel Registration

Motor Vehicle Commission, Certified Information Unit, PO Box 146, Trenton, NJ 08666; 609-292-6500, 888-486-3339 (In-state), 8AM-5PM. www.state.nj.us/mvc/cit_title/v_title.html ✉ 🖥

Accident Reports

New Jersey State Police, Criminal Justice Records Section, PO Box 7068, West Trenton, NJ 08628-0068; 609-882-2000 x2234, 8AM-5PM. www.njsp.org ✉ 🖥

Voter Registration

Access to Records is Restricted
Dept of Law and Public Safety, Division of Elections, PO Box 304, Trenton, NJ 08625; 609-292-3760, Fax: 609-777-1280, 8:30AM-5PM. www.njelections.org Commissioner of Registration maintains these records, but they can only be accessed at the county level. While these county agencies may permit individual look-ups, records in mass may only be purchased for political purposes.

GED Certificates

GED Testing Program, Dept. of Education - Bureau Adult Ed. & Literacy, PO Box 500, Trenton, NJ 08625; 609-777-0577, 609-777-1050-forms, Fax: 609-984-0573, 9AM-4PM. www.state.nj.us/njded/students/ged ✉

Hunting License and Fishing License Information

Records not maintained by a state level agency.
They do not have a central database. You must contact the vendor where the license was purchased. Plans are underway to implement a computerized database.

New Mexico

Governor's Office
   State Capitol, Room 400   505-476-2200
   Santa Fe, NM 87503   Fax 505-676-3026
   www.governor.state.nm.us   8AM-5PM

Attorney General's Office
   PO Drawer 1508   505-827-6000
   Santa Fe, NM 87504-1508   Fax 505-827-5826
   www.ago.state.nm.us   8AM-5PM

State Website: www.state.nm.us

Legislative Records
   505-986-4600   http://legis.state.nm.us

State Archives
   505-476-7908   www.nmcpr.state.nm.us

Capital: Santa Fe, in Santa Fe County

Search Unclaimed Property Online
   https://ec3.state.nm.us/ucp/SearchUCP.htm

Key: Access state agency records by:. phone-☎ mail-✉ fax-**Fax** in person-✋ online-🖥 email-**Email**

Criminal Records

Department of Public Safety, Criminal Records Bureau, PO Box 1628, Santa Fe, NM 87504-1628 (4491 Cerrillos Rd, Santa Fe, NM 87504); 505-827-9181, Fax: 505-827-3388, 8AM-5PM. www.dps.nm.org ✉ ✋ 🖥

Statewide Court Records

Administrative Office of the Courts, 237 Don Gaspar, Rm 25, Santa Fe, NM 87501; 505-827-4800, Fax: 505-827-4246, 8AM-5PM. www.nmcourts.com 🖥

Sexual Offender Registry

Department of Public Safety, Records Bureau, PO Box 1628, Santa Fe, NM 87504-1628 (4491 Cerrillos Rd, Santa Fe, NM 87504); 505-827-9297, 505-827-9193, Fax: 505-827-3388, 8AM-5PM. www.nmsexoffender.dps.state.nm.us/ ✉ ☎ ✋ 🖥

Incarceration Records

Corrections Department, Central Records Unit, PO Box 27116, Santa Fe, NM 87502; 505-827-8674, Fax 505-827-8801, 8AM-5PM. http://corrections.state.nm.us/ ✉ ☎ 🖥

Corporation Records, Limited Liability Company Records

New Mexico Public Regulation Commission, Corporations Bureau, PO Box 1269, Santa Fe, NM 87504-1269 (1120 Paseo de Peralta, Pera Bldg 4th Fl, Rm 413, Santa Fe, NM 87501); 505-827-4502 (Main Number), 800-947-4722 (In-state Only), 505-827-4510 (Good Standing), 505-827-4513 (Copy Request), Fax: 505-827-4387, 8AM-N; 1PM-5PM. www.nmprc.state.nm.us/corporations/corpshome.htm ✉ ☎ Fax ✋ 🖥

Trademarks/Servicemarks, Trade Names

Secretary of State, Trademarks Division, 325 Don Gaspar, #301, Santa Fe, NM 87503; 505-827-3609, Fax 505-827-3611, 8-5PM. www.sos.state.nm.us/trade.htm ✉ ☎ Fax ✋

Uniform Commercial Code

UCC Division, Secretary of State, 325 Don GasparSt #300, Santa Fe, NM 87503; 505-827-3610, Fax 505-827-3611, 8-5pm.

www.sos.state.nm.us/ucc/ucchome.htm ✉ ✋ 🖥

Federal and State Tax Liens

Records not maintained by a state level agency.
Records are filed with the Clerk at the county level.

Sales Tax Registrations

Taxation & Revenue Department, Tax Administrative Services Division, PO Box 5374, Santa Fe, NM 87504 (Montoya Bldg, 1200 St Francis Drive, Santa Fe, NM 87501); 505-827-0700, Fax: 505-827-0614, 8-5PM. www.state.nm.us/tax ✉ ✋

Birth Certificates, Death Records

Department of Health, Bureau of Vital Records, PO Box 26110, Santa Fe, NM 87502 (1105 South St Francis Dr, Santa Fe, NM 87502); 505-827-0121, 505-827-2338 (Information), 877-284-0963 (Order), Fax: 505-984-1048, 8AM-5:00PM (Counter Service: 9AM-4PM). www.health.state.nm.us ✉ ☎ Fax ✋ 🖥

Marriage Certificates, Divorce Records

Records not maintained by a state level agency.
Marriage and Divorce records are found at county of issue.

Workers' Compensation Records

Access to Records is Restricted
Workers Compensation Administration, PO Box 27198, Albuquerque, NM 87125-7198 (2410 Centre Ave, SE, Albuquerque, NM 87106); 505-841-6000, 800-255-7965 (In-State Toll Free), Fax: 505-841-6060, 8AM-5PM. www.state.nm.us/wca/ The subject must write the agency, provide proof of ID with a driver's license, and request the record, and pay a copy. Most records are confidential but access is permitted for all parties to a case and other cases involving a worker. ✉ ✋

Driver Records

Motor Vehicle Division, Driver Services Bureau, PO Box 1028, Santa Fe, NM 87504-1028 (Joseph M. Montoya Bldg, 1100 S St. Francis Dr, 2nd Fl, Santa Fe);

505-827-2214, Fax: 505-827-2792, 8AM-5PM. www.state.nm.us/tax/mvd ✉ ✋ 🖥

Vehicle Ownership, Vehicle Identification, Vessel Ownership, Vessel Registration

Motor Vehicle Division, Vehicle Services Bureau, PO Box 1028, Santa Fe, NM 87504-1028 (Joseph M. Montoya Bldg, 1100 S St. Francis Dr, 2nd Fl, Santa Fe, NM 87504); 505-827-4636, 505-827-1004, Fax: 505-827-0395, 8AM-5PM. www.state.nm.us/tax/mvd ✉ ✋ 🖥

Accident Reports

Department of Public Safety, Attn: Records, PO Box 1628, Santa Fe, NM 87504-1628 (New Mexico State Police Complex, 4491 Cerrillos Rd, Santa Fe, NM 87504); 505-827-9181, Fax: 505-827-9189, 8AM-5PM. www.dps.nm.org ✉ ☎ ✋ 🖥

Voter Registration

Access to Records is Restricted
Secretary of State, Bureau of Elections, 325 Don Gaspar, #300, Santa Fe, NM 87503; 505-827-3620, 800-477-3632, Fax: 505-827-8403, 8AM-5PM. www.sos.state.nm.us/ELECTNET.HTM Individual look-ups must be done at the county clerk level. This agency maintains a limited database, not all counties upload data in a timely manner. Agency does sell statewide lists for restricted (political) purposes, and not commercial purposes.

GED Certificates

Department of Education, GED Testing Program, 300 Don Gaspar, Rm 122, Santa Fe, NM 87501-2786; 505-827-6702, Fax: 505-827-6616, 8AM-5PM. www.sde.state.nm.us/div/ais/assess/ged/ ✉ Fax ✋

Hunting License and Fishing License Information

NM Dept of Game & Fish, PO Box 25112, Santa Fe, NM 87504 (#1 Wildlife Way, Santa Fe); 505-476-8000, 800-862-9310, Fax: 505-827-7915, 8AM-12PM; 1-5PM. www.wildlife.state.nm.us ✉ ✋

New York

Governor's Office
Executive Chamber, State Capitol   518-474-8390
Albany, NY 12224   9AM-5PM
www.state.ny.us/governor

Attorney General's Office
State Capitol   518-474-7330
Albany, NY 12224-0341   Fax 518-473-9909
www.oag.state.ny.us   9AM-5:30PM

State Website: www.state.ny.us

Legislative Records
518-455-3216   www.senate.state.ny.us

State Archives: 518-474-8955
www.nysarchives.org/gindex.shtml

Capital: Albany, in Albany County

> **Search Unclaimed Property Online**
> www.osc.state.ny.us/cgi-bin/db2www/ouffrm.d2w/input

Criminal Records

Access to Records is Restricted
Division of Criminal Justice Services, 4 Tower Place, Albany, NY 12203; 518-457-6043, Fax: 518-457-6550, 8AM-5PM. www.criminaljustice.state.ny.us Records only released pursuant to court order, subpoena, to entities authorized by statute, or to person of record. The public must search at the county court level.

Statewide Court Records

NY State Office of Court Administration, New York City Office, 25 Beaver St, New York, NY 10004; 212-428-2100, 212-428-2990, Fax: 212-428-2190, 9AM-5PM. www.courts.state.ny.us ✉️ 🖥️

Sexual Offender Registry

Division of Criminal Justice Srvs, Sexual Offender Registry, 4 Tower Place, Rm 604, Albany, NY 12203; 518-457-6326 x1, 800-262-3257 x2 (Verification), Fax: 518-485-5805, 8AM-5PM. www.criminaljustice.state.ny.us/nsor/search_disclaimer.htm ✉️ ☎️Fax🖥️

Incarceration Records

New York Department of Correctional Services, Building 2, 1220 Washington Ave, Albany, NY 12226-2050; 518-457-5000, 518-457-8126 (Contact phone), Fax: 518-485-9502, 8AM-4PM. www.docs.state.ny.us ✉️ ☎️Fax🖥️

Trademarks/Servicemarks

Department of State, Miscellaneous Records Unit, 41 State St, Albany, NY 12231; 518-474-4770, Fax: 518-473-0730, 8AM-4:30PM. http://dos.state.ny.us ✉️ ☎️Fax🖐️

Corporation Records, Limited Partnership Records, Limited Liability Company Records, Limited Liability Partnerships

Division of Corporations, Department of State, 41 State St, Albany, NY 12231; 518-473-2492 (General Information), 900-835-2677 (Corporate Searches), Fax: 518-474-1418, 8AM-4:30PM. www.dos.state.ny.us ✉️ ☎️Fax🖐️🖥️

Uniform Commercial Code, Federal and State Tax Liens

Department of State, UCC Unit - Records, 41 State Street, Albany, NY 12231-0001; 518-474-4763, 518-474-5418, Fax: 518-474-4478, 8AM-4:30PM. www.dos.state.ny.us/corp/uccfaq.html ✉️ 🖐️🖥️

Sales Tax Registrations

Sales Tax Registration Bureau, WA Harriman Campus, Building 8, Rm 957, Albany, NY 12227; 800-972-1233, 7AM-5PM. www.nystax.gov/ ✉️ ☎️Fax🖐️

Birth Certificates, Death Records, Marriage Certificates, Divorce Records

Vital Records Section, Certification Unit, 800 N Pearl St, Albany, NY 12204-1842; (PO Box 2602, Albany, NY 12220-2602); 518-474-3038, 518-474-3077, 877-854-4481 (Searching), Fax: 877-854-4607, 8:30-4:30PM. www.health.state.ny.us/nysdoh/consumer/vr.htm ✉️ ☎️Fax🖐️

Birth Certificate-New York City, and Death Record-New York City

Department of Health, Bureau of Vital Records, 125 Worth St, Rm 133, New York, NY 10013; 212-788-4520, 212-442-1999, Fax: 212-962-6105, 9-4PM. www.nyc.gov/html/doh/ ✉️ ☎️Fax🖐️🖥️

Marriage Certificate-New York City

City Clerk's Office, Department of Records & Information Services, 1 Centre Street, Rm 252, New York, NY 10007; 212-669-8090, 8:30AM-3PM M-F. ✉️ 🖐️

Divorce Records-New York City

New York County Clerk's Office, Divorce Records, 60 Centre Street, Rm 141B, New York, NY 10007; 212-374-4376, 9AM-3PM, M-F. ✉️ 🖐️

Workers' Compensation Records

NY Workers' Compensation Board, Office of General Counsel, 20 Park Street # 401, Albany, NY 12207; 518-474-6670, 9AM-5PM. www.wcb.state.ny.us ✉️ 🖐️🖥️

Driver Records

Department of Motor Vehicles, MV-15 Processing, 6 Empire State Plaza, Room 430, Albany, NY 12228; 518-473-5595, 800-225-5368 (In-state), 8AM-5PM. www.nydmv.state.ny.us ✉️ ☎️🖐️🖥️

Key: Access state agency records by:. phone-☎️   mail-✉️   fax-Fax   in person-🖐️   online-🖥️   email-Email

Vehicle Ownership, Vehicle Identification, Vessel Ownership, Vessel Registration

Department of Motor Vehicles, Customer Service Center, 6 Empire State Plaza, Room 430, Albany, NY 12228; 518-474-0710, 518-474-8510, 8AM-5PM. www.nydmv.state.ny.us ✉ 🖐 💻

Accident Reports

DMV Certified Document Center, Accident Report Section, 6 Empire State Plaza, Swan St Bldg, Albany, NY 12228; 518-474-0710, 8AM-4:30PM. www.nysdmv.com ✉ ☎ Fax

Voter Registration

Records not maintained by a state level agency. Records may only be viewed or purchased at the county level. Purchases are restricted for political purposes only.

GED Certificates

NY State Education Dept, GED Testing, PO Box 7348, Albany, NY 12224-0348; 518-474-5906, Fax: 518-474-3041, www.emsc.nysed.gov/workforce/ged 10AM-N, 1PM-3PM. ✉ ☎

Hunting License and Fishing License Information

Records not maintained by a state level agency.

North Carolina

Governor's Office
20301 Mail Service Center   919-733-4240
Raleigh, NC 27699-0301   Fax 919-715-3175
www.governor.state.nc.us   8AM-6PM

Attorney General's Office
Justice Department   919-716-6400
PO Box 629   Fax 919-716-6750
Raleigh, NC 27602-0629   8AM-5PM
www.jus.state.nc.us

State Website: www.ncgov.com

Legislative Records
919-733-7779   www.ncleg.net

State Archives
919-733-7305   www.ah.dcr.state.nc.us

Capital: Raleigh, in Wake County

> Search Unclaimed Property Online

https://www.treasurer.state.nc.us/dstmcmsweb/escheats/pages/forms/search.asp

Criminal Records

Access to Records is Restricted
State Bureau of Investigation, Identification Section, PO Box 29500, Raleigh, NC 27626 (3320 Garner Rd, Raleigh, NC 27626-0500); 919-662-4500 x6302, Fax: 919-662-4380, 8AM-5PM. http://sbi.jus.state.nc.us This agency and the Administrative Office of the Courts implemented a computer-to-computer interface. Employers are denied access unless subject is in a business designated to receive records (ie. health or child care)

Statewide Court Records

Administrative Office of Courts, PO Box 2448, Raleigh, NC 27602-2448 (2 E Morgan St, Raleigh, NC 27602-2448); 919-733-7107, Fax: 919-715-5779, 8AM-5PM. www.nccourts.org/Courts/ 💻

Sexual Offender Registry

State Bureau of Investigation, Division of Criminal Information-SOR Unit, PO Box 29500, Raleigh, NC 27626 (3320 Garner Rd, Raleigh, NC 27626-0500); 919-662-

4500 x6257, Fax: 919-662-4619, 8AM-5PM. http://sbi.jus.state.nc.us ✉ 🖐 💻

Incarceration Records

Department of Corrections, Combined Records, 2020 Yonkers Road, 4226 MSC, Raleigh, NC 27699-4226; 919-716-3200, Fax: 919-716-3986, 8AM-4:30PM. www.doc.state.nc.us/ ✉ ☎ Fax 💻

Corporation Records, Limited Partnerships, Limited Liability Company Records, Trademarks/Servicemarks

Secretary of State, Corporations Division, PO Box 29622, Raleigh, NC 27626-0622 (2 S Salisbury, Raleigh, NC 27601); 919-807-2225 (Corporations), 919-807-2162 (Trademarks), 888-246-7636, Fax: 919-807-2039, 8-5. www.secstate.state.nc.us/ ✉ ☎ Fax 🖐 💻

Uniform Commercial Code, Federal Tax Liens

UCC Division, Secretary of State, PO Box 29626, Raleigh, NC 27626-0626 (2 South Salisbury St, Raleigh, NC 27602); 919-807-2111, Fax: 919-807-2120, 8-5PM. www.secretary.state.nc.us/UCC ✉ 🖐 💻

State Tax Liens

Records not maintained by a state level agency.
Tax lien data is found at the county level.

Sales Tax Registrations

Access to Records is Restricted
Revenue Department, Sales & Use Tax Division, PO Box 25000, Raleigh, NC 27640 (501 N Wilmington Street, Raleigh, NC 27604); 919-733-3661, Fax: 919-715-6086, 8-5PM. www.dor.state.nc.us ✉ 💻

Birth Certificates, Death Records, Marriage Certificates, Divorce Records

Center for Health Statistics, Vital Records Branch, 1903 Mail Service Center, Raleigh, NC 27699-1903 (225 N McDowell St, Raleigh, NC 27603); 919-733-3526, 800-669-8310 (Credit Card Orders), Fax: 919-829-1359, 8AM-4PM. http://vitalrecords.dhhs.state.nc.us/ ⊠☎🖐

Workers' Compensation Records

NC Industrial Commission, Worker's Comp Records, 4340 Mail Service Center, Raleigh, NC 27699-4340; 919-807-2500, 800-688-8349 (Claims Questions), Fax: 919-715-0282, www.comp.state.nc.us 8AM-5PM. ⊠🖐🖥

Driver Records

Division of Motor Vehicles, Driver's License Section, 3113 MSC, Raleigh, NC 27699 (1100 New Bern Ave, Raleigh, NC 27697); 919-715-7000, 8AM-5PM. www.ncdot.org/dmv/driver_services/ ⊠🖐🖥

Vehicle Ownership, Vehicle Identification

Division of Motor Vehicles, Registration/Correspondence Unit, 1100 New Bern Ave, Rm 100, Raleigh, NC 27697-0001; 919-715-7000, 8AM-5PM. www.dmv.dot.state.nc.us ⊠🖐

Accident Reports

Division of Motor Vehicles, Traffic Records Section, 3105 Mail Service Center, Raleigh, NC 27699-3105; 919-861-3098, Fax: 919-733-9605, 8-5PM. www.ncdot.org/dmv/other_services/recor dsstatistics/copyCrashReport.html ⊠🖐

Vessel Ownership, Vessel Registration

North Carolina Wildlife Resources Commission, Transaction Management, 1709 Mail Service Center, Raleigh, NC 27699-1709 (322 Chapanoke Road, Raleigh); 800-628-3773, Fax: 919-662-4379, 8-5PM. http://216.27.49.98/ ⊠Fax

Voter Registration

State Board of Elections, PO Box 27255, Raleigh, NC 27611-7255; 919-733-7173, Fax: 919-715-0135, 8AM-5PM. www.sboe.state.nc.us ⊠☎Fax🖐🖥

GED Certificates

Department of Community Colleges, GED Office, 50164 Mail Service Center, Raleigh, NC 27699-5016; 919-733-7051 x744, Fax: 919-715-5351, 8AM-5PM. www.ncccs.cc.nc.us ⊠Fax🖐

Hunting License and Fishing License Information

Wildlife Resource Commission, Archdale Bldg, 512 N Salisbury Street, Raleigh, NC 27604-0118; 919-662-4370, Fax: 919-661-4878, 8AM-5PM. http://216.27.49.98 ⊠Fax

North Dakota

Governor's Office
  State Capitol
  600 E Boulevard Ave, 1st Fl
  Bismarck, ND 58505-0001
  www.governor.state.nd.us

701-328-2200
Fax 701-328-2205
8AM-5PM

Attorney General's Office
  State Capitol - Dept 125
  600 E Boulevard Ave
  Bismarck, ND 58505-0040
  www.ag.state.nd.us

701-328-2210
Fax 701-328-2226
8AM-5PM

State Website: http://discovernd.com

Legislative Records
  701-328-2916 www.state.nd.us/lr

State Archives
  701-328-2666 www.state.nd.us/hist/sal.htm

Capital: Bismark, in Burleigh County

Search Unclaimed Property Online

www.land.state.nd.us/abp/abphome.htm

Criminal Records

Bureau of Criminal Investigation, Criminal Records Section, PO Box 1054, Bismarck, ND 58502-1054 (4205 N State St, Bismarck, ND 58501); 701-328-5500, Fax: 701-328-5510, 8AM-5PM. www.ag.state.nd.us ⊠🖐

Statewide Court Records

Court Administrator, North Dakota Supreme Court, 600 E Blvd Ave, Dept 180, Bismarck, ND 58505-0530; 701-328-

4216, Fax: 701-328-2092, 8AM-5PM. www.ndcourts.com/ 🖥

Sexual Offender Registry

Bureau of Criminal Investigation, SOR Unit, PO Box 1054, Bismarck, ND 58502-1054 (4205 N State St, Bismarck); 701-328-5500, Fax: 701-328-5510, 8-5PM. www.ndsexoffender.com/ ⊠☎🖐🖥

Incarceration Records

Department of Corrections and Rehabilitation, Records Clerk, PO Box 5521, Bismarck, ND 58506 (3100 E Railroad Ave, Bismarck, ND 58506); 701-328-6122, Fax: 701-328-6640, 8AM-5PM. www.state.nd.us/docr/ ⊠☎Fax

Key: Access state agency records by:. phone-☎ mail-⊠ fax-Fax in person-🖐 online-🖥 email-Email

Uniform Commercial Code, Federal and State Tax Liens

UCC Division, Secretary of State, 600 E Boulevard Ave Dept 108, Bismarck, ND 58505; 701-328-3662, Fax: 701-328-4214, 8AM-5PM. www.state.nd.us/sec ✉☎Fax🖐🖥

Corporation Records, Limited Liability Company Records, Limited Partnership Records, Limited Liability Partnership Records, Trademarks, Servicemarks, Fictitious Name, Assumed Name

Secretary of State, Business Information/Registration, 600 E Boulevard Ave, Dept 108, Bismarck, ND 58505-0500; 701-328-4284, 800-352-0867, Fax: 701-328-2992, 8AM-5PM. www.state.nd.us/sec ✉☎Fax🖐🖥

Sales Tax Registrations

Office of State Tax Commissioner, Sales & Special Taxes Division, State Capitol, 600 E Boulevard Ave, Bismarck, ND 58505; 701-328-3470, Fax: 701-328-3700, 8AM-5PM. www.state.nd.us/taxdpt ✉☎Fax🖥

Birth Certificates, Death Records, Marriage Certificates

ND Department of Health, Vital Records, State Capitol, 600 E Blvd, Dept 301, Bismarck, ND 58505-0200; 701-328-2360, Fax: 701-328-1850, 7:30AM-5PM. www.vitalnd.com ✉Fax🖐🖥

Divorce Records

Access to Records is Restricted
Department of Health, Vital Records, State Capitol, 600 E Blvd, Dept 301, Bismarck, ND 58505-0200; 701-328-2360, Fax: 701-328-1850, 7:30AM-5PM. www.vitalnd.com This agency can direct you to the county with the records. Call or email to vitalrec@state.nd.us.

Workers' Compensation Records

Workforce Safety & Insurance, Workers' Compensation Records, PO Box 5585, Bismarck ND 58506-5585 (1600 East Century Avenue, Suite 1); 701-328-3800, 800-777-5033, Fax: 701-328-3750, 7:30-5PM. www.workforcesafety.com/ ✉

Driver Records

Department of Transportation, Driver License & Traffic Safety Division, 608 E Boulevard Ave, Bismarck, ND 58505-0700; 701-328-2603, Fax: 701-328-2435, 8AM-5PM. www.state.nd.us/dot ✉🖐🖥

Vehicle Ownership, Vehicle Identification

Department of Transportation, Records Section/Motor Vehicle Div., 608 E Boulevard Ave, Bismarck, ND 58505-0780; 701-328-2725, 701-328-1285 (TTY), Fax: 701-328-1487, 8AM-4:50PM. www.state.nd.us/dot/ ✉Fax🖐

Accident Reports

Driver License & Traffic Safety Division, Traffic Records Section, 608 E Boulevard Ave, Bismarck, ND 58505-0780; 701-328-4397, 701-328-2601, Fax: 701-328-2435, 8-5PM. www.state.nd.us/dot ✉🖐

Vessel Ownership, Vessel Registration

North Dakota Game & Fish Department, Boat Registrations, 100 N Bismarck Expressway, Bismarck, ND 58501; 701-328-6335, Fax: 701-328-6374, 8-5PM. www.state.nd.us/gnf ✉☎Fax🖐🖥

Voter Registration

Records not maintained by a state level agency. Records are maintained in poll books at county level by County Auditors. Records are open to the public.

GED Certificates

Dept. of Public Instruction, GED Testing, 600 E Blvd Ave, Bismarck, ND 58505-0440; 701-328-2393, Fax: 701-328-4770, 8-4:30 www.dpi.state.nd.us ✉Fax🖐🖥

Hunting License and Fishing License Information

Game & Fish Department, 100 N Bismarck Expressway, Bismarck, ND 58501-5095; 701-328-6300, 701-328-6335 (Licensing), Fax: 701-328-6352, 8-5PM. www.state.nd.us/gnf ✉Fax🖐🖥

Ohio

Governor's Office
  77 S High St, 30th Floor   614-466-3555
  Columbus, OH 43215   Fax 614-466-9354
  http://governor.ohio.gov   8AM-5PM

Attorney General's Office
  State Office Tower   614-466-4320
  30 E Broad St, 17th Floor   Fax 614-644-6135
  Columbus, OH 43215-3428   8AM-5PM
  www.ag.state.oh.us

State Website: http://ohio.gov

Legislative Records
  614-466-9745 www.legislature.state.oh.us
State Archives
  614-297-2300 www.ohiohistory.org/ar_tools.html
Capital: Columbus, in Franklin County

Search Unclaimed Property Online

www.unclaimedfundstreasurehunt.ohio.gov

Key: Access state agency records by:. phone-☎ mail-✉ fax-Fax in person-🖐 online-🖥 email-Email

Ohio Criminal Records

Ohio Bureau of Investigation, Civilian Background Section, PO Box 365, London, OH 43140 (1560 State Rte 56, London, OH 43140); 740-845-2000 (General Info), 740-845-2375 (civilian checks), Fax: 740-845-2633, 8-4:45PM. www.webcheck.ag.state.oh.us ✉🖥

Statewide Court Records

Administrative Director, Supreme Court of Ohio, 65 S Front Street, Columbus, OH 43215-3431; 614-387-9000, 800-826-9010, 8-5PM. www.sconet.state.oh.us 🖥

Sexual Offender Registry

Access to Records is Restricted
Ohio Bureau of Investigation, Sexual Offender Registry, PO Box 365, London, OH 43140 (1560 State Rte 56 SW, London, OH); 740-845-2221, 740-845-2223, Fax: 740-845-2633, 8AM-4:45PM. www.esorn.ag.state.oh.us/Secured/p1.asp x O.R.C. 2950.13 requires that the public eSORN database contain information on every person convicted as an adult and registered in the state registry of sex offenders and child-victim offenders.🖥

Incarceration Records

Ohio Department of Rehabilitation and Correction, Bureau of Records Management, 1050 Freeway Drive, N., Columbus, OH 43229; 614-752-1076, Fax: 614-752-1086, 8:30AM-5PM M-F. www.drc.state.oh.us/ ✉☎Fax🖥

Corporation Records, Fictitious Name, Limited Partnership Records, Assumed Name, Trademarks, Servicemarks, Limited Liability Company Records

Secretary of State, Corporate Records Access, PO Box 130, Columbus, OH 43215 (180 E Broad Street, 16th Fl, Columbus); 877-767-3453, 614-466-3910, Fax: 614-466-3899, 8AM-5PM. www.sos.state.oh.us/sos/ ✉☎Fax🖐🖥

Uniform Commercial Code

UCC Records, Secretary of State, PO Box 2795, Columbus, OH 43216 (180 E Broad Street, 16th Fl); 877-767-3453, 614-466-3910, Fax 614-466-2892, 8AM-5PM. www.sos.state.oh.us/sos/ucc/index.html ✉☎Fax🖐🖥

Federal and State Tax Liens

Records not maintained by a state level agency. You must search at the local county recorder offices.

Sales Tax Registrations

Access to Records is Restricted
Taxation Department, Sale & Use Tax Division, 30 E Broad St, 20th Fl, Columbus, OH 43215; 614-466-7351, 888-405-4039, Fax: 614-466-4977, 8AM-5PM M-F. http://tax.ohio.gov This agency refuses to release any information about registrants.

Birth Certificates, Death Records

Department of Health, Bureau of Vital Statistics, PO Box 15098, Columbus, OH 43215-0098 (246 N High St, 1st Fl, Revenue Room, Columbus); 614-466-2531, 877-828-3101, Fax: 877-553-2439, www.odh.state.oh.us/VitStats/birth1.htm 7:45AM-4:30PM. ✉Fax🖐

Marriage Certificates, Divorce Records

Access to Records is Restricted
Dept of Health, Bureau of Vital Statistics, PO Box 15098, Columbus, OH 43215; www.odh.state.oh.us/VitStats/searchpro.htm 614-466-2531. Marriage and Divorce records are found at county of issue. This agency will only do a search of the index from 1953 forward. ✉🖐

Workers' Compensation Records

Bureau of Workers Compensation, Customer Contact Center, 30 W Spring St, Fl 10, Columbus, OH 43215-2241; 800-644-6292, Fax: 877-520-6446, 7:30AM-5:30PM. www.ohiobwc.com ✉☎Fax🖐🖥

Driver Records

Department of Public Safety, Bureau of Motor Vehicles, 1970 W Broad St, Columbus, OH 43223-1102; 614-752-7600, Fax: 614-752-7987, 8AM-5:30PM M-T-W; 8AM-4:30PM TH-F. www.ohiobmv.com/ ✉☎Fax🖐🖥

Vehicle Ownership, Vehicle Identification

Bureau of Motor Vehicles, Motor Vehicle Title Records, 1970 W Broad St, Columbus, OH 43223-1102; 614-752-7671, Fax: 614-752-8929, 7:30-4:45PM. www.ohiobmv.com ✉☎Fax🖐🖥

Accident Reports

Department of Public Safety, OSHP Central Records, 1st Fl, PO Box 182074, Columbus, OH 43218-2074; 614-752-1583, Fax: 614-644-9749, 8AM-4:45PM. http://statepatrol.ohio.gov/crash.htm ✉🖐🖥

Vessel Ownership, Vessel Registration

NRD-Division of Watercraft, Titles and Registration, 4435 Fountain Square Dr Bldg A, Columbus, OH 43224-1362; 614-265-6480, 877-426-2837 (Titles), Fax: 614-267-8883, 8AM-5PM. www.dnr.state.oh.us/watercraft/ ✉☎Fax🖐🖥

Voter Registration

Secretary of State, Elections Division, 180 E Broad St, 15th Fl, Columbus, OH 43215; 614-466-2585, Fax: 614-752-4360, 8-5PM. www.state.oh.us/sos ✉🖐

GED Certificates

GED Transcript Office, 25 S Front St, 1st Fl, Columbus, OH 43215-4183; 614-466-1577, Fax: 614-752-9445, 8AM-4:30PM. www.ode.state.oh.us/curriculum-assessment/assessment/ged ✉Fax🖐

Hunting License and Fishing License Information

Dept of Natural Resources, Division of Wildlife, 1840 Belcher Drive, Columbus, OH 43224; 614-265-6300, 8AM-5PM. www.dnr.state.oh.us/wildlife/default.htm ✉

Key: Access state agency records by:. phone-☎ mail-✉ fax-**Fax** in person-🖐 online-🖥 email-**Email**

Oklahoma

Governor's Office
  State Capitol, Suite 212   405-521-2342
  Oklahoma City, OK 73105   Fax 405-521-3353
  www.governor.state.ok.us   8AM-5PM

Attorney General's Office
  2300 N Lincoln, #112   405-521-3921
  Oklahoma City, OK 73105   Fax 405-521-6246
  www.oag.state.ok.us/explorer.index.html

State Website: www.state.ok.us

Legislative Records
  Bill Status Info-Rm B-30, 405-521-5642
  www.lsb.state.ok.us

State Archives
  405-522-3577   www.odl.state.ok.us

Capital: Oklahoma City, in Oklahoma County

Search Unclaimed Property Online
  www.youroklahoma.com/unclaimed

Criminal Records

State Bureau of Investigation, Criminal History Reporting, 6600 N Harvey, Oklahoma City, OK 73116; 405-848-6724, Fax: 405-879-2503, 8AM-5PM. www.osbi.state.ok.us ✉**Fax**✋

Statewide Court Records

Administrative Director of Courts, 1915 N Stiles, #305, Oklahoma City, OK 73105; 405-521-2450, Fax: 405-521-6815, 8AM-5PM. www.oscn.net 🖥

Sexual Offender Registry

Dept. of Corrections, Sex Offender Registry, PO Box 11400, Oklahoma City, OK 73136-0400; 405-962-6104, 8-5PM. www.doc.state.ok.us/DOCS/offender_info.htm ✉🖥

Incarceration Records

Department of Corrections, Offender Records, PO Box 11400, Oklahoma City, OK 73136 (3400 Martin Luther King Avenue, Oklahoma City, OK 73136); 405-425-2500, Fax: 405-425-2608, 8AM-4:30. www.doc.state.ok.us/ ✉☎**Fax**🖥

Uniform Commercial Code

UCC Central Filing Office, Oklahoma County Clerk, 320 R.S. Kerr Ave, County Office Bldg, Rm 105, Oklahoma City, OK 73102; 405-713-1521, Fax 405-713-1810, www.oklahomacounty.org/countyclerk 8AM-5PM. ✉✋🖥

Federal and State Tax Liens

Records not maintained by a state level agency. All state tax liens and federal tax liens are filed at the local level.

Federal tax liens on businesses are filed with the Clerk of Oklahoma County.

Corporation Records, Limited Liability Company Records, Limited Partnerships, Trademarks/Servicemarks, Limited Liability Partnerships

Secretary of State, Business Records Department, 2300 N Lincoln Blvd, Rm 101, Oklahoma City, OK 73105-4897; 405-522-4582 (Records), 900-825-2424 (Records), Fax: 405-521-3771, 8-5PM. www.sos.state.ok.us/ ✉☎**Fax**✋🖥

Sales Tax Registrations

Taxpayer Assistance, Sales Tax Regis. Records, 2501 N Lincoln Blvd, Oklahoma City, OK 73194; 405-521-3160, 405-521-3200, Fax: 405-521-3826, 7:30-4:30PM. www.oktax.state.ok.us/salesuse.html ✉☎✋

Birth Certificates, Death Records

State Department of Health, Vital Records Service, PO Box 53551, Oklahoma City, OK 73152-3551 (1000 NE 10th St); 405-271-4040, 405-271-1646 (Order Line), Fax: 405-232-3311, 8:30AM-4PM. www.health.state.ok.us/program/vital/brec.html ✉☎**Fax**✋

Marriage Certificates, Divorce Records

Records not maintained by a state level agency. Marriage and Divorce records are found at county level.

Workers' Compensation Records

Workers Compensation Court, Records, 1915 N Stiles Ave, Oklahoma City, OK 73105-4918; 405-522-8600, 405-522-8640 (Records Dept), 800-269-5353 (Enforcement), Fax: 405-552-8647, 8AM-5PM. www.owcc.state.ok.us ✉✋

Driver Records

MVR Desk, Records Management Division, PO Box 11415, Oklahoma City, OK 73136-0415 (3600 Martin Luther King Blvd, Rm 206, Oklahoma City, OK 73111); 405-425-2262, 8AM-4:45PM. www.dps.state.ok.us/dls ✉✋🖥

Vehicle Ownership, Vehicle Identification, Vessel Ownership, Vessel Registration

Oklahoma Tax Commission, Motor Vehicle Division, Attn: Research, 2501 N Lincoln Blvd, Oklahoma City, OK 73194; 405-521-3770, 7:30AM-4:30PM. www.oktax.state.ok.us/mvhome.html ✉✋

Accident Reports

Department of Public Safety, Records Management Division, PO Box 11415, Oklahoma City, OK 73136 (3600 Martin Luther King Blvd, Room 206, Oklahoma City, OK 73111); 405-425-2192, Fax: 405-425-2046,   8AM-4:45PM. www.dps.state.ok.us ✉☎✋

Voter Registration

State Election Board, PO Box 53156, Oklahoma City, OK 73152 (State Capitol-Rm B6, Oklahoma City, OK 73105); 405-

521-2391, Fax: 405-521-6457, 8-5PM. www.elections.state.ok.us ✉☎**Fax**✋

GED Certificates

State Dept of Education, Lifelong Learning, 2500 N Lincoln Blvd, Rm 115, Oklahoma City, OK 73105; 405-521-

3321, Fax: 405-522-5394. http://sde.state.ok.us ✉☎**Fax**✋

Hunting License and Fishing License Information

Access to Records is Restricted
Department of Wildlife Conservation, Fish & Game Records, PO Box 53465,

Oklahoma City, OK 73152; 405-521-3852, Fax: 405-521-6535, 8AM-4:30PM. www.wildlifedepartment.com They have a central database, but do not release information to the public.

Oregon

Governor's Office
  State Capitol Bldg.
  900 Court St NE
  Salem, OR 97301-4047
  www.governor.state.or.us

503-378-4582
Fax 503-378- 4863
8AM-5PM

Attorney General's Office
  Department of Justice
  1162 Court St NE
  Salem, OR 97310
  www.doj.state.or.us

503-378-4400
Fax 503-378-4017
8AM-5PM

State Website: www.oregon.gov

Legislative Records
  503-986-1180 www.leg.state.or.us

State Archives
  503-373-0701 http://arcweb.sos.state.or.us

Capital: Salem, in Marion County

| Search Unclaimed Property Online |

http://statelands.dsl.state.or.us/upframe.htm

Criminal Records

Oregon State Police, Unit 11, Identification Services Section, PO Box 4395, Portland, OR 97208-4395 (3772 Portland Rd NE, Bldg C, Salem, OR); 503-378-3070, Fax: 503-378-2121, 8AM-5PM. www.osp.state.or.us ✉**Fax**💻

Statewide Court Records

Court Administrator, Supreme Court Bldg, 1163 State St, Salem, OR 97301-2563; 503-986-5500, Fax: 503-986-5503, 8AM-5PM. www.ojd.state.or.us/osca 💻

Sexual Offender Registry

Oregon State Police, SOR Unit, 255 Capitol St NE, 4th Fl, Salem, OR 97310; 503-378-3720, Fax: 503-363-5475, 8AM-5PM. www.osp.state.or.us ✉☎**Fax**

Incarceration Records

Oregon Department of Corrections, Offender Information & Sentence Computation, PO Box 5670, Wilsonville, OR 97070-5670 (24499 SW Grahams Ferry Rd, Bldg Z, Wilsonville, OR 97070); 503-570-6900, Fax: 503-570-6902, 8AM-5PM. www.doc.state.or.us/ ✉☎**Fax**💻

Corporation Records, Limited Partnership Records, Trademarks, Servicemarks, Fictitious Name, Assumed Name, Limited Liability Company Records

Corporation Division, Public Service Building, 255 Capital St NE, #151, Salem, OR 97310-1327; 503-986-2317, Fax: 503-378-4381, 8AM-5PM. www.filinginoregon.com ✉☎**Fax**✋💻

Uniform Commercial Code, Federal and State Tax Liens

UCC Division, Attn: Records, 255 Capitol St NE, Suite 151, Salem, OR 97310-1327; 503-986-2200 x6, Fax: 503-373-1166, www.filinginoregon.com/ucc/index.htm 8AM-5PM. ✉**Fax**✋💻

Sales Tax Registrations

State does not impose sales tax.

Birth Certificates, Death Records, Marriage Certificates, Divorce Records

Department of Human Services, Vital Records, PO Box 14050, Portland, OR 97293-0050 (800 NE Oregon St, #205, Portland, OR 97232); 503-731-4108, 503-731-4095 (info message), Fax: 503-234-8417, 8-4:30. www.ohd.hr.state.or.us/chs/ ✉☎**Fax**✋💻

Workers' Compensation Records

Department of Consumer & Business Srvs, Workers Compensation Division, PO Box 14480, Salem, OR 97309-0405 (350 Winter Street NE Rm 27, Salem, OR 97301-3879); 503-947-7818, 503-947-7993 (TTY), Fax: 503-945-7630, 8AM-5PM www.oregonwcd.org ✉**Fax**✋💻

Driver Records

Driver and Motor Vehicle Services, Record Services, 1905 Lana Ave, NE, Salem, OR 97314; 503-945-5000, Fax: 503-945-5425, 8AM-5PM. www.oregondmv.com ✉☎**Fax**

Key: Access state agency records by:. phone-☎ mail-✉ fax-**Fax** in person-✋ online-💻 email-**Email**

Vehicle Ownership, Vehicle Identification

Driver and Motor Vehicle Services, Record Services Unit, 1905 Lana Ave, NE, Salem, OR 97314; 503-945-5000, Fax: 503-945-5425, 8AM-5PM. www.oregondmv.com ✉☎**Fax**

Accident Reports

Driver & Motor Vehicle Services Division, Accident Reports & Information, 1905 Lana Ave, NE, Salem, OR 97314; 503-945-5098, Fax: 503-945-5267, 8AM-5PM. www.oregondmv.com ✉☎**Fax**✋

Vessel Ownership, Vessel Registration

State Marine Board, Records, PO Box 14145, Salem, OR 97309 (435 Commercial St NE, #400, Salem, OR); 503-378-8587, Fax: 503-378-4597, 8AM-5PM www.boatoregon.com ✉☎**Fax**✋

Voter Registration

Records not maintained by a state level agency.
Records are maintained at the county level and cannot be purchased for commercial reasons. State plans on having a statewide voter registration database in 2006.

GED Certificates

Dept of Community Colleges/ Workforce Development, GED Program, 255 Capitol St NE, Salem, OR 97310; 503-378-8648 x369, Fax: 503-378-8434, 8AM-5PM M-F. www.odccwd.state.or.us ✉☎**Fax**✋

Hunting License and Fishing License Information

Fish & Wildlife Department, Licensing Division, 3406 Cherry Ave NE, Salem, OR 97303; 503-947-6100, Fax: 503-947-6117, 8AM-5PM. www.dfw.state.or.us ✉**Fax**✋

Pennsylvania

Governor's Office
  225 Main Capitol Bldg
  Harrisburg, PA 17120
  www.governor.state.pa.us/
  717-787-2500
  Fax 717-772-8284
  9AM-4:30PM

Attorney General's Office
  Strawberry Square, 16th Floor
  Harrisburg, PA 17120
  www.attorneygeneral.gov
  717-787-3391
  Fax 717-787-1190

State Website: www.state.pa.us

Legislative Records
  717-787-2342 www.legis.state.pa.us

State Archives
  717-783-3281 www.phmc.state.pa.us

Capital: Harrisburg, in Dauphin County

Search Unclaimed Property Online
  www.treasury.state.pa.us/Unclaimed/Search.html

Criminal Records

State Police, Central Repository- 164, 1800 Elmerton Ave, Harrisburg, PA 17110; 717-783-5494, 717-783-9973, www.psp.state.pa.us/psp/site/default.asp 8:15AM-4:15PM. ✉🖥

Statewide Court Records

Administrative Office of PA Courts, PO Box 229, Mechanicsburg, PA 17055; 717-795-2062 (communications), 717-795-2000 (main), Fax: 717-795-2050, 9AM-5PM. www.courts.state.pa.us ✉🖥

Sexual Offender Registry

State Police Central Repository, Megan's Law Unit, 1800 Elmerton Ave, Harrisburg, PA 17110; 717-783-4363, 717-783-9973, Fax 717-705-8839, 7-3PM www.psp.state.pa.us/psp/site/default.asp 🖥

Incarceration Records

Pennsylvania Department of Corrections, Inmate Records Office, PO Box 598, Camp Hill, PA 17001-0598; 717-737-6538, Fax: 717-731-7159, 8AM-4PM. www.cor.state.pa.us ✉☎**Fax**🖥

Corporation Records, Limited Partnership Records, Trademarks, Servicemarks, Fictitious Name, Assumed Name, Limited Liability Company Records, Limited Liability Partnerships

Corporation Bureau, Department of State, PO Box 8722, Harrisburg, PA 17105-8722 (206 North Bldg, Harrisburg); 717-787-1057, Fax: 717-783-2244, 8-5PM. www.dos.state.pa.us/corps/site/default.asp ✉☎**Fax**✋🖥

Uniform Commercial Code

UCC Division, Department of State, PO Box 8721, Harrisburg, PA 17105-8721 (North Office Bldg, Rm 206, Harrisburg); 717-787-1057 x3, Fax: 717-783-2244, www.dos.state.pa.us/DOS/site/default.asp 8AM-5PM. ✉**Fax**✋🖥

Federal and State Tax Liens

Records not maintained by a state level agency.
All federal and state tax liens are filed at the Prothonotary of each county.

Sales Tax Registrations

Revenue Department, Sales Tax Registration Division, Dept 280905, Harrisburg, PA 17128; 717-783-9360, Fax: 717-787-3708, 7:30AM-4:30PM. www.revenue.state.pa.us ✉☎**Fax**

Birth Certificates, Death Records

Department of Health, Division of Vital Records, PO Box 1528, New Castle, PA 16103-1528 (101 S Mercer St, Room 401, New Castle, PA); 724-656-3100 (Message Phone), Fax: 724-652-8951, 8AM-4PM. http://webserver.health.state.pa.us/health/cwp/view.asp?a=168&Q=229939 ✉ ☎ Fax ✋ 💻

Marriage Certificates, Divorce Records

Records not maintained by a state level agency.
Marriage and divorce records are found at county level at Prothonotary of issue.

Workers' Compensation Records

Bureau of Workers' Compensation, Physical Records Section, 1171 S Cameron St, Rm 103, Harrisburg, PA 17104; 717-772-4447, 7:30AM-4PM. www.dli.state.pa.us/landi/site/default.asp ✉

Driver Records

Department of Transportation, Driver Record Services, PO Box 68695, Harrisburg, PA 17106-8695 (1101 S Front Street, 3rd Fl, Harrisburg); 717-391-6190, 800-932-4600-in-state only. 7:30AM-4:30PM. www.dmv.state.pa.us ✉ ✋ 💻

Vehicle Ownership, Vehicle Identification

Department of Transportation, Vehicle Record Services, PO Box 68691, Harrisburg, PA 17106-8691 (1101 South Front St, Harrisburg, PA 17104); 717-391-6190, 800-932-6000 (In-state), 7:30-4:30PM. www.dmv.state.pa.us ✉

Accident Reports

State Police Headquarters, Crash Reports Unit, 1800 Elmerton Ave, Harrisburg, PA 17110; 717-783-5516, 8AM-4PM. www.psp.state.pa.us ✉

Vessel Ownership, Vessel Registration

Access to Records is Restricted
Fish and Boat Commission, Licensing & Registration Section, PO Box 68900, Harrisburg, PA 17106-8900; 717-705-7940, Fax: 717-705-7931, 8AM-4PM. www.fish.state.pa.us Boat registration and ownership information is not open to the public. Liens filed at UCC filing locations

Voter Registration

Records not maintained by a state level agency.
State is in the process of implementing a statewide database (SURE Project). Until it is available, search at the county level.

GED Certificates

Commonwealth Diploma Program, GED Testing, 333 Market St 12th Fl, Harrisburg, PA 17126; 717-787-6747, www.paadulted.org/able/site/default.asp 8:30AM-4:30PM. ✉ ✋

Hunting License Information

Access to Records is Restricted
Game Commission, Hunting License Division, 2001 Elmerton Ave, Harrisburg, PA 17110-9797; 717-787-2084 (Hunting License Division), Fax: 717-787-2613, www.theoutdoorshop.state.pa.us/fbg/ 8AM-4PM. Hunting license information is not released to the public.

Fishing License Information

Access to Records is Restricted
Fish & Boat Commission, Fishing License Division, PO Box 67000, Harrisburg, PA 17106 (1601 Elmerton, Harrisburg, PA); 717-705-7930 (Fishing License Division), Fax: 717-705-7931, 8AM-4PM. ✉ ✋

Rhode Island

Governor's Office
222 State House
Providence, RI 02903
www.governor.state.ri.us

401-222-2080
Fax 401-222-5894
8:30AM-4:30PM

Attorney General's Office
150 S Main St
Providence, RI 02903
www.riag.state.ri.us

401-274-4400
Fax 401-222-1331
8:30AM-4:30PM

State Website: www.state.ri.us

Legislative Records
Secretary of State; 401-222-3983
www.rilin.state.ri.us

State Archives
401-222-2353 www.state.ri.us/archives

Capital: Providence, in Providence County

Search Unclaimed Property Online

www.treasury.ri.gov/moneylst.htm

Criminal Records

Department of Attorney General, Bureau of Criminal Identification, 150 S Main Street, Providence, RI 02903; 401-274-4400 x2353, Fax: 401-222-1331, 8:30AM-4:30PM. www.riag.ri.gov ✉ ✋

Statewide Court Records

Court Administrator, Supreme Court, 250 Benefit St, Providence, RI 02903; 401-222-3272, Fax: 401-222-3599, 8:30AM-4:30PM. www.courts.state.ri.us ✉ ✋ 💻

Sexual Offender Registry

Access to Records is Restricted
Department of Attorney General, BCI Unit, 150 S Main Street, Providence, RI 02903; 401-274-4400, 8:30AM-4:30PM. www.riag.state.ri.us Statewide Sexual

Offender Registry is not available to the public. Must search at the local level.

Incarceration Records

Rhode Island Department of Corrections, Assistant to the Director, 40 Howard Avenue, Cranston, RI 02920; 401-462-3900, Fax: 401-464-2630, 8AM-4:30PM. www.doc.state.ri.us

Corporation Records, Fictitious Name, Limited Partnerships, Limited Liability Companys, Limited Liability Partnerships, Not For Profit Entities

Secretary of State, Corporations Division, 100 N Main St, Providence, RI 02903-1335; 401-222-3040, Fax: 401-222-1309, http://155.212.254.78/corporations.htm 8:30AM-4:30PM.

Trademarks/Servicemarks

Secretary of State, Trademark Section, 100 N Main St, Providence, RI 02903; 401-222-1487, Fax: 401-222-3879, www.corps.state.ri.us/trademarks.htm 8:30AM-4:30PM.

Uniform Commercial Code

UCC Section, Secretary of State, 100 North Main St, Providence, RI 02903; 401-222-3040, Fax: 401-222-3879, http://155.212.254.78/corporations.htm 8:30AM-4:30PM.

Federal and State Tax Liens

Records not maintained by a state agency. Records located at county level.

Sales Tax Registrations

Taxation Division, Sales & Use Tax Office, One Capitol Hill, Providence, RI 02908; 401-222-2937, Fax: 401-222-6288, www.tax.state.ri.us **Fax**

Birth Certificates, Death Records, Marriage Certificates

State Department of Health, Division of Vital Records, 3 Capitol Hill, Room 101, Providence, RI 02908-5097; 401-222-2812, 401-222-2811, 8:30AM-4:30PM. www.healthri.org

Divorce Records

Records not maintained by a state level agency. Divorce records are found at one of the 4 county Family Courts.

Workers' Compensation Records

Dept. of Labor & Training, Division of Workers' Compensation, PO Box 20190, Cranston, RI 02920 (1511 Pontiac Ave); 401-462-8100, Fax: 401-462-8105, 8:30-4PM. www.dlt.state.ri.us **Fax**

Driver Records

Div. of Motor Vehicles, Driving Record Clerk, Operator Control, 286 Main Street, Pawtucket, RI 02860; 401-721-2650, 8:30-4:30. www.dmv.state.ri.us

Vehicle Ownership, Vehicle Identification

Registry of Motor Vehicles, Vehicle Records, 100 Main Street, Pawtucket, RI 02860; 401-588-3020 x2552 (Regis.),

401-588-3018 (titles), Fax 401-721-2697, 8:30-3:30PM. www.dmv.state.ri.us

Accident Reports

Rhode Island State Police, Accident Record Division, 311 Danielson Pike, North Scituate, RI 02857; 401-444-1143, Fax: 401-444-1133, 10AM-4PM M,T,F; till 6:30PM on Wed. www.risp.state.ri.us

Vessel Ownership, Vessel Registration

Dept of Environmental Management, Boat Registration/Licensing, 235 Promenade, Rm 360, Providence, RI 02908; 401-222-6647, Fax: 401-222-1181, 8:30AM-3:30PM. www.state.ri.us/dem

Voter Registration

Records not maintained by a state level agency. There is no central state database of voters yet. The Local Board of Canvassers keeps records at the town and city level. Records may not be purchased for commercial purposes.

GED Certificates

Department of Education, GED Testing, 255 Westminster, Providence, RI 02908; 401-222-4600 x2181, 7:30-4.

Hunting License and Fishing License Information

Boat Registration & Licensing, Licensing Division, 235 Promenade St, Rm 360, Providence, RI 02908; 401-222-3576, Fax: 401-222-1181, 8:30AM-3:30PM. www.state.ri.us/dem **Fax**

South Carolina

Governor's Office
  PO Box 11829   803-734-9400
  Columbia, SC 29211   Fax 803-734-9413
  www.state.sc.us/governor   8AM-6PM

Attorney General's Office
  PO Box 11549   803-734-3970
  Columbia, SC 29211   Fax 803-734-4323
  www.scattorneygeneral.org   8:30AM-5:30PM

State Website: www.myscgov.com

Legislative Records
  803-734-2060 www.scstatehouse.net

State Archives
  803-896-6100 www.state.sc.us/scdah

Capital: Columbia, in Richland County

Search Unclaimed Property Online

http://webprod.cio.sc.gov/SCSTOWeb/mainFrame.do

Key: Access state agency records by:. phone- ☎ mail- ✉ fax-**Fax** in person- 🖐 online- 🖥 email-**Email**

Criminal Records

South Carolina Law Enforcement Division (SLED), Criminal Records Section, PO Box 21398, Columbia, SC 29221 (4400 Broad River Rd, Columbia); 803-896-7043, Fax: 803-896-7022, 8:30-5PM. www.sled.state.sc.us ✉ ✋ 💻

Statewide Court Records

Court Administration, 1015 Sumter St, 2nd Fl, Columbia, SC 29201; 803-734-1800, Fax: 803-734-1355, 8:30AM-5PM M-F. www.sccourts.org/ 💻

Sexual Offender Registry

Sex Offender Registry, c/o SLED, PO Box 21398, Columbia, SC 29221 (4400 Broad River Rd, Columbia, SC 29210); 803-896-7043, Fax: 803-896-7022, 8:30-5PM. www.sled.state.sc.us ✉ ☎ 💻

Incarceration Records

Department of Corrections, Inmate Records Branch, 4444 Broad River Rd, Columbia, SC 29221-1787; 803-896-8531, 877-846-3472 (Automated Information), Fax: 803-896-1217, 8AM-5PM. www.state.sc.us/scdc/ ✉ ☎ 💻

Corporation Records, Trademarks/Servicemarks, Limited Partnerships, Limited Liability Companys, Limited Liability Partnerships

Corporation Division, Capitol Complex, PO Box 11350, Columbia, SC 29211 (Edgar A. Brown Bldg, Room 525, 1205 Pendleton St, Columbia); 803-734-2158, Fax: 803-734-1614, 8:30PM-5PM. www.scsos.com/ ✉ ☎ ✋ 💻

Fictitious Name, Assumed Name, Trade Names

Records not maintained by a state level agency.
Records are found at the county level.

Annual Reports, Directors and Officers

Dept. of Revenue, Office Services/ Records, Photocopy Section, Columbia, SC 29214; 803-898-5751, Fax: 803-898-5888, www.sctax.org/DOR/default.htm 8:30AM-5PM. ✉ Fax ✋

Uniform Commercial Code

UCC Division, Secretary of State, PO Box 11350, Columbia, SC 29211 (Edgar Brown Bldg, 1205 Pendelton St #525, Columbia, SC 29201); 803-734-1961, Fax: 803-734-2164, 8:30AM-5PM. www.scsos.com/Uniform_Commercial_Code.htm ✉ Fax ✋ 💻

Federal and State Tax Liens

Records not maintained by a state level agency.
Tax lien data is found at the county level.

Sales Tax Registrations

Revenue Dept, Sales Tax Registration Records, PO Box 125, Columbia, SC 29214 (301 Gervais St); 803-898-5872, Fax: 803-898-5888, 8:30AM-4:45PM. www.sctax.org/default.htm ✉ ☎ Fax ✋

Birth Certificates, Death Records, Marriage Certificates, Divorce Records

South Carolina DHEC, Vital Records, 2600 Bull St, Columbia, SC 29201-1797; 803-898-3630, 803-898-3631-order line, 877-284-1008-expedite line, Fax: 803-898-3761, www.scdhec.net/vr/index.htm 8:30AM-4:30PM. ✉ ☎ Fax ✋

Workers' Compensation Records

Workers Compensation Commission, PO Box 1715, Columbia, SC 29202 (1612 Marion St, Columbia, SC 29201); 803-737-5700, Fax: 803-737-5768, 8:30AM-5PM. www.wcc.state.sc.us ✉ Fax ✋

Driver License Information, Driver Records

Department of Motor Vehicles, Driver Records Section, PO Box 1498, Columbia, SC 29216-0035 (10311 Wilson Blvd, Blythewood, SC 29216); 803-737-4000, Fax: 803-737-1077, 8:30AM-5PM. www.scdmvonline.com/ ✉ ☎ Fax ✋ 💻

Vehicle Ownership, Vehicle Identification

Division of Motor Vehicles, Title and Registration Records Section, PO Box 1498, Columbia, SC 29216 (955 Park St, Columbia, SC 29201); 803-737-4000, Fax: 803-737-1112, 8:30AM-5PM. www.state.sc.us/dps/dmv ✉ ☎ Fax ✋

Accident Reports

Accident Reports, Financial Responsibilty Office, PO Box 1498, Columbia, SC 29216-0040 (955 Park St, Columbia, SC 29201); 803-737-4000, Fax: 803-737-4483, 8:30AM-5PM. ✉ ✋

Vessel Ownership, Vessel Registration

Dept of Natural Resources, Registration & Titles, PO Box 167, Columbia, SC 29202 (1000 Assembly St, Room 104, Columbia); 803-734-3857, Fax: 803-734-4138, 8:30-5. www.dnr.state.sc.us ✉ ✋

Voter Registration

State Election Commission, Records, PO Box 5987, Columbia, SC 29250; 803-734-9060, Fax: 803-734-9366, 8:30AM-5PM. www.state.sc.us/scsec ✉ ☎ Fax ✋

GED Certificates

GED Testing Office, 1429 Senate St, #402, Columbia, SC 29201; 803-734-8347 x5, Fax: 803-734-8336, 8:30AM-5PM www.sde.state.sc.us/ ✉ Fax ✋

Hunting License and Fishing License Information

Records not maintained by a state level agency.
Licenses are kept on file within the License Division by the county and agent where the license was sold, however the records are not open to the public.

South Dakota

Governor's Office
    State Capitol, 500 E Capitol Ave   605-773-3212
    Pierre, SD 57501-5070   Fax 605-773-4711
    www.state.sd.us/governor/   8AM-5PM

Attorney General's Office
    State Capitol, 500 E Capitol Ave   605-773-3215
    Pierre, SD 57501-5070   Fax 605-773-4106
    www.state.sd.us/attorney/index.htm   8AM-5PM

State Website: www.state.sd.us

Legislative Records
    605-773-3251   http://legis.state.sd.us

State Archives
    605-773-3804   www.sdhistory.org

Capital: Pierre, in Hughes County

Time Zone: CST*

> * South Dakota's 18 western-most counties are MST: They
> are: Bennett, Butte, Corson, Custer, Dewey, Fall River,
> Haakon, Harding, Jackson, Lawrence, Meade, Mellette,
> Pennington, Perkins, Shannon, Stanley, Todd, Ziebach.

> **Search Unclaimed Property Online**
> www.missingmoney.com/main/index.cfm

Criminal Records

Division of Criminal Investigation,
Identification Section, 500 E Capitol,
Pierre, SD 57501-5070; 605-773-3331,
Fax: 605-773-4629, 8AM-5PM.
http://dci.sd.gov/ ✉

Statewide Court Records

State Court Administrator, State Capitol
Bldg, 500 E Capitol Ave, Pierre, SD
57501; 605-773-3474, Fax 605-773-5627,
8AM-5PM. www.sdjudicial.com ✉**Fax**

Sexual Offender Registry

Division of Criminal Investigation,
Identification Section - SOR Unit, 500 E
Capitol, Pierre, SD 57501-5070 (3444
East Highway 34, Pierre); 605-773-3331,
605-773-4614, Fax 605-773-2596, 8-5pm.
http://dci.sd.gov/administration/id/sexoffe
nder/index.asp 💻

Incarceration Records

SD Department of Corrections, Central
Records Office, 3200 E. Highway 34, 500
E. Capitol Avenue, Pierre, SD 57501-
5070 (1600 North Dr, Pierre); 605-773-
3478, (605-367-5190 Sioux Falls records),
Fax: 605-773-3194, 8AM-4PM. www.st
ate.sd.us/corrections/corrections.html ☎

Corporation Records,
Limited Partnerships,
Limited Liability Company
Records,
Trademarks/Servicemarks

Corporation Division, Secretary of State,
500 E Capitol Ave, Suite B-05, Pierre, SD

57501-5070; 605-773-4845, 605-773-
3539 (Trademarks), Fax: 605-773-4550,
8AM-5PM. www.sdsos.gov/corporations/
✉☎**Fax**✋💻

Fictitious Name,
Assumed Name

**Records not maintained by a state
level agency.**
Records are located at the county level.

Uniform Commercial Code,
Federal Tax Liens

UCC Division, Secretary of State, 500
East Capitol, Pierre, SD 57501-5077; 605-
773-4422, Fax: 605-773-4550, 8-5PM.
www.sdsos.gov/ucc ✉☎**Fax**✋💻

State and Federal Tax Liens

**Records not maintained by a state
level agency.** State and federal tax liens
on individuals are filed at county level.

Sales Tax Registrations

Department of Revenue and Regulation,
Business Tax Division, 445 E Capitol,
Pierre, SD 57501-3100; 605-773-3311,
Fax: 605-773-6729, 8AM-5PM.
www.state.sd.us/drr2/revenue.html
✉☎**Fax**✋

Birth Certificates,
Death Records,
Marriage Certificates,
Divorce Records

Department of Health, Vital Records, 600
E Capitol, Pierre, SD 57501-2536; 605-
773-4961, Fax: 605-773-5683, 8-5PM.

www.state.sd.us/doh/VitalRec/index.htm
✉☎✋💻

Workers' Compensation
Records

Labor Department, Workers Comp Div.,
700 Governors Dr, Pierre, SD 57501; 605-
773-3681, Fax: 605-773-4211, 8AM-
5PM. www.state.sd.us/dol/dlm/dlm-
home.htm ✉

Driver Records

Dept of Public Safety, Office of Driver
Licensing, 118 W Capitol, Pierre, SD
57501; 605-773-6883, Fax 605-773-3018,
www.state.sd.us/dps/dl/sddriver.htm
8AM-5PM. ✉☎✋💻

Vehicle Ownership,
Vehicle Identification,
Vessel Ownership,
Vessel Registration

Division of Motor Vehicles, Information
Section, 445 E Capitol Ave, Pierre, SD
57501; 605-773-3541, Fax 605-773-2550,
8AM-5PM.
www.state.sd.us/drr2/motorvcl.htm ✉✋

Accident Reports

Department of Public Safety, Accident
Records, 118 W Capitol Ave, Pierre, SD
57501-2000; 605-773-3868, Fax: 605-
773-6893, 8AM-5PM. ✉✋

Voter Registration

**Records not maintained by a state
level agency.** The Secretary of State and
County Auditors have compiled a

statewide voter registration file of the official voter registration files in each county auditor's office. Name searching should be done at the county level.

GED Certificates

Department of Labor, AEL/GED/Literacy, 700 Governors Drive, Pierre, SD 57501-

2291; 605-773-3101, Fax: 605-773-6184, www.state.sd.us/dol/GED/index.html 8AM-5PM. ✉Fax✍

Hunting License and Fishing License Information

Game, Fish & Parks Department, License Division, 412 W Missouri, Pierre, SD

57501; 605-773-3926, Fax: 605-773-5842, 8AM-5PM. www.state.sd.us/gfp ✍

Tennessee

Governor's Office
    State Capitol, 1st Floor
    Nashville, TN 37243-0001
    www.state.tn.us/governor

615-741-2001
Fax 615-532-9711
8AM-5PM

Attorney General's Office
    PO Box 20207
    Nashville, TN 37202-0207
    www.attorneygeneral.state.tn.us

615-741-3491
Fax 615-741-2009
8AM-4:30PM

State Website: www.state.tn.us

Legislative Records
    615-741-3511 www.legislature.state.tn.us

State Archives: 615-741-7996

www.state.tn.us/sos/statelib/tslahome.htm

Capital: Nashville, in Davidson County

Time Zone: CST*

    * Tennessee's twenty-nine eastern-most counties are EST: They are: Anderson, Blount, Bradley, Campbell, Carter, Claiborne, Cocke, Grainger, Greene, Hamilton, Hancock, Hawkins, Jefferson, Johnson, Knox, Loudon, McMinn, Meigs, Monroe, Morgan, Polk, Rhea, Roane, Scott, Sevier, Sullivan, Unicoi, Union, Washington.

Search Unclaimed Property Online

www.tennesseeanytime.org/unclp/

Criminal Records

Tennessee Bureau of Investigation, Records and Identification Unit, 901 R S Gass Blvd, Nashville, TN 37216; 615-744-4000 x1, Fax: 615-744-4651, 24 hours daily. www.tbi.state.tn.us ✉Fax

Statewide Court Records

Administrative Office of the Courts, Nashville City Center, 511 Union St, Suite 600, Nashville, TN 37219; 615-741-2687, Fax: 615-741-6285, 8AM-4:30PM. www.tsc.state.tn.us 🖥

Sexual Offender Registry

Tennessee Bureau of Investigation, Sexual Offender Registry, 901 R S Gass Blvd., Nashville, TN 37216; 888-837-4170, Fax: 615-744-4655, 24 hours daily. www.ticic.state.tn.us/ ☎🖥

Incarceration Records

Tennessee Department of Corrections, Rachel Jackson Building, 2nd Fl, 320 6th Avenue, N., Nashville, TN 37243; 615-741-1000, Fax 615-532-1497, 8AM-5PM. www.state.tn.us/correction/ ✉☎Fax🖥

Corporation Records, Limited Partnership Records, Fictitious Name, Assumed Name, Limited Liability Company Records

Secretary of State: Corporations, William R Snodgrass Tower, 312 8th Ave. N, 6th Fl, Nashville, TN 37243; 615-741-2286, 615-741-6488 (for copies), Fax: 615-741-7310, www.state.tn.us/sos/service.htm 8AM-4:30PM. ✉☎✍🖥

Trademarks/Servicemarks, Trade Names

Secretary of State, Trademarks/Tradenames Division, 312 8th Ave North, 6th Fl, Nashville, TN 37243-0306; 615-741-0531, Fax: 615-741-7310, 8AM-4:30PM. www.state.tn.us/sos/service.htm ✉☎✍🖥

Uniform Commercial Code

TN Sec of State - UCC Records, William R Snodgrass Tower, 312 Eighth Ave N, 6th Fl, Nashville, TN 37243; 615-741-

3276, Fax: 615-741-7310, 8AM-4:30PM. www.state.tn.us/sos ✉✍🖥

Federal and State Tax Liens

Records not maintained by a state level agency.
State and federal tax liens are filed at the county level with the Register of Deeds where the lienee or its property is located.

Sales Tax Registrations

Access to Records is Restricted
Revenue Department, Sales Tax Registration, Andrew Jackson Bldg, 500 Deaderick St, Nashville, TN 37242; 615-741-3580, 615-253-0600, Fax: 615-253-6299, 8-4:30. www.state.tn.us/revenue/ This agency refuses to make any information about registrants available.

Birth Certificates, Death Records, Marriage Certificates, Divorce Records

Department of Health, Office of Vital Records, 421 5th Ave North, 1st Fl, Nashville, TN 37247; 615-741-1763, 615-

741-0778 (Credit card orders), Fax: 615-726-2559, 8-4PM. http://www2.state.tn.us/health/vr/index.htm ✉☎Fax✋💻

Workers' Compensation Records

Department of Labor, Workers Compensation Division, 710 James Robertson Pkwy, 2nd Fl, Nashville, TN 37243; 615-253-1842, Fax 615-532-1942, 8AM-4:30PM. www.state.tn.us/labor-wfd/wcomp.html ✉Fax✋

Driver Records

Dept. of Safety, Financial Responsibility Section, Attn: Driving Records, 1150 Foster Ave, Nashville, TN 37210; 615-741-3954, Fax: 615-253-2093, 8-4:30PM. www.tennessee.gov/safety/ ✉✋💻

Vehicle Ownership, Vehicle Identification

Title and Registration Div, Information Unit, 44 Vantage Way #160, Nashville, TN 37243; 615-741-3101 (Titles), 888-

871-3171, Fax 615-253-4259, 8-4:30PM. www.tennessee.gov/safety/nav2.html ✉✋💻

Accident Reports

Financial Responsibility Section, Records Unit, 1150 Foster Avenue, Nashville, TN 37210; 615-741-3954, Fax: 615-253-2093, 8AM-4:30PM. www.tennessee.gov/safety/ ✉✋

Vessel Ownership, Vessel Registration

Wildlife Resources Agency, Boating Division, PO Box 40747, Nashville, TN 37204; 615-781-6585, Fax 615-741-4606, 8AM-4:30PM. www.state.tn.us/twra ✉☎Fax✋

Voter Registration

Access to Records is Restricted
Secretary of State, Division of Elections, 312 8th Avenue North, 9th Fl, Nashville, TN 37243; 615-741-7956, Fax: 615-741-1278, www.state.tn.us/sos/election.htm

8AM-4:30PM. The statewide database cannot be accessed. Records are held by the Administrator of Elections at the county level. Records can only be purchased for politically-related purposes.

GED Certificates

Department of Labor & Workforce Development, GED Records - Davy Crockett Tower, 500 James Robertson Parkway, 11th Fl, Nashville, TN 37245; 615-741-7054, Fax: 615-532-4899, 8AM-4:30PM. www.state.tn.us/labor-wfd/AE/aeged.htm ✉Fax✋

Hunting License and Fishing License Information

Wildlife Resources Agency, Sportsman License Division, PO Box 40747, Nashville, TN 37204; 615-781-6585, Fax: 615-781-5277, 8AM-4:30PM. www.state.tn.us/twra/ ✉☎Fax✋

Texas

Governor's Office
PO Box 12428
Austin, TX 78711-2428
www.governor.state.tx.us
512-463-2000
Fax 512-463-1849
7:30AM-5:30PM

Attorney General's Office
PO Box 12548
Austin, TX 78711-2548
www.oag.state.tx.us
512-463-2100
Fax 512-463-2063
7:30AM-5:30PM

State Website: www.state.tx.us

Legislative Records
512-463-1252 www.lrl.state.tx.us

State Archives
512-463-5455 www.tsl.state.tx.us

Capital: Austin, in Travis County

Time Zone: CST*

   * Texas' two western-most counties are MST: They are: El Paso and Hudspeth.

   Search Unclaimed Property Online

https://txcpa.cpa.state.tx.us/up/Search.jsp

Criminal Records

Dept of Public Safety, Correspondence Section, Crime Records Service, PO Box 15999, Austin, TX 78761-5999 (5805 N Lamar, Bldg G, Austin, TX 78752); 512-424-2474, Fax: 512-424-5011, 8-5PM. http://records.txdps.state.tx.us ✉✋💻

Statewide Court Records

Office of Court Administration, PO Box 12066, Austin, TX 78711-2066 (205 W

14th St, Ste. 600, Austin, TX 78711); 512-463-1625, Fax: 512-463-1648, 8AM-5PM. www.courts.state.tx.us/oca 💻

Sexual Offender Registry

Dept of Public Safety, Sex Offender Registration, PO Box 4143, Austin, TX 78765-4143; 512-424-2478, 8AM-5PM. http://records.txdps.state.tx.us ✉💻

Incarceration Records

Texas Department of Criminal Justice, Bureau of Classification and Records, PO Box 99, Huntsville, TX 77342-5099; 936-295-6371, 800-535-0283 (Parole Status line), 8AM-5PM. www.tdcj.state.tx.us ✉☎💻

Corporation Records, Fictitious Name, Limited Partnership Records, Limited Liability Company Records, Assumed Name, Trademarks/Servicemarks

Secretary of State, Corporation Section, PO Box 13697, Austin, TX 78711-3697 (J Earl Rudder Bldg, 1019 Brazos, B-13, Austin, TX 78701); 512-463-5555 (Information), 512-463-5578 (Copies), Fax: 512-463-5643, 8AM-5PM. www.sos.state.tx.us ⊠☎Fax⚕🖥

Uniform Commercial Code, Federal Tax Liens

UCC Section, Secretary of State, PO Box 13193, Austin, TX 78711-3193 (1019 Brazos St, Rm B-13, Austin, TX 78701); 512-475-2705, Fax: 512-475-2812, 8AM-5PM. www.sos.state.tx.us/ucc/index.shtml ⊠☎Fax⚕🖥

State Tax Liens

Records not maintained by a state agency. Records located at county level.

Sales Tax Registrations

Comptroller of Public Accounts, Sales Tax Permits, PO Box 13528, Austin, TX 78711-3528 (LBJ Office Bldg, 111 E 17th St, Austin, TX 78774); 800-531-5441 x66013, 800-252-1386 (Other Business Searches), Fax: 512-475-1610, 8-5PM. www.window.state.tx.us/taxinfo/sales/ ⊠☎Fax⚕🖥

Birth Certificates, Marriage Certificates, Death & Divorce Records

Department of Health, Bureau of Vital Statistics, PO Box 12040, Austin, TX 78711-2040 (1100 W 49th St, Austin); 512-758-7366, Fax: 512-758-7711, 8AM-5PM. www.tdh.state.tx.us/bvs ⊠Fax⚕

Workers' Compensation Records

Workers' Compensation Commission, 7551 Metro Center Dr, #100,, Austin, TX 78744; 512-804-4000, 512-804-4990 (Reprographics Dept.), Fax: 512-804-4993, www.twcc.state.tx.us ⊠Fax🖥

Driver Records

Department of Public Safety, Driver Records Section, PO Box 149246, Austin, TX 78714-9246 (5805 N Lamar Blvd, Austin, TX 78752); 512-424-2032, 512-424-2600, Fax: 512-424-7285, 8AM-5PM. www.txdps.state.tx.us ⊠⚕🖥

Vehicle Ownership, Vehicle Identification

Department of Transportation, Vehicle Titles and Registration Division, 4000 Jackson Ave, Austin, TX 78731; 512-465-7611, Fax: 512-465-7736, 8AM-5PM. www.dot.state.tx.us ⊠☎🖥

Accident Reports

Texas Department of Public Safety, Accident Records Bureau, PO Box 15999, Austin, TX 78761-5999 (5805 N Lamar Blvd, Austin, TX 78752); 512-424-2600, 8AM-5PM. www.txdps.state.tx.us ⊠⚕

Vessel Ownership, Vessel Registration

Parks & Wildlife Dept, 4200 Smith School Rd, Austin, TX 78744; 512-389-4828, 800-262-8755, Fax: 512-389-4900, www.tpwd.state.tx.us/boat/boat.htm 8AM-5PM. ⊠⚕

Voter Registration

Access to Records is Restricted
Secretary of State, Elections Division, PO Box 12060, Austin, TX 78711-2060; 800-252-8683, Fax: 512-475-2811, 8AM-5PM. www.sos.state.tx.us To do individual look-ups, one must go to the Tax Assessor-Collector at the county level. The state will sell the entire database, for non-commercial purposes, in a variety of media and sort formats.

GED Certificates

Texas Education Agency, GED Unit CC:350, PO Box 13817, Austin, TX 78711 (1701 N Congress Ave, Austin); 512-463-9292, Fax: 512-305-9493, 8-5 www.tea.state.tx.us/ged ⊠☎Fax⚕

Hunting License and Fishing License Information

TX Parks & Wildlife Department, License Section, 4200 Smith School Rd, Austin, TX 78744; 512-389-4820, Fax: 512-389-4330, 8AM-5PM. www.tpwd.state.tx.us ⊠Fax⚕

Utah

Governor's Office
210 State Capitol
Salt Lake City, UT 84114
www.governor.utah.gov

801-538-1000
Fax 801-538-1528
8AM-5PM

Attorney General's Office
236 State Capitol
Salt Lake City, UT 84114
http://attorneygeneral.utah.gov

801-538-9600
Fax 801-538-1121
8AM-5:30PM

State Website: www.utah.gov/main/index

Legislative Records
801-538-1588 http://le.utah.gov

State Archives
801-538-3012 www.archives.state.ut.us

Capital: Salt Lake City, in Salt Lake County

Search Unclaimed Property Online
https://www.up.state.ut.us/asp/search.asp

Key: Access state agency records by:. phone-☎ mail-⊠ fax-**Fax** in person-⚕ online-🖥 email-**Email**

Utah Criminal Records

Bureau of Criminal Identification, Records Supervisor, Box 148280, Salt Lake City, UT 84114-8280 (3888 West 5400 South, Salt Lake City, UT 84119); 801-965-4445, Fax: 801-965-4749, 8AM-5PM. http://bci.utah.gov ⊠Fax

Statewide Court Records

Court Administrator, PO Box 140241, Salt Lake City, UT 84114-0241 (450 S State, Salt Lake City, UT 84114); 801-578-3800, 801-238-7832 (Search Request Info), Fax: 801-578-3859, 8AM-5PM. www.utcourts.gov ⊠Fax🖥

Sexual Offender Registry

Sex Offenders Registration Program, Records, 14717 S Minuteman Dr, Draper, UT 84020; 801-545-5908, Fax: 801-545-5911, 8-5PM. www.corrections.utah.gov/ ⊠☎✋🖥

Incarceration Records

Utah Department of Corrections, DIQ Records, PO Box 250, Draper, UT 84020 (14717 S Minuteman Dr, Draper, UT 84020); 801-576-7791, Fax: 801-572-7794, 8AM-4PM. www.cr.ex.state.ut.us ⊠☎Fax

Corporation Records, Limited Liability Company Records, Fictitious Name, Limited Partnership Records, Assumed Name, Trademarks/Servicemarks

Commerce Department, Corporate Division, PO Box 146705, Salt Lake City, UT 84114-6705 (160 E 300 S, 2nd fl, Salt Lake City, UT 84111); 801-530-4849 (Call Center), Fax: 801-530-6111, 8-5PM. www.commerce.utah.gov ⊠☎Fax✋🖥

Uniform Commercial Code

Department of Commerce, UCC Division, Box 146705, Salt Lake City, UT 84114-6705 (160 E 300 South, Heber M Wells Bldg, 2nd Fl); 801-530-4849, 877-526-3994-in state, Fax: 801-530-6438, 8-5PM. www.commerce.utah.gov/cor/uccpage.htm ⊠Fax✋🖥

Federal and State Tax Liens

Records not maintained by a state level agency.
Records are found at the local level.

Sales Tax Registrations

Taxpayer Services, Technical Research, 210 N 1950 W, Salt Lake City, UT 84134; 801-297-2200, Fax: 801-297-7697, 8-5 http://tax.utah.gov/sales/index.html ⊠✋

Birth Certificates, Death Records, Marriage Certificates, Divorce Records

Department of Health, Office of Vital Records & Statistics, Box 141012, Salt Lake City, UT 84114-1012 (288 N 1460 W, Salt Lake City, UT 84114); 801-538-6105 (This Agency), 801-538-6380 (Vitalchek), Fax: 801-538-9467, 9AM-5PM (walk-in counter closes at 4:30 PM). http://health.utah.gov/vitalrecords/ ⊠☎Fax✋🖥

Workers' Compensation Records

Labor Commission, Division of Industrial Accidents, PO Box 146610, Salt Lake City, UT 84114-6610 (160 E 300 S, 3rd Fl, Salt Lake City, UT 84114); 801-530-6800, Fax: 801-530-6804, 8AM-5PM. www.laborcommission.utah.gov ⊠Fax✋

Driver Records

Dept. of Public Safety, Driver License Division, Customer Service Section, PO Box 30560, Salt Lake City, UT 84130-0560 (4501 South 2700 West, 3rd Floor South, Salt Lake City); 801-965-4437, Fax: 801-965-4496, 8AM-5PM. http://driverlicense.utah.gov ⊠Fax✋🖥

Vehicle Ownership, Vehicle Identification, Vessel Ownership, Vessel Registration

State Tax Commission, Motor Vehicle Records Section, 210 North 1950 West, Salt Lake City, UT 84134; 801-297-3507, Fax: 801-297-3578, 8AM-5PM. http://dmv.utah.gov/ ⊠☎✋🖥

Accident Reports

Driver's License Division, Accident Reports Section, PO Box 30560, Salt Lake City, UT 84130-0560 (4501 South 2700 West, 3rd Floor South, Salt Lake City, UT 84119); 801-965-4428, Fax: 801-964-4536, 8AM-5PM. ⊠Fax✋

Voter Registration

Access to Records is Restricted
Elections Office, Utah Capitol Complex, East Office Bldg - #E325, Salt Lake City, UT 84114; 801-538-1041, Fax: 801-538-1133, 8AM-5PM. http://elections.utah.gov Individual record requests are referred to the county clerk offices. Records that have not been secured by the registrant are open to the public. The entire state voter registration database (current records only) can be purchased from this office.

GED Certificates

Utah State Office of Education, GED Testing Records, PO Box 144200, Salt Lake City, UT 84114-4200; 801-538-7921, Fax: 801-538-7868, 8AM-4PM. www.usoe.k12.ut.us/adulted/ged/index.html ⊠Fax✋

Hunting License and Fishing License Information

Utah Division of Wildlife Resources, PO Box 146301, Salt Lake City, UT 84114-6301 (1594 West North Temple, #2110, Salt Lake City, UT 84116); 801-538-4700, 877-592-5169, Fax: 801-538-4709, 8-5PM. www.wildlife.utah.gov/ ⊠Fax

Vermont

Governor's Office
109 State St
Montpelier, VT 05609-0101
www.vermont.gov/governor/

802-828-3333
Fax 802-828-3339
7:45AM-4:30PM

Attorney General's Office
109 State St
Montpelier, VT 05609-1001
www.atg.state.vt.us/

802-828-3171
Fax 802-828-2154
7:45AM-4:30PM

State Website: http://vermont.gov

Legislative Records
802-828-2231 www.leg.state.vt.us

State Archives
802-828-2308 http://vermont-archives.org

Capital: Montpelier, in Washington County

Search Unclaimed Property Online
www.missingmoney.com/main/index.cfm

Criminal Records

Access to Records is Restricted
State Repository, Vermont Criminal Information Center, 103 S. Main St., Waterbury, VT 05671-2101; 802-244-8727, Fax: 802-241-5552, 8AM-4:30PM. www.dps.state.vt.us Records are not publicly available and can only be accessed by those authorized by law and by subject for personal review.✉

Statewide Court Records

Court Administrator, Administrative Office of Courts, 109 State St, Montpelier, VT 05609-0701; 802-828-3278, Fax: 802-828-3457 www.vermontjudiciary.org 💻

Sexual Offender Registry

Access to Records is Restricted
State Repository, Vermont Criminal Information Center, 103 S. Main St., Waterbury, VT 05671-2101; 802-244-8727, Fax: 802-241-5552, 8AM-4:30PM. www.dps.state.vt.us/cjs/s_registry.htm Records are not publicly available and can only be access by those authorized by law or the subject. Search at local level.

Incarceration Records

Vermont Department of Corrections, Inmate Information Request, 103 S. Main Street, Waterbury, VT 05671-1001; 802-241-2276, Fax: 802-241-2565, 8-4:30PM. www.doc.state.vt.us ✉ ☎Fax💻

Voter Registration

Records not maintained by a state agency. Records are at municipal level.

Corporation Records, Limited Liability Company Records, Limited Liability Partnerships, Limited Partnerships, Trademarks/Servicemarks

Secretary of State, Corporation Div, 81 River St, Drawer 9, Montpelier, VT 05609; 802-828-2386, Fax 802-828-2853, 7:45AM-4:30PM.   www.sec.state.vt.us/ ✉☎Fax💻

Uniform Commercial Code

UCC Division, Secretary of State, 81 River St, Drawer 4, Montpelier, VT 05609; 802-828-2386, Fax 802-828-2853, www.sec.state.vt.us/corps/corpindex.htm 7:45AM-4:30PM. ✉Fax💻

Federal and State Tax Liens

Records not maintained by a state agency. Records at local town level.

Sales Tax Registrations

Administrative Agency/Tax Department, Taxpayers Services Division, 109 State St, Montpelier, VT 05609-1401; 802-828-2551, Fax: 802-828-5787, 7:45AM-4:30PM. www.state.vt.us/tax/ ✉☎Fax

Birth Certificates, Marriage Certificates, Death & Divorce Records

Reference & Research, Vital Records Section, US Rte 2, Drawer 33, Montpelier, VT 05633-7601; 802-828-3286, Fax: 802-828-3710, 8AM-4PM. www.bgs.state.vt.us/gsc/pubrec/referen ✉☎Fax💻

Workers' Compensation Records

Labor & Industry, Workers Compensation Division, Drawer 20, Montpelier, VT 05620-3401 (National Life Bldg, Montpelier, VT 05620); 802-828-2286, Fax: 802-828-2195, 7:45AM-4:30PM. www.state.vt.us/labind/wcindex.htm ✉Fax💻

Driver Records, Driver License Information

Dept. of Motor Vehicles, DI - Records Unit, 120 State St, Montpelier, VT 05603; 802-828-2050, Fax: 802-828-2098. www.aot.state.vt.us/dmv/dmvhp.htm 7:45AM-4:30PM✉💻💻

Vehicle Ownership, Vehicle Identification, Vessel Ownership, Vessel Registration

Dept. of Motor Vehicles, Registration & License Information/Records, 120 State St, Montpelier, VT 05603; 802-828-2000, Fax: 802-828-2872, 7:45-4:30PM; Weds 1-4:30PM. www.dmv.state.vt.us ✉💻

Accident Reports

Dept. of Motor Vehicles, Accident Report Section, 120 State St, Montpelier, VT 05603; 802-828-2050, 7:45-4PM. ✉💻

GED Certificates

Dept. of Education, GED Testing, 120 State St, Montpelier, VT 05620; 802-828-5161, Fax: 802-828-3146, 8AM-4:30PM. www.vermontcareers.org ✉☎Fax💻

Key: Access state agency records by:. phone-☎ mail-✉ fax-**Fax** in person-💻 online-💻 email-**Email**

Vermont Hunting and Fishing License Information

Records not maintained by a state level agency. Although they maintain a central database on computer, the records are not open to the public.

Virginia

Governor's Office
Capitol Bldg, 3rd Floor
Richmond, VA 23219   804-786-2211
www.governor.virginia.gov   Fax 804-371-6351
                           8:30AM-5:30PM

Attorney General's Office
900 E Main St
Richmond, VA 23219   804-786-2071
www.oag.state.va.us   Fax 804-786-1991
                           8:30AM-5PM

State Website: www.myvirginia.org

Legislative Records
804-698-1500 http://legis.state.va.us

State Archives
804-692-3500 www.lva.lib.va.us

Capital: Richmond in Richmond City County

Search Unclaimed Property Online

https://www.trs.virginia.gov/propertysearchdotnet/Default.aspx

Criminal Records

State Police, CCRE, PO Box C-85076, Richmond, VA 23261-5076 (7700 Midlothian Turnpike, Richmond); 804-323-2277, Fax: 804-323-0861, 8AM-5PM. www.vsp.state.va.us ✉🖥

Statewide Court Records

Executive Secretary, Administrative Office of Courts, 100 N 9th St, 3rd Fl, Richmond, VA 23219; 804-786-6455, Fax: 804-786-4542, 8AM-5PM. www.courts.state.va.us 🖥

Sexual Offender Registry

Virginia State Police, Sex Offender and Crimes Against Minors Registry, PO Box 85076, Richmond, VA 23261-5076 (7700 Midlothian Turnpike, Richmond, VA 23235); 804-323-2153, Fax: 804-323-0862, 8AM-5PM. http://sex-offender.vsp.state.va.us/cool-ICE/ ✉🖥

Incarceration Records

Virginia Department of Corrections, Central Criminal Records Section, PO Box 26963, Richmond, VA 23261-6963 (6900 Atmore Drive, Richmond, VA 23225); 804-323-2153, Fax: 804-323-0462, 8AM-5PM. www.vadoc.state.va.us ✉☎🖥

State Tax Liens

Records not maintained by a state level agency. All information is found at the local city or county level.

Corporation Records, Limited Liability Company, Fictitious Name, Limited Partnership, Business Trust Records

State Corporation Commission, Clerks Office, PO Box 1197, Richmond, VA 23218-1197 (Tyler Bldg, 1st Fl, 1300 E Main St, Richmond, VA 23219); 804-371-9733, Fax: 804-371-9133, 8:15AM-5PM. www.state.va.us/scc/division/clk/index.htm ✉☎Fax🖐🖥

Trademarks, Service Marks

State Corporation Commission, Securities Division, PO Box 1197 (1300 Main St, 9th Fl), Richmond, VA 23218 (1300 Main St, 9th Fl, Richmond, VA 23219); 804-371-9187, Fax: 804-371-9911, 8:15-5PM. www.state.va.us/scc/index.html ✉☎Fax🖐🖥

Uniform Commercial Code, Federal Tax Liens

UCC Division, State Corporation Commission, PO Box 1197, Richmond, VA 23218-1197 (1300 E Main St, 1st Fl, Richmond, VA 23219); 804-371-9733, Fax: 804-371-9744, 8:15AM-5PM. www.state.va.us/scc/division/clk/index.htm ✉☎Fax🖐🖥

Sales Tax Registrations

Taxation Department, Sales Tax Licenses, PO Box 1115, Richmond, VA 23218-1115 (2220 W Broad St, Richmond); 804-

367-8037, Fax: 804-786-2670, 8:30AM-4:30PM. www.tax.state.va.us/ ✉

Birth Certificates, Death Records, Marriage Certificates, Divorce Records

State Health Department, Office of Vital Records, PO Box 1000, Richmond, VA 23218-1000 (1601 Willow Lawn Drive, #275, Richmond, VA 23220); 804-662-6200, 8AM-4:45PM, Closed on major holidays.www.vdh.state.va.us/vitalrec/ ✉☎Fax🖐

Workers' Compensation Records

Workers' Compensation Commission, 1000 DMV Dr, Richmond, VA 23220; 804-367-8633, 877-664-2566, Fax: 804-367-9740, 8:15AM-5PM. www.vwc.state.va.us/ ✉🖐

Driver Records

Motorist Records Services, Attn: Records Request Work Center, PO Box 27412, Richmond, VA 23269; 804-367-0538, 8:30AM-5:30PM M-F; 8:30AM-12:30PM S. www.dmv.state.va.us ✉🖐🖥

Vehicle Ownership, Vehicle Identification

Department of Motor Vehicles, Vehicle Records Work Center, PO Box 27412, Richmond, VA 23269; 804-367-0538, 8:30AM-5:30PM M-F; 8:30AM-12:30PM S. www.dmv.state.va.us ✉🖐🖥

Accident Reports

Department of Motor Vehicles, Driver Records Work Center, Rm 516, PO Box 27412, Richmond, VA 23269; 804-367-0538, 866-368-5463, Fax: 804-367-0390, 8:30AM-5:30PM M-F; 8:30AM-12:30PM S. www.dmv.state.va.us ✉**Fax**👋

Vessel Ownership, Vessel Registration

Game & Inland Fisheries Dept, 4010 W Broad St, Richmond, VA 23230; 804-367-

6135, 877-898-2628, Fax: 804-367-1064, 8:15-5. www.dgif.virginia.gov ✉👋💻

Voter Registration

Access to Records is Restricted

State Board of Elections, 200 N 9th Street, #101, Richmond, VA 23219; 804-786-6551, Fax: 804-371-0194, 8:30AM-5PM. www.sbe.state.va.us Individual searches must be done at the county or city level with the General Registrars. The state will sell all or portions of its statewide database (95 counties, 40 cities) to

organizations promoting voter registration and participation.

GED Certificates

Dept of Education, GED Services, PO Box 2120, Richmond, VA 23218-2120; 804-786-4642, Fax: 804-225-3352, 8:15AM-5PM. www.pen.k12.va.us ✉👋

Hunting License and Fishing License Information

Records not maintained by a state level agency.

Washington

Governor's Office
 PO Box 40002
 Olympia, WA 98504-0002
 www.governor.wa.gov

360-902-4111
Fax 360-753-4110
8AM-5PM

Attorney General's Office
 PO Box 40100
 Olympia, WA 98504-0100
 www.atg.wa.gov

360-753-6200
Fax 360-586-7671
8AM-5PM

State Website: http://access.wa.gov

Legislative Information Center
 360-786-7573 www1.leg.wa.gov/legislature
State Archives
 360-753-5485 www.secstate.wa.gov/archives

Capital: Olympia, in Thurston County

Search Unclaimed Property Online

http://ucp.dor.wa.gov/default.asp?link=FIF

Criminal Records

Washington State Patrol, Identification and Criminal History Section, PO Box 42633, Olympia, WA 98504-2633 (3000 Pacific Ave. SE #204, Olympia, WA 98501); 360-705-5100, Fax: 360-570-5275, 8-5PM. www.wsp.wa.gov ✉👋💻

Statewide Court Records

Administrative Office of Courts, Temple of Justice, PO Box 41174, Olympia, WA 98504-1174 (1206 Quince St SE, Olympia, WA 98504); 360-357-2121, Fax: 360-357-2127, 8AM-5PM. www.courts.wa.gov 💻

Sexual Offender Registry

Washington State Patrol, SOR, PO Box 42633, Olympia, WA 98504-2633 (3000 Pacific Ave. SE #204, Olympia, WA 98501); 360-705-5100 x3, Fax: 360-570-5275, 8AM-5PM. www.wsp.wa.gov 💻

Incarceration Records

Washington Department of Corrections, Office of Correctional Operations, 410 W.

5th, MS-41118, Olympia, WA 98504-1118; 360-753-3317 (Basic info), 360-586-3492 (Public Disclosure), 8AM-5PM M-F. www.doc.wa.gov ✉☎💻

Corporation Records, Trademarks/Servicemarks, Limited Partnerships, Limited Liability Company Records

Secretary of State, Corporations Division, PO Box 40234, Olympia, WA 98504-0234 (Dolliver Bldg, 801 Capitol Way South, Olympia, WA 98501); 360-753-7115, Fax: 360-664-8781, 8AM-5PM. www.secstate.wa.gov/corps/ ✉☎👋💻

Trade Names

Master License Service, Business & Professions Div, PO Box 9034, Olympia, WA 98507-9034 (405 Black Lake Blvd, Olympia, WA 98507); 360-664-1400, 900-463-6000 (Trade Name Search phone), Fax: 360-570-7875, 8AM-4:30PM. www.dol.wa.gov/ ✉☎👋

Uniform Commercial Code, Federal Tax Liens

Department of Licensing, UCC Records, PO Box 9660, Olympia, WA 98507-9660 (405 Black Lake Blvd, Olympia); 360-664-1530, Fax: 360-586-4414, 8-5PM. www.dol.wa.gov/unfc/uccfront.htm ✉💻

State Tax Liens

Records not maintained by a state level agency.
State tax liens are filed at the county level.

Sales Tax Registrations

Department of Revenue, Taxpayer Services, PO Box 47478, Olympia, WA 98504-7478; 360-486-2345, 800-647-7706, Fax: 360-486-2159, 8AM-5PM. www.dor.wa.gov ✉☎**Fax**👋💻

Workers' Compensation Records

Labor and Industries, Public Disclosure Unit, PO Box 44632, Olympia, WA

98504-4632 (7273 Linderson Way SW, Tumwater, WA 98501); 360-902-5542, Fax: 360-902-5529, 8AM-5PM. www.lni.wa.gov/ ⊠**Fax**✍

Birth Certificates, Death Records, Marriage Certificates, Divorce Records

Department of Health, Vital Records, PO Box 9709, Olympia, WA 98507-9709 (101 Israel Rd SE, Tumwater, WA 98501); 360-236-4300 (Main Number), 360-236-4313 (Credit Card Ordering), Fax: 360-352-2586, 9AM - 4PM. www.doh.wa.gov ⊠☎**Fax**✍💻

Driver Records

Department of Licensing, Driver Record Section, PO Box 9030, Olympia, WA 98507-9030 (1125 Washington Street SE, Olympia, WA 98504); 360-902-3921, 360-902-3900 (General Information),

Fax: 360-586-9044, 8AM-4:30PM. www.dol.wa.gov ⊠✍💻

Vehicle Ownership, Vehicle Identification, Vessel Ownership, Vessel Registration

Department of Licensing, Vehicle Records, PO Box 2957, Olympia, WA 98507-2957 (1125 S Washington MS-48001, Olympia, WA 98504); 360-902-3780, Fax: 360-902-3827, 8AM-5PM. www.dol.wa.gov ⊠☎✍💻

Accident Reports

State Patrol, Collision Reports, PO Box 47382, Olympia, WA 98504; 360-570-2355, Fax: 360-570-2400, 8AM-5PM. www.wsp.wa.gov/ ⊠✍

Voter Registration

Access to Records is Restricted
Secretary of State, Office of Elections Division, PO Box 40220, Olympia, WA

98504 360-902-4180, Fax: 360-664-4619, 8-5PM. www.secstate.wa.gov/elections/ All voter information is kept at the local level by the County Auditor (except King County where records are kept by the Dept of Records and Elections).

GED Certificates

State Board for Community & Technical Colleges, GED Records, PO Box 42495, Olympia, WA 98504-2495 (319 7th Ave, Olympia, WA 98504); 360-704-4410, Fax: 360-664-8808, 8AM-5PM. www.sbctc.ctc.edu ⊠**Fax**✍

Hunting License and Fishing License Information

Department of Fish & Wildlife, Attn: Public Disclosure Officer, 600 Capitol Way, N, Olympia, WA 98501-1091; 360-902-2253, Fax: 360-902-2171, 8AM-5PM. http://wdfw.wa.gov ⊠**Fax**✍💻

West Virginia

Governor's Office
1900 Kanawha Blvd, East
Charleston, WV 25305-0370
www.state.wv.us/governor

304-558-2000
Fax 304-342-7025
8AM-6PM M-TH;

Attorney General's Office
1900 Kanawha Blvd. Rm 26E
Charleston, WV 25305-9924
www.wvs.state.wv.us/wvag/

304-558-2021
Fax 304-558-0140
8:30AM-5PM

State Website: www.wv.gov

Legislative Records
304-347-4830 www.legis.state.wv.us
State Archives 304-558-0220
www.wvculture.org/history/wvsamenu.html

Capital: Charleston, in Kanawha County

Search Unclaimed Property Online
www.missingmoney.com/main/index.cfm

Criminal Records

State Police, Criminal Records Section, 725 Jefferson Rd, South Charleston, WV 25309; 304-746-2277, Fax 304-746-2402, 8:30-4:30. www.wvstatepolice.com ⊠

Statewide Court Records

Administrative Office, State Supreme Court of Appeals, 1900 Kanawha Blvd, Bldg 1, Rm E 100, Charleston, WV 25305; 304-558-0145, Fax 304-558-1212, 9AM-5PM. www.state.wv.us/wvsca 💻

Sexual Offender Registry

State Police Headquarters, Sexual Offender Registry, 725 Jefferson Rd,

South Charleston, WV 25309; 304-746-2133, Fax: 304-746-2403, 8:30-4:30PM. www.wvstatepolice.com/sexoff/ 💻

Incarceration Records

Division of Corrections, Records Room, 112 California Ave. 3rd Fl, Charleston, WV 25305; 304-558-2037, Fax: 304-558-5934, www.wvf.state.wv.us/wvdoc/ 8AM-5PM. ⊠☎**Fax**💻

Federal and State Tax Liens

Records not maintained by a state agency. Tax liens filed at county level.

Corporation Records, Limited Liability Company Records, Limited Partnerships, Trademarks/Servicemarks, Limited Liability Partnerships

Secretary of State, Corporation Division, State Capitol Bldg, Room W151, Charleston, WV 25305-0776; 304-558-8000, Fax: 304-558-5758, 8:30AM-5PM. www.wvsos.com ⊠☎**Fax**✍💻

Key: Access state agency records by:. phone-☎ mail-⊠ fax-**Fax** in person-✍ online-💻 email-**Email**

Uniform Commercial Code

UCC Division, Secretary of State, Bldg 1, West Wing, Rm 157K, Charleston, WV 25305-0440; 304-558-6000, Fax: 304-558-0900, www.wvsos.com/ucc/main.htm 8:30AM-4:30PM. ✉☎Fax🖑

Sales Tax Registrations

WV State Tax Department, Office of Business Registration, 1001 E Lee St E, Charleston, WV 25301; 304-558-8500, Fax: 304-558-8754, 8:30AM-4:30PM. www.state.wv.us/taxrev/ ✉☎Fax🖑

Birth Certificates, Death Records, Marriage Certificates

Bureau of Public Health, Vital Records, 350 Capitol St, Rm 165, Charleston, WV 25305-3701; 304-558-2931, Fax: 304-558-1051, www.wvdhhr.org/bph/oehp/hsc 8:30AM-5PM. ✉☎🖑

Divorce Records

Records not maintained by a state agency. Records maintained by the Clerk of Court in the county of divorce.

Workers' Comp. Records

Workers Compensation Division, Records Management, PO Box 3151, Charleston, WV 25332; 304-558-5587, 304-926-3400, Fax: 304-558-1908, 8AM-4:30PM. www.state.wv.us/scripts/bep/wc/ ✉🖑

Driver License Information, Driver Records

Div. of Motor Vehicles, 1800 Kanawha Blvd, Building 3, Rm 124, State Capitol Complex, Charleston, WV 25317; 304-558-0238, 304-558-5362, Fax: 304-558-0037, www.wvdot.com/6_motorists/dmv/6G_DMV.HTM 8:30-4:30. ✉🖑💻

Vehicle Ownership, Vehicle Identification, Vessel Registration

Division of Motor Vehicles, Information Services, 1606 Washington St East, Charleston, WV 25311; 304-558-0282,

Fax: 304-558-1012, 8:30AM-4:30PM. www.wvdot.com/6_motorists/dmv/6g2_re gistration.htm ✉🖑

Accident Reports

Department of Public Safety, Traffic Records Section, 725 Jefferson Rd, South Charleston, WV 25309-1698; 304-746-2128, Fax: 304-746-2206, 8:30AM-5PM. www.wvstatepolice.com ✉☎Fax🖑

GED Certificates

Dept of Education, GED Office, 1900 Kanawha Blvd E, Bldg 6, Rm 250, Charleston, WV 25305-0330; 304-558-6315, Fax: 304-558-4874, 8AM-4PM. www.wvabe.org/ged/ ✉Fax

Hunting License and Fishing License Information

Natural Resources Department, Licensing Division, 1900 Kanawha Blvd E, Bldg 3, Room 624, Charleston, WV 25305; 304-558-2758, Fax: 304-558-6208, 8:30AM-4:30PM. www.wvweb.com/www/hunting ✉Fax🖑

Wisconsin

Governor's Office
PO Box 7863   608-266-1212
Madison, WI 53707-7863   Fax 608-267-8983
www.wisgov.state.wi.us   8AM-5PM

Attorney General's Office
Justice Department, PO Box 7857   608-266-1221
Madison, WI 53707-7857   Fax 608-267-2779
www.doj.state.wi.us   8AM-5PM

State Website: www.wisconsin.gov

Legislative Records
608-266-0341 www.legis.state.wi.us
State Archives 608-264-6460
www.wisconsinhistory.org/libraryarchives/

Capital: Madison, in Dane County

Search Unclaimed Property Online

http://prd1.state.wi.us/servlet/trdUnclaimProperty or
www.missingmoney.com/main/index.cfm

Criminal Records

Department of Justice, Crime Information Bureau, Record Check Unit, PO Box 2688, Madison, WI 53701-2688 (17 W Main St); 608-266-5764, 608-266-7780 (Online Questions), Fax: 608-267-4558, 8-4:30. www.doj.state.wi.us ✉Fax🖑💻

Statewide Court Records

Director of State Courts, Supreme Court, PO Box 1688, Madison, WI 53701-1688;

608-266-6828, Fax: 608-267-0980, 8AM-5PM. http://wicourts.gov 💻

Sexual Offender Registry

Department of Corrections, Sex Offender Registry Program, PO Box 7925, Madison, WI 53707 (3099 E Washington Ave.); 608-240-5830, Fax: 608-240-3355 http://offender.doc.state.wi.us/public/ 7:45-4:30PM. ✉💻

Incarceration Records

Wisconsin Department of Corrections, Bureau of Technology Management, PO Box 8980, Madison, WI 53708-8980 (3099 E Washington Ave); 608-240-5741, Fax: 608-240-3385, 7:30AM-4PM. www.wi-doc.com ✉☎Fax💻

Trademarks/Servicemarks,

Secretary of State TradenamesTrademarks Div., PO Box 7848, Madison, WI 53707-7848 (30 W Mifflin St, 10th Fl, Madison);

Key: Access state agency records by:. phone-☎ mail-✉ fax-Fax in person-🖑 online-💻 email-Email

608-266-5653, Fax: 608-266-3159, http://badger.state.wi.us/agencies/sos 7:45AM-4:30PM. ☒ ☎ **Fax** ✋

Corporation Records, Limited Partnership Records, Limited Liability Company Records, Limited Liability Partnerships

Division of Corporate & Consumer Services, Corporation Record Requests, PO Box 7846, Madison, WI 53707-7846 (345 W Washington Ave, 3rd Fl, Madison); 608-261-7577, Fax: 608-267-6813, 7:45AM-4:30PM. www.wdfi.org ☒ ☎ **Fax** ✋ 🖥

Uniform Commercial Code, Federal and State Tax Liens

Department of Financial Institutions, CCS/UCC, PO Box 7847, Madison, WI 53707-7847 (345 W Washington Ave 3rd Fl, Madison, WI 53703); 608-261-9548, Fax: 608-264-7965, 7:45AM-4:30PM. www.wdfi.org ☒ ☎ **Fax** ✋ 🖥

Sales Tax Registrations

Revenue Department, Income, Sales, & Excise Tax Division, PO Box 8902, Madison, WI 53708-8902 (3125 Rimrock Rd, Madison, WI 53713); 608-266-2776, Fax: 608-267-1030, 7:45AM-4:30PM. www.dor.state.wi.us ☒ ☎ **Fax** ✋

Birth Certificates, Death Records, Marriage Certificates, Divorce Records

Bureau of Health Information, Vital Records, PO Box 309, Madison, WI 53701-0309 (One W Wilson St, #158); 608-266-1373, 608-267-7820-genealogy, Fax: 608-255-2035, 8AM-4:15PM. www.dhfs.state.wi.us/VitalRecords ☒ **Fax** ✋ 🖥

Workers' Compensation Records

Dept of Workforce Development, Worker's Compensation Division, PO Box 7901, Madison, WI 53707-7901 (201 E Washington Ave, Madison); 608-266-1340, Fax: 608-267-0394, 7:45AM-4:30PM. www.dwd.state.wi.us/wc ☒ ✋

Driver Records

Division of Motor Vehicles, Records & Licensing Info. Section, PO Box 7995, Madison, WI 53707-7995 (4802 Sheboygan Ave, #350); 608-266-2353, Fax: 608-267-3636, 7:30AM-5:15PM. www.dot.wisconsin.gov ☒ ☎ 🖥

Vehicle Ownership, Vehicle Identification

Department of Transportation, Vehicle Records Section, PO Box 7911, Madison, WI 53707-7911 (4802 Sheboygan Ave, Room 102, Madison, WI 53707); 608-266-3666, 608-266-1466-registration laws, Fax: 608-267-6966, 7:30AM-4:30PM. www.dot.wisconsin.gov ☒ ☎

Accident Reports

Division of Motor Vehicles, Traffic Accident Section, PO Box 7919, Madison, WI 53707-7919 (4802 Sheboygan Ave, Room 804, Madison, WI 53707); 608-266-8753, Fax: 608-267-0606, 7:30AM-4:30PM. www.dot.wisconsin.gov/ ☒ ☎

Vessel Ownership, Vessel Registration

Department of Natural Resources, Boat Registration, PO Box 7921, Madison, WI 53707 (101 S Webster, Madison, WI 53703); 608-266-2621, Fax: 608-264-6130, 7:45AM-4:30PM. www.dnr.wi.gov ☒ ☎ **Fax** ✋

Voter Registration

Records not maintained by a state level agency.
This agency is in the process of creating a statewide voter registration list. All records are maintained at the municipal level. Although records are open to the public, be advised that not all municipalities maintain voter lists.

GED Certificates

Department of Public Instruction, GED Program, PO Box 7841, Madison, WI 53707-7841 (125 S Webster, Madison, WI 53707); 608-267-9245, 800-441-4563, Fax: 608-264-9552, 8AM-4:30PM. www.dpi.state.wi.us ☒ ☎ **Fax** ✋

Hunting License and Fishing License Information

Access to Records is Restricted
Fish & Game Licensing Division, Records Manager - CS/G3, PO Box 7924, Madison, WI 53707 (101 S Webster St, Madison, WI 53703); 608-266-2621, 608-261-0770 (List Sales), Fax: 608-261-4380, 8AM-4:30PM. www.dnr.state.wi.us They do not provide name searching, but will sell lists by license type.

Wyoming

Governor's Office
  State Capitol Building, Rm 124   307-777-7434
  Cheyenne, WY 82002-0010   Fax 307-632-3909
  www.wyoming.gov/governor/governor_home.asp

Attorney General's Office
  200 W 24thth Street   307-777-7841
  Cheyenne, WY 82002   Fax 307-777-6869
  http://attorneygeneral.state.wy.us   8AM-5PM

State Website: http://wyoming.gov

Legislative Records
  307-777-7881 http://legisweb.state.wy.us
State Archives: 307-777-7826
  http://wyoarchives.state.wy.us/index.htm
Capital: Cheyenne, in Laramie County

Search Unclaimed Property Online

http://treasurer.state.wy.us/search.asp

Wyoming Criminal Records

Division of Criminal Investigation, Criminal Record Unit, 316 W 22nd St, Cheyenne, WY 82002; 307-777-7523, Fax: 307-777-7252, 8AM to 5PM. http://attorneygeneral.state.wy.us/dci/index.html ✉ ✋

Sexual Offender Registry

Division of Criminal Investigation, ATTN: WSOR, 316 W 22nd St, Cheyenne, WY 82002-0001; 307-777-7809, Fax: 307-777-7252, 8AM to 5PM. http://attorneygeneral.state.wy.us/dci/index.html 🖳

Statewide Court Records

Court Administrator, Supreme Court Bldg, 2301 Capitol Ave, Cheyenne, WY 82002; 307-777-7583, Fax: 307-777-3447, 8-5PM. www.courts.state.wy.us 🖳

Incarceration Records

Wyoming Department of Corrections, 700 W. 21st Street,, Cheyenne, WY 82002; 307-777-7405, Fax: 307-777-7479, 8-5. http://doc.state.wy.us/corrections.asp ✉ ☎ Fax 🖳

Corporation Records, Limited Liability Company Records, Limited Partnership Records, Fictitious Name, Trademarks/Servicemarks

Corporations Division, Attn: Records, 200 W 24th Street, Rm 110, Cheyenne, WY 82002; 307-777-7311, Fax: 307-777-5339, 8AM-5PM. http://soswy.state.wy.us ✉ ☎ Fax ✋ 🖳

Uniform Commercial Code, Federal Tax Liens

Secretary of State, UCC Division - Records, 200 W 24th Street, Room 110, Cheyenne, WY 82002-0020; 307-777-5372, Fax: 307-777-5988, 8AM-5PM.

http://soswy.state.wy.us/uniform/uniform.htm ✉ Fax ✋ 🖳

State Tax Liens

Records not maintained by a state level agency.
There is no state income tax. All other state tax liens are filed at the county level.

Sales Tax Registrations

Department of Revenue, Excise Tax Division, Herschler Bldg, 122 W 25th St, Cheyenne, WY 82002-0110; 307-777-5200, Fax: 307-777-3632, 8AM-5PM. http://revenue.state.wy.us ✉ ☎ ✋

Birth Certificates, Death Records, Marriage Certificates, Divorce Records

Wyoming Department of Health, Vital Records Services, Hathaway Bldg, Cheyenne, WY 82002; 307-777-7591, Fax: 307-635-4103, 8AM-5PM. http://wdhfs.state.wy.us/vital_records ✉ Fax ✋

Workers' Compensation Records

Employment Department, Workers Compensation Division, 1510 E Pershing Blvd, Cheyenne, WY 82002; 307-777-7159, Fax: 307-777-5946, 8AM-4:30PM. http://wydoe.state.wy.us/doe.asp?ID=9 ✉ Fax

Driver License Information, Driver Records

Wyoming Department of Transportation, Driver Services, 5300 Bishop Blvd, Cheyenne, WY 82009-3340; 307-777-4800, Fax: 307-777-4773, 8AM-5PM. www.dot.state.wy.us ✉ ✋ 🖳

Vehicle Ownership, Vehicle Identification

Wyoming Dept. of Transportation, Motor Vehicle Services, 5300 Bishop Blvd, Cheyenne, WY 82009-3340 (5300 Bishop Blvd, Cheyenne, WY 82002); 307-777-4851, Fax: 307-777-4772, 8AM-5PM. http://wydotweb.state.wy.us/web/vehicle_services/index.html ✉ Fax ✋

Accident Reports

Highway Safety Program, Accident Records Section, 5300 Bishop Blvd, Cheyenne, WY 82009; 307-777-4450, Fax: 307-777-4250, 8AM-5PM. ✉ ☎ ✋

Vessel Ownership, Vessel Registration

Wyoming Game & Fish Dept, Watercraft Section, 5400 Bishop Blvd, Cheyenne, WY 82006; 307-777-4575, Fax: 307-777-4610, 8AM-5PM http://gf.state.wy.us ✉ ☎ Fax ✋

Voter Registration

Secretary of State, Election Division, Wyoming State Capitol, Cheyenne, WY 82002-0020; 307-777-7186, Fax: 307-777-7640, 8AM-5PM. http://soswy.state.wy.us/election/election.htm ✉ ✋

GED Certificates

Department of WorkForce Services, GED Program, 122 W 25th Street, Cheyenne, WY 82002; 307-777-6911, Fax: 307-777-7106, www.wyomingworkforce.org 8AM-5PM ✉ Fax ✋

Hunting License and Fishing License Information

Game & Fish Department, License Section, 5400 Bishop Blvd, Cheyenne, WY 82006; 307-777-4600 (Licensing Section), Fax: 307-777-4679, 8AM-5PM. http://gf.state.wy.us ✉ ☎ Fax ✋

Chapter 5

Recording Offices

Combined, there are 4,266 local recording offices where recorded documents are maintained. Real estate records such as deeds and mortgages usually come to mind, but, depending on the state, there are an assortment of record types to be found in connection with a county courthouse including Uniform Commercial Code filings, liens, vital records, assessment data, voter registration rolls, and court documents such as judgments.

The Lowdown on Recorded Documents

Documents filed and recorded at local county, parish, city or town offices represent some of the best opportunities to gain access to open public records, more so if they are available for searching online by name. In fact, recorded documents are one of the most available types of public records that can be viewed online and obtained over the Internet, either for free or at a reasonable fee. Even better, if you are lucky enough to live in close proximity, you can visit your local office and view complete records and acquire copies. Viewing is free. There is a fee for copies.

Real Estate

Real estate records are public so that everyone can know who owns what property. Liens on real estate must be public so a buyer knows all the facts. The county (or parish, borough, or city) recording office is the source. Access to real estate-related records is also available from many private companies that purchase entire county record databases and create their own database for commercial purposes.

Uniform Commercial Code (UCC)

UCC filings are to personal property what mortgages are to real estate property. UCCs are in the category of financial records that must be fully open to public scrutiny so that other potential lenders are on notice about which assets of the borrower have been pledged as collateral.

As with tax liens, UCC recordings are filed, according to state law, either at the state or local (county, town, parish) level. Until June 30, 2001, liens on certain types of companies required dual filing (must file at BOTH locations, thus records can be searched at BOTH locations). As of July 1, 2001, UCC filings other than those that go into real estate records are no longer filed at the local filing offices in most states, but older filings can still be located there until 2008. As with real estate records, there are a number of private companies who have created their own databases for commercial resale.

A Great Source of Information

Although recorded documents are a necessity to making an informed business-related decision, they are also a virtual treasure trove of data. UCC filing documents give you the names and addresses of creditors and debtors, describe the asset offered for collateral, the date of the filing, and whether or not the loan has been satisfied. This information contained on the statements can lead an experienced investigator to other avenues along the information trail. For example, if the collateral is a plane or a vessel, this will lead to registration records; if the debtor is a business, other names on the filing may lead to other traceable business partners or ventures.

How the Recording Offices Section is Organized

In this book, the mailing address, telephone, business hours, and fax number are listed for each office as well as if online access is available. Included are the categories of information offered online from this or a related agency such as tax assessor information, vital records, liens, licenses, etc. If a mailing address is a post office box, a physical address may also be given in parenthesis.

An introduction to each state Recording Offices section contains a summary of the facts about where and how real estate records are maintained as well as indicating information about Uniform Commercial Code (UCC) and tax lien filings. The introductions mention any unusual conditions pertaining to real estate, tax lien, and UCC searching in that state. A list of some of the other liens that are filed at the local level is also included. To aid in searching, statewide or regional databases are explained.

Recording Office Searching Rules

The general rules for background searching of UCC records are as follows:

- Except in local filing states, a search at the state level is adequate to locate all UCC records on a subject.
- Mortgage record searches will include any real estate related UCC filings.
- See the sections below for discussions of special collateral rules.

Due diligence searching, however, usually demands searching the local records in dual filing states, especially for older UCC records.

Special Categories of Collateral

Real Estate Related UCC Collateral

A specific purpose of lien statutes under both the UCC and real estate laws is to put a buyer or potential secured creditor on notice that someone has a prior security interest in real or personal property. UCC financing statements are to personal property what mortgages or deeds of trust are to real property.

One problem addressed by the UCC is that certain types of property have the characteristics of both real and personal property. In those instances, it is necessary to have a way to provide lien notice to two different categories of interested parties: those who deal with the real estate aspect of the property and those who deal with the "personal" aspect of the property.

In general, our definition of real estate related UCC collateral is any property that in one form is attached to land, but that in another form is not attached. For the sake of simplicity, we can define the characteristics of two broad types of property that meet this definition:

1. Property that is initially attached to real property, but then is separated.
   Three specific types of collateral have this characteristic: minerals (including oil and gas), timber, and crops. These things are grown on or extracted from land. While they are on or in the ground they are thought of as real property, but once they are harvested or extracted they become personal property. Some states have a separate central filing system for crops.

2. Property that is initially personal property, but then is attached to land, is generally called fixtures.
   Equipment such as telephone systems or heavy industrial equipment permanently affixed to a building are examples of fixtures. It is important to realize that what is a fixture, like beauty, is in the eye of the beholder, since "fixtures" is a somewhat vague definition.

UCC financing statements applicable to real estate related collateral must be filed where the real estate and mortgage records are kept, which is generally at the county level — except in Connecticut, Rhode Island and Vermont where the Town/City Clerk maintains these records. The summary in front of each state gives the titles of the local official who maintains these records.

Consumer Goods

Among the state-to-state variations, some states required filing where real estate is filed for certain consumer goods. However, as of July 1, 2001 all non-realty related UCC filings in most states, including consumer goods, now go only to the central filing office in the state.

Equipment Used in Farming Operations

33 states required only local filing for equipment used in farming operations. However as of July 1, 2001, all non-realty-related UCC filing has been centralized.

Searching Note

If you are looking for information on subjects that might have these types of filings against them, a search of county records may still be revealing even if you would normally search only at the state level.

The Importance of Revised Article 9

Revised Article 9

On July 1, 2001, Revised Article 9 became law in 46 states and the District of Columbia, with 4 states adopting the law later; Alabama (January 1, 2002), Connecticut (October 1, 2001), Florida (January 1, 2002) and Mississippi (January 1, 2002). Under this new law, most UCC filings will go to the state where a business is organized, not where the collateral or chief executive offices are located. Thus, you will find new filings against IBM only in Delaware (IBM and many other public companies are Delaware corporations), and not in New York or in any other states where it has branch offices. Therefore, you will need to know where a company is organized in order to know where to find new UCC filings against it.

The place to file against individuals is the state where the person resides.

However, the new law does not apply to federal tax liens, which are still generally filed where the chief executive office is located. IBM's chief executive offices, for example, may still be in New York state.

As stated above, realty-related UCC filings continue to go to land recording offices where the property is located.

How to Search for Filings Under Old Article 9

Under old Article 9, Uniform Commercial Code financing statements and changes to them might be filed at two or three government agencies in each state, depending upon the type of collateral involved in the transaction. Each state's UCC statute containes variations on a nationally recommended Model Act. Each variation is explained below. The charts appear later in this chapter.

You will still need to know about where UCC filings are located under old Article 9 because the transition period to Revised Article 9 is five years long. UCC filings on record before July 1, 2001 remain effective until they lapse, which is generally five years from initial filing date.

A lot of UCC filings against IBM, for example, made before July 1, 2001 will still be on record in New York's central filing office, and may also be found in county filing offices since New York was a dual filing state, as explained below.

Under old Article 9, 33 states were central filing states. Central filing states are those where most types of personal property collateral require filing of a UCC financing statement only at a central filing location within that state.

Under old Article 9, five states had statewide UCC database systems. Some of these systems are still in effect under Revised Article 9. Minnesota and Wisconsin were central filing states with a difference: UCC financing statements filed at the county level are also entered into a statewide database. In North Dakota UCC financing statements may be filed at either the state or county level, and all filings are entered into a statewide database. In Louisiana, Nebraska, and Georgia, UCC financing statements may be filed with any county (parish). Under Revised Article 9, Minnesota has established a county/state system like North Dakota in all but six county offices, and Nebraska is now a central filing state. In each of these six states the records are entered into a central, statewide database that is available for searching in each county, as well as at the state agency (no state agency in Louisiana or Georgia).

Under old Article 9, eight states required dual filing of certain types of UCC financing statements. The usual definition of a dual filing state is one in which financing statements containing collateral such as inventory, equipment or receivables must be filed in both a central filing office, usually with the Secretary of State, and in a local (county) office where the collateral or business is located. The three states below were also dual filing states, with a difference. Under Revised Article 9, no dual filing is required within a state

Under old Article 9, the filing systems in three states, MA, NH, and PA, can be described as triple filing because the real estate portion of the filings goes to an office separate from the UCC filing offices. In Massachusetts and New Hampshire, UCC filings were submitted to the town/city while real estate filings go to the county. In Pennsylvania, county government was separated into the Prothonotary for UCC filings and the Recorder for real estate filings. The local filing offices for non-realty-related UCC filings no longer take filings under Revised Article 9, but they will continue to perform searches of the old records.

Some counties in other states do have separate addresses for real estate recording, but this is usually just a matter of local departmentalization.

Under old Article 9, Kentucky and Wyoming were the only local filing only states. In both of these states a few filings were also found at the state level because filings for out of state debtors went to the Secretary of State. And in Wyoming, filings for Wyoming debtor accounts receivable and farm products require dual filing. However, under Revised Article 9, all filings have been centralized.

The Old Article 9 UCC Locator Chart

This chart will tell you at a glance where UCC and real estate records are filed under old Article 9 on a state-by-state basis. Under Revised Article 9, effective July 1, 2001 except as noted later for Alabama, Connecticut, Florida and Mississippi, all new personal property filings go to the central filing office.

| State | Most Personal Property | | All Real Property |
	Central Filing Office	Local Filing Office	Filing Office
AK	Department of Natural Resources		District Recorder
AL	Secretary of State		Judge of Probate
AR	Secretary of State	and Circuit Clerk	Circuit Clerk
AZ	Secretary of State		County Recorder
CA	Secretary of State		County Recorder
CO	Secretary of State	or any County Recorder (as of July 1, 1996)	County Clerk & Recorder
CT	Secretary of State		Town/City Clerk
DC	County Recorder		County Recorder
DE	Secretary of State		County Recorder
FL	Secretary of State		Clerk of Circuit Court
GA	None	Clerk Superior Court	Clerk of Superior Court
HI	Bureau of Conveyances		Bureau of Conveyances
IA	Secretary of State		County Recorder
ID	Secretary of State		County Recorder
IL	Secretary of State		County Recorder
IN	Secretary of State		County Recorder
KS	Secretary of State		Register
KY	Secretary of State (Out of state only)	County Clerk	County Clerk
LA	None	Clerk of Court	Clerk of Court

MA	Secretary of the Commonwealth	and Town/City Clerk	Register of Deeds
MD	Department of Assessments & Taxation	and Clerk of Circuit Court (until 7/1/95)	Clerk of Circuit Court
ME	Secretary of State		County Register
MI	Secretary of State		County Register
MN	Secretary of State or Recorder		County Recorder
MO	Secretary of State	and County Recorder	County Recorder
MS	Secretary of State	and Chancery Clerk	Chancery Clerk
MT	Secretary of State		Clerk & Recorder
NC	Secretary of State	and Register of Deeds	Register of Deeds
ND	Secretary of State or County Register		County Register
NE	Secretary of State (Out of state only)	County Clerk	County Register
NH	Secretary of State	and Town/City Clerk	County Register
NJ	Secretary of State		County Clerk/Register
NM	Secretary of State		County Clerk
NV	Secretary of State		County Recorder
NY	Secretary of State	and County Clerk (Register)	County Clerk (Register)
OH	Secretary of State	and County Recorder	County Recorder
OK	Oklahoma County Clerk		County Clerk
OR	Secretary of State		County Clerk
PA	Department of State	and Prothonotary	County Recorder
RI	Secretary of State		County Clerk & Recorder
SC	Secretary of State		County Register/Clerk
SD	Secretary of State		County Register
TN	Secretary of State		County Register
TX	Secretary of State		County Clerk
UT	Division of Corporations & Commercial Code		County Recorder
VA	Corporation Commission	and Clerk of Circuit Court	Clerk of Circuit Court
VT	Secretary of State	and Town/City Clerk (until 7/1/95)	Town/City Clerk
WA	Department of Licensing		County Auditor
WI	Dept. of Financial Institutions		County Register
WV	Secretary of State		County Clerk
WY	Secretary of State (Out of state and A/R only)	County Clerk	County Clerk

Alabama

Organization: 67 counties, 71 recording offices. The recording officer is the Judge of Probate. Four counties have two recording offices: Barbour, Coffee, Jefferson, and St. Clair. See the notes under each county regarding how to determine which office is appropriate to search. The entire state is in the Central Time Zone (CST).

Real Estate Records: Most counties do not perform real estate searches. Copy fees vary. Certification fees vary. Tax records are located at the Assessor's Office.

UCC Records: Alabama has adopted Revised Article 9 effective 01/01/2002. Financing statements are filed at the state level; real estate related collateral with the County Judge of Probate. Prior to 01/01/2002, consumer goods and farm collateral were filed with the county Judge of Probate. Only one-third of counties will perform UCC searches. Use search request form UCC-11. Search fees vary from $5.00 to $12.00 per debtor name. Copies usually cost $1.00 per page.

Tax Lien Records: Federal and state tax liens on personal property of businesses are filed with the Secretary of State. Other federal and state tax liens are filed with the county Judge of Probate. Counties do not perform separate tax lien searches although the liens are usually filed in the same index with UCC statements. Other Liens: Mechanics, judgment, lis pendens, hospital, vendor.

Online Access: There is no statewide system, but a limited number of counties offer free online access to recorded documents.

Autauga Judge of Probate 176 W. 5th St., Prattville, AL 36067-3041 **334-361-3731** Fax: 334-361-3740. 8:30AM-5PM. Property, Assessor, Map records online.

Baldwin Judge of Probate PO Box 459, Bay Minette, AL 36507 (1 Courthouse Sq). **251-937-0230** Fax: 251-580-2563. 8-4:30 www.probate.co.baldwin.al.us Property, Deed, Recording, UCC records online.

Barbour - Clayton Division Judge of Probate PO Box 158, Clayton, AL 36016 (Court Sq). **334-775-8371** Fax: 334-775-1126. 8AM-5PM.
Eufaula Division Judge of Probate PO Box 758, Eufaula, AL 36072 (303 E. Broad St, Rm 101). **334-687-1530** Fax: 334-687-0921. 8AM-5PM.

Bibb Judge of Probate 8 Court Sq W, #A, Centreville, AL 35042 **205-926-3104** Fax: 205-926-3131. 8AM-4:30PM.

Blount Judge of Probate 220 2nd Ave East, Oneonta, AL 35121 **205-625-4180** Fax: 205-625-4206. 8AM-4PM.

Bullock Judge of Probate PO Box 71, Union Springs, AL 36089 (217 N. Prairie). **334-738-2250** Fax: 334-738-3839. 8-4:30PM.

Butler Judge of Probate PO Box 756, Greenville, AL 36037 (700 Court Sq). **334-382-3512** Fax: 334-382-5489. 8AM-4PM M,T,Th,F; 8AM-Noon W.

Calhoun Judge of Probate 1702 Noble St, #102, Anniston, AL 36201 **256-241-2825** Fax: 256-231-1728. 8AM-4:30PM.

Chambers Judge of Probate Courthouse, Lafayette, AL 36862 **334-864-4384** Fax: 334-864-4394. 8AM-4:30PM. Real Estate, UCC records online.

Cherokee Judge of Probate 100 Main St #204, Centre, AL 35960 **256-927-3363** Fax: 256-927-6949. 8AM-4PM; 8AM-N Sat.

Chilton Judge of Probate PO Box 270, Clanton, AL 35046 (500 2nd Ave North). **205-755-1555** Fax: 205-280-7204. 8-4PM.

Choctaw Judge of Probate 117 S. Mulberry, Courthouse, Butler, AL 36904 **205-459-2417** Fax: 205-459-4248. 8-4:30PM.

Clarke Judge of Probate PO Box 10, Grove Hill, AL 36451 (117 Court St, Courthouse). **251-275-3251** Fax: 251-275-8517. 8-5PM.

Clay Judge of Probate PO Box 1120, Ashland, AL 36251 (Courthouse). **256-354-3006** Fax: 256-354-4778. 8AM-4:30PM.

Cleburne Judge of Probate 120 Vickery St, Rm 101, Heflin, AL 36264 **256-463-5655** Fax: 256-463-1044. 8AM-5PM.

Coffee - Elba Division Judge of Probate 230-P N. Court Ave, Elba, AL 36323 **334-897-2211** Fax: 334-897-2028. 8-4:30PM.
Enterprise Division Judge of Probate PO Box 311247, Enterprise, AL 36331 (99 S Edwards St). **334-347-2688** Fax: 334-347-2095. 8AM-4:30PM.

Colbert Judge of Probate PO Box 47, Tuscumbia, AL 35674 (Probate Judge, 201 Main St, Basement). **256-386-8546** Fax: 256-386-8547. 8AM-4:30PM.

Conecuh Judge of Probate PO Box 149, Evergreen, AL 36401 (Jackson St, Court Sq) **251-578-1221** Fax 251-578-7034. 8-4:30

Coosa Judge of Probate PO Box 218, Rockford, AL 35136 (Highway 231 & 22, Courthouse). **256-377-4919** Fax: 256-377-1549. 8AM-4PM.

Covington Judge of Probate PO Box 789, Andalusia, AL 36420-0789 (1 Court Sq). **334-428-2518/2519** Fax: 334-428-2563. 8AM-5PM. Real Estate records online.

Crenshaw Judge of Probate PO Box 328, Luverne, AL 36049-0328 (29 S. Glenwood Ave). **334-335-6568** Fax: 334-335-4749. 8AM-4:30PM.

Cullman Judge of Probate PO Box 970, Cullman, AL 35055 (200 2nd Ave SW **256-775-4807** Fax: 256-775-4813. 8AM-4:30.

Dale of Probate PO Box 580, Ozark, AL 36361-0580 (Courthouse). **334-774-2754** Fax: 334-774-0468. 8AM-5PM.

Dallas Judge of Probate PO Box 987, Selma, AL 36702-0987 (105 Lauderdale St). **334-874-2516** 8:30-4:30.

De Kalb Judge of Probate 300 Grand SW #100, Courthouse, Fort Payne, AL 35967 **256-845-8510** Fax: 256-845-8514. 7:45AM-4:15. Property, Assessor, Mapping records online.

Elmore Judge of Probate PO Box 280, Wetumpka, AL 36092 (200 Commerce St). **334-567-1143** Fax: 334-567-1144. 8-4:30.

Escambia Judge of Probate PO Box 557, Brewton, AL 36427 (318 Belleville Ave, Rm 205). **251-867-0206** Fax: 251-867-0284. 8AM-4PM. www.clerk.co.escambia.fl.us Property Appraiser records online.

Etowah Judge of Probate PO Box 187, Gadsden, AL 35902 (800 Forrest Ave). **256-**

549-5341 Fax: 256-546-1149. 8-5. Property Appraisal, Property Tax records online.

Fayette Judge of Probate PO Box 670, Fayette, AL 35555 (113 Temple Ave North **205-932-4519** Fax: 205-932-7600. 8-4PM.

Franklin Judge of Probate PO Box 70, Russellville, AL 35653 (410 N Jackson St). **256-332-8801** Fax: 256-332-8423. 8AM-5PM; 8AM-Noon Sat.

Geneva Judge of Probate PO Box 430, Geneva, AL 36340 (200 N. Commerce St.). **334-684-5647** Fax: 334-684-5602. 8-5PM.

Greene Judge of Probate PO Box 790, Eutaw, AL 35462-0790 (400 Morrow Ave). **205-372-3340** Fax: 205-372-0499. 8-4PM.

Hale Judge of Probate 1001 Main St, Courthouse, Greensboro, AL 36744 **334-624-8740** Fax: 334-624-8725. 8AM-4PM.

Henry Judge of Probate 101 Court Sq, #A, Abbeville, AL 36310 (101 Court Sq, #A, 101 Court Sq). **334-585-3257** Fax: 334-585-3610. 8AM-4:30PM.

Houston Judge of Probate PO Drawer 6406, Dothan, AL 36302 (462 N. Oates, 2nd Fl). **334-677-4723** Fax: 334-677-4733. 8-4:30.

Jackson Judge of Probate PO Box 128, Scottsboro, AL 35768 (Courthouse Sq). **256-574-9292** Fax: 256-574-9318. 8-4:30PM.

Jefferson - Bessemer Judge of Probate 1801 3rd Ave., Bessemer, AL 35020 **205-481-4100**. **Birmingham Judge of Probate** 716 N. 21st St, Courthouse, Birmingham, AL 35203 **205-325-5112** Fax: 205-325-1437. 8AM-4:45PM. Property Tax, Unclaimed Property, Inmate records online.

Lamar Judge of Probate PO Box 338, Vernon, AL 35592 (44690 Hwy 17). **205-695-9119** Fax: 205-695-9253. 8AM-5PM M,T,Th,F; 8AM-Noon W,Sat.

Lauderdale Judge of Probate PO Box 1059, Florence, AL 35631-1059 (200 S. Court St). **256-760-5800** Fax: 256-760-5807. 8AM-5PM. Real Estate, Appraisal, Property Tax records online.

Lawrence Judge of Probate PO Box 310, Moulton, AL 35650 (14330 Court St, #102). **256-974-2440** Fax: 256-974-3188. 8AM-4PM.

Lee Judge of Probate PO Drawer 2266, Opelika, AL 36803 (215 S. 9th). **334-745-9761** Fax: 334-745-5082. 8:30AM-4:30PM. Real Estate, Appraisal, Property Tax, Sex Offender records online.

Limestone Judge of Probate PO Box 1145, Athens, AL 35612 (200 W. Washington St, Courthouse, 2nd Fl). **256-233-6427** Fax 256-233-6474. 8AM-4:30PM.

Lowndes Judge of Probate PO Box 5, Hayneville, AL 36040 (1 Washington St) **334-548-2365** Fax: 334-548-5398. 8-4:30PM

Macon Judge of Probate 101 E. Northside St., #101, Tuskegee, AL 36083-1731 **334-724-2611** Fax: 334-724-2512. 8:30-4:30PM.

Madison Judge of Probate 100 Northside Sq, Rm 101, Huntsville, AL 35801-4820 **256-532-3339** Fax: 256-532-3338. 8:30-5PM.

Marengo Judge of Probate PO Box 480668, Linden, AL 36748 (101 E. Coats Ave). **334-295-2210** Fax: 334-295-2254. 8-4:30PM.

Marion Judge of Probate PO Box 1687, Hamilton, AL 35570 (Military St). **205-921-2471** Fax: 205-921-5109. 8AM-N, 1-5PM. Property Tax, Land, Mapping records online.

Marshall Judge of Probate 425 Gunter Ave, Guntersville, AL 35976 **256-571-7767** Fax: 256-571-7732. 8AM-4:30PM. Property, GIS Mapping records online.

Mobile County Judge of Probate PO Box 7, Mobile, AL 36601 (101 Government St). **251-574-8497** Fax: 251-690-4939. 8AM-5PM. www.mobile-county.net/probate/ Deed, UCC, Property, Incs, Marriage, Estate Claim, Mortgage, Real/Personal Property, Voter Registration records online.

Monroe Judge of Probate PO Box 665, Monroeville, AL 36461-0665 (65 N. Alabama Ave) **251-743-4107** Fax: 251-575-4756. 8AM-5PM M,T,W,F; 8AM-N Th.

Montgomery Judge of Probate PO Box 223, Montgomery, AL 36195 (Rm 206, 100 S. Lawrence). **334-832-1237** 8AM-5PM. Unclaimed Property records online.

Morgan Judge of Probate PO Box 848, Decatur, AL 36602-0848 (302 Lee St). **256-351-4680** 8-4:30. Property, Appraisal, Assessor, Tax payment records online.

Perry Judge of Probate PO Box 478, Marion, AL 36756 (300 Washington St). **334-683-2210** Fax 334-683-2211. 8-4:30PM.

Pickens Judge of Probate PO Box 370, Carrollton, AL 35447 (Probate Bldg.). **205-367-2010** Fax: 205-367-2011. 8AM-4PM.

Pike Judge of Probate 120 W Church St, Troy, AL 36081 **334-566-1246** Fax: 334-566-8585. 8AM-5PM.

Randolph Judge of Probate PO Box 249, Wedowee, AL 36278 (1 Main St.). **256-357-4933** Fax: 256-357-9053. 8AM-5PM.

Russell Judge of Probate PO Box 700, Phenix City, AL 36868-0700 (501 14th St). **334-298-7979** Fax: 334-298-7979. 8:30-5.

Shelby Judge of Probate PO Box 825, Columbiana, AL 35051 (Main St). **205-669-3720** Fax: 205-669-3714. 8AM-4:30PM. www.shelbycountyalabama.com Recording, Land, Judgment, Deed, UCC, Notary, Fictitious Name, Marriage, Probate, Property Tax records online.

St. Clair - Northern District Judge of Probate PO Box 220, Ashville, AL 35953 (Admin. Bldg., 129 5th Ave). **205-594-2124** Fax: 205-594-2125. 8AM-5PM. www.stclairco.com/index.php Property, Appraisal, Assessor records online. **Southern District Judge of Probate** 1815 Cogswell Ave, #212, Pell City, AL 35125 **205-338-9449** Fax: 205-884-1182. 8-5PM. Property, Appraisal, Assessor records online.

Sumter Judge of Probate PO Box 1040, Livingston, AL 35470-1040 (Courthouse Sq). **205-652-7281** Fax: 205-652-6206. 8-4.

Talladega Judge of Probate PO Box 737, Talladega, AL 35161 (Courthouse) **256-362-4175** Fax: 256-761-2128

Tallapoosa Judge of Probate 125 N. Broadnax St., Courthouse, Rm 126, Dadeville, AL 36853 **256-825-1090** Fax: 256-825-1604.

Tuscaloosa Judge of Probate PO Box 20067, Tuscaloosa, AL 35402-0067 (714 Greensboro). **205-349-3870 x205/6** 8:30-5PM. www.tuscco.com Real Estate, Lien, UCC, Grantor/Grantee, Probate, Marriage, Mortgage, Incorporation, Property, Jail, Sex Offender, Most Wanted records online.

Walker Judge of Probate PO Box 502, Jasper, AL 35502 (1803 3rd Ave. S.W., Rm 102). **205-384-7282** Fax: 205-384-7005. 8AM-4PM. Sex Offender records online.

Washington Judge of Probate PO Box 549, Chatom, AL 36518 (403 Court St). **251-847-2201** Fax: 251-847-3677. 8AM-4:30PM. Real Estate records online.

Wilcox Judge of Probate PO Box 668, Camden, AL 36726 (100 Broad St, Courthouse). **334-682-4883** Fax: 334-682-9484. 8-11:30AM, N-4:30PM.

Winston Judge of Probate PO Box 27, Double Springs, AL 35553 (11 Blake St, Rm 7). **205-489-5219** Fax: 205-489-5135. 8-4:30PM (8AM-N 1st Sat of every month).

Alaska

Organization: The 23 Alaskan counties are called boroughs. However, real estate recording is done under a system of 34 recording districts that was established at the time of the Gold Rush. Some of the Districts are identical in geography to boroughs, such as the Aleutian Islands, but other boroughs and districts overlap. Therefore you need to know which recording district any given town or city is located in. A helpful website is www.dnr.state.ak.us/recorders/findYourDistrict.htm.

The entire state except the Aleutian Islands is in the Alaska Time Zone (AK).

Real Estate Records: Districts do not perform real estate searches. Certification fees are usually $5.00 per document. Copies usually cost $1.25 for the first page, $.25 per additional page.

UCC Records: Financing statements are filed at the state level, except for real estate related collateral, which are filed with the District Recorder. However, prior to 07/2001, consumer goods and farm collateral were filed at the District Recorder and can be searched there. All districts will perform UCC searches now at $15.00 per debtor name for information and $25.00 with copies. Use search request form UCC-11. Copies ordered separately usually cost $2.00 per financing statement.

Tax Lien Records: state and federal tax liens are filed with the District Recorder. Districts do not perform separate tax lien searches.

Online Access: Online access to the state recorder's office database from the Dept. of Natural Resources is available free at www.dnr.state.ak.us/recorders/search. This includes property information, liens, deeds, bankruptcies and more. Images are not available although the index goes as far back as the mid-1970's depending on the recording district involved. Also, a DNR "land records" database is searchable at www.dnr.state.ak.us/cgi-bin/lris/landrecords

---

Aleutian Islands District Recorder 550 W 7th Ave, #1200, #1140, Anchorage, AK 99501 **907-269-8899** 8AM-3:30PM. Real Estate, UCC records online.

Anchorage District Recorder 550 W 7th Ave, #1200, #1140, Anchorage, AK 99501 **907-269-8879** 8-3:30PM. Real Estate, UCC, Property Tax, Most Wanted, Stolen Vehicle records online.

Barrow District Recorder 1648 S Cushman St. #201, Fairbanks, AK 99701-6206 **907-452-3521** Fax: 907-452-2951. 8:00AM-4PM. Real Estate, UCC records online.

Bethel District Recorder PO Box 426, Bethel, AK 99559 (311 Willow St., City Office Bldg.). **907-543-3391** Fax: 907-543-7053. 9:15AM-Noon, 1-3:15PM. Real Estate, UCC records online.

Bristol Bay District Recorder 550 W 7th Ave, #1200, #1140, Anchorage, AK 99501 **907-269-8879** 8AM-3:30PM. Real Estate, UCC records online.

Cape Nome District Recorder Box 431, Nome, AK 99762 (Front St, 3rd Fl, Old Federal Bldg.). **907-443-5178** Fax: 907-452-2951. 8AM-12:30PM. Real Estate, UCC records online.

Chitina District Recorder Box 2023, Valdez, AK 99686 (213 Meals Ave, #30). **907-835-2266** 8:30AM-4PM. Real Estate, UCC, Deed records online.

Cordova District Recorder 550 W 7th Ave, #1200, #1140, Anchorage, AK 99501 **907-269-8879** 8AM-3:30PM. Real Estate, UCC records online.

Fairbanks District Recorder 1648 S Cushman St. #201, Fairbanks, AK 99701-6206 **907-452-3521** Fax: 907-269-8912. 8:00AM-3:30pm. www.co.fairbanks.ak.us Real Estate, UCC, Cemetery records online.

Fort Gibbon District Recorder 1648 S Cushman St. #201, Fairbanks, AK 99701 **907-452-3521** Fax: 907-452-2951. 8:30AM-4PM. Real Estate, UCC records online.

Haines District Recorder 400 Willoughby, 3rd Fl, Juneau, AK 99801 **907-465-3449** 8:30-4PM. Real Estate, UCC records online.

Homer District Recorder 195 E Bunnell Ave., #A, Homer, AK 99603 **907-235-8136** 8:30AM-12:00, 1-4PM. Real Estate, UCC, Assessor records online.

Iliamna District Recorder 550 W 7th Ave, #1200, #1140, Anchorage, AK **907-269-8899** 8-3:30PM. Real Estate, UCC records online.

Juneau District Recorder 400 Willoughby, 3rd Fl, Juneau, AK 99801 **907-465-3449** 8:30-4. www.juneau.org/cbj/index.php Real Estate, UCC, Assessor records online.

Kenai District Recorder 120 Trading Bay Rd #230, #230, Kenai, AK 99611 **907-283-3118** 8:30AM-4PM. Assessor, Real Estate, UCC records online.

Ketchikan District Recorder 415 Main St, Rm 310, Ketchikan, AK 99901 **907-225-3142** Fax: 907-247-3142. 8:30AM-4PM; closed for lunch. Real Estate, UCC records online.

Kodiak District Recorder 204 Mission Rd, Rm 110, Kodiak, AK 99615 **907-486-9432** Fax: 907-486-9432. 8:00AM-Noon, 1-4PM. Real Estate, UCC, Assessor records online.

Kotzebue District Recorder 1648 S. Cushman St. #201, Fairbanks, AK 99701-6206 **907-452-3521** Fax: 907-452-2951. 8:00-4PM. Real Estate, UCC records online.

Kuskokwim District Recorder PO Box 426, Bethel, AK 99559 (311 Willow St.). **907-543-3391** Fax: 907-543-7053. 9:15AM-N, 1-3:15PM. Real Estate, UCC records online.

Kvichak District Recorder 550 W 7th Ave, #1200, Anchorage, AK 99501 **907-269-8899** 8-3:30PM. Real Estate, UCC records online.

Manley Hot Springs District Recorder 1648 S Cushman St. #201, Fairbanks, AK 99701-6206 **907-452-3521** Fax: 907-452-2951. 8:30-4PM. Real Estate, UCC records online.

Mount McKinley District Recorder 1648 S Cushman St. #201, Fairbanks, AK 99701 **907-452-3521** Fax: 907-452-2951. 8:30AM-4PM. Real Estate, UCC records online.

Nenana District Recorder 1648 S Cushman St. #201, Fairbanks, AK 99701-6206 **907-452-3521** Fax: 907-452-2951. 8:30AM-4PM. Real Estate, UCC records online.

Nulato District Recorder 1648 S Cushman St. #201, Fairbanks, AK 99701-6206 **907-452-3521** Fax: 907-452-2951. 8:30AM-4PM. Real Estate, UCC records online.

Palmer District Recorder 1800 Glenn Hwy #7, Palmer, AK 99645 **907-745-3080** Fax:

907-745-0958. 8:30-4PM. Real Estate, UCC records online.

Petersburg District Recorder 415 Main St, Rm 310, Ketchikan, AK 99901 **907-225-3142** Fax: 907-247-3142. 8:30AM-4PM; closed for lunch. Real Estate, UCC records online.

Rampart District Recorder 1648 S. Cushman St. #201, Fairbanks, AK 99701-6206 **907-452-3521** Fax: 907-452-2951. 8AM-4PM. Real Estate, UCC records online.

Seldovia District Recorder 195 E Bunnell Ave., #A, Homer, AK 99603 **907-235-8136**

8:30-12.:00AM, 1-4PM. Real Estate, UCC, Assessor records online.

Seward District Recorder Box 246, Seward, AK 99664 (302 Railway #131). **907-224-3075** Fax: 907-224-7192. 8:30AM-4PM. Real Estate, UCC, Assessor records online.

Sitka District Recorder 210C Lake St, Sitka, AK 99835 **907-747-3275** 8:30AM-N, 1-4 M-Th. Real Estate, UCC records online.

Skagway District Recorder 400 Willoughby, 3rd Fl, Juneau, AK 99801 **907-465-3449** 8:30-4PM. Real Estate, UCC records online.

Talkeetna District Recorder 1800 Glenn Hwy #7, Palmer, AK 99645 **907-745-3080** Fax: 907-745-0958. 8:30AM-4PM. Real Estate, UCC records online.

Valdez District Recorder Box 2023, Valdez, AK 99686 (213 Meals Ave). **907-835-2266** 8:30AM-N, 1-4PM. Real Estate, UCC records online.

Wrangell District Recorder 415 Main St, Rm 310, Ketchikan, AK 99901 **907-225-3142** Fax: 907-247-3142. 8:30AM-4PM; closed for lunch. Real Estate, UCC records online.

Arizona

Organization: 15 counties, 16 recording offices. The Navajo Nation is profiled here. The recording officer is the County Recorder. Recordings are usually placed in a Grantor/Grantee index. The entire state is in the Mountain Time Zone (MST), and does not change to daylight savings time. Note that no less than four new telephone area codes have added in recent years: 480 and 623 for east and west Phoenix Metro area respectively, 520 for south and southeastern state, and 924 for west and north of state.

Real Estate Records: Counties do not perform real estate searches. Copy fees are usually $1.00 per page. Certification fees are usually $3.00 per document.

UCC Records: Financing statements are filed at the state level, except for real estate related collateral, which are filed with the County Recorder. However, prior to 07/2001, consumer goods and farm collateral were filed at the County Recorder and these older records can be searched there. All counties will perform UCC searches. Use search request form UCC-3. Search fees are generally $10.00 per debtor name. Copies usually cost $1.00 per page.

Tax Lien Records: Federal and state tax liens on personal property of businesses are filed with the Secretary of State. Other federal and state tax liens are filed with the County Recorder. Several counties will do a separate tax lien search. Other Liens: Executions, judgments, labor.

Online Access: A number of county assessor offices offer online access. The Secretary of State offers online access to UCC records at www.sosaz.com/scripts/UCC_Search.dll.

Apache County Recorder PO Box 425, St. Johns, AZ 85936 (75 W. Cleveland). **928-337-7515** Fax: 928-337-7676. 8AM-5PM. www.co.apache.az.us/Recorder/ Real Estate, Recording, Deed, Judgment, Lien records online.

Cochise County Recorder PO Box 184, Bisbee, AZ 85603 (4 Ledge Ave.). **520-432-8350** Fax: 520-432-8368. 8-5PM. www.co.cochise.az.us Treasurer Back Tax, Restaurant Inspection records online.

Coconino County Recorder 110 E. Cherry Ave, Flagstaff, AZ 86001 **928-779-6585** Fax: 928-779-6739. 8AM-5PM. http://co.coconino.az.us/recorder/ Recording, Grantor/Grantee, Real Estate records online.

Gila County Recorder 1400 E. Ash St, Globe, AZ 85501 (1400 E. Ash St). **928-425-3231** Fax: 928-425-9270. 8AM-5PM. http://recorder.co.gila.az.us Recording, Deed, Lien, Grantor/Grantee records online.

Graham County Recorder 921 Thatcher Blvd., Safford, AZ 85546 **928-428-3560** Fax: 928-348-8625. www.graham.az.gov Assessor, Property, Most Wanted, Recording, Deed, Divorce, Judgment, Lien records online.

Greenlee County Recorder PO Box 1625, Clifton, AZ 85533-1625 (211 5th St). **928-865-2632** Fax: 928-865-4417. 8AM-5PM. www.thecountyrecorder.com Real Estate, Deed, Lien, Judgment, Vital Statistic, Recording records online.

La Paz County Recorder 1112 Joshua Ave, #201, Parker, AZ 85344 **928-669-6136** Fax: 928-669-5638. 8AM-5PM. Recorder, Deed, Judgment, Lien records online.

Maricopa County Recorder 111 S. 3rd Ave #103, Phoenix, AZ 85003 **602-506-3535** Fax: 602-506-3273. http://recorder.maricopa.gov Real Estate, Lien, Property, Assessor records online. 8AM- 5PM.

Mohave County Recorder PO Box 70, Kingman, AZ 86402-0070 (315 Oak St). **928-753-0701** Fax: 928-753-0727. 8AM-5PM. www.co.mohave.az.us Real Estate, Grantor/Grantee, Lien, Assessor, Most Wanted, Sex Offender records online.

Navajo County Recorder PO Box 668, Holbrook, AZ 86025-0668 (100 E. Carter Dr). **928-524-4194** Fax: 928-524-4308. 8AM-5PM. www.co.navajo.az.us Property, Assessor, Grantor/Grantee, Recording, UCC, Tax Lien, Death, Tax Sale records online.

Navajo Nation County Recorder State Rd 264 W, Window Rock, AZ 86515 **928-871-7365** Fax: 928-871-7381. 8AM-5PM. www.co.navajo.az.us Property, Assessor, Grantor/Grantee, Recording, UCC, Tax Lien, Death, Tax Sale records online.

Pima County Recorder 115 N. Church Ave, Tucson, AZ 85701 **520-740-4350** Fax: 520-623-1785. 8-5. www.recorder.co.pima.az.us

Assessor, Real Estate, Lien, Recording, Deed, Most Wanted, Sex Offender records online.

Pinal County Recorder PO Box 848, Florence, AZ 85232-0848 (383 N Main St.). **520-866-7100** Fax: 520-866-7170. http://co.pinal.az.us Grantor/Grantee, Tax Bill, Tax Lien, Tax Sale, Assessor records online.

Santa Cruz County Recorder 2150 N. Congress, County Complex, Nogales, AZ 85621 **520-375-7990** Fax: 520-761-7938. 8-5. Assessor, Property records online.

Yavapai County Recorder 1015 Fair St, Rm 228, Prescott, AZ 86305 **928-771-3244** Fax: 928-771-3258. 8-5pm. www.co.yavapai.az.us

Assessor, Real Estate, Recording, Inmate/ Offender records online.

Yuma County Recorder 410 S Maiden Lane, Yuma, AZ 85364-2311 **928-373-6020** Fax: 928-373-6024. Property, Assessor records online.

 # Arkansas

Organization: 75 counties, 85 recording offices. The recording officer is the Clerk of Circuit Court, who is Ex Officio Recorder. Ten counties have two recording offices - Arkansas, Carroll, Clay, Craighead, Franklin, Logan, Mississippi, Prairie, Sebastian, and Yell. See the notes under each county for how to determine which office is appropriate to search. Is in Central Time Zone (CST).

Real Estate Records: Most counties do not perform real estate searches. Copy fees and certification fees vary.

UCC Records: Prior to 07/01 this was a dual filing state. Financing statements were filed at the state level and with the Circuit Clerk, except for consumer goods, farm and real estate related collateral that were filed only with the Circuit Clerk. Now all financing statements are filed at the state level, except for real estate related collateral that is still filed with the Circuit Clerk. Most counties will perform UCC searches. Use search request form UCC-11. Search fees usually $10.00 per debtor name. Copy fees vary.

Tax Lien Records: Federal tax liens on personal property of businesses are filed with the Secretary of State. Other federal and all state tax liens are filed with the Circuit Clerk. Many counties will perform separate tax lien searches. Search fees are usually $6.00 per name. Other Liens: Mechanics, lis pendens, judgments, hospital, child support, materialman.

Online Access: There is no statewide access. Benton county offers records via their website. Also, there is a commercial system available for a limited number of participating counties. Registration and logon is required, the signup fee is $200 minimum plus $.10 per minute usage. For signup or information call 479-631-8054 or visit www.arcountydata.com.

Arkansas County - Northern District Circuit Clerk 302 S. College St., Stuttgart, AR 72160 (302 S. College). **870-673-2056** Fax: 870-673-3869. 8AM-4:30PM. Assessor, Property records online.
Southern District Circuit Clerk 101 Court Sq, De Witt, AR 72042 (101 Court Sq). **870-946-4219** Fax: 870-946-1394. 8AM-Noon,12:30-4:30PM.

Ashley Circuit Clerk 205 E. Jefferson St, Courthouse, Hamburg, AR 71646 **870-853-2030** Fax: 870-853-2034. 8AM-4:30PM.

Baxter Circuit Clerk 1 E. 7th St #103, Courthouse Sq, Mountain Home, AR 72653 **870-425-3475** Fax: 870-424-5105. 8AM-4:30PM. Assessor, Property, Real Estate Recording records online.

Benton Circuit Clerk 215 E. Central St, #6, Bentonville, AR 72712 **479-271-1017** Fax: 479-271-5719. 8-4:30. www.co.benton.ar.us Real Estate, Deed, Circuit Court, Lien, Plat, Property Tax, Judgment, Medical Lien, Inmate, Personal Property records online.

Boone Circuit Clerk 100 N Main, Courthouse, #200, Harrison, AR 72601 **870-741-5560** Fax: 870-741-4335. 8AM-4:30PM. Real Estate Recording, Assessor, Property records online.

Bradley Circuit Clerk 101 E. Cedar St, Courthouse, Warren, AR 71671 **870-226-2272** Fax: 870-226-8401. 8AM-4:30PM.

Calhoun Circuit Clerk PO Box 1175, Hampton, AR 71744 (309 W. Main St, **870-798-2517** Fax: 870-798-2428. 8AM-4:30.

Carroll County - Eastern District Circuit Clerk PO Box 71, Berryville, AR 72616 (210 W. Church). **870-423-2422** Fax: 870-423-4796. 8:30AM-4:30PM. Assessor, Property, Jail records online.
Western District Circuit Clerk PO Box 109, Eureka Springs, AR 72632 (2nd Fl, 44 S. Main). **479-253-8646** Fax: 479-253-6013. 8:30AM-4:30PM. Assessor, Property, Jail records online.

Chicot Circuit Clerk 108 Main St, Courthouse, Lake Village, AR 71653 **870-265-8010** Fax: 870-265-8012. 8-4:30PM.

Clark Circuit Clerk PO Box 576, Arkadelphia, AR 71923 (Courthouse Sq). **870-246-4281** Fax: 870-846-1416. 8:30AM-4:30PM. Real Estate Recording online.

Clay County - Eastern District Circuit Clerk 151 S Second St, Piggott, AR 72454 **870-598-2524** Fax: 870-598-1107. 8AM-N, 1-4:30PM.

Western District Circuit Clerk 800 W. Second St., Corning, AR 72422 **870-857-3271** Fax: 870-857-9201. 8AM-N, 1PM-4:30PM.

Cleburne Circuit Clerk PO Box 543, Heber Springs, AR 72543 (301 W. Main St). **501-362-8149** Fax: 501-362-4650. 8:30-4:30PM.

Cleveland Circuit Clerk PO Box 368, Rison, AR 71665 (Courthouse, 20 Magnolia). **870-325-6521** Fax: 870-325-6144. 8-4:30PM.

Columbia Circuit Clerk PO Box 327, Magnolia, AR 71753 **870-235-3700** Fax: 870-235-3786. 8AM-4:30PM.

Conway Circuit Clerk 115 S. Moose St, County Courthouse, Rm 206, Morrilton, AR 72110 **501-354-9617** Fax: 501-354-9612. 8-5.

Craighead County - Eastern Circuit Clerk PO Box 537, Lake City, AR 72437 (405 Court St). **870-237-4342** Fax: 870-237-8174. 8AM-5PM.
Western Circuit Clerk PO Box 120, Jonesboro, AR 72401 (511 S. Main). **870-933-4530** Fax: 870-933-4534. 8AM-5PM. Assessor, Property, Personal Property, Assessor, Real Estate records online.

Crawford Circuit Clerk 300 Main, Courthouse - Rm 22, Van Buren, AR 72956-5799 **479-474-1821** 8AM-5PM. Real Estate Recording records online.

Crittenden Circuit Clerk 100 Court St., Marion, AR 72364 **870-739-3248** Fax: 870-739-3072. 8AM-4:30PM. Assessor, Property records online.

Cross Circuit Clerk 705 E Union, Rm 9, Wynne, AR 72396 **870-238-5720** Fax: 870-238-5739. 8AM-4PM.

Dallas Circuit Clerk 206 W 3rd St, Courthouse, Fordyce, AR 71742-3299 **870-352-2307** Fax: 870-352-7179. 8:30-4:30PM.

Desha County Circuit Clerk PO Box 309, Arkansas City, AR 71630 (Robert Moore Dr, Arkansas City Courthouse). **870-877-2411** Fax: 870-877-3407. 8AM-4PM. Real Estate, Recording records online.

Drew Circuit Clerk 210 S. Main, Monticello, AR 71655 **870-460-6250** Fax: 870-460-6246. 8AM-4:30PM. Real Estate, Deed, Circuit Court, Lien, Judgment records online.

Faulkner Faulkner County Circuit Clerk PO Box 9, Conway, AR 72033 (801 Locust St). **501-450-4911** Fax: 501-450-4948. 8AM-4:30PM. Assessor, Property records online.

Franklin County - Charleston District Circuit Clerk 607 E Main St, Charleston, AR 72933 **479-965-7332** Fax: 479-965-9322. 8AM-Noon, 12:30-4:30PM.
Ozark District Circuit Clerk PO Box 1112, Ozark, AR 72949 (211 W. Commercial). **479-667-3818** Fax: 479-667-5174. 8-4:30.

Fulton Circuit Clerk PO Box 485, Salem, AR 72576-0485 (123 S Main). **870-895-3310** Fax: 870-895-3383. 8AM-4:30PM. Assessor, Property records online.

Garland Circuit Clerk Courthouse - Rm207, Quachita & Hawthorn Sts, Hot Springs, AR 71901 **501-622-3630** Fax: 501-609-9043. 8AM-5PM. Sex Offender records online.

Grant Circuit Clerk 101 W. Center, Rm 106, Courthouse, Sheridan, AR 72150 **870-942-2631** Fax: 870-942-3564. 8AM-4:30PM.

Greene Circuit Clerk 320 W. Court St, Rm 124, Paragould, AR 72450 **870-239-6330** Fax: 870-239-3550. 8AM-4:30PM. Assessor, Property records online.

Hempstead County Circuit Clerk PO Box 1420, Hope, AR 71802 (4th & Washington Sts, Courthouse). **870-777-2384** Fax: 870-777-7827. 8AM-4PM.

Hot Spring Circuit Clerk PO Box 1220, Malvern, AR 72104 (210 Locust St, Courthouse). **501-332-2281** 8AM-4:30PM.

Howard Circuit Clerk 421 N. Main St, Rm 7, Nashville, AR 71852 **870-845-7506** 8AM-4:30PM.

Independence Circuit Clerk PO Box 2155, Batesville, AR 72503 (192 Main St). **870-793-8865** Fax: 870-793-8888. 8AM-4:30. Real Estate Recording records online.

Izard Circuit Clerk PO Box 95, Melbourne, AR 72556 (Main & Lunen Sts, **870-368-4316** Fax: 870-368-4748. 8:30AM-4:30PM. Assessor, Property records online.

Jackson Circuit Clerk 208 Main St, Courthouse, Newport, AR 72112 **870-523-7423** Fax: 870-523-3682. 8AM-4:30PM.

Jefferson Circuit Clerk PO Box 7433, Pine Bluff, AR 71611 (Main & Barraque, Rm 101). **870-541-5309** 8:30AM-5PM.

Johnson Circuit Clerk PO Box 189, Clarksville, AR 72830-0189 (Main St Courthouse). **479-754-2977** Fax: 479-754-4235. 8AM-4:30PM. Assessor, Property records online.

Lafayette Circuit Clerk 3 Courthouse Sq, Third & Spruce, Lewisville, AR 71845 (3 Courthouse Sq, Third & Spruce). **870-921-4878** Fax: 870-421-4879. 8AM-4:30PM.

Lawrence Circuit Clerk PO Box 581, Walnut Ridge, AR 72476 (315 W. Main St, Rm 7). **870-886-1112** Fax: 870-886-1128. 8AM-4:30PM.

Lee County Circuit Clerk 15 E. Chestnut St, Courthouse, Marianna, AR 72360 (15 E. Chestnut St). **870-295-7710** Fax: 870-295-7712. 8:30AM-4:30PM.

Lincoln Circuit Clerk 300 S. Drew St, Star City, AR 71667 (300 S. Drew St). **870-628-3154** Fax: 870-628-5546. 8AM-5.

Little River Circuit Clerk PO Box 575, Ashdown, AR 71822-0575 (351 N. Second). **870-898-7211** Fax: 870-898-7207. 8:30AM-4:30PM.

Logan County - Northern Circuit Clerk 25 W. Walnut, Courthouse, Paris, AR 72855 **479-963-2164** Fax: 479-963-3304. 8-4:30.
Southern Circuit Clerk 366 N Broadway #2, Courthouse, Booneville, AR 72927 **479-675-2894** Fax: 479-675-0577. 8AM-N, 1-4:30.

Lonoke Circuit Clerk PO Box 219, Lonoke, AR 72086-0219 (Courthouse). **501-676-2316** 8AM-4:30PM. Assessor, Property records online.

Madison Circuit Clerk PO Box 416, Huntsville, AR 72740 (Main St Courthouse). **479-738-2215** Fax: 479-738-1544. 8AM-4:30PM.

Marion Circuit Clerk PO Box 385, Yellville, AR 72687 (Hwy 62 Courthouse). **870-449-6226** Fax: 870-449-4979. 8-4:30.

Miller Circuit Clerk 412 Laurel St., County Courthouse, #109, Texarkana, AR 71854 **870-774-4501** Fax: 870-772-5293. 8AM-4:30. Land, Deed records online.

Mississippi County - Chickasawba Circuit Clerk PO Box 1498, Blytheville, AR 72316-1498 (2nd & Walnut St). **870-762-2332** Fax: 870-762-8148. 9AM-4:30PM.
Osceola Circuit Clerk PO Box 466, Osceola, AR 72370 (Courthouse). **870-563-6471** Fax: 870-563-5063. 9AM-4:30PM.

Monroe Circuit Clerk 123 Madison St, Clarendon, AR 72029 **870-747-3615** Fax: 870-747-3710. 8AM-4:30PM.

Montgomery Circuit Clerk PO Box 369, Mount Ida, AR 71957-0369 (105 Hwy 270 East). **870-867-3521** Fax: 870-867-2177. 8AM-4:30PM.

Nevada Circuit Clerk PO Box 204, Prescott, AR 71857 (215 E. Second St). **870-887-2511** Fax: 870-887-1911. 8AM-5PM.

Newton Circuit Clerk PO Box 410, Jasper, AR 72641 **870-446-5125** Fax: 870-446-5755. 8AM-4:30PM.

Ouachita Circuit Clerk PO Box 667, Camden, AR 71701 (145 Jefferson St). **870-837-2230** Fax: 870-837-2252. 8-4:30.

Perry Circuit Clerk PO Box 358, Perryville, AR 72126 (310 W Main St Rm 105, Courthouse Sq). **501-889-5126** Fax: 501-889-5759. 8AM-4:30PM.

Phillips Circuit Clerk 620 Cherry St., Courthouse, #206, Helena, AR 72342 **870-338-5515** Fax: 870-338-5513. 8AM-4:30. Real Estate Recording records online.

Pike Circuit Clerk PO Box 219, Murfreesboro, AR 71958 (1 Courthouse Sq). **870-285-2231** Fax: 870-285-3281. 8-4:30PM. Assessor, Property records online.

Poinsett Circuit Clerk PO Box 46, Harrisburg, AR 72432-0046 (401 Market St. **870-578-4420** Fax: 870-578-4427. 8:30AM-4:30PM. Assessor, Property records online.

Polk Circuit Clerk 507 Church, Courthouse, Mena, AR 71953 **479-394-8100** Fax: 479-394-8170. 8AM-4:30PM. Real Estate, Deed, Circuit Court, Lien, Judgment records online.

Pope Circuit Clerk 100 W. Main, 3rd Fl, County Courthouse, Russellville, AR 72801 **479-968-7499** Fax: none. 8AM-5. Assessor, Property records online.

Prairie County - Northern Circuit Clerk PO Box 1011, Des Arc, AR 72040 (200 Court Sq). **870-256-4434** Fax: 870-256-4434. 8AM-4:30PM.

Southern Circuit Clerk PO Box 283, De Valls Bluff, AR 72041-0283 (200 Court Sq, Prairie & Magnolia). **870-998-2314** Fax: 870-998-2314. 8AM-N, 1-4:30PM.

Pulaski Circuit Clerk 401 W. Markham St, Rm S216, Little Rock, AR 72201 **501-340-8433** Fax: 501-340-8889. 8:30AM-4:30PM. Assessor, Property, Personal Property online.

Randolph Circuit Clerk 107 W. Broadway, Pocahontas, AR 72455 **870-892-5522** Fax: 870-892-8794. 8AM-4:30PM.

Saline Circuit Clerk 200 N. Main St. #113, Benton, AR 72018 **501-303-5615** Fax: 501-303-5675. 8AM-4:30. Assessor, Property, Real Estate Recording records online.

Scott Circuit Clerk PO Box 2165, Waldron, AR 72958 (190 W. First, Courthouse). **479-637-2642** Fax: 479-637-0124. 8-4:30PM.

Searcy Circuit Clerk PO Box 998, Marshall, AR 72650 (Courthouse, Town Sq). **870-448-3807** Fax: 870-448-5005. 8-4:30PM.

Sebastian County - Fort Smith Clerk and Recorder PO Box 1089, Fort Smith, AR 72902-1089 (35 S 6th St, Rm 103). **479-782-5065** Fax: 479-784-1567. 8AM-5PM. www.sebastiancountyonline.com Assessor, Property records online.

Southern District County Clerk PO Box 428, Greenwood, AR 72936 (301 E Center Rm 104, **479-996-4195** Fax: 479-996-4165. 8-5PM. Assessor, Property records online.

Sevier County Circuit Clerk 115 N. 3rd St, De Queen, AR 71832 **870-584-3055** Fax 870-642-3119. 8AM-4:30PM.

Sharp Circuit Clerk PO Box 307, Ash Flat, AR 72513 (718 Ash Flat Dr, Courthouse). **870-994-7361** Fax: 870-994-7712. 8-4. Assessor, Property, Real Estate records online.

St. Francis Circuit Clerk PO Box 1775, Forrest City, AR 72336-1775 (313 S. Izard St). **870-261-1715** Fax: 870-261-1723. 8-4:30PM. Assessor, Property records online.

Stone Circuit Clerk 107 W Main #D, Mountain View, AR 72560 **870-269-3271** Fax: 870-269-2303. 8AM-4:30PM. Assessor, Property records online.

Union Circuit Clerk PO Box 1626, El Dorado, AR 71731-1626 (101 N. Washington, Rm 201). **870-864-1940** Fax: 870-864-1994. 8:30AM-5PM. Real Estate, Deed, Circuit Court, Lien, Judgment records online.

Van Buren Circuit Clerk 451 Main St. #2, Clinton, AR 72031-9806 (Courthouse, Main

& Griggs). **501-745-4140** Fax: 501-745-7400. 8AM-5PM. Real Estate Recording records online.

Washington Circuit Clerk 280 N. College, #302, Courthouse, Fayetteville, AR 72701 **479-444-1538** Fax: 479-444-1537. 8AM-4:30PM. www.co.washington.ar.us Real Estate, Lien, UCC, Recording, Court, Inmate, Vital Statistic records online.

White Circuit Clerk White County Courthouse, 300 N. Spruce, Searcy, AR 72143 (Spring St./East Entrance). **501-279-6203** Fax: 501-279-6233. 8AM-4:30PM. Assessor, Property records online.

Woodruff Circuit Clerk PO Box 492, Augusta, AR 72006 (500 N. Third St). **870-347-2391** Fax: 870-347-8703. 8AM-4PM. Real Estate Recording records online.

Yell County - Danville Circuit Clerk PO Box 219, Danville, AR 72833 (East 5th & Main). **479-495-4850** Fax: 479-495-4875. 8AM-4PM.

Dardanelle Circuit Clerk PO Box 457, Dardanelle, AR 72834 (Union St Courthouse). **479-229-4404** Fax: 479-229-5634. 8AM-4PM.

California

Organization: 58 counties, 58 recording offices. The recording officer is the County Recorder. Recordings are usually located in a Grantor/Grantee or General index. The entire state is in the Pacific Time Zone (PST).

Real Estate Records: Most counties do not perform real estate name searches. Copy fees and certification fees vary.

UCC Records: Financing statements are filed at the state level, except for real estate related collateral, which are filed with the County Recorder. However, prior to 07/2001, consumer goods and farm collateral were also filed at the County Recorder and these older records can be searched there. All counties will perform UCC searches. Use search request form UCC-11. Search fees are usually $15.00 per debtor name. Copy costs vary.

Tax Lien Records: Federal and state tax liens on personal property of businesses are filed with the Secretary of State. Other federal and state tax liens are filed with the County Recorder. Some counties will perform separate tax lien searches. Fees vary for this type of search. Other Liens: Judgment (Note - Many judgments are also filed with Secretary of State), child support, mechanics.

Online Access: A number of counties offer online access to assessor and real estate information. The system in Los Angeles is a commercial subscription system.

Alameda Recorder 1106 Madison St, 1st Fl, Oakland, CA 94607 **510-272-6362** Fax: 510-272-6382. 8:30-4:30. www.co.alameda.ca.us Assessor, Recording, Deed, Mortgage, Lien, Fictitious Name, Property Tax records online.

Alpine Recorder PO Box 217, Markleeville, CA 96120 (Admin. Bldg., 99 Water St.). **530-694-2286** Fax: 530-694-2491. 9AM-Noon,1-4PM.

Amador Recorder 500 Argonaut Lane, Jackson, CA 95642 **209-223-6468** Fax: 209-223-6204. 8-5PM. www.co.amador.ca.us/depts/recorder/index.htm Recording, Deed, Lien, Judgment, Fictitious name, Tax Sale records online.

Butte Recorder 25 County Ctr Dr, Oroville, CA 95965-3375 **530-538-7691** Fax: 530-538-7975. 9AM-5PM; Recording hours: 9AM-4PM. http://clerk-recorder.buttecounty.net

Real Estate, Recording, Fictitious Business Name, Inmate records online.

Calaveras Recorder 891 Mountain Ranch Rd, Government Ctr, San Andreas, CA 95249 **209-754-6372** Fax: 209-754-6733. 8-4. Property Tax, Assessor records online.

Colusa Recorder 546 Jay St #200, Colusa, CA 95932 **530-458-0500** Fax: 530-458-0512. 8:30AM-5PM. www.colusacountyclerk.com

Contra Costa Recorder PO Box 350, Martinez, CA 94553 (730 Las Juntas). **925-646-2360** Fax: 925-646-2135. 8AM-4PM. www.co.contra-costa.ca.us/depart/elect/Rindex.html Recording, Fictitious Name, Deed, Lien, Judgment, Real Estate, Most Wanted records online.

Del Norte Recorder 981 H St #160, Crescent City, CA 95531 **707-464-7216** Fax: 707-464-0321. 8AM-N, 1-5. Tax Sale records online.

El Dorado Recorder 360 Fair Lane, Placerville, CA 95667-4197 **530-621-5490** Fax: 530-621-2147. 8AM-5PM Real Estate, Personal Property, Vital Statistic, Fictitious Name records online.

Fresno Recorder PO Box 766, Fresno, CA 93712 (2281 Tulare St., Rm 302 / Hall of Records). **559-488-3471** Fax: 559-488-6774. www.co.fresno.ca.us/0420/recorders_web/index.htm Recorder, Property, Birth, Death, Marriage, Lien, Deed, Mortgage, Inmate records online. 9AM-4PM.

Glenn Recorder 526 W. Sycamore St, Willows, CA 95988 **530-934-6412** Fax: 530-934-6305. 8AM-5PM.

Humboldt Recorder 825 Fifth St, 5th Fl, Eureka, CA 95501 **707-445-7593** Fax: 707-445-7324. www.co.humboldt.ca.us/recorder/ Inmate, Offender records online. 8:30-5PM.

Imperial Recorder 940 Main St, Rm 202, El Centro, CA 92243-2865 **760-482-4272** 9AM-4:30PM. Inmate, Offender, Most Wanted records online.

Inyo Recorder PO Box F, Independence, CA 93526 (168 N. Edwards). **760-878-0222** Fax: 760-878-1805. 9-N,1-5PM. Recording, Fictitious Business Name records online.

Kern Recorder 1655 Chester Ave, Hall of Records, Bakersfield, CA 93301 **661-868-6400** Fax: 661-868-6401. 8AM-5PM. www.co.kern.ca.us/recorder Assessor, Property Tax, Fictitious Business Name, Vital Statistic, Recording, Real Estate, Tax Collector, Unclaimed Property records online.

Kings Recorder 1400 W. Lacey Blvd., Hanford, CA 93230 **559-582-3211 x2470** Fax: 559-582-6639. www.countyofkings.com Inmate records online. 8AM-3PM.

Lake Recorder 255 N. Forbes, Rm 223, Lakeport, CA 95453 **707-263-2293** Fax: 707-263-3703.

Lassen Recorder 220 S. Lassen St, #5, Susanville, CA 96130 **530-251-8234** Fax: 530-257-3480. Public Hours: 10AM-N, 1-3PM; phone hours 8AM-N. http://clerk.lassencounty.org Real Estate, Recording, Tax Sale records online.

Los Angeles Recorder PO Box 53195, Real Estate Records Section, Los Angeles, CA 90053-0115 (Registrar-Recorder/County Clerk, 12400 E. Imperial Highway, Rm 1007). **562-462-2125, 800-815-2666** Fax: 562-864-1250 for record requests.. 8AM-5PM. http://regrec.co.la.ca.us Assessor, Fictitious Name, Inmate, Property Tax, Sex Offender, Most Wanted records online.

Madera Recorder 209 W. Yosemite, Madera, CA 93637 **559-675-7724** Fax: 559-675-7870. 8AM-3:30PM. www.madera-county.com

Marin Recorder PO Box C, San Rafael, CA 94913 (3501 Civic Ctr Dr, Rm 232). **415-499-6092** Fax: 415-499-7893. 9AM-4PM research & copies; 9AM-3PM Recording. www.co.marin.ca.us/depts/AR/main/index.cfm Real Estate, Property Tax, Grantor/Grantee, Recording, Vital Statistic, Business Name, Booking Log records online.

Mariposa Recorder PO Box 35, Mariposa, CA 95338 (4982 10th St). **209-966-5719** 8AM-5PM (Recording: 8AM-3:30PM).

Mendocino Recorder 501 Low Gap Rd, Rm 1020, Ukiah, CA 95482 **707-463-4376** Fax: 707-463-4257. www.co.mendocino.ca.us Inmate, Offender records online. 8AM-5PM.

Merced Recorder 2222 M St, Merced, CA 95340 **209-385-7627** Fax: 209-385-7626. 8AM-4:30PM. http://web.co.merced.ca.us/recorder/ Recorder, Grantor/ Grantee, Deed, Real Estate, Most Wanted, Missing Person, Sex Offender records online.

Modoc Recorder 204 Court St, Alturas, CA 96101 **530-233-6205** Fax: 530-233-6666. 8:30AM-N, 1-5PM. Recording, Fictitious Business Name, Tax Sale records online.

Mono Recorder PO Box 237, Bridgeport, CA 93517 (Annex II, Bryant St.). **760-932-5530** Fax: 760-932-5531. 9AM-5PM.

Monterey Recorder PO Box 29, Salinas, CA 93902 (240 Church St, Rm 305). **831-755-5041** Fax: 831-755-5064. 8AM-5PM. www.co.monterey.ca.us/recorder/ Inmate, Offender, Wanted, Tax Sale records online.

Napa Recorder PO Box 298, Napa, CA 94559-0298 (900 Coombs St, Rm 116). **707-253-4246** Fax: 707-259-8149. 8-5PM. www.mynapa.info/Gov/Departments/DeptDefault.asp?DID=28000 Property Tax, Tax Sale, Grantor/Grantee, Property, Recording, Deed, Judgment, Lien, Inmate records online.

Nevada Recorder 950 Maidu Ave, Nevada City, CA 95959 **530-265-1221** Fax: 530-265-1497. http://recorder.co.nevada.ca.us Recording, Fictitious Name, Property Tax, GIS, Real Estate records online. 9AM-4PM.

Orange Recorder PO Box 238, Santa Ana, CA 92702-0238 (12 Civic Ctr Plaza, Rm 101). **714-834-2887** Fax: 714-834-2675. www.oc.ca.gov/recorder Grantor/Grantee, Deed, Lien, Judgment, Fictitious Business Name, Property Tax, Wanted, Missing Person, Inmate, Arrest records online. 8AM-4:30PM.

Placer Recorder 2954 Richardson Dr., Auburn, CA 95603 **530-886-5600** Fax: 530-886-5687. 8AM-5PM (Recording: 9AM-4PM). www.placer.ca.gov/clerk/clerk.htm Recording, Fictitious Name, Marriage, Most Wanted, Missing Person, Jail, Assessor, Property Tax records online.

Plumas Recorder 520 Main St, Rm 102, Quincy, CA 95971 **530-283-6218** Fax: 530-283-6155. 8AM-5PM.

Riverside Recorder PO Box 751, Attn: County Recorder/Clerk, Riverside, CA 92502-0751 (2724 Gateway Dr.). **951-486-7000** Fax: 951-486-7007. 8AM-4:30PM http://riverside.asrclkrec.com Assessor, Prop. Tax, Fictitious Name, Grantor/ Grantee, Wanted, Missing Person records online.

Sacramento Recorder PO Box 839, Sacramento, CA 95812-0839 (600 8th St, Corner of 8th & F Sts). **916-874-6334; 800-313-7133** 8AM-5PM (recording 8AM-3PM). www.saccounty.net Assessor, Grantor/Grantee, Deed, Business License, Wanted Suspect, Inmate records online.

San Benito Recorder 440 Fifth St, Rm 206, Hollister, CA 95023 **831-636-4046** Fax: 831-636-2939. 8AM-5PM (Recording hours 9AM-4PM). Most Wanted records online.

San Bernardino Recorder 222 W. Hospitality Ln., 1st Fl, San Bernardino, CA 92415-0022 **909-387-8306** Fax: 909-386-9050. 8AM-4:30PM. www.co.san-bernardino.ca.us Recorder, Assessor, Fictitious Name, Grantor/Grantee, Inmate, Property Tax records online.

San Diego Recorder PO Box 121750, San Diego, CA 92112 (1600 Pacific Highway, Rm 260). **619-238-8158** Fax: 619-557-4155. 8AM-5PM. www.sdarcc.com Assessor, Fictitious Name, Real Estate, Grantor/Grantee, Inmates, Most Wanted, Warrant, Sex Offender, Pet, Missing Children, Tax Sale records online.

San Francisco Recorder 1 Dr. Carlton E. Goodlet Pl., City Hall, Rm 190, San Francisco, CA 94102 **415-554-4176** Fax: 415-554-4179. 8AM-4PM. www.sfgov.org Assessor, Property, Fictitious Business Name, Birth, Death records online.

San Joaquin Recorder PO Box 1968, Stockton, CA 95201 (24 S Hunter St, Rm

304). **209-468-3939** Fax: 209-468-8040. 8AM-5PM. www.co.san-joaquin.ca.us Property, Most Wanted, Missing Person records online.

San Luis Obispo Recorder 1144 Monterey St, #C, San Luis Obispo, CA 93408 **805-781-5080** Fax: 805-781-1111. 8AM-5PM. www.sloclerkrecorder.org Grantor/Grantee, Deed, Judgment, Lien, Real Estate, Mortgage, Divorce, Fictitious Name, Missing Person, Most Wanted, Bad Check records online.

San Mateo Recorder 555 County Ctr, 1st Fl, Redwood City, CA 94063 **650-363-4713** Fax: 650-363-4843. www.care.co.sanmateo.ca.us Property Tax, Fictitious Name records online.

Santa Barbara Recorder PO Box 159, Santa Barbara, CA 93102-0159 (1100 Anacapa St, Hall of Records). **805-568-2250** Fax: 805-568-2266. 8AM-4:30PM. www.sb-democracy.com Assessor, Recorder, Real Estate, Lien, Deed, Vital Statistic, Judgment, Property Tax, Most Wanted records online.

Santa Clara Clerk/Recorder 70 W. Hedding St, 1st Fl, East Wing, County Gov't Ctr, San Jose, CA 95110 **408-299-2481** Fax: 408-280-1768. 8-4:30. www.clerkrecordersearch.org Recording, Grantor/Grantee, Fictitious Business Name, Assessor, Tax Collector records online.

Santa Cruz Recorder 701 Ocean St, Rm 230, Rm 230, Santa Cruz, CA 95060 **831-454-2800** Fax: 831-454-3169. www.co.santa-cruz.ca.us/rcd/ Assessor, Property Tax, Fictitious Business Name, Recording, Deed, Judgment, Vital Statistic, Inmate records online. 8AM-4PM.

Shasta Recorder 1500 Court St, Rm 102, Redding, CA 96001 **530-225-5671** Fax: 530-225-5152. 8AM-5PM. www.co.shasta.ca.us Assessor, Recorder, Real Estate, Vitals online.

Sierra Recorder PO Drawer D, Downieville, CA 95936 (100 Courthouse Sq). **530-289-3295** Fax: 530-289-3300. 9AM-N,1-4PM. www.sierracounty.ws Tax Sale records online.

Siskiyou Recorder PO Box 8, Yreka, CA 96097 (311 Fourth St). **530-842-8065** Fax: 530-842-8077. 8AM-4PM. Recording, Deed, Lien, Land, Fictitious Business Name, Tax Sale records online.

Solano Recorder 701 Texas St, Fairfield, CA 94533 **707-421-6290** Fax: 707-421-6911. 8-4. www.solanocounty.com Property Tax, Recording, Grantor/Grantee, Deed, Judgment, Lien, Death, Inmate records online.

Sonoma Recorder PO Box 1709, Santa Rosa, CA 95406-1709 (585 Fiscal Drive, Rm 103F). **707-565-2651** Fax: 707-565-3905. 8AM-4:30. www.sonoma-county.org

Stanislaus Recorder PO Box 1008, Modesto, CA 95353 (1021 "I" St. Rm 101). **209-525-5260** Fax: 209-525-5207. 8AM-Noon,1-4PM. www.co.stanislaus.ca.us Recording, Fictitious Name, Deed, Lien, Land, Most Wanted, Missing Person records online.

Sutter Recorder PO Box 1555, Yuba City, CA 95992-1555 (433 Second St). **530-822-7134** Fax: 530-822-7214. 8AM-5PM. www.suttercounty.org Recorder, Grantor/Grantee, Real Estate, Fictitious Names online.

Tehama Recorder PO Box 250, Red Bluff, CA 96080 (633 Washington St, Rm 11).

530-527-3350 Fax: 530-527-1745. 8AM-5PM. www.tehamacountyadmin.org Inmate records online.

Trinity Recorder PO Box 1215, Weaverville, CA 96093-1258 (101 Court St). **530-623-1215** Fax: 530-623-8398. 8AM-5PM. www.trinitycounty.org/Departments/assessor-clerk-elect/clerkrecorder.htm Fictitious Business Name records online.

Tulare Recorder 221 S. Mooney Blvd., County Civic Ctr, Rm 103, Visalia, CA 93291-4593 **559-733-6377** Fax: 559-740-4329. 8AM-5PM. www.co.tulare.ca.us Recording, Deed, Judgment, Lien, Vital Statistic, Fictitious Names online.

Tuolumne Recorder 2 S. Green St, County Admin. Ctr, Sonora, CA 95370 **209-533-5531** Fax: 209-533-6543. 8AM-5PM.

Ventura Recorder 800 S. Victoria Ave, Government Ctr, Ventura, CA 93009 **805-654-2292** Fax: 805-654-2392. 8AM-4PM. www.countyofventura.org Recording, Birth Fictitious Name, Death, Marriage, Most Wanted, Property Tax records online.

Yolo Recorder PO Box 1130, Woodland, CA 95776-1130 (625 Court St, Rm 105). **530-666-8130** Fax: 530-666-8109. 8AM-4PM. www.yolocounty.org/org/Recorder Assessor, Birth, Death, Marriage, Fictitious Business Name, Davis Cemetery records online.

Yuba Recorder 915 8th St #107, Marysville, CA 95901 **530-741-6547** Fax: 530-749-7854. 8AM-5PM.

Colorado

Organization: 63 counties, 63 recording offices. The recording officer is the County Clerk and Recorder. The entire state is in the Mountain Time Zone (MST).

November 15, 2001, Broomfield City and County came into existence, derived from portions of Adams, Boulder, Jefferson and Weld counties. County offices are located at 1 Descombes Dr, Broomfield, CO 80020; 303-469-3301; hours 8AM-5PM. To determine if an address is in Broomfield, parcel search by address at www.co.broomfield.co.us/centralrecords/assessor.shtml.

Real Estate Records: Counties do not perform real estate searches. Copy fees are usually $1.25 per page and certification fees are usually $1.00 per document. Tax records are located in the Assessor's Office.

UCC Records: Financing statements are filed at the state level, except for real estate related collateral, which are filed with the County Clerk & Recorder. However, prior to 07/2001, consumer goods and farm collateral were also filed at the County Clerk & Recorder and these older records can be searched there. Nearly all counties perform UCC searches. Use search request form UCC-11. Search fees are usually $5.00 per debtor name for the first year and $2.00 for each additional year searched (or $13.00 for a five year search). Copies usually cost $1.25 per page.

Tax Lien Records: Federal and some state tax liens on personal property are filed with the Secretary of State. Other federal and state tax liens are filed with the County Clerk and Recorder. Many counties will perform tax lien searches, usually at the same fees as UCC searches. Copies usually cost $1.25 per page Other Liens: Judgments, motor vehicle, mechanics.

Online Access: To date, over 20 Colorado Counties offer free access to property assessor records. Also, the state archives provides limited inheritance tax records for 14 Colorado Counties at www.colorado.gov/dpa/doit/archives/inh_tax/index.html; generally records extend forward only to the 1940s.

At the state level, the Secretary of State offers web access to UCCs, and the Department of Revenue offers trade name searches. See the State Agencies section for details.

Adams Clerk & Recorder 450 S. 4th Ave, Admin. Bldg., Brighton, CO 80601-3197 **303-654-6020** Fax: 303-654-6009. 8AM-4:30PM. www.co.adams.co.us Assessor, Property records online.

Alamosa Clerk & Recorder PO Box 630, Alamosa, CO 81101 (402 Edison St). **719-589-6681** Fax: 719-589-6118. 8AM-4:30.

Arapahoe Clerk & Recorder 5334 S. Prince St, Adminstration Bldg, Littleton, CO 80166-0060 **303-795-4200** Fax: 303-794-4625. 7AM-4:30PM. www.co.arapahoe.co.us Assessor, Property Tax, Real Estate, Deed, Judgment, Lien, Recording, Personal Property records online.

Archuleta Clerk & Recorder PO Box 2589, Pagosa Springs, CO 81147-2589 (449 San Juan St). **970-264-8350** Fax: 970-264-8357. 8AM-4PM.

Baca Clerk & Recorder 741 Main St, Courthouse, Springfield, CO 81073 **719-523-4372** Fax: 719-523-4881. 8:30-4:30. www.bacacounty.net

Bent Clerk & Recorder PO Box 350, Las Animas, CO 81054 (725 Bent St). **719-456-2009** Fax: 719-456-0375. 8:30AM-4:30PM.

Boulder Clerk & Recorder 1750 33rd St #201, Boulder, CO 80301 **303-413-7770** 8AM-5PM. www.co.boulder.co.us/clerk Assessor, Property Tax, Voter Registration, Recording, Grantor/Grantee, Deed, Judgment, Lien, Most Wanted records online.

Broomfield County/City Clerk & Recorder One DesCombes Dr, Broomfield, CO 80020 **303-469-3301** Fax: 303-438-6252. 8AM-5PM. www.co.broomfield.co.us Real Estate, Assessor, Voter Registration records online.

Chaffee Clerk & Recorder PO Box 699, Salida, CO 81201 (104 Crestone Ave.). **719-539-6913** Fax: 719-539-8588. 8AM-4PM Recording; 8AM-5PM Researching.

Cheyenne Clerk & Recorder PO Box 567, Cheyenne Wells, CO 80810 (51 S. 1st St). **719-767-5685** Fax: 719-767-5540. 8-4PM.

Clear Creek Clerk & Recorder PO Box 2000, Georgetown, CO 80444-2000 (405 Argentine St, Courthouse). **303-679-2339** Fax: 303-679-2416. 8:30AM-4:30PM. www.co.clear-creek.co.us/depts/clerk.htm

Conejos Clerk & Recorder PO Box 127, Conejos, CO 81129-0127 (6683 Cty Rd 13). **719-376-5422** Fax: 719-376-5661. 8-4:30.

Costilla Clerk & Recorder PO Box 308, San Luis, CO 81152 (354 Main St). **719-672-3301** Fax: 719-672-3962. 8AM-N, 1-5PM.

Crowley Clerk & Recorder 631 Main #104, Ordway, CO 81063-1092 **719-267-4643** Fax: 719-267-4608. 8AM-4.

Custer Clerk & Recorder PO Box 150, Westcliffe, CO 81252 (205 S. 6th St). **719-783-2441** Fax: 719-783-2885. 8AM-4PM.

Delta Clerk & Recorder 501 Palmer St, #211, Delta, CO 81416 **970-874-2150** Fax: 970-874-2161. 8:30AM-4:30PM.

Denver County Clerk & Recorder 201 W Colfax Ave Dept 101, Denver, CO 80202 **720-865-8400** Fax: 720-865-8580. 9AM-4PM. www.denvergov.org Assessor, Real Estate, Property Tax, Personal Property, Contract, Inmate, Solicitation Arrest, Restaurant records online.

Dolores Clerk & Recorder PO Box 58, Dove Creek, CO 81324-0058 (409 N. Main St). **970-677-2381** Fax: 970-677-2815. 8:30AM-4:30PM.

Douglas Clerk & Recorder PO Box 1360, Castle Rock, CO 80104 (301 Wilcox St). **303-660-7446** Fax: 303-814-2776. 8AM-4:30PM. www.douglas.co.us/recording Deed, Grantor/Grantee, Judgment, Lien, Mortgage, UCC, Vital Statistic, Assessor, Property records online.

Eagle Clerk & Recorder PO Box 537, Eagle, CO 81631 (500 Broadway). **970-328-8710** Fax: 970-328-8716. 8AM-5PM. www.eagle-county.com Assessor, Property, Grantor/Grantee, Property Sale, wanted records online.

El Paso Clerk & Recorder PO Box 2007, Colorado Springs, CO 80901-2007 (200 S. Cascade Ave). **719-520-6200** Fax: 719-520-6230. 8AM-5PM. www.car.elpasoco.com/ Assessor, Public Trustee Sale, Inmate, Contractor, Granter-Grantee records online.

Elbert Clerk & Recorder PO Box 37, Kiowa, CO 80117 (215 Comanche St). **303-621-3129, 303-621-3116** Fax: 303-621-3168. 8AM-4:30PM.

Fremont Clerk & Recorder 615 Macon Ave, Rm 102, Canon City, CO 81212-3311 **719-276-7336** Fax: 719-275-1594. 8:30-

4:30PM. Assessor, Property, Property Sale records online.

Garfield Clerk & Recorder 109 8th St, #200, Glenwood Springs, CO 81601 **970-945-2377** Fax: 970-947-1078. 8:30-5. Assessor, Treasurer records online.

Gilpin Clerk & Recorder PO Box 429, Central City, CO 80427 (203 Eureka St). **303-582-5321** Fax: 303-582-3086. 8AM-5PM. Marriage records online.

Grand Clerk & Recorder PO Box 120, Hot Sulphur Springs, CO 80451 (308 Byers Ave). **970-725-3347 x273** Fax: 970-725-0100. www.gcgovernment.com Property, Assessor, Grantor/Grantee, Recording records online. 8:30AM-5PM.

Gunnison Clerk & Recorder 221 N Wisconsin #C, Courthouse, Gunnison, CO 81230 **970-641-1516** Fax: 970-641-7690. 8AM-5PM. www.co.gunnison.co.us

Hinsdale Clerk & Recorder PO Box 9, Lake City, CO 81235 (317 Henson St). **970-944-2228** Fax: 970-944-2202. 7AM-5:30PM.

Huerfano Clerk & Recorder 410 Main St., Courthouse, #204, Walsenburg, CO 81089 **719-738-2380** Fax: 719-738-2364. 8-4PM.

Jackson Clerk & Recorder PO Box 337, Walden, CO 80480-0337 (396 LaFever St). **970-723-4334** Fax: 970-723-3214. 8-5PM.

Jefferson Clerk & Recorder 100 Jefferson County Parkway, #2530, Golden, CO 80419-2530 **303-271-8121** Fax: 303-271-8180. 8:30AM-4:30PM. http://co.jefferson.co.us/e xt/dpt/officials/clkrec/index.htm Assessor, Property, Grantor/Grantee, Deed, Judgment, Recording records online.

Kiowa Clerk & Recorder PO Box 37, Eads, CO 81036-0037 (1305 Goff St). **719-438-5421** Fax: 719-438-5327. 8AM-4:30PM.

Kit Carson Clerk & Recorder PO Box 249, Burlington, CO 80807-0249 (251 16th St, #203). **719-346-8638** Fax: 719-346-7242. 8AM-4PM.

La Plata Clerk & Recorder PO Box 519, Durango, CO 81302-0519 (Courthouse, Rm 134, 1060 E. 2nd Ave.). **970-382-6294** Fax: 970-382-6299. http://co.laplata.co.us Real Estate, Sale, Property records online. 8-5PM.

Lake Clerk & Recorder PO Box 917, Leadville, CO 80461 (505 Harrison Ave). **719-486-4131** Fax: 719-486-3972. 9-5PM.

Larimer Clerk & Recorder PO Box 1280, Fort Collins, CO 80522-1280 (200 W. Oak, 1st Fl). **970-498-7860** Fax: 970-498-7830. 7:30AM-4:30PM. www.larimer.org Property Tax, Assessor, Treasurer, UCC, Lien, Deed, Judgment, Recording, Voter Registration, Most Wanted records online.

Las Animas Clerk & Recorder PO Box 115, Trinidad, CO 81082 (200 E 1st.St. Rm 205). **719-846-3314** Fax: 719-845-2573. 8-4.

Lincoln Clerk & Recorder PO Box 67, Hugo, CO 80821-0067 (103 3rd Ave). **719-743-2444** Fax: 719-743-2524. 8AM-4:30.

Logan Clerk & Recorder 315 Main St #3, Logan County Courthouse, Sterling, CO 80751 **970-522-1544** Fax: 970-522-2063. www.loganco.gov/departments.htm 8-5PM. Assessor, Real Estate records online.

Mesa Clerk & Recorder PO Box 20000-5007, Grand Junction, CO 81502-5007 (544 Rood Ave). **970-244-1679** Fax: 970-256-1588. 8:30AM-4:30PM. www.co.mesa.co.us Grantor/Grantee, Judgment, Lien, Real Estate, Assessor, Real Estate, Property Tax, Voter Registration records online.

Mineral Clerk & Recorder PO Box 70, Creede, CO 81130 (1201 N. Main St). **719-658-2440** Fax: 719-658-2931. 8AM-4PM.

Moffat Clerk & Recorder 221 W. Victory Way, Craig, CO 81625-2716 **970-824-9104** Fax: 970-824-4975. 8AM-4PM. Wanted records online.

Montezuma Clerk & Recorder 109 W. Main St, Rm #108, Cortez, CO 81321 **970-565-3728** Fax: 970-564-0215. 8:30AM-4:30PM. www.co.montezuma.co.us/ Property Tax, Property Sale records online.

Montrose Clerk & Recorder PO Box 1289, Montrose, CO 81402 (320 S. First St #101). **970-249-3362** Fax: 970-249-0757. 8:30AM-4:30PM. Property, Assessor records online.

Morgan Clerk & Recorder PO Box 1399, Fort Morgan, CO 80701 (231 Ensign St, Admin. Bldg.). **970-542-3521** Fax: 970-542-3520. 8AM-4PM. Assessor records online.

Otero Clerk & Recorder PO Box 511, La Junta, CO 81050-0511 (13 W. 3rd St. Rm 210, Courthouse). **719-383-3020** Fax: 719-383-3026. 8AM-5. Assessor records online.

Ouray Clerk & Recorder PO Bin C, Ouray, CO 81427 (541 Fourth St) **970-325-4961** Fax: 970-325-0452. 9-5. http://co.ouray.co.us

Park Clerk & Recorder PO Box 220, Fairplay, CO 80440 (501 Main St). **719-836-4222** Fax: 719-836-4348. 7AM-5PM. www.parkco.org Assessor, Property Tax, Divorce records online.

Phillips Clerk & Recorder 221 S. Interocean, Holyoke, CO 80734 **970-854-3131** Fax: 970-854-4745. 8AM-4:30PM.

Pitkin Clerk & Recorder 530 E. Main St., #101, Aspen, CO 81611 **970-920-5180** Fax: 970-920-5196. www.aspenpitkin.com Assessor, Inmates, Divorce, Probate, Grantor/Grantee records online. 8:30AM-4:30PM.

Prowers Clerk & Recorder 301 S. Main St #210, Lamar, CO 81052 **719-336-8011** Fax: 719-336-5306. 8:30AM-4:30PM.

Pueblo Clerk & Recorder PO Box 878, Pueblo, CO 81002-0878 (215 W. 10th St). **719-583-6625** Fax: 719-583-4625. 8AM-4:30PM. www.co.pueblo.co.us/clerk/ Assessor, Real Estate, Property Sale, Registered Voter records online.

Rio Blanco Clerk & Recorder PO Box 1067, Meeker, CO 81641 (555 Main St). **970-878-5068** 8AM-5PM.

Rio Grande Clerk & Recorder PO Box 160, Del Norte, CO 81132 (Annex Bldg., 965 6th St.). **719-657-3334** Fax: 719-657-2621. 8AM-4PM. www.qpublic.net/riogrande/ Property Tax, Assessor, Sale records online.

Routt Clerk & Recorder PO Box 773598, Steamboat Springs, CO 80477 (522 Lincoln Ave. **970-870-5556** Fax: 970-870-1329. 8AM-4:30PM; Recording Hours: 8AM-4PM. www.co.routt.co.us Real Estate, Assessor, Treasurer, Deed, Judgment, Property Sale records online.

Saguache Clerk & Recorder PO Box 176, Saguache, CO 81149-0176 (501 4th St.). **719-655-2512** Fax: 719-655-2730. 8AM-4PM. Recording, Real Estate, Deed, Lien, Death, Marriage records online.

San Juan Clerk & Recorder PO Box 466, Silverton, CO 81433-0466 (1557 Greene). **970-387-5671** Fax: 970-387-5671. 9AM-5.

San Miguel Clerk & Recorder PO Box 548, Telluride, CO 81435-0548 (305 W. Colorado Ave). **970-728-3954** Fax: 970-728-4808. 9AM-5PM. Wanted records online.

Sedgwick Clerk & Recorder PO Box 50, Julesburg, CO 80737 (315 Cedar St). **970-474-3346** Fax: 970-474-0954. 8AM-4PM.

Summit Clerk & Recorder PO Box 1538, Breckenridge, CO 80424 (208 E. Lincoln). **970-453-3475** Fax: 970-453-3540. 8AM-5PM. www.co.summit.co.us Property, GIS-mapping records online.

Teller Clerk & Recorder PO Box 1010, Cripple Creek, CO 80813-1010 (101 W. Bennett Ave). **719-689-2951** Fax: 719-689-3524. 8AM-4:30PM. www.co.teller.co.us Real Estate, Grantor/Grantee, Assessor, Property Tax records online.

Washington Clerk & Recorder PO Box L, Akron, CO 80720-0380 (150 Ash). **970-345-6565** Fax: 970-345-6607. 8AM-4:30PM.

Weld Clerk & Recorder PO Box 459, Greeley, CO 80632-0459 (1402 N. 17th Ave.). **970-304-6530** Fax: 970-353-1964. 8AM-5PM. www.co.weld.co.us Real Estate, Assessor, Treasurer, Property Tax, Most Wanted, Sex Offender records online.

Yuma Clerk & Recorder 310 Ash St, #F, Wray, CO 80758 **970-332-5809** Fax: 970-332-5919. 8:30AM-4:30PM.

 # Connecticut

Organization: 8 counties and 170 towns/cities. There is no county recording in this state. The recording officer is the Town/City Clerk. Be careful not to confuse searching in the following towns/cities as equivalent to a countywide search: Fairfield, Hartford, Litchfield, New Haven, New London, Tolland, and Windham. The entire state is in the Eastern Time Zone (EST).

Real Estate Records: Many towns do not perform real estate searches. Copy fees are usually $1.00 per page. Certification fees are usually $1.00 per document or per page.

UCC Records: Connecticut adopted Revised Article 9 on October 1, 2001. Financing statements are filed at the state level, except for real estate related collateral, which are filed only with the Town/City Clerk. Some towns will perform UCC searches. Copies usually cost $1.00 per page.

Tax Lien Records: All federal and state tax liens on personal property are filed with the Secretary of State. Federal and state tax liens on real property are filed with the Town/City Clerk. Towns will not perform tax lien searches. Other Liens: Mechanics, judgments, lis pendens, municipal, welfare, carpenter, sewer & water, city/town.

Online Access: A number of towns offer free access to assessor information. The State's Municipal Public Access Initiative has produced a website of Town and Municipality general information at www.munic.state.ct.us.

Andover Town Clerk 17 School Rd., Andover, CT 06232-0328 **860-742-0188** Fax: 860-742-7535. M 8:3AM-7PM; Tues-Th 8:30AM-3PM; F 8:30AM-12PM.

Ansonia City Clerk 253 Main St, City Hall, Ansonia, CT 06401 **203-736-5980** 8AM-5:30PM, M, T, W, F; 8AM-6:30PM, TH.

Ashford Town Clerk 25 Pompey Hollow Rd, Ashford, CT 06278 **860-429-7044** Fax: 860-487-2025. 8:30-3 M-W, F; 7-9PM W.

Avon Town Clerk 60 W. Main St, Avon, CT 06001 **860-409-4310** Fax: 860-677-8428. 8:30AM-4:30PM (Summer: 8AM-4:45 M-Th). Property Assessor records online.

Barkhamsted Town Clerk 67 Ripley Hill Rd., Pleasant Valley, CT 06063 **860-379-8665** Fax: 860-379-9284. 9AM-4PM (F til 1PM).

Beacon Falls Town Clerk 10 Maple Ave, Beacon Falls, CT 06403 **203-729-8254** Fax: 203-720-1078. 9AM-Noon, 1-4PM.

Berlin Town Clerk 240 Kensington Rd, Kensington, CT 06037 **860-828-7075** Fax: 860-828-8628. M-W, 8:30-4:30; Th 8:30-7; F 8:30-1. www.town.berlin.ct.us Real Estate, Marriage, Recorder, Assessor records online.

Bethany Town Clerk 40 Peck Rd, Bethany, CT 06524-3338 **203-393-2100 x104, x105** Fax: 203-393-0821. 9:00-4:30.

Bethel Town Clerk 1 School St., Bethel, CT 06801 **203-794-8505** Fax: 203-794-8588. 9-5.

Bethlehem Town Clerk PO Box 160, Bethlehem, CT 06751 (36 Main St. So.). **203-266-7510** Fax: 203-266-7670. 9AM-N T,W,Th,F,Sat. www.ci.bethlehem.ct.us

Bloomfield Town Clerk PO Box 337, Bloomfield, CT 06002 (800 Bloomfield Ave, Town Hall). **860-769-3506** Fax: 860-769-3597. 9AM-5PM.

Bolton Town Clerk 222 Bolton Ctr Rd, Bolton, CT 06043-7698 **860-649-8066** Fax: 860-643-0021. 9AM-4PM M,W,Th; 9AM-5PM, 6-8PM T; 9AM-3PM F.

Bozrah Town Clerk I River Rd, Bozrah, CT 06334 **860-889-2689** Fax: 860-887-5449. 9AM-4PM T,W; 9-4 Th; 9AM-Noon Fri.

Branford Town Clerk PO Box 150, Branford, CT 06405 (1019 Main St, Town Hall). **203-488-6305** Fax: 203-481-5561. 9AM-4:30PM (9AM-4PM Recording hours). Assessor records online.

Bridgeport Town Clerk 45 Lyon Terrace, City Hall, Rm 124, Bridgeport, CT 06604 **203-576-7207** 9AM-4:30; Recording 4PM.

Bridgewater Town Clerk PO Box 216, Bridgewater, CT 06752-0216 (Main St, Town Hall). **860-354-5102** Fax: 860-350-5944. 8AM-Noon M,W,F; 8AM-5PM T.

Bristol City Clerk PO Box 114, Bristol, CT 06011-0114 (111 N. Main St, City Hall). **860-584-7600** 8:30AM-5PM.

Brookfield Town Clerk PO Box 5106, Brookfield, CT 06804-5106 (Brookfield Town Hall). **203-775-7314** Fax: 203-775-5231. 8:30AM-4:30PM; Most Th to 7PM. www.brookfield.org Assessor records online.

Brooklyn Town Clerk PO Box 356, Brooklyn, CT 06234 (4 Wolf Den Rd, Town Hall). **860-774-9543** Fax: 860-779-3744. M-W 9AM-4:30PM; Th 9AM-6PM; F 9AM-1PM. www.brooklynct.org

Burlington Town Clerk 200 Spielman Highway, Burlington, CT 06013 **860-673-2108** Fax: 860-675-9312. 8:30AM-4PM.

Canaan Town Clerk PO Box 47, Falls Village, CT 06031 (107 Main St) **860-824-0707** Fax: 860-824-4506. 9AM-3PM.

Canterbury Town Clerk PO Box 27, Canterbury, CT 06331-0027 (1 Municipal Dr,). **860-546-9377** Fax: 860-546-9295. 9-4PM M-W; 9AM-6:30 TH; 9-1:30PM F.

Canton Town Clerk PO Box 168, Collinsville, CT 06022 (4 Market St). **860-693-7870** Fax: 860-693-7840. 8:30-4:30.

Chaplin Town Clerk PO Box 286, Chaplin, CT 06235 (495 Phoenixville Rd, Town Hall). **860-455-9455** Fax: 860-455-0027. 9am-3pm M, W, Th; 1pm-7pm Tues.

Cheshire Town Clerk 84 S. Main St, Town Hall, Cheshire, CT 06410 **203-271-6601** 8:30AM-4PM www.cheshirect.org

Chester Town Clerk PO Box 218, Chester, CT 06412-0218 (65 Main St). **860-526-0013 x511** Fax: 860-526-0004. 9AM-N, 1-4PM M,W,Th; 9AM-N, 1-7PM T; 9AM-N Fri.. www.chesterct.com Assessor records online.

Clinton Town Clerk 54 E. Main St, Clinton, CT 06413 **860-669-9101** 9AM-4PM. Assessor records online.

Colchester Town Clerk 127 Norwich Ave, Colchester, CT 06415 **860-537-7215** Fax: 860-537-0547. 8:30AM-4:30PM M-W & F; 8:30-7PM Th. www.colchesterct.net Assessor records online.

Colebrook Town Clerk PO Box 5, Colebrook, CT 06021 (562 Colebrook Rd, Rte 183, Town Hall). **860-379-3359 ext 213** Fax: 860-379-7215. 9AM-12:00-1-4:30PM. Assessor records online.

Columbia Town Clerk 323 Jonathan Trumbull Hwy, Columbia, CT 06237 **860-228-3284** Fax: 860-228-2335. 8:30AM-3PM M-W; 9AM-7PM Th; 8AM-Noon Fri.

Cornwall Town Clerk PO Box 97, Cornwall, CT 06753-0097 (26 Pine St.). **860-672-2709** 9AM-4PM M-Th.

Coventry Town Clerk 1712 Main St, Coventry, CT 06238 **860-742-7966** Fax: 860-742-8911. 8:30-4:30 M-W; 8:30-6:30 Th; 8:30AM-1:30PM.

Cromwell Town Clerk 41 West St, Cromwell, CT 06416-2100 **860-632-3440** Fax: 860-632-3425. 8:30AM-4PM. www.cromwellct.com

Danbury City Town Clerk 155 Deer Hill Ave, City Hall, Danbury, CT 06810 **203-797-4531** 8:30-4:30PM. www.ci.danbury.ct.us Assessor, Land, Permit, Water Information records online.

Darien Town Clerk 2 Renshaw Rd, Darien, CT 06820-5397 **203-656-7307** 8:30-4:30.

Deep River Town Clerk 174 Main St, Town Hall, Deep River, CT 06417 **860-526-6024** Fax: 860-526-6023. 9AM-Noon,1-4PM.

Derby City Town Clerk 35 Fifth St, Derby, CT 06418-1897 **203-736-1462** Fax: 203-736-1458. 9AM-5PM.

Durham Town Clerk PO Box 428, Durham, CT 06422 (30 Town House Rd, Town Hall). **860-349-3452** Fax: 860-349-0547. 9AM-4:30PM M-F, 10AM-N Sat except holidays. http://townofdurhamct.org

East Granby Town Clerk PO Box TC, East Granby, CT 06026-0459 (9 Center St, Town Hall). **860-653-6528** Fax: 860-653-4017. 8:30AM-N, 1-4PM M-Th; 8:30-1PM F.

East Haddam Town Clerk PO Box K, Town Office Bldg, East Haddam, CT 06423 (Goodspeed Plaza, Town Office Bldg.). **860-873-5027** 9AM-4PM M,W,Th; 9AM-N F (Tu until 7PM). http://easthaddam.org

East Hampton Town Clerk 20 E. High St, Town Hall, East Hampton, CT 06424 **860-267-2519** Fax: 860-267-1027. 8AM-4PM M,W,Th; 8-7:30PM T; 8AM-12:30PM F.

East Hartford Town Clerk 740 Main St, East Hartford, CT 06108-3126 **860-291-7230** Fax: 860-289-0831. 8:30AM-4:30PM. www.ci.east-hartford.ct.us

East Haven Town Clerk 250 Main St, East Haven, CT 06512-3034 **203-468-3201** Fax: 203-468-3372. 8:30AM-4:15.

East Lyme Town Clerk PO Box 519, Niantic, CT 06357 (108 Pennsylvania Ave). **860-739-6931** Fax: 860-739-6930. 8:30AM-4:30PM. Assessor records online.

East Windsor Town Clerk PO Box 213, Broad Brook, CT 06016-0213 (11 Rye St) **860-623-9467** Fax: 860-623-4798. 8:30-4:30 M,T,W; 8:30-7:30PM Th; 8:30-12:30P F.

Eastford Town Clerk PO Box 273, Eastford, CT 06242 (16 Westford Rd). **860-974-1885** Fax: 860-974-0624. 10AM-N, 1-4PM T,W.

Easton Town Clerk PO Box 61, Easton, CT 06612 (225 Center Rd). **203-268-6291** Fax: 203-261-6080. 9AM-2PM.

Ellington Town Clerk PO Box 187, Ellington, CT 06029-0187 (55 Main St). **860-870-3105** 9AM-7 M; 9AM-4:30 T-F.

Enfield Town Clerk 820 Enfield St, Enfield, CT 06082-2997 **860-253-6440** 9AM-5PM. www.enfield.org Tax Sale records online.

Essex Town Clerk PO Box 98, Essex, CT 06426 (29 West Ave). **860-767-4344 x129** Fax: 860-767-4560. 9AM-4PM. Property, Assessor records online.

Fairfield Town Clerk 611 Old Post Rd, Fairfield, CT 06430-6690 **203-256-3090** 8:30AM-4:30PM Assessor records online.

Farmington Town Clerk 1 Monteith Drive, Farmington, CT 06032-1053 **860-673-8247** Fax: 860-675-7140. 8:30AM-4:30PM. Assessor, Property records online.

Franklin Town Clerk 7 Meeting House Hill Rd, Town Hall, Franklin, CT 06254 **860-642-7352** Fax: 860-642-6606. 8:30AM-3PM M-Th; 6PM-8PM T.

Glastonbury Town Clerk 2155 Main St, Glastonbury, CT 06033 **860-652-7616** Fax: 860-652-7639. 8-4:30PM. www.glasct.org Property, Assessor records online.

Goshen Town Clerk PO Box 54, Goshen, CT 06756-0054 (42 North St, Town Office Bldg.). **860-491-3647** 9AM-N,1-4PM M-Th; 9-1PM F. Assessor records online.

Granby Town Clerk 15 N. Granby Rd, Granby, CT 06035 **860-844-5308** 9AM-Noon,1-4PM. Assessor records online.

Greenwich Town Clerk PO Box 2540, Greenwich, CT 06836 (101 Field Point Rd, Town Hall). **203-622-7897** 8AM-4PM.

Griswold Town Clerk PO Box 369, Jewett City, CT 06351 (28 Main St). **860-376-7060 x100** Fax: 860-376-7070. 8:30-4 M,T,Th,F; 8:30AM-N Wed. www.griswold-ct.org

Groton Town Clerk 45 Fort Hill Rd, Groton, CT 06340 **860-441-6642** 8:30-4:30 M-W & F; 9AM-4:30PM Th.

Guilford Town Clerk 31 Park St, Town Hall, Guilford, CT 06437 (**203-453-8001**) 8:30AM-4:30PM. www.ci.guilford.ct.us

Haddam Town Clerk PO Box 87, Haddam, CT 06438 (30 Field Park Drive) **860-345-8531** Fax: 860-345-3730. 9AM-4PM M,T,W; 9AM-7PM Th; 9AM-Noon F.

Hamden Town Clerk 2372 Whitney Ave, Memorial Town Hall, Hamden, CT 06518 **203-287-2510** Fax: 203-287-2518. 9AM-4PM. Assessor records online.

Hampton Town Clerk PO Box 143, Hampton, CT 06247-0143 (Town Office Bldg., 164 Main St.). **860-455-9132** Fax: 860-455-0517. 9AM-4 T,Th; 6-8PM Th.

Hartford City Clerk 550 Main St, Hartford, CT 06103-2992 **860-543-8580** Fax: 860-772-8041. 8:30AM-4:30 PM.

Hartland Town Clerk PO Box 297, East Hartland, CT 06027 (Town Office Bldg., 22 S. Rd). **860-653-0285** Fax: 860-653-0452. 10AM-N, 1-4PM M,T,W. www.munic.state.ct.us/hartland/hartland.htm

Harwinton Town Clerk 100 Bentley Drive, Town Hall, Harwinton, CT 06791 **860-485-9613** Fax: 860-485-0051. 8:30AM-4PM.

Hebron Town Clerk PO Box 156, Hebron, CT 06248 (15 Gilead St). **860-228-5971 x124** Fax: 860-228-4859. 8-4 M-W; 8AM-6 Th; 8AM-1:00 F. www.hebronct.com

Kent Town Clerk PO Box 678, Kent, CT 06757-0678 (41 Kent Green Blvd., Town Hall). **860-927-3433** Fax: 860-927-4541. 9AM-4. Assessor, Property records online.

Killingly Town Clerk PO Box 6000, Danielson, CT 06239 (172 Main St). **860-779-5307** Fax: 860-779-5394. 8:30-4:30.

Killingworth Town Clerk 323 Route 81, Killingworth, CT 06419-1298 **860-663-1616** Fax: 860-663-3305. 9AM-Noon,1-4PM.

Lebanon Town Clerk 579 Exeter Rd, Town Hall, Lebanon, CT 06249 **860-642-7319** 9AM-4PM M,T,F; 9AM-7PM Th. Assessor, Property records online.

Ledyard Town Clerk 741 Col. Ledyard Highway, Ledyard, CT 06339 **860-464-3259** Fax: 860-464-1126. 8:30AM-4:30PM Mon-Fri. www.town.ledyard.ct.us

Lisbon Town Clerk 1 Newent Rd, RD 2 Town Hall, Lisbon, CT 06351-9802 **860-376-2708** Fax: 860-376-6545. 9AM-4PM M-Th; 6PM-8PM W; 9AM-2PM F; 9AM-N Sat.

Litchfield Town Clerk PO Box 488, Litchfield, CT 06759-0488 (74 West St). **860-567-7561** 9AM-4:30PM.

Lyme Town Clerk 480 Hamburg Rd., Town Hall, Lyme, CT 06371 **860-434-7733** Fax: 860-434-2989. 9AM-4PM. Assessor, Property records online.

Madison Town Clerk 8 Campus Dr., Madison, CT 06443-2538 **203-245-5672** Fax: 203-245-5613. 8:30-4. www.madisonct.org Assessor, Property records online.

Manchester Town Clerk PO Box 191, Manchester, CT 06045-0191 (41 Center St). **860-647-3037** Fax: 860-647-3029. 8:30-5. www.ci.manchester.ct.us/Town_Clerk/index.htm Assessor records online.

Mansfield Town Clerk 4 S. Eagleville Rd, Mansfield, CT 06268 **860-429-3302** 8:15AM-4:30PM M-W; 8:15AM-6:30PM Th; 8AM-Noon F. www.mansfieldct.org/

Marlborough Town Clerk PO Box 29, Marlborough, CT 06447 (26 N. Main St). **860-295-6206** Fax: 860-295-0317. 8AM-4:30PM M-Th; 8AM-7PM T; 8AM-N F.

Meriden City Clerk 142 E. Main St, Meriden, CT 06450-8022 **203-630-4030** Fax: 203-630-4059. 9AM-7PM M; 9AM-5PM T-F. www.cityofmeriden.org/government/

Middlebury Town Clerk PO Box 392, Middlebury, CT 06762-0392 (1212 Whittemore Rd.). **203-758-2557** Fax: 203-758-2915. 9-N,1-5. www.middlebury-ct.org

Middlefield Town Clerk PO Box 179, Middlefield, CT 06455 (393 Jackson Hill

Rd). **860-349-7116** Fax: 860-349-7115. 9-5 M; 9-4 T-Th; 9-3 F. www.munic.state.c t.us/MIDDLEFIELD/contents.htm Assessor records online.

Middletown City Clerk PO Box 1300, Middletown, CT 06457 (245 DeKoven Drive). **860-344-3459** Fax: 860-344-3591. 8:30AM-4:30PM. www.cityofmiddleto wn.com/Departments.htm

Milford City Clerk 70 W River St, Milford, CT 06460-3364 **203-783-3210** 8:30-5PM. www.ci.milford.ct.us Assessor records online.

Monroe Town Clerk 7 Fan Hill Rd, Monroe, CT 06468-1800 **203-452-5417** Fax: 203-261-6197. 9AM-5PM.

Montville Town Clerk 310 Norwich-New London Tpke., Town Hall, Uncasville, CT 06382 **860-848-1349** Fax: 860-848-1521. 9AM-5PM.

Morris Town Clerk PO Box 66, Morris, CT 06763-0066 (3 East St). **860-567-7433** Fax: 860-567-7432. 9AM-Noon, 1-4PM.

Naugatuck Town Clerk 229 Church St, Town Hall, Naugatuck, CT 06770 **203-720-7000** Fax: 203-720-7099. 8:30AM-4PM. Assessor records online.

New Britain Town Clerk 27 W. Main St, New Britain, CT 06051 **860-826-3344** Fax: 860-826-3348. 8:15AM-3:45PM M-W & F; 8:15-6:45 Th. Assessor records online.

New Canaan Town Clerk 77 Main St, Town Hall, New Canaan, CT 06840 **203-594-3070** Fax: 203-594-3130. www.newcanaan.info Assessor, Property records online. 8:30-4:30.

New Fairfield Town Clerk 4 Brushhill Rd, New Fairfield, CT 06812 **203-312-5616** 8:30AM-5PM T-F; 8:30AM-Noon Sat.

New Hartford Town Clerk PO Box 426, New Hartford, CT 06057 (530 Main St, Town Hall). **860-379-5037** Fax: 860-379-1367. 9AM-N, 12:40-4 M,T,Th; 9AM-N, 1-6 W;. www.town.new-hartford.ct.us/home .html Assessor, Property records online.

New Haven City Clerk 200 Orange St, Rm 202, New Haven, CT 06510 **203-946-8339** Fax: 203-946-6974. 9AM-5PM. Assessor records online.

New London City Clerk 181 State St, New London, CT 06320 **860-447-5205** Fax: 860-447-1644. 8:30AM-3:50PM. www.ci.new-london.ct.us Assessor records online.

New Milford Town Clerk 10 Main St, New Milford, CT 06776 **860-355-6020** Fax: 860-355-6002. 9AM-5. Assessor records online. www.newmilford.org/agencies/home.htm

Newington Town Clerk 131 Cedar St, Newington, CT 06111-2696 **860-665-8545** 8:30-4:30. www.ci.newington.ct.us

Newtown Town Clerk 45 Main St, Newtown, CT 06470 **203-270-4210** 8-4:30.

Norfolk Town Clerk PO Box 552, Norfolk, CT 06058-0552 (19 Maple Ave). **860-542-5679** 8:30-N, 1-4PM M-Th, 8:30AM-N F.

North Branford Town Clerk PO Box 287, North Branford, CT 06471-0287 (1599 Foxon Rd). **203-484-6015** 8:30-4:30PM.

North Canaan Town Clerk PO Box 338, North Canaan, CT 06018 (100 Pease St, Town Hall). **860-824-3138** Fax: 860-824-3139. 9:30AM-Noon, 1-4PM; Fri till 1PM.

North Haven Town Clerk 18 Church St, Town Hall, North Haven, CT 06473 **203-239-5321 x541** 8:30AM-4:30PM.

North Stonington Town Clerk 40 Main St, North Stonington, CT 06359 **860-535-2877 x21** Fax: 860-535-4554. 9AM-4PM. www.munic.state.ct.us/N_Stonington/

Norwalk City Town Clerk PO Box 5125, Norwalk, CT 06856-5125 (125 East Ave, City Hall). **203-854-7746** Fax: 203-854-7817. 8:30AM-4:30PM M T W F; 8:30 AM-7PM Th. www.norwalkct.org Property, Assessor records online.

Norwich City Clerk 100 Broadway, City Hall, Rm 215, Norwich, CT 06360 **860-823-3732** Fax: 860-823-3790. 8:30AM-4:30PM. www.norwichct.org Assessor, Real Estate records online.

Old Lyme Town Clerk 52 Lyme St, Old Lyme, CT 06371 **860-434-1605 x221** Fax: 860-434-9283. 9AM-N,1-4PM. Assessor records online.

Old Saybrook Town Clerk 302 Main St, Old Saybrook, CT 06475 **860-395-3135** Fax: 860-395-5014. www.oldsaybrookct.com Real Estate records online. 8:30-4:30.

Orange Town Clerk 617 Orange Center Rd., Town Hall, Orange, CT 06477 **203-891-2122** Fax: 203-891-2185. 8:30AM-4:30PM.

Oxford Town Clerk 486 Oxford Rd, Oxford, CT 06478 **203-888-2543** Fax: 203-888-2136. 9AM-5PM M-Th; 7-9PM Mon & Th.

Plainfield Town Clerk 8 Community Ave, Town Hall, Plainfield, CT 06374 **860-564-4075** 8:30AM-4:30PM M,T,W; 8:30AM-6:30PM Th; 8:30AM-1PM.

Plainville Town Clerk 1 Central Sq, Municipal Ctr, Plainville, CT 06062 **860-793-0221** 8:30AM-4:30PM.

Plymouth Town Clerk 80 Main St, Town Hall, Terryville, CT 06786 **860-585-4039** Fax: 860-585-4015. 8:30-4:30PM.

Pomfret Town Clerk 5 Haven Rd, Pomfret Center, CT 06259 **860-974-0343** Fax: 860-974-3950. 9-4. Assessor records online.

Portland Town Clerk PO Box 71, Portland, CT 06480 (265 Main St). **860-342-6743** Fax: 860-342-0001. 9AM-4:30PM.

Preston Town Clerk 389 Route 2, Town Hall, Preston, CT 06365-8830 **860-887-9821** Fax: 860-885-1905. 9AM-4:30PM T-F; Th until 6:30. Assessor records online.

Prospect Town Clerk 36 Center St, Prospect, CT 06712-1699 **203-758-4461** Fax: 203-758-4466. 8:30AM-4PM.

Putnam Town Clerk 126 Church St, Putnam, CT 06260 **860-963-6807** Fax: 860-963-2001. 8:30-N 1-4:30. www.putnamct.us Assessor, Property records online.

Redding Town Clerk PO Box 1028, Redding, CT 06875-1028 (Route 107, 100 Hill Rd., Town Office Bldg.). **203-938-2377** Fax: 203-938-8816. 9AM-4:30PM.

Ridgefield Town Clerk 400 Main St, Ridgefield, CT 06877 **203-431-2783** Fax: 203-431-2722. 8:30-4:30. www.ridgefieldct .org/government/townclerk/townclerk.htm

Rocky Hill Town Clerk 761 Old Main St., Rocky Hill, CT 06067 **860-258-2705** 8:30-4:30. Land, Marriage, Death, Trade Name, Recording records online.

Roxbury Town Clerk 29 North St., Roxbury, CT 06783-1405 **860-354-3328** Fax: 860-354-0560. 9AM-Noon, 1-4PM T & Th; 9AM-Noon F. Assessor, Property records online.

Salem Town Clerk 270 Hartford Rd, Town Office Bldg., Salem, CT 06420 **860-859-3873 x170** Fax: 860-859-1184. 8AM-4PM M-W; 8-5PM Th; 8AM-N Fri. www.salemct.gov

Salisbury Town Clerk PO Box 548, Salisbury, CT 06068 (27 Main St) **860-435-5182** Fax: 860-435-5172. 9AM-4PM.

Scotland Town Clerk PO Box 122, Scotland, CT 06264 (9 Devotion Rd., Town Hall). **860-423-9634** Fax: 860-423-3666. 9-3 M,T,Th- Noon-8PM W; Closed Friday.

Seymour Town Clerk 1 First St, Town Hall, Seymour, CT 06483-2817 **203-888-0519** 9AM-5PM (No Recording after 4:15PM).

Sharon Town Clerk PO Box 224, Sharon, CT 06069 (63 Main St, Town Hall). **860-364-5224** Fax: 860-364-5224. M- Th 8:30AM-Noon, 1-4PM ; Fri 8:30AM-Noon. Assessor records online.

Shelton City Clerk PO Box 364, Shelton, CT 06484-0364 (54 Hill St). **203-924-1555** Fax: 203-924-1721. www.cityofshelton.org

Sherman Town Clerk PO Box 39, Sherman, CT 06784-0039 (9 Route 39 North, Town Hall). **860-354-5281** Fax: 860-350-5041. 9AM-N, 1-4PM T,W,Th,F; 9AM-N Sat.

Simsbury Town Clerk PO Box 495, Simsbury, CT 06070 (933 Hopmeadow St). **860-658-3243** Fax: 860-658-3206. 8:30AM-4:30PM.

Somers Town Clerk PO Box 308, Somers, CT 06071 (600 Main St). **860-763-8206** Fax: 860-763-8228. 8:30AM-4:30PM M-W,F; 8:30AM-7PM Th. www.somersnow.com

South Windsor Town Clerk 1540 Sullivan Ave, South Windsor, CT 06074 **860-644-2511 x225** Fax: 860-644-3781. 8-4:30. w.vw.southwindsor.org Property Transfer records online.

Southbury Town Clerk 501 Main St South, Southbury, CT 06488-2295 **203-262-0657** Fax: 203-264-9762. 8:30AM-4:30PM.

Southington Town Clerk PO Box 152, Southington, CT 06489 (75 Main St) **860-276-6211** Fax: 860-276-6229. 8:30-4PM M, T, W, F; 8:30-7 TH. www.southington.org Most Wanted records online.

Sprague Town Clerk PO Box 162, Baltic, CT 06330 (1 Main St). **860-822-3001** Fax: 860-822-3013. 8:00AM-4:30PM M-T (W Open til 5:30PM).

Stafford Town Clerk PO Box 11, Stafford Springs, CT 06076 (Warren Town Hall, 1 Main St.). **860-684-1765** Fax: 860-684-1765. 8:15AM-4PM M-W; 8:15AM-6:30PM Th; 8AM-Noon F.

Stamford City Clerk PO Box 10152, Stamford, CT 06904 (888 Washington Blvd). **203-977-4054** Fax: 203-977-4943. 8:00AM-3:45PM. www.cityofstamford.org/ Welcome.htm Assessor, Real Estate, Personal Property, City Businesses records online.

Sterling Town Clerk PO Box 157, Oneco, CT 06373-0157 (1114 Plainfield Pike). **860-564-2657** Fax: 860-564-1660. 8:30AM-3:30-M,T,TH; 8AM-6PM-W; 8AM-N F.

Stonington Town Clerk PO Box 352, Stonington, CT 06378 (152 Elm St). **860-535-5060** Fax: 860-535-5062. 8:30AM-4PM. www.townofstonington.com

Stratford Town Clerk 2725 Main St, Rm 101, Stratford, CT 06615 **203-385-4020** Fax: 203-385-4005. 8AM-4:30PM. www.townofstratford.com

Suffield Town Clerk 83 Mountain Rd, Town Hall, Suffield, CT 06078 (83 Mountain Rd,

Town Hall). **860-668-3880** Fax: 860-668-3898. 8:30AM-4:30PM; Summer: 8-4:30 M-Th; 8-1PM F. www.suffieldtownhall.com Assessor records online.

Thomaston Town Clerk 158 Main St, Thomaston, CT 06787 **860-283-4141** Fax: 860-283-1013. 9-4:30PM.

Thompson Town Clerk PO Box 899, No. Grosvenor Dale, CT 06255 (815 Riverside Drive). **860-923-9900** Fax: 860-923-3836. 9AM-5PM. Assessor records online.

Tolland Town Clerk 21 Tolland Green, Hicks Memorial Muni. Ctr, Tolland, CT 06084 **860-871-3630** Fax: 860-871-3663. 8:30AM-4PM MTW; 8:30AM-7:30PM TH; 8:30 AM-Noon F.

Torrington City Clerk 140 Main St, City Hall, Torrington, CT 06790 **860-489-2236** Fax: 860-489-2548. www.torrington-ct.org Assessor, Property records online. 8-4:30.

Trumbull Town Clerk 5866 Main St, Trumbull, CT 06611 **203-452-5035** Fax: 203-452-5094. 9AM-5PM.

Union Town Clerk 1043 Buckley Highway, Route 171, Union, CT 06076-9520 **860-684-3770** Fax: 860-684-8830. 9AM-Noon T,Th; 9AM-Noon, 1-3PM W.

Vernon Town Clerk 14 Park Pl, Rockville, CT 06066 **860-870-3662** Fax: 860-870-3683. 8:30AM-4:30PM M-W; 8:30-7 Th; 8:30-1PM F. www.munic.state.ct.us/VERNON/

Voluntown Town Clerk PO Box 96, Voluntown, CT 06384-0096 (115 Main St, Town Hall). **860-376-4089** Fax: 860-376-3295. 9AM-2PM; 6-8PM T Evening. www.voluntown.gov

Wallingford Town Clerk Omit PO Box, Wallingford, CT 06492 (45 S. Main St, Municipal Bldg, Rm 108). **203-294-2145** Fax: 203-294-2150. 9AM-5PM.

Warren Town Clerk 7 Sackett Hill Rd, Town Hall, Warren, CT 06754 **860-868-0090** Fax: 860-868-7746. 10-4 W,Th; 10-N M,F.

Washington Town Clerk PO Box 383, Washington Depot, CT 06794 (2 Bryan Plaza). **860-868-2786** Fax: 860-868-3103. 9AM-Noon, 1-4:45PM.

Waterbury City Clerk 235 Grand St, City Hall, Waterbury, CT 06702 **203-574-6806** Fax: 203-574-6887. 8:30-4:30. Assessor, Property, Real Estate Sale records online.

Waterford Town Clerk 15 Rope Ferry Rd, Waterford, CT 06385 **860-444-5831** Fax: 860-437-0352. 8-4PM.

Watertown Town Clerk 37 DeForest St, Watertown, CT 06795 **860-945-5230** Fax: 860-945-2706. 9-5. www.watertownct.org

West Hartford Town Clerk 50 S. Main St, Rm 313 Town Hall Common, West Hartford, CT 06107-2431 **860-523-3148** Fax: 860-523-3522. 8:30AM-4:30PM. Assessor, Property records online.

West Haven City Clerk PO Box 526, West Haven, CT 06516 (355 Main St). **203-937-3534** Fax: 203-937-3706. 9AM-5PM. Assessor records online.

Westbrook Town Clerk 866 Boston Post Rd, Westbrook, CT 06498-1881 **860-399-3044** Fax: 860-399-3092. 9-4PM M-W & F; 9-7PM Th; 9AM-N F.

Weston Town Clerk PO Box 1007, Weston, CT 06883 (56 Norfield). **203-222-2616** Fax: 203-222-8871. 9AM-4:30PM. www.weston-ct.com Land, Marriage, Death, Trade Name, Grantor/Grantee records online.

Westport Town Clerk PO Box 549, Westport, CT 06881 (110 Myrtle Ave, 105). **203-341-1110** Fax: 203-341-1112. 8:30-4:30PM www.ci.westport.ct.us/govt/services Assessor records online.

Wethersfield Town Clerk 505 Silas Deane Highway, Wethersfield, CT 06109 **860-721-2880** Fax: 860-721-2994. 8AM-4:30PM. www.wethersfieldct.com/govt.htm Assessor, Property records online.

Willington Town Clerk 40 Old Farms Rd, Willington, CT 06279 **860-487-3121** Fax: 860-487-3103. 9AM-2PM (M 6-8PM). www.willingtonct.org

Wilton Town Clerk 238 Danbury Rd, Wilton, CT 06897 **203-563-0106** Fax: 203-563-0130. 8:30-4:30. www.munic.state.ct.us /wilton/wilton.htm Assessor records online.

Winchester Town Clerk 338 Main St, Town Hall, Winsted, CT 06098-1697 **860-738-6963** Fax: 860-738-6595. 8AM-4PM M-W, 8AM-7PM Th, 8AM-noon F. www.townofwinchester.org Property, Assessor records online.

Windham Town Clerk PO Box 94, Willimantic, CT 06226 (979 Main St). **860-465-3013** Fax: 860-465-3012. 8AM-5PM M-W; 8AM-7:30PM Th; 8AM-Noon F. www.windhamct.com

Windsor Locks Town Clerk 50 Church St, Town Office Bldg., Windsor Locks, CT 06096 **860-627-1441** 8-4 M-W; 8-6 Th; 8AM-1PM F. Assessor records online.

Windsor Town Clerk PO Box 472, Windsor, CT 06095-0472 (275 Broad St). **860-285-1902** Fax: 860-285-1909. 8-5 M,W-F; 8-6 T.

www.townofwindsorct.com Assessor, Real Estate records online.

Wolcott Town Clerk 10 Kenea Ave, Town Hall, Wolcott, CT 06716 **203-879-8100** Fax: 203-879-8105. 8:30-4:30 (Recording 4PM).

Woodbridge Town Clerk 11 Meetinghouse Lane, Woodbridge, CT 06525 **203-389-3422**

Fax: 203-389-3473. 8-4. www.munic.state.c t.us/woodbridge/townclerk.html Assessor records online.

Woodbury Town Clerk PO Box 369, Woodbury, CT 06798-3407 (275 Main St South). **203-263-2144** Fax: 203-263-4755. 8:30AM-4:30PM (Summer 8AM-4PM).

Woodstock Town Clerk 415 Route 169, Town Hall, Woodstock, CT 06281 **860-928-6595** Fax: 860-963-7557. 8:30AM-4:30PM M,T,Th; 8:30AM-6PM W; 8:30-3PM F.

Delaware

Organization: Delaware has 3 counties and 3 recording offices. The recording officer is the County Recorder in both jurisdictions. Delaware is in the Eastern Time Zone (EST).

Real Estate Records: Counties do not perform real estate searches, but will provide copies.

UCC Records: Financing statements are filed at the state level, except for real estate related collateral, which are filed only with the County Recorder. All counties perform UCC searches. Copy and certification fees vary.

Tax Lien Records: Federal tax liens on personal property of businesses are filed with the Secretary of State. Other federal and all state tax liens on personal property are filed with the County Recorder. Copy and certification fees vary.

Online Access: There is no statewide access to recorder or assessor information.

Kent County Recorder of Deeds 414 Federal St., County Admin. Bldg, Rm 218, Dover, DE 19901 **302-744-2314** Fax: 302-736-2035. 8:30AM-4:30PM. Sheriff Sale, Most Wanted records online.

New Castle County Recorder of Deeds 800 French St, 4th Fl, Wilmington, DE 19801 **302-395-7700** Fax: 302-395-7732. 9AM-5PM. www.ncc-deeds.com Real Estate, Property Assessor, Recorder, Deed, Marriage, Incs, Sex Offender, Wanted records online.

Sussex County Recorder of Deeds PO Box 827, Georgetown, DE 19947-0827 (Admin. Bldg, Lower Level). **302-855-7785** Fax: 302-855-7787. 8:30AM-4:30PM. Real Estate, Property Tax, Sheriff Sale records online.

District of Columbia

Organization: District of Columbia is in the Eastern Time Zone (EST).

Real Estate Records: The District does not perform real estate searches.

UCC Records: Financing statements are filed with the Recorder, including real estate related collateral. UCC searches performed for $30.00 per debtor name. Copies cost $2.25 per page.

Tax Lien Records: Federal tax liens on personal property of businesses are filed with the Secretary of State. Other federal and all state tax liens on personal property are filed with the Recorder.

Online Access: Search the recorders database at http://countyrecords.landata.com/WashDC. Registration is required; images are available for free, temporarily. Also, search the real property tax database for free at http://cfo.washingtondc.gov/services/tax/property/database.shtm.

District of Columbia Recorder of Deeds 515 D St NW, Rm 203, Washington, DC 20001 **202-727-5374, 202-727-7110** 8:30AM-4:30PM. Real Estate, Assessor, Recording, Deed, Judgment, Lien, UCC, Legislation, Most Wanted, Missing records online.

Florida

Organization: 67 counties, 67 recording offices. The recording officer is the Clerk of the Circuit Court. All transactions are recorded in the "Official Record," a grantor/grantee index. Some counties will search by type of transaction while others will return everything on the index. 57 counties are in the Eastern Time Zone (EST) and 10 are in the Central Time Zone (CST).

Real Estate Records: Any name searched in the "Official Records" will usually include all types of liens and property transfers for that name. Most counties will perform searches. In addition to the usual $1.00 per page copy fee, certification of documents usually cost $1.00 per document. Tax records are located at the Property Appraiser Office.

UCC Records: Financing statements are filed at the state level, and real estate related collateral at the Clerk of the Circuit Court. Until 1/2002, farm related financing was also filed at the clerk's office. All but a few counties will perform UCC searches. Use search request form UCC-11. Search fees are usually $1.00 per debtor name per year searched and include all lien and real estate transactions on record. Copies usually cost $1.00 per page.

Tax Lien Records: Federal tax liens on personal property of businesses are filed with the Secretary of State. All other federal and state tax liens on personal property are filed with the county Clerk of Circuit Court. Usually tax liens on personal property are filed in the same index with UCC financing statements and real estate transactions. Most counties will perform a tax lien as part of a UCC search. Copies usually cost $1.00 per page. Other Liens: Judgments, hospital, mechanics, sewer, ambulance.

Online Access: There are numerous county agencies that provide online access to records. Online access to the 51 county's Circuit Clerks of Courts is available free at www.myfloridacounty.com/services/officialrecords_intro.shtml.

On or after October 1, 2002, any person preparing or filing a document for recording in the Official Record may not include a Social Security Number in such document unless required by law. The Clerk of the Circuit Court cannot place an image or copy of the following documents on a publicly available Internet website for general public display: Military discharges; Death certificates; Court files, records or papers relating to Family Law, Juvenile Law or Probate Law cases.

Any person has the right to request the Clerk/County Recorder to redact/remove his Social Security Number from an image or copy of an Official Record that has been placed on such Clerk/County Recorder's publicly available Internet website.

Alachua County Clerk of Circuit Court PO Box 600, Gainesville, FL 32602 (12 S.E. 1st St., County Admin. Bldg.-Rm 151). **352-374-3625** Fax: 352-491-4649. 8:30AM-5PM. www.clerk-alachua-fl.org Property Appraiser, Real Estate, Lien, Vital Statistic, Recording, Traffic Citation records online.

Baker County Clerk of Circuit Court 339 E. MacClenny Ave, MacClenny, FL 32063 **904-259-0208** Fax: 904-259-4176. 8:30-5. Real Estate, Lien, Recording, Property online.

Bay County Clerk of Circuit Court PO Box 2269, Panama City, FL 32402 (300 E. 4th St, Courthouse). **850-747-5104** Fax: 850-747-5199. 8AM-4:30PM. www.baycoclerk.com Property Tax, Real Estate, Tax Lien, Recording, Appraiser, Property Sale online.

Bradford County Clerk of Circuit Court PO Drawer B, Starke, FL 32091 (945 N. Temple Ave). **904-966-6283** Fax: 904-964-4454. 8-5PM. www.myfloridacounty.com Real Estate, Appraisal, Deed, Judgment, Marriage, Lien, Court records online.

Brevard County Clerk of Circuit Court PO Box 2767, Titusville, FL 32781 (700 S. Park Ave., Bldg. #2). **321-264-5244/5350** Fax: 321-264-5246. www.clerk.co.brevard.fl.us Real Estate, Lien, Marriage, Recording, Tax Sale, Property Appraiser, Personal Property records online.

Broward County Director of County Records 115 S Andrews Ave, Rm 114, Records Division, Fort Lauderdale, FL 33301 **954-357-7281** Fax: 954-357-7267. 7:30AM-5PM. www.broward.org/records Property, Appraiser, Real Estate, Lien, Recording, Occ. License, Most Wanted, Arrest, Missing, Sex Offender records online.

Calhoun County Clerk of Circuit Court 20859 SE Central Ave, Rm 130, Blountstown, FL 32424 (425 E Central Ave, Rm 130). **850-674-4545** Fax: 850-674-5553. 8-4PM. www.calhounclerk.com Real Estate, Lien, Deed, Judgment, Recording records online.

Charlotte County Clerk of Circuit Court PO Box 510156, Punta Gorda, FL 33951-0156 (350 E Marion Ave). **941-637-2245** F-941-637-2172. 8-5. www.co.charlotte.fl.us Property Appraiser, Real Estate, Lien, Recording, Property Sale, Arrest, Most Wanted, Sex Offender records online.

Citrus County Clerk of Circuit Court 110 N. Apopka Ave. Rm101, Inverness, FL 34450-4299 **352-341-6468** Fax: 352-341-6477. 8AM-5PM. www.clerk.citrus.fl.us Property Appraiser, Real Estate, Lien, Deed,

Recording, Marriage, Property Tax, Sex Offender records online.

Clay County Clerk of Circuit Court PO Box 698, Green Cove Springs, FL 32043-0698 (825 N Orange Ave.). **904-284-6317** Fax: 904-284-6390. 8:30AM-4:30PM. http://clerk.co.clay.fl.us Appraiser, Real Estate, Lien, Recording, Tangible Personal Property, Property Tax, Most Wanted, Sex Offender records online.

Collier County Clerk of Circuit Court PO Box 413044, Naples, FL 34101-3044 (3301 Tamiami Trail East, Admin. Bldg, 4th Fl). **239-732-2646** Fax: 239-774-8003. 8AM-5PM (No recording after 4:30PM). www.clerk.collier.fl.us Property Appraiser, Real Estate, Lien, UCC, Vital Statistic, Recording, Tax Sale, Wanted, Missing Person, Property Tax records online.

Columbia County Clerk of Circuit Court PO Box 2069, Lake City, FL 32056-2069 (145 N. Hernando St). **386-758-1342** Fax: 386-758-1337.. www.columbiaclerk.com Real Estate, Lien, Recording, Probate, Property Tax, Appraiser, GIS, Occ License records online.

Dade County Clerk of Circuit Court 22 N.W. 1st St, Miami, FL 33128 **305-275-1155** Fax: 305-372-7775. www.metro-dade.com/c

lerk Real Estate, Recording, Judgment, Lien, Marriage, Tax Deed Sale, Property Appraiser, Property Tax records online.

De Soto County Clerk of Circuit Court 115 E. Oak St, Arcadia, FL 34266 (115 E. Oak St). **863-993-4876** Fax: 863-993-4669. 8AM-5PM. Real Estate, Lien, Recording, Property Tax, Inmate, Wanted records online.

Dixie County Clerk of Circuit Court PO Box 1206, Cross City, FL 32628 (Courthouse, 150 NE Cedar St.). **352-498-1200** Fax: 352-498-1201. 9AM-N,1-5PM. Real Estate, Lien, Recording records online.

Duval County Clerk of Circuit Court 330 E. Bay St #103, Courthouse, Jacksonville, FL 32202 **904-630-2043** Fax: 904-630-2959. 8:30AM-4:30PM. www.coj.net Property Appraiser, Real Estate, Lien, Recording, Grantor/Grantee, Vital Statistic, Occ. License records online.

Escambia County Clerk of Circuit Court 223 Palafox Pl, Old Courthouse, Pensacola, FL 32501 **850-595-3930** Fax: 850-595-4827. 8-5PM. www.clerk.co.escambia.fl.us Property Appraiser, Real Estate, Grantor/Grantee, Lien, Recording, Vital Statistic, Property Tax, Tax Sale records online.

Flagler County Clerk of Circuit Court PO Box 787, Recording Division, Bunnell, FL 32110 (Rm 115, 200 E. Moody Blvd.). **386-437-7433** Fax: 386-437-7406. 8AM-5PM. http://clerk.co.flagler.fl.us Appraiser, Recording, Real Estate, Lien, Most Wanted, Sex Offender, Property Sale records online.

Franklin County Clerk of Circuit Court 33 Market St #203, Apalachicola, FL 32320 **850-653-8861 x108 or x109** Fax: 850-653-2261. 8:30AM-4:30PM. www.franklinclerk.com Real Estate, Lien, Recording records online.

Gadsden County Clerk of Circuit Court PO Box 1649, Quincy, FL 32353-1649 (10 E. Jefferson St). **850-875-8601** Fax: 850-875-8612. www.clerk.co.gadsden.fl.us Real Estate, Recording, Judgment, Deed, Lien, Vital Statistic, Property Appraiser records online.

Gilchrist County Clerk of Circuit Court PO Box 37, Trenton, FL 32693 (112 S. Main St.). **352-463-3170** Fax: 352-463-3166. www.co.gilchrist.fl.us/cophone Real Estate, Property Appraiser, Lien, Recording, Deed, Judgment, Marriage, Death records online.

Glades County Clerk of Circuit Court PO Box 10, Moore Haven, FL 33471 (Highway 27 & 5th St, 500 Ave. J #102). **863-946-6010** Fax: 863-946-0560. 8AM-5PM. http://gladesclerk.com/ Real Estate, Lien, Recording records online.

Gulf County Clerk of Circuit Court 1000 Cecil G. Costin, Sr. Blvd. Rm. 148, Port St. Joe, FL 32456 **850-229-6112** Fax: 850-229-6174. 9AM-5PM. www.gulfclerk.com Real Estate, Lien, Deed, Judgment, Marriage, Death, Recording records online.

Hamilton County Clerk of Circuit Court 207 NE 1st St, Rm 106, Jasper, FL 32052 **386-792-1288** Fax: 386-792-3524. 8:30-4:30. Real Estate, Lien, Recording records online.

Hardee County Clerk of Circuit Court PO Drawer 1749, Wauchula, FL 33873 (417 W. Main St). **863-773-4174** Fax: 863-773-3295. 8AM-5PM; 8AM-4PM Recording hours. www.hardeeclerk.com Real Estate, Recording, Lien, Appraiser, Most Wanted, Arrest, Inmate, Warrant records online.

Hendry County Clerk of Circuit Court PO Box 1760, La Belle, FL 33975-1760 (25 E Hickapoochee Ave). **863-675-5217** Fax: 863-675-5238 www.hendryclerk.org 8:30-5. Real Estate, Recording, Lien records online.

Hernando County Clerk of Circuit Court 20 N. Main, Rm 215, Brooksville, FL 34601 **352-540-6768** Fax: 352-754-4243. www.clerk.co.hernando.fl.us Real Estate, Property Appraiser, Lien, Marriage, Recording, Wanted, Arrest records online.

Highlands Clerk of Circuit Court 590 S. Commerce Ave, Sebring, FL 33870 **863-402-6590** 8-5PM. www.clerk.co.highlands.fl.us Property Appraiser, Personal Property, Real Estate, Lien, Recording records online.

Hillsborough County Clerk of Circuit Court PO Box 3249, Tampa, FL 33601-1110 (419 Pierce St, Rm 114-K). **813-276-8100 x4367** Fax: 813-276-2114. 8AM-5PM. www.hillsclerk.com Property Appraiser, Personal Property, Real Estate, Lien, Deed, Recording, Warrant, Inmate, Repo/Impound records online.

Holmes County Clerk of Circuit Court PO Box 397, Bonifay, FL 32425 (201 N. Oklahoma St). **850-547-1102** Fax: 850-547-6630. 8AM-4PM. www.holmesclerk.com Real Estate, Lien, Recording records online.

Indian River County Clerk of Circuit Court PO Box 1028, Vero Beach, FL 32961-1028 (2000 16th Ave.). **772-770-5185 x184** 8:30-5PM. http://indian-river.fl.us Property Appraiser, Real Estate, Lien, Vital Statistic, Inmate, Criminal History records online.

Jackson County Clerk of Circuit Court PO Drawer 510, Marianna, FL 32447 (4445 E. Lafayette St). **850-482-9552** Fax: 850-482-7849. 8-4:30PM. www.jacksonclerk.com Real Estate, Lien, Recording, Marriage, Death, Probate, Property Tax records online.

Jefferson County Clerk of Circuit Court Courthouse, Rm 10, Monticello, FL 32344 **850-342-0218 x27** Fax: 850-342-0222. 8AM-5PM. http://co.jefferson.fl.us Property, Real Estate, Lien, Recording records online.

Lafayette County Clerk of Circuit Court PO Box 88, Mayo, FL 32066 (Main & Fletcher Sts). **386-294-1600** Fax: 386-294-4231. 8AM-5PM. www.lafayetteclerk.com Real Estate, Lien, Recording records online.

Lake County Clerk of Circuit Court PO Box 7800, Tavares, FL 32778-7800 (550 W. Main St). **352-253-2600** Fax: 352-253-2616. 8:30AM-5PM www.lakecountyclerk.org Property Appraiser, Recording, Real Estate, Lien, Marriage, Death records online.

Lee County Clerk of Circuit Court PO Box 2278, Fort Myers, FL 33902-2278 (2115 Second St, 2nd Fl). **239-335-2283** 7:45AM-5PM. http://leeclerk.org/index.asp Property Appraiser, Real Estate, Occ. License, Lien, Recording, Business Property records online.

Leon County Clerk of Circuit Court PO Box 726, Tallahassee, FL 32302 (301 S. Monroe St, Rm 123). **850-577-4030** Fax: 850-921-1310. www.clerk.leon.fl.us Property Appraiser, Real Estate, Lien, Marriage, Recording, Permit, Foreclosure, Contractor, Most Wanted records online.

Levy County Clerk of Circuit Court PO Drawer 610, Bronson, FL 32621 (355 N. Court St.). **352-486-5229** Fax: 352-486-5166. 8AM-5PM. www.levyclerk.com Real Estate, Lien, Recording, Property Tax, Property Appraiser, Warrant records online.

Liberty County Clerk of Circuit Court PO Box 399, Bristol, FL 32321 (10818 NW S.R. 20, Courthouse). **850-643-2215** Fax: 850-643-2866. 8AM-5PM. www.libertyclerk.com Real Estate, Lien, Recording records online.

Madison County Clerk of Circuit Court PO Box 237, Madison, FL 32341 (101 S. Range St, Rm 108). **850-973-1500** Fax: 850-973-2059. 8AM-5PM. www.madisonclerk.com Real Estate, Lien, Recording, Property, Appraiser, Sale records online.

Manatee County Clerk of Circuit Court PO Box 25400, Bradenton, FL 34206 (1115 Manatee Ave West). **941-741-4041** Fax: 941-741-4082. www.manateeclerk.com Property Appraiser, Real Estate, Lien, Recording, Deed, Judgment, Death, Marriage, Condominium, Foreclosure, Tax Deed Sale, Most Wanted records online. 8:30AM-5PM.

Marion County Clerk of Circuit Court PO Box 1030, Ocala, FL 34478-1030 (110 N.W. First Ave). **352-620-3925** Fax: 352-620-3930. 8-5PM. www.marioncountyclerk.org

Property Appraiser, Real Estate, Recording, Tax Collector, Tax Deed Sale, Inmate, Sex Offender records online.

Martin County Clerk of Circuit Court PO Box 9016, Stuart, FL 34995 (100 E. Ocean Blvd, 3rd Fl). **772-288-5554** Fax: 772-223-7920. 8AM-5PM. www.martin.fl.us/GOVT Property Appraiser, Real Estate, Lien, Recording, Personal Property records online.

Monroe County Clerk of Circuit Court PO Box 1980, Key West, FL 33041-1980 (500 Whitehead St, Courthouse). **305-292-3540** Fax: 305-295-3623. 8:30AM-4:45PM. www.co.monroe.fl.us Real Estate, Recording, Deed, Lien, Property Tax, Occ. License, Arrest, Inmate, Warrant records online.

Nassau County Clerk of Circuit Court PO Box 456, Fernandina, FL 32035 (191 Nassau Pl). **904-548-4600** Fax: 904-548-4508. 9AM-5PM (Recording Hours: 9AM-4PM). www.nassauclerk.com Real Estate, Lien, Recording records online.

Okaloosa County Clerk of Circuit Court PO Drawer 1359, Crestview, FL 32536 (101 E. James Lee Blvd.). **850-689-5847** Fax: 850-689-5886. 8-5PM. www.clerkofcourts.cc Property Appraiser, Real Estate, Lien, Recording, Vital Statistic, Property Tax, Occ. License records online.

Okeechobee Clerk of Circuit Court 304 N.W. 2nd St, Rm 101, Okeechobee, FL 34972 **863-763-2131** www.clerk.co.okeechobee.fl.us Property, Recording, Appraiser, GIS, Personal Property, Property Sale records online.

Orange County Comptroller PO Box 38, Official Records Dept., Orlando, FL 32802-0038 (401 S. Rosaland Ave.). **407-836-5115** Fax: 407-836-5120. 7:30AM-4:30PM. www.occompt.com Property Appraiser, Recording, Real Estate, Lien, Vital Statistic, Land Sale, Personal Property, Property Tax, Contractor records online.

Osceola County Clerk of Circuit Court 2 Courthouse Sq, #2000, Kissimmee, FL 34741-5491 **407-343-3500 x3517** Fax: 407-343-3534. 8:30-5PM; www.osceolaclerk.com Real Estate, Property Tax, Appraiser, Occ. License, Inmate records online.

Palm Beach County Clerk of Circuit Court PO Box 4177, West Palm Beach, FL 33402 (205 N. Dixie Highway, Rm 4.2500). **561-355-2991** Fax: 561-355-2633. 8AM-5PM. www.pbcountyclerk.com Property Appraiser, Real Estate, Deed, Lien, Judgment, Recording, Vital Statistic, Property Tax, Personal Property, Occ License, Warrant, Sexual Predator, Sheriff Booking records online.

Pasco County Clerk of Circuit Court 38053 Live Oak Ave, Rm 205, Dade City, FL 33523-3894 **352-521-4469 or 4408** 8:30-5. www.pascoclerk.com Property Appraiser, Real Estate, Lien, Vital Statistic, Recording, Occ License, Personal Property, Wanted, Sexual Predator, Cont'r/Permit records online.

Pinellas County Clerk of Circuit Court 315 Court St, Rm 150, Clearwater, FL 33756 **727-464-4876** Fax: 727-464-4383. 8-5PM. http://clerk.co.pinellas.fl.us Property Appraiser, Real Estate, Lien, Judgment, Recording, Traffic/Boating Fine, Tax Collector, Personal Property, Tax Deed Sale, Accident Report records online.

Polk County Clerk of Circuit Court PO Box 9000 Drawer CC-8, Bartow, FL 33831-9000 (255 N. Broadway). **863-534-4516** Fax: 863-534-4008. 8AM-4:30PM. www.polkcountyclerk.net Property Appraiser, Real Estate, Lien, Vital Statistic, Recording, Personal Property, Occ License Account, Tax Collector, Tax Deed Sale, Warrant, Most Wanted records online.

Putnam County Clerk of Circuit Court PO Box 758, Palatka, FL 32178-0758 (410 St. Johns Ave). **386-329-0361** Fax: 386-329-0888. 8:30AM-5PM. www.putnam-fl.com/clk/ Real Estate, Lien, Recording, Tax Appraiser, Property, Occ License, Warrant, Jail Log, Most Wanted records online.

Santa Rosa County Clerk of Circuit Court PO Box 472, Milton, FL 32572 (Clerk of Courts Recording Dept, 6495 Caroline St). **850-983-1966** Fax: 850-983-1991. 8-4:30. www.co.santa-rosa.fl.us/santa_rosa/clerk/ Property Appraiser, Real Estate, Lien, Deed, Recording, Marriage, Death, Judgment, Tax Collector, Fugitive records online.

Sarasota Clerk of Circuit Court PO Box 3079, Sarasota, FL 34230 (2000 Main). **941-861-7400** 8:30-5. www.sarasotaclerk.com Real Estate, Lien, Vital Statistic, Recording, Appraiser, Personal Property, records online.

Seminole County Clerk of Circuit Court PO Box 8099-Attn Recording Dept, Sanford, FL 32772-8099 (301 N. Park Ave, Rm A-132). **407-665-4336** 8AM-4:30PM. www.seminoleclerk.org Property Appraiser, Real Estate, Lien, Recording records online.

St. Johns County Clerk of Circuit Court PO Drawer 300, St. Augustine, FL 32085-0300 (4010 Lewis Speedway). **904-819-3600** Fax: 904-819-3661. 8AM-5PM (No Recording after 4:15PM). www.co.st-johns.fl.us Property Appraiser, Real Estate, Lien, Recording, Civil, Probate, UCC,

Property Tax, Occ. License, Most Wanted, Sex Offender records online.

St. Lucie County Clerk of Circuit Court PO Box 700, Fort Pierce, FL 34954 (221 S. Indian River Dr). **772-462-6928** Fax: 772-462-1283. 8AM-5PM. www.stlucieco.gov Property Appraiser, Real Estate, Lien, Recording, Marriage, Fictitious Name, Personal Property, sex offender records online.

Sumter County Clerk of Circuit Court 209 N. Florida St, Rm 106, Bushnell, FL 33513 **352-793-0215** Fax: 352-793-0218. 8:30AM-5PM. Real Estate, Lien, Recording, Property Tax, Occ License records online.

Suwannee County Clerk of Circuit Court 200 S. Ohio Ave, Live Oak, FL 32060 **386-362-0554** Fax: 386-362-0548. 8:30AM-4:45PM. www.suwclerk.org Real Estate, Lien, Deed, Recording, Property Tax, Marriage, Inmate, Wanted records online.

Taylor County Clerk of Circuit Court PO Box 620, Perry, FL 32348 (108 N. Jefferson St). **850-838-3506** Fax: 850-838-3549. 8AM-5PM. www.taylorclerk.com Recording, Deed, Lien, Judgment, Commissioner records online.

Union County Clerk of Circuit Court State Rd 100, Courthouse Rm 103, Lake Butler, FL 32054 **386-496-3711** Fax: 386-496-1718. 8AM-5PM. Real Estate, Lien, Recording, Property, GIS records online.

Volusia County Clerk of Circuit Court PO Box 6043, Deland, FL 32721 (101 N Alabama). **386-736-5912** Fax: 386-740-5104. 8AM-4:30PM. www.clerk.org Property Appraiser, Real Estate, Lien, Vital Statistic, Recording, Citation Violation, Arrest, Property Sale, GIS, Inmate, Tax Deed Sale, Court, Personal Property records online.

Wakulla County Clerk of Circuit Court 3056 Crawfordville Hwy, County Court House, Crawfordville, FL 32327 **850-926-0905** Fax: 850-926-0938. 8AM-4PM. Real Estate, Lien, Recording, Property Appraiser records online.

Walton County Clerk of Circuit Court PO Box 1260, De Funiak Springs, FL 32433 (571 US Highway 90 East). **850-892-8115** Fax: 850-892-7551 www.co.walton.fl.us/clerk 8-4. Real Estate, Lien, Vital Statistic, Grantor/Grantee, Property Tax records online.

Washington County Clerk of Circuit Court PO Box 647, Chipley, FL 32428 (1293 Jackson Ave, Bldg 100). **850-638-6285** Fax: 850-638-6297. 8AM-4PM. Recording, Deed, Judgment, Lien, Appraiser, Property Tax, Property Sale records online.

Georgia

Organization: 159 counties, 159 recording offices. The recording officer is the Clerk of Superior Court. All transactions are recorded in a "General Execution Docket." The entire state is in the Eastern Time Zone (EST).

Real Estate Records: Most counties will not perform real estate searches. Copy fees are the same as for UCC. Certification fees are usually $2.00 per document - $1.00 for seal and $1.00 for stamp - plus $.50 per page.

UCC Records: There is no central state agency office for UCC. Financing statements are filed only with the Clerk of Superior Court and one can file in any county. Their system, as of January 1, 1995, merges all new UCC filings into a central statewide database, and allows statewide searching for new filings only from any county office. However, filings prior to that date will remain at the county offices. Only a few counties will perform local UCC searches. Use search request form UCC-11 for local searches. Search fees vary from $2.50 to $25.00 per debtor name. Copies usually cost $.25 per page if you make it and $1.00 if the county makes it.

Tax Lien Records: All tax liens on personal property are filed with the county Clerk of Superior Court in a "General Execution Docket" (grantor/grantee) or "Lien Index." Most counties will not perform tax lien searches. Copy fees are the same as for UCC. Other Liens: Judgments, hospital, materialman, county tax, lis pendens, child support, labor, mechanics.

Online Access: The Georgia Superior Court Clerk's Cooperative Authority (GSCCCA) at www.gsccca.org/search offers free access to three state indices. The Real Estate Index contains property transactions from all counties since 01/01/99. The Lien Index includes lines filed on real and personal property. As we go to press, all but 9 counites on on this system, but eventually this will be a statewide system. Throughput varies, but is generally form 01/10/2002 forward. The UCC Index contains UCC financing statement data from all counties since January 1, 1995, and can be searched by name, taxpayer ID, file date and file number. Additionally, the actual image of the corresponding UCC statement can be downloaded for a fee. Go to the website for details.

Appling Superior Court Clerk PO Box 269, Baxley, GA 31513 (110 Tippins St.). **912-367-8126** Fax: 912-367-8180. 8AM-5PM. RE Deed, Lien, UCC records online.

Atkinson Superior Court Clerk PO Box 6, Pearson, GA 31642 (Highway 441 South). **912-422-3343** Fax: 912-422-7025. 8AM-N, 1-5PM. RE Deed, UCC records online.

Bacon Superior Court Clerk PO Box 376, Alma, GA 31510 (502 W 12th St, #304). **912-632-4915** Fax: 912-632-6545. 9AM-5PM. RE Deed, Lien, UCC records online.

Baker Superior Court Clerk PO Box 10, Newton, GA 39870 (Courthouse Way). **229-734-3004** Fax: 229-734-7770. 9AM-5PM. RE Deed, Lien, UCC records online.

Baldwin Superior Court Clerk PO Drawer 987, Milledgeville, GA 31059 (121 N. Wilkinson St. #209). **478-445-4007** Fax: 478-445-1404. 8:30AM-5PM. RE Deed, Lien, UCC records online.

Banks Superior Court Clerk 144 Yonah Homer Rd #8, Homer, GA 30547-2614 **706-677-6243** Fax: 706-677-6294. 8AM-5PM. RE Deed, UCC, Lien records online.

Barrow Superior Court Clerk PO Box 1280, Winder, GA 30680 (30 N. Broad St). **770-307-3035** 8AM-5PM. RE Deed, Lien, UCC records online.

Bartow Superior Court Clerk 135 W. Cherokee Ave., #233, Cartersville, GA 30120 **770-387-5025** 8AM-5PM. RE Deed, UCC, Lien records online.

Ben Hill Superior Court Clerk PO Box 1104, Fitzgerald, GA 31750-1104 (401 E. Central Ave). **229-426-5135** Fax: 229-426-5487. 8:30AM-4:30PM. RE Deed, UCC, Lien records online.

Berrien Superior Court Clerk 101 E. Marion Ave. #3, Nashville, GA 31639 **229-686-5506** 8AM-5PM. RE Deed, Lien, UCC records online.

Bibb Superior Court Clerk PO Box 1015, Macon, GA 31202-1015 (601 Mulberry St). **478-621-6527** Fax: 478-621-6033. 8:30AM-5PM. RE Deed, UCC, Property, Lien, Finance Statement records online.

Bleckley Superior Court Clerk 306 SE 2nd St, Cochran, GA 31014 **478-934-3210** Fax: 478-934-6671. 8:30AM-5PM. RE Deed, Lien, UCC records online.

Brantley Superior Court Clerk PO Box 1067, Nahunta, GA 31553 (117 Brantley St.). **912-462-5635** Fax: 912-462-5538. 8AM-5. RE Deed, Lien, UCC records online.

Brooks Superior Court Clerk PO Box 630, Quitman, GA 31643 (Screven St Courthouse). **229-263-4747** Fax: 229-263-5050. 8AM-5PM. RE Deed, Lien, UCC records online.

Bryan Superior Court Clerk PO Box 670, Pembroke, GA 31321 (151 S. College St). **912-653-3872** Fax: 912-653-3805. 8AM-5PM. RE Deed, UCC, Lien, Notary, Plat records online.

Bulloch Superior Court Clerk 20 Siebald St, Judicial Annex, Statesboro, GA 30458 **912-764-9009** Fax: 912-764-5953. 8AM-5PM. RE Deed, Lien, UCC records online.

Burke Superior Court Clerk PO Box 803, Waynesboro, GA 30830-0803 (111 E. 6th St. Rm 107). **706-554-2279** Fax: 706-554-7887. 9AM-5PM. RE Deed, UCC, Lien, Plat records online.

Butts Superior Court Clerk PO Box 320, Jackson, GA 30233 (26 Third St). **770-775-8215** Fax: 770-504-1359. 8AM-5PM. RE Deed, UCC, Lien records online.

Calhoun Superior Court Clerk PO Box 69, Morgan, GA 39866 (Courthouse Sq, 111 School St). **229-849-2715** Fax: 229-849-0072. 8-5. RE Deed, UCC records online.

Camden Superior Court Clerk PO Box 578, Woodbine, GA 31569-0578 (200 E. 4th St., Courthouse Sq). **912-576-5622** 9AM-5PM. RE Deed, Lien, UCC records online.

Candler Superior Court Clerk PO Drawer 830, Metter, GA 30439 (355 S. Broad St, West). **912-685-5257** Fax: 912-685-2160. 8:30-5. RE Deed, Lien, UCC records online.

Carroll Superior Court Clerk PO Box 1620, Carrollton, GA 30112 (311 Newnan St, Rm 203). **770-830-5830** Fax: 770-214-3584. 8AM-5PM. RE Deed, UCC, Notary Public, Lien records online.

Catoosa Superior Court Clerk 875 Lafayette St, Courthouse, Ringgold, GA 30736 **706-935-4231** Fax: none. 8:30AM-5PM. RE Deed, Lien, UCC records online.

Charlton Superior Court Clerk PO Box 760, Folkston, GA 31537 (100 S. Third St.). **912-496-2354** Fax: 912-496-3882. 8AM-5PM. RE Deed, Lien, UCC records online.

Chatham Superior Court Clerk PO Box 10227, Savannah, GA 31412 (133 Montgomery St, Rm. 304). **912-652-7214** Fax: 912-652-7380. 8AM-5PM. www.chathamcourts.org RE Deed, Lien, UCC records online.

Chattahoochee Superior Court Clerk PO Box 120, Cusseta, GA 31805-0120 (Broad St Courthouse). **706-989-3424** Fax: 706-989-0396. 8AM-5PM. RE Deed, Lien, UCC records online.

Chattooga Superior Court Clerk PO Box 159, Summerville, GA 30747 (Commerce St Courthouse). **706-857-0706** Fax: 706-857-0686. 8:30AM-5PM. RE Deed, Lien, UCC records online.

Cherokee Superior Court Clerk 90 North St, #G-170, Canton, GA 30114 (90 North St, #G-170). **678-493-6531** 8AM-5PM. www.cherokeega.org RE Deed, UCC, Sex Offender, Inmate records online.

Clarke Superior Court Clerk PO Box 1805, Athens, GA 30603 (325 E. Washington St, Rm 100). **706-613-3196** Fax: 706-613-3189. 8AM-5PM. RE Deed, UCC, Property, Inmate records online.

Clay Superior Court Clerk PO Box 550, Fort Gaines, GA 39851 (210 Washington St). **229-768-2631** Fax: 229-768-3047. 8AM-4:30. RE Deed, UCC, Lien records online.

Clayton Superior Court Clerk 9151 Tara Blvd, Rm 202, Jonesboro, GA 30236 (physical address #1CL25). **770-477-3395** Fax: 770-477-3490. 8-5. www.co.clayton.ga.us/superior_court/clerk_of_courts/ Real Estate, UCC, Lien, Property Tax records online.

Clinch Superior Court Clerk PO Box 433, Homerville, GA 31634 (Courthouse). **912-487-5854** Fax: 912-487-3083. 8AM-5PM. RE Deed, Lien, UCC records online.

Cobb Superior Court Clerk PO Box 3490, Marietta, GA 30061 (10 E. Park Sq). **770-528-1363** Fax: 770-528-1325. 8AM-5PM. www.cobbgasupctclk.com Real Estate, Grantor/Grantee, UCC, Deed, Property Tax records online.

Coffee Superior Court Clerk 101 S. Peterson Ave., Courthouse, Douglas, GA 31533 (#218-B). **912-384-2865** 8:30AM-5PM. RE Deed, Lien, UCC records online.

Colquitt Superior Court Clerk PO Box 2827, Moultrie, GA 31776-2827 (Rm 214, #9 S. Main St.). **229-616-7420** Fax: 229-616-7029. 8-5. RE Deed, UCC, Lien, Notary, Public records online.

Columbia Superior Court Clerk PO Box 2930, Evans, GA 30809 (640 Ronald Regan Dr). **706-312-7139** 8-5. RE Deed, UCC, Lien, Sex Offender, Property records online.

Cook Superior Court Clerk 212 N. Hutchinson Ave, Adel, GA 31620-2497 **229-896-7717** 8:30AM-4:30PM. RE Deed, Lien, UCC records online.

Coweta Superior Court Clerk 200 Court Sq, Courthouse, First Fl, Newnan, GA 30263 **770-254-2690** Fax: 770-254-3700. 8AM-5PM. RE Deed, UCC, Lien records online.

Crawford Superior Court Clerk PO Box 1037, Roberta, GA 31078-1037 (100 GA Hwy 42 South). **478-836-3328** 9AM-5. RE Deed, Lien, UCC records online.

Crisp Superior Court Clerk PO Box 747, Cordele, GA 31010-0747 (210 7 St South). **229-276-2616** Fax: 229-273-5730. 8:30AM-5PM. RE Deed, Lien, UCC records online.

Dade Superior Court Clerk PO Box 417, Trenton GA 30752 (Main St-US Hiway 11) **706-657-4778** Fax: 706-657-8284. 8:30AM-5PM. RE Deed, Lien, UCC records online.

Dawson Superior Court Clerk 25 Tucker Ave, #106, Dawsonville, GA 30534-0222 **706-344-3510** Fax: 706-344-3511. 8AM-5PM. RE Deed, UCC, Lien records online.

De Kalb Superior Court Clerk 556 N. McDonough St, Rm 208, Decatur, GA 30030 **404-371-2836** 7:30AM-6PM. RE Deed, UCC, Property Tax, records online.

Decatur Superior Court Clerk PO Box 336, Bainbridge, GA 39818 (112 W Water St). **229-248-3025** Fax: 229-248-3029. 8AM-5PM. RE Deed, Lien, UCC records online.

Dodge Superior Court Clerk PO Box 4276, Eastman, GA 31023-4276 (Anson Ave). **478-374-2871** Fax: 478-374-3035. 9AM-N, 1-5PM. RE Deed, Lien, UCC records online.

Dooly Superior Court Clerk PO Box 326, Vienna, GA 31092-0326 (104 Second St, Rm 12). **229-268-4234** Fax: 229-268-6142. 8:30-5. RE Deed, Lien, UCC records online.

Dougherty Superior Court Clerk PO Box 1827, Albany, GA 31701 (225 Pine Ave, Rm 126). **229-431-2198** Fax: 229-431-2850. 8:30AM-5PM. www.albany.ga.us Real Estate, Personal Property, Tax, Court, Deed, Mortgage, Tax Assessor, Personal Property, UCC, Death, Divorce, Trade Name records online.

Douglas Superior Court Clerk 8700 Hospital Dr., Courthouse, Douglasville, GA 30134 **770-920-7449** 8AM-5PM. RE Deed, Lien, UCC records online.

Early Superior Court Clerk PO Box 849, Blakely, GA 39823 (Courthouse, Court Sq). **229-723-3033** Fax: 229-723-4411. 8AM-5PM. RE Deed, Lien, UCC records online.

Echols Superior Court Clerk PO Box 213, Statenville, GA 31648 (110 Highway 94 East). **229-559-5642** Fax: 229-559-5792. 8AM-Noon, 1-4:30PM. RE Deed, Lien, UCC records online.

Effingham Superior Court Clerk PO Box 387, Springfield, GA 31329-0387 (901 N. Pine St). **912-754-2118** 8:30AM-5PM. RE Deed, UCC, Lien records online.

Elbert Superior Court Clerk PO Box 619, Elberton, GA 30635 (12 Oliver St). **706-283-2005** Fax: 706-213-7286. 8-5. RE Deed, UCC, Lien, Plat Recording records online.

Emanuel Superior Court Clerk PO Box 627, Swainsboro, GA 30401 (Court St). **478-237-8911** Fax: 478-237-2173. 8AM-5PM. RE Deed, UCC records online.

Evans Superior Court Clerk PO Box 845, Claxton, GA 30417 (123 W. Main St). **912-739-3868** Fax: 912-739-2504. 8AM-5PM. RE Deed, Lien, UCC records online.

Fannin Superior Court Clerk PO Box 1300, Blue Ridge, GA 30513 (420 W. Main St., Courthouse). **706-632-2039** 9AM-5PM. RE Deed, Lien, UCC records online.

Fayette Superior Court Clerk PO Box 130, Fayetteville, GA 30214 (1 Center Dr, 1st Fl). **770-716-4290** Fax: 770-716-4868. 8-4:30. www.admin.co.fayette.ga.us Assessor, Real Estate, UCC, Lien records online.

Floyd Superior Court Clerk PO Box 1110, Rome, GA 30162-1110 (3 Gov't Plaza, #103). **706-291-5190** Fax: 706-233-0035. 8-5. RE Deed, Lien, UCC records online.

Forsyth Superior Court Clerk 100 Courthouse Sq, Rm 010, Cumming, GA 30040 **770-781-2120** Fax: 770-886-2858. 8:30AM-5PM. www.forsythco.com RE Deed, Lien, UCC records online.

Franklin Superior Court Clerk PO Box 70, Carnesville, GA 30521 (9592 Lavonia Rd.). **706-384-2514** Fax: 706-384-4384. 8AM-5PM. RE Deed, Lien, UCC records online.

Fulton Superior Court Clerk 136 Pryor St, Atlanta, GA 30303 **404-730-5300** 8:30AM-

5PM. www.fcclk.org RE Deed, Lien, UCC records online.

Gilmer Superior Court Clerk 1 West Side Sq, Courthouse, Box #30, Ellijay, GA 30540 **706-635-4462** Fax: 706-635-1462. 8:30AM-5PM. RE Deed, Lien, UCC records online.

Glascock Superior Court Clerk PO Box 231, Gibson, GA 30810 (62E Main St) **706-598-2084** Fax: 706-598-2577. 8AM-Noon,1-5PM. RE Deed, UCC, Lien records online.

Glynn Superior Court Clerk PO Box 1355, Brunswick, GA 31521-1355 (701 H St). **912-554-7313** Fax: 912-267-5625. 8:30AM-5PM. Assessor, Property, Recording, UCC, Lien records online.

Gordon Superior Court Clerk 100 Wall St., Courthouse, #102, Calhoun, GA 30701 **706-629-9533** Fax: 706-629-2139. 8:30AM-5PM. RE Deed, Lien, UCC records online.

Grady Superior Court Clerk Box 8, 250 N. Broad St, Cairo, GA 39828 **229-377-2912** 8:30-5. RE Deed, Lien, UCC records online.

Greene Superior Court Clerk 113 N Main St, Courthouse, #109, Greensboro, GA 30642-1107 **706-453-3340** Fax: 706-453-9179. 8-5PM. RE Deed, UCC, Lien records online.

Gwinnett Superior Court Clerk PO Box 880, Lawrenceville, GA 30046 (75 Langley Dr). **770-822-8100** 8AM-5PM. www.gwinnettcourts.com Property, Deed, UCC, Judgment, Lien records online.

Habersham Superior Court Clerk 555 Monroe St, Unit 35, Clarkesville, GA 30523 **706-754-2923** Fax: 706-754-8779. 8AM-5PM. RE Deed, UCC, Lien records online.

Hall Superior Court Clerk PO Box 1336, Gainesville, GA 30503-1336 (Courthouse, 111 Spring St.). **770-531-7052** Fax: 770-536-0702. 8AM-5PM. www.hallcounty.org RE Deed, UCC, Lien, Plat records online.

Hancock Superior Court Clerk PO Box 451, Sparta, GA 31087 **706-444-6644** Fax: 706-444-5685. 9AM-5PM. RE Deed, Lien, UCC records online.

Haralson Superior Court Clerk PO Drawer 849, Buchanan, GA 30113 (4485 State Highway 120 East). **770-646-2005** Fax: 770-646-2035. 8:30AM-5PM. RE Deed, Lien, UCC records online.

Harris Superior Court Clerk PO Box 528, Hamilton, GA 31811 (102 College St, Highway 27). **706-628-5570** Fax: 706-628-7039. 8AM-5PM. RE Deed, Lien, UCC records online.

Hart Superior Court Clerk PO Box 386, Hartwell, GA 30643 (185 W. Franklin St,

Rm 1). **706-376-7189** Fax: 706-376-1277. 8:30-5. RE Deed, Lien, UCC records online.

Heard Superior Court Clerk PO Box 249, Franklin, GA 30217 (215 E. Court Sq.). **706-675-3301** Fax: 706-675-0819. 8:30AM-5PM. RE Deed, Lien, UCC records online.

Henry Superior Court Clerk #1 Courthouse Sq, McDonough, GA 30253 **770-954-2121** 8AM-5PM. www.co.henry.ga.us RE Deed, UCC, Property Tax, Assessor records online.

Houston Superior Court Clerk 201 N Perry Pkwy, Perry, GA **478-987-2170** Fax: 478-987-3252. www.houstoncountyga.com Assessor, RE deed, Plat, Lien records online.

Irwin Superior Court Clerk 113 N Irwin Ave, Ocilla, GA 31774 **229-468-5356** Fax: 229-468-9753. 8AM-5PM. RE Deed, UCC records online.

Jackson Superior Court Clerk PO Box 7, Jefferson, GA 30549 (85 Washington St). **706-367-6360** Fax: 706-367-2468. 8AM-5PM. RE Deed, Lien, UCC records online.

Jasper Superior Court Clerk Courthouse, Monticello, GA 31064. **706-468-4901** Fax: 706-468-4946. 8AM-5PM. RE Deed, UCC, Lien records online.

Jeff Davis Superior Court Clerk PO Box 429, Hazlehurst, GA 31539 (Jeff Davis St). **912-375-6615** Fax: 912-375-6637. 8AM-5PM. RE Deed, Lien, UCC records online.

Jefferson Superior Court Clerk PO Box 151, Louisville, GA 30434 (202 E. Broad St). **478-625-7922** Fax: 478-625-9589. 9AM-5PM. RE Deed, Lien, UCC records online.

Jenkins Superior Court Clerk PO Box 659, Millen, GA 30442 (Harvey St Courthouse). **478-982-4683** Fax: 478-982-1274. 8:30AM-1-5PM. RE Deed, Lien, UCC records online.

Johnson Superior Court Clerk PO Box 321, Wrightsville, GA 31096 **478-864-3484** Fax: 478-864-1343. 9AM-5PM. RE Deed, Lien, UCC records online.

Jones Superior Court Clerk PO Box 39, Gray, GA 31032 (Jefferson St). **478-986-6671** 8:30AM-4:30PM. RE Deed, Lien, UCC records online.

Lamar Superior Court Clerk 326 Thomaston St, Courthouse, Barnesville, GA 30204-1669 **770-358-5145** Fax: 770-358-5814. 8AM-5PM. RE Deed, Lien, UCC records online.

Lanier Superior Court Clerk 100 Main St, County Courthouse, Lakeland, GA 31635 **229-482-3594** Fax: 229-482-8333. 8AM-N, 1-5PM. RE Deed, Lien, UCC records online.

Laurens Superior Court Clerk PO Box 2028, Dublin, GA 31040 (101 N. Jefferson). **478-272-3210** Fax: 478-275-2595. 8:30-5:30. RE Deed, Lien, UCC records online.

Lee Superior Court Clerk PO Box 49, Leesburg, GA 31763 (100 Leslie Highway). **229-759-6018** Fax: 229-759-6049. 8AM-5PM. RE Deed, UCC, Lien records online.

Liberty Superior Court Clerk PO Box 50, Hinesville, GA 31310 (100 Main St.). **912-876-3625** Fax: 912-369-5463. 8AM-5PM. www.libertyco.com RE Deed, UCC, Lien records online.

Lincoln Superior Court Clerk PO Box 340, Lincolnton, GA 30817 (210 Humphrey St, Rm 103). **706-359-5505** 9AM-Noon, 1PM-5PM. RE Deed, UCC records online.

Long Superior Court Clerk PO Box 458, Ludowici, GA 31316 (49 S MacDonald St). **912-545-2123** Fax: 912-545-2020. 8:30AM-5PM. RE Deed, Lien, UCC records online.

Lowndes Superior Court Clerk PO Box 1349, Valdosta, GA 31601-1349 (108 E. Central Ave.). **229-333-5125** Fax: 229-333-7637. 8AM-5PM. RE Deed, Lien, UCC records online.

Lumpkin Superior Court Clerk 99 Courthouse Hill, #D, Dahlonega, GA 30533-0541 **706-864-3736** Fax: 706-864-5298. 8-5. RE Deed, UCC, Lien records online.

Macon Superior Court Clerk PO Box 337, Oglethorpe, GA 31068 (121 Sumter St). **478-472-7661** Fax: 478-472-4775. 8:30AM-5PM. RE Deed, Lien, UCC records online.

Madison Superior Court Clerk PO Box 247, Danielsville, GA 30633 (Courthouse Sq, Hwy 29). **706-795-3352** Fax: 706-795-2209. 8AM-5PM. RE Deed, Lien, UCC records online.

Marion Superior Court Clerk PO Box 41, Buena Vista, GA 31803 (100 N Broad St). **229-649-7321** Fax: 229-649-7931. 9AM-5PM. RE Deed, Lien, UCC records online.

McDuffie Superior Court Clerk PO Box 158, Thomson, GA 30824-0150 (337 Main St, Rm 101). **706-595-2134** Fax: 706-595-9150. 8AM-5PM. RE Deed, Lien, UCC records online.

McIntosh Superior Court Clerk PO Box 1661, Darien, GA 31305 (310 Northway). **912-437-6641** Fax: 912-437-6673. 8AM-4:30PM. Deed (2000-present), UCC, Notary, Lien records online.

Meriwether Superior Court Clerk PO Box 160, Greenville, GA 30222-0160 (100 Court

Sq). **706-672-4416** Fax: 706-672-9465. 8:30-5PM. RE Deed, Lien, UCC records online.

Miller Superior Court Clerk PO Box 66, Colquitt, GA 39837 (155 First St). **229-758-4102** Fax: 229-758-6585. 9AM-5PM. RE Deed, Lien, UCC records online.

Mitchell Superior Court Clerk PO Box 427, Camilla, GA 31730 (11 Broad St.). **229-336-2022** Fax: 229-336-2003. 8:30AM-5PM. RE Deed, Lien, UCC records online.

Monroe Superior Court Clerk PO Box 450, Forsyth, GA 31029-0450 (1 Courthouse Sq). **478-994-7022** Fax: 478-994-7053. 8:30AM-4:30. RE Deed, UCC, Lien records online.

Montgomery Superior Court Clerk PO Box 311, Mount Vernon, GA 30445 (Highway 221 & 56). **912-583-4401** 9AM-5PM. RE Deed, Lien, UCC records online.

Morgan Superior Court Clerk PO Box 130, Madison, GA 30650 **706-342-3605** 9AM-5PM. RE Deed, Lien, UCC records online.

Murray Superior Court Clerk PO Box 1000, Chatsworth, GA 30705 (121 N 3rd Ave) **706-695-2932** Fax: 706-517-9672. 8:30-5. RE Deed, Lien, UCC records online.

Muscogee Superior Court Clerk PO Box 2145, Columbus, GA 31902-2145 (100 10th St). **706-653-4358** Fax: 706-653-4359. 8:30-5PM. RE Deed, Lien, UCC records online.

Newton Superior Court Clerk 1132 Usher St, 3rd Fl, Newton County Judicial Ctr, Covington, GA 30014 **770-784-2035** 8AM-5PM. RE Deed, Lien, UCC records online.

Oconee Superior Court Clerk PO Box 1099, Watkinsville, GA 30677 (23 N. Main St). **706-769-3940** Fax: 706-769-3948. 8AM-5PM. RE Deed, UCC, Lien records online.

Oglethorpe Superior Court Clerk PO Box 68, Lexington, GA 30648-0068 (111 W. Main St). **706-743-5731** Fax: 706-743-5335. 8AM-5PM. UCC, Real Estate records online.

Paulding Superior Court Clerk 11 Courthouse Sq., Rm G-2, Dallas, GA 30132 **770-443-7527** 8AM-5PM. RE Deed, Lien, UCC records online.

Peach Superior Court Clerk PO Box 389, Fort Valley, GA 31030 (205 W. Church St). **478-825-5331** 8:30AM-5PM. RE Deed, Lien, UCC records online.

Pickens Superior Court Clerk PO Box 130, Jasper, GA 30143 (52 N. Main St, Annex). **706-253-8763** 8AM-5PM. RE Deed, Lien, UCC records online.

Pierce Superior Court Clerk PO Box 588, Blackshear, GA 31516 (Highway 84). **912-**449-2020** Fax: 912-449-2106. 9AM-5PM. RE Deed, Lien, UCC records online.

Pike Superior Court Clerk PO Box 10, Zebulon, GA 30295 (Highways 18 & 19). **770-567-2000** 8AM-5PM. RE Deed, UCC, Lien records online.

Polk Superior Court Clerk PO Box 948, Cedartown, GA 30125 (Courtnouse #1, Rm 106, 100 Pryor St.). **770-749-2114** Fax: 770-749-2148. 9AM-5PM. RE Deed, Lien, UCC records online.

Pulaski Superior Court Clerk PO Box 60, Hawkinsville, GA 31036 (350 Commerce St). **478-783-1911** Fax: 478-892-3308. 8AM-5PM. RE Deed, Lien, UCC records online.

Putnam Superior Court Clerk 100 S Jefferson St, Eatonton, GA 31024-1087 **706-485-4501** Fax: 706-485-2875. 8AM-5PM. RE Deed, UCC, Lien records online.

Quitman Superior Court Clerk PO Box 307, Georgetown, GA 39854 (Main St Courthouse). **229-334-2578** Fax: 229-334-3991. 8AM-Noon, 1-5PM. RE Deed, Lien, UCC records online.

Rabun Superior Court Clerk 25 Courthouse Sq #105, Clayton, GA 30525 **706-782-3615** Fax: 706-782-7588. 8:30AM-5PM. RE Deed, Lien, UCC records online.

Randolph Superior Court Clerk PO Box 98, Cuthbert, GA 39840 (208 Court St). **229-732-2216** Fax: 229-732-5881. 8AM-5PM. RE Deed, Lien, UCC records online.

Richmond Superior Court Clerk PO Box 2046, Augusta, GA 30903 (530 Green St, 5th Fl, Rm 503). **706-821-2460** Fax: 706-821-2448. 8:30AM-5PM. RE Deed, Lien, UCC records online.

Rockdale Superior Court Clerk PO Box 937, Conyers, GA 30012 (922 Court St, Rm 101). **770-929-4068** Fax: 770-860-0381. 8:15AM-4:45PM. RE Deed, UCC, Lien records online.

Schley Superior Court Clerk PO Box 7, Ellaville, GA 31806-0007 (14 S Broad St). **229-937-5581** Fax: 229-937-5588. 8-N,1-5PM. RE Deed, Lien, UCC records online.

Screven Superior Court Clerk PO Box 156, Sylvania, GA 30467 (216 Mims Rd). **912-564-2614** Fax: 912-564-2622. 8AM-5PM. RE Deed, Lien, UCC records online.

Seminole Superior Court Clerk PO Box 672, Donalsonville, GA 39845 (200 S. Knox St.). **229-524-2525** Fax: 229-524-8883. 9-5PM. RE Deed, Lien, UCC records online.

Spalding Superior Court Clerk PO Box 1046, Griffin, GA 30224 (132 E. Solomon St). **770-467-4356** 8AM-5PM. RE Deed, UCC, Lien records online.

Stephens Superior Court Clerk 205 N. Alexander St, Rm 202, Courthouse, Toccoa, GA 30577-2310 **706-886-9496** Fax: 706-886-5710. 8AM-5PM. RE Deed, UCC, Lien records online.

Stewart Superior Court Clerk PO Box 910, Lumpkin, GA 31815-0910 (Main St). **229-838-6220** Fax: 229-838-4505. 8AM-4:30. RE Deed, Lien, UCC records online.

Sumter Superior Court Clerk PO Box 333, Americus, GA 31709 (Lamar St Courthouse). **229-928-4537** 9AM-5PM. RE Deed, UCC, Lien records online.

Talbot Superior Court Clerk PO Box 325, Talbotton, GA 31827-0325 (26 Washington St). **706-665-3239** Fax: 706-665-8637. 9AM-5PM. RE Deed, Lien, UCC records online.

Taliaferro Superior Court Clerk PO Box 182, Crawfordville, GA 30631 (Monument St Courthouse). **706-456-2123** Fax: 706-456-2749. 9AM-Noon, 1-5PM. RE Deed, Lien, UCC records online.

Tattnall Superior Court Clerk PO Box 39, Reidsville, GA 30453 (108 Brazell St). **912-557-6716** Fax: 912-557-4552. 8AM-4:30. RE Deed, Lien, UCC records online.

Taylor Superior Court Clerk PO Box 248, Butler, GA 31006 **478-862-5594** Fax: 478-862-5334. 8AM-5PM. RE Deed, Lien, UCC records online.

Telfair Superior Court Clerk 128 E Oak St, #2, Courthouse, McRae, GA 31055-1604 **229-868-6525** Fax: 229-868-7956. 8:30AM-4:30PM. RE Deed, UCC records online.

Terrell Superior Court Clerk PO Box 189, Dawson, GA 39842 (513 S Main). **229-995-2631** 8:30AM-5PM. RE Deed, Lien, UCC records online.

Thomas Superior Court Clerk PO Box 1995, Thomasville, GA 31799 (225 N. Broad St). **229-225-4108** Fax: 229-225-4110. 8AM-5PM. www.thomascoclerkofcourt.org RE Deed, UCC, Lien records online.

Tift Superior Court Clerk PO Box 354, Tifton, GA 31793 (Corner of Tift Ave & 2nd St). **229-386-7810** Fax: 229-386-7807. 9-5PM. RE Deed, Lien, UCC records online.

Toombs Superior Court Clerk PO Drawer 530, Lyons, GA 30436 (100 Courthouse Sq). **912-526-3501** Fax: 912-526-1015. 8:30-5PM. RE Deed, Lien, UCC records online.

Towns Superior Court Clerk 48 River St., Courthouse, #E, Hiawassee, GA 30546 **706-**

896-2130 8:30AM-4:30PM. Real Estate, Deed, UCC records online.

Treutlen Superior Court Clerk PO Box 356, Soperton, GA 30457 (200 Georgia Ave.). **912-529-4215** Fax: none. 8AM-5PM. RE Deed, Lien, UCC records online.

Troup Superior Court Clerk PO Box 866, LaGrange, GA 30241-0866 (Courthouse, 118 Ridley Ave). **706-883-1740** 8AM-5PM. RE Deed, Lien, UCC records online.

Turner Superior Court Clerk PO Box 106, Ashburn, GA 31714 (219 E. College Ave). **229-567-2011** Fax: 229-567-0450. 8AM-5PM. RE Deed, UCC records online.

Twiggs Superior Court Clerk PO Box 228, Jeffersonville, GA 31044-0228 (425 Railroad St.). **478-945-3350** Fax: 478-945-6751. 8-5. RE Deed, UCC records online.

Union Superior Court Clerk 114 Courthouse St #5, Blairsville, GA 30512 **706-439-6022** Fax: 706-439-6026. 8AM-5PM. RE Deed, Lien, UCC records online.

Upson Superior Court Clerk PO Box 469, Thomaston, GA 30286 (116 W. Main St) **706-647-7835** Fax: 706-647-8999. 8AM-5PM. RE Deed, Lien, UCC records online.

Walker Superior Court Clerk PO Box 448, La Fayette, GA 30728 (South Duke St). **706-638-1742** Fax: 706-638-1779. 8AM-5PM. RE Deed, Lien, UCC records online.

Walton Superior Court Clerk PO Box 745, Monroe, GA 30655 (116 S. Broad St. Judicial Bldg.). **770-267-1304** Fax: 770-267-1441. 8:30AM-5PM. RE Deed, UCC, Lien records online.

Ware Superior Court Clerk PO Box 776, Waycross, GA 31502-0776 (800 Church St). **912-287-4340** Fax: 912-287-2498. 9AM-5PM. RE Deed, Lien, UCC records online.

Warren Superior Court Clerk PO Box 227, Warrenton, GA 30828 (Community Services Bldg., 100 Main St, Rm 201). **706-465-2262** Fax: 706-465-0232. 8AM-N, 1-5PM. RE Deed, Lien, UCC records online.

Washington Superior Court Clerk PO Box 231, Sandersville, GA 31082-0231 (Courthouse). **478-552-3186** 9AM-5PM. RE Deed, Lien, UCC records online.

Wayne Superior Court Clerk PO Box 920, Jesup, GA 31598-0920 (262 E. Walnut). **912-427-5930** Fax: 912-427-5939. 8:30AM-5PM. RE Deed, Lien, UCC records online.

Webster Superior Court Clerk PO Box 117, Preston, GA 31824 **229-828-3525** Fax: 229-828-6961. 8AM-Noon, 12:30PM-4:30PM. RE Deed, UCC, Lien records online.

Wheeler Superior Court Clerk PO Box 38, Alamo, GA 30411-0038 (119 W. Pearl St.). **912-568-7137** Fax: 912-568-7453. 8AM-4PM. RE Deed, Lien, UCC records online.

White Superior Court Clerk 59 S. Main St, Courthouse, #B, Cleveland, GA 30528 **706-865-2613** Fax: 706-865-2613. 8:30AM-5PM. RE Deed, Lien, UCC records online.

Whitfield Superior Court Clerk PO Box 868, Dalton, GA 30722 (300 W. Crawford St). **706-275-7450** Fax: 706-275-7456. 8AM-5PM. RE Deed, Lien, UCC records online.

Wilcox Superior Court Clerk 103 N Broad St Courthouse, Abbeville, GA 31001-1000 **229-467-2442** Fax: 229-467-2886. 9AM-5PM. RE Deed, UCC, Lien records online.

Wilkes Superior Court Clerk 23 E. Court St, Rm 205, Washington, GA 30673 (23 E. Court St, Rm 205). **706-678-2423** Fax: 706-678-2115. 9AM-5PM. RE Deed, Lien, UCC records online.

Wilkinson Superior Court Clerk & Juvenile Court PO Box 250, Irwinton, GA 31042-0250 (100 Bacon St, Courthouse). **478-946-2221** Fax: 478-946-1497. 8AM-5PM. RE Deed, Lien, UCC records online.

Worth Superior Court Clerk 201 N. Main St, Courthouse, Rm 13, Sylvester, GA 31791 **229-776-8205** Fax: 229-776-8237. 8AM-5PM. RE Deed, Lien, UCC records online.

Hawaii

Organization: All UCC financing statements, tax liens, and real estate documents are filed centrally with the Bureau of Conveyances located in Honolulu. The entire state is in the Hawaii Time Zone (HT).

Online Access: There is no statewide access to recorder or assessor information.

Bureau of Conveyances Bureau of Conveyances PO Box 2867, Honolulu, HI 96803 (Dept. of Land & Natural Resources, 1151 Punchbowl St, Rm 120). **808-587-0154** Fax: 808-587-4380. 7:45AM-4:30PM. www.hawaii.gov/dlnr/bc Property records online.

Idaho

Organization: 44 counties, 44 recording offices. The recording officer is the County Recorder. Many counties utilize a grantor/grantee index containing all transactions recorded with them. 34 counties are in the Mountain Time Zone (MST), and 10 are in the Pacific Time Zone (PST).

Real Estate Records: Most counties will not perform name searches. Certification of copies usually costs $1.00 per document.

UCC Records: Financing statements are filed at the state level except for real estate related filings. All counties will perform UCC searches. Use search request form UCC-4. Search fees are usually $6.00 per debtor name for a listing of filings and $12.00 per debtor name for a listing plus copies at no additional charge. Separately ordered copies usually cost $1.00 per page.

Tax Lien Records: Until 07/01/98, state tax liens were filed at the local county recorder. Now they are filed with the Secretary of State who has all active case files. Federal tax liens on personal property of businesses are filed with the Secretary of State. Other federal tax liens are filed with the county recorder. Some counties will perform a combined tax lien search for $5.00 while others will not perform tax lien searches. Other Liens: Judgments, hospital, labor, mechanics.

Online Access: Two counties have web access to assessor records. Also, the Secretary of State's office offers online access to UCCs.

Adams da Clerk & Recorder 200 W Front St, Rm 1207, Boise, ID 83702 **208-287-6845** Fax: 208-287-6459. 8:30AM-4:30PM. Assessor, Property, Inmate records online.

Adams Clerk & Recorder PO Box 48, Council, ID 83612 (Michigan St.). **208-253-4561** Fax: 208-253-4880. 8AM-N, 1-5PM.

Bannock Clerk & Recorder 624 E. Center, Courthouse, Rm 211, Pocatello, ID 83201 **208-236-7340** Fax: 208-236-7345. 8-5PM.

Bear Lake Clerk & Recorder PO Box 190, Paris, ID 83261 (7th E. Center). **208-945-2212** Fax: 208-945-2780. 8:30AM-5PM.

Benewah Clerk & Recorder 701 College, St. Maries, ID 83861 **208-245-3212** Fax: 208-245-3046. 9AM-5PM.

Bingham Clerk & Recorder 501 N. Maple #205, Blackfoot, ID 83221 **208-785-5005** Fax: 208-785-4131. 8AM-5PM.

Blaine Clerk & Recorder 206 1st Ave. South #200, Hailey, ID 83333 **208-788-5505** Fax: 208-788-5501. 9-5PM. www.co.blaine.id.us

Boise Clerk & Recorder PO Box 1300, Idaho City, ID 83631 (420 Main, Auditor). **208-392-4431** Fax: 208-392-4473. 8-5PM.

Bonner Clerk & Recorder 215 S. First, Sandpoint, ID 83864 **208-265-1432** Fax: 208-265-1447. 9AM-5PM.

Bonneville Clerk & Recorder 605 N. Capital Ave, Idaho Falls, ID 83402-3582 **208-529-1350** Fax: 208-529-1353. 8AM-5PM. www.co.bonneville.id.us

Boundary Clerk & Recorder PO Box 419, Bonners Ferry, ID 83805 (6452 Kootenai, Courthouse). **208-267-2242** Fax: 208-267-7814. 9AM-5PM. www.boundary-idaho.com

Butte Clerk & Recorder PO Box 737, Arco, ID 83213 (248 W. Grand). **208-527-3021** Fax: 208-527-3295. 9AM-5PM.

Camas Clerk & Recorder PO Box 430, Fairfield, ID 83327-0430 (Corner of Soldier & Willow). **208-764-2242** Fax: 208-764-2349. 8:30AM-N, 1-5PM.

Canyon Recorder 1115 Albany St, Caldwell, ID 83605 **208-454-7556** 8:30AM-5PM. www.canyoncounty.org Assessor, Property records online.

Caribou Clerk & Recorder PO Box 775, Soda Springs, ID 83276-0775 (159 S. Main). **208-547-4324** Fax: 208-547-4759. 9-5PM.

Cassia Clerk & Recorder 1459 Overland Ave, Rm 105, Burley, ID 83318 **208-878-5240** Fax: 208-878-1003. 8:30AM-5PM.

Clark Clerk & Recorder PO Box 205, Dubois, ID 83423 (320 W. Main). **208-374-5304** Fax: 208-374-5609. 9AM-5PM.

Clearwater Clerk & Recorder PO Box 586, Orofino, ID 83544-0586 (150 Michigan Ave). **208-476-5615** Fax: 208-476-9315. 8AM-5PM. www.clearwatercounty.org

Custer Clerk & Recorder PO Box 385, Challis, ID 83226 (801 Main St). **208-879-2360** Fax: 208-879-5246. 8AM-5PM.

Elmore Clerk & Recorder 150 S. 4th East, ##3, Mountain Home, ID 83647-3097 **208-587-2130** Fax: 208-587-2159. 9AM-5PM. www.elmoreco.org

Franklin Clerk & Recorder 39 W. Oneida, Preston, ID 83263 **208-852-1090** Fax: 208-852-1094. 9AM-5PM.

Fremont Clerk & Recorder 151 W. 1st N. Rm12, St. Anthony, ID 83445 **208-624-3148** Fax: 208-624-7335. 9AM-5PM. www.co.fremont.id.us/departments/index.htm

Gem Clerk & Recorder 415 E. Main, Emmett, ID 83617 **208-365-4561** Fax: 208-365-7795. 8AM-5PM.

Gooding Clerk & Recorder PO Box 417, Gooding, ID 83330 (624 Main St). **208-934-4841** Fax: 208-934-5085. 9AM-5PM.

Idaho Clerk & Recorder 320 W. Main, Rm 5, Grangeville, ID 83530 **208-983-2751** Fax: 208-983-1428. 8:30AM-5PM.

Jefferson Clerk & Recorder PO Box 275, Rigby, ID 83442 (134 N. Clark). **208-745-7756** Fax: 208-745-6636. 9AM-5PM.

Jerome Clerk & Recorder 300 N. Lincoln, Courthouse, Rm 301, Jerome, ID 83338 **208-324-8811** Fax: 208-324-2719. 8:30-4:30PM.

Kootenai Clerk & Recorder PO Box 9000, Coeur d'Alene, ID 83816-9000 (451 Gov't Way). **208-446-1480** 9AM-5PM. www.co.kootenai.id.us/default.asp Property, Recording, Unclaimed Property online.

Latah Clerk & Recorder PO Box 8068, Moscow, ID 83843-0568 (Rm 101, 5th & Van Buren). **208-882-8580 x3379** Fax: 208-883-7203. 8AM-5PM. www.latah.id.us

Lemhi Clerk & Recorder 206 Courthouse Drive, Salmon, ID 83467 **208-756-2815** Fax: 208-756-8424. 8AM-5PM.

Lewis Clerk & Recorder PO Box 39, Nezperce, ID 83543 (510 Oak St). **208-937-2661** Fax: 208-937-9234. 9AM-5PM.

Lincoln Clerk & Recorder PO Drawer A, Shoshone, ID 83352 (111 W. B St). **208-886-7641** Fax: 208-886-2707. 8:30-5PM.

Madison Clerk & Recorder PO Box 389, Rexburg, ID 83440 (134 E. Main, Admin.

Bldg). **208-359-6200 x1** Fax: 208-356-8396. 9AM-5PM. www.co.madison.id.us

Minidoka Clerk & Recorder PO Box 368, Rupert, ID 83350-0474 (715 G St). **208-436-9511** Fax: 208-436-0737. 8:30AM-5PM.

Nez Perce Clerk & Recorder PO Box 896, Lewiston, ID 83501-0896 (1230 Main St, Rm 100). **208-799-3020** Fax: 208-799-3070. 8AM-5PM. www.co.nezperce.id.us

Oneida Clerk & Recorder 10 Court St, Malad, ID 83252 **208-766-4116 x100** Fax: 208-766-2448. 9AM-5PM.

Owyhee Clerk & Recorder PO Box 128, Murphy, ID 83650 (20381 State Hiway 78). **208-495-2421** Fax 208-495-1173. 8:30-5PM.

Payette Clerk & Recorder 1130 3rd Ave. North, #104, Payette, ID 83661 **208-642-6000** Fax: 208-642-6011. 9AM-5PM.

Power Clerk & Recorder 543 Bannock, American Falls, ID 83211 **208-226-7611** Fax: 208-226-7612. 9-5PM. www.co.power.id.us

Shoshone Clerk & Recorder 700 Bank St, Courthouse, #120, Wallace, ID 83873-2348 **208-752-1264** Fax: 208-753-2711. 9-5PM.

Teton Clerk & Recorder 89 N. Main #1, Driggs, ID 83422 **208-354-2905** Fax: 208-354-8410. 9AM-5PM.

Twin Falls Clerk & Recorder PO Box 126, Twin Falls, ID 83303-0126 (425 Shoshone St North). **208-736-4004** Fax: 208-736-4182. 8AM-5PM. www.twinfallscounty.org

Valley Clerk & Recorder PO Box 1350, Cascade, ID 83611-1350 (219 N. Main). **208-382-7100** Fax 208-382-7107. 9-5PM.

Washington Clerk & Recorder PO Box 670, Weiser, ID 83672-0670 (256 E. Court St). **208-549-2092** Fax: 208-549-3925. 8:30AM-5PM.

Illinois

Organization: 102 counties, 103 recording offices. Cook County had separate offices for real estate recording and UCC filing until June 30, 2001. As of that date the UCC filing office only searches for pre-existing UCCs and no longer takes new UCC filings. The recording officer is the Recorder of Deeds. Many counties utilize a grantor/grantee index containing all transactions. The entire state is in the Central Time Zone (CST).

Real Estate Records: Most counties will not perform real estate searches. Cost of certified copies varies widely, but many counties charge the same as the cost of recording the document. Tax records are usually located at the Treasurer's Office.

UCC Records: Financing statements are filed at the state level except for real estate related filings which are filed with the County Recorder. (See above regarding Cook County.) Most counties will perform UCC searches. Use search request form UCC-11. Search fees are usually $10.00 per debtor name/address combination. Copies usually cost $1.00 per page.

Tax Lien Records: Federal tax liens on personal property of businesses are filed with the Secretary of State. Other federal and all state tax liens on personal property are filed with the County Recorder. Some counties will perform tax lien searches for $5.00-$10.00 per name (state and federal are separate searches in many of these counties) and $1.00 per page of copy. Other Liens: Judgments, mechanics, contractor, medical, lis pendens, oil & gas, mobile home.

Online Access: A number of counties offer online access. There is no statewide system.

Adams County Recorder PO Box 1067, Quincy, IL 62306 (507 Vermont St). **217-277-2125** 8:30AM-4:30PM. Assessor, Real Estate records online.

Alexander County Recorder 2000 Washington Ave, Cairo, IL 62914 **618-734-7000** Fax: 618-734-7002. 8AM-N, 1-4PM.

Bond County Recorder 203 W. College Ave, Greenville, IL 62246 **618-664-0449** Fax: 618-664-9414. 8AM-4PM.

Boone County Recorder 601 N. Main St, #202, Belvidere, IL 61008 **815-544-3103** Fax: 815-547-8701. www.boonecountyil.org Real Estate records online. 8:30AM-5PM.

Brown County Recorder Courthouse - Rm4, #1 Court St, Mount Sterling, IL 62353-1285 **217-773-3421** Fax: 217-773-2233. 8:30AM-4:30PM.

Bureau County Recorder 700 S. Main St., Courthouse, Princeton, IL 61356 **815-875-3239** Fax: 815-879-4803. 8AM-4PM.

Calhoun County Clerk & Recorder PO Box 187, Hardin, IL 62047 **618-576-2351** Fax: 618-576-2895. 8:30AM-4:30PM.

Carroll County Recorder PO Box 152, Mount Carroll, IL 61053 (301 N. Main). **815-244-0223** Fax: 815-244-3709. 8:30AM-4:30AM.

Cass County Recorder 100 E Springfield St, Virginia, IL 62691 **217-452-7217** Fax: 217-452-7219. 8:30AM-4:30PM.

Champaign County Recorder 1776 E. Washington, Urbana, IL 61802 **217-384-3774** Fax: 217-344-1663. 8AM-4:30PM. Property records online.

Christian County Recorder PO Box 647, Taylorville, IL 62568 (Courthouse on the Sq). **217-824-4960** Fax: 217-824-5105. 8AM-4PM. UCC, Property records online.

Clark County Recorder Courthouse, Marshall, IL 62441 (Courthouse). **217-826-8311** 8AM-4PM.

Clay County Recorder PO Box 160, Louisville, IL 62858-0160 (County Bldg. Rm 106). **618-665-3626** Fax: 618-665-3607. 8AM-4PM.

Clinton County Recorder PO Box 308, Carlyle, IL 62231 (Rm 230 (upstairs) Courthouse). **618-594-2464** Fax: 618-594-0195. 8AM-4PM. www.clintonco.org Property records online.

Coles County Recorder 651 Jackson Ave, Rm 122, Charleston, IL 61920 **217-348-7325** Fax: 217-348-7337. 8:30AM-4:30PM.

Cook County - Recorder of Deeds 118 N. Clark St, Rm 120, Chicago, IL 60602-1387 **312-603-7524** Fax: 312-603-5063. 9AM-5PM. www.ccrd.info Property Tax records online.

County Recorder 118 N. Clark St. #120, Rm 230, Chicago, IL 60602 **312-603-5134, 312-603-5050** Fax: 312-603-5063. 8AM-4:55PM. www.ccrd.info Real Estate, Recorder, Deed, Grantor/ Grantee, Heir records online.

Crawford County Recorder PO Box 616, Robinson, IL 62454-0602 (100 Douglas St). **618-546-1212** Fax: 618-546-0140. 8AM-4PM. www.crawfordcountyclerk.com

Cumberland County Recorder PO Box 146, Toledo, IL 62468 (140 Courthouse Sq). **217-849-2631** Fax: 217-849-2968. 8-4PM.

De Kalb County Recorder 110 E. Sycamore St, Sycamore, IL 60178 **815-895-7156** 8:30-4:30PM. Real Estate, Lien records online.

De Witt County Recorder PO Box 439, Clinton, IL 61727-0439 (201 W. Washington St). **217-935-2119** Fax: 217-935-4596. 8:30AM-4:30PM.

Douglas County Recorder PO Box 467, Tuscola, IL 61953-0467 (401 S Center St, 2nd Fl). **217-253-4410** Fax: 217-253-2233. 8:30AM-4:30PM.

Du Page County Recorder PO Box 936, Wheaton, IL 60189 (421 N County Farm Rd). **630-407-5400** Fax: 630-407-5300. 8AM-4:30PM. www.dupageco.org/recorder/ Real Estate, Lien, Tax Assessor online.

Edgar County Clerk and Recorder 115 W. Court St, Rm J, Paris, IL 61944-1785 **217-466-7433** Fax: 217-466-7430. 8AM-4PM.

Edwards County Recorder 50 E. Main St, Courthouse, Albion, IL 62806-1294 **618-445-2115** Fax: 618-445-4941. 8AM-4PM.

Effingham County Clerk & Recorder PO Box 628, Effingham, IL 62401-0628 (101 N. 4th St, #201). **217-342-6535** Fax: 217-342-3577. 8AM-4PM. http://co.effingham.il.us

Fayette County Recorder PO Box 401, Vandalia, IL 62471 (221 S. 7th St). **618-283-5000** Fax: 618-283-5004. 8AM-4PM.

Ford County Recorder 200 W. State St, Rm 101, Paxton, IL 60957 **217-379-2721** Fax: 217-379-3258. 8:30-4:30 www.prairienet.org

Franklin County Clerk & Recorder PO Box 607, Benton, IL 62812 (Courthouse). **618-438-3221** Fax: 618-435-3405. 8-4PM.

Fulton County Recorder PO Box 226, Lewistown, IL 61542 (100 N. Main). **309-547-3041** 8AM-4PM.

Gallatin County Recorder PO Box 550, Shawneetown, IL 62984 (West Lincoln Blvd). **618-269-3025** Fax: 618-269-3343. 8AM-4PM. Property records online.

Greene County Recorder 519 N. Main St, Courthouse, Carrollton, IL 62016-1033 **217-942-5443** Fax: 217-942-9323. 8AM-4PM.

Grundy County Recorder PO Box 675, Morris, IL 60450-0675 (111 E. Washington St). **815-941-3224** Fax: 815-942-2222. 8AM-4:30PM.

Hamilton County Recorder Courthouse, 100 S Jackson St, Rm 2, McLeansboro, IL 62859-1489 **618-643-2721** 8AM-4:30PM.

Hancock County Recorder PO Box 39, Carthage, IL 62321-0039 (500 Blk Main St, 2nd Fl). **217-357-3911** 8AM-4PM.

Hardin County Recorder PO Box 187, Elizabethtown, IL 62931 (Courthouse). **618-287-2251** Fax: 618-287-2661. 8AM-4PM.

Henderson County Recorder PO Box 308, Oquawka, IL 61469-0308 (4th & Warren Sts). **309-867-2911** Fax: 309-867-2033. 8AM-4PM.

Henry County Recorder 307 W Center St, Henry County Courthouse, Cambridge, IL 61238 **309-937-3486** Fax: 309-937-2796. www.henrycty.com/recorder/index.html Assessor records online. 8AM-4:30PM.

Iroquois County Recorder 1001 E. Grant St, Watseka, IL 60970 **815-432-6962** Fax: 815-432-3894. 8:30AM-4:30PM.

Jackson County Recorder 1001 Walnut, The Courthouse, Murphysboro, IL 62966 **618-687-7360** 8AM-4PM.

Jasper County Recorder 204 W Washington St #2, Newton, IL 62448 **618-783-3124** Fax: 618-783-4137. 8AM-4:30PM.

Jefferson County Recorder 100 S. 10th St, Rm 105, Courthouse, Mount Vernon, IL 62864 **618-244-8020** 8AM-5PM.

Jersey County Recorder 200 N Lafayette #2, Jerseyville, IL 62052 (**618-498-5571 x117/8** Fax: 618-498-6128. 8:30AM-4:30PM.

Jo Daviess County Recorder 330 N. Bench St, Galena, IL 61036 (**815-777-9694** Fax: 815-777-3688. 8AM-4PM.

Johnson County Recorder PO Box 96, Vienna, IL 62995 (Courthouse). **618-658-3611** Fax: 618-658-2908. 8AM-N,1-4PM.

Kane County Recorder PO Box 71, Geneva, IL 60134 (719 S. Batavia Ave, Bldg C). **630-232-5935** Fax: 630-232-5945. 8:30AM-4:30PM. www.co.kane.il.us Real Estate records online.

Kankakee County Recorder 189 E. Court St, Kankakee, IL 60901 **815-937-2980** Fax: 815-937-3657. 8:30AM-4:30PM.

Kendall County Recorder 111 W. Fox St, Yorkville, IL 60560 **630-553-4112** Fax: 630-553-5283. 8AM-4:30PM. Real Estate records online..

Knox County Recorder 200 S. Cherry, County Courthouse, Galesburg, IL 61401 **309-345-3818** Fax: 309-343-3842. 8:30AM-4:30PM.

La Salle County Recorder PO Box 189, Ottawa, IL 61350 (707 Etna Rd, Gov.t Ctr Rm 269). **815-434-8226** Fax: 815-434-8260. www.lasallecounty.org/Final/contents2.htm Real Estate, Assessor records online.

Lake County Recorder 18 N. County St, Courthouse - 2nd Fl, Waukegan, IL 60085-4358 **847-377-2575** Fax: 847-625-7200. 8:30AM-5PM. www.co.lake.il.us/recorder Real Estate records online.

Lawrence County Recorder 1100 State St, Courthouse, Lawrenceville, IL 62439 **618-943-5126** Fax: 618-943-5205. 9AM-5PM.

Lee County Recorder PO Box 329, Dixon, IL 61021-0329 (112 E. Second St.). **815-288-3309** Fax: 815-288-6492. 8:30-4:30PM.

Livingston County Recorder 112 W. Madison, Courthouse, Pontiac, IL 61764-1871 **815-844-2006** Fax: 815-842-1844. 8AM-4:30PM. www.livingstoncounty-il.org

Logan County Recorder PO Box 278, Lincoln, IL 62656 (Courthouse, 601 Broadway Rm 20). **217-732-4148** Fax: 217-732-6064. www.co.logan.il.us/county_clerk/ Real Estate records online. 8:30-4:30PM.

Macon County Recorder 141 S. Main St, Rm 201, Decatur, IL 62523-1293 **217-424-1359** Fax: 217-428-2908. 8:30AM-4:30PM.

Macoupin County Recorder PO Box 107, Carlinville, IL 62626 (Courthouse). **217-854-3214** Fax: 217-854-7347. 8:30AM-4:30PM.

Madison County Recorder PO Box 308, Edwardsville, IL 62025-0308 (157 N. Main, #211, Admin. Bldg.). **618-692-7040 x4775** Fax: 618-692-9843. 8AM-5PM.

Marion County Recorder PO Box 637, Salem, IL 62881 (100 E. Main St, Rm 201). **618-548-3400** Fax: 618-548-2226. 8-4PM.

Marshall County Recorder PO Box 328, Lacon, IL 61540 (122 N. Prairie). **309-246-6325** Fax: 309-246-3667. 8:30AM-4:30PM.

Mason County Recorder PO Box 77, Havana, IL 62644 (100 N. Broadway). **309-543-6661** Fax: 309-543-2085. 8AM-4PM.

Massac County Recorder PO Box 429, Metropolis, IL 62960 (Courthouse, Rm 2-A, Superman Sq). **618-524-5213** Fax: 618-524-8514. 8AM-4PM.

McDonough County Recorder 1 Courthouse Sq, Macomb, IL 61455 **309-833-2474** Fax: 309-836-3368. 8AM-4PM.

McHenry County Recorder 2200 N. Seminary Ave, Rm A280, Woodstock, IL 60098 **815-334-4110** Fax: 815-338-9612.. www.co.mchenry.il.us/countydpt/recorder Assessor/Treasurer, Property, Foreclosure records online. 8AM-4:30PM

McLean County Recorder PO Box 2400, Bloomington, IL 61702-2400 (104 W. Front St, Rm 708). **309-888-5170** Fax: 309-888-5927. 8AM-4:30PM. www.mclean.gov/Recorder, Deed, UCC, Lien, Vital Statistic, Assessor, Property, Treasurer Tax Bill, Sex Offender, Assumed Name, Elected Official records online.

Menard County Recorder PO Box 465, Petersburg, IL 62675 (102 S. Seventh St). **217-632-2415** Fax: 217-632-4301. 8:30AM-4:30PM.

Mercer County Recorder PO Box 66, Aledo, IL 61231 (100 S.E. 3rd St, 2nd Fl). **309-582-7021** Fax: 309-582-7022. 8-4PM.

Monroe County Recorder 100 S. Main, Courthouse, Waterloo, IL 62298-1399 (100 S. Main). **618-939-8681** Fax: 618-939-8639. 8AM-4:30PM.

Montgomery County Recorder 1 Court house Sq, Historic Courthouse, Hillsboro, IL 62049-1196 **217-532-9532** Fax: 217-532-9581. 8AM-4PM. www.montgomeryco.com

Morgan County Recorder PO Box 1387, Jacksonville, IL 62651 (300 W. State St). **217-243-8581** Fax: 217-243-8368. 8:30AM-4:30PM.

Moultrie County Recorder 10 S Main, #6, Courthouse, Sullivan, IL 61951 **217-728-4389** Fax: 217-728-8178. 8:30AM-4:30PM.

Ogle County Recorder PO Box 357, Oregon, IL 61061 (4th & Washington Sts). **815-732-1115 x269/1** 8:30AM-4:30PM. Land, Recorder, Deed, UCC records online.

Peoria County Recorder 324 Main St, County Courthouse, Rm G04, Peoria, IL 61602 **309-672-6090** 9AM-5PM. www.co.peoria.il.us/ Assessor, Property, Recording records online.

Perry County Recorder PO Box 438, Pinckneyville, IL 62274 (3764 St Rt 13/127). **618-357-5116** Fax: 618-357-3194. 8AM-4PM. www.perrycountyil.org

Piatt County Recorder PO Box 558, Monticello, IL 61856 (101 W. Washington, Rm 110). **217-762-9487** Fax: 217-762-7563. 8:30AM-4:30PM. www.piattcounty.org

Pike County Recorder 100 E. Washington St., Courthouse, Pittsfield, IL 62363 **217-285-6812** Fax: 217-285-5820. 8:30AM-4PM.

Pope County Recorder PO Box 216, Golconda, IL 62938 (Courthouse). **618-683-4466** Fax: 618-683-4466. 8AM-N, 1-4PM.

Pulaski County Recorder PO Box 118, Mound City, IL 62963 (Corner of 2nd & High). **618-748-9360** Fax: 618-748-9305. 8AM-N, 1-4PM.

Putnam County Recorder PO Box 236, Hennepin, IL 61327 (120 N. 4th St). **815-925-7129** Fax: 815-925-7549. 9AM-4PM.

Randolph County Recorder 1 Taylor St, Rm 202, Chester, IL 62233-0309 **618-826-5000 x191** Fax: 618-826-3750. 8AM-4:00PM. Property records online.

Richland County Recorder 103 W. Main, Courthouse, Olney, IL 62450 **618-392-3111** Fax: 618-393-4005. 8AM-4PM.

Rock Island County Recorder PO Box 3067, Rock Island, IL 61204 (210 15th St, 2nd Fl). **309-558-3360** Fax: 309-558-3642. 8AM-4:30PM. www.co.rock-island.il.us Property, Assessor records online.

Saline County Recorder 10 E. Poplar, #17, Harrisburg, IL 62946 **18-253-8197** Fax: 618-252-3073. 8AM-4PM.

Sangamon County Recorder PO Box 669, Springfield, IL 62705-0669 (200 S. 9th St., Rm 211). **217-535-3150** Fax: 217-535-3159. 8:30AM-5PM. www.co.sangamon.il.us Property records online.

Schuyler County Recorder PO Box 200, Rushville, IL 62681 (102 S. Congress). **217-322-4734** Fax: 217-322-6164. 8AM-4PM.

Scott County Recorder Courthouse, Winchester, IL 62694 **217-742-3178** Fax: 217-742-5853. 8AM-4PM.

Shelby County Recorder PO Box 230, Shelbyville, IL 62565 (301 E. Main St.). **217-774-4421** Fax: 217-774-5291. 8-4PM.

St. Clair County Recorder PO Box 543, Belleville, IL 62220 (10 Public Sq, County Bldg, 5th Fl). **618-277-6600** 8:30AM-5PM. www.stclaircountyrecorder.com Recorder, Grantor/Grantee, Real Estate, Divorce, Lien, Judgment records online.

Stark County Recorder PO Box 97, Toulon, IL 61483 (130 W. Main). **309-286-5911** Fax: 309-286-4039. www.starkcourt.org 8:30AM-4:30PM. Unclaimed Funds records online.

Stephenson County Recorder 15 N. Galena Ave, #1, Freeport, IL 61032 **815-235-8385** Fax: none. 8:30AM-4:30PM.

Tazewell County Recorder PO Box 36, Pekin, IL 61555-0036 (Arcade Bldg., 13 S. Capitol St.). **309-477-2210** Fax: 309-477-2321. 8:30AM-5PM.

Union County Recorder 309 W. Market, Jonesboro, IL 62952 **618-833-5711** Fax: 618-833-8712. 8AM-4PM.

Vermilion County Recorder 6 N. Vermilion St, Danville, IL 61832-5877 **217-554-6041** Fax: 217-554-6047. 8AM-4:30PM.

Wabash County Recorder PO Box 277, Mount Carmel, IL 62863 (401 Market St). **618-262-4561** 8AM-5PM.

Warren County Recorder 100 W Broadway, Courthouse, Monmouth, IL 61462-1797 **309-734-8592** Fax: 309-734-7406. 8AM-4:30PM.

Washington County Recorder 101 E. St. Louis St, County Courthouse, Nashville, IL 62263-1105 **618-327-4800 x300** Fax: 618-327-3582. 8AM-4PM.

Wayne County Recorder PO Box 187, Fairfield, IL 62837 (301 E. Main). **618-842-5182** Fax: 618-842-6427. 8AM-4:30PM. http://assessor.wayne.il.us Assessor, Property records online.

White County Recorder PO Box 339, Carmi, IL 62821 (301 E. Main St). **618-382-7211** 8AM-4PM.

Whiteside County Recorder 200 E. Knox, Morrison, IL 61270 **815-772-5241** Fax: 815-772-5244. 8:30-4:30PM. www.whiteside.org

Will County Recorder 58 E Clinton, #100, Joliet, IL 60432 **815-740-4637** Fax: 815-740-4697. 8:30AM-4:30PM. Assessor, Appraiser, Property, Voter Registration, Deed, Lien, Mortgage records online.

Williamson County Recorder PO Box 1108, Marion, IL 62959-1108 (200 W. Jefferson). **618-997-1301 X121** Fax: 618-993-2071. 8AM-4PM.

Winnebago County Recorder 404 Elm St, Rm 405, Rockford, IL 61101 **815-987-3100** Fax: 815-961-3261. 8AM-4PM. Property, UCC records online.

Woodford County Recorder 115 N. Main, Courthouse, Rm 202, Eureka, IL 61530-1273 **309-467-2822** 8AM-5PM.

Indiana

Organization: 92 counties, 92 recording offices. The recording officer is the County Recorder (or the Circuit Clerk for state tax liens on personal property). Many counties utilize a "Miscellaneous Index" for tax and other liens. 81 counties are in the Eastern Time Zone (EST), and 11 are in the Central Time Zone (CST).

Real Estate Records: Most counties will not perform real estate name searches. Copies usually cost $1.00 per page, and certification usually costs $5.00 per document.

UCC Records: Financing statements are filed at the state level, except for real estate related collateral, which are filed with the County Recorder. However, prior to 07/2001, consumer goods collateral were also filed at the County Recorder and these older records can be searched there. Starting 07/2002, farm collateral will change from local to state centralized filing. All counties will perform UCC searches. Use search request form UCC-11. Search fees are usually $1.00 per debtor name. Copies usually cost $.50 per page. Most counties also charge $.50 for each financing statement reported on a search.

Tax Lien Records: All federal tax liens on personal property are filed with the County Recorder. State tax liens on personal property are filed with the Circuit Clerk who is in a different office from the Recorder. Refer to the County Court section for information about Indiana Circuit Courts. Most counties will not perform tax lien searches. Other Liens: Judgments, mechanics, hospital, sewer, utility, innkeeper.

Online Access: A growing number of county agencies offer online access. The most notable is the subscription service offered by Marion County at www.civicnet.net.

Adams County Recorder 313 W. Jefferson, Rm 240, Adams County Service Complex, Decatur, IN 46733 **260-724-5343** Fax: 260-724-5344. 8AM-4:30PM.

Allen County Recorder 1 E. Main St, City County Bldg, Rm 206, Fort Wayne, IN 46802-1890 **260-449-7165** Fax: 260-449-3261. 8AM-4:30PM.

Bartholomew County Recorder PO Box 1121, Columbus, IN 47202-1121 (440 3rd St, #203). **812-379-1520** Fax: 812-375-5440. 8AM-5PM. www.bartholomewco.com Property, GIS records online.

Benton County Recorder 706 E. 5th St, #24, Fowler, IN 47944-1556 **765-884-1630** Fax: 765-884-2013. 8:30AM-4PM.

Blackford County Recorder 110 W. Washington St, Courthouse, Hartford City, IN 47348 **765-348-2207** Fax: 765-348-7222. 8AM-4PM.

Boone County Recorder 202 Courthouse Sq, Lebanon, IN 46052 **765-482-3070** 8-4PM.

Brown County Recorder PO Box 86, Nashville, IN 47448 (120 Gould St.). **812-988-5462** Fax: 812-988-5520. 8AM-4PM.

Carroll County Recorder 101 W. Main St, Court House, Delphi, IN 46923-1522 **765-564-2124** Fax: 765-564-2576. 8AM-5PM M,T,Th,F; 8AM-N W.

Cass County Recorder 102 Cass County Gov't Bldg., Logansport, IN 46947 **574-753-7810** 8AM-4PM M-TH; 8AM-5PM F. www.in-map.net/counties/CASS/recorder/

Clark County Recorder 501 E. Court Ave, Rm 105, Jeffersonville, IN 47130 **812-285-6236** 8:30AM-4:30PM.

Clay County Recorder 609 E National Ave., Courthouse, Rm 111, Brazil, IN 47834 **812-448-9005** Fax: 812-446-5095. 8AM-4PM.

Clinton County Recorder 270 Courthouse Sq, Frankfort, IN 46041-1957 **765-659-6320** Fax: 765-659-6391. 8-4PM (noon on Thur).

Crawford County Recorder PO Box 214, English, IN 47118-0214 (South Court St). **812-338-2615** Fax: 812-338-2507. 8AM-4PM M & F; 8AM-6PM T,Th; Closed W.

Daviess County Recorder PO Box 793, Washington, IN 47501 (200 E. Walnut). **812-254-8675** Fax: 812-254-8647. 8-4PM.

Dearborn County Recorder 215 B, W. High St, Lawrenceburg, IN 47025 **812-537-8837** Fax: none. 8:30AM-4:30PM.

Decatur County Recorder 150 Courthouse Sq, #121, Greensburg, IN 47240 **812-663-4681** Fax: 812-663-2407. 8AM-4PM (F open until 5PM).

DeKalb County Recorder PO Box 810, Auburn, IN 46706 (1st Fl, 100 S. Main St.). **260-925-2112** Fax: 260-925-5126. 8:30-4:30.

Delaware County Recorder PO Box 1008, Muncie, IN 47308 (100 W. Main St, Rm 209). **765-747-7804** Fax: 765-284-1875. 8:30AM-4:30PM.

Dubois County Recorder 1 Courthouse Sq, Rm 101, Jasper, IN 47546 **812-481-7067** Fax: 812-481-7044. 8AM-4PM.

Elkhart County Recorder PO Box 837, Goshen, IN 46527 (117 N. 2nd St, Rm 205). **574-535-6754** 8-5PM M-Th, 8-4PM F. www.elkhartcountygov.com/administrative Real Estate, Lien, Tax Assessor online.

Fayette County Recorder PO Box 324, Connersville, IN 47331-0324 (401 Central Ave). **765-825-3051** 8:30AM-4PM. www.co.fayette.in.us

Floyd County Recorder PO Box 878, New Albany, IN 47151-0878 (311 W. 1st St, Rm 115). **812-948-5430** Fax: 812-949-7727. 8AM-4PM. Recording, Real Estate records online.

Fountain County Recorder PO Box 55, Covington, IN 47932 (301 4th St). **765-793-2431** Fax: 765-793-6211. 8AM-4PM.

Franklin County Recorder 459 Main St, Brookville, IN 47012-1486 **765-647-5131** 8:30AM-4PM.

Fulton County Recorder 125 E 9th St, Rochester, IN 46975 **574-223-2914** Fax: 574-223-4734. 8AM-4PM (F 8AM-5PM).

Gibson County Recorder PO Box 1078, Princeton, IN 47670 (101 N. Main). **812-385-3332** Fax: 812-386-9502. 8AM-4PM.

Grant County Recorder 401 S. Adams St, Marion, IN 46953 **765-668-8871** 8AM-4PM. www.grantcounty.net Recorder, Deed, UCC, Mortgage, Assessor, Property Tax, Voter Registration, Sex Offender records online.

Greene County Recorder PO Box 309, Bloomfield, IN 47424 (Courthouse, Rm

109). **812-384-2020** Fax: 812-384-2044. 8AM-4PM. www.co.greene.in.us

Hamilton County Recorder 33 N. 9th St, #309, Courthouse, Noblesville, IN 46060 **317-776-9618** Fax: 317-776-8200. 8AM-4:30PM. Inmate, Offender records online.

Hancock County Recorder 9 E. Main St, Rm 204, Greenfield, IN 46140 **317-477-1142** 8-4PM. www.hancockcoingov.org/recorder Sale Disclosure records online.

Harrison County Recorder 300 Capitol Ave, Courthouse, Rm 204, Corydon, IN 47112 **812-738-3788** Fax: 812-738-1153. 8AM-4PM M,T,Th,F; 8AM-N W & Sat.

Hendricks County Recorder 355 S Washington, Danville, IN 46122 **317-745-9224** 8AM-4PM. www.co.hendricks.in.us Property, GIS-Mapping records online.

Henry County Recorder PO Box K, New Castle, IN 47362 (101 S Main St). **765-529-4304** Fax: 765-521-7017. 8AM-4PM.

Howard County Recorder PO Box 733, Kokomo, IN 46903-0733 (Admin. Bldg., 230 N Main Rm 330). **765-456-2210** Fax: 765-456-2056. 8AM-4PM.

Huntington County Recorder 201 N. Jefferson St., Rm 101, Huntington, IN 46750-2841 **260-358-4848** 8AM-4:30PM.

Jackson County Recorder PO Box 75, Brownstown, IN 47220 (101 S. Main - Main Fl). **812-358-6113** 8AM-4:30PM.

Jasper County Recorder 115 W. Washington, Courthouse Box 4, Rensselaer, IN 47978-2891 (2nd Fl). **219-866-4923** 8AM-4PM.

Jay County Recorder 120 W. Main St, Portland, IN 47371 **260-726-6940** 8:30AM-4:30PM.

Jefferson County Recorder 300 E Main St, Courthouse - Rm 104, Madison, IN 47250 **812-265-8902** 8AM-4PM.

Jennings County Recorder PO Box 397, Vernon, IN 47282-0397 (200 E Brown St). **812-352-3053** Fax: 812-352-3000. 8-4PM.

Johnson County Recorder PO Box 489, Franklin, IN 46131 (86 W. Court St). **317-736-3718** Fax: 317-736-4776. 8-4:30PM.

Knox County Recorder 101 N 7th St, Courthouse, Vincennes, IN 47591 **812-885-2508** Fax: 812-886-2414. 8AM-4PM.

Kosciusko County Recorder 100 W. Center St, Rm 14, Warsaw, IN 46580 **574-372-2360** Fax: 574-372-2469. 8AM-4:30PM. http://kcgov.com Property, GIS Mapping records online.

La Porte County Recorder 813 Lincolnway, La Porte, IN 46350-3488 **219-326-6808** Fax: 219-326-0828. www.laportecounty.org 8:00-4PM. Property records online.

LaGrange County Recorder PO Box 214, LaGrange, IN 46761 (114 W. Michigan St). **260-499-6320** 8-4 M-Th; 8AM-5PM F.

Lake County Recorder 2293 N Main St, Bldg. A, 2nd Fl, Crown Point, IN 46307 **219-755-3730** Fax: 219-755-3257. 8:30-4:30PM.

Lawrence County Recorder 916 15th St, Rm 21, Rm 21, Bedford, IN 47421 **812-275-3245** Fax: 812-275-4138. 8:30AM-4:30PM.

Madison County Recorder 16 E. 9th St, Anderson, IN 46016 **765-641-9618** Fax: 765-641-9617. 8AM-4PM.

Marion County Recorder 200 E. Washington, City-County Bldg, #721, Indianapolis, IN 46204 **317-327-4020** Fax: 317-327-3942. 8AM-4:30PM. www.indygov.org/recorder Real Estate, Lien, Deed, UCC, Inmate records online.

Marshall County Recorder 112 W. Jefferson St, Rm 201, Plymouth, IN 46563 **574-935-8515** Fax: 574-935-5099. 8-4PM.

Martin County Recorder PO Box 147, Shoals, IN 47581 (111 Main St). **812-247-2420** Fax: 812-247-2756. 8AM-4PM.

Miami County Recorder 25 N. Broadway #205, Peru, IN 46970 **765-472-3901** Fax: 765-472-1412. 8AM-4PM.

Monroe County Recorder PO Box 1634, Bloomington, IN 47402 (Courthouse, Rm 122). **812-349-2520** 8AM-4PM.

Montgomery County Recorder PO Box 865, Crawfordsville, IN 47933 (100 E. Main St). **765-364-6415** Fax: 765-364-6404. 8-4.

Morgan County Recorder PO Box 1653, Martinsville, IN 46151 (180 S. Main, #125). **765-342-1077** 8AM-4PM (8AM-5PM F).

Newton County Recorder 201 N 3rd St, Kentland, IN 47951 **219-474-6081** 8-4PM.

Noble County Recorder 101 N. Orange St, Rm 210, Albion, IN 46701 **260-636-2672** Fax: 260-636-3264. 8AM-4PM. www.noblecountyrecorder.com

Ohio County Recorder 413 Main St, Courthouse, Rising Sun, IN 47040 **812-438-3369** Fax: 812-438-4590. 9AM-4PM M,T,Th,F; 9AM-12 Sat; Closed W.

Orange County Recorder 205 E Main St, Courthouse, Paoli, IN 47454 **812-723-3600** 8AM-4PM.

Owen County Recorder Courthouse, Spencer, IN 47460 **812-829-5013** Fax: 812-829-5014. 8AM-4PM.

Parke County Recorder 116 W. High St., Rm 102, Rockville, IN 47872-1787 **765-569-3419** Fax: 765-569-4037. 8AM-4PM.

Perry County Recorder 2219 Payne St, Rm W2, Tell City, IN 47586-2830 **812-547-4261** Fax: 812-547-6428. 8AM-4PM.

Pike County Recorder 801 E Main St, Courthouse, Petersburg, IN 47567-1298 **812-354-6747** Fax: 812-354-9431. 8AM-4PM.

Porter County Recorder 155 Indiana Ave, #210, Valparaiso, IN 46383 **219-465-3465** Fax: 219-465-3592. 8:30AM-4:30PM.

Posey County Recorder 126 E 3rd St #215, Mount Vernon, IN 47620 **812-838-1314** Fax: 812-838-8563. 8AM-4PM.

Pulaski County Recorder 112 E Main St, Courthouse - Rm 220, Winamac, IN 46996 **574-946-3844** 8AM-4PM.

Putnam County Recorder Courthouse Sq, Rm 25, Greencastle, IN 46135 **765-653-5613** 8AM-4PM.

Randolph County Recorder 100 S Main St, Courthouse, Rm 101, Winchester, IN 47394-1899 **765-584-7300** 8AM-4PM.

Ripley County Recorder PO Box 404, Versailles, IN 47042 (115 N. Main St.). **812-689-5808** Fax: 812-689-0048. 8AM-4PM.

Rush County Recorder Courthouse, Rm 208, Rushville, IN 46173 **765-932-2388** 8AM-4PM.

Scott County Recorder 1 E. McClain St, #100, Scottsburg, IN 47170 **812-752-8442** Fax: 812-752-2678. 8:30AM-4:30PM.

Shelby County Recorder 407 S. Harrison, Courthouse, Shelbyville, IN 46176 **317-392-6370** Fax: 317-392-6393. 8AM-4PM.

Spencer County Recorder 200 Main, Courthouse, Rockport, IN 47635 **812-649-6013** Fax: 812-649-6005. 8AM-4PM.

St. Joseph County Recorder 227 W Jefferson, Rm 321, South Bend, IN 46601 **574-235-9525** Fax: 574-235-5170. 8AM-4:30PM. Land, Most Wanted records online.

Starke County Recorder PO Box 1, Knox, IN 46534 (53 E. Mound). **574-772-9110** Fax: 574-772-9178. 8:30AM-4PM.

Steuben County Recorder PO Box 397, Angola, IN 46703 (317 S. Wayne St., #2F). **260-668-1000 x1700** Fax: 260-665-8483. 8AM-4:30PM.

Sullivan County Recorder 100 Court House Sq, Rm 205, Sullivan, IN 47882-1565 **812-268-4844** Fax: 812-268-0521. 8AM-4PM.

Switzerland County Recorder 212 W Main, Courthouse, Vevay, IN 47043 **812-427-2544** 8AM-3:30PM.

Tippecanoe County Recorder 20 N. 3rd St, Lafayette, IN 47901 **765-423-9353** Fax: 765-423-9158. http://county.tippecanoe.in.us 8AM-4:30PM. Property records online.

Tipton County Recorder 101 E. Jefferson St., Courthouse, Tipton, IN 46072 **765-675-4614** Fax: 765-675-3893. 8AM-4PM.

Union County Recorder 26 W. Union St, Liberty, IN 47353 **765-458-5434** Fax: 765-458-5263. 8AM-4PM.

Vanderburgh County Recorder PO Box 1037, Evansville, IN 47708 (231 City-County Admin. Bldg., 1 NW MLK, Jr. Blvd.). **812-435-5215** Fax: 812-435-5580.

8AM-4:30PM. www.assessor.evansville.net Property records online.

Vermillion County Recorder PO Box 145, Newport, IN 47966-0145 (Rm 202, 255 S. Main). **765-492-5003** 8AM-4PM.

Vigo County Recorder 199 Oak St, Terre Haute, IN 47807 **812-462-3301** Fax: 812-232-2219. 8AM-4PM.

Wabash County Recorder One W. Hill St., Courthouse, Wabash, IN 46992 **260-563-0661 x253** 8AM-4PM.

Warren County Recorder 125 N. Monroe, Courthouse - #10, Williamsport, IN 47993-1162 **765-762-3174** Fax: 765-762-7222. 8AM-4PM.

Warrick County Recorder PO Box 28, Boonville, IN 47601-0028 (107 W Locust St, #230). **812-897-6165** Fax: 812-897-6168. www.warrickcounty.gov/departments/recorde r.htm Assessor, Property, Tax Bill records online. 8AM-4PM.

Washington County Recorder Courthouse, Salem, IN 47167 **812-883-4001** Fax: 812-883-4020. 8:30AM-4PM (F 8:30-6PM).

Wayne County Recorder 401 E Main St, County Admin. Bldg., Richmond, IN 47374 **765-973-9235** Fax: 765-973-9341. 8:30AM-5PM M; 8:30AM-4:30 PM T-F. www.co.wayne.in.us/offices Property, Assessor, Marriage records online.

Wells County Recorder 102 W Market St, Courthouse #203, Bluffton, IN 46714 **260-824-6507** Fax: 260-824-1238. 8-4:30PM.

White County Recorder PO Box 127, Monticello, IN 47960 (Main & Broadway Courthouse). **574-583-5912** Fax: 574-583-1521. 8AM-4PM.

Whitley County Recorder Courthouse, 2nd Fl - Rm 18, Columbia City, IN 46725 **260-248-3106** Fax: 260-248-3163. 8AM-4:30PM M-Th; 8AM-6PM F.

Iowa

Organization: 99 counties, 100 recording offices. Lee County has two recording offices. The recording officer is the County Recorder. Many counties utilize a grantor/grantee index containing all transactions recorded with them. See the notes under the county for how to determine which office is appropriate to search. The entire state is in the Central Time Zone (CST).

Real Estate Records: Most counties are hesitant to perform real estate searches, but some will provide a listing from the grantor/grantee index with the understanding that it is not certified in the sense that a title search is. Certification of copies usually costs $2.00-5.00 per document.

UCC Records: Financing statements are filed at the state level, except for real estate related collateral, which are filed with the County Recorder. However, prior to 07/2001, consumer goods were also filed at the County Recorder and these older records can be searched there. All counties will perform UCC searches. Use search request form UCC-11. Search fees are usually $5.00 per debtor name ($6.00 if the standard UCC-11 form is not used). Copies usually cost $1.00 per page.

Tax Lien Records: Federal tax liens on personal property of businesses are filed with the Secretary of State. Other federal and all state tax liens on personal property are filed with the County Recorder. County search practices vary widely but most provide some sort of tax lien search for $6.00 per name. Other Liens: Home improvement, job service.

Online Access: There is no statewide access to county recorder data, however assessor records for 40 counties, plus Ames, Cedar Rapids, Iowa City, and Souix City are available free at www.iowaassessors.com.

A statewide Property Tax lookup and payment page is available at www.iowatreasurers.org/county_locator.cfm?ID=1. First, select the county, then follow prompts to search page where you can first look-up the name, then parcel info.

Adair County Recorder 400 Public Sq, Courthouse, Greenfield, IA 50849 **641-743-2411** Fax: 641-743-2565. 8AM-4:30PM.

Adams County Recorder PO Box 28, Corning, IA 50841 (500 9th St.). **641-322-3744** Fax: 641-322-3744. 8:30AM-4:30PM.

Allamakee County Recorder 110 Allamakee St, Courthouse, Waukon, IA 52172-1794 **563-568-2364** Fax: 319-568-6419. 8AM-4PM.

Appanoose County Recorder Courthouse, Centerville, IA 52544 **641-856-6103** Fax: 641-856-8023. 8:30AM-4:30PM.

Audubon County Recorder 318 Leroy St. #7, Audubon, IA 50025-1255 **712-563-2119** Fax: 712-563-4766. 8AM-4:30PM.

Benton County Recorder Courthouse, Vinton, IA 52349 (111 E 4th St) **319-472-3309** Fax: 319-472-3309. 8AM-4:30PM.

Black Hawk County Recorder 316 E. 5th St, Courthouse, Rm 208, Waterloo, IA 50703-4774 **319-833-3171** Fax: 319-833-3170. 8-5PM. Assessor, Property records online.

Boone County Recorder 201 State St, Boone, IA 50036-3987 **515-433-0514** Fax: 515-432-8102. 8AM-4:30PM. Assessor, Property records online.

Bremer County Recorder 415 E Bremer Ave, Waverly, IA 50677 **319-352-0401** Fax: 319-352-0518. 8AM-4:30PM.

Buchanan County Recorder PO Box 298, Independence, IA 50644-0298 (210 5th Ave NE). **319-334-4259** Fax: 319-334-7453. 8AM-4:30PM.

Buena Vista County Recorder PO Box 454, Storm Lake, IA 50588 **712-749-2539** Fax: 712-749-2539. 8AM-4:30PM. Property Assessor, Ag Sale, Inmate, Accident, Incident records online.

Butler County Recorder PO Box 346, Allison, IA 50602 (428 6th St). **319-267-2735** Fax: 319-267-2675. 8AM-4PM.

Calhoun County Recorder 416 4th St. #3, Calhoun County Courthouse, Rockwell City, IA 50579 **712-297-8121** 8:30AM-4:30PM. Treasurer, Property, Death, Assessor, Real Estate Sale records online.

Carroll County Recorder PO Box 782, Carroll, IA 51401-0782 (114 E 6th). **712-792-3328** Fax: 712-792-9493. 8AM-4:30PM. Assessor, Property records online.

Cass County Recorder 5 W. 7th, Atlantic, IA 50022-1492 **712-243-1692** Fax: 712-243-6660. 8AM-4:30PM.

Cedar County Recorder 400 Cedar St, Courthouse, Tipton, IA 52772-1752 **563-886-2230** Fax: 563-886-2120. 8AM-4PM.

Cerro Gordo County Recorder 220 N. Washington, Mason City, IA 50401 **641-421-3056** Fax: 641-421-3154. 8AM-4:30PM. www.co.cerro-gordo.ia.us Real Estate, Property, Assessor records online.

Cherokee County Recorder Drawer G, Cherokee, IA 51012 (520 W. Main). **712-225-6735** Fax: 712-225-6754. 8-4:30PM.

Chickasaw County Recorder PO Box 14, New Hampton, IA 50659 (8 E. Prospect). **641-394-2336** Fax: 641-394-2816. 8:30AM-4:30PM. www.chickasawcoia.org

Clarke County Recorder 100 S Main, Courthouse, Osceola, IA 50213 **641-342-3313** Fax: 641-342-3313. 8:30AM-4:30PM.

Clay County Recorder 300 W. 4th St, #3, Admin. Bldg, Spencer, IA 51301-3806 **712-262-1081** Fax: 712-264-3983. 8AM-4:30PM. www.co.clay.ia.us Real Estate, Recording, Grantor/Grantee, Tax Sale Certificate, Mortgage, Assessor, Property records online.

Clayton County Recorder PO Box 278, Elkader, IA 52043 (111 High St, 1st Fl). **563-245-2710** Fax: 319-245-2353. 8AM-4:30PM. www.claytoncountyiowa.net

Clinton County Recorder PO Box 2957, Clinton, IA 52733-2957 (1900 N. 3rd St.). **563-244-0565 x0544** Fax: 563-242-8412. 8AM-4:30PM. www.clintoncountyiowa.com

Crawford County Recorder 1202 Broadway, Denison, IA 51442 **712-263-3643** Fax: 712-263-3413. 8AM-4:30PM. http://crawfordcounty.org

Dallas County Recorder PO Box 38, Adel, IA 50003-0038 (801 Court St, Rm 203). **515-993-5804** Fax: 515-933-5970. 8AM-4:30PM. Assessor, Property records online.

Davis County Recorder 100 Courthouse Sq #7, Bloomfield, IA 52537 **641-664-2321** Fax: 641-664-3082. 7:30AM-4:30PM. www.daviscountyassessor.org Real Estate, Assessor, Property Tax records online.

Decatur County Recorder 207 N. Main St, Leon, IA 50144 **641-446-4322** Fax: 641-446-7159. 8AM-4:30PM.

Delaware County Recorder 301 E Main, Courthouse, Manchester, IA 52057 **563-927-4665** Fax: 319-927-3641. 8AM-4:30PM.

Des Moines County Recorder PO Box 277, Burlington, IA 52601-0277 (513 N. Main St). **319-753-8221** Fax: 319-753-8721. 8AM-4:30PM. www.co.des-moines.ia.us/

Dickinson County Recorder PO Box O.E., Spirit Lake, IA 51360 (Hill & 18th Sts). **712-336-1495** Fax: 712-336-2677. 8AM-4:30PM. Assessor, Property records online.

Dubuque County Recorder 720 Central #9, Courthouse, Dubuque, IA 52001 **563-589-4434** Fax: 319-589-4484. 8:30AM-5PM. www.dubuquecounty.org Assessor, Property records online.

Emmet County Recorder 609 1st Ave North, Estherville, IA 51334 **712-362-4115** Fax: 712-362-7454. 8AM-4:30PM. Real Estate, Assessor, Property records online.

Fayette County Recorder PO Box 226, West Union, IA 52175-0226 (114 N. Vine St.). **563-422-3687** Fax: 563-422-3739. 8-4PM.

Floyd County Recorder 101 S Main, Courthouse, Charles City, IA 50616 **641-257-6154** Fax: 641-228-6458. 8AM-4:30PM. Assessor, Property records online.

Franklin County Recorder PO Box 26, Hampton, IA 50441 (12 1st Ave NW). **641-456-5675** Fax: 641-456-6009. 8AM-4PM.

Fremont County Recorder PO Box 295, Sidney, IA 51652. **712-374-2315** Fax: 712-374-2826. 8AM-4:30PM.

Greene County Recorder 114 N. Chestnut, Courthouse, Jefferson, IA 50129 **515-386-**

3716 Fax: 515-386-5274. 8AM-4:30PM. Assessor, Property records online.

Grundy County Recorder 706 G Ave, Grundy Center, IA 50638-1447 **319-824-3234** 8-4:30. Assessor, Property records online.

Guthrie County Recorder 200 N. 5th, Courthouse, Guthrie Center, IA 50115 **641-747-3412** Fax: 641-747-3081. 8-4:30PM.

Hamilton County Recorder PO Box 126, Webster City, IA 50595-0126 (2300 Superior St). **515-832-9535** Fax: 515-832-8620. 8AM-4:30PM. Assessor, Property records online.

Hancock County Recorder 855 State St, Garner, IA 50438 **641-923-2464** Fax: 641-923-3912. 8AM-4PM.

Hardin County Recorder PO Box 443, Eldora, IA 50627 (1215 Edgington Ave.). **641-939-8178** Fax: 641-939-8245. 8AM-4:30PM.

Harrison County Recorder Courthouse, Logan, IA 51546 **712-644-2545** Fax: 712-644-3157. 8AM-4:30PM. Assessor, Property records online.

Henry County Recorder PO Box 106, Mount Pleasant, IA 52641 (100 E. Washington). **319-385-0765** Fax: 319-385-3601. 8AM-4:30PM.

Howard County Recorder 137 N Elm, Court House, Cresco, IA 52136 **563-547-3621** Fax: 319-547-1103. 8AM-4:30PM.

Humboldt County Recorder PO Box 100, Dakota City, IA 50529-0100 (203 Main St). **515-332-3693** Fax: 515-332-1738. 8AM-4:30PM.

Ida County Recorder 401 Moorehead, Courthouse, Ida Grove, IA 51445 **712-364-2220** Fax: 712-364-3939. 8AM-4:30PM.

Iowa County Recorder PO Box 185, Marengo, IA 52301 (901 Court Ave.). **319-642-3622** Fax: 319-642-5562. 7:30-4:30PM.

Jackson County Recorder 201 W. Platt, Courthouse, Maquoketa, IA 52060 **563-652-2504** Fax: 563-652-6460. 8:00AM-4:30PM. www.jacksoncountyiowa.com

Jasper County Recorder PO Box 665, Newton, IA 50208 (Courthouse, Rm 205). **641-792-5442** Fax: 641-791-3680. 8AM-5PM. Assessor, Property records online.

Jefferson County Recorder 51 W. Briggs, Fairfield, IA 52556-2820 **641-472-4331** Fax: 641-472-6695. 8AM-4:30PM. Assessor, Property records online.

Johnson County Recorder 913 S. Dubuque St, #202, Iowa City, IA 52240-4207 **319-356-**

6093 Fax: 319-339-6181. 8AM-4PM MWF; 8AM-5:30PM T,Th. Assessor, Property records online. www.johnson-county.com

Jones County Recorder 500 W Main, Courthouse, Rm 116, Anamosa, IA 52205-1632 **319-462-2477** Fax: 319-462-5802. 8AM-4:30PM. www.co.jones.ia.us/recorder.html

Keokuk County Recorder 101 S. Main St., Courthouse, Sigourney, IA 52591 **641-622-2540** Fax: 641-622-3789. 8AM-4:30PM. www.keokukcountyia.com

Kossuth County Recorder 114 W. State, Algona, IA 50511 **515-295-5660** Fax: 515-295-3071. 8AM-4PM. Assessor, Property records online.

Lee County (Northern District) County Recorder PO Box 322, Fort Madison, IA 52627-0322 (933 Avenue H). **319-372-4662** Fax: 319-372-7033. 8:30AM-4:30PM. www.leecounty.org

Lee County (Southern District) County Recorder PO Box 160, Keokuk, IA 52632 (25 N. 7th). **319-524-1126** Fax: 319-524-1544. 8:30AM-4:30PM. www.leecounty.org

Linn County Recorder PO Box 1406, Cedar Rapids, IA 52406-1406 (930 First St S.W.). **319-892-5420** Fax: 319-892-5459. 8-5PM. www.linncountyrecorder.com Assessor, Property records online.

Louisa County Recorder PO Box 264, Wapello, IA 52653-0264 (117 S. Main St). **319-523-5361** Fax: 319-523-5362. 8-4:30.

Lucas County Recorder 916 Braden, Courthouse, Chariton, IA 50049 **641-774-2413** Fax: 641-774-1619. 8AM-4PM.

Lyon County Recorder 206 Second Ave, Courthouse, Rock Rapids, IA 51246 **712-472-2381** Fax: 712-472-2381. 8AM-4:30PM. Assessor, Property records online.

Madison County Recorder PO Box 152, Winterset, IA 50273-0152 (112 N. John Wayne Dr). **515-462-3771** Fax: 515-462-5881. 8AM-4:30PM; 9AM-N Last Sat of the month. www.madisoncoia.us Assessor, Property records online.

Mahaska County Recorder 106 S.1st. St, Courthouse, Oskaloosa, IA 52577 **641-673-8187** 8AM-4:30PM. Assessor, Property records online.

Marion County Recorder 214 E. Main St., Knoxville, IA 50138 **641-828-2211** Fax: 641-828-3538. 8AM-4:30PM. Assessor, Property records online.

Marshall County Recorder PO Box 573, Marshalltown, IA 50158-0573 (3rd Fl, 1 E. Main St.). **641-754-6355** Fax: 641-754-6349. 8AM-4:30PM. www.co.marshall.ia.us Assessor, Property records online.

Mills County Recorder 418 Sharp St, Courthouse, Glenwood, IA 51534 **712-527-9315** 8AM-4:30PM. Assessor, Property records online.

Mitchell County Recorder 508 State St, Osage, IA 50461-1250 **641-732-5861** Fax: 641-732-5218. 8AM-4:30PM.

Monona County Recorder PO Box 53, Onawa, IA 51040 (610 Iowa Ave). **712-423-2575** Fax: 712-423-3034. 8AM-4:30PM.

Monroe County Recorder 10 Benton Ave. East, Courthouse, Albia, IA 52531 **641-932-5164** Fax: 641932-2863. 8AM-4PM.

Montgomery County Recorder PO Box 469, Red Oak, IA 51566 (105 E Coolbaugh St). **712-623-4363** Fax: 712-623-8915. 8AM-4:30PM. Assessor, Property records online.

Muscatine County Recorder 401 E. 3rd St, Courthouse, Muscatine, IA 52761-4166 **563-263-7741** Fax: 563-263-7248. 8AM-4:30PM. www.co.muscatine.ia.us Property, GIS-mapping records online.

O'Brien County Recorder PO Box 340, Primghar, IA 51245-0340 (155 S Hayes). **712-957-3045** Fax: 712-957-3046. 8-4:30. www.obriencounty.com/government/recorder.htm

Osceola County Recorder 300 7th St, Courthouse, Sibley, IA 51249-1695 (300 7th St). **712-754-3345** Fax: 712-754-3743. 8AM-4:30PM. www.osceolaclerkcourt.org

Page County Recorder 112 E. Main St., Courthouse, Clarinda, IA 51632 (112 E. Main St). **712-542-3130** Fax: 712-542-3636. 8AM-4:30PM.

Palo Alto County Recorder PO Box 248, Emmetsburg, IA 50536 (1010 Broadway). **712-852-3701** Fax: 712-852-3704. 8-4PM.

Plymouth County Recorder 215 4th Ave. SE, Courthouse, Le Mars, IA 51031 **712-546-4020** 8-5. Assessor, Property records online.

Pocahontas County Recorder 99 Court Sq, Pocahontas, IA 50574-1621 **712-335-4404** Fax: 712-335-4502. 8AM-4PM.

Polk County Recorder 111 Court Ave, Rm 250, County Admin. Bldg., Des Moines, IA 50309 **515-286-3160** Fax: 515-323-5393. 8AM-4:30PM. www.co.polk.ia.us Assessor, Property, Real Estate Sale, Recording, Deed, Lien, UCC records online.

Pottawattamie County Recorder 227 S. Sixth St, Council Bluffs, IA 51501 **712-328-5612** Fax: 712-328-4738. 8AM-4PM.

www.pottcounty.com Real Estate, Property, Residential Sale, Assessor records online.

Poweshiek County Recorder PO Box 656, Montezuma, IA 50171-0656 (302 E. Main St). **641-623-5434** Fax: 641-623-2875. 8AM-4PM. Assessor, Property records online.

Ringgold County Recorder 109 W Madison #204, Mount Ayr, IA 50854 **641-464-3231** Fax: 641-464-2568. 8AM-4PM.

Sac County Recorder 100 NW State St., Sac City, IA 50583 **712-662-7789** Fax: 712-662-6298. 8AM-4:30PM. www.saccounty.org

Scott County Recorder 428 Western Ave, 5th Fl, Davenport, IA 52801-1187 **563-326-8621** Fax: 563-328-3225. 8AM-4:30PM. www.scottcountyiowa.com Assessor, Property, Restaurant Inspection, Most Wanted records online.

Shelby County Recorder PO Box 67, Harlan, IA 51537-0067 (612 Court St, Rm 201). **712-755-5640** Fax: 712-755-7556. 8AM-4:30PM. www.shco.org Real Estate Recording, Assessor, Property records online.

Sioux County Recorder PO Box 48, Orange City, IA 51041 (210 Central Ave SW). **712-737-2229** Fax: 712-737-2230. 8AM-4:30PM. www.siouxcounty.org Property Tax records online.

Story County Recorder PO Box 55, Nevada, IA 50201-0055 (900 6th St, Admin. Bldg.). **515-382-7230** Fax: 515-382-7326. 8AM-5PM (No recording after 3:30PM). www.storycounty.com/departments.html Assessor, Property Tax, Grantor/Grantee, Deed, Mortgage, UCC, Sheriff Sale, Most Wanted records online.

Tama County Recorder PO Box 82, Toledo, IA 52342 (High St). **641-484-3320** 8AM-4:30PM.

Taylor County Recorder 405 Jefferson St., Courthouse, Bedford, IA 50833 **712-523-2275** Fax: 712-523-2274. 8AM-4:30PM.

Union County Recorder 300 N. Pine St, Creston, IA 50801 **641-782-1725** Fax: 641-782-1709. 8:30AM-4:30PM.

Van Buren County Recorder PO Box 455, Keosauqua, IA 52565 (Dodge & 4th Sts). **319-293-3240** Fax: 319-293-3828. 8-4:30PM.

Wapello County Recorder 101 W. 4th St, Ottumwa, IA 52501 **641-683-0045** Fax: 641-683-0019. 8AM-4:30PM.

Warren County Recorder 301 N Buxton, #109, Indianola, IA 50125 **515-961-1089** 8-4:30. Assessor, Property records online.

Washington County Recorder PO Box 889, Washington, IA 52353-0889 (224 W. Main St.). **319-653-7727** 8AM-4:30PM. Assessor, Property records online.

Wayne County Recorder PO Box 435, Corydon, IA 50060 (Highways 2 & 14, Courthouse). **641-872-1676** Fax: 641-872-2843. 8AM-4PM.

Webster County Recorder PO Box 1253, Fort Dodge, IA 50501 (701 Central Ave, 2nd Fl). **515-576-2401** Fax: 515-574-3723.

8AM-4:30PM. www.webstercountyia.org Assessor, Property, Real Estate records online.

Winnebago County Recorder 126 S. Clark St #1, Courthouse, Forest City, IA 50436-1706 **641-585-2094** Fax: 641-585-2891. 8AM-4:30PM.

Winneshiek County Recorder 201 W. Main St, Decorah, IA 52101 **563-382-3486** Fax: 319-387-4083. 8AM-4PM.

Woodbury County Auditor & Recorder 620 Douglas St, Rm 106, Sioux City, IA

51101 **712-279-6528** Fax: 712-233-8946. 8AM-4:30PM. Assessor, Property, Real Estate records online.

Worth County Recorder 1000 Central Ave, Northwood, IA 50459 **641-324-2734** Fax: 641-324-3682. 8AM-4PM.

Wright County Recorder PO Box 187, Clarion, IA 50525 (115 N. Main). **515-532-3204** Fax: 515-532-2669. 8AM-4PM. www.wrightcounty.org/county_offices.htm

Kansas

Organization: 105 counties, 105 recording offices. The recording officer is the Register of Deeds. Many counties utilize a "Miscellaneous Index" for tax and other liens, separate from real estate records. 100 counties are in the Central Time Zone (CST) and 5 are in the Mountain Time Zone (MST).

Real Estate Records: Most counties will not perform real estate searches, although some will do as an accommodation with the understanding that they are not "certified." Some counties will also do a search based upon legal description to determine owner. Copy fees vary, and certification fees are usually $1.00 per document. Tax records are located at the Appraiser's Office.

UCC Records: Financing statements are filed at the state level, except for real estate related collateral, which are filed with the Register of Deeds. However, prior to 07/2001, consumer goods collateral were also filed at the Register of Deeds and these older records can be searched there. All counties will perform UCC searches. Use search request form UCC-3. Search fees are usually $15.00 per debtor name. Copies usually cost $1.00 per page.

Tax Lien Records: Federal tax liens on personal property of businesses are filed with the Secretary of State. Other federal tax liens and all state tax liens on personal property are filed with the county Register of Deeds. Most counties automatically include tax liens on personal property with a UCC search. Tax liens on personal property may usually be searched separately for $8.00 per name. Other Liens: Mechanics, harvesters, lis pendens, threshers.

Online Access: A few counties have online access, there is no statewide system.

Allen Register of Deeds 1 N. Washington Ave, Iola, KS 66749 **620-365-1412** Fax: 620-365-1414. 8AM-5PM. www.ksrods.org

Anderson Register of Deeds 100 E 4th St, Courthouse, Garnett, KS 66032-1503 **785-448-3715** Fax: 785-448-5621. 8AM-5PM. Marriage records online.

Atchison Register of Deeds 423 N. 5th St., Courthouse, Atchison, KS 66002-1861 **913-367-2568** Fax: 913-367-8441. 8:30-5PM.

Barber Register of Deeds 120 E. Washington St, Courthouse, Medicine Lodge, KS 67104 **620-886-3981** Fax: 620-886-5045. 8:30AM-5PM.

Barton Register of Deeds 1400 Main St, Courthouse, #205, Great Bend, KS 67530-4037 **620-793-1849** Fax: 620-793-1981. 8AM-5PM. www.bartoncounty.org Assessor records online.

Bourbon Register of Deeds 210 S. National, Fort Scott, KS 66701 **620-223-3800 x17** Fax: 620-223-5241. 8:30AM-4:30PM.

Brown Register of Deeds 601 Oregon, Courthouse, Hiawatha, KS 66434 **85-742-3741** Fax: 785-742-3255. 8AM-5PM. www.brown.kansasgov.com

Butler Register of Deeds 205 W. Central, Courthouse, #104, El Dorado, KS 67042 **316-322-4113** Fax: 316-321-1011. 8AM-5PM. www.bucoks.com Appraiser, Real Estate Value records online.

Chase Register of Deeds PO Box 529, Cottonwood Falls, KS 66845-0529 (Courthouse Plaza). **620-273-6398** Fax: 620-273-6617. 8AM-5PM.

Chautauqua Register of Deeds 215 N. Chautauqua, Courthouse, Sedan, KS 67361 **620-725-5830** Fax: 620-725-5831. 8AM-N, 1-4PM.

Cherokee Register of Deeds PO Box 228, Columbus, KS 66725 (110 W. Maple, Rm 121). **620-429-3777** Fax: 620-429-1362. 9AM-5PM.

Cheyenne Register of Deeds PO Box 907, St. Francis, KS 67756-0907 (212 E. Washington). **785-332-8820** Fax: 785-332-8825. 8AM-N,1-5PM.

Clark Register of Deeds PO Box 222, Ashland, KS 67831-0222 (913 Highland). **620-635-2812** Fax: 620-635-2393. 8:30AM-4:30PM.

Clay Register of Deeds PO Box 63, Clay Center, KS 67432 (712 5th St.). **785-632-3811** Fax: 785-632-2736. 8AM-5PM.

Cloud Register of Deeds PO Box 96, Concordia, KS 66901-0096 (811 Washington St). **785-243-8121** Fax: 785-243-8123. www.cloudcountyks.org Assessor, Property records online. 8AM-4:30PM.

Coffey Register of Deeds 110 S 6th St, Rm 205 - Courthouse, Burlington, KS 66839 **620-364-2423** 8-5PM. Marriage records online.

Comanche Register of Deeds PO Box 576, Coldwater, KS 67029-0576 (201 S. New

York). **620-582-2152** Fax: 620-582-2390. 9AM-N,1-5PM.

Cowley Register of Deeds PO Box 741, Winfield, KS 67156-0471 (311 E. 9th). **620-221-5461** Fax: 620-221-5463. 8AM-N,1-5.

Crawford Register of Deeds PO Box 44, Girard, KS 66743 (Courthouse, 2nd Fl). **620-724-8218** Fax: 620-724-8823. 8:30AM-4:30PM.

Decatur Register of Deeds PO Box 167, Oberlin, KS 67749-0167 (120 E. Hall). **785-475-8105** Fax: 785-475-8150. 8AM-N,1-5.

Dickinson Register of Deeds PO Box 517, Abilene, KS 67410 (First & Buckeye, Court house). **785-263-3073** Fax: 785-263-0428. 8-5PM. Property, Assessor records online.

Doniphan Register of Deeds PO Box 73, Troy, KS 66087 (120 E. Chestnut St.). **785-985-3932** Fax: 785-985-3723. 8AM-5PM. www.dpcountyks.com

Douglas Register of Deeds 1100 Massachusetts, Courthouse, Lawrence, KS 66044-3097 **785-832-5283** Fax: 785-330-2807. 8AM-5PM. www.douglas-county.com Property Appraiser, Real Estate, Recording, Deed, Lien records online.

Edwards Register of Deeds PO Box 264, Kinsley, KS 67547-0364 (312 Massachusetts). **620-659-3131** Fax: 620-659-2583. 8AM-5PM.

Elk Register of Deeds PO Box 476, Howard, KS 67349-0476 (127 N. Pine). **620-374-2472** Fax: 620-374-2771. 8AM-4:30PM.

Ellis Register of Deeds PO Box 654, Hays, KS 67601 (1204 Fort St). **785-628-9450** Fax: 785-628-9451. 8-5. www.ksrods.org

Ellsworth Register of Deeds 210 N. Kansas #7, Courthouse, Ellsworth, KS 67439-3110 **785-472-3022** Fax: 785-472-4912. 8-5PM.

Finney Register of Deeds PO Box M, Garden City, KS 67846 (311 N. 9th). **620-272-3520** Fax: 620-272-3624. 8AM-5PM. www.finneycounty.org

Ford Register of Deeds PO Box 1352, Dodge City, KS 67801-1352 (100 Gunsmoke, 4th Fl, East Office, Gov't Ctr). **620-227-4565** Fax: 620-227-4566. 9-5PM.

Franklin Register of Deeds 315 S. Main, Courthouse, Rm 103, Ottawa, KS 66067-2335 **785-229-3440** Fax: 785-229-3419. 8AM-4:30PM. Marriage records online.

Geary Register of Deeds PO Box 927, Junction City, KS 66441-2591 (200 E. 8th). **785-238-5531** Fax: 785-762-2642. 8:30-5.

Gove Register of Deeds PO Box 116, Gove, KS 67736 (520 Washington St). **785-938-4465** Fax: 785-938-4486. 8AM-N, 1-5PM.

Graham Register of Deeds 410 N. Pomeroy, Hill City, KS 67642 **785-421-2551** Fax: 785-421-2784. 8AM-5PM.

Grant Register of Deeds 108 S. Glenn, Lower Level, Courthouse, Ulysses, KS 67880 **620-356-1538** Fax: 620-356-5379. 9-5PM.

Gray Register of Deeds PO Box 487, Cimarron, KS 67835-0487 (300 S. Main). **620-855-3835** Fax: 620-855-3107. 8-5PM.

Greeley Register of Deeds PO Box 12, Tribune, KS 67879 (616 Second St). **620-376-4275** Fax: 620-376-2294. 9AM-5PM.

Greenwood Register of Deeds 311 N Main, Courthouse, Eureka, KS 67045-1311 **620-583-8162** Fax: 620-583-8178. 8AM-5PM.

Hamilton Register of Deeds PO Box 1167, Syracuse, KS 67878 **620-384-6925** Fax: 620-384-5853. 8AM-N, 1-4:30PM.

Harper Register of Deeds 201 N Jennings, Courthouse, Anthony, KS 67003 **620-842-5336** Fax: 620-842-3455. 8AM-N,1-5PM. www.harpercounty.org/departments.htm

Harvey Register of Deeds PO Box 687, Newton, KS 67114-0687 (8th & Main). **316-284-6950** Fax: 316-284-6951. 8AM-5PM.

Haskell Register of Deeds PO Box 656, Sublette, KS 67877 (300 S. Inman). **620-675-8343** 9AM-N,1-5PM.

Hodgeman Register of Deeds PO Box 505, Jetmore, KS 67854-0505 (500 Main St). **620-357-8536** Fax: 620-357-6161. 9AM-12:00-1-5PM.

Jackson Register of Deeds 415 New York, Courthouse, Rm 203, Holton, KS 66436 **785-364-3591** Fax: 785-364-3420. 8-4:30PM.

Jefferson Register of Deeds PO Box 352, Oskaloosa, KS 66066-0352 (310 Jefferson St). **785-863-2243** Fax: 785-863-2602. 8AM-6:30PM M; 8AM-4PM T-F.

Jewell Register of Deeds 307 N. Commercial St, Courthouse, Mankato, KS 66956-2093 **785-378-4070** Fax: 785-378-4075. 8:30AM-N, 1-4:30PM.

Johnson Register of Deeds PO Box 700, Olathe, KS 66051 (111 S. Cherry St, #1300). **913-715-2300 x5375** Fax: 913-715-2310. 8AM-5PM. www.jocoks.com Property Appraiser, Tax Sale, Land records online.

Kearny Register of Deeds PO Box 42, Lakin, KS 67860 (304 N. Main). **620-355-6241** Fax: 620-355-7382. 8AM-5PM.

Kingman Register of Deeds 130 N Spruce, Kingman, KS 67068 **620-532-3211** Fax: 620-532-2037. 8AM-N,1-5PM.

Kiowa Register of Deeds 211 E Florida, Greensburg, KS 67054 **620-723-2441** Fax: 620-723-1033. 8:30AM-N, 1-5PM. www.kiowacounty.us

Labette Register of Deeds 521 Merchant, Courthouse, Oswego, KS 67356 **620-795-4931** Fax: 620-795-2928. 8:30AM-5PM.

Lane Register of Deeds PO Box 805, Dighton, KS 67839-0805 (144 South Lane). **620-397-2803** Fax: 620-397-5937. 8AM-N,1-5PM.

Leavenworth Register of Deeds 300 Walnut, Rm 103, Courthouse, Leavenworth, KS 66048 **913-684-0424** Fax: 913-684-0406. 8AM-5PM.

Lincoln Register of Deeds 216 E. Lincoln, Lincoln, KS 67455-2056 **785-524-4657** Fax: 785-524-5008. 8AM-N,12:30-4:30PM.

Linn Register of Deeds PO Box 350, Mound City, KS 66056-0350 (315 Main St). **913-795-2226** Fax: 913-795-2889. 8AM-N, 12:30-4:30PM.

Logan Register of Deeds 710 W. 2nd St, Courthouse, Oakley, KS 67748 **785-672-4224** Fax: 785-672-3517. 8AM-5PM.

Lyon Register of Deeds 430 Commercial St, Emporia, KS 66801 **620-341-3241** Fax: 620-341-3438. 8AM-5PM.

Marion Register of Deeds PO Box 158, Marion, KS 66861-0158 (Courthouse Sq). **620-382-2151** Fax: 620-382-3420. 8:30AM-5PM.

Marshall Register of Deeds 1201 Broadway, Courthouse, Marysville, KS 66508 **785-562-3226** Fax: 785-562-5685. 8:30AM-5PM.

McPherson Register of Deeds PO Box 86, McPherson, KS 67460 (119 N. Maple). **620-241-5050** Fax: 620-245-0749. 8AM-5PM. www.mcphersoncountyks.us

Meade Register of Deeds PO Box 399, Meade, KS 67864-0399 (200 N. Fowler). **620-873-8705** Fax: 620-873-8713. 8-5PM.

Miami Register of Deeds 201 S. Pearl St. #101, Paola, KS 66071 **913-294-3716** Fax: 913-294-9515. 8AM-4:30PM.

Mitchell Register of Deeds PO Box 6, Beloit, KS 67420 (111 S. Hersey). **785-738-3854** Fax: 785-738-5844. 8:30AM-5PM.

Montgomery Register of Deeds PO Box 647, Independence, KS 67301 (217 E.Myrtle St. #102). **620-330-1140** Fax: 620-330-1144. 8:30AM-5PM.

Morris Register of Deeds Courthouse, Council Grove, KS 66846 **620-767-5614** Fax: 620-767-6712. 8AM-5PM.

Morton Register of Deeds PO Box 756, Elkhart, KS 67950-0756 (1025 Morton). **620-697-2561** Fax: 620-697-4386. 9-5PM.

Nemaha Register of Deeds PO Box 211, Seneca, KS 66538 (607 Nemaha). **785-336-2120** Fax: 785-336-3373. 8AM-4:30PM.

Neosho Register of Deeds PO Box 138, Erie, KS 66733-0138 (100 Main). **620-244-3858** Fax: 620-244-3860. 8AM-4:30PM.

Ness Register of Deeds PO Box 127, Ness City, KS 67560 (202 W. Sycamore). **785-798-3127** Fax: 785-798-3829. 8AM-N, 1-5.

Norton Register of Deeds PO Box 70, Norton, KS 67654 (Courthouse). **785-877-5765** Fax: 785-877-5703. 8AM-N, 1-5PM.

Osage Register of Deeds PO Box 265, Lyndon, KS 66451-0265 (717 Topeka Ave). **785-828-4523** Fax: 785-828-4749. 8AM-5PM. www.osageco.org Appraiser, Property records online.

Osborne Register of Deeds PO Box 160, Osborne, KS 67473-0160 (423 W. Main). **785-346-2452** Fax: 785-346-5252. 8:30AM-N, 1-5PM. www.osbornecounty.org Property, Appraiser records online.

Ottawa Register of Deeds 307 N Concord, Courthouse - #220, Minneapolis, KS 67467-2140 **785-392-2078** Fax: 785-392-3605. 8AM-N,1-5PM. www.ottawacounty.org Appraiser, Property Tax records online.

Pawnee Register of Deeds 715 Broadway St., Courthouse, 2nd Fl, Larned, KS 67550-3097 **620-285-3276** Fax: 620-285-3802. 8:30-5.

Phillips Register of Deeds 310 State St, Courthouse, Phillipsburg, KS 67661 **785-543-6875** Fax: 785-999-9999. 8AM-5PM.

Pottawatomie Register of Deeds PO Box 186, Westmoreland, KS 66549 (207 N. 1st). **785-457-3471** Fax: 785-457-3577. 8AM-4:30PM. www.pottcounty.org

Pratt Register of Deeds PO Box 873, Pratt, KS 67124 (3rd & Ninnescah). **620-672-4140** Fax: 620-672-9541. 8AM-N,1-5PM. www.prattcounty.org

Rawlins Register of Deeds PO Box 201, Atwood, KS 67730 (607 Main). **785-626-3172** Fax: 785-626-9481. 9AM-N,1-5PM.

Reno Register of Deeds 206 W. First, Hutchinson, KS 67501 **620-694-2942** Fax: 620-694-2944. 8AM-5PM.

Republic Register of Deeds PO Box 429, Belleville, KS 66935 (1815 M St.). **785-527-7238** Fax: 785-527-2659. 8AM-5PM.

Rice Register of Deeds 101 W. Commercial, Lyons, KS 67554 **620-257-2931** Fax: 620-257-3039. 8:00AM-5PM.

Riley Register of Deeds 5th & Humboldt Sts., 110 Courthouse Plaza, Manhattan, KS 66502-6018 **785-537-6340** Fax: 785-537-6343. 8AM-5PM. www.co.riley.ks.us/register/

Rooks Register of Deeds 115 N. Walnut St., Stockton, KS 67669 **785-425-6291** Fax: 785-425-6497. 8AM-N,1-5PM.

Rush Register of Deeds PO Box 117, La Crosse, KS 67548 (715 Elm). **785-222-3312** Fax: 785-222-3559. 8:30AM-N, 1-5PM.

Russell Register of Deeds PO Box 191, Russell, KS 67665 (4th & Main). **785-483-4612** Fax: 785-483-5725. 8AM-5PM.

Saline Register of Deeds PO Box 5040, Salina, KS 67402-5040 (300 W. Ash, Rm 212). **785-309-5855** Fax: 785-309-5856. 8AM-5PM. www.co.saline.ks.us

Scott Register of Deeds 303 Court St., Courthouse, Scott City, KS 67871 **620-872-3155** Fax: 620-872-7145. 8AM-5PM. www.scott.kansasgov.com

Sedgwick Register of Deeds PO Box 3326, Wichita, KS 67201-3326 (525 N. Main, 4th Fl, Rm 415). **316-660-9400** Fax: 316-383-8066. www.sedgwickcounty.org/deeds/ Real Estate, Lien, Recorder, Assessor, Property Sale, Property Tax, Treasurer, Delinquent Tax records online. 8AM-5PM.

Seward Register of Deeds 415 N. Washington, #105, Courthouse, Liberal, KS 67901 **620-626-3220** Fax: 620-626-3362. 8AM-5PM. www.seward.kansasgov.com

Shawnee Register of Deeds 200 E. 7th St, #108, Topeka, KS 66603-3932 **785-233-8200 x4020** Fax: 785-291-4950. 8AM-4:30PM. www.co.shawnee.ks.us Property Appraiser, Personal Property records online.

Sheridan Register of Deeds PO Box 899, Hoxie, KS 67740-0899 (925 9th St). **785-675-3741** Fax: 785-675-3050. 8AM-N,1-5.

Sherman Register of Deeds 813 Broadway, Rm 104, Goodland, KS 67735-3097 **785-899-4845** Fax: 785-899-4848. 7AM-N,1-4PM.

Smith Register of Deeds 218 S. Grant, Smith Center, KS 66967 **785-282-5160** Fax: 785-282-6257. 8AM-N, 1-5PM.

Stafford Register of Deeds 209 N. Broadway, County Courthouse, St. John, KS 67576 **620-549-3505** 8AM-N,1-5PM.

Stanton Register of Deeds PO Box 716, Johnson, KS 67855 (201 N. Main). **620-492-2190** Fax: 620-492-2688. 8:30AM-N, 1-5.

Stevens Register of Deeds 200 E. 6th, Hugoton, KS 67951 **620-544-2630** Fax: 620-544-4081. 9AM-5PM.

Sumner Register of Deeds PO Box 469, Wellington, KS 67152 (500 Block N. Washington, #103). **620-326-2041** Fax: 620-326-8172. 8AM-5PM.

Thomas Register of Deeds 300 N. Court, Colby, KS 67701 **785-462-4535** Fax: 785-462-4512. 8AM-N, 1PM-5PM.

Trego Register of Deeds 216 Main, WaKeeney, KS 67672-2189 **785-743-6622** Fax: 785-743-2461. 8:30AM-5PM.

Wabaunsee Register of Deeds PO Box 278, Alma, KS 66401-0278 (215 Kansas Ave). **785-765-3822** Fax: 785-765-3824. 8AM-4:30PM. www.wabaunsee.kansasgov.com Property Tax, Treasurer, Property, Assessor records online.

Wallace Register of Deeds PO Box 10, Sharon Springs, KS 67758-9998 (313 N. Main). **785-852-4283** Fax: 785-852-4783. 8AM-N, 1-5PM.

Washington Register of Deeds 214 C St, Courthouse, Washington, KS 66968-1928 **785-325-2286** Fax: 785-325-2830. 8-5PM.

Wichita Register of Deeds PO Box 472, Leoti, KS 67861-0472 (206 S. 4th). **620-375-2733** Fax: 316-375-4350. 8AM-N,1-5PM.

Wilson Register of Deeds Courthouse, Rm 106, Fredonia, KS 66736-1396 **620-378-3662** Fax: 620-378-4762. 8:30AM-5PM.

Woodson Register of Deeds 105 W. Rutledge, Rm 101, Yates Center, KS 66783-1499 **620-625-8635** Fax: 620-625-8670. 8AM-N,1-5PM. www.woodsoncounty.net

Wyandotte Register of Deeds 710 N. 7th St., Courthouse, Kansas City, KS 66101-3084 **913-573-2841** Fax: 913-321-3075. 8AM-5PM. Real Estate, Lien, Property Appraisal, Personal Property, Recording, Deed, Judgment records online.

Kentucky

Organization: 120 counties, 122 recording offices. The recording officer is the County Clerk. Kenton County has two recording offices. Jefferson County had a separate office for UCC filing until June 30, 2001; that office now only searches for filings up to that date. 80 counties are in the Eastern Time Zone (EST) and 40 are in the Central Time Zone (CST).

Real Estate Records: Most counties will not perform real estate searches. Copy fees vary. Certification fee is usually $5 per document. Tax records are maintained by the Property Valuation Administrator, designated "Assessor" in this section.

UCC Records: Under revised Article 9, Kentucky changes from a "local filing state" to a "central filing state" with the Secretary Of State's office. Collateral on non-resident debtors were always filed at the state level. Rela estate related UCC is still found at the County Clerk's offcie. Many counties will not perform UCC searches. Use search request form UCC-11. Search fees are usually $5.00 per debtor name, and copy fees vary widely.

Tax Lien Records: All federal and state tax liens on personal property are filed with the County Clerk, often in an "Encumbrance Book." Most counties will not perform tax lien searches. Other Liens: Judgments, motor vehicle, mechanics, lis pendens, bail bond

Online Access: A few counties offer free access to assessor records. Several other counties offer commercial systems. There is no statewide system.

Adair County Clerk 424 Public Sq, Columbia, KY 42728 **270-384-2801** Fax: 270-384-4805. 7:30AM-4PM.

Allen County Clerk 201 W. Main St, Rm 6, Scottsville, KY 42164 **270-237-3706** Fax: 270-237-9206. 8:00-4:30PM, 8AM-N Sat.

Anderson County Clerk 151 S. Main, Lawrenceburg, KY 40342 **502-839-3041** Fax: 502-839-3043. 8:30AM-5PM M-Th; 8:30AM-6PM F.

Ballard County Clerk PO Box 145, Wickliffe, KY 42087 (132 N 4th St). **270-335-5168** Fax: 270-335-3081. 8AM-4PM M-F; 8AM-5:30PM Last Friday of month.

Barren County Clerk 117 N Public Sq #1A, Glasgow, KY 42141-2869 **270-651-5200** Fax: 270-651-1083. 8AM-4:30AM.

Bath County Clerk PO Box 609, Owingsville, KY 40360 17 Main St). **606-674-2613** Fax: 606-674-9526. 8AM-4PM.

Bell County Clerk PO Box 156, Pineville, KY 40977 (Courthouse Sq). **606-337-6143** Fax: 606-337-5415. 8AM-4 M-F; 8-N Sat.

Boone County Clerk PO Box 874, Burlington, KY 41005 (2950 E. Washington Sq, 1st Fl). **859-334-2137** Fax: 859-334-2193. 8:30-4:30 M, W-F; 8:30-6 T. www.boonecountyclerk.com Real estate, lien, UCC, Assessor, Marriage records online.

Bourbon County Clerk PO Box 312, Paris, KY 40362-0312 (Main St). **859-987-2142** Fax: 859-987-5660. 8:30AM-4:30PM M-Th; 8:30AM-6PM F.

Boyd County Clerk PO Box 523, Catlettsburg, KY 41129 (2800 Louisa St). **606-739-5116** Fax: 606-739-6357. 8:30AM-

4PM Main Office; 9AM-4:30PM & 9AM-N Sat. Real Estate, Lien records online.

Boyle County Clerk 321 W. Main St., Rm 123, Danville, KY 40422-1837 **859-238-1112** Fax: 859-238-1114. 8:30AM-5PM M; 8:30AM-4PM T-F.

Bracken County Clerk PO Box 147, Brooksville, KY 41004-0147 **606-735-2952** Fax: 606-735-2687. 8AM-4PM M,T,Th,F; 8AM-N W,Sat.

Breathitt County Clerk 1137 Main St, Jackson, KY 41339 **606-666-3810** Fax: 606-666-3807. 8AM-4PM M,T,Th,F; 8AM-N W; 9AM-N Sat.

Breckinridge County Clerk PO Box 538, Hardinsburg, KY 40143 (Main St.). **270-756-6166** Fax: 270-756-1569. 8-4PM, 8-N Sat.

Bullitt County Clerk PO Box 6, Shepherdsville, KY 40165-0006 (Annex, 149 N. Walnut St.). **502-543-2513** Fax: 502-543-9121. 8AM-4PM M,T,W,F; 8AM-6PM Th. www.bullittcountyclerk.ky.gov

Butler County Clerk PO Box 449, Morgantown, KY 42261 **270-526-5676** Fax: 270-526-2658. 8AM-4:30PM.

Caldwell County Clerk 100 E Market St, Rm 3, Courthouse - Rm 3, Princeton, KY 42445 **270-365-6754** Fax: 270-365-7447. 8AM-4PM.

Calloway County Clerk 101 S. 5th St, Murray, KY 42071-2569 **270-753-3923** Fax: 270-759-9611. 8AM-4:30PM.

Campbell County Clerk 4th & York Sts, Courthouse, Newport, KY 41071 **859-292-3850** Fax: 859-292-3887. 8:30AM-6PM M;

8:30AM-4PM T-F; 9AM-N Sat. Property, Appraiser records online.

Carlisle County Clerk PO Box 176, Bardwell, KY 42023 (W. Court St). **270-628-3233** Fax: 270-628-0191. 8:30-4PM.

Carroll County Clerk 440 Main St, Court House, Carrollton, KY 41008 **502-732-7005** Fax: 502-732-7007. 8:30AM-4:30PM M,T,Th,F; 8:30AM-N W,Sat.

Carter County Clerk 300 W. Main St, Rm 232, Grayson, KY 41143 **606-474-5188** Fax: 606-474-6883. 8:30AM-4PM; 8:30-N Sat.

Casey County Clerk Box 310, Liberty, KY 42539 (614 Campbellsville St.). **606-787-6471** Fax: 606-787-9155. 8AM-4:30PM M-F; 8AM-N Sat.

Christian County Clerk 511 S. Main, Hopkinsville, KY 42240 **270-887-4105** Fax: 270-887-4186. 8AM-4:30PM.

Clark County Clerk PO Box 4060, Winchester, KY 40392 (34 S. Main St). **859-745-0280** Fax: 859-745-4251. 8AM-5PM M; 8AM-4PM T-F.

Clay County Clerk 123 Town Sq #3, Manchester, KY 40962 **606-598-2544** Fax: 606-599-0603. 8AM-4:30PM; 8AM-N Sat.

Clinton County Clerk 212 Washington St, Courthouse, Albany, KY 42602 **606-387-5943** Fax: 606-387-5258. 8AM-4:30PM; 8AM-N Sat.

Crittenden County Clerk 107 S. Main, Courthouse, #203, Marion, KY 42064 **270-965-3403** Fax: 270-965-3447. 8AM-4:30PM M,T,Th,F; 8AM-N W,Sat.

Cumberland County Clerk PO Box 275, Burkesville, KY 42717 (Public Sq, Rm 6).

270-864-3726 Fax: 270-864-5884. 8AM-4:30PM; 8AM-N Sat.

Daviess County Clerk PO Box 609, Owensboro, KY 42302 (212 St. Ann St). **270-685-8420** Fax: 270-685-2431. 8AM-4PM M-Th; 8AM-6PM F.

Edmonson County Clerk PO Box 830, Brownsville, KY 42210-0830 (108 Main St, Community Ctr). **270-597-2624** Fax: 270-597-9714. 8AM-5PM M,T,W,F; 8-N Sat.

Elliott County Clerk PO Box 225, Sandy Hook, KY 41171-0225 (Main St). **606-738-5421** Fax: 606-738-4462. 8AM-4PM; 9AM-N Sat.

Estill County Clerk PO Boc 59, Irvine, KY 40336 **606-723-5156** Fax: 606-723-5108. 8AMN, 1-4PM M,T,Th,F; 8AM-N W,Sat.

Fayette County Clerk 162 E. Main St, Lexington, KY 40507-1334 **859-253-3344** 8-4:30. Property, Crime Map records online.

Fleming County Clerk Court Sq, Rm 101, Flemingsburg, KY 41041 **606-845-8461** Fax: 606-845-0212. 8:30AM-4:30PM M-F; 8:30AM-N Sat.

Floyd County Clerk PO Box 1089, Prestonsburg, KY 41653-5089 (Rm 1, 149 S. Central). **606-886-3816** Fax: 606-886-8089. 8AM-4:30PM M,T,W,Th; 8AM-6PM F;9AM-N Sat.

Franklin County Clerk PO Box 338, Frankfort, KY 40602 (315 W. Main St). **502-875-8703** Fax: 502-875-8718. 8AM-4:30PM. www.franklincountyclerk.org

Fulton County Clerk PO Box 126, Hickman, KY 42050 (Wellington St, Johnson Annex). **270-236-2061** Fax: 270-236-2522. 8AM-4PM.

Gallatin County Clerk PO Box 1309, Warsaw, KY 41095 (16 Main St). **859-567-5411** Fax: 859-567-5444. 8AM-6PM M; 8AM-4:30PM T-F; 8AM-12 Sat..

Garrard County Clerk 15 Public Sq, #5, Courthouse Bldg., Lancaster, KY 40444 **859-792-3071** Fax: 859-792-6751. 8AM-4PM M,T,Th,F; 8AM-N W,Sat.

Grant County Clerk 101 N Main St, Courthouse Basement, Rm 15, Williamstown, KY 41097 **859-824-3321** Fax: 859-824-3367. 8:30AM-4PM M-F; 8:30AM-N Sat.

Graves County Clerk Courthouse, Mayfield, KY 42066 (**270-247-1676** Fax: 270-247-1274. 8AM-4:30PM M-Th; 8AM-6PM F.

Grayson County Clerk 10 Public Sq, Leitchfield, KY 42754 **270-259-5295** Fax: 270-230-0881. 8-5 M,T,W,F; 8-N Th,Sat.

Green County Clerk 203 W. Court St, Greensburg, KY 42743 **270-932-5386** Fax: 270-932-6241. 8-4 M-W,F; 8-N Th,Sat.

Greenup County Clerk PO Box 686, Greenup, KY 41144-0686 (Main St). **606-473-7396** Fax: 606-473-5354. 9AM-4:30PM

Hancock County Clerk PO Box 146, Hawesville, KY 42348 (225 Main & Cross St). **270-927-6117** Fax: 270-927-8639. 8AM-4PM M-W,F; 8AM-5:30PM Th.

Hardin County Clerk PO Box 1030, Elizabethtown, KY 42702 (14 Public Sq). **270-765-4116** Fax: 270-769-2682. 8AM-4:30PM. www.hccoky.org Recording, Will, Deed, Mortgage, Real Estate, Marriage, Assumed Name records online.

Harlan County Clerk PO Box 670, Harlan, KY 40831-0670 (210 E. Central St., #205). **606-573-3636** Fax: 606-573-0064. 8:30AM-4:30PM M-W & F; 8:30AM-6PM Th.

Harrison County Clerk 313 Oddville Rd, Cynthiana, KY 41031 **859-234-7130** Fax: 859-234-8049. 8:30AM-4:30PM M T W F; 8:30AM-6PM T Th.

Hart County Clerk PO Box 277, Munfordville, KY 42765 (Main St Courthouse). **270-524-2751** Fax: 270-524-0458. 8AM-4PM (8AM-N Sat).

Henderson County Clerk PO Box 374, Henderson, KY 42419-0374 (20 N. Main St.). **270-826-3906** Fax: 270-826-9677. 8AM-4:30PM M-Th; 8AM-6PM F.

Henry County Clerk PO Box 615, New Castle, KY 40050-0615 (27 S. Property Rd.). **502-845-5705** Fax: 502-845-5708. 8AM -5PM; M ; 8AM-4PM,T,W,Th F.

Hickman County Clerk 110 E Clay, Courthouse, Clinton, KY 42031 **270-653-2131** Fax: 270-653-4248. 8:30AM-4PM.

Hopkins County Clerk 10 S Main St, Madisonville, KY 42431 **270-821-7361** Fax: 270-825-7000. 8AM-4PM.

Jackson County Clerk PO Box 339, McKee, KY 40447 (Main St, Rm 108 Courthouse Sq.). **606-287-7800** Fax: 606-287-4505. 8AM-4PM; 8:30AM-N Sat.

Jefferson County Clerk County Clerk PO Box 35339, Louisville, KY 40232-5339 (531 Court Pl, Rm 204A). **502-574-6427** Fax: 502-574-6041. 8AM-4:30PM. Property, Assessor records online.

Jefferson County Recorder County Clerk 527 W Jefferson St, Rm 204, Louisville, KY 40202 **502-574-5785** Fax: 502-574-8130. www.countyclerk.jefferson.ky.us 8AM-4:45. Land records online.

Jessamine County Clerk 101 N. Main St, Nicholasville, KY 40356-1270 **859-885-4161** Fax: 859-885-5837. 8AM-5PM M; 8AM-4PM T,W,F; 8AM-N Th; 9am-N Sat.

Johnson County Clerk 230 Court St. Courthouse, Paintsville, KY 41240 **606-789-2557** Fax: 606-789-2559. 8AM-4:30PM , 8:30AM-N Sat.

Kenton County (1st District) County Clerk PO Box 1109, Covington, KY 41012 (3rd & Court Sts, Rm 102). **859-392-1600** Fax: 859-392-1639. 8:30AM-4PM M-Th; 8:30AM-6PM F. www.kentonpva.com Property Appraiser records online.

Kenton County (2nd District) County Clerk PO Box 38, Independence, KY 41051 (5272 Madison). **859-392-1692** Fax: 859-392-1681. 8:30AM-4PM M,T,Th,F; 8:30AM-6PM W. www.kentonpva.com Property Appraiser records online.

Knott County Clerk PO Box 446, Hindman, KY 41822 (54 W.Main St). **606-785-5651** Fax: 606-785-0996. 8AM-4PM , 8-N Sat.

Knox County Clerk 401 Court Sq, #102, Barbourville, KY 40906 **606-546-3568** Fax: 606-546-3589. 8:30AM-4PM.

Larue County Clerk 209 W. High St., Hodgenville, KY 42748 **270-358-3544** Fax: 270-358-4528. 8AM-4:30PM M,T,Th,F; 8AM-N W,Sat.

Laurel County Clerk 101 S. Main, Rm 203, Courthouse, London, KY 40741 **606-864-5158** Fax: 606-864-7369. 8AM-4:30; 8:30-N Sat. Property Appraiser records online.

Lawrence County Clerk 122 S. Main Cross St, Louisa, KY 41230 **606-638-4108** Fax: 606-638-0638. 8:30AM-4PM; 8:30-N Sat.

Lee County Clerk PO Box 551, Beattyville, KY 41311 (Main St Rm 11). **606-464-4115** Fax: 606-464-4102. 8AM-4PM.

Leslie County Clerk PO Box 916, Hyden, KY 41749 (22010 Main St). **606-672-2193** Fax: 606-672-4264. 8AM-5PM; 8-N Sat.

Letcher County Clerk 156 Main St. #102, Whitesburg, KY 41858 **606-633-2432** Fax: 606-632-9282. 8:30AM-4PM; 8:30AM-N 1st Sat of month.

Lewis County Clerk PO Box 129, Vanceburg, KY 41179-0129 (514 2nd St, 2nd Fl). **606-796-3062** Fax: 606-796-6511. 8:30AM-4:30PM M T Th F; 8:30-N W.

Lincoln County Clerk 102 E. Main, Courthouse, Stanford, KY 40484 **606-365-4570** Fax: 606-365-4572. 8AM-4PM M-F; 9AM-N Sat.

Livingston County Clerk PO Box 400, Smithland, KY 42081-0400 (335 Court St). **270-928-2162** Fax: 270-928-2162. 8AM-4PM; 8AM-6PM M.

Logan County Clerk PO Box 358, Russellville, KY 42276-0358 (229 W. 3rd St.). **270-726-6061** Fax: 270-726-4355. 8:30AM-4:30PM.

Lyon County Clerk PO Box 310, Eddyville, KY 42038 (Dale Ave Courthouse). **270-388-2331** Fax: 270-388-0634. 8:30-4PM.

Madison County Clerk 101 W. Main St, County Court House, Richmond, KY 40475-1415 **859-624-4704** Fax: 859-624-8474. 8AM-4PM M-F; 8AM-6:30PM Th.

Magoffin County Clerk PO Box 530, Salyersville, KY 41465 (Courthouse). **606-349-2216** Fax: 606-349-2328. 8:30AM-4PM; 8:30AM-N Sat.

Marion County Clerk 120 W Main St, Courthouse, #3, Lebanon, KY 40033 **270-692-2651** Fax: 270-692-9811. 8:30AM-4:30PM; 8:30AM-N Sat.

Marshall County Clerk 1101 Main St, Courthouse, Benton, KY 42025 **270-527-4740** Fax: 270-527-4738. 8AM-4:30PM.

Martin County Clerk PO Box 460, Inez, KY 41224-0485 (Main St Courthouse). **606-298-2810** Fax: 606-298-0143. 8-5; 8-N Sat.

Mason County Clerk PO Box 234, Maysville, KY 41056 (W. Third St). **606-564-3341** Fax: 606-564-8979. 9AM-5PM; 9-11:30AM Sat.

McCracken County Clerk PO Box 609, Paducah, KY 42002-0609 (7th St between Washington & Clark). **270-444-4700** Fax: 270-444-4704. 8:30AM-4:30PM (M open until 5:30PM).

McCreary County Clerk PO Box 699, Whitley City, KY 42653 (1 Main St). **606-376-2411** Fax: 606-376-3898. 8:30AM-4:30PM M-F; 9AM-N Sat.

McLean County Clerk PO Box 57, Calhoun, KY 42327-0057 (210 Main St). **270-273-3082** Fax: 270-273-5084. 8AM-4:30PM; 9AM-N Sat.

Meade County Clerk PO Box 614, Brandenburg, KY 40108 (516 Fairway Drive). **270-422-2152** Fax: 270-422-2158. 8AM-4:30PM; 9AM-N Sat.

Menifee County Clerk PO Box 123, Frenchburg, KY 40322-0123 (12 Walnut St). **606-768-3512** Fax: 606-768-6738. 8:30-4PM M,T,W,F; 8:30-11:30AM Th,Sat.

Mercer County Clerk PO Box 426, Harrodsburg, KY 40330 (235 S. Main St). **859-734-6313** Fax: 859-734-6309. 8-4:30.

Metcalfe County Clerk PO Box 25, Edmonton, KY 42129 (100 E. Stockton St, #1). **270-432-4821** Fax: 270-432-5176. 8AM-4PM.

Monroe County Clerk 200 N. Main St. #D, Tompkinsville, KY 42167-1548 (Main St Courthouse). **270-487-5471** Fax: 270-487-5976. 8AM-4:30PM M-F; 8AM-N Sat.

Montgomery County Clerk PO Box 414, Mount Sterling, KY 40353 (Court St). **859-498-8700** Fax: 859-498-8729 or 498-8738. 8:30AM-4PM M-TH; 8:30-6PM F.

Morgan County Clerk PO Box 26, West Liberty, KY 41472 (505 Prestonsburg St). **606-743-3949** Fax: 606-743-2111. 8AM-4PM; 8AM-N Sat.

Muhlenberg County Clerk PO Box 525, Greenville, KY 42345 (1st Fl, 100 Court Row). **270-338-1441** Fax: 270-338-1774. 8AM-4PM; 8AM-6PM F.

Nelson County Clerk PO Box 312, Bardstown, KY 40004 (113 E. Stephen Foster Ave). **502-348-1830** Fax: 502-348-1822. 8:30AM-4:30PM M-F; 8AM-11:45AM Sat.

Nicholas County Clerk PO Box 227, Carlisle, KY 40311 (Main St Courthouse). **859-289-3730** Fax: 859-289-3709. 8AM-4:30PM; 8-11:30AM Sat.

Ohio County Clerk PO Box 85, Hartford, KY 42347 (301 S. Main St). **270-298-4422** Fax: 270-298-4425. 8AM-4:30PM M-Th; 8AM-6PM F; 8AM-N Sat.

Oldham County Clerk 100 W. Jefferson St, LaGrange, KY 40031 **502-222-9311** Fax: 502-222-3208. 8:30AM-4PM M-W,F; 8:30-6 Th. http://oldhamcounty.state.ky.us Real Estate, Lien, UCC, Assessor, Marriage records online.

Owen County Clerk 135 W Bryan St, Owenton, KY 40359-0338 **502-484-2213** Fax: 502-484-1002. 8AM-4PM M T TH F; 8am-N W SAT, Closed on WED.

Owsley County Clerk PO Box 500, Booneville, KY 41314 (Courthouse, Main St.). **606-593-5735** Fax: 606-593-5737. 8AM-4PM; 8AM-12 Sat.

Pendleton County Clerk PO Box 112, Falmouth, KY 41040 (233 Main St, Rm 1). **859-654-3380** Fax: 859-654-5600. 8:30AM-4PM M-F; 8:30AM-N Sat.

Perry County Clerk PO Box 150, Hazard, KY 41702 (Main St Courthouse). **606-436-4614** Fax: 606-439-0557. 8AM-4PM.

Pike County Clerk PO Box 631, Pikeville, KY 41502-0631 (146 Main St). **606-432-6240** Fax: 606-432-6222. 8:30AM-4:30 M,T,W,Th; 8:30-6PM F; 8:30AM-N Sat..

Powell County Clerk PO Box 548, Stanton, KY 40380 (130 Washington St). **606-663-6444** Fax: 606-663-6406. 9AM-4PM M-W; 9AM-N Th; 9AM-4PM F; 9AM-N Sat.

Pulaski County Clerk PO Box 724, Somerset, KY 42502 (Main St). **606-679-3652** Fax: 606-678-0073. 8AM-4:30PM.

Robertson County Clerk PO Box 75, Mount Olivet, KY 41064 (Courthouse). **606-724-5212** Fax: 606-724-5022. 8:30-N, 1-4PM M,T,Th,F; 8:30AM-N W, Sat.

Rockcastle County Clerk 205 E Main St #6, Mount Vernon, KY 40456 **606-256-2831** Fax: 606-256-4302. 8:30-4PM; 8:30-N Sat.

Rowan County Clerk 627 E. Main St, Courthouse - 2nd Fl, Morehead, KY 40351 **606-784-5212** Fax: 606-784-2923. 8AM-4PM M-TH; 8AM-6PM F.

Russell County Clerk PO Box 579, Jamestown, KY 42629-0579 (Courthouse). **270-343-2125** Fax: 270-343-4700. 8AM-4PM; 8AM-11:00 Sat.

Scott County Clerk 101 E Main St, Courthouse, Georgetown, KY 40324-1794 **502-863-7875** Fax: 502-863-7898. 8:30AM-4:30PM M-Th; 8:30AM-6PM F.

Shelby County Clerk PO Box 819, Shelbyville, KY 40066-0819 (501 Washington). **502-633-4410** Fax: 502-633-7887. 8:30AM-4:30PM M,T,W,F; 8:30-6PM Th. www.shelbycountyclerk.com Real Estate, Deed, Recording records online.

Simpson County Clerk PO Box 268, Franklin, KY 42135 (103 W. Cedar St). **270-586-8161** Fax: 270-586-6464. 8AM-4PM.

Spencer County Clerk PO Box 544, Taylorsville, KY 40071 (2 W. Main St). **502-477-3215** Fax: 502-477-3216. 8AM-4:30PM M-F; 8AM-11:30 Sat.

Taylor County Clerk 203 N. Court St, ## 5, Campbellsville, KY 42718-2298 **270-465-6677** Fax: 270-789-1144. 8AM-4:30PM M-Th; 8AM-5PM F.

Todd County Clerk PO Box 307, Elkton, KY 42220 (200 Washington St.). **270-265-2363** Fax: 270-265-2588. 8AM-4:30PM.

Trigg County Clerk PO Box 1310, Cadiz, KY 42211 (38 Main St.). **270-522-6661** Fax: 270-522-6662. 8AM-4PM M-Th; 8-5PM F.

Trimble County Clerk PO Box 262, Bedford, KY 40006-0262 (Courthouse). **502-255-7174** Fax: 502-255-7045. 8:30AM-4:30PM M,T,Th,F; 8:30AM-N Sat.

Union County Clerk PO Box 119, Morganfield, KY 42437-0119 (100 W.Main). **270-389-1334** Fax: 270-389-9135. 8AM-4PM.

Warren County Clerk PO Box 478, Bowling Green, KY 42102-0478 (429 E. 10th St). **270-842-9416** Fax: 270-843-5319.

8:30-4:30PM. http://warrencounty.state.ky.us Real Estate, Lien, UCC, Assessor, Marriage records online.

Washington County Clerk PO Box 446, Springfield, KY 40069 (Cross Main Annex Bldg.). **859-336-5425** Fax: 859-336-5408. 9AM-4:30PM; 9AM-N Sat.

Wayne County Clerk PO Box 565, Monticello, KY 42633 (109 N. Main St, First Fl). **606-348-6661** Fax: 606-348-8303. 8AM-4:30PM; 8AM-N Sat.

Webster County Clerk PO Box 19, Dixon, KY 42409-0019 (Courthouse, 25 US 41A).

270-639-7006 Fax: 270-639-7029. 8AM-4PM M; 8AM-4PM T-F.

Whitley County Clerk PO Box 8, Williamsburg, KY 40769 (Main St Courthouse, Rm 2). **606-549-6002** Fax: 606-549-2790. 7:30AM-4PM; 7:30AM-N Sat.

Wolfe County Clerk PO Box 400, Campton, KY 41301 (1st Fl, 10 Court St.). **606-668-3515** Fax: 606-668-3492. 8AM-4PM M,T,Th,F; 8AM-N W & Sat.

Woodford County Clerk 103 S Main St, Courthouse - Rm 120, Versailles, KY 40383 **859-873-3421** Fax: 859-873-6985. 8AM-4PM M,T,W,Th; 8AM-5:45PM F.

Louisiana

Organization: 64 parishes (not counties), 64 recording offices. One parish, St. Martin, has two non-contiguous segments. The recording officer is the Clerk of Court. Many parishes include tax and other non-UCC liens in their mortgage records. The entire state is in the Central Time Zone (CST).

Real Estate Records: Most parishes will perform a mortgage search. Some will provide a record owner search. Copy and certification fees vary widely.

UCC Records: Financing statements are filed with the Clerk of Court in any parish in the state and are entered onto a statewide computerized database of UCC financing statements available for searching at any parish office. All parishes perform UCC searches for $15.00 per debtor name. Use search request form UCC-11. Copy fees are $.50-1.00 per page.

Tax Lien Records: All federal and state tax liens are filed with the Clerk of Court. Parishes usually file tax liens on personal property in their UCC or mortgage records, and most will perform tax lien searches for varying fees. Some parishes will automatically include tax liens on personal property in a mortgage certificate search. Other Liens: Judgments, labor, material, hospital.

Online Access: A number of Parishes offer online access to recorded documents, most are commercial fee systems.

Acadia Parish Clerk of Court PO Box 922, Crowley, LA 70526 (Parkerson Ave, Court house). **337-788-8881** Fax: 337-788-1048. 8:30AM-4:30. www.acadiaparishclerk.com

Allen Parish Clerk of Court PO Box 248, Oberlin, LA 70655 (400 W 6th Ave). **337-639-4351** Fax: 337-639-2030. 8-4:30PM.

Ascension Parish Clerk of Court PO Box 192, Donaldsonville, LA 70346 (300 Houmas St). **225-473-9866** Fax: 225-473-8641. 8:30AM-4:30PM.

Assumption Parish Clerk of Court PO Drawer 249, Napoleonville, LA 70390 (4809 LA Hwy 1). **985-369-6653** Fax: 985-369-2032. 8:30AM-4:30PM.

Avoyelles Parish Clerk of Court PO Box 196, Marksville, LA 71351 (301 E Mark St). **318-253-7523** Fax: 318-253-4614. 8:30AM-4:30PM.

Beauregard Parish Clerk of Court PO Box 100, De Ridder, LA 70634 (214 W. First St). **337-463-8595** Fax: 337-462-3916. 8-4:30.

Bienville Parish Clerk of Court 100 Courthouse Dr, Rm 100, Arcadia, LA 71001-3600 **318-263-2123** Fax: 318-263-7426. 8:30-4:30PM. www.bienvilleparish.org/clerk

Bossier Parish Clerk of Court PO Box 430, Benton, LA 71006 (200 Burt Blvd). **318-965-2336** Fax: 318-965-2713. 8:30AM-4:30PM. www.bossierclerk.com

Caddo Parish Clerk of Court 501 Texas St, Shreveport, LA 71101-5408 **318-226-6780** Fax: 318-227-9080. 8:30AM-5PM. www.caddoclerk.com Real Estate, Lien, Marriage records online.

Calcasieu Parish Clerk of Court PO Box 1030, Lake Charles, LA 70601-1030 (1000 Ryan St). **337-437-3550** Fax: 337-437-3350. 8:30AM-4:30PM.

Caldwell Parish Clerk of Court PO Box 1327, Columbia, LA 71418 (200 Main St). **318-649-2272** Fax: 318-649-2037. 8-4:30.

Cameron Parish Clerk of Court PO Box 549, Cameron, LA 70631 (119 Smith Circle,

Rm 21). **337-775-5316** Fax: 337-775-7172. 8:30AM-4:30PM.

Catahoula Parish Clerk of Court PO Box 654, Harrisonburg, LA 71340 (301 Bushley St, Courthouse Sq). **318-744-5497** Fax: 318-744-5488. 8:30AM-4:30PM.

Claiborne Parish Clerk of Court PO Box 330, Homer, LA 71040 (512 E. Main St). **318-927-9601** Fax: 318-927-2345. 8:30-4:30.

Concordia Parish Clerk of Court PO Box 790, Vidalia, LA 71373 (4001 Carter St. #5). **318-336-4204** Fax: 318-336-8777. 8:30AM-4:30PM.

De Soto Parish Clerk of Court PO Box 1206, Mansfield, LA 71052 (210 Texas St). **318-872-3110** Fax: 318-872-4202. 8-4:30.

East Baton Rouge Parish Clerk of Court PO Box 1991, Baton Rouge, LA 70821-1991 (222 St. Louis St). **225-389-3960** Fax: 225-389-3392. www.ebrclerkofcourt.org Real Estate, Lien records online. 7:30-5:30PM.

East Carroll Parish Clerk of Court 400 First St, Lake Providence, LA 71254 **318-559-2399** Fax: 318-559-1502. 8:30AM-4:30PM.

East Feliciana Parish Clerk of Court PO Drawer 599, Clinton, LA 70722 (12305 St. Helena St). **225-683-5145** Fax: 225-683-3556. www.eastfelicianaclerk.com/ Real Estate, Lien, Mortgage, Marriage, Civil Court records online. 8:30AM-4:30PM.

Evangeline Parish Clerk of Court PO Drawer 347, Ville Platte, LA 70586 (200 Court St #104). **337-363-5671** Fax: 337-363-5780. 8AM-4:30PM.

Franklin Parish Clerk of Court PO Box 1564, Winnsboro, LA 71295 (6550 Main St). **318-435-5133** Fax: 318-435-5134. 8:30AM-4:30PM.

Grant Parish Clerk of Court PO Box 263, Colfax, LA 71417 (200 Main St). **318-627-3246** Fax: 318-627-3201. 8:30AM-4:30PM.

Iberia Parish Clerk of Court PO Drawer 12010, New Iberia, LA 70562-2010 (300 Iberia St). **337-365-7282** Fax: 337-365-0737. 8:30AM-4:30PM. Real Estate, Lien, Marriage, Divorce records online.

Iberville Parish Clerk of Court PO Box 423, Plaquemine, LA 70765-0423 (58050 Meriam St). **225-687-5160** Fax: 225-687-5260. 8:30AM-4:30PM.

Jackson Parish Clerk of Court PO Drawer 370, Jonesboro, LA 71251 (500 E. Court Ave). **318-259-2424** Fax: 318-395-0386. 8:30AM-4:30PM.

Jefferson Davis Parish Clerk of Court PO Box 799, Jennings, LA 70546-0799 (300 State St). **337-824-1160/1161** Fax: 337-824-1354. 8:30AM-4:30PM.

Jefferson Parish Clerk of Court PO Box 10, Gretna, LA 70054 (200 Derbigny St, 6th Fl). **504-364-2900** Fax: 504-364-3780. 7:30-4:30 www.clerkofcourt.co.jefferson.la.us Real Estate, Assessor, Marriage, Civil online.

La Salle Parish Clerk of Court PO Box 1316, Jena, LA 71342 (1050 Courthouse St). **318-992-2158** Fax: 318-992-2157. 8:30AM-4:30PM.

Lafayette Parish Clerk of Court PO Box 2009, Lafayette, LA 70502 (800 S. Buchanan St). **337-291-6400** Fax: 337-291-6392. www.lafayetteparishclerk.com Real Estate, Lien records online. 8:30-4:30PM.

Lafourche Parish Clerk of Court PO Box 818, Thibodaux, LA 70302 (303 W. Third St). **985-447-4841** Fax: 985-447-5800. 8:30AM-4:30PM.

Lincoln Parish Clerk of Court PO Box 924, Ruston, LA 71273-0924 (100 W. Texas Ave, Rm 100). **318-251-5130** Fax: 318-255-6004. 8:30AM-4:30PM.

Livingston Parish Clerk of Court PO Box 1150, Livingston, LA 70754 (20180 Iowa St). **225-686-2216** Fax: 225-686-1867. 8AM-4:30PM.

Madison Parish Clerk of Court PO Box 1710, Tallulah, LA 71282 (100 N. Cedar St). **318-574-0655** Fax: 318-574-3961. 8:30AM-4:30PM.

Morehouse Parish Clerk of Court PO Box 1543, Bastrop, LA 71221-1543 (100 E Madison St). **318-281-3343** Fax: 318-281-3775. 8:30AM-4:30PM.

Natchitoches Parish Clerk of Court PO Box 476, Natchitoches, LA 71458-0476 (200 Church St, Rm 104). **318-352-8152** Fax: 318-352-9321. 8:30AM-4:30PM.

Orleans Parish Clerk of Court 421 Loyola Ave, B-1 #402, New Orleans, LA 70112 **504-592-9100** Fax: 504-592-9128. 9AM-4PM. www.orleanscdc.gov Real Estate, Mortgage, Lien, Birth, Death records online.

Ouachita Parish Clerk of Court PO Box 1862, Monroe, LA 71210-1862 (300 St. John St, #104). **318-327-1444** Fax: 318-327-1462. 8:30AM-5PM.

Plaquemines Parish Clerk of Court PO Box 40, Belle Chasse, LA 70037-0040 (8346 Hwy 23, Region 1 Bldg, 2nd Fl). **504-392-4969** 8:30AM-4:30PM.

Pointe Coupee Parish Clerk of Court PO Box 86, New Roads, LA 70760 (201 E. Main St). **225-638-9596** Fax: 225-638-9590. 8:30AM-4:30PM.

Rapides Parish Clerk of Court PO Box 952, Alexandria, LA 71309 (701 Murray St.). **318-473-8153** Fax: 318-473-4667. 8:30-4:30.

Red River Parish Clerk of Court PO Box 485, Coushatta, LA 71019-0485 (615 E. Carroll St). **318-932-6741** Fax: 318-932-3126. 8:30AM-4:30PM.

Richland Parish Clerk of Court PO Box 119, Rayville, LA 71269 (708 Julia St, #103). **318-728-4171** Fax: 318-728-7020. 8:30AM-4:30PM.

Sabine Parish Clerk of Court PO Box 419, Many, LA 71449 (400 S Capital Rm 102). **318-256-6223** Fax: 318-256-9037. 8-4:30.

St. Bernard Parish Clerk of Court PO Box 1746, Chalmette, LA 70044 (1101 W St. Bernard Hwy). **504-271-3434** 8:30-4:30.

St. Charles Parish Clerk of Court PO Box 424, Hahnville, LA 70057 (15045 River Rd). **985-783-6632** Fax: 985-783-2005. 8:30AM-4:30PM.

St. Helena Parish Clerk of Court PO Box 308, Greensburg, LA 70441-0308 (369 Sitman St). **225-222-4514** Fax: 225-222-3443. 8:30AM-4:30PM.

St. James Parish Clerk of Court PO Box 63, Convent, LA 70723 (5800 LA Highway 44). **225-562-7496** Fax: 225-562-2383. 8AM-4:30PM.

St. John the Baptist Parish Clerk of Court PO Box 280, Edgard, LA 70049-0280 (2393 Hwy 18). **985-497-3331** Fax: 985-497-3972. 8:30AM-4:30PM.

St. Landry Parish Clerk of Court PO Box 750, Opelousas, LA 70571 (118 S. Court St., #109). **337-942-5606** Fax: 337-948-7265. 8AM-4:30PM. www.stlandry.org/index.htm

St. Martin Parish Clerk of Court PO Box 308, St. Martinville, LA 70582 (415 S. Main St). **337-394-2210** Fax: 337-394-7772. 8:30AM-4:30PM.

St. Mary Parish Clerk of Court PO Drawer 1231, Franklin, LA 70538 (500 Main St). **318-828-4100 x200** Fax: 318-828-2509. 8:30AM-4:30PM.

St. Tammany Parish Clerk of Court PO Box 1090, Covington, LA 70434 (510 E Boston St). **985-898-2430** 8:30-4:30PM. www.sttammanyclerk.org/main/index.asp Recorder, Real Estate, Mortgage, Lien, Assessor, Property Tax records online.

Tangipahoa Parish Clerk of Court PO Box 667, Amite, LA 70422 (110 N. Bay St, #100). **985-748-4146** Fax: 985-748-6746. 8:30AM-4:30PM. www.tangiclerk.org Real Estate, Lien, Recording, Civil, Marriage, Mortgage records online.

Tensas Parish Clerk of Court PO Box 78, St. Joseph, LA 71366 (Hancock St, Court house Sq). **318-766-3921** Fax: 318-766-3926.

Terrebonne Parish Clerk of Court PO Box 1569, Houma, LA 70361 (7856 Main St) **985-868-5660** Fax: 985-868-5143. 8:30AM-4:30PM.

Union Parish Clerk of Court 100 E. Bayou St, #105, Courthouse, Farmerville, LA 71241 **318-368-3055** Fax: 318-368-3861. 8:30AM-4:30PM.

Vermilion Parish Clerk of Court 100 N State St #101, Courthouse Bldg, Abbeville, LA 70510 **337-898-1992** Fax: 337-898-0404. 8:30AM-4:30PM.

Vernon Parish Clerk of Court PO Box 40, Leesville, LA 71496-0040 (201 S 4th St). **337-238-1384** Fax: 337-238-9902. 8-4:30.

Washington Parish Clerk of Court PO Box 607, Franklinton, LA 70438 (Courthouse, Washington at Main St). **985-839-7821** Fax: 985-839-7851. 8AM-4:30PM.

Webster Parish Clerk of Court PO Box 370, Minden, LA 71058-0370 (410 Main). **318-371-0366** Fax 318-371-0226. 8:30-4:30.

West Baton Rouge Parish Clerk of Court PO Box 107, Port Allen, LA 70767 (850 8th St). **225-383-0378** Fax: 225-383-3694. 8:30AM-4:30PM.

West Carroll Parish Clerk of Court PO Box 1078, Oak Grove, LA 71263 (305 E Main). **318-428-2369** Fax: 318-428-9896. 8:30-4:30.

West Feliciana Parish Clerk of Court PO Box 1843, St. Francisville, LA 70775 (4789 Prosperity St) **225-635-3794** Fax: 225-635-3770. 8:30AM-4:30PM.

Winn Parish Clerk of Court PO Box 137, Winnfield, LA 71483 (119 W Main) **318-628-3515** Fax: 318-628-3527. 8-4:30.

Maine

Organization: 16 counties, 17 recording offices. The recording officer is the County Register of Deeds. Counties maintain a general index of all transactions recorded. Aroostock and Oxford Counties each have two recording offices. There are no county assessors; each town has its own. The entire state is in the Eastern Time Zone (EST).

Real Estate Records: Counties do not usually perform real estate name searches, but some will look up a name informally. Copy and certification fees vary widely. Assessor and tax records are located at the town/city level.

UCC Records: Financing statements are filed at the state level, except for real estate related filings, which are filed only with the Register of Deeds. Counties do not perform UCC searches. Copy fees are usually $1.00 per page.

Tax Lien Records: All tax liens on personal property are filed with the Secretary of State. All tax liens on real property are filed with the Register of Deeds. Other Liens: Municipal, bail bond, mechanics.

Online Access: There is no statewide system. Several counties have developed their own system and a private vendor has placed assessor records from a number of towns on the Internet. Visit http://data.visionappraisal.com.

Androscoggin Register of Deeds 2 Turner St, Courthouse, Auburn, ME 04210-5978 **207-782-0191** Fax: 207-784-3163. 8AM-5PM. http://142.167.64.12/alis/ww400r.pgm Real estate, Deed, Lien, Assessor records online.

Aroostook County - Northern Register of Deeds PO Box 47, Fort Kent, ME 04743 (22 Hall St, #201). **207-834-3925** Fax: 207-834-3138. www.aroostook.me.us/deeds.html Deed records online. 8AM-4:30PM.

Southern District Register of Deeds 26 Court St, #102, Houlton, ME 04730 **207-532-1500** Fax: 207-532-7319. 8AM-4:30PM. www.aroostook.me.us/indexhome.html

Cumberland Register of Deeds PO Box 7230, Portland, ME 04112 (142 Federal St). **207-871-8389** Fax: 207-772-4162. 8:30AM-4:30. Assessor, Property Sale records online.

Franklin Register of Deeds 140 Main St, Courthouse, Farmington, ME 04938-1818 **207-778-5889** Fax: 207-778-5899. 8:30-4.

Hancock Register of Deeds 50 State St #9, Ellsworth, ME 04605 **207-667-8353** Fax: 207-667-1410. www.co.hancock.me.us Real Estate, Deed, Lien, UCC, Recording records online. 8:30AM-4PM.

Kennebec Register of Deeds PO Box 1053, Augusta, ME 04332-1053 (1 Weston Court, 2nd Fl). **207-622-0431** Fax: 207-622-1598. 8AM-4PM. Assessor, Property, Deed, Recording records online.

Knox Register of Deeds PO Box 943, Rockland, ME 04841 (62 Union St). **207-594-0422** Fax: 207-594-0446. 8AM-4PM. www.knoxcounty.midcoast.com Property records online.

Lincoln Register of Deeds PO Box 249, Wiscasset, ME 04578-0249 (32 High St). **207-882-7515** Fax: 207-882-4061. 8-4PM. Deed, Property, Recording records online.

Oxford Register of Deeds PO Box 179, South Paris, ME 04281-0179 (126 Western Ave). **207-743-6211** Fax: 207-743-2656. 8-4.

Penobscot Register of Deeds PO Box 2070, Bangor, ME 04402-2070 (97 Hammond St). **207-942-8797** Fax: 207-945-4920. 8AM-4:30PM. Real Estate, Deed, Recording, Assessor, Property records online.

Piscataquis Register of Deeds 159 E. Main St, Dover-Foxcroft, ME 04426 **207-564-2411** Fax: 207-564-7708. 8:30AM-4PM. Deed, Land, Judgment records online.

Sagadahoc Register of Deeds PO Box 246, Bath, ME 04530 (752 High St). **207-443-8214** Fax: 207-443-8216. 8:30AM-4:30PM. www.cityofbath.com Recording, Grantor/Grantee, Real Estate, Assessor, Most Wanted records online.

Somerset Register of Deeds PO Box 248, Skowhegan, ME 04976-0248 (Court & High St). **207-474-3421** Fax: 207-474-2793. 8:30AM-4:30PM.

Waldo Register of Deeds PO Box D, Belfast, ME 04915 (137 Church St). **207-338-1710** Fax: 207-338-6360. 8AM-4PM.

Washington Register of Deeds PO Box 297, Machias, ME 04654-0297 (47 Court St). **207-255-6512** Fax: 207-255-3838. 8-4PM.

York Register of Deeds PO Box 339, Alfred, ME 04002-0339 (45 Kennebunk Rd.). **207-324-1576** Fax: 207-324-2886. 8:30-4:30. Real Estate, Deed, Recording, Assessor, Property records online.

Maryland

Organization: 23 counties and one independent city -- 24 total recording offices. The recording officer is the Clerk of the Circuit Court. Baltimore City has a recording office separate from the county of Baltimore. See the City/County Locator section at the end of this chapter for ZIP Codes that include both the city and the county. The entire state is in the Eastern Time Zone (EST).

Real Estate Records: Counties will not perform estate searches. Copies usually cost $.50 per page, and certification fees $5.00 per document.

UCC Records: This was a dual filing state until July 1995. As of July 1995, all new UCC filings except for consumer goods, farm related and real estate related filings were submitted only to the central filing office. Starting July 2001, only real estate related filing are submitted to the Clerk of Circuit Court,

Tax Lien Records: All tax liens are filed with the county Clerk of Circuit Court. Counties will not perform tax lien name searches. Other Liens: Judgment, mechanics, county, hospital, condominium.

Online Access: Search statewide property records data free online at http://sdatcert3.resiusa.org/rp_rewrite/. There is no name searching.The Maryland State Dept. of Planning offers MDPropertyview with property maps/parcels and assessments on the web or CD-Rom. Registration required; visit www.mdp.state.md.us or call 410-767-4614 or 410-767-4474. There is no name searching. Also, vendors provide online access in several places. County tax records are at www.taxrecords.com. Land survey, condominium and survey plats is available free by county at www.plats.net. Use username "Plato" and password "plato#". No name searching.

Allegany Clerk of Circuit Court 30 Washington St, Cumberland, MD 21502-2948 **301-777-5922** Fax: 301-777-2100. 8AM-4:30PM. Real Property, Land Survey/Plat records online.

Anne Arundel Clerk of Circuit Court PO Box 71, Annapolis, MD 21404 (7 Church Circle St, Rm 21). **410-222-1425** Fax: 410-222-1087. 8:30AM-4:30PM. Real Property, Land Survey/Plat records online.

Baltimore City Clerk 100 N. Calvert St, Rm 610, Baltimore, MD 21202 **410-333-3760** 8AM-4:30PM. Real Property, Land Survey/Plat, Property Tax records online.

Baltimore County Clerk of Circuit Court PO Box 6754, Baltimore, MD 21285 (401 Bosley Ave). **410-887-2652** Fax: 410-887-3062. 8:30AM-4:30PM. Real Property, Land Survey/Plat records online.

Calvert Clerk of Circuit Court 175 Main St, Courthouse, Prince Frederick, MD 20678 **410-535-1660** 8:30AM-4:30PM. Real Property, Land Survey/Plat records online.

Caroline Clerk of Circuit Court PO Box 458, Denton, MD 21629 (109 Market St). **410-479-1811** Fax: 410-479-1142. 8:30AM-4:30PM. Real Property, Land Survey/Plat records online.

Carroll Clerk of Circuit Court 55 N. Court St, Rm G8, Westminster, MD 21157 **410-386-2022** Fax: 410-876-0822. 8:30-4:30PM. Real Property, Land Survey/Plat records online.

Cecil Clerk of Circuit Court 129 E. Main St., Rm 108, Elkton, MD 21921-5971 **410-996-5375** 8:30AM-4:30PM. Real Property, Land Survey/Plat records online.

Charles Clerk of Circuit Court PO Box 970, La Plata, MD 20646 (200 Charles St). www.courts.state.md.us/clerks/charles **301-932-3201** 8:30AM-4:30PM. Real Property, Land Survey/Plat, Treasurer, Property Tax records online.

Dorchester Clerk of Circuit Court PO Box 150, Cambridge, MD 21613 (206 High St). **410-228-0481** Fax: 410-228-1860. 8:30AM-4:30PM. Real Property, Land Survey/Plat records online.

Frederick Clerk of Circuit Court 100 W. Patrick St, Frederick, MD 21701 **301-694-1964** Fax: 301-846-2245. 8:30-4:30PM. Real Property, Land Survey/Plat records online.

Garrett Clerk of Circuit Court PO Box 447, Oakland, MD 21550-0447 (203 S. Fourth St). **301-334-1937** Fax: 301-334-5017. 8:30AM-4:30PM. Real Property, Land Survey/Plat records online.

Harford Clerk of Circuit Court 20 W. Courtland St, Bel Air, MD 21014 **410-638-3244** 8:30AM-4PM. Real Property, Land Survey/Plat records online.

Howard Clerk of Circuit Court 9250 Bendix Rd, Columbia, MD 21045 **410-313-6117** 8:30AM-4:30PM. Real Property, Land Survey/Plat records online.

Kent Clerk of Circuit Court 103 N. Cross St., Chestertown, MD 21620 **410-778-7431** 8:30AM-4:30PM. Real Property, Land Survey/Plat records online.

Montgomery Clerk of Circuit Court 50 Maryland Ave, Rm 122A, County Courthouse, Rockville, MD 20850 **240-777-9466** Fax: 240-777-9486. 8:30AM-4:30PM. www.montgomerycountymd.gov/mc/judicial/ Real Property, Land Survey/Plat, Property Tax, Assessor records online.

Prince George's Clerk of Circuit Court 14735 Main St, Upper Marlboro, MD 20772 **301-952-3352** 8:30AM-3PM. www.co.pg.md.us Real Property, Land Survey/Plat, Property Tax records online.

Queen Anne's Clerk of Circuit Court 100 Court House Sq, Centreville, MD 21617 **410-758-1773** 8:30AM-4:30PM. Real Property, Land Survey/Plat records online.

Somerset Clerk of Circuit Court PO Box 99, Princess Anne, MD 21853 (30512 Prince William St). **410-651-1555** Fax: 410-651-1048. 8:30AM-4:30PM. Real Property, Land Survey/Plat records online.

St. Mary's Clerk of Circuit Court PO Box 676, Leonardtown, MD 20650 (41605 Courthouse Dr.). **301-475-4567** 8:30AM-4:30PM. Real Property, Land Survey/Plat records online.

Talbot Clerk of Circuit Court PO Box 723, Easton, MD 21601 (11 N. Washington St). **410-822-2611** Fax: 410-820-8168. 8:30AM-4:30PM. www.courts.state.md.us Real Property, Land Survey/Plat records online.

Washington Clerk of Circuit Court PO Box 229, Hagerstown, MD 21741-0229 (95 W. Washington St., #212). **301-733-8660** Fax: 301-791-1151. 8:30AM-4:30PM.

www.courts.state.md.us/washington.html Real Property, Land Survey/Plat records online.

Wicomico Clerk of Circuit Court PO Box 198, Salisbury, MD 21803-0198 (101 N. Division St., Rm 105). **410-543-6551**

8:30AM-4:30PM. Real Property, Land Survey/Plat records online.

Worcester Clerk of Circuit Court PO Box 40, Snow Hill, MD 21863-0040 (1 W. Market St., Rm 104). **410-632-5500**

8:30AM-4:30PM. Real Property, Land Survey/Plat records online.

 # Massachusetts

Organization: 14 counties, 312 towns, and 39 cities; 21 recording offices and 365 UCC filing offices. Each town/city profile indicates the county in which the town/city is located. Filing locations vary depending upon the type of document, as noted below. Berkshire and Bristol counties each have three recording offices. Essex, Middlesex and Worcester counties each have two recording offices. Cities/towns bearing the same name as a county are Barnstable, Essex, Franklin, Hampden, Nantucket, Norfolk, Plymouth, and Worcester. Some UCC financing statements on personal property collateral were submitted to cities/towns until June 30, 2001, while real estate recording continues to be handled by the counties. The recording officers are Town/City Clerk (UCC), County Register of Deeds (real estate), and Clerk of US District Court (federal tax liens). Entire state is in the Eastern Time Zone (EST).

Real Estate Records: Real estate records are located at the county level. Each town/city profile indicates the county in which the town/city is located. Counties will not perform searches. Copy fee with certification is usually $.75 per page. Each town also has Assessor/Tax Collector/Treasurer offices from which real estate ownership and tax information is available.

UCC Records: This was a dual filing state. Until July 1, 2001, financing statements were usually filed both with the Town/City clerk and at the state level, except for real estate related collateral, which is recorded at the county Register of Deeds. Now, all filing are at the state except for the real estate related collateral. Most all recording offices perform searches. Use search request form UCC-11. Search fees are usually $10.00 per debtor name. Copy fees vary widely.

Tax Lien Records: Federal tax liens on personal property were filed with the Town/City Clerks prior to 1970. Since that time federal tax liens on personal property are filed with the US District Court in Boston as well as with the towns/cities. Following is how to search the central index for federal tax liens - Address: US District Court, 1 Courthouse Way, Boston, MA 02110 (617-748-9152)

The federal tax liens are indexed here on a computer system. Searches are available by mail or in person. Do not use the telephone. The court suggests including the Social Security number and/or address of individual names in your search request in order to narrow the results. A mail search costs $15.00 and will take about two weeks. Copies are included. Make your check payable to Clerk, US District Court. You can do the search yourself at no charge on their public computer terminal.

State tax liens on personal property are filed with the Town/City Clerk or Tax Collector. All tax liens against real estate are filed with the county Register of Deeds. Some towns file state tax liens on personal property with the UCC index and include tax liens on personal property automatically with a UCC search. Others will perform a separate state tax lien search usually for a fee of $10.00 plus $1.00 per page of copies. Other Liens: Medical, town/city tax, child support.

Online Access: A large number of towns and several counties offer online access to assessor records via the Internet for no charge. Also, a private vendor has placed assessor records from a number of towns on the Internet. Visit http://data.visionappraisal.com.

Abington Town Clerk 500 Gliniewicz Way, Abington, MA 02351 **781-982-2112** Fax: 781-982-2138. www.abingtonmass.com

Acton Town Clerk 472 Main St, Town Hall, Acton, MA 01720 **978-264-9615** Fax: 978-264-9630. www.town.acton.ma.us

Acushnet Town Clerk 122 Main St, Town Hall, Acushnet, MA 02743 **508-998-0215** Fax: 508-998-0203. 8AM-4PM.

Adams Town Clerk 8 Park St, Adams, MA 01220 **413-743-8320** Fax: 413-743-8316.

Agawam Town Clerk 36 Main St., Agawam, MA 01001-1837 **413-786-0400 x215** Fax: 413-786-9927. Property Assessor, Real Estate, Recording, Lien records online.

Alford Town Clerk 5 Alford Center Rd, Town Hall, Alford, MA 01230-8914 **413-528-4536** Fax: 413-528-4581. 4:30-7:30PM Th.

Amesbury Town Clerk 62 Friend St, Town Hall, Amesbury, MA 01913 **978-388-8100** Fax: 978-388-8150. 8AM-4PM M-Th; 5PM-8PM Th; 8AM-N F. Property Assessor records online.

Amherst Town Clerk 4 Boltwood Ave., Amherst, MA 01002 **413-256-4035** Fax: 413-256-2504. www.town.amherst.ma.us Property Assessor records online.

Andover Town Clerk 36 Bartlet St, Andover, MA 01810-3882 **978-623-8256** Fax: 978-623-8221. www.town.andover.ma.us Assessor, Land, Grantor/ Grantee, Recording online.

Arlington Town Clerk 730 Mass Ave, Town Hall, Arlington, MA 02476-9109 **781-316-3073** Fax: 781-316-3079. 9-5 Assessor records online. www.town.arlington.ma.us

Ashburnham Town Clerk 54 Willard Rd., Ashburnham, MA 01430 **978-827-4102** Fax: 978-827-4105. 9AM-5PM (7-9PM 1st & 3rd Mon of month).

Ashby Town Clerk 895 Main St., Ashby, MA 01431 **978-386-2424** Fax: 978-386-2490. 9AM-2PM, 6-8PM W. Property, Assessor records online.

Ashfield Town Clerk PO Box 560, Ashfield, MA 01330-0595 (412 Main St.). **413-628-4441** Fax: 413-628-4588. 9AM-12:30PM, 1:30-5PM M-W,F; 7-9PM F.

Ashland Town Clerk 101 Main St, Town Hall, Ashland, MA 01721 **508-881-0101** Fax: 508-881-0102. www.ashlandmass.com

Athol Town Clerk 584 Main St, Athol, MA 01331 **978-249-4551** Fax: 978-249-2491. 8-5 M,W,Th; 8AM-8PM T; Closed Fri..

Attleboro City Clerk 77 Park St, City Hall, Attleboro, MA 02703 **508-223-2222** Fax: 508-222-3046. 8:30AM-4:30PM.

Auburn Town Clerk 104 Central St, Auburn, MA 01501 **508-832-7701** Fax: 508-832-7702. 8AM-4PM; extended hours 2nd & 4th Mon. 8AM-7PM. www.auburnguide.com

Avon Town Clerk Buckley Ctr, Avon, MA 02322 **508-588-0414** Fax: 508-559-0209.

Ayer Town Clerk PO Box 308, Ayer, MA 01432 (1 Main St.). **978-772-8215** Fax: 978-772-8222. 8:30AM-5PM. Property, Assessor records online.

Barnstable County Register of Deeds PO Box 368, Barnstable, MA 02630 (3195 Main St, Route 6A). **508-362-7733** Fax: 508-362-5065. www.bcrd.co.barnstable.ma.us Real Estate, Lien, Deed records online.

Barnstable Town Clerk 367 Main St., Hyannis, MA 02601 **508-862-4044** Fax: 508-790-6326. www.town.barnstable.ma.us 8:30AM-4:30PM. Assessor records online.

Barre Town Clerk PO Box 418, Barre, MA 01005 (2 Exchange St.). **978-355-5003** Fax: 978-355-5032. 7-9PM M,W; 9AM-N, 1-4PM T,Th.

Becket Town Clerk 557 Main St., Jeanne W Pryor, Becket, MA 01223 **413-623-8934** Fax: 413-623-6036. 12-4:30PM M; 8:30AM-1PM T F; Noon-8PM W.

Bedford Town Clerk 10 Mudge Way, Town Hall, Bedford, MA 01730-0083 **781-275-0083** Fax: 781-687-6157. 8AM-4PM. www.town.bedford.ma.us

Belchertown Town Clerk PO Box 629, Belchertown, MA 01007-0607 (2 Jabish St). **413-323-0281** Fax: 413-323-0107. 8AM-5PM. www.belchertown.org

Bellingham Town Clerk PO Box 367, Bellingham, MA 02019-0367 (2 Mechanic St). **508-966-5827** Fax: 508-966-5804. 8:30-4:30PM T,W,Th; 8:30AM-1PM F; 8:30AM-7PM M. www.bellinghamma.org

Belmont Town Clerk 455 Concord Ave, Town Hall, Belmont, MA 02178-2514 **617-489-8201** Fax: 617-489-2185. 8AM-4PM. www.town.belmont.ma.us Assessor, Property records online.

Berkley Town Clerk 1 N. Main St, Berkley, MA 02779 **508-822-3348** Fax: 508-822-3511. 9-3PM. Property, Assessor records online.

Berkshire County - Middle District Register of Deeds 44 Bank Row, Pittsfield, MA 01201 **413-443-7438** Fax: 413-448-6025. 8:30AM-4:30PM (No Recording after 3:59PM). Real Estate, Lien records online.
Northern District - Register of Deeds 65 Park St, #1, Adams, MA 01220 **413-743-0035** Fax: 413-743-1003. 8:30AM-4:30PM. Real Estate, Lien records online.
Southern District Register of Deeds 334 Main St, Great Barrington, MA 01230 **413-528-0146** Fax: 413-528-6878. 8:30AM-4:30PM. Real Estate, Lien records online.

Berlin Town Clerk 23 Linden St, Box 8, Berlin, MA 01503 **978-838-2931** Fax: 978-838-0014. 12-3PM T,Th; 7-9PM W.

Bernardston Town Clerk PO Box 504, Bernardston, MA 01337-0435 (38 Church St). **413-648-5400** Fax: 413-648-5408. 9AM-2PM. Property Assessor records online.

Beverly City Clerk 191 Cabot St, Beverly, MA 01915-1031 **978-921-6000 x164** Fax: 978-921-8511. 8:30AM-4:30PM M,T,W; 8:30AM-7:30PM Th; 8:30AM-1PM. www.beverlyma.gov

Billerica Town Clerk 365 Boston Rd, Town Hall, Billerica, MA 01821-1885 **978-671-0924** Fax: 978-663-6510. 8:30AM-4PM.

Blackstone Town Clerk 15 St Paul St, Municipal Ctr, Blackstone, MA 01504-2295 **508-883-1500 x146** Fax: 508-883-7043. 9AM-4:30PM M-F, 5:30-7:30PM Tues..

Blandford Town Clerk PO Box 101, Blandford, MA 01008 (102 Main St). **413-848-2747** Fax: 413-848-0908. 6-8PM Mon Evening. Real Estate, Recording, Lien records online.

Bolton Town Clerk PO Box 278, Bolton, MA 01740 (663 Main St., Rear). **978-779-2771** Fax: 978-779-5461. 9-1PM W,Th; 7-9PM T; 9-4PM F. www.townofbolton.com Real Estate, Deed records online.

Boston City Clerk 1 City Hall Plaza, City Hall, Rm 601, Boston, MA 02201 **617-635-4600** Fax: 617-635-4658. 9AM-5PM. www.ci.boston.ma.us/assessing Assessor records online.

Bourne Town Clerk 24 Perry Ave, Town Hall, Buzzards Bay, MA 02532 **508-759-0613** Fax: 508-759-8026. 8:30AM-4:30PM.

Boxborough Town Clerk 29 Middle Rd, Boxborough, MA 01719-1499 **978-263-1116** Fax: 978-264-3127. 10AM-2PM; Closed T; 7-9PM Mon; 10AM-1PM Thurs. www.town.boxborough.ma.us

Boxford Town Clerk 7A Spofford Rd, Boxford, MA 01921 **978-887-6000 x501** Fax: 978-887-3546. 8AM-4:30PM M-Th.

Boylston Town Clerk 221 Main St, Boylston, MA 01505 **508-869-2234** Fax: 508-869-6210. 8AM-2PM M,T; (til 1PM W,TH); 6-8PM M; 9AM-2PM T-Th.

Braintree Town Clerk 1 JFK Memorial Drive, Braintree, MA 02184-6498 **781-794-8000 x8241** Fax: 781-794-8259.

Brewster Town Clerk 2198 Main St, Brewster, MA 02631 **508-896-4506** Fax: 508-896-8089. 8:30AM-4PM.

Bridgewater Town Clerk 64 Central Sq, Town Hall, Bridgewater, MA 02324 **508-697-0921** Fax: 508-697-0941. 8AM-4PM M-Th; 8AM-1PM F. www.bridgewaterma.org

Brimfield Town Clerk PO Box 508, Brimfield, MA 01010 (21 Main St.). **413-245-4101** Fax: 413-245-4107. 6:30PM-8PM T; 9-11AM Sat. Real Estate, Recording, Lien records online.

Bristol County - Fall River District Register of Deeds 441 N. Main St, Fall River, MA 02720 **508-673-1651** Fax: 508-673-7633. 8AM-4:30PM. www.fr-registry.com Real Estate, Lien records online.
Northern District Register of Deeds 11 Court St, Taunton, MA 02780-0248 **508-822-0502** Fax: 508-880-4975. 8AM-4:30PM. Real Estate, Lien records online.
Southern District Register of Deeds 25 N. 6th St, New Bedford, MA 02740 **508-993-2603** Fax: 508-997-4250. 8:30AM-4:30PM. www.newbedforddeeds.com Real Estate, Lien records online.

Brockton City Clerk 45 School St, Brockton, MA 02401 **508-580-7114** Fax: 508-580-7104. 8:30AM-4:30PM.

Brookfield Town Clerk 6 Central St., Brookfield, MA 01506 **508-867-2930 X12** Fax: 508-867-5091. 9AM-3PM Tu. Th, 7-8PM Tu.. www.brookfieldma.us Property, Assessor records online.

Brookline Town Clerk 333 Washington St, Town Hall, Brookline, MA 02445 **617-730-2010** Fax: 617-730-2043. 8AM-5PM M-W, 8AM-8PM Th, 8AM-12:30PM F. www.town.brookline.ma.us/Assessors Assessor, Property records online.

Buckland Town Clerk PO Box 159, Buckland, MA 01338 (17 State St). **413-625-8572** Fax: 413-625-8570. 10-3PM M-Th.

Burlington Town Clerk 29 Center St, Town Hall, Burlington, MA 01803 **781-270-1660**

Fax: 781-270-1608. 8:30AM-4:30PM. www.burlington.org/clerk

Cambridge City Clerk 795 Massachusetts Ave., City Hall, Rm 103, Cambridge, MA 02139 **617-349-4260** Fax: 617-349-4269. 8:30AM-8PM M; 8:30AM-5PM T-TH; 8:30-N F. Assessor records online. http://www2.ci.cambridge.ma.us/assessor

Canton Town Clerk 801 Washington St, Memorial Hall, Canton, MA 02021 **781-821-5013** Fax: 781-821-5016. 9AM-5PM.

Carlisle Town Clerk 66 Westford St, Carlisle, MA 01741 **978-369-6155** Fax: 978-371-0594. 9AM-3PM.

Carver Town Clerk 108 Main St, Carver, MA 02330 **508-866-3403** Fax: 508-866-3408. 8AM-4PM M-Th; 8AM-N F, Tues. 8AM-4PM; 5-8PM.

Charlemont Town Clerk PO Box 605, Charlemont, MA 01339-0605 (Linda Wagner, 2023 Route 2). **413-625-6157** Fax: 413-339-0320. By appointment.

Charlton Town Clerk 37 Main St, Charlton, MA 01507 **508-248-2249** Fax: 508-248-2073. 10AM-3PM M-Th; 1st & 3rd Tues of month 6-8PM.

Chatham Town Clerk 549 Main St, Chatham, MA 02633 **508-945-5101** Fax: 508-945-3550. www.town.chatham.ma.us

Chelmsford Town Clerk 50 Billerica Rd, Chelmsford, MA 01824 **978-250-5205** Fax: 978-840-5208. www.townofchelmsford.us

Chelsea City Clerk 500 Broadway, City Hall, Rm 209, Chelsea, MA 02150 **617-889-8226** Fax: 617-889-8367. 8-4PM M,W,Th; 8AM-7PM T; 8AM-N F. Assessor records online.

Cheshire Town Clerk PO Box S, 80 Church St, Cheshire, MA 01225 **413-743-1690** Fax: 413-743-0389. 9-3PM M,T,W; 9AM-N Th.

Chester Town Clerk Town Hall, Chester, MA 01011 **413-354-6603** Fax: 413-354-2268. 7-9PM M. Property, Assessor, Real Estate, Recording, Lien records online.

Chesterfield Town Clerk 422 Main St, Davenport Bldg, Chesterfield, MA 01012-0013 **413-296-4741** Fax: 413-296-4394. 7-9PM M or by Appointment.

Chicopee City Clerk 17 Springfield St, City Hall, Chicopee, MA 01013 **413-594-1466** Fax: 413-594-2057. 8AM-5PM. Real Estate, Recording, Lien records online.

Chilmark Town Clerk PO Box 119, Chilmark, MA 02535-0119 (401 Middle Rd.). **508-645-2107** Fax: 508-645-2110. 9AM-N. www.ci.chilmark.ma.us

Clarksburg Town Clerk 111 River Rd, Town Hall, Clarksburg, MA 01247 **413-663-8247** Fax: 413-664-6575. 9AM-2PM W-F.

Clinton Town Clerk 242 Church St, Clinton, MA 01510 **978-365-4119** Fax: 978-895-4130. 8:30AM-4PM.

Cohasset Town Clerk 41 Highland Ave, Cohasset, MA 02025-1814 **781-383-4100** Fax: 781-383-1561. 8:30AM-4:30PM M,W,Th; 8:30-7PM Tu; 8:30AM-1PM F.

Colrain Town Clerk PO Box 31, Colrain, MA 01340-0031 (55 Main Rd.). **413-624-3454** Fax: 413-624-8852. 9AM-4PM M-Th.

Concord Town Clerk PO Box 535, Concord, MA 01742 (22 Monument Sq). **978-318-3080** Fax: 978-318-3093. 8:30AM-4:30PM. www.concordnet.org Property Assessor records online.

Conway Town Clerk PO Box 240, Conway, MA 01341 (32 Main St.). **413-369-4235** Fax: 413-369-4237. 9AM-N T,Th,F.

Cummington Town Clerk 585 Berkshire Trail, Cummington, MA 01026 **413-634-5458** Fax: 413-634-5568. 6-8PM W.

Dalton Town Clerk 462 Main St, Town Hall, Dalton, MA 01226 **413-684-6103 x14** Fax: 413-684-6129. 8-4PM M-W; 8-6PM Th.

Danvers Town Clerk 1 Sylvan St, Town Hall, Danvers, MA 01923 **978-777-0001** Fax: 978-777-1025. 8AM-5PM M-W; 8-7:30PM Th; 8AM-1:30PM F. www.danvers-ma.org

Dartmouth Town Clerk PO Box 79399, Dartmouth, MA 02747 (400 Slocum Rd). **508-910-1800** Fax: 508-910-1894. 8:30AM-4:30PM. www.town.dartmouth.ma.us/town_hall.htm Assessor records online.

Dedham Town Clerk PO Box 306, Dedham, MA 02027 (High St Courthouse). **781-751-9200** Fax: 781-751-9109. 8:30AM-4:30PM. Assessor records online.

Deerfield Town Clerk 8 Conway St., South Deerfield, MA 01373 **413-665-2130** Fax: 413-665-7275. www.town.deerfield.ma.us

Dennis Town Clerk PO Box 1419, South Dennis, MA 02660-1419 (485 Main St). **508-760-6115** Fax: 508-394-8309. 8:30AM-4:30PM. www.town.dennis.ma.us/ Assessor, Property records online.

Dighton Town Clerk 979 Somerset Ave, Dighton, MA 02715-0465 **508-669-5411** Fax: 508-669-5932. 8:00AM-4PM M,T,Th; 8AM-5PM W; 8AM-N Fri.. www.dighton-ma.gov/Home/

Douglas Town Clerk 29 Depot St., Municipal Ctr, Douglas, MA 01516 **508-476-4000 x355** Fax: 508-476-4012. 9AM-1PM, 1:30-4PM M-Th; 6-8PM T.

Dover Town Clerk PO Box 250, Dover, MA 02030-0250 (5 Springdale Ave). **508-785-0032** Fax: 508-785-2341. 9AM-1 M,W,F; 9-4 T,Th. Property, Assessor records online. http://doverma.org/townclerk.shtml

Dracut Town Clerk 62 Arlington St, Rm 4, Dracut, MA 01826 **978-453-0951** Fax: 978-452-7924. Assessor records online.

Dudley Town Clerk 40 Schofield Ave, Town Hall #17, Dudley, MA 01571 **508-949-8004** Fax: 508-949-7115. 8AM-N, 12:30-4:30 PM M-Th; 6-8PM Th; 8AM-1PM F. www.dudleyma.gov Assessor records online.

Dukes County Register of Deeds PO Box 5231, Edgartown, MA 02539 (81 Main St). **508-627-4025** Fax: 508-627-7821. 8:30-4:30.

Dunstable Town Clerk 511 Main St., Dunstable, MA 01827 **978-649-4514** Fax: 978-649-2205. M 6PM-9PM; TWTH 9AM-2PM; F 9AM-N.

Duxbury Town Treasurer 878 Tremont St, Duxbury, MA 02332-4499 **781-934-1100** Fax: 781-934-9278. 8AM-N,1-4PM. Property Assessor records online.

East Bridgewater Town Clerk PO Box 387, East Bridgewater, MA 02333 (175 Central St.). **508-378-1606** Fax: 508-378-1638. 8:30AM-8PM Tu-Th; 8:30AM-4:30PM M; 8:30AM-N F.

East Brookfield Town Clerk Town Hall, East Brookfield, MA 01515 **508-867-6769** Fax: 508-867-4190. 9AM-12 M; 11AM-1PM F. Assessor, Property records online.

East Longmeadow Town Clerk 60 Center Sq, East Longmeadow, MA 01028-2446 **413-525-5400 x410** Fax: 413-525-0022. 8AM-4PM. www.eastlongmeadow.org Real Estate, Recording, Lien records online.

Eastham Town Clerk 2500 State Highway, Eastham, MA 02642 **508-240-5900 x223**

Easthampton City Clerk 50 Payson Ave #100, Easthampton, MA 01027 **413-529-1460** Fax: 413-529-1488. 8AM-4PM M-F; 7-8PM W. Propety Assessor records online.

Easton Town Clerk 136 Elm St, North Easton, MA 02356-0129 **508-230-0530** Fax: 508-230-0539. 8:30AM-8:30PM M; 7AM-4:30PM T Th; 8:30AM-12:30PM F. www.easton.ma.us

Edgartown Town Clerk PO Box 35, Edgartown, MA 02539-0035 (70 Main St.).

508-627-6110 Fax: 508-627-6123. Real Estate, Property Tax records online.

Egremont Town Clerk PO Box 56, North Egremont/ So. Egremont, MA 01258-0056 (Route 71, Town Hall). **413-528-0182** Fax: 413-528-5465. Hours- 7-9PM Tues. Property, Assessor records online.

Erving Town Clerk 12 E Main St, Town Hall, Erving, MA 01344 **413-422-2800** Fax: 413-422-2808. 2-5PM, 6-9PM M.

Essex County - Northern District Register of Deeds 381 Common St, Lawrence, MA 01840 **978-683-2745** Fax: 978-681-5409. 8AM-4:30PM (recording until 4PM). www.lawrencedeeds.com Real Estate, Lien, Grantor/Grantee, Recording records online. **Southern District Register of Deeds** 36 Federal St, Salem, MA 01970 **978-741-0201** Fax: 978-744-5865. 8AM-4PM. www.salemdeeds.com Real Estate, Lien, Deed records online.

Essex Town Clerk Martin St., Town Hall, Essex, MA 01929 **978-768-7111** 8:30AM-1PM M,W; 1-4PM T & Th; Closed F.

Everett City Clerk City Hall, Rm 10, Everett, MA 02149 **617-394-2225** Fax: 617-387-5770. M 8AM-7:30PM; 8AM-4PM T-Th; 8-11:30AM Fri..

Fairhaven Town Clerk 40 Center St, Fairhaven, MA 02719-2999 **508-979-4025** Fax: 508-979-4079. 8:30AM-4:30PM.

Fall River City Clerk One Government Ctr, Fall River, MA 02722 **508-324-2220** Fax: 508-324-2211. 9AM-5PM.

Falmouth Town Clerk PO Box 904, Falmouth, MA 02541 (59 Town Hall Sq). **508-548-7611** Fax: 508-457-2511. Assessor records online. www.town.falmouth.ma.us

Fitchburg City Clerk 718 Main St, Fitchburg, MA 01420-3198 **978-345-9592** Fax: 978-345-9595. 8:30AM-4:30PM.

Florida Town Clerk 20 South St, Town Hall, Drury, MA 01343 **413-664-6685** Fax: 413-664-8640. By Appointment.

Foxborough Town Clerk 40 South St, Foxborough, MA 02035-2397 **508-543-1208** Fax: 508-543-6278. 8:30AM-4PM M,W,Th; 8:30-4PM, 5-8PM T; 8:30-N

Framingham Town Clerk 150 Concord St, Memorial Bldg. - Rm 105, Framingham, MA 01702-8374 **508-620-4863** Fax: 508-628-1358. 8:30AM-5PM M; 8:30AM-5PM T-F. www.framinghamma.org

Franklin County Register of Deeds PO Box 1495, Greenfield, MA 01302-1495 (425 Main St). **413-772-0239** Fax: 413-774-7150.

8:30AM-4:30PM (Recording until 4PM). Real Property, Recording, Lien, Deed, Judgment records online.

Franklin Town Clerk 355 Easr Central St., Municipal Bldg., Franklin, MA 02038 **508-520-4900** Fax: 508-520-4903. 8AM-4PM M,T,Th, 8AM-6PM,W ,8am -1PM,F.

Freetown Town Clerk PO Box 438, Assonet, MA 02702 (3 N. Main St). **508-644-2203** Fax: 508-644-9826. 9AM-7PM M, 9-4PM F T-F. http://town.freetown.ma.us/tg/

Gardner City Clerk 95 Pleasant St, City Hall, Rm 118, Gardner, MA 01440 **978-630-4008** Fax: 978-630-2520. 8AM-4:30PM; F 8AM-4PM. Property Assessor records online.

Georgetown Town Clerk 1 Library St, Georgetown, MA 01833 **978-352-5711** Fax: 978-352-5725. M&W 9AM-N,T&Th 9AM-4PM; Closed Fri..

Gill Town Clerk 325 Main Rd, Town Clerk's Office, Gill, MA 01376 **413-863-8103** Fax: 413-863-7775. 10AM-4PM W-F.

Gloucester City Clerk 9 Dale Ave, Gloucester, MA 01930-5998 **978-281-9720** Fax: 978-281-8472. 8:30AM-4PM M-W,F Winter; 8:30AM-6:30PM Th. www.ci.gloucester.ma.us

Goshen Town Clerk PO Box 124, Goshen, MA 01032 (40 Main St.). **413-268-8236** Fax: 413-268-8237. 7-8:30PM Monday.

Gosnold Town Clerk Town Hall, Gosnold, MA 02713 **508-990-7408** Fax: 508-990-7408. By Appointment.

Grafton Town Clerk 30 Providence Rd, Municipal Ctr, Grafton, MA 01519-1186 **508-839-4722** Fax: 508-839-4602. 8:30AM-4:30PM (T 8:30AM-7PM). Property, Assessor records online.

Granby Town Clerk 250 State St., Kellogg Hall, Granby, MA 01033 **413-467-7178** Fax: 413-467-2080. 9AM-3PM M,T,W,Th; 9AM-N F; 7-9PM 1st & 3rd M.

Granville Town Clerk PO Box 247, Granville, MA 01034-0247 (707 Main Rd). **413-357-8585** Fax: 413-357-6002. 9-11AM, 7-9PM M. Real Estate, Recording, Lien records online.

Great Barrington Town Clerk 334 Main St, Great Barrington, MA 01230-1802 **413-528-3140** Fax: 413-528-2290. 8:30AM-4PM.

Greenfield Town Clerk 14 Court Sq, Town Hall, Greenfield, MA 01301 **413-772-1555 x112** Fax: 413-772-1542. 8:30AM-5PM.

Groton Town Clerk 173 Main St., Town Hall, Groton, MA 01450 **978-448-1100** Fax:

978-448-2030. 8:30AM-7PM M; 8:30AM-4:30PM T-Th; 9-4 F; 9-1 Sat.

Groveland Town Clerk Town Hall, Groveland, MA 01830 **978-372-6861** Fax: 978-469-5006. 9-1PM M,T,Th,F; 9-N W.

Hadley Town Clerk 100 Middle St, Hadley, MA 01035-9517 **413-584-1590** Fax: 413-586-5661. 9AM-4PM. www.hadleyma.org

Halifax Town Clerk 499 Plymouth St, Halifax, MA 02338-1395 **781-293-7970** Fax: 781-294-7684. 7AM-4PM; 6:30-8:30PM Tues (closed Fri).

Hamilton Town Clerk PO Box 429, Hamilton, MA 01936 (577 Bay Rd). **978-468-5570** Fax: 978-468-2682. 8AM-4:30PM (Fri open until Noon); 4:30-7PM M Eve.. www.town.hamilton.ma.us

Hampden County Register of Deeds 50 State St, Hall of Justice, Springfield, MA 01103 **413-755-1722** Fax: 413-731-8190. 8:30AM-4:30PM; 9AM-4PM(Recording). http://registryofdeeds.co.hampden.ma.us Real Estate, Lien, Recording records online.

Hampden Town Clerk PO Box 215, Hampden, MA 01036 (625 Main St.). **413-566-3214** Fax: 413-566-2010. 9AM-1PM M-Th; Closed F. www.hampden.org Real Estate, Recording, Lien records online.

Hampshire County Register of Deeds 33 King St, Hall of Records, Northampton, MA 01060 **413-584-3637** Fax: 413-584-4136. 8:30AM-4:30PM (Recording ends at 4PM). Real Estate, Lien records online.

Hancock Town Clerk 3650 Hancock Rd., Hancock, MA 01237-1097 **413-738-5225** Fax: 413-738-5310. 7-9PM T; 9AM-N Th; 9-11AM 1st Sat of the month.

Hanover Town Clerk 550 Hanover St, Hanover, MA 02339-2217 **781-826-2691** Fax: 781-826-5950. 8AM-4PM.

Hanson Town Clerk 542 Liberty St., Town Hall, Hanson, MA 02341 **781-293-2772** Fax: 781-294-0884. 8AM-5PM M,T,W,Th; 7-9PM Tue.

Hardwick Town Clerk PO Box 575, Gilbertville, MA 01031-0575 (307 Main St.). **413-477-6197** Fax: 413-477-6703. 6:30-8:30PM M; 9AM-N Sat. Property, Assessor records online.

Harvard Town Clerk 13 Ayer Rd, Town Hall, Harvard, MA 01451-1458 **978-456-4100** Fax: 978-456-4113. 8:30AM-4PM M-Th. www.harvard.ma.us/townclerk.htm

Harwich Town Clerk 732 Main St, Harwich, MA 02645-2717 **508-430-7516** Fax: 508-432-5039. 8:30AM-4PM.

Hatfield Town Clerk 59 Main St, Hatfield, MA 01038-970. **413-247-0492** Fax: 413-347-5029. 8:30AM-4PM (F 8:30AM-12).

Haverhill City Clerk 4 Summer St, City Hall, Rm 118, Haverhill, MA 01830-5880 **978-374-2312** Fax: 978-373-8490. 8AM-4PM. www.ci.haverhill.ma.us

Hawley Town Clerk Town Hall, Hawley, MA 01339-9624 **413-339-5518** Fax: 413-339-4959. 1-5PM Wed.

Heath Town Clerk 1 E Main St, Town Hall, Heath, MA 01346 **413-337-4934** Fax: 413-337-8542. 9AM-2PM M-Th. Property, Assessor records online.

Hingham Town Clerk 210 Central St, Hingham, MA 02043 **781-741-1410** Fax: 781-740-0239. 8:30AM-4:30PM. Propert, Assessor records online.

Hinsdale Town Clerk PO Box 803, Hinsdale, MA 01235 (Town Hall). **413-655-2301** Fax: 413-655-8807. 1-3PM, 6:30-8PM W; 12:45-3PM Th.

Holbrook Town Clerk Town Hall, Holbrook, MA 02343-1502 **781-767-4314** Fax: 781-767-9054. 8AM-4PM.

Holden Town Clerk 1196 Main St, Town Hall, Holden, MA 01520-1092 **508-829-0265** Fax: 508-829-0281. 8:30AM-4:30PM; Summer Hr 8AM-4Pm. Real Estate, Property Tax records online.

Holland Town Clerk 27 Sturbridge Rd, Holland, MA 01521-9712 **413-245-7108** Fax: 413-245-7037. 9AM-N, 1-4PM M,W,Th; 9AM-N, 1-5PM, 7-8:30PM. Real Estate, Recording, Deed, Lien records online.

Holliston Town Clerk 703 Washington St, Holliston, MA 01746 **508-429-0601** Fax: 508-429-0684. www.townofholliston.us Property, Assessor records online. 8:30AM-4:30PM.

Holyoke City Clerk 536 Dwight St, Holyoke, MA 01040 (City Hall, Rm 2). **413-322-5520** Fax: 413-322-5521. 8:30AM-4:30PM. www.ci.holyoke.ma.us Assessor, Property, Real Estate, Recording, Lien records online.

Hopedale Town Clerk PO Box 7, Hopedale, MA 01747 (78 Hopedale St.). **508-634-2203** Fax: 508-634-2200. 9AM-2PM M-Th.

Hopkinton Town Clerk 18 Main St, Hopkinton, MA 01748-1260 **508-497-9710** Fax: 508-497-9702. 8:30AM-4PM.

Hubbardston Town Clerk PO Box H, Hubbardston, MA 01452 (Town Hall). **978-928-5244** Fax: 978-928-1402. 2-8PM M; 8AM-4PM T-Th.

Hudson Town Clerk 78 Main St, Town Hall, Hudson, MA 01749 **978-568-9615** 8AM-4:30PM. www.townofhudson.org Property, Assessor records online.

Hull Town Clerk Town Hall, 253 Atlantic Ave, Hull, MA 02045 **781-925-2262** Fax: 781-925-0224. 8AM-4PM M,W; 8:30AM-7:30PMT, Th.

Huntington Town Clerk PO Box 523, Office of Town Clerk, Huntington, MA 01050 (24 Russell Rd). **413-667-3186** Fax: 413-667-3507. 9AM-N M.; 6-8PM Wed.

Ipswich Town Clerk 25 Green St, Ipswich, MA 01938-2357 **978-356-6600** Fax: 978-356-6616. 8AM-7PM M; 8AM-4PM T,W,Th; 8AM-N F. www.town.ipswich.ma.us/

Kingston Town Clerk 26 Evergreen St., Kingston, MA 02364 **781-585-0502** Fax: 781-585-0542. 8:30AM-N, 1-4:30PM. www.kingstonmass.org

Lakeville Town Clerk 346 Bedford St, Lakeville, MA 02347 **508-946-8814** Fax: 508-946-3970. 9AM-4PM.

Lancaster Town Clerk Box 97, Town Hall, Lancaster, MA 01523-0097 (695 Main St.). **978-365-2542** Fax: 978-368-4005. 9-6PM M; 9-4PM T-TH. Property, Assessor records online. www.ci.lancaster.ma.us

Lanesborough Town Clerk PO Box 1492, Lanesborough, MA 01237 (83 N. Main St). **413-442-1351** Fax: 413-443-5811. 8-1PM.

Lawrence City Clerk 200 Common St, Lawrence, MA 01840 **978-794-5803** Fax: 978-557-0285. 8:30AM-4:30PM. www.cityoflawrence.com/Departments.asp Land, Grantor/Grantee, Recording records online.

Lee Town Clerk 32 Main St, Town Hall, Lee, MA 01238 **413-243-5505** Fax: 413-243-5507. 8:30AM-4PM.

Leicester Town Clerk 3 Washburn Sq, Leicester, MA 01524 **508-892-7011** Fax: 508-892-7070. 8:30AM-4PM.

Lenox Town Clerk 6 Walker St, Town Hall, Lenox, MA 01240-2718 **413-637-5506** Fax: 413-637-5518. 9AM-4PM.

Leominster City Clerk 25 West St, Leominster, MA 01453 **978-534-7536** Fax: 978-534-7546. 8:30AM-4PM M-W & F; 8:30AM-5:30PM Th. www.ci.leominster.us Assessor records online.

Leverett Town Clerk PO Box 178, Leverett, MA 01054 (9 Montague Rd.). **413-548-9150** Fax: 413-548-9150. 7PM-9PM M; 9AM-N W,Th.

Lexington Town Clerk 1625 Massachusetts Ave, Town Office Bldg., Lexington, MA 02420 **781-862-0500 x270** Fax: 781-861-2754. 8:30-4:30PM. http://ci.lexington.ma.us Assessor records online.

Leyden Town Clerk Town Hall, Leyden, MA 01337 **413-774-7769** Fax: 413-772-0146. 10AM-1PM W-F.

Lincoln Town Clerk PO Box 6353, Lincoln Center, MA 01773-6353 (16 Lincoln Rd). **781-259-2607** Fax: 781-259-1677. 8:30AM-4:30PM. www.state.ma.us/cc/lincoln.html

Littleton Town Clerk PO Box 1305, Littleton, MA 01460 (37 Shattuck St.). **978-952-2314** Fax: 978-952-2321. 9AM-3PM M,T,W,F; 9-9PM Th. www.littletonma.org

Longmeadow Town Clerk 20 Williams St, Town Hall, Longmeadow, MA 01106 **413-567-1066** Fax: 413-565-4112. 8:15AM-4:30PM. www.longmeadow.org Assessor, Real Estate, Recording, Lien records online.

Lowell City Clerk 375 Merrimack St, City Hall, Lowell, MA 01852 **978-970-4161** Fax: 978-970-4162. www.ci.lowell.ma.us Assessor records online. 8AM-5PM.

Ludlow Town Clerk 488 Chapin St, Ludlow, MA 01056 **413-583-5610** Fax: 413-583-5603. 8:30AM-4:30PM. www.ludlow.ma.us/clerk/ Real Estate, Recording, Lien records online.

Lunenburg Town Clerk PO Box 135, Lunenburg, MA 01462 (17 Main St). **978-582-4131** Fax: 978-582-4148. 8AM-6:30PM M,W,Th; 8AM-4:00 PM Tu.

Lynn City Clerk 3 City Hall Sq, Lynn, MA 01901 **781-598-4000** Fax: 781-477-7032. 8:30AM-4PM M,W,Th; 8:30AM-8PM T; 8:30AM-12:30PM F.

Lynnfield Town Clerk 55 Summer St, Lynnfield, MA 01940-1823 **781-334-3128** Fax: 781-334-0014. 8AM-4:30PM (F 8-1).

Malden City Clerk 200 Pleasant St, City Hall, Malden, MA 02148 **781-397-7116** Fax: 781-388-0610. 8AM-4PM M,W,Th; 8AM-7PM T; 8AM-N F.

Manchester-by-the-Sea Town Clerk 10 Central St, Town Hall, Manchester-by-the Sea, MA 01944-1399 **978-526-2040** Fax: 978-526-2001. 9AM-5PM M-W; 9AM-8PM Th. www.manchester.ma.us Property Assessor records online.

Mansfield Town Clerk 6 Park Row, Town Hall, Mansfield, MA 02048-2433 **508-261-7345** Fax: 508-261-1083. 8AM-4PM M, T, Th; 8AM-8PM W; 8AM-N F.

Marblehead Town Clerk Abbot Hall, Marblehead, MA 01945 **781-631-0528** Fax:

781-631-8571. 8AM-5PM, M, T, Th; 7:30AM-7:30PM, W; 8AM-1PM F. www.marblehead.org Assessor, Property records online.

Marion Town Clerk 2 Spring St, Marion, MA 02738 **508-748-3502** Fax: 508-748-2845. 8AM-4:30PM M-Th; 8AM-3:30PM F. www.townofmarion.org Property Assessor records online.

Marlborough City Clerk 140 Main St, Marlborough, MA 01752-3812 **508-460-3775** Fax: 508-624-6504. 8:30AM-5PM. Property Assessor records online.

Marshfield Town Clerk Town Hall, Marshfield, MA 02050 **781-834-5540** Fax: 781-837-7163. 8:30AM-4:30PM.

Mashpee Town Clerk 16 Great Neck Rd. N., Town Hall, Mashpee, MA 02649 **508-539-1400 x561** Fax: 508-539-1403. 9AM-4PM. www.ci.mashpee.ma.us Assessor online

Mattapoisett Town Clerk PO Box 89, Mattapoisett, MA 02739-0089 (16 Main St.). **508-758-4103** Fax: 508-758-3030. 8AM-4PM. www.mattapoisett.net Property, Assessor records online.

Maynard Town Clerk 195 Main St, Town Hall, Maynard, MA 01754-2575 **978-897-1000** Fax: 978-897-8457. 8AM-4PM.

Medfield Town Clerk 459 Main St, Town Hall, Medfield, MA 02052 **508-359-8505** Fax: 508-359-6182. 8:30AM-4:30PM M-W; 8:30AM-7:30PM Th; 8:30AM-1PM F. www.town.medfield.net

Medford City Clerk 85 George P. Hassett Drive, City Clerk, Medford, MA 02155 **781-393-2425** Fax: 781-391-1895. 8:30AM-4:30PM M,T,Th; 8:30AM-7:30PM W; 8:30AM-12:3. www.medford.org Property Assessor records online.

Medway Town Clerk 155 Village St., Medway, MA 02053 **508-533-3204** Fax: 508-533-3287. 8AM-7:30PM M; 8AM-4PM Tu-Th; 8AM-1PM F.

Melrose City Clerk 562 Main St, Melrose, MA 02176 **781-979-4114** Fax: 781-665-6877. 8AM-4:30PM (July-Aug: 8-4:30PM M-Th; 8AM-1PM F. www.cityofmelrose.org

Mendon Town Clerk PO Box 54, Mendon, MA 01756-0054 (20 Main St). **508-473-1085** Fax: 508-478-8241. 8AM-3:30PM M-Th, 6:30-9PM M; Closed F.

Merrimac Town Clerk 2 School St, Merrimac, MA 01860 **978-346-8013** Fax: 978-346-0522. 9AM-4PM M-Th.

Methuen City Clerk 41 Pleasant St, Rm 112, Methuen, MA 01844 **978-794-3213** Fax: 978-

794-3215. 8:30AM-5:30PM M-TH; 8:30AM-Noon F. www.ci.methuen.ma.us Property Assessor, Land, Grantor/Grantee, Recording records online.

Middleborough Town Clerk 20 Centre St, 1st Fl, Middleborough, MA 02346 (**508-946-2415** Fax: 508-946-2308. 8:45AM-5PM.

Middlefield Town Clerk PO Box 265, Middlefield, MA 01243 (Town Hall). **413-623-8966** Fax: 413-623-6108. 7PM-9PM; 9AM-N Sat.

Middlesex County - Northern District Register of Deeds 360 Gorham St, Lowell, MA 01852 **978-322-9000** Fax: 978-322-9001. 8:30AM-4:15PM. www.lowelldeeds.com **Southern District Registery of Deeds** 208 Cambridge St, Cambridge, MA 02141 **617-679-6300** 8AM-4PM. Real Estate, Lien records online.

Middleton Town Clerk Memorial Hall, Middleton, MA 01949 **978-774-6927** Fax: 978-774-6167. 9-4PM M-W-Th; 9-1PM F; 6-8PM T. www.townofmiddleton.org

Milford Town Clerk 52 Main St, Milford, MA 01757 **508-634-2307** Fax: 508-634-2324. 8:30AM-4:30PM.

Millbury Town Clerk 127 Elm St, Municipal Office Bldg., Millbury, MA 01527 **508-865-9110** 9AM-4PM. Property, Assessor online.

Millis Town Clerk 900 Main St., Millis, MA 02054-1512 **508-376-7046** Fax: 508-376-7053. 8:30AM-4:30PM. Assessor online.

Millville Town Clerk PO Box 703, Millville, MA 01529-0703 (8 Central St.). **508-883-5849** Fax: 508-883-2994. M-Th 8:30-1PM; 6-8PM W. http://millvillema.org Real Estate, Deed, Tax Lien records online.

Milton Town Clerk 525 Canton Ave, Town Hall, Milton, MA 02186 **617-696-5414** 8:30AM-5PM.

Monroe Town Clerk PO Box 6, Monroe, MA 01350 (Town Hall). **413-424-5272** Fax: 413-424-7580.

Monson Town Clerk 110 Main St. #4, Monson, MA 01057-1332 **413-267-4115** Fax: 413-267-3726. 9AM-12:30 PM, 1:30-4PM (3:30 on Tu). Real Estate, Recording, Lien records online.

Montague Town Clerk 1 Avenue A, Turners Falls, MA 01376-1128 **413-863-3211** Fax: 413-863-3224. 8:30AM-4:30PM.

Monterey Town Clerk Town Hall, Monterey, MA 01245 **413-528-5175** Fax: 413-528-9452. 9:30AM-12:30PM Sat, or by appointment.

Montgomery Town Clerk Town Hall, 161 Main Rd, Montgomery, MA 01085 **413-862-3386** Fax: 413-862-3204. by appointment. Real Estate, Recording, Lien records online.

Mt. Washington Town Clerk 118 East St., Mt. Washington, MA 01258 **413-528-2839** Fax: 413-528-2839. 8-9PM M-Town Clerk; 8:30AM-1:30PM M-T for Town Sec.

Nahant Town Clerk Town Hall, Nahant, MA 01908-0075 (**781-581-0018** Fax: 781-593-0340. 9AM-N.

Nantucket County Register of Deeds 16 Broad St, Nantucket, MA 02554 **508-228-7250** Fax: 508-325-5331. 8AM-4PM; Recording Hours: 8AM-N, 1-3:45PM. www.nantucketdeeds.com Real estate, Deed, Recording, Lien records online.

Nantucket Town Clerk 16 Broad St, Town & County Bldg., Nantucket, MA 02554 **508-228-7217** Fax: 508-325-5313. 8AM-4PM. www.town.nantucket.ma.us

Natick Town Clerk 13 E. Central St, Natick, MA 01760 **508-647-6430** Fax: 508-655-6715. 8AM-5PM. www.natickma.org Assessor, Property records online.

Needham Town Clerk PO Box 663, Needham, MA 02192 (1471 Highland Ave). **781-455-7510** Fax: 781-449-4569. 8:30AM-5PM. www.town.needham.ma.us Property, Assessor records online.

New Ashford Town Clerk 142 Beach Hill Rd, New Ashford, MA 01237 **413-458-5461** Fax: 413-458-5461. By appointment.

New Bedford City Clerk 133 William St, New Bedford, MA 02740 **508-979-1450** Fax: 508-991-6225. 8AM-4PM. www.ci.new-bedford.ma.us/Nav3.htm Property, Assessor records online.

New Braintree Town Clerk 20 Memorial Dr Rm 5, New Braintree, MA 01531. **508-867-4952** Fax: 508-867-6316. 7AM-9PM M; 9AM-1PM F. www.newbraintree.net

New Marlborough Town Clerk PO Box 99, Mill River, MA 01244 (Mill River-Southfield Rd.). **413-229-8116** Fax: 413-229-6674. 9AM-2PM. www.new-marlborough.ma.us

New Salem Town Clerk 15 S Main St, Town Hall, New Salem, MA 01355 **978-544-2731** Fax: 978-544-5775. 6-8PM M; 9-11AM W.

Newbury Town Clerk 25 High Rd, Newbury, MA 01951-4799 **978-462-2332** Fax: 978-465-3064. 8-3:30PM M,T,W,Th; 8AM-1PM F. www.townofnewbury.org Assessor, Property Tax records online.

Newburyport City Clerk 60 Pleasant St, Newburyport, MA 01950 **978-465-4407** Fax: 978-462-79236. 8-4PM M,T,W; 8AM-8PM Th; 8AM-N F. Assessor records online.

Newton City Clerk 1000 Commonwealth Ave, Newton Center, MA 02159 **617-796-1200** Fax: 617-964-2333. 8:30AM-5PM M; 8:30AM-8:00PM T; 8:30AM-5PM W. www.ci.newton.ma.us Assessor online.

Norfolk County Register of Deeds PO Box 69, Dedham, MA 02027-0069 (649 High St). **781-461-6122** Fax: 781-326-4742. 8:30-4:45PM. www.norfolkdeeds.org Real Estate, Lien, Deed, Judgment records online.

Norfolk Town Clerk 1 Liberty Lane, Norfolk, MA 02056 **508-528-1400** Fax: 508-541-3363. 9-4PM. www.virtualnorfolk.org

North Adams City Clerk 10 Main St, North Adams, MA 01247 **413-662-3015** 8-4:30.

North Andover Town Clerk 120 Main St, North Andover, MA 01845 **978-688-9502** Fax: 978-688-9556. 8:30AM-4:30PM. www.townofnorthandover.com Land, Grantor/Grantee, Recording records online.

North Attleborough Town Clerk PO Box 871, North Attleborough, MA 02761-0871 (43 S. Washington St). **508-699-0108** Fax: 508-699-2354. 8AM-4PM (Th 8AM-7PM). Assessor records online.

North Brookfield Town Clerk 185 N Main St., North Brookfield, MA 01535 **508-867-0203** Fax: 508-867-0249. Noon-2:30PM 6PM-8PM T; Noon-2:30PM Th; 9AM-N F. Property, Assessor records online.

North Reading Town Clerk 235 N. St, North Reading, MA 01864-1294 **978-664-6030** Fax: 978-664-6048. 8AM-4PM M-Th; 8AM-1PM F.

Northampton City Clerk 210 Main St, Northampton, MA 01060 **413-587-1224** Fax: 413-587-1264. 8:30AM-4:30PM.

Northborough Town Clerk 63 Main St, Northborough, MA 01532-1994 **508-393-5001** Fax: 508-393-6996. 8AM-4PM M,W,Th; 8AM-7PM T; 7AM-N F. www.town.northborough.ma.us

Northbridge Town Clerk 7 Main St, Town Hall, Whitinsville, MA 01588 **508-234-2001** Fax: 508-234-2001. 8:30AM-7PM M; 8:30AM-4:30PM T-Th; 8:30AM-1PM F. www.northbridgemass.org

Northfield Town Clerk Town Hall, Northfield, MA 01360 (69 Main St.). **413-498-2901** Fax: 413-498-5103. 8:30AM-4PM M-Tu; 9-N 4-N;12-8PM W.

Norton Town Clerk 70 E. Main St, Town Hall, Norton, MA 02766 **508-285-0231** Fax: 508-285-0297. 8:30AM-4:30PM M,T,W,F; 8:30AM-8PM Th.

Norwell Town Clerk PO Box 295, Norwell, MA 02061-0295 (345 Main St). **781-659-8072** Fax: 781-659-7795. 8AM-4PM. www.townofnorwell.net

Norwood Town Clerk PO Box 40, Norwood, MA 02062 (566 Washington St.). **781-762-1240 x193** Fax: 781-762-0954. 8:15AM-4:30PM.

Oak Bluffs Town Clerk PO Box 2490, Oak Bluffs, MA 02557-2490 (Town Hall). **508-693-5515** Fax: 508-696-7736. 8:30AM-4PM. Assessor records online.

Oakham Town Clerk PO Box 222, Oakham, MA 01068-0222 (2 Coldbrook Rd.). **508-882-5549** Fax: 508-882-3060. 5:30-7PM T; 9AM-11:30AM,Th. Property, Assessor records online.

Orange Town Clerk 6 Prospect St, Orange, MA 01364 **978-544-2254** Fax: 978-544-1120. 8AM-4PM M-Th; 8AM-1PM F.

Orleans Town Clerk 19 School Rd, Orleans, MA 02653-3699 **508-240-3700** Fax: 508-240-3388. 8:30AM-4:30PM.

Otis Town Clerk PO Box 237, Otis, MA 01253 (1 N. Main.). **413-269-0101** Fax: 413-269-0111. 7:30-2:30PM M-F; 9AM-N Sat.

Oxford Town Clerk 325 Main St, Oxford, MA 01540 **508-987-6032** Fax: 508-987-6048. 9AM-4:30PM. www.town.oxford.ma.us Property Assessor records online.

Palmer Town Clerk 4417 Main St., Palmer, MA 01069. **413-283-2608** Fax: 413-283-2637. 9AM-4:30PM. Real Estate, Recording, Lien records online.

Paxton Town Clerk 697 Pleasant St, Paxton, MA 01612 **508-799-7347 x13** Fax: 508-797-0966. 8AM-2PM M-Th. Assessor online.

Peabody City Clerk 24 Lowell St, City Hall, Peabody, MA 01960 **978-538-5900** Fax: 978-538-5985. 8:30AM-4PM M-W; 8:30AM-7PM Th; 8:30AM-12:30PM F. www.ci.peabody.ma.us

Pelham Town Clerk 351 Amherst Rd., Rhodes Bldg, Pelham, MA 01002-9753 **413-253-7129** Fax: 413-256-1061. 8:30AM-4:30PM M-Th. www.townofpelham.org

Pembroke Town Clerk 100 Center St, Pembroke, MA 02359 **781-293-7211** Fax: 781-293-4650. 8:30AM-4:30PM.

Pepperell Town Clerk 1 Main St, Town Hall, Pepperell, MA 01463-1644 **978-433-0339** Fax: 978-433-0338. 8AM-4:30PM. www.town.pepperell.ma.us

Peru Town Clerk PO Box 564, Peru, MA 01235 (4 North Rd). **413-655-8326** Fax: 413-655-8312. 6-8PM Mondays.

Petersham Town Clerk PO Box 486, Petersham, MA 01366 (3 S. Main St.). **978-724-6649** Fax: 978-724-3501. 6-8PM Mon.

Phillipston Town Clerk 50 The Common, Phillipston, MA 01331 **978-249-1733** Fax: 978-249-3356. 12-2PM, 6-8PM M; 5-7PM W; 8:30AM-10AM SAT.

Pittsfield City Clerk 70 Allen St, City Hall Rm 103, Pittsfield, MA 01201 **413-499-9361** Fax: 413-499-9363. 8:30AM-4PM. www.pittsfield-ma.org

Plainfield Town Clerk 12 Broom St, Plainfield, MA 01070 **413-634-5582** 10AM-Noon Sat.

Plainville Town Clerk PO Box 1717, Plainville, MA 02762 (142 South St). **508-695-3142 x20** Fax: 508-695-1857. 8-4PM.

Plymouth County Registry of Deeds PO Box 3535, Plymouth, MA 02361 (7 Russell St). **508-830-9200** Fax: 508-830-9280. 8:15AM-4:30PM (Recording 8:30AM-4PM). www.regdeeds.co.plymouth.ma.us Real Estate, Lien, Judgment records online.

Plymouth Town Clerk 11 Lincoln St, Plymouth, MA 02360-3386 **508-830-4050** Fax: 508-830-4062. 8AM-4:30PM. www.townofplymouth.org

Plympton Town Clerk PO Box 153, Plympton, MA 02367-0153 (5 Palmer Rd. Rte 58). **781-585-3220** Fax: 781-582-1505. 9AM-2PM, 7-9PM M; 9AM-2PM T-Th.. http://town.plympton.ma.us

Princeton Town Clerk 6 Town Hall Drive, Princeton, MA 01541-1137 **978-464-2103** Fax: 978-464-2106. 8:30AM-3:30PM. http://town.princeton.ma.us

Provincetown Town Clerk 260 Commercial St, Provincetown, MA 02657 **508-487-7013** Fax: 508-487-9560. 8AM-5PM. Assessor, Property Sale records online. www.provincetowngov.org

Quincy City Clerk 1305 Hancock St, City Hall, Quincy, MA 02169 **617-376-1136** Fax: 617-376-1139 8:30AM-4:30 PM www.ci.quincy.ma.us

Randolph Town Clerk 41 S. Main St., Randolph, MA 02368 **781-961-0900** Fax: 781-961-0919. 8:30AM-4:30PM.

Raynham Town Clerk 53 Orchard St, Raynham, MA 02767-1320 **508-824-2700**

Fax: 508-823-1812. 8:30-4:30PM M-Th; 8:30AM-N F. www.town.raynham.ma.us

Reading Town Clerk 16 Lowell St, Reading, MA 01867 **781-942-9050** Fax: 781-942-9070. 8:30AM-5PM. www.ci.reading.ma.us Assessor records online.

Rehoboth Town Clerk 148 Peck St, Rehoboth, MA 02769-3099 **508-252-6502** Fax: 508-252-5342. 9AM-4PM.

Revere City Clerk 281 Broadway, City Hall, Revere, MA 02151-5087 **781-286-8160** Fax: 781-286-8135. 8:15AM-4PM M-Th; 8:15AM-N F. Assessor records online.

Richmond Town Clerk PO Box 81, Richmond, MA 01254 (1529 State Rd). **413-698-3315** Fax: 413-698-3272. 9AM-Noon T,Th-Sat.

Rochester Town Clerk 1 Constitution Way, Town Hall, Rochester, MA 02770 **508-763-3871** Fax: 508-763-4892. 7-9PM M.

Rockland Town Clerk 242 Union St, Rockland, MA 02370 **781-871-1892** 8:30AM-4:30PM.

Rockport Town Clerk PO Box 429, Rockport, MA 01966 (34 Broadway). **978-546-6894** Fax: 978-546-3562. 8AM-4PM. www.town.rockport.ma.us

Rowe Town Clerk Town Hall, Rowe, MA 01367 **413-339-5520** Fax: 413-339-5316. 8-11AM W.

Rowley Town Clerk PO Box 351, Rowley, MA 01969-0351 (139 Main St, 1A Rt.). **978-948-2081** Fax: 978-948-2162. By appointment. Property Assessor online.

Royalston Town Clerk 94 Athol Rd, Royalston, MA 01368-0118 **978-249-0493** Fax: 978-575-0493. 9:30AM-2:30PM Tuesdays. Assessor, Property records online.

Russell Town Clerk 65 Main St, Town Hall, Russell, MA 01071 **413-862-3265** Fax: 413-862-3103. 4:30-6:30PM T; 4-6PM F. Real Estate, Recording, Lien records online.

Rutland Town Clerk 250 Main St, Rutland, MA 01543 **508-886-4104** Fax: 508-886-2929. 7:30AM-4PM M,W,Th; 7:30AM-7PM T. Assessor, Property records online.

Salem City Clerk 93 Washington, City Hall, Salem, MA 01970-3593 **978-745-9595** Fax: 978-740-9209. 8AM-4PM M-W; 8AM-7PM Th; 8AM-N F.

Salisbury Town Clerk 5 Beach Rd, Salisbury, MA 01952 **978-462-7591** Fax: 978-462-4176. 8:30AM-4PM, 7-9PM M; 8:30AM-4PM T-Th; 8:30AM-1PM F.

Sandisfield Town Clerk PO Box 163, Sandisfield, MA 01255 (3 Silverbrook Rd.). **413-258-4711** Fax: 413-258-4225. 10AM-2PM, 6-8PM M; 10-2PM Th or by Appt.

Sandwich Town Clerk 145 Main St, Sandwich, MA 02563 **508-888-0340** Fax: 508-888-2497. 8:30AM-4:30PM. www.sandwichmass.org

Saugus Town Clerk 298 Central St, Town Hall, Saugus, MA 01906 **781-231-4101** Fax: 781-231-4109. 8:30AM-7PM M; 8:30AM-5PM T,W,Th; 8:30AM-12:30PM F;. www.saugus.net

Savoy Town Clerk 720 Main Rd., Town Office, Savoy, MA 01256 **413-743-3759** Fax: 413-743-4292. 1-5PM Tu, Th; 7-9PM Tu by appointment only.

Scituate Town Clerk 600 C. J. Cushing Way, Town Hall, Scituate, MA 02066 **781-545-8744** Fax: 781-545-8704. 8:30AM-4:45PM M,W,Th; 8:30-7:30 Tu, 8:30-11:45AM F. www.town.scituate.ma.us

Seekonk Town Clerk 100 Peck St, Seekonk, MA 02771 **508-336-2920** Fax: 508-336-0764. 9AM-4:30PM. www.ci.seekonk.ma.us

Sharon Town Clerk 90 S. Main St, Town Hall, Sharon, MA 02067 **781-784-1505** Fax: 781-784-1503. 8:30AM-5PM M-W; 8:30AM-8PM Th; 8:30AM-12:30PM F.

Sheffield Town Clerk PO Box 175, Sheffield, MA 01257 (21 Depot Sq). **413-229-8752** Fax: 413-229-7010. 9AM-4PM.

Shelburne Town Clerk 51 Bridge St, Town Hall, Shelburne, MA 01370 **413-625-0301** Fax: 413-625-0312. 9-5PM T; 5-8PM Th.

Sherborn Town Clerk 19 Washington St, Sherborn, MA 01770 **508-651-7853** Fax: 508-651-7854. 9AM-1PM M-Th & Tues eves 6-8PM. www.sherbornma.org

Shirley Town Clerk PO Box 782, Shirley, MA 01464 (7 Keady Way). **978-425-2610** Fax:978-425-2602 8-3PM (6-9PM M Eve).

Shrewsbury Town Clerk 100 Maple Ave, Town Hall, Shrewsbury, MA 01545 **508-841-8507** Fax: 508-842-0587. 8AM-4:30PM.

Shutesbury Town Clerk PO Box 264, Shutesbury, MA 01072-0264 (1 Cooleyville Rd.). **413-259-1204** Fax: 413-259-1107. 9AM-1PM M-Th. www.shutesbury.org

Somerset Town Clerk 140 Wood St, Somerset, MA 02726 **508-646-2818** Fax: 508-646-2802. 8:30AM-4PM. Property, Assessor records online.

Somerville City Clerk 93 Highland Ave, Somerville, MA 02143 **617-625-6600 x4100** Fax: 617-625-4239. 8:30-4:30PM M-W;

8:30-7:30PM Th; 8:30-12:30PM F. www.ci.somerville.ma.us Assessor online.

South Hadley Town Clerk 116 Main St, South Hadley, MA 01075-2833 **413-538-5023** Fax: 413-538-7565. 8:30AM-4:30PM.

Southampton Town Clerk PO Box 276, Southampton, MA 01073 (8 East St.). **413-527-8392** Fax: 413-529-1006. 8:30AM-4PM M-Th. Assessor records online.

Southborough Town Clerk 17 Common St, Town Hall, Southborough, MA 01772-9109 **508-485-0710** Fax: 508-480-0161. 9AM-5PM.

Southbridge Town Clerk 41 Elm St, Southbridge, MA 01550 **508-764-5408** Fax: 508-764-5425. 8AM-4PM M-W; 8AM-8PM Th; 8AM-Noon Fri. www.ci.southbridge.ma.us

Southwick Town Clerk 454 College Hwy, Southwick, MA 01077 **413-569-5504** Fax: 413-569-0667. 8:30AM-4:30PM. www.southwickma.org Assessor, Real Estate, Recording, Lien records online.

Spencer Town Clerk 157 Main St, Town Hall, Spencer, MA 01562-2197 **508-885-7500** Fax: 508-885-7528. 8AM-4PM, 6-8PM M; 8AM-4PM TTh; 8AM-N, 1PM-4PM W.

Springfield City Clerk 36 Court St, Springfield, MA 01103 **413-787-6094** 9AM-4PM (Th open until 6PM). Real Estate, Recording, Lien records online.

Sterling Town Clerk 1 Park St, Mary Ellen Butterick Muni. Bldg, Sterling, MA 01564 **978-422-8111** Fax: 978-422-0289. 8-4:30.

Stockbridge Town Clerk PO Box 417, Stockbridge, MA 01262-0417 (6 Main St.). **413-298-4568** Fax: 413-298-4485. 9AM-N M, Tu, Th, F; 1-4PM W. www.townofstockbridge.com

Stoneham Town Clerk 35 Central St, Stoneham, MA 02180 (35 Central St). **781-279-2650** Fax: 781-279-2653. 8AM-4PM M,W-Th; 8AM-7PM T; 8AM-N F.

Stoughton Town Clerk 10 Pearl St, Town Hall, Stoughton, MA 02072 (10 Pearl St). **781-341-1300** Fax: 781-341-1032. 8:30AM-4:30PM M-W; 8:30AM-7PM Th; 8:30AM-1PM F. www.stoughton.org

Stow Town Clerk 380 Great Rd, Town Bldg., Stow, MA 01775 **978-897-4514** Fax: 978-897-4534. 8AM-7PM M; 8AM-12:30PM T; 8AM-4PM W-F.

Sturbridge Town Clerk 308 Main, Sturbridge, MA 01566 **508-347-2510** Fax: 508-347-5886. www.town.sturbridge.ma.us

8AM-N, 1-4PM, 6-8PM M; 8AM-N, 1-4PM T-F. Real Estate, Deed records online.

Sudbury Town Clerk 322 Concord Rd, Sudbury, MA 01776-1800 **978-443-8891 x351** Fax: 978-443-0264. 9AM-5PM. www.town.sudbury.ma.us/services Assessor, Property records online.

Suffolk County Register of Deeds PO Box 9660, Boston, MA 02114-9660 (24 New Chardon St.). **617-788-8575** Fax: 617-720-4163. 8AM-4:30PM. www.suffolkdeeds.com Real Estate, Lien, Deed, Property Assessor records online.

Sunderland Town Clerk 12 School St., Sunderland, MA 01375-9503 **413-665-1442** Fax: 413-665-1446. 9AM-3PM M-Th.

Sutton Town Clerk 4 Uxbridge Rd., Town Hall, Sutton, MA 01590 **508-865-8725** Fax: 508-865-8721. 9AM-4PM M,T,W,Th; 7-9PM T; 9AM-N F.

Swampscott Town Clerk 22 Monument Ave, Town Hall, Swampscott, MA 01907 **(781-596-8856** Fax: 781-596-8870. 8:30AM-4:30PM M-Th; 8AM-12:30PM F. www.town.swampscott.ma.us Assessor, Real Estate records online.

Swansea Town Clerk 81 Main St, Town Hall, Swansea, MA 02777 **508-678-9389** 9AM-4PM M,T,Th,F; 9AM-5PM W. Property, Assessor records online.

Taunton City Clerk 15 Summer St, City Hall, Taunton, MA 02780 **508-821-1024** Fax: 508-821-1098. www.ci.taunton.ma.us Assessor records online. 9AM-5PM.

Templeton Town Clerk 9 Main St., Town Office Bldg., Baldwinville, MA 01436 **978-939-8466** Fax: 978-939-8327. 8AM-7 PM M; 8AM-4PM T,TH; 8AM-1PM Fri (Closed Wed). Assessor records online.

Tewksbury Town Clerk 1009 Main St, Town Hall, Tewksbury, MA 01876-2796 **978-640-4355** Fax: 978-640-4302. 8:30AM-4:30PM. www.tewksbury.info

Tisbury Town Clerk PO Box 606, Tisbury, MA 02568-0606 (51 Spring St). **508-696-4215** Fax: 508-693-5876. 8:30AM-4:30PM. www.ci.tisbury.ma.us Assessor records online.

Tolland Town Clerk 241 W. Granville Rd, Tolland, MA 01034 **413-259-4794** Fax: 413-258-4048. 2-7PM Mondays. Real Estate, Recording, Lien records online.

Topsfield Town Clerk 8 W. Common St, Town Hall, Topsfield, MA 01983 **978-887-1505** Fax: 978-887-1502. 8:30AM-4PM M-Th (Summer Hours: 8AM-N).

Town of Aquinnah Town Clerk 65 State Rd, Aquinnah, MA 02535 **508-645-2306** Fax: 508-645-2310. By Appointment.

Townsend Town Clerk 272 Main St, Memorial Hall, Townsend, MA 01469 **978-597-1704** Fax: 978-597-8135. 9AM-4PM; 9AM-8PM Tu; 9AM-N 1st & 3rd Sat..

Truro Town Clerk PO Box 2012, Truro, MA 02666-2012 (24 Town Hall Rd.). **508-349-7004 ext 14** Fax: 508-349-7720. 8AM-4PM.

Tyngsborough Town Clerk 25 Bryants Lane, Tyngsborough, MA 01879 **978-649-2300 x129** Fax: 978-649-2301. 8AM-7PM M; 8AM-4PM Tu-Th; 8AM-12:30PM F. www.tyngsboroughmass.com Assessor, Property records online.

Tyringham Town Clerk Main Rd, Tyringham, MA 01264 **413-243-1749** Fax: 413-243-4942. 9AM-1PM or by app't. www.tyngsboroughmass.com/clerk.htm

Upton Town Clerk Box 969, Upton, MA 01568 (1 Main St). **508-529-3565** Fax: 508-529-1010. MW9-3; TTh9-1 & 6-8; F9 -1. www.upton.ma.us

Uxbridge Town Clerk 21 S. Main St, Uxbridge, MA 01569 **508-278-3156** Fax: 508-278-3154. 9AM-4PM.

Wakefield Town Clerk 1 Lafayette St, Town Hall, Wakefield, MA 01880-2383 **781-246-6383** Fax: 781-246-4155. 8:30AM-5PM.

Wales Town Clerk PO Box 834, Wales, MA 01081-0834 (3 Hollow Rd.). **413-245-7571** Fax: 413-245-3261. 9AM-3PM Mon/Tues. Real Estate, Recording, Lien records online.

Walpole Town Clerk 135 School St, Town Hall, Walpole, MA 02081-2898 **508-660-7297** Fax: 508-660-7303. 8AM-4PM; M-F; 7-9PM T. www.walpole.ma.us Property Assessor records online.

Waltham City Clerk 610 Main St, 2nd Fl, Waltham, MA 02452 **781-314-3120** Fax: 781-314-3130. www.city.waltham.ma.us Assessor, Property records online. 8:30AM-4:30PM.

Ware Town Clerk 126 Main St, Ware, MA 01082 **413-967-4471** Fax: 413-967-9600. 8:30AM-4:30PM.

Wareham Town Clerk 54 Marion Rd, Wareham, MA 02571 **508-291-3140** Fax: 508-291-3116. 8:30AM-4:30PM. Assessor records online.

Warren Town Clerk PO Box 603, Warren, MA 01083-0603 (48 High St.). **413-436-5702** Fax: 413-436-9754. 9AM-3:30PM M-W,F; 5-8PM Th.

Warwick Town Clerk 12 Athol Rd, Town Hall, Warwick, MA 01378 **978-544-8304** Fax: 978-544-6499. 8AM-2PM, M.

Washington Town Clerk 8 Summit Hill Rd., GA094, Washington, MA 01223 **413-623-8878** Fax: 413-623-2116. 7PM-9PM M or by appointment.

Watertown Town Clerk 149 Main St, Admin. Bldg., Watertown, MA 02472 **617-972-6486** Fax: 617-972-6595. 8:30AM-5PM. www.ci.watertown.ma.us Assessor records online.

Wayland Town Clerk 41 Cochituate Rd, Wayland, MA 01778-2697 **508-358-3630 or 3631** Fax: 508-358-3627. 8:30AM-4:30PM. www.wayland.ma.us Assessor records online.

Webster Town Clerk 350 Main St, Webster, MA 01570 **508-949-3850** Fax: 508-949-3888. 8AM-4PM, Closed F.

Wellesley Town Clerk 525 Washington St, Wellesley, MA 02482 **781-431-1019 x250** Fax: 781-239-1043. 8AM-5PM. www.ci.wellesley.ma.us/town/index.html Assessor, Town By-Law, Zoning By-Law, Election results records online.

Wellfleet Town Clerk 300 Main St, Wellfleet, MA 02667 **508-349-0301** Fax: 508-349-0317. 8AM-4PM.

Wendell Town Clerk 270 Wendell Depot Rd., Wendell Depot, MA 01380 **978-544-6682** By Appt..

Wenham Town Clerk 138 Main St., Town Hall, Wenham, MA 01984 **978-468-5520** Fax: 978-468-6164. 9AM-4:30PM M,W,Th; 9AM-7PM T; 9AM-1PM F.

West Boylston Town Clerk 120 Prescott St, West Boylston, MA 01583 **508-835-6240** Fax: 508-835-4102. 9-3:30PM M,T,Th,F; 5-9PM W. www.westboylston.com

West Bridgewater Town Clerk 65 N. Main St, Town Hall, West Bridgewater, MA 02379-1734 **508-894-1200** Fax: 508-894-1210. 8AM-4PM; 1st & 3rd W 7PM-9PM. www.town.west-bridgewater.ma.us

West Brookfield Town Clerk PO Box 766, West Brookfield, MA 01585 (2 E. Main). **508-867-1415** Fax: 508-867-1401. 9AM-N.

West Newbury Town Clerk 381 Main St., Town Office Bldg, West Newbury, MA 01985-1499 **978-363-1100 x15** Fax: 978-363-1117. 8AM-4:30PM M-Th; 8AM-N F. www.town.west-newbury.ma.us

West Springfield Town Clerk 26 Central St, Town Hall, West Springfield, MA 01089-2779 **413-263-3012** Fax: 413-263-3046. 8AM-4:30PM. www.west-springfield.ma.us

Assessor, Real Estate, Recording, Lien records online.

West Stockbridge Town Clerk PO Box 163, West Stockbridge, MA 01266 (9 Main St). **413-232-0300** Fax: 413-232-0318. 1-6PM Mon; 10AM-3PM Tu TH. www.weststockbridgetown.com

West Tisbury Town Clerk Box 278, West Tisbury, MA 02575-0278 (Town Hall). **508-696-0148** Fax: 508-696-0103. 8:30AM-1:30PM. Assessor records online.

Westborough Town Clerk 34 W. Main St, Town Hall, Westborough, MA 01581-1998 **508-366-3020** Fax: 508-366-3099. 8AM-5PM M W TH; 8AM-8PM T; 7:30-N Fri.

Westfield City Clerk 59 Court St, Westfield, MA 01085-3574 **413-572-6235** Fax: 413-564-3114. 9AM-5PM. www.cityofwestfield.org Real Estate, Recording, Lien, Assessor records online.

Westford Town Clerk 55 Main St, Town Hall, Westford, MA 01886 **978-692-5515** Fax: 978-399-2555. 8-4. www.westford.com

Westhampton Town Clerk Town Hall, Westhampton, MA 01027 **413-527-0463** Fax: 413-527-8655. 7PM-8:30PM M.

Westminster Town Clerk PO Box 456, Westminster, MA 01473 (3 Bacon St.). **978-874-7406** Fax: 978-874-7411. 8AM-1PM, 2-4:30PM M-Th; 8AM-1PM F. www.westminster-ma.org

Weston Town Clerk PO Box 378, Weston, MA 02493 (Town House Rd). **781-893-7320** Fax: 781-891-3697. 8:30AM-5PM. www.weston.org

Westport Town Clerk 816 Main Rd., Town Hall, Westport, MA 02790 **508-636-1000** Fax: 508-636-1147. 8:30-N, 12:30-4PM.

Westwood Town Clerk 580 High St, Westwood, MA 02090 **781-326-3964** Fax:

781-329-8030. 8:30AM-4:30PM M,W,Th; 8:30AM-7PM T; 8:30AM-1PM F.

Weymouth Town Clerk 75 Middle St, Town Hall, East Weymouth, MA 02189 **781-335-2000** Fax: 781-335-3283. 8:30AM-4:30PM.

Whately Town Clerk 218 Chestnut Plain Rd., Whately, MA 01093-0002 **413-665-0054** Fax: 413-665-9560. Noon-7PM M; 9AM-1PM Th.

Whitman Town Clerk PO Box 426, Whitman, MA 02382 (54 South Ave). **781-618-9710** Fax: 781-618-9791. 8AM-4PM M,W,Th-F; 8AM-7:30PM T.

Wilbraham Town Clerk 240 Springfield St, Wilbraham, MA 01095 **413-596-2809** Fax: 413-596-2830. 8:30AM-4:30PM. Real Estate, Recording, Lien records online.

Williamsburg Town Clerk PO Box 447, Haydenville, MA 01039-0447 (141 Main St.). **413-268-8402** Fax: 413-268-8409. 11-3 M, 9:15-3 & 6:30-8 Tu, 11-1 W, 9:15-3 Th. www.burgy.org

Williamstown Town Clerk 31 North St, Williamstown, MA 01267 **413-458-9341** Fax: 413-458-4839. 8:30AM-5PM. www.williamstown.net

Wilmington Town Clerk 121 Glen Rd, Town Hall, Wilmington, MA 01887 **978-658-2030** Fax: 978-658-3334. 8:30AM-4:30PM. www.town.wilmington.ma.us

Winchendon Town Clerk 109 Front St, Winchendon, MA 01475 **978-297-2766** Fax: 978-297-1616. 8:30AM-6PM M; 8:30AM-4:30PM T-Th; 8:30AM-N F.

Winchester Town Clerk 71 Mount Vernon St, Town Hall, Winchester, MA 01890 **781-721-7130** Fax: 781-721-1153. 8AM-4PM.

Windsor Town Clerk 3 Hinsdale Rd., Windsor, MA 01270 **413-684-3977** Fax: 413-684-1585. 5-7PM Monday or by app't..

Winthrop Town Clerk Town Hall, Winthrop, MA 02152-3156 **617-846-1742** Fax: 617-539-5814. 8AM-7PM M; 8AM-4PM T-Th; 8AM-N F.

Woburn City Clerk 10 Common St, Woburn, MA 01801-4197 **781-932-4453** Fax: 781-932-4455. 9-4:30PM M-W; 9-7PM Th; 9AM-1PM F. www.cityofwoburn.com Property Assessor records online.

Worcester City Clerk 455 Main St, City Hall, Rm 206, Worcester, MA 01608 **508-799-1121** Fax: 508-799-1194. 8:45AM-4:15PM T,W,Th,F; 8:45AM-5PM M. Real Estate, Lien, Assessor records online.

Worcester County - Northern District Register of Deeds PO Box 983, Fitchburg, MA 01420 (84 Elm St.). **978-342-2132** Fax: 978-345-2865. 8:30AM-4:30PM; www.state.ma.us/nwrod Real Estate, Lien records online.

Worcester District Register of Deeds 2 Main St, Courthouse, Worcester, MA 01608 **508-798-7717** Fax: 508-753-1338. 8:15AM-4:30PM (Recording Hours: 9AM-N, 1-4PM). www.worcesterdeeds.com Real Estate, Deed, Lien, Grantor/Grantee, Judgment, Property Tax records online.

Worthington Town Clerk Town Hall, Worthington, MA 01098-0247 **413-238-5578** Fax: 413-238-5579. 10AM-N Saturday.

Wrentham Town Clerk 100 Stonewall Blvd, Wrentham, MA 02093 **508-384-5415** Fax: 508-384-5434. 8AM-4PM M-Th; 8AM-1:30PM F.

Yarmouth Town Clerk 1146 Route 28, Town Hall, South Yarmouth, MA 02664 **508-398-2231** Fax: 508-398-2365. 8:30AM-4:30PM. Assessor records online.

Michigan

Organization: 83 counties, 83 recording offices. The recording officer is the County Register of Deeds. 79 counties are in the Eastern Time Zone (EST). 4 counties that border Wisconsin (Gogebic, Iron, Dickinson, Menominee) are in the Central Time Zone (CST).

Real Estate Records: Some counties will perform real estate searches. Copies usually cost $1.00 per page. and certification fees vary. Ownership records are located at the Equalization Office, designated "Assessor" in this section. Tax records are located at the Treasurer's Office.

UCC Records: Financing statements are filed at the state level, except for real estate related collateral, which are filed with the County Register. However, prior to 07/2001, consumer goods and farm collateral were also filed at the County Register and these older records can be searched there. All counties will perform UCC searches. Use search request form UCC-11. Search fees are usually $3.00 per debtor name if federal tax identification number or Social Security Number are given, or $6.00 without the number. Copies usually cost $1.00 per page.

Tax Lien Records: Federal and state tax liens on personal property of businesses are filed with the Secretary of State. Other federal and state tax liens are filed with the Register of Deeds. Most counties search each tax lien index separately. Some charge one fee to search both, while others charge a separate fee for each one. When combining a UCC and tax lien search, total fee is usually $9.00 for all three searches. Some counties require tax identification number as well as name to do a search. Copy fees are usually $1.00 per page. Other Liens: Construction, lis pendens.

Online Access: There is no statewide online access, but a number of counties, including Wayne, offer free access to assessor and register of deeds records.

Alcona Register of Deeds PO Box 269, Harrisville, MI 48740-0269 (5th St Courthouse). **989-724-6802** Fax: 989-724-5684. 8:30AM-4:30PM.

Alger Register of Deeds PO Box 538, Munising, MI 49862 (101 Court St). **906-387-2076** Fax: 906-387-2156. 8AM-4PM.

Allegan Register of Deeds 113 Chestnut St, County Court House, Allegan, MI 49010-1360 **269-673-0390** Fax: 269-673-0289. 8AM-5PM. www.allegancounty.org/ Real Estate records online.

Alpena Register of Deeds 720 W. Chisholm St, Courthouse, Alpena, MI 49707-2487 **989-354-9547** Fax: 989-354-9646. 8:30-4:30PM.

Antrim Register of Deeds PO Box 376, Bellaire, MI 49615 (203 E. Cayuga St). **231-533-6683** Fax: 231-533-8317. 8:30AM-5PM. www.antrimcounty.org Most Wanted records online.

Arenac Register of Deeds PO Box 296, Standish, MI 48658 (120 Grove St). **989-846-9201** 8:30AM-5PM.

Baraga Register of Deeds 16 N. 3rd St., Courthouse, L'Anse, MI 49946-1085 **906-524-6183** Fax: 906-524-6186. 8:30AM-N, 1-4:30PM.

Barry Register of Deeds PO Box 7, Hastings, MI 49058-0007 (220 W State St). **269-948-4824** Fax: 269-948-4820. 8AM-5PM. www.barrycounty.org Property, Assessor, Delinquent Tax records online.

Bay Register of Deeds 515 Center Ave, Bay City, MI 48708-5994 **989-895-4228** Fax: 989-895-4296. 8AM-5PM (June-September 7:30AM-4PM). www.co.bay.mi.us/ Property Tax records online.

Benzie Register of Deeds PO Box 377, Beulah, MI 49617 (448 Court Pl). **231-882-0016** Fax: 231-882-0167. 8AM-N, 1-5PM.

Berrien Register of Deeds 701 Main St., Berrien County Admin. Ctr, St. Joseph, MI 49085 **616-983-7111 x8562** Fax: 616-982-8659. 8:30-5PM. www.berriencounty.org/

Branch Register of Deeds 570 Marshall Rd, #C, Coldwater, MI 49036 **517-279-4320** 9AM-N, 1-5PM. www.co.branch.mi.us/ Vital Statistic, Business Name, DBA records online.

Calhoun Register of Deeds 315 W. Green St, Marshall, MI 49068 **269-781-0718** Fax: 269-781-0721. 8-5PM. http://co.calhoun.mi.us

Cass Register of Deeds PO Box 355, Cassopolis, MI 49031-0355 (120 N. Broadway, #123). **269-445-4464** Fax: 269-445-4406. 8-5PM. www.casscountymi.org

Charlevoix Register of Deeds 301 State St, County Bldg., Charlevoix, MI 49720 **231-547-7204** Fax: 231-547-7246. 9AM-5PM. Birth, Marriage, Obituary, Cemetery, Birth records online.

Cheboygan Register of Deeds PO Box 70, Cheboygan, MI 49721 (870 S. Main St). **231-627-8866** Fax: 231-627-8453. 8:30-5.

Chippewa Register of Deeds 319 Court St, Courthouse, Sault Ste. Marie, MI 49783 **906-635-6312** Fax: 906-635-6855. 8AM-5PM. www.sault.com/~chippewa

Clare Register of Deeds PO Box 586, Harrison, MI 48625 (225 W. Main St.). **989-539-7131** Fax: 989-539-6616. 8-4:30PM. www.claremi.com/local_contacts.html

Clinton Register of Deeds PO Box 435, St. Johns, MI 48879-0435 (100 E State St, #2500). **989-224-5270** Fax: 989-227-6473. 8AM-5PM. www.clinton-county.org/

Crawford Register of Deeds 200 W. Michigan, Grayling, MI 49738 **989-348-2841** Fax: 989-344-3223. 8:30AM-4:30PM. www.crawfordco.us/deeds/deeds.htm Most Wanted records online.

Delta Register of Deeds 310 Ludington St, #104, Escanaba, MI 49829-4039 **906-789-5116** Fax: 906-789-5196. 8AM-4PM.

Dickinson Register of Deeds PO Box 609, Iron Mountain, MI 49801 (705 S. Stephenson Ave). **906-774-0955** Fax: 906-774-4660. 8AM-4:30PM.

Eaton Register of Deeds 1045 Independence Blvd., Rm 104, Charlotte, MI 48813-1095 **517-543-7500 x232** Fax: 517-543-7377. 8-5PM. www.co.eaton.mi.us/cntsrv/online.htm Assessor, Tax, Recorder, Marriage, Divorce records online.

Emmet Register of Deeds 200 Division, Petoskey, MI 49770 **231-348-1761** Fax: 231-348-0633. 8:30AM-5PM.

Genesee Register of Deeds 1101 Beach St, Admin. Bldg., Flint, MI 48502 **810-257-3060** Fax: 810-768-7965. www.co.genesee.mi.us Recording, Property, Deed, Marriage, Death records online. 8AM-5PM.

Gladwin Register of Deeds 401 W. Cedar Ave, #7, Gladwin, MI 48624-2093 **989-426-7551** Fax: 989-426-6902. 8:30AM-4:30PM.

Gogebic Register of Deeds 200 N. Moore St., Courthouse, Bessemer, MI 49911 **906-667-0381** Fax: 906-663-4660. 8:30AM-4:30PM.

Grand Traverse Register of Deeds 400 Boardman Ave, Traverse City, MI 49684-2577 **231-922-4750** Fax: 231-922-2770. 8AM-5PM (Vault closes at 4:30PM). Marriage, Death records online.

Gratiot Register of Deeds PO Box 5, Ithaca, MI 48847 (214 E. Center St). **989-875-5217** 8AM-N-1PM-4:30PM.

Hillsdale Register of Deeds 29 N Howell, Rm 3, Courthouse, Hillsdale, MI 49242 **517-437-2231** Fax: 517-437-3139. 8:30AM-5PM. www.co.hillsdale.mi.us

Houghton Register of Deeds 401 E. Houghton Ave, Houghton, MI 49931 **906-482-1311** Fax: 906-483-0364. 8-4:30PM.

Huron Register of Deeds 250 E Huron Ave, Bad Axe, MI 48413 **989-269-9941** Fax: 989-269-8786. 8:30AM-5PM.

Ingham Register of Deeds PO Box 195, Mason, MI 48854-0195 (341 S. Jefferson). **517-676-7216** Fax: 517-676-7287. 8-5PM. www.ingham.org/rd/rodindex.htm Assumed Business Name, Recording, Deed, Grantor/Grantee, Assessor, Property, Delinquent Tax, Marriage Applicant records online.

Ionia Register of Deeds PO Box 35, Ionia, MI 48846 (100 Main St). **616-527-5320** Fax: 616-527-5380. 8:30AM-N, 1-5PM. www.ioniacounty.org

Iosco Register of Deeds PO Box 367, Tawas City, MI 48764 (422 W. Lake St). **989-362-2021** Fax: 989-984-1101. 9AM-5PM. www.iosco.net

Iron Register of Deeds 2 S. Sixth St, #11, Courthouse Annex, #11, Crystal Falls, MI 49920-1413 **906-875-3321** Fax: 906-875-0658. 8AM-N, 12:30-4PM.

Isabella Register of Deeds 200 N. Main St, Mt. Pleasant, MI 48858 **989-772-0911 x253** Fax: 989-953-7219. 8AM-4:30PM. www.isabellacounty.org

Jackson Register of Deeds 120 W. Michigan Ave, 11th Fl, Jackson, MI 49201 **517-788-4350** Fax: 517-788-4686. 8AM-5PM. www.co.jackson.mi.us/rod/ Real Estate, Lien, Deed, Grantor/Grantee, Foreclosed Property Sale records online.

Kalamazoo Register of Deeds 201 W. Kalamazoo Ave, #102, Kalamazoo, MI 49007 **269-383-8970** 8AM-4:30PM.

Kalkaska Register of Deeds 605 N. Birch St, Kalkaska, MI 49646 **231-258-3315** Fax: 231-258-3345. 9AM-5PM.

Kent Register of Deeds 300 Monroe Ave NW, Grand Rapids, MI 49503-2286 **616-336-3558** Fax: 616-336-8938. 8AM-5PM. www.co.kent.mi.us/YourGovernment/Registe rofDeeds/deeds_index.htm Recording, Deed, Lien, Assessor, Property, Accident Report, Vital Statistic, Treasurer records online.

Keweenaw Register of Deeds HC 1 Box 607, Eagle River, MI 49950-9744 (5095 4th St). **906-337-2229** Fax: 906-337-2795. 9AM-4PM.

Lake Register of Deeds 800 Tenth St. #200, Baldwin, MI 49304 **231-745-4641** Fax: 231-745-2241. 8:30AM-N, 1-5PM. www.michigan.gov

Lapeer Register of Deeds 279 N. Court St, Lapeer, MI 48446 **810-667-0211** Fax: 810-667-0293. www.county.lapeer.org/deeds

Leelanau Register of Deeds PO Box 595, Leland, MI 49654 (301 E. Cedar). **231-256-9682** Fax: 231-256-8149. 9AM-5PM. www.leelanaucounty.com

Lenawee Register of Deeds 301 N. Main St., Adrian, MI 49221 **517-264-4538** Fax: 517-264-4543. 8AM-4:30PM.

Livingston Register of Deeds PO Box 197, Howell, MI 48844 (200 E Grand River). **517-546-0270** Fax: 517-546-5966. 8AM-5PM. Real Estate, Lien, Tax Assessor, Death records online.

Luce Register of Deeds County Gov't Bldg., Newberry, MI 49868 **906-293-5521** Fax: 906-293-0050. 8AM-4PM.

Mackinac Register of Deeds 100 Marley St, Saint Ignace, MI 49781 **906-643-7306** Fax: 906-643-7302. 8:30AM-4:30PM.

Macomb Register of Deeds 10 N. Main, Mt. Clemens, MI 48043 **586-469-5342** Fax: 586-469-5130. www.co.macomb.mi.us Recorder, Deed, Business Registration, Death,

Campaign Committee/Candidate, Most Wanted, Sex Offender records online.

Manistee Register of Deeds 415 Third St, Courthouse, Manistee, MI 49660-1606 **231-723-2146** Fax: 231-398-3544. 8:30-N, 1-5.

Marquette Register of Deeds 234 W. Baraga Ave, C-105, Marquette, MI 49855 **906-225-8415** Fax: 906-225-8420. 8AM-5PM. www.co.marquette.mi.us Warrant List records online.

Mason Register of Deeds PO Box 57, Ludington, MI 49431-0057 (300 E. Ludington Ave). **231-843-4466** Fax: 231-845-7977. 9AM-5PM.

Mecosta Register of Deeds PO Box 718, Big Rapids, MI 49307 (400 Elm St). **231-592-0148** 8:30AM-5PM. Assessor, Property records online.

Menominee Register of Deeds 839 10th Ave, Courthouse, Menominee, MI 49858 **906-863-2822** Fax: 906-863-8839. 8AM-4:30PM. www.menomineecounty.com Land, Deed, Recording records online.

Midland Register of Deeds 220 W. Ellsworth St, County Services Bldg., Midland, MI 48640-5194 **989-832-6820** Fax: 989-832-6608. 8AM-5PM.

Missaukee Register of Deeds PO Box 800, Lake City, MI 49651 (111 S. Canal St.). **231-839-4967** Fax: 231-839-3684. 9AM-5PM. www.missaukee.org

Monroe Register of Deeds 51 S Macomb St, Monroe, MI 48161 **734-240-7390** 8:30-5PM.

Montcalm Register of Deeds PO Box 188, Stanton, MI 48888 (211 W. Main St). **989-831-7337** Fax: 989-831-7320. 8AM-N, 1-5PM. Real Estate, Lien records online.

Montmorency Register of Deeds PO Box 789, Atlanta, MI 49709 (12265 M-32). **989-785-8079** Fax: 989-785-8080. 8:30AM-N, 1-4:30PM.

Muskegon Register of Deeds 990 Terrace St., 2nd Fl, Muskegon, MI 49442 **231-724-6271** Fax: 231-724-6842. 8AM-5PM; www.co.muskegon.mi.us/deeds/ Death records online.

Newaygo Register of Deeds PO Box 885, White Cloud, MI 49349 (1087 Newell St) **231-689-7246** Fax: 231-689-7271. 8-N, 1-5.

Oakland Register of Deeds 1200 N. Telegraph Rd, Bldg 12 East, Pontiac, MI 48341-0480 **248-858-0605** 8AM-4:30PM. www.co.oakland.mi.us/clerkrod/ Real Estate, Property Tax, Tax Lien, Most Wanted, Foreclosure records online.

Oceana Register of Deeds PO Box 111, Hart, MI 49420 (100 State St). **231-873-4158** Fax: 231-873-9218. 9AM-5PM.

Ogemaw Register of Deeds 806 W. Houghton Ave, Rm 104, West Branch, MI 48661 **989-345-0728** Fax: 989-345-6221. 8:30AM-4:30PM.

Ontonagon Register of Deeds 725 Greenland Rd, Ontonagon, MI 49953-1492 **906-884-4255** Fax: 906-884-6796. 8:30AM-4:30PM.

Osceola Register of Deeds 301 W Upton Ave., Reed City, MI 49677-0208 **231-832-6113** 9AM-5PM.

Oscoda Register of Deeds PO Box 399, Mio, MI 48647 (310 Morenci St). **989-826-1116** Fax: 989-826-1136. 8:30AM-12PM, 1PM-4.30PM.

Otsego Register of Deeds 225 W. Main St, Rm 110, Rm 108, Gaylord, MI 49735 **989-731-7550 x301/2** Fax: 989-731-7519. 8AM-N, 1-4:30PM.

Ottawa Register of Deeds PO Box 265, Grand Haven, MI 49417-0265 (414 Washington Ave, Rm 305). **616-846-8240** Fax: 616-846-8131. 8AM-5PM. www.co.ottawa.mi.us Property, Mapping, Deed, UCC, Judgment records online.

Presque Isle Register of Deeds PO Box 110, Rogers City, MI 49779-0110 (151 E. Huron St). **989-734-2676** Fax: 989-734-0506. 8:30AM-4:30PM.

Roscommon Register of Deeds PO Box 98, Roscommon, MI 48653 (500 Lake St). **989-275-5931** Fax: 989-275-8640. 8:30-4:30PM.

Saginaw Register of Deeds 111 S. Michigan Ave, Saginaw, MI 48602 **989-790-5270** Fax: 989-790-5278. www.saginawcounty.com Assessor, Assumed Business Name, Marriage, Death, Election, Notary, Grantor/Grantee, Recording, Obituary records online.

Sanilac Register of Deeds Box 168, Sandusky, MI 48471-0168 (60 W. Sanilac). **810-648-2313** Fax: 810-648-5461. 8AM-N, 1-4:30PM.

Schoolcraft Register of Deeds 300 Walnut St, Rm 164, Manistique, MI 49854 **906-341-3618** Fax: 906-341-5680. 8AM-4PM.

Shiawassee Register of Deeds PO Box 103, Corunna, MI 48817 (208 N. Shiawassee). **989-743-2216** Fax: 989-743-2459. 8-5PM.

St. Clair Register of Deeds 200 Grand River Blvd, Rm 105, Port Huron, MI 48060 **810-989-6930** Fax: 810-985-4297. 8AM-4:30PM. Marriage, Death records online.

St. Joseph Register of Deeds PO Box 388, Centreville, MI 49032-0388 (125 W. Main). **269-467-5552 x552** Fax: 269-467-5592. 9AM-5PM. www.stjosephcountymi.org Assessor records online.

Tuscola Register of Deeds 440 N. State St, Caro, MI 48723 **989-672-3840** Fax: 989-672-4266. 8-N, 1-4:30. www.tuscolacounty.org

Van Buren Register of Deeds 219 Paw Paw St, #102, Paw Paw, MI 49079 **269-657-8242**

Fax: 269-657-7573. 8:30AM-5PM. www.vbco.org/government0104.asp Real Estate records online.

Washtenaw Register of Deeds PO Box 8645, Ann Arbor, MI 48107 (200 N Main #110). **734-222-6710** Fax: 734-222-6819. 8:30AM-5PM. www.ewashtenaw.org/government/clerk_register Property, Vital Statistic, Business Name, Deed records online.

Wayne Register of Deeds 400 Monroe, Rm 620, Detroit, MI 48226 (**313-224-5860/5860**

Fax: 313-224-5884. 8AM-4:30PM. www.waynecounty.com/register/ Assessor, Recording, Deed, Judgment, Lien, Assumed Name,Delinquent Property records online.

Wexford Register of Deeds 437 E. Division St, PO Box 303, Cadillac, MI 49601 **231-779-9455** Fax: 231-779-0292. 8:30AM-5PM www.wexfordcounty.org/services_deeds.php Real Estate records online.

Minnesota

Organization: 87 counties, 87 recording offices. The recording officer is the County Recorder. State is in Central Time Zone (CST).

Real Estate Records: Many Minnesota counties will perform real estate searches, especially short questions over the telephone. Copy fees vary, but do not apply to certified copies. Certification fees are usually $1.00 per page with a minimum of $5.00.

UCC Records: Until July 2001, Minnesota maintained a centralized database of financing statements filed at the state level and all counties entered all non-real estate filings into the central statewide database which was accessible from any county office. Now, the only filings recorded by the County Recorder are real estate related collateral. All counties will perform UCC searches. Use search request form UCC-11. Search fees are usually $20.00 per debtor name. A UCC search can include tax liens. Copies usually cost $1.00 per page.

Tax Lien Records: Federal and state tax liens on personal property of businesses are filed with the Secretary of State. Other federal and state tax liens are filed with the County Recorder. A special search form UCC-12 is used for separate tax lien searches. Some counties search each tax lien index separately. Some charge one $15.00 or $20.00 fee to search both indexes, but others charge a separate fee for each index searched. Search and copy fees vary widely. Other Liens: Mechanics, hospital, judgment, attorneys.

Online Access: There is no statewide system, but a number of counties offer web access to assessor data and recorded deeds.

Aitkin County Recorder 209 Second St NW, Rm 205, Aitkin, MN 56431 **218-927-7336** Fax: 218-927-7324. 8AM-4:30PM.

Anoka County Recorder 2100 3rd Ave., Anoka, MN 55303-2265 **763-323-5416** Fax: 763-323-5421. 8-4:30. www.co.anoka.mn.us Real Estate, Tax Assessor records online.

Becker County Recorder PO Box 787, Detroit Lakes, MN 56502 (913 Lake Ave). **218-846-7304** Fax: 218-846-7323. 8AM-4:30PM. www.beckercounty.com Property Tax, Assessor records online.

Beltrami County Recorder 619 Beltrami Ave NW, Courthouse, Bemidji, MN 56601 **218-333-4170** Fax: 218-333-4527. 8-4:30.

Benton County Recorder PO Box 129, Foley, MN 56329 (531 Dewey St). **320-968-5037** Fax: 320-968-5329. 8AM-4:30PM. www.co.benton.mn.us/departments/recorder/

Big Stone County Recorder PO Box 218, Ortonville, MN 56278 (20 SE 2nd St.). **320-839-2308** Fax: 320-839-2308. 8-4:30PM.

Blue Earth County Recorder PO Box 3567, Mankato, MN 56002-3567 (410 Jackson St). **507-389-8251** Fax: 507-389-8808. 8AM-

5PM. www.co.blue-earth.mn.us Property records online.

Brown County Recorder PO Box 248, New Ulm, MN 56073-0248 (14 S. State St). **507-233-6653** Fax: 507-233-6668. 8AM-5PM. www.co.brown.mn.us

Carlton County Recorder Box 70, Carlton, MN 55718 (301 Walnut St.). **218-384-9122** Fax: 218-384-9157. 8AM-4PM.

Carver County Recorder 600 E Fourth St, Carver County Govt Ctr, Admin Bldg, Chaska, MN 55318-2158 (**952-361-1930** Fax: 952-361-1931. 8-4:30. www.co.carver.mn.us Real Estate, Grantor/Grantee, Lien, Property Tax records online.

Cass County Recorder PO Box 3000, Walker, MN 56484 (2nd Fl, 300 Minnesota Ave.). **218-547-7381** Fax: 218-547-7292. 8AM-4:30PM. www.co.cass.mn.us Property, GIS, Warrant, Most Wanted records online.

Chippewa County Recorder 629 No. 11th St., Montevideo, MN 56265 **320-269-9431** Fax: 320-269-7168. 8AM-4:30PM.

Chisago County Recorder 313 N Main St., Government Ctr, Rm/Box 277, Center City,

MN 55012-9663 **651-213-0438** Fax: 651-213-0454. 8AM-4:30PM.

Clay County Recorder PO Box 280, Moorhead, MN 56561-0280 (807 N. 11th St, 2nd Fl). **218-299-5031** Fax: 218-299-7500. 8AM-4:30PM. www.co.clay.mn.us Real Estate records online.

Clearwater County Recorder 213 Main Ave North, Dept. 207, Bagley, MN 56621 **218-694-6129** Fax: 218-694-6179. 8-4:30PM.

Cook County Recorder 411 W. 2nd St., Grand Marais, MN 55604-2307 **218-387-3660** Fax: 218-387-3043. 8AM-4PM.

Cottonwood County Recorder PO Box 326, Windom, MN 56101 (900 Third Ave, Rm 6). **507-831-1458** Fax: 507-831-3675. 8AM-4:30PM.

Crow Wing County Recorder PO Box 383, Brainerd, MN 56401 (326 Laurel St). **218-824-1280** Fax: 218-824-1281. 8AM-5PM.

Dakota County Recorder 1590 Highway 55, Hastings, MN 55033 **651-438-4355** Fax: 651-438-8176. 8-4:30PM. www.co.dakota.mn.us Real Estate, Assessor records online.

Dodge County Recorder PO Box 128, Mantorville, MN 55955-0128 (22 6th St. East, Dept. 101). **507-635-6250** Fax: 507-635-6265. 8-4:30PM. www.co.dodge.mn.us

Douglas County Recorder 305 8th Ave West, Courthouse, Alexandria, MN 56308 **320-762-3877** Fax: 320-762-2389. 8AM-4:30PM. www.co.douglas.mn.us Assessor records online.

Faribault County Recorder PO Box 130, Blue Earth, MN 56013 (415 N. Main St). **507-526-6252** Fax: 507-526-6227. 8AM-4:30PM. Property records online.

Fillmore County Recorder Box 465, Preston, MN 55965-0465 (101 Fillmore St.). **507-765-3852** Fax: 507-765-4571. 8AM-4:30PM.

Freeborn County Recorder 411 S. Broadway, Court House, Albert Lea, MN 56007-4506 **507-377-5130** Fax: 507-377-5265. www.co.freeborn.mn.us/recorder.html

Goodhue County Recorder Box 408, Red Wing, MN 55066 (5th & West Ave Courthouse). **651-385-3149** Fax: 651-385-3119. 8AM-4:30PM.

Grant County Recorder PO Box 1007, Elbow Lake, MN 56531-4300 (10 Second St NE). **218-685-4133** Fax: 218-685-4521.

Hennepin County Recorder 300 S. 6th St, 8-A Gov't Ctr, Minneapolis, MN 55487 **612-348-3049** 8AM-4:30PM. Real Estate, Lien, Most Wanted records online. www.co.hennepin.mn.us

Houston County Recorder PO Box 29, Caledonia, MN 55921-0029 (304 S. Marshall St). **507-725-5813** Fax: 507-725-2647. 8AM-4:30PM.

Hubbard County Recorder 301 Court Ave, Park Rapids, MN 56470 (1st Fl). **218-732-3552** Fax: 218-732-3645. 8AM-4:30PM. www.co.hubbard.mn.us/Recorder.htm Property, GIS records online.

Isanti County Recorder 555 18th Ave SW, Courthouse, Cambridge, MN 55008 **763-689-1191** 8AM-4:30PM. www.co.isanti.mn.us

Itasca County Recorder 123 NE 4th St, Grand Rapids, MN 55744-2600 **218-327-2856** Fax: 218-327-0689. 8AM-4:30PM. www.co.itasca.mn.us Property, Auditor records online.

Jackson County Recorder PO Box 209, Jackson County Recorder, Jackson, MN 56143 (405 4th St.). **507-847-2580** Fax: 507-847-6824. 8AM-4:30PM.

Kanabec County Recorder 18 N. Vine St, Mora, MN 55051 **320-679-6466** Fax: 320-679-6431. 8AM-4:30PM.

Kandiyohi County Recorder PO Box 736, Willmar, MN 56201-0736 (400 Benson Ave. SW). **320-231-6223** Fax: 320-231-6284.. www.co.kandiyohi.mn.us Property, Assessor records online. 8AM-4:30PM

Kittson County Recorder 410 Fifth St #202, Hallock, MN 56728 **218-843-2842** Fax: 218-843-2538. 8:30AM-4:30PM.

Koochiching County Recorder 715 4th St., Courthouse, International Falls, MN 56649 **218-283-1193** Fax: 218-283-1194. 8AM-5PM. www.co.koochiching.mn.us Property, Auditor records online.

Lac qui Parle County Recorder PO Box 132, Madison, MN 56256-0132 (600 6th St). **320-598-3724** 8:30AM-4:30PM.

Lake County Recorder 601 Third Ave, Two Harbors, MN 55616 **218-834-8347** Fax: 218-834-8493. 8-4:30PM. www.co.lake.mn.us Assessor, Property, Warrant records online.

Lake of the Woods County Recorder PO Box 808, Baudette, MN 56623 (206 SE 8th Ave). **218-634-1902** Fax: 218-634-2509. 7:30AM-4PM.

Le Sueur County Recorder 88 S. Park Ave, Courthouse, Le Center, MN 56057-1620 **507-357-2251** Fax: 507-357-6375. 8-4:30PM.

Lincoln County Recorder PO Box 119, Ivanhoe, MN 56142 (319 N. Rebecca). **507-694-1360** Fax: 507-694-1198. 8:30-4:30PM.

Lyon County Recorder 607 W. Main St, Marshall, MN 56258 **507-537-6722** Fax: 507-537-7988. 8:30AM-4:30PM. Property records online.

Mahnomen County Recorder PO Box 380, Mahnomen, MN 56557 (311 N. Main). **218-935-5528** Fax: 218-935-5946. 8-4:30 M-T.

Marshall County Recorder 208 E Colvin, Warren, MN 56762 **218-745-4801** Fax: 218-745-5013. 8AM-4:30PM.

Martin County Recorder PO Box 785, Fairmont, MN 56031-0785 (201 Lake Ave). **507-238-3213** Fax: 507-235-8537. 8-5PM. www.co.martin.mn.us Property records online.

McLeod County Recorder 2389 Hennepin Ave N, Glencoe, MN 55336 (2391 N Hennepin Ave, North Complex). **320-864-1327** Fax: 320-864-1295. 8AM-4:30PM. Property records online.

Meeker County Recorder 325 N. Sibley Ave, Courthouse, Litchfield, MN 55355 **320-693-5440** Fax: 320-693-5444. 8-4:30PM.

Mille Lacs County Recorder 635 2nd St S.E., Milaca, MN 56353 **320-983-8308** Fax: 320-983-8388. 8AM-4:30PM.

Morrison County Recorder 213 SE 1st Ave., Admin. Bldg., Little Falls, MN 56345 **320-632-0145** Fax: 320-632-0141. 8-4:30. www.co.morrison.mn.us/wsite/index.htm

Mower County Recorder 201 First St NE, Austin, MN 55912-3475 **507-437-9446** Fax: 507-437-9471. www.co.mower.mn.us

Murray County Recorder PO Box 57, Slayton, MN 56172-0057 (2500 28th St). **507-836-6148 x144** Fax: 507-836-8904. 8:30AM-N, 1-5PM.

Nicollet County Recorder PO Box 493, St. Peter, MN 56082-0493 (501 S. Minnesota Ave). **507-934-0320** Fax: 507-934-4487. www.co.nicollet.mn.us/dept.php3?id=16

Nobles County Recorder PO Box 757, Worthington, MN 56187 (315 10th St). **507-372-8236** 8AM-4:30PM.

Norman County Recorder PO Box 146, Ada, MN 56510 (16 E. 3rd Ave). **218-784-5481** Fax: 218-784-2399. 8:30AM-4:30PM. Assessor records online.

Olmsted County Property Records & Licensing 151 4th St. SE, Rochester, MN 55904 **507-285-8194** Fax: 507-287-7186. 8AM-5PM. www.olmstedcounty.com Probate records online.

Otter Tail County Recorder PO Box 867, Fergus Falls, MN 56538 (565 W Fur). **218-739-2271** 8AM-5PM. Property Tax records online.

Pennington County Recorder PO Box 616, Thief River Falls, MN 56701 (1st & Main St Courthouse). **218-683-7027** Fax: 218-683-7026. 8AM-4:30PM.

Pine County Recorder 315 Main St S. #3, Courthouse, Pine City, MN 55063 **320-629-5665** Fax: 320-629-5765. 8AM-4:30PM.

Pipestone County Recorder 416 Hiawatha Ave. S., Pipestone, MN 56164 **507-825-6755** Fax: 507-825-6767. 8AM-4:30PM.

Polk County Recorder PO Box 397, Crookston, MN 56716 (612 Broadway, #213). **218-281-3464** Fax: 218-281-1636. 8AM-4:30PM.

Pope County Recorder 130 E. Minnesota Ave., Glenwood, MN 56334 **320-634-5723** Fax: 320-634-5717. 8AM-4:30PM.

www.mncounties.org/pope/ Property records online.

Ramsey County Recorder 50 W. Kellogg Blvd., #812 RCGC-W, St. Paul, MN 55102-1693 **651-266-2060** 8AM-4:30PM. Property Assessor records online.

Red Lake County Recorder Box 3, Red Lake Falls, MN 56750-0003 (124 Main Ave North). **218-253-2997** Fax: 218-253-2052. 9AM-5PM.

Redwood County Recorder PO Box 130, Redwood Falls, MN 56283 (Courthouse Sq, Main Fl). **507-637-4032** Fax: 507-637-4064. 8AM-4:30PM.

Renville County Recorder 500 E. DePue, 2nd Fl, Olivia, MN 56277 **320-523-3669** Fax: 320-523-3679. 8-4:30PM. Assessor records online. www.co.renville.mn.us/dept.html

Rice County Recorder 320 NW 3rd St, #10, Faribault, MN 55021-6146 **507-332-6114** Fax: 507-332-5999. 8AM-4:30PM. www.co.rice.mn.us Property Assessor, Property Sale records online.

Rock County Recorder PO Box 509, Luverne, MN 56156 (204 E. Brown). **507-283-5014** Fax: 507-283-1343. 8AM-5PM. Assessor records online.

Roseau County Recorder 606 5th Ave. SW, Rm 170, Roseau, MN 56751-1477 **218-463-2061** Fax: 218-463-4294. 8AM-4:30PM.

Scott County Recorder 200 Fourth Ave West, Shakopee, MN 55379 **952-496-8150** Fax: 952-496-8138. 8AM-4:30PM. www.co.scott.mn.us Real Estate, Recorder, Property Tax, Assessor, GIS records online.

Sherburne County Recorder 13880 Highway 10, Elk River, MN 55330 **763-241-**2915 Fax: 763-241-2995. 8AM-4:30PM. www.co.sherburne.mn.us Real Estate, Tax Assessor, Most Wanted records online.

Sibley County Recorder PO Box 44, Gaylord, MN 55334-0044 (400 Court St, Rm 26). **507-237-4306** Fax: 507-237-4062. 8AM-5PM. http://co.sibley.mn.us

St. Louis County Recorder PO Box 157, Duluth, MN 55801-0157 (100 N. 5th Ave West, Rm 101). **218-726-2677** Fax: 218-725-5052. 8AM-4:30PM. www.stlouiscounty.org/recordersoffice/recordersoffice.htm Real Estate, Property Tax, Auditor records online.

Stearns County Recorder 705 Courthouse Sq, Admin. Ctr, Rm 131, St. Cloud, MN 56303 **320-656-3855** Fax: 320-656-3916. 8AM-4:30PM. www.co.stearns.mn.us Real Estate, Tax Assessor records online.

Steele County Recorder PO Box 890, Owatonna, MN 55060 (630 Florence Ave.). **507-444-7450** Fax: 507-444-7470. 8AM-5PM. Property Tax records online.

Stevens County Recorder PO Box 530, Morris, MN 56267 (5th & Colorado). **320-589-7414** Fax: 320-589-7112. 8:30AM-4:30PM (Summer Hours 8AM-4PM). Assessor records online.

Swift County Recorder PO Box 246, Benson, MN 56215 (301 14th St North). **320-843-3377** Fax: 320-843-2275. 8-4:30.

Todd County Recorder 221 First Ave South, #300, Long Prairie, MN 56347-1391 **320-732-4428** Fax: 320-732-4001. 8AM-4:30PM. www.co.todd.mn.us/Recorder/recorder.htm Property, GIS-Mapping records online.

Traverse County Recorder PO Box 487, Wheaton, MN 56296-0487 (702 2nd Ave.

North). **320-563-4622** Fax: 320-563-4424. 8AM-4:30PM.

Wabasha County Recorder 625 Jefferson Ave, Wabasha, MN 55981 **651-565-3623** Fax: 651-565-2774. 8AM-4PM.

Wadena County Recorder 415 Jefferson St S, Wadena, MN 56482 **218-631-7622** Fax: 218-631-5709. 8AM-4:30PM. www.co.wadena.mn.us

Waseca County Recorder 307 N. State St, Waseca, MN 56093 **507-835-0670** Fax: 507-835-0633. 8AM-4:30PM.

Washington County Recorder 14900 N. 61st St, PO Box 6, Stillwater, MN 55082 **651-430-6755** Fax: 651-275-7060. 7:30AM-5PM. www.co.washington.mn.us Real Estate Tract records online.

Watonwan County Recorder PO Box 518, St. James, MN 56081 (Courthouse). **507-375-1216** 8:30AM-N, 1-5PM.

Wilkin County Recorder PO Box 29, Breckenridge, MN 56520 (300 S. 5th St). **218-643-7164** Fax: 218-643-7170. 8AM-4:30PM. www.co.wilkin.mn.us/recorder.asp

Winona County Recorder 177 Main St, Winona, MN 55987 **507-457-6340** Fax: 507-454-9371. 8AM-4:30PM.

Wright County Recorder 10 2nd St NW, Rm 210, Buffalo, MN 55313-1196 **763-682-7357** Fax: 763-684-4558. 8AM-4:30PM. www.co.wright.mn.us Recorder, Land, Lien, Grantor/Grantee, Property Tax records online.

Yellow Medicine County Recorder 415 9th Ave, Courthouse, Granite Falls, MN 56241 **320-564-2529** Fax: 320-564-3670. 8AM-4PM. http://yellowmedicine.govoffice.com

Mississippi

Organization: 82 counties, 92 recording offices. The recording officers are the Chancery Clerk and the Clerk of Circuit Court (state tax liens). Ten counties have two separate recording offices - Bolivar, Carroll, Chickasaw, Craighead, Harrison, Hinds, Jasper, Jones, Panola, Tallahatchie, and Yalobusha. See the notes under each county for how to determine which office is appropriate to search. The entire state is in the Central Time Zone (CST).

Real Estate Records: A few counties will perform real estate searches. Copies usually cost $.50 per page and certification fees $1.00 per document. The Assessor maintains tax records.

UCC Records: This was a dual filing state. Until 07/2001, financing statements were filed both at the state level and with the Chancery Clerk, except for consumer goods, farm related and real estate related filings, which were filed only with the Chancery Clerk. Now, only real estate related filings are filed at the county level. Nearly all counties will perform UCC searches. Use search request form UCC-11. Search fees are usually $5.00 per debtor name. Copy fees vary from $.25 to $2.00 per page.

Tax Lien Records: Federal tax liens on personal property of businesses are filed with the Secretary of State. Federal tax liens on personal property of individuals are filed with the county Chancery Clerk. State tax liens on personal property are filed with the county Clerk of Circuit Court. Refer to the County Court section for information about Mississippi Circuit Courts. State tax liens on real property are filed with the Chancery Clerk. Most Chancery Clerk offices will perform a federal tax lien search for a fee of $5.00 per name. Copy fees vary. Other Liens: Mechanics, lis pendens, judgment (Circuit Court), construction.

Online Access: A limited number of counties offer online access to records. There is no statewide system except for the Secretary of State's UCC access - see State Agencies section. A vendor provides access to thirteen counties at http://deltacomputersystems.com.

Adams Chancery Clerk PO Box 1006, Natchez, MS 39121 (1 Courthouse Sq). **601-446-6684** Fax: 601-445-7913. 8AM-5PM.

Alcorn Chancery Clerk PO Box 69, Corinth, MS 38835-0069 (501 Waldron St). **662-286-7700** Fax: 662-286-7706. 8AM-5PM. Property Tax, Appraisal records online.

Amite Chancery Clerk PO Box 680, Liberty, MS 39645-0680 (243 W. Main St). **601-657-8022** Fax: 601-657-8288. 8AM-5PM.

Attala Chancery Clerk 230 W. Washington St., Chancery Court Bldg., Kosciusko, MS 39090 **662-289-2921** Fax: 662-289-7662. 8AM-5PM.

Benton Chancery Clerk PO Box 218, Ashland, MS 38603 (190 Ripley St). **662-224-6300** Fax: 662-224-6303. 8AM-5PM.

Bolivar County - 1st District Chancery Clerk PO Box 238, Rosedale, MS 38769-0238 (801 Main St). **662-759-3762** Fax: 662-759-3467. 8AM-N, 1-5PM.
2nd District Chancery Clerk PO Box 789, Cleveland, MS 38732 (Court St Court house). **662-843-2071** Fax: 662-846-2940.

Calhoun Chancery Clerk PO Box 8, Pittsboro, MS 38951 (103 W Main St). **662-412-3117** Fax: 662-412-3128. 8AM-5PM.

Carroll County - 1st District Chancery Clerk PO Box 60, Carrollton, MS 38917 (Courthouse). **662-237-9274** Fax: 662-237-9642. 8AM-12:00-1-5PM.
2nd District Chancery Clerk PO Box 6, Vaiden, MS 39176 (101 Highway 51). **662-464-5476** Fax: 662-464-5407. 8AM-5PM.

Chickasaw County - 1st District Chancery Clerk Courthouse, 1 Pinson Sq, Houston, MS 38851 **662-456-2513** Fax: 662-456-5295. 8AM-12:00-1-5PM.
2nd District Chancery Clerk 234 Main St, Rm 201, Okolona, MS 38860-1438 **662-447-2092** Fax: 662-447-5024.

Choctaw Chancery Clerk PO Box 250, Ackerman, MS 39735-0250 (22 E.Quinn St). **662-285-6329** Fax: 662-285-3444. 8-5.

Claiborne Chancery Clerk PO Box 449, Port Gibson, MS 39150 (410 Main St). **601-437-4992** Fax: 601-437-3731. 8AM-5PM.

Clarke Chancery Clerk PO Box 689, Quitman, MS 39355 (Archusa St Courthouse). **601-776-2126** Fax: 601-776-2756. 8AM-5PM.

Clay Chancery Clerk PO Box 815, West Point, MS 39773 (205 Court St). **662-494-3124** 8AM-5PM.

Coahoma Chancery Clerk PO Box 98, Clarksdale, MS 38614 (115 First St). **662-624-3000** Fax: 662-624-3040. 8AM-5PM.

Copiah Chancery Clerk PO Box 507, Hazlehurst, MS 39083-0507 (100 Caldwell Dr). **601-894-3021** Fax: 601-894-3026.

Covington Chancery Clerk PO Box 1679, Collins, MS 39428 (101 S. Elm St.). **601-765-4242** Fax: 601-765-5016. 8AM-5PM.

De Soto Chancery Clerk PO Box 949, Hernando, MS 38632 (2535 Highway 51 South, Rm 104). **662-429-1318** Fax: 662-449-1420. 8AM-5PM. www.desotoms.info Property Tax, Assessor, Grantor/Grantee, Deed, Recording, Voter Registration records online.

Forrest Chancery Clerk PO Box 951, Hattiesburg, MS 39403 (641 Main St). **601-545-6014** Fax: 601-545-6095. 8AM-5PM.

Franklin Chancery Clerk PO Box 297, Meadville, MS 39653 (36 Main St E.). **601-384-2330** Fax: 601-384-5864. 8AM-5PM.

George Chancery Clerk 355 Cox St, Lucedale, MS 39452 **601-947-4801** Fax: 601-947-1300. 8AM-5PM; 9AM-N Sat. Assessor, Property records online.

Greene Chancery Clerk PO Box 610, Leakesville, MS 39451 (400 Main St.). **601-394-2377** 8AM-5PM.

Grenada Chancery Clerk PO Drawer 1208, Grenada, MS 38902-1208 (59 Green St). **662-226-1821** Fax: 662-227-2860. 8-5PM.

Hancock Chancery Clerk PO Box 429, Bay Saint Louis, MS 39520 (152 Main St). **228-467-5404** Fax: 228-467-3159. 8AM-5PM.

Harrison County - 1st District Chancery Clerk PO Drawer CC, Gulfport, MS 39502 (1801 23rd Ave). **228-865-4195** Fax: 228-868-1480. http://co.harrison.ms.us Property, Deed, Recording, UCC, Voter Registration, Deed, Grantor/Grantee, Marriage, Inmate, Court records online. 8AM-5PM.
2nd District Chancery Clerk PO Box 544, Biloxi, MS 39533 (730 Martin Luther King Jr. Blvd.). **228-435-8220** Fax: 228-435-8292. 8AM-5PM. http://co.harrison.ms.us Property, Deed, Recording, UCC, Voter Registration,

Deed, Grantor/Grantee, Marriage, Inmate, Court records online.

Hinds County - 1st District Chancery Clerk PO Box 686, Jackson, MS 39205-0686 (316 S. President St). **601-968-6508** Fax: 601-973-5535. 8AM-5PM. www.co.hinds.ms.us/pgs/elected/chanceryclerk.asp Real Estate, Grantor/Grantee, Judgment, Lien, Assessor, Condominium, Acreage records online.
2nd District Chancery Clerk PO Box 88, Raymond, MS 39154 (Main St, Courthouse Annex). **601-857-8055** 8AM-5PM. www.co.hinds.ms.us Real Estate, Assessor, Grantor/Grantee, Judgment records online.

Holmes Chancery Clerk PO Box 239, Lexington, MS 39095 (2 Court Sq). **662-834-2508** Fax: 662-834-3020.

Humphreys Chancery Clerk PO Box 547, Belzoni, MS 39038 (102 Castleman). **662-247-1740** Fax: 662-247-0101. 8-N, 1-5PM.

Issaquena Chancery Clerk PO Box 27, Mayersville, MS 39113-0027 (129 Court St). **662-873-2761** Fax: 662-873-2061. 8-N; 1-5.

Itawamba Chancery Clerk PO Box 776, Fulton, MS 38843 (201 W. Main St). **662-862-3421** Fax: 662-862-3421.

Jackson Chancery Clerk PO Box 998, Pascagoula, MS 39568 (650 Delmas Ave). **228-769-3131** Fax: 228-769-3135. 8-5PM.

Jasper County - 1st District Chancery Clerk PO Box 38, Paulding, MS 39348-0038 (1782 Highway 503). **601-727-4941** Fax: 601-727-4475. 8AM-5PM.
2nd District Chancery Clerk PO Box 1047, Bay Springs, MS 39422 (Court St, 27 W 8th St). **601-764-3026** Fax: 601-764-3999. 8-5.

Jefferson County Chancery Clerk PO Box 145, Fayette, MS 39069 (307 Main). **601-786-3021** Fax: 601-786-6009. 8AM-5PM.

Jefferson Davis County Chancery Clerk PO Box 1137, Prentiss, MS 39474 (1025 3rd St.). **601-792-4204** Fax: 601-792-2894.

Jones County - 1st District Chancery Clerk 101 N. Court St, Jones County Courthouse, Ellisville, MS 39437 **601-477-3307** Fax: 601-477-1240. 8-12:00-1-5PM.
2nd District Chancery Clerk PO Box 1468, Laurel, MS 39441 (415 N. 5th Ave). **601-428-0527** Fax: 601-428-3602. 8AM-5PM.

Kemper Chancery Clerk PO Box 188, De Kalb, MS 39328 (Courthouse Sq). **601-743-2460** Fax: 601-743-2789. 8AM-5PM.

Lafayette Chancery Clerk PO Box 1240, Oxford, MS 38655 (Courthouse). **662-234-2131** Fax: 662-234-5038. 8AM-5PM. Property Tax, Appraisal records online.

Lamar Chancery Clerk PO Box 247, Purvis, MS 39475 (403 Main St). **601-794-8504** Fax: 601-794-3903. 8AM-5PM. Property Tax, Appraisal records online.

Lauderdale Chancery Clerk PO Box 1587, Meridian, MS 39302-1587 (500 Constitution Ave, 1st Fl). **601-482-9701** 8AM-5PM. www.lauderdalecounty.org Property Tax, Appraisal records online.

Lawrence Chancery Clerk PO Box 821, Monticello, MS 39654 (517 E. Broad St.). **601-587-7162** Fax: 601-587-0767. 8-5PM.

Leake Chancery Clerk PO Box 72, Carthage, MS 39051 (Courthouse, Court Sq). **601-267-7371** Fax: 601-267-6137.

Lee Chancery Clerk PO Box 7127, Tupelo, MS 38802 (200 Jefferson St). **662-841-9100** Fax: 662-680-6091. Property Tax, Appraisal records online.

Leflore Chancery Clerk PO Box 250, Greenwood, MS 38935-0250 (310 W. Market, Courthouse). **662-455-7913** Fax: 662-455-7965.

Lincoln Chancery Clerk PO Box 555, Brookhaven, MS 39602 (300 S. First St). **601-835-3411** 8AM-5PM. Real Estate, Grantor/Grantee, Deed records online.

Lowndes Chancery Clerk PO Box 684, Columbus, MS 39703 (515 2nd Ave North). **662-329-5800** 8AM-5PM.

Madison Chancery Clerk PO Box 404, Canton, MS 39046 (146 W. Center St, Courtyard Sq). **601-859-1177** 8AM-5PM. http://mcatax.com Property Tax, Appraisal records online.

Marion Chancery Clerk 250 Broad St, #2, Columbia, MS 39429 (250 Broad St, #2). **601-736-2691** Fax: 601-441-0538. 8-5PM.

Marshall Chancery Clerk PO Box 219, Holly Springs, MS 38635 (Court Sq). **662-252-4431** Fax: 662-252-0004. Property Tax, Appraisal records online.

Monroe Chancery Clerk PO Box 578, Aberdeen, MS 39730 (201 W. Commerce St) **662-369-8143** Fax: 662-369-7928. 8-5PM

Montgomery Chancery Clerk PO Box 71, Winona, MS 38967 (614 Summit St). **662-283-2333** Fax: 662-283-2233. 8AM-5PM.

Neshoba Chancery Clerk 401 Beacon St, #107, Philadelphia, MS 39350 **601-656-3581** 8AM-5PM. Property Tax, Appraisal records online.

Newton Chancery Clerk PO Box 68, Decatur, MS 39327 (92 W. Broad St.). **601-635-2367** Fax: 601-635-3210.

Noxubee Chancery Clerk PO Box 147, Macon, MS 39341 (505 S. Jefferson). **662-726-4243** Fax: 662-726-2272. 8AM-5PM.

Oktibbeha Chancery Clerk 101 E. Main, Courthouse, Starkville, MS 39759 **662-323-5834** Fax: 662-338-1064. 8AM-5PM.

Panola County - 1st District Chancery Clerk PO Box 130, Sardis, MS 38666 (215 S. Pocahontas St). **662-487-2070** Fax: 662-487-3595. 8AM-12:00-1-5PM.
2nd District Chancery Clerk 151 Public Sq, Batesville, MS 38606 **662-563-6205** Fax: 662-563-8233. 8AM-5PM.

Pearl River Chancery Clerk PO Box 431, Poplarville, MS 39470 (200 S. Main St.). **601-403-2317** Fax: 601-403-2318. 8AM-5PM. Property Tax, Appraisal records online.

Perry Chancery Clerk PO Box 198, New Augusta, MS 39462 (103 Main St). **601-964-8398** Fax: 601-964-8265.

Pike Chancery Clerk PO Box 309, Magnolia, MS 39652 (East Bay). **601-783-3362** Fax: 601-783-2001. www.co.pike.ms.us Real Estate, Grantor/Grantee, Deed records online.

Pontotoc Chancery Clerk PO Box 209, Pontotoc, MS 38863 (11 E. Washington St.). **662-489-3900** Fax: 662-489-3940. 8AM-5PM.

Prentiss Chancery Clerk PO Box 477, Booneville, MS 38829 (100 N. Main St). **662-728-8151** Fax: 662-728-2007. 8-5PM.

Quitman Chancery Clerk Chestnut St, Courthouse, Marks, MS 38646 **662-326-2661** Fax: 662-326-8004.

Rankin Chancery Clerk PO Box 700, Brandon, MS 39043 (#D, 211 E Government St.). **601-825-1469** Fax: 601-824-7116. www.rankincounty.org Real Estate, Tax Assessor, Voter Regis. records online.

Scott Chancery Clerk PO Box 630, Forest, MS 39074 (100 Main St). **601-469-1922** Fax: 601-469-5180. 8AM-5PM.

Sharkey Chancery Clerk PO Box 218, Rolling Fork, MS 39159 (400 Locust St.are). **662-873-2755** Fax: 662-873-6045. 8AM-5PM.

Simpson Chancery Clerk PO Box 367, Mendenhall, MS 39114 (111 W Pine Ave, #3). **601-847-2626** Fax: 601-847-7016. 8AM-5PM.

Smith Chancery Clerk PO Box 39, Raleigh, MS 39153 (123 Main St.). **601-782-9811** Fax: 601-782-4690. 8AM-5PM.

Stone Chancery Clerk PO Drawer 7, Wiggins, MS 39577 (323 Cavers Ave). **601-928-5266** 8-5PM.

Sunflower Chancery Clerk PO Box 988, Indianola, MS 38751-0988 (200 Main St.). **662-887-4703** Fax: 662-887-7054.

Tallahatchie County - 1st District Chancery Clerk PO Box 350, Charleston, MS 38921 (Courthouse). **662-647-5551** Fax: 662-647-8490. 8AM-N,1-5PM.
2nd District Chancery Clerk PO Box 180, Sumner, MS 38957 (Main St Courthouse). **662-375-8731** Fax: 662-375-7252. 8-5PM.

Tate Chancery Clerk 201 Ward St, PO Box 309, Senatobia, MS 38668 **662-562-5661** Fax: 662-560-6205. 8AM-5PM.

Tippah Chancery Clerk PO Box 99, Ripley, MS 38663 (Courthouse). **662-837-7374** Fax: 662-837-7148.

Tishomingo Chancery Clerk 1008 Battleground Dr., Courthouse, Iuka, MS 38852 **662-423-7010** Fax: 662-423-7005. 8-5.

Tunica Chancery Clerk PO Box 217, Tunica, MS 38676 (1300 School St). **662-363-2451** Fax: 662-357-5934. 8AM-N, 1-5PM.

Union Chancery Clerk PO Box 847, New Albany, MS 38652 (Courthouse). **662-534-1900** Fax: 662-534-1907. 8AM-5PM.

Walthall Chancery Clerk PO Box 351, Tylertown, MS 39667 (200 Ball Ave). **601-876-3553** Fax: 601-876-6026. www.walthallcountychamber.org/

Warren Chancery Clerk PO Box 351, Vicksburg, MS 39181 (1009 Cherry St). **601-636-4415** Fax: 601-634-4815. www.co.warren.ms.us Property Tax, Appraisal records online.

Washington Chancery Clerk PO Box 309, Greenville, MS 38702-0309 (900 Washington Ave). **662-332-1595** Fax: 662-334-2725. 8AM-5PM. Property Tax, Appraisal records online.

Wayne Chancery Clerk 609 Azalea Dr., Wayne County Courthouse, Waynesboro, MS 39367 **601-735-2873** Fax: 601-735-6224. 8AM-5PM.

Webster Chancery Clerk PO Box 398, Walthall, MS 39771 (Highway 9 North Courthouse). **662-258-4131** Fax: 662-258-6657. 8-5PM.

Wilkinson Chancery Clerk PO Box 516, Woodville, MS 39669 (525 Main St). **601-888-4381** Fax: 601-888-6776. 8AM-5PM.

Winston Chancery Clerk PO Drawer 69, Louisville, MS 39339 (South Court St). **662-773-3631** Fax: 662-773-8814. 8AM-5PM.

Yalobusha County - 1st District Chancery Clerk PO Box 260, Coffeeville, MS 38922 (Courthouse). **662-675-2716** Fax: 662-675-8004.

Yalobusha County - 2nd District Chancery Clerk PO Box 664, Water Valley, MS 38965 (132 Blackmur Dr). **662-473-2091** Fax: 662-473-3622. 8AM-5PM.

Yazoo Chancery Clerk PO Box 68, Yazoo City, MS 39194 (211 E. Broadway). **662-746-2661** Fax: 662-746-3893. 8AM-5PM.

 # Missouri

Organization: 114 counties and one independent city -- 115 recording offices. The recording officer is the Recorder of Deeds. The City of St. Louis has its own recording office. See the City/County Locator section at the end of this chapter for ZIP Codes that cover both the city and county of St. Louis. The entire state is in the Central Time Zone (CST).

Real Estate Records: A few counties will perform real estate searches. Copy and certification fees vary.

UCC Records: Missouri was a dual filing state. Until 07/2001, financing statements were filed both at the state level and with the Recorder of Deeds, except for consumer goods, farm related and real estate related filings, which were filed only with the Recorder. Now only real estate relating filings are filed at the county level. Most all counties will perform UCC searches. Use search request form UCC-11. Search fees are usually $14.00 per debtor name without copies and $28.00 with copies. Copies usually cost $.50 per page.

Tax Lien Records: All federal and state tax liens are filed with the county Recorder of Deeds. They are usually indexed together. Some counties will perform tax lien searches. Search and copy fees vary widely. Other Liens: Mechanics, judgment, child support.

Online Access: A handful of counties offer online access. UCCs are available from the Secretary of State.

Adair Recorder of Deeds 106 W. Washington St., Courthouse, Kirksville, MO 63501 **660-665-3890** Fax: 660-785-3212. 8:30AM-N, 1-4:30PM.

Andrew Recorder of Deeds PO Box 208, Savannah, MO 64485 (Courthouse, 5th & Main). **816-324-4221** Fax: 816-324-5667. 8AM-5PM.

Atchison Recorder of Deeds Box 280, Rock Port, MO 64482 (400 Washington St.). **660-744-2707** Fax: 660-744-5705. 8:30AM-N, 1-4:30PM. www.morecorders.com

Audrain Recorder of Deeds 101 N Jefferson, Rm 105, Audrain County Courthouse, Mexico, MO 65265 **573-473-5830** Fax: 573-581-8087. 8AM-5PM.

Barry Recorder of Deeds PO Box 340, Cassville, MO 65625 (Courthouse). **417-847-2914** Fax: 417-847-2914. 8AM-4PM.

Barton Recorder of Deeds 1004 Gulf, Courthouse, Rm 107, Lamar, MO 64759 **417-682-2110** Fax: 417-682-4102. 8:30AM-N, 12:30-4:30PM.

Bates Recorder of Deeds Box 186, Butler, MO 64730 (1 N. Delaware). **660-679-3611** 8:30AM-4:30PM.

Benton Recorder of Deeds PO Box 37, Warsaw, MO 65355 (Van Buren St Courthouse). **660-438-5732** Fax: 660-438-3652. 8AM-N, 1-4:30PM.

Bollinger Recorder of Deeds Box 49, Marble Hill, MO 63764 (204 High St.). **573-238-1900 ext 301** Fax: 573-238-4511. 8-4PM.

Boone Recorder of Deeds 801 E. Walnut, Rm 132, Boone County Gov't Ctr, Columbia, MO 65201-7728 **573-886-4345** Fax: 573-886-4359. x www.showmeboone.com/recorder/ Real Estate, Lien, Marriage, UCC, Real Property, Personal Property records online.

Buchanan Recorder of Deeds 411 Jules Sts, Courthouse, St. Joseph, MO 64501-1789 **816-271-1437** Fax: 816-271-1582. 8AM-4:30PM. www.co.buchanan.mo.us

Butler Recorder of Deeds 100 N. Main St, Courthouse, Poplar Bluff, MO 63901 **573-686-8086** 8AM-4PM. Death Index records online.

Caldwell Recorder of Deeds PO Box 65, Kingston, MO 64650 (49 E. Main St.). **816-586-3080** 8AM-4:30PM.

Callaway Recorder of Deeds PO Box 406, Fulton, MO 65251 (10 E. 5th St). **573-642-0787** Fax: 573-642-7929. 8AM-5PM. Death records online.

Camden Recorder of Deeds 1 Court Circle, Camdenton, MO 65020 **573-346-4440** Fax: 573-346-8367. 8:30AM-4:30PM.

Cape Girardeau Recorder of Deeds PO Box 248, Jackson, MO 63755 (1 Barton Sq). **573-243-8123** Fax: 573-204-2477. 8-4:30PM.

Carroll Recorder of Deeds PO Box 245, Carrollton, MO 64633 (Courthouse). **660-542-1466** Fax: 660-542-1444. 8:30AM-4:30PM.

Carter Recorder of Deeds PO Box 1107, Van Buren, MO 63965 (105 Main St). **573-323-9656** Fax: 573-323-4885. 8AM-N, 1-4PM.

Cass Recorder of Deeds 102 E. Wall St, Cass County Court House, Harrisonville, MO 64701 **816-380-8117** Fax: 816-380-8165. 8AM-4:30PM. www.casscounty.com/cassfr.htm

Cedar Recorder of Deeds PO Box 607, Stockton, MO 65785 (113 South St.). **417-276-6700 x246** Fax: 417-276-5001. 8AM-N, 1-4PM.

Chariton Recorder of Deeds PO Box 112, Keytesville, MO 65261 (Highway 24 West). **660-288-3602** Fax: 660-288-3763. 8:30AM-N, 1-4:30PM.

Christian Recorder of Deeds PO Box 358, Ozark, MO 65721 (100 W Church St, Rm #104). **417-581-9941** Fax: 417-581-9943. 8AM-4:30PM.

Clark Recorder of Deeds 111 E. Court #2, Courthouse, Kahoka, MO 63445 **660-727-3292** Fax: 660-727-1051. 8AM-N,1-4PM.

Clay Recorder of Deeds PO Box 238, Liberty, MO 64069 (1 Courthouse Sq, Admin. Bldg.). **816-792-7641** Fax: 816-792-7777. 8-4PM. http://recorder.co.clay.mo.us Real Estate, Marriage, Military Discharge, UCC, Recording records online.

Clinton Recorder of Deeds PO Box 275, Plattsburg, MO 64477 (207 N. Main St.). **816-539-3719** Fax: 816-539-3893. 8AM-N, 1-5PM.

Cole Recorder of Deeds PO Box 353, Jefferson City, MO 65102 (311 E. High). **573-634-9115** 8AM-4:30PM. Death records online.

Cooper Recorder of Deeds 200 Main St, Courthouse, Rm 26, Boonville, MO 65233-1276 **660-882-2232** Fax: 660-882-2043. 8:30AM-5PM.

Crawford Recorder of Deeds PO Box 177, Steelville, MO 65565 (Main St). **573-775-5048** Fax: 573-775-3365. 8AM-4:30PM.

Dade Recorder of Deeds Courthouse, Greenfield, MO 65661 **417-637-5373** Fax: 417-637-5055. 8AM-4PM.

Dallas Recorder of Deeds PO Box 373, Buffalo, MO 65622 (Rm 14, 108 S Maple). **417-345-2242** Fax: 417-345-5539. 8AM-N,1-4PM.

Daviess Recorder of Deeds PO Box 132, Gallatin, MO 64640 (102 N Main, 2nd Fl). **660-663-3183** Fax: 660-663-3376. 8AM-N, 1-4:30PM.

De Kalb Recorder of Deeds PO Box 248, Maysville, MO 64469-0248 (Rm 1, 109 W. Main). **816-449-2602** Fax: 816-449-2440. 8:30AM-N, 1-4:30PM.

Dent Recorder of Deeds 112 E. 5th St, Salem, MO 65560-1444 **573-729-3931** Fax: 573-729-9414. 8AM-4:30PM.

Douglas Recorder of Deeds PO Box 249, Ava, MO 65608 (203 SE 2nd Ave). **417-683-4713** Fax: 417-683-2794. 8-4:30PM.

Dunklin Recorder of Deeds PO Box 389, Kennett, MO 63857 (Courthouse Sq, Rm 204). **573-888-3468** 8:30AM-N, 1-4:30PM.

Franklin Recorder of Deeds 300 E Main St #101, Union, MO 63084 **636-583-6367** Fax: 636-583-7330. 8-4:30. www.franklinmo.org.

Gasconade Recorder of Deeds 119 E.1st St, Rm 6, Hermann, MO 65041-1182 **573-486-2632** Fax: 573-486-5812. 8AM-4:30PM.

Gentry Recorder of Deeds PO Box 27, Albany, MO 64402 (200 W. Clay). **660-726-3618** Fax: 660-726-4102. 8AM-4:30PM.

Greene Recorder of Deeds 940 Boonville, Rm 100, Springfield, MO 65802 **417-868-4068** Fax: 417-868-4807. 8AM-4:30PM. www.greenecountymo.org Assessor, Property, Deed, Lien, UCC, Recording, Death, Divorce records online.

Grundy Recorder of Deeds PO Box 196, Trenton, MO 64683 (700 Main St.). **660-359-5409** Fax: 660-359-6604. 8:30AM-4:30PM.

Harrison Recorder of Deeds PO Box 189, Bethany, MO 64424 (1515 Main St) **660-425-6425** Fax: 660-425-3772. 8-N, 1-4:30.

Henry Recorder of Deeds 100 W. Franklin #4, Courthouse, Clinton, MO 64735 **660-885-6963 x7209** Fax: 660-885-2264. 8:30AM-4:30PM.

Hickory Recorder of Deeds PO Box 101, Hermitage, MO 65668 (Courthouse). **417-745-6421** Fax: 417-745-6670. 8AM-N, 12:30-4:30PM.

Holt Recorder of Deeds PO Box 318, Oregon, MO 64473 (100 W. Nodaway). **660-446-3301** 8:30AM-N, 1-4:30PM.

Howard Recorder of Deeds 1 Courthouse Sq, Fayette, MO 65248 **660-248-2194** Fax: 660-248-1075. 8:30AM-4:30PM.

Howell Recorder of Deeds PO Box 967, West Plains, MO 65775 (Courthouse). **417-256-3750** 8AM-4:30PM.

Iron Recorder of Deeds PO Box 24, Ironton, MO 63650 (250 S. Main). **573-546-2811** Fax: 573-546-2166. 8AM-4:30PM.

Jackson County (Kansas City) Recorder of Deeds 415 E. 12th St, Rm 104, Kansas City, MO 64106 **816-881-3192** Fax: 816-881-3719. 8AM-5PM. www.co.jackson.mo.us Property, Tax Assessor, Recording, Marriages, Grantor/Grantee, Deed, Lien, Judgment, UCC records online.

Jasper Recorder of Deeds PO Box 387, Carthage, MO 64836-0387 (116 W Second). **417-358-0432** 8:30AM-4:30PM. www.jaspercounty.org/recorder/

Jefferson Recorder of Deeds PO Box 100, Hillsboro, MO 63050 (729 Maple St, Rm 126). **636-797-5414** 8:00AM-5:00PM. www.jeffcomo.org Real Estate, Recording, Judgment, Assessor, Prop. Tax records online.

Johnson Recorder of Deeds PO Box 32, Warrensburg, MO 64093 (300 N Holden St #305). **660-747-6811** 8:30AM-4:30PM.

Knox Recorder of Deeds PO Box 116, Edina, MO 63537 (Courthouse). **660-397-2305** Fax: 660-397-3331. 8:30AM-N; 1-4.

Laclede Recorder of Deeds 200 N Adams, Lebanon, MO 65536-3046 **417-532-4011** Fax: 417-532-3852. 8AM-4PM. http://laclede.county.missouri.org/recorder/

Lafayette Recorder of Deeds PO Box 416, Lexington, MO 64067 (11th and Main). **660-259-6178** Fax: 660-259-2918. 8:30AM-4:30PM.

Lawrence Recorder of Deeds PO Box 449, Mount Vernon, MO 65712 (Courthouse on the Sq). **417-466-2670** Fax: 417-466-4995. 9AM-N, 1-5PM.

Lewis Recorder of Deeds PO Box 97, Monticello, MO 63457-0097 (1 Courthouse Sq). **573-767-5440** Fax: 573-767-5378. 8AM-N,1-4PM.

Lincoln Recorder of Deeds 201 Main St, Troy, MO 63379 **636-528-6300** Fax: 636-528-2665. 8AM-4:30PM.

Linn Recorder of Deeds PO Box 151, Linneus, MO 64653 (Courthouse, Rm 204). **660-895-5216** Fax: 660-895-5379. 9AM-N, 1-4:30PM.

Livingston Recorder of Deeds 700 Webster St, Courthouse, #6, Chillicothe, MO 64601 **660-646-0166** 8:30AM-N, 1-4:30PM.

Macon Recorder of Deeds PO Box 382, Macon, MO 63552 (101 E. Washington, Bldg 2). **660-385-2732** Fax: 660-385-4235. 8:30AM-4PM.

Madison Recorder of Deeds PO Box 470, Fredericktown, MO 63645-0470 (Courthouse). **573-783-2102** Fax: 573-783-2715. 8AM-5PM.

Maries Recorder of Deeds PO Box 213, Vienna, MO 65582 (211 Fourth St.). **573-422-3338** Fax: 573-422-3976. 8AM-4PM.

Marion Recorder of Deeds PO Box 392, Palmyra, MO 63461 (100 S. Main Rm 103). **573-769-2550** Fax: 573-769-6012. 8:30AM-5PM.

McDonald Recorder of Deeds PO Box 157, Pineville, MO 64856 (Highway W, Courthouse). **417-223-7523** Fax: 417-223-4125. 8AM-4PM.

Mercer Recorder of Deeds 802 E Main St, Princeton, MO 64673 **660-748-4335** Fax: 660-748-4339. 8:30AM-N, 1-4:30PM.

Miller Recorder of Deeds PO Box 11, Tuscumbia, MO 65082 (256 High St.). **573-369-1935** Fax: 573-369-1939. 8:30AM-4:30PM.

Mississippi Recorder PO Box 369, Charleston, MO 63834 (200 N Main). **573-683-2146** Fax: 573-683-7696. 8AM-5PM. Real Estate Recording records online.

Moniteau Circuit Clerk and Recorder 200 E. Main St, California, MO 65018 **573-796-2071** Fax: 573-796-2591. 8AM-4:30PM.

Monroe Recorder of Deeds PO Box 246, Paris, MO 65275 (300 Main St). **660-327-1131** Fax: 660-327-1130. 8AM-4:30PM.

Montgomery Recorder of Deeds 211 E. 3rd St, Montgomery City, MO 63361 **573-564-3157** 8AM-4:30PM. Death records online.

Morgan Recorder 100 E. Newton St, Courthouse, Versailles, MO 65084 **573-378-4029** Fax: 573-378-6431. 8AM-4:30PM.

New Madrid Recorder of Deeds PO Box 217, New Madrid, MO 63869 (450 Main St). **573-748-5146** 8:30AM-N, 1-4:30PM. Real Estate Recording records online.

Newton Recorder of Deeds PO Box 604, Neosho, MO 64850-0130 (101 S Wood St). **417-451-8224** Fax: 417-451-8273. 8:30AM-5PM. www.ncrecorder.org Deed, Mortgage, UCC, Lien, Vital Statistic records online.

Nodaway Recorder of Deeds 305 N. Main, Rm 104, Maryville, MO 64468 **660-582-5711** Fax: 660-582-5282. 8:30AM-4:30PM.

Oregon Recorder of Deeds PO Box 406, Alton, MO 65606 (Courthouse). **417-778-7460** Fax: 417-778-7206. 8:00AM-4:00PM.

Osage Recorder of Deeds PO Box 825, Linn, MO 65051-0825 (106 E. Main St.). **573-897-3114** Fax: 573-897-4075. 8AM-4:30PM.

Ozark Circuit Clerk & Recorder PO Box 36, Gainesville, MO 65655 (Courthouse). **417-679-4232** Fax: 417-679-4554. 8AM-N 12:30PM-4:30PM.

Pemiscot Recorder of Deeds 610 Ward Ave, #1A, Pemiscot County Courthouse, Caruthersville, MO 63830 **573-333-2204** 8:30AM-4:30PM. Real Estate Recording records online.

Perry Recorder of Deeds 15 W. Ste. Marie St, #1, Perryville, MO 63775 **573-547-1611** Fax: 573-547-3879. 8AM-5PM.

Pettis Recorder of Deeds 415 S. Ohio, Sedalia, MO 65301 **660-826-1136** Fax: 660-829-4479. 8:00AM-5:00PM.

Phelps Recorder of Deeds 200 N Main, Courthouse, Rolla, MO 65401 **573-364-1891** Fax: 573-364-1419. 8AM-5PM. www.phelpscounty.org/cthouse.html

Pike Recorder of Deeds 115 W. Main St, Bowling Green, MO 63334 **573-324-5567** 8AM-4:30PM.

Platte Chief Deputy 415 3rd St, #70, Platte City, MO 64079 **816-858-3323** Fax: 816-858-2379. www.co.platte.mo.us/recorder.html

Polk Recorder of Deeds 102 E. Broadway, Courthouse, Bolivar, MO 65613-1502 **417-326-4924** Fax: 417-326-6898. 8AM-5PM.

Pulaski Recorder of Deeds 301 Historic Route 66 E., Courthouse #202, Waynesville, MO 65583 **573-774-4760** Fax: 573-774-6967. 8AM-4:30PM.

Putnam Recorder of Deeds Courthouse, Rm 202, Unionville, MO 63565-1659 **660-947-2071** Fax: 660-947-2320. 8AM-N, 1-5PM.

Ralls Recorder of Deeds PO Box 444, New London, MO 63459-0444 (311 S. Main St.). **573-985-5631** 8:30AM-N, 1-4:30PM.

Randolph Recorder of Deeds 110 S. Main St., Courthouse, Huntsville, MO 65259 **660-277-4718** Fax: 660-277-3246. 8AM-4PM.

Ray Recorder of Deeds PO Box 167, Richmond, MO 64085 (Courthouse, 2nd Fl). **816-776-4500** 8AM-N, 1-4PM.

Reynolds Recorder of Deeds PO Box 76, Centerville, MO 63633-0076 (Courthouse). **573-648-2494** Fax: 573-648-2503. 8-4PM.

Ripley Recorder of Deeds 100 Courthouse Sq, #3, Doniphan, MO 63935 **573-996-2818** Fax: 573-966-5014.

Saline Recorder of Deeds Courthouse, Rm 206, Marshall, MO 65340 **660-886-2677** Fax: 660-886-2603. 8AM-4:30PM.

Schuyler Recorder of Deeds PO Box 186, Lancaster, MO 63548 (Courthouse, Highway 136 East). **660-457-3784** Fax: 660-457-3016. 8AM-4PM.

Scotland Recorder of Deeds 117 S. Market St, #106, Memphis, MO 63555-1449 **660-465-8605** Fax: 660-465-8673. 8AM-4PM.

Scott Recorder of Deeds PO Box 78, Benton, MO 63736 (Courthouse, Highway 61). **573-545-3551** 8:30AM-5PM. Real Estate Recording records online.

Shannon Recorder of Deeds PO Box 148, Eminence, MO 65466 (Courthouse, 113 Main St.). **573-226-3315** Fax: 573-226-5321. 8AM-12:00-12:30-4:30PM.

Shelby Recorder of Deeds PO Box 176, Shelbyville, MO 63469 (Courthouse). **573-633-2151** Fax: 573-633-1004. 8-4:30PM.

St. Charles Recorder of Deeds PO Box 99, St. Charles, MO 63302-0099 (201 N

Second, Rm 338). **636-949-7505** Fax: 636-949-7512. 8-5. www.saintcharlescounty.org Assessor, Property records online.

St. Clair Recorder of Deeds PO Box 323, Osceola, MO 64776-0493 (Courthouse Sq). **417-646-2950** 8AM-4:30PM.

St. Francois Recorder of Deeds Courthouse, Farmington, MO 63640 **573-756-2323** 8AM-4PM.

St. Genevieve Recorder of Deeds 55 S.3rd St. RM 3, Court House, Ste. Genevieve, MO 63670 **573-883-2706** Fax: 573-883-5312. 8AM-4:30PM.

St. Louis City Recorder of Deeds Tucker & Market Sts, City Hall, Rm 127, St. Louis, MO 63103 **314-622-4328** Fax: 314-622-4175. Property records online.

St. Louis County Recorder of Deeds 41 S. Central Ave, 4th Fl, Clayton, MO 63105 **314-615-2500** Fax: 314-615-4964. 8AM-5PM.

Stoddard Recorder of Deeds PO Box 217, Bloomfield, MO 63825-0217 (Courthouse Sq, Prairie St.). **573-568-3444** Fax: 573-568-2545.

Stone Recorder of Deeds PO Box 18, Galena, MO 65656 (Courthouse Sq). **417-357-6362** Fax: 417-357-8131. 8AM-4PM.

Sullivan Recorder of Deeds Courthouse, Milan, MO 63556 (Courthouse). **660-265-3630** Fax: 660-265-5071. 9AM-N; 1PM-4:30PM.

Taney Recorder of Deeds PO Box 428, Forsyth, MO 65653 (138 Shoit St). **417-546-7234** 8AM-5PM. www.co.taney.mo.us Property records online.

Texas County Recorder of Deeds PO Box 287, Houston, MO 65483 (210 N. Grand). **417-967-3742** Fax: 417-967-4220.

Vernon Recorder of Deeds 100 W. Cherry, Courthouse, Nevada, MO 64772 **417-448-2520** Fax: 417-448-2524. 8:30-N, 1-4:30.

Warren Recorder of Deeds 104 W Boone's Lick Rd., Warrenton, MO 63383 **636-456-9800** 8AM-4:30PM.

Washington Recorder of Deeds 102 N. Missouri St., Potosi, MO 63664 **573-438-5023** Fax: 573-438-7900. 8AM-4:30PM.

Wayne Recorder of Deeds PO Box 78, Greenville, MO 63944 (106 Walnut). **573-224-3041** Fax: 573-224-3015. 8:30AM-N; 1:00PM-4:30PM.

Webster Recorder of Deeds PO Box 546, Marshfield, MO 65706 (Courthouse). **417-859-5882** Fax: 417-468-3843. 8AM-5PM.

Worth Recorder of Deeds PO Box 14, Grant City, MO 64456 (Courthouse on the Sq). **660-564-2484** Fax: 660-564-2432. 8-4PM.

Wright Recorder PO Box 39, Hartville, MO 65667 (Courthouse Sq). **417-741-7322** Fax: 417-741-7504. 8AM-4:30PM.

 # Montana

Organization: 57 counties, 56 recording offices. The recording officer is the County Clerk and Recorder (it is the Clerk of District Court for state tax liens). Yellowstone National Park is considered a county but is not included as a filing location. The entire state is in the Mountain Time Zone (MST).

Real Estate Records: Many Montana counties will perform real estate searches. Search and copy fees vary. Certification usually costs $2.00 per document.

UCC Records: Financing statements are filed at the state level, except for real estate related collateral, which are filed with the Clerk and Recorder. However, prior to 07/2001, consumer goods collateral were also filed at the county and these older records can be searched there. All counties will perform UCC searches. Use search request form UCC-11. Search fees are usually $7.00 per debtor name. Copy fees vary.

Tax Lien Records: Federal tax liens on personal property of businesses are filed with the Secretary of State. Other federal tax liens are filed with the county Clerk and Recorder. State tax liens are filed with the Clerk of District Court. Usually tax liens on personal property filed with the Clerk and Recorder are in the same index with UCC financing statements. Most counties will perform tax lien searches, some as part of a UCC search and others for a separate fee, usually $7.00 per name. Copy fees vary. Other Liens: Mechanics, thresherman, judgment, lis pendens, construction, logger.

Online Access: Search for a for a Montana property owner by name and county on the Montana Cadastral Mapping Project GIS mapping database at http://gis.doa.state.mt.us.

Beaverhead Clerk and Recorder 2 South Pacific, Dillon, MT 59725-2799 **406-683-2642** Fax: 406-683-5776. 8AM-5PM. Property records online.

Big Horn Clerk and Recorder PO Box 908, Hardin, MT 59034 (121 W. 3rd St). **406-665-9730** Fax: 406-665-9738. 8:00AM-5:00PM. Property records online.

Blaine Clerk and Recorder PO Box 278, Chinook, MT 59523-0278 (400 Ohio St). **406-357-3240** Fax: 406-357-2199. 8AM-5PM. Property records online.

Broadwater Clerk and Recorder 515 Broadway, Townsend, MT 59644 **406-266-3443** Fax: 406-266-3674. 8AM-5PM. Property records online.

Carbon Clerk and Recorder PO Box 887, Red Lodge, MT 59068 (17 W. 11th St). **406-446-1220** Fax: 406-446-2640. 7AM-5:30PM. Property records online.

Carter Clerk and Recorder PO Box 315, Ekalaka, MT 59324-0315 (214 Park St). **406-775-8749** Fax: 406-775-8750. 8AM-N, 1-5PM. Property records online.

Cascade Clerk and Recorder PO Box 2867, Great Falls, MT 59403-2867 (415 2nd Ave North). **406-454-6800** Fax: 406-454-6802. 8AM-5PM. www.co.cascade.mt.us Property records online.

Chouteau Clerk and Recorder PO Box 459, Fort Benton, MT 59442-0459 (1308 Franklin). **406-622-5151** Fax: 406-622-3012. 8AM-5PM. Property records online.

Custer Clerk and Recorder 1010 Main St, Miles City, MT 59301-1010 **406-874-3343** Fax: 406-874-3452. 8AM-5PM. Property records online.

Daniels Clerk and Recorder PO Box 247, Scobey, MT 59263 (213 Main St). **406-487-5561** 8AM-5PM. Property records online.

Dawson Clerk and Recorder 207 W. Bell, Glendive, MT 59330 **406-377-3058** Fax: 406-377-1717. www.dawsoncountymontana.org Property records online. 8AM-5PM.

Deer Lodge Clerk and Recorder 800 Main St., Courthouse, Anaconda, MT 59711-2999 **406-563-4060** Fax: 406-563-4001. Property records online.

Fallon Clerk and Recorder PO Box 846, Baker, MT 59313-0846 (10 W. Fallon Ave). **406-778-7106** Fax: 406-778-2048. 8:00AM-5:00PM. Property records online.

Fergus Clerk and Recorder 712 W. Main, Lewistown, MT 59457 **406-538-5242** Fax: 406-538-9023. 8AM-5PM. Property records online.

Flathead Clerk and Recorder 800 S. Main, 2nd Fl, Courthouse, Kalispell, MT 59901-5400 **406-758-5526** Fax: 406-758-5865.

8AM-5PM. www.co.flathead.mt.us Property records online.

Gallatin Clerk and Recorder 311 W. Main, Rm 204, Rm 204, Bozeman, MT 59715 **406-582-3050** Fax: 406-582-3037. 8AM-5PM. www.co.gallatin.mt.us/webtax/default.asp Property, Tax, Treasurer records online.

Garfield Clerk and Recorder PO Box 7, Jordan, MT 59337-0007 (700 Kramer). **406-557-2760** Fax: 406-557-2625. 8AM-5PM. Property records online.

Glacier Clerk and Recorder 512 E. Main, Cut Bank, MT 59427 **406-873-5063 x22** Fax: 406-873-2125. 8AM-5PM. Property records online.

Golden Valley Clerk and Recorder PO Box 10, Ryegate, MT 59074 (107 Kemp). **406-568-2231** Fax: 406-568-2598. 8AM-5PM. Property records online.

Granite Clerk and Recorder PO Box 925, Philipsburg, MT 59858 (220 N. Sansome). **406-859-3771** Fax: 406-859-3817. 8AM-5PM. Property records online.

Hill Clerk and Recorder 315 4th St, Courthouse, Havre, MT 59501 **406-265-5481** Fax: 406-265-2445. 8AM-5PM. http://co.hill.mt.us Property records online.

Jefferson Clerk and Recorder PO Box H, Boulder, MT 59632 (Centennial & Washington). **406-225-4020** Fax: 406-225-

4149. 8AM-N, 1-5PM. http://co.jeffers on.mt.us Property records online.

Judith Basin Clerk and Recorder PO Box 427, Stanford, MT 59479 (Courthouse). **406-566-2277** Fax: 406-566-2211. 8AM-5PM. Property records online.

Lake Clerk and Recorder 106 4th Ave East, Polson, MT 59860 **406-883-7210** Fax: 406-883-7283. 8AM-5PM. www.lakecounty-mt.org Property records online.

Lewis and Clark Clerk and Recorder PO Box 1721, Helena, MT 59624 (316 North Park Ave). **406-447-8337** Fax: 406-457-8598. 8AM-5PM. www.co.lewis-clark.mt.us Grantor/Grantee, Real Estate, Lien, Recording, Property records online.

Liberty Clerk and Recorder PO Box 459, Chester, MT 59522-0459 (101 1st St East). **406-759-5365** Fax: 406-759-5395. 8AM-5PM. Property records online.

Lincoln Recorder 512 California Ave, Libby, MT 59923 **406-293-7781** Fax: 406-293-8577. 8AM-5PM. Property records online.

Madison Clerk and Recorder PO Box 366, Virginia City, MT 59755 (110 W. Wallace). **406-843-4270** 8AM-N,1-5PM. Property records online.

McCone Clerk and Recorder PO Box 199, Circle, MT 59215-0199 (1004 C Ave.). **406-485-3505** Fax: 406-485-2689. 8AM-5PM. Property records online.

Meagher Deputy Clerk & Recording PO Box 309, White Sulphur Springs, MT 59645 (15 W. Main). **406-547-3612** Fax: 406-547-3388. 9AM-4PM. Property records online.

Mineral Clerk and Recorder PO Box 550, Superior, MT 59872-0550 (300 River St). **406-822-3520** Fax: 406-822-3579. 8AM-5PM. Property records online.

Missoula Clerk and Recorder 200 W. Broadway, Missoula, MT 59802-4292 **406-528-4752** Fax: 406-523-2812. 8AM-5PM. www.co.missoula.mt.us Property, Assessor records online.

Musselshell Clerk and Recorder 506 Main St, Courthouse, Roundup, MT 59072 (**406-323-1104** Fax: 406-323-3303. 8AM-5PM. Property records online.

Park Clerk and Recorder 414 E. Callendar, Livingston, MT 59047 **406-222-4110** Fax: 406-222-4199. 8AM-5PM. Property records online.

Petroleum Clerk and Recorder PO Box 226, Winnett, MT 59087 (201 E. Main). **406-429-5311** Fax: 406-429-6328. 8AM-5PM. Property records online.

Phillips Recorder PO Box 360, Malta, MT 59538 (314 S. 2nd Ave West). **406-654-2423** Fax: 406-654-2429. 8AM-5PM. Property records online.

Pondera Clerk and Recorder 20 4th Ave S.W., Conrad, MT 59425 **406-271-4000** Fax: 406-271-4070. 8AM-5PM. http://ponderacountymontana.org

Powder River Clerk and Recorder PO Box 270, Broadus, MT 59317-0270 (Courthouse Sq). **406-436-2361** Fax: 406-436-2151. 8AM-5PM. Property records online.

Powell Clerk and Recorder 409 Missouri Ave, Deer Lodge, MT 59722 **406-846-3680** Fax: 406-846-2784. 8AM-5PM. Property records online.

Prairie Clerk and Recorder PO Box 125, Terry, MT 59349 (217 W. Park). **406-635-5575** Fax: 406-635-5576. Property records online.

Ravalli Clerk and Recorder 215 S 4th St #C, Hamilton, MT 59840 **406-375-6212** Fax: 406-375-6326. 9AM-5PM. www.co.ravalli.mt.us Property records online.

Richland Clerk and Recorder 201 W. Main St, Sidney, MT 59270 **406-433-1708** Fax: 406-433-3731. www.richland.org Property records online. 8AM-5PM.

Roosevelt Clerk and Recorder 400 Second Ave South, Wolf Point, MT 59201 **406-653-6250** Fax: 406-653-6289. 8AM-5PM. Property records online.

Rosebud Clerk and Recorder PO Box 47, Forsyth, MT 59327 (1200 Main St). **406-346-2251** Fax: 406-346-7551. Property records online.

Sanders Clerk and Recorder PO Box 519, Thompson Falls, MT 59873 (1111 Main St.). **406-827-6922** Fax: 406-827-4388. Property records online.

Sheridan Clerk and Recorder 100 W. Laurel Ave, Plentywood, MT 59254 **406-765-3403** Fax: 406-765-2609. 8AM-5PM. www.co.sheridan.mt.us Property records online.

Silver Bow Clerk and Recorder 155 W Granite St #208, Butte, MT 59701 **406-497-6335** Fax: 406-497-6328. www.co.silverbow.mt.us/clerk_and_recorder. htm Property records online.

Stillwater Clerk and Recorder PO Box 149, Columbus, MT 59019 (400 3rd Ave North). **406-322-8000** Fax: 406-322-8007. 8AM-5PM. Property records online.

Sweet Grass Clerk and Recorder PO Box 888, Big Timber, MT 59011 (200 W. 1st Ave.). **406-932-5152** Fax: 406-932-5177. 8AM-5PM. Property records online.

Teton Clerk and Recorder PO Box 610, Choteau, MT 59422 (Courthouse). **406-466-2693** Fax: 406-466-2138. www.tetoncomt.org Property records online.

Toole Clerk and Recorder 226 1st St South, Shelby, MT 59474 **406-424-8300** Fax: 406-424-8301. 8AM-5PM. Property records online.

Treasure Clerk and Recorder PO Box 392, Hysham, MT 59038 (307 Rapelje Ave.). **406-342-5547** Fax: 406-342-5445. 8AM-N,1-5PM. Property records online.

Valley Clerk and Recorder Box 2, 501 Court Sq, Glasgow, MT 59230 **406-228-6220** Fax: 406-228-9027. 8AM-5PM. Property records online.

Wheatland Clerk and Recorder PO Box 1903, Harlowton, MT 59036 (Courthouse). **406-632-4891** Fax: 406-632-4880. 8-12; 1-5. Property records online.

Wibaux Clerk and Recorder PO Box 199, Wibaux, MT 59353-0199 (200 S. Wibaux St). **406-796-2481** Fax: 406-796-2625. 8AM-5PM. Property records online.

Yellowstone Clerk and Recorder PO Box 35001, Billings, MT 59107 (217 N. 27th, Rm 401). **406-256-2785** Fax: 406-256-2736. 8AM-5PM. www.co.yellowst one.mt.us/clerk Assessor, Tax, Grantor/Grantee, Property records online.

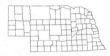

Nebraska

Organization: 93 counties, 109 recording offices. The recording officers are County Clerk (UCC and some state tax liens) and Register of Deeds (real estate and most tax liens). Most counties have a combined Clerk/Register office, which are designated "County Clerk" in this section. Sixteen counties have separate offices for County Clerk and for Register of Deeds - Adams, Cass, Dakota, Dawson, Dodge, Douglas, Gage, Hall, Lancaster, Lincoln, Madison, Otoe, Platte, Sarpy, Saunders, and Scotts Bluff. In combined offices, the Register of Deeds is frequently a different person from the County Clerk. 74 counties are in the Central Time Zone (CST) and 19 are in the Mountain Time Zone (MST).

Real Estate Records: Some Nebraska counties will perform real estate searches, including owner of record from the legal description of the property. Address search requests and make checks payable to the Register of Deeds, not the County Clerk. Fees vary.

UCC Records: Financing statements are filed at the state level, and real estate related collateral are filed with the County Clerk. Previously, financing statements could be filed at any county. All non-real estate UCC filings are entered into a statewide database that is accessible from any county office. All but a few counties will perform UCC searches. Use search request form UCC-11. The UCC statute allows for telephone searching. Search fees are usually $4.50 per debtor name. Copy fees vary.

Tax Lien Records: All federal and some state tax liens are filed with the County Register of Deeds. Some state tax liens on personal property are filed with the County Clerk. Most counties will perform tax lien searches, some as part of a UCC search, and others for a separate fee, usually $4.50 per name in each index. Copy fees vary. Other Liens: Mechanics, artisans, judgment, motor vehicle, agricultural.

Online Access: Nebrask@online offers online access to Secretary of State's UCC database; registration and a usage fee is required. For information, visit www.nebraska.gov/business/egov.phtml. The state treasurer's unclaimed property database is searchable free at www.treasurer.state.ne.us/ie/uphome.asp.

Adams County - County Clerk PO Box 2067, Hastings, NE 68902 (500 W. 4th, #109). **402-461-7107** Fax: 402-461-7185. **Register of Deeds** PO Box 203, Hastings, NE 68902 (500 N Denver). **402-461-7148** Fax: 402-461-7154. www.adamscounty.org

Antelope County Clerk PO Box 26, Neligh, NE 68756-0026 (501 Main St, Rm #6). **402-887-4410** Fax: 402-887-4719. 8:30-5PM.

Arthur County Clerk Box 126, Arthur, NE 69121-0126 (205 Fir St). **308-764-2203** Fax: 308-764-2216. 8-12:00-1-4PM.

Banner County Clerk PO Box 67, Harrisburg, NE 69345 (204 State St). **308-436-5265** Fax: 308-436-4180. 8-N, 1-5PM.

Blaine County Clerk PO Box 136, Brewster, NE 68821 (Lincoln Ave Courthouse). **308-547-2222** Fax: 308-547-2228. 8AM-4PM.

Boone County Clerk 222 S. 4th St, Albion, NE 68620-1247 **402-395-2055** Fax: 402-395-6592. 8:30AM-5PM. www.co.boone.ne.us

Box Butte County Clerk Box 678, Alliance, NE 69301-0678 (5th Box Butte, #203). **308-762-6565** Fax: 308-762-2867. 8AM-4:30PM. www.co.box-butte.ne.us/

Boyd County Clerk PO Box 26, Butte, NE 68722 (Thayer St Courthouse). **402-775-2391** Fax: 402-775-2146. 8:15AM-4PM.

Brown County Clerk 148 W. 4th St., Courthouse, Ainsworth, NE 69210 **402-387-2705** Fax: 402-387-0918. 8AM-5PM.

Buffalo County Register of Deeds PO Box 1270, Kearney, NE 68848-1270 (16th & Central Ave, 1512). **308-236-1239** Fax: 308-236-1291. 8AM-5PM.

Burt County Clerk PO Box 87, Tekamah, NE 68061 (111 N. 13th St.). **402-374-2955** Fax: 402-374-2956. 8AM-4:30PM.

Butler County Deputy Clerk PO Box 289, David City, NE 68632-0289 (451 5th St). **402-367-7430** Fax: 402-367-3329. 8:30AM-5PM. www.nol.org/butler

Cass County - County Clerk 346 Main St., Courthouse, Rm 202, Plattsmouth, NE 68048-1964 **402-296-9300** Fax: 402-296-9332. 8AM-5PM.
Register of Deeds 346 Main St., County Courthouse, Plattsmouth, NE 68048-1964 **402-296-9330** Fax: 402-296-9331. 8AM-5PM. www.cassne.org

Cedar County Clerk PO Box 47, Hartington, NE 68739 (Courthouse). **402-254-7411** Fax: 402-254-7410. www.co.cedar.ne.us

Chase County Clerk Box 1299, Imperial, NE 69033-1299 (921 Broadway). **308-882-5266** Fax: 308-882-5390. 8:00AM-4:00PM.

Cherry County Clerk Box 120, Valentine, NE 69201-0120 (365 N. Main). **402-376-2771** Fax: 402-376-3095. 8:30-N, 1-4:30.

Cheyenne County Clerk PO Box 217, Sidney, NE 69162-0217 (1000 10th Ave).

308-254-2141 Fax: 308-254-5049. 8AM-5PM. www.co.cheyenne.ne.us

Clay County Clerk 111 W. Fairfield St, Clay Center, NE 68933-1499 **402-762-3463** Fax: 402-762-3250. 8:30AM-5PM M-F.

Colfax County Clerk 411 E. 11th St, Schuyler, NE 68661 **402-352-8504** Fax: 402-352-8515. 8:30AM-5PM. www.state.ne.us/colfax/

Cuming County Clerk Box 290, West Point, NE 68788 (200 S. Lincoln). **402-372-6002** Fax: 402-372-6013. www.co.cuming.ne.us

Custer County Clerk 431 S. 10th, Broken Bow, NE 68822 **308-872-5701** 9AM-5PM.

Dakota County Register of Deeds PO Box 511, Dakota City, NE 68731 (1601 Broadway). **402-987-2166** 8AM-4:30PM.

Dawes County Clerk 451 Main St, Courthouse, Chadron, NE 69337-2698 **308-432-0100** Fax: 308-432-5179. 8:30-4:30PM.

Dawson County - County Clerk PO Box 370, Lexington, NE 68850-0370 (700 N. Washington St). **308-324-2127** Fax: 308-324-6106.
Register of Deeds 700 N. Washington, Courthouse, Lexington, NE 68850 (700 N. Washington). **308-324-4271** 8AM-N, 1-5.

Deuel County Clerk PO Box 327, Chappell, NE 69129 (718 3rd St. & Vincent). **308-874-3308** Fax: 308-874-3472. 8AM-4PM.

Dixon County Clerk Box 546, Ponca, NE 68770-0546 (302 Third St.). **402-755-2208** Fax: 402-755-4276. 8AM-4:30PM.

Dodge County - County Clerk 435 North Park, Courthouse - Rm 102, Fremont, NE 68025-4967 **402-727-2767** Fax: 402-727-2764. 8:30AM-4:30PM.
Register of Deeds 435 North Park, Rm 201, Fremont, NE 68025 **402-727-2735** Fax: 402-727-2734. www.registerofdeeds.com Real Estate records online. 8:30AM-4:30PM.

Douglas County - County Clerk 1819 Farnam St., Rm H09, Omaha, NE 68183-0008 **402-444-7159** Fax: 402-444-6456. http://co.douglas.ne.us/explorer.shtml
Register of Deeds 1819 Farnam, Rm H09, Omaha, NE 68183 **402-444-7194** Fax: 402-444-6693. www.co.douglas.ne.us Property, Assessor, Marriage records online. 8-4:30.

Dundy County Clerk PO Box 506, Benkelman, NE 69021-0506 (Courthouse). **308-423-2058** 8AM-5PM.

Fillmore County Register of Deeds PO Box 307, Geneva, NE 68361-0307 (900 G st.). **402-759-4931** Fax: 402-759-4307. 8-5PM. www.fillmorecounty.org/government/gov1.html

Franklin County Clerk PO Box 146, Franklin, NE 68939 (405 15th Ave). **308-425-6202** Fax: 308-425-6093. 8:30-4:30PM.

Frontier County Clerk PO Box 40, Stockville, NE 69042--004 (1 Wellington St). **308-367-8641** Fax: 308-367-8730. 8:30AM-N, 1-5PM. www.co.frontier.ne.us

Furnas County Clerk PO Box 387, Beaver City, NE 68926 (912 R St). **308-268-4145** 8AM-4PM.

Gage County - County Clerk PO Box 429, Beatrice, NE 68310-0429 (612 Grant St). **402-223-1300** Fax: 402-223-1371. 8AM-5PM. www.nol.org/gage/ Property, Assessor records online.
Register of Deeds PO Box 337, Beatrice, NE 68310 (612 Grant St.). **402-223-1361** 8AM-4:30PM.

Garden County Clerk PO Box 486, Oshkosh, NE 69154 (611 Main St). **308-772-3924** Fax: 308-772-4143. 8AM-4PM.

Garfield County Clerk Box 218, Burwell, NE 68823 (250 S. 8th St). **308-346-4161** 9AM-N, 1-5PM.

Gosper County Clerk PO Box 136, Elwood, NE 68937-0136 (507 Smith Ave.). **308-785-2611** Fax: 308-785-2300. 8:30AM-4:30PM. www.co.gosper.ne.us

Grant County Clerk PO Box 139, Hyannis, NE 69350-0139 (Harrison Av Courthouse). **308-458-2488** Fax: 308-458-2485. 8-4PM.

Greeley County Clerk PO Box 287, Greeley, NE 68842 (Courthouse). **308-428-3625** Fax: 308-428-3022.

Hall County - County Clerk 121 S. Pine, Grand Island, NE 68801 **308-385-5080** Fax: 308-385-5084. 8:30AM-5PM.
Register of Deeds PO Box 1692, Grand Island, NE 68802-1692 (121 S. Pine). **308-385-5040** 8:30AM-5PM. www.grand-island.com Real Estate, Grantor/Grantee, Deed, Lien, Judgment records online.

Hamilton County Clerk, Register of Deeds 1111 13th St, #1, Courthouse, Aurora, NE 68818-2017 **402-694-3443** Fax: 402-694-2396. 8AM-5PM. www.co.hamilton.ne.us

Harlan County Clerk PO Box 698, Alma, NE 68920-0698 (706 W. 2nd St). **308-928-2173** Fax: 308-928-2079. 8:30AM-4:30PM.

Hayes County Clerk PO Box 370, Hayes Center, NE 69032-0370 (Troth St Courthouse). **308-286-3413** Fax: 308-286-3208. 8AM-4PM.

Hitchcock County Clerk PO Box 248, Trenton, NE 69044 (229 E. D). **308-334-5646** Fax: 308-334-5398. 8:30AM-4PM. www.co.hitchcock.ne.us

Holt County Clerk PO Box 329, O'Neill, NE 68763-0329 (204 N. 4th). **402-336-2250** Fax: 402-336-1762. 8-4:30PM.

Hooker County Clerk PO Box 184, Mullen, NE 69152 (303 NW 1st). **308-546-2244** Fax: 308-546-2490. 8:30AM-N, 1-4:30PM.

Howard County Clerk PO Box 25, St. Paul, NE 68873 (612 Indian St). **308-754-4343** Fax: 308-754-4125. 8AM-5PM.

Jefferson County Clerk 411 4th, Courthouse, Fairbury, NE 68352-1619 **402-729-5201** Fax: 402-729-2016.

Johnson County Clerk PO Box 416, Tecumseh, NE 68450 (Courthouse). **402-335-6300** Fax: 402-335-6311. 8AM-12:30PM, 1-4:30PM.

Kearney County Clerk PO Box 339, Minden, NE 68959-0339 (424 N. Colorado). **308-832-2723** Fax: 308-832-2729. 8:30-5.

Keith County Clerk PO Box 149, Ogallala, NE 69153 (511 N. Spruce). **308-284-4726** Fax: 308-284-6277.

Keya Paha County Clerk PO Box 349, Springview, NE 68778 (310 Courthouse Dr). **402-497-3791** Fax: 402-497-3799. 8AM-N,1-5PM. www.co.keya-paha.ne.us/

Kimball County Clerk 114 E. Third St, Kimball, NE 69145-1296 **308-235-2241** Fax: 308-235-3654. 8AM-5PM M-Th, 8AM-4PM F. www.co.kimball.ne.us

Knox County Clerk PO Box 166, Center, NE 68724-0166 (206 Main St). **402-288-5604** Fax: 402-288-5605. 8:30AM-4:30PM. www.co.knox.ne.us

Lancaster County - County Clerk 555 S. 10th St, County-City Bldg., Lincoln, NE 68508-2867 **402-441-7482** Fax: 402-441-8728. http://interlinc.ci.lincoln.ne.us Assessor, Recording, Grantor/Grantee, Deed, Judgment, Dog Tag, Treasurer, Marriage, Accident, Parking Ticket, Building Permit records online. 7:30AM-4:30PM.
Register of Deeds 555 S. 10th St, Lincoln, NE 68508 **402-441-7577** Fax: 402-441-7012. www.ci.lincoln.ne.us/cnty/co_agenc.htm Real Estate, Lien, Grantor/Grantee, Assessor, Treasurer records online. 7:30AM-4:30PM.

Lincoln County - County Clerk 301 N. Jeffers, Rm 101, North Platte, NE 69101 **308-534-4350** Fax: 308-535-3522. 9AM-5PM. www.co.lincoln.ne.us
Register of Deeds County Clerk 301 N. Jeffers, Rm 103, North Platte, NE 69101-3931 **308-534-4350** Fax: 308-534-5287. 9-5PM.

Logan County Clerk PO Box 8, Stapleton, NE 69163 (317 Main St). **308-636-2311** 8:30-4:30PM M,T,W,Th; 8:30-4PM F.

Loup County Clerk PO Box 187, Taylor, NE 68879-0187 (Courthouse). **308-942-3135** Fax: 308-942-6015. 8:30AM-N, 1-5PM M,T,W,Th; 8:30AM-N F.

Madison County - County Clerk PO Box 290, Madison, NE 68748-0290 (110 Clara Davis Dr). **402-454-3311 x137** Fax: 402-454-6682. 8:30AM-5PM.
Register of Deeds PO Box 229, Madison, NE 68748 (110 Clara Davis Dr). **402-454-3311** Fax: 402-454-6682. 8:30AM-5PM.

McPherson County Clerk PO Box 122, Tryon, NE 69167-0122 (5th & Anderson). **308-587-2363** Fax: 308-587-2363. 8:30-4:30.

Merrick County Clerk PO Box 27, Central City, NE 68826 (Courthouse). **308-946-2881** Fax: 308-946-2332. 8AM-5PM.

Morrill County Clerk PO Box 610, Bridgeport, NE 69336 (6th & L St). **308-262-0860** Fax: 308-262-1469. 8-4:30PM.

Nance County Clerk PO Box 338, Fullerton, NE 68638 (209 Esther St). **308-536-2331** Fax: 308-536-2742.

Nemaha County Clerk 1824 N St, Courthouse, Auburn, NE 68305-2399 **402-274-4213** Fax: 402-274-4389. 8AM-5PM.

Nuckolls County Clerk PO Box 366, Nelson, NE 68961-0366 (150 S. Main). **402-225-4361** Fax: 402-225-4301. 8:30AM-4:30PM.

Otoe County - County Clerk PO Box 249, Nebraska City, NE 68410 (1021 Central Ave). **402-873-9505** Fax: 402-873-9506. 8-4:30PM. www.co.otoe.ne.us/deeds.html
Register of Deeds 1021 Central Ave., Rm 203, Nebraska City, NE 68410 **402-873-9530** Fax: 402-873-9507. 8AM-4:30PM.

Pawnee County Clerk PO Box 431, Pawnee City, NE 68420 (625 6th St). **402-852-2962** Fax: 402-852-2963. 8AM-4PM.

Perkins County Clerk PO Box 156, Grant, NE 69140-0156 (200 Lincoln Ave). **308-352-4643** Fax: 308-352-2455. 8AM-4PM.

Phelps County Clerk PO Box 404, Holdrege, NE 68949-0404 (Courthouse). **308-995-4469** Fax: 308-995-4368. 9AM-5PM.

Pierce County Clerk 111 W. Court, Courthouse - Rm 1, Pierce, NE 68767-1224 **402-329-4225** Fax: 402-329-6439. 8:30AM-4:30PM. www.co.pierce.ne.us

Platte County - County Clerk 2610 14th St, Columbus, NE 68601 **402-563-4904** Fax: 402-564-4614. www.plattecounty.net Warrant records online. 8AM-5PM.
Register of Deeds 2610 14th St, Columbus, NE 68601 **402-563-4911** 8AM-5PM.

Polk County Clerk PO Box 276, Osceola, NE 68651-0276 (Courthouse Sq). **402-747-5431** Fax: 402-747-2656. 8AM-5PM.

Red Willow County Clerk 502 Norris Ave, McCook, NE 69001 **308-345-1552** Fax: 308-345-4460. www.nol.org/red_willow 8-4PM.

Richardson County Clerk 1700 Stone St., Courthouse, Falls City, NE 68355 **402-245-**

2911 Fax: 402-245-2946. 8:30-5PM. www.nol.org/richardson
Rock County Clerk PO Box 367, Bassett, NE 68714 (400 State St). **402-684-3933** 9AM-N, 1-5PM.

Saline County Real Estate-County Clerk PO Box 865, Wilber, NE 68465 (215 S. Court). **402-821-2374** Fax: 402-821-3381. 8AM-5PM.

Sarpy County - County Clerk 1210 Golden Gate Drive, #1118, Papillion, NE 68046-2895 (**402-593-2114** Fax: 402-593-4360. 8AM-4:45PM M,T,Th,F; 8AM-6PM W. www.sarpy.com Real Estate records online.
Register of Deeds 1210 Golden Gate Drive #1109, Papillion, NE 68046 **402-593-2186** Fax: 402-593-2338. 8AM-5PM.

Saunders County - County Clerk PO Box 61, Wahoo, NE 68066-0187 (433 N. Chestnut). **402-443-8101** Fax: 402-443-5010.
Register of Deeds PO Box 184, Wahoo, NE 68066 (5th & Chestnut). **402-443-8111** Fax: 402-443-5010. 8AM-5PM.

Scotts Bluff County - County Clerk 1825 10th St, Admin. Office Bldg., Gering, NE 69341 **308-436-6601** Fax: 308-436-3178.
Register of Deeds 1825 10th St, Admin. Office Bldg., Gering, NE 69341 **308-436-6607** Fax: 308-436-6609. 8AM-4:30PM.

Seward County Clerk PO Box 190, Seward, NE 68434-0190 (529 Seward St). **402-643-2883** Fax: 402-643-9243. 8AM-5PM. http://connectseward.org/cs/

Sheridan County Clerk PO Box 39, Rushville, NE 69360 (301 E. 2nd St). **308-327-5650** 8:30AM-4:30PM.

Sherman County Clerk PO Box 456, Loup City, NE 68853-0456 (630 "O" St). **308-745-1513** Fax: 308-745-1820.

Sioux County Clerk PO Box 158, Harrison, NE 69346 (325 Main St). **308-668-2443** Fax: 308-668-2443. 8AM-4:30PM.

Stanton County Register of Deeds PO Box 347, Stanton, NE 68779-0347 (804 Ivy St). **402-439-2222** Fax: 402-439-2200. 8:30-4:30.

Thayer County Clerk PO Box 208, Hebron, NE 68370 (225 N. 4th). **402-768-6126** 8AM-4:30PM.

Thomas County Clerk PO Box 226, Thedford, NE 69166-0226 (503 Main St). **308-645-2261** Fax: 308-645-2623. 8AM-N, 1-4PM M-Th; 8AM-N, 1-3PM F.

Thurston County Clerk PO Box G, Pender, NE 68047 (106 S. 5th St). **402-385-2343** Fax: 402-385-3544. 8:30AM-5PM.

Valley County Clerk 125 S. 15th, Ord, NE 68862-1499 **308-728-3700** 8AM-5PM.

Washington County Clerk PO Box 466, Blair, NE 68008 (1555 Colfax St). **402-426-6822** Fax: 402-426-6825. 8AM-4:30PM.

Wayne County Clerk PO Box 248, Wayne, NE 68787-0248 (510 Pearl St). **402-375-2288** Fax: 402-375-2288. 8:30AM-5PM. http://county.waynene.org Sheriff Sale, Warrant List records online.

Webster County Clerk PO Box 250, County Clerk Office, Red Cloud, NE 68970 (621 N. Cedar). **402-746-2716** Fax: 402-746-2710. 8:30AM-4:30PM.

Wheeler County Clerk PO Box 127, Bartlett, NE 68622 (3rd and Main Sts). **308-654-3235** Fax: 308-654-3470. 9AM-N, 1-5PM.

York County Clerk 510 Lincoln Ave., Courthouse, York, NE 68467 **402-362-7759** Fax: 402-362-2651.

Nevada

Organization: 16 counties and one independent city, 17 recording offices. The recording officer is the County Recorder. Carson City has a separate filing office. The entire state is in the Pacific Time Zone (PST).

Real Estate Records: Most counties will not provide real estate searches. Copies cost $1.00 per page and certification fees are usually $4.00 per document.

UCC Records: Financing statements are filed at the state level, except for real estate related collateral, which are filed with the County Recorder. However, prior to 07/2001, consumer goods and farm collateral were also filed at the County Recorder and these older records can be searched there. All recording offices will perform UCC searches. Search fees are $15.00 per debtor name using the approved UCC-3 request form and $20.00 using a non-standard form. Copies cost $1.00 per page.

Tax Lien Records: Federal tax liens on personal property of businesses are filed with the Secretary of State. Federal tax liens on personal property of individuals are filed with the County Recorder. Although not called state tax liens, employment withholding judgments have the same effect and are filed with the County Recorder. Most counties will provide tax lien searches for a fee of $15.00 per name - $20.00 if the standard UCC request form is not used. Other Liens: Mechanics

Online Access: Clark County has many searchable databases online. A private company, GoverNet, offers online access to Assessor, Treasurer, Recorder and other county databases. Registration is required, sliding monthly and per-hit fees apply. Counties online are Churchill, Clark, Elko, Esmeralda, Eureka, Humboldt, Lander, Lyon, Mineral, Nye, Pershing, Storey, Washoe, and White Pine. Warning: not all counties provide update information consistently. System includes access to Secretary of State's Corporation, Partnership, UCC, Fictitious Name, and Federal Tax Lien records. For more information, visit www.governet.net/SurfNV/ or call 208-522-1225.

Carson City Recorder 885 E. Musser St, #1028, Carson City, NV 89701-4775 **775-887-2260** Fax: 775-887-2146. 8AM-5PM. www.carson-city.nv.us/clerk Assessor, Recorder, Treasurer, Real Estate, Marriage, Vital Statistic records online.

Churchill County Recorder 155 N. Taylor, #131, Fallon, NV 89406-2748 **775-423-6001** Fax: 775-423-8933. 8AM-5PM. www.churchillcounty.org Assessor, Treasurer, Recording, Grantor/Grantee, Deed, Real Estate, Property Tax records online.

Clark County Recorder PO Box 551510, Las Vegas, NV 89155-1510 (500 S. Grand Central Pkwy, 2nd Fl). **702-455-4336** Fax: 702-455-5644. Real Estate, Lien, Deed, UCC, Vitals, Marriage, Property Assessor, Fictitious name, Business license, Inmate records online. www.co.clark.nv.us/recorder/recindex.htm

Douglas County Recorder PO Box 218, Minden, NV 89423 (1616 8th St). **775-782-9025** Fax: 775-783-6413. 9AM-5PM. http://recorder.co.douglas.nv.us Assessor, Real Estate, Property Tax, Recorder, Deed records online.

Elko County Recorder 571 Idaho St., Rm 103, Elko, NV 89801-3770 **775-738-6526** Fax: 775-738-3299. 9AM-5PM. Assessor,

Treasurer, Recording, Marriage, Personal Property, Property Tax records online.

Esmeralda County Recorder PO Box 458, Goldfield, NV 89013 (233 Crook St). **775-485-6337** Fax: 775-485-3524. 8AM-5PM. Assessor, Treasurer, Recording records online.

Eureka County Recorder PO Box 556, Eureka, NV 89316 (10 S. Main St). **775-237-5263** Fax: 775-237-5614. 8AM-N, 1-5PM. www.co.eureka.nv.us Assessor, Treasurer, Recorder, Deed, Lien, Judgment, Vital Statistic records online.

Humboldt County Recorder 25 W. 4th St, Winnemucca, NV 89445 **775-623-6414** Fax: 775-623-6337. 8AM-5PM. www.hcnv.us Inmate records online.

Lander County Recorder 315 S. Humboldt, Battle Mountain, NV 89820 **775-635-5173** Fax: 775-635-8272. 8AM-5PM. Assessor, Recorder records online.

Lincoln County Recorder PO Box 218, Pioche, NV 89043 (1 Main St). **775-962-5495** Fax: 775-962-5180.

Lyon County Recorder 27 S Main St, Yerington, NV 89447-0927 **775-463-6581** Fax: 775-463-6585. 8AM-5PM. www.lyon-county.org Assessor, Recorder, Treasurer records online.

Mineral County Recorder PO Box 1447, Hawthorne, NV 89415-1447 (105 South A St). **775-945-3676** Fax: 775-945-1749. 8AM-5PM. Assessor, Treasurer, Recording records online.

Nye County Recorder PO Box 1111, Tonopah, NV 89049-1111 (101 Radar Rd.). **775-482-8116** Fax: 775-482-8111. Assessor, Treasurer, Recording, Deed, Pahrump Business records online.

Pershing County Recorder PO Box 736, Lovelock, NV 89419-0736 (398 Main St). **775-273-2408** Fax: 775-273-1039. 8-5. Assessor, Treasurer, Recording records online.

Storey County Recorder PO Box 493, Virginia City, NV 89440 (B St Courthouse). **775-847-0967** Fax: 775-847-1009. 9-5PM. Assessor, Treasurer, Recording records online.

Washoe County Recorder PO Box 11130, Reno, NV 89520-0027 (1001 E. 9th St). **775-328-3661** Fax: 775-325-8010. 8AM-5PM. www.co.washoe.nv.us/recorder Assessor, Treasurer, Recording, Grantor/Grantee, Real Estate, Inmate records online.

White Pine County Recorder 801 Clark St, #1, Ely, NV 89301 **775-289-4567** Fax: 775-289-9686. 9AM-5PM. Assessor, Recorder records online.

New Hampshire

Organization: 238 cities/towns and 10 counties, 10 recording offices and 242 UCC filing offices. The recording officers are Town/City Clerk (UCC) and Register of Deeds (real estate only). Each town/city profile indicates the county in which the town/city is located. Be careful to distinguish the following names that are identical for both a town/city and a county - Grafton, Hillsborough, Merrimack, Strafford, and Sullivan. Many towns are so small that their mailing addresses are within another town. The following unincorporated towns do not have a Town Clerk, so all liens are located at the corresponding county: Cambridge (Coos), Dicksville (Coos), Green's Grant (Coos), Hale's Location (Carroll), Millsfield (Coos), and Wentworth's Location (Coos). The entire state is in the Eastern Time Zone (EST).

Real Estate Records: Real estate transactions are recorded at the county level, and property taxes are handled at the town/city level. Local town real estate ownership and assessment records are usually located at the Selectman's Office. Each town/city profile indicates the county in which the town/city is located. Most counties will not perform real estate searches. Copy fees vary. Certification fees generally are $2.00 per document.

UCC Records: This was a dual filing state until Revised Article 9. Previously, financing statements were filed at the state level and with the Town/City Clerk, except for consumer goods and farm related collateral, which were filed only with the Town/City Clerk, and real estate related collateral, which was and still is filed with the county Register of Deeds. Most recording offices will perform UCC searches. Use search request form UCC-11. Search fees are usually $5.00 per debtor name using the standard UCC-11 request form and $7.00 using a non-standard form. Copy fees are usually $.75 per page.

Tax Lien Records: Federal and state tax liens on personal property of businesses are filed with the Secretary of State. Other federal and state tax liens on personal property are filed with the Town/City Clerk. Federal and state tax liens on real property are filed with the county Register of Deeds. There is wide variation in indexing and searching practices among the recording offices. Where a search fee of $7.00 is indicated, it refers to a non-standard request form such as a letter. Other Liens: Condominium, town tax, mechanics, welfare.

Online Access: The New Hampshire Counties Registry of Deeds website allows free searching of real estate-related records for Belknap, Cheshire, Hillsborough and Strafford counties at www.nhdeeds.com. Also, a private vendor has placed on the Internet the assessor records from a number of towns. Visit http://data.visionappraisal.com.

Acworth Town Clerk PO Box 37, Town Clerk, Acworth, NH 03601 **603-835-6879** 6:30-8PM M-W; 9-11AM Sat.

Albany Town Clerk 19728 NH Route 16, Conway, NH 03818 **603-447-2877** Fax: 603-447-2877. 8AM-N M; 4PM-7PM W; 9AM-N Sat.

Alexandria Town Clerk 45 A Washburn Rd, Alexandria, NH 03222 (**603-744-3288** Fax: 603-744-8577. 8AM-5:30PM M T F, Noon-7PM Th, Closed Wed.

Allenstown Town Clerk 16 School St, Allenstown, NH 03275 **603-485-4276** Fax: 603-485-8669. M 8:30-1 & 3-7; T/W 8:30-1, 3-5; Th 8:30-3. www.allenstown.org

Alstead Town Clerk Box 65, Alstead, NH 03602 (15 Mechanic St.). **603-835-2242** Fax: 603-835-2986. 8AM-4PM,Closed F.

Alton Town Clerk Box 637, Alton, NH 03809 (1 Monument Sq.). **603-875-2101** Fax: 603-875-3894. 8:30AM-4:30PM.

Amherst Town Clerk PO Box 960, Amherst, NH 03031 (2 Main St). **603-673-6041** Fax: 603-673-6794. 9AM-3PM M-F; 5:30-8PM Mon. Property Assessor records online.

Andover Town Clerk PO Box 61, Andover, NH 03216 (31 School St). **603-735-5332** Fax: 603-735-6975. 10AM-1PM T Th, 6:30PM-8:30PM W, 9AM-N Sat.

Antrim Town Clerk PO Box 517, Antrim, NH 03440 (66 Main St.). **603-588-6785** Fax: 603-588-2969. 8AM-4PM M-Th.

Ashland Town Clerk PO Box 517, Ashland, NH 03217 (20 Highland St). **603-968-4432** Fax: 603-968-3776. 8AM-4PM. Assessor records online.

Atkinson Town Clerk 21 Academy Ave, Town Hall, Atkinson, NH 03811-2204 **603-362-4920** Fax: 603-362-5305. 8:30AM-6:30PM M; 8:30AM-4PM T-F. www.town-atkinsonnh.com Property, Real Estate Transfer records online.

Auburn Town Clerk PO Box 309, Auburn, NH 03032-0309 (47 Chester Rd). **603-483-2281** Fax: 603-483-0518. 8AM-2PM, M,W,TH; 8AM-12PM, F; 6-8PM M Eve.

Barnstead Town Clerk PO Box 11, Center Barnstead, NH 03225 (108 S. Barnstead Rd.). **603-269-4631** Fax: 603-269-4072.

Barrington Town Clerk 41 Province Lane, Barrington, NH 03825 **603-664-5476** Fax: 603-664-5179. 8AM-4:15PM M T TH; 4-6PM W; 8AM-Noom F. Property, Deed, Grantor/Grantee records online.

Bartlett Town Clerk RFD 1 Box 50, Intervale, NH 03845 (Town Hall Rd). **603-356-2300** Fax: 603-356-2300. 8AM-4PM M-W & F; 8-11AM Sat.

Bath Town Clerk PO Box 165, Bath, NH 03740 (West Bath Rd). **603-747-2454** Fax: 603-747-0497. 8AM-12, 1PM-4PM M,W,Th; 8AM-12, 5:30-8:30PM T.

Bedford Town Clerk 24 N. Amherst Rd, Bedford, NH 03110 **603-472-3550** Fax: 603-472-4573. 8AM-4:30PM M,W,Th,F; 7:00-4:30PM Tu. www.ci.bedford.nh.us Assessor records online.

Belknap County Register of Deeds PO Box 1343, Laconia, NH 03247-1343 (64 Court St.). **603-527-5420** Fax: 603-527-5429. 8AM-4PM. www.nhdeeds.com Real Estate, Deed, Mortgage, Lien records online.

Belmont Town Clerk PO Box 310, Belmont, NH 03220 (143 Main St). **603-267-8302** Fax: 603-267-8305. 7:30AM-4PM. Assessor, Property records online.

Bennington Town Clerk 7 School St, #101, Bennington, NH 03442 **603-588-2189** Fax: 603-588-8005. 9AM-N M & S.;8:30AM-12:30PM Tu.; 4:30-8:30PM Th.. http://townofbennington.com/

Benton Town Clerk 110 Flanders Rd, Benton, NH 03785-6402 (547 Bradley Hill Rd.). **603-787-6541** Fax: 603-787-6646. 6:30-8:30PM Monday night.

Berlin City Clerk 168 Main St, City Hall, Berlin, NH 03570 **603-752-2340** Fax: 603-752-1654. 8:30-12:00-1-4:30.

Bethlehem Town Clerk PO Box 189, Bethlehem, NH 03574 (2155 Main St.). **603-869-2293** Fax: 603-869-2280. 4:30-7PM M,W; 9AM-1PM T,Th.

Boscawen Town Clerk 116 N. Main St., Boscawen, NH 03303 **603-753-9188** Fax:

603-753-9183. M, Th 8am-11am; 12-4:30; T & W 8-11am; 12-6:30pm.

Bow Town Clerk 10 Grandview Rd, Bow, NH 03304-3410 **603-225-2683** Fax: 603-225-5428. 7:30AM-4:10PM. Property Assessor records online.

Bradford Town Clerk/Tax Collector PO Box 607, Bradford, NH 03221-0607 (75 Main St). **603-938-2288** Fax: 603-938-2094. N-7PM Mon.; 7AM-5PM T; 8-5PM Fri..

Brentwood Town Clerk 1 Dalton Rd, Brentwood, NH 03833 **603-642-6400 x14** Fax: 603-642-6310. 9AM-4:30PM M-F; 7-9PM T; 9AM-N Sat Sept-May.

Bridgewater Town Clerk PO Box 419, Plymouth, NH 03264 (955 River Rd.). **603-968-7911** Fax: 603-968-3506. 6PM-8:30PM T- W; 8:30-10AM 3rd Sat.

Bristol Town Clerk 230 Lake St, #A, Bristol, NH 03222-1120 **603-744-8478** Fax: 603-744-2521. 8:30AM-4:00PM.

Brookfield Town Clerk PO Box 756, Sanbornville, NH 03872 (2 Piney Rd., Cedar Park). **603-522-3231** Fax: 603-522-6245. 1-8PM M.

Brookline Town Clerk PO Box 336, Brookline, NH 03033 (Main St). **603-673-8855 x218** Fax: 603-673-8136. 8AM-2PM M-F, 6PM-9PM W, 9AM-N Last SAT of month. www.brookline.nh.us

Campton Town Clerk 1307 NH Rte 175, Campton, NH 03223 **603-726-3223** Fax: 603-726-9817. 9AM-3:30PM.

Canaan Town Clerk PO Box 38, Canaan, NH 03741-0038 (1169 US Rte 4). **603-523-7106** Fax: 603-523-4526. 9AM-12 1PM-4PM M,W,F; 9AM-12 T TH. http://town.canaan.nh.us

Candia Town Clerk 74 High St, Candia, NH 03034-2713 **603-483-5573** Fax: 603-483-0252. 8:30-11 M, 5PM-8PM T TH, 9AM-1PM W F. Assessor records online.

Canterbury Town Clerk PO Box 500, Canterbury, NH 03224 (10 Hackleboro Rd). **603-783-9955** Fax: 603-783-0501. 10AM-2PM M; 11AM-6PM T; 5-8:30PM Th.

Carroll County Register of Deeds PO Box 163, Ossipee, NH 03864-0163 (Route 171, 95 Water Village Rd.). **603-539-4872** Fax: 603-539-5239. 9AM-5PM.

Carroll Town Clerk PO Box 88, Twin Mountain, NH 03595-0088 (School Rd). **603-846-5494** Fax: 603-846-5713. 9AM-N M; 9AM-3PM T,W,Th.

Center Harbor Town Clerk PO Box 140, Center Harbor, NH 03226 (Main St). **603-253-4561** Fax: 603-253-8420. 9AM-3PM.

Charlestown Town Clerk PO Box 834, Charlestown, NH 03603 (26 Railroad St). **603-826-5821** Fax: 603-826-5181. 8AM-1PM, 1:30-4PM (til 6PM on Fri)

Chatham Town Clerk 1681 Main Rd, Chatham, NH 03813 (Route 113 North Chatham). **603-694-2043** Fax: 603-694-2043. 5-7PM T.

Cheshire County Register of Deeds PO Box 584, Keene, NH 03431 (33 West St). **603-352-0403** Fax: 603-352-7678. 8:30AM-4:30PM. www.nhdeeds.com Real Estate, Deed, Mortgage, Lien records online.

Chester Town Clerk PO Box 275, Chester, NH 03036 (1 Chester St). **603-887-3636** 8AM-12:30PM M,T,Th,F; 8AM-4PM W.

Chesterfield Town Clerk PO Box 64, Chesterfield, NH 03443-0064 (504 Route 63). **603-363-8071** Fax: 603-363-8047. 9AM-5:30PM M,W; 5-8PM Th. www.nhchesterfield.com

Chichester Town Clerk 54 Main St., Chichester, NH 03258 (54 Main St.). **603-798-5808** Fax: 603-798-3170.

Claremont City Clerk 58 Tremont Sq, City Hall, Finance Office, Claremont, NH 03743 **603-542-7001** Fax: 603-542-7014. 9AM-12:30PM, 1:30-5. www.claremontnh.com

Clarksville Town Clerk 408 NH Route 145, Clarksville, NH 03592 **603-246-7751** Fax: 603-246-3480. 1-6:30PM M; 9AM-4PM T, Th; 12:30-6:30PM W; 9AM-N F.

Colebrook Town Assessor 10 Bridge St, Colebrook, NH 03576 **603-237-9173** Fax: 603-237-5086. 8AM-4PM. www.colebrook-nh.com

Columbia Town Clerk PO Box 157, Colebrook, NH 03576 (1919 US Rte 3). **603-237-5255** Fax: 603-237-8270. 10AM-5PM, M,W; 8AM-3PM, T, F.

Concord City Clerk 41 Green St, Rm 2, Concord, NH 03301-4255 **603-225-8500** Fax: 603-225-8592. www.onconcord.com Property Assessor records online. 8AM-4:30PM.

Conway Town Clerk 1634 E. Main St., Center Conway, NH 03813 **603-447-3822** Fax: 603-447-1348. 9AM-5PM. http://conwaynh.org

Coos County Register of Deeds 55 School St, #103, Coos County Courthouse, Lancaster, NH 03584 **603-788-2392** Fax: 603-788-4291. 8AM-4PM.

Cornish Town Clerk PO Box 183, Cornish Flat, NH 03746 (488 Townhouse Rd.). **603-675-5207** Fax: 603-675-5605. 9MA-N M Th F; 4PM-7PM M TH;.

Croydon Town Clerk 879 NH Rte 10, Newport, NH 03773 **603-863-7830** Fax: 603-863-2601. 9AM-1 M-Th; 6-8PM W&Th.

Dalton Town Clerk 741 Dalton Rd, Dalton, NH 03598 **603-837-2096** Fax: 603-837-9642. 11AM-5:45PM M; 7AM-5PM T,W,Th.

Danbury Town Clerk 23 High St., Danbury, NH 03230 **603-768-5448** Fax: 603-768-3313. 8AM-4PM M&W; 1-7PM T.

Danville Town Clerk PO Box 11, Danville, NH 03819 (127 Pine St.). **603-382-8253** Fax: 603-382-3363. 9AM-1PM M; 4-8PM T & Th; 8:30AM-2:30PM W.

Deerfield Town Clerk PO Box 159, Deerfield, NH 03037 (8 Raymond Rd). **603-463-8811** Fax: 603-463-2820. 8AM-2:30PM T-F; 8AM-7PM M. www.ci.deerfield-nh.us

Deering Town Clerk 762 Deering Ctr Rd., Deering, NH 03244 **603-464-3224** Fax: 603-464-3804. www.deering.nh.us

Derry Town Clerk 14 Manning St, Derry, NH 03038 (**603-432-6105** Fax: 603-432-6131. 7AM-4PM M-F; 7AM-7PM W. www.derry.nh.us Assessor, Property, Sale records online.

Dorchester Town Clerk 368 N Dorchester Rd, Dorecester, NH 03266 **603-786-9076** 9-11AM M; 3-6PM W; 9-11AM last Sat..

Dover City Clerk 288 Central Ave, City Hall, Dover, NH 03820 **603-743-6021** Fax: 603-516-6666. 8AM-4PM. www.ci.dover.nh.us Property, Deed, Grantor/Grantee online.

Dublin Town Clerk Box 62, Dublin, NH 03444 (Main St, Town Hall). **603-563-8859** Fax: 603-563-9221. 8:30AM-4PM M-Th.

Dummer Town Clerk 1420 East Side River Rd., Dummer, NH 03588 **603-449-3408** Fax: 603-449-3349. By appointment.

Dunbarton Town Clerk 1011 School St., Dunbarton, NH 03045 **603-774-3547** Fax: 603-774-5541. 8:30AM-4PM.

Durham Town Clerk/Tax Collector 15 Newmarket Rd, Town Hall, Durham, NH 03824 **603-868-5577** Fax: 603-868-8033. www.ci.durham.nh.us/DEPARTMENTS/town_clerk/clerk.html Property, Deed, Grantor/Grantee, Assessor records online. 8-5PM.

East Kingston Town Clerk PO Box 249, East Kingston, NH 03827-0249 (24 Depot Rd.). **603-642-8794** Fax: 603-642-8406. M 6-8PM; T-F 8AM-2PM; Thur eve. 6-8PM.

Easton Town Clerk PO Box 741, Franconia, NH 03580 (1060 Easton Valley Rd). **603-823-8017** Fax: 603-823-7780. 10AM-N M; 4PM-6PM Th.

Eaton Town Clerk Box 118, Eaton Center, NH 03832 (Rt. 153). **603-447-2840** Fax: 603-447-2560. 9AM-11AM, M; 7PM-9PM T or by appointment.

Effingham Town Clerk PO Box 117, Effingham, NH 03882 (30 Townhouse Rd). **603-539-7551** Fax: 603-539-7799. 8AM-N, 3PM-7PM T; 8AM-5PM TH; 8AM-N Sat.

Ellsworth Town Clerk 12 Ellsworth Pond Rd, c/o Donna O'Brien, Plymouth, NH 03223 **603-726-3551** Fax: 603-726-8994. by appointment only.

Enfield Town Clerk PO Box 373, Enfield, NH 03748-0373 (23 Main St). **603-632-5001** Fax: 603-632-5182. 8:30-3:30PM M-W & F; 9:30AM-4:30PM T. www.enfield.nh.us

Epping Town Clerk 157 Main St, Epping, NH 03042 **603-679-8288** Fax: 603-679-3002.

Epsom Town Clerk PO Box 10, Epsom, NH 03234 (27 Black Hall Rd). **603-736-4825** Fax: 603-736-8539. 8-1PM;4:30-6:30PM, M;10-3PM T; 8-3PM TH;8-3PM F.

Errol Town Clerk PO Box 100, Errol, NH 03579 (Town Hall). **603-482-3351** Fax: 603-482-3804. 9AM-11AM, M;5PM-7:30PM, T; 8:30AM-11AM, TH.

Exeter Town Clerk 10 Front St, Exeter, NH 03833 **603-778-0591** Fax: 603-772-4709. 8:30-3:30www.exeternh.org/tnclk/index.html

Farmington Town Clerk 41 S Main St, Town Hall, Farmington, NH 03835 **603-755-3657** Fax: 603-755-9128. 8:30-5PM M-W, 8:30-7PM Th, 8:30-12:30 PM F. Property, Deed, Grantor/Grantee records online.

Fitzwilliam Town Clerk PO Box 504, Fitzwilliam, NH 03447 (13 NH Rte. 119 West). **603-585-7791** Fax: 603-585-7744.

Francestown Town Clerk PO Box 67, Francestown, NH 03043-0067 (27 Main St). **603-547-6251** Fax: 603-547-2622. 8AM-N M-Th; 6-8PM M.

Franconia Town Clerk PO Box 900, Franconia, NH 03580 (421 Main St.). **603-**

823-5237 Fax: 603-823-5581. 8AM-2PM Tues.; 1-7PM Th.

Franklin City Clerk 316 Central St, Franklin, NH 03235 **603-934-3109** Fax: 603-934-7413. 8AM-5PM.

Freedom Town Clerk PO Box 457, Freedom, NH 03836 (33 Old Portland Rd). **603-539-6323** Fax: 603-539-8270. 6:30-8PM Mon & Wed; 9AM-N Sat..

Fremont Town Clerk PO Box 120, Fremont, NH 03044 (295 Main St). **603-895-8693** Fax: 603-895-3149. 9:30AM-N, 1-4PM T,W,F; 3-8PM Th; 3rd Sat 9:30AM-N. http://fremont.nh.gov

Gilford Town Clerk 47 Cherry Valley Rd, Town Hall, Gilford, NH 03246 **603-527-4713** Fax: 603-527-4719.

Gilmanton Town Clerk/Tax Collector PO Box 550, Gilmanton, NH 03237-0550 (503 Province Rd, Academy Bldg.). **603-267-6726** Fax: 603-267-6701. 9AM-N 7-8:30PM M; 9AM-4PM W F; 9AM-N TH.

Gilsum Town Clerk PO Box 36, Gilsum, NH 03448 (650 Route 10). **603-357-0320** Fax: 603-352-0845. 6-8PM Tu; 8-N Sat..

Goffstown Town Clerk 16 Main St, Goffstown, NH 03045 **603-497-3613** Fax: 603-497-8993. 8:30AM-4:30PM M,T,F; 8:30AM-N W; 8:30AM-6PM Th. www.ci.goffstown.nh.us

Gorham Town Clerk 20 Park St, Gorham, NH 03581-1694 **603-466-2744** Fax: 603-466-3100. 8:30AM-N, 1-5PM M,W,F; 8:30-1PM, 2-5PM T,Th. www.gorhamnh.org

Goshen Town Clerk PO Box 58, Goshen, NH 03752 (54 Mill Village Rd N). **603-863-5655** Fax: 603-863-6139. 8:30AM-N, 1-5PM M,W,F.

Grafton County Registry of Deeds 3785 Dartmouth College Hwy, Box 2, North Haverhill, NH 03774-9700 **603-787-6921** Fax: 603-787-2363. 7:30AM-4:30PM. Real Estate, Lien records online.

Grafton Town Clerk PO Box 297, Grafton, NH 03240 (Library Rd.). **603-523-7270** Fax: 603-523-4397.

Grantham Town Clerk PO Box 135, Grantham, NH 03753-0135 (34 Dunbar Hill Rd). **603-863-5608** Fax: 603-863-4499. 7:30AM-4:30PM M-Th; 7-9PM Tu-W. http://granthamnh.net/

Greenfield Town Clerk PO Box 256, Greenfield, NH 03047 (Francestown Rd). **603-547-2782** Fax: 603-547-3004. 6AM-7:30PM M-Th; 2nd & 4th Sat. 9AM-N. http://greenfieldnh.org

Greenland Town Clerk PO Box 100, Greenland, NH 03840-0100 (575 Portsmouth Ave). **603-431-7111** Fax: 603-430-3761. 12:00-8PM,M; 9AM-4:30PM T-F. Property Assessor records online.

Greenville Town Clerk PO Box 354, Greenville, NH 03048-0354 (46 Main St). **603-878-4155** Fax: 603-878-4951. 10AM-12:00-1-4PM,T,TH; 10AM-N,1-3PM W.

Groton Town Clerk 63-1 N. Groton Rd, Groton, NH 03241 **603-744-8849** 10AM-6PM M,F; 10AM-2PM 1st & last Sat.

Hampstead Town Clerk PO Box 298, Hampstead, NH 03841 (11 Main St). **603-329-4100** Fax: 603-329-7174. 8AM-7PM, M; 8AM-4PM, T,W,TH; 8AM-12PM, F.

Hampton Falls Town Clerk 1 Drinkwater Rd, Town Hall, Hampton Falls, NH 03844 **603-926-4618** Fax: 603-926-1848. 9AM-N, 1-4PM M,T,Th.

Hampton Town Clerk 100 Winnacunnet Rd, Hampton, NH 03842 **603-926-0406** Fax: 603-929-5917. 9AM-4PM. Assessor, Property records online.

Hancock Town Clerk PO Box 6, Hancock, NH 03449 (50 Main St). **603-525-4441** Fax: 603-525-4427. 9AM-4PM.

Hanover Town Clerk PO Box 483, Hanover, NH 03755-0483 (41 S. Main St). **603-643-4123** Fax: 603-643-1720. 8:30AM-4:30PM.

Harrisville Town Clerk PO Box 284, Harrisville, NH 03450 (705 Chesham Rd.). **603-827-5546** Fax: 603-827-2917. 2-7PM, T; 4-6:30PM, W; 9-11:30AM Th..

Hart's Location Town Clerk 5 Forest Rd, Hart's Location, NH 03812 **603-374-2436** By Appointment.

Haverhill Town Clerk 2975 Dartmouth College Hwy, N. Haverhill, NH 03774 **603-787-6200** Fax: 603-787-2226. 9-4:30PM.

Hebron Town Clerk HC 58 Box 286, East Hebron, NH 03242 (Town Hall). **603-744-7999** Fax: 603-744-7999. 6-8PM Tu; 9:30-11:30AM Sat..

Henniker Town Clerk 2 Depot Hill Rd, Henniker, NH 03242 **603-428-3240** Fax: 603-428-4366. 8AM-5:30PM, M; 8AM-N, T; 8AM-4:30PM, W, F.

Hill Town Clerk PO Box 251, Hill, NH 03243 (30 Crescent St). **603-934-3951** Fax: 603-934-3951. Mon/Wed 9AM-12; Tues. 9AM-12 & 6-9PM; Th. 9AM-3PM.

Hillsborough County Registrar of Deeds PO Box 370, Nashua, NH 03061-0370 (19 Temple St). **603-882-6933** Fax: 603-594-4137. 8AM-3:45PM. www.nhdeeds.com

Real Estate, Deed, Mortgage, Lien, Grantor/Grantee records online.

Hillsborough Town Clerk PO Box 1699, Hillsborough, NH 03244 (29 School St). **603-464-5571** Fax: 603-464-4270. 9-5PM.

Hinsdale Town Clerk PO Box 31, Hinsdale, NH 03451. **603-336-5719** Fax: 603-366-5711. 11-4 M-W, 1:30-6:30 1st 2nd TH, other TH 11-4. Assessor, Property records online.

Holderness Town Clerk PO Box 203, Holderness, NH 03245 (Route 3, Town Hall). **603-968-7536** Fax: 603-968-9954. 8:30AM-4:30PM. www.holderness-nh.gov/

Hollis Town Clerk 7 Monument Sq, Hollis, NH 03049-6568 (3 Hallis Village Marketplace). **603-465-2064** Fax: 603-465-2964. M-W-F 8AM-1PM; Mon Eve. 7-9; 1st Sat. 8-11AM. Assessor records online.

Hooksett Town Clerk 16 N. Main St, Hooksett, NH 03106 **603-485-9534** Fax: 603-485-4423. 8AM-4:30PM; 8AM-6:30PM W. www.hooksett.org

Hopkinton Town Clerk PO Box 446, Contoocook, NH 03229-0446 (846 Main St). **603-746-3180** Fax: 603-746-4011. 8AM-4:30PM. www.hopkintonnh.us

Hudson Town Clerk 12 School St, Hudson, NH 03051-4294 **603-886-6003** 8:30-4:30.

Jackson Town Clerk PO Box 336, Jackson, NH 03846-0336 (54 Main St). **603-383-6248** 8:30AM-12:30PM T,W,F.

Jaffrey Town Clerk 10 Goodnow St., Jaffrey, NH 03452 **603-532-7861** Fax: 603-532-7862.

Jefferson Town Clerk 84 Stag Hollow Rd, Jefferson, NH 03583 **603-586-4553** Fax: 603-586-4553.

Keene City Clerk 3 Washington St, Keene, NH 03431 **603-352-0133** Fax: 603-357-9884. 8AM-5PM. www.keenenh.com

Kensington Town Clerk 95 Amesbury Rd, Rte 150, Town Hall, Kensington, NH 03833 **603-772-5423** Fax: 603-772-6841. http://town.kensington.nh.us

Kingston Town Clerk PO Box 657, Kingston, NH 03848-0657 (163 Main St). **603-642-3112** Fax: 603-642-3204. 8:30AM-N, 1-4PM M-F; 7-9PM M, T.

Laconia City Clerk PO Box 489, Laconia, NH 03247 (45 Beacon St East). **603-527-1265** Fax: 603-524-1766. 8:30AM-4:30PM. Property Assessor records online.

Lancaster Town Clerk 25 Main St, Lancaster, NH 03584 **603-788-2306** Fax: 603-

788-2114. 8:30AM-5PM M-TH; 8:30AM-4:30PM F.

Landaff Town Clerk PO Box 125, Landaff, NH 03585 (23 Jim Noyes Hill Rd.). **603-838-6220** Fax: 603-838-6220. 9AM-11AM & 5PM-7PM T.

Langdon Town Clerk 5 Walker Hill Rd, Langdon Town Hall, Langdon, NH 03602 **603-835-2389** Fax: 603-835-2389. 10AM-N, 3-6PM T.

Lebanon City Clerk 51 N. Park St, Lebanon, NH 03766 **603-448-3054** Fax: 603-448-4891. 8AM-5PM. www.lebcity.com Property Assessor records online.

Lee Town Clerk 7 Mast Rd, Town Hall, Lee, NH 03824 **603-659-2964** Fax: 603-659-7202. 8AM-4PM M, W, F. Property, Deed, Grantor/Grantee records online.

Lempster Town Clerk PO Box 33, East Lempster, NH 03605-0033 (856 US Route 10). **603-863-3213** Fax: 603-863-8105. 9AM-N M-F; 5-7PM W.

Lincoln Town Clerk PO Box 39, Lincoln, NH 03251 (148 Main St). **603-745-8971** Fax: 603-745-6743. 8AM-4PM.

Lisbon Town Clerk 46 School St, Lisbon, NH 03585 **603-838-2862** Fax: 603-838-6790. 9AM-12,1-4:30PM.

Litchfield Town Clerk 2 Liberty Way, #3, Litchfield, NH 03052 **603-424-4045** 10AM-6PM, M; 9-4PM, T; 8AM-3PM, W TH F.

Littleton Town Clerk 125 Main St, 2nd Fl, Littleton, NH 03561 **603-444-3995 x20** Fax: 603-444-1715. 8:30AM-12:30PM, 1-4PM. www.townoflittleton.org Property, Map records online.

Londonderry Town Clerk 50 Nashua Rd, #100, Londonderry, NH 03053 **603-432-1100 x195** Fax: 603-432-1142. 8:30AM-5PM. www.londonderry.org

Loudon Town Clerk PO Box 7837, Loudon, NH 03301 (29 S Village Rd). **603-798-4542** Fax: 603-798-4546.

Lyman Town Clerk 65 Parker Hill Rd, Lyman, NH 03585 **603-838-6113** Fax: 603-838-6818.

Lyme Town Clerk PO Box 342, Lyme, NH 03768 (38 Union St). **603-795-2535** Fax: 603-795-4637. 9AM-12:00PM,M,T,F,.

Lyndeborough Town Clerk PO Box 164, Lyndeborough, NH 03082 (Clerk's Office, Citizens Hall Rd). **603-654-9653** Fax: 603-654-5777. 8AM-1PM, 2-7PM M; 8AM-1PM, 2-3PM W.

Madbury Town Clerk 13 Town Hall Rd, Madbury, NH 03820-9510 **603-742-5131** Fax: 603-742-2505. Property, Deed, Grantor/Grantee records online.

Madison Town Clerk PO Box 248, Madison, NH 03849 (26 Rte. 113 West). **603-367-9931** Fax: 603-367-4547. 8-4PM M,T,W,F.

Manchester City Clerk One City Hall Plaza, Manchester, NH 03101 **603-624-6455** Fax: 603-624-6481. 9-5. www.manchesternh.gov

Marlborough Town Clerk PO Box 487, Marlborough, NH 03455-0487 (236 E. Main St). **603-876-4529** Fax: 603-876-4703. 9AM-4:30 M T TH; 9AM-N W, 9AM-2PM F. www.marlboroughnh.org

Marlow Town Tax Collector PO Box 184, Marlow, NH 03456 (Town Hall). **603-446-2245** Fax: 603-446-3806. Tues. evening 5-7.

Mason Town Clerk 16 Darling Hill Rd., Mason, NH 03048-4717 **603-878-2070** Fax: 603-878-4892. 1-4PM T; 9-N, 7-9PM TH.

Meredith Town Clerk 41 Main St, Meredith, NH 03253-9704 **603-279-4538** Fax: 603-279-1042. 8AM-5PM. http://meredithnh.org/

Merrimack County Register of Deeds PO Box 248, Concord, NH 03302-0248 (163 N. Main St.). **603-228-0101** Fax: 603-226-0868. www.merrimackcounty.nh.us.landata.com Real Estate, Grantor/Grantee, Deed, Real Estate records online. 8AM-4:30PM.

Merrimack Town Clerk PO Box 27, Merrimack, NH 03054 (6 Baboosic Lake Rd). **603-424-3651** Fax: 603-424-0461. 8:30AM-4:30PM M-F; 2nd & 4th M 8:30AM-7PM. www.ci.merrimack.nh.us

Middleton Town Clerk 182 Kings Highway, Middleton Town Offices, Middleton, NH 03887 **603-473-2576** Fax: 603-473-2577. Property, Deed, Grantor/Grantee online.

Milan Town Clerk PO Box 158, Milan, NH 03588 (20 Bridge St). **603-449-3461** Fax: 603-449-2624. 9AM-N;1-4PM M/evenings6-8PM;9AM-N;1-5PM T-Th.

Milford Town Clerk 1 Union Sq, Milford, NH 03055 **603-673-3514, 673-3403** Fax: 603-673-2273. 8-4. www.milfordnh.com/town/

Milton Town Clerk PO Box 180, Milton, NH 03851-0180 (599 White Mountain Hwy). **603-652-9414** Fax: 603-652-4120. www.miltonnh-us.com Property, Deed, Grantor/Grantee records online.

Monroe Town Treasurer PO Box 63, Monroe, NH 03771-0063 (50 Main St). **603-638-2644** Fax: 603-638-2021.

Mont Vernon Town Clerk PO Box 417, Mont Vernon, NH 03057 (Clerk's Office,

McCollom Bldg.-Main St.). **603-673-9126** Fax: 603-672-9021. 5-8PM M & W; 9AM-N T & Th.

Moultonborough Town Clerk PO Box 15, Moultonborough, NH 03254 (36 Holland St.). **603-476-2347** Fax: 603-476-5835. 9AM-N 1-4PM M W F; 9AM-1PM T.

Nashua City Clerk 229 Main St, Nashua, NH 03061-2019 **603-589-3010** Property Assessor records online.

Nelson Town Clerk 7 Nelson Common Rd., Nelson, NH 03457 (Nelson Village, Old Brick Schoolhouse). **603-847-9043** Fax: 603-847-9043. 9AM-N Tu.; 5-8PM W; 9AM-1PM Th.

New Boston Town Clerk PO Box 250, New Boston, NH 03070-0250 (7 Meeting House Hill). **603-487-5504 x106** Fax: 603-487-2975. 9AM-7PM M, 9AM-4PM W F, 4PM-8PM TH. www.new-boston.nh.us

New Castle Town Clerk PO Box 367, New Castle, NH 03854-0367 (49 Main St.). **603-431-6710** Fax: 603-433-6198. 9AM-1PM M W; 12PM-5PM Th.

New Durham Town Clerk PO Box 207, New Durham, NH 03855 (4 Main St). **603-859-2091** Fax: 603-859-6644. 9AM-4PM Property, Deed, Grantor/Grantee online.

New Hampton Town Clerk/Tax Collector PO Box 538, New Hampton, NH 03256 (6 Pinnacle Hill Rd). **603-744-8454** Fax: 603-744-5106. 7:30AM-11:45PM/12:45PM-4:15 PM M T W F; 1-7:30PM Th. www.new-hampton.nh.us

New Ipswich Town Clerk 661 Turnpike Rd., New Ipswich, NH 03071 **603-878-3567** Fax: 603-878-3855. 9-4PM M,W,Th; 1-7PM T.

New London Town Clerk PO Box 314, New London, NH 03257-0314 (120 Main St). **603-526-4046** Fax: 603-526-9494. 8:30AM-4PM. Property Appraiser records online.

Newbury Town Clerk PO Box 253, Newbury, NH 03255 (Route 103, Old Newbury School). **603-763-5326** 6PM-9PM M; 8:30AM-3:30PM T-F. Assessor, Property records online.

Newfields Town Clerk PO Box 300, Newfields, NH 03856-0300 (65 Main St.). **603-772-5070** Fax: 603-772-9004. 8:30AM-2:30PM.

Newington Town Clerk 205 Nimble Hill Rd, Town Offices, Newington, NH 03801 **603-436-7640** Fax: 603-436-7188. 9AM-4:30PM T,W,Th.

Newmarket Town Clerk 186 Main St, Town Hall, Newmarket, NH 03857 **603-659-3073**

Fax: 603-659-3441. 8AM-4:30PM, till 6PM 1st & last Thursdays. Assessor, Property records online.

Newport Town Clerk 15 Sunapee St, Newport, NH 03773 **603-863-2224** Fax: 603-863-8008. 8AM-4:30PM.

Newton Town Tax Collector Box 375, Newton, NH 03858-0375 (South Main St). **603-382-4096** Fax: 603-382-9140. 8AM-4PM M-W.

North Hampton Town Clerk PO Box 141, North Hampton, NH 03862-0141 (237 Atlantic Ave). **603-964-6029** Fax: 603-964-1514. www.northhampton-nh.gov Assessor, Property records online. 8:30AM-2:00PM

Northfield Town Clerk 21 Summer St, Northfield, NH 03276 **603-286-4482** Fax: 603-286-3328. 8:30AM-5PM, Closed T.

Northumberland Town Clerk 2 State St, Groveton, NH 03582 **603-636-1451** Fax: 603-636-1450. 8:30-N, 1-4PM; to 6PM on Th.

Northwood Town Clerk 818 First NH Turnpike, Northwood, NH 03261-0314 (**603-942-5586 X201** Fax: 603-942-9107.

Nottingham Town Clerk PO Box 114, Nottingham, NH 03290 (139 Stage Rd). **603-679-9598** Fax: 603-679-9598. 4-8PM M,W; 1-5PM T; 9AM-1PM Th,Sat.

Orford Town Clerk 59 Archer Town Rd., Clerk's Office, Orford, NH 03777 **603-353-4404** 2-7PM T; 6-8PM W; 8-11AM Th.

Ossipee Town Clerk PO Box 67, Center Ossipee, NH 03814 (55 Main St.). **603-539-2008** Fax: 603-539-4183. 8:30AM-4:30PM.

Pelham Town Clerk 6 Village Green, Pelham, NH 03076 **603-635-2040** Fax: 603-508-3096. 8:00AM-4PM M,W,Th.,F; 8:00AM-7:00PM Tu..

Pembroke Town Clerk 311 Pembroke St, Pembroke, NH 03275 (**603-485-4747** Fax: 603-485-3967. 8-4PM, Th 5PM-8PM. Assessor records online.

Peterborough Town Tax Collector 1 Grove St, Peterborough, NH 03458 **603-924-8010** Fax: 603-924-8001. 8AM-4:30 M-F; 5-7PM Th.. www.townofpeterborough.com

Piermont Town Clerk PO Box 27, Piermont, NH 03779 (573 Route 25C). **603-272-4840** Fax: 603-272-4947. 1-7PM Tu,W.

Pittsburg Town Clerk 1526 Main St, Pittsburg, NH 03592 **603-538-6699** Fax: 603-538-6697. 8:30AM-5:30PM.

Pittsfield Town Clerk Box 98, Pittsfield, NH 03263-0098 (85 Main St.). **603-435-6773** Fax: 603-435-7922. 8AM-6PM M; 8AM-

2:30PM T; 8AM-1PM W TH; 2PM-5PM F. www.pittsfield-nh.com

Plainfield Town Clerk Box 380 Town Clerk's Office, Meriden, NH 03770 (Town Clerk Office). **603-469-3201** Fax: 603-469-3642. 8AM-4PM M-Th, closed F.

Plaistow Town Clerk 145 Main St, Town Hall, #2, Plaistow, NH 03865 **603-382-8129** Fax: 603-382-7183. 8:30AM-7PM M, 8:30AM-4:30PM T-F. www.plaistow.com

Plymouth Town Clerk 6 PO Sq, Town Hall, Plymouth, NH 03264 **603-536-1732** Fax: 603-536-0036. 8:30AM-4PM.

Portsmouth City Clerk 1 Junkins Ave, Portsmouth, NH 03802-0628 **603-431-2000** Fax: 603-427-1526. 8AM-4:30PM. www.cityofportsmouth.com/cityclerk/index.htm Property Assessor records online.

Randolph Town Hall 130 Durand Rd., Randolph, NH 03593 **603-466-5771** Fax: 603-466-9856. 9-11AM M; 7-9PM W.

Raymond Town Clerk Epping St, Town Office Bldg., Raymond, NH 03077 **603-895-4735 X110** Fax: 603-895-0903. 8:00AM-7:00PM M; 8:00AM-4:30PM T-F. Property Assessor records online.

Richmond Town Clerk 105 Old Homestead Hwy, Richmond, NH 03470 **603-239-6202** 9AM-N, 1-4PM, 6-8PM M; 9AM-N T,Th; 9AM-N, 1-4 W.

Rindge Town Clerk PO Box 11, Rindge, NH 03461 (49 Payson Hill Rd.). **603-899-5181 x107** Fax: 603-899-2101. 9AM-1PM M-Th; 6-8PM Th Eve; 9AM-1PM F. www.town.rindge.nh.us

Rochester City Clerk 31 Wakefield St, City Hall, Rochester, NH 03867-1917 **603-332-2130** Fax: 603-335-7565. 8AM-5PM. www.rochesternh.net Property, Deed, Grantor/Grantee records online.

Rockingham County Register of Deeds PO Box 896, Kingston, NH 03848 (10 Route 125). **603-642-5526** Fax: 603-642-8548/5930. 8AM-4PM. www.nhdeeds.com Real Estate, Most Wanted, Inmate records online.

Rollinsford Town Clerk PO Box 309, Rollinsford, NH 03869 (667 Main St). **603-742-2510** Fax: 603-740-0254. 9AM-1PM M,T,W,F; 3-7PM Th. Property, Deed, Grantor/Grantee records online.

Roxbury Town Clerk 404 Branch Rd., Roxbury NH 03431 **603-352-4903** 7-8pm M.

Rumney Town Clerk PO Box 275, Rumney, NH 03266 (79 Depot St). **603-786-2237** Fax: 603-786-2237. 4PM-8PM, M; 9AM-2PM, T, W, TH, F.

Rye Town Clerk 10 Central Rd, Rye, NH 03870 **603-964-8562** Fax: 603-964-4132. Property Assessor records online.

Salem Town Clerk 33 Geremonty Drive, Municipal Bldg., Salem, NH 03079-3390 **603-890-2110** Fax: 603-898-1223. 8:30AM-5PM. www.ci.salem.nh.us Property Assessor records online.

Salisbury Town Clerk Box 180, Salisbury, NH 03268-0180 (70 Franklin Rd.). **603-648-2473** Fax: 603-648-6658. 8:30AM-N, 5:30-8:30PM T; 2PM-6PM W.

Sanbornton Town Clerk PO Box 124, Sanbornton, NH 03269 (573 Sanborn Rd.). **603-286-4034** Fax: 603-286-9544. Assessor, Property records online.

Sandown Town Clerk 320 Main St, Town Hall, PO Box 583, Sandown, NH 03873-2627 **603-887-4870** Fax: 603-887-5163. M 8-12PM/2-8PM; T-Th 8-12PM/12:30-3PM; F 8-12PM. www.sandown.us

Sandwich Town Clerk PO Box 194, Center Sandwich, NH 03227 (8 Maple St.). **603-284-7113** Fax: 603-284-6819. Mon. evenings 7-9PM.

Seabrook Town Clerk PO Box 476, Seabrook, NH 03874 (99 Lafayette Rd.). **603-474-3152** Fax: 603-474-8007. 9-4PM.

Sharon Town Clerk 432 Route 123, Sharon, NH 03458 **603-924-9250** Fax: 603-924-9250. 6-8PM T.

Shelburne Town Clerk 881 N. Rd, Philbrook Farm Inn, Shelburne, NH 03581 **603-466-3831** By appointment.

Somersworth City Clerk 1 Government Way, Somersworth, NH 03878-9574 **603-692-4262** Fax: 603-692-9574. 9AM-5PM M,W,F; 8AM-5PM T,Th. Property, Deed, Grantor/Grantee records online.

South Hampton Town Clerk 3 Hilldale Ave., South Hampton, NH 03827 (304 Main Ave.). **603-394-7696** 7-8:30PM M,T; 12:30-2PM W; 9:30-11:30AM F.

Springfield Town Clerk PO Box 22, Springfield, NH 03284 (759 Main St). **603-763-4805** Fax: 603-763-3336. 9AM-N, 1-4PM M-F; 6-8PM W; 4-8PM Th.

Stark Town Clerk 1189 Stark Hwy., Stark, NH 03582 **603-636-2118** Fax: 603-636-6199. 10AM-4PM T,Th.

Stewartstown Town Clerk PO Box 35, West Stewartstown, NH 03597-0035 (High St). **603-246-3329** Fax: 603-246-3329. 9:30AM-2PM Tu.;, 9AM-4PM W-F.

Stoddard Town Clerk 2175 Route 9, Stoddard, NH 03464 **603-446-2203** Fax: 603-446-2203. 9AM-2PM 4PM-6PM T TH.

Strafford County Register of Deeds PO Box 799, Dover, NH 03820 (259 County Farm Rd). **603-742-1741** Fax: 603-749-5130. www.nhdeeds.com/stfd/web/start.htm Real Estate, Deed, Mortgage, Lien, Grantor/Grantee records online.

Strafford Town Clerk PO Box 169, Strafford, NH 03884-0169 (Town Hall). **603-664-2192** Fax: 603-664-7276. 9AM-1PM M; 9-2:30PM Tu.,Wed.; 9-N Th.. Property, Deed, Grantor/Grantee records online.

Stratford Town Clerk PO Box 366, North Stratford, NH 03590 (Fire Station). **603-922-5598** Fax: 603-922-3317. 9AM-N 5PM-8PM, M; 9AM-N, 4PM-7PM, W.

Stratham Town Clerk 10 Bunker Hill Ave, Stratham, NH 03885 **603-772-4741** Fax: 603-775-0517. 8:30-4PM. www.strathamnh.org

Sugar Hill Town Clerk Box 574, Sugar Hill, NH 03585 (1411 Rt. 117). **603-823-8516** Fax: 603-823-8446. 4PM-6PM M; 9AM-1PM T TH.

Sullivan County Register of Deeds PO Box 448, Newport, NH 03773 (14 Main St, 2nd Fl). **603-863-2110** Fax: 603-863-0013. 8AM-4PM. www.nhdeeds.com/ Real Estate, Grantor/Grantee, Deed records online.

Sullivan Town Clerk 522 South Rd, Sullivan, NH 03445 **603-352-1495** 8-9AM.

Sunapee Town Clerk PO Box 303, Sunapee, NH 03782-0303 (23 Edgemont Rd). **603-763-2449** Fax: 603-763-4608. 9AM-5PM M,T,Th,F; 9AM-1PM W.

Surry Town Tax Collector 1 Village Rd., Surry, NH 03431 **603-352-3075** Fax: 603-357-4890.

Sutton Town Clerk PO Box 487, North Sutton, NH 03260-0487 (93 Main St.). **603-927-4575** Fax: 603-927-4631. 8AM-4PM T-Th; Noon-7PM M; 9AM-N last Sat..

Swanzey Town Clerk PO Box 10009, Swanzey, NH 03446 (620 Old Homestead). **603-352-7411** Fax: 603-352-6250. 9AM-5PM. Assessor records online.

Tamworth Town Clerk PO Box 279, Tamworth, NH 03886 (84 Main St). **603-323-7971** Fax: 603-323-2347. 8AM-N 1PM-4:30PM T-F.

Temple Town Clerk Box 69, Temple, NH 03084 (Rte. 45). **603-878-3873** Fax: 603-878-5067. 9AM-2PM- T,W,Th..

Thornton Town Clerk 16 Merrill Access Rd, Thornton, NH 03223 **603-726-4232** Fax: 603-726-2078.

Tilton Town Clerk 257 Main St, Tilton, NH 03276-1207 **603-286-4425** Fax: 603-286-3519. 8:30AM-4:15PM. www.tiltonnh.org

Troy Town Clerk PO Box 249, Troy, NH 03465-0249 (16 Central Sq). **603-242-3845** Fax: 603-242-3430. 9-4:30 M-W; 1-7PM Th; 9AM-1:30PM F. www.town.troy.nh.us

Tuftonboro Town Clerk PO Box 98, Center Tuftonboro, NH 03816 (Town Hall). **603-569-4539** Fax: 603-569-4328. 9AM-4PM,M,T,W,F; 9AM-12:00PM Th.

Unity Town Clerk 13 Center Rd., Unity, NH 03603 **603-542-9665** Fax: 603-542-9736. M & T 9-5PM; Wed 9AM-6PM; Th 8AM-N.

Wakefield Town Clerk 2 High St., Sanbornville, NH 03872 **603-522-6205 x306** Fax: 603-522-6794. 8:30-4 T TH F,8:30-12-W, 8:30-1:30 Sat. www.wakefieldnh.com

Walpole Town Clerk PO Box 756, Walpole, NH 03608 (Town Clerk Office, 34 Elm St.). **603-756-3514** Fax: 603-756-4153. 7AM-4PM T,W,F; 6-7PM W.

Warner Town Clerk PO Box 265, Warner, NH 03278-0265 (Main St.). **603-456-3362** Fax: 603-456-3576. 8AM-3PM M-TH; 5-7PM T. www.warner.nh.us/departments.htm

Warren Town Clerk PO Box 66, Warren, NH 03279 (Water St). **603-764-9463** Fax: 603-764-9315. 4PM-8PM M; 6-8PM W.

Washington Town Clerk PO Box 109, Washington, NH 03280-0109 (Clerk's Office). **603-495-3667** Fax: 603-495-3299. 9AM-3PM F.

Waterville Valley Town Clerk Box 500, Waterville Valley, NH 03215 (Clerk's

Office). **603-236-4730** Fax: 603-236-2056. 8AM-4PM.

Weare Town Clerk PO Box 190, Weare, NH 03281-0190 (15 Flanders Memorial Dr.). **603-529-7575** Fax: 603-529-7571. 8AM-4PM M, T, Th, F; 8AM-7PM W. www.town.weare.nh.us

Webster Town Clerk 945 Battle St, Rte 127, Webster, NH 03303 **603-648-2538** Fax: 603-648-6055. 9-N, 1-4PM M,W; 7-9PM Mon.

Wentworth Town Clerk PO Box 2, Wentworth, NH 03282 (Municipal Bldg.). **603-764-5244** Fax: 603-764-9362. 12-7PM Tu; 8:30AM-3PM W,Th..

Westmoreland Town Clerk 108 Pierce Lane, Westmoreland, NH 03467 **603-399-7211** 7-8:30PM M; 10-1PM F; 1-3 Tu ,W

Whitefield Town Clerk 7 Jefferson Rd, Whitefield, NH 03598 **603-837-9871** Fax: 603-837-3148.

Wilmot Town Clerk PO Box 94, Wilmot, NH 03287 (9 Kearsarge Valley Rd.). **603-526-9639** Fax: 603-526-2523. 8:30AM-1:30PM T,Th; 4-7PM W.

Wilton Town Clerk PO Box 83, Wilton, NH 03086 (42 Main St). **603-654-9451** Fax: 603-654-6663. 9AM-4PM,M,T,F, closed W,9-7PM Th. www.ci.wilton.nh.us

Winchester Town Clerk 1 Richmond Rd, Winchester, NH 03470 **603-239-6233** Fax: 603-239-4146. 8AM-5PM.

Windham Town Clerk PO Box 120, Windham, NH 03087 (3 N Lowell Rd). **603-434-5075** Fax: 603-425-6582. 8-4PM (8AM-7PM M) www.windhamnewhampshire.com

Windsor Town Clerk 14 White Pond Rd, Windsor, NH 03244 **603-478-3292** Fax: 603-478-3213. 7PM-9PM W.

Wolfeboro Town Clerk Box 1207, Wolfeboro, NH 03894 (84 S. Main St). **603-569-5328** Fax: 603-569-8167. 8AM-1:00; 2-4PM. Assessor, Property records online.

Woodstock Town Tax Collector PO Box 146, North Woodstock, NH 03262 (Clerk Office, 165 Lost River Rd.). **603-745-9233** Fax: 603-745-2393. 8AM-4PM T-Th.

New Jersey

Organization: 21 counties, 21 recording offices. The recording officer title varies depending upon the county. It is either Register of Deeds or County Clerk. The Clerk of Circuit Court records the equivalent of some state's tax liens. The entire state is in the Eastern Time Zone (EST).

Real Estate Records: No counties will provide real estate searches. Copy and certification fees vary. Assessment and tax offices are at the municipal level.

UCC Records: Financing statements are filed at the state level, except for real estate related collateral, which are filed with the County Clerk. However, prior to 07/2001, consumer goods and farm collateral were also filed at the County Clerk and these older records can be searched there. About half of the recording offices will perform UCC searches. Use search request form UCC-11. Search fees are usually $25.00 per debtor name and copy fees vary.

Tax Lien Records: All federal tax liens are filed with the County Clerk/Register of Deeds and are indexed separately from all other liens. State tax liens comprise two categories - certificates of debt are filed with the Clerk of Superior Court (some, called docketed judgments are filed specifically with the Trenton court), and warrants of execution are filed with the County Clerk/Register of Deeds. Few counties will provide tax lien searches. Refer to the County Court section for information about New Jersey Superior Courts. Other Liens: Judgment, mechanics, bail bond.

Online Access: There is no statewide government database online, but a statewide database of property tax records can be accessed from a private vendor at at http://taxrecords.com.

Atlantic County Clerk 5901 Main St, Courthouse, CN 2005, Mays Landing, NJ 08330-1797 **609-625-4011** Fax: 609-625-4738. 8:30 AM-6:30 PM M W; 8:30AM-4:30 T TH F. www.atlanticcountyclerk.org Property, Assessor, Inmate records online.

Bergen County Clerk One Bergen County Plaza, Hackensack, NJ 07601 **201-336-7007** 9-4PM. Property, Assessor records online.

Burlington County Clerk PO Box 6000, Mount Holly, NJ 08060 (49 Rancocas Rd, 1st Fl). **609-265-5122** Fax: 609-265-0696. Property, Assessor records online.

Camden County Clerk 520 Market St, Courthouse Rm 102, Camden, NJ 08102-1375 **856-225-5300** Fax: 856-225-7100. 8AM-4PM. Property, Assessor records online.

Cape May County Clerk PO Box 5000, Cape May Court House, NJ 08210-5000 (7 N. Main St, DN 109). **609-465-1010** Fax: 609-465-8625. 8:30AM-4:30PM. www.capemaycountygov.net Real Estate, Recording, Property records online.

Cumberland County Clerk PO Box 716, Bridgeton, NJ 08302 (60 W. Broad St., Rm A137). **856-453-4864** Fax: 856-455-1410. 8:30-4PM. Property, Assessor records online.

Essex County Register of Deeds 465 Martin Luther King Blvd, Hall of Records, Rm 130, Newark, NJ 07102 **973-621-4960** Fax: 973-621-6114. www.essexregister.com Property, Assessor records online. 9AM-4PM.

Gloucester County Clerk PO Box 129, Woodbury, NJ 08096-0129 (1 N. Broad St).

856-853-3230 Fax: 856-853-3327. 8:30AM-4PM. www.co.gloucester.nj.us Recording, Real Estate, Deed, Lien, UCC, Mortgage, Assessor, Property Tax records online.

Hudson County Clerk 595 Newark Ave, Rm 105, Jersey City, NJ 07306 **201-795-6571** Fax: 201-795-5177. 9AM-5PM. Property, Assessor records online.

Hunterdon County Clerk 71 Main St, Hall of Records, Flemington, NJ 08822 **908-788-1221** Fax: 908-782-4068. 8:30AM-4PM. Property records online.

Mercer County Clerk 209 S. Broad St, Courthouse, Rm 100, Trenton, NJ 08650 **609-989-6466** Fax: 609-989-1111. 8:30AM-4:30PM. www.mercercounty.org Property records online.

Middlesex County Clerk PO Box 1110, New Brunswick, NJ 08903 (75 Bayard St., 4th Fl). **732-745-3204** 8:30AM-4PM. Recording, Deed, Lien, Judgment, Mortgage, Property records online.

Monmouth County Clerk PO Box 1251, Freehold, NJ 07728 (Market Yard). **732-431-7324** www.co.monmouth.nj.us Real Estate, Deed, Mortgage, Grantor/Grantee, Property Tax, Assessor records online. 8:30-4:30PM.

Morris County Clerk PO Box 315, Morristown, NJ 07963-0315 (Admin. & Records Bldg., Court St). **973-285-6135** Fax: 973-285-5231. 8AM-4M M-F; 8AM-8PM W. Property, Assessor records online.

Ocean County Clerk PO Box 2191, Toms River, NJ 08754 (118 Washington St, 1st Fl

Rm 114). **732-929-2018** Fax: 732-349-4336. 8:30AM-4PM. www.oceancountyclerk.com Property Tax, Real Estate, Deed records online.

Passaic County Clerk Registry Division 77 Hamilton St, Courthouse, Paterson, NJ 07505 **973-881-4777** 8:30AM-4:30PM; Vault Hours: 7:45AM-5:45PM.

Salem County Clerk 92 Market St, Salem, NJ 08079-1911 **856-935-7510 x8218** Fax: 856-935-8882. Property, Assessor records online.

Somerset County Clerk PO Box 3000, Somerville, NJ 08876 (20 Grove St.). **908-231-7006** Fax: 908-253-8853. 8:15AM-4PM. www.co.somerset.nj.us Real Estate, Recording, Deed, Property Tax, Assessor records online.

Sussex County Clerk 4 Park Pl, Hall of Records, Newton, NJ 07860-1795 **973-579-0900** Fax: 973-383-7493. 8:30AM-4:30PM. www.sussexcountyclerk.com Property, Assessor, Real Estate, Recording, Deed records online.

Union County Clerk 2 Broad St, Courthouse, Rm 115, Elizabeth, NJ 07207 **908-527-4794** Fax: 908-558-2589. 8:30AM-4:30PM. www.unioncountynj.org/constit/clerk/record.html Real Estate, Deed, Property Tax, Assessor records online.

Warren County Clerk 413 Second St, Courthouse, Belvidere, NJ 07823-1500 **908-475-6211** 8:30AM-4PM. Property, Assessor records online.

New Mexico

Organization: 33 counties, 33 recording offices. The recording officer is the County Clerk. Most counties maintain a grantor/grantee index and a miscellaneous index. The entire state is in the Mountain Time Zone (MST).

Real Estate Records: Most counties will not perform real estate searches. Copy and certification fees vary.

UCC Records: Financing statements are filed at the state level, except for real estate related collateral, which are filed with the County Clerk. However, prior to 07/2001, consumer goods and farm collateral were also filed at the County Clerk and these older records can be searched there. Only a few recording offices will perform UCC searches. Use search request form UCC-11. Search and copy fees vary, but search fee is usually $5.00.

Tax Lien Records: All federal and state tax liens are filed with the County Clerk. Most counties will not provide tax lien searches. Other Liens: Judgment, mechanics, lis pendens, contractors, hospital.

Online Access: Several counties offer online access, but there is no statewide system.

Bernalillo County Clerk PO Box 542, Albuquerque, NM 87103 (1 Civic Plaza NW, 6th Fl). **505-768-4090** Fax: 505-768-4190. 8-5. www.bernco.gov/live/depts_and_offices.asp Real Estate, Property Assessor records online.

Catron County Clerk PO Box 197, Reserve, NM 87830-0197 (Main St). **505-533-6400** Fax: 505-533-6400. 8AM-4:30PM.

Chaves County Clerk Box 580, Roswell, NM 88202-0580 (# 1 St. Mary Pl). **505-624-6614** Fax: 505-624-6523. 7AM-5PM.

Cibola County Clerk PO Box 190, Grants, NM 87020 (515 W. High St). **505-287-2539** Fax: 505-285-2562. 8AM-5PM.

Colfax County Clerk PO Box 159, Raton, NM 87740-0159 (Third St & Savage Ave). **505-445-5551** Fax: 505-445-4031. 8-5PM.

Curry County Clerk PO Box 1168, Clovis, NM 88102-1168 (700 N. Main St, #7). **505-763-5591** Fax: 505-763-4232. 8AM-5PM. www.currycounty.org/clerk's.html

De Baca County Clerk PO Box 347, Fort Sumner, NM 88119 (514 Ave. C). **505-355-2601** Fax: 505-355-2441. 8-N, 1-4:30PM.

Dona Ana County Clerk 251 W. Amador, Rm 103, Las Cruces, NM 88005-2893 **505-647-7421** Fax: 505-647-7464. 8AM-5PM. www.co.dona-ana.nm.us Assessor, Real Estate, Personal Property, Voter Registration records online.

Eddy County Clerk 101 W. Greene St, Rm 312, Carlsbad, NM 88220 **505-885-3383** Fax: 505-234-1793. 8AM-5PM.

Grant County Clerk PO Box 898, Silver City, NM 88062 (201 N. Cooper). **505-574-0042** Fax: 505-574-0076. 8AM-5PM.

Guadalupe County Clerk 420 Parker Ave, Courthouse, #1, Santa Rosa, NM 88435 **505-472-3791** Fax: 505-472-3735. 8AM-5PM.

Harding County Clerk PO Box 1002, Mosquero, NM 87733-1002 (Third & Pine). **505-673-2301** Fax: 505-673-2922. 8-4PM.

Hidalgo County Clerk 300 Shakespeare St, Lordsburg, NM 88045 **505-542-9213** Fax: 505-542-3193. 8AM-5PM.

Lea County Clerk PO Box 1507, Lovington, NM 88260 (100 Main St). **505-396-8614** Fax: 505-396-3293. www.leacounty-nm.org

Lincoln County Clerk PO Box 338, Carrizozo, NM 88301 (300 Central Ave). **505-648-2394** Fax: 505-648-2576. 8AM-5PM. Assessor, Property records online.

Los Alamos County Clerk PO Box 30, Los Alamos, NM 87544 (2300 Trinity Drive, Rm 100). **505-662-8010** Fax: 505-662-8008.

Luna County Clerk PO Box 1838, Deming, NM 88031-1838 (700 S. Silver). **505-546-0491** Fax: 505-546-4708. 8AM-5PM.

McKinley County Clerk PO Box 1268, Gallup, NM 87301 (207 W. Hill Ave). **505-863-6866** Fax: 505-863-1419. 8AM-5PM.

Mora County Clerk PO Box 360, Mora, NM 87732-0360 (Main St). **505-387-2448** Fax: 505-387-9023. 8AM-N, 1-5PM.

Otero County Clerk 1000 New York Ave, Rm 108, Alamogordo, NM 88310-6932 **505-437-4942** Fax: 505-443-2922. 7:30AM-6PM. www.oteroclerk@co.otero.nm.us

Quay County Clerk PO Box 1225, Tucumcari, NM 88401-1225 (301 S. Third St). **505-461-0510** Fax: 505-461-0513. 8-5.

Rio Arriba County Clerk PO Box 158, Tierra Amarilla, NM 87575 (Courthouse, 7 Main St). **505-588-7724** Fax: 505-588-7418.

Roosevelt County Clerk 101 W. First, Rm 106, Portales, NM 88130 **505-356-8562** Fax: 505-356-3560. www.rooseveltcounty.com

San Juan County Clerk PO Box 550, Aztec, NM 87410 (100 S. Oliver Dr. #200). **505-334-9471** Fax: 505-334-3635. 7AM-5:30PM. www.co.san-juan.nm.us Real Estate, Assessor records online.

San Miguel County Clerk Courthouse, Las Vegas, NM 87701 **505-425-9331** Fax: 505-454-1799. 8AM-5PM.

Sandoval County Clerk PO Box 40, Bernalillo, NM 87004 (711 Camino Del Pueblo, 2nd Fl). **505-867-7572** Fax: 505-771-8610. 8AM-5PM.

Santa Fe County Clerk PO Box 1985, Santa Fe, NM 87504-1985 (102 Grant Ave). **505-986-6280** Fax: 505-995-2767. 8AM-4PM. Assessor, Property records online.

Sierra County Clerk 100 Date St, Truth or Consequences, NM 87901 **505-894-2840** Fax: 505-894-2516. 8AM-5PM.

Socorro County Clerk PO Box I, Socorro, NM 87801 (200 Church St). **505-835-3263** Fax: 505-835-1043. 8AM-5PM.

Taos County Clerk 105 Albright St, #D, Taos, NM 87571 **505-737-6380** Fax: 505-737-6390. 8AM-5PM.

Torrance County Clerk PO Box 48, Estancia, NM 87016 (9th & Allen Sts). **505-384-2221** Fax: 505-384-4080. 8AM-5PM.

Union County Clerk PO Box 430, Clayton, NM 88415 (200 Court St). **505-374-9491** Fax: 505-374-2763. 9AM-5PM.

Valencia County Clerk PO Box 969, Los Lunas, NM 87031 (444 Luna Ave). **505-866-2073** Fax: 505-866-2023. 8-4:30PM. www.co.valencia.nm.us/CntyAgencies.htm

New York

Organization: 62 counties, 62 recording offices. The recording officer is the County Clerk (it is the New York City Register in the counties of Bronx, Kings, New York, and Queens). The entire state is in the Eastern Time Zone (EST).

Real Estate Records: Some counties will perform real estate searches. Certified copy fees are usually $1.00 per page with a $4.00 minimum. Tax records are located at the Treasurer's Office.

UCC Records: This was a dual filing state. Financing statements werefiled both at the state level and with the County Clerk, except for consumer goods, cooperatives (as in cooperative apartments), farm related and real estate related collateral, which were filed only with the County Clerk. Effective 07/2001, only real estate related collateral is filed at the county, but searches may still be done on all the records prior to 07/2001. All counties will perform UCC searches. Use search request form UCC-11. Search fees are $25.00 per debtor name. Copies usually cost $5.00 per document.

Tax Lien Records: Federal tax liens on personal property of businesses are filed with the Secretary of State. Other federal tax liens are filed with the County Clerk. State tax liens are filed with the County Clerk, with a master list - called state tax warrants - available at the Secretary of State's office. Federal tax liens are usually indexed with UCC Records. State tax liens are usually indexed with other miscellaneous liens and judgments. Some counties include federal tax liens as part of a UCC search, and others will search tax liens for a separate fee or not at all. Search fees and copy fees vary. Other Liens: Judgment, mechanics, welfare, hospital, matrimonial, wage assignment, lis pendens.

Online Access: A handful of counties and towns offering free Internet access to assessor records, and the number is growing. The NYC Register now offers free access to borough real estate records.

Albany County Clerk County Courthouse, Rm 128, Albany, NY 12207 **518-487-5120** Fax: 518-487-5099. 9AM-4:45PM. www.albanycounty.com/departments Naturalization, Property, Deed, Morgages, Recording, Assessor records online.

Allegany County Clerk 7 Court St, Courthouse, Belmont, NY 14813-0087 **585-268-9270** Fax: 585-268-9659. 9AM-5PM (June-Aug. 8:30-4). www.alleganyco.com Property records online.

Bronx Borough City Register 1932 Arthur Ave, Bronx, NY 10457 **718-579-6827** 9AM-4PM. Real Estate, Lien, Deed, Judgment, UCC, Deed, Mortgage, Tax Assessor, Property records online.

Broome County Clerk PO Box 2062, Binghamton, NY 13902-2062 (44 Hawley St). **607-778-2451** Fax: 607-778-2243. 8AM-5PM (Memorial Day to Labor Day-7:30AM-4PM). www.gobroomecounty.com/clerk/index.php Property, Deed, Mortgage records online.

Cattaraugus County Clerk 303 Court St, Little Valley, NY 14755 **716-938-9111** Fax: 716-938-6009. 9AM-5PM, M-F. www.cattco.org Real Estate, Tax Assessor, Most Wanted, Warrant, Land records online.

Cayuga County Clerk 160 Genesee St, Auburn, NY 13021 **315-253-1271** Fax: 315-253-1653. www.co.cayuga.ny.us/clerk

Property, Assessor, Real Estate, Deed, Lien records online.

Chautauqua County Clerk PO Box 170, Mayville, NY 14757-0170 (1 N. Erie St). **716-753-4980** Fax: 716-753-4310. 8:30AM-4:30PM. www.co.chautauqua.ny.us Property records online.

Chemung County Clerk PO Box 588, Elmira, NY 14902-0588 (210 Lake St). **607-737-2920** Fax: 607-737-2897. 8:30Am-4:30PM. www.chemungcounty.com Property records online.

Chenango County Clerk 5 Court St, Norwich, NY 13815 **607-337-1452** 8:30AM-5PM. www.co.chenango.ny.us Property records online.

Clinton County Clerk 137 Margaret St, Government Ctr, Plattsburgh, NY 12901-2974 **518-565-4700** Fax: 518-565-4718. 8-5PM. www.co.clinton.ny.us/Departments/CC/CCHome.htm Property records online.

Columbia County Clerk 560 Warren St., Hudson, NY 12534 **518-828-3339** Fax: 518-828-5299. 9-5PM. Property records online.

Cortland County Clerk 46 Greenbush St #101, Cortland, NY 13045-3702 **607-753-5021** Fax: 607-758-5500. 9AM-5PM. http://www2.cortland-co.org Property records online.

Delaware County Clerk PO Box 426, Delhi, NY 13753 (Court House Sq). **607-746-2123**

Fax: 607-746-6924. 8:30AM-5PM. Property records online.

Dutchess County Clerk 22 Market St, Poughkeepsie, NY 12601 **845-486-2120** Fax: 845-486-2138. 9AM-4:45PM. www.dutchessny.gov Property records online.

Erie County Clerk 25 Delaware Ave, County Hall, Buffalo, NY 14202 (**716-858-6724** Fax: 716-858-6550. http://ecclerk.erie.gov Recording, Deed, Mortgage, Judgment, Property records online.

Essex County Clerk PO Box 247, Elizabethtown, NY 12932 (7559 Court St). **518-873-3601** Fax: 518-873-3548. 8-5PM. www.co.essex.ny.us Property records online.

Franklin County Clerk PO Box 70, Malone, NY 12953 (355 W. Main St). **518-481-1681** Fax: 518-483-9143. 8AM-PM June-Aug; 9-5PM Sept-May. Property records online.

Fulton County Clerk PO Box 485, Johnstown, NY 12095 (223 W. Main St). **518-736-5555** Fax: 518-762-3839. 9AM-5PM. Auditor, Real Estate, Deed, UCC records online.

Genesee County Clerk PO Box 379, Batavia, NY 14021-0379 (15 Main St). **585-344-2550 x2443** Fax: 585-344-8551. 8:30AM-5PM. Property records online.

Greene County Clerk PO Box 446, Catskill, NY 12414 (320 Main St). **518-943-2050**

Fax: 518-943-2146. 9AM-5PM (June-Aug 8:30AM-4:30PM). Property records online.

Hamilton County Clerk PO Box 204, Lake Pleasant, NY 12108 (Clerk's Office Bldg., Rte. 8). **518-548-7111** Fax: 518-548-9740. 8:30AM-4:30PM. Property records online.

Herkimer County Clerk 109 Mary St, #1111, Herkimer, NY 13350 **315-867-1137** Fax: 315-867-1349. 9AM-5PM. Property records online.

Jefferson County Clerk 175 Arsenal St, Watertown, NY 13601-2555 **315-785-3081** Fax: 315-785-5145. 9AM-5PM; 8:30AM-4PM July-Aug. Property records online.

Kings Borough Clerk 210 Joralemon St, Municipal Bldg, 1st Fl, Rm 2, Brooklyn, NY 11201 **718-802-3589** Fax: 718-802-3745. 9AM-4PM. Real Estate, Lien, Deed, Judgment, UCC, Deed, Mortgage, Tax Assessor, Property records online.

Lewis County Clerk PO Box 232, Lowville, NY 13367-0232 (7660 State St). **315-376-5333** Fax: 315-376-3768. 8:30AM-4:30PM. Property records online.

Livingston County Clerk 6 Court St, Rm 201, Government Ctr, Geneseo, NY 14454-1043 **585-243-7010** Fax: 585-243-7928. 8:30AM-4:30PM Oct 1-May 30; 8AM-4 June 1-Sept 30. Property records online.

Madison County Clerk PO Box 668, Wampsville, NY 13163 (North Court St, County Office Bldg.). **315-366-2261** Fax: 315-366-2615. 9AM-4:45PM. Property records online.

Monroe County Clerk 39 W. Main St, Rochester, NY 14614 **585-428-5151** Fax: 585-428-5447. www.co.monroe.ny.us Land, Judgment, UCC, Lien, Court, Property records online. 9AM-5PM.

Montgomery County Clerk PO Box 1500, Fonda, NY 12068-1500 (County Office Bldg.). **518-853-8115** 8:30AM-4PM. Property records online.

Nassau County Clerk 240 Old Country Rd, Mineola, NY 11501 **516-571-2272** Fax: 516-742-4099. 9AM-4:45PM. Real Estate, Assessor, Recording, Property records online. www.co.nassau.ny.us/clerk/index.html

New York Borough City Register 66 John St, Rm 202, New York, NY 10007 **212-361-7550** 9AM-4PM. Real Estate, Lien, Judgment, UCC, Deed, Mortgage, Tax Assessor, Most Wanted, Missing Person, Restaurant Insp. records online.

Niagara County Clerk PO Box 461, Lockport, NY 14095 (175 Hawley St). **716-439-7022** Fax: 716-439-7066. 9AM-5PM

(Summer 8:30AM-4:30PM). Real Estate, Recording, Deed, Mortgage, Lien, Judgment records online.

Oneida County Clerk 800 Park Ave, Utica, NY 13501 **315-798-5792** Fax: 315-798-6440. www.oneidacounty.org/index1.htm Property records online. 8:30AM-5PM.

Onondaga County Clerk 401 Montgomery St, Rm 200, Syracuse, NY 13202 **315-435-8200** Fax: 315-435-3455. 8AM-5PM. Property records online.

Ontario County Clerk 20 Ontario St., Ontario County Muni. Bldg., Canandaigua, NY 14424 **585-396-4200** Fax: 585-393-2951. 8:30AM-5PM. www.co.ontario.ny.us Property records online.

Orange County Clerk 255 Main St, Goshen, NY 10924 **845-291-2690** Fax: 845-291-2691. 9AM-5PM. www.co.orange.ny.us Property records online.

Orleans County Clerk 3 S. Main St, Courthouse Sq, Albion, NY 14411-1498 **585-589-5334** Fax: 585-589-0181. 8:30AM-4PM July-Aug; 9AM-5PM Sept-June. Property records online.

Oswego County Clerk 46 E. Bridge St, Oswego, NY 13126 **315-349-8385** Fax: 315-343-8383. 9-5PM. Property records online.

Otsego County Clerk PO Box 710, Cooperstown, NY 13326-0710 (197 Main St). **607-547-4278** Fax: 607-547-7544. 9AM-5PM Sept-June; 9AM-4PM July-Aug.. Property records online.

Putnam County Clerk 40 Gleneida Ave., Carmel, NY 10512 (**845-225-3641** Fax: 845-228-0231. 9AM-5PM (Summer 8AM-4PM). Real Estate, UCC, Lien, Property records online.

Queens Borough City Register 144-06 94th Ave., Jamaica, NY 11435 **718-298-7000** 9AM-4PM. Real Estate, Lien, Deed, Judgment, UCC, Deed, Mortgage, Tax Assessor records online.

Rensselaer County Clerk Courthouse, Congress & 2nd St, Troy, NY 12180 **518-270-4080** Fax: 518-271-7998. 8:30AM-5PM. Property, Assessor, Deed, Lien, Real Estate records online.

Richmond Borough Clerk 130 Stuyvesant Pl, Staten Island, NY 10301 **718-390-5386** 9AM-5PM. Real Estate, Lien, Deed, Judgment, UCC, Deed, Mortgage, Tax Assessor records online.

Rockland County Clerk 1 S. Main St #100, New City, NY 10956 **845-638-5070** Fax: 845-638-5647. 7AM-7PM M-Th; 7AM-6PM F.

www.rocklandcountyclerk.com Real Estate, Lien, Deed, Court, Recording records online.

Saratoga County Clerk 40 McMaster St, Ballston Spa, NY 12020 **518-885-2213 ext 4411** Fax: 518-884-4726. Search hours: 8AM-5PM; Recording & Filing hours: 8. Property records online.

Schenectady County Clerk 620 State St, Schenectady, NY 12305-2114 **518-388-4220** Fax: 518-388-4224. 9-5PM. www.scpl.org Real Estate, Tax Assessor, Property records online.

Schoharie County Clerk PO Box 549, Schoharie, NY 12157 (284 Main St). **518-295-8316** Fax: 518-295-8338. 8:30AM-5PM. Property records online.

Schuyler County Clerk 105 Ninth St Unit 8, County Office Bldg., Watkins Glen, NY 14891 **607-535-8133** 9AM-5PM. Property records online.

Seneca County Clerk 1 DiPronio Drive, Waterloo, NY 13165 **315-539-1771** Fax: 315-539-3789. 8:45AM-4:45PM. Property records online.

St. Lawrence County Clerk 48 Court St, Canton, NY 13617-1198 **315-379-2237** Fax: 315-379-2302. 8:30AM-4:30PM. www.co.st-lawrence.ny.us/CoTOC2.htm Property records online.

Steuben County Clerk 3 E. Pulteney Sq, County Office Bldg., Bath, NY 14810 **607-776-9631 x3210** Fax: 607-776-7158. 8:30AM-5PM. www.steubencony.org Tax Assessor, Property records online.

Suffolk County Clerk's Office 310 Center Drive, Riverhead, NY 11901-3392 **631-852-2038** Fax: 631-852-2004. 8AM-5PM. Property, Most Wanted records online.

Sullivan County Clerk PO Box 5012, Monticello, NY 12701 (100 North St). **845-794-3000 x3152** 9AM-5PM. Property records online.

Tioga County Clerk PO Box 307, Owego, NY 13827 (16 Court St). **607-687-8660** Fax: 607-687-8686. 9-5. Property records online.

Tompkins County Clerk 320 N. Tioga St, Main Courthouse, Ithaca, NY 14850-4284 **607-274-5431** Fax: 607-274-5445. 8:30-5. www.tompkins-co.org Real Estate, Assessor, Tentative Assessment records online.

Ulster County Clerk PO Box 1800, Kingston, NY 12402-0800 (240-244 Fair St). **845-340-3288** Fax: 845-340-3299. 9AM-4:45PM. www.co.ulster.ny.us Real Estate, Lien, Property Tax, Voter Registration, Court records online.

Warren County Clerk 1340 State Route 9, Municipal Ctr, Lake George, NY 12845 **518-761-6426** Fax: 518-761-6551. 9-5PM. Property records online.

Washington County Clerk 383 Broadway, Bldg A, Fort Edward, NY 12828 **518-746-2170** Fax: 518-746-2166. 8:30AM-4:30PM. Property records online.

Wayne County Clerk PO Box 608, Lyons, NY 14489-0608 (9 Pearl St). **315-946-7470**

Fax: 315-946-5978. 9AM-5PM. www.co.wayne.ny.us Property records online.

Westchester County Clerk 110 Dr. Martin Luther King Jr. Blvd., White Plains, NY 10601 **914-995-3098** Fax: 914-995-3172. 8AM-4:30PM. Property, Recordings, Deed, Land, Fictitious Names, Judgment, Lien, UCC records online.

Wyoming County Clerk 143 N Main St, #104, Warsaw, NY 14569 **585-786-8810** Fax:

585-786-3703. 9AM-5PM. Real Estate, Recording, Property records online.

Yates County Clerk 417 Liberty St, Penn Yan, NY 14527 **315-536-5120** Fax: 315-536-5545. www.yatescounty.org Property records online. 9AM-5PM.

North Carolina

Organization: 100 counties, 100 recording offices. The recording officers are the Register of Deeds and the Clerk of Superior Court (tax liens). The entire state is in the Eastern Time Zone (EST).

Real Estate Records: Counties will not perform real estate searches. Copy fees are usually $1.00 per page. Certification usually costs $3.00 for the first page and $1.00 for each additional page of a document.

UCC Records: This was a dual filing state. Financing statements are were both at the state level and with the Register of Deeds, except for consumer goods, farm related and real estate related collateral. As of 7/1/2001, only real estate related collateral is filed at the county elvel. All counties will perform UCC searches on the records recorded prior to 7/1/2001. Use search request form UCC-11. Search fees were raised in 2001 to $30.00 per debtor name. Copies usually cost $1.00 per page.

Tax Lien Records: Federal tax liens on personal property of businesses are filed with the Secretary of State. Other federal and all state tax liens are filed with the county Clerk of Superior Court, not with the Register of Deeds. (Oddly, even tax liens on real property are also filed with the Clerk of Superior Court, not with the Register of Deeds.) Refer to The Sourcebook of County Court Records for information about North Carolina Superior Courts. Other Liens: Judgment, mechanics (all at Clerk of Superior Court).

Online Access: A growing number of counties offer free access to assessor and real estate records via the web.

Alamance Register of Deeds PO Box 837, Graham, NC 27253 (118 W. Harden St). **336-570-6565** 8AM-5PM.

Alexander Register of Deeds 75 First St SW, #1, Taylorsville, NC 28681-2504 **828-632-3152** Fax: 828-632-1119. 8AM-5PM.

Alleghany Register of Deeds PO Box 186, Sparta, NC 28675 (12 N. Main St). **336-372-4342** Fax: 336-372-2061. 8AM-5PM. www.allcorod.com Real Estate, Grantor/Grantee, Property, GIS records online.

Anson Register of Deeds PO Box 352, Wadesboro, NC 28170-0352 (Green St Courthouse). **704-694-3212** Fax: 704-694-6135. www.co.anson.nc.us/services.php 8:30-5PM. Assessor, Real Estate, 911 Address Converter, Tax Collection records online.

Ashe Register of Deeds 150 Government Circle, #2300, Jefferson, NC 28640 **336-219-2540** Fax: 336-219-2564. 8AM-4:30PM. Assessor, Real Estate, Grantor/Grantee, Property records online.

Avery Register of Deeds PO Box 87, Newland, NC 28657 (200 Montezuma St.). **828-733-8260** Fax: 828-733-8261. 8AM-

4:30PM. www.averyrod.com Recording, Grantor/Grantee, Property records online.

Beaufort Register of Deeds PO Box 514, Washington, NC 27889 (112 W. Second St). **252-946-2323** 8:30AM-5PM.

Bertie Register of Deeds PO Box 340, Windsor, NC 27983 (King & Dundee Sts). **252-794-5309** Fax: 252-794-5374. 8:30-5.

Bladen Register of Deeds PO Box 247, Elizabethtown, NC 28337 (Courthouse Drive). **910-862-6710** Fax: 910-862-6714.

Brunswick Register of Deeds PO Box 87, Bolivia, NC 28422-0087 (75 Courthouse Dr.). **877-625-9310, 910-253-2690** Fax: 910-253-2703. http://rod.brunsco.net Recording, Deed, Lien, Property Tax records online.

Buncombe Register of Deeds 60 Court Plaza, Rm 110, Asheville, NC 28801-3563 **828-250-4300** Fax: 828-255-5829. 8:30AM-5PM. www.buncombecounty.org Assessor, Property Tax, Real Estate, Recording, Marriage, Death, Corporation, Fictitious Name, Deed records online.

Burke Register of Deeds PO Box 936, Morganton, NC 28680 (201 S. Green St). **828-438-5450** Fax: 828-438-5463. 8AM-

5PM. www.co.burke.nc.us Property, Assessor records online.

Cabarrus Register of Deeds PO Box 707, Concord, NC 28026 (65 Church St S.E.). **704-920-2112** Fax: 704-920-2898. 8AM-5PM. www.co.cabarrus.nc.us Assessor, Real Estate, Recorder, Deed, Lien, Grantor/Grantee, UCC, Tax Roll records online.

Caldwell Register of Deeds 905 West Ave N.W., County Office Bldg., Lenoir, NC 28645 (**828-757-1399** Fax: 828-757-1294. 8:00AM-5:00PM. www.co.caldwell.nc.us Property, Assessor, Real Estate, Birth, Death, Marriage, Notary, Business Name records online.

Camden Register of Deeds PO Box 190, Camden, NC 27921 (117 North 343). **252-338-1919** 8AM-5PM.

Carteret Register of Deeds Courthouse Sq, Beaufort, NC 28516-1898 **252-728-8474** Fax: 252-728-7693. 8AM-5PM.

Caswell Register of Deeds PO Box 98, Yanceyville, NC 27379 (139 E. Church St). **336-694-4197** Fax: 336-694-1405. 8-5PM.

Catawba Register of Deeds PO Box 65, Newton, NC 28658-0065 (100 S. West Blvd.). **828-465-1573** 8AM-5PM.

www.co.catawba.nc.us Assessor, Property, Grantor/Grantee, Real Estate, Deeds online.

Chatham Register of Deeds PO Box 756, Pittsboro, NC 27312 (12 East St.). **919-542-8235** 8AM-4:30PM.

Cherokee Register of Deeds 53 Peachtree St, Murphy, NC 28906 **828-837-2613** Fax: 828-837-8414. www.cherokeecounty-nc.org Real Estate records online.

Chowan Register of Deeds PO Box 487, Edenton, NC 27932-0487 (101 S. Broad St). **252-482-2619** 8AM-5PM.

Clay Register of Deeds PO Box 118, Hayesville, NC 28904 (54 Church St.). **828-389-0087** Fax: 828-389-9749. 8AM-5PM.

Cleveland Register of Deeds PO Box 1210, Shelby, NC 28151-1210 (311 E. Marion St). **704-484-4834** Fax: 704-484-4909. 8AM-5PM. www.clevelandcounty.com Real Estate, Assessor, Real Estate, Grantor/Grantee records online.

Columbus Register of Deeds PO Box 1086, Whiteville, NC 28472-1086 (Courthouse). **910-640-6625** Fax: 910-640-2547. 8:30AM-5PM. Recording, Deed, Lien, Real Estate, Assumed Name, Corporation, UCC records online.

Craven Register of Deeds 226 Pollock St, New Bern, NC 28560 **252-636-6617** Fax: 252-636-1937. 8AM-5PM. www.co.craven.nc.us Real Estate, Recording, Deed, Tax Assessor, Boat, Mobile Home, Foreclosure, GIS records online.

Cumberland Register of Deeds PO 2039, Fayetteville, NC 28302-2039 (117 Dick St, Rm 114). **910-678-7775** Fax: 910-323-1456. 8AM-5PM. www.ccrod.org Land, Deed, Recording, UCC, Property Tax, Assessor records online.

Currituck Register of Deeds PO Box 71, Currituck, NC 27929 (2801 Caratoke Hwy.). **252-232-3297** Fax: 252-232-3906. 8AM-5PM.

Dare Register of Deeds PO Box 70, Manteo, NC 27954 (300 Queen Elizabeth Ave). **252-473-3438** 8:30AM-5PM. www.co.dare.nc.us Assessor, Real Estate, Marriage, UCC records online.

Davidson Register of Deeds PO Box 464, Lexington, NC 27293-0464 (203 W. Second St). **336-242-2150** Fax: 336-238-2318. 8AM-5PM. www.co.davidson.nc.us Property, Assessor, Real Estate records online.

Davie Register of Deeds 123 S. Main St, Mocksville, NC 27028 **336-634-2513** 8:30AM-5PM. www.co.davie.nc.us Real Estate, GIS-mapping records online.

Duplin Register of Deeds PO Box 970, Kenansville, NC 28349 (118 Duplin St). **910-296-2108** Fax: 910-296-2344. 8AM-5PM. http://rod.duplincounty.org Real Property, Deed, Lien, Judgment, Mortgage, Marriage, Death, Notary, Military Discharge records online.

Durham Register of Deeds PO Box 1107, Durham, NC 27702 (200 E. Main St). **919-560-0494** Fax: 919-560-0497. 8:30AM-5PM. www.co.durham.nc.us/rgds Real Estate, Deed, Judgment, Recording, Voter Registration records online.

Edgecombe Register of Deeds PO Box 386, Tarboro, NC 27886 (301 St. Andrew St). **252-641-7924** Fax 252-641-1771. 7:30-5PM.

Forsyth Register of Deeds PO Box 20639, Winston-Salem, NC 27120-0639 (102 W. Third St, Upper Plaza). **336-727-2903** Fax: 336-727-2341. 8AM-5PM. Real Estate, Land, Lien records online.

Franklin Register of Deeds PO Box 545, Louisburg, NC 27549-0545 (113 S. Main St). **919-496-3500** Fax: 919-496-1457. 8AM-5PM. www.co.franklin.nc.us Real Property records online.

Gaston Register of Deeds PO Box 1578, Gastonia, NC 28053 (325 N. Marietta St.). **704-862-7681** Fax 704-862-7519. 8:30-5PM.

Gates Register of Deeds PO Box 471, Gatesville, NC 27938-0471 (202 Court St). **252-357-0850** Fax: 252-357-0850. 9-5PM.

Graham Register of Deeds PO Box 406, Robbinsville, NC 28771 (Main St Court house). **828-479-7971** Fax: 828-479-7988.

Granville Register of Deeds PO Box 427, Oxford, NC 27565 (101 Main St). **919-693-6314** . 8:30AM-5PM.

Greene Register of Deeds PO Box 86, Snow Hill, NC 28580 (Greene St Courthouse). **252-747-3620** 8AM-5PM.

Guilford Register of Deeds PO Box 1467, High Point, NC 27261-1467 (505 E. Green St, Rm 132). **336-845-7931** 8AM-5PM. www.co.guilford.nc.us Recorder, Assessor, Property, UCC, Vital Statistic, Military Discharge records online.

Halifax Register of Deeds PO Box 67, Halifax, NC 27839-0067 (357 Ferrell Lane). **252-583-2101** Fax: 252-583-1273. 8:30AM-5PM. www.halifaxnc.com/halinav.html

Harnett Register of Deeds PO Box 279, Lillington, NC 27546 (729 Main St). **910-893-7540** Fax: 910-814-3841. 8AM-5PM. www.harnett.org/harnett/departments/rod.html Real Estate, Grantor/Grantee, Vital Statistic, Military Discharge, UCC records online.

Haywood Register of Deeds 215 N Main St, Courthouse, Waynesville, NC 28786 **828-452-6635** Fax: 828-452-6762. 8AM-5PM. Real Estate, Deed, Property, GIS-mapping records online.

Henderson Register of Deeds 200 N. Grove St, #129, Hendersonville, NC 28792 **828-697-4901** 9AM-5PM. Real Estate, GIS-mapping records online.

Hertford Register of Deeds PO Box 36, Winton, NC 27986 (Courthouse). **252-358-7850** Fax: 252-358-7806. 8:30AM-5PM.

Hoke Register of Deeds 113 Campus Ave, Raeford, NC 28376 **910-875-2035** Fax: 910-875-9554. 8AM-5PM.

Hyde Register of Deeds PO Box 294, Swanquarter, NC 27885 (Courthouse Sq). **252-926-4181** Fax: 252-926-3082. Real Property, Grantor/Grantee records online.

Iredell Register of Deeds PO Box 904, Statesville, NC 28687 (221 Water St). **704-872-7468** Fax: 704-878-3055. 8AM-5PM. www.co.iredell.nc.us

Jackson Register of Deeds 401 Grindstaff Cove Rd. #103, Sylva, NC 28779 **828-586-7530** Fax: 828-586-6879. 8:30AM-5PM. www.jacksonnc.org

Johnston Register of Deeds PO Box 118, Smithfield, NC 27577 (Market St, Courthouse Sq). **919-989-5160** Fax: 919-989-5728. 8AM-5PM. www.johnstonnc.com Real Estate, UCC, Deed records online.

Jones Register of Deeds PO Box 189, Trenton, NC 28585-0189 (101 Market St.). **252-448-2551** Fax: 252-448-1357. 8AM-5PM. www.jonesrod.com

Lee Register of Deeds PO Box 2040, Sanford, NC 27331-2040 (1408 S. Horner Blvd.). **919-774-4821** Fax: 919-774-5063. 8AM-5PM. www.leencrod.org Real Estate, Grantor/Grantee, Deed, Lien records online.

Lenoir Register of Deeds PO Box 3289, Kinston, NC 28502 (101 N. Queen St.). **252-559-6420** Fax: 252-523-6139. 8:30-5.

Lincoln Register of Deeds PO Box 218, Lincolnton, NC 28093-0218 (Courthouse). **704-736-8530** Fax: 704-732-9049. 8AM-5PM. www.co.lincoln.nc.us/ Real Estate, Deed, Lien, Mapping, UCC, Property Tax records online.

Macon Register of Deeds 5 W. Main St, Franklin, NC 28734 **828-349-2095** Fax: 828-349-6382. Property, Deed Image records online.

Madison Register of Deeds PO Box 66, Marshall, NC 28753 (75 Blannahassett Island). **828-649-3131** 8:30AM-5PM.

Martin Register of Deeds PO Box 348, Williamston, NC 27892 (305 E. Main St). **252-792-1683** Fax: 252-792-1684. 8-5PM.

McDowell Register of Deeds 21 S. Main St, Courthouse, Marion, NC 28752-3992 **828-652-4727** Fax: 828-652-1537. 8:30AM-5PM. Land, Deed records online.

Mecklenburg Register of Deeds 720 E. 4th St, #103, Charlotte, NC 28202 **704-336-2443** Fax: 704-336-7699. 8:30AM-4:30PM. http://meckrod.hartic.com Assessor, Real Estate, Grantor/Grantee, Judgment, Lien, Vital Statistic, Personal Property, Accident Report records online.

Mitchell Register of Deeds 26 Crimson Laurel Cir. #4, Bakersville, NC 28705-9510 **828-688-2139** Fax: 828-688-3666. 8-5PM.

Montgomery Register of Deeds PO Box 695, Troy, NC 27371-0695 (102 E. Spring St.). **910-576-4271** Fax: 910-576-2209. 8AM-5PM.

Moore Register of Deeds PO Box 1210, Carthage, NC 28327 (100 Dowd St). **910-947-6370** Fax: 910-947-6396. 8AM-5PM. www.co.moore.nc.us Real Estate, Lien, Grantor/Grantee, Vital Statistic, DD214, Property Tax, Land Record, Restaurant Grade records online.

Nash Register of Deeds PO Box 974, Nashville, NC 27856 (120 W. Washington St). **252-459-9836** Fax: 252-459-9889. 8AM-4:30PM. www.deeds.co.nash.nc.us/resolution

New Hanover Register of Deeds 216 N. 2nd St., Wilmington, NC 28401 **910-798-4530** Fax: 910-798-4586. 8AM-5PM. www.nhcgov.com Real Estate, Assessor, Grantor/Grantee, Lien, UCC, Judgment, Marriage, Military Discharge records online.

Northampton Register of Deeds PO Box 128, Jackson, NC 27845 (Courthouse). **252-534-2511** Fax: 252-534-1580. 8AM-5PM.

Onslow Register of Deeds 109 Old Bridge St, Jacksonville, NC 28540 **910-347-3451** Fax: 910-347-3340. 8AM-5PM. http://co.onslow.nc.us/register_of_deeds Real Estate records online.

Orange Register of Deeds PO Box 8181, Hillsborough, NC 27278-8181 (200 S. Cameron St). **919-732-8181** Fax: 919-644-3018. www.co.orange.nc.us/deeds/ Property records online.

Pamlico Register of Deeds PO Box 433, Bayboro, NC 28515 (Courthouse). **252-745-4421** 8AM-5PM.

Pasquotank Register of Deeds PO Box 154, Elizabeth City, NC 27907-0154 (206 E. Main St, Rm D102). **252-335-4367** Fax: 252-335-5106. summerourd@co.pasquuotank.nc.us. Property, Assessor records online.

Pender Register of Deeds PO Box 43, Burgaw, NC 28425 (#300, Courthouse). **910-259-1225** Fax: 910-259-1299. 8AM-5PM. Property records online.

Perquimans Register of Deeds PO Box 74, Hertford, NC 27944 (128 N. Church St). **252-426-5660** Fax: 252-426-7443. 8-5PM.

Person Register of Deeds Courthouse Sq, Roxboro, NC 27573 (Courthouse Sq). **336-597-1733** www.personcounty.net Real Estate, Recording, Grantor/Grantee records online.

Pitt Register of Deeds PO Box 35, Greenville, NC 27835-0035 (3rd & Evans Sts Courthouse). **252-830-4128** 8AM-5PM. www.co.pitt.nc.us/depts/ Property, Tax Sale records online.

Polk Register of Deeds PO Box 308, Columbus, NC 28722 (102 Courthouse St). **828-894-8450** Fax: 828-894-5781. 8:30-5PM. www.polkrod.com

Randolph Register of Deeds PO Box 4066, Asheboro, NC 27204 (158 Worth St). **336-318-6960** www.co.randolph.nc.us Real Property records online. 8AM-5PM.

Richmond Register of Deeds 114 E Franklin St., #101, Rockingham, NC 28379-3601 **910-997-8250** Fax: 910-997-8499. 8AM-5PM. Property records online.

Robeson Register of Deeds Box 22 Courthouse-Rm102, Lumberton, NC 28358 (500 N. Elm St). **910-671-3046** Fax: 910-671-3041. 8:15AM-5:15PM.

Rockingham Register of Deeds PO Box 56, Wentworth, NC 27375-0056 (Courthouse, #99, 1086 NC 65). **336-342-8820** Fax: 336-342-6209. www.rockinghamcorod.org Land, Grantor/Grantee, Judgment, Tax Sale, Property, GIS records online. 8AM-5PM.

Rowan Register of Deeds PO Box 2568, Salisbury, NC 28145 (402 N. Main St). **704-638-3102** www.co.rowan.nc.us/rod Real Estate, Recording, Property records online.

Rutherford Register of Deeds PO Box 551, Rutherfordton, NC 28139 (Rm A-202, 229 N. Main St.). **828-287-6155** Fax: 828-287-1229. 8:30AM-5PM.

Sampson Register of Deeds PO Box 256, Clinton, NC 28329 (Main St. Courthouse, Rm 109). **910-592-8026** Fax: 910-592-1803. 8AM-5:15PM. www.sampsonrod.org Real

Estate, Recorder, Deed, Grantor/Grantee records online.

Scotland Register of Deeds PO Box 769, Laurinburg, NC 28353 (212 Biggs St, Rm 250). **910-277-2575** Fax: 910-277-3133. 8AM-5PM.

Stanly Register of Deeds PO Box 97, Albemarle, NC 28002-0097 (201 S. Second St). **704-986-3640** 8:30AM-5PM. www.co.stanly.nc.us Real Estate, Assessor records online.

Stokes Register of Deeds PO Box 67, Danbury, NC 27016 (1014 Main St). **336-593-2811** Fax: 336-593-9360. 8:30AM-5PM. www.stokescorod.org Grantor/Grantee, Deed, UCC, Property records online.

Surry Register of Deeds PO Box 303, Dobson, NC 27017-0303 (201 E. Kapp St). **336-401-8150** Fax: 336-401-8151. 8:15AM-5PM. www.co.surry.nc.us Tax Map records online.

Swain Register of Deeds PO Box 1183, Bryson City, NC 28713 (101 Mitchell St). **828-488-9273 x207** Fax: 828-488-6947. 8AM-5PM. www.swaincounty.org/page5.html

Transylvania Register of Deeds 12 E Main St, Courthouse, Brevard, NC 28712 **828-884-3162** 8:30AM-5PM. www.landofsky.org

Tyrrell Register of Deeds PO Box 449, Columbia, NC 27925 (403 Main St). **252-796-2901** Fax: 252-796-0148. 9AM-5PM. www.tyrrellrod.com Real Estate, Grantor/Grantee, Deed records online.

Union Register of Deeds PO Box 248, Monroe, NC 28111-0248 (500 N. Main St, Rm 205). **704-283-3727** 8AM-5PM.

Vance Register of Deeds 122 Young St, Courthouse, #F, Henderson, NC 27536 **252-738-2110** 8:30AM-5PM.

Wake Register of Deeds PO Box 1897, Raleigh, NC 27602 (300 S. Salisbury St, Rm 104). **919-856-5460** Fax: 919-856-5467. http://web.co.wake.nc.us/rdeeds/ Real Estate, Assessor, Deed, Judgment, Lien, Voter Registration records online. 8:30-5:15PM.

Warren Register of Deeds PO Box 506, Warrenton, NC 27589 (109 Main St). **252-257-3265** Fax: 252-257-7011. 8:30-5PM.

Washington Register of Deeds PO Box 1007, Plymouth, NC 27962 (120 Adams St). **252-793-2325** Fax: 252-793-6982. 8:30AM-5PM. www.washingtoncountygov.com

Watauga Register of Deeds 842 W. King St, #9, Boone, NC 28607-3585 **828-265-8052** Fax: 828-265-7632. 8AM-5PM.

www.wataugacounty.org/deeds/index.html Grantor/Grantee, Deed, UCC, Assessor, Property records online.

Wayne Register of Deeds PO Box 267, Goldsboro, NC 27533-0267 (William St Courthouse). **919-731-1449** Fax: 919-731-1441. 8AM-5PM. www.waynegov.com Real Estate, Deed, Grantor/Grantee records online.

Wilkes Register of Deeds 500 Courthouse Dr, #1000, Wilkesboro, NC 28697 **336-651-7351** 8:30AM-5PM. Property, GIS-mapping records online.

Wilson Register of Deeds PO Box 1728, Wilson, NC 27893 (101 N. Goldsboro St.). **252-399-2935** Fax: 252-399-2942. 8-5PM. www.wilson-co.com/rod.html Assessor, Real

Estate, Voter Registration, Property, Deed records online.

Yadkin Register of Deeds PO Box 211, Yadkinville, NC 27055 (101 State St). **336-679-4225** Fax: 336-679-3239. 8AM-5PM. www.yadkincounty.gov/RegDeed.htm

Yancey Register of Deeds Courthouse, Rm #4, 110 Town Sq, Burnsville, NC 28714 **828-682-2174** Fax: 828-682-4520. 8:30-5PM.

North Dakota

Organization: 53 counties, 53 recording offices. The recording officer is the Register of Deeds. State is in Central Time Zone (CST).

Real Estate Records: Some counties will perform real estate searches by name or by legal description. Copy fees are usually $1.00 per page. Certified copies usually cost $5.00 for the first page and $2.00 for each additional page. Copies may be faxed.

UCC Records: Since 07/1/2001, all financing statements must be filed at the state level, except for real estate related collateral, which are filed only with the Register of Deeds. Previously, the state was a dual filing state and reocrd could be filed at either place. The good news is that all counties access a statewide computer database of filings and will perform UCC searches. Use search request form UCC-11. Various search options are available, including by federal tax identification number or Social Security number The search with copies costs $7.00 per debtor name, including three pages of copies and $1.00 per additional page. Copies may be faxed for an additional fee of $3.00.

Tax Lien Records: Federal tax liens on personal property of businesses are filed with the Secretary of State. Other federal and all state tax liens are filed with the county Register of Deeds. All counties will perform tax lien searches. Some counties automatically include business federal tax liens as part of a UCC search because they appear on the statewide database. (Be careful - federal tax liens on individuals may only be in the county lien books, not on the statewide system.) Separate searches are usually available at $5.00-7.00 per name. Copy fees vary. Copies may be faxed. Other Liens: Mechanics, judgment, hospital, repair, egg cutter.

Online Access: The North Dakota Recorders Information Network (NDRIN) is a electronic central repository representing a number of ND counties participating in Internet access to to records. There is a $200 set-up fee and $50 monthly with $1.00 charge per image printed. Register or request information via the website at www.ndrin.com.

Adams County Recorder PO Box 469, Hettinger, ND 58639-0469 (602 Adams Ave). **701-567-2460** Fax: 701-567-2910. 8:30AM-N, 1-5PM.

Barnes County Register of Deeds 230 4th St NW, #201, Valley City, ND 58072 **701-845-8506** Fax: 701-845-8538. 8AM-5PM.

Benson County Recorder PO Box 193, Minnewaukan, ND 58351 (Courthouse). **701-473-5332** Fax: 701-473-5571.

Billings County Recorder PO Box 138, Medora, ND 58645-0138 (495 4th St.). **701-623-4491** Fax: 701-623-4896. 9AM-N; 1PM-5PM.

Bottineau County Recorder 314 W. 5th St, Bottineau, ND 58318-1265 **701-228-2786** Fax: 701-228-3658. 8:30AM-5PM.

Bowman County Recorder PO Box 379, Bowman, ND 58623 (104 W. 1st St). **701-523-3450** Fax: 701-523-5443. 8-4:30PM.

Burke County Register of Deeds PO Box 219, Bowbells, ND 58721-0219 (Main St

Courthouse). **701-377-2818** Fax: 701-377-2020. 8:30AM-5PM.

Burleigh County Recorder PO Box 5518, Bismarck, ND 58506-5518 (221 N. 5th St). **701-222-6749** Fax: 701-222-6717. 8AM-5PM. www.ndrin.com Real Estate, Treasurer/Auditor, Property records online.

Cass County Register of Deeds PO Box 2806, Fargo, ND 58108-2806 (211 Ninth St South). **701-241-5620** Fax: 701-241-5621. 8AM-5PM. Real Estate records online.

Cavalier County Register of Deeds 901 3rd St #13, Langdon, ND 58249 **701-256-2136** Fax: 701-256-2566. 8:30AM-4:30PM.

Dickey County Register of Deeds PO Box 148, Ellendale, ND 58436 (309 N. 2nd). **701-349-3249** Fax: 701-349-4639. 8AM-4:30PM.

Divide County Register of Deeds PO Box 68, Crosby, ND 58730 (300 N.Main St.). **701-965-6661** Fax: 701-965-6943. 8:30-12:00-1-5PM.

Dunn County Register of Deeds PO Box 106, Manning, ND 58642-0106 (205 Owens St.). **701-573-4443** Fax: 701-573-4444. 8AM-N, 12:30 PM-4:30PM. www.ndrin.com Real Estate, Mortgage records online.

Eddy County Register of Deeds 524 Central Ave, New Rockford, ND 58356-1698 **701-947-2813** Fax: 701-947-2067. 8:00AM-N; 12:30PM-4:00PM.

Emmons County Recorder PO Box 905, Linton, ND 58552 (Courthouse). **701-254-4812** Fax: 701-254-4012. 8:30AM-N, 1PM-5PM.

Foster County Recorder PO Box 76, Carrington, ND 58421 (1000 5th Ave N). **701-652-2491** Fax: 701-652-2173. 8:30AM-4:30PM.

Golden Valley County Recorder PO Box 130, Beach, ND 58621-0130 (150 1st Ave S.E.). **701-872-3713** Fax: 701-872-4383. 8AM-N, 1PM-4PM.

Grand Forks County Register of Deeds PO Box 5066, Grand Forks, ND 58206 (151 S. 4th St.). **701-780-8259** Fax: 701-780-8212. 8AM-5PM. www.co.grand-forks.nd.us/homepage.htm Real Estate, Recording, Deed, Death, Judgment, Lien records online.

Grant County Register of Deeds PO Box 258, Carson, ND 58529 (Courthouse). **701-622-3544** Fax: 701-622-3717. 8AM-4PM.

Griggs County Register of Deeds PO Box 237, Cooperstown, ND 58425 (Courthouse 45th & Rollins). **701-797-2771** Fax: 701-797-3587. 8AM-1200-1-4:30.

Hettinger County Recorder PO Box 668, Mott, ND 58646 (336 Pacific Ave.). **701-824-2545/2645** Fax: 701-824-2717.

Kidder County Recorder PO Box 66, Steele, ND 58482 (120 E..Broadway). **701-475-2632** Fax: 701-475-2202. 9AM-N; 1-5PM.

La Moure County Recorder PO Box 128, La Moure, ND 58458-0128 (202 4th Ave. N.E.). **701-883-5301 x6** Fax: 701-883-4220. 9AM-N, 1-5PM (Sum. 8AM-N, 1-4PM). http://lamoco.drtel.net/countyrecorder.html

Logan County Register of Deeds PO Box 6, Napoleon, ND 58561-0006 (Highway 3 Courthouse). **701-754-2751** Fax: 701-754-2270. 8:30AM-N, 1-4:30PM.

McHenry County Recorder PO Box 149, Towner, ND 58788 (407 S. Main, Rm 206). **701-537-5634** Fax: 701-537-5969. 8AM-N, 1-4:30PM. www.state.nd.us Deed, Mortgage records online.

McIntosh County Recorder PO Box 179, Ashley, ND 58413 (112 N. East 1st). **701-288-3589/3450** Fax: 701-288-3671. 8-4:30.

McKenzie County Recorder PO Box 523, Watford City, ND 58854 (201 W. 5th St). **701-444-3453** Fax: 701-844-3902. 8:30AM-5PM. www.4eyes.net/county.htm & www.ndrin.com Real Estate records online.

McLean County Recorder PO Box 1108, Washburn, ND 58577-1108 (712 5th Ave). **701-462-8541 x226/5** Fax: 701-462-3633. www.visitmcleancounty.com Real Estate records online. 8AM-N, 12:30-4:30PM.

Mercer County Recorder PO Box 39, Stanton, ND 58571 (1021 Arthur St). **701-745-3272** Fax: 701-745-3364. 8AM-4PM.

Morton County Register of Deeds 210 2nd Ave, Mandan, ND 58554 **701-667-3305** Fax: 701-667-3453. 8AM-5PM.

Mountrail County Register of Deeds PO Box 69, Stanley, ND 58784 (101 N Main). **701-628-2945** Fax: 701-628-2276.

Nelson County Coounty Recorder 210 B Ave. West, #203, Lakota, ND 58344 (210 W. B Ave. #203). **701-247-2433** Fax: 701-247-2412. 8AM-N, 1PM-4:30PM.

Oliver County Register of Deeds PO Box 125, Center, ND 58530 (Courthouse). **701-794-8777** Fax: 701-794-3476. 8AM-N, 1-4.

Pembina County Clerk/Recorder 301 Dakota St W. #10, Cavalier, ND 58220 **701-265-4373** Fax: 701-265-4876. 8AM-5PM. www.pembinacountynd.gov Real Estate records online.

Pierce County Register of Deeds 240 S.E. 2nd St, Rugby, ND 58368 **701-776-5206** Fax: 701-776-5707. 9AM-5PM.

Ramsey County Register of Deeds 524 4th Ave #30, Devils Lake, ND 58301 (**701-662-7018** Fax: 701-662-7093. 8AM-5PM. www.co.ramsey.nd.us

Ransom County Recorder PO Box 666, Lisbon, ND 58054-0666 (Courthouse). **701-683-5823** Fax: 701-683-5827. 8:30AM-5PM. Real Estate, Recorder records online.

Renville County Register of Deeds PO Box 68, Mohall, ND 58761-0068 (205 Main St East). **701-756-6398** Fax: 701-756-7158. 9AM-4:30PM. www.renvillecounty.org

Richland County Recorder 418 2nd Ave North, Courthouse, Wahpeton, ND 58075-4400 **701-642-7800** Fax: 701-642-7820. 8:00AM-5:00PM.

Rolette County Recorder PO Box 276, Rolla, ND 58367 (102 NE 2nd). **701-477-3166** Fax: 701-477-5770. 8:30AM-4:30PM.

Sargent County Register of Deeds PO Box 176, Forman, ND 58032-0176 (655 Main St). **701-724-6241** Fax: 701-724-6244.

Sheridan County Register of Deeds PO Box 668, McClusky, ND 58463-0668 (215 2nd St). **701-363-2207** Fax: 701-363-2953. 9AM-N, 1-5PM.

Sioux County Register of Deeds PO Box L, Fort Yates, ND 58538 (Courthouse). **701-854-3853** Fax: 701-854-3854. 8-4:30PM.

Slope County Recorder PO Box JJ, Amidon, ND 58620-0445 (Courthouse). **701-879-6275** Fax: 701-879-6278.

Stark County Recorder PO Box 130, Dickinson, ND 58601 (Sims & 3rd Ave). **701-456-7645** Fax: 701-456-7628. 8AM-5PM. Real Estate records online.

Steele County Register of Deeds PO Box 296, Finley, ND 58230 (201 Washington St). **701-524-2152** Fax: 701-524-1325. 8AM-12:00-1-4:30PM. Real Estate records online.

Stutsman County Recorder 511 2nd Ave S.E., Courthouse, Jamestown, ND 58401 **701-252-9034** Fax: 701-251-1603. 8AM-5PM.

Towner County Recorder PO Box 517, Cando, ND 58324 (315 2nd St). **701-968-4340 x5** Fax: 701-968-4344.

Traill County Recorder PO Box 399, Hillsboro, ND 58045 (13 1st St NW). **701-636-4457** Fax: 701-636-4457. 8AM-N 12:30PM-4:30PM.

Walsh County Recorder 600 Cooper Ave, Courthouse, Grafton, ND 58237 **701-352-2380** Fax: 701-352-3340. 8AM-N, 12:30PM-4:30PM. Real Estate records online.

Ward County Register of Deeds PO Box 5005, Minot, ND 58705-5005 (315 S.E. Third St). **701-857-6410** Fax: 701-857-6414. 8AM-4:30PM. Real Estate, Property Tax records online.

Wells County Recorder PO Box 125, Fessenden, ND 58438 (700 Court St). **701-547-3141** Fax: 701-547-3719. 8-N, 12:30-4PM. http://mylocalgov.com/wellscountynd Real Estate records online.

Williams County Recorder PO Box 2047, Williston, ND 58802-2047 (205 E. Broadway). **701-577-4540** Fax: 701-577-4535. 8AM-5PM. www.williamsnd.com Property Tax, Treasurer records online.

Ohio

Organization: 88 counties, 88 recording offices. The recording officers are the County Recorder and Clerk of Common Pleas Court (state tax liens). The entire state is in the Eastern Time Zone (EST).

Real Estate Records: Counties will not perform real estate searches. Copy fees are usually $1.00 per page. Certification usually costs $.50 per document. Tax records are located at the Auditor's Office.

UCC Records: This was a dual filing state. Financing statements were filed both at the state level and with the County Recorder, except for consumer goods, farm related and real estate related collateral, which were filed only with the County Recorder. As of 7/1/2001, only real estate related collateral is filed at the county level. All counties will perform UCC searches. Use search request form UCC-11. Search fees are usually $20.00 per debtor name. Copies usually cost $1.00 per page.

Tax Lien Records: Federal tax liens are filed with the County Recorder. All state tax liens are filed with the Clerk of Common Pleas Court. Refer to County Court section for information about Ohio courts. Federal tax liens are filed in the "Official Records" of each county. Most counties will not perform a federal tax lien search. Other Liens: Mechanics, workers compensation, judgment.

Online Access: A growing number of Ohio counties offer online access via the Internet to assessor and real estate data.

Adams County Recorder 110 W. Main, Courthouse, West Union, OH 45693 **937-544-2513** Fax: 937-544-4616. 8AM-4PM. Property Tax, Sex Offender records online.

Allen County Recorder PO Box 1243, Lima, OH 45802 (301 N. Main St, Rm 204). **419-223-8517** Fax: 419-222-8427. 8:30AM-4:30PM. www.co.allen.oh.us/rec.php Property, Auditor, Property Sale, Cemetery, War Casualty, Death records online.

Ashland County Recorder 142 W. 2nd St., Courthouse, Ashland, OH 44805-2193 **419-282-4238** Fax: 419-281-5715. 8AM-4PM. www.ashlandcounty.org/recorder/index.htm Real Estate, Auditor, Property Sale, Sex Offender records online.

Ashtabula County Recorder 25 W. Jefferson St, Jefferson, OH 44047 **440-576-3762** Fax: 440-576-3231. 8AM-4:30PM. www.co.ashtabula.oh.us Real Estate, Auditor, Property Sale records online.

Athens County Recorder 15 S Court St, Rm 236, Athens, OH 45701 **740-592-3228** Fax: 740-592-3229. 8AM-4PM. www.athenscountygovernment.com Property, Deed, UCC, Inmate, Mapping records online.

Auglaize County Recorder 209 S Blackhoof St, Rm 103, Wapakoneta, OH 45895-1972 **419-739-6735** Fax: 419-739-6736. Property, Sex Offender records online.

Belmont County Recorder 101 Main St, Courthouse, Rm 105, St. Clairsville, OH 43950 **740-699-2121** Fax: 740-699-2140 x198. 8:30-4:30PM. www.belmontcountyohio.org/recorder/index.html Deed, Property records online.

Brown County Recorder PO Box 149, Georgetown, OH 45121 (800 Mt. Orab

Pike). **937-378-6478** Fax: 937-378-2848. 84PM. Property, Deed, UCC records online.

Butler County Recorder 130 High St, Hamilton, OH 45011 **513-887-3192** Fax: 513-887-3198. 8AM-4:30PM. www.butlercountyohio.org/recorder Property, Deed, UCC, Probate, Voter Registration, Tax Sale, Sex Offender records online.

Carroll County Recorder PO Box 550, Carrollton, OH 44615-0550 (119 Public Sq). **330-627-4545** Fax: 330-627-4295. 8AM-4PM. www.ohiorecorders.com Auditor, Property records online.

Champaign County Recorder 512 S US Hwy 68 #B200, Urbana, OH 43078. **937-652-2263** Fax: 937-652-1515. www.co.champaign.oh.us/auditor/ Real Estate records online.

Clark County Recorder PO Box 1406, Springfield, OH 45501 (31 N Limestone St). **937-328-2445** Fax: 937-328-4620. 8AM-4:30PM. www.co.clark.oh.us/ Property, Deed, UCC, Sheriff Real Estate Sale, Tax Sale, Sex Offender records online.

Clermont County Recorder 101 E. Main St, Batavia, OH 45103-2958 **513-732-7236** Fax: 513-732-7891. 8AM-4:30PM. http://recorder.co.clermont.oh.us/ Property, Deed, UCC, Property Tax, Auditor, Sex Offender, Child Support records online.

Clinton County Recorder 46 S. South St, Courthouse, Wilmington, OH 45177 **937-382-2067** Fax: 937-382-8097. 8AM-4PM. www.co.clinton.oh.us/default.htm Auditor, Property records online.

Columbiana County Recorder 105 S. Market St., County Courthouse, Rm 104, Lisbon, OH 44432 **330-424-9517 x641** Fax:

330-424-5067. 8am-4pm M-F. Real Estate, Auditor, Forfeited Land Sale records online.

Coshocton County Recorder PO Box 817, Coshocton, OH 43812 (349 Main St). **740-622-2817** Fax: 740-295-7352. 8AM-4PM. www.co.coshocton.oh.us/ Property, Deed, UCC, Auditor, Property Tax, Sex Offender records online.

Crawford County Recorder PO Box 788, Bucyrus, OH 44820-0788 (112 E. Mansfield St). **419-562-6961** Fax: 419-562-6061. 8:30-4:30PM. Auditor, Real Estate, Dog Tag records online.

Cuyahoga County Recorder 1219 Ontario St, Rm 220, Cleveland, OH 44113 **216-443-7316** Fax: 216-443-8193. 8:30AM-4:30PM. www.recorder.cuyahogacounty.com Auditor, Probate, Marriage, Real Estate, Tax Lien, Recording, Cemetery, Most Wanted, Sexual Predator records online.

Darke County Recorder 504 S Broadway, Courthouse, Greenville, OH 45331 **937-547-7390** www.co.darke.oh.us/links.htm Real Estate, Deed, UCC, Property Tax records online. 8:30AM-4:30PM.

Defiance County Recorder 221 Clinton St, Courthouse, Defiance, OH 43512 **419-782-4741** Fax: 419-782-3421. 8:30AM-4:30PM. www.defiance-county.com/recorder.html Auditor, Real Estate records online.

Delaware County Recorder 91 N. Sandusky St, Courthouse, Delaware, OH 43015 **740-833-2460** Fax: 740-833-2459. 8:30AM-4:30PM. www.co.delaware.oh.us Real Estate, Deed, UCC Auditor, Property Sale, Sheriff Sale, Most Wanted, Sex Offender, DUI records online.

Erie County Recorder 247 Columbus Ave., Erie County Office Bldg, Rm 225, Sandusky, OH 44870-2635 **419-627-7686** Fax: 419-627-6639. 8AM-4PM. www.erie-county-ohio.net/officials.htm Auditor, Property, Recording, Deed records online.

Fairfield County Recorder PO Box 2420, Lancaster, OH 43130-5420 (210 E Main St). **740-687-7100** Fax: 740-687-7104. 8AM-4PM. www.co.fairfield.oh.us Property, Deed, UCC, Auditor, Property Sale, Inmate, Sex Offender records online.

Fayette County Recorder 133 S Main St, Courthouse Bldg., Washington Court House, OH 43160-1393 **740-335-1770** Fax: 740-333-3521. 9AM-4PM. www.fayette-co-oh.com/ Recorder, Deed, Lien, Judgment, Birth, Auditor, Property, Sale, Sex Offender, Sheriff Sale records online.

Franklin County Recorder 373 S. High St, 18th Fl, Columbus, OH 43215-6307 **614-462-3930, 614-462-3378** Fax: 614-462-4312, 614-462-4299. www.co.franklin.oh.us/recorder/ Recorder, Property, Auditor, Unclaimed Funds, Marriage, Treasurer Refund, Most Wanted, Sheriif Sale, Sex Offender records online. 8:AM-5PM.

Fulton County Recorder 152 S Fulton St #175, Wauseon, OH 43567 **419-337-9232** Fax: 419-337-9282. 8:30AM-4:30PM. www.fultoncountyoh.com Property, Deed, Recorder, UCC, Auditor, Real Estate records online.

Gallia County Recorder 18 Locust St, Rm 1265, Gallipolis, OH 45631-1265 **740-446-4612 x248** Fax: 740-446-4804. 8AM-4PM. www.galliacounty.org/government/governme nt.html Property, Real Estate, Most Wanted, Sex Offender, Inmate records online.

Geauga County Recorder 231 Main St, #1C, Courthouse Annex, Chardon, OH 44024-1235 **440-285-2222 x3680** 8AM-4:30PM. www.co.geauga.oh.us Delinquent Property Tax, Tax Sale, Auditor, Property, Most Wanted, Sex Offender records online.

Greene County Recorder PO Box 100, Xenia, OH 45385-0100 (69 Greene St, 3rd Fl). **937-376-5270** Fax: 937-376-5386. 8AM-4:30PM. www.co.greene.oh.us/recorder.htm Real Estate, Auditor, Recording, Deed, Mortgage, Grantor/Grantee, Sheriff Sale, Sex Offender records online.

Guernsey County Recorder 801 Wheeling Ave, Courthouse D-202, Cambridge, OH 43725 **740-432-9275** Fax: 740-439-6258. 8AM-4PM. Sex Offender records online.

Hamilton County Recorder 138 E Court St, Rm 101-A, Cincinnati, OH 45202 **513-946-4570** Fax: 513-946-4577. 8AM-4PM. www.recordersoffice.hamilton-co.org Real Estate, Lien, Recording, Lien, Deed, Mortgage, UCC, Auditor, Sex Offender, Most Wanted, Missing, Sheriff Sale. Marriage records online.

Hancock County Recorder 300 S. Main St, Courthouse, Findlay, OH 45840 **419-424-7091** Fax: 419-423-3017. 8:30AM-4:30PM. http://co.hancock.oh.us/recorder/recorder.htm Property, Auditor, Sex Offender, Real estate, Recorder, Deed, UCC records online.

Hardin County Recorder One Courthouse Sq, #220, Kenton, OH 43326 **19-674-2250** Fax: 419-675-2802. 8:30AM-4PM; 8:30-5PM Fri. www.co.hardin.oh.us Auditor, Property, Sex Offender records online.

Harrison County Recorder 100 W. Market St, Courthouse, Cadiz, OH 43907 **740-942-8869** Fax: 740-942-4693. 8:30AM-4:30PM. www.harrisoncountyohio.org/

Henry County Recorder 660 N. Perry St., Courthouse, Rm 202, Napoleon, OH 43545-1747 **419-592-1766** Fax: 419-592-1652. 8:30AM-4:30PM. www.ohiorecorders.com Sheriff Sale, Sex Offender records online.

Highland County Recorder PO Box 804, Hillsboro, OH 45133 (119 Governor Foraker Pl, #108). **937-393-9954** Fax: 937-393-5855. 8:30AM-4PM. www.ohiorecorders.com Property, Deed, UCC, Auditor, Property Sale, Sex Offender, Sheriff Sale records online.

Hocking County Recorder PO Box 949, Logan, OH 43138-0949 (1 E. Main St). **740-385-2031** Fax: 740-385-0377. 8:30AM -4PM. www.co.hocking.oh.us/ Property, Auditor, Sexual Offender, Inmate records online.

Holmes County Recorder PO Box 213, Millersburg, OH 44654 (75 E. Clinton St, #101). **330-674-5916** Fax: none. 8-4:30PM. Property, Auditor, Sale records online.

Huron County Recorder PO Box 354, Norwalk, OH 44857 (2 E. Main St). **419-668-1916** Fax: 419-663-4052. 8-4:30PM. Property, Auditor, Sale records online.

Jackson County Recorder 226 E. Main St., Courthouse, #1, Jackson, OH 45640 **740-286-1919** 8AM-4PM. Inmates, Sex Offender records online.

Jefferson County Recorder 301 Market St., Steubenville, OH 43952 **740-283-8566** Fax: none. 8:30AM-4:30PM. Property, Auditor records online.

Knox County Recorder 117 E. High St, Mount Vernon, OH 43050 **740-393-6755** 8AM-4PM. www.knoxcountyohio.org/CountyOffices.htm Property, Auditor, Court records online.

Lake County Recorder PO Box 490, Painesville, OH 44077-0490 (105 Main St). **440-350-2510** Fax: 440-350-5940. 8-4PM. www.lakecountyrecorder.org Recording, Lien, Deed, UCC, Land Bank Sale records online.

Lawrence County Recorder PO Box 77, Ironton, OH 45638 (111 S. 4th St). **740-533-4314** Fax: 740-533-4411. 8AM-4PM. http://63.239.104.62 Auditor, Property, Real Estate, Deed, Lien, Recording records online.

Licking County Recorder PO Box 520, Newark, OH 43058 (20 S Second St, 3rd Fl). **740-349-6060** Fax: 740-349-1415. 8:30AM-4:30PM. www.lcounty.com/rec/ Real Estate, Tax Lien, Recording, Property Tax, Cemetery, Genealogy, Sex Offender records online.

Logan County Recorder 100 S Madriver, #A, Bellefontaine, OH 43311-2075 **937-599-7201** Fax: 937-599-7287. 8:30AM-4:30PM. www.co.logan.oh.us/Recorder/index.html Real Estate, Auditor, Recording, Deed, Lien, Jail Inmate, Sex Offender records online.

Lorain County Recorder 226 Middle Ave, Elyria, OH 44035 **440-329-5148** Fax: 440-329-5477. www.loraincounty.com/recorder Real Estate, Lien, Auditor, Property Sale, Unclaimed Funds, Sheriff Sale, Sex Offender records online. 8AM-4:30PM.

Lucas County Recorder 1 Government Ctr #700, Jackson St, Toledo, OH 43604 **419-213-4400** Fax: 419-213-4284. 8AM-5PM. www.co.lucas.oh.us/ Real Estate, Auditor, Unclaimed Funds, Sheriff Sale, Sex Offender records online.

Madison County Recorder 1 N Main St, Rm 40, Courthouse, London, OH 43140 **740-852-1854** Fax: 740-845-1776. 8AM-4PM. www.co.madison.oh.us Real Estate, Auditor, Deed, UCC, Recording, Sex Offender, Sheriff Sale records online.

Mahoning County Recorder PO Box 928, Youngstown, OH 44501 (120 Market St). **330-740-2345** Fax: 330-740-2006. www.mahoningcountyauditor.org Real Estate, Auditor, Property Sale, Deed, UCC, Lien, Judgment, Recording records online.

Marion County Recorder 222 W Center St, Marion, OH 43302-3646 **740-223-4100** 8:30AM-4:30PM. www.co.marion.oh.us Real Estate, Auditor records online.

Medina County Recorder 144 N. Broadway, County Admin. Bldg, Medina, OH 44256-2295 **330-725-9782** 8AM-4:30PM.

www.recorder.co.medina.oh.us Real Estate, Auditor, Property Transfer, Sex Offender, records online.

Meigs County Recorder 100 E. Second St, Courthouse, Pomeroy, OH 45769 **740-992-3806** Fax: 740-992-2867. 8:30AM-4:30PM.

Mercer County Recorder 101 N. Main St, Courthouse Sq, Rm 203, Celina, OH 45822 **419-586-4232** Fax: 419-586-3541. 8:30AM-5PM M; 8:30AM-4PM T-F. www.mercercountyohio.org Real Estate, Auditor, Property Sale, Sex Offender records online.

Miami County Recorder PO Box 653, Troy, OH 45373 (201 W. Main St). **937-332-6893** Fax: 937-332-6806. 7:30AM-4:30PM.

Monroe County Recorder PO Box 152, Woodsfield, OH 43793-0152 (101 N. Main St, Rm 20). **740-472-5264** Fax: 740-472-2523. 8AM-4PM. Property, Auditor records online.

Montgomery County Recorder PO Box 972, Dayton, OH 45422 (451 W Third St, 5th Fl). **937-225-4275** Fax: 937-225-5980. www.mcohio.org/departments.html Property, Real Estate, Lien, Recording, Auditor records online. 8AM-4:30PM.

Morgan County Recorder 155 E Main St, RM 160, McConnelsville, OH 43756 **740-962-4051** Fax: 740-962-3364. 8AM-4PM. Property, Auditor, Inmate records online.

Morrow County Recorder 48 E. High St, Mount Gilead, OH 43338 **419-947-3060** Fax: 419-947-3709. 8AM-4PM. www.morrowcounty.info/morrowoff.htm Real Estate, Appraisal, Property Sale records online.

Muskingum County Recorder PO Box 2333, Zanesville, OH 43702-2333 (4th & Main Courthouse). **740-455-7107** Fax: 740-455-7943. 8:30-4:30. Real Estate, Assessor, Sheriff Sale, Sex Offender records online.

Noble County Recorder 260 Courthouse, Rm 2E, Caldwell, OH 43724 **740-732-4319** 8AM-4PM M-W; 8AM-NTh; 8AM-6PM.

Ottawa County Recorder 315 Madison St, Rm 204, Port Clinton, OH 43452 (**419-734-6730** Fax: 419-734-6919. 8:30AM-4:30PM. Property, Auditor, Cemetery, Sex Offender records online.

Paulding County Recorder 115 N Williams St, Paulding, OH 45879 **419-399-8275** Fax: 419-399-2862. 8AM-4PM.

Perry County Recorder PO Box 147, New Lexington, OH 43764 (105 Main St). **740-342-2494** Fax: 740-342-5539. 8:30AM-4:30PM. Inmate records online.

Pickaway County Recorder 207 S. Court St, Circleville, OH 43113 **740-474-5826** Fax: 740-477-6361. 8AM-4PM. Property, Auditor, Real Estate, Recorder, Deed, UCC records online.

Pike County Recorder 230 Waverly Plaza #500, Courthouse, Waverly, OH 45690 **740-947-2622** Fax: 740-947-7997. 8:30AM-4PM. Recorder, Deed, Lien, UCC, Real Estate, Auditor, Inmate records online.

Portage County Recorder 449 S. Meridian St, Ravenna, OH 44266 **330-297-3554** Fax: 330-297-7349. 8-4:30. www.co.portage.oh.us Property, Auditor, Property Sale, Sheriff Sale, Sex Offender records online.

Preble County Recorder PO Box 371, Eaton, OH 45320-0371 (101 E Main St.). **937-456-8173** 8AM-4:30PM. www.ohiorecorders.com Real Estate, Auditor, Obituary records online.

Putnam County Recorder 245 E. Main St, Courthouse - #202, Ottawa, OH 45875-1959 **419-523-6490** Fax: 419-523-4403. 8:30AM-4:30PM. Property, Auditor, Property Sale records online.

Richland County Recorder 50 Park Ave East, Mansfield, OH 44902 **419-774-5602/5600** Fax: 419-774-5603. 8AM-4PM. www.richlandcountyauditor.org Real Estate, Auditor, Deed, UCC, Property Sale, Sheriff Sale, Sex Offender records online.

Ross County Recorder PO Box 6162, Chillicothe, OH 45601 (2 N. Paint St, #E). **740-702-3000** Fax: 740-702-3006. 8:30AM-4:30PM. www.co.ross.oh.us/ Property, Deed, UCC, Auditor, Recorder records online.

Sandusky County Recorder 100 N. Park Ave., Courthouse, Fremont, OH 43420-2477 **419-334-6226** 8AM-4:30PM. www.sandusky-county.org/County_Recorder.asp Property, Auditor, Treasurer records online.

Scioto County Recorder 602 7th St, Rm 110, Rm 110, Portsmouth, OH 45662-3950 **740-355-8304** Fax: 740-353-7358. 8-4:30PM. www.sciotocountyohio.com Property, Auditor records online.

Seneca County Recorder 109 S. Washington St #2104, Tiffin, OH 44883 **419-447-4434** 8:30AM-4:30PM. Property, Most Wanted, Missing Person records online.

Shelby County Recorder 129 E. Court St, Shelby County Annex, Sidney, OH 45365 **937-498-7270** Fax: 937-498-7272. 7:30AM-4:30PM. www.co.shelby.oh.us/Recorder.asp Sheriff Sale, Sex Offender records online.

Stark County Recorder 110 Central Plaza South, #170, Canton, OH 44702-1409 **330-451-7443** Fax: 330-451-7394. 8:30AM-4:30PM (Recording: 8:30AM-4PM). www.co.stark.oh.us Real Estate, Deed, Recording, Auditor, Property, Sheriff Sale, Delinquent Taxpayer, Sex Offender, Unclaimed Funds records online.

Summit County Fiscal Officer, Recording Department 175 S Main St, Akron, OH 44308-1355 **330-643-2720** 7:30AM-4PM. www.co.summit.oh.us/fiscaloffice Real Estate, Auditor, Property Tax, Recording, Deed, Sex Offender, Most Wanted, Sheriff Sale records online.

Trumbull County Recorder 160 High St NW, Warren, OH 44481 **330-675-2401, 330-393-2707** Fax: 330-675-2404. 8:30AM-4:30PM. www.tcrecorder.co.trumbull.oh.us Auditor, Property Tax, Recording, Deed, Mortgage, Lien, Unclaimed Funds, Warrant records online.

Tuscarawas County Recorder 125 E. High Ave, New Philadelphia, OH 44663 **330-365-3284** 8-4:30PM. www.co.tuscarawas.oh.us Real Estate, Delinquent Tax List, Unclaimed Fund records online.

Union County Recorder 233 W. Sixth St., Marysville, OH 43040 **937-645-3032** Fax: 937-642-3397. 8:30AM-4PM. www.co.union.oh.us/Recorder/recorder.html Auditor, Property Tax, Real Estate, Recording, Delinquent Taxpayer records online.

Van Wert County Recorder 121 E Main St, Courthouse - Rm 206, Van Wert, OH 45891-1729 **419-238-2558** Fax: 419-238-5410. 8:30AM-5PM M; 8:30AM-4PM T-F. www.ohiorecorders.com Property, Deed, UCC, Recording, Auditor records online.

Vinton County Recorder 100 E Main St, McArthur, OH 45651 **740-596-4314** Fax: 740-596-2265. 8:30AM-4PM. Inmate records online.

Warren County Recorder 406 Justice Dr., Lebanon, OH 45036. **513-695-1382** Fax: 513-695-2949. www.co.warren.oh.us Property, Auditor, Mapping, Sex Offender records online. 8AM-4:30PM.

Washington County Recorder 205 Putnam St, Courthouse, Marietta, OH 45750 **740-373-6623 x235 or 236** Fax: 740-373-9643. 8AM-5PM. www.ohiorecorders.com Property, Auditor, Deed, UCC, Recorder, Real Estate records online.

Wayne County Recorder 428 W Liberty St, Wooster, OH 44691-5097 **330-287-5460** Fax: 330-287-5685. 8-4:30. www.co.wayne.oh.us

Property, Auditor, Sex Offender, Late Taxpayer records online.

Williams County Recorder 1 Courthouse Sq, Bryan, OH 43506 (**419-636-3259** 8:30AM-4:30PM. Property, Auditor, Property Sale records online.

Wood County Recorder 1 Courthouse Sq, Bowling Green, OH 43402 **419-354-9140** 8:30-4:30PM. www.co.wood.oh.us/recorder Property, Auditor, Obituary, Treasurer Tax records online.

Wyandot County Recorder 109 S. Sandusky Ave., Courthouse, Upper Sandusky, OH 43351 **419-294-1442** Fax: 419-294-6405. 8:30AM-4:30PM. Property, Auditor records online.

Oklahoma

Organization: 77 counties, 77 recording offices. The recording officer is the County Clerk. State is in the Central Time Zone (CST).

Real Estate Records: Many counties will perform real estate searches by legal description. Copy fees are usually $1.00 per page. Certification usually costs $1.00 per document.

UCC Records: Financing statements are filed centrally with the County Clerk of Oklahoma County. Prior to 7/2001, consumer goods, farm related, and real estate related collateral were dual filed with the local County Clerk as well as the County Clerk of Oklahoma County. Now only rela estate related collateral is filed at the local level. All counties will perform UCC searches. Use search request form UCC-4. Search fees are usually $5.00 per debtor name for a written request and $3.00 per name by telephone. Copies usually cost $1.00 per page.

Tax Lien Records: Federal tax liens on personal property of businesses are filed with the County Clerk of Oklahoma County, which is the central filing office for the state. Other federal and all state tax liens are filed with the County Clerk. Usually state and federal tax liens on personal property are filed in separate indexes. Some counties will perform tax lien searches. Search fees vary. Other Liens: Judgment, mechanics, physicians, hospital.

Online Access: Very little is available online.

Adair County Clerk PO Box 169, Stilwell, OK 74960 (Division St & Highway 59). **918-696-7198** Fax: 918-696-2603. 8-4:30.

Alfalfa County Clerk 300 S. Grand, Cherokee, OK 73728 **580-596-3158** 8:30AM-4:30PM.

Atoka County Clerk 200 E. Court St, Atoka, OK 74525 **580-889-5157** Fax: 580-889-5063. 8:30AM-4:30PM.

Beaver County Clerk PO Box 338, Beaver, OK 73932-0338 (111 W. Second St). **580-625-3141** Fax: 580-625-3430. 8AM-5PM.

Beckham County Clerk PO Box 428, Sayre, OK 73662 (Rm 102, 302 E. Main St.). **580-928-3383** Fax: 580-928-5220. 9AM-5PM.

Blaine County Clerk PO Box 138, Watonga, OK 73772 (212 N. Weigel). **580-623-5890** Fax: 580-623-5009. 8AM-4PM.

Bryan County Clerk PO Box 1789, Durant, OK 74702 (402 W. Evergreen). **580-924-2202** Fax: 580-924-2289. 8AM-5PM.

Caddo County Clerk PO Box 68, Anadarko, OK 73005 (SW Second & Oklahoma). **405-247-6609** Fax: 405-247-6510. 8:30-4:30PM.

Canadian County Clerk PO Box 458, El Reno, OK 73036 (201 N. Choctaw). **405-262-1070 ext123** Fax: 405-422-2411. www.canadiancounty.org Land, Grantor/ Grantee, Deed, Lien, Judgment records online.

Carter County Clerk PO Box 1236, Ardmore, OK 73402 (#20 "B" Street SW, Rm 102, 1st Fl). **580-223-8162** 8AM-5PM. www.brightok.net/chickasaw/ardmore/county/ coclerk.html Assessor, Unsolved Case records online.

Cherokee County Clerk 213 W. Delaware, Rm 200, Tahlequah, OK 74464 **918-456-3171** Fax: 918-458-6508. 8AM-4:30PM.

Choctaw County Clerk 300 E, Duke, Courthouse, Hugo, OK 74743 **580-326-3778** Fax: 580-326-6787. 8AM-4PM.

Cimarron County Clerk PO Box 145, Boise City, OK 73933 (Courthouse Sq). **580-544-2251** Fax: 580-544-2251. 8AM-N, 1-5PM.

Cleveland County Clerk 641 E Robinson #300, Norman, OK 73071 **405-366-0240** Fax: 405-366-0229. 8:15AM-4:45PM. www.okclev.cogov.net Recording, Lien, Judgment, UCC, Fictitious Name, Military Discharge records online.

Coal County Clerk 4 N. Main, #1, Coalgate, OK 74538 **580-927-2103** Fax: 580-927-4003. 8AM-4PM.

Comanche County Clerk 315 SW 5th, Rm 304, Lawton, OK 73501-4347 **580-355-5214** 8:30AM-5PM.

Cotton County Clerk 301 N. Broadway, Walters, OK 73572 **580-875-3026** Fax: 580-875-3756. 8AM-4PM.

Craig County Clerk PO Box 397, Vinita, OK 74301 (Courthouse). **918-256-2507** Fax: 918-256-3617. 8:30AM-4:30PM.

Creek County Clerk 317 E. Lee, 1st Fl, Sapulpa, OK 74066 **918-227-6306** 8-5PM.

Custer County Clerk PO Box 300, Arapaho, OK 73620 (675 W. "B" St). **580-323-1221** Fax: 580-323-4421. 8AM-4PM.

Delaware County Clerk PO Box 309, Jay, OK 74346 (327 S. 5th St). **918-253-4520** Fax: 918-253-8352. 8AM-4:30PM. Real Estate, Deed records online.

Dewey County Clerk PO Box 368, Taloga, OK 73667 (Broadway & Ruble). **580-328-5361** Fax: 580-328-5652. 8AM-4PM.

Ellis County PO Box 197, Arnett, OK 73832 (100 Courthouse Sq). **580-885-7301** Fax: 580-885-7258. 8:30AM-4:30PM.

Garfield County Clerk PO Box 1664, Enid, OK 73702-1664 (114 W. Broadway). **580-237-0226** Fax: 580-249-5951. 8-4:30PM.

Garvin County Clerk PO Box 926, Pauls Valley, OK 73075 (201 W. Grant). **405-238-2772** Fax: 405-238-6283. 8:30-4:30PM.

Grady County Clerk PO Box 1009, Chickasha, OK 73023 (4th & Choctaw). **405-224-7388** Fax: 405-222-4506. 8AM-4:30PM. www.gradycounty.net

Grant County Clerk PO Box 167, Medford, OK 73759-0167 (112 E. Guthrie). **580-395-2274** Fax: 580-395-2086. 8AM-4:30PM.

Greer County Clerk PO Box 207, Mangum, OK 73554 (Courthouse Sq). **580-782-3664** Fax: 580-782-3803. 8AM-4PM.

Harmon County Clerk 14 W Hollis, Courthouse, Hollis, OK 73550 **580-688-3658** 8-12:00-1-5PM.

Harper County Clerk PO Box 369, Buffalo, OK 73834 (311 SE First St). **580-735-2012** Fax: 580-735-2612. 8AM-4PM.

Haskell County Clerk 202 E. Main, Courthouse, Stigler, OK 74462 **918-967-2884** Fax: 918-967-2885. 8AM-4:30PM.

Hughes County Clerk 200 N. Broadway ST. #5, Holdenville, OK 74848-3400 **405-379-5487** Fax: 405-379-6890. 8AM-4:30PM.

Jackson County Clerk PO Box 515, Altus, OK 73522 (Main & Broadway, Rm 203). **580-482-4070** 8AM-4PM.

Jefferson County Clerk 220 N. Main, Courthouse - Rm 103, Waurika, OK 73573 **580-228-2029** Fax: 580-228-3418. 8-4PM.

Johnston County Clerk 414 W. Main, Rm 101, Tishomingo, OK 73460 **580-371-3184** Fax: 580-371-3662. 8:30AM-4:30PM.

Kay County Clerk PO Box 450, Newkirk, OK 74647-0450 (201 S. Main). **580-362-2537** Fax: 580-362-3300. 8AM-4:30PM.

Kingfisher County Clerk 101 S. Main, Rm #3, Kingfisher, OK 73750 **405-375-3887** Fax: 405-375-6033. 8AM-4:30PM.

Kiowa County Clerk PO Box 73, Hobart, OK 73651-0073 (316 S. Main). **580-726-5286** Fax: 580-726-6033. 9AM-5PM.

Latimer County Clerk 109 N Central, Rm 103, Wilburton, OK 74578 **918-465-3543** Fax: 918-465-4001. 8AM-4:30PM.

Le Flore County Clerk PO Box 218, Poteau, OK 74953-0218 (100 S. Broadway). **918-647-5738** Fax: 918-647-8930. 8AM-4:30PM. Real Estate, Deed records online.

Lincoln County Clerk PO Box 126, Chandler, OK 74834-0126 (800 Manvel Ave.). **405-258-1264** 8:30AM-4:30PM. Real Estate Recording records online.

Logan County Clerk 301 E. Harrison, #102, Guthrie, OK 73044-4999 **405-282-0266** Fax: 405-282-0267. 8:30AM-4:30PM.

Love County Clerk 405 W. Main, Rm 203, Marietta, OK 73448 **580-276-3059** 8AM-N, 12:30-4:30PM.

Major County Clerk PO Box 379, Fairview, OK 73737-0379 (9th & Broadway). **580-227-4732** Fax: 580-227-2736. 8:30AM-4:30PM.

Marshall County Clerk Courthouse, Rm 101, Madill, OK 73446 **580-795-3220** Fax: 580-795-7596. 8:30AM-N, 12:30-5PM.

Mayes County Clerk 1 Court Place #120, Pryor, OK 74361 **918-825-2426** Fax: 918-825-3803. 9AM-5PM.

McClain County Clerk PO Box 629, Purcell, OK 73080-0629 (121 N Washington, #303). **405-527-3360** Fax: 405-5 27-5242. 8AM-4:30PM.

McCurtain County Clerk PO Box 1078, Idabel, OK 74745 (108 N. Central). **580-286-2370** Fax: 580-286-7040. 8AM-4PM.

McIntosh County Clerk PO Box 110, Eufaula, OK 74432-0110 (110 N. 1st St). **918-689-5419** Fax: 918-689-3385. 8-4PM.

Murray County Clerk PO Box 442, Sulphur, OK 73086 (10th & Wyandotte). **580-622-3920** Fax: 580-622-6209. 8-4:30.

Muskogee County Clerk PO Box 1008, Muskogee, OK 74401 (400 W Broadway). **918-682-7781** 8AM-4:30PM.

Noble County Clerk 300 Courthouse Dr, Box 11, Courthouse, Rm 201, Perry, OK 73077 **580-336-2141** Fax: 580-336-2481. 8AM-4:30PM.

Nowata County Clerk 229 N. Maple, Nowata, OK 74048 **918-273-2480** Fax: 918-273-2481. 8AM-4:30PM.

Okfuskee County Clerk PO Box 108, Okemah, OK 74859-0108 (3rd & Atlanta). **918-623-1724** Fax: 918-623-0739. 8-4PM.

Oklahoma County Clerk 320 Robert S. Kerr Ave, UCC Filing Ofc - Rm 107, Oklahoma City, OK 73102 **405-713-1522** Fax: 405-713-1810. 8AM-5PM. www.oklahomacounty.org Real Estate, Assessor, Grantor/Grantee, UCC, Property Tax, Inmate, Sex Offender, Wanted records online.

Okmulgee County Clerk PO Box 904, Okmulgee, OK 74447-0904 (7th & Seminole). **918-756-0788** Fax: 918-758-1261. 8AM-4:30PM.

Osage County Clerk PO Box 87, Pawhuska, OK 74056 (6th & Grandview). **918-287-3136** Fax: 918-287-4979. 8:30AM-5PM.

Ottawa County Clerk 102 E. Central, #203, Miami, OK 74354-7043 **918-542-3332** Fax: 918-542-8260. 9AM-N, 1-5PM; Recording until 4:00PM.

Pawnee County Clerk 500 Harrison St., Courthouse, Rm 202, Pawnee, OK 74058 **918-762-2732** Fax: 918-762-6404. 8-4:30.

Payne County Clerk 315 W 6th Ave #202, Stillwater, OK 74074 **405-747-8310** 8AM-5PM. Real Estate, Deed records online.

Pittsburg County Clerk PO Box 3304, McAlester, OK 74502 (115 E. Carl Albert Parkway). **918-423-6865** Fax: 918-423-7304. 8AM-5PM.

Pontotoc County Clerk PO Box 1425, Ada, OK 74820 (100 W. 13th, Rm 205). **580-332-1425** Fax: 580-332-9509. 8AM-5PM. www.pontotoccountyclerk.org Recording, Land, UCC, Judgment, Lien, Military records online.

Pottawatomie County Clerk PO Box 576, Shawnee, OK 74802 (325 N. Broadway). **405-273-8222** Fax: 405-275-6898. 8:30AM-5PM.

Pushmataha County Clerk 302 SW 'B', Antlers, OK 74523 **580-298-3626** Fax: 580-298-8452. 8AM-4:30PM.

Roger Mills County Clerk PO Box 708, Cheyenne, OK 73628 (Broadway & L.L. Males Ave). **580-497-3395** Fax: 580-497-3488. 9AM-4:30PM.

Rogers County Clerk PO Box 1210, Claremore, OK 74018 (219 S. Missouri, Rm 1-104). **918-341-2518** Fax: 918-341-4529. 8AM-5PM. www.rogerscounty.org Assessor, Property Tax, Treasurer, Tax Roll, Real Estate Recording records online.

Seminole County Clerk PO Box 1180, Wewoka, OK 74884 (110 S. Wewoka, Courthouse). **405-257-2501** Fax: 405-257-6422. 8AM-4PM.

Sequoyah County Clerk 120 E. Chickasaw, Sallisaw, OK 74955 **918-775-4516** Fax: 918-775-1218. 8-4.

Stephens County Clerk 101 S. 11th St, Rm 203, Duncan, OK 73533-4758 **580-255-0977** Fax: 580-255-0991. 8:30AM-4:30PM. Real Estate, Deed records online.

Texas County Clerk PO Box 197, Guymon, OK 73942-0197 (319 N. Main). **580-338-3141** Fax: 580-338-4311. 9AM-5PM.

Tillman County Clerk PO Box 992, Frederick, OK 73542 (10th & Gladstone). **580-335-3421** Fax: 580-335-3795. 8AM-4PM. www.oklahomacounty.org/countyclerk

Tulsa County Clerk 500 S. Denver Ave, County Admin. Bldg, Rm 112, Tulsa, OK 74103-3832 **918-596-5801** Fax: 918-596-5867. 8:30AM-5PM. www.tulsacounty.org

Assessor, Treasurer, Recording, Deed, Property, Inmate records online.

Wagoner County Clerk PO Box 156, Wagoner, OK 74477 (307 E Cherokee). **918-485-2216** Fax: 918-485-7709. 8-4:30.

Washington County Clerk 420 S Johnstone, #100, Bartlesville, OK 74003 **918-337-2840**

Fax: 918-337-2894. 8AM-5PM. www.countycourthouse.org Land, Deed, Mortgage, Lien, Sex Offender records online.

Washita County Clerk PO Box 380, Cordell, OK 73632 (100 E. Main). **580-832-3548** 8AM-4PM.

Woods County Clerk PO Box 386, Alva, OK 73717-0386 (Courthouse, 407 Government St). **580-327-0998** Fax: 580-327-6222. 9AM-5PM.

Woodward County Clerk 1600 Main St, #8, Woodward, OK 73801-3051 **580-254-6800** Fax: 580-254-6840. 9AM-5PM.

 # Oregon

Organization: 36 counties, 36 recording offices. The recording officer is the County Clerk. 35 counties are in the Pacific Time Zone (PST) and one is in the Mountain Time Zone (MST).

Real Estate Records: Some counties will not perform real estate searches. Search fees vary. Many counties will search all liens together for $12.50 per name. Copy fees are usually $.25 per page. Certification usually costs $3.75 per document. The Assessor keeps tax and ownership records.

UCC Records: Financing statements are filed at the state level, except for real estate related collateral. Many county clerks will perform UCC searches, fees vary from $3.50 to $13.50, we suggest to call first.

Tax Lien Records: All federal and state tax liens on personal property are filed with the Secretary of State. Other federal and state tax liens are filed with the County Clerk. Most counties will perform tax lien searches and include both with a UCC search for an extra $7.50 per name. Search fees vary widely. Other Liens: County tax, public utility, construction, judgment, hospital.

Online Access: A few counties offer Internet access to assessor records. There is no statewide system available.

Baker County Clerk 1995 Third St, #150, Baker, OR 97814-3398 **541-523-8207** Fax: 541-523-8240. 8-5. www.bakercounty.org Property, Assessor records online.

Benton County Clerk 120 NW 4th St, Rm 4, Corvallis, OR 97330 **541-766-6831** Fax: 541-766-6675. 8AM-5PM. www.co.benton.or.us Real Estate, Assessor, Property, Inmate, 30-day Released Inmate, Wanted records online.

Clackamas County Clerk 2051 Kaen Rd, Oregon City, OR 97045 (2nd Fl). **503-655-8551** 8:30AM-5PM M,T,Th,F; 9:30AM-5PM W. www.co.clackamas.or.us/clerk Real Property, Most Wanted records online.

Clatsop County Clerk PO Box 178, Astoria, OR 97103-0178 (749 Commercial). **503-325-8511** Fax: 503-325-9307. 8:30AM-4:00PM. www.co.clatsop.or.us

Columbia County Clerk Courthouse, St. Helens, OR 97051-2041 **503-397-3796** Fax: 503-397-7266. Recording hrs 9pm-4pm..

Coos County Clerk 250 N Baxter, Courthouse, Coquille, OR 97423-1899 **541-396-3121** Fax: 541-396-6551. 8AM-5PM (Closed to public: Noon-1PM). www.co.coos.or.us Assessor, Property, Sale records online.

Crook County Clerk 300 E. Third, Prineville, OR 97754 **541-447-6553** Fax: 541-416-2145. 8AM-5PM.

Curry County Clerk PO Box 746, Gold Beach, OR 97444 (29821 Ellensburg Ave.). **541-247-3295** Fax: 541-247-6440. 8:30AM-4PM. www.co.curry.or.us

Deschutes County Clerk 1300 NW Wall St. #200, Bend, OR 97701 **541-388-6549** Fax: 541-389-6830. 8AM-4PM http://recordings.co.deschutes.or.us Real Estate, Deed, Mortgage, Lien, Assessor, Property Tax records online.

Douglas County Clerk PO Box 10, Roseburg, OR 97470 (1036 SE Douglas, Rm 221). **541-440-4322** Fax: 541-440-4408. 8-4PM. Assessor, Property records online.

Gilliam County Clerk PO Box 427, Condon, OR 97823 (221 S. Oregon St). **541-384-2311** Fax: 541-384-2166. 8:30-N, 1-5PM.

Grant County Clerk 201 S. Humbolt, #290, Canyon City, OR 97820 **541-575-1675** Fax: 541-575-2248.

Harney County Clerk 450 N. Buena Vista, Burns, OR 97720 **541-573-6641** Fax: 541-573-8370. 8:30AM-5PM (closed 1 hr for lunch). www.co.harney.or.us/

Hood River County Clerk 601 State St., Hood River, OR 97031-1871 **541-386-1442/or/6849** Fax: 541-387-6864. 8-5PM.

Jackson County Clerk 10 S. Oakdale, Rm 216A, Medford, OR 97501 **541-774-6147**

Fax: 541-774-6714. 8AM-4PM. www.jacksoncounty.org

Jefferson County Clerk 66 S.E. D St, #C, Madras, OR 97741 **541-475-4451** Fax: 541-325-5018.

Josephine County Clerk PO Box 69, Grants Pass, OR 97528 (6 & C Sts). **541-474-5240** Fax: 541-476-5246. 9AM-4PM.

Klamath County Clerk 305 Main St., Klamath Falls, OR 97601 (**800-377-6094, 541-883-5134** Fax: 541-885-6757. 8AM-5PM; Recording Hours: 8AM-4PM. www.co.klamath.or.us

Lake County Clerk 513 Center St, Lakeview, OR 97630-1539 **541-947-6006** Fax: 541-947-6015. 8:30AM-5PM.

Lane County Clerk 125 E. 8th Ave, Eugene, OR 97401 **541-682-3654** Fax: 541-682-3330. 8AM-5PM; Recording 9AM-N, 1-4PM. Assessor, Real Estate, Property records online.

Lincoln County Clerk 225 W. Olive St, Rm 201, Newport, OR 97365-3869 **541-265-4131** Fax: 541-265-4950. 8:30AM-5PM.

Linn County Clerk PO Box 100, Albany, OR 97321 (300 SW 4th St. Rm 207). **541-967-3829** Fax: 541-926-5109. 8:30AM-5PM. www.co.linn.or.us Assessor, Real Estate, Property Sale records online.

Malheur County Clerk 251 B St West, #4, Vale, OR 97918 **541-473-5151** Fax: 541-473-5523. 8:30AM-5PM. www.malheurco.org

Marion County Clerk PO Box 14500, Salem, OR 97309 (100 High St NE, Rm 1331). **503-588-5225** Fax: 503-588-5237. http://clerk.co.marion.or.us/records 8:30-5. Jail Inmate, Sex Offender records online.

Morrow County Chief Deputy Clerk PO Box 338, Heppner, OR 97836 (100 Court St, Rm. 102). **541-676-9061** Fax: 541-676-9876. www.rootsweb.com/~ormorrow/MorrowCountyCourthouse.htm

Multnomah County Clerk PO Box 5007, Portland, OR 97208-5007 (Rm 158, 501 SE Hawthorne St, 1st Fl). **503-988-3034** Fax: 503-988-3330. 8AM-5PM; www.co.multnomah.or.us/dss/at/index.html Real Property, Released Inmate, Restaurant Inspection records online.

Polk County Clerk 850 Main St, Rm 201, Courthouse, Dallas, OR 97338-3179 **503-623-9217** Fax: 503-623-0717. 8AM-5PM. www.co.polk.or.us

Sherman County Deputy Clerk PO Box 365, Moro, OR 97039 (500 Court St). **541-565-3606** Fax: 541-565-3312. 8AM-5PM.

Tillamook County Clerk 201 Laurel Ave, Tillamook, OR 97141 **503-842-3402** Fax: 503-842-1599. 8AM-N; 1PM-5PM. www.co.tillamook.or.us/gov/clerk/default.htm Assessor, Real Estate records online.

Umatilla County Clerk PO Box 1227, Pendleton, OR 97801-1227 (216 SE 4th St, Rm 108). **541-278-6236** Fax: 541-278-6345. Jail records online.

Union County Clerk 1001 4th St, #"D", La Grande, OR 97850 **541-963-1006** Fax: 541-963-1013. 8:30-5PM M-Th; 9:00-4PM F.

Wallowa County Clerk 101 S. River, Rm 100 Door 16, Enterprise, OR 97828 **541-426-4543 x15** Fax: 541-426-5901. 8:30AM-5PM.

Wasco County Clerk 511 Washington St., Courthouse, The Dalles, OR 97058-2237 **541-296-6159** Fax: 541-298-3607. 10AM-4PM.

Washington County Clerk 155 N. First Ave, Mail Stop 9, Hillsboro, OR 97124 (#130). **503-846-8752** www.co.washington.or.us Real Estate records online. 8:30AM-4:30PM.

Wheeler County Clerk PO Box 327, Fossil, OR 97830-0327 (701 Adams St, Rm 204). **541-763-2400** Fax: 541-763-2026. 8:30-4.

Yamhill County Clerk 535 NE 5th St, Rm 119, McMinnville, OR 97128-4593 **503-434-7518** Fax: 503-434-7520. 9AM-5PM. www.co.yamhill.or.us/clerk Property records online.

 Pennsylvania

Organization: 67 counties, 67 recording offices and 134 UCC filing offices. Each county has two different recording offices: the Prothonotary - their term for "Clerk" - who accepted UCC and tax lien filings until 07/01/2001, and the Recorder of Deeds who maintains real estate records. The entire state is in the Eastern Time Zone (EST).

Real Estate Records: County Recorders of Deeds will not perform real estate searches. Copy fees and certification fees vary.

UCC Records: This was a dual filing state. Until 07/1/2001, Financing statements were filed both at the state level and with the Prothonotary, except for real estate related collateral, which were filed with the Recorder of Deeds. Now, only real estate related collateral is filed locally. Some county offices will not perform UCC searches. Use search request form UCC-11. Search fees are usually $59.00 per debtor name. Copies usually cost $.50-$2.00 per page. Counties also charge $5.00 per financing statement found on a search.

Tax Lien Records: All federal and state tax liens on personal property and on real property are filed with the Prothonotary. Usually, tax liens on personal property are filed in the judgment index of the Prothonotary. Some Prothonotaries will perform tax lien searches. Search fees are usually $5.00 per name. Other Liens: Judgment, municipal, mechanics.

Online Access: A number of counties provide web access to assessor data. The Infocon County Access System provides Internet and direct dial-up access to recorded record information for 15 Penn. counties - Armstrong, Bedford, Blair, Butler, Clarion, Clinton, Erie, Franklin, Huntingdon, Juaniata, Lawrence, Mercer, Mifflin, Pike, and Potter. Fees are involved. Document images are available. For information, call Infocon at 814-472-6066 or visit www.ic-access.com.

Adams County Prothonotary 111-117 Baltimore St, Gettysburg, PA 17325 **717-334-6781** Fax: 717-334-0532. 8AM-4:30PM.
Recorder of Deeds 111-117 Baltimore St, County Courthouse, Rm 102, Gettysburg, PA 17325 **717-337-9826** Fax: 717-334-1758. 8AM-4:30PM.

Allegheny County Prothonotary 414 Grant St, City County Office Bldg, Pittsburgh, PA 15219 **412-350-4200** Fax: 412-350-5260. http://www2.county.allegheny.pa.us/realestate / Civil Court, UCC, Tax Lien, Real Estate, Assessor records online. 8:30AM-4:30PM.
Recorder of Deeds 542 Forbes Ave, 101 County Office Bldg., Pittsburgh, PA 15219-

2947 **412-350-4226** Fax: 412-350-6877. www.county.allegheny.pa.us Recorder, Deed, Mortgage, Real Estate records online.

Armstrong County Prothonotary 500 E Market St, County Courthouse, Kittanning, PA 16201 **724-543-2500** Fax: 724-548-3351. www.geocities.com/acprothonotary Tax Lien records online. 8:00AM-4:30PM.
Recorder of Deeds 500 Market St, County Courthouse, Kittanning, PA 16201-1495 **724-548-3256** Fax: 724-548-3236. Real Estate, Marriage, Probate records online.

Beaver County Prothonotary 810 Third St, County Courthouse, Beaver, PA 15009 **724-**

728-3934 x11279 Fax: 724-728-3360. http://co.beaver.pa.us/prothonotary
Recorder of Deeds 810 3rd St, County Courthouse, Beaver, PA 15009 **724-728-5700** Fax: 724-728-8479. 8:30AM-4:30PM. www.co.beaver.pa.us Real Estate, Deed, Mortgage, Assessor records online.

Bedford County Prothonotary County Courthouse, Corner of Penn & Julliana, Bedford, PA 15522 **814-623-4833** Fax: 814-623-4831. 8:30AM-4:30PM. Tax Lien records online.
County Recorder 200 S. Juliana St, County Courthouse, Bedford, PA 15522 **814-623-4836** Fax: 814-624-0488. 8:30AM-4:30PM.

www.bedford.net/regrec/home.html Real Estate, Assessor, Probate, Marriages online.

Berks County Prothonotary 633 Court St., Reading, PA 19601 **610-478-6980** Fax: 610-478-6969. www.berksprothy.com Judgment, Lien, UCC, Civil Court records online.
Recorder of Deeds 633 Court St, 3rd Fl, Reading, PA 19601 **610-478-3380** Fax: 610-478-3359. www.berksrecofdeeds.com Vital Statistic, Probate, DR Warrant records online.

Blair County Prothonotary 423 Allegheny St #144, Hollidaysburg, PA 16648 **814-693-3080** 8AM-4PM. Tax Lien records online.
Recorder of Deeds 423 Allegheny St, #145, Hollidaysburg, PA 16648 **814-693-3095** Fax: 814-693-3093. 8AM-4PM. Real Estate, Marriage, Probate records online.

Bradford County Prothonotary 301 Main St, Courthouse, Towanda, PA 18848 **570-265-1705** Fax: 570-265-1735. 9AM-5PM.
Recorder of Deeds 301 Main St, Courthouse, Towanda, PA 18848 **570-265-1702** Fax: 570-265-1721. 9AM-5PM. Real Estate, Deed, Mortgage, Will records online.

Bucks County Prothonotary 55 E. Court St., Courthouse, Doylestown, PA 18901 **215-348-6191** Fax: 215-348-6184. 8:00AM-4:15PM. www.buckscounty.org/courts/ Recording, Judgment, Court, Voter Registration, Vital Statistic records online.
Recorder of Deeds 55 E. Court St., Courthouse, Doylestown, PA 18901-4367 **215-348-6209** www.buckscounty.org/depart ments/registerofwills/index.html Assessor, Recorder, Real Estate, Tax Lien, Probate, Court, Will records online. 8:15-4:15PM

Butler County Prothonotary PO Box 1208, Butler, PA 16003-1208 (300 S. Main St). **724-284-5314** 8:30AM-4:30PM.
Recorder of Deeds PO Box 1208, Butler, PA 16003-1208 (124 W. Diamond St, Fl L, County Gov't Bldg.). **724-284-5340** Fax: 724-285-9099. www.co.butler.pa.us Marriage, Probate records online.

Cambria County Prothonotary 200 S. Center St., Ebensburg, PA 15931 **814-472-1637** Fax: 814-472-5632. 9AM-4PM.
Recorder of Deeds 200 S. Center St., Cambria County Courthouse, Ebensburg, PA 15931 **814-472-1473** Fax: 814-472-1412. 9AM-4PM. www.co.cambria.pa.us

Cameron County Prothonotary 20 E. 5th St, Emporium, PA 15834 **814-486-3349** Fax: 814-486-0464. 8:30AM-4PM.
Recorder of Deeds 20 E. 5th St, Emporium, PA 15834 **814-486-3349** Fax: 814-486-0464.

Carbon County Prothonotary PO Box 130, Jim Thorpe, PA 18229-0127 (2 Broadway).

570-325-2481 Fax: 570-325-8047. 8:30AM-4:30PM. Tax Lien, UCC records online.
Recorder of Deeds PO Box 87, Jim Thorpe, PA 18229 (Annex, Rte. 209 & Hazard Sq). **570-325-2651** Fax: 570-325-2726. 8:30AM-4:30PM. Real Estate, Probate, Grantor/ Grantee records online.

Centre County Prothonotary Allegheny & High, County Courthouse, Bellefonte, PA 16823 **814-355-6796** 8:30AM-5PM.
Recorder of Deeds 414 Holmes Ave. #1, Bellefonte, PA 16823 **814-355-6801** 8:30-5PM. www.co.centre.pa.us/133.htm Domestic Relations Warrants, Tax Assessment, Tax Claims, GIS records online.

Chester County Prothonotary PO Box 2748, West Chester, PA 19380-0991 (2 N High St #130). **610-344-6111** Fax: 610-344-5903. www.chesco.org/prothy.html Court Docket, Property Tax, Warrant, Lien, Assessor records online. 8:30AM-4:30PM.
Recorder of Deeds PO Box 2748, West Chester, PA 19380-0991 (121 N Walnut St #100). **610-344-6330** Fax: 610-344-6408. 8:30AM-4:30PM, recording rm opens 7:30AM Monday. www.chesco.org/recorder Recording, Deed, Court, Vital Statistic, Archive records online.

Clarion County Prothonotary Main St, Courthouse, Clarion, PA 16214-1092 **814-226-4000** Fax: 814-226-8069. Tax Lien records online.
Recorder of Deeds Courthouse, Corner of 5th Ave. & Main St., Clarion, PA 16214 **814-226-4000 x2500** Fax: 814-226-1117. Assessor, Real Estate, Voter Registration records online.

Clearfield County Prothonotary PO Box 549, Clearfield, PA 16830 (2nd & Market Sts). **814-765-2641** Fax: 814-765-7659. 8:30AM-4PM. www.clearfieldco.org
Recorder of Deeds PO Box 361, Clearfield, PA 16830 (2nd & Market Sts, #103). **814-765-2641 x1350** Fax: 814-765-6089. 8:30AM-4PM. www.clearfieldco.org Real Estate, Deed, Mortgage, Will records online.

Clinton County Prothonotary 230 E. Water St., Courthouse, Lock Haven, PA 17745 **570-893-4007** Fax: 570-893-4288. 8AM-5PM M,T,Th,F; 8AM-12:30PM Wed. www.clintoncountypa.com
Recorder of Deeds PO Box 943, Lock Haven, PA 17745 (Water & Jay Sts Courthouse). **570-893-4010** Fax: 570-893-4273. 8:30AM-5PM. Real Estate, Probate, Property records online.

Columbia County Prothonotary PO Box 380, Bloomsburg, PA 17815 (35 W. Main St). **570-389-5614** 8AM-4:30PM.
Recorder of Deeds PO Box 380, Bloomsburg, PA 17815 (35 W. Main St).

570-389-5632 Fax: 570-389-5636. 8-4:30. www.columbiapa.org/county/offices.html

Crawford County Prothonotary 903 Diamond Park, County Courthouse, Meadville, PA 16335 **814-333-7324** Fax: 814-337-5416. 8:30AM-4:30PM.
Recorder of Deeds 903 Diamond Park, Courthouse, Meadville, PA 16335 **814-373-2537** Fax: 814-337-5296. 8:30AM-4:30PM. www.co.crawford.pa.us

Cumberland County Prothonotary 1 Courthouse Sq, County Courthouse, Carlisle, PA 17013, **717-240-7832** 8AM-4:30PM. Civil Court, Judgment records online.
Recorder of Deeds 1 Courthouse Sq, County Courthouse, Carlisle, PA 17013 **717-240-6370** Fax: 717-240-6490. 8AM-4:30PM. Property Tax, Assessor, Cemetery records online.

Dauphin County Prothonotary PO Box 945, Harrisburg, PA 17108 (Front & Market Sts, Rm 101). **717-780-6520** 8AM-4:30PM. www.dauphincounty.org
Recorder of Deeds PO Box 12000, Harrisburg, PA 17108 (Front & Market Sts). **717-780-6560** Fax: 717-780-6482. 8AM-4:30PM. Property, Assessor, Property Sale records online.

Delaware County Prothonotary 201 W. Front St, Rm 127, Delaware County Gov't Ctr Bldg., Media, PA 19063 **610-891-5009** 8:30AM-4:30PM.
Recorder of Deeds 201 W. Front St, Rm 107, Government Ctr. Bldg., Media, PA 19063 **610-891-4260** http://www2.co.delaware.pa.u s/pa/default.htm Assessor, Deed, Real Estate, Judgment, Court records online. 8:30-4:30.

Elk County Prothonotary PO Box 237, Ridgway, PA 15853-0237 (Main St Courthouse). **814-776-5344** Fax: 814-776-5303. 8:30AM-4PM.
Recorder of Deeds PO Box 314, Ridgway, PA 15853-0314 (Main & Court Sts). **814-776-5349** Fax: 814-776-5382. 8:30-4PM.

Erie County Prothonotary 140 W. 6th St, Rm 120, Erie, PA 16501-1080 **814-451-6078** 8:30AM-4:30PM. Tax Lien records online.
Recorder of Deeds PO Box 1849, Erie, PA 16507-0849 (140 W. 6th St). **814-451-6246** Fax: 814-451-6213. 8:30AM-4:30PM. Real Estate, Marriage, Probate records online.

Fayette County Prothonotary 61 E. Main St, Courthouse, Uniontown, PA 15401 **724-430-1272** 8AM-4:30PM.
Recorder of Deeds 61 E. Main St, Courthouse, Uniontown, PA 15401-3389 **724-430-1238** Fax: 724-430-1238. 8AM-4:30PM. Property, Assessor records online.

Forest County Prothonotary 526 Elm St #2, Tionesta, PA 16353 **814-755-3526** Fax: 814-755-8837. 9AM-4PM. www.co.forest.pa.us
Recorder of Deeds 526 Elm St #2, Tionesta, PA 16353 **814-755-3526** Fax: 814-755-8837. 9AM-4PM. www.co.forest.pa.us

Franklin County Prothonotary 157 Lincoln Way East, County Court House, Chambersburg, PA 17201 **717-261-3860** Fax: 717-264-6772. 8:30AM-5PM. Tax Lien records online.
Recorder of Deeds 157 Lincoln Way East, Chambersburg, PA 17201 **717-264-4125** Fax: 717-263-5717. 8:30AM-4:30PM. Real Estate, Probate records online.

Fulton County Prothonotary 201 N. 2nd St, Fulton County Courthouse, McConnellsburg, PA 17233 **717-485-4212** 8:30AM-4:30PM.
Recorder of Deeds 201 N. Second St, Fulton County Courthouse, McConnellsburg, PA 17233 **717-485-4212** 8:30AM-4:30PM.

Greene County Prothonotary 10 E. High St, Rm 105, Waynesburg, PA 15370 **724-852-5289** 8:30AM-4:30PM.
Recorder of Deeds 10 E High St, Courthouse, Waynesburg, PA 15370 **724-852-5283** 8:30AM-4:30PM. http://county.greenepa.net

Huntingdon County Prothonotary PO Box 39, Huntingdon, PA 16652-1486 (223 Penn St). **814-643-1610** Fax: 814-643-4271. 8:30AM-4:30PM. Tax Lien records online.
Recorder of Deeds 223 Penn St, Courthouse, Huntingdon, PA 16652 **814-643-2740** Fax: 814-643-8152. 8:30AM-4:30PM. Real Estate, Marriage, Probate records online.

Indiana County Prothonotary & Clerk of Courts 825 Philadelphia St, Courthouse, 1st Fl, Indiana, PA 15701-3934 **724-465-3855** Fax: 724-465-3968. 8AM-4PM.
Recorder of Deeds 825 Philadelphia St, Courthouse, Indiana, PA 15701 **724-465-3860** Fax: 724-465-3863. 8AM-4PM.

Jefferson County Prothonotary & Clerk of Courts 200 Main St, Court House, Rm 102, Brookville, PA 15825 **814-849-1606** Fax: 814-849-1625. 8:30AM-4:30PM.
Recorder of Deeds 200 Main St, Courthouse, Brookville, PA 15825 (**814-849-1610** Fax: 814-849-1677. 8:30AM-4:30PM.

Juniata County Prothonotary Courthouse, Mifflintown, PA 17059 **717-436-7715** Fax: 717-436-7734. 8AM-4:30PM.
Recorder of Deeds PO Box 68, Mifflintown, PA 17059 (Courthouse). **717-436-7709** Fax: 717-436-7756. 8AM-4:30PM. Real Estate, Marriage, Probate records online.

Lackawanna County Prothonotary/ Clerk of Judicial Records 200 N. Washington Ave, Scranton, PA 18503 **70-963-6723** Fax: none.

Recorder of Deeds 200 N. Washington, Courthouse, Scranton, PA 18503 **570-963-6775**, 9AM-4PM.

Lancaster County Prothonotary PO Box 83480, Lancaster, PA 17608-3480 (50 N. Duke St). **717-299-8282** Fax: 717-293-7210. 8:30AM-5PM. www.co.lancaster.pa.us
Recorder of Deeds PO Box 83480, Lancaster, PA 17608 (50 N. Duke St). **717-299-8238** Fax: 717-299-8393. 8:30AM-5PM www.co.lancaster.pa.us Assessor, Real Estate, Recording, Tax Lien, UCC records online.

Lawrence County Prothonotary 430 Court St, Government Ctr, New Castle, PA 16101-3593 **724-656-1943** Fax: 724-656-1988. 8AM-4PM. Tax Lien records online.
Recorder of Deeds 430 Court St, Government Ctr, New Castle, PA 16101 **724-656-2127** Fax: 724-656-1966. 8AM-4PM. Real Estate, Assessor, Marriage, Probate records online.

Lebanon County Prothonotary 400 S. 8th St, Rm 104, Lebanon, PA 17042 **717-274-2801** 8:30AM-4:30PM.
Recorder of Deeds 400 S. 8th St, Rm 107, Lebanon PA 17042, **717-274-2801**, 8:30AM-4PM. www.lebcounty.org

Lehigh County Prothonotary 455 W. Hamilton St., Allentown, PA 18101-1614 **610-782-3148** Fax: 610-770-3840. 8:30AM-4:30PM. Judgment, Deed, Lien, Voter Registration, Assessor, Occ License, Will, Civil/Criminal Court, Grantor/Grantee, Tax Sale records online.
Recorder of Deeds 17 S 7th St, Rm 350, Allentown, PA 18101 **610-782-3162** Fax: 610-782-3116. 8am-4pm. Assessor, Real Estate, Tax Lien, Marriage records online.

Luzerne County Prothonotary 200 N. River St, County Court House, Wilkes-Barre, PA 18711, **570-825-1745** Fax: 570-825-1757.
Recorder of Deeds 200 N. River St, Courthouse, Wilkes-Barre, PA 18711 **570-825-1641** Fax: 570-970-4580. 9-4:30PM. Recorder, Deed, Land records online.

Lycoming County Prothonotary 48 W. Third St, Williamsport, PA 17701 **570-327-2251** 8:30AM-5PM.
Recorder of Deeds 48 W. Third St, Williamsport, PA 17701 **570-327-2263** Fax: 570-327-2511. 8:30AM-5PM.

McKean County Prothonotary PO Box 273, Smethport, PA 16749 (500 Main St). **814-887-3271** Fax: 814-887-3219. 8:30-4:30.
Recorder of Deeds 500 W. Main St., Smethport, PA 16749 **814-887-3253** Fax: 814-887-3255. 8:30AM-4:30PM.

Mercer County Prothonotary 105 Courthouse, Mercer, PA 16137-0066 **724-**

662-3800 x2261 Fax: none. 8:30AM-4:30PM. Tax Lien records online.
Recorder of Deeds 109 Courthouse, Mercer, PA 16137-1293 **724-662-3800** Fax: 724-662-2096. 8:30AM-4:30PM. Real Estate, Assessor records online.

Mifflin County Prothonotary 20 N. Wayne St, Lewistown, PA 17044 **717-248-8146** Fax: 717-248-5275. 8AM-4:30PM. Tax Lien records online.
Recorder of Deeds 20 N. Wayne St, Lewistown, PA 17044 **717-242-1449** Fax: 717-248-2503. www.co.mifflin.pa.us Real Estate, Assessor, Probate, GIS Mapping records online. 8AM-4:30PM.

Monroe County Prothonotary N. 7th & Monroe St, Courthouse, Rm 303, Stroudsburg, PA 18360-2190 **570-420-3570** Fax: 570-420-3582. 8:30AM-4:30PM.
Recorder of Deeds 7th & Monroe St, Courthouse, Stroudsburg, PA 18360-2185 **570-420-3530** Fax: 570-420-3537. 8:30AM-4:30PM. Real Estate, Deed, Will, Mortgage records online.

Montgomery County Prothonotary PO Box 311, Norristown, PA 19404 (Swede & Airy Sts, Rm 100). **610-278-3360** Fax: 610-278-5994. 8:30AM-4:15PM.
Recorder of Deeds PO Box 311, Norristown, PA 19404-0311 (1 Montgomery Plaza, #303, Swede & Airy Sts.). **610-278-3289** Fax: 610-278-3869. 8:30AM-4:15PM. www.montcopa.org Assessor, Real Estate, Recording, Deed, Tax Lien, Owner Name, Estate, Tax Claim Property records online.

Montour County Prothonotary 29 Mill St, Courthouse, Danville, PA 17821 **570-271-3010** Fax: 570-271-3089. 9AM-4PM. www.montourco.org/montour/site/default.asp Will records online.
Register & Recorder 29 Mill St, Courthouse, Danville, PA 17821 **570-271-3012** Fax: 570-271-3071. www.montourco.org Deed, Will, Marriage records online.

Northampton County Prothonotary 669 Washington St., 2nd Fl, Rm 207, Easton, PA 18042-7498 **610-559-3060** 8:30-4:30PM.
Recorder of Deeds 669 Washington St, Government Ctr, Easton, PA 18042 **610-559-3077** Fax: 610-559-3103. 8:30AM-4:30PM. Real Estate, Deed, Mortgage, Misc. Recording, Property, Assessor records online.

Northumberland County Prothonotary 201 Market St, Courthouse, Rm 7, Sunbury, PA 17801-3468 **570-988-4151** 9AM-4:30PM (Monday-open until 5PM).
Recorder of Deeds 201 Market St, Court House, Sunbury, PA 17801 **570-988-4140** 9AM-4:30PM.

Perry County Prothonotary PO Box 325, New Bloomfield, PA 17068-0325 (Courthouse). **717-582-2131** 8AM-4PM.
Recorder of Deeds PO Box 223, New Bloomfield, PA 17068, **717-582-2131** 8AM-4PM. Real Estate, Deed records online.

Philadelphia County Prothonotary Broad & Market Sts, City Hall, Rm 271, Philadelphia, PA 19107 **215-686-6664** 9AM-3PM. Judgment, Lien, Civil Court records online.
County Recorder of Deeds Broad & Market Sts, City Hall, Rm 153, Philadelphia, PA 19107 **215-686-2260** 8AM-2PM. Property, Assessor, Death records online.

Pike County Prothonotary 412 Broad St, Milford, PA 18337 **570-296-7231** Fax: none. 8:30AM-4:30PM. Tax Lien records online.
Recorder of Deeds 506 Broad St, Milford, PA 18337 **570-296-3508** Fax: 570-296-3514. 8:30AM-4:30PM. Probate records online.

Potter County Prothonotary 1 E. 2nd St, Rm 23, Courthouse, Coudersport, PA 16915 **814-274-9740** Fax: 814-274-3361. 8:30AM-4:30PM. Tax Lien records online.
Recorder of Deeds Courthouse, Rm 20, Coudersport, PA 16915 **814-274-8370** Fax: 814-274-3360. 8:30AM-4:30PM. Real Estate, Assessor, Probate records online.

Schuylkill County Prothonotary 401 N. Second St., Pottsville, PA 17901-2520 **570-628-1270** Fax: 570-628-1261.
Recorder of Deeds 401 N. 2nd St.., Pottsville, PA 17901 **570-628-1480** 8:30AM-4:30PM.

Snyder County Prothonotary PO Box 217, Middleburg, PA 17842-0217 (9 W. Market St). **570-837-4202** Fax: 570-837-4275.
Recorder of Deeds PO Box 217, Middleburg, PA 17842-0217 (9 W. Market St). **570-837-4225** Fax: 570-837-4299. 8:30AM-4PM.

Somerset County Prothonotary 111 E. Union St, #190, Somerset, PA 15501 **814-445-1428** Fax: 814-444-9270. 8:30-4PM.

Recorder of Deeds 300 N Center Ave, #400, #140, Somerset, PA 15501 **814-445-1547** Fax: 814-445-1563. 8:30AM-4PM.

Sullivan County Prothonotary Main St, Courthouse, Laporte, PA 18626 **570-946-7351** Fax: 570-946-7105. 8:30AM-4PM.
Recorder of Deeds Main St, Courthouse, Laporte, PA 18626 **570-946-7351** Fax: 570-946-7105. 8:30AM-4PM.

Susquehanna County Prothonotary PO Box 218, Montrose, PA 18801-0218 (11 Maple St). **570-278-4600 x121** Fax: 570-278-4191. 9AM-4:30PM. Prothonotary records online.
Recorder of Deeds PO Box 218, Montrose, PA 18801 (Courthouse). **570-278-4600 x112/3** Fax: 570-278-2963. 8:30-4:30PM.

Tioga County Prothonotary 116 Main St, Courthouse, Wellsboro, PA 16901 **570-724-9281** 9AM-4:30PM.
Recorder of Deeds 116 Main St, Courthouse, Wellsboro, PA 16901 **570-724-9260** 9AM-4:30. Real Estate, Deed, Will records online.

Union County Prothonotary 103 S. 2nd St, Courthouse, Lewisburg, PA 17837 **570-524-8751** Fax: 570-524-1628. 8:30AM-4:30PM. www.unionco.org
Recorder of Deeds 103 S. 2nd St, Courthouse, Lewisburg, PA 17837-1996 **570-524-8761** 8:30-4:15PM. www.unionco.org

Venango County Prothonotary Courthouse, Franklin, PA 16323. **814-432-9577** Fax: 814-432-9579. 8:30AM-4:30PM.
Recorder of Deeds PO Box 831, Franklin, PA 16323 (1168 Liberty St.). **814-432-9539** Fax: 814-432-9569. 8:30AM-4:30PM. www.co.venango.pa.us/Directory/index.htm

Warren County Prothonotary 4th & Market Sts, Courthouse, Warren, PA 16365 **814-723-7550** Fax: 814-728-3459. 8:30AM-4:30PM.
Recorder of Deeds 204 Fourth Ave, Courthouse, Warren, PA 16365 **814-723-7550** 8:30AM-3:30PM.

Washington County Prothonotary 1 S. Main St, #1001, Courthouse, Washington, PA 15301 **724-228-6770** Fax: 724-229-5913. 9AM-4:30PM.
Recorder of Deeds 1 S. Main St, Rm 1006, Washington County Courthouse, Washington, PA 15301 **724-228-6806** Fax: 724-228-6737. 9AM-4:30PM. www.co.washington.pa.us Assessor, Real Estate records online.

Wayne County Prothonotary 925 Court St, Courthouse, Honesdale, PA 18431-1996 **570-253-5970 x200/3** Fax: 570-253-0687. 8:30AM-4:30PM.
Recorder of Deeds 925 Court St, Honesdale, PA 18431-1996 (**570-253-5970 x212** www.co.wayne.pa.us/recorder.asp

Westmoreland County Prothonotary PO Box 1630, Greensburg, PA 15601 (2 N.Main St, Rm 501). **724-830-3516** 8:30AM-4PM.
County Recorder 2 N Main St #203, Greensburg, PA 15601 **724-830-3734** Fax: 724-850-3979. www.co.westmoreland.pa.us Real Estate, Tax Lien, Mortgage, UCC, Deed records online.

Wyoming County Prothonotary 1 Courthouse Sq, Wyoming County Courthouse, Tunkhannock, PA 18657-1219 **717-836-3200** 8:30AM-4PM.
Recorder of Deeds 1 Courthouse Sq, Tunkhannock, PA 18657 **570-996-2361** 8:30AM-4PM.

York County Prothonotary 28 E. Market St, York, PA 17401 **717-771-9611** Fax: 717-771-4629. 8AM-5PM. www.york-county.org
Recorder of Deeds 28 E. Market St, York, PA 17401 **717-771-9295** Fax: 717-771-9582. 8AM-4:30PM. www.york-county.org/depar tments/deeds/deeds.htm Assessor, Real Estate, Deed, Death, Inmate, Naturalization records online.

 # Rhode Island

Organization: 5 counties and 39 towns, 39 recording offices. The recording officer is the Town/City Clerk (Recorder of Deeds). The Town/City Clerk usually also serves as the Recorder of Deeds. There is no county administration in Rhode Island that handles recording. The entire state is in the Eastern Time Zone (EST). Be aware that the recordings in the counties of Bristol, Newport, and Providence can relate to property located in other cities/ towns even though each city bears the same name as the county.

Real Estate Records: Towns will not perform real estate searches. Copy fees are usually $1.50 per page. Certification usually costs $3.00 per document.

UCC Records: Financing statements are filed at the state level, except for farm related and real estate related collateral, which are filed with the Town/City Clerk. Most recording offices will not perform UCC searches. Use search request form UCC-11. Copy fees are usually $1.50 per page. Certification usually costs $3.00 per document.

Tax Lien Records: All federal and state tax liens on personal property and on real property are filed with the Recorder of Deeds. Towns will not perform tax lien searches. Other Liens: Mechanics, municipal, lis pendens.

Online Access: A number of towns have property records available. A private vendor has placed on the Internet the assessor records from several towns. Visit http://data.visionappraisal.com.

Barrington Town Clerk 283 County Rd, Town Hall, Barrington, RI 02806 **401-247-1900** Fax: 401-245-5003. 8:30AM-4:30PM.

Bristol Town Clerk 10 Court St, Town Hall, Bristol, RI 02809 **401-253-7000** Fax: 401-253-3080. 8:30-4. www.onlinebristol.com Real Estate records online.

Burrillville Town Clerk 105 Harrisville Main St, Town Hall, Harrisville, RI 02830-1499 **401-568-4300** Fax: 401-568-0490. 8:30AM-4:30PM M-W; 8:30AM-7PM Th; 8:30AM-12:30PM F. www.burrillville.org Property, Tax Assessor records online.

Central Falls City Clerk 580 Broad St, City Hall, Central Falls, RI 02863 **401-727-7400** Fax: 401-727-7406. 8:30AM-4:30PM. www.centralfallsri.us Property, Assessor records online.

Charlestown Town Clerk 4540 South County Trail, Charlestown, RI 02813 **401-364-1200** Fax: 401-364-1238. 8:30AM-4:30PM. www.charlestownri.org

Coventry Town Clerk 1670 Flat River Rd, Town Hall, Coventry, RI 02816-8911 **401-822-9174** Fax: 401-822-9132. Assessor, Property records online.

Cranston City Clerk 869 Park Ave, City Hall, Cranston, RI 02910 **401-461-1000 x3130** 8:30AM-4:30PM. Assessor, Property records online.

Cumberland Town Clerk PO Box 7, Cumberland, RI 02864-0808 (45 Broad St). **401-728-2400** Fax: 401-724-1103. 8:30AM-4:30PM. www.cumberlandri.org Property, Assessor records online.

East Greenwich Town Clerk PO Box 111, East Greenwich, RI 02818 (125 Main St.). **401-886-8603** Fax: 401-886-8625. 8:30AM-4:30PM. www.eastgreenwichri.com Property records online.

East Providence City Town Clerk 145 Taunton Ave, City Hall, East Providence, RI 02914 **401-435-7500** Fax: 401-435-4630. 8AM-3:30PM. www.eastprovidence.com Assessor, Property records online.

Exeter Town Deputy Town Clerk 675 Ten Rod Rd, Town Hall, Exeter, RI 02822 **401-294-3891** Fax: 401-295-1248. 9AM-4PM. www.town.exeter.ri.us Assessor, Property records online.

Foster Town Clerk 181 Howard Hill Rd, Town Hall, Foster, RI 02825-1227 **401-392-9200** Fax: 401-392-9201. 9AM-3:30PM.

Glocester Town Clerk PO Drawer B, Glocester/ Chepachet, RI 02814-0702 (1145 Putnam Pike). **401-568-6206** Fax: 401-568-5850. www.glocesterri.org/townclerk.htm

Hopkinton Town Clerk 1 Town House Rd, Town Hall, Hopkinton, RI 02833 **401-377-7777** Fax: 401-377-7788. 8:30AM-4:30PM. Property, Assessor records online.

Jamestown Town Clerk 93 Narragansett Ave, Town Hall, Jamestown, RI 02835 **401-423-7200** Fax: 401-423-7230. 8AM-4:30PM. www.jamestownri.net Real Estate records online.

Johnston Town Clerk 1385 Hartford Ave, Town Hall, Johnston, RI 02919 **401-351-6618** Fax: 401-331-4271. 8:30AM-4:30PM. www.johnston-ri.com Assessor, Property records online.

Lincoln Town Clerk PO Box 100, Lincoln, RI 02865 (100 Old River Rd). **401-333-1100** Fax: 401-333-3648. www.lincolnri.net Property, Assessor records online.

Little Compton Town Clerk PO Box 226, Little Compton, RI 02837-0226 (40 Commons). **401-635-4400** Fax: 401-635-2470. 8AM-4PM.

Middletown Town Clerk 350 E. Main Rd, Town Hall, Middletown, RI 02842 **401-847-0009** Fax: 401-848-0500. 8AM-5PM. www.ci.middletown.ri.us Assessor, Property records online.

Narragansett Town Clerk 25 5th Ave, Town Hall, Narragansett, RI 02882 (**401-789-1044** Fax: 401-783-9637. 8:30AM-4:30PM. Assessor, Property records online.

New Shoreham Town Clerk PO Drawer 220, Block Island, RI 02807 (16 Old Town Rd). **401-466-3200** Fax: 401-466-3219. 9-3PM. Assessor, Property records online.

Newport City Recorder of Deeds 43 Broadway, Town Hall, Newport, RI 02840-2798 **401-846-9600** Fax: 401-849-8757. 8:30AM-5PM (Recording Hours 8:30AM-4PM). www.cityofnewport.com Assessor, Property records online.

North Kingstown Town Clerk 80 Boston Neck Rd, Town Hall, North Kingstown, RI 02852 **401-294-3331** www.northkingstown.org Assessor, Property records online.

North Providence Town Clerk 2000 Smith St, Town Hall, North Providence, RI 02911 **401-232-0900** Fax: 401-233-1409. 8:30AM-4:30PM (Summer hours 8:30 AM-4PM).

North Smithfield Town Clerk 575 Smithfield Rd, Town Hall, North Smithfield, RI 02896 **401-767-2200** Fax: 401-356-4057. 8AM-4PM M-W; 8AM-7PM Th; 8AM-N F. Assessor, Property records online.

Pawtucket City Clerk 137 Roosevelt Ave, City Hall, Pawtucket, RI 02860 **401-728-0500** Fax: 401-728-8932. 8:30AM-3:30PM. www.pawtucketri.com Recording, Deed, Real Estate records online.

Portsmouth Town Clerk PO Box 155, Portsmouth, RI 02871 (2200 E. Main Rd). **401-683-2101** 9AM-3:45PM. www.portsmouthri.com/frames.htm Assessor, Property records online.

Providence City Clerk 25 Dorrance St, City Hall, Providence, RI 02903 **401-421-7740 x312** 8:30AM-4:30PM.

Richmond Town Clerk 5 Richmond Townhouse Rd., Town Hall, Wyoming, RI 02898 **401-539-2497** Fax: 401-539-1089. 9AM-4PM. www.richmondri.com

Scituate Town Clerk PO Box 328, North Scituate, RI 02857-0328 (195 Danielson Pike). **401-647-2822** Fax: 401-647-7220. 8:30AM-4PM. www.scituateri.org/townhall.htm Property, Assessor records online.

Smithfield Town Clerk 64 Farnum Pike, Town Hall, Esmond, RI 02917 **401-233-1000** Fax: 401-232-7244. M-F 8:30-4:30PM. www.smithfieldri.com Property, Assessor records online.

South Kingstown Town Clerk PO Box 31, Wakefield, RI 02880 (180 High St). **401-789-9331** Fax: 401-788-9792. 8:30AM-4:30PM, recording stops at 4PM.. www.southkingstownri.com Real Estate, Assessor records online.

Tiverton Town Clerk 343 Highland Rd, Town Hall, Tiverton, RI 02878 **401-625-6700** Fax: 401-625-6705. 8:30AM-4PM. Assessor, Property records online.

Warren Town Clerk 514 Main St, Town Hall, Warren, RI 02885 **401-245-7340** Fax: 401-245-7421. 9AM-4PM. Property records online.

Warwick City Clerk 3275 Post Rd, Warwick, RI 02886 **401-738-2000** Fax: 401-738-6639. www.warwickri.com Tax Assessor records online. 8:30AM-4:30PM.

West Greenwich Town Clerk 280 Victory Highway, Town Hall, West Greenwich, RI

02817 **401-397-5016** Fax: 401-392-3805. 9AM-4PM M-F; 7-9PM W.

West Warwick Town Clerk 1170 Main St, Town Hall, West Warwick, RI 02893-4829 **401-822-9201** Fax: 401-822-9266. 8:30AM-4:30PM.

Westerly Town Clerk 45 Broad St, Town Hall, Westerly, RI 02891 **401-348-2500** Fax: 401-348-2571. 8:30AM-4:30PM M-F.

Woonsocket City Town Clerk 169 Main St, City Hall, Woonsocket, RI 02895 **401-762-6400** Fax: 401-765-4569.

 # South Carolina

Organization: 46 counties, 46 recording offices. The recording officer is the Register of Mesne Conveyances or Clerk of Court (the title varies by county). The entire state is in the Eastern Time Zone (EST).

Real Estate Records: Most counties will not perform real estate searches. Copy and certification fees vary. The Assessor keeps tax records.

UCC Records: Financing statements are filed at the state level, except for real estate related collateral, which are filed with the Register. However, prior to 07/2001, consumer goods and farm collateral were also filed at the Register and these older records can be searched there. As a general rule, all recording offices will perform UCC searches. Searches fees are usually $5.00 per debtor name. Copy fees are usually $1.00 per page.

Tax Lien Records: All federal and state tax liens on personal property and on real property are filed with the Register of Mesne Conveyances (Clerk of Court). Some counties will perform tax lien searches. Search fees and copy fees vary.

Online Access: There is no statewide system, buy several counties have placed free record data on their websites.

Abbeville County Clerk of Court PO Box 99, Abbeville, SC 29620 (Court Sq). **864-459-5074** Fax: 864-459-9188. 9AM-5PM.

Aiken Register of Mesne Conveyances PO Box 537, Aiken, SC 2980 (828 Richland Ave West). **803-642-2072** 8:30AM-5PM.

Allendale County Clerk of Court PO Box 126, Allendale, SC 29810 (611A W. Mulberry St). **803-584-2737** Fax: 803-584-7058. 9AM-5PM.

Anderson Register of Deeds PO Box 8002, Anderson, SC 29622 (100 S. Main St). **864-260-4054** Fax: 864-260-4443. 8:30AM-5PM. www.andersoncountysc.org Real Estate, Property Tax, Sale, Assessor, Marriage, Estate, Guardianship, Vehicle, Permit, Court records online.

Bamberg County Clerk of Court PO Box 150, Bamberg, SC 29003 (110 N. Main St). **803-245-3025** Fax: 803-245-3088. 9-5PM.

Barnwell County Clerk of Court PO Box 723, Barnwell, SC 29812(Courthouse Bldg., Rm 114). **803-541-1020** Fax: 803-541-1025.

Beaufort County Clerk of Court PO Box 1128, Beaufort, SC 29901 (102 Ribaut Rd., Rm 208). **843-470-5218** Fax: 843-470-5248. www.co.beaufort.sc.us Assessor, Property records online.

Berkeley County Clerk of Court 223 N. Live Oak Drive, Moncks Corner, SC 29461 **843-719-4084** Fax: 843-719-4851. 8AM-

5PM. www.co.berkeley.sc.us Property, Assessor, Personal Property, Vehicle Tax, Real Estate, Recording, UCC records online.

Calhoun County Clerk of Court 902 F.R. Huff Drive, St. Matthews, SC 29135 **803-874-3524** Fax: 803-874-1942. 9AM-5PM.

Charleston County Clerk of Court PO Box 726, Charleston, SC 29402 (2 Courthouse Sq, #201, Meeting St). **843-958-4800** Fax: 843-958-4803. www.charlestoncounty.org Real Estate, Deed, Mortgage, Property Tax, Judgment, Marriage, Will/Estate, Guardianship, Conservatorship records online.

Cherokee County Clerk of Court PO Drawer 2289, Gaffney, SC 29342 (Courthouse, E. Floyd Baker Blvd.). **864-487-2571** Fax: 864-487-2754. 8:30-5PM.

Chester County Clerk of Court PO Drawer 580, Chester, SC 29706 (140 Main St). **803-385-2605** Fax: 803-581-7975.

Chesterfield County Clerk of Court PO Box 529, Chesterfield, SC 29709 (200 W. Main St). **843-623-2574** Fax: 843-623-6944. 8:30AM-5PM.

Clarendon County Clerk of Court-Register of Deeds PO Box 136, Manning, SC 29102 (Boyce St Courthouse). **803-435-4443** Fax: 803-435-8258. 8:30AM-5PM.

Colleton Register of Deeds PO Box 620, Walterboro, SC 29488 (31 Klein St, 1st Fl). **843-542-2745** Fax: 843-542-2749. 8-5PM.

Darlington County Clerk of Court PO Box 1177, Darlington, SC 29540 (Courthouse). **843-398-4330** Fax: 843-393-6871. 8:30-5.

Dillon County Clerk of Court PO Drawer 1220, Dillon, SC 29536 (401 W. Main St, #201). **843-774-1425** Fax: 843-841-3706. 8:30AM-5PM.

Dorchester County Clerk of Court PO Box 38, St. George, SC 29477 (201 Johnston St.). **843-563-0106** Fax: 843-563-0182. 8:30AM-5PM.

Edgefield County Clerk of Court PO Box 34, Edgefield, SC 29824 (129 Courthouse Sq). **803-637-4080** Fax: 803-637-4117. 8:30AM-5PM.

Fairfield County Clerk of Court PO Drawer 299, Winnsboro, SC 29180 (101 S.Congress St). **803-712-6526** 9AM-5PM.

Florence County Clerk of Court MSC-E City/County Complex, Florence, SC 29501 (180 N Irby). **843-665-3031** Fax: 843-665-3097. 8:30AM-5PM.

Georgetown Register of Deeds PO Box 421270, Georgetown, SC 29442 (715 Prince St). **843-545-3088** 8:30AM-5PM. Property, GIS, Recording, Real Estate, Deed, UCC records online. www.georgetowncountysc.org

Greenville Register of Deeds 301 University Ridge, #1300, County Sq #1300, Greenville, SC 29601 **864-467-7240** Fax: 864-467-7107. 8:30AM-5PM. www.greenvillecounty.org

Real Property, Deed, Vehicle, Property Tax, Most Wanted, Missing Person records online.

Greenwood County Clerk of Court 528 Monument St., Courthouse, Greenwood, SC 29646 **864-942-8551** Fax: 864-942-8693. 8:30AM-5PM. www.co.greenwood.sc.us Assessor, Property records online.

Hampton County Clerk of Court PO Box 7, Hampton, SC 29924 (1 Elm St). **803-943-7510** Fax: 803-943-7596. 8AM-5PM.

Horry Register of Deeds PO Box 470, Conway, SC 29528 (1301 2nd Ave.). **843-915-5000** Fax: 843-915-6430. 8AM-5PM. www.horrycounty.org Recorder, Deed, Lien, Real Property records online.

Jasper County Clerk of Court PO Box 248, Ridgeland, SC 29936 (305 Russell St). **843-726-7710** Fax: 843-726-7782. 9AM-5PM.

Kershaw Register of Deeds 515 Walnut St #180, Camden, SC 29020 **803-425-1500** Fax: 803-425-7673. 8:30AM-5PM.

Lancaster County Clerk of Court 101 N Main St, Lancaster, SC 29720 **803-285-1581** Fax: 803-416-9388.

Laurens County Clerk of Court PO Box 287, Laurens, SC 29360 (100 Hillcrest Sq #B). **864-984-3538** Fax: 864-984-7023. 9AM-5PM.

Lee Register of Deeds PO Box 387, Bishopville, SC 29010 (123 S. Main St). **803-484-5341** Fax: 803-484-1632. 9-5PM.

Lexington Register of Deeds 212 S Lake Drive, Lexington, SC 29072 **803-359-8168** Fax: 803-359-8189. 8AM-5PM. www.lex-co.com/my_lex.html Assessor, Property records online.

Marion County Clerk of Court PO Box 295, Marion, SC 29571 (100 W. Court St). **843-423-8240** Fax: 843-423-8306. 8:30-5.

Marlboro County Clerk of Court PO Drawer 996, Bennettsville, SC 29512 (Main St Courthouse). **843-479-5613** Fax: 843-479-5640. 8:30AM-5PM.

McCormick County Clerk of Court 133 S. Mine St Rm102, Courthouse, Rm 102, McCormick, SC 29835 **864-465-2195** Fax: 864-465-0071. 9AM-5PM.

Newberry County Court Clerk PO Drawer 10, Newberry, SC 29108 (Rm 5, 1226 College St.). **803-321-2110** Fax: 803-321-2111. 8:30-5. Assessor, Real Estate, Auditor, Property Tax, Treasurer records online.

Oconee Register of Deeds 415 S Pine St, Walhalla, SC 29691 **864-638-4285** 8:30AM-5PM. www.oconeesc.com Land, Deed, Mortgage, Plat records online.

Orangeburg Register of Deeds Box 9000, Orangeburg, SC 29116-9000 (190 Gibson St., Rm 108). **803-533-6236** Fax: 803-535-2354. 8:30AM-5PM. Assessor, Property records online.

Pickens Register of Deeds 222 McDaniel Ave. B-5, Pickens, SC 29671 **864-898-5868**

Fax: 864-898-5924. www.co.pickens.sc.us Assessor, Property, Voter Registration, Most Wanted, Property Tax records online.

Richland Register of Deeds PO Box 192, Columbia, SC 29202 (1701 Main St). **803-576-1910** Fax: 803-576-1922. 8:30AM-5PM. Assessor, Property records online.

Saluda County Clerk of Court Courthouse, Saluda, SC 29138 **864-445-3303** Fax: 864-445-3772. 8:30AM-5PM.

Spartanburg Register of Mesne Conveyances 366 N. Church St, County Admin. Offices, Spartanburg, SC 29303 **864-596-2514** 8:30AM-5PM.

Sumter Register of Deeds 141 N. Main St., Courthouse, Rm 202, Sumter, SC 29150 **803-436-2177** www.sumtercountysc.org Real Estate, Recording, Deed, Property Tax records online. 8:30AM-5PM.

Union County Clerk of Court PO Box 703, Union, SC 29379 (210 W. Main St). **864-429-1630** Fax: 864-429-1715. 9AM-5PM. www.judicial.state.sc.us/clerks/union

Williamsburg County Clerk of Court 125 W. Main St, Kingstree, SC 29556 **843-355-9321 ext552** Fax: 843-355-7821. 8AM-5PM.

York County Clerk of Court PO Box 649, York, SC 29745 (2 S. Congress). **803-684-8510** 8AM-5PM. Property, GIS, Recorder, Real Estate, Deed, UCC records online.

South Dakota

Organization: 66 counties, 66 recording offices. The recording officer is the Register of Deeds. 48 counties are in the Central Time Zone (CST) and 18 are in the Mountain Time Zone (MST).

Real Estate Records: Many counties will perform real estate searches. Search fees and copy fees vary. Certification usually $1.00.

UCC Records: Financing statements are filed at the state level, except for real estate related collateral, which are filed with the Register of Deeds. All recording offices will perform UCC searches. All counties have access to a statewide database of UCC filings. Use search request form UCC-11. Searches fees are usually $12.00 per debtor name, $10.00 if online. Copy fees are usually $1.00 per page. Certification is $5.00.

Tax Lien Records: Federal and state tax liens on personal property of businesses are filed with the Secretary of State. Other federal and state tax liens are filed with the county Register of Deeds. Most counties will perform tax lien searches. Search fees and copy fees vary. Other Liens: Mechanics, motor vehicle, materials.

Online Access: Access to UCC records is available online through the SOS's Fast File Internet Access System at https://www.state.sd.us/sos/ucc.htm. Registration and annual fee is required. A certified search is also available. A new system named "Expa" is soon to be available for the occasional user.

Aurora Register of Deeds PO Box 397, Plankinton, SD 57368 (401 N. Main St.). **605-942-7161** Fax: 605-942-7751. 8-N, 1-5.

Beadle Register of Deeds PO Box 55, Huron, SD 57350-0055 (450-3rd St. SW). **605-353-8412** Fax: 605-353-8402. 8AM-5PM.

Bennett Register of Deeds PO Box 433, Martin, SD 57551-0433 (202 Main St). **605-685-6054** Fax: 605-685-6311. 8AM-N, 12:30-4:30AM.

Bon Homme Register of Deeds PO Box 3, Tyndall, SD 57066 (Cherry St Courthouse). **605-589-4217** 8AM-4:30PM.

Brookings Register of Deeds 314 6th Ave, Courthouse, Brookings, SD 57006-2084 **605-696-8240** Fax: 605-696-8245. 8AM-5PM.

Brown Register of Deeds PO Box 1307, Aberdeen, SD 57402-1307 (25 Market St). **605-626-7140** Fax: 605-626-4010.

Brule Register of Deeds 300 S. Courtland, #110, Chamberlain, SD 57325 **605-734-4434** Fax: 605-234-4434. 8AM-N,1-5PM.

Buffalo Register of Deeds PO Box 174, Gannvalley, SD 57341 (Courthouse Sq.). **605-293-3239** Fax: 605-293-3240. 9-5PM.

Butte Register of Deeds 839 Fifth Ave, Belle Fourche, SD 57717 **605-892-2912** Fax: 605-829-4525. 8AM-5PM.

Campbell Register of Deeds PO Box 148, Mound City, SD 57646-0148 (111 2nd St. East). **605-955-3505** Fax: 605-955-3308. 8AM-N; 1-5PM.

Charles Mix Register of Deeds PO Box 206, Lake Andes, SD 57356-0206 (400 E. Main). **605-487-7141** Fax: 605-487-7221. 8-4:30.

Clark Register of Deeds PO Box 294, Clark, SD 57225-0294 (202 N. Commercial St.). **605-532-5363** Fax: 605-532-5931. 8-5PM.

Clay Register of Deeds 211 W. Main St, #202, Vermillion, SD 57069 **605-677-7130**.

Codington Register of Deeds 14 1st Ave S.E., Watertown, SD 57201-3695 **605-882-6278** Fax: 602-882-5230. 8AM-5PM.

Corson Register of Deeds PO Box 256, McIntosh, SD 57641-0256 (Courthouse). **605-273-4395** Fax: 605-273-4233. 8-N, 1-5.

Custer Register of Deeds 420 Mount Rushmore Rd, Custer, SD 57730-1934 **605-673-8171** Fax: 605-673-8148. 8-5PM M-Th..

Davison Register of Deeds 200 E. 4th, Courthouse, Mitchell, SD 57301-2692 **5-995-8616** Fax: 605-995-8648. 8AM-5PM. www.davisoncounty.org/registerofdeeds.html

Day Register of Deeds 711 W. First St, Webster, SD 57274-1396 **605-345-9506** Fax: 605-345-9507. 8AM-N 1PM-5PM.

Deuel Register of Deeds PO Box 307, Clear Lake, SD 57226 (408 4th St. W) **605-874-2268** Fax: 605-874-1306. 8AM-5PM.

Dewey Register of Deeds PO Box 117, Timber Lake, SD 57656 (710 C St). **605-865-3661** Fax: 605-865-3691. 8AM-N; 1-5.

Douglas Register of Deeds PO Box 267, Armour, SD 57313-0267 (1st & Braddock (Hwy 281)). **605-724-2204** Fax: 605-724-2204. 8AM-12, 1PM-5PM.

Edmunds Register of Deeds PO Box 386, Ipswich, SD 57451-0386 (Courthouse). **605-426-6431** Fax: 605-426-6257. 8AM-N,1-5.

Fall River Register of Deeds 906 N. River St, Hot Springs, SD 57747 **605-745-5139** Fax: 605-745-6835.

Faulk Register of Deeds PO Box 309, Faulkton, SD 57438 (Courthouse). **605-598-6228** Fax: 605-598-6680. 8AM-N,1-5PM.

Grant Register of Deeds PO Box 587, Milbank, SD 57252 (210 E. Fifth Ave). **605-432-4752** Fax: 605-432-9004. 8AM-5PM.

Gregory Register of Deeds PO Box 437, Burke, SD 57523 (221 E.8th St.). **605-775-2624** Fax: 605-775-9116. 8AMN,1-5PM.

Haakon Register of Deeds PO Box 100, Philip, SD 57567-0100 (130 S. Howard). **605-859-2785** 8AM-N,1-5PM.

Hamlin Register of Deeds PO Box 56, Hayti, SD 57241 (300 4th St.). **605-783-3206** 8AM-N, 1-5PM.

Hand Register of Deeds 415 W. 1st Ave, Miller, SD 57362-1346 **605-853-3512** Fax: 605-853-2769. 8AM-5PM.

Hanson Register of Deeds PO Box 500, Alexandria, SD 57311 (720 5th St). **605-239-4512** Fax: 605-239-4296. 8AM-N; 1-5PM.

Harding Register of Deeds PO Box 101, Buffalo, SD 57720 (Courthouse). **605-375-3321** Fax: 605-375-3318. 8AM-N, 1-5PM.

Hughes Register of Deeds 104 E. Capital, Pierre, SD 57501 **605-773-7495** Fax: 605-773-7479. 8AM-5PM. www.sdcounties.org

Hutchinson Register of Deeds 140 Euclid St, Rm 37, Olivet, SD 57052-2103 **605-387-4217** Fax: 605-387-4209. 8AM-N 1-5PM.

Hyde Register of Deeds PO Box 342, Highmore, SD 57345 (412 Commercial SE). **605-852-2517** 8-12:00-1-5PM.

Jackson Register of Deeds PO Box 248, Kadoka, SD 57453 (Main St Courthouse). **605-837-2420** 8AM-5PM.

Jerauld Register of Deeds PO Box 452, Wessington Springs, SD 57382-0452 (205 S Wallace). **605-539-1221** 8AM-12, 1-5PM.

Jones Register of Deeds PO Box 446, Murdo, SD 57559 (310 Main St). **605-669-7104** 8AM-5PM.

Kingsbury Register of Deeds PO Box 146, De Smet, SD 57231 (202 2nd St SE). **605-854-3591** Fax: 605-854-3833. 8AM-N, 1-5.

Lake Register of Deeds PO Box 266, Madison, SD 57042 (200 E. Center). **605-256-7614** Fax: 605-256-7622. 8AM-5PM.

Lawrence Register of Deeds PO Box 565, Deadwood, SD 57732 (90 Sherman St). **605-578-3930** 8AM-5PM.

Lincoln Register of Deeds 100 E. 5th, Canton, SD 57013-1789 (100 E. 5th). **605-764-5661** Fax: 605-764-5932. 8AM-5PM.

Lyman Register of Deeds PO Box 98, Kennebec, SD 57544 (100 Main St). **605-869-2297** Fax: 605-869-2203. 8AM-N; 1-5.

Marshall Register of Deeds PO Box 130, Britton, SD 57430 (911 Vander Horck Ave). **605-448-2352** Fax: 605-448-2116.

McCook Register of Deeds PO Box 338, Salem, SD 57058 (130 W. Essex Ave.). **605-425-2701** Fax: 605-425-2534. 8:30-4:30.

McPherson Register of Deeds PO Box 129, Leola, SD 57456 (Main St Courthouse). **605-439-3151** Fax: 605-439-3394.

Meade Register of Deeds 1425 Sherman St, Sturgis, SD 57785 **605-347-2356** Fax: 347-5925. 8AM-5PM.

Mellette Register of Deeds PO Box 183, White River, SD 57579-0183 **605-259-3371** Fax: 605-259-3194. 8AM-N,1-5PM.

Miner Register of Deeds PO Box 546, Howard, SD 57349 (North Main St Courthouse). **605-772-5621** Fax: 605-772-4148. 8AM-N, 1-5PM.

Minnehaha Register of Deeds 415 N Dakota Ave, Sioux Falls, SD 57104-2465 \ **605-367-4223** Fax: 605-367-8314. 8AM-5PM. www.minnehahacounty.org/depts/register_deeds/register_deeds.asp Property Tax records online.

Moody Register of Deeds PO Box 247, Flandreau, SD 57028-0247 (Pipestone Ave Courthouse). **605-997-3151** Fax: 605-997-9996. 8AM-5PM.

Pennington Register of Deeds 315 St. Joe St, Rapid City, SD 57701 **605-394-2177** 8AM-5PM. Property Tax, Assessor records online.

Perkins Register of Deeds PO Box 127, Bison, SD 57620 (100 E. Main St.). **605-244-5620** Fax: 605-244-7289. 8AM-5PM.

Potter Register of Deeds 201 S. Exene, Gettysburg, SD 57442 **605-765-9467** Fax: 605-765-2836. 8AM-5PM.

Roberts Register of Deeds 411 E. 2nd Ave, Sisseton, SD 57262 **605-698-7152** 8-5PM.

Sanborn Register of Deeds PO Box 295, Woonsocket, SD 57385 (604 W 6th St.). **605-796-4516** Fax: 605-796-4509. 8-5PM.

Shannon Register of Deeds 906 N. River St, Hot Springs, SD 57747 **605-745-5139**.

Spink Register of Deeds 210 E. 7th Ave, Redfield, SD 57469-**605-472-0150** Fax: 605-472-2410. 8AM-5PM.

Stanley Register of Deeds PO Box 596, Fort Pierre, SD 57532 (8 E. 2nd Ave). **605-223-7786** Fax: 605-223-7788. 8AM-N,1-5PM.

Sully Register of Deeds PO Box 265, Onida, SD 57564 (700 Ash Ave). **605-258-2331** Fax: 605-258-2884.

Todd Register of Deeds 200 E 3rd St, Winner, SD 57580-1806 **605-842-2208** Fax: 605-842-1116. 8AM-5PM.

Tripp Register of Deeds 200 E 3rd St, Courthouse, Winner, SD 57580-1806 **605-842-2208** Fax: 605-842-3621. 8AM-5PM.

Turner Register of Deeds PO Box 485, Parker, SD 57053-0485 (400 S. Main St). **605-297-3443** Fax: 605-297-5556.

Union Register of Deeds PO Box 490, Elk Point, SD 57025-0490 (200 E. Main). **605-356-2191** Fax: 605-356-3047. 8:30AM-5PM. Property records online.

Walworth Register of Deeds PO Box 159, Selby, SD 57472-0159 (4304 4th St). **605-649-7057** Fax: 605-649-7867. 8AM-N,1-5PM.

Yankton Register of Deeds PO Box 694, Yankton, SD 57078 (321 W 3rd). **605-260-4400 x5** Fax: 605-668-9682. 9AM-5PM.

Ziebach Register of Deeds PO Box 68, Dupree, SD 57623 (Courthouse). **605-365-5165** Fax: 605-365-5204. 8AM-5PM.

Tennessee

Organization: 95 counties, 96 recording offices. The recording officer is the Register of Deeds. Sullivan County has two offices. 66 counties are in the Central Time Zone (CST) and 29 are in the Eastern Time Zone (EST).

Real Estate Records: Counties will not perform real estate searches. Certified copies usually cost $1.00 per page. Tax records are kept at the Assessor's Office.

UCC Records: Financing statements are filed at the state level, except for real estate related collateral, which are filed with the Register of Deeds. However, prior to 07/2001, consumer goods and farm collateral were also filed at the Register of Deeds and these older records can be searched there. Many recording offices will not perform UCC searches. Use search request form UCC-11. Search fee is usually $12-15, the copy fee is $1.00.

Tax Lien Records: Federal tax liens are filed with the county Register of Deeds. State tax liens are filed with the Secretary of State or the Register of Deeds. Counties will not perform tax lien searches. Other Liens: Judgment, materialman, mechanics, trustee.

Online Access: The State Comptroller of the Treasury Real Estate Assessment Database can be searched free at http://170.142.31.248/. Select a county then search by name for real property information. Counties not on the system are Davidson, Hamilton, Knox, Shelby, and Unicoi.

Online access to over 40 counties' property and deeds indexes and images is available via a private company at http://auth.titlesearcher.com/ts/ts.asp or email support@TitleSearcher.com. Registration, login, and monthly $35 fee per county required, plus $20. set up. A $5 per day plan is also available. Also, online access to 22 counties' property, deeds, judgment, liens, and UCCs is available via a private company at www.ustitlesearch.com or call 615-223-5420. Registration, login, and monthly $25 fee required, plus $50 set up. Use DEMO username to try system. Finally, www.tnrealestate.com offers free and fee services for real estate information from all Tennessee counties.

Anderson Register of Deeds 100 N Main St, Courthouse, Rm 205, Clinton, TN 37716-3688 **865-457-5400** Fax: 865-457-1638. 8:30AM-4:30PM. Land, Property Assessor, Recorder, Deed records online.

Bedford Register of Deeds 108 Northside Sq, Shelbyville, TN 37160 **931-684-5719** Fax: 931-685-2086. http://titlesearcher.com Land, Property Assessor, Recorder, Deeds online.

Benton Register of Deeds 1 E. Court Sq, #105, Camden, TN 38320-2070 **731-584-6661** 8AM-4PM; 8AM-5PM F. Real Estate, Deed, Judgment, Lien, UCC, Property Assessor records online.

Bledsoe Register of Deeds PO Box 385, Pikeville, TN 37367 (Main St Courthouse). **423-447-2020** Fax: 423-447-6856. 8AM-4PM. Land, Property Assessor, Recording records online.

Blount Register of Deeds 349 Court St, Maryville, TN 37804-5906 **865-273-5880** Fax: 865-273-5890. 8AM-4:30PM. Property Assessor records online.

Bradley Register of Deeds PO Box 579, Cleveland, TN 37364-0579 (155 N. Ocoee, Rm 102). **423-476-0513** Fax: 423-478-8888. 8:30AM-4:30PM. Land, Property Assessor, Deed, Recording records online.

Campbell Register of Deeds PO Box 85, Jacksboro, TN 37757 (#302, 570 Main St). **423-562-3864** Fax: 423-562-9833. 8AM-4:30PM. Land, Deed, Property Assessor, Deed, Recording records online.

Cannon Register of Deeds Courthouse, Woodbury, TN 37190 **615-563-2041** Fax: 615-563-5696. 8AM-4PM. Real Estate, Deed, Judgment, Lien, UCC, Property Assessor records online.

Carroll Register of Deeds 625 High St, #104, Carroll County Office Complex, Huntingdon, TN 38344 **731-986-1952** Fax: 731-986-1955. 8AM-4PM. Real Estate, Deed, Judgment, Lien, UCC, Property Assessor records online.

Carter Register of Deeds 801 E. Elk Ave, Elizabethton, TN 37643 **423-542-1830** 8:30AM-5PM. Land, Property Assessor, Deed, Recording records online.

Cheatham Register of Deeds PO Box 453, Ashland City, TN 37015 (210 S. Main, #109). **615-792-4317** Fax: 615-792-2039. 8AM-4PM. Real Estate, Deed, Judgment, Lien, UCC, Property Assessor records online.

Chester Register of Deeds PO Box 292, Henderson, TN 38340 (Main St Courthouse). **731-989-4991** 8AM-4PM. Real Estate, Deed, Judgment, Lien, UCC, Property Assessor records online.

Claiborne Register of Deeds PO Box 117, Tazewell, TN 37879 (1740 Main St). **423-626-3325** 8:30AM-4PM. Land, Property Assessor, Deed, Recording records online.

Clay Register of Deeds PO Box 430, Celina, TN 38551 (East Lake Ave). **931-243-3298** Fax: 931-243-6723. 8AM-4PM M,T,Th,F; 8AM-N Sat. Land, Property Assessor, Deed, Recording records online.

Cocke Register of Deeds 111 Court Ave, Rm 102, Courthouse, Newport, TN 37821-3102 **423-623-7540** 8AM-4:30PM M,T,Th,F; 8AM-N W,Sat. Land, Property Assessor, Deed, Recording records online.

Coffee Register of Deeds PO Box 178, Manchester, TN 37349 (1341 McArthur St, #2). **931-723-5130** Fax: 931-723-8232. Land, Property Assessor, Deed, Recording online.

Crockett Register of Deeds 1 S Bells St #2, County Courthouse, Alamo, TN 38001 **731-696-5455** Fax: 731-696-3028. 8AM-4PM. Real Estate, Deed, Judgment, Lien, UCC, Property Assessor records online.

Cumberland Register of Deeds 2 N. Main St, #204, Crossville, TN 38555-4583 **931-484-5559** 8AM-4PM. Land, Property Assessor, Deed, Recording records online.

Davidson Register of Deeds 103 Metro Courthouse, Nashville, TN 37201 (501 Broadway #501). **615-862-6790** Fax: 615-880-2039. 8AM-4:25PM. Property, Inmates online. www.registerofdeeds.nashville.org

De Kalb Register of Deeds One Public Sq, Rm 201, Smithville, TN 37166 **615-597-4153** Fax: 615-597-7420. 8AM-4:30PM. Property Assessor records online.

Decatur Register of Deeds PO Box 488, Decaturville, TN 38329 (Main St Courthouse). **731-852-3712** 8-4 M,T,Th,F; 8AM-N W,Sat. Land, Property Assessor, Deed, Recording records online.

Dickson Register of Deeds PO Box 130, Charlotte, TN 37036 (Court Sq). **615-789-5123** Fax: 615-789-3893. 8AM-4PM. Real Estate, Deed, Judgment, Lien, UCC, Property Assessor records online.

Dyer Register of Deeds PO Box 1360, Dyersburg, TN 38025-1360 (1 Veteran's Sq). **731-286-7806** Fax: 731-288-7724. 8:30AM-4:30PM. www.co.dyer.tn.us Real Estate, Deed, Judgment, Lien, UCC, Property Tax records online.

Fayette Register of Deeds PO Box 99, Somerville, TN 38068-0099 (16755 Hwy 64 #108). **901-465-5251** Land, Property Assessor, Deed, Recording records online.

Fentress Register of Deeds PO Box 341, Jamestown, TN 38556 (101 Main St, Hwy 127). **931-879-7818** Fax: 931-879-4502. 8AM-4PM. Land, Property Assessor, Deed, Recording records online.

Franklin Register of Deeds 1 S Jefferson St, Rm #6, Franklin County Courthouse, Winchester, TN 37398-0101 **931-967-2840** 8-4:30PM; 8AM-N Sat. Land, Property Assessor, Deed, Recorder records online.

Gibson Register of Deeds 1 Court Sq, Courthouse, Trenton, TN 38382 **731-855-7628** Fax: 731-855-7650. 8-4:30PM M-F; 8AM-N Sat.. Real Estate, Deed, Judgment, Lien, UCC, Property Assessor records online.

Giles Register of Deeds PO Box 678, Pulaski, TN 38478 (Courthouse). **931-363-5137** Fax: 931-424-6101. 8AM-4PM. Land, Property Assessor, Deed, Recording records online. www.usit.net/giles/Government/register.htm

Grainger Register of Deeds PO Box 174, Rutledge, TN 37861 (8095 Rudledge Pike, Highway 11W). **865-828-3511** Fax: 865-828-4300. 8:30-4:30PM. Land, Property Assessor, Deed, Recording records online.

Greene Register of Deeds 101 S. Main St. #201, Courthouse, Greeneville, TN 37743 **423-798-1726** 8AM-4:30PM. Land, Property Assessor, Deed, Recording records online.

Grundy Register of Deeds PO Box 35, Altamont, TN 37301-0035 (Highway 56 & 108, City Hall). **931-692-3621** Fax: 931-692-3627. www.tngenweb.org/grundy/ Real Estate, Deed, Judgment, Lien, UCC, Property Assessor records online.

Hamblen Register of Deeds 511 W. 2nd North St, Morristown, TN 37814 **423-586-6551** Fax: 423-587-9798. 8:00AM-4:00PM M-F. Land, Property Assessor, Deed, Recording records online.

Hamilton Register of Deeds PO Box 1639, Chattanooga, TN 37401-1639 (625 Georgia Ave. Rm 400). **423-209-6560** Fax: 423-209-6561. www.hamiltontn.gov/register Real Estate, Recording, Deed, Property Assessor, Delinquent Tax records online. 7:30-5PM.

Hancock Register of Deeds PO Box 347, Sneedville, TN 37869 (Main St. Courthouse). **423-733-4545** 8:30AM-4PM; 8:30AM-N W,Sat. Real Estate, Deed, Judgment, Lien, UCC, Property Assessor records online.

Hardeman Register of Deeds Courthouse, 100 N Main St., Bolivar, TN 38008 **731-658-3476** Fax: 731-658-3075. 8:30AM-4:30PM; 8:30AM-5PM F. Real Estate, Deed, Judgment, Lien, UCC, Property Assessor records online.

Hardin Register of Deeds Courthouse, Savannah, TN 38372 (601 Main St). **731-925-4936** 8AM-4:30PM M,T,Th,F; 8AM-N W. Real Estate, Deed, Judgment, Lien, UCC, Property Assessor records online.

Hawkins Register of Deeds PO Box 235, Rogersville, TN 37857 (110 E. Main St, Annex Rm 202). **423-272-8304** Fax: 423-921-3170. 8AM-4PM; W & Sat 8AM-N. Land, Property Assessor, Deed, Recording records online.

Haywood Register of Deeds 1 N. Washington, Courthouse, Brownsville, TN 38012 **731-772-1432** 8:30AM-5PM. Property Assessor records online..

Henderson Register of Deeds Courthouse, Lexington, TN 38351 **731-968-2941** 8AM-4:30PM; closed on Sat.. Real Estate, Deed, Judgment, Lien, UCC, Property Assessor records online.

Henry Register of Deeds PO Box 44, Paris, TN 38242 (213 W. Washington St, 2nd Fl). **731-642-4081** Fax: 731-642-2123. 8:30AM-4:30PM. Real Estate, Deed, Judgment, Lien, UCC, Property Assessor records online.

Hickman Register of Deeds #1 Courthouse, Centerville, TN 37033-1639 **931-729-4882** 7:30AM-4PM. Land, Property Assessor, Deed, Recording records online.

Houston Register of Deeds PO Box 388, Erin, TN 37061 (100 Main St, Court Sq). **931-289-3141** Fax: 931-289-4240. Real Estate, Deed, Judgment, Lien, UCC, Property Assessor records online.

Humphreys Register of Deeds 102 Thompson St, Courthouse Annex, Rm 3, Waverly, TN 37185 **931-296-7681** 8AM-4:30PM. Land, Property Assessor, Deed, Recording records online.

Jackson Register of Deeds PO Box 301, Gainesboro, TN 38562 (6 E. Hull Ave.). **931-268-9012** 8AM-4PM M,T,Th,F; 8AM-2PM W; 8AM-N Sat. Land, Property Assessor, Deed, Recording records online.

Jefferson Register of Deeds PO Box 58, Dandridge, TN 37725 (202 W. Main St). **865-397-2918** 8AM-4PM; 8-11AM Sat. Land, Property Assessor, Deed, Recording records online.

Johnson Register of Deeds 222 W Main St, Mountain City, TN 37683 **423-727-7841** Fax: 423-727-7047. 8:30-5PM. Land, Property Assessor, Deed, Recording records online.

Knox Register of Deeds 400 W. Main Ave, Rm 225, Knoxville, TN 37902 **865-215-2330** Fax: 865-215-2332. 8AM-4:30PM. www.knoxcounty.org/register/index.html Real Estate, Property Tax records online.

Lake Register of Deeds 229 Church St, Box 5, Courthouse, Tiptonville, TN 38079 **731-253-7462** Fax: 731-253-6815. 8AM-4PM. Real Estate, Deed, Judgment, Lien, UCC, Property Assessor records online.

Lauderdale Register of Deeds Courthouse, Ripley, TN 38063 **731-635-2171** Fax: 731-635-9682. Real Estate, Deed, Judgment, Lien, UCC, Property Assessor records online.

Lawrence Register of Deeds 240 W. Gaines St, N.B.U. #18, Lawrenceburg, TN 38464 **931-766-4100** Fax: 931-766-5602. 8AM-4:30. www.titlesearcher.com Land, Property Assessor, Deed, Recording records online.

Lewis Register of Deeds 110 N Park Ave, Rm 104, Hohenwald, TN 38462 **931-796-2255** 8AM-4:30PM. Real Estate, Deed, Judgment, Lien, UCC, Property Assessor records online.

Lincoln Register of Deeds 112 Main Ave S, Rm 104, Fayetteville, TN 37334 **931-433-5366** Fax: 931-433-9312. 8AM-4PM. Land, Property Assessor, Deed, Recording online.

Loudon Register of Deeds PO Box 395, Loudon, TN 37774 (101 Mulberry St.). **865-458-2605** Fax: 865-458-9028. 8AM-4:30PM. Land, Property Assessor, Deed, Recording records online.

Macon Register of Deeds Courthouse, Rm 102, Lafayette, TN 37083 **615-666-2353** Fax: 615-666-2691. 8-4:30 M,T,W,F; 8-4 TH. www.maconcountytn.com/register_of_deeds.htm Land, Property Assessor, Deed, Recording records online.

Madison Register of Deeds 100 Main St, Courthouse, Rm 109, Jackson, TN 38301 **731-423-6028** Fax: 731-422-1171. Land, Property Assessor, Deed, Recording records online.

Marion Register of Deeds PO Box 789, Jasper, TN 37347 (Highway 41 Courthouse). **423-942-2573** 8AM-4PM M-F. Land, Property Assessor, Deed, Recording records online.

Marshall Register of Deeds 1103 Courthouse Annex, Lewisburg, TN 37091 **931-359-4933** 8AM-4PM. Real Estate, Deed, Judgment, Lien, UCC, Property Assessor records online.

Maury Register of Deeds PO Box 769, Columbia, TN 38402-0769 (1 Public Sq). **931-381-3690** x358 8AM-4PM. www.titlesearcher.com Land, Property Assessor, Deed, Recording, Sexual Offender Registry records online.

McMinn Register of Deeds PO Box 1074, Athens, TN 37371-1074 (6 E. Madison). **423-745-1232** Fax: 423-745-0095. 8:30-4:00 M-F. Real Estate, Deed, Judgment, Lien, UCC, Property Assessor records online.

McNairy Register of Deeds PO Box 158, Selmer, TN 38375 (Court Ave Courthouse). **731-645-3656** Fax: 731-645-3656. 8AM-4:30PM M,T,Th,F; 8AM-N Sat. Real Estate, Deed, Judgment, Lien, UCC, Property Assessor records online.

Meigs Register of Deeds PO Box 245, Decatur, TN 37322 (Courthouse). **423-334-5228** Fax: 423-334-5228. 8AM-5PM M,T,Th,F; 8AM-N Sat. Property Assessor records online.

Monroe Register of Deeds 103 College St -#4, Madisonville, TN 37354 **423-442-2440** 8:30AM-4:30PM M,T,Th,F; 8:30AM-N W & Sat. Land, Property Assessor, Deed, Recording records online.

Montgomery Register of Deeds PO Box 1124, Clarksville, TN 37041 (622 Madison St. #C). **931-648-5713** Fax: 931-553-5157. 8AM-4:30PM. Real Estate, Deed, Judgment, Lien, UCC, Property Assessor records online.

Moore Register of Deeds PO Box 206, Lynchburg, TN 37352 (Courthouse). **931-759-7913** Fax: 931-759-6394. 8AM-4:30PM; Closed Th; 8AM-N Sat. Property Assessor records online.

Morgan Register of Deeds PO Box 311, Wartburg, TN 37887 (Courthouse Sq, Rm 102). **423-346-3105** 8AM-4PM. Real Estate, Deed, Judgment, Lien, UCC, Property Assessor records online.

Obion Register of Deeds PO Box 514, Union City, TN 38261 (5 Bill Burnett Circle). **731-885-9351** Fax: 731-885-7515. 8:AM-4:30PM. Property Assessor records online.

Overton Register of Deeds 317 E. University St, Rm 150, Livingston, TN 38570 **931-823-4011** 8AM-4:30PM. Property Assessor records online.

Perry Register of Deeds PO Box 62, Linden, TN 37096-0062 (121 E.Main St). **931-589-2210** Fax: 931-589-2215. 8AM-4PM. Land, Property Assessor, Deed, Recording online.

Pickett Register of Deeds PO Box 5, Byrdstown, TN 38549 (Main Sq 1). **931-**

864-3316 Fax: 931-864-6615. 8AM-11:00-N-4PM. Property Assessor records online.

Polk Register of Deeds PO Box 293, Benton, TN 37307 (411 Highway Courthouse). **423-338-4537** 8:30AM-4:30PM. land, Property Assessor, Deed, Recording records online.

Putnam Register of Deeds PO Box 487, Cookeville, TN 38503-0487 (300 E. Spring St, Rm 3). **931-526-7101** 8AM-4PM. Real Estate, Deed, Judgment, Lien, UCC, Property Assessor records online.

Rhea Register of Deeds 375 Church St #106, Dayton, TN 37321 **423-775-7841** 8AM-4:30PM. Land, Property Assessor online.

Roane Register of Deeds PO Box 181, Kingston, TN 37763 (200 Race St, #6). **865-376-4673** 8:30AM-6PM M; 8:30AM-4:30PM T-F. Land, Property Assessor, Deed, Recording records online.

Robertson Register of Deeds 525 S. Brown St., Springfield, TN 37172 **615-384-3772** 8AM-4:30PM. Real Estate, Deed, Judgment, Lien, UCC, Property Assessor records online.

Rutherford Register of Deeds PO Box 5050, Murfreesboro, TN 37133-5050 (319 N. Maple St, Rm 133). **615-898-7870** Fax: 615-898-7987. 8AM-4PM. Real Estate, Deed, Judgment, Lien, UCC, Property Assessor records online.

Scott Register of Deeds PO Box 61, Huntsville, TN 37756 (283 Court St, Rm 217). **423-663-2417** 8AM-4:30PM. Property Assessor records online.

Sequatchie Register of Deeds PO Box 174, Dunlap, TN 37327 (307 E. Cherry St, 307E). **423-949-2512** Fax: 423-949-6554. 8AM-5PM. Land, Property Assessor, Deed, Recording records online.

Sevier Register of Deeds 125 Court Ave, Courthouse #209W, Sevierville, TN 37862 **865-453-2758** 8AM-4:30PM M-Th; 8AM-6PM F. www.titlesearcher.com Land, Property Assessor, Deed, Recording records online.

Shelby Register of Deeds 160 N. Main St, Rm 519, Memphis, TN 38173-0823. **901-545-4366** Fax: 901-545-3837. 8AM-4:30PM. http://register.shelby.tn.us Real Estate, Lien, Recording, Judgment, Lien records online.

Smith Register of Deeds 122 Turner High Circle, #113, Carthage, TN 37030 (**615-735-1760** Fax: 615-735-8263. 8AM-4PM. Land, Property Assessor, Deed, Recording records online.

Stewart Register of Deeds PO Box 57, Dover, TN 37058 (225 Donelson Parkway). **931-232-5990** 8AM-4:30PM. Real Estate,

Deed, Judgment, Lien, UCC, Property Assessor records online.

Sullivan County - Blountville Register of Deeds 3411 Hwy 126, #101, Blountville, TN 37617 **423-323-6420** Fax: 423-279-2771. 8AM-5PM. Property Assessor records online.
Bristol Register of Deeds 801 Anderson St., Bristol, TN 37620 **423-989-4370** 8AM-5PM. Property Assessor records online.

Sumner Register of Deeds PO Box 299, Gallatin, TN 37066-0299 (355 N. Belvedere Dr Rm 201). **615-452-3892** 8AM-4:30PM. www.deeds.sumnertn.org Real Estate, Recording, Deed, Property Tax records online.

Tipton Register of Deeds PO Box 644, Covington, TN 38019-0644 (Courthouse, Rm 105). **901-476-0204** Fax: 901-476-0227. 8AM-5PM. Real Estate, Deed, Judgment, Lien, UCC, Property Assessor records online.

Trousdale Register of Deeds 200 E. Main St. #8, Hartsville, TN 37074-1706 **615-374-2921** Fax: 615-374-1100. 8AM-4:30PM. Real Estate, Deed, Judgment, Lien, UCC, Property Assessor records online.

Unicoi Register of Deeds PO Box 305, Erwin, TN 37650-0305 (100 Main, 1st Fl).

423-743-6104 Fax: 423-743-6278. 9AM-5PM; 9AM-N Sat. www.titlesearcher.com Land, Deed, Recording records online.

Union Register of Deeds 901 Main St #108, Maynardville, TN 37807 **865-992-8024** 8AM-4PMM,T,Th.F; 8AM-N W,Sat. Land, Lien, Will, Deed, Judgment, Recorder, Property Assessor records online.

Van Buren Register of Deeds PO Box 9, Spencer, TN 38585 (Courthouse Sq). **931-946-7363** Fax: 931-946-7363. 8AM-4PM M-Th, 8AM-5PM F. www.titlesearcher.com Land, Property Assessor, Deed, Recording records online.

Warren Register of Deeds PO Box 128, McMinnville, TN 37111 (111 S. Court Sq). **931-473-2926** Fax: 931-474-2114. 8AM-4:30PM M-Th; 8AM-5PM F. Real Estate, Deed, Judgment, Lien, UCC, Property Assessor records online.

Washington Register of Deeds PO Box 69, Jonesboro, TN 37659 (Main St Courthouse). **423-753-1644** Fax: 423-753-1743. 8AM-5PM. Real Estate, Deed, Judgment, Lien, UCC, Property Assessor records online.

Wayne Register of Deeds PO Box 465, Waynesboro, TN 38485 (Court Sq). **931-722-5518** Fax: 931-722-5518. 8AM-4PM M T TH F; 8AM-N W & Sat. Land, Property Assessor, Deed, Recording records online.

Weakley Register of Deeds PO Box 45, Dresden, TN 38225-0045 (Courthouse, Rm 102). **731-364-3646** Fax: 731-364-5284. 8:30AM-4:30PM. Land, Property Assessor, Deed, Judgment records online.

White Register of Deeds PO Box 86, Sparta, TN 38583-0086 (Rm 118, 1 E.Bockman Way). **931-836-2817** Fax: 931-836-8418. www.tennesseeanytime.org/local/white.html Land, Property Assessor, Deed, Recording records online.

Williamson Register of Deeds PO Box 808, Franklin, TN 37065-0808 (1320 W. Main St, Rm 201). **615-790-5706** 8AM-4:30PM. Deed, Property, Tax Assessor, Recording records online.

Wilson Register of Deeds PO Box 176, Lebanon, TN 37087 (228 E.Main St.). **615-443-2611** Fax: 615-443-3288. 8AM-4PM. www.wilsondeeds.com Real Estate, Lien, Recording, Property Assessor records online.

Texas

Organization: 254 counties, 254 recording offices. The recording officer is the County Clerk. 252 counties are in the Central Time Zone (CST) and 2 are in the Mountain Time Zone (MST).

Real Estate Records: Some counties will perform real estate searches. Copy fees are usually $1.00 per page. Certification usually costs $5.00 per document. Each county has an "Appraisal District" which is responsible for collecting taxes.

UCC Records: Financing statements are filed at the state level, except for real estate related collateral, which are filed with the County Clerk. Most all recording offices will perform UCC searches. Searches fees are usually $10.00 per debtor name using the approved UCC-11 request form, plus $15.00 for using a non-Texas form. Copy fees are usually $1.00-2.00 per page with a minimum copy fee of $5.00.

Tax Lien Records: Federal tax liens on personal property of businesses are filed with the Secretary of State. Other federal and all state tax liens are filed with the County Clerk. All counties will perform tax lien searches. Search fees and copy fees can vary, but records are usually provided as part of the UCC search. Other Liens: Mechanics, judgment, hospital, labor, lis pendens.

Online Access: Numerous counties offer online access to assessor and recordered document data. There are now several private companies that offer access via the web to multiple countys' tax assessor data. Visit www.txcountydata.com or www.taxnetusa.com. Also, a search at the State Archives' TRAIL website at http://www2.tsl.state.tx.us/trail/ lets you locate information from over 180 Texas state agency web servers.

Anderson County Clerk 500 N. Church St, Palestine, TX 75801 **903-723-7432** Fax: 903-723-7801. 8AM-5PM. Appraiser, Property Tax, Land, Judgment, Lien, Grantor/Grantee records online.

Andrews County Clerk PO Box 727, Andrews, TX 79714 (215 N.W. 1st St, Rm 121A). **432-524-1426** Fax: 432-524-1473.

Angelina County Clerk PO Box 908, Lufkin, TX 75902-0908 (215 E. Lufkin Ave). **936-634-8339** Fax: 936-634-8460. 8AM-4:30PM. Appraiser, Property Tax online.

Aransas County Clerk 301 N. Live Oak, Rockport, TX 78382 **361-790-0122** Fax: 361-790-0119. 8AM-4:30PM. Real Estate, Deed, Lien, Judgment, Birth, Death, Appraiser, Property Tax records online.

Archer County Clerk PO Box 427, Archer City, TX 76351 (112 E Walnut). **940-574-4302** Fax: 940-574-4625. 8:30AM-5PM. Property Tax records online.

Armstrong County Clerk PO Box 309, Claude, TX 79019-0309 (Trice St, Courthouse). **806-226-2081** Fax: 806-226-5301. 8AM-N, 1-5PM.

Atascosa County Clerk #1 Courthouse Circle #102, Jourdanton, TX 78026 (Rm 6-1). **830-767-2511** Fax: 830-769-1021. 8AM-5PM. Appraiser, Property Tax records online.

Austin County Clerk 1 E. Main, Bellville, TX 77418-1551 **979-865-5911** Fax: 979-865-0336. 8AM-5PM. Appraiser, Property Tax, Land, Judgment, Lien, Grantor/Grantee records online..

Bailey County Clerk 300 S. First, #200, Muleshoe, TX 79347 **806-272-3044** Fax: 806-272-3538. 8:30AM-N 1-5PM. Property, Appraiser records online.

Bandera County Clerk PO Box 823, Bandera, TX 78003 (500 Main St). **830-796-3332** Fax: 830-796-8323. 8:30AM-4:30PM. Property, Personal Property, Appraiser online.

Bastrop County Clerk PO Box 577, Bastrop, TX 78602 (803 Pine St). **512-332-7234** Fax: 512-332-7241. 8AM-5PM. Appraiser, Property Tax, Land, Judgment, Lien, Grantor/Grantee records online.

Baylor County Clerk PO Box 689, Seymour, TX 76380-0689 (101 S. Washington). **940-889-3322** Fax: 940-889-4300. 8:30-5PM.

Bee County Clerk 105 W. Corpus Christi St, Rm 103, Beeville, TX 78102 **361-362-3245** Fax: 361-362-3247. 8AM-N, 1-5PM. Property Tax records online.

Bell County Clerk PO Box 480, Belton, TX 76513-0480 (550 E. 2nd Ave). **254-933-5174** Fax: 254-933-5176. 8-5PM. www.bellcountytx.com/countyclerk/index.htm

Bexar County Clerk 100 Dolorosa, Rm 108, Bexar County Courthouse, San Antonio, TX 78205-3083 **210-335-2581, 335-2273, 335-3041** www.countyclerk.bexar.landata.com Grantor/Grantee, Marriage, UCC, Assumed Name, Recording, Property Tax, Appraiser, Probate records online.

Blanco County Clerk PO Box 65, Johnson City, TX 78636 (101 E Pecan St). **830-868-7357** Fax: 830-868-4158. 8AM-4:30PM. Appraiser, Property Tax records online.

Borden County Clerk PO Box 124, Gail, TX 79738-0124 (117 E Wasson). **806-756-4312** Fax: 806-756-4405. 8AM-N, 1-5PM.

Bosque County Clerk PO Box 617, Meridian, TX 76665 (103 River St). **254-435-2201** Fax: 254-435-2152. 8AM-5PM.

Bowie County Clerk PO Box 248, New Boston, TX 75570 (710 James Bowie Dr). **903-628-6740** Fax: 903-628-6729. 8AM-5PM. Property Tax, Appraiser records online.

Brazoria County Clerk 111 E. Locust, #200, Angleton, TX 77515 **979-849-5711** Fax: 979-864-1358. www.brazoria.tx.us.landata.com Appraiser, Property Tax, Land, Grantor/Grantee records online. 8AM-4:30PM

Brazos County Clerk 300 E. 26th St, #120, Bryan, TX 77803 **979-361-4132** Fax: 979-361-4125. 8AM-5PM. Appraiser, Property Tax records online.

Brewster County Clerk PO Box 119, Alpine, TX 79831 (201 West Ave E). **432-837-3366** Fax: 432-837-6217. 8:30AM-5PM. Property, Appraiser records online.

Briscoe County Clerk PO Box 555, Silverton, TX 79257 (415 Main St). **806-823-2134** Fax: 806-823-2359. 8AM-5PM.

Brooks County Clerk PO Box 427, Falfurrias, TX 78355 (110 E. Miller). **361-325-5604** Fax: 361-325-4944.

Brown County Clerk 200 S. Broadway, Courthouse, Brownwood, TX 76801 **325-643-2594** 8:30AM-5PM. Appraiser, Property Tax records online.

Burleson County Clerk 100 W Buck St #203, Caldwell, TX 77836 **979-567-2329** Fax: 979-567-2376. 8AM-5PM. Appraiser, Property Tax records online.

Burnet County Clerk 220 S. Pierce St, Burnet, TX 78611 **512-756-5406** Fax: 512-756-5410. 8AM-5PM. Appraiser, Property Tax, Land, Grantor/Grantee records online.

Caldwell County Clerk PO Box 906, Lockhart, TX 78644-0906 (110 S. Main). **512-398-1804** 8:30AM-N, 1-5PM. Appraiser, Property Tax, Personal Property records online.

Calhoun County Clerk 211 S. Ann, Port Lavaca, TX 77979 **361-553-4411** Fax: 361-553-4420. Land, Grantor/Grantee, Judgment, Lien, Grantor/Grantee records online.

Callahan County Clerk 100 W. 4th, #104, Courthouse, Baird, TX 79504 **325-854-1217** Fax: 325-854-1227. 8AM-5PM.

Cameron County Clerk PO Box 2178, Brownsville, TX 78520 (964 E. Harrison). **956-544-0815** Fax: 956-544-0813. 8AM-5PM. Appraiser, Property Tax records online.

Camp County Clerk 126 Church St, Rm 102, Pittsburg, TX 75686 **903-856-2731** Fax: 903-856-2309. 8AM-5PM.

Carson County Clerk PO Box 487, Panhandle, TX 79068 (5th & Main St). **806-537-3873** Fax: 806-537-3623. 8AM-N, 1-5.

Cass County Clerk PO Box 449, Linden, TX 75563 (Main & Houston). **903-756-5071** Fax: 903-756-5732. 8AM-5PM.

Castro County Clerk 100 E. Bedford, Rm 101, Dimmitt, TX 79027-2643 **806-647-3338**

Chambers County Clerk PO Box 728, Anahuac, TX 77514 (404 Washington St). **409-267-8309** Fax: 409-267-8315. 8AM-5PM. Property Tax, Appraiser records online.

Cherokee County Clerk PO Box 420, Rusk, TX 75785 (402 N. Main). **903-683-2350** Fax: 903-683-5931. Land, Grantor/Grantee, Judgment, Lien, Property Tax, Appraiser records online.

Childress County Clerk Courthouse Box 4, Childress, TX 79201 (100 Ave E NW). **940-937-6143** Fax: 940-937-3479. 8:30-5PM.

Clay County Clerk PO Box 548, Henrietta, TX 76365 (100 N Bridge). **940-538-4631** 8AM-5PM. Property Tax records online.

Cochran County Clerk 100 N. Main, Courthouse, Morton, TX 79346-2598 (100 N. Main). **806-266-5450** Fax: 806-266-9027.

Coke County Clerk PO Box 150, Robert Lee, TX 76945 (13 E. 7th St). **325-453-2631** Fax: 325-453-2650. 8AM-5PM.

Coleman County Clerk PO Box 591, Coleman, TX 76834 (Courthouse). **325-625-2889** 8AM-5PM.

Collin County Clerk 200 S. McDonald, Annex "A", #120, McKinney, TX 75069 **972-548-4134** 8AM-5PM (8AM-4PM Land Recording). www.co.collin.tx.us Appraiser, Property Tax, Business Personal Property, Deed, Lien, Judgment, Vital Statistic, Mortgage records online.

Collingsworth County Clerk 800 West Ave, Box 10, Wellington, TX 79095 **806-447-2408** Fax: 806-447-5418. 9AM-5PM.

Colorado County Clerk PO Box 68, Columbus, TX 78934 (400 Spring St). **979-732-2155** Fax: 979-732-8852. 8AM-5PM. Land, Grantor/Grantee, Judgment, Lien, Grantor/Grantee, Cemetery records online.

Comal County Clerk 150 N Seguin, #101, #104, New Braunfels, TX 78130 **830-620-5513** Fax: 830-620-3410. 8AM-4:30PM. www.co.comal.tx.us

Comanche County Clerk Courthouse, Comanche, TX 76442 **325-356-2655** Fax: 325-356-5764. 8:30-5PM. Appraiser, Property Tax records online.

Concho County Clerk PO Box 98, Paint Rock, TX 76866 (152 N. Roberts). **325-732-4322** Fax: 325-732-2040. 8:30-5PM.

Cooke County Clerk Courthouse, Gainesville, TX 76240 **940-668-5420** Fax: 940-668-5440. 8AM-5PM. Property, Appraiser records online.

Coryell County Clerk PO Box 237, Gatesville, TX 76528 (Courthouse). **254-865-5911** Fax: 254-865-8631. Property, Appraiser, Recording, Real Estate online.

Cottle County Clerk PO Box 717, Paducah, TX 79248 (9th & Richards). **806-492-3823** 9AM-12, 1-5PM.

Crane County Clerk PO Box 578, Crane, TX 79731 (201 W. 6th St. Rm 110). **432-558-3581** 9AM-N, 1-5PM.

Crockett County Clerk PO Drawer C, Ozona, TX 76943 (907 Ave D). **325-392-2022** Fax: 325-392-3742.

Crosby County Clerk 201 W Aspen St, Rm 102, Crosbyton, TX 79322 (**806-675-2334** 8AM-N, 1-5PM.

Culberson County Clerk PO Box 158, Van Horn, TX 79855 (301 La Caverna). **432-283-2058** Fax: 432-283-9234. 8AM-12, 1-5.

Dallam County Clerk PO Box 1352, Dalhart, TX 79022 (101 E. 5th). **806-249-4751** Fax: 806-249-2252.

Dallas County Clerk 509 Main St., Records Bldg, 2nd Fl, Dallas, TX 75202-3502 **214-653-7275** Fax: 214-653-7082. 8AM-4:30PM. www.dallascounty.org/html/citizen-serv/county-clerk/ Property Tax, Personal Property, Voter Registration, Marriage, UCC, Assumed Name, Probate records online.

Dawson County Clerk PO Drawer 1268, Lamesa, TX 79331 (200 N. 1st St). **806-872-3778** Fax: 806-872-2473. 8:30AM-5PM.

De Witt County Clerk 307 N. Gonzales, Courthouse, Cuero, TX 77954 **361-275-3724** Fax: 361-275-8994. 8AM-N, 1-5PM.

Deaf Smith County Clerk 235 E. 3rd, Rm 203, Hereford, TX 79045-5542 **806-363-7077** Fax: 806-363-7023. 8AM-5PM.

Delta County Clerk 200 W. Dallas Ave, Cooper, TX 75432 **903-395-4400** Fax: 903-395-2178. 8AM-5PM.

Denton County Clerk PO Box 2187, Denton, TX 76202-2187 (1450 E McKinney). **940-349-2010** Fax: 940-349-2013/Non-filings. 8AM-5PM; 8AM-4:30, W. www.dentoncounty.com/dept/ccl.htm Real Estate, Property, Recording, Voter Registration, Wanted, Parollee, Sex Offender, Bond, Jail, Conviction records online.

Dickens County Clerk PO Box 120, Dickens, TX 79229 (Montgomery St. & Hwy 82). **806-623-5531** Fax: 806-623-5319. 8AM-N, 1-5PM.

Dimmit County Clerk 103 N. 5th St, Carrizo Springs, TX 78834 **830-876-2323 x233** Fax: 830-876-4205. 8AM-5PM.

Donley County Clerk PO Drawer U, Clarendon, TX 79226 (300 S. Sully). **806-874-3436** Fax: 806-874-5146. 8AM-N, 1-5PM. Property, Appraiser records online.

Duval County Clerk PO Box 248, San Diego, TX 78384 (400 E. Gravis on Highway 44). **361-279-3322 x271/2** Fax: 361-279-3159. 8AM-N, 1-5PM.

Eastland County Clerk PO Box 110, Eastland, TX 76448-0110 (100 W. Main, #102). **254-629-1583** Fax: 254-629-8125. 8AM-5PM. Vital Statistic records online.

Ector County Clerk PO Box 707, Odessa, TX 79760 (300 Grant Ave, Rm 111). **432-498-4130** Fax: 432-498-4177. 8AM-4:30PM. Real Estate, Appraiser, Personal Property records online.

Edwards County Clerk PO Box 184, Rocksprings, TX 78880-0184 (400 Main). **830-683-2235** Fax: 830-683-5376. 8-5PM.

El Paso County Clerk 500 E. San Antonio, Rm 105, El Paso, TX 79901-2496 **915-546-2074** 8AM-4:45PM. Assumed Name, Property Tax, Real Estate, Vital Statistic records online.

Ellis County Clerk PO Box 250, Waxahachie, TX 75168 (Records Bldg., 117 W. Franklin). **972-923-5070** Fax: 972-923-5075. 8AM-4:30PM. Appraiser, Property Tax records online.

Erath County Clerk 100 W. Washington St., Courthouse, Stephenville, TX 76401 **254-965-1482** Fax: 254-965-5732. 8AM-4PM. Property Tax, Appraiser records online.

Falls County Clerk PO Box 458, Marlin, TX 76661 (Corner of Business Hwy 6 & Hwy 7). **254-883-1408** Fax: 254-883-1406. 8AM-N, 1-5PM.

Fannin County Clerk 101 E. Sam Rayburn Dr., Courthouse, #102, Bonham, TX 75418-4346 **903-583-7488** Fax: 903-583-9598. Appraiser, Property Tax records online.

Fayette County Clerk PO Box 59, La Grange, TX 78945 (246 W Colorado). **979-968-3251** Fax: 979-968-8531. 8AM-N, 1-5PM. www.co.fayette.tx.us

Fisher County Clerk PO Box 368, Roby, TX 79543-0368 (Highway 180 & 70, Courthouse). **325-776-2401** Fax: 325-776-3274. 8AM-5PM.

Floyd County Clerk 105 Main St, Courthouse, Rm 101, Floydada, TX 79235

806-983-4900 Fax: 806-983-4909. 8:30AM-12, 1-5PM.

Foard County Clerk PO Box 539, Crowell, TX 79227 (100 Main & Commerce). **940-684-1365** Fax: 940-684-1918. 9AM-4:30PM.

Fort Bend County Clerk 301 Jackson, #101, Richmond, TX 77469 **281-341-8685** Fax: 281-341-8669. 8AM-4PM. www.co.fort-bend.tx.us Real Estate, Lien, Grantor/Grantee, Appraiser, UCC, Marriage, Death, Birth, Probate records online.

Franklin County Clerk PO Box 68, Mount Vernon, TX 75457-0068 (Dallas & Kaufman Sts). **903-537-4252 x6** Fax: 903-537-2982. www.co.franklin.tx.us/ Property Tax records online.

Freestone County Clerk PO Box 1010, Fairfield, TX 75840 (103 E. Main St, #1). **903-389-2635** 8AM-5PM M-Th; 8AM-4:30PM F. Appraiser records online.

Frio County Clerk 500 E. San Antonio St, # 6, Pearsall, TX 78061 **830-334-2214** Fax: 830-334-0021. 8AM-N; 1-5PM.

Gaines County Clerk 101 S. Main, Rm 107, Seminole, TX 79360 **432-758-4003** Fax: 432-758-1442. 8AM-5PM.

Galveston County Clerk PO Box 2450, Galveston, TX 77553-2450 (722 Moody Ave, 1st Fl). **409-766-2200** 8AM-5PM. www.co.galveston.tx.us/County_Clerk/ Real Estate, Lien, Appraiser, Grantor/Grantee, Property Tax, Personal Property, Sheriff Sale, Most Wanted records online.

Garza County Clerk PO Box 366, Post, TX 79356-0366 (300 W. Main). **806-495-4430** Fax: 806-495-4431. 8AM-N, 1-5PM.

Gillespie County Clerk 101 W. Main, Rm 109, Unit #13, Fredericksburg, TX 78624 **830-997-6515** Fax: 830-997-9958. 8AM-4PM. Appraiser, Property Tax records online.

Glasscock County Clerk PO Box 190, Garden City, TX 79739 (E. Currie). **432-354-2371** Fax: 432-354-2348. 8AM-4PM.

Goliad County Clerk PO Box 50, Goliad, TX 77963 (127 N. Courthouse Sq). **361-645-3294** Fax: 361-645-3858. 8AM-N, 1PM-5PM. Real estate, Grantor/Grantee, Judgment, Lien, Property records online.

Gonzales County Clerk PO Box 77, Gonzales, TX 78629 (1709 Sarah DeWitt Dr.). **830-672-2801** Fax: 830-672-2636.

Gray County Clerk PO Box 1902, Pampa, TX 79066-1902 (205 N. Russell). **806-669-8004** Fax: 806-669-8054. 8:30AM-N, 1-5.

Grayson County Clerk 100 W. Houston #17, Sherman, TX 75090 **903-813-4243** Fax: 903-870-0829. 8AM-5PM. www.co.grayson.tx.us/main.htm Property Tax, Bad Check, Sheriff Sale, Sheriff Bond, Jail, Appraiser records online.

Gregg County Clerk PO Box 3049, Longview, TX 75606 (100 E. Methvin, #200). **903-236-8430** Fax: 903-237-2574. 8AM-5PM. www.co.gregg.tx.us Property Tax, Real Estate, Grantor/Grantee, Deed, Mortgage, Vital Statistic, UCC records online.

Grimes County Clerk PO Box 209, Anderson, TX 77830 (100 Main St.). **936-873-2111** Fax: 936-873-3308. 8-N, 1-4:45.

Guadalupe County Clerk PO Box 990, Seguin, TX 78156-0990 (101 E. Court St, Rm 209). **830-303-4188 x236** Fax: 830-401-0300. 8AM-4:30PM. Property Tax, Appraiser records online.

Hale County Clerk 500 Broadway #140, Plainview, TX 79072-8030 **806-291-5261** Fax: 806-291-9810. 8AM-N,1-5PM. Property, Appraiser records online.

Hall County Clerk Courthouse, Box 8, Memphis, TX 79245 **806-259-2627** Fax: 806-259-5078. 8:30AM-5PM.

Hamilton County Clerk Main St, Courthouse, Hamilton, TX 76531 **254-386-3518** Fax: 254-386-8727. 8AM-5PM.

Hansford County Clerk 15 N.W. Court, Spearman, TX 79081 (1 N.W. Court St). **806-659-4110** Fax: 806-659-4168. 8AM-5PM. Property, Appraiser, Personal Property records online.

Hardeman County Clerk PO Box 30, Quanah, TX 79252-0030 (300 Main St). **940-663-2901** Fax: 940-663-5161. 8:30-5.

Hardin County Clerk PO Box 38, Kountze, TX 77625 (Courthouse Sq, Highway 326). **409-246-5185** 8AM-5PM.

Harris County Clerk PO Box 1525, Houston, TX 77251-1525 (1001 Preston, 4th Fl). **713-755-6405** Fax: 713-755-4977. 8AM-4:30PM. www.co.harris.tx.us/cclerk Real Estate, Lien, Appraiser, Voter, UCC, Assumed Name, Grantor/Grantee, Vital Statistic, Personal Property, Delinquent Tax records online.

Harrison County Clerk PO Box 1365, Marshall, TX 75671 (W. Houston & S. Wellington Sts). **903-935-4858** Fax: 903-935-4877. Property Tax records online.

Hartley County Clerk PO Box Q, Channing, TX 79018 (9th & Railroad). **806-235-3582** Fax: 806-235-2316. 8:30-N, 1-5. Property, Appraiser, Personal Property records online.

Haskell County Clerk PO Box 725, Haskell, TX 79521-0725 (1 Ave. D). **940-864-2451** Fax: 940-864-6164. 8AM-5PM.

Hays County Clerk 137 N. Guadalupe, County Records Bldg., San Marcos, TX 78666 (**512-393-7329** Fax: 512-393-7337. 8AM-5PM. www.co.hays.tx.us Appraiser, Property Tax records online.

Hemphill County Clerk PO Box 867, Canadian, TX 79014 (400 Main St). **806-323-6212** 8AM-5PM.

Henderson County Clerk PO Box 632, Athens, TX 75751-0632 (Courthouse Sq, S. Side, First Fl). **903-675-6140** Fax: 903-675-6105. 8AM-5PM. Property, Appraiser records online.

Hidalgo County Clerk PO Box 58, Edinburg, TX 78540 (100 N. Closner). **956-318-2100** Fax: 956-318-2105. 7:30AM-5:30PM. www.hidalgo.tx.us.landata.com/ Appraiser, Property Tax records online.

Hill County Clerk PO Box 398, Hillsboro, TX 76645 (1 Courthouse Sq). **254-582-4030** 8AM-5PM. Property, Appraiser, Personal Property records online.

Hockley County Clerk 800 Houston St, #213, Levelland, TX 79336 **806-894-3185**.

Hood County Clerk PO Box 339, Granbury, TX 76048-0339 (Rm 5, 100 E Pearl). **817-579-3222** Fax: 817-579-3227. 8AM-5PM. Appraiser, Property Tax records online.

Hopkins County Clerk PO Box 288, Sulphur Springs, TX 75483 (411 College, Annex). **903-438-4074** Fax: 903-438-4110. 8AM-5PM. www.hopkinscountytx.org

Houston County Clerk PO Box 370, Crockett, TX 75835-0370 (Courthouse Sq, 401 E. Houston). **936-544-3255** Fax: 936-544-1954. 8AM-4:30PM.

Howard County Clerk PO Box 1468, Big Spring, TX 79721-1468 (300 Main). **432-264-2213** Fax: 432-264-2215. 8AM-5PM. www.howard-county.net

Hudspeth County Clerk PO Drawer A, Sierra Blanca, TX 79851 (FM 1111, Courthouse Sq). **915-369-2301** Fax: 915-369-2361.

Hunt County Clerk PO Box 1316, Greenville, TX 75403-1316 (2500 Lee St, 2nd Fl east end). **903-408-4130** 8AM-5PM. Appraiser, Property Tax records online.

Hutchinson County Clerk PO Box 1186, Stinnett, TX 79083 (6th & Main). **806-878-4002** 9AM-5PM.

Irion County Clerk PO Box 736, Mertzon, TX 76941-0736 (209 N. Parkview). **325-835-2421** Fax: 325-835-2008. 8AM-N; 1-5.

Jack County Clerk 100 Main St, Jacksboro, TX 76458 **940-567-2111** 8AM-5PM.

Jackson County Clerk 115 W. Main, Rm 101, Edna, TX 77957 **361-782-3563** Fax: 361-782-3132. Real Estate, Grantor/Grantee, Judgment, Lien records online.

Jasper County Deputy Clerk PO Box 2070, Jasper, TX 75951 (Courthouse, Rm 103, Main at Lamar St.). **409-384-2632** Fax: 409-384-7198. 8AM-4:30PM.

Jeff Davis County Clerk PO Box 398, Fort Davis, TX 79734 (100 Woodward Ave). **432-426-3251** Fax: 432-426-3760.

Jefferson County Clerk PO Box 1151, Beaumont, TX 77704-1151 (1149 Pearl St). **409-835-8475** Fax: 409-839-2394. 8AM-5PM. www.co.jefferson.tx.us Recording, Deed, Lien, Judgment, Property Tax, Marriage, UCC, Assumed Names online.

Jim Hogg County Clerk PO Box 878, Hebbronville, TX 78361 (102 E. Tilley). **361-527-4031** Fax: 361-527-5843. 9-5PM.

Jim Wells County Clerk PO Box 1459, Alice, TX 78333 (200 N. Almond St). **361-668-5702** 8AM-N, 1-5PM.

Johnson County Clerk PO Box 662, Cleburne, TX 76033-0662 (2 N. Main, Rm 101). **817-556-6314** Fax: 817-556-6326. 8-N, 1-4:30PM. www.johnsoncountytx.org Appraiser, Property Tax records online.

Jones County Clerk PO Box 552, Anson, TX 79501-0552 (12th & Commercial Sts). **325-823-3762** Fax: 325-823-4223. 8-5PM.

Karnes County Clerk 101 N. Panna Maria Ave., Courthouse #9, Karnes City, TX 78118-2929 **830-780-3938** Fax: 830-780-4576. Property, Appraiser records online.

Kaufman County Clerk Courthouse, Kaufman, TX 75142 **972-932-4331** Fax: 972-932-7628. 8-5PM. www.kaufmancounty.net Appraiser, Property Tax, Real Estate, Grantor/Grantee, Deed, Lien records online.

Kendall County Clerk 201 E. San Antonio, #127, Boerne, TX 78006 **830-249-9343** Fax: 830-249-3472. 8AM-5PM. Appraiser, Property Tax records online.

Kenedy County Clerk PO Box 227, Sarita, TX 78385-0227 (101 Mallory St). **361-294-5220** Fax: 361-294-5218. 8:30-N, 1-4:30.

Kent County Clerk PO Box 9, Jayton, TX 79528-0009 (Courthouse). **806-237-3881** Fax: 806-237-2632. 8:30AM-N, 1-5PM.

Kerr County Clerk 700 Main, Courthouse, Rm 122, Kerrville, TX 78028-5389 **830-792-2255** Fax: 830-792-2274. 8AM-5PM. www.ktc.com Appraiser, Property Tax records online.

Kimble County Clerk 501 Main St, Junction, TX 76849 **325-446-3353** Fax: 325-446-2986. 8AM-N, 1-5PM.

King County Clerk PO Box 135, Guthrie, TX 79236 (Courthouse, Highway 82). **806-596-4412** Fax: 806-596-4664. 9AM-N, 1-5.

Kinney County Clerk PO Drawer 9, Brackettville, TX 78832 (501 Ann St). **830-563-2521** Fax: 830-563-2644. 8AM-N; 1-5.

Kleberg County Clerk PO Box 1327, Kingsville, TX 78364 (700 E. Kleberg St, 1st Fl). **361-595-8548** Fax: 361-593-1355. 8AM-N, 1-5. Property Tax records online.

Knox County Clerk PO Box 196, Benjamin, TX 79505 (Highway 6 & 82). **940-454-2441** Fax: 940-454-2005. 8AM-12, 1-5PM.

La Salle County Clerk 101 Courthouse Squ #107, Cotulla, TX 78014 **830-879-4432** Fax: 830-879-2933. 8AM-12; 1PM-5PM. Property, Appraiser records online.

Lamar County Clerk 119 N. Main #109, Courthouse, Paris, TX 75460 **903-737-2420** Fax: 903-782-1100. Inmate, Sheriff Bond, Sex Offender, Death records online.

Lamb County Clerk 100 6th Dr., Rm 103 Box 3, Littlefield, TX 79339-3366 **806-385-4222 x210** Fax: 806-385-6485. 8:30AM-5PM. Appraiser, Property Tax records online.

Lampasas County Clerk PO Box 347, Lampasas, TX 76550 (400 Live Oak St). **512-556-8271** 8AM-5PM.

Lavaca County Clerk PO Box 326, Hallettsville, TX 77964-0326 (109 N. LaGrange St). **361-798-3612** 8AM-5PM.

Lee County Clerk PO Box 419, Giddings, TX 78942 (898 E. Richmond). **979-542-3684** Fax: 979-542-2623. 8AM-5PM.

Leon County Clerk PO Box 98, Centerville, TX 75833 (Cass & St. Mary Sts, Courthouse Sq). **903-536-2352** 8AM-5PM. Property, Appraiser records online.

Liberty County Clerk PO Box 369, Liberty, TX 77575 (1923 Sam Houston, Rm 209). **936-336-4673** 8AM-5PM. Appraiser, Property Tax records online.

Limestone County Clerk PO Box 350, Groesbeck, TX 76642 (200 W. State St). **254-729-5504** Fax: 254-729-2951. 8AM-5PM. Appraiser, Property Tax records online.

Lipscomb County Clerk PO Box 70, Lipscomb, TX 79056 (Main St Courthouse). **806-862-3091** Fax: 806-862-3004. 8AM-12 1-5PM. Property, Appraiser records online.

Live Oak County Clerk PO Box 280, George West, TX 78022 (301 Houston). **361-449-2733 x3** 8AM-N, 1-5PM.

Llano County Clerk PO Box 40, Llano, TX 78643-0040 (107 W. Sandstone). **325-247-4455** Fax: 325-247-2406. 8AM-5PM. Appraiser, Property Tax records online.

Loving County Clerk PO Box 194, Mentone, TX 79754 (100 Bell St.). **432-377-2441** Fax: 432-377-2701. 9AM-N, 1-5PM.

Lubbock County Clerk PO Box 10536, Lubbock, TX 79408-0536 (904 Broadway, 2nd Fl Rm 207). **806-775-1060** Fax: 806-775-1660. www.co.lubbock.tx.us Election, Appraiser, Property Tax records online.

Lynn County Clerk PO Box 937, Tahoka, TX 79373 (Courthouse). **806-561-4750** Fax: 806-561-4988. 8:30AM-5PM.

Madison County Clerk 101 W. Main, Rm 102, Madisonville, TX 77864 **936-348-2638** Fax: 936-348-5858. 8AM-4:30PM.

Marion County Clerk PO Box 763, Jefferson, TX 75657 (102 W. Austin, Rm 206). **903-665-3971** Fax: 903-665-8732. 8AM-N, 1-5PM.

Martin County Clerk PO Box 906, Stanton, TX 79782 (301 N St. Peter St). **432-756-3412** Fax: 432-607-2212. 8AM-5PM.

Mason County Clerk PO Box 702, Mason, TX 76856-0702 (201 Ft. McKavitt). **325-347-5253** Fax: 325-347-6868. 8AM-N, 1-4.

Matagorda County Clerk 1700 7th St, Rm 202, Bay City, TX 77414 **979-244-7680** Fax: 979-244-7688. M-F 8AM-5PM. Property, Appraiser records online.

Maverick County Clerk 500 Quarry St, #2, Eagle Pass, TX 78852 **830-773-2829** Fax: 830-752-4479. 8AM-12, 1-5PM. Appraiser, Property Tax records online.

McCulloch County Clerk Courthouse, Brady, TX 76825 **325-597-0733** Fax: 325-597-1731. 8AM-12; 1PM-5PM. Criminal Record, Misdemeanor Record, Felony Record records online.

McLennan County Clerk PO Box 1727, Waco, TX 76703-1727 (215 N. 5th). **254-757-5078** Fax: 254-757-5146. Appraiser, Property Tax, Real Estate, Grantor/Grantee, Real Estate Recording records online.

McMullen County Clerk PO Box 235, Tilden, TX 78072-0235 (River & Elm Sts Courthouse). **361-274-3215** Fax: 361-274-3618. 8AM-4PM.

Medina County Clerk 16th St Courthouse, Rm 109, Hondo, TX 78861 **830-741-6041** Fax: 830-741-6015.

Menard County Clerk PO Box 1038, Menard, TX 76859 (210 E. San Saba). **325-396-4682** Fax: 325-396-2047. 8AM-N; 1-5.

Midland County Clerk PO Box 211, Midland, TX 79702 (200 W Wall St, #105). **432-688-4401** Fax: 432-688-8914. 8AM-5PM. www.co.midland.tx.us Property Appraiser, Voter Registration records online.

Milam County Clerk 100 S. Fannin, Cameron, TX 76520-3939 **254-697-6596** Fax: 254-697-7055. 8AM-5PM. Appraiser, Property Tax, Land, Grantor/Grantee, Judgment, Lien records online.

Mills County Clerk PO Box 646, Goldthwaite, TX 76844-0646 (1011 4th St). **325-648-2711** Fax: 325-648-3251. 8AM-N, 1-5PM.

Mitchell County Clerk 349 Oak St. #103, Colorado City, TX 79512-6213 **325-728-3481** Fax: 325-728-5322. 8AM-N 1-5PM.

Montague County Clerk PO Box 77, Montague, TX 76251-0077 (Rush & Washington Sts Courthouse). **940-894-2461** Fax: 940-894-3110. 8AM-5PM.

Montgomery County Clerk PO Box 959, Conroe, TX 77305 (210 W. Davis, #103). **936-539-7893** Fax: 936-760-6990. 8:30AM-4:30PM. www.co.montgomery.tx.us Grantor/Grantee, Judgment, Lien, Recordings online.

Moore County Clerk 715 Dumas Ave, Rm 105, Dumas, TX 79029 **806-935-2009** Fax: 806-935-9004. 8:30AM-5PM.

Morris County Clerk 500 Broadnax St, Daingerfield, TX 75638 **903-645-3911** Fax: 903-645-4026. 8AM-5PM.

Motley County Clerk PO Box 660, Matador, TX 79244 (Main & Dundee Courthouse). **806-347-2621** Fax: 806-347-2220. 8:30-5.

Nacogdoches County Clerk 101 W. Main, Rm 205, Nacogdoches, TX 75961 **936-560-7733** Fax: 936-559-5926. 8AM-5PM. www.co.nacogdoches.tx.us Real Estate, Lien, Judgment, Deed, Vital Statistic, Property Tax records online.

Navarro County Clerk PO Box 423, Corsicana, TX 75151 (300 W. Third Ave, #101). **903-654-3035** 8AM-5PM. Appraiser, Property Tax records online.

Newton County Clerk PO Box 484, Newton, TX 75966-0484 (Courthouse Sq). **409-379-**

5341 Fax: 409-379-9049. 8AM-4:30PM. Appraiser, Property Tax, Death records online.

Nolan County Clerk 100 E 3rd St #108, Sweetwater, TX 79556-0098 (100 E. 3rd, East Wing, Rm 100-A). **325-235-2462** Fax: 325-236-9416. 8:30AM-N, 1-5PM.

Nueces County Clerk PO Box 2627, Corpus Christi, TX 78403 (901 Leopard St, Rm.201). **361-888-0111** Fax: 361-888-0329. 8AM-5PM. www.co.nueces.tx.us Real Estate, Recording, Deed, Judgment, Lien, Appraiser, Property Tax records online.

Ochiltree County Clerk 511 S. Main, Perryton, TX 79070 **806-435-8039** Fax: 806-435-2081. 8:30AM-N, 1-5PM. Property, Appraiser records online.

Oldham County Clerk PO Box 360, Vega, TX 79092 (Highway 385 & Main St). **806-267-2667** 8:30AM-5PM.

Orange County Clerk PO Box 1536, Orange, TX 77631-1536 (801 Division). **409-882-7055** Fax: 409-882-7012. 8AM-5PM. www.co.orange.tx.us Property, Appraiser records online.

Palo Pinto County Clerk PO Box 219, Palo Pinto, TX 76484 (520 Oak St). **940-659-1277** Fax: 940-659-3628. 8:30AM-4:30PM.

Panola County Clerk Sabine & Sycamore, Courthouse Bldg, Rm 201, Carthage, TX 75633 **903-693-0302** Fax: 903-693-2726.

Parker County Clerk PO Box 819, Weatherford, TX 76086 (1112 Santa Fe Dr). **817-599-6185** Fax: 817-598-6183. 8AM-4PM. Appraiser, Property Tax records online.

Parmer County Clerk PO Box 356, Farwell, TX 79325 (400 Third St). **806-481-3691** Fax: 806-481-9154. 8:30AM-5PM.

Pecos County Clerk 103 W. Callaghan St, Fort Stockton, TX 79735 **432-336-7555** Fax: 432-336-7557. 8AM-5PM.

Polk County Clerk PO Drawer 2119, Livingston, TX 77351 (101 W. Church St). **936-327-6804** Fax: 936-327-6874. 8-5PM.

Potter County Clerk PO Box 9638, Amarillo, TX 79105 (500 S. Fillmore, Rm 205). **806-379-2275** Fax: 806-379-2296. 8AM-5PM. www.prad.org Appraiser, Property Tax records online.

Presidio County Clerk PO Box 789, Marfa, TX 79843 (320 N. Highland). **432-729-4812** Fax: 432-729-4313. 8AM-N; 1-4PM.

Rains County Clerk PO Box 187, Emory, TX 75440 (220 W Quitman St). **903-474-9999** Fax: 903-474-9390. 8AM-5PM.

Randall County Clerk PO Box 660, Canyon, TX 79015 (401 15th St). **806-468-5505** Fax: 806-656-6430. www.randallcounty.org Appraiser, Property Tax, Business Personal Property, Sheriff Sale records online.

Reagan County Clerk PO Box 100, Big Lake, TX 76932 (3rd at Plaza, Courthouse). **325-884-2442** Fax: 325-884-1503. 8:30-5.

Real County Clerk PO Box 750, Leakey, TX 78873-0750 (Courthouse Sq). **830-232-5202** Fax 830-232-6888. www.realcountytexas.com

Red River County Clerk 200 N. Walnut, Courthouse Annex, Clarksville, TX 75426-3075 **903-427-2401** Fax: 903-427-3589. 8:30-5. Property, Appraiser records online.

Reeves County Clerk PO Box 867, Pecos, TX 79772 (100 E. 4th St, Rm 101). **432-445-5467** Fax: 432-445-3997. 8AM-5PM.

Refugio County Clerk PO Box 704, Refugio, TX 78377 (808 Commerce, Rm.112). **361-526-2233** Fax: 361-526-1325. Marriage, Birth, Death, Divorce records online.

Roberts County Clerk PO Box 477, Miami, TX 79059-0477 (Highway 60 & Kiowa Sts). **806-868-2341** Fax: 806-868-3381. 8AM-N; 1-5PM.

Robertson County Clerk PO Box 1029, Franklin, TX 77856 (Courthouse Sq on Center St, Rm 104). **979-828-4130** Fax: 979-828-1260. 8AM-5PM.

Rockwall County Clerk 1101 Ridge Rd, S-101, Rockwall, TX 75087 **972-882-0220** Fax: 972-882-0229. 8AM-5PM. Appraiser, Property Tax, Deed records online.

Runnels County Clerk PO Box 189, Ballinger, TX 76821-0189 (600 Courthouse Sq). **325-365-2720** Fax: 325-365-3408. 8:30AM-N, 1-5PM.

Rusk County Clerk PO Box 758, Henderson, TX 75653-0758 (115 N. Main). **903-657-0330** 8AM-5PM. Property Tax, Real Estate, Grantor/Grantee, Judgment, Lien records online.

Sabine County Clerk PO Drawer 580, Hemphill, TX 75948-0580 (Oak & Main Sts Courthouse). **409-787-3786** Fax: 409-787-2044. 8AM-4:30PM.

San Augustine County Clerk 100 W. Columbia, #106 Courthouse, San Augustine, TX 75972-1335 **936-275-2452** Fax: 936-275-9579. 8AM-4:30PM.

San Jacinto County Clerk PO Box 669, Coldspring, TX 77331 (Church & Byrd Sts). **936-653-2324** Fax: 936-653-2324. Appraiser, Property Tax records online.

San Patricio County Clerk PO Box 578, Sinton, TX 78387 (400 W. Sinton St, Rm 124). **361-364-6290** Fax: 361-364-6112. 8AM-5PM. Appraiser, Property Tax, Personal Property records online.

San Saba County Clerk 500 E. Wallace, San Saba, TX 76877 **325-372-3614** Fax: 325-372-5746. 8-4:30PM. www.sansabacounty.org

Schleicher County Clerk PO Drawer 580, Eldorado, TX 76936 (Highway 277, Courthouse Sq). **325-853-2833 ext 72** Fax: 325-853-2768. 9AM-12:00-1-5PM.

Scurry County Clerk 1806 25th St, #300, Snyder, TX 79549-2530 **325-573-5332** Fax: 325-573-7396. 8:30AM-5PM.

Shackelford County Clerk PO Box 247, Albany, TX 76430 (225 S. Main). **325-762-2232** 8:30AM-N, 1-5PM.

Shelby County Clerk PO Box 1987, Center, TX 75935 (200 San Augustine St., #A). **936-598-6361** Fax: 936-598-3701. 8-4:30.

Sherman County Clerk PO Box 270, Stratford, TX 79084 (701 N. 3rd St). **806-366-2371** Fax: 806-366-5670. 8AM-N,1-5.

Smith County Clerk PO Box 1018, Tyler, TX 75710 (200 E Ferguson St #300). **903-535-0630** Fax: 903-535-0684. 8AM-5PM. Property, Appraiser records online.

Somervell County/District Clerk PO Box 1098, Glen Rose, TX 76043 (107 N.E. Vernon St.). **254-897-4427** Fax: 254-897-3233. 8AM-5PM. Appraiser, Property Tax records online.

Starr County Clerk Courthouse, Rio Grande City, TX 78582 **956-487-8032** Fax: 956-487-8624. 8AM-5PM.

Stephens County Clerk Courthouse, Breckenridge, TX 76424 **254-559-3700**.

Sterling County Clerk PO Box 55, Sterling City, TX 76951-0055 (609 4th St). **325-378-5191** Fax: 325-378-2266. 8AM-4PM M-Th; 8AM-1:30PM Fri..

Stonewall County Clerk PO Drawer P, Aspermont, TX 79502 (510 S. Broadway). **940-989-2272** 8AM-4:30PM.

Sutton County Clerk 300 E. Oak, #3, Sutton County Annex, Sonora, TX 76950 **325-387-3815** 8:30AM-4:30PM.

Swisher County Clerk 119 S. Maxwell, Courthouse, Tulia, TX 79088 **806-995-3294** Fax: 806-995-4121. 8AM-5PM. Appraiser, Property Tax records online.

Tarrant County Clerk 100 W. Weatherford, Courthouse, Rm 130, Ft. Worth, TX 76196 **817-884-1060** 8AM-4:30PM.

www.tarrantcounty.com/tc_countyclerk/site/d efault.asp Property Tax, Appraiser, Real Estate, Grantor/Grantee, Lien records online.

Taylor County Clerk PO Box 5497, Abilene, TX 79608 (300 Oak St). **325-674-1202** Fax: 325-674-1279. www.taylorcad.org Appraiser, Property Tax, Personal Property, Unclaimed Property records online.

Terrell County Clerk PO Drawer 410, Sanderson, TX 79848 (108 Hackberry). **432-345-2391** Fax: 432-345-2740. 9AM-5PM. Property, Appraiser records online.

Terry County Clerk 501 W. Main, Rm 105, Brownfield, TX 79316-4398 **806-637-8551** Fax: 806-637-4874. 8:30AM-5PM.

Throckmorton County Clerk PO Box 309, Throckmorton, TX 76483 (105 Minter St). **940-849-2501** Fax: 940-849-3220. 8AM-N; 1:00-5:00PM.

Titus County Clerk 100 W. 1 St., 2nd Fl, #204, Mount Pleasant, TX 75455 **903-577-6796** Fax: 903-572-5078. 8AM-5PM. Property, Appraiser records online.

Tom Green County Clerk 124 W. Beauregard, San Angelo, TX 76903-5835 **325-659-6552** Fax: 325-659-3251. 8-4:30.

Travis County Clerk PO Box 149325, Austin, TX 78714-9325 (1000 Guadalupe). **512-854-9188** Fax: 512-854-4526. 8AM-5PM. www.traviscad.org Appraiser, Property Tax, Business Property, Voter Registration, Grantor/Grantee, Recording, UCC, Marriage, Probate records online.

Trinity County Clerk PO Box 456, Groveton, TX 75845 (162 W First St). **936-642-1208** Fax: 936-642-3004. 8AM-5PM.

Tyler County Clerk 110 W. Bluff, Rm 110, Woodville, TX 75979 **409-283-2281** 8AM-4:30PM. Property, Appraiser records online.

Upshur County Clerk PO Box 730, Gilmer, TX 75644 (Highway 154 Courthouse). **903-843-4014** Fax: 903-843-5492. Appraiser, Property Tax, Real Estate, Grantor/Grantee, Lien, Judgment records online.

Upton County Clerk PO Box 465, Rankin, TX 79778 (205 E. 10th St). **432-693-2861** Fax: 432-693-2129. www.co.upton.tx.us

Uvalde County Clerk PO Box 284, Uvalde, TX 78802-0284 (Main & Getty Sts). **830-278-6614** 8AM-5PM. Property, Appraiser records online.

Val Verde County Clerk PO Box 1267, Del Rio, TX 78841-1267 (400 Pecan). **830-774-7564** 8AM-4:30PM.

Van Zandt County Clerk 121 E. Dallas St, Courthouse - Rm 202, Canton, TX 75103 **903-567-6503** Fax: 903-567-6722. 8AM-5PM. Property Appraisal, Land, Grantor/Grantee, Judgment, Lien records online.

Victoria County Clerk PO Box 1968, Victoria, TX 77902 (115 N. Bridge St #103). **361-575-1478** Fax: 361-575-6276. Appraiser, Property Tax, Land, Grantor/Grantee, Judgment, Lien records online.

Walker County Clerk PO Box 210, Huntsville, TX 77342-0210 (1100 University Ave). **936-436-4922** Fax: 936-436-4928. 8AM-4:45PM. Property, Appraiser records online.

Waller County Clerk 836 Austin St, Rm 217, Hempstead, TX 77445 **979-826-7711** 8AM-N, 1-5PM. Appraiser, Property Tax records online.

Ward County Clerk Corner of 4 & Allen, Monahans, TX 79756 (400 S. Allen St.). **432-943-3294** 8AM-5PM.

Washington County Clerk 100 E. Main, #102, Brenham, TX 77833 **979-277-6200** Fax: 979-277-6278. 8AM-5PM. www.co.washington.tx.us/cclerk/index.html Recording, Land, Marriage, Death, Birth, Military Discharge, Grantor/Grantee, Judgment, Lien records online.

Webb County Clerk PO Box 29, Laredo, TX 78042 (1110 Victoria St, #201). **956-523-4622** Fax: 956-523-5035. 8AM-5PM. www.webbcounty.com Appraiser, Property Tax records online.

Wharton County Clerk PO Box 69, Wharton, TX 77488 (309 E Milam #700). **979-532-2381** Fax: 979-532-8426. Appraiser, Property Tax, Real Estate, Grantor/Grantee, Judgment, Lien records online.

Wheeler County Clerk PO Box 465, Wheeler, TX 79096 (400 Main St). **806-826-5544** Fax: 806-826-3282. 8AM-5PM.

Wichita County Clerk PO Box 1679, Wichita Falls, TX 76307-1679 (900 7th St, Rm 250). **940-766-8144** Fax: 940-716-8554. Property, Appraisal records online.

Wilbarger County Clerk 1700 Main St. #15, Courthouse, Vernon, TX 76384 **940-552-5486** Fax: 940-553-2320. Property Tax, Personal Property records online.

Willacy County Clerk 540 W. Hidalgo Ave, Courthouse Bldg, First Fl, Raymondville, TX 78580 **956-689-2710** Fax: 956-689-0937. 8AM-N, 1-5PM. Proeprty, Appraiser, Real Estate, Grantor/Grantee, Judgment, Lien records online.

Williamson County Clerk PO Box 18, Georgetown, TX 78627-0018 (1st Fl, 710 S. Main St.). **512-943-1515** Fax: 512-943-1616. 8AM-5PM. www.wilco.org Appraiser, Property Tax, Tax Sale, Land, Grantor/Grantee, Judgment, Lien, Jail, Sheriff Bond records online.

Wilson County Clerk PO Box 27, Floresville, TX 78114 (1420 3rd St). **830-393-7308** Fax: 830-393-7334. 8AM-5PM. Property Tax, Appraiser records online.

Winkler County Clerk PO Box 1007, Kermit, TX 79745 (100 E. Winkler St). **432-586-3401** 8AM-5PM.

Wise County Clerk PO Box 359, Decatur, TX 76234 (200 N. Trinity, Records Bldg.). **940-627-3351** Fax: 940-627-2138. 8AM-5PM. Property, Appraiser records online.

Wood County Clerk PO Box 1796, Quitman, TX 75783 (1 Main St). **903-763-2711** Fax: 903-763-5641. www.co.wood.tx.us

Yoakum County Clerk PO Box 309, Plains, TX 79335 (Cowboy Way & Avenue G). **806-456-2721** Fax: 806-456-2258. 8-5PM.

Young County Clerk 516 Fourth St #104, Graham, TX 76450-3063 **940-549-8432** Fax: 940-521-0305. 8:30AM-5PM. Property, Appraiser records online.

Zapata County Clerk PO Box 789, Zapata, TX 78076 (7th Ave & Hidalgo St). **956-765-9915** Fax: 956-765-9933. 8AM-5PM. Property, Appraiser records online.

Zavala County Clerk Zavala Courthouse, Crystal City, TX 78839 **830-374-2331** Fax: 830-374-5955. 8AM-5PM.

Utah

Organization: 29 counties 29 recording offices. The recording officers are the County Recorder and the Clerk of District Court (state tax liens). The entire state is in the Mountain Time Zone (MST).

Real Estate Records: County Recorders will not perform real estate searches. Copy fees vary. certification fees are usually $2.00.

UCC Records: Financing statements are filed at the state level, except for real estate related collateral, which are filed with the Register of Deeds (and at the state level in certain cases). Many filing offices will not perform UCC searches. Copy fees vary, but is usually $1.00. Certification usually costs $2.00 per document.

Tax Lien Records: All federal tax liens are filed with the County Recorder. They do not perform searches. All state tax liens are filed with Clerk of District Court, many of which have online access.

Online Access: A number of counties offer online access; some are fee-based.

Beaver County Recorder PO Box 431, Beaver, UT 84713 (105 E. Center). **435-438-6480** Fax: 435-438-6481. 9AM-5PM.

Box Elder County Recorder 1 S. Main, Courthouse, Brigham City, UT 84302-2599 **435-734-2031** Fax: 435-734-2038. 8AM-5PM. www.boxeldercounty.org

Cache County Recorder 179 N. Main St #101, Logan, UT 84321 **435-716-7180** Fax: 435-716-7187. 8-5. Recording, Grantor/Grantee, Lien, Property records online.

Carbon County Recorder 120 E Main, Courthouse Bldg., Price, UT 84501 **435-636-3244** Fax: 435-637-6757. 8AM-5PM.

Daggett County Recorder PO Box 219, Manila, UT 84046 (95 N. 1st West). **435-784-3210** Fax: 435-784-3335. 9AM-N; 1-5.

Davis County Recorder PO Box 618, Farmington, UT 84025 (28 E. State, Rm 119). **801-451-3225** Fax: 801-451-3141. 8:30AM-5PM. www.co.davis.ut.us Real Estate, Lien records online.

Duchesne County Recorder PO Box 916, Duchesne, UT 84021 (734 N. Center). **435-738-1160** Fax: 435-738-5522. 8:30-5PM.

Emery County Recorder PO Box 698, Castle Dale, UT 84513-0698 (95 E. Main). **435-381-2414** Fax: 435-381-2614. 8:30AM-5:00PM. www.emerycounty.com Plat records online.

Garfield County Recorder PO Box 77, Panguitch, UT 84759 (55 S. Main). **435-676-1112 x112** Fax: 435-676-8239. 9-N; 1-5PM.

Grand County Recorder & Deputies 125 E. Center St., Moab, UT 84532 **435-259-1331** Fax: 435-259-1320.

Iron County Recorder PO Box 506, Parowan, UT 84761 (68 S. 100 East). **435-477-8350** 8:30AM-5PM.

Juab County Recorder 160 N. Main, Nephi, UT 84648 **435-623-3430** 8:30AM-5PM.

Kane County Recorder 76 N. Main St, #14, Kanab, UT 84741 **435-644-2360** 8-N, 1-5.

Millard County Recorder 50 S. Main, Fillmore, UT 84631 **435-743-6210** Fax: 435-743-4221. 8AM-5PM.

Morgan County Recorder PO Box 886, Morgan, UT 84050 (48 W. Young St). **801-829-3277** Fax: 801-845-4066. 8AM-5PM. www.morgan-county.net

Piute County Recorder PO Box 116, Junction, UT 84740 (Courthouse). **435-577-2505** Fax: 435-577-2433. 9AM-5PM.

Rich County Recorder PO Box 322, Randolph, UT 84064 (20 S. Main). **435-793-2005** 9AM-N,1-5PM.

Salt Lake County Recorder 2001 S. State St, Rm N-1600, Salt Lake City, UT 84190-1150 **801-468-3391** 8AM-5PM. www.co.slc.ut.us Assessor, Property Tax, Land records online.

San Juan County Recorder PO Box 789, Monticello, UT 84535 (117 S. Main, Rm 103). **435-587-3228** Fax: 435-587-2425. 8AM-5PM.

Sanpete County Recorder 160 N. Main, Manti, UT 84642 **435-835-2181** Fax: 435-835-2182. 8:30AM-5PM.

Sevier County Recorder 250 N. Main, Richfield, UT 84701 **435-896-9262 x210** Fax: 435-896-8888. 8AM-5PM.

Summit County Recorder PO Box 128, Coalville, UT 84017 (54 N. Main). **435-336-3238** Fax: 435-336-3055. 8AM-5PM M-F.

Tooele County Recorder 47 S. Main St, Rm 213, Tooele, UT 84074-2194 (47 S. Main St, Rm 213). **435-843-3180** Fax: 435-882-7317. 8:30AM-5PM. www. co.tooele.ut.us Property Tax records online.

Uintah County Recorder 147 E. Main St., County Bldg., Vernal, UT 84078 (147 E. Main St., County Bldg.). **435-781-5461** Fax: 435-781-5319. www.co.uintah.ut.us

Utah County Recorder PO Box 122, Provo, UT 84603 (Admin. Bldg.-Rm 1300, 100 E.Center). **801-370-8179** Fax: 801-370-8181. 8:30AM-5PM. www.utahcountyonline.org Recorder, Deed, Real Estate, Lien, Assessor, Delinquent Tax, Property Tax records online.

Wasatch County Recorder 25 N. Main, Heber, UT 84032 **435-657-3210** 8AM-5PM. www.co.wasatch.ut.us/d/recorder.html Real Property, Grantor/Grantee, Marriages online.

Washington County Recorder 87 N 200 E, #101, St. George, UT 84770 **435-634-5709** Fax: 435-652-5895. www.washco.state.ut.us Property, Tax Roll records online.

Wayne County Recorder PO Box 187, Loa, UT 84747-0187 (18 S. Main). **435-836-1303** Fax: 435-836-2479. www.waynecnty.com

Weber County Recorder 2380 Washington Blvd, #370, Ogden, UT 84401 **801-399-8441** 8AM-5PM. http://www1.co.weber.ut.us Real Estate records online.

Vermont

Organization: 14 counties and 246 towns/cities, 246 recording offices. The recording officer is the Town/City Clerk. There is no county administration in Vermont. Many towns are so small that their mailing addresses are in different towns. Four towns/cities have the same name as counties - Barre, Newport, Rutland, and St. Albans. The entire state is in the Eastern Time Zone (EST).

Many towns are now charging a $2.00 per hour vault time fee for in-person searchers.

Real Estate Records: Most towns/cities will not perform real estate searches. Copy fees and certification fees vary. Certified copies are generally very expensive at $6.00 per page total. Deed copies usually cost $2.00 flat.

UCC Records: This was a dual filing state until 12/31/94. From 01/01/95, only consumer goods and real estate related collateral were filed with Town/City Clerks. Starting 07/01/2001, only real estate collateral is filed at the local level. Most recording offices will perform UCC searches. Use search request form UCC-11. Search fees are usually $10.00 per name, and copy fees vary.

Tax Lien Records: All federal and state tax liens on personal property and on real property are filed with the Town/City Clerk in the lien/attachment book and indexed in real estate records. Most towns/cities will not perform tax lien searches. Other Liens: Mechanics, local tax, judgment, foreclosure.

Online Access: There is virtually no online access to county recorded documents. State recorded UCC data is available online from the Vermont Secretary of State.

Addison Town Clerk 7099 VT Rte 22A, Addison, VT 05491 (65 Route 17 West). **802-759-2020** Fax: 802-759-2233. 8:30AM-N, 1PM-4:30PM.

Albany Town Clerk PO Box 284, Albany, VT 05820-0284 (Main St.). **802-755-6100** 9AM-4PM T,Th; 9AM-7PM W.

Alburg Town Clerk PO Box 346, Alburg, VT 05440-0346 (16 S Main St). **802-796-3468** Fax: 802-796-3939. 9:00-N; 1-5PM.

Andover Town Clerk 953 Weston-Andover Rd., Andover, VT 05143 **802-875-2765** Fax: 802-875-6647. 9AM-1PM (11-3PM Wed).

Arlington Town Clerk PO Box 304, Arlington, VT 05250 (3828 Rt 7A, Town Hall). **802-375-2332** 9AM-2PM.

Athens Town Clerk 56 Brookline Rd., Athens, VT 05143 **802-869-3370** Fax: 802-869-3370. 9AM-1PM or by appointment.

Bakersfield Town Clerk Box 203, Bakersfield, VT 05441 (Town Rd 3). **802-827-4495** Fax: 802-527-3106.

Baltimore Town Clerk 1902 Baltimore Rd., Baltimore, VT 05143 (49 Harris Rd.). **802-263-5419** Fax: 802-263-9423. 10-N Sat.

Barnard Town Clerk PO Box 274, Barnard, VT 05031-0274 (North Rd.). **802-234-9211** 8AM-3:30PM M-W.

Barnet Town Clerk Box 15, Barnet, VT 05821-0015 (US Route 5, Main St). **802-633-2256** Fax: 802-633-4315. 9-N, 1-4:30.

Barre City Town Clerk Box 418, Barre, VT 05641 (12 N. Main St). **802-476-0242** Fax: 802-476-0264. 8AM-4PM.

Barre Town Clerk PO Box 124, Websterville, VT 05678-0124 (149 Websterville Rd). **802-479-9391** Fax: 802-479-9332. 8AM-4:30 www.barretown.org

Barton Town Clerk PO Box 657, Barton, VT 05822-1386 (34 Main St.). **802-525-6222** Fax: 802-525-8856. 7:30AM-4PM.

Belvidere Town Clerk 3996 Vermont Rt 109, Belvidere Center, VT 05492 **802-644-6621** 8:30AM-3:30PM T W Th.

Bennington Town Clerk 205 South St, Bennington, VT 05201 **802-442-1043** Fax: 802-442-1068. 8-5. Property, Assessor records online. www.bennington.com

Benson Town Clerk PO Box 163, Benson, VT 05731-0163 (2760 Stage Rd.). **802-537-2611** Fax: 802-537-2612. 9AM-N, 1-5PM.

Berkshire Town Clerk RFD 1 Box 2560, Enosburg Falls, VT 05450 (Town Hall). **802-933-2335** Fax: 802-933-5913. 9AM-N, 1-4PM M,T,Th,F; 9AM-N W.

Berlin Town Clerk 108 Shed Rd., Berlin, VT 05602 **802-229-9298** Fax: 802-229-9530. 8:30-N,1-4:30PM (July-Aug 8:30-N, 1-3)

Bethel Town Clerk PO Box 404, Bethel, VT 05032 (134 S Main St). **802-234-9722** Fax: 802-234-6840. 8AM-4PM, M, TH; 8AM-N, T, F.

Bloomfield Town Clerk PO Box 336, No. Stratford, NH, VT 03590 (3399 VT Route 102). **802-962-5191** Fax: 802-962-5191. 9AM-3PM Tues & Thurs.

Bolton Town Clerk RD 1 Box 445, Waterbury, VT 05676 (3045 Theodore Roosevelt Hwy). **802-434-3064** Fax: 802-434-6404. 7AM-4PM M-TH.

Bradford Town Clerk PO Box 339, Bradford, VT 05033-0339 (172 N. Main St.). **802-222-4727** Fax: 802-222-3520.

Braintree Town Clerk 932 VT Route 12A, Braintree, VT 05060 **802-728-9787** Fax: 802-728-9787. 8AM-N 1-5PM Tu & Th; 1-5PM Wed..

Brandon Town Clerk 49 Center St, Brandon, VT 05733 **802-247-5721** Fax: 802-247-5481. 8AM-4PM. www.town.brandon.vt.us

Brattleboro Town Clerk 230 Main St #108, Brattleboro, VT 05301-2885 **802-254-4541** Fax: 802-257-2312. 8:30AM-5PM. www.brattleboro.org

Bridgewater Town Clerk PO Box 14, Bridgewater, VT 05034 (Route 4, Clerk's Office). **802-672-3334** Fax: 802-672-5395. 8AM-4PM M-Th; 8AM-N F.

Bridport Town Clerk Box 27, Bridport, VT 05734-0027 (Town Hall). **802-758-2483** 9AM-4PM M T F; 9AM-N 1-4PM W.

Brighton Town Clerk PO Box 377, Island Pond, VT 05846 (49 Mill St Extension). **802-723-4405** Fax: 802-723-4405. 8:00-3:30PM M-F.

Bristol Town Clerk Box 249, Bristol, VT 05443 (1 South St). **802-453-2486** Fax: 802-453-5188. 8AM-4:30PM.

Brookfield Town Clerk PO Box 463, Brookfield, VT 05036-0463 (Ralph Rd.). **802-276-3352** Fax: 802-276-3926. 8:30AM-4:30PM M,T,F.

Brookline Town Clerk PO Box 403, Brookline, VT 05345 (Town Hall). **802-365-4648** Fax: 802-365-4648. 9AM-2PM Wed..

Brownington Town Clerk 509 Dutton Brook Ln, Orleans, VT 05860 **802-754-8401** Fax: 802-754-8401. 8:30-11AM M; 9AM-3:30PM W; 9AM-N Th.

Brunswick Town Clerk RFD 1, Box 470, 4495 Vermont Rte. 102, Brunswick, VT 05905 **802-962-5283** M-Sat by app't.

Burke Town Clerk 212 School St, West Burke, VT 05871 **802-467-3717** Fax: 802-467-8623. 8AM-4PM.

Burlington City Town Clerk 149 Church St, City Hall, Rm 20, Burlington, VT 05401 **802-865-7135** Fax: 802-865-7014. 8-4:30PM.

Cabot Town Clerk PO Box 36, Cabot, VT 05647-0036 (Main St, Town Hall). **802-563-2279** Fax: 802-563-2423. 9AM-5PM M-Th; 9AM-1PM F.

Calais Town Clerk 668 W. County Rd., Calais, VT 05648 **802-223-5952** 8AM-5PM M,T,Th; 8AM-N Sat.

Cambridge Town Clerk PO Box 127, Jeffersonville, VT 05464 (Clerks Office). **802-644-2251** Fax: 802-644-8348. 8-4PM.

Canaan Town Clerk PO Box 159, Canaan, VT 05903-0159 (318 Christian Hill). **802-266-3370** Fax: 802-266-7085. 9AM-3PM.

Castleton Town Clerk PO Box 727, Castleton, VT 05735 (Main St, Town Hall). **802-468-2212** Fax: 802-468-5482. 8-N, 1-4.

Cavendish Town Clerk PO Box 126, Cavendish, VT 05142-0126 (High St, Town Hall). **802-226-7292** Fax: 802-226-7790. 9AM-N, 1PM-4:30PM.

Charleston Town Clerk 5063 Vermont Rt 105, West Charleston, VT 05872-7902 **802-895-2814** Fax: 802-895-2814. 9AM-3PM (Closed Wed).

Charlotte Town Clerk PO Box 119, Charlotte, VT 05445-0119 (159 Ferry Rd). **802-425-3071** Fax: 802-425-4241. 8AM-4PM. www.vermont-towns.org/charlotte

Chelsea Town Clerk PO Box 266, Chelsea, VT 05038 (Main St, Town Hall). **802-685-4460** Fax: 802-685-4460. 8AM-N, 1-4PM.

Chester Town Clerk PO Box 370, Chester, VT 05143 (556 Elm St.). **802-875-2173** Fax: 802-875-2237. 8AM-5PM.

Chittenden Town Clerk PO Box 89, Chittenden, VT 05737 (337 Holden Rd). **802-483-6647** 1:30-5PM.

Clarendon Town Clerk PO Box 30, North Clarendon, VT 05759-0030 (Middle Rd). **802-775-4274** Fax: 802-775-4274.

Colchester Town Clerk PO Box 55, Colchester, VT 05446 (172 Blakely Rd). **802-655-0812** Fax: 802-654-0757. 8AM-4PM. www.colchestervt.org

Concord Town Clerk PO Box 317, Concord, VT 05824-0317 (374 Main St.). **802-695-2220** Fax: 802-695-2220. 7:30AM-3:30PM.

Corinth Town Clerk PO Box 461, Corinth, VT 05039 (Cookeville Rd Town Hall). **802-439-5850** Fax: 802-439-5850. M 8:30AM-3:30PM;Tu 11AM-3PM;Th 10AM-3PM;F 8:30-3PM.

Cornwall Town Clerk 2629 Route 30, Cornwall, VT 05753-9299 **802-462-2775** Fax: 802-462-2606.

Coventry Town Clerk PO Box 104, Coventry, VT 05825 (Community Center, E. Fremont). **802-754-2288** Fax: 802-754-6274. 8AM-N M,T,Th, F; 7AM-4PM, W.

Craftsbury Town Clerk Box 55, Craftsbury, VT 05826 (85 Craftsbury Rd). **802-586-2823** Fax: 802-586-2823.

Danby Town Clerk Box 231, Danby, VT 05739-0231 (Brook Rd). **802-293-5136** Fax: 802-293-5311. 9AM-N, 1-4PM M-Th.

Danville Town Clerk PO Box 183, Danville, VT 05828 (36 Rte 2 West). **802-684-3352** Fax: 802-684-9606.

Derby Town Clerk PO Box 25, Derby, VT 05829 (124 Main St). **802-766-4906** Fax: 802-766-2027. 8AM-4PM.

Dorset Town Clerk 112 Mad Tom Rd, Town Hall, East Dorset, VT 05253 **802-362-1178** Fax: 802-362-5156.

Dover Town Clerk PO Box 527, Dover, VT 05356-0527 (102 Route 100). **802-464-5100** Fax: 802-464-8721. 9AM-5PM.

Dummerston Town Clerk 1523 Middle Rd., E. Dummerston, VT 05346 **802-257-1496** Fax: 802-257-4671.

Duxbury Town Clerk 3316 Crossett Hill Rd, Waterbury, VT 05676 **802-244-6660** Fax: 802-244-5442. 8AM-4PM M-Th.

East Haven Town Clerk PO Box 10, East Haven, VT 05837-0010 (17 Maple St.). **802-467-3772** 1-6PM T; 8-1PM Th or by appt.

East Montpelier Town Clerk PO Box 157, East Montpelier, VT 05651-0157 (40 Kelton Rd, Town Bldg.). **802-223-3313** Fax: 802-223-3314. 9AM-5PM M-Th; 9AM-N F.

Eden Town Clerk 71 Old Schoolhouse Rd., Eden Mills, VT 05653 **802-635-2528** Fax: 802-635-1724. 8-12:30; 1-4:30 M-Th.

Elmore Town Clerk PO Box 123, Lake Elmore, VT 05657 (Town Hall). **802-888-2637** Fax: 802-888-2637. 9-3PM T,W,Th.

Enosburgh Town Clerk PO Box 465, Enosburg Falls, VT 05450 (239 Main St). **802-933-4421** Fax: 802-933-4832. 8AM4PM (closed on Wednesdays).

Essex Town Clerk 81 Main St, Essex Junction, VT 05452 **802-879-0413** Fax: 802-878-1353. 7:30AM-4:30PM. www.essex.org

Fair Haven Town Clerk 3 N. Park Pl, Fair Haven, VT 05743 **802-265-3610** Fax: 802-265-2158. M-F 8-4PM.

Fairfax Town Clerk PO Box 27, Fairfax, VT 05454 (67 Hunt St, Town Office). **802-849-6111** 9AM-4PM, M-F.

Fairfield Town Clerk PO Box 5, Fairfield, VT 05455 (Town Hall). **802-827-3261** 10AM-2PM.

Fairlee Town Clerk PO Box 95, Fairlee, VT 05045-0095 (75 Town Common Rd). **802-333-4363** Fax: 802-333-9214. 8:30AM-4:30PM M-T, 10AM-6PM W, or app't.

Fayston Town Clerk 866 N. Fayston Rd., No. Fayston, VT 05660 **802-496-2454** Fax: 802-496-9850. 9AM-N, 12:30-3:30PM.

Ferrisburgh Town Clerk PO Box 6, Ferrisburgh, VT 05456-0006 (6 Little Chicago Rd). **802-877-3429** Fax: 802-877-6757. 8AM-4PM.

Fletcher Town Clerk 215 Cambridge Rd, Cambridge, VT 05444 **802-849-6616** Fax: 802-849-2500. 9AM-3:30PM.

Franklin Town Clerk PO Box 82, Franklin, VT 05457-0082 (5167 Main St, Haston Library). **802-285-2101** 9AM-4PM M,T,F; 9AM-7PM Th; 9AM-N W.

Georgia Town Clerk 47 Town Common Rd North, St. Albans, VT 05478 **802-524-3524** Fax: 802-524-3543. 8:00AM-5PM M-Th; 8:00AM-4:00PM Fri..

Glover Town Clerk 51 Bean Hill, Glover, VT 05839 **802-525-6227** Fax: 802-525-4115. 8AM-4PM, M-F.

Goshen Town Clerk 50 Carlisle Hill Rd., Goshen, VT 05733 **802-247-6455** 9AM-1PM Tues.

Grafton Town Clerk PO Box 180, Grafton, VT 05146 (Main St) **802-843-2419** 9AM-N, 1-4PM M,T,Th,F.

Granby Town Clerk PO Box 56, Granby, VT 05840 (9005 Granby Rd). **802-328-3611** Fax: 802-328-3611. By appointment only..

Grand Isle Town Clerk Town Clerk PO Box 49, Grand Isle, VT 05458 (9 Hyde Rd). **802-372-8830** Fax: 802-372-8815. 8:30AM-3:30PM.

Granville Town Clerk PO Box 66, Granville, VT 05747-0066 (4801 Route 100). **802-767-4403** Fax: 802-767-3968. 9AM-3PM M-Th.

Greensboro Town Clerk Box 119, Greensboro, VT 05841 (Town Hall). **802-533-2911** 8:30AM-N, 1-4PM.

Groton Town Clerk 314 Scott Highway, Groton, VT 05046 **802-584-3276** Fax: 802-584-3276. 7AM-N, 12:30-3:30PM M-Th.

Guildhall Town Clerk PO Box 10, Guildhall, VT 05905 (Route 102). **802-676-3797** Fax: 802-676-3518. 9AM-12:00PM, T, TH, or by Appt..

Guilford Town Clerk 236 School Rd., Guilford, VT 05301-8319 **802-254-6857** Fax: 802-257-5764. 9AM-4PM M T TH F; 09AM-N & 6:30-8:00 PM W.

Halifax Town Clerk PO Box 45, West Halifax, VT 05358 (246 Branch Rd.). **802-368-7390** Fax: 802-368-7390. 9AM-4PM M,T,F; 9AM-N Sat.

Hancock Town Clerk PO Box 100, Hancock, VT 05748 (48 Rt 125). **802-767-3660** Fax: 802-767-3660. 8AM-3PM T-TH; Monday by appt. only; Sat 8-10AM.

Hardwick Town Clerk Box 523, Hardwick, VT 05843 (2 Church St). **802-472-5971** Fax: 802-472-3793. 9AM-4PM.

Hartford Town Clerk 171 Bridge St, White River Junction, VT 05001-1920 **802-295-2785** 8AM-N, 1-5PM. www.hartford-vt.org

Hartland Town Clerk PO Box 349, Hartland, VT 05048-0349 (1 Queechee Rd.). **802-436-2444** Fax: 802-436-2444. 8-4PM.

Highgate Town Clerk PO Box 67, Highgate Center, VT 05459 (Municipal Bldg., Route 78). **802-868-4697** 8:30-N, 1PM-4:30PM.

Hinesburg Town Clerk PO Box 133, Hinesburg, VT 05461 (Town Hall). **802-482-2281** Fax: 802-482-5404.

Holland Town Clerk 120 School Rd., Holland/Derby Line, VT 05830 **802-895-4440** Fax: 802-895-4440. 9-2PM (closed Wed).

Hubbardton Town Clerk 1831 Monument Hill Rd, Castleton, VT 05735 **802-273-2951** Fax: 802-273-3729. 9AM-2PM M,W,F.

Huntington Town Clerk 4930 Main Rd., Huntington, VT 05462 **802-434-2032** Fax:

802-434-4731. 8AM-4PM M,W; 7AM-2PM Tu,F; 8AM-6PM Th.

Hyde Park Town Clerk PO Box 98, Hyde Park, VT 05655-0098 (344 VT 15 West). **802-888-2300** Fax: 802-888-6878. 8-4PM.

Ira Town Clerk 808 Route 133, West Rutland, VT 05777 **802-235-2745** 9AM-2:30PM M; 2-7PM T.

Irasburg Town Clerk Box 51, Irasburg, VT 05845 (Route 58). **802-754-2242** 9AM-3PM M,W,Th.

Isle La Motte Town Clerk PO Box 250, Isle La Motte, VT 05463 (Rt 129, Town Hall). **802-928-3434** Fax: 802-928-3002. 8AM-3PM Tu,Th; 8AM-N Sat..

Jamaica Town Clerk PO Box 173, Jamaica, VT 05343 (White Bldg. in center of Jamaica Village). **802-874-4681** 9AM-N, 1-4PM T,W,Th,F.

Jay Town Clerk 1036 Vermont Rte. 242, Jay, VT 05859-9820 **802-988-2996** Fax: 802-988-2996. 7AM-4PM (Closed M).

Jericho Town Clerk PO Box 67, Jericho, VT 05465 (67 VT Route 15). **802-899-4936** Fax: 802-899-5549. 8-5 M-TH, 8-3 F. www.jerichovt.gov

Johnson Town Clerk PO Box 383, Johnson, VT 05656 (293 Lower Main West). **802-635-2611** Fax: 802-635-9523. 7:30-4PM.

Killington Town Clerk PO Box 429, Killington, VT 05751-0429 (2706 River Rd). **802-422-3243** Fax: 802-422-3030. 9-3PM. www.killingtontown.com/staff.htm

Kirby Town Clerk 346 Town Hall Rd., Town of Kirby, Lyndonville, VT 05851-9802 **802-626-9386** Fax: 802-626-9386. 8AM-3PM; T,TH.

Landgrove Town Clerk Box 508, Londonderry, VT 05148 (Casey Henson, Red Pine Dr.-End of Landgrove Hollow Rd). **802-824-3716** Fax: 802-824-3716. 9AM-1PM.

Leicester Town Clerk 44 Schoolhouse Rd., Leicester, VT 05733 **802-247-5961** 1-4M-W.

Lemington Town Clerk 2549 River Rd, VT 102, Lemington, VT 05903 **802-277-4814** 11AM-2PM W.

Lincoln Town Clerk 62 Quaker St., Lincoln, VT 05443 **802-453-2980** Fax: 802-453-2975. 9AM-N, 1PM-4PM T-F; 9AM-N Sat, Closed Monday.

Londonderry Town Clerk PO Box 118, South Londonderry, VT 05155-0118 (Old School St.). **802-824-3356** 9AM-3PM T-F; 9AM-12 Sat.

Lowell Town Clerk 2170 VT Rt. 100, Lowell, VT 05847-0007 **802-744-6559** Fax: 802-744-2357. 9AM-2:30PM Mon & Th.

Ludlow Town Clerk PO Box 307, Ludlow, VT 05149 (37 Depot St). **802-228-3232** Fax: 802-228-8399. 8:30AM-4:30PM.

Lunenburg Town Clerk PO Box 54, Lunenburg, VT 05906 (Main St.). **802-892-5959** Fax: 802-892-5100. 8:30-N, 1-4PM.

Lyndon Town Clerk PO Box 167, Lyndonville, VT 05851 (119 Park Ave). **802-626-5785** Fax: 802-626-1265. 7:30AM-4:30PM.

Maidstone Town Clerk PO Box 118, Maidstone, VT 05905-0118 (1174 State Rt. 102). **802-676-3210** Fax: 802-676-3210. 9AM-11AM M-TH.

Manchester Town Clerk PO Box 830, Manchester Center, VT 05255 (6039 Main St.). **802-362-1315** Fax: 802-362-1315. 8:30AM-1PM, 2-4:30PM M-T-Th-F; 10AM-6PM W. www.town.manchester.vt.us

Marlboro Town Clerk PO Box E, Marlboro, VT 05344 (510 South Rd). **802-254-2181** Fax: 802-257-2447. 9AM-4PM M,W,Th.

Marshfield Town Clerk 122 School St, Rm 1, Marshfield, VT 05658 **802-426-3305** Fax: 802-426-3045.

Mendon Town Clerk 34 US Route 4, Mendon, VT 05701 **802-775-1662** Fax: 802-773-9682. 8AM-3PM,M-W; 8AM-1PM,TH; Closed F.

Middlebury Town Clerk 94 Main St, Middlebury, VT 05753-1334 **802-388-4041** Fax: 802-388-4364. 8:30AM-4:30PM.

Middlesex Town Clerk 5 Church St., Middlesex, VT 05602 **802-223-5915** Fax: 802-223-0569. M-Th 8:30-N 1:00-4:30PM. www.middlesex-vt.org/

Middletown Springs Town Clerk PO Box 1232, Middletown Springs, VT 05757-1197 (10 Park St). **802-235-2220** Fax: 802-235-2066. 9AM-N, 1-4PM M, Tu; 1-4PM F,9AM-12:00PM.

Milton Town Clerk PO Box 18, Milton, VT 05468 (43 Bombardier Rd.). **802-893-4111** Fax: 802-893-1005. 8AM-5PM.

Monkton Town Clerk 280 Yorkton Ridge, North Ferrisburg, VT 05473-9509 **802-453-3800** 8AM-1PM M,T,Th,F; 8:30-N Sat.

Montgomery Town Clerk PO Box 356, Montgomery Center, VT 05471-0356 (98 Main St). **802-326-4719** Fax: 802-326-4939. 9AM-N 1PM-4PM M T TH F; 9AM-N W. www.vermont-towns.org/montgomery'

Montpelier City Clerk 39 Main St, City Hall, Montpelier, VT 05602 **802-223-9500** Fax: 802-223-9523.

Moretown Town Clerk PO Box 666, Moretown, VT 05660 (Route 100B). **802-496-3645** 9AM-N, 1-4:30PM M-Th; 9AM-3:30PM F.

Morgan Town Clerk PO Box 45, Morgan, VT 05853-0045 (41 Meade Hill Rd). **802-895-2927** Fax: 802-895-4204. 9AM-3PM M,T,Th; 8AM-5PM Wed; 9AM-N Fri..

Morristown Town Clerk PO Box 748, Morrisville, VT 05661-0748 (18 Lower Main St.). **802-888-6370** Fax: 802-888-6375. 8:30AM-4:30PM, M-Th, F; 8:30AM-12:30PM, W. www.morristownvt.org

Mount Holly Town Clerk PO Box 248, Mount Holly, VT 05758 (50 School St). **802-259-2391** Fax: 802-259-2391. 8:30AM-4PM M-TH.

Mount Tabor Town Clerk PO Box 245, Mt. Tabor, VT 05739 (Brooklyn Rd., Town Office). **802-293-5282** Fax: 802-293-5287. Tues & Wed 9AM-12PM.

New Haven Town Clerk 78 North St., New Haven, VT 05472 **802-453-3516** Fax: 802-453-3516. 9-3PM. www.newhavenvt.com

Newark Town Clerk 1336 Newark St, Newark, VT 05871 **802-467-3336** 9AM-4PM M,W,Th.

Newbury Town Clerk PO Box 126, Newbury, VT 05051 (Main St.). **802-866-5521** Fax: 802-866-5301. 8:30AM-2:30PM, M-F; 2:30-6PM T. www.cohase.org

Newfane Town Clerk PO Box 36, Newfane, VT 05345-0036 (555 VT Rte. 30). **802-365-7772** Fax: 802-365-7692. 9AM-3PM.

Newport City Town Clerk 222 Main St, Newport, VT 05855 **802-334-2112** Fax: 802-334-5632. 8:30AM-4:30PM. Assessor, Property records online.

Newport Town Clerk PO Box 85, Newport Center, VT 05857 (102 Vance Hill). **802-334-6442** Fax: 802-334-6442. 7AM-4:30PM,M-Th, Closed F.

North Hero Town Clerk PO Box 38, North Hero, VT 05474 (2681 US Rte. 2). **802-372-6926** Fax: 802-372-3806. 9AM-4PM.

Northfield Town Clerk 51 S. Main St, Northfield, VT 05663 **802-485-5421** Fax: 802-485-8426.

Norton Town Clerk VT Route 1145, Norton, VT 05907 (347 Nelson Rd.). **802-822-9935** Fax: 802-822-9935. Appointment Only.

Norwich Town Clerk PO Box 376, Norwich, VT 05055 (300 Main St.). **802-649-1419** Fax: 802-649-0123. 8:30-4:30 8:30-4:30,M,T,W,F, 8:30-7PM Th.

Orange Town Clerk PO Box 233, East Barre, VT 05649 (US Rte 302, (3 miles east of E Barre)). **802-479-2673** Fax: 802-479-2673. 8AM-N, 1-4PM.

Orwell Town Clerk PO Box 32, Orwell, VT 05760-0032 (436 Main St.). **802-948-2032** 9:30AM-N, 1-3:30PM M, T, Th, F.

Panton Town Clerk PO Box 174, Vergennes, VT 05491-0174 (3176 Jersey St). **802-475-2333** Fax: 802-475-2785. 9AM-5PM M,Th; 9AM-2PM Tu, F; 4-7PM W.

Pawlet Town Clerk PO Box 128, Pawlet, VT 05761-0128 (122 School St). **802-325-3309** Fax: 802-325-6109. 9:00AM-3:00PM T-TH; 9:00AM-N F.

Peacham Town Clerk Box 244, Peacham, VT 05862 (79 Church St.). **802-592-3218** Fax: 802-592-3011. 8:30AM-N T,W,Th,F; 4:30PM-7:30PM W.. www.peacham.net

Peru Town Clerk Box 127, Peru, VT 05152 (402 Main St.). **802-824-3065** Fax: 802-824-3065. 8:30AM-4PM T, Th.

Pittsfield Town Clerk PO Box 556, Pittsfield, VT 05762-0556 (40 Village Green). **802-746-8170** Noon-6PM T; 9AM-3PM W,Th.

Pittsford Town Clerk PO Box 10, Pittsford, VT 5763 (Town Hall). **802-483-2931** Fax: 802-483-6612. 8AM-4:30PM.

Plainfield Town Clerk PO Box 217, Plainfield, VT 5667 (Town Hall). **802-454-8461** Fax: 802-454-8461. 7:30-4PM M,W,F.

Plymouth Town Clerk 68 Town Office Rd., Plymouth, VT 05056 **802-672-3655** Fax: 802-672-5466. 8:30-11:30AM, 12:30-3:30PM.

Pomfret Town Clerk PO Box 64, South Pomfret, VT 05067 (5188 Pomfret Rd). **802-457-3861** 8:30AM-2:30PM M,W,F.

Poultney Town Clerk 9 Main St, #2, Poultney, VT 05764 **802-287-5761** 8:30AM-12:30, 1:30-4PM.

Pownal Town Clerk PO Box 411, Pownal, VT 05261 (467 Center St.). **802-823-7757** Fax: 802-823-0116. 9-2.

Proctor Town Clerk 45 Main St, Proctor, VT 05765 **802-459-3333** Fax: 802-459-2356. 8-4.

Putney Town Clerk PO Box 233, Putney, VT 05346 (127 Main St). **802-387-5862** 9AM-2PM M, Th, F; 9AM-2PM, 7-9PM W; 9AM-N Sat.

Randolph Town Clerk Drawer B, Randolph, VT 05060 (7 Summer St). **802-728-5682** Fax: 802-728-5818. 8AM-N, 1-4:30PM. www.randolphvt.com

Reading Clerk PO Box 72, Reading, VT 05062 (799 Route 106). **802-484-7250** Fax: 802-454-7250. www.readingvt.govoffice.com

Readsboro Town Clerk PO Box 187, Readsboro, VT 05350 (301 Phelps Lane). **802-423-5405** Fax: 802-423-5423. 8AM-2PM M,T; 6-8PM M Eve; 8AM-1PM W,Th; Closed F.

Richford Town Clerk PO Box 236, Richford, VT 05476-0236 (Main St. Town Hall). **802-848-7751** Fax: 802-848-7752. 8:30AM-4PM. www.richfordvt.com

Richmond Town Clerk PO Box 285, Richmond, VT 05477 (203 Bridge St.). **802-434-2221** 8AM-6PM M; 8AM-4PM T-Th, 8AM-1PM F.

Ripton Town Clerk Box 10, Ripton, VT 05766-0010 (Rte 125). **802-388-2266** 2-6PM M; 9AM-1PM T,W,Th,F.

Rochester Town Clerk PO Box 238, Rochester, VT 05767-0238 (School St.). **802-767-3631** Fax: 802-767-6028. 8AM-4PM T-F, 8AM-N Sat..

Rockingham Town Clerk PO Box 339, Bellows Falls, VT 05101-0339 (7 Village Sq). **802-463-4336** Fax: 802-463-1228. 8:30AM-4:30PM.

Roxbury Town Clerk Box 53, Roxbury, VT 05669 (1664 Roxbury Rd). **802-485-7840** Fax: 802-485-7860. 9AM-N; 1-4PM T-F.

Royalton Town Clerk PO Box 680, South Royalton, VT 05068-0680 (Basement - Royalton Memorial Library, 23 Alexander Pl #1). **802-763-7207** Fax: 802-763-7307. www.royaltonvt.com

Rupert Town Clerk Box 140, West Rupert, VT 05776 (187 E. St). **802-394-7728** Fax: 802-394-2524. 2-7PM M; 12-5PM W; 10AM-3PM Th.

Rutland City Clerk PO Box 969, Rutland, VT 05702 (1 Strongs Ave). **802-773-1801** 9AM-4:45PM. www.rutlandcity.com

Rutland Town Clerk PO Box 225, Center Rutland, VT 05736 (Route 4 West). **802-773-2528** Fax: 802-773-7295. 8-4:30PM.

Ryegate Town Clerk PO Box 332, Ryegate, VT 05042 (Town Highway #1, 18 S. Bayley-Hazen Rd). **802-584-3880** Fax: 802-584-3880. 1-5PM M,T,W; 9AM-1PM F..

Salisbury Town Clerk PO Box 66, Salisbury, VT 05769-0066 (25 Schoolhouse Rd.). **802-352-4228** Fax: 802-352-9832. 9AM-3PM T-F; 1st/3rd Sat 9AM-N.

Sandgate Town Clerk 3266 Sandgate Rd., Sandgate, VT 05250 **802-375-9075** Fax: 802-375-8350. 10AM-4PM T; 9AM-3PM W.

Searsburg Town Clerk PO Box 157, Wilmington, VT 05363 (Route 9). **802-464-8081** 8AM-N M,T,F.

Shaftsbury Town Clerk PO Box 409, Shaftsbury, VT 05262 (61 Buck Hill Rd). **802-442-4038** Fax: 802-442-0955. 9AM-5PM, M ;9AM-3:00PM T-F.

Sharon Town Clerk PO Box 250, Sharon, VT 05065 (69 Rt 132). **802-763-8268** Fax: 802-763-7392. 7AM-12PM,1-6PM M,T,Th; 6:30AM-1PM W.

Sheffield Town Clerk PO Box 165, Sheffield, VT 05866-0165 (Town Highway #32). **802-626-8862** 8AM-2PM,MWF, Closed T,Th.

Shelburne Town Clerk PO Box 88, Shelburne, VT 05482 (5376 Shelburne Rd.). **802-985-5116** Fax: 802-985-9550. 8:30AM-4:30PM. www.shelburneVT.org

Sheldon Town Clerk PO Box 66, Sheldon, VT 05483 (1640 Main St.). **802-933-2524** Fax: 802-933-4951. 8AM-3PM.

Shoreham Town Clerk 297 Main St., Shoreham, VT 05770-9759 **802-897-5841** Fax: 802-897-2545. 9-4PM; closed Thurs..

Shrewsbury Town Clerk 9823 Cold River Rd., Shrewsbury, VT 05738 **802-492-3511** Fax: 802-492-3511. 10AM-3PM M-TH.

South Burlington City Town Clerk 575 Dorset St, South Burlington, VT 05403 **802-846-4105** 8AM-4:30PM, M T TH F; 8am-6:30PM, W.

South Hero Town Clerk PO Box 175, South Hero, VT 05486 (333 Rt.2). **802-372-5552** 8:30AM-N, 1-4:30PM M-W; 8:30AM-N,1-5PM Th.

Springfield Town Clerk 96 Main St, Springfield, VT 05156 **802-885-2104** Fax: 802-885-1617. 8AM-4:30PM.

St. Albans City Clerk PO Box 867, St. Albans, VT 05478-0867 (100 N. Main). **802-524-1501** 7:30AM-4PM.

St. Albans Town Clerk PO Box 37, St. Albans Bay, VT 05481 (579 Lake Rd). **802-524-2415** Fax: 802-524-9609. 8AM-4PM; closed Wednesdays.

St. George Town Clerk 1 Barber Rd., St. George, VT 05495 **802-482-5272** Fax: 802-482-5548. M-F 8-12PM.

St. Johnsbury Town Clerk 1187 Main St, #2, St. Johnsbury, VT 05819-2288 **802-748-**

4331 Fax: 802-748-1268. 8AM-5PM, Summer 7-4. www.town.st-johnsbury.vt.us

Stamford Town Clerk 986 Main Rd., Stamford, VT 05352-9601 **802-694-1361** 11AM-4PM T & W; Noon-4PM, 7-9PM Th; Noon-4PM F.

Stannard Town Clerk PO Box 94, Greensboro Bend, VT 05842-0094 (Town Hall). **802-533-2577** 8AM-N W.

Starksboro Town Clerk PO Box 91, Starksboro, VT 05487-0091 (3056 VT Route 116). **802-453-2639** Fax: 802-453-7293. 8:30AM-4:30PM M-Th.

Stockbridge Town Clerk PO Box 39, Stockbridge, VT 05772-0039 (1722 Vt Rte 100). **802-746-8400** Fax: 802-746-8400. 8AM-4:30PM T W TH; 8AM-N F.

Stowe Town Clerk PO Box 248, Stowe, VT 05672 (67 Main St.). **802-253-6133** Fax: 802-253-6143. 7:30AM-4:30PM.

Strafford Town Clerk PO Box 27, Strafford, VT 05072 (227 Justin Morrill Highway). **802-765-4411** Fax: 802-765-9621. 8AM-5PM T,W; 8AM-7PM Th; 8AM-N F.

Stratton Town Clerk PO Box 166, West Wardsboro, VT 05360 (West Jamaica Rd.). **802-896-6184** Fax: 802-896-6630. 9:00AM-3:00PM M-TH.

Sudbury Town Clerk 36 Blacksmith Ln., Sudbury, VT 05733 **802-623-7296** Fax: 802-623-7296. 9AM-4PM M; 7PM-9PM W,9AM-3PM F..

Sunderland Town Clerk PO Box 295, East Arlington, VT 05252 (181 South Rd.). **802-375-6106** 8AM-2PM M,T,Th,; 8AM-N, 6-8PM W.

Sutton Town Clerk Box 106, Sutton, VT 05867 (State Aid #1). **802-467-3377** Fax: 802-467-1052. 9AM-5PM,M,T,Th, F; 9am-12:00PM, W.

Swanton Town Clerk PO Box 711, Swanton, VT 05488 (1 Academy St). **802-868-4421** Fax: 802-868-4957. 8AM-4PM.

Thetford Town Clerk PO Box 126, Thetford Center, VT 05075-0126 (3910 Rt. 113). **802-785-2922** Fax: 802-785-2031. 8:30-3PM.

Tinmouth Town Clerk 515 North End Rd., Tinmouth, VT 05773 **802-446-2498** Fax: 802-446-2498. 8AM-12, 1-5PM M & Th & 8AM-N Sat Jan-May only..

Topsham Town Clerk PO Box 69, Topsham, VT 05076 (6 Harts Rd). **802-439-5505** Fax: 802-439-5505. 1-6PM Mon.; 9AM-4PM T-F.

Townshend Town Clerk PO Box 223, Townshend, VT 05353-0223 (Rte 30, Town Hall). **802-365-7300** 9AM-4PM M-W & F.

Troy Town Clerk PO Box 80, North Troy, VT 05859 (Main St). **802-988-2663** Fax: 802-988-4692. 8AM-N, 1-4PM.

Tunbridge Town Clerk PO Box 6, Tunbridge, VT 05077 (Main St.). **802-889-5521** Fax: 802-889-3744. 8AM-N 1-4PM.

Underhill Town Clerk PO Box 32, Underhill, VT 05490 (12 Pleasant Valley Rd.). **802-899-4434** Fax: 802-899-2137. 8AM-4PM M T TH F; 8AM-6PM W.

Vergennes City Town Clerk PO Box 35, Vergennes, VT 05491-0035 (120 Main St.). **802-877-2841** Fax: 802-877-1160. 8-4:30.

Vernon Town Clerk 567 Governor Hunt Rd., Vernon, VT 05354 **802-257-0292** Fax: 802-254-3561. 8AM-4PM.

Vershire Town Clerk 6894 Vermont Rte. 113, Vershire, VT 05079 **802-685-2227** 8:30AM-3PM T-Th.

Victory Town Clerk PO Box 609, North Concord, VT 05858 (Ruth Neborsky). **802-328-2400** Fax: 802-328-2400. 10-4PM T-F.

Waitsfield Town Clerk 9 Bridge St, Waitsfield, VT 05673-0390 **802-496-2218** Fax: 802-496-9284. 9AM-4PM.

Walden Town Clerk 12 Vt. Rte. 215, West Danville, VT 05873 **802-563-2220** Fax: 802-563-3008. 9AM-3PM.

Wallingford Town Clerk PO Box 327, Wallingford, VT 05773 (75 School St.). **802-446-2336** Fax: 802-446-3174. 8AM-4:30PM M-Th; 8AM-N F. www.wallingfordvt.com

Waltham Town Clerk PO Box 175, Vergennes, VT 05491 (Maple St Ext.). **802-877-3641** Fax: 802-877-3641. 9AM-3PM T; 9AM-3PM F.

Wardsboro Town Clerk PO Box 48, Wardsboro, VT 05355-0048 (71 Main St.). **802-896-6055** Fax: 802-896-1000. 9AM-N, 1-4:30PM M-Th.

Warren Town Clerk PO Box 337, Warren, VT 05674 (42 Cemetary Rd). **802-496-2709** Fax: 802-496-2418. 9AM-4:30PM.

Washington Town Clerk 2895 Rte. 110, Clerk's Office, Washington, VT 05675 **802-883-2218** 8:30AM-2PM M,T.

Waterbury Town Clerk 51 S. Main St, Waterbury, VT 05676 **802-244-8447** Fax: 802-244-1014. www.waterburyvt.com

Waterford Town Clerk PO Box 56, Lower Waterford, VT 05848 (532 Maple St.). **802-**

748-2122 Fax: 802-748-8196. 8:30AM-3:30PM, M, TH, F; Noon-6PM, T.

Waterville Town Clerk PO Box 31, Waterville, VT 05492 (850 Vt. Rte. 109). **802-644-8865** Fax: 802-644-8865. 9AM-1:30PM M,T,Th; closed W & F.

Weathersfield Town Clerk PO Box 550, Weathersfield, VT 05030-0304 (5259 Rt 5, Ascutney Village at Martin Mem. Hall). **802-674-2626** 9-4PM M-T-W; 9-5PM Th.

Wells Town Clerk PO Box 585, Wells, VT 05774 (138 Vermont Rt.30). **802-645-0486** Fax: 802-645-0464. 8:30AM-4PM.

West Fairlee Town Clerk Box 615, West Fairlee, VT 05083 (Rt 113). **802-333-9696** Fax: 802-333-9611. 10AM-4PM M,W,F.

West Haven Town Clerk 2919 Main Rd., West Haven, VT 05743-9610 **802-265-4880** Fax: 802-265-4880. 1PM-3:30PM.

West Rutland Town Clerk 35 Marble St., West Rutland, VT 05777 **802-438-2204** Fax: 802-438-5133. 9AM-4PM M-Th.; Fri. by appointment.. www.wrutland.net

West Windsor Town Clerk Box 6, Brownsville, VT 05037 (22 Brownsville-Hartland Rd). **802-484-7212** Fax: 802-484-3518.

Westfield Town Clerk 1257 Vermont Rte. 100, Westfield, VT 05874 **802-744-2484** Fax: 802-744-2484. 8AM-5PM M & W; 10AM-5PM Tu;.

Westford Town Clerk 1713 Vermont Route 128, Westford, VT 05494 **802-878-4587** Fax: 802-879-6503. 8:30AM-4:30PM.

Westminster Town Clerk PO Box 147, Westminster, VT 05158-0147 (3651 US Route 5). **802-722-4091** Fax: 802-722-9816. 8:30-4PM. http://westminster.govoffice.com

Westmore Town Clerk 54 Hinton Hill Rd., Orleans, VT 05860 **802-525-3007** Fax: 802-525-3007. M 9AM-N;1-7PM, T&Th 9AM-N; 1-4PM, F 9AM-12PM.

Weston Town Clerk PO Box 98, Weston, VT 05161 (12 Lawrence Hill Rd.). **802-824-6645** Fax: 802-824-4121. 9AM-1PM.

Weybridge Town Clerk 1727 Quaker Village Rd., Weybridge, VT 05753 **802-545-2450** Fax: 802-545-2624. 9-2PM M,T,TH,F.

Wheelock Town Clerk PO Box 1328, Lyndonville, VT 05851-1328 (Rt.122). **802-626-9094** Fax: 802-626-9094. 8AM-4PM M-W, 10AM-6PM Th.

Whiting Town Clerk 29 S. Main St., Whiting, VT 05778 **802-623-7813** 9AM-N M,W,F and by App't.

Whitingham Town Clerk PO Box 529, Jacksonville, VT 05342 (2948 VT Rte 100). **802-368-7887** Fax: 802-368-7519. 9AM-2PM, 5:30-7:30PM Wed.

Williamstown Town Clerk PO Box 646, Williamstown, VT 05679 (2470 VT Rte. 14). **802-433-5455** Fax: 802-433-2160. 8AM-N,12:30-4:30PM M; 8AM-N T-F. www.williamstownvt.org

Williston Town Clerk 7900 Williston Rd., Williston, VT 05495 **802-878-5121** Fax: 802-764-1140. 8AM-4:30PM.

Wilmington Town Clerk PO Box 217, Wilmington, VT 05363-0217 (Main St). **802-**

464-5836 Fax: 802-464-1238. 8:30-N, 1-4PM M-W; 8:30AM-4PM Th; 8:30AM-6:30PM F. www.wilmingtonvermont.us

Windham Town Clerk 5976 Windham Hill Rd, Windham, VT 05039 **802-874-4211** Fax: 802-874-4144. 10AM-3PM T,Th,F.

Windsor Town Clerk PO Box 47, Windsor, VT 05089 (147 Main St). **802-674-5610** Fax: 802-674-1017. 8AM-4:30PM M,W,Th; 8AM-6PM Tues; 8AM-2PM F.

Winhall Town Clerk Box 389, Bondville, VT 05340 (#3 River Rd). **802-297-2122** 9AM-N (Closed Th).

Winooski City Town Clerk 27 W. Allen St, Winooski, VT 05404 **802-655-6419** Fax: 802-655-6414. 8-4PM.

Wolcott Town Clerk PO Box 100, Wolcott, VT 05680-0100 (4186 VT Rte. 15). **802-888-2746** Fax: 802-888-2746. 8AM-4PM T-F; Tues Evening 6-8PM.

Woodbury Town Clerk PO Box 123, Woodbury, VT 05681 (Rte 14, Town Clerk). **802-456-7051** 8:30AM-1PM T-W-Th; 6-8PM Th evening.

Woodford Town Clerk 1391 Vermont Rte. 9, Bennington, VT 05201 **802-442-4895** Fax: 802-442-4816. 8:30AM-N.

Woodstock Town Clerk 31 The Green, Woodstock, VT 05091 **802-457-3611** Fax: 802-457-2329. 8:00AM-N, 1:00-4:30PM. www.townofwoodstock.org

Worcester Town Clerk Drawer 161, Worcester, VT 05682-0161 (20 Worcester Village Rd.). **802-223-6942** Fax: 802-229-5216. 8AM-4PM M,T,Th; 8AM-1PM F.

Virginia

Organization: 95 counties and 41 independent cities, 123 recording offices. The recording officer is the Clerk of Circuit Court. Fifteen independent cities share the Clerk of Circuit Court with the county - Bedford, Covington (Alleghany County), Emporia (Greenville County), Fairfax, Falls Church (Arlington or Fairfax County), Franklin (Southhampton County), Galax (Carroll County), Harrisonburg (Rockingham County), Lexington (Rockbridge County), Manassas and Manassas Park (Prince William County), Norton (Wise County), Poquoson (York County), South Boston (Halifax County), and Williamsburg (James City County). Charles City and James City are counties, not cities. The City of Franklin is not in Franklin County, the City of Richmond is not in Richmond County, and the City of Roanoke is not in Roanoke County. The entire state is in the Eastern Time Zone (EST).

Real Estate Records: Only a few Clerks of Circuit Court will perform real estate searches. Copy fees and certification fees vary. The independent cities may have separate Assessor Offices.

UCC Records: This was a dual filing state. Until 07/2001, financing statements were filed at the state level and with the Clerk of Circuit Court, except for consumer goods, farm and real estate related collateral, which were filed only with the Clerk of Circuit Court. Now, only real estate related collateral is filed at the county level. Some recording offices will perform UCC searches. Use search request form UCC-11. Searches fees and copy fees vary.

Tax Lien Records: Federal tax liens on personal property of businesses are filed with the State Corporation Commission. Other federal and all state tax liens are filed with the county Clerk of Circuit Court. They are usually filed in a "Judgment Lien Book." Most counties will not perform tax lien searches. Other Liens: Judgment, mechanics, hospital, lis pendens.

Online Access: A growing number of Virginia counties and cities provide free access to real estate-related information via the Internet. A limited but growing private company network named VarnaNet provides free residential, commercial and vacant property and tax records for nine Virginia jurisdictions at www.vamanet.com/cgi-bin/LOCS - at the website, click on the county name at left.

Accomack County Clerk of Circuit Court PO Box 126, Accomac, VA 23301-0126 (23316 Courthouse Ave). **757-787-5776** Fax: 757-787-1849. 9AM-5PM.

Albemarle County Clerk of Circuit Court 501 E. Jefferson St., Rm 225, Charlottesville, VA 22902 **434-972-4083** Fax: 434-293-0298.

Alexandria City Clerk of Circuit Court 520 King St, Rm 307, Alexandria, VA 22314 **703-838-4044** www.ci.alexandria.va.us Assessor, Property records online. 9AM-5PM.

Alleghany County Clerk of Circuit Court PO Box 670, Covington, VA 24426-0670 (266 W. Main St). **540-965-1730** Fax: 540-965-1732. www.alleghanycountyclerk.com

Amelia County Clerk of Circuit Court PO Box 237, Amelia Court House, VA 23002-0237 (16441 Court St). **804-561-2128** 8:30AM-4:30PM.

Amherst County Clerk of Circuit Court PO Box 462, Amherst, VA 24521 (113 Taylor St.). **434-946-9321** 8AM-5PM.

Appomattox County Clerk of Circuit Court PO Box 672, Appomattox, VA 24522 (Courthouse Sq, Court St). **434-352-5275** Fax: 434-352-2781. 8:30AM-4:30PM.

Arlington County Clerk of Circuit Court 1425 N. Courthouse Rd, 6th Fl, Arlington, VA 22201 **703-228-4369** 8AM-4PM. www.co.arlington.va.us Real Estate, Assessor, Trade Name records online.

Augusta County Clerk of Circuit Court PO Box 689, Staunton, VA 24402-0689 (1 E. Johnson St). **540-245-5321** Fax: 540-245-5318. 8AM-5PM. Property, Appraisal, Most Wanted records online.

Bath County Clerk of Circuit Court PO Box 180, Warm Springs, VA 24484 (Courthouse Hill Rd., Rm 123). **540-839-7226** 8:30AM-4:30PM.

Bedford County Clerk of Circuit Court 123 E Main St, Bedford, VA 24523 **540-586-7632** Fax: 540-586-6197. 8:30AM-5PM. Property Tax records online.

Bland County Clerk of Circuit Court PO Box 295, Bland, VA 24315-0295 (1 Courthouse Sq). **276-688-4562** Fax: 276-688-2438. 8AM-6PM.

Botetourt County Clerk of Circuit Court PO Box 219, Fincastle, VA 24090 (Main & Roanoke Sts). **540-473-8274** 8:30-4:30PM.

Bristol City Clerk of Circuit Court 497 Cumberland St, Rm 210, Bristol, VA 24201 **276-645-7321** Fax: 276-645-7345. 9-5PM.

Brunswick County Clerk of Circuit Court 216 N. Main St., Lawrenceville, VA 23868 **434-848-2215** Fax: 434-848-4307. 8:30-5.

Buchanan County Clerk of Circuit Court PO Box 929, Grundy, VA 24614 (Main & Walnut Sts, 2nd Fl). **276-935-6567** Fax: 276-935-6574. 8:30AM - 5PM.

Buckingham County Clerk of Circuit Court PO Box 107, Buckingham, VA 23921 (Highway 60 Courthouse). **434-969-4734** Fax: 434-959-2043. 8:30AM-4:30PM.

Buena Vista City Clerk of Circuit Court 2039 Sycamore Ave., Buena Vista, VA 24416 **540-261-8627** Fax: 540-261-8623. 8:30-5.

Campbell County Clerk of Circuit Court PO Box 7, Rustburg, VA 24588 (732 Village Hwy). **434-592-9517** 8:30AM-4:30PM.

Caroline County Clerk of Circuit Court PO Box 309, Bowling Green, VA 22427-0309 (Main St. & Courthouse Ln). **804-633-5800** 8:30AM-4PM Appraiser, Property records online.

Carroll County Clerk of Circuit Court PO Box 218, Hillsville, VA 24343-0218 (515 N. Main St). **276-728-3117** Fax: 276-728-0255. 8AM-5PM. www.chillsnet.org Real Estate, Judgment, UCC, Plat records online.

Charles City Clerk of Circuit Court PO Box 86, Charles City, VA 23030-0086 (10700 Courthouse Rd; Rts 5 & 155). **804-829-9212** Fax: 804-829-5647.

Charlotte County Clerk of Circuit Court PO Box 38, Charlotte Court House, VA 23923 (Courthouse). **434-542-5147** Fax: 434-542-4336. 8:30AM-4:30PM.

Charlottesville City Clerk of Circuit Court 315 E. High St, Charlottesville, VA 22902 **434-295-3182** 8:30AM-4:30PM.

Chesapeake City Clerk of Circuit Court 307 Albemarle Dr, #300, Chesapeake, VA 23322 (300 Cedar Rd). **757-382-3031** Fax: 757-382-3034. http://cityofchesapeake.net

Property Appraiser, Inspection, Most Wanted records online. 8:30AM-5PM

Chesterfield County Clerk of Circuit Court PO Box 125, Chesterfield, VA 23832 (9500 Courthouse Rd). **804-748-1241** Fax: 804-796-5625. www.chesterfield.gov Assessor, Property Tax, Property Sale records online.

Clarke County Clerk of Circuit Court PO Box 189, Berryville, VA 22611 (102 N. Church St). **540-955-5116** Fax: 540-955-0284. 9AM-5PM. Property, Appraiser records online.

Clifton Forge City Clerk of Circuit Court c/o Alleghany County, PO Box 670, Clifton Forge, VA 24426 (266 W Main St). **540-965-1730** Fax: 540-965-1732. 9AM-5PM.

Colonial Heights City Clerk of Circuit Court PO Box 3401, Colonial Heights, VA 23834 (401 Temple Ave). **804-520-9364** Fax: 804-524-8726. 8:30AM-5PM.

Craig County Clerk of Circuit Court PO Box 185, New Castle, VA 24127-0185 (303 Main St). **540-864-6141** 9AM-5PM.

Culpeper County Clerk of Circuit Court 135 W. Cameron St, Rm 103, Culpeper, VA 22701 **540-727-3438** 8:30AM-4:30PM.

Cumberland County Clerk of Circuit Court PO Box 8, Cumberland, VA 23040 (County Office Bldg., 1). **804-492-4442** Fax: 804-492-4876. 8:30AM-4:30PM.

Danville City Clerk of Circuit Court PO Box 3300, Danville, VA 24543 (401 Patton St.). **434-799-5168** Fax: 434-799-6502. www.danville-va.gov/home.asp Property, Tax Assessor records online. 9AM-4:30PM.

Dickenson County Clerk of Circuit Court PO Box 190, Clintwood, VA 24228 (Main St Courthouse). **276-926-1616** Fax: 276-926-6465. www.dickensonctyva.com Real Estate, Property Tax records online. 8:30-4:30

Dinwiddie County Clerk of Circuit Court PO Box 63, Dinwiddie, VA 23841 (14008 Boydton Plank Rd.). **804-469-4540**

Essex County Clerk of Circuit Court PO Box 445, Tappahannock, VA 22560 (305 Prince St). **804-443-3541** Fax: 804-445-1216. 8:30AM-5PM.

Fairfax County Clerk of Circuit Court 4110 Chain Bridge Rd, 3rd Fl, Fairfax, VA 22030 **703-691-7320** 8AM-4PM. www.fairfaxcounty.gov/courts/circuit/land_re cords_info.htm Real Estate, Property Tax, Tax Sale records online.

Fauquier County Clerk of Circuit Court 40 Culpeper St, 1st Fl, Warrenton, VA 20186 **540-347-8608** 8-4:30PM. www.fauquiercoun ty.gov/government/departments/circuitcourt

Floyd County Clerk of Circuit Court 100 E. Main St, Rm 200, Floyd, VA 24091 **540-745-9330** 8:30AM-4:30PM; 8:30AM-N Sat.

Fluvanna County Clerk of Circuit Court PO Box 550, Palmyra, VA 22963-0299 (132 Main St). **434-591-1970** Fax: 434-591-1971. 8-4:30. Appraiser, Property records online.

Franklin County Clerk of Circuit Court PO Box 567, Rocky Mount, VA 24151 (275 S Main St #212). **540-483-3065** Fax: 540-483-3042. 9AM-4:30PM.

Frederick County Clerk of Circuit Court 5 N. Kent St, Winchester, VA 22601 **540-667-5770** Fax: 540-545-8711. 9AM-5PM. www.winfredclerk.com/standard.htm

Fredericksburg City Clerk of Circuit Court PO Box 359, Fredericksburg, VA 22404 (815 Princess Anne St). **540-372-1066** 8-4PM.

Giles County Clerk of Circuit Court PO Box 502, Pearisburg, VA 24134-0501 (501 Wenonah Ave). **540-921-1722** Fax: 540-921-3825. 9AM-4PM. Appraiser, Property records online.

Gloucester County Clerk of Circuit Court PO Box 2118, Gloucester, VA 23061-0570 (7400 Justice Dr Rm 330). **804-693-2502** Fax: 804-693-2186. www.courts.state.va.us Judgment records online. 8AM-4:30PM.

Goochland County Clerk of Circuit Court PO Box 196, Goochland, VA 23063 (2938 River Rd West, Bldg G). **804-556-5353** 8:30AM-5PM.

Grayson County Clerk of Circuit Court PO Box 130, Independence, VA 24348-0130 (129 Davis St). **276-773-2231** Fax: 276-773-3338. 8AM-5PM. Real Estate records online.

Greene County Clerk of Circuit Court PO Box 386, Stanardsville, VA 22973-0386 (Courthouse, Court Sq). **434-985-5208** Fax: 434-985-6723. 8:15AM-4:30PM.

Greensville County Clerk of Circuit Court PO Box 631, Emporia, VA 23847 (308 S. Main St). **434-348-4215** Fax: 434-348-4020. 9-5PM. Appraiser, Property records online.

Halifax County Clerk of Circuit Court PO Box 729, Halifax, VA 24558 (Courthouse

Sq). **434-476-6211** Fax: 434-476-2890. Property records online.

Hampton City Clerk of Circuit Court PO Box 40, Hampton, VA 23669-0040 (101 Kingsway Mall). **757-727-2440** Fax: 757-728-3505. 8:30AM-5PM.

Hanover County Clerk of Circuit Court PO Box 39, Hanover, VA 23069-0039 (7507 Library Dr, 2nd Fl). **804-537-6150** 8:30AM-4:30PM. www.co.hanover.va.us

Henrico County Clerk of Circuit Court PO Box 27032, Richmond, VA 23273 (4301 E. Parham Rd). **804-501-4202** 8AM-4PM; www.co.henrico.va.us/clerk/

Henry County Clerk of Circuit Court 3160 Kings Mountain Rd. #B, Martinsville, VA 24112 **276-634-4880** 9AM-5PM. http://henrycounty.neocom.net Property records online.

Highland County Clerk of Circuit Court PO Box 190, Monterey, VA 24465-0190 (Spruce St Courthouse). **540-468-2447** Fax: 540-468-3447. 8:30AM-4:30PM.

Hopewell City Clerk of Circuit Court PO Box 310, Hopewell, VA 23860 (100 E. Broadway, Rm 251). **804-541-2239** Fax: 804-541-2438. 8:30AM-4PM. Court Appeals Granted, Docket records online.

Isle of Wight County Clerk of Circuit Court PO Box 110, Isle of Wight, VA 23397 (17122 Monument Circle, Hwy 258). **757-355-6233** Fax: 757-357-0884. 9AM-5PM. Judgment records online.

James City Clerk of Circuit Court 5201 Monticello Ave #6, Williamsburg, VA 23188. **757-564-2242** Fax: 757-564-2329. 8:30-4. www.jccegov.com/resources/clerkofcircrt/ind ex.html Real Estate records online.

King and Queen County Clerk of Circuit Court PO Box 67, King and Queen Court House, VA 23085 (234 Allen's Circle). **804-785-5984** Fax: 804-785-5698. 9AM-5PM.

King George County Clerk Circuit Court 9483 Kings Highway, #3, King George, VA 22485 **540-775-3322** 8:30AM-4:30PM.

King William County Clerk of Circuit Court PO Box 216, King William, VA 23086 (Route 619, 227 Courthouse Ln). **804-769-4936** Fax: 804-769-4991. 8:30AM-4:30PM.

Lancaster County Clerk of Circuit Court PO Box 99, Lancaster, VA 22503 (8311 Maryball Rd.). **804-462-5611** Fax: 804-462-9978. 8:30AM-4:30PM. www.lancova.com Chancery, Law records online.

Lee County Clerk of Circuit Court PO Box 326, Jonesville, VA 24263 (Main St Court house). **276-346-7763** Fax: 276-346-3440.

Loudoun County Clerk of Circuit Court PO Box 550, Leesburg, VA 20178 (18 E. Market St.). **703-777-0270** 8:30AM-4:30PM. www.loudoun.gov/government/ Property, Assessor records online.

Louisa County Clerk of Circuit Court PO Box 37, Louisa, VA 23093 (100 W. Main St). **540-967-5312** 8:30AM-5PM (Stop Recording 4:15PM).

Lunenburg County Clerk of Circuit Court 11435 Courthouse Rd., Lunenburg, VA 23952 **434-696-2230** 8:30AM-4:30PM.

Lynchburg City Clerk of Circuit Court PO Box 4, Lynchburg, VA 24505 (900 Court St). **434-455-2620** Fax: 434-847-1864. 8:15AM-4:45PM.

Madison County Clerk of Circuit Court PO Box 220, Madison, VA 22727-0220 (1 Main St.). **540-948-6888** Fax: 540-948-3759. 8:30AM-4:30PM.

Martinsville City Clerk PO Box 1206, Martinsville, VA 24114-1206 (55 W. Church St). **276-403-5106** Fax: 276-403-5232. www.ci.martinsville.va.us/Circuitclerk Property, Deed, Judgment, Will, Marriage, Delinquent Tax records online.

Mathews County Clerk of Circuit Court PO Box 463, Mathews, VA 23109-0463 (Courthouse Sq). **804-725-2550** 8AM-4PM.

Mecklenburg County Clerk of Circuit Court PO Box 530, Boydton, VA 23917-0530 (393 Washington St). **434-738-6191** Fax: 434-738-6861. 8:30AM-5PM.

Middlesex County Clerk of Circuit Court PO Box 158, Saluda, VA 23149 (Route 17 Courthouse). **804-758-5317** 8:30-4:30PM.

Montgomery County Clerk of Circuit Court PO Box 6309, Christiansburg, VA 24068 (1 E.Main #B5). **540-382-5760** Fax: 540-382-6937. 8:30AM-4:30PM. Real Estate, Property Tax records online.

Nelson County Clerk of Circuit Court PO Box 10, Lovingston, VA 22949 (84 Courthouse Sq). **434-263-5733** Fax: 434-263-8313. 9AM-5PM.

New Kent County Clerk of Circuit Court PO Box 98, New Kent, VA 23124-0098 (12001 Courthouse Circle). **804-966-9520** Fax: 804-966-9528. 8:30AM-4:30PM. Assessor, Property records online.

Newport News Clerk of Circuit Court 2500 Washington Ave, Courthouse, Newport News, VA 23607 **757-926-8561** Fax: 757-926-8531.

www.newport-news.va.us Assessor, Real Estate records online.

Norfolk City Clerk of Circuit Court 100 St. Paul's Blvd., Norfolk, VA 23510-2773 **757-664-4380** http://norfolkgov.com/home.asp Real Estate, Assessor, Sex Offender Registry records online. 8:45AM-4:45PM.

Northampton County Clerk of Circuit Court PO Box 36, Eastville, VA 23347-0036 (16404 Courthouse Rd). **757-678-0465** Fax: 757-678-5410.

Northumberland County Clerk of Circuit Court PO Box 217, Heathsville, VA 22473 (Highway 360, 39 Judicial Pl). **804-580-3700** 8:30AM-4:45PM.

Nottoway County Clerk of Circuit Court PO Box 25, Nottoway, VA 23955 (State Route 625 Courthouse). **434-645-9043** Fax: 434-645-2201. 8:30AM-4:30PM.

Orange County Clerk of Circuit Court PO Box 230, Orange, VA 22960 (127 Belleview Ave). **540-672-4030** Fax: 540-672-2939.

Page County Clerk of Circuit Court 116 S. Court St, #A, Luray, VA 22835. **540-743-4064** Fax: 540-743-2338. 9AM-5PM.

Patrick County Clerk of Circuit Court PO Box 148, Stuart, VA 24171-0148 (101 W. Blue Ridge St.). **276-694-7213** Fax: 276-694-6943.

Petersburg City Clerk of Circuit Court 7 Courthouse Ave., Petersburg, VA 23803 **804-733-2367** Fax: 804-732-5548. 8AM-4PM. www.courts.state.va.us

Pittsylvania County Clerk of Circuit Court PO Drawer 31, Chatham, VA 24531 (1 N. Main St). **434-432-7887** Fax: 434-432-7913. 8:30-5. Real Estate, Assessor records online.

Portsmouth City Clerk of Circuit Court PO Drawer 1217, Portsmouth, VA 23705 (601 Crawford St). **757-393-8671** Fax: 757-399-4826. 8:30AM-5PM.

Powhatan County Clerk Circuit Court PO Box 37, Powhatan, VA 23139-0037 (3880 Old Buckingham Rd). **804-598-5660** 8:30-5PM. Appraiser, Property records online.

Prince Edward County Clerk of Circuit PO Box 304, Farmville, VA 23901 (111 South St.). **434-392-5145** 8:30AM-4:30PM.

Prince George County Clerk of Circuit Court PO Box 98, Prince George, VA 23875-0098 (6601 Courts Dr.). **804-733-2640** Recording Hours 8:30AM-4:30PM.

Prince William County Clerk of Circuit Court 9311 Lee Ave, Rm 300, Manassas, VA 20110-5598 **703-792-6035** Fax: 703-792-

6083. www.pwcgov.org/ccourt Land, Property Assessor records online.

Pulaski County Clerk of Circuit Court 45 3rd St. NW, #101, Pulaski, VA 24301 **540-980-7825** Fax: 540-980-7835. 8:30AM-4:30PM. Property, GIS records online.

Radford City Clerk of Circuit Court 619 Second St, Courthouse, Radford, VA 24141 **540-731-3610** Fax: 540-731-3612. 8:30AM-5PM (No machine receipts after 4:30PM). Property records online.

Rappahannock County Clerk of Circuit Court PO Box 517, Washington, VA 22747-1517 (238 Gay St, Clerk's Office). **540-675-5350** Fax: 540-675-5351. 8:30-4:30PM.

Richmond City Clerk of Circuit Court 400 N. 9th St., Richmond, VA 23219 **804-646-6505** 8:45AM-4:45PM. Property, Assessor records online.

Richmond County Clerk of Circuit Court PO Box 1000, Warsaw, VA 22572-1000 (101 Court Circle). **804-333-3781** Fax: 804-333-5396. 9AM-5PM. www.co.richmond.va.us

Roanoke City Clerk of Circuit Court Box 2610, Roanoke, VA 24010-2610 (315 Church Ave SW, Rm 357). **540-853-6702** 8:30AM-4:30PM. www.ci.roanoke.va.us Property, GIS records online.

Roanoke County Clerk of Circuit Court PO Box 1126, Salem, VA 24153-1126 (305 E. Main St). **540-387-6205** Fax: 540-387-6145. 8:30AM-4:30PM.

Rockbridge County Clerk of Circuit Court 2 S. Main St, Court House, Lexington, VA 24450, **540-463-2232** Fax: 540-463-3850. 8:30-4:30PM. Property, Appraiser online.

Rockingham County Clerk of Circuit Court Courthouse, Harrisonburg, VA 22801 **540-564-3110** Fax: 540-564-3127. Real Estate, Deed, Lien records online.

Russell County Clerk of Circuit Court PO Box 435, Lebanon, VA 24266 (Main St Courthouse). **276-889-8023** Fax: 276-889-8003. 8:30AM-5PM.

Salem City Clerk of Circuit Court PO Box 891, Salem, VA 24153 (2 E. Calhoun St). **540-375-3067** Fax: 540-375-4039. 8-5PM.

Scott County Clerk of Circuit Court 104 E. Jackson St, Courthouse, #2, Gate City, VA 24251-3417 **276-386-3801** 8:30-5:00PM.

Shenandoah County Clerk of Circuit Court PO Box 406, Woodstock, VA 22664-0406 (112 S. Main St). **540-459-6150** Fax: 540-459-6155. 9AM-5PM M-F.

Smyth County Clerk of Circuit Court 109 W Main St #144, Marion, VA 24354-2510

276-782-4044 Fax: 276-782-4045. 9AM-4:30. Property records online.

Southampton County Clerk of Circuit Court PO Box 190, Courtland, VA 23837 (22350 Main St, Rm 106). **757-653-9245**

Spotsylvania County Clerk of Circuit Court PO Box 96, Spotsylvania, VA 22553-0096 (9113 Courthouse Rd). **540-582-7090** Fax: 540-582-2169.

Stafford County Clerk of Circuit Court PO Box 69, Stafford, VA 22555 (1300 Courthouse Rd.). **540-659-8752** 8-4PM.

Staunton City Clerk PO Box 1286, Staunton, VA 24402 (113 E. Beverly St, 3rd Fl). **540-332-3874** Fax: 540-332-3970. www.staunton.va.us/cityhall/spinhall.htm

Suffolk City Clerk of Circuit Court PO Box 1604, Suffolk, VA 23439-1604 (150 N. Main St.). **757-923-2251** 8:30AM-5PM.

Surry County Clerk of Circuit Court PO Box 203, Surry, VA 23883-0203 (28 Colonial Trail East). **757-294-3161**

Sussex County Clerk of Circuit Court PO Box 1337, Sussex, VA 23884 (Route 735, 15088 Courthouse Rd). **434-246-5511 x3274** Fax: 434-246-2203. 9AM-5PM.

Tazewell County Clerk of Circuit Court PO Box 968, Tazewell, VA 24651-0968 (101 Main St). **276-988-7541** Fax: 276-988-7585. 8-AM-4:30PM. Property records online.

Virginia Beach Clerk of Circuit Court 2425 Nimmo Prky, Judicial Ctr, Virginia Beach, VA 23456-9017 **757-427-8818** Fax: 757-426-5686. www.vbgov.com Real Estate, Property Tax, Assessor, Marriage, Judgment, UCC, Will, Business Name records online.

Warren County Clerk of Circuit Court 1 E. Main St, Front Royal, VA 22630-3382 **540-635-2435** Fax: 540-636-3274. 9AM-5PM. www.courts.state.va.us Recording, Deed, Land, Lien, Court, Will, Marriage, UCC records online.

Washington County Clerk of Circuit Court PO Box 289, Abingdon, VA 24212 (189 E. Main St.). **276-676-6226** Fax: 276-676-6218. 7:30AM-5PM.

Waynesboro City Clerk of Circuit Court PO Box 910, Waynesboro, VA 22980 (250 S. Wayne Ave). **540-942-6616** 8:30AM-5PM. Porperty, Appraiser records online.

Westmoreland County Clerk of Circuit Court PO Box 307, Montross, VA 22520 (15803 Kings Hwy). **804-493-0108**

Winchester City Clerk of Circuit Court 5 N. Kent St, Winchester, VA 22601 **540-667-**

5770 Fax: 540-667-6638. 9AM-5PM. www.winfredclerk.com

Wise County Clerk of Circuit Court PO Box 1248, Wise, VA 24293 (206 E. Main St). **276-328-6111** Fax: 276-328-0039. www.courtbar.org Assessor, Real Estate, Lien,

Probate, Marriage, Property Tax, Appraisal, Wanted, Fugitive records online.

Wythe County Clerk of Circuit Court 225 S. Fourth St, Rm 105, Wytheville, VA 24382 **276-223-6050** Fax: 276-223-6057. 8:30-5.

York County Clerk of Circuit Court PO Box 371, Yorktown, VA 23690 (300 Ballard St.). **757-890-3350** Fax: 757-890-3364. www.yorkcounty.gov/circuitcourt Property records online.

Washington

Organization: 39 counties, 39 recording offices. The recording officer is the County Auditor. County records are usually combined in a Grantor/Grantee index. The entire state is in the Pacific Time Zone (PST).

Real Estate Records: Many County Auditors will perform real estate searches, including record owner. Search fees and copy fees vary. Copies usually cost $1.00 per page and $2.00 for certification per document. If the Auditor does not provide searches, contact the Assessor for record owner information. Contact the Treasurer (Finance Department in King County) for information about unpaid real estate taxes.

UCC Records: Financing statements are filed at the state level, except for real estate related collateral, which are filed with the County Auditor. Most recording offices will perform UCC searches. Use search request form UCC-11R. Searches fees vary, copy fee is usually $1.00.

Tax Lien Records: All federal tax liens on personal property are filed with the Dept. of Licensing. Other federal and all state tax liens are filed with the County Auditor. Most counties will perform tax lien searches. Search fees are usually $8.00 or $10.00 per hour.

Online Access: A number of counties including the larger population counties offer online access to assessor or real estate records.

Adams County Auditor 210 W Broadway, Ritzville, WA 99169 **509-659-3247** Fax: 509-659-3254. www.co.adams.wa.us Property, Sale records online.

Asotin County Auditor PO Box 129, Asotin, WA 99402 (135 2nd St). **509-243-2084** Fax: 509-243-2087. www.co.asotin.wa.us

Benton County Auditor PO Box 470, Prosser, WA 99350 (620 Market St). **509-786-5616** Fax: 509-786-5528. 8AM-5PM. Assessor, Property records online.

Chelan County Auditor PO Box 400, Wenatchee, WA 98807 (350 Orondo 3rd Fl). **509-667-6815** Fax: 509-667-6244. 9AM-5PM. www.co.chelan.wa.us Grantor/Grantee, Property, Marriage records online.

Clallam County Recording Dept 223 E. Fourth St #1, Port Angeles, WA 98362 **360-417-2220** Fax: 360-417-2517. 8:30AM-4:30PM. www.clallam.net Property, Assessor records online.

Clark County Auditor PO Box 5000, Vancouver, WA 98666-5000 (12th & Franklin). **360-397-2208** Fax: 360-397-6007. 8AM-5PM. www.co.clark.wa.us/auditor/ Real Estate, Lien, Vital Statistic, Recording, Most Wanted, Sex Offender records online.

Columbia County Auditor 341 E. Main St., Dayton, WA 99328-1361 **509-382-4541** Fax: 509-382-4830. www.columbiaco.com

Cowlitz County Auditor 207 4th Ave North, Kelso, WA 98626 **360-577-3006** Fax: 360-414-5552. www.co.cowlitz.wa.us/auditor/ Most Wanted, Missing Person records online.

Douglas County Auditor PO Box 456, Waterville, WA 98858 (213 S. Rainier). **509-745-8527** Fax: 509-745-8812. 8:30AM-4PM. www.douglascountywa.net Assessor, Plat, Property records online.

Ferry County Auditor 350 E. Delaware #2, Republic, WA 99166 **509-775-5200** Fax: 509-775-5208. 8AM-4PM.

Franklin County Auditor PO Box 1451, Pasco, WA 99301 (1016 N. 4th St). **509-545-3536** Fax: 509-545-3529. 8:30AM-5PM. Assessor, Property, Sex Offender records online.

Garfield County Auditor PO Box 278, Pomeroy, WA 99347-0278 (Corner of 8th & Main). **509-843-1411** Fax: 509-843-3941. 8:30AM-5PM.

Grant County Auditor PO Box 37, Ephrata, WA 98823 (1st & C Street NW). **509-754-2011 x336** 8AM-5PM.

Grays Harbor County Auditor 101 W. Broadway, #2, Montesano, WA 98563 **360-249-4232 x331** Fax: 360-249-3330. Assessor, Treasurer, Property Tax records online.

Island County Deputy Auditor PO Box 5000, Coupeville, WA 98239 (6th & Main). **360-679-7366** Fax: 360-240-5553. 8-4:30.

www.islandcounty.net/auditor/index.htm Sex Offender records online.

Jefferson County Auditor PO Box 563, Port Townsend, WA 98368 (1820 Jefferson St). **360-385-9116** Fax: 360-385-9228. 8-5PM. www.co.jefferson.wa.us/auditor/recording/Recording.asp Assessor, Real Estate, Recording, Vital Statistic, Grantor/Grantee, Lien, Deed, UCC, Permit, Voter Registration. online.

King County Superintendent of Records 500 4th Ave, Admin. Bldg, Rm 311, Seattle, WA 98104 **206-296-1570** Fax: 206-205-8396. 8:30AM-4:30PM. www.metrokc.gov Real Estate, Lien, Marriage, Recorder, Deed, Judgment, Vital Statistic records online.

Kitsap County Auditor 614 Division St, Rm 106 /MS 31, Port Orchard, WA 98366 **360-337-4935** Fax: 360-337-4645. 8-4:30PM. www.kitsapgov.com/aud/default.htm Auditor, Property Tax, Grantor/Grantee, Recording, Deed, Lien, Vital Statistic, Judgments online.

Kittitas County Auditor 205 W. 5th, RM #105, Ellensburg, WA 98926-3129 **509-962-7504** Fax: 509-962-7687. 9AM-5PM. www.co.kittitas.wa.us/

Klickitat County Auditor 205 S. Columbus Ave, MS-CH-2, Goldendale, WA 98620 **509-773-4001** Fax: 509-773-4244. 9AM-5PM. www.klickitatcounty.org

Lewis County Auditor PO Box 29, Chehalis, WA 98532-0029 (351 NW North St). **360-740-1163** Fax: 360-740-1421. 8AM-5PM.

Lincoln County Auditor PO Box 28, Davenport, WA 99122 (450 Logan). **509-725-4971** Fax: 509-725-0820. 8AM-5PM.

Mason County Auditor PO Box 400, Shelton, WA 98584 (411 N. 5th St). **360-427-9670** Fax: 360-427-8425. 8:30AM - 4:30PM. http://auditor.co.mason.wa.us Assessor, Property records online.

Okanogan County Auditor PO Box 1010, Okanogan, WA 98840 (149 N Third). **509-422-7240** Fax: 509-422-7163. 8:30AM-5PM. Assessor, Property records online.

Pacific County Auditor PO Box 97, South Bend, WA 98586-9903 (300 Memorial Dr). **360-875-9318** Fax: 360-875-9333. 8:30AM-4:30PM. www.co.pacific.wa.us/directory.htm

Pend Oreille County Auditor PO Box 5015, Newport, WA 99156 (West 625 4th St). **509-447-3185** Fax: 509-447-2475. 8-4:30.

Pierce County Auditor 2401 S. 35th St, Rm 200, Tacoma, WA 98409 **253-798-7440** Fax: 253-798-2761. 8:30-4:30PM. Assessor, Real Estate, Recording, Deed, Lien, Vital Statistic, Judgment, Assumed Name, Inmate records online. www.piercecountywa.org/auditor

San Juan County Auditor PO Box 638, Friday Harbor, WA 98250 (350 Court St).

360-378-2161 Fax: 360-378-6256. 8AM-4:30PM. www.co.san-juan.wa.us Assessor, Property Tax, Auditor, Real Estate, Deed, Lien records online.

Skagit County Auditor PO Box 1306, Mount Vernon, WA 98273-1306 (700 So. 2nd St., 2nd Fl). **360-336-9420** Fax: 360-336-9429. www.skagitcounty.net Recording, Property Tax, Assessor, Treasurer, Deed, Lien, Vital Statistic records online.

Skamania County Auditor PO Box 790, Stevenson, WA 98648-0790 (240 Vancouver Ave). **509-427-9420** Fax: 509-427-4165. 8:30AM-5PM. www.wacounties.org/waco/county/skamania.html

Snohomish County Auditor 3000 Rockefeller Ave, Dept. R, M/S #204, Everett, WA 98201 **425-388-3483 press 0** Fax: 425-259-2777. http://www1.co.snohomish.wa.us/Departments/Auditor/ Real Estate, Assessor, Recording, Marriage, Jail, Offender, Jail Booking records online. 9AM-5PM.

Spokane County Auditor W 1116 Broadway, Spokane, WA 99260 **509-477-2270** Fax: 509-477-6451. 8:30AM-5:00PM. www.spokanecounty.org/auditor Property Tax, Land records online.

Stevens County Auditor 215 S. Oak St., Colville, WA 99114 **509-684-7512** Fax: 509-684-8310. 8AM-4:30PM.

Thurston County Auditor 2000 Lakeridge Drive SW, Olympia, WA 98502 **360-786-5405** Fax: 360-786-5223. 8AM-4:30PM. www.co.thurston.wa.us/auditor Assessor, Real Estate, Auditor, Recording records online.

Wahkiakum County Auditor PO Box 543, Cathlamet, WA 98612 (64 Main St). **360-795-3219** Fax: 360-795-0824. 8AM-4PM. www.cwcog.org/wahkiakum.html Property Sale, Sheriff Warrant records online.

Walla Walla County Auditor PO Box 1856, Walla Walla, WA 99362-0356 (315 W. Main St). **509-527-3204** Fax: 509-526-4806. 9AM-4:30PM. www.co.walla-walla.wa.us/Departments/auditor/auditor.htm Property Tax, Assessor, Resi. Sale, Farm Sale records online.

Whatcom County Auditor 311 Grand Ave #103, Bellingham, WA 98225 **360-676-6740** Fax: 360-738-4556. 8:30AM-4:30PA. www.co.whatcom.wa.us/auditor Assessor, Real Estate, Voter Registration records online.

Whitman County Auditor PO Box 350, Colfax, WA 99111-0350 (North 404 Main, 2nd Fl). **509-397-6270** Fax: 509-397-6351. 9AM-5PM www.whitmancounty.org

Yakima County Auditor 128 N. 2nd St, #117, Yakima, WA 98901 **509-574-1330** Fax: 509-574-1341. www.pan.co.yakima.wa.us Assessor, Real Estate, Property Tax records online. 9AM-4:30PM.

West Virginia

Organization: 55 counties, 55 recording offices. The recording officer is County Clerk. Entire state is in Eastern Time Zone (EST).

Real Estate Records: Most County Clerks will not perform real estate searches. Copy fees are usually $1.50 up to two pages and $1.00 for each additional page. Certification usually costs $1.00 per document.

UCC Records: Financing statements are filed at the state level, except for real estate related collateral, which are filed only with the Register of Deeds. Previous to 07/2001, collateral on consumer goods were are filed in both places, now they are only filed at the state level. Many recording offices will perform UCC searches. Use search request form UCC-11. Searches and copy fees vary.

Tax Lien Records: All federal and state tax liens are filed with the County Clerk. Most counties will not perform tax lien searches. Other Liens: Judgment, mechanics, lis pendens

Online Access: There is no statewide system open to public. One county – Monongalia – offers online access to assessor records.

Barbour County Clerk 8 N. Main St, Courthouse, Philippi, WV 26416 **304-457-2232** 8:30AM-4:30PM.

Berkeley County Clerk 100 W. King St, Rm 1, Martinsburg, WV 25401 **304-264-1927** Fax: 304-267-1794.

Boone County Clerk 200 State St, Madison, WV 25130 **304-369-7337** Fax: 304-369-7329.

Braxton County Clerk PO Box 486, Sutton, WV 26601-0728 (300 Main St). **304-765-2833** Fax: 304-765-2093. 8AM-4PM.

Brooke County Clerk 632 Main St, Courthouse, Wellsburg, WV 26070 **304-737-3661** Fax: 304-737-4023. 9AM-5PM, M-F; 9AM-12, SAT.

Cabell County Clerk 750 Fifth Ave, Rm 108, Cabell County Courthouse, Huntington,

WV 25701-2083 **304-526-8625** Fax: 304-526-8632. 8:30AM-4:30PM.

Calhoun County Clerk PO Box 230, Grantsville, WV 26147-0230 (Main St,Courthouse). **304-354-6725** Fax: 304-354-6725. 8:30AM-4:00 PM.

Clay County Clerk PO Box 190, Clay, WV 25043 (207 Main St.). **304-587-4259** Fax: 304-587-7329. 8AM-4PM.

Doddridge County Clerk 118 E. Court St, Rm 102, West Union, WV 26456-1297 **304-873-2631** 8:30AM-4PM.

Fayette County Clerk PO Box 569, Fayetteville, WV 25840 (Courthouse). **304-574-4226** Fax: 304-574-4335. 8AM-4PM.

Gilmer County Clerk 10 Howard St, Courthouse, Glenville, WV 26351 **304-462-7641** Fax: 304-462-5134. 8AM-4PM.

Grant County Clerk 5 Highland Ave, Petersburg, WV 26847 **304-257-4550** Fax: 304-257-4207. 8:30AM-4:30PM.

Greenbrier County Clerk PO Box 506, Lewisburg, WV 24901 (200 N. Court St). **304-647-6602** Fax: 304-647-6694. 8:30-4:30.

Hampshire County Clerk PO Box 806, Romney, WV 26757-0806 (Main St Courthouse). **304-822-5112** Fax: 304-822-4039. 9AM-4PM (F open until 8PM).

Hancock County Clerk PO Box 367, New Cumberland, WV 26047 (102 Court St). **304-564-3311 x279** Fax: 304-564-5941. 8:30AM-4:30PM.

Hardy County Clerk 204 Washington St, Courthouse - Rm 111, Moorefield, WV 26836 **304-538-2929** Fax: 304-538-6832. 9-4. Deed, Mortgage, Grantor/Grantee records online.

Harrison County Clerk 301 W. Main St, Courthouse, Clarksburg, WV 26301 **304-624-8612** Fax: 304-624-8575. 8:30AM-4:30PM.

Jackson County Clerk PO Box 800, Ripley, WV 25271 (Court & Main Sts). **304-372-2011** Fax: 304-372-5259. 9AM-4PM M-F; 9AM-N Sat..

Jefferson County Clerk PO Box 208, Charles Town, WV 25414 (100 E. Washington St). **304-728-3215** Fax: 304-728-1957. 9AM-5PM (F open until 7PM).

Kanawha County Clerk PO Box 3226, Charleston, WV 25332 (409 Virginia St East). **304-357-0130** Fax: 304-357-0585.

Lewis County Clerk PO Box 87, Weston, WV 26452 (110 Center Ave). **304-269-8215** Fax: 304-269-8202. 8:30AM-4:30PM.

Lincoln County Clerk PO Box 497, Hamlin, WV 25523 (8000 Court Ave). **304-824-3336** Fax: 304-824-7972.

Logan County Clerk Stratton & Main St, Courthouse, Rm 101, Logan, WV 25601 (Stratton & Main St, Rm 101). **304-792-8600** Fax: 304-792-8621. 8:30AM-4:30PM.

Marion County Clerk PO Box 1267, Fairmont, WV 26555 (217 Adams St). **304-367-5441** Fax: 304-367-5448. 8:30-4:30PM.

Marshall County Clerk PO Box 459, Moundsville, WV 26041 (7th St & Tomlinson Ave). **304-845-1220** Fax: 304-845-5891. 8:30AM-4:30PM.

Mason County Clerk 200 6th St, Point Pleasant, WV 25550 **304-675-1997** Fax: 304-675-2521. 8:30AM-4:30PM.

McDowell County Clerk 90 Wyoming St, #109, Welch, WV 24801-2487 **304-436-8544** Fax: 304-436-8576. 9Am-5PM.

Mercer County Clerk 1501 Main St., Princeton, WV 24740 **304-487-8312** Fax: 304-487-8351. 8:30AM-4PM.

Mineral County Clerk 150 Armstrong St, Keyser, WV 26726 **304-788-3924** Fax: 304-788-4109. 8:30AM-5PM.

Mingo County Clerk PO Box 1197, Williamson, WV 25661 (75 E. 2nd Ave.). **304-235-0330** Fax: 304-235-0565. 8:30-4:30.

Monongalia County Clerk 243 High St, Courthouse Rm 123, Morgantown, WV 26505-5491 **304-291-7230** Fax: 304-291-7233. Assessor, Real Estate records online.

Monroe County Clerk PO Box 350, Union, WV 24983 (216 Main St). **304-772-3096** 8:30AM-4:30PM.

Morgan County Clerk 77 Fairfax St, #1A, #100, Berkeley Springs, WV 25411 **304-258-8547** Fax: 304-258-8545. 9AM-5PM M,T,Th; 9AM-1PM W; 9AM-7PM F.

Nicholas County Clerk 700 Main St, #2, Summersville, WV 26651 **304-872-7820** Fax: 304-872-9600. 8:30AM-4:30PM.

Ohio County Clerk 1500 Chapline St Rm 205, Wheeling, WV 26003 **304-234-3656** Fax: 304-234-3829. 8:30AM-5PM.

Pendleton County Clerk PO Box 1167, Franklin, WV 26807-0089 (Main St Courthouse). **304-358-2505** Fax: 304-358-2473. 8:30AM-4PM.

Pleasants County Clerk 301 Court Lane, Rm 101, Courthouse, St. Marys, WV 26170 **304-684-3542** Fax: 304-684-7569. 8:30-4:30PM.

Pocahontas County Clerk 900C 10th Ave, Marlinton, WV 24954 **304-799-4549** 8:30AM-4:30PM.

Preston County Clerk 101 W. Main St, Rm 201, Kingwood, WV 26537 **304-329-0070** Fax: 304-329-0198. 9AM-5PM (F open until 7PM).

Putnam County Clerk 3389 Winfield Rd., Winfield, WV 25213-9705 **304-586-0202** Fax: 304-586-0280. 8AM-4PM.

Raleigh County Clerk 215 Main St, Courthouse, Beckley, WV 25801 **304-255-9123** Fax: 304-255-9352. 8:30AM-4PM.

Randolph County Clerk PO Box 368, Elkins, WV 26241 (2 Randolph Ave). **304-636-0543** 8AM-4:30PM.

Ritchie County Clerk 115 E. Main St, Courthouse Rm 201, Harrisville, WV 26362 **304-643-2164** Fax: 304-643-2906. 8-4PM.

Roane County Clerk PO Box 69, Spencer, WV 25276 (200 Main St). **304-927-2860** Fax: 304-927-2489. 8:30AM-4PM M-F; 9AM-N Sat..

Summers County Clerk PO Box 97, Hinton, WV 25951-0097 (120 Ballengee St). **304-466-7104** Fax: 304-466-7146. 8:30-4:30PM.

Taylor County Clerk 214 W. Main St, Rm 101, Courthouse, Grafton, WV 26354 **304-265-1401** Fax: 304-265-3016. 8:30- 4:30.

Tucker County Clerk 215 First St. #3, Parsons, WV 26287 (215 First St.). **304-478-2414** Fax: 304-478-4464. 8AM-4PM.

Tyler County Clerk PO Box 66, Middlebourne, WV 26149 (121 Main). **304-758-2102** Fax: 304-758-2126. 8AM-4PM.

Upshur County Clerk 40 W. Main St, Courthouse Rm 101, Buckhannon, WV 26201 **304-472-1068** Fax: 304-472-1029. 8AM-4PM (til 6:30 on Th).

Wayne County Clerk of County Commission PO Box 248, Wayne, WV 25570 (Rm 108, 700 Hendricks St). **304-272-5974** Fax: 304-272-5318. 8AM-4PM MTWF; 8AM-8PM TH.

Webster County Clerk 2 Court Sq, Courthouse Rm G-1, Webster Springs, WV 26288-1054 **304-847-2508** Fax: 304-847-5780. 8:30AM-4PM.

Wetzel County Clerk PO Box 156, New Martinsville, WV 26155-0156 (200 Main St). **304-455-8224** Fax: 304-455-5256. 9AM-4:40 M,T,W,F; 9AM-4PM Th; 9-N Sat..

Wirt County Clerk PO Box 53, Elizabeth, WV 26143 (Courthouse Sq). **304-275-4271** Fax: 304-275-3418. 8:30AM-4PM.

Wood County Clerk PO Box 1474, Parkersburg, WV 26102-1474 (3rd & Market Sts, Rm 201). **304-424-1850** Fax: 304-424-1864. 8:30AM-4:30PM. www.woodcountywv.com Recording, Deed, Will, Death, Birth records online.

Wyoming County Clerk PO Box 309, Pineville, WV 24874 (Main St Courthouse). **304-732-8000** Fax: 304-732-9659.

Wisconsin

Organization: 72 counties, 72 recording offices. The recording officers are the Register of Deeds and the Clerk of Court (state tax liens). The entire state is in the Central Time Zone (CST).

Real Estate Records: Registers will not perform real estate searches. Copy fees and certification fees vary. Assessor telephone numbers are for local municipalities or for property listing agencies. Counties do not have assessors. Copies usually cost $2.00 for first page and $1.00 each additional. Certification usually costs $.25 per document. The Treasurer maintains property tax records.

UCC Records: Financing statements are filed at the state level, except for real estate related collateral, which are filed with the Register of Deeds. However, prior to 07/2001, consumer goods and farm collateral were also filed at the Register of Deeds and these older records can be searched there. Nearly all recording offices will perform UCC searches, and many will accept a search by phone. Use search request form UCC-11 for mail-in searches. Searches fees are usually $10.00 per debtor name. Copy fees are usually $2.00 1st page and $1.00 each add'l page.

Tax Lien Records: Federal tax liens on personal property of businesses are filed with the Secretary of State. Only federal tax liens on real estate are filed with the county Register of Deeds. State tax liens are filed with the Clerk of Court, and at the State Treasurer at the Dept. of Revenue. Refer to the County Court Records section for information about Wisconsin courts. Most but not all Registers will perform federal tax lien searches. Search fees vary, but copy fees are $2.00 1st page and $1.00 each add'l page. Other Liens: Judgment, mechanics, breeders.

Online Access: A number of cities and a few counties offer online access to assessor and property records.

Adams Register of Deeds PO Box 219, Friendship, WI 53934-0219 (402 Main St). **608-339-4206** 8AM-4:30PM.

Ashland Register of Deeds 201 W. Main St, Rm 206, Ashland, WI 54806 **715-682-7008** Fax: 715-682-7035. 8AM-4PM.

Barron Register of Deeds 330 E. LaSalle, Rm 201, Barron, WI 54812 **715-537-6210** Fax: 715-537-6277. www.co.barron.wi.us Land, Assessor records online.

Bayfield Register of Deeds PO Box 813, Washburn, WI 54891 (117 E. 5th). **715-373-6119** 8AM-4PM.

Brown Register of Deeds PO Box 23600, Green Bay, WI 54305-3600 (305 E. Walnut, Rm 260). **920-448-4470** Fax: 920-448-4449. 8AM-4:30PM. www.co.brown.wi.us/rod Real Estate, Recording records online.

Buffalo Register of Deeds PO Box 28, Alma, WI 54610-0028 (407 Second St). **608-685-6230** Fax: 608-685-6213. Land records online.

Burnett Register of Deeds 7410 County Rd K #103, Siren, WI 54872 **715-349-2183** Fax: 715-349-2037. www.burnettcounty.com Property, Tax Assessor records online.

Calumet Register of Deeds 206 Court St, Chilton, WI 53014 **920-849-1441** Fax: 920-849-1469. www.co.calumet.wi.us Assessor, Property Tax records online. 8AM-4:30PM.

Chippewa Register of Deeds 711 N Bridge St, Chippewa Falls, WI 54729-1876 **715-726-7994** Fax: 715-726-4582. 8AM-4:30 PM. www.co.chippewa.wi.us/Departments/Registe

rDeeds Recording, Deed, Judgment, Real Estate records online.

Clark Registrar PO Box 384, Neillsville, WI 54456-0384 (517 Court St, Rm 303). **715-743-5162** Fax: 715-743-5154. 8AM-4:30PM. www.co.clark.wi.us Assessor, Property records online.

Columbia Register of Deeds PO Box 133, Portage, WI 53901 (400 DeWitt St). **608-742-9677** Fax: 608-742-9875. Property Tax, Land records online.

Crawford Register of Deeds 220 N. Beaumont Rd, Prairie du Chien, WI 53821 **608-326-0219** Fax: 608-326-0220. http://crawfordcounty-wi-us.org

Dane Register of Deeds PO Box 1438, Madison, WI 53701 (210 Martin Luther King Jr. Blvd., Rm 110). **608-266-4141** www.co.dane.wi.us/regdeeds/rdhome.htm Fax: 608-267-3110. 7:45-4PM. Assessor, Real Estate, Property Tax records online.

Dodge Register of Deeds 127 E. Oak St, Admin. Bldg., Juneau, WI 53039-1391 **920-386-3720** Fax: 920-386-3902. 8-4:30PM.

Door Register of Deeds PO Box 670, Sturgeon Bay, WI 54235-0670 (421 Nebraska St). **920-746-2270** Fax: 920-746-2525. 8AM-4:30PM.

Douglas Register of Deeds PO Box 847, Superior, WI 54880 (1313 Belknap St, Rm 108). **715-395-1463** Fax: 715-395-1553. 8AM-4:30PM. www.douglascountywi.org

Dunn Register of Deeds 800 Wilson Ave, Menomonie, WI 54751 **715-232-1228** Fax: 715-232-1229. 8AM-4:30PM.

Eau Claire Register of Deeds PO Box 718, Eau Claire, WI 54702 (721 Oxford Ave, Rm 1310). **715-839-4745** 8AM-5PM. www.co.eau-claire.wi.us/ Warrant, Most Wanted records online.

Florence Register of Deeds PO Box 410, Florence, WI 54121-0410 (501 Lake Ave). **715-528-4252** Fax: 715-528-5470. 8:30-4.

Fond du Lac Register of Deeds PO Box 509, Fond du Lac, WI 54935-0509 (160 S. Macy St). **920-929-3018** Fax: 920-929-3293. 7:45-4:30. www.co.fond-du-lac.wi.us Property, Assessor, GIS Mapping records online.

Forest Register of Deeds 200 E. Madison St, Crandon, WI 54520 **715-478-3823** 8:30AM-N, 1-4:30PM.

Grant Register of Deeds PO Box 391, Lancaster, WI 53813-0391 (111 S. Jefferson). **608-723-2727** Fax: 608-723-4048. 8-4:30. Land, Assessor records online.

Green Register of Deeds 1016 16th Ave, Courthouse, Monroe, WI 53566 **608-328-9439** Fax: 608-328-2835. 8AM-5PM.

Green Lake Register of Deeds PO Box 3188, Green Lake, WI 54941-3188 (492 Hill St). **920-294-4021** Fax: 920-294-4165. 8AM-4:30PM. www.co.green-lake.wi.us

Iowa Register of Deeds 222 N. Iowa St, Dodgeville, WI 53533 **608-935-0396** Fax: 608-935-3024. 8:30AM-4:30PM.

Iron Register of Deeds 300 Taconite St, Hurley, WI 54534 **715-561-2945** Fax: 715-561-2928.

Jackson Register of Deeds 307 Main, Black River Falls, WI 54615 **715-284-0205** Fax: 715-284-0204. 8AM-4PM.

Jefferson Register of Deeds PO Box 356, Jefferson, WI 53549 (320 S. Main St, Rm 102). **920-674-7235** 8AM-4:30PM. www.co.jefferson.wi.us Grantor/Grantee, Treasurer, GIS-Mapping, Assessor Property Tax records online.

Juneau Register of Deeds 220 E. State St. #212, Mauston, WI 53948-1379 **608-847-9325** Fax: 608-847-9402. 8-N, 12:30-4:30.

Kenosha Register of Deeds 1010 56 St., Kenosha, WI 53140 **262-653-2444** Fax: 262-653-2564. 8AM-5PM. Real Estate, Lien, Vital Statistic, Assessor records online.

Kewaunee Register of Deeds 613 Dodge St, Kewaunee, WI 54216-1398 **920-388-7126** Fax: 920-388-7195. www.kewauneeco.org Grantor/Grantee, Deed, Tract & Image, GIS Mapping, Property Tax records online.

La Crosse Register of Deeds 400 N. 4th St, Rm 1220, Admin. Ctr, La Crosse, WI 54601-3200 **608-785-9644** Fax: 608-785-9643. www.co.la-crosse.wi.us/Departments/depart ments.htm Land, Deed, Property Owner records online.

Lafayette Register of Deeds PO Box 170, Darlington, WI 53530 (626 Main St). **608-776-4838** Fax: 608-776-4991. 8AM-4:30PM. Land, Deed records online.

Langlade Register of Deeds 800 Clermont St, Antigo, WI 54409 **715-627-6209** Fax: 715-627-6303. 8:30AM-4:30PM.

Lincoln Register of Deeds 1110 E. Main, Courthouse, Merrill, WI 54452 **715-536-0318** Fax: 715-536-0360. www.co.lincoln.wi.us Land records online.

Manitowoc Register of Deeds PO Box 421, Manitowoc, WI 54221-0421 (1010 S. 8th St). **920-683-4010** Fax: 920-683-2702. www.manitowoc-county.com Assessor, Real Estate records online.

Marathon Register of Deeds 500 Forest St, Courthouse, Wausau, WI 54403-5568 **715-261-1470** Fax: 715-261-1488. www.co.marathon.wi.us Land records online.

Marinette Register of Deeds 1926 Hall Ave, Courthouse, Marinette, WI 54143 **715-732-7550** Fax: 715-732-7532. 8:30AM-4:30PM.

Marquette Register of Deeds PO Box 236, Montello, WI 53949-0236 (77 W. Park St).

608-297-9132 Fax: 608-297-7606. 8AM-N, 12:30-4:30PM.

Menominee Register of Deeds PO Box 279, Keshena, WI 54135-0279 (Courthouse Lane). **715-799-3312** Fax: 715-799-1322. 8AM-4:30PM.

Milwaukee Register of Deeds 901 N. 9th St, Rm 103, Milwaukee, WI 53233 **414-278-4011** Fax: 414-223-1257. www.co.milwaukee.wi.us Assessor, Real Estate, Property Sale records online.

Monroe Register of Deeds 202 S. "K" St, Rm 2, Sparta, WI 54656 **608-269-8716** Fax: 608-269-8715. www.co.monroe.wi.us

Oconto Register of Deeds 301 Washington St, Rm 2035, Oconto, WI 54153-1699 **920-834-6807** 8AM-4PM. www.co.oconto.wi.us Property, Assessor records online.

Oneida Register of Deeds PO Box 400, Rhinelander, WI 54501 (Oneida Ave, 1 Courthouse Sq). **715-369-6150** Fax: 715-369-6222. 8AM-4:30PM.

Outagamie Register of Deeds 410 S. Walnut St, CAB 205, Appleton, WI 54911-5999 **920-832-5095** Fax: 920-832-2177. 8AM-4:30PM; Summer hours: 7AM-3:30PM. www.co.outagamie.wi.us Inmate, Offender records online.

Ozaukee Register of Deeds PO Box 994, Port Washington, WI 53074-0994 (121 W. Main St). **262-284-8260** Fax: 262-284-8100. 8:30AM-5:00PM. www.co.ozaukee.wi.us Recording, Real Estate, Grantor/Grantee, Vital Statistic, Property Tax, Tracts, Civil Court records online.

Pepin Register of Deeds PO Box 39, Durand, WI 54736 (740 7th Ave West). **715-672-8856** Fax: 715-672-8677. 8:30- 4:30.

Pierce Register of Deeds PO Box 267, Ellsworth, WI 54011-0267 (414 W. Main St). **715-273-3531 x418** Fax: 715-273-6861. 8AM-5PM. www.co.pierce.wi.us Real Estate, Assessor, Property Tax records online.

Polk Register of Deeds PO Box 335, Balsam Lake, WI 54810-0335 (100 Polk County Plaza, #160). **715-485-9240** Fax: 715-485-9202. 8:30AM-4:30PM. www.co.polk.wi.us

Portage Register of Deeds 1516 Church St, County-City Bldg., Stevens Point, WI 54481 **715-346-1428** Fax: 715-345-5361. 7:30-4:30. www.co.portage.wi.us Property Tax, Assessor, Recording, Land, Deed, Criminal Complaint records online.

Price Register of Deeds 126 Cherry, Phillips, WI 54555 **715-339-2515** 8AM-N, 1-4:30.

Racine Register of Deeds 730 Wisconsin Ave, Racine, WI 53403 **262-636-3208** Fax: 262-636-3851. 8-5PM. www.goracine.org

Richland Register of Deeds PO Box 337, Richland Center, WI 53581 (Seminary St Courthouse). **608-647-3011** 8:30-4:30PM.

Rock Register of Deeds 51 S. Main St, Janesville, WI 53545 **608-757-5657** Fax: 608-757-5563. 8AM-5PM. Assessor, Real Estate records online. www.co.rock.wi.us/departm ents/reg_deeds.htm

Rusk Register of Deeds 311 Miner Ave. Rm #N132, Ladysmith, WI 54848-0311 **715-532-2139** Fax: 715-532-2194. 8:00AM-4:30PM. Land records online.

Sauk Register of Deeds 505 Broadway St., Baraboo, WI 53913 **608-355-3288** Fax: 608-355-3292. 8AM-4:30PM. Property, Assessor records online.

Sawyer Register of Deeds PO Box 686, Hayward, WI 54843-0686 (10610 Main). **715-634-4867** Fax: 715-634-6839. 8AM-4PM. http://sawyercountygov.org

Shawano Register of Deeds 311 N. Main, Shawano, WI 54166 **715-524-2129** Fax: 715-524-5157.

Sheboygan Register of Deeds 508 New York Ave, 2nd Fl, Sheboygan, WI 53081 **920-459-3023** 8AM-5PM. Land, Deed, Real Estate, Tax Lien records online.

St. Croix Register of Deeds 1101 Carmichael Rd., Hudson, WI 54016 **715-386-4652** Fax: 715-386-4687. www.co.saint-croix.wi.us

Taylor Register of Deeds 224 S 2nd St, Medford, WI 54451-1811 **715-748-1483** Fax: 715-748-1446. 8:30AM-4:30PM. www.co.taylor.wi.us/departments/registerofde eds/rodmain.htm Real Estate records online.

Trempealeau Register of Deeds PO Box 67, Whitehall, WI 54773 (36245 Main St.). **715-538-2311** www.tremplocounty.com Real Estate, Assessor records online.

Vernon Register of Deeds PO Box 46, Viroqua, WI 54665 (400 Court House Sq St). **608-637-3571** Fax: 608-637-5304.

Vilas Register of Deeds 330 Court St., Eagle River, WI 54521 **715-479-3660** Fax: 715-479-3695. 8AM-4PM. http://co.vilas.wi.us

Walworth Register of Deeds PO Box 995, Elkhorn, WI 53121-0995 (Rm 102, 100 W. Walworth St.). **262-741-4214** Fax: 262-741-4947. 8AM-5PM. www.co.walworth.wi.us Property Tax, Recording, Grantor/Grantee, Deed records online.

Washburn Register of Deeds PO Box 607, Shell Lake, WI 54871 (10 4th Ave). **715-468-4616** Fax: 715-468-4658. 8-4:30PM.

Washington Register of Deeds PO Box 1986, West Bend, WI 53095-7986 (432 E. Washington St, Rm 2084). **262-335-4318** Fax: 262-335-6866. 8AM-4:30PM. www.co.washington.wi.us/departments/default.htm

Waukesha Register of Deeds 1320 Pewaukee Rd, Rm 110, Waukesha, WI 53188

262-548-7863 8AM-4:30PM. Property, Assessor, Recording, Deed, Lien, Marriage, UCC records online. www.waukeshacounty.gov/departments/register

Waupaca Register of Deeds PO Box 307, Waupaca, WI 54981 (811 Harding St). **715-258-6250** Fax: 715-258-6212. 8AM-4PM. Property Tax, Assessor, Register of Deed, Land records online.

Waushara Register of Deeds PO Box 338, Wautoma, WI 54982 (209 S. St. Marie). **920-787-0444** Fax: 920-787-0425. 8-4:30.

Winnebago Register of Deeds PO Box 2808, Oshkosh, WI 54903-2808 (Rm 30, 415 Jackson St). **920-236-4883** Fax: 920-303-3025. Assessor, Real Estate records online.

Wood Register of Deeds PO Box 8095, Wisconsin Rapids, WI 54495 (400 Market St). **715-421-8450** www.co.wood.wi.us

 # Wyoming

Organization: 23 counties, 23 recording offices. The recording officer is the County Clerk. Is in the Mountain Time Zone (MST).

Real Estate Records: County Clerks will not perform real estate searches. Copy fees are usually $1.00 per page, and certification fees are usually $2.00 per document. The Assessor maintains property tax records.

UCC Records: Since 07/1/2001, all filings have been centralized at the state. Prior, financing statements were usually filed with the County Clerk and accounts receivable and farm products require dula filing at the state level as well. All recording offices will perform UCC searches. Use search request form UCC-11. Searches fees are usually $10.00 per debtor name. Copy fees vary.

Tax Lien Records: Federal tax liens on personal property of businesses are filed with the Secretary of State. Other federal and all state tax liens are filed with the County Clerk. Most counties perform tax lien searches. Search fees are usually $10.00 per name.

Online Access: Teton county offers online access to the County Clerk's database of recorded documents.

Albany County Clerk 525 Grand Ave. Rm202, Laramie, WY 82070 **307-721-2547** Fax: 307-721-2544. 9AM-5PM.

Big Horn County Clerk PO Box 31, Basin, WY 82410 (420 W. C St). **307-568-2357** Fax: 307-568-9375. 8-5. www.state.wy.us

Campbell County Clerk PO Box 3010, Gillette, WY 82717-3010 (500 S. Gillette Ave, #220). **307-682-7285** Fax: 307-687-6455. 8AM-5PM.

Carbon County Clerk 415 W. Pine, PO Box 6, Courthouse, Rawlins, WY 82301 **307-328-2679** Fax: 307-328-2690. 8AM-5PM.

Converse County Clerk 107 North 5th St, #114, Douglas, WY 82633-0990. **307-358-2244** Fax: 307-358-5998. 8AM-5PM.

Crook County Clerk PO Box 37, Sundance, WY 82729 (309 Cleveland St). **307-283-1323** Fax: 307-283-3038. 8AM-5PM.

Fremont County Clerk 450 N. 2nd St, Rm 220, Lander, WY 82520 **307-332-2405** Fax: 307-332-1132. www.fremontcounty.org

Goshen County Clerk PO Box 160, Torrington, WY 82240 (2125 E. A St). **307-532-4051** Fax: 307-532-7375. 7:30AM-4PM. www.state.wy.us

Hot Springs County Clerk 415 Arapahoe St, Courthouse, Thermopolis, WY 82443-2783 **307-864-3515** Fax: 307-864-3333. 8-5PM.

Johnson County Clerk 76 N. Main St, Buffalo, WY 82834 **307-684-7272** Fax: 307-684-2708. 8AM-5PM.

Laramie County Clerk PO Box 608, Cheyenne, WY 82003 (Rm 1600, 309 W. 20th St.). **307-633-4351** Fax: 307-633-4240. 8AM-5PM. www.laramiecountyclerk.com

Lincoln County Clerk PO Box 670, Kemmerer, WY 83101-0670 (925 Sage). **307-877-9056** Fax: 307-877-3101.

Natrona County Clerk PO Box 863, Casper, WY 82602 (200 N. Center). **307-235-9270** Fax 307-235-9367. www.natronacounty-wy.gov

Niobrara County Clerk PO Box 420, Lusk, WY 82225 (424 S. Elm). **307-334-2211** Fax: 307-334-3013. 8AM-4PM.

Park County Clerk 1002 Sheridan Ave., Courthouse, Cody, WY 82414 **307-527-8600** Fax: 307-527-8626.

Platte County Clerk PO Drawer 728, Wheatland, WY 82201 (800 9th St). **307-322-2315** Fax: 307-322-2245. 7AM-4PM.

Sheridan County Clerk 224 S. Main St, #B-2, Sheridan, WY 82801-9998 **307-674-2500** Fax: 307-674-2529. 8AM-5PM.

Sublette County Clerk PO Box 250, Pinedale, WY 82941-0250 (21 S. Tyler Ave). **307-367-4372** Fax: 307-367-6396.

Sweetwater County Clerk PO Box 730, Green River, WY 82935 (80 W. Flaming Gorge Way). **307-872-6400** Fax: 307-872-6337. 9AM-5PM. www.co.sweet.wy.us/clerk

Teton County Clerk PO Box 1727, Jackson, WY 83001 (200 S. Willow). **307-733-4433** Fax: 307-739-8681. www.tetonwyo.org/clerk/ Real Estate, Lien, Recording records online.

Uinta County Clerk PO Box 810, Evanston, WY 82931-0810 (225 9th St). **307-783-0308** Fax: 307-783-0511. www.uintacounty.com

Washakie County Clerk Box 260, Worland, WY 82401-0260 (10th & Big Horn). **307-347-3131** Fax: 307-347-9366. 8AM-5PM. www.washakiecounty.net

Weston County Clerk 1 W. Main, Newcastle, WY 82701 **307-746-4744** Fax: 307-746-9505. 8AM-5PM.

Chapter 6

County Courts

The purpose of the County Court Records Sections is to provide quick yet detailed access information on the more than 5,000 major courts that have jurisdiction over significant criminal and civil cases under state law.

Included in *Find Public Records Fast* are all state felony courts, large and small claim civil courts, and probate courts in the United States. In addition, each state section begins with an introduction that summarizes where other major categories of court cases — misdemeanor, limited civil action, small claims, DUI, preliminary hearings, and juvenile cases — can be found.

The term "County Courts" – as used in this publication – refers to those courts of original jurisdiction (trial courts) within each state's court system that handle…

- Felonies – Generally defined as crimes punishable by one year or more of jail time
- Civil Actions – For money damages (usually greater than $3,000)
- Probate – Estate matters
- Misdemeanors – Generally defined as minor infractions with a fine or minimal jail time
- Evictions – Landlord/tenant actions
- Small Claims – Actions for minor money damages (generally under $3,000)

Useful Applications

The County Court Record Sections are especially useful for four kinds of applications—

- **General litigation searching/background searching**… Combined with the Federal Court section (Chapter 7), you have complete coverage of all important courts in the United States.
- **Employment background checking**… Included is full coverage of local criminal courts at the felony level, and many misdemeanor courts as well.
- **Tenant background checking**… Courts where landlord/tenant cases are filed are indicated in the state introduction charts, and most of the courts handling such cases are profiled.
- **Asset searching**… The probate courts have records of wills and estate matters that can be used to determine assets, related parties, and useful addresses.

Some Court Basics

Before trudging into a courthouse and demanding to view a document, you should first be aware of some basic court procedures. Whether the case is filed in a state, municipal, or federal court, each case follows a similar process.

Civil Cases

A **civil** case usually commences when a plaintiff files a complaint with a court against defendants. The defendants respond to the complaint with an answer. After this initial round, there may be literally hundreds of activities before the court issues a judgment. These activities can include revised complaints and their answers, motions of various kinds, discovery proceedings (including depositions) to establish the documentation and facts involved in the case. All of these activities are listed on a docket sheet, which may be a piece of paper or a computerized index.

Once the court issues a judgment, either party may appeal the ruling to an appellate division or court. In the case of a money judgment, the winning side can usually file it as a judgment lien with the county recorder. Appellate divisions usually deal only with legal issues and not the facts of the case.

Criminal Cases

In a **criminal** case, the plaintiff is a government jurisdiction. The Government brings the action against the defendant for violation of one or more of its statutes.

There are three distinct categories of criminal record cases. The text below, written by Mr. Les Rosen, author of *The Safe Hiring Manual* by Facts of Demand Press, gives an excellent description of these categories. A special thank you to Mr. Rosen for allowing us to reprint this material!

1. *A **Felony** is a serious offense that is punishable by state prisons. Note the use of the word **punishable**, as opposed to actually **punished**. The distinction is important because a person can be convicted of a felony but may not go to prison. How does that work? Depending upon the state and the crime, there are certain felonies where a judge can give a defendant FELONY PROBATION. This typically occurs with a relatively less serious felony committed by a relatively less serious offender. An example may be a first time felony drug offender convicted of a less serious drug offense, such as possession of a small amount of drugs for sale.*

   If a defendant received felony probation, the court can still sentence him to custody but in the local county jail. If the defendant violates his probation, the court then has the option of sending the defendant to state prison. That obviously creates a great deal of incentive for a felony defendant to not violate probation.

2. *A **Misdemeanor** is a less serious offense that is only punishable by local jail time at the county level. Typically a misdemeanor is punishable by up to one year in the county jail in the custody of the local county sheriff and a fine up to $1,000. A court can also impose terms and conditions of probation such as discussed above.*

3. *An **Infraction** is a public offense punishable only by a fine. This is typically a traffic violation, such as an illegal left turn or speeding.*

Actually there is a fourth category—Wobblers. The term designated an offense that can be either a misdemeanor or a felony offense, depending upon how the prosecuting attorney chooses to file the charges or how a judge views the offense. In California for example, a commercial burglary can be either a misdemeanor or a felony.

* * *

Other Case Types

In a **bankruptcy** case, which can be heard only in federal courts, there is neither defendant nor plaintiff. Instead, the debtor files voluntarily for bankruptcy protection against creditors, or creditors file against the debtor in order to force the debtor into involuntary bankruptcy. See the Federal Courts Section.

In a **probate** case the court oversees the fulfillment of wills, estate administrations, trusts, guardianships of incompetent adults and minors, commitment hearings for the mentally ill and mentally challenged, adoptions, birth corrections, name changes, delayed birth registrations, and custodial accounts, etc.

State Court Structure

The secret to determining where a state court case is located is to understand how the court system is structured in that particular state. The general structure of all state court systems has four parts:

Appellate courts	**Limited jurisdiction trial courts**
Intermediate appellate courts	**General jurisdiction trial courts**

The two highest levels, appellate and intermediate appellate courts, only hear cases on appeal from the trial courts. Opinions of these appellate courts are of interest primarily to attorneys seeking legal precedents for new cases.

General jurisdiction trial courts usually handle a full range of civil and criminal litigation. These courts usually handle felonies and larger civil cases.

Limited jurisdiction trial courts come in two varieties. First, many limited jurisdiction courts handle smaller civil claims (usually $10,000 or less), misdemeanors, and pretrial hearing for felonies. Second, some of these courts –sometimes called special jurisdiction courts – are limited to one type of litigation, for example the Court of Claims in New York which only handles liability cases against the state.

Some states, for instance Iowa, have consolidated their general and limited jurisdiction court structure into one combined court system. In other states there may be a further distinction between state-supported courts and municipal courts.

Generalizations should not be made about where specific types of cases are handled in the various states. Misdemeanors, probate, landlord/tenant (eviction), domestic relations, and juvenile cases may be handled in either or both the general and limited jurisdiction courts. To help you locate the correct court to perform your search in, this book specifically lists the types of cases handled in a state's courts.

Types of Litigation in Trial Courts

Criminal

Criminal cases are categorized as felonies or misdemeanors. A general rule, a felony involves a jail term of one year or more, whereas a misdemeanor may only involve a monetary fine.

Civil

Civil cases are categorized as tort, contract, and real property rights. Torts can include automobile accidents, medical malpractice, and product liability cases. Actions for small money damages, typically under $3,000, are known as small claims.

Other

Other types of cases that frequently are handled by separate courts or specialized divisions of courts include juvenile, probate (wills and estates), and domestic relations (or family courts). Note that, in many states, access to juvenile court and family court records is restricted.

How Courts Maintain Records

Case Numbering

When a case is filed, it is assigned a case number. This is the primary indexing method in every court. In searching for case records, you will need to know — or find — the applicable case number. If you have the case number in good form already, your search should be fast and reasonably inexpensive.

Be aware that case numbering procedures are not consistent throughout a state court system. One district may assign numbers by district while another may assign numbers by location (division) within the district, or by judge. Remember: case numbers appearing in legal text citations may not be adequate for searching unless they appear in the proper form for the particular court in which you are searching.

All basic civil case information is entered onto **docket sheets**.

Docket Sheet

Information from cover sheets and from documents filed as a case goes forward is recorded on the docket sheet. The docket sheet then contains an outline of the case history from initial filing to its current status. While docket sheets differ somewhat in format, the basic information contained on a docket sheet is consistent from court to court. All docket sheets contain:

- Name of court, including location (division) and the judge assigned;
- Case number and case name;
- Names of all plaintiffs and defendants/debtors;
- Names and addresses of attorneys for the plaintiff or debtor;
- Nature and cause (e.g., statute) of action.

Computerization

Most courts are computerized, which means the docket sheet data is entered into a computer system. Within a state or judicial district, the courts may be linked together via a single computer system.

Docket sheets from cases closed before the advent of computerization may not be in the computer system. For pre-computer cases, most courts keep summary case information on microfilm, microfiche, or index cards.

Case documents are not generally available on computer because courts are still experimenting with and developing electronic filing and imaging of court documents. Generally, documents are only available to be copied by contacting the court where the case records are located.

Restricted Records

Most courts have a certain case records which are not released without a court order. Examples include juvenile, adoption, and sealed records. This practice will vary from state-to-state or county-to-county.

Watch for Name Variations From State to State

Do not assume that the structure of the court system in another state is anything like your own. In one state, the Circuit Court may be the highest trial court whereas in another it is a limited jurisdiction court. Examples are: New York, where the Supreme Court is not very "supreme" and the downstate court structure varies from upstate; and Tennessee, where circuit courts are in districts.

Record Searching Guidelines

Basic Information in this Book

The 3,140 U.S. counties (and where applicable, parishes, boroughs, independent cities, etc.) are listed in alphabetical order within each state. When a county has more than one court profiled, the courts appear in order beginning with the court of general jurisdiction, then proceeding down to more limited jurisdictions. Each profile specifically lists the types of cases handled by that court. If a level of court has divisions, generally civil courts are listed before criminal courts. Note that when more than one court of the same type is located in a county, the courts are not listed in alphabetical order.

In addition to the address and telephone number you will find hours of operation and fax numbers given for most courts.

Access Methods and Indexing

Each court profile includes icons which show the acceptable searching methods, be it phone☎, **FAX**, mail✉, in person✋, and online🖥.

As for the actual records, criminal courts index their records by defendant name and/or case number. Some courts do so by year. Most civil courts index their records by the plaintiff name as well as by defendant name. A plaintiff search is useful, for example, to determine if someone is especially litigious.

During the past decade, thousands of courts have installed computerized indexing systems. Computerized systems are considerably faster and easier to search, allowing for more indexing capability than the microfilm and card indexes that preceded them. Many courts provide public access computer terminals within the courthouse. Sometimes the programs on these terminals are the same programs the clerks use to do name or case look-ups. However, usually all or part of the DOB and SSN are cloaked. This means it is necessary to check the case file to determine the true identity of the proper person, as the actual case file should have the needed identifiers.

Other Record Searching Hints

Here are some more useful searching hints to keep in mind—

- When a county has multiple courts of the same level, general information is provided to help determine which office to search in, depending upon the subject's address.

- In many instances two types of courts within a county (e.g., circuit and district) are combined. When phoning or writing these courts, we recommend that your request specifically state that you want both courts included in the search.

- If sending your request by mail, we recommend including a SASE (self-addressed, stamped envelope) to make sure the results are returned to you.

- Be aware that the number of courts that no longer conduct name searches has risen. For these courts, you must hire a local retriever, directly or through a search company, to search for you. It should be noted that usually these courts still take specific document copy requests by mail. Because of long mail turnaround times and court fees, local retrievers are frequently used even when the court will honor a request by mail. You may search online for a professional document retriever who is a member of the Public Record Retriever Network (PRRN) at www.brbpub.com/PRRN/search.asp. Also, an exhaustive list of 2500+ local document retrievers is available in the *The National Directory of Local Court and County Record Retriever* by BRB Publications (www.brbpub.com/books)

Additional State Court Resources

The National Center for State Courts

www.ncsconline.org

NASCIO

https://www.nascio.org/aboutNascio/profiles/   - Click on a state then the Judicial Link

Alabama

State Court Administration (All County Circuit & District Courts): Director of Courts, 300 Dexter Ave, Montgomery, AL, 36104; 334-242-0300, Fax: 334-242-2099. http://www.alacourt.gov/

Court Structure: Circuit Courts are the courts of general jurisdiction; District Courts have limited jurisdiction in civil matters. These courts are combined in all but eight larger counties. Barbour, Coffee, Jefferson, St. Clair, Talladega, and Tallapoosa Counties have two court locations within the county.

Jefferson County (Birmingham), Madison (Huntsville), Marshall, and Tuscaloosa Counties have separate criminal divisions for Circuit and/or District Courts. Misdemeanors committed with felonies are tried with the felony. The Circuit Courts are appeals courts for misdemeanors.

District Courts can receive guilty pleas in felony cases.

Probate Courts: All counties have separate probate courts. Probate court telephone numbers are generally included with the Circuit or District Court entry although the court location may be different.

Online Access: The state has a remote access program called (SJIS), but it is only open to government agencies. Searchers are now reccommended by this agency to contact a commercial vendor at www.alacourt.com. Note that fees are involved. State Supreme Court and Appellette decisions are available at www.alalinc.net and at website above.

Additional Information: Although in most counties Circuit and District courts are combined, each index may be separate. Therefore, when you request a search of both courts, be sure to state that the search is to cover "both the Circuit and District Court records." Several offices do not perform searches. Some offices do not have public access computer terminals.

Autauga County

Circuit & District Court *Felony, Misdemeanor, Civil, Eviction, Small Claims* 134 N Court St, #114, Prattville, AL 36067-3049. 8AM-5PM. Civil: 334-361-3736, Crim: 334-361-3737. ✉️🖥️✋

Probate Court 176 W 5th, Prattville, AL 36067 8:30AM-5PM **334-361-3728/4842** Fax: 334-361-3740.

Baldwin County

Circuit & District Court *Felony, Misdemeanor, Civil, Eviction, Small Claims* 312 Courthouse Sq #10, Bay Minette, AL 36507. 8AM-4:30PM. **251-937-0370**, Civil: 251-937-0299, Crim: 251-937-0280. 🖥️✋

Probate Court PO Box 459, Bay Minette, AL 36507. 8AM-4:30PM. **251-937-9561**, Fax: 251-937-0252. Access probate property records www.deltacomputersystems.com/al/al05/probatea.html.

Barbour County

Circuit & District Court - Clayton Division *Felony, Misdemeanor, Civil, Eviction, Small Claims, Probate* PO Box 219, Clayton, AL 36016. 8AM-4:30PM. **334-775-8366**, Fax: 334-775-1125, Probate: 334-775-8371. Probate is a separate court. ✉️🖥️✋

Circuit & District Court - Eufaula Division *Misdemeanor, Civil, Eviction, Small Claims, Probate* 303 E Broad St, Rm 201, Eufaula, AL 36027. 8AM-4:30PM. **334-687-1515/16**, Fax: 334-687-1599, Probate: 334-687-1530. Probate is a separate court at Rm 101. 🖥️✋

Bibb County

Circuit & District Court *Felony, Misdemeanor, Civil, Eviction, Small Claims, Probate* Bibb County Courthouse PO Box 185, Centreville, AL 35042. 8AM-4:30PM. **205-926-3103** Civil (Circuit), Fax: 205-926-3132. Civil phone: 205-926-3100 (Dist), Crim: 205-926-3107, Probate: 205-926-3108. Probate is a separate court. ✉️🖥️✋

Blount County

Circuit & District Court *Felony, Misdemeanor, Civil, Eviction, Small Claims* 220 2nd Ave East Rm 208, Oneonta, AL 35121. 8AM-5PM. **205-625-4153**. ✉️🖥️✋

Probate Court 220 2nd Ave E, Oneonta, AL 35121. 8AM-5PM. **205-625-4191/4180**, Fax: 205-625-4206.

Bullock County

Circuit & District Court *Felony, Misdemeanor, Civil, Eviction, Small Claims, Probate* PO Box 230, Union Springs, AL 36089. 8AM-4:30PM. **334-738-2280**, Fax: 334-738-2282, Probate: 334-738-2250. Probate is a separate court. ☎️Fax✉️🖥️✋

Butler County

Circuit & District Court *Felony, Misdemeanor, Civil, Eviction, Small Claims, Probate* PO Box 236, Greenville, AL 36037. 7:30AM-4:30PM. **334-382-3521**, Fax: 334-382-7488, Probate: 334-382-3512. Probate is a separate court. ✉️🖥️✋

Calhoun County

Circuit Court *Felony, Civil Actions Over $10,000* 25 W 11th St, #300, Anniston, AL 36201. 8AM-4:30PM. **256-231-1750**, Fax: 256-231-1826. 🖥️✉️✋

District Court *Misdemeanor, Civil Actions Under $10,000, Eviction, Small Claims* 25 W 11th St Box 9, Anniston, AL 36201. 8AM-4:30PM. **256-231-1850**, Fax: 256-231-1863. 🖥️✋

Probate Court 1702 Noble St, #102, Anniston, AL 36201. 8AM-4:30PM. **256-241-2825**.

Chambers County

Circuit & District Court *Felony, Misdemeanor, Civil, Eviction, Small Claims, Probate* Chambers County

Courthouse - Clerks Office, Lafayette, AL 36862. 8AM-4:30PM. **334-864-4348**, Probate: 334-864-4372. Probate is a separate court. ✉️🖥✋

Cherokee County

Circuit & District Court *Felony, Misdemeanor, Civil, Eviction, Small Claims* 100 Main St, Rm 203, Centre, AL 35960-1532. 8AM-4:30PM. **256-927-3340**. ✉️🖥✋

Probate Court 100 Main St, Rm 204, Centre, AL 35960. 8-4PM M-F, 8AM-N Sat. **256-927-3363**, Fax: 256-927-6949.

Chilton County

Circuit & District Court *Felony, Misdemeanor, Civil, Eviction, Small Claims, Probate* PO Box 1946, Clanton, AL 35046. 8AM-5PM. **205-755-4275 Dist; 280-1844 Dist.**, Probate: 205-755-1555. Probate is a separate court. 🖥✋

Choctaw County

Circuit & District Court *Felony, Misdemeanor, Civil, Eviction, Small Claims, Probate* Choctaw County Courthouse, #10 PO Box 428, Butler, AL 36904. 8AM-4:30PM. **205-459-2155**, Probate: 205-459-2417. Probate is a separate court. 🖥✋

Clarke County

Circuit & District Court *Felony, Misdemeanor, Civil, Eviction, Small Claims, Probate* PO Box 921, Grove Hill, AL 36451. 8AM-5PM. **251-275-3363**, Probate: 251-275-3251. Probate is a separate court. ✉️✋

Clay County

Circuit & District Court *Felony, Misdemeanor, Civil, Eviction, Small Claims, Probate* PO Box 816, Ashland, AL 36251. 8AM-4:30PM. **256-354-7926**, Probate: 256-354-2198. Probate is a separate court. ✉️🖥✋

Cleburne County

Circuit & District Court *Felony, Misdemeanor, Civil, Eviction, Small Claims, Probate* 120 Vickery St Rm 202, Heflin, AL 36264. 8AM-4:30PM. **256-463-2651**, Fax: 256-463-2257, Probate: 256-463-5655. Probate is a separate court. ✉️🖥✋

Coffee County

Circuit & District Court - Enterprise Division *Felony, Misdemeanor, Civil, Eviction, Small Claims* PO Box 311284, Enterprise, AL 36331. 8AM-5PM. **334-347-2519**. ✉️🖥✋

Circuit & District Court - Elba Division *Felony, Misdemeanor, Civil, Eviction, Small Claims, Probate* 230 M Court Ave, Elba, AL 36323. 8:30AM-N, 1-4:30PM. **334-897-2954**. ✉️🖥✋

Probate Court - Enterprise Division *Probate* PO Box 311247, Enterprise, AL 36331. 8AM-4:30PM. **334-347-2688**, Fax: 334-347-2095.

Colbert County

Circuit Court *Felony, Civil Actions Over $10,000, Probate* Colbert County Courthouse 201 N Main St, Tuscumbia, AL 35674. 8AM-4:30PM. **256-386-8512**, Probate: 256-386-8542. Probate is a separate court. 🖥✋

District Court *Misdemeanor, Civil Actions Under $10,000, Eviction, Small Claims* Colbert County Courthouse 201 N Main St, Tuscumbia, AL 35674. 8AM-N; 1PM-4:30PM. **256-386-8518**. 🖥✋

Conecuh County

Circuit & District Court *Felony, Misdemeanor, Civil, Eviction, Small Claims, Probate* PO Box 107, Evergreen, AL 36401. 8AM-4:30PM. **251-578-2066**, Probate: 251-578-1221. Probate is a separate court. ✋

Coosa County

Circuit & District Court *Felony, Misdemeanor, Civil, Eviction, Small Claims, Probate* PO Box 98, Rockford, AL 35136. 8AM-4:30PM. **256-377-4988**, Fax: 256-377-1599, Probate: 256-377-4919. Probate is a separate court. 🖥✋Fax✉️

Covington County

Circuit & District Court *Felony, Misdemeanor, Civil, Eviction, Small Claims, Probate* Covington County Courthouse, Andalusia, AL 36420. 8AM-5PM. **334-428-2520**, Probate: 334-428-2510. Probate is a separate court. 🖥✋

Crenshaw County

Circuit & District Court *Felony, Misdemeanor, Civil, Eviction, Small Claims, Probate* PO Box 167, Luverne,

AL 36049. 8AM-4:30PM. **334-335-6575**, Fax: 334-335-2076, Probate: 334-335-6568. Porbate Court address is PO Box 328, Luverne 36049. ✉️🖥✋

Cullman County

Circuit Court *Felony, Civil Actions Over $10,000, Probate* Cullman County Courthouse, Rm 303 500 2nd Ave SW, Cullman, AL 35055. 8-4:30PM. **256-775-4654**, Probate: 256-775-4652. ✉️🖥✋

District Court *Misdemeanor, Civil Actions Under $10,000, Eviction, Small Claims* 500 2nd Ave SW Courthouse Rm 211, Cullman, AL 35055-4197. 8AM-4:30PM. **256-775-4660**. ✉️🖥✋

Dale County

Circuit & District Court *Felony, Misdemeanor, Civil, Eviction, Small Claims, Probate* PO Box 1350, Ozark, AL 36361. 8AM-4:30PM. **334-774-5003**, Probate: 334-774-2754. Probate is a separate court. 🖥✋

Dallas County

Circuit Court *Felony, Civil Actions Over $10,000, Probate* PO Box 1148, Selma, AL 36702. 8AM-5PM. **334-874-2523**. Probate is a separate court, and can be contacted 334-876-4830. ☎️✉️🖥✋

District Court *Misdemeanor, Civil Actions Under $10,000, Eviction, Small Claims* PO Box 1148, Selma, AL 36702. 8AM-5PM. **334-874-2523**. Probate court is separate form this court and can be reached at 334-876-4830. ✉️🖥✋

De Kalb County

Circuit & District Court *Felony, Misdemeanor, Civil, Eviction, Small Claims, Probate* PO Box 681149, Fort Payne, AL 35968. 8AM-4PM. **256-845-8525**, Probate: 256-845-8510. Probate is a separate court. ✉️🖥✋

Elmore County

Circuit & District Court - Civil Division *Civil, Probate* PO Box 310, Wetumpka, AL 36092. 8AM-4:30PM. **334-567-1123**, Fax: 334-567-5957, Probate: 334-567-1139. Probate is a separate court. Access civil records by 🖥✋.

Circuit Court - Criminal Division *Felony, Misdemeanor* PO Box 310 8935 US Hwy 23, Wetumpka, AL 36092.

8AM-4:30PM. **334-567-1123**, Fax: 334-567-5957. 💻✋

Escambia, County

Circuit & District Court *Felony, Misdemeanor, Civil, Eviction, Small Claims, Probate* PO Box 856, Brewton, AL 36427. 8AM-4:30PM. **251-867-0305**, Fax: 251-867-0365, Probate: 251-867-0201. Probate is a separate court. ✉**Fax**💻✋

Etowah County

Circuit & District Court *Felony, Misdemeanor, Civil, Eviction, Small Claims* 801 Forrest Ave #202, Gadsden, AL 35901. 8:30AM-4:30PM. **256-549-2150/5430**, Probate: 256-549-5333. Probate is a separate court. ✉💻✋

Probate Court 801 Forest Ave, #202, Gadsden, AL 35901. **256-549-2150**, Fax: 256-546-1149.

Fayette County

Circuit & District Court *Felony, Misdemeanor, Civil, Eviction, Small Claims, Probate* PO Box 906, Fayette, AL 35555. 8AM-4:30PM. **205-932-4617**, Probate: 205-932-4519. Probate is a separate court. 💻✉**Fax**✋

Franklin County

Circuit & District Court *Felony, Misdemeanor, Civil, Eviction, Small Claims, Probate* PO Box 160, Russellville, AL 35653. 8AM-4:30PM. **256-332-8861**, Probate: 256-332-8802. Probate is a separate court; Probate address is PO Box 70. ✉💻✋

Geneva County

Circuit & District Court *Felony, Misdemeanor, Civil, Eviction, Small Claims, Probate* PO Box 86, Geneva, AL 36340. 8AM-5PM. **334-684-5620**, Fax: 334-684-5605, Probate: 334-684-5640. Probate is a separate court. ✉💻✋

Greene County

Circuit & District Court *Felony, Misdemeanor, Civil, Eviction, Small Claims, Probate* PO Box 307, Eutaw, AL 35462. 8AM-12:00, 1-4:30PM. **205-372-3598**, Probate: 205-372-3340. Probate is a separate court. ✉💻✋

Hale County

Circuit & District Court *Felony, Misd., Civil, Eviction, Small Claims, Probate* Hale County Courthouse, Rm 8 PO

Drawer 99, Greensboro, AL 36744. 8AM-4:30PM. **334-624-4334**, Probate: 334-624-8740. Probate is a separate court. ✉💻✋

Henry County

Circuit & District Court *Felony, Misdemeanor, Civil, Eviction, Small Claims, Probate* 101 W Court St, #J, Abbeville, AL 36310-2135. 8AM-4:30PM. **334-585-2753**, Fax: 334-585-5006, Probate: 334-585-3257. Probate is a separate court. ✉💻✋

Houston County

Circuit & District Court *Felony, Misdemeanor, Civil, Eviction, Small Claims, Probate* PO Drawer 6406, Dothan, AL 36302. 7:30AM-4:30PM. **334-677-4800/4872**, Civil: Circ-334-677-4858; Dist-334-677-4868, Crim: Circ-334-677-4863; Dist-334-677-4872, Probate: 334-677-4719. Probate is a separate court. ✉💻✋

Jackson County

Circuit & District Court *Felony, Misdemeanor, Civil, Eviction, Small Claims, Probate* PO Box 397, Scottsboro, AL 35768. 8AM-4:30PM. **256-574-9320**, Fax: 256-259-9981. Civil phone: 256-574-9320, Crim: 256-574-9320, Probate: 256-574-9290. Probate court is a separate office at the courthouse (PO Box 128) and can be contacted at the telephone number above or 256-574-9295. ✉**Fax**💻✋

Jefferson County

Circuit Court - Bessemer Division *Felony, Civil Actions Over $10,000* Rm 606, Courthouse Annex, Bessemer, AL 35020. 8AM-5PM. **205-481-4165**. 💻✋

District Court - Bessemer Division *Misdemeanor, Civil Actions Under $10,000, Eviction, Small Claims* Rm 506, Courthouse Annex, Bessemer, AL 35020. 8AM-5PM. **205-481-4187**. 💻✋✉

Circuit Court - Birmingham Civil Division *Civil Actions Over $10,000 (Over $5,000 if jury trial)* 716 N 21st St, Rm 400, Birmingham, AL 35263. 8AM-5PM. **205-325-5355**. Access civil records by☎✉💻✋.

Circuit Court - Birmingham Criminal Division *Felony* 801 Richard Arrington Blvd Rm 901, Birmingham, AL 35263. 8AM-4:55PM. **205-325-5285**. 💻✋

District Court - Birmingham Civil Division *Civil Actions Under $10,000, Eviction, Small Claims* 716 Richard Arrington BLVD N, Birmingham, AL 35203. 8AM-5PM. **205-325-5331**. Access civil records by☎✉💻✋.

District Court - Birmingham Criminal Division *Misdemeanor* 801 Richard Arrington Blvd N, Rm 207, Birmingham, AL 35203. 8AM-5PM. **205-325-5309**. ✉💻✋

Probate Court 716 Richard Arrington Jr Blvd N., Birmingham, AL 35203. 8AM-4:45PM. **205-325-5420/ 5411**, Fax: 205-325-4885.

Lamar County

Circuit & District Court *Felony, Misdemeanor, Civil, Eviction, Small Claims, Probate* PO Box 434, Vernon, AL 35592. 8AM-4:30PM. **205-695-7193**, Fax: 205-695-1871, Probate: 205-695-9119. Probate is a separate court. ✉**Fax**💻✋

Lauderdale County

Circuit Court *Felony, Civil Actions Over $10,000, Probate* PO Box 795, Florence, AL 35631. 8AM-N, 1-5PM. **256-760-5710**, Crim: 256-760-5713, Probate: 256-760-5800. Probate is a separate court. 💻✋

District Court *Misdemeanor, Civil Actions Under $10,000, Eviction, Small Claims* PO Box 776, Florence, AL 35631. 8AM-N, 1-5PM. **256-760-5726**, Fax: 256-760-5727. Civil phone: 256-760-5722, Crim: 256-760-5724. ✉**Fax**💻✋

Lawrence County

Circuit & District Court *Felony, Misdemeanor, Civil, Eviction, Small Claims, Probate* PO Box 249, Moulton, AL 35650. 8AM-4PM. **256-974-2432**, Civil: 256-974-2435, Crim: 256-974-2436, Probate: 256-974-2439. Probate is a separate court. 💻✋

Lee County

Circuit & District Court *Felony, Misdemeanor, Civil, Eviction, Small Claims* 2311 Gateway Dr, Rm 104, Opelika, AL 36801. 8:30AM-4:30PM. **334-749-7141**, Fax: 334-737-3520. Probate is a separate court; Probate phone is 334-745-9761; address-Lee County Courthouse, 215 S 9 St, Opelika, AL 36801. ☎✉💻✋

Limestone County

Circuit & District Court *Felony, Misdemeanor, Civil, Eviction, Small Claims, Probate* 200 Washington St West, Athens, AL 35611. 8AM-4:30PM. **256-233-6406**, Probate: 256-233-6427. Probate is a separate court. ⊠ ✋ 🖥

Lowndes County

Circuit & District Court *Felony, Misdemeanor, Civil, Eviction, Small Claims, Probate* PO Box 876, Hayneville, AL 36040. 8AM-4:30PM. **334-548-2252**, Probate: 334-548-2365. Probate is a separate court. ⊠🖥✋

Macon County

Circuit & District Court *Felony, Misdemeanor, Civil, Eviction, Small Claims, Probate* PO Box 830723, Tuskegee, AL 36083. 8AM-12:00; 1-4:30PM. **334-724-2614**, Probate: 334-724-2611. Probate is a separate court. ⊠🖥✋

Madison County

Circuit Court - Civil *Civil Actions Over $10,000, Probate* 100 N Side Square, Courthouse, Huntsville, AL 35801. 8AM-5PM. **256-532-3381**, Probate: 256-532-3330. Probate is a separate court. Access civil records by🖥✋.

Circuit Court - Criminal *Felony* 100 N Side Square, Courthouse, Huntsville, AL 35801-4820. 8:30AM-5PM. **256-532-3386**. 🖥✋

District Court *Misdemeanor, Civil Actions Under $10,000, Eviction, Small Claims* 100 N Side Square, Rm 822 Courthouse, Huntsville, AL 35801. 8:30AM-5PM. Fax: 256-532-6972. Civil phone: 256-532-3622, Crim: 256-532-3373. 🖥✋

Marengo County

Circuit & District Court *Felony, Misdemeanor, Civil, Eviction, Small Claims, Probate* PO Box 480566, Linden, AL 36748. 8AM-4:30PM. **334-295-2220**. ⊠🖥✋

Marion County

Circuit & District Court *Felony, Misdemeanor, Civil, Eviction, Small Claims, Probate* PO Box 1595, Hamilton, AL 35570. 8AM-5PM. **205-921-7451**, Probate: 205-921-2471. Probate is a separate court. ⊠🖥✋

Marshall County

Circuit & District Court - Albertville Division *Felony, Misdemeanor, Civil, Eviction, Small Claims* 133 S.Emmet St., Albertville, AL 35950. 8AM-4:30PM. **256-878-4522/4521/4515**. ✋

Circuit Court - Guntersville Civil Division *Civil Actions Over $10,000, Small Claims, Probate* 424 Blount Ave #201, Guntersville, AL 35976. 8AM-12:00; 1-4:30PM. **256-571-7788**, Probate: 256-571-7764. Probate is a separate court. Access civil records by 🖥✋.

Circuit Court - Guntersville Criminal Division *Felony, Misdemeanor* 424 Blount Ave #201, Guntersville, AL 35976. 8AM-12:00 1-4:30PM. **256-571-7791**. 🖥✋

Mobile County

Circuit Court *Felony, Civil Actions Over $10,000* 205 Government St #C-913, Mobile, AL 36644-2913. 8AM-5PM. **251-574-8786**. 🖥✋

District Court *Misdemeanor, Civil Actions Under $10,000, Eviction, Small Claims, Probate* 205 Government St, Mobile, AL 36644. 8AM-5PM. **251-574-8520, 251-690-8525 (small claims)**, Fax: 251-574-4840. Civil phone: 251-574-8526, Crim: 251-574-8511, Probate: 251-574-8502. Probate court is a separate court. ☎Fax⊠🖥✋

Monroe County

Circuit & District Court *Felony, Misdemeanor, Civil, Eviction, Small Claims, Probate* County Courthouse 65 N Alabama Ave, Monroeville, AL 36460. 8AM-5PM. **251-743-2283**, Probate: 251-743-4107. Probate is a separate court. ⊠🖥✋

Montgomery County

Circuit Court *Felony, Civil Actions Over $10,000, Probate* PO Box 1667, Montgomery, AL 36102-1667. 8AM-1100-11:30-4PM. **334-832-1260**, Probate: 334-832-1237. Probate is a separate court. ⊠🖥✋

District Court *Misdemeanor, Civil Actions Under $10,000, Eviction, Small Claims* PO Box 1667, Montgomery, AL 36102. 8AM-11:30AM, 12:30PM-4PM. **334-832-4950**. ⊠🖥✋

Morgan County

Circuit Court *Felony, Civil Actions Over $10,000, Probate* PO Box 668, Decatur, AL 35602. 8AM-4:30PM. **256-351-4790**, Probate: 256-351-4675. Probate is a separate court. 🖥✋

District Court *Misdemeanor, Civil Actions Under $10,000, Eviction, Small Claims* PO Box 668, Decatur, AL 35602. 8:30-4:30PM. **256-351-4649**. 🖥✋⊠

Perry County

Circuit & District Court *Felony, Misdemeanor, Civil, Eviction, Small Claims, Probate* PO Box 505, Marion, AL 36756. 8AM-4:30PM. **334-683-6106**, Probate: 334-683-2210. Probate is a separate court. ⊠🖥✋

Pickens County

Circuit & District Court *Felony, Misdemeanor, Civil, Eviction, Small Claims, Probate* PO Box 418, Carrollton, AL 35447. 8AM-4:30PM. **205-367-2050**, Probate: 205-367-2010. ⊠🖥✋

Pike County

Circuit & District Court *Felony, Misdemeanor, Civil, Eviction, Small Claims, Probate* 120 W Church St, Troy, AL 36081. 8AM-5PM. **334-566-4622**, Probate: 334-566-1246. Probate is a separate court. ⊠🖥✋

Randolph County

Circuit & District Court *Felony, Misdemeanor, Civil, Eviction, Small Claims, Probate* PO Box 328, Wedowee, AL 36278. 8AM-N, 1-5PM. **256-357-4551**, Probate: 256-357-4933. Probate is a separate court. 🖥✋

Russell County

Circuit & District Court *Felony, Misdemeanor, Civil, Eviction, Small Claims, Probate* PO Box 518, Phenix City, AL 36868. 8:30AM-4:PM. **334-298-0516**, Fax: 334-297-6250, Probate: 334-298-7979. ⊠🖥

St. Clair County

Circuit & District Court - Ashville Division *Felony, Misdemeanor, Civil, Eviction, Small Claims, Probate* www.stclairco.com/ PO Box 1569, Ashville, AL 35953. 8AM-5PM. **205-594-2184**, Probate: 205-594-2120. Probate is a separate court. ⊠🖥✋

Key: Symbols refer to criminal records access unless otherwise noted. phone-☎ mail-⊠ fax-**Fax** in person-✋ online-🖥 email-**Email**

Circuit & District Court - Pell City Division *Felony, Misdemeanor, Civil, Eviction, Small Claims, Probate* 1815 Cogswell Ave, #217, Pell City, AL 35125. 8AM-5PM. **205-338-2511; Circuit: 205-338-7224 District**, Probate: 205-338-9449. Probate is separate court. ✉️🖥️✋

Shelby County

Circuit & District Court *Felony, Misdemeanor, Civil, Eviction, Small Claims, Probate* PO Box 1810, Columbiana, AL 35051. 8AM-4:30PM. **205-669-3760**, Probate: 205-669-3711. Probate is a separate court. ✉️**Fax**🖥️✋

Sumter County

Circuit & District Court *Felony, Misdemeanor, Civil, Eviction, Small Claims* PO Box 936 (115 Franklin St), Livingston, AL 35470. 8-4:30PM. **205-652-2291**, prob: 205-652-7281. ✉️🖥️✋

Probate Court PO Box 1040, Livingston, AL 35470. 8AM-4PM. **205-652-7281**, Fax: 205-652-2606 Access civil records by✉️✚✋

Talladega County

Circuit & District Court - Northern Division *Felony, Misd., Civil, Eviction, Small Claims Probate* PO 6137 148 E. St N, Talladega, AL 35161. 8AM-5PM. **256-761-2102**. 🖥️✋

District Court - Southern Division *Misdemeanor, Civil Actions Under $10,000, Eviction, Small Claims* PO Box 183, Sylacauga, AL 35150. 7:30AM-4:30AM. **256-245-4352**. Access ✉️🖥️✋

Probate Court PO Box 737, Talladega, AL 35161. 8AM-5PM. **256-362-4175**, Fax: 256-761-2128.

Tallapoosa County

Circuit & District Court - Eastern Division *Felony, Misdemeanor, Civil, Eviction, Small Claims, Probate* Tallapoosa County Courthouse, Dadeville, AL 36853. 8AM-5PM. **256-825-1098**, Probate: 256-825-4266. Probate is a separate court. ✉️🖥️✋

Circuit & District Court - Western Division *Felony, Misdemeanor, Civil, Eviction, Small Claims* PO Box 189, Alexander City, AL 35011. 8AM-5PM. **256-329-8123/234-4361**. Access ✉️🖥️✋

Tuscaloosa County

Circuit Court - Civil *Civil Actions over $10,000.* 714 Greensboro Ave, Tuscaloosa, AL 35401. 8:30AM-5PM. **205-349-3870**, Civil: Circ-205-349-3870 X260; Dist: X357, Probate: 205-349-3870 X203. Probate is a separate court. Access civil records by🖥️✋.

District Courts - Civil *Civil Actions Under $10,000, Probate* 714 Greensboro Ave, Tuscaloosa, AL 35401. 8:30AM-5PM. **205-349-3870**, Civil: 205-349-3870 x355, Probate: 205-349-3870 x203. Probate is a separate court. Access civil records by🖥️✋

Circuit Court - Criminal *Felony* 714 Greensboro Ave, 3rd Fl, Tuscaloosa, AL 35401. 8AM-5PM. **205-349-3870 X326**. ✉️🖥️✋

District Court - Criminal Division *Misdemeanor* PO Box 1687, Tuscaloosa, AL 35403. 8:30AM-5PM. **205-349-3870 X357**. ☎️✉️🖥️✋

Walker County

Circuit & District Court *Felony, Misdemeanor, Civil, Eviction, Small Claims, Probate* PO Box 749, Jasper, AL 35502. 8AM-4:30PM. **205-384-7268**, Fax: 205-384-7271. Probate is a separate court; Probate address- PO Box 502; Probate phone- 205-384-7281. 🖥️✋

Washington County

Circuit & District Court *Felony, Misd., Civil, Eviction, Small Claims, Probate* www.millry.net/~spgrimes PO Box 548, Chatom, AL 36518. 8AM-4:30PM. **251-847-2239**. 🖥️✋

Wilcox County

Circuit & District Court *Felony, Misdemeanor, Civil, Eviction, Small Claims, Probate* PO Box 608, Camden, AL 36726. 8AM-N, 1-5PM. **334-682-4126**, Probate: 334-682-4883. Probate is a separate court. ✉️🖥️✋

Winston County

Circuit & District Court *Felony, Misdemeanor, Civil, Eviction, Small Claims, Probate* PO Box 309, Double Springs, AL 35553. 8AM-4:30PM. **205-489-5533**, Fax: 205-489-1225, Probate: 205-489-5219. Probate is a separate court. 🖥️✋

Alaska

State Court Administration: Office of the Administrative Director, 820 W 4th Ave, Anchorage, AK, 99501; 907-264-8269, Fax: 907-264-8291. http://www.state.ak.us/courts/

Court Structure: Alaska is not organized into counties, but rather into 15 boroughs (3 unified home rule municipalities that are combination borough and city, and 12 boroughs) and 12 home rule cities, which do not directly coincide with the 4 Judicial Districts into which the judicial system is divided. In other words, judicial boundaries cross borough boundaries. It is a unified, centrally administered, and totally state-funded judicial system. Municipal governments do not maintain separate court systems.

The four levels of courts in the Alaska Court System are the supreme court, the court of appeals, the superior court and the district court. The supreme court and the court of appeals are appellate courts, while the superior and district courts are trial courts. Probate is handled by the superior courts. The superior court is the trial court of general jurisdiction. There are 34 superior court judgeships located throughout the state. The district court is a trial court of limited jurisdiction. The district court currently has 17 judges in the state. The superior court serves as an appellate court for appeals from civil and criminal cases which have been tried in the district court.

We have listed the courts by their borough or home rule city in keeping with a convenient alphabetical format. You should search through the city court location names to determine the correct court for your search. The First District encompasses all of S.E.

Key: Symbols refer to criminal records access unless otherwise noted. phone-☎️ mail-✉️ fax-**Fax** in person-✋ online-🖥️ email-**Email**

Alaska. Magistrates act as judicial officers. This 1st District has five trial courts/Superior courts: Ketchikan, Wrangell, Petersburg, Sitka and Juneau. District Magistrate Courts are Haines, Skagway, Yakutat, Angoon, Kake, Hoona, Craig.

Online Access: You may do a name search of a nearly statewide Alaska Trial Courts database index at www.state.ak.us/courts/names.htm. Search results give case number, file date, disposition date, charge, and sentence. The index gives the name used on the first pleading only. The index is updated every 90 days. This search in and by itself is not FCRA-compliant for employment screening purposes. The civil/criminal name index is available to anyone who sends a blank CD-ROM each quarter to the Administrative Director. The home web page gives access to Appellate opinions.

Additional Information: Documents may not be filed by fax in any Alaska court location without prior authorization of a judge.

The fees established by court rules for Alaska courts are: search fee - $15.00 per hour or fraction thereof; certification fee - $5.00 per document and $2.00 per additional copy of the document; copy fee - $.25 per page.

Magistrate Courts vary widely in how records are maintained and their hours of operation (some open only a few hours per week)

Aleutian Islands

Unalaska District Court (3rd District)
Felony, Misdemeanor, Civil PO Box 245, Unalaska, AK 99685-0245. 8AM-4:30PM. **907-581-1266**, Fax: 907-581-2809. 🖐✉🖥

Anchorage Borough

Superior & District Court (3rd District)
Felony, Misd., Civil, Eviction, Small Claims, Probate 825 W4th, Anchorage, AK 99501-2004. 8AM-4:30PM. **907-264-0491**, Fax: 907-264-0873, Probate: 907-264-0436. Fax✉🖐

Bethel District

Aniak District Court (4th District)
Misdemeanor, Civil Actions Under $7,500, Small Claims PO Box 147, Aniak, AK 99557-0147. 8AM-4:30PM. **907-675-4325**, Fax: 907-675-4278. 📞✉Fax🖐

Superior & District Court (4th District)
Felony, Misd., Civil, Eviction, Small Claims, Probate PO Box 130, Bethel, AK 99559-0130. 8AM-4:30PM,9-4:30 W. **907-543-2298**, Fax 907-543-4419. Access records by Fax✉🖐🖥

Bristol Bay Borough

Naknek Magistrate Court (3rd District)
Felony, Misdemeanor, Civil Actions Under $7,500, Small Claims PO Box 229, Naknek, AK 99633-0229. 8:30AM-4PM. **907-246-6151**, Fax: 907-246-7418. Naknek is 3NA on the state court record numbers. Some Lake and Peninsula cases heard here. ✉🖐🖥

Denali Borough

Healy Magistrate Court (4th District)
Misd., Civil Actions Under $7,500, Small Claims PO Box 298, Healy, AK 99743-0298. 8AM-4:30PM. **907-683-2213**, Fax: 907-683-1383. Felony cases are at

Fairbanks Superior & District Court. 📞✉Fax🖐🖥

Dillingham

Dillingham Superior Court (3rd District) *Felony, Misd., Civil, Small Claims* PO Box 909, Dillingham, AK 99576-0909. 8AM-4:30PM. **907-842-5215**, Fax: 907-842-5746. 🖐✉🖥

Fairbanks North Star

Superior & District Court (4th District)
Felony, Misd., Civil, Eviction, Small Claims, Probate 101 Lacey St, Fairbanks, AK 99701-4761. 8AM-4:30PM. **907-452-9277**, Fax: 907-452-9330. Civil phone: 907-452-9267, Crim: 907-452-9289, Probate: 907-452-9256. Access by 🖐🖥

Haines Borough

District Court (1st District) *Misd., Civil Actions Under $50,000, Small Claims* PO Box 169, Haines, AK 99827-0169. 8AM-N, 1-4:30PM. **907-766-2801**, Fax: 907-766-3148. Felony cases are at Juneau Superior & District Court. 📞Fax✉🖐🖥

Juneau Borough

Superior & District Court (1st District)
Felony, Misd., Civil, Eviction, Small Claims, Probate Dimond Courthouse PO Box 114100, Juneau, AK 99811-4100. 8AM-4:30PM,M-Th, 9AM-4:30 F. **907-463-4700**, Fax: 907-463-3788. Fax✉🖐🖥

Kenai Peninsula Borough

Superior & District Court (3rd District)
Felony, Misd., Civil, Eviction, Small Claims, Probate 125 Trading Bay Dr, #100, Kenai, AK 99611. 8AM-4:30PM. **907-283-3110**, Fax: 907-283-8535. ✉🖐🖥

District Court (3rd District) *Misd., Civil Actions Under $50,000, Small Claims*

3670 Lake St, #400, Homer, AK 99603-9647. 8AM-4:30PM. **907-235-8171**, Fax: 907-235-4257. 📞Fax✉🖐🖥

Seward Magistrate Court (3rd District)
Misd., Civil Actions Under $7,500, Small Claims PO Box 1929 5th and Adams Strs, Seward, AK 99664-1929. 8AM-4:30PM. **907-224-3075**, Fax: 907-224-7192. 🖐✉🖥

Ketchikan Gateway Borough

Superior & District Court (1st District)
Felony, Misd., Civil, Eviction, Small Claims, Probate 415 Main, Rm 400, Ketchikan, AK 99901-6399. 8AM-4:30PM M-Th, 9AM-4:30PM Fridays. **907-225-3195**, Fax: 907-225-7849. Fax✉🖐🖥

Kodiak Island Borough

Superior & District Court (3rd District)
Felony, Misd., Civil, Eviction, Small Claims, Probate 204 Mission Road, Rm 10, Kodiak, AK 99615-7312. 8AM-4:30PM M,T,Th,F; 9AM-4:30PM W. **907-486-1600**, Fax: 907-486-1660. ✉Fax🖐🖥

Matanuska-Susitna

Superior & District Court (3rd District)
Felony, Misd., Civil, Eviction, Small Claims, Probate 435 S Denali, Palmer, AK 99645-6437. 8AM-4:30PM. Fax: 907-746-4151. Civil phone: 907-746-8108, Crim: 907-746-8104. ✉🖐🖥

Nome

Superior & District Court (2nd District) *Felony, Misdemeanor, Civil, Eviction, Small Claims, Probate* PO Box 1110, Nome, AK 99762-1110. 8AM-4:30PM. **907-443-5216**, Fax: 907-443-2192. Fax✉🖐🖥

Unalakleet Magistrate Court (2nd District) *Misdemeanor, Civil Actions*

Key: Symbols refer to criminal records access unless otherwise noted. phone-📞 mail-✉ fax-Fax in person-🖐 online-🖥 email-Email

Under $7,500, Small Claims PO Box 250, Unalakleet, AK 99684-0250. 8AM-4PM. **907-624-3015**, Fax: 907-624-3118. This is a one-person court. 🤚✉️**Fax**

North Slope Borough

Superior & District Court (2nd District) *Felony, Misdemeanor, Civil, Eviction, Small Claims, Probate* PO Box 270, Barrow, AK 99723-0270. 8AM-4:30PM. **907-852-4800 X80**, Fax: 907-852-4804. **Fax**✉️🤚🖥️

Northwest Arctic Borough

Superior & District Court (2nd District) *Felony, Misdemeanor, Civil, Eviction, Small Claims, Probate* PO Box 317 605 3rd Ave, Kotzebue, AK 99752-0317. 8AM-4:30PM. **907-442-3208**, Fax: 907-442-3974. This court holds records for the closed Magistrate Court formerly in Ambler. ✉️**Fax**🤚🖥️

Prince of Wales-Outer Ketchikan

Craig Magistrate Court (1st District) *Misd., Civil Actions Under $7,500, Small Claims* PO Box 646, Craig, AK 99921-0646. 8AM-4:30PM. **907-826-3316/3306**, Fax: 907-826-3904. Felony cases are at Ketchican Superior & District Court. 🤚☎️**Fax**✉️🖥️

Sitka Borough

Superior & District Court (1st District) *Felony, Misd., Civil, Eviction, Small Claims, Probate* 304 Lake St, Rm 203, Sitka, AK 99835-7759. 8AM-4:30PM. **907-747-3291**, Fax: 907-747-6690. ☎️**Fax**✉️🤚🖥️

Skagway-Yakutat-Angoon

Hoonah District Court (1st District) *Misd., Civil Actions Under $50,000, Small Claims* PO Box 430, Hoonah, AK 99829-0430. 8AM-N, 1-4:30PM. **907-945-3668**, Fax: 907-945-3637. Felony cases are at Juneau Superior & Dist. Court. ✉️🤚

Skagway District Magistrate Court *Misdemeanor, Civil Actions Under $7,500, Small Claims* PO Box 495, Skagway, AK 99840-0495. 8AM-N, 1-4PM M-T-W; 8AM-N, 1-3:30PM Thurs. **907-983-2368**, Fax: 907-983-3801. Hours will vary from Summer to Winter. Summer hours-M-Tu 8:30-4; W-8:45-4; Th-9-4; F-8:15-10AM, closed 12-1PM for lunch. Felony cases are at Juneau Superior & Dist. Court. 🤚**Fax**✉️

Yakutat Magistrate Court (1st District) *Misdemeanor, Civil Actions Under $7,500, Small Claims* PO Box 426, Yakutat, AK 99689-0426. 9AM-4:30PM M-Th. **907-784-3274** (phone number subject to change), Fax: 907-784-3257. Felony cases are at Juneau Superior & Dist. Court. ✉️**Fax**🤚**Email**

Angoon Magistrate Court (1st District) *Misdemeanor, Civil Actions Under $7,500, Small Claims* PO Box 250, Angoon, AK 99820-0123. 1PM-4:30PM. **907-788-3229**, Fax: 907-788-3108. Felony cases are at Sitka Superior & Dist. Court. ☎️✉️**Fax**🤚

Southeast Fairbanks

Delta Junction Magistrate Court (4th District) *Misdemeanor, Civil Actions Under $7,500, Small Claims* PO Box 401, Delta Junction, AK 99737-0401. 8AM-N, 1-4:30PM. **907-895-4211**, Fax: 907-895-4204. Felony cases are at Fairbanks Superior & District Court. ☎️✉️**Fax**🤚🖥️

Tok Magistrate Court (4th District) *Misd, Civil Actions Under $7,500, Small Claims* PO Box 187, Tok, AK 99780-0187. 8AM-N; 1PM-4:30PM. **907-883-5171**, Fax: 907-883-4367. Felony cases are at Fairbanks Superior & District Court. 🤚☎️✉️🖥️

Valdez-Cordova

Superior & District Court (3rd District) *Felony, Misd., Civil, Eviction, Small Claims, Probate* PO Box 127 213 Meals, Valdez, AK 99686-0127. 8AM-4:30PM. **907-835-2266**, Fax: 907-835-3764. **Fax**✉️🤚🖥️

Cordova Court (3rd District) *Felony, Misdemeanor, Civil, Small Claims, Probate* PO Box 898, Cordova, AK 99574-0898. 8-4:30PM. **907-424-3378**, Fax: 907-424-7581. ☎️✉️**Fax**🤚🖥️

Glennallen District Court (3rd District) *Misdemeanor, Civil, Small Claims* PO Box 86, Glennallen, AK 99588-0086. 8AM-4:30PM. **907-822-3405**. ✉️🤚🖥️

Wade Hampton

St Mary's Magistrate Court (Bethel Area) *Misdemeanor, Civil Actions Under $10,000, Small Claims* PO Box 269, St Mary's, AK 99658-0183. 8AM-N, 1-4:30PM. **907-438-2912**, Fax: 907-438-2819. Felony cases are at Bethel Superior & District Court. 🤚✉️

Chevak Magistrate Court (Bethel Area) *Misdemeanor, Civil Actions Under $7,500, Small Claims* PO Box 238, Chevak, AK 99563-0238. 8AM-4:30PM. **907-858-7231**, Fax: 907-858-7230. Felony cases at Bethel Superior & District Court. ✉️**Fax**🤚

Emmonak Magistrate Court (Bethel Area) *Misdemeanor, Civil Actions Under $15,000, Small Claims* PO Box 176, Emmonak, AK 99581-0176. 8AM-4:30PM. **907-949-1748**, Fax: 907-949-1535. Felony cases are at Bethel Superior & District Court. 🤚✉️

Wrangell-Petersburg

Wrangell Superior & District Court (1st District) *Felony, Misdemeanor, Civil, Eviction, Small Claims, Probate* PO Box 869, Wrangell, AK 99929-0869. 8AM-4:30PM. **907-874-2311**, Fax: 907-874-3509. The TDD office can be reached at 907-874-2313. ☎️**Fax**✉️🤚🖥️

Petersburg Superior & District Court (1st District) *Felony, Misdemeanor, Civil, Eviction, Small Claims, Probate* PO Box 1009, Petersburg, AK 99833-1009. 8AM-4:30PM. **907-772-3824**, Fax: 907-772-3018. ☎️**Fax**✉️🤚🖥️

Kake Magistrate Court (1st District) *Misdemeanor, Civil Actions Under $7,500, Small Claims* PO Box 100, Kake, AK 99830-0100. 8AM-N. **907-785-3651**, Fax: 907-785-3152. 🤚✉️

Yukon-Koyukuk

Galena Magistrate Court (4th District) *Misdemeanor, Civil Actions Under $7,500, Small Claims* PO Box 167, Galena, AK 99741-0167. 8AM-4:30PM. **907-656-1322**, Fax: 907-656-1546. Felony cases are at Fairbanks Superior & District Court. 🤚✉️

Nenana Magistrate Court (4th District) *Misd., Civil Actions Under $7,500, Small Claims* PO Box 449, Nenana, AK 99760-0449. 8:30AM-4PM. **907-832-5430**, Fax: 907-832-5841. Felony cases are at Fairbanks Superior & District Court. 🤚☎️🖥️

Fort Yukon Magistrate Court (4th District) *Misdemeanor, Civil Actions Under $7,500, Small Claims* PO Box 211, Fort Yukon, AK 99740-0211. 9:30AM-3PM. **907-662-2336**, Fax: 907-662-2824. Felony cases are at Fairbanks Superior & District Court. ✉️🤚**Fax**

Tanana Magistrate Court (4th District) *Misd., Civil Actions Under $7,500, Small Claims* PO Box 449, Nenana, AK 99777. Th-F 2nd full week each month. **907-366-7243**, Fax: 907-832-5841. Magistrate may also be contacted by phone at 907-832- 5430. Felony cases at Fairbanks Superior & District Court. 🖐☎✉

Arizona

State Court Administration: Administrative Office of the Courts, Arizona Supreme Court Bldg, 1501 W Washington, Phoenix, AZ, 85007; 602-542-9301, Fax: 602-542-9484. http://www.supreme.state.az.us

Court Structure: The Superior Court is the court of general jurisdiction. Justice, and Municipal courts generally have separate jurisdiction over case types as indicated in the text. Most courts will search their records by plaintiff or defendant. Estate cases are handled by Superior Court. Fees are the same as for civil and criminal case searching.

Online Access: The Arizona Judicial Branch offers Public Access to Court Case Information, a valuable online service providing a resource for information about court cases from 137 out of 180 superior, justice, and municipal courts in Arizona. Access information includes: detailed case information, i.e., case type, charges, filing and disposition dates; the parties in the case, not including victims and witnesses; and the court mailing address and location. Go to http://www.supreme.state.az.us/publicaccess/.

The Maricopa and Pima county courts maintain their own systems, but will also, under current planning, be part of ACAP. These two counties provide ever-increasing online access to the public.

Additional Information: Public access to all Maricopa County court case indexes is available at a central location - 1 W Madison Ave in Phoenix. Copies, however, must be obtained from the court where the case is heard.

Many offices do not perform searches due to personnel and/or budget constraints. As computerization of record offices increases across the state, more record offices are providing public access computer terminals.

Fees across all jurisdictions, as established by the Arizona Supreme Court and State Legislature, are as follows as of August 9, 2001: search - Superior Court: $18.00 per name; lower courts: $17.00 per name; certification - Superior Court: $18.00 per document; lower courts: $17.00 per document; copies - $.50 per page. Courts may choose to charge no fees.

As of Fall, 2001, Justice Courts accept civil actions up to $10,000; the increase is due to higher value claims in landlord/tenant cases. Civil cases between $5,000 and $10,000 may be filed at either Justice or Superior Courts.

Apache County

Superior Court *Felony, Civil Over $5,000, Probate* www.co.apache.az.us/clerk/ PO Box 365, St Johns, AZ 85936. 8AM-5PM. **928-337-7550**, Fax: 928-337-2771. ✉🖐💻

Puerco Justice Court *Misdemeanor, Civil Actions Under $10,000, Eviction, Small Claims* PO Box 610, Sanders, AZ 86512. 8AM-N, 1-5PM. **928-688-2954**, Fax: 928-688-2244. ✉🖐💻

Chinle Justice Court *Misdemeanor, Civil Actions Under $10,000, Eviction, Small Claims* PO Box 888, Chinle, AZ 86503. 8AM-5PM. **928-674-5922**, Fax: 928-674-5926. ✉🖐💻Fax

St Johns Justice Court *Misdemeanor, Civil Actions Under $10,000, Eviction, Small Claims* PO Box 308, St Johns, AZ 85936. 8AM-5PM. **928-337-7558**, Fax: 928-337-2683. ✉🖐💻

Round Valley Justice Court *Misdemeanor, Civil Actions Under $10,000, Eviction, Small Claims* PO Box 1356, Springerville, AZ 85938. 8AM-N, 1-5PM. **928-333-4613**, Fax: 928-333-4205. ☎Fax✉🖐💻

Cochise County

Superior Court *Felony, Civil Over $5,000, Probate* www.co.cochise.az.us/Court/Crtclerk.htm PO Box CK, Bisbee, AZ 85603. 8AM-5PM. **520-432-8604**, Fax: 520-432-4850. Access-Fax✉🖐email💻

Douglas Justice Court *Misdemeanor, Civil Actions Under $10,000, Eviction, Small Claims* 661 G Ave, Douglas, AZ 85607. 8AM-5PM. **520-805-5640**, Fax: 520-364-3684. Fax✉🖐💻

Bowie Justice Court *Misdemeanor, Civil Actions Under $10,000, Eviction, Small Claims* PO Box 317, Bowie, AZ 85605. 8AM-5PM. **520-847-2303**, Fax: 520-847-2242. ☎Fax✉🖐💻

Benson Justice Court *Misdemeanor, Civil Actions Under $10,000, Eviction, Small Claims* 126 W 5th St, #1, Benson, AZ 85602. 8AM-5PM. **520-586-8100**, Fax: 520-586-9647. Fax✉🖐💻

Willcox Justice Court *Misdemeanor, Civil Actions Under $10,000, Eviction, Small Claims* 450 S Haskell, Willcox, AZ 85643. 8AM-5PM. **520-384-7000**, Fax: 520-384-4305. ☎Fax✉🖐💻

Bisbee Justice Court *Misdemeanor, Civil Actions Under $10,000, Eviction, Small Claims* 207 N Judd Dr, Bisbee, AZ 85603. 8AM-5PM. **520-432-9542**, Fax: 520-432-9594. Fax✉🖐💻

Sierra Vista Justice Court *Misdemeanor, Civil Actions Under $10,000, Eviction, Small Claims* 4001 E Foothills Dr, Sierra Vista, AZ 85635. 8AM-5PM. **520-803-3801**, Fax: 520-439-9106. Fax✉🖐💻

Coconino County

Superior Court *Felony, Civil Actions Over $5,000, Probate* 200 N San Francisco St, Flagstaff, AZ 86001. 8AM-5PM. **928-779-6535**. ✉🖐💻

Page Justice Court *Misdemeanor, Civil Actions Under $10,000, Eviction, Small Claims* PO Box 1565, Page, AZ 86040. 8AM-5PM. **928-645-8871**, Fax: 928-645-1869. ✉✋🖥

Fredonia Justice Court *Misdemeanor, Civil Actions Under $10,000, Eviction, Small Claims* PO Box 559 112 N Main, Fredonia, AZ 86022-0559. 8AM-5PM. **928-643-7472**, Fax 928-643-7491. ✉✋

Flagstaff Justice Court *Misdemeanor, Civil Actions Under $10,000, Eviction, Small Claims* 200 N San Franciso St., Flagstaff, AZ 86001. 8AM-5PM. **928-779-6806**. ✉✋🖥

Williams Justice Court *Misdemeanor, Civil Actions Under $10,000, Eviction, Small Claims* 700 W Rail Road Ave, Williams, AZ 86046. 8AM-N; 1-5PM. **928-635-2691**. ✉✋🖥

Gila County

Superior Court *Felony, Civil Actions Over $5,000, Probate* 1400 E Ash, Globe, AZ 85501. 8AM-5PM. **928-425-3231 X8553**. ✉✋🖥

Payson Justice Court *Misdemeanor, Civil Actions Under $10,000, Eviction, Small Claims* 714 S Beeline Hwy, #103, Payson, AZ 85541. 8AM-5PM. **928-474-5267**, Fax: 928-474-6214. This court holds the records for the Pine Justice Court which is closed. ☎Fax✉✋🖥

Globe Regional Justice Court *Misdemeanor, Civil Actions Under $10,000, Eviction, Small Claims* Globe/Miami Magistrate Court 1400 E Ash, Globe, AZ 85501. 8AM-5PM. **928-425-3231 x8545**, Fax: 928-425-4773. This courts holds the records for the justice courts formally located in Miami and Hayden/Winkelman. ✉Fax✋🖥

Graham County

Superior Court *Felony, Civil Actions Over $5,000, Probate* 800 Main St, Safford, AZ 85546-3803. 8AM-5PM. **928-428-3100**, Fax: 928-428-0061. ☎Fax✉✋🖥

Justice Court Precinct #1 *Misdemeanor, Civil Actions Under $10,000, Eviction* 800 W Main St, Safford, AZ 85546. 8AM-5PM. **928-428-1210**, Fax: 928-428-3523. ✉✋🖥

Pima Justice Court Precinct #2 *Misdemeanor, Civil Actions Under $10,000, Eviction, Small Claims* PO Box 1159, 136 W Center St, Pima, AZ 85543. 8AM-5PM. **928-485-2771**, Fax: 928-485-9961. Fax✉✋🖥

Greenlee County

Superior Court *Felony, Civil Actions Over $5,000, Probate* PO Box 1027, Clifton, AZ 85533. 8AM-5PM. **928-865-4242**, Fax: 928-865-5358. ✉✋🖥

Justice Court Precinct #2 *Misdemeanor, Civil Actions Under $10,000, Eviction, Small Claims* PO Box 208, **Duncan**, AZ 85534. 9AM-5PM. **928-359-2536**, Fax: 928-359-1936. ✉✋🖥

Justice Court Precinct #1 *Misdemeanor, Civil Actions Under $10,000, Eviction, Small Claims* PO Box 517, **Clifton**, AZ 85533. 9AM-5PM. **928-865-4312**, Fax: 928-865-5644. ✉✋🖥

La Paz County

Superior Court *Felony, Civil Actions Over $5,000, Probate* www.co.la-paz.az.us/courts.htm 1316 Kofa Ave, #607, Parker, AZ 85344. 8AM-5PM. **928-669-6131**, Fax: 928-669-2186. ✉✋🖥

Parker Justice Court *Misdemeanor, Civil Actions Under $10,000, Eviction, Small Claims* 1105 Arizona Ave, Parker, AZ 85344. 8AM-5PM. **928-669-2504**, Fax: 928-669-2915. ✉✋🖥

Quartzsite Justice Court *Misdemeanor, Civil Actions Under $10,000, Eviction, Small Claims* PO Box 580, Quartzsite, AZ 85346. 8AM-5PM. **928-927-6313**, Fax: 928-927-4842. Fax✉✋🖥

Salome Justice Court *Misdemeanor, Civil Actions Under $10,000, Eviction, Small Claims* PO Box 661, Salome, AZ 85348. 8AM-5PM. **928-859-3871**, Fax: 928-859-3709. ✉✋🖥

Maricopa County

Superior Court *Felony, Civil Over $5,000, Probate* www.superiorcourt.maricopa.gov 601 W Jackson St., Phoenix, AZ 85003. 8AM-5PM. **602-506-3360**, Fax: 602-506-7619. Fax✉🖥✋

Maricopa Cty. Justice Courts www.superiorcourt.maricopa.gov/justiceCourts/

Chandler Justice Court *Misd., Civil Actions $10,000, Eviction, Small Claims* 2051 W Warner Rd, #20, Chandler, AZ 85224. 8AM-5PM. **480-963-6691**. ✉✋

Buckeye Justice Court *Misd., Civil Under $10,000, Eviction, Small Claims* 100 N Apache Rd, Buckeye, AZ 85326. 8AM-5PM. **623-386-4289**, Fax: 623-386-5796. ✉✋

South Phoenix Justice Court *Misdemeanor, Civil Actions Under $10,000, Eviction, Small Claims* 217 E Olympic Dr, Phoenix, AZ 85040. 8-5PM. **602-243-0318**, Fax: 602-243-6389. ✋

East Tempe Justice Court *Misd., Civil Under $10,000, Eviction, Small Claims* 1845 E Broadway, #8, Tempe, AZ 85282. 8AM-5PM. **480-967-8856**, Fax: 480-921-7413. ✉✋

Scottsdale Justice Court *Misd., Civil Under $10,000, Eviction, Small Claims* 8230 E Butherus Dr, Scottsdale, AZ 85260. 8AM-5PM. **480-443-6600**, Fax: 480-443-5981. ☎✉✋

Northwest Phoenix Justice Court *Misdemeanor, Civil Actions Under $10,000, Eviction, Small Claims* 8230 E Butherus Dr, Scottsdale, AZ 85260. 8AM-5PM. **602-395-0293**, Fax: 602-678-4508. Court is co-located with the Scottsdale Justice Court. ✉✋

East Mesa Justice Court *Misd., Civil Under $10,000, Eviction, Small Claims* 4811 E Julep, #128, Mesa, AZ 85205. 8AM-5PM. **480-985-0188**, Fax: 480-396-6327. ✉✋

Tolleson Justice Court *Misd., Civil Under $10,000, Eviction, Small Claims* 9550 W Van Buren, #6, Tolleson, AZ 85353. 8AM-5PM. **623-936-1449**, Fax: 623-936-4859. ✉✋

Wickenburg Justice Court *Misdemeanor, Civil Actions Under $10,000, Eviction, Small Claims* 155 N Tegner, #D, Wickenburg, AZ 85390. 8AM-5PM. **602-506-1554**, Fax: 928-684-9639. Town Court telephone number is 928-684-5451. ✉✋

Northeast Phoenix Justice Court *Misdemeanor, Civil Under $10,000, Eviction, Small Claims* 10255 N 32nd St, Phoenix, AZ 85028. 8AM-5PM. **602-494-0620**, Fax: 602-953-2315. ☎✉✋

Gila Bend Justice Court *Misd., Civil Under $10,000, Eviction, Small Claims* PO Box 648 (209 E Pima St), Gila Bend, AZ 85337. 8AM-5PM. **928-683-2651**, Fax: 928-683-6412. Access by ✉✋

North Valley Justice Court *Misdemeanor, Civil Actions Under $10,000, Eviction, Small Claims* 5222 W

Glendale, Glendale, AZ 85301. 8AM-5PM. **623-915-2877**, Fax: 623- 463-0670. ✉✋

East Phoenix Justice Court #2 *Misdemeanor, Civil Actions Under $10,000, Eviction, Small Claims* 4109 N 12th St, Phoenix, AZ 85014. 8AM-5PM. **602-266-3741**, Fax 602-277-9442. ✉✋

East Phoenix Justice Court #1 *Misdemeanor, Civil Actions Under $10,000, Eviction, Small Claims* 1 W Madison St, #1, Phoenix, AZ 85003. 8AM-5PM. **602-254-1599**, Fax: 602-254-1603. ☎✉✋

Central Phoenix Justice Court *Misdemeanor, Civil Actions Under $10,000, Eviction, Small Claims* 1 W Madison St, Phoenix, AZ 85003. 8AM-5PM. **602-254-1488**, Fax: 602-254-1496. ✉**Fax**✋

West Phoenix Justice Court *Misdemeanor, Civil Actions Under $10,000, Eviction, Small Claims* 1 W Madison St, Phoenix, AZ 85003. 8-5PM. **602-256-0292**, Fax: 602-256-7959. ✋

South Mesa/Gilbert Justice Court *Misdemeanor, Civil Actions Under $10,000, Eviction, Small Claims* 55 E Civic Center Dr, #102, Gilbert, AZ 85296-3468. 8AM-5PM. **480-926-3051**, Fax: 480-545-1638. Access records✉✋

Glendale Justice Court *Misd., Civil Under $10,000, Eviction, Small Claims* 5222 W Glendale, Glendale, AZ 85301. 8AM-5PM. **623-939-9477**, Fax: 623-842-2260. ✉✋

West Mesa Justice Court *Misd., Civil Under $10,000, Eviction, Small Claims* 2050 W University Dr, Mesa, AZ 85201. 8AM-5PM. **480-964-2958**, Fax: 480-969-1098. ✋✉

North Mesa Justice Court *Misd., Civil Under $10,000, Eviction, Small Claims* 1837 S Mesa St, #A-201, Mesa, AZ 85210. 8AM-5PM. **480-926-9731**, Fax: 480-926-7763. **Fax**✉✋

Maryvale Justice Court *Misd., Civil Under $10,000, Eviction, Small Claims* 4622 W Indian School Rd, Bldg D, Phoenix, AZ 85031. 8AM-5PM. **623-245-0432**, Fax: 623-245-1216. ✉✋

West Tempe Justice Court *Misdemeanor, Civil Actions Under $10,000, Eviction, Small Claims* 8240 S Kyrene Rd, #113 Bldg A, Tempe, AZ 85284. 8AM-5PM. **480-705-7349**, Fax: 480-785-4577. ✉✋

Peoria Justice Court *Misdemeanor, Civil Under $10,000, Eviction, Small Claims* 11601 N 19th Ave, Phoenix, AZ 85029. 8AM-5PM. **602-395-0294**. ☎**Fax**✉✋

Mohave County
www.mohavecourts.com

Superior Court *Felony, Civil Over $5,000, Probate* PO Box 7000, Kingman, AZ 86402-7000. 8AM-5PM. **928-753-0713**, Fax: 928-753-0781. ☎**Fax**✉✋

Moccasin Justice Court *Misdemeanor, Civil Actions Under $10,000, Eviction, Small Claims* HC-65, PO Box 90, Moccasin, AZ 86022. 8AM-5PM. **928-643-7104**, Fax: 928-643-6206. This court is also the Magistrate Court for Colorado City. ✉✋

Lake Havasu Consolidated Court *Misdemeanor, Civil Actions Under $10,000, Eviction, Small Claims* 2001 College Dr, #148, Lake Havasu City, AZ 86403. 8AM-5PM. **928-453-0705**, Fax: 928-680-0193. **Fax**✉✋

Kingman/Cerbat Justice Court *Misdemeanor, Civil Actions Under $10,000, Eviction, Small Claims* 524 W Beale St PO Box 29, Kingman, AZ 86401-0029. 8AM-5PM. **928-753-0710**, Fax: 928-753-7840. Access-☎**Fax**✉✋

Bullhead City Justice Court *Misdemeanor, Civil Actions Under $10,000, Eviction, Small Claims* 2225 Trane Rd, Bullhead City, AZ 86442. 8AM-5PM. **928-758-0709 x2015**, Fax: 928-753-7840. ✉✋

Navajo County

Superior Court *Felony, Civil Actions Over $5,000, Probate* PO Box 668, Holbrook, AZ 86025. 8AM-5PM. **928-524-4188**, Fax: 928-524-4261. ☎**Fax**✉✋🖥

Snowflake Justice Court *Misdemeanor, Civil Actions Under $10,000, Eviction, Small Claims* 145 S Main St, #D, Snowflake, AZ 85937. 8AM-5PM. **928-536-4141**, Fax: 928-536-3511. **Fax**✉✋🖥

Kayenta Justice Court *Misdemeanor, Civil Actions Under $10,000, Eviction, Small Claims* PO Box 38, Kayenta, AZ 86033. 8AM-N,1-5PM. **928-697-3522**, Fax: 928-697-3528. If planning to make an in-person search, call to make an appointment. ✉✋🖥

Winslow Justice Court *Misdemeanor, Civil Actions Under $10,000, Eviction, Small Claims* Box 808, Winslow, AZ 86047. 8AM-5PM. **928-289-6840**, Fax: 928-289-6847. Access **Fax**✉✋🖥

Holbrook Justice Court *Misdemeanor, Civil Actions Under $10,000, Eviction, Small Claims* PO Box 366, Holbrook, AZ 86025. 8AM-5PM. **928-524-4720**, Fax: 928-524-4725. ✉✋🖥

Show Low Justice Court *Misdemeanor, Civil Actions Under $10,000, Eviction, Small Claims* PO Box 3085 (561 E Duece of Clubs), Show Low, AZ 85902-3085. 8AM-5PM. **928-532-6030**, Fax: 928-532-6035. **Fax**✉✋🖥

Pinetop-Lakeside Justice Court *Misdemeanor, Civil Actions Under $10,000, Eviction, Small Claims* PO Box 2020 (1360 Neils Hansen Dr), Lakeside, AZ 85929. 8AM-5PM. **928-368-6200**, Fax: 928-368-8674. Access-**Fax**✉✋🖥

Pima County

Superior Court *Felony, Civil Over $5,000, Probate* www.cosc.co.pima.az.us 110 W Congress, Tucson, AZ 85701. 8AM-5PM. **520-740-3240**, Fax: 520-798-3531. Address correspondence to attention of civil or criminal section. ✉✋🖥

Ajo Justice Court *Misdemeanor, Civil Actions Under $10,000, Eviction, Small Claims* 111 La Mina, Ajo, AZ 85321. 8AM-5PM. **520-387-7684**. ✉✋🖥**Fax**

Green Valley Justice Court *Misdemeanor, Civil Actions Under $10,000, Eviction, Small Claims* 601 N LaCanada, Green Valley, AZ 85614. 8AM-5PM. **520-648-0658**, Fax: 520-648-2235. ✉✋🖥

Pima County Consolidated Justice Court *Misdemeanor, Civil Actions Under $10,000, Eviction, Small Claims* http://jp.co.pima.az.us 115 N Church Ave, Tucson, AZ 85701. 8AM-4:30PM, M-F, 7:30-noon Sat. **520-740-3171**, Fax: 520-884-0346. **Fax**✉🖥✋

Pinal County

Superior Court *Felony, Civil Over $5,000, Probate* www.co.pinal.az.us/cl

erksc PO Box 2730, Florence, AZ 85232-2730. 8AM-5PM. **520-866-5300**, Fax: 520-866-5320. ☎☒👆💻

http://co.pinal.az.us/JusticeCourts/

Eloy Justice Court *Misdemeanor, Civil Actions Under $10,000, Eviction, Small Claims* http://co.pinal.az.us/JusticeCourts/ PO Box 586, Eloy, AZ 85231. 8AM-N, 1-5PM. **520-466-9221**, Fax: 520-466-4473. ☒👆💻

Superior/Kearny Justice Court *Misdemeanor, Civil Actions Under $10,000, Eviction, Small Claims* 60 E Main St, Superior, AZ 85273. 8AM-N, 1-5PM. **520-689-5871**, Fax: 520-689-2369. **Fax**☒👆💻

Mammoth Justice Court *Misdemeanor, Civil Under $10,000, Eviction, Small Claims* PO Box 777, Mammoth, AZ 85618. 8AM-5PM. **520-487-2262**, Fax: 520-866-7839. ☒👆💻

Casa Grande Justice Court *Misdemeanor, Civil Actions Under $10,000, Eviction, Small Claims* 820 E Cottonwood Ln, Bldg B, Casa Grande, AZ 85222. 8AM-5PM. **520-836-5471**, Fax: 520-866-7404. Access ☒👆💻

Oracle Justice Court *Misdemeanor, Civil Actions Under $10,000, Eviction, Small Claims* PO Box 3924, Oracle, AZ 85623. 8AM-5PM. **520-896-9250**, Fax: 520-868-7812. ☒👆💻

Apache Junction Justice Court *Misdemeanor, Civil Actions Under $10,000, Eviction, Small Claims* 575 N Idaho, #200, Apache Junction, AZ 85219. 8AM-5PM. **480-982-2921**, Fax: 520-866-6153. Area code for the fax number is different than the voice number. **Fax**☒👆💻

Maricopa Justice Court *Misdemeanor, Civil Under $10,000, Eviction, Small Claims* 44625 W Garvey Rd, Maricopa, AZ 85239. 8AM-5PM. **520-568-2451**, Fax: 520-568-2924. Access **Fax**☒👆💻

Florence Justice Court *Misdemeanor, Civil Under $10,000, Eviction, Small Claims* PO Box 1818, Florence, AZ 85232. 8AM-5PM. **520-866-7194**, Fax: 520-866-7190. ☒👆💻

Santa Cruz County

Superior Court *Felony, Civil Over $5,000, Probate* http://sccazcourts.org PO Box 1265, Nogales, AZ 85628. 8AM-5PM. **520-375-7700**, Fax: 520-761-7857. ☒**Fax**👆💻

Santa Cruz Justice Court *Misdemeanor, Civil Actions Under $10,000, Eviction, Small Claims* www.sccazcourts.org PO Box 1150, Nogales, AZ 85628. 8AM-5PM. **520-761-7853**, Fax: 520-761-7929. **Fax**☒👆💻

East Santa Cruz County Justice Court - Precinct #2 *Misdemeanor, Civil Actions Under $10,000, Eviction, Small Claims* PO Box 100, Patagonia, AZ 85624. 8:30AM-5PM. **520-455-5796**, Fax: 520-455-5513 (Attn: Justice Court). ☒👆💻

Yavapai County

www.co.yavarai.az.us

Superior Court *Felony, Civil Actions Over $1,000, Probate* Yavapai County Courthouse, Prescott, AZ 86301. 8AM-5PM. **928-771-3312**, Fax: 928-771-3111. **Fax**☒👆💻

Prescott Justice Court *Misdemeanor, Civil Actions Under $10,000, Eviction, Small Claims* Yavapai County Courthouse 120 S Cortez, Rm 103, Prescott, AZ 86301. 8AM-5PM. **928-771-3300**, Fax: 928-771-3302. **Fax**☒👆

Yarnell Justice Court *Misdemeanor, Civil Actions Under $10,000, Eviction, Small Claims* PO Box 65 Justice Court Bldg, Yarnell, AZ 85362. 8AM-5PM. **928-427-3318**, Fax: 928-771-3362. ☒👆💻

Verde Valley Justice Court *Misdemeanor, Civil Actions Under $10,000, Eviction, Small Claims* 10 S 6th St, Cottonwood, AZ 86326. 8AM-5PM. **928-639-5820**, Fax: 928-639-5828. ☒👆💻

Seligman Justice Court *Misdemeanor, Civil Actions Under $10,000, Eviction, Small Claims* PO Box 56, Seligman, AZ 86337-0056. 8AM-5PM. **928-422-3281**, Fax: 928-422-3282. ☎**Fax**☒👆💻

Bagdad Justice Court *Misdemeanor, Civil Actions Under $10,000, Eviction, Small Claims* PO Box 243, Bagdad, AZ 86321. 8AM-5PM M; 8:00AM-4:00PM T-Th (MST). **928-633-2141**, Fax: 928-633-4451. ☒👆💻

Mayer Justice Court *Misdemeanor, Civil Actions Under $10,000, Eviction, Small Claims* PO Box 245, Mayer, AZ 86333. 8AM-5PM. **928-771-3355**. ☒👆💻

Yuma County

Superior Court *Felony, Civil Actions Over $5,000, Probate* 168 S 2nd Ave, Yuma, AZ 85364. 8AM-5PM. **928-329-2164**, Fax: 928-329-2007. Civil phone: 928-329-2164, Crim: 928-329-2167, Probate: 928-329-2163. **Fax**☒👆💻

Wellton Justice Court *Misdemeanor, Civil Actions Under $10,000, Eviction, Small Claims* PO Box 384, Wellton, AZ 85356. 8AM-5PM. **928-785-3321**, Fax: 928-785-4933. Access ☎**Fax**☒👆💻

Yuma Justice Court *Misdemeanor, Civil Actions Under $10,000, Eviction, Small Claims* 168 S 2nd Ave, Yuma, AZ 85364. 8AM-5PM. **928-329-2180**, Fax: 928-329-2005. ☒👆💻

Somerton Justice Court *Misdemeanor, Civil Actions Under $10,000, Eviction, Small Claims* www.somertoncourts.com PO Box 458 350 W Main St, Somerton, AZ 85350. 8AM-5PM. **928-627-2722**, Fax 928-627-1076. access ☎**Fax**☒👆💻

Arkansas

State Court Administration: Administrative Office of Courts, 625 Marshall St, 1100 Justice Bldg, Little Rock, AR, 72201; 501-682-9400, Fax: 501-682-9410. http://www.courts.state.ar.us/

Court Structure: Circuit Courts are the courts of general jurisdiction and are arranged in 28 circuits. Circuit courts consist of five subject matter divisions: criminal, civil, probate, domestic relations, and juvenile. The Circuit Clerk handles the records and recordings; however, some counties have a County Clerk that handles probate. District courts, formerly known as municipal courts before passage of Amendment 80 to the Arkansas Constitution, exercise county-wide jurisdiction over misdemeanor cases, preliminary felony cases, and civil cases in matters of less than $5,000, including small claims. The City Courts operate in smaller communities where District Courts do not exist and exercise city-wide jurisdiction.

Probate Courts: Probate is handled by the Chancery and Probate Courts.

Online Access: There is a very limited internal online computer system at the Administrative Office of Courts. The home web page gives online access to Supreme and Appellate opinions.

Additional Information: Many courts that allow written search requests require an SASE. Fees vary widely across jurisdictions as do prepayment requirements.

Arkansas County

Circuit Court - Northern District *Felony, Civil Actions, Probate* 302 S College St, Stuttgart, AR 72160. 8AM-4:30PM. **870-673-2056**, Fax: 870-673-3869, Probate: 870-673-7311. Probate has a different Clerk. 🖐

Circuit Court - Southern District *Felony, Civil Actions Over $5,000* 101 Courthouse Sq, De Witt, AR 72042. 8AM-4:30PM (closed 12 to 12:30). **870-946-4219**, Fax: 870-946-1394. **Fax**✉🖐

Stuttgart District Court *Misdemeanor, Civil Actions Under $5,000, Eviction, Small Claims* PO Box 848 514 S. Main, Stuttgart, AR 72160. 8-4:30PM. **870-673-7951**, Fax: 870-673-6522. ☎✉**Fax**🖐

Ashley County

Circuit Court *Felony, Civil Actions Over $5,000, Probate* Ashley County Courthouse 205 E Jefferson, Hamburg, AR 71646. 8AM-4:30PM. **870-853-2030**, Fax: 870-853-2034. ✉🖐

Hamburg District Court *Misdemeanor, Civil Actions Under $5,000, Eviction, Small Claims* PO Box 72, Hamburg, AR 71646. 8AM-4:30PM. **870-853-8326**, Fax: 870-853-8600. ✉🖐

Baxter County

Circuit Court *Felony, Civil Actions Over $5,000, Probate* 1 E 7th St Courthouse Square, Mountain Home, AR 72653. 8AM-4:30PM. **870-425-3475**, Fax: 870-424-5105. ✉🖐

District Court *Misdemeanor, Civil Actions Under $5,000, Eviction, Small Claims* 720 S Hickory, Mountain Home, AR 72653. 8AM-4:30PM. **870-425-3140**, Fax: 870-425-8470. Civil phone: 870-425-8910. 🖐✉

Benton County

Circuit Court *Felony, Civil Actions Over $5,000, Probate* www.co.benton.ar.us 102 NE "A" St, Bentonville, AR 72712. 8AM-4:30PM. **479-271-1015**, Fax: 479-271-5719, Prob: 479-271-5727. ☎✉💻🖐

District Court *Misdemeanor, Civil Actions Under $5,000, Small Claims* 117 W Central, Bentonville, AR 72712. 8AM-4:30PM. **479-271-3120**, Fax: 479-271-3134. 🖐✉

Boone County

Circuit Court *Felony, Civil Actions Over $5,000* 100 N Main St #200, Harrison, AR 72601. 8AM-4:30PM. **870-741-5560**, Fax: 870-741-4335. Probate records in the County Clerk's office, 870-741-8428. ✉🖐

District Court *Misdemeanor, Civil Actions Under $5,000, Eviction, Small Claims* PO Box 968, Harrison, AR 72602. 8AM-4:30PM. **870-741-2788**, Fax: 870-741-4329. 🖐✉

Bradley County

Circuit Court *Felony, Civil Actions Over $5,000, Probate* Bradley County Courthouse - Records 101 E Cedar, Warren, AR 71671. 8AM-4:30PM. **870-226-2272**, Fax: 870-226-8401, Probate: 870-226-3464. ✉🖐

District Court *Misdemeanor, Civil Actions Under $5,000, Eviction, Small Claims* PO Box 352, Warren, AR 71671. 8AM-4:30PM. **870-226-2567**, Fax: 870-226-2567. 🖐✉

Calhoun County

Circuit Court *Felony, Civil Actions Over $5,000, Probate* PO Box 1175, Hampton, AR 71744. 8AM-4:30PM. **870-798-2517**. ✉🖐

District Court *Misdemeanor, Civil Actions Under $5,000, Eviction, Small Claims* PO Box 783, Hampton, AR 71744. 8AM-4:30PM. **870-798-2753**, Fax: 870-798-3665. Civil phone: 870-798-2165. Municipal Clerk at the city is 870-798-3201. 🖐✉

Carroll County

Berryville Circuit Court - Eastern District *Felony, Civil Actions Over $5,000, Eviction, Probate* Carroll County Circuit Court PO Box 71, Berryville, AR 72616. 8:30AM-4:30PM. **870-423-2422**, Fax: 870-423-4796, Probate: 870-423-2022. **Fax**✉🖐

Eureka Springs Circuit Court - Western District *Felony, Civil Actions Over $5,000, Eviction, Probate* 44 S Main, PO Box 109, Eureka Springs, AR 72632. 8:30AM-4:30PM. **479-253-8646**. ☎✉🖐

Key: Symbols refer to criminal records access unless otherwise noted. phone-☎ mail-✉ fax-**Fax** in person-🖐 online-💻 email-**Email**

Eureka Springs District Court *Misd., Civil Under $5,000, Small Claims* www.cityofeurekasprings.org/muncourt.html Courthouse, 44 S Main, Eureka Springs, AR 72632. 8AM-5PM. **479-253-8574**, Fax: 479-253-6887. ☎✉✋

Berryville District Court *Misdemeanor, Civil Actions Under $5,000, Small Claims* 103 S Springs, Berryville, AR 72616. 8AM-4:30PM. **870-423-6247**, Fax: 870-423-7069. ✋✉

Chicot County

Circuit Court *Felony, Civil Actions Over $5,000, Probate* 108 Main St County Courthouse, Lake Village, AR 71653. 8AM-4:30PM. **870-265-8010**, Fax: 870-265-8012, Probate: 870-265-8000. Probate is located here in a separate office. ✉✋

Lake Village District Court *Misdemeanor, Civil Actions Under $5,000, Eviction, Small Claims* PO Box 832, Lake Village, AR 71653. 9AM-5PM. **870-265-3283**. ✉✋

Clark County

Circuit Court *Felony, Civil Actions Over $5,000, Probate* PO Box 576, Arkadelphia, AR 71923. 8:30AM-4:30PM. **870-246-4281**. ✉✋

District Court *Misdemeanor, Civil Actions Under $5,000, Eviction, Small Claims* PO Box 449, Arkadelphia, AR 71923. 8:30AM-4:30PM. **870-246-9552**. ☎✉**Fax**✋

Clay County

Piggott Circuit Court *Felony, Civil Actions Over $5,000* 151 S 2nd, Piggott, AR 72454. 8AM-4:30PM. **870-598-2524**, Fax: 870-598-2524, Probate: 870-598-2813. ✋

Corning Circuit Court *Felony, Civil Actions Over $5,000, Probate* 800 SW 2nd St, Corning, AR 72422-2715. 8AM-4:30PM. **870-857-3271**, Fax: 870-857-9201. ✋

District Court *Misdemeanor, Civil Actions Under $5,000, Eviction, Small Claims* 151 S 2nd Ave, Piggott, AR 72454. 8AM-4:30PM. **870-598-2265**. Office open 20 hours per week only. For eviction info the court says to contact Clay County Sheriff, 151 S 2nd St, Piggott, AR 72454, 870-598-2266. ✉✋

Cleburne County

Circuit Court *Felony, Civil Actions Over $5,000, Probate* PO Box 543, Heber Springs, AR 72543. 8:30AM-4:30PM. **501-362-8149**, Fax: 501-362-4650. ☎✉✋

District Court *Misdemeanor, Civil Actions Under $5,000, Small Claims, Eviction* 102 E Main, Heber Springs, AR 72543. 8:30AM-4:30PM. **501-362-6585**, Fax: 501-362-4661. ☎✉**Fax**✋

Cleveland County

Circuit Court *Felony, Civil Actions Over $5,000, Probate* PO Box 368, Rison, AR 71665. 8AM-4:30PM. **870-325-6521**, Fax: 870-325-6144. ✉✋

District Court *Misdemeanor, Civil Actions Under $5,000, Eviction, Small Claims* PO Box 405, City Hall, Rison, AR 71665. 8AM-4PM. **870-325-7382**, Fax: 870-325-6152. ✋

Columbia County

Circuit Court *Felony, Civil Actions Over $5,000, Probate* 1 Court Sq #3, Magnolia, AR 71753-3595. 8AM-4:30PM. **870-235-3700**, Fax: 870-235-3786. ✉✋

Magnolia District Court *Misdemeanor, Civil Actions Under $5,000, Eviction, Small Claims* 121 S Jefferson, Magnolia, AR 71753. 8-5PM. **870-234-7312**. ✉✋

Conway County

Circuit Court *Felony, Civil Actions Over $5,000, Probate* Conway County Courthouse, Rm 206, Morrilton, AR 72110. 8AM-5PM. **501-354-9617**, Fax: 501-354-9612, Probate: 501-354-9621. ☎✉✋

District Court *Misdemeanor, Civil Actions Under $5,000, Eviction, Small Claims* Conway County Courthouse PO Box 127, Morrilton, AR 72110. 8AM-4:30PM. **501-354-9615**, Fax: 501-354-9633. ✋✉

Craighead County

Jonesboro Circuit Court *Felony, Civil Actions Over $5,000, Probate* PO Box 120, Jonesboro, AR 72403. 8AM-5PM. **870-933-4530**, Fax: 870-933-4534. **Fax**✉✋

Lake City Circuit Court *Felony, Civil Actions Over $5,000, Probate* PO Box 537, Lake City, AR 72437. 8AM-5PM.

870-237-4342, Fax: 870-237-8174. ✉**Fax**✋

District Court *Misdemeanor, Civil Actions Under $5,000, Eviction, Small Claims* 410 W Washington, Jonesboro, AR 72401. 8AM-5PM. **870-933-4508**, Fax: 870-933-4582. Access by ✋✉

Crawford County

Circuit Court *Felony, Civil Actions Over $5,000, Probate* www.crawford-county.org/circuit_court.htm County Courthouse, 300 Main St, Rm 22, Van Buren, AR 72956. 8AM-5PM. **479-474-1821**, Fax: 479-471-0622, Probate: 479-474-1312. ✉✋

District Court *Misdemeanor, Civil Actions Under $5,000, Eviction, Small Claims* 1003 Broadway, Van Buren, AR 72956. 8AM-5PM. **479-474-1671**, Fax: 479-471-5010. ✋✉

Crittenden County

Circuit Court *Felony, Civil Actions Over $5,000, Probate* 100 Court St, Marion, AR 72364. 8AM-4:30PM. **870-739-3248**, Fax: 870-739-3287. ✋

District Court *Misdemeanor, Civil Actions Under $5,000, Eviction, Small Claims* PO Box 766, West Memphis, AR 72303. 8AM-5PM. **870-732-7560**, Fax: 870-732-7538/7566. Civil phone: 870-732-7563. ☎✉✋

Cross County

Circuit Court *Felony, Civil Actions Over $5,000, Probate* County Courthouse 705 E Union, Rm 9, Wynne, AR 72396. 8AM-4PM. **870-238-5720**, Probate: 870-238-5735. ✋

District Court *Misdemeanor, Civil Actions Under $5,000, Eviction, Small Claims* 205 Mississippi St, Wynne, AR 72396. 8AM-4PM. **870-238-9171**, Fax: 870-238-3930. ✉✋

Dallas County

Circuit Court *Felony, Civil Actions Over $5,000, Probate* Dallas County Courthouse, Fordyce, AR 71742. 8:30AM-4:30PM. **870-352-2307**, Fax: 870-352-7179. ✋

District Court *Misdemeanor, Civil Actions Under $5,000, Eviction, Small Claims* 202 W 3rd St, Fordyce, AR 71742. 8AM-4:30PM. **870-352-2332**, Fax: 870-352-3414. ✋

Desha County

Circuit Court *Felony, Civil Actions Over $5,000, Probate* PO Box 309, Arkansas City, AR 71630. 8AM-4PM. **870-877-2411**, Fax: 870-877-3407, Probate: 870-877-2323. **Fax**✉✋

District Court *Misdemeanor, Civil Actions Under $5,000, Eviction, Small Claims* PO Box 157, Dumas, AR 71639-2226. 8AM-4:30PM. **870-382-6972**, Fax: 870-382-1106. ✋✉

Drew County

Circuit Court *Felony, Civil Actions Over $5,000, Probate* 210 S Main, Monticello, AR 71655. 8AM-4:30PM. **870-460-6250**, Fax: 870-460-6246. ✋

District Court *Misdemeanor, Civil Actions Under $5,000, Eviction, Small Claims* PO Box 505, Monticello, AR 71655. 8AM-4:30PM. **870-367-4420**, Fax: 870-460-9056. ✉**Fax**✋

Faulkner County

Circuit Court *Felony, Civil Actions Over $5,000, Probate* PO Box 9, Conway, AR 72033. 8AM-4:30PM. **501-450-4911**, Fax: 501-450-4948. **Fax**✉✋

District Court *Misdemeanor, Civil Actions Under $5,000, Small Claims* 810 Parkway, Conway, AR 72032. 8AM-4:30PM. **501-450-6112**, Fax: 501-450-6184. ✉**Fax**✋

Franklin County

Charleston Circuit Court *Felony, Civil Actions Over $5,000, Probate* 607 E main, Charleston, AR 72933. 8AM-4:30PM. **479-965-7332**, Probate: 479-965-2129. ✉✋

Ozark Circuit Court *Felony, Civil Actions Over $5,000, Probate* PO Box 1112 211 W Commercial, Ozark, AR 72949. 8AM-4:30PM. **479-667-3818**, Fax: 479-667-5174, Probate: 479-667-3607. Probate is maintained at the County Clerk's Office. **Fax**✉✋

District Court *Misdemeanor, Civil Actions Under $5,000, Small Claims* PO Box 426, Charleston, AR 72933. 8AM-5PM. **479-965-7455**, Fax: 479-965-9980. ✉**Fax**✋

Fulton County

Circuit Court *Felony, Civil Actions Over $5,000, Probate* PO Box 485, Salem, AR 72576. 8AM-4:30PM. **870-895-3310**, Fax: 870-895-3383. Access by ✉✋

District Court *Misdemeanor, Civil Actions Under $5,000, Eviction, Small Claims* PO Box 928, Salem, AR 72576. 8AM-4:30PM. **870-895-4136**, Fax: 870-895-4114. ✋✉☎

Garland County

Circuit Court *Felony, Civil Actions Over $5,000, Probate* Garland County Courthouse 501 Ouachita Ave, Rm 207, Hot Springs, AR 71901. 8AM-5PM. Fax: 501-609-9043. Civil phone: 501-622-3630, Crim: 501-622-3640, Probate: 501-622-3610. Probate records are handled by the County Clerk. **Fax**✉✋

District Court *Misdemeanor, Civil Actions Under $5,000, Eviction, Small Claims* 607 Ouachita, Hot Springs, AR 71901. 8AM-4:30PM. **501-321-6765**, Fax: 501-321-6764. ✋✉

Grant County

Circuit Court *Felony, Civil Actions Over $5,000, Probate* Grant County Courthouse 101 W Center, Rm 106, Sheridan, AR 72150. 8AM-4:30PM. **870-942-2631**, Fax: 870-942-3564. ✋

District Court *Misdemeanor, Civil Actions Under $5,000, Eviction, Small Claims* PO Box 603, Sheridan, AR 72150. 8AM-4:15PM. **870-942-3464**, Fax: 870-942-8885. ✋✉

Greene County

Circuit Court *Felony, Civil Actions Over $5,000, Probate* 320 W Court #124, Paragould, AR 72450. 8AM-4:30PM. **870-239-6330**, Fax: 870-239-3550. **Fax**✉✋

District Court *Misdemeanor, Civil Actions Under $5,000, Eviction, Small Claims* www.gccourt.com 320 W Court, Rm 227, Paragould, AR 72450. 8AM-4:30PM. **870-239-7507**, Fax: 870-239-7506. ✋✉

Hempstead County

Circuit Court *Felony, Civil Actions Over $5,000, Probate* PO Box 1420, Hope, AR 71802. 8AM-4PM. **870-777-2384**, Fax: 870-777-7827, Probate: 870-777-2241. Probate is handled by the County Clerk at same address. ☎**Fax**✉✋

District Court *Misdemeanor, Civil Actions Under $5,000, Eviction, Small Claims* PO Box 1420, Hope, AR 71802-1420. 8AM-4PM. **870-777-2525**, Fax: 870-777-7830. ✉✋

Hot Spring County

Circuit Court *Felony, Civil Actions Over $5,000* 210 Locust St, PO Box 1200, Malvern, AR 72104. 8:00AM-4:30PM. **501-332-2281**, Probate: 501-332-2291. ✉✋

Malvern District Court *Misdemeanor, Civil Actions Under $5,000, Eviction, Small Claims* 305 Locust St, Rm 201, Malvern, AR 72104. 8AM-4:30PM. **501-332-7604**, Fax: 501-332-3144. Formerly known as Malvern Municipal Court before 7/1/01. ✉**Fax**✋

Howard County

Circuit Court *Felony, Civil Actions Over $5,000, Probate* 421 N Main, Rm 7, Nashville, AR 71852. 8AM-4:30PM. **870-845-7506**, Probate: 870-845-7503. Probate is handled by the County Clerk at this address. ✋

District Court *Misdemeanor, Civil Actions Under $5,000, Eviction, Small Claims* 426 N Main, ##7, Nashville, AR 71852-2009. 8AM-4:30PM. **870-845-7522**, Fax: 870-845-3705. ✋✉

Independence County

Circuit Court *Felony, Civil Actions Over $5,000* PO Box 2155 (192 E.Main and Broad St), Batesville, AR 72503. 8AM-4:30PM. **870-793-8833**, Fax: 870-793-8888. ✋✉

District Court *Misdemeanor, Civil Actions Under $5,000, Eviction, Small Claims* 368 E Main, Rm 205, Batesville, AR 72501. 8AM-4:30PM. **870-793-8817**, Fax: 870-793-8875. ✋✉

Izard County

Circuit Court *Felony, Civil Actions Over $5,000, Probate* PO Box 95, Melbourne, AR 72556. 8:30AM-4:30PM. **870-368-4316**, Fax: 870-368-4748. **Fax**✉✋

District Court *Misdemeanor, Civil Actions Under $5,000, Small Claims* PO Box 337, Melbourne, AR 72556. 8:30AM-4:30PM. **870-368-4390**, Fax: 870-368-2267. ✉ **Fax**✋

Jackson County

Circuit Court *Felony, Civil Actions Over $5,000, Probate* Jackson County Courthouse 208 Main St, Newport, AR 72112. 8AM-4:30PM. **870-523-7423**, Fax: 870-523-3682. ✋📩

District Court *Misdemeanor, Civil Actions Under $5,000, Eviction, Small Claims* 615 3rd St, Newport, AR 72112. 8AM-4:30PM. **870-523-9555**, Fax: 870-523-4365. Civil phone: Ext 118, Crim: Ext 119, Probate: Ext 120. 📩**Fax**✋

Jefferson County

Circuit Court *Felony, Civil Actions Over $5,000, Probate* PO Box 7433, Pine Bluff, AR 71611. 8:30PM-5PM. Civil: 870-541-5307, Crim: 870-541-5306. ✋

District Court *Misdemeanor, Civil Actions Under $5,000, Eviction, Small Claims* 200 E 8th Ave, Pine Bluff, AR 71601. 8AM-5PM. **870-543-1860 Div.I; 850-7584 Div. II**, Fax: 870-543-1889. ✋📩

Johnson County

Circuit Court *Felony, Civil Actions Over $5,000, Probate* PO Box 189, Clarksville, AR 72830-0189. 8AM-4:30PM. **479-754-2977**, Fax: 479-754-4235, Probate: 479-754-3967. Probate is handled by County Clerk, PO Box 57. Access by 📩✋

District Court *Misdemeanor, Civil Actions Under $5,000, Eviction, Small Claims* PO Box 581, Clarksville, AR 72830. 8AM-4PM. **479-754-8533**, Fax: 479-754-6014. ✋📩

Lafayette County

Circuit Court *Felony, Civil Actions Over $5,000, Probate* #3 Courthouse Square, Lewisville, AR 71845. 8AM-4:30PM. **870-921-4878**, Fax: 870-921-4879 (Crim), Probate: 870-921-4633. Civil fax is 870-921-4879. Probate is located at #2 Courthouse Square. Access by 📩✋

District Court *Misdemeanor, Civil Actions Under $5,000, Eviction, Small Claims* 110 E Fourth, #1, Lewisville, AR 71845. 8AM-4:30PM. **870-921-5555**, Fax: 870-921-4256. ✋

Lawrence County

Circuit Court *Felony, Civil Actions Over $5,000, Probate* PO Box 581 315 W. Main St., Rm 7, Walnut Ridge, AR 72476. 8AM-4:30PM. **870-886-1112**,

Fax: 870-886-1128, Probate: 870-886-1111. 📩✋

Walnut Ridge District Court *Misdemeanor, Civil Actions Under $5,000, Eviction, Small Claims* 201 SW 2nd St, Walnut Ridge, AR 72476. 8AM-4:30PM. **870-886-3905**. Access by ✋📩

Lee County

Circuit Court *Felony, Civil Actions Over $5,000, Probate* 15 E Chestnut, Marianna, AR 72360. 8:30AM-4:30PM. **870-295-7710**, Fax: 870-295-7766. ✋

District Court *Misdemeanor, Civil Actions Under $5,000, Eviction, Small Claims* 45 W Mississippi, Marianna, AR 72360. 8AM-N; 1-5PM. **870-295-3813**, Fax: 870-295-5726. Access by ✋📩

Lincoln County

Circuit Court *Felony, Civil Actions Over $5,000, Probate* Courthouse, 300 S Drew, Star City, AR 71667. 8AM-4:30PM. **870-628-3154**, Fax: 870-628-5546, Probate: 870-628-5114. ✋

Lincoln County District Court *Misdemeanor, Civil Actions Under $5,000, Eviction, Small Claims* 300 S Drew St, Star City, AR 71667. 8AM-4:30PM. **870-628-4904**, Civil: 870-628-4166. 📩✋

Little River County

Circuit Court *Felony, Civil Actions Over $5,000, Probate* PO Box 575, Ashdown, AR 71822. 8AM-4:30PM. **870-898-7211**, Fax: 870-898-5783, Probate: 870-898-7210. ✋

District Court *Misdemeanor, Civil Actions Under $5,000, Eviction, Small Claims* 351 N 2nd St, #8, Ashdown, AR 71822. 8:30AM-4:30PM. **870-898-7230**, Fax: 870-898-7262. Access by ✋📩

Logan County

Circuit Court *Felony, Civil Actions Over $5,000, Probate* Courthouse 25 W Walnut, Paris, AR 72855. 8AM-4:30PM. **479-963-2164**, Fax: 479-963-3304, Probate: 479-963-2618. Access by ✋

Paris District Court *Misdemeanor, Civil Actions Under $5,000, Eviction, Small Claims* Paris Courthouse, Paris, AR 72855. 8:30AM-4:30PM. **479-963-3792**, Fax: 479-963-2762. Access by ✋📩

Lonoke County

Circuit Court *Felony, Civil Actions Over $5,000, Probate* PO Box 218 Attn: Circuit Clerk, Lonoke, AR 72086. 8AM-4:30PM. **501-676-2316**, Probate: 501-676-2368. 📩✋

Lonoke District Court *Misdemeanor, Civil Actions Under $5,000, Eviction, Small Claims* 107 W 2nd St, Lonoke, AR 72086-2701. 8AM-4:30PM. **501-676-3585**, Fax: 501-676-2500. 📩✋

Madison County

Circuit Court *Felony, Civil Actions Over $5,000, Probate* PO Box 416 (Courthouse), Huntsville, AR 72740. 8AM-4:30PM. **479-738-2215**, Fax: 479-738-2735, Probate: 479-738-2747. Probate in County Clerk's office, PO Box 37; phone- 479-738-1544 Access by ✋

District Court *Misdemeanor, Civil Actions Under $5,000, Eviction, Small Claims* PO Box 549, Huntsville, AR 72740. 8AM-4:30PM. **479-738-2911**, Fax: 479-738-6846. ✋📩**Fax**

Marion County

Circuit Court *Felony, Civil Actions Over $5,000, Probate* PO Box 385, Yellville, AR 72687. 8AM-4:30PM. **870-449-6226**, Fax: 870-449-4979. Access by 📩✋

District Court *Misdemeanor, Civil Actions Under $5,000, Small Claims* PO Box 301, Yellville, AR 72687. 8AM-4:30PM. **870-449-6030**. Access by 📩✋

Miller County

Circuit Court *Felony, Civil Actions Over $5,000, Probate* 412 Laurel St Rm 109, Texarkana, AR 71854. 8AM-4:30PM. **870-774-4501**, Fax: 870-772-5293. Probate is at the County Clerk's office. 📩✋🖥

District Court *Misdemeanor, Eviction* 2300 East St, Texarkana, AR 71854. 8AM-4:30PM. **870-772-2780**, Fax: 870-773-3595. ✋📩

Mississippi County

Osceola Circuit Court *Felony, Civil Actions Over $5,000, Probate* County Courthouse PO Box 466 (200 W Hale), Osceola, AR 72370. 9AM-4:30PM. **870-563-6471**. ✋

Blytheville Circuit Court *Felony, Civil Actions Over $5,000, Probate* PO Box 1498, Blytheville, AR 72316. 9AM-

4:30PM. **870-762-2332**, Fax: 870-763-8148. ✋

Blytheville District Court *Misdemeanor, Civil Actions Under $5,000, Small Claims* 121 N 2nd St, #104, Blytheville, AR 72315. 8AM-5PM. **870-763-7513**, Fax: 870-762-0433. ✉**Fax**✋

Osceola District Court *Misdemeanor, Civil Actions Under $5,000, Small Claims* 397 W Keiser, Osceola, AR 72370. 8AM-4PM. **870-563-1303**, Fax: 870-563-8439. ✉✋

Monroe County

Circuit Court *Felony, Civil Actions Over $5,000, Probate* 123 Madison St, Courthouse, Clarendon, AR 72029. 8AM-4:30PM. **870-747-3615**, Fax: 870-747-3710. ✋

District Court *Misdemeanor, Civil Actions Under $5,000, Small Claims* City Hall, 270 Madison St, Clarendon, AR 72029. 8AM-5PM. **870-747-5200**, Fax: 870-747-9969. ✉✋

Montgomery County

Circuit Court *Felony, Civil Actions Over $5,000, Probate* PO Box 369, Courthouse, Mount Ida, AR 71957. 8AM-4:30PM. **870-867-3521**, Fax: 870-867-2177. ✋

District Court *Misdemeanor, Civil Actions Under $5,000, Eviction, Small Claims* PO Box 548, Mount Ida, AR 71957. 8AM-4:30PM M-Th, other days hours may vary. **870-867-2221**. ✋✉

Nevada County

Circuit Court *Felony, Civil Actions Over $5,000, Probate* PO Box 204, Prescott, AR 71857. 8AM-5PM. **870-887-2511**, Fax: 870-887-1911. Access by ✋✉

District Court *Misdemeanor, Civil Actions Under $5,000, Small Claims* PO Box 22, Prescott, AR 71857. 8AM-5PM. **870-887-6016**, Fax: 870-887-3244. ☎✉**Fax**✋

Newton County

Circuit Court *Felony, Civil Actions Over $5,000, Probate* PO Box 410, Jasper, AR 72641. 8AM-4:30PM. **870-446-5125**, Fax: 870-446-5155. **Fax**✉✋

District Court *Misdemeanor, Civil Actions Under $5,000, Eviction, Small Claims* PO Box 550, Jasper, AR 72641.

8AM-4:30PM. **870-446-5335**, Fax: 870-446-2234. ☎✉**Fax**✋

Ouachita County

Circuit Court *Felony, Civil Actions Over $5,000, Probate* PO Box 667, Camden, AR 71701. 8AM-4:30PM. **870-837-2230** (Circuit), Fax: 870-837-2252, Probate: 870-837-2220. ✋

District Court *Misdemeanor, Civil Actions Under $5,000, Eviction, Small Claims* 213 Madison St, Camden, AR 71701. 8AM-4:30PM. **870-836-0331**, Fax: 870-837-5530. ✉**Fax**✋

Perry County

Circuit Court *Felony, Civil Actions Over $5,000, Probate* PO Box 358, Perryville, AR 72126. 8AM-4:30PM. **501-889-5126**, Fax: 501-889-5759. ✋

District Court *Misdemeanor, Civil Actions Under $5,000, Eviction, Small Claims, Traffic* PO Box 186, Perryville, AR 72126. 8AM-4:30PM. **501-889-5296**, Fax: 501-889-5835. Access by ✋✉

Phillips County

Circuit Court *Felony, Civil Actions Over $5,000, Probate* Courthouse, 620 Cherry St #206, Helena, AR 72342. 8AM-4:30PM. **870-338-5515**, Fax: 870-338-5513, Probate: 870-338-5505. ✉✋

District Court *Misdemeanor, Civil Actions Under $5,000, Eviction, Small Claims* 226 Perry ST, City Hall, Helena, AR 72342. 8AM-4:30PM. **870-338-8825**, Fax: 870-338-8676. Access by ✋✉

Pike County

Circuit Court *Felony, Civil Actions Over $5,000, Probate* PO Box 219, Murfreesboro, AR 71958. 8AM-4:30PM. **870-285-2231**, Fax: 870-285-3281. **Fax**✉✋

District Court *Misdemeanor, Civil Actions Under $5,000, Eviction, Small Claims* PO Box 197, Murfreesboro, AR 71958. 8:30AM-4:30PM. **870-285-3865**, Fax: 870-285-3865. ✋✉

Poinsett County

Circuit Court *Felony, Civil Actions Over $5,000, Probate* PO Box 46, Harrisburg, AR 72432. 8:30AM-4:30PM. **870-578-4420**, Fax: 870-578-4427. ✉✋

Lepanto District Court *Misdemeanor, Civil Actions Under $5,000, Eviction, Small Claims* PO Box 610, Lepanto, AR 72354. 8AM-4:30PM. **870-475-2415**, Fax: 870-475-3161. Access by ✉✋

Marked Tree District Court *Misdemeanor, Civil Actions Under $5,000, Eviction, Small Claims* #1 Elm St, Marked Tree, AR 72365. 8AM-4:30PM. **870-358-2024**, Fax: 870-358-7867. ✉✋

Harrisburg District Court *Misd., Civil Actions Under $5,000, Eviction, Small Claims* 202 N East St, Harrisburg, AR 72432. 8AM-4:30PM. **870-578-4110**, Fax: 870-578-4123. ✉✋

Trumann District Court *Misdemeanor, Civil Actions Under $5,000, Eviction, Small Claims* PO Box 120, Trumann, AR 72472. 8AM-4:30PM. **870-483-7771**, Fax: 870-483-2620. ✉✋

Tyronza District Court *Misdemeanor, Civil Actions Under $5,000, Eviction, Small Claims* PO Box 275, Tyronza, AR 72386. 8AM-4:30PM. **870-487-2168**, Fax: 870-487-2729. Access by ✉✋

Polk County

Circuit Court *Felony, Civil Actions Over $5,000, Probate* 507 Church St, Mena, AR 71953. 8AM-4:30PM. **479-394-8100**, Probate: 479-394-8123. Probate is handled separately from the court. ✉✋

District Court *Misdemeanor, Civil Actions Under $5,000, Eviction, Small Claims* Courthouse, 507 Church St, Mena, AR 71953. 8AM-4:30PM. **479-394-8140**, Fax: 479-394-6199. ✋

Pope County

Circuit Court *Felony, Civil Actions Over $5,000* 100 W Main, Russellville, AR 72801. 8AM-5PM. **479-968-7499**, Probate: 479-968-6064. Access by ✋

District Court *Misdemeanor, Civil Actions Under $5,000, Small Claims* 205 W Second, Russellville, AR 72801. 8AM-5PM. **479-968-1393**, Fax: 479-968-4166. ☎**Fax**✉✋

Prairie County

Circuit Court - Southern District *Felony, Civil Actions Over $5,000, Probate* PO Box 283, De Valls Bluff, AR 72041. 8AM-4:30PM. **870-998-2314**, Fax: 870-998-2314. Access- ☎**Fax**✉✋

Key: Symbols refer to criminal records access unless otherwise noted. phone-☎ mail-✉ fax-**Fax** in person-✋ online-💻 email-**Email**

Circuit Court - Northern District *Felony, Civil Actions Over $5,000, Probate* PO Box 1011, Des Arc, AR 72040. 8AM-4:30PM. **870-256-4434**, Fax: 870-256-4434. Access by ✉ ✋

Des Arc District Court *Misdemeanor, Civil Actions Under $5,000, Eviction, Small Claims* PO Box 389, Des Arc, AR 72040. 8AM-4:30PM. **870-256-3011**, Fax: 870-256-4612. Access by ✋✉

Pulaski County

District Court *Misdemeanor, Civil Actions Under $5,000, Eviction, Small Claims* 3001 W Roosevelt, Little Rock, AR 72204. 8AM-4:30PM. **501-340-6824**, Fax: 501-340-6899. ☎✉✋

Circuit Court *Felony, Civil Actions Over $5,000, Probate* Courthouse, Rm 102 401 W Markham St, #102, Little Rock, AR 72201. 8:30AM-4:30PM. **501-340-8431**, Fax: 501-340-8420, Probate: 501-340-8411. ✋

Randolph County

Circuit Court *Felony, Civil Actions Over $5,000, Probate* 107 W Broadway, Pocahontas, AR 72455. 8AM-4:30PM. **870-892-5522**, Fax: 870-892-8794, Probate: 870-892-5822. Probate records are located at same address, right down the hall. ✉✋

District Court *Misdemeanor, Civil Actions Under $5,000, Eviction, Small Claims* 1510 Pace Rd, Pocahontas, AR 72455. 8:00AM-4:30PM. **870-892-4033**, Fax: 870-892-4392. Access by ✋✉

St. Francis County

Circuit Court *Felony, Civil Actions Over $5,000, Probate* PO Box 1775, Forrest City, AR 72336. 8AM-4:30PM. **870-261-1715**, Fax: 870-261-1723. ✉✋

District Court *Misdemeanor, Civil Actions Under $5,000, Eviction, Small Claims* 615 E Cross, Forrest City, AR 72335. 8AM-4:30PM. **870-261-1410**, Fax: 870-261-1411. Access by ✋✉

Saline County

Circuit Court *Felony, Civil Actions Over $5,000, Probate* www.salinecounty.org 200 N Main St, Benton, AR 72015. 8AM-4:30PM. **501-303-5615**, Fax: 501-303-5675, Probate: 501-303-5630. Probate-215 N Main, Benton, AR 72015. ✋

Benton District Court *Misdemeanor, Civil Actions Under $5,000, Eviction, Small Claims* 1605 Edison Ave #19, Benton, AR 72015. 8AM-4:30PM. **501-303-5670/1 & 5975**, Fax: 501-776-5696. ✋✉

Scott County

Circuit Court *Felony, Civil Actions Over $5,000, Probate* PO Box 2165 190 W First St Box 10, Waldron, AR 72958. 8-4:30PM. **479-637-2642**. ☎✉Fax✋

District Court *Misdemeanor, Civil Actions Under $5,000, Eviction, Small Claims* 100 W 1st St, Box 15, Waldron, AR 72958. 8AM-4:30PM. **479-637-4694**, Fax: 479-637-4712. Access by ✋✉

Searcy County

Circuit Court *Felony, Civil Actions Over $5,000, Probate* PO Box 998, Marshall, AR 72650. 8-4:30PM. **870-448-3807**. ✋

District Court *Misdemeanor, Civil Actions Under $5,000, Eviction, Small Claims* PO Box 885, Marshall, AR 72650. 9AM-5PM. **870-448-5411**, Fax: 870-448-5927. ✋✉

Sebastian County

Circuit Court - Greenwood Division *Felony, Civil Actions Over $5,000, Probate* www.sebastiancountyonline.com PO Box 310, County Courthouse, Greenwood, AR 72936. 8AM-5PM. **479-996-4175**, Fax: 479-996-6885. Records from both Circuit Courts-Fort Smith and Greenwood-are on the same computer system, but copies of case files must be pulled from the individual courts. ✉✋

Circuit Court - Fort Smith *Felony, Civil Actions Over $5,000, Probate* www.sebastiancountyonline.com 35 S 6th St,Rm 203 PO Box 1179, Fort Smith, AR 72902. 8AM-5PM. **479-782-1046**. Records from both Circuit Courts-Fort Smith and Greenwood-are on the same computer system, but copies of case files must be pulled from the individual courts. Closed files in this Circuit are maintained at 40 S 4th St in Fort Smith. Fax✉✋

Fort Smith District Court *Misdemeanor, Civil Actions Under $5,000, Traffic, Small Claims* Courthouse, 35 S 6th St, Fort Smith, AR 72901. 8:30AM-5PM. **479-784-2420**, Fax: 479-784-2438. ☎Fax✉✋

Sevier County

Circuit Court *Felony, Civil Actions Over $5,000, Probate* 115 N 3rd, Courthouse, De Queen, AR 71832. 8AM-4:30PM. **870-584-3055**, Fax: 870-642-3119, Probate: 870-642-2852. Probate court is located in the same building at County Clerk. ✋

District Court *Misdemeanor, Civil Actions Under $5,000, Eviction, Small Claims* 115 N 3rd St, Rm 215, De Queen, AR 71832. 8AM-4:30PM. **870-584-7311**, Fax: 870-642-6651. Access by ✋✉

Sharp County

Circuit Court *Felony, Civil Actions Over $5,000, Probate* PO Box 307, Ash Flat, AR 72513. 8AM-4PM. **870-994-7361**, Fax: 870-994-7712. Access by ✋🖥

District Court *Misdemeanor, Civil Actions Under $5,000, Eviction, Small Claims* PO Box 2, Ash Flat, AR 72513. 8AM-4PM. **870-994-2745**, Fax: 870-994-7901. ✋✉

Stone County

Circuit Court *Felony, Civil Actions Over $5,000, Probate* www.16thdistrictark.org/ 107 W Mail #D, Mountain View, AR 72560. 8AM-4:30PM. **870-269-3271**, Fax: 870-269-2303. ✋

District Court *Misdemeanor, Civil Actions Under $5,000, Eviction, Small Claims* 107 W Main, #H, Mountain View, AR 72560. 8AM-4:30PM. **870-269-3465**. Access by ☎Fax✉✋

Union County

Circuit Court *Felony, Civil Actions Over $5,000, Probate* PO Box 1626, El Dorado, AR 71730. 8:30AM-5PM. **870-864-1940**. ✋🖥

District Court *Misdemeanor, Civil Actions Under $5,000, Eviction, Small Claims* 250 American #A, El Dorado, AR 71730. 8:30AM-5PM. **870-864-1950**, Fax: 870-864-1955. ✋Fax✉

Van Buren County

Circuit Court *Felony, Civil Actions Over $5,000, Probate* 451 Main St, Clinton, AR 72031. 8-5PM. **501-745-4140**. ✉✋

District Court *Misdemeanor, Civil Actions Under $5,000, Small Claims* PO Box 181, Clinton, AR 72031. 8AM-5PM. **501-745-8894**, Fax: 501-745-5810. ☎✉Fax✋

Washington County

Circuit Court *Felony, Civil Actions Over $5,000, Probate* www.co.washington.ar.us/ 280 N College, #302, Fayetteville, AR 72701. 8AM-4:30PM. **479-444-1538**, Fax: 479-444-1537, Probate: 479-444-1711. **Fax**✉✍🖥

Fayetteville District Court *Misd., Civil Actions Under $5,000, Small Claims* www.co.washington.ar.us 100 B WRock, Fayetteville, AR 72701. 8AM-5PM. **479-587-3596**, Fax: 479-444-3480. ✍✉

White County

Circuit Court *Felony, Civil Actions Over $5,000, Probate* 301 W Arch, Searcy, AR 72143. 8AM-4:30PM. **501-279-6223**, Fax: 501-279-6218, Probate: 501-279-6204. ✉✍

Searcy District Court *Misdemeanor, Civil Actions Under $5,000, Small Claims* 311 N Gum, Searcy, AR 72143. 8:00AM-4:30PM. **501-268-7622/279-1040**, Fax: 501-207-5712. ✍☎**Fax**✉

Woodruff County

Circuit Court *Felony, Civil Actions Over $5,000* PO Box 492, Augusta, AR 72006. 8AM-4PM. **870-347-8703**, Fax: 870-347-2915, Probate: 870-347-2871. Probate is handled by the County Clerk. ☎✉✍

District Court *Misdemeanor, Civil Actions Under $5,000, Eviction, Small Claims* PO Box 381, Augusta, AR 72006. 8:30AM-5PM. **870-347-2790**, Fax: 870-347-2436. ✍✉

Yell County

Danville Circuit Court *Felony, Civil Actions Over $5,000, Probate* PO Box 219, Danville, AR 72833. 8AM-4PM. **479-495-4850**, Fax: 479-495-4875. ✉**Fax**✍

Dardanelle Circuit Court *Felony, Civil Actions Over $5,000, Probate* County Courthouse PO Box 457, Dardanelle, AR 72834. 8AM-4PM. **501-229-4404**. ✉✍

District Court *Misdemeanor, Civil Actions Under $5,000, Eviction, Small Claims* County Courthouse, Dardanelle, AR 72834. 8AM-4PM. **501-229-1389**. ✍✉

California

State Court Administration: Administrative Office of Courts, 455 Golden Gate Ave, San Francisco, CA, 94102; 415-865-4200, Fax: 415-865-4205. www.courtinfo.ca.gov

Court Structure: In July, 1998, the judges in individual counties were given the opportunity to vote on unification of superior and municipal courts within their respective counties. By late 2000, all counties had voted to unify these courts. Courts that were formally Municipal Courts are now known as Limited Jurisdiction Superior Courts. In some counties, superior and municipal courts were combined into one superior court. Civil under $25,000 is a Limited Civil Court, over $25,000 is an Unlimited Civil Court, and if both are over and under, then the court is a Combined Civil Court.

It is important to note that Limited Courts may try minor felonies not included under our felony definition.

Due to its large number of courts, the Los Angeles County section is arranged uniquely in this book. Each Branch or Division of the Los Angeles Superior Court is given by name, which usually indicates a court's general jurisdictional and geographic boundary (the actual jurisdiction area is noted in the text). The court name is followed by the District it is located in - South Central, West, Northeast, Central, etc. Also, a court name may mention whether its jurisdiction is "Civil" only or "Criminal" only.

Online Access: There is no statewide online computer access available, internal or external. However, a number of counties have developed their own online access sytems and provide Internet access at no fee. The site at www.courtinfo.ca.gov offers access to all opinions from the Supreme and Appeals courts from 1850 to present. Opinions not certified for publications are available for last 60 days. This site also contains very useful information about the state court system, inlcluding opinions form the Supreme and Appeals courts.

Los Angeles County - As of 2003, all felony and misdemeanor defendant records in Los Angeles County are available online at www.lasuperiorcourt.org/criminalindex. Search fee is $4 to $5. Historical Superior Court felony indices go back to 1973; misdemeanor cases vary - some go back to 1982, others only until 1991. Case disposition information also varies; generally, if the entire criminal case was automated at the time of sentencing, then an accurate case disposition should be included, but if it was not automated or the electronic data was somehow compromised, then the case disposition will not be available online. Keep in mind this is a new system that is still being tested.

Additional Information: If there is more than one court of a type within a county, where the case is tried and where the record is held depends on how a citation is written, where the infraction occurred, or where the filer chose to file the case.

Some courts now require signed releases from the subject in order to perform criminal searches and will no longer allow the public to conduct such searches.

Personal checks are acceptable by state law.

Key: Symbols refer to criminal records access unless otherwise noted.　phone-☎　mail-✉　fax-**Fax**　in person-✍　online-🖥　email-**Email**

Although fees are set by statute, courts interpret them differently. For example, the search fee is supposed to be $6.00 per name per year searched, but many courts charge only $5.00 per name. Generally, certification is $6.60 per document and copies are usually $.75 per page, but can range from $.50 to $1.10, and in Los Angeles County copies are $.57 each.

Alameda County

www.co.alameda.ca.us/courts/index.shtml

Superior Court - Criminal *Felony* 1225 Fallon St, Rm 107, Oakland, CA 94612. 8:30AM-4PM. **510-272-6777**, Fax: 510-835-4850. Located at the Rene C Davidson Alameda County Courthouse. ✉✋

Superior Court South Branch/Hayward - Civil *Civil, Probate* 24405 Amador St, Rm 108, Hayward, CA 94544. 8:30AM-5PM. **510-670-5060**. Located at the Hayward Hall of Justice. Access civil records by✉✋💻

Superior Court - Civil *Civil Actions Over $25,000, Probate* 1225 Fallon St, Rm 109, Oakland, CA 94612. 8:30AM-4:30PM. **510-272-6503**. Access civil records by✉✋💻

Pleasanton Superior Court *Misdemeanor, Civil Actions over $25,000, Eviction, Small Claims, Probate* 5672 Stoneridge Dr Hall of Justice, Pleasanton, CA 94588. 8:30AM-4PM. **925-803-7123**, Fax: 925-803-7979 (civ) 925-551-6862 (crim). Civil phone: 925-551-6886, Crim: 925-803-7995, Probate: 925-551-6886. Includes the cities of Livermore, Dublin, Sunol and Pleasanton and all areas east to San Joaquin County line, north of Highway 580 to Contra Costa line. Located at the Gale/Schenone Hall of Justice. ✉✋

Berkeley/Albany Superior Court - Civil *Civil Actions Under $25,000, Eviction, Small Claims* 2000 Center St, Rm 202, Berkeley, CA 94704. 8:30AM-4:00PM. **510-644-6423**. Co-extensive with the city limits of Berkeley and Albany. Access civil records by✉✋💻

Hayward Superior Court *Misd., Civil Under $25,000, Eviction, Small Claims* 24405 Amador St, Hayward, CA 94544. 8:30AM-4PM. Fax: 510-670-5953. Civil phone: 510-670-5059, Crim: 510-670-6434. Located at the Hayward Hall of Justice. Formerly San Leandro/Hayward Superior Ct. Now includes the cities of San Leandro, Hayward and adjoining unincorporated areas of Castro Valley and San Lorenzo. ✉✋

Oakland/Piedmont/Emeryville Superior Court - Civil *Civil Actions Under* $25,000, Eviction, Small Claims 600 Washington St 4th Fl, #4020, Oakland, CA 94607. 8:30AM-4PM. **510-268-4222**, Fax: 510-268-7807. Located at the Allen E Broussard Justice Center. Comprises the cities of Oakland, Piedmont and Emeryville. by✉✋💻

Oakland/Piedmont/Emeryville Superior Court - Criminal *Misdemeanor, Felony* 661 Washington St 2nd Fl, Oakland, CA 94607. 8:30AM-5PM. **510-268-7700**, Fax: 510-268-7705. Located at the Wiley W Manuel Courthouse. Comprises the cities of Oakland, Piedmont and Emeryville, Albany and Berkeley. ✉✋

Fremont Superior Court *Misd., Civil Under $25,000, Eviction, Small Claims* 39439 Paseo Padre Pky, Fremont, CA 94538. 8:30AM-5PM. Fax: 510-795-2349. Civil phone: 510-795-2360, Crim: 510-795-2300. Located at the Fremont Hall of Justice. Jurisdiction includes Fremont, Newark and Union City. ✉✋

Alameda Branch Superior Court *Felony, Misdemeanor, Civil Actions Under $25,000, Eviction, Small Claims* 2233 Shoreline Dr, Alameda, CA 94501. 8:30AM-5:00PM. **510-268-4209**, Fax: 510-268-4273. Civil phone: 510-268-4219, Crim: 510-268-7494. Co-extensive with the city limits of Alameda only. Located at the George E McDonald Hall of Justice. ✉✋

Alpine County

Superior Court *Felony, Misdemeanor, Civil, Eviction, Small Claims, Probate* www.alpine.courts.ca.gov PO Box 518, Markleeville, CA 96120. 8AM-N, 1-5PM. **530-694-2113** Fax: 530-694-2119. ✉✋

Amador County

Superior Court *Felony, Misdemeanor, Civil, Eviction, Small Claims, Probate* www.amadorcourt.org 108 Court St, Jackson, CA 95642. 9.:3AM-4PM. Civil: 209-223-6463, Crim: phone 209-223-6320. ✉✋

Butte County

Superior Court *Felony, Misdemeanor, Small Claims, Eviction* www.courtinfo.ca.gov/courts/trial/butte One Court St, Oroville, CA 95965. 8:30AM-4PM. **530-532-7002**, Fax: 530-892-8516. Civil phone: 530-532-7009, Crim: 530-532-7012, Probate: 530-532-7017. This courthouse physically holds most criminal court files for the county; however, one can search the countywide computer index at any court. Civil cases were transferred to the Chico court in 2003. ✉✋💻

Chico Branch - Superior Court *Misdemeanor, Civil Actions, Eviction, Small Claims, Probate* 655 Oleander Ave, Chico, CA 95926. 8:30AM-4PM. 530-892-9407 (Traffic), Civil: 530-892-0849, Crim: 530-532-7011. This court handles civil cases previously handled by Oroville court. Active county Probate case records are located here; closed cases are archived in the basement at the main Superior Court in Oroville. ✉✋💻

Gridley Branch - Superior Court *Misdemeanor-Traffic, Eviction, Small Claims* 239 Sycamore, Gridley, CA 95948. 8AM-1PM 1st & 3rd Tuesday of month. **530-846-5701 or 538-7551**. Only open cases are found at this location. Closed cases must be searched at either Chico or Oroville. When court is closed (all but 2 days a month) calls are routed to the Oroville court. ✉💻

Paradise Branch - Superior Court *Misdemeanor-Traffic, Eviction, Small Claims* 747 Elliott Rd, Paradise, CA 95969. 8:30AM-4PM. **530-532-7018**.

Calaveras County

Superior Ct *Misd., Civil, Small Claims, Probate* www.co.calaveras.courts.ca.gov 891 Mt Ranch Rd, San Andreas, CA 95249. 8AM-4PM. **209-754-6311 info**, Fax: 209-754-6689. Civil phone: 209-754-6310, Crim: 209-754-6338, Probate: 209-754-6310. ✉✋

Colusa County

www.colusa.courts.ca.gov

Superior Court *Felony, Civil Actions Over $25,000, Probate* 532 Oak St, Colusa, CA 95932. 8:30AM-5PM. **530-458-5149**, Fax: 530-458-2230. Since 1995, the records have been combined for both courts in this county; search prior records at the individual courts. Dept. 1's courtroom is at 547 Market St. ✉✋

Colusa Superior Court *Felony, Misdemeanor, Civil, Eviction, Small*

Claims 532 Oak St, Colusa, CA 95932. 8:30AM-5PM. **530-458-5149**, Fax: 530-458-2230. Since 1995, records from both courts in this county have been combined; prior records must be searched at the individual courts. ✉ 🖐

Contra Costa County

www.co.contra-costa.ca.us

Superior Court *Felony, Civil Actions Over $25,000, Probate* www.cc-courts.org 725 Court St, Martinez, CA 94553. 8AM-3PM. **925-646-2950**, Civil: 925-646-2951, Crim: 925-646-2440. Family Law Center can be reached at 925-957-7866. ✉ 🖐

Walnut Creek Branch - Superior Court *Felony, Misdemeanor, Civil Actions Under $25,000, Eviction, Small Claims* 640 Ygnacio Valley Rd, Walnut Creek, CA 94596-3820. 8AM-3PM. Civil: 925-646-6579, Crim: 925-646-6572. Includes Alamo, Canyon, Danville, Lafayette, Moraga, Orinda, Rheem, San Ramon, St Mary's College, Walnut Creek and Ygnacio Valley. Effective 01/01/99, this court has all civil records formerly at the municipal court in Concord. ✉ 🖐

Richmond Superior Court *Misd., Civil Actions Under $25,000, Eviction, Small Claims* 100 37th St, Rm 185, Richmond, CA 94805. 8AM-3PM. Civil: 510-374-3137, Crim: 510-374-3158. Includes Crockett, El Cerrito, El Sobrante, Hercules, Kensington, North Richmond, Pinole, Point Richmond, Port Costa, Richmond, Rodeo, Rollingwood and San Pablo. ✉ 🖐

Pittsburg Branch - Superior Court *Felony, Misdemeanor, Civil Actions $25,000 and under, Eviction, Small Claims* 45 Civic Ave, Pittsburg, CA 94565-0431. 8AM-3PM;. Civil: 925-427-8159, Crim: 925-427-8173. Includes Antioch, Bay Pt., Bradford Island, Brentwood, Byron, Discovery Bay, Knightsen, Oakley, Pittsburg. ✉ 🖐

Del Norte County

Superior Court *Felony, Misdemeanor, Civil, Eviction, Small Claims, Probate* 450 "H" St, Rm 209, Crescent City, CA 95531. 8AM-5PM. **707-464-8115**, Fax: 707-465-4005. ✉**Fax** 🖐

El Dorado County

http://eldocourtweb.eldoradocourt.org

South Lake Tahoe Branch - Superior Court - Criminal *Felony, Misdemeanor*

1354 Johnson Blvd, #1, South Lake Tahoe, CA 96150. 8AM-2PM. **530-573-3044**, Fax: 530-542-9102. ✉ 🖐

Placerville Branch - Superior Ct *Felony* http://eldocourtweb.eldoradocourt.org/ 495 Main St, Placerville, CA 95667. 8AM-2PM. **530-621-6426**, Fax: 530-622-9774. Criminal phone: 530-622-6427. ✉ 🖐

South Lake Tahoe Branch - Superior Court - Civil *Civil, Eviction, Probate* 1354 Johnson Blvd, #2, South Lake Tahoe, CA 96150. 8AM-2PM. **530-573-3075**, Fax: 530-544-6532 Access civil records by ✉ 🖐

Cameron Park Branch - Superior Court *Civil, Probate* 3321 Cameron Park Dr, Cameron Park, CA 95682. 8AM-3PM. **530-621-5867**, Fax: 530-672-2413. This is a Trial and Law & Motion court. Only records after 2000 are housed here. Records from 1999 and prior are available at the Placerville Branch Superior Court. Access civil records by ✉ 🖐.

Westen Slope Branch Superior Court *Misdemeanor, Small Claims, Evictions* 2850 Fairlane Ct, Bldg C, Placerville, CA 95667. 8AM-3PM. Civil: 530-621-7470, Crim: 530-621-7464. Also known as the Fairlane Branch. Also hears felony arraignments. ✉ 🖐

Fresno County

www.co.fresno.ca.us/2810/

Superior Court *Felony, Misdemeanor, Civil, Small Claims, Probate* 1100 Van Ness Ave, #401, Fresno, CA 93724. 8AM-3PM; clerk open to researcher 9AM-3PM. Fax: 559-488-1976 civ; 559-488-6799 felony fax; 488-1654 misd. Fax. Civil phone: 559-488-3453, Crim: 559-488-3142 misd.; 559-488-3388 felony, Probate: 559-488-3618. Felony is B-102; Misdemeanor: Rm 402; Civil unlimited: RM 401. ☎**Fax** ✉ 🖐

Kerman Division - Superior Court *Misdemeanor, Civil Actions Under $25,000, Eviction, Small Claims* 719 S Madera Ave, Kerman, CA 93630. 8AM-3PM. **559-846-7371/7372**, Fax: 559-846-5751. The court holds preliminary hearings for felonies. Includes Biola, Biola Junction, Cantua, Five Points, Helm, Kerman, Rolinda, San Joaquin, and Tranquility. ☎ ✉ 🖐

Firebaugh Division - Superior Court *Misdemeanor, Civil Actions Under*

$25,000, Eviction, Small Claims 1325 "O" St, Firebaugh, CA 93622. 8AM-3PM. **559-659-2011/2012**, Fax: 559-659-6228. Includes Firebaugh and Mendota. ☎**Fax** ✉ 🖐

Clovis Division - Superior Court *Traffic, Misdemeanor, Civil Actions Under $25,000, Eviction, Small Claims* 1011 5th St, Clovis, CA 93612. 8AM-3PM. **559-299-4964**, Fax: 559-299-2595. Includes Alder Springs, Auberry, Big Creek, Burroughs Valley, Clovis, Friant, Huntington Lake, Millerton Lake, Pine Ridge, Prather, Shaver, Tollhouse, and Watts. Does felony welfare fraud cases only. ✉ 🖐

Fowler Division - Superior Court *Misdemeanor, Civil Actions Under $25,000, Eviction, Small Claims* PO Box 400, Fowler, CA 93625. 8AM-3PM. **559-834-3215**, Fax: 559-834-1645. This court holds the records for the closed courts in Caruthers, Parlier, and Selma (no criminal) as well as cases from the cities of Bowles, Del Rey, Fowler, Kinopburg, Monmouth, and Raisin City (no criminal). ✉ 🖐

Reedley Division - Superior Court *Misdemeanor, Civil Actions Under $25,000, Eviction, Small Claims* 815 "G" St, Reedley, CA 93654. 8AM-3PM. **559-638-3114**, Fax: 559-637-1534. Includes Badger, Cedarbrook, Cedar Pines, Centerville, Dunlap, Hume, Kings River Canyon, Navalencia, Minkler, Miramonte, Orange Cove, Piedra, Reedley, Sanger, Squaw Valley, Trimmer Springs, and Wahtoke. Access by ✉ 🖐

Kingsburg Division - Superior Court *Felony, Misdemeanor* 1600 California St, Kingsburg, CA 93631. 8AM-3PM. **559-897-2241**, Fax: 559-897-1419. This court includes records from the branch court closed in Riverdale, Selma/Parlick/Fowler (criminal only), and cases from the cities of Burrel, Camden, Kingsburg, Lanare, Laton, and Riverdale. Access by ✉ 🖐

Coalinga Division - Superior Court *Misdemeanor, Civil Actions Under $25,000, Eviction, Small Claims* 160 W Elm St, Coalinga, CA 93210. 8AM-3PM. **559-935-2017/2018**, Fax: 559-935-5324. Includes Coalinga and Huron. ✉ 🖐

Glenn County

Superior Court *Felony, Misdemeanor, Civil, Small Claims, Probate* 526 W

Sycamore, Willows, CA 95988. 8AM-5PM. **530-934-6446**, Fax: 530-934-6728. Records from the municipal court were combined with this court when the courts were consolidated. Records-530-934-6461 ✉🖐

Humboldt County

Superior Court *Felony, Civil, Probate* 825 5th St, 421 I St, Eureka, CA 95501. 10AM-4PM. **707-445-7256**. Countywide searching can be done from this court, records computerized for 10 years. The former Eureka, Eel River, and North Humboldt Municipal Ct Divisions have been combined with this court. ✉🖐

Imperial County

There is no countywide database in this county. All record searching for Imperial county must be done at each location.

Imperial Branch - Superior Court *Felony, Misdemeanor, Civil, Eviction, Small Claims, Probate* 939 W Main St, El Centro, CA 92243. 8AM-4PM. Fax: 760-482-4219/Cri760-482-4918. Civil phone: 760-482-4217, Crim phone: 760-482-4256. ✉🖐

Brawley Branch - Superior Court *Misdemeanor, Civil Actions Under $25,000, Eviction, Small Claims* 220 Main St., Brawley, CA 92227. 8AM-4PM. **760-351-2840**, Fax: 760-351-7703. ☎Fax✉🖐

Calexico Branch - Superior Court *Misdemeanor, Civil Actions Under $25,000, Eviction, Small Claims* 415 4th St, Calexico, CA 92231. 8AM-4PM. **760-357-3726**, Fax: 760-357-6571. Fax✉🖐

Inyo County

There is no countywide database, each branch court must be searched separately.

Superior Court *Felony, Civil Actions Over $25,000, Probate* PO Drawer U 168 N Edwards St, Independence, CA 93526. 8AM- 4PM. **760-878-0218**. ✉🖐

Bishop Branch - Superior Court *Misdemeanor, Civil Actions Under $25,000, Eviction, Small Claims* 301 W Line St, Bishop, CA 93514. 8AM-4PM (open 12-1). **760-872-4971**. ✉🖐

Independence Limited Branch - Superior Court *Misdemeanor, Civil Actions Under $25,000, Eviction, Small Claims* PO Drawer 518 168 N Edwards St, Independence, CA 93526. 9AM-5PM. **760-878-0319**, Fax 760-878-0334. ✉🖐

Kern County

www.co.kern.ca.us/courts/

Superior Court *Felony, Civil Actions, Eviction, Small Claims* 1415 Truxtun Ave, Bakersfield, CA 93301. 8AM-5PM. **661-868-5393**, Fax: 800-487-4567 (civ only) Crim: 661-868-4888. ✉🖐

Ridgecrest Branch Superior Court - East Division *Misdemeanor, Civil Actions Under $25,000, Eviction, Small Claims* 132 E Coso St, Ridgecrest, CA 93555. 8AM-5PM. **760-384-5900**, Fax: 760-384-5899;. Civil phone: 760-384-5986. Includes the communities of Ridgecrest, Inyokern, China Lake, Johanesburg, and Randsburg. ✉🖐☎Fax

Shafter/Wasco Branch Superior Court - North Division *Misdemeanor, Civil Actions Under $25,000, Eviction, Small Claims* 325 Central Valley Hwy, Shafter, CA 93263. 8AM-5PM. **661-746-7500**, Fax: 661-746-0545. Access records✉🖐

Delano/McFarland Branch Superior Court - North Division *Misdemeanor, Civil Actions Under $25,000, Eviction, Small Claims* 1122 Jefferson St, Delano, CA 93215. 8AM-5PM. **661-720-5800**, Fax: 661-721-1237. Criminal phone: x3. ✉🖐

Taft Branch Superior Court - South Division *Misdemeanor, Civil Actions Under $25,000, Eviction, Small Claims* 311 N Lincoln St, Taft, CA 93268. 8AM-N,1-5PM. **661-763-8531**, Fax: 661-763-2439. ☎✉🖐

Lamont/Arvin Branch Superior Court - South Division *Misdemeanor, Civil Actions Under $25,000, Eviction, Small Claims* 12022 Main St, Lamont, CA 93241. 8AM-5PM. **661-868-5800**, Fax: 661-845-9142. Fax✉🖐

Kern River Branch Superior Court - East Division *Misdemeanor, Civil Actions Under $25,000, Eviction, Small Claims* 7046 Lake Isabella Blvd, Lake Isabella, CA 93240. 8AM-4PM M-Th 8AM-5PM F. **760-549-2000**, Fax: 760-549-2120. Includes the communities of Lake Isabella, Kern River, Weldon, Onxy, and Mt Mesa. ☎✉🖐

Mojave Branch Superior Court - East Division *Misdemeanor, Civil Actions Under $25,000, Eviction, Small Claims* 1773 Hwy 58, Mojave, CA 93501. 8AM-5PM. **661-824-7100**, Fax: 661824-7089. Includes California City, Edwards AFB, Mojave, Boron, Rosemond, Cantil, and Tehachapi. ✉Fax🖐

Superior Court Metropolitan Division *Misdemeanor*, 1215 Truxtun Ave, Bakersfield, CA 93301. 8AM-5PM. **661-868-2482**, Fax: 661-868-2695. Formerly Bakersfield Municipal Court. Includes Bakersfield, Oildale, Edison, Glenville, Woody. ✉🖐

Kings County

Superior Court - Criminal *Felony, Misdemeanor* 1426 South Dr, Hanford, CA 93230. 8AM-5PM. **559-582-3211 X4838**, Fax: 559-584-7054. ✉🖐

Superior Court - Civil *Civil Actions, Eviction, Small Claims, Probate* 1426 South Dr, Hanford, CA 93230. 8AM-5PM. **559-582-3211 X2430**, Fax: 559-584-0319 Access civil records by ✉🖐

Corcoran Division Superior Court *Misdemeanor, Civil Actions Under $25,000, Eviction, Small Claims* 1000 Chittenden Ave, Corcoran, CA 93212. 8AM-5PM. **559-992-5193/5194**, Fax: 559-992-5933. ✉🖐

Lemoore Division Superior Court *Misdemeanor, Civil Actions Under $25,000, Eviction, Small Claims* 449 "C" St, Lemoore, CA 93245. 8AM-5PM. **559-924-7757**, Fax: 559-925-0319. Court says to search records at Hanford court; see above. Criminal ✉🖐

Avenal Division Superior Court *Misdemeanor, Civil Actions Under $25,000, Eviction, Small Claims* 501 E Kings St, Avenal, CA 93204. 8AM-5PM. **559-386-5225**, Fax: 559-386-9452. Fax✉🖐

Lake County

Superior Court *Felony, Misdemeanor, Civil, Eviction, Small Claims, Probate* www.courtinfo.ca.gov/courts/trial/lake/lakeport.htm 255 N Forbes St, Lakeport, CA 95453. 8AM-1PM. **707-263-2374**, Fax: 707-262-1327. This court holds the records for the former Northlake Municipal Court. Please note that there are also felony records at the South Lake Division, and both courts should be checked when doing a criminal record search. ✉🖐

South Lake Division - Superior Court *Felony, Misdemeanor, Civil Actions Under $25,000, Eviction, Small Claims* 7000 S Center Dr, Clearlake, CA 95422.

8AM-1PM; Phone hours 8:30AM-12:30PM. **707-994-4859**, Fax: 707-994-1625. Civil phone: 707-994-8262, Crim: 707-994-6598. There are some felony cases here that will not be on the computer index at the Superior Court in Lakeport. The court recommends searching both courts when doing criminal record searches. ✉✋

Lassen County

Superior Court *Felony, Misdemeanor, Civil, Eviction, Small Claims, Probate* www.lassencourt.org/ 220 S Lassen St, #2, Susanville, CA 96130. 7:30AM-5:30PM. **530-251-8189 (dept 1); 251-8205 (dept 2)**. ☎✉✋

Los Angeles County

www.lasuperiorcourt.org

Los Angeles Superior Court - Central District - Felony *Felony, Misdemeanor* 210 W Temple St, Rm M-6, Los Angeles, CA 90012. 8:30AM-4:30PM. **213-974-5259**, Fax: 213-617-1224 (for agencies only) Crim: 213-974-6535 Felony; 974-6141 Misd. This court now handles felonies and misdemeanors; they can do misdemeanor searches for the Central District area of downtown LA, East LA, and Hollywood. ✉✋🖥

Los Angeles Superior Court - Central District - Civil *Civil Actions, Eviction, Small Claims* 110 N Grand Ave, Rm 426, Los Angeles, CA 90012. 8:30AM-4:30PM. **213-974-6135 (974-5171 if over $25,000)**, Fax: 213-621-2701. Any civil cases here under $25,000 are co-extensive with the city limits of Los Angeles and includes the City of San Fernando and sections designated as San Pedro, West Los Angeles, Van Nuys, Venice and the county area known as Florence. Access civil records ☎✉🖥✋.

Los Angeles Superior Court - Probate Dept. www.lasuperiorcourt.org/probate 111 N Hill St, Rm 258, Los Angeles, CA 90012. 8AM-4PM. **213-974-5471**. Case summaries (notes) available free at website; search by case number. Also, probate for current cases in Central Dist., Burbank, Compton, Glendale, Lancaster, Long Beach, Pasadena, Pomona, San Fernando, Santa Monica, Torrance District Courts.

Santa Clarita Superior Court - North Valley District *Misdemeanor, Civil*

Actions Under $25,000, Eviction, Small Claims 23747 W Valencia Blvd, Santa Clarita, CA 91355. 8AM-4:30PM. **661-253-7316**, Fax: 661-254-4107. Civil phone: 661-253-7313, Crim: 661-253-7384. Formerly known as Newhall Sup. Court, it includes Saugus, Valencia, Santa Clarita and unincorporated area bound by Ventura County line (west), Kern County line (north), Agua Dulce on the east, and Glendale and Los Angeles city limits (south). ✉✋🖥

San Pedro Superior Court - South District *Civil Actions, Eviction, Small Claims, Traffic* 505 S Centre St, Rm 202, San Pedro, CA 90731. 8:30AM-4:30PM (civ, sm claims & criminal); 8AM-4:30PM (traffic). **310-519-6014; 519-6016** Traffic, Civil: 310-519-6015. Includes San Pedro, Wilmington and a county strip in Torrance extending up to Western Ave. Access civil records by✉🖥✋.

Alhambra Superior Court - Northeast District *Misdemeanor, Civil Actions Under $25,000, Eviction, Small Claims* 150 W Commonwealth Ave, Alhambra, CA 91801. 8AM-4:30PM. Civil: 626-308-5521, Crim: 626-308-5525. Includes cities of Alhambra, Monterey Park, San Gabriel, Temple City and the unincorporated County area known as South San Gabriel. Address the specific division (criminal, civil, small claims) in correspondence. ✉✋🖥

San Fernando Superior Court - North Valley District *Felony, Misdemeanor, Small Claims* 900 3rd St, #1137, San Fernando, CA 91340. 8:30AM-4:30PM. **818-898-2401**, Crim: 818-898-2655 Felony, 818-898-2407 Misc. Includes Granada Hills, Northridge, Chatsworth, Sunland, Tujunga, Pacoima, Mission Hills, Sylmar, Arleta, Lake View Terrace, Sun Valley and City of San Fernando. They merged with the Newhall Court to become North Valley Court. ✉🖥✋

Beverly Hills Superior Court - West District *Misdemeanor, Civil Actions Under $25,000, Eviction, Small Claims* 9355 Burton Way, Beverly Hills, CA 90210. 8:30AM-4:30PM. **310-860-0070**. Includes cities of Beverly Hills and West Hollywood. Access records☎✉✋🖥

Pomona Superior Court - East District *Misdemeanor, Civil Actions Under $25,000, Eviction, Small Claims* 350 W

Mission Blvd, Pomona, CA 91766. 8AM-4:30PM; Phone Hours: 8AM-N, 2-4PM. **909-802-9944**, Fax: 909-865-6767. Includes cities of Pomona, Claremont, La Verne, Walnut, San Dimas and unincorporated area including Diamond Bar. ✉✋🖥

Airport Superior Court - West District *Felony, Misdemeanor* 11701 S La Cienega Blvd, Los Angeles, CA 90045. 8:30AM-4:30PM. **310-727-6020**, Crim: 310-727-6100. New Court in 2000, includes the areas of Palms, Mar Vista, Rancho Park, Marina del Rey, Venice, Playa del Rey, and Sawtelle. Holds records for the former West LA Court covering Culver, El Segundo, Hawthorne. Access by ✋🖥

Long Beach Superior Court - South District *Misdemeanor, Civil Actions Under $25,000, Eviction, Small Claims* 415 W Ocean Blvd, Long Beach, CA 90802. 8:30AM-4:30PM. **562-491-6201**, Fax: 562-437-0147 (Criminal). Civil phone: 562-491-6234; 562-491-6235 Sm Claims, Crim: 562-491-6226/6227, Probate: 562-491-5928. Includes cities of Long Beach and Signal Hill and adjoining unincorporated area. Address requests to civil or criminal division. ✉✋🖥

Metropolitan Branch Superior Court - Central District *Misdemeanor* 1945 S Hill St, Rm 200, Los Angeles, CA 90007. 8AM-4:30PM. **213-744-4023**, Fax: 213-744-1879. Vehicle Code misdemeanor and traffic citations for the incorporated City of Los Angeles excluding the areas known as San Pedro, West Los Angeles and communities of San Fernando Valley and the unincorporated County area more commonly known as Florence. ✉✋🖥

Culver City Superior Court - West District *Civil Under $25,000, Eviction, Small Claims* 4130 Overland Ave, Culver City, CA 90230. 8:30AM-4:30PM. **310-202-3181**, Fax: 310-836-8345. Civil phone: 310-202-3160. Includes Culver City and surrounding unincorporated areas including Angelus Vista, portions of Marina del Rey, View Park and Windsor Hills, all surrounded by the City of Los Angeles, on south bounded by Inglewood. No longer handles misdemeanors as of 2000. Access civil records by✉🖥✋.

Malibu Superior Court - West District *Misdemeanor, Civil Actions Under $25,000, Eviction, Small Claims* 23525

W Civic Center Way, Malibu, CA 90265. 8AM-4:30PM. **310-317-1335**, Fax: 310-456-0194. Includes Malibu, Agoura Hills, Calabasas, Westlake Village, Hidden Hills and unincorporated areas known as Topanga and Chatsworth Lake, bounded by Ventura County on the west and north, Pacific Ocean on the south and City of Los Angeles on the east. ✉✋🖥

Torrance Superior Court - Southwest District *Misd., Civil, Traffic, Eviction, Small Claims* 825 Maple Ave, Torrance, CA 90503-5058. 8:30AM-4:30PM. **310-222-6505, 222-6501 Admin.**, Fax: 310-783-5108 Crim; 310-782-7326 Civil fax. Civil phone: 310-222-8809 Civ, 222-6400 Sm Claims, Crim: 310-222-6506, Probate: 310-222-8803. Includes cities of Torrance, Gardena, Rolling Hills, Rolling Hills Estates, Manhattan Beach, Lomita, Redondo Beach, Hermosa Beach, Palos Verdes Estates, Rancho Palos Verdes, and Lawndale. ✉✋🖥

Whittier Superior Court - Southeast District *Misdemeanor, Civil Actions Under $25,000, Eviction, Small Claims* 7339 S Painter Ave, Whittier, CA 90602. 8AM-4:30PM. Civil: 562-907-3127, Crim: 562-907-3113. Includes cities of Whittier, Santa Fe Springs, Pico Rivera, La Habra Heights plus unincorporated territory in the Whittier area including areas designated as Los Nietos and South Whittier. ✉✋🖥

Hollywood Superior Court - Central District *Misdemeanor* 5925 Hollywood Blvd, Los Angeles, CA 90028. 8:30AM-4:30PM. **323-856-5747**. High-grade and low-grade Misdemeanors for the Hollywood area. ✉✋🖥

Compton Superior Court - South Central District *Felony, Misdemeanor, Civil Actions, Eviction, Small Claims* 200 W Compton Blvd, Compton, CA 90220. 8:30AM-4:30PM. Fax: 310-223-5941. Civil phone: 310-603-7812, Crim: 310-603-7112. Includes cities of Carson, Compton, Lynwood and Paramount and the unincorporated portions of county that surround them. ✉✋🖥

Redondo Beach Superior Court - Southwest District *Civil Actions over $25,000* 117 W Torrance Blvd, Redondo Beach, CA 90277-3638. 8:15AM-4:30PM. **310-798-6875**, Fax: 310-376-4051. Also known as the Southwest District South Bay Court - Beach Cities Branch. Access civil records by✉🖥✋.

Norwalk Superior Court - Southeast District *Felony, Civil Actions Over $25,000, Probate* 12720 Norwalk Blvd, Norwalk, CA 90650. 8:30AM-4:30PM. **562-807-7340**. ✉✋🖥

Santa Monica Superior Court - West District *Misdemeanor, Civil Actions Under $25,000, Eviction, Small Claims* 1725 Main St, Rm 224, Santa Monica, CA 90401. 8:30AM-4:30PM. **310-260-3522**, Fax: 310-576-1399. Civil phone: 310-587-2442. Limited/Sm Claims; 310-587-2442. Unlim., Crim: 310-587-2442. Probate: 310-260-3771. Includes City of Santa Monica and the unincorporated territory of the Veteran's Administration facilities located at West Los Angeles. ✉✋🖥

El Monte Superior Court - East District *Misdemeanor, Civil Actions Under $25,000, Eviction, Small Claims* 11234 E Valley Blvd, El Monte, CA 91731. 8AM-4:30PM. Fax: 626-444-9029. Civil phone: 626-575-4117, Crim: 626-575-4121. Includes cities of El Monte, South El Monte, La Puente, Rosemead and adjacent unincorporated county area. ☎✉✋🖥

Pasadena Superior Court - Northeast District *Misdemeanor, Civil Actions Under $25,000, Eviction, Small Claims* 300 E Walnut, Pasadena, CA 91101. 8:30AM-4:30PM. Fax: 626-568-3903. Civil phone: 626-356-5695, Crim: 626-356-5254. Includes cities of Pasadena, South Pasadena, San Marino, Sierra Madre and the area of Altadena and East Pasadena. ✉✋🖥

Downey Superior Court - Southeast District *Misdemeanor, Civil Actions Under $25,000, Eviction, Small Claims* 7500 E Imperial Hwy, Downey, CA 90242. 8:30AM-4:30PM T-F; 8:30AM-6PM M. Civil: 562-803-7052, Crim: 562-803-7049. Comprises the cities of Downey, Norwalk and La Mirada. ✉✋🖥

Huntington Park Superior Court - Southeast District *Misdemeanor, Civil Actions Under $25,000, Eviction, Small Claims* 6548 Miles Ave, Huntington Park, CA 90255. 8AM-4:30PM. Fax: 323-589-6769. Civil phone: 323-586-6365, Crim: 323-586-6362. Includes cities of Bell, Bell Gardens, Cudahy, Huntington Park, Maywood and Vernon. Also includes South Gate, Hollydale and area of Walnut Park from closed court at South Gate. ☎✉✋🖥

Inglewood Superior Court - Southwest District *Misdemeanor, Civil Actions Under $25,000, Eviction, Small Claims* 1 Regent St, Inglewood, CA 90301. 8AM-4:30PM. **310-419-5132**, Fax: 310-674-4862 (680-7055 Civ. Fax). Civil phone: 310-419-5132, Crim: 310-419-5128. Includes cities of Inglewood, Hawthorne, El Segundo, Lennox and adjoining unincorporated area. Access by ✉✋

East Los Angeles Superior Court - Central District *Misdemeanor, Civil Actions Under $25,000, Eviction, Small Claims* 214 S Fetterly Ave, Los Angeles, CA 90022. 8AM-4:30PM. Civil: 323-780-2017, Crim: 323-780-2025. Includes cities of Montebello and Commerce and adjacent territory bordering Monterey Park on the north and Los Angeles on the west. ✉✋🖥

Van Nuys Superior Court - Northwest District - Civil *Civil Actions, Eviction, Small Claims, Family Law, Probate* 6230 Sylmar St, Van Nuys, CA 91401. 8:30AM-4:30PM. **818-374-2208**. Small Claims for Sherman Oaks, Van Nuys, Reseda, North Hollywood, Woodland Hills, Canoga Park, Tarzana, Porter Ranch, Winnetka and Panorama City. Civil jurisdiction depends on whether limited or general. Access civil records by✉🖥✋.

Burbank Superior Court - North Central District *Felony, Misdemeanor, Civil Actions, Eviction, Small Claims*. 300 E Olive Ave, Burbank, CA 91502-1215. 8:15AM-4:30PM. Fax: 818-953-9455 Civil. Civil phone: 818-557-3482 Civ; 818-557-3461 Sm Claims, Crim: 818-557-3466. ✉✋🖥

Bellflower Superior Court - Southeast District *Misdemeanor, Civil Actions Under $25,000, Eviction, Small Claims* 10025 E Flower St, Bellflower, CA 90706. 8AM-4:30PM. **562-804-8025**, Civil: 562-804-8011, Crim: 562-804-8018. Includes Artesia, Bellflower, Hawaiian Gardens, Lakewood and Cerritos. Specify civil or criminal search request. Small claims phone is 562-804-8011. ✉✋🖥

West Covina Superior Court - East District *Misdemeanor, Civil Actions Under $25,000, Eviction, Small Claims* 1427 W Covina Pky, West Covina, CA 91790. 8AM-4:30PM. Fax: 626-338-7364. Civil phone: 626-813-3236 Civ, 626-813-3226 Sm Claims, Crim: 626-813-3239. Formerly known as Citrus Court, this includes cities of Azusa, Baldwin Park, Covina, Glendora, Industry, Irwindale, Valinda, West Covina and surrounding unincorporated County area. ✋💻

West Los Angeles Superior Court - West District *Civil Actions Under $25,000, Eviction, Small Claims* 1633 Purdue Ave, Los Angeles, CA 90025. 8:30AM-4:30PM. **310-914-7477**, Fax: 310-312-2902. Includes the areas of Palms, Mar Vista, Rancho Park, Marina del Rey, Venice, Playa del Rey and Sawtelle. Holds records for the former Robertson branch. Criminal felony and misdemeanors are at the new Airport Court. ✉️✋💻

Van Nuys Superior Court - Northwest District - Criminal *Felony, Misdemeanor* 14400 Erwin St, Mall, 2nd Fl, Van Nuys, CA 91401. 8:30AM-4:30PM. **818-374-2903**. Misdemeanors for that part of city known as Sherman Oaks, Van Nuys, Reseda, North Hollywood, Woodland Hills, Canoga Park, Tarzana, Proter Ranch, Winnetka and Panorama City. ☎️✉️✋💻

Lancaster Superior Court - North District *Felony, Misd., Civil, Small Claims, Probate* 42011 4th St, Lancaster, CA 93534. 8AM-4:30PM. **661-974-7200**. Formerly Antelope; includes Lancaster, City of Palmdale, and unincorporated County territory including Acton, Agua Dulce, Fairmont, Lake Hughes, Llano, Leona Valley, Littlerock, Pearblossom, Quartz Hill, Roosevelt, Green Valley Big Pines, Lake Elizabeth. Access-✉️✋💻

Glendale Superior Court - North Central District *Misdemeanor, Civil Actions Under $25,000, Eviction, Small Claims* Los Angeles Superior Court 600 E Broadway, Glendale, CA 91206. 8:15AM-4:30PM. Fax: 818-548-0486 Civ; 548-0236 Crim. Civil phone: 818-500-3551, Crim: 818-500-3530. Includes cities of Glendale, LaCanada-Flintridge and unincorporated county are known as Montrose, La Crescenta, Verdugo City, Highway Highlands, and Kogel Canyon. ✉️✋💻

Santa Anita Superior Court - Northeast District *Civil Under $25,000, Eviction, Small Claims* 300 W Maple Ave, Monrovia, CA 91016. 8AM-4:30PM. **626-301-4056**, Fax: 626-357-7825. Civil phone: 626-301-4050, Crim: 626-301-

4051. Includes cities of Monrovia, Arcadia, Duarte, Bradbury and unincorporated county territory in surrounding area. This court no longer handles misdemeanor records, cases refered to Alhambra court. Access civil records by ✉️💻✋

Madera County

Superior Court *Felony, Civil, Probate, Eviction, Small Claims* 209 W Yosemite Ave, Madera, CA 93637. 8AM-4PM. **559-675-7944**, Fax: 559-675-0701. Civil phone: 559-675-7996, Crim: 559-675-7734. The Superior and Municipal courts located in the City of Madera have combined into a consolidated court. There is no countywide database of records; each court must be searched. ✉️**Fax**✋

Sierra Division - Superior Court *Felony, Misdemeanor, Civil Actions Under $25,000, Eviction, Small Claims, Probate* 40601 Road 274, Bass Lake, CA 93604. 8:30AM-4:30PM. **559-642-3235**, Fax: 559-642-3445. There is no countywide database of records. Each court must be searched. Access by ✉️✋

Marin County

Superior Court *Felony, Misdemeanor, Civil, Eviction, Small Claims, Probate* www.co.marin.ca.us/courts PO Box 4988, San Rafael, CA 94913-4988. 8:30AM-4PM. Civil: 415-473-6407, Crim: 415-473-6225. ✉️✋💻

Mariposa County

Superior Court *Felony, Misdemeanor, Civil, Small Claims, Eviction, Probate* www.mariposacourts.org 5088 Bullion St (PO Box 28), Mariposa, CA 95338. 8:30AM-4PM. **209-966-2005**, Fax: 209-742-6860. Civil phone: 209-966-6599, Crim: 209-966-2005, Probate: 209-966-6599. This former municipal court is now known as Department 2. ☎️**Fax**✉️✋

Mendocino County

www.mendocino.courts.ca.gov/

Superior Court *Felony, Civil Actions Over $25,000, Probate* 100 N State & Perkins Sts (PO Box 996 Civ; PO Box 337 Crim), Ukiah, CA 95482. 8AM-2:30 PM (noon on F). Fax: 707-463-4655. Civil phone: 707-463-4481, Crim: 707-463-4486. ✉️✋💻

Ten Mile Branch - Superior Court *Felony, Misd., Civil Actions, Eviction,*

Small Claims www.mendocino.co urts.ca.gov/fortbragg.html 700 S Franklin St, Fort Bragg, CA 95437. 8AM-2:30PM (Noon on Friday). **707-964-3192**, Fax: 707-961-2611. ✉️✋💻

Willits Branch - Superior Court *Felony, Misdemeanor, Civil Actions Under $25,000, Eviction, Small Claims* 125 E Commercial St, Rm 100, Willits, CA 95490. 8AM-2 :30PM (Noon on Friday). **707-459-7800**, Fax: 707-459-7818. ✉️✋💻

Merced County

Superior Court *Felony, Civil Actions Over $25,000, Probate* 627 W 21st St, Merced, CA 95340. 8AM-4PM. **209-385-7531**, Fax: 209-725-9223. Access-✉️✋

Los Banos Branch - Superior Court *Misdemeanor, Civil Actions Under $25,000, Eviction, Small Claims* 445 "I" St, Los Banos, CA 93635. 8AM-4PM. **209-725-4124**, Fax: 209-725-4125. This court was combined with the old Dos Palos and Gustine Municipal Courts. ✉️✋

4, 5, 7 & 8 Divisions - Merced Limited Superior Court *Misdemeanor, Civil Actions Under $25,000, Eviction, Small Claims* 670 W 22nd St, Merced, CA 95340. 8AM-4PM M-F (civil); N-4PM M-F (civ only). **209-725-4113**, Fax: 209-725-4114. Civil phone: 209-385-7337, Crim: 209-385-7335. Access by ✉️✋

Modoc County

Superior Court *Felony, Misdemeanor, Civil, Small Claims, Eviction, Probate* 205 S East St, Alturas, CA 96101. 8:30AM-5PM. **530-233-6515/6**, Fax: 530-233-6500. **Fax**✉️✋

Mono County

Superior Court - Bridgeport Branch *Felony, Civil, Probate* PO Box 537, Bridgeport, CA 93517. 8:30AM-5PM. **760-932-5239**. ✉️✋

Mammoth Lakes Division - Superior Court *Felony, Misd., Civil, Eviction, Small Claims* www.monosuperiorcourt.c a.gov/ PO Box 1037, Mammoth Lakes, CA 93546. 9AM-5PM. **760-924-5444**, Fax: 760-924-5419. ✉️✋

Monterey County

www.co.monterey.ca.us/court **Superior Court - Monterey Branch** *Civil,*

Probate, http://65.119.109.232/ 1200 Aguajito Rd 1st Fl, Monterey, CA 93940. 9:30AM-4PM. **831-647-5800**. This court holds the civil records from the city of Salinas. Criminal records for Monterey are held in Salinas. Access civil records by ✉ ✋

Superior Court - Salinas Division *Felony, Misdemeanor* 240 Church St, Rm 318, PO Box 1819, Salinas, CA 93902. 8AM-4PM. **831-755-5400**. All criminal records are filed at the Salinas courthouse. All civil, probate, and family law cases are files at the Monterey courthouse. ✉ ✋ 💻

King City Division - Consolidated Trial Court *Felony, Misdemeanor, Civil Actions Under $25,000, Eviction, Small Claims* 250 Franciscan Way (PO Box 647), King City, CA 93930. 8AM-5PM; Public Hours: 9:30AM-4PM. **831-386-5200**. Encompasses the cities of King City, Greenfield, Soledad, areas south of King City to the San Luis Obispo County line. ✉ ✋ 💻

Napa County
www.napa.courts.ca.gov
Superior Court - Criminal Div. *Felony, Misdemeanor* 1111 3rd St, Napa, CA 94559. 8AM-5PM. **707-299-1180**, Fax: 707-253-4673. ✉ ✋**Fax**💻

Superior Court - Civil Division *Civil, Eviction, Small Claims, Probate* 825 Brown St, Napa, CA 94559. 8AM-5PM. **707-299-1130**, Fax: 707-253-4229. Criminal phone: 702-299-1180 Access civil records by ✉ ✋

Nevada County
www.court.co.nevada.ca.us
Superior Court - Criminal *Felony, Misdemeanor* 201 Church St, #7, Nevada City, CA 95959. 8AM-5PM. **530-265-1311**, Fax: 530-478-1938. ☎✉ ✋💻

Superior Court - Civil Division *Civil, Eviction, Small Claims* 201 Church St, #5, Nevada City, CA 95959. 8AM-5PM. Civil: 530-265-1294, Crim: 530-265-1311, Probate: 530-265-1293. Evictions and Small Claims: 530-265-1294. Access civil records by☎✉ ✋💻

Truckee Branch - Superior Court *Misdemeanor, Civil, Eviction, Small Claims* 10075 Levon Ave, #301, Truckee, CA 96161. 8AM-5PM. Fax: 530-582-7875. Civil phone: 530-582-7837, Crim: 530-582-7835. ✉ ✋💻

Orange County
www.occourts.org
Superior Court - Civil *Civil Actions, Small Claims* 700 Civic Center Dr W, Santa Ana, CA 92701. 8AM-4PM. **714-834-2200**. This court handles civil actions over $25,000 countywide, but holds only limited civil and small claims cases for this central jurisdiction venue (Santa Ana area). Access civil records by ✉ ✋

Superior Court - Criminal Operations *Felony, Misdemeanor* 700 Civic Center Dr W, Santa Ana, CA 92701. 8AM-4PM. **714-834-2200**, Crim: 714-834-2266. ✉ ✋

West Orange County Superior Court *Misdemeanor, Civil Actions Under $25,000, Eviction, Small Claims* 8141 13th St, Westminster, CA 92683. 8AM-4PM. **714-896-7181**, Fax: 714-896-7404 (civ); 896-7219 (criminal). Civil phone: 714-896-7191, Crim: 714-896-7351. Includes the cities of Cypress, Fountain Valley, Garden Grove, Huntington Beach, Los Alamitos, Rossmore, Seal Beach, Stanton, Sunset Beach, Surfside, Westminster and adjoining unincorporated territory. ✉ ✋

North Orange County Superior Court *Felony, Misdemeanor, Civil Actions Under $25,000, Eviction, Small Claims* 1275 N Berkeley Ave PO Box 5000, Fullerton, CA 92838-0500. 7:30AM-4PM. **714-773-4555**; 773-4667 (Small Claims). Civil phone: 714-773-4664, Crim: 714-773-4668. Includes the cities of Anaheim, Brea, Buena Park, Fullerton, La Habra, La Palma, Placentia, Yorba Linda and surrounding unincorporated area including Anaheim Hills. Traffic phone: 714-773-4615. ✉ ✋

Central Orange County Superior Court - Limited Jurisdiction *Misdemeanor, Civil Actions Under $25,000, Eviction, Small Claims* PO Box 1138 700 Civic Ctr Dr W, Santa Ana, CA 92702. 8AM-4PM. Fax: 714-953-9032. Civil phone: 714-834-3580, Crim: 714-834-3575. Includes cities of Santa Ana, Orange, Tustin and surrounding unincorporated territories including Cowan Heights, El Modena, Tustin Marine Air Base, Lemon Heights, Modjeska, Orange Park Acres, Silverado Canyon, and Villa Park. ✉ ✋

Harbor - Laguna Niguel Superior Court - Criminal Division *Misdemeanor* 30143 Crown Valley Pky Justice Center,

Laguna Niguel, CA 92677. 8AM-4PM. **949-249-5000**. Also known as South Orange County Superior Court. Includes Capistrano Bch, Coto De Caza, Dana Pt, Laguna Hills, Laguna Niguel, Mission Viejo, Rancho St. Margarita, San Clemente, San Juan Capistrano, Trabuco Canyon. ✉ ✋

Harbor - Laguna Hills Superior Court - Civil Division *Civil Actions Under $25,000, Eviction, Small Claims* 23141 Moulton Pky, Laguna Hills, CA 92653. 8AM-4PM. **949-472-6964**. Formerly known as South Orange, this includes Aliso Viejo, Capistrano Bch, Coto De Caza, Dana Pt, Laguna (various), Lake Forest, Mission Viejo, Rancho St. Margarita, San Clemente, San Juan Capistrano, Trabuco Canyon. Access civil records by ✉ ✋

Harbor - Newport Beach Superior Court *Misdemeanor, Civil Actions Under $25,000, Eviction, Small Claims* 4601 Jamboree Rd, #104, Newport Beach, CA 92660-2595. 8AM-4PM. **949-476-4699**. Includes Balboa Island, Corona Del Mar, Costa Mesa, Newport Beach, Irvine, Santa Ana Heights, John Wayne/Orange Co Airport, Lido Isle and surrounding unincorporated areas. ✉ ✋

Orange County Probate Court 341 The City Dr, Orange, CA 92868. 8AM-5PM. **714-935-8043**. Search court calendars free at www.occourts.org/calendars/calendarsprob.asp.

Placer County
www.placercourts.org
Superior Court *Felony, Civil, Eviction, Probate* 101 Maple St, Auburn, CA 95603. 8AM-3PM. Civil: 530-889-6550, Crim: 530-886-1200. ☎✉ ✋

Tahoe Division - Superior Court *Misdemeanor, Civil, Eviction, Small Claims* PO Box 5669, Tahoe City, CA 96145. 8AM-3PM. **530-581-6336**, Fax: 530-581-6344. This court does all areas of law with the exception of Adoptions and Probate. ✉ ✋

Auburn Branch - Superior Ct *Felony, Misdemeanor* 11532 "B" Ave, Auburn, CA 95603. 8AM-3PM Office (8AM-3PM phone hours). **530-886-1200**, Fax: 530-886-1209. Includes Auburn, Penryn, Newcastle, Bowman, Colfax, Weimar, Alta, Dutch Flat, Loomis. Also includes criminal for Roseville, Rocklin, Lincoln criminal as of 12/8/97. ✉ ✋

Key: Symbols refer to criminal records access unless otherwise noted. phone-☎ mail-✉ fax-**Fax** in person-✋ online-💻 email-**Email**

Plumas County

www.plumascourt.ca.gov
Superior Court - Criminal Div. *Felony, Misdemeanor* 520 Main St, Rm 104, Quincy, CA 95971. 8AM-5PM. **530-283-6232**, Fax: 530-283-6415. ✉✋

Superior Court - Civil Division *Civil, Small Claims, Probate* 520 Main St, Rm 104, Quincy, CA 95971. 8AM-5PM. **530-283-6305**, Fax: 530-283-6415. Criminal phone: 530-283-6232 Access civil records by ☎Fax✉✋

Portola Branch - Superior Court *Civil Actions Under $25,000, Eviction, Small Claims, Traffic* 161 Nevada St (PO Box 1054), Portola, CA 96122. 8AM-3:30PM. **530-832-4286**, Fax: 530-832-5838. ☎✉✋

Chester Branch - Superior Court *Civil Actions Under $25,000, Eviction, Small Claims* www.psln.com/pccourt 1st & Willow Way (PO Box 722), Chester, CA 96020. 8AM-4PM. **530-258-2646**, Fax: 530-258-2652 Access civil by ☎ ✉ ✋

Riverside County

www.courts.co.riverside.ca.us/
Superior Court - Civil Division *Civil Actions, Small Claims, Probate* 4050 Main St, Riverside, CA 92501. 8AM-4PM. **951-955-1960**, Fax: 909-955-1751, Probate: 951-955-1970. All Superior Court Files and Limited Jurisdiction files except for those cases filed within the Mt. San Jacinto Judicial District and Three Lakes Judicial District. Access civil records by ☎Fax✉🖥✋.

Superior Court - Criminal Div. *Felony, Misdemeanor.* 4100 Main St, Riverside, CA 92501. 7:30AM-4PM. **951-955-2300**, Fax: 951-955-4007. ☎Fax✉🖥✋

Blythe Division - Superior Court *Felony, Misdemeanor, Civil Actions, Eviction, Small Claims* 265 N Broadway, Blythe, CA 92225. 7:30AM-4PM. Fax: 760-921-7941 civ.; 921-7942 crim. Civil phone: 760-921-7981, Crim: 760-921-7828 (incl: traffic). Includes Blythe, Ripley. Phone for Family Law is 760-921-7982. ☎Fax✉🖥✋

Temecula Branch - Superior Court *Civil Under $25,000, Eviction, Small Claims* 41002 County Center Dr, Temecula, CA 92591. 7:30AM-4PM. **951-600-6400**, Fax: 951-600-6423. Civil records for the former Lake Elsinore and

Perris Branches are stored here. Includes Perris, Sun City, Romoland, Homeland, Lakeview, Glenn Valley, Mead Valley, Quail Valley, Nuevo. Access civil records ☎✉🖥✋

Hemet Division - Superior Court *Civil Actions Under $25,000, Eviction, Small Claims* 880 N State St, Hemet, CA 92543. 7:30AM-4PM. **951-766-2322**, Fax: 951-766-2317. Includes Aguanga, Anza, Gilman Hot Springs, Hemet, Idylwild, Mountain Center, Pine Cove, Redec, Sage, San Jacinto, Sobba Hot Spring, Valle Vista and Winchester. Access civil records by ✉🖥✋.

Banning Division - Superior Court *Felony, Misdemeanor, Civil Actions Under $25,000, Eviction, Small Claims* 155 E Hays St, Banning, CA 92220. 7:30AM-4PM. Fax: 909-922-7160 civ; 909-922-7150 crim. Civil phone: 909-922-7155, Crim: 909-922-7145. Includes Banning, Cabazon, Highland Springs, Poppet Flatt, Silent Valley, Beaumont, Calimesa, Cherry Valley and Whitewater. ☎Fax✉🖥✋

Southwest Justice Center - Superior Court *Felony, Misdemeanor, Family Law* 30755 "D" Auld Rd, #1226, Murrieta, CA 92563. 7:30AM-4PM. **951-304-5000**, Fax: 951-304-5250. This is a new court (01/01/03) that took in the criminal court cases from the closed Superior Courts in Lake Elsinore and Perris. Fax✉🖥✋

Indio Division - Superior Court *Misdemeanor, Civil Actions Under $25,000, Eviction, Small Claims, Probate* 46-200 Oasis St, Indio, CA 92201. 7:30AM-4PM. **760-863-8426**, Fax: 760-863-8707. Civil phone: 760-863-8208, Crim: 760-863-8206, Probate: 760-863-8207. Includes Desert Center, Eagle Mountain, Indio, La Quinta, Coachella, Bermuda Dunes, Mecca, North Shore, Pinyon Pines, Palm Springs, Salton Sea, Oasis, Thermal. Most Palm Springs records are here. ☎Fax✉🖥✋

Sacramento County

Superior Court *Felony, Misdemeanor, Civil* www.saccourt.com 720 9th St, Rm 102, Sacramento, CA 95814. 8:30AM-4:30PM. **916-874-5522**, Fax: 916-874-5620. Civil phone: 916-874-6868, Crim: 916-874-5744. Probate is located at 3341 Power Inn Rd, Sacramento 95826 (916-875-3400). Galt, Elk Grove, and Walnut

Grove branches are closed. This court now holds their records. ☎✉🖥✋

San Benito County

Superior Court *Felony, Misdemeanor, Civil, Small Claims, Eviction, Probate* www.sanbenito.courts.ca.gov Courthouse, 440 5th St, Rm 205, Hollister, CA 95023. 8AM-4PM. **831-636-4057**, Fax: 831-636-2046. As of 11/2000, Small Claims, Family Law, and Eviction records are located at the Limited Jurisdiction Court, 390 5th St, Hollister. Phone: 831-630-5115. Fax: 831-636-4117. Same search requirements as stated below. ✉✋

San Bernardino County

www.sbcounty.gov/courts/
Victorville District - Superior Court *Felony, Misdemeanor, Civil, Eviction, Small Claims, Probate* 14455 Civic Dr, Victorville, CA 92392. 8AM-4PM. Fax: 760-243-8790 (civil); 8794 (criminal). Civil phone: 760-245-6215, Crim: 760-245-6215. Includes the Cities of Victorville, Adelanto Hesperia and the areas of Apple Valley, El Mirage, Helendale, Lucerne Valley, Oro Grande, Phelan, Pinon Hill and Wrightwood. ✉✋🖥

Barstow District - Superior Court *Felony, Misdemeanor, Civil, Eviction, Small Claims* www.sbcounty.gov/courts/ 235 E Mountain View, Barstow, CA 92311. 8AM-4PM. **760-256-4814**, Civil: 760-256-4907, Crim: 760-256-4785. Includes the City of Barstow and the unincorporated areas of Yermo, Lenwood, Daggett, Hinkley and Baker. ✉✋🖥

Central District - Superior Court *Felony, Misdemeanor, Civil, Eviction, Small Claims, Probate* 351 N Arrowhead Ave, San Bernardino, CA 92415. 8AM-4PM. Fax: 909-387-4428 (387-4993 criminal). Civil phone: 909-387-3922, Crim: 909-384-1888. ✉✋🖥

Rancho Cucamonga District - Superior Court *Felony, Misdemeanor, Civil, Eviction, Small Claims, Probate* www.co.san-bernardino.ca.us/courts/ 8303 N Haven Ave, Rancho Cucamonga, CA 91730. 8AM-4PM. **909-945-4131 info.**, Fax: 909-945-4154. Civil phone: 909-945-4131, Crim: 909-350-9764. Formerly West District Superior Ct. Includes cities of Montclair, Ontario, Upland, Rancho Cucamonga, Alta Loma, Etiwanda, Guasti

---

Key: Symbols refer to criminal records access unless otherwise noted. phone-☎ mail-✉ fax-Fax in person-✋ online-🖥 email-**Email**

and surrounding unincorporated area of Mt Baldy. ☎Fax☒✍🖳

Joshua Tree District - Superior Court
Felony, Misdemeanor, Civil, Eviction, Small Claims 6527 White Feather Rd (PO Box 6602), Joshua Tree, CA 92252. 8AM-4PM. **760-366-5770**, Fax: 760-366-4156. Civil phone: 760-366-5770, Crim: 760-366-5775. Includes the incorporated area of City of Twenty-Nine Palms, Town of Yucca Valley and unincorporated areas of Morongo Valley, Pioneertown, Landers, Johnson Valley and Wonder Valley. ☒✍🖳

Big Bear Lake District - Superior Court
Misdemeanor, Civil Actions Under $25,000, Eviction, Small Claims PO Box 2806 (477 Summit Blvd), Big Bear Lake, CA 92315. 8AM-4PM. **909-866-0150**, Fax: 909-866-0160. ☒✍🖳

Central Division Branch - Superior Court *Misdemeanor, Civil Actions, Eviction, Small Claims, Probate* 351 N Arrowhead, San Bernardino, CA 92415-0220. 8AM-4PM. Fax: 909-387-4428. Civil phone: 909-885-0139, Crim: 909-384-1888, Probate: 909-387-3952. Includes the City of Bernardino, cities of Grand Terrace, Loma Linda, Colton and Highland and the unincorporated area of Del Rosa, Devore, Muscoy, Patton, Verdemont. Specify which city you are searching in. ☒✍🖳

Twin Peaks District - Superior Court
Traffic Misdemeanor, Civil under $25,000, Eviction, Small Claims 26010 State Hwy 189 (PO Box 394), Twin Peaks, CA 92391. 8AM-4:30PM Monday only. **909-336-0620**, Fax: 909-336-0683. Felony and misdemeanors are now heard at the San Bernardino District Courthouse. For information on Twin Peaks cases Tuesdays to Fridays, call the San Bernardino District Courthouse. ☒✍🖳

Needles District - Superior Court
Felony, Misdemeanor, Civil Actions Under $25,000, Eviction, Small Claims 1111 Bailey Ave, Needles, CA 92363. 8AM-4PM. **760-326-9245**, Fax: 760-326-9254. ☒✍🖳

Fontana Division - Superior Court
Felony, Misdemeanor, Civil Actions Under $25,000, Traffic 17780 Arrow Hwy, Fontana, CA 92335. 8AM-4PM. **909-350-9322**. Includes the Cities of Fontana, Rialto, Crestmore and the unincorporated areas of Lytle Creek Canyon and Bloomington. ☒✍🖳

Chino Division - Superior Court
Felonies, Misdemeanor, Eviction, Small Claims 13260 Central Ave, Chino, CA 91710. 8AM-4PM. **909-356-5337**, Fax: 909-465-5221. Criminal phone: 909-465-5260. Includes City of Chino and surrounding unincorporated area. Rancho Cucamonga Courts handles all civil cases since 01/01/99. ☒✍🖳

Redlands District - Superior Court
Traffic Misdemeanor, Eviction, Small Claims 216 Brookside Ave, Redlands, CA 92373. 8AM-4PM. Fax: 909-798-8588. Civil phone: 909-888-4260, Crim: 909-885-1269. All felonies and non-traffic misdemeanors are filed at Central Dist. Court. This Court's district includes Redlands, Yucaipa and the unincorporated areas of Angeles Oaks, Barton Flats, Colton, Forest Home, Grand Terrace, Highland, Loma Linda and Mentone. ☒✍🖳

San Diego County

For any San Diego County requests, always specify which division - Central, East, North, or South.

www.sandiego.courts.ca.gov/superior/
Superior Court - Criminal *Felony, Misdemeanor* PO Box 120128 (220 W Broadway), San Diego, CA 92112-0128. 8:30AM-4:30PM. **619-531-3040** Misd. phone. Both General and Limited Criminal records are located here. ☒✍

Superior Court - Civil *Civil, Probate, Eviction, Small Claims, Probate* Hall of Justice PO Box 120128 (330 W Broadway), San Diego, CA 92112-0128. 8:30AM-4:30PM. Civil: 619-531-3141, Probate: 619-236-3781. Now has Central Division Limited Jurisdiction civil cases. Probate is located at the Madge Bradley Bldg, 1409 4th Ave, 92101. Access civil records by☒✍🖳

North County Branch - Superior Court
Felony, Misdemeanor, Civil Actions, Eviction, Small Claims, Probate 325 S Melrose Dr, Vista, CA 92081. 8:30AM-4:30PM. **760-726-9595**, Probate: 760-806-6150. Includes Cities of Oceanside, Del Mar, Carlsbad, Solana Beach, Encinitas, Escondido, San Marcos, Vista and unincorporated towns of Del Dios, Olivenhain, San Luis Rey, San Pasqual, Rancho Santa Fe, Valley Ctr., Bonsall, Palomar Mt., Borrego Spr., Pala, etc. ☒✍🖳

South County Branch - Superior Court
Felony, Misdemeanor, Civil Actions, Probate, Eviction, Small Claims 500-C 3rd Ave, Chula Vista, CA 91910. 8:30AM-4:30PM. Fax: 619-691-4969 (Civil) 4864 is Criminal. Civil phone: 619-691-4439, Crim: 619-691-4726. Includes National City, Chula Vista, Coronado, Imperial Beach and that portion of the City of San Diego lying south of the City of Chula Vista and contiguous unincorporated areas. ☎Fax☒✍🖳

East County Division - Superior Court
Felony, Misd., Civil, Small Claims, Eviction 250 E Main St, El Cajon, CA 92020. 8AM-4:30PM. **619-441-4100**, Civil: 619-441-4461, Crim: 619-441-4342, Probate: 619-441-6770 (family law). Court now houses the former municipal court records. Includes El Cajon, La Mesa, Lemon Grove, Santee and unincorporated towns of Alpine, Boulevard, Campo, Dulzura, Grossmont, Jacumba, Jamul, Julian, Lakeside, Mesa Grande, Ramona, Spring Valley, Tecate. Access by ☒✍🖳

Ramona Branch - East Division
Misdemeanor, Civil Actions Under $25,000, Eviction, Small Claims 1428 Montecito Rd, Ramona, CA 92065. 8AM-4:30PM. **760-738-2435**. Jurisdiction over the northeast area of the county. Closed noon to 1PM T, W, TH. ☒✍🖳

San Francisco County

Superior Court - Criminal Div. *Felony* http://sfgov.org/site/courts_page.asp?id=3664 850 Bryant St, #101 & 102, San Francisco, CA 94107/94103. 8AM-4:30PM. **415-553-1159/9394**. Misd. records- 415-553-1665. Court manager- 415-553-1897. ☒✍

Superior Court - Civil Division *Civil, Small Claims, Eviction, Probate* http://sfgov.org/site/courts_index.asp 400 McAllister St, #103, San Francisco, CA 94102. 8AM-4PM daily, except Wed. 10AM-N. **415-551-4000 (general info)**, Civil: 415-551-3888, Probate: 415-551-3892 Access civil records by☒✍🖳

Limited Superior - Civil Division *Civil Actions Under $25,000, Eviction, Small Claims* www.sfgov.org/courts 400 McAllister St, #103, San Francisco, CA 94107. 8AM-4:30PM, Wed 8Am-3PM. **415-551-3802 (Records Section)**, Fax: 415-551-3801. Civil phone: 415-551-4000. Includes all County including former municipal court on Folsom St. Access civil records by ✉ 🖐 🖥️

Superior Court - Misdemeanor Division
Misdemeanor www.ci.sf.ca.us/courts 850 Bryant St, Rm 101, San Francisco, CA 94103. 8AM-4:30PM. **415-553-1665 (Records Dept)**, Crim: 415-553-9395. Includes all County. ✉ 🖐 🖥️

San Joaquin County
www.stocktoncourt.org/courts/
Superior Court - Civil *Civil Actions, Eviction, Small Claims, Probate* 222 E Weber Ave, Rm 303, Stockton, CA 95202-2709. 7:30AM-4PM (office); 8AM-5PM; (phones). **209-468-2355**, Fax: 209-468-0539. Civil phone: 209-468-2933, Probate: 209-468-2843. Includes City of Stockton and suburban areas Farmington and Linden, Delta area and surrounding unincorporated areas. Access civil records by ✉ 🖐 🖥️

Superior Court - Criminal Div *Felony, Misd.* 222 E Weber Ave, Rm 101, Stockton, CA 95202. 7:30AM-5PM. **209-468-2935**, Crim: 209-468-2935. ✉ 🖐 🖥️

Lodi Division - Superior Court
Misdemeanor (Traffic), Civil Actions Under $25,000, Eviction, Small Claims 315 W Elm St (Civil) 230 W Elm St (Criminal), Lodi, CA 95240. 8AM-4PM. **209-331-2104**, Fax: 209-331-2135. Civil phone: 209-331-2101, Crim: 209-331-2121. Includes City of Lodi, eight mile road to Sacramento County line, towns of Acampo, Clements, Lockeford, Terminous, Thornton, Woodbridge. ☎ ✉ Fax 🖐 🖥️

Manteca Branch - Superior Court
Felony, Misdemeanor, Civil Actions Under $25,000, Eviction, Small Claims 315 E Center St, Manteca, CA 95336. 8AM-4PM. Civil: 209-239-9188, Crim: 209-239-1316. Includes Cities of Manteca, Ripon, Escalon, French Camp, Lathrop and surrounding unincorporated areas. ✉ 🖐 🖥️

Tracy Branch - Superior Court *Felony, Misdemeanor, Civil Actions Under $25,000, Eviction, Small Claims* 475 E 10th St, Tracy, CA 95376. 8AM-4PM. Fax: 209-831-5919. Civil phone: 209-831-5902, Crim: 209-831-5900. Includes Cities of Tracy, Banta, portion of Vernalis and surrounding unincorporated area. ✉ 🖐 🖥️

San Luis Obispo County
www.slocourts.net
Superior Court - Civil Division *Civil Actions, Small Claims, Eviction, Probate* 1035 Palm St, Rm 385 Government Ctr, San Luis Obispo, CA 93408. 8:30AM-4PM. **805-781-5677**, Probate: 805-781-5242. Has jurisdiction over all County for Civil actions over $25,000, and also the current and former "limited jurisdiction" (under $25,000) civil cases in immediate area. Access civil records by ✉ 🖐

Superior Court - Criminal Division *Felony, Misdemeanor* Gov't Center, Rm 220 1050 Monterey St., San Luis Obispo, CA 93408. 8:30AM-4PM. **805-781-5670**. This court now handles misdemeanor cases formerly handled by the limited jurisdiction court. ✉ 🖐

Grover Beach Branch - Superior Court *Misdemeanor, Civil Actions Under $25,000, Eviction, Small Claims* 214 S 16th St, Grover Beach, CA 93433-2299. 8:30AM-4PM. Civil: 805-473-7077, Crim: 805-473-7072. Includes Nipomo, Grover Beach, Arroyo Grande, Pismo Beach, Oceano, South Coast areas. ☎☎ ✉ 🖐

Paso Robles Branch - Superior Court *Misdemeanor, Civil Actions Under $25,000, Eviction, Small Claims* 549 10th St, Paso Robles, CA 93446-2593. 8:30AM-4PM. Civil: 805-237-3079, Crim: 805-237-3080. Includes Atascadero, Templeton, Paso Robles, San Miguel, Shandon, Cholame, areas north & east of Cuesta Grade. ☎ ✉ 🖐

San Mateo County
www.sanmateocourt.org
Superior Court *Felony, Civil Actions Over $25,000, Probate* 400 County Center, Redwood City, CA 94063. 8AM-4PM. Fax: 650-363-4914. Civil phone: 650-363-4711, Crim: 650-363-4302. Southern Area Limited Criminal, lower-value civil actions, evictions and small claims also located here. Access by ✉ 🖐

Superior Court - Southern Branch *Misdemeanor, Civil, Eviction, Small Claims* 400 County Center, Redwood City, CA 94063. 8AM-4PM. Civil: 650-363-4576, Crim: 650-363-4203. Limited Criminal - Includes Atherton, Belmont, Foster City, Half Moon Bay, Menlo Park, Portola Valley, Redwood City, San Carlos, Woodside, East Palo Alto and

unincorporated areas including La Honda, Pescadera, and San Gregorio. ✉ 🖐

Northern Branch - Superior Court *Misdemeanor, Small Claims, Traffic* 1050 Mission Rd, South San Francisco, CA 94080. 8AM-4PM. **650-877-5773**. Includes Brisbane, Daly City (including Westlake), Pacifica, San Bruno, South San Francisco, the northern coastal towns and all unincorporated areas in the north end of the county including Colma, Bart and Broadmoor. Small Claims phone-650-877-5778. ✉ 🖐

Santa Barbara County
www.sbcourts.org
Superior Court - Civil - Anacapa Division *Civil, Eviction, Small Claims, Probate* Box 21107 (1100 Anacapa St), Santa Barbara, CA 93121. 8AM-4PM; closed on mandatory furlough days. **805-568-2220**, Fax: 805-568-2219. Civil phone: 805-568-2238, Crim: 805-568-2753. Also known as the Anacapa Division. Includes the City of Santa Barbara, Goleta, and adjacent unincorporated areas, Carpenteria and Montecito. Access civil records by ☎ Fax ✉ 🖐

Superior Court - Criminal - Figueroa Division *Felony, Misdemeanor* 118 E Figueroa St, Santa Barbara, CA 93101. 7:45AM-4PM; closed on mandatory furlough days. **805-568-2735**, Fax: 805-568-3208. Civil phone: 805-568-2238, Crim: 805-568-2752/2753. Includes the City of Santa Barbara, Goleta and adjacent areas, Carpenteria, Montecito. For civil cases call Anacapa Division at 805-568-2220. ✉ 🖐

Santa Maria Miller Division - Superior Court *Felony, Misdemeanor, Traffic.* 312-M E Cook St, Bldg E, Santa Maria, CA 93454-5165. 8AM-3PM; closed on mandatory furlough days. **805-346-7590**, Fax: 805-346-7591. Criminal phone: 805-346-7565. Miller Division is in the same building complex as the Cook Division, which handles civil, small claims, family cases. Miller includes the same jurisdictional area as Cook Division. ✉ Fax 🖐

Santa Maria Cook Division - Superior Court *Civil Actions Under $25,000, Probate, Eviction, Small Claims* 312-C E Cook St (PO Box 5369), Santa Maria, CA 93454-5369. 7:30AM-4PM; closed on mandatory furlough days. **805-346-7414**,

Fax: 805-346-7616. Civil phone: 805-346-7405. This Cook Division handles Civil; its sister court (Miller Division) handles Criminal. Includes Betteravia, Casmalia, Cuyama, Guadalupe, Gary, Los Alamos, New Cuyama, Orcutt, Santa Maria, Sisquoc, Tepusquet and sections of the Vandenburg Air Force Base. by📧🖐

Lompoc Division - Superior Court *Felony. Misdemeanor, Civil Actions Under $25,000, Eviction, Small Claims* 115 Civic Center Plz, Lompoc, CA 93436. 8:30AM-4PM; closed on mandatory furlough days. Fax: 805-737-7786. Civil phone: 805-737-7796, Crim: 805-737-7790. Includes Lompoc and adjacent unincorporated areas including sections of Vandenburg Air Force Base. 📧🖐

Solvang Division - Superior Court *Misdemeanor, Small Claims, Traffic* 1745 Mission Dr, #C, Solvang, CA 93463. 8AM-3PM; closed on mandatory furlough days. **805-686-5040**, Fax: 805-686-5079. Includes the City of Solvang, Buelton, and adjacent unicorported areas, Los Olivos and Santa Ynez. 📧🖐

Santa Clara County

www.sccsuperiorcourt.org
Superior Court - Criminal *Felony, Misdemeanor* 191 N 1st St, San Jose, CA 95113-1001. 8:30AM-4PM. **408-808-6600**, Crim: 408-808-6600. Includes the Cities of Alviso, Campbell, Los Gatos, Milpitas, Monte Sereno, San Jose, Santa Clara, Saratoga. 📧🖐

Superior Court - Civil *Civil, Eviction, Probate* www.sccsuperiorcourt.org 191 N 1st St, San Jose, CA 95113. 8:30AM-4PM. **408-882-2100**. Handles cases for San Jose, Milpitas, Santa Clara, Los Gatos and Campbell areas. Access civil records by📧🖐🖥

South County Facility - Superior Court *Felony, Misdemeanor, Civil Actions Under $25,000, Eviction, Small Claims* http://sccsuperiorcourt.org 12425 Monterey Rd, San Martin, CA 95046-9590. 8:30AM-4PM. **408-695-5000**, Civil: 408-695-5012, Crim: 408-695-5014. Jurisdiction includes the Cities of Gilroy, Morgan Hill, San Martin and surrounding unincorporated areas. Traffic case phone number is 408-695-5011. 📧🖐

Palo Alto Facility - Superior Court *Felony, Misdemeanor, Small Claims* www.sccsuperiorcourt.org 270 Grant Ave, Palo Alto, CA 94306. 8:30AM-4PM. **650-462-3800**. Includes Palo Alto, Mountain View, Los Altos, Los Altos Hills, Stanford University, Sunnyvale and the surrounding unincorporated areas. 📧🖐

Sunnyvale Facility - Superior Court *Felony, Misd.* www.sccsuperiorcourt.org 270 Grant Ave, #204, Palo Alto, CA 94306. 8:30AM-3PM. **408-462-3800**. Court closed; records now at Palo Alto Court facility; address/phone given here.

Santa Cruz County

www.santacruzcourt.org
Superior Court - Civil *Civil, Probate* 701 Ocean St, Rm 110, Santa Cruz, CA 95060. 8AM-4PM. **831-454-2020**. This court also handles Family Law. Access civil records by☎📧🖐🖥

Superior Court - Criminal *Felony, Misdemeanor* 701 Ocean St, Rm 120, Santa Cruz, CA 95060. 8AM-4PM. **831-454-2230**, Fax: 831-454-2215. **Fax**📧🖐

Watsonville Division - Superior Court *Misdemeanor, Civil Actions Under $25,000, Eviction, Small Claims* 1430 Freedom Blvd, Watsonville, CA 95076. 8AM-4PM. **831-763-8060**. Includes all of Santa Cruz County. Access by 📧🖐

Shasta County

www.shastacourts.com
Superior Court *Felony, Misdemeanor, Civil, Small Claims, Eviction, Probate* 1500 Court St, Redding, CA 96001. 8:30AM-4:30PM. **530-245-6789**, Fax: 530-225-5564 Civil; 245-6483 Criminal. Address #319 for civil division and #219 for criminal. 📧🖐🖥

Burney Branch - Superior Court *Misd., Civil, Eviction, Small Claims* 20509 Shasta St, Burney, CA 96013. 8AM-N, 1-4:30PM. **530-335-3571**, Fax: 530-225-5684. Civil actions handled by Redding Branch since 1992. Prior civil limited jurisdiction records maintained here. 📧🖐🖥

Sierra County

Superior Court *Felony, Misdemeanor, Civil, Eviction, Small Claims, Probate* www.sierracourt.org PO Box 476, Courthouse Sq, Downieville, CA 95936. 8AM-N, 1-5PM. **530-289-3698**, Fax: 530-289-0205. ☎**Fax**📧🖐

Siskiyou County

www.siskiyou.courts.ca.gov
Superior Court *Felony, Misdemeanor, Civil, Probate* 311 4th St, PO Box 1026, Yreka, CA 96097. 8AM-5PM; 8AM-3PM (phone hours). Fax: 530-842-0164(Civ); 530-842-8178(Crim). Civil phone: 530-842-8196, Crim: 530-842-8195. 📧🖐🖥

Weed Branch - Superior Court *Misdemeanor, Small Claims* 550 Main St, Weed, CA 96094. 8AM-4PM. **530-938-2483**, Fax: 530-842-0109. Civil phone: 530-842-0107. 📧**Fax**🖐🖥

Dorris Branch - Superior Court *Civil Actions Under $25,000, Eviction, Small Claims* PO Box 828 324 N Pine St, Dorris, CA 96023. 8AM-N, 1-4PM. **530-397-3161**, Fax: 530-397-3169. New misdemeanor cases referred to Weed, CA Branch. This court only maintains a few criminal records for a year. Access civil records by📧🖐🖥

Solano County

www.solanocourts.com
Superior Court - Civil *Civil, Eviction, Probate* 600 Union Ave, Fairfield, CA 94533. 8AM-3PM. **707-421-6053**, Fax: 707-435-2950, Probate: 707-421-6471. Probate is a separate office at the same address. Probate fax: 707-421-6961. Small claims: 707-421-7435. Includes Fairfield, Suisun, Vacaville, Dixon, Rio Vista, and surrounding area. Access civil records by☎📧🖥🖐.

Superior Court - Criminal *Felony, Misdemeanor* 530 Union Ave, #200, Fairfield, CA 94533. 8AM-3PM. **707-421-7440; 421-7834 Sup Court Records**, Fax: 707-421-7439. This court includes Fairfield, Suisun, Vacaville, Dixon, Rio Vista and the adjacent unincorporated areas. 📧🖐🖥

Vallejo Branch - Superior Court *Misdemeanor, Civil, Eviction, Small Claims,Felony,Probate* 321 Tuolumne St, Vallejo, CA 94590. 8AM-3PM. Fax: 707-553-5661. Civil phone: 707-553-5346, Crim: 707-553-5341. Includes Cities of Vallejo and Benicia and adjacent areas. 📧🖐🖥

Sonoma County

www.sonomasuperiorcourt.com
Superior Court - Criminal *Felony, Misd, Probate* 600 Administration Dr, Rm 105J, Santa Rosa, CA 95403-0281. 8AM-3PM, M,W,F; 8-6PM Th. **707-565-1100**. ☎📧🖐

Superior Court - Civil Division *Civil, Eviction, Small Claims* 600 Administration Dr Rm 107J, Santa Rosa,

---

Key: Symbols refer to criminal records access unless otherwise noted. phone-☎ mail-📧 fax-**Fax** in person-🖐 online-🖥 email-**Email**

CA 95403. 8AM-3PM M,T,W,F; till 6PM TH. **707-565-1100**. Access civil records by✉✋

Stanislaus County

http://www.stanct.org
Superior Court - Criminal *Felony, Misd.* PO Box 1098 800 11 St, Rm 140, 95354, Modesto, CA 95353. 8AM-N, 1-4PM. **209-558-6000**. ✉✋

Superior Court - Civil *Civil, Eviction, Small Claims, Probate* 1100 "I" St, PO Box 828, Modesto, CA 95353. 8AM-3PM. **209-558-6000**, Fax: 209-525-4348 (civil). Ceres Branch has been closed and records transferred here. Access civil records by✉**Fax**✋🖥.

Sutter County

www.suttercourts.com
Superior Court - Civil Division *Civil, Eviction, Small Claims, Probate* 463 2nd St, Rm 211 Courthouse East, 2nd Fl, Yuba City, CA 95991. 8AM-5PM. **530-822-7352**, Fax: 530-822-7192 Access civil records by✉✋

Superior Court - Criminal Division *Felony, Misd.* 446 2nd St, Yuba City, CA 95991. 8AM-5PM. **530-822-7360**, Fax: 530-822-7159. **Fax**✉✋

Tehama County

Superior Court - Civil Division *Civil, Small Claims, Eviction, Probate, Family Law* PO Box 310, Red Bluff, CA 96080. 8AM-5PM. **530-527-6441** Access civil records by✉✋

Superior Court - Criminal Division *Felony, Misdemeanor* 445 Pine St, PO Box 1170, Red Bluff, CA 96080. 8AM-5PM. **530-527-3563**, Fax: 530-527-0956. Criminal phone: 530-527-7314. ✉✋

Corning Branch - Superior Court *Misdemeanor, Civil Actions Under $25,000, Eviction, Small Claims* 720 Hoag St, Corning, CA 96021. 8AM-5PM. **530-824-4601**, Fax: 530-824-6457. ✉✋

Trinity County

Superior Court *Felony, Misdemeanor, Civil, Eviction, Small Claims, Probate*

101 Court St, PO Box 1258, Weaverville, CA 96093. 9AM-4PM. **530-623-1208**, Fax: 530-623-3762. Access by ✉✋

Tulare County

Superior Court *Felony, Civil, Eviction, Small Claims, Probate* www.tularesuperiorcourt.ca.gov Courthouse 221 S Mooney, Visalia, CA 93291. 8AM-4PM. Fax: 559-737-4547. Civil phone: 559-733-6454, Crim: 559-733-6830. This court has records from Exeter, Woodlake, Goshen, Farmersville and Three Rivers. Address criminal record requests to Rm. 124 and civil to Rm. 201. ✉✋

Porterville Division - Superior Court *Misdemeanor, Civil Actions Under $25,000, Eviction, Small Claims* 87 E Morton Ave, Porterville, CA 93257. 8AM-4PM. **559-782-4710**, Fax: 559-782-4805. Includes Porterville, Springville, Camp Nelson, Johnsondale, Terra Bella, Ducor, Richgrove, Poplar, Strathmore and surrounding areas. Access by ✉✋

Dinuba Division - Superior Court *Felony, Misdemeanor, Civil Actions Under $25,000, Eviction, Small Claims* http:www.tularesuperiorcourt.ca.gov 640 S Alta Dinuba, Dinuba, CA 93618. 8AM-4PM. **559-591-5815**. Includes Dinuba, Cutler, Orosi, Seville, Traver, London, Delf, Orange Cove. ✉✋

Tulare/Pixley Division - Superior Court *Misdemeanor, Civil Actions Under $25,000, Eviction, Small Claims* 425 E Kern St (PO Box 1136), Tulare, CA 93275. 8AM-4PM. **559-685-2556**, Fax: 559-685-2663. Includes Tulare, Pixley, Tipton, Earlimart, Alpaugh, Allensworth, Woodville, Waukena and surrounding areas. ✉**Fax**✋

Tuolumne County

www.courtinfo. ca.gov/courts/trial/tuolumne
Superior Court - Civil *Civil, Eviction, Small Claims, Probate* 41 W Yaney, Sonora, CA 95370. 8AM-5PM. **209-533-5555**, Fax: 209-533-6944. Departments 1, 2, and 5. Small claims court: 209-533-6509. Access civil records by✉✋

Superior Court - Criminal *Felony, Misd,* 60 N Washington St, Sonora, CA 95370.

8AM-4PM. **209-533-5563**, Fax: 209-533-5581. Departments 3 and 4. Traffic court: 209-533-5671. ✉✋

Ventura County

http://courts.countyofventura.org
Ventura Superior Court *Felony, Misd., Civil, Eviction, Small Claims, Probate* 800 S Victoria Ave, PO Box 6489, Ventura, CA 93006-6489. 8AM-5PM. Fax: 805-650-4032. Civil phone: 805-654-2609, Crim: 805-654-2611, Probate: 805-654-2264. ☎✉🖥✋

East County Superior Court *Misd., Civil, Eviction, Small Claims,* PO Box 1200 (3855F Alamo St), Simi Valley, CA 93062-1200. 8AM-11:30AM; 1:30PM-5PM. Civil: 805-582-8086, Criminal 805-582-8080. Eviction 582-8086; Small Claims 582-8078; Family Law 582-8086. ☎✉✋🖥

Yolo County

Superior Court *Felony, Misdemeanor, Civil, Eviction, Small Claims, Probate* www.yolocourts.com 725 Court St, Rm 308, Woodland, CA 95695. 8AM-3PM. **800-944-0990, 530-666-8598**, Fax: 530-666-8576. Civil phone: 530-666-8170, Crim: 530-666-8050. Phone numbers may change; see www.yolocourts.com for new numbers. Address civil requests to Rm 103 and criminal to Rm 111. Small claims phone is 530-666-8060. Access ☎✉✋

Yuba County

Superior Court *Felony, Misdemeanor, Civil, Small Claims, Probate* 215 5th St, #200, Marysville, CA 95901. 8:30AM-4:30PM. **530-749-7600**, Fax: 530-749-7351. ✉✋

Marysville Civil Limited Superior Court *Civil Actions Under $25,000, Eviction, Small Claims* 215 5th St, #200, Marysville, CA 95901. 8:30AM-4:30PM. **530-749-7600**, Fax: 530-749-7354 Access civil records by✉✋

Colorado

State Court Administration: State Court Administrator, 1301 Pennsylvania St, Suite 300, Denver, CO, 80203; 303-861-1111, Fax: 303-837-2340. www.courts.state.co.us

Court Structure: As of 9/1/2001, the maximum civil claim in County Courts was increased to $15,000. The District and County Courts have overlapping jurisdiction over civil cases involving less than $15,000 ($10,000 prior to 9/1/2001). Fortunately, District and County Courts are combined in most counties. Combined courts usually search both civil or criminal indexes for a single fee, except as indicated in the profiles. Municipal courts only have jurisdiction over traffic, parking, and ordinance violations.

Probate Courts: Denver is the only county where Probate Court is separate from the District Court.

Online Access: There is no official government system, but we can mention a unique commercial system. As a result of an initiative of the Colorado Judicial Branch, all district courts and all county courts are available on the Internet at www.cocourts.com. Real-time records include civil, civil water, small claims, domestic, felony, misdemeanor, and traffic cases and can be accessed by name or case number. Court records go as far back as 1995. There is a fee for this subscription Internet access, generally $6.00 per search (as of March 17, 2003) and there are discounts for volume users. Contact Jeff Mueller, Major Accounts, by telephone at 866-COCOURT, or by email at Jeffm@cocourts.com.

Additional Information: November 15, 2001, Broomfield City & County came into existence, derived from the counties of Adams, Boulder, Jefferson and Weld. A District and County Court (presumed to be 17th Judicial District) was established.

Co-located with seven district courts are divisions known as Water Courts. The Water Courts are located in Weld, Pueblo, Alamosa, Montrose, Garfield, Routt, and La Plata counties.

Adams County

District and County courts combined, but records are searched separately unless requester asks to search both courts.

17th District Court *Felony, Civil Actions Over $10,000, Probate* www.17thjudicialdistrict.com 1100 Judicial Center Dr, Brighton, CO 80601. 8AM-5PM; closed from N-1pm. **303-659-1161**, Fax: 303-654-3216. Civil phone: 303-654-3237, Crim: 303-654-3314, Probate: 303-654-3237. ⊠ ✍ 🖥

County Court *Misdemeanor, Civil Actions Under $15,000, Eviction, Small Claims* www.17thjudicialdistrict.com/ 1100 Judicial Center Dr, Brighton, CO 80601. 8AM-5PM; closed from Noon-1PM. **303-659-1161**, Civil: 303-654-3335, Crim: 303-654-3314. ⊠ ✍ 🖥

Alamosa County

Alamosa Combined Court *Felony, Misdemeanor, Civil, Eviction, Small Claims, Probate* 702 4th St, Alamosa, CO 81101. 8AM-N, 1-4PM. **719-589-4996**, Fax: 719-589-4998. ⊠ ✍ 🖥

Arapahoe County

18th District Court *Felony, Civil Over $15,000, Probate* www.courts.state.co.us/d istrict/18th/18dist.htm 7325 S Potomac St, Centennial, CO 80112. 8AM-N, 1:15-4PM. **303-649-6355**. ☎ ⊠ ✍ 🖥

Arapahoe County Court Division B *Misdemeanor, Civil Actions Under $15,000, Eviction, Small Claims* www.courts.state.co.us/district/18th/18dist.ht m 15400 E 14th Pl, Aurora, CO 80011. 8AM-N, 1:15-4PM. **303-363-8004**, Fax: 303-363-7155. ☎ ⊠ ✍ 🖥

Arapahoe County Court Division A *Misdemeanor, Civil Actions Under $15,000, Eviction, Small Claims* www.courts.state.co.us/district/18th/18dist.ht m 1790 W Littleton Blvd, Littleton, CO 80120-2060. 8AM-N-1:30-4PM. **303-798-4591**. ⊠ ✍ 🖥

Archuleta County

Archuleta Combined Courts *Felony, Misdemeanor, Civil, Eviction, Small Claims, Probate* PO Box 148, Pagosa Springs, CO 81147. 8AM-4PM. **970-264-2400**, Fax: 970-264-2407. ⊠ ✍ 🖥

Baca County

Baca County District & County Courts *Felony, Misd., Civil, Eviction, Small Claims, Probate* www.courts.state.co.us/ district/15th/15dist.htm 741 Main St, Springfield, CO 81073. 8AM-5PM. **719-523-4555**. ⊠ ✍ 🖥

Bent County

16th District Court *Felony, Misd., Civil, Eviction, Small Claims, Probate* www.courts.state.co.us/district/16th/16dist.ht m Bent County Courthouse 725 Bent, Las Animas, CO 81054. 8AM-12, 1-5PM. **719-456-1353**, Fax: 719-456-0040. ⊠ ✍ 🖥

Boulder County

20th District & County Courts *Felony, Misdemeanor, Civil, Eviction, Small Claims, Probate* 6th & Canyon, 1777 6th St, Boulder, CO 80306. 8AM-4PM. **303-441-3750**. ⊠ ✍ 🖥

Broomfield County

Broomfield Municipal Court (District & County) *Felony, Misdemeanor, Civil, Eviction, Small Claims, Probate* www.co.broomfield.co.us 17 DesCombes Dr, Broomfield, CO 80020. 8AM-5PM. **720-887-2100**, Fax: 720-887-2122. This is a new county created in late 2001, record keeping is limited. Older records should be searched in Adams, Boulder, Jefferson or Weld counties. This court holds Municipal court records prior to county organization. ⊠ ✍ 🖥

Chaffee County

11th District & County Courts *Felony, Misd., Civil, Eviction, Small Claims, Probate* www.courts.state.co.us/district/11 th/dist11.htm PO Box 279, Salida, CO 81201. 8AM-5PM. **719-539-2561/6031**, Fax: 719-539-6281. This court combined in 2002; formerly two courts. ☎ ⊠ ✍ 🖥

Cheyenne County

District & County Courts *Felony, Misd., Civil, Eviction, Small Claims, Probate* www.courts.state.co.us/district/15th/15dist.htm PO Box 696, Cheyenne Wells, CO 80810. 8AM-4PM, till noon on Fri. **719-767-5649**. ✉✋💻

Clear Creek County

Clear Creek Combined Courts *Felony, Misdemeanor, Civil, Eviction, Small Claims, Probate* PO Box 367, Georgetown, CO 80444. 8AM-4PM. **303-569-3273**, Fax: 303-569-3274. ✉✋💻

Conejos County

12th District & County Courts *Felony, Misd., Civil, Eviction, Small Claims, Probate* 6683 County Road 13, Conejos, CO 81129. 8AM-4PM. **719-376-5466**, Fax: 719-376-5939. ✉✋💻

Costilla County

12th District & County Courts *Felony, Misd., Civil, Eviction, Small Claims, Probate* www.courts.state.co.us/district/12th/12dist.htm PO Box 301, San Luis, CO 81152. 8AM-N, 1-4PM. **719-672-3681**, Fax: 719-672-4493. Access **Fax**✉✋💻

Crowley County

16th District & County Courts *Felony, Misd., Civil, Eviction, Small Claims, Probate* www.courts.state.co.us/district/16th/16dist.htm 110 E 6th St, #303, Ordway, CO 81063. 8AM-5PM. **719-267-4468**, Fax: 719-267-3753. Access-✉**Fax**✋💻

Custer County

11th District & County Courts *Felony, Misd., Civil, Eviction, Small Claims, Probate* www.courts.state.co.us/district/11th/dist11.htm PO Box 60, Westcliffe, CO 81252. 8AM-2PM. **719-783-2274**, Fax: 719-783-2995. ✉✋💻

Delta County

District & County Courts *Felony, Misdemeanor, Civil, Eviction, Small Claims, Probate* www.7thjudicialdistrictco.org/delta.html 501 Palmer St, Rm 338, Delta, CO 81416. 9AM-4PM. **970-874-6280**. ✉✋💻

Denver County

2nd District Court *Felony, Civil Over $10,000* www.courts.state.co.us/district/02nd/02dist.htm 1437 Bannock Office of the Court Clerk, Denver, CO 80202. 8AM-4PM. **720-865-8301**. ✉✋💻

County Court - Civil Division *Civil Under $15,000, Eviction, Small Claims* www.courts.state.co.us/district/counties.htm 1515 Cleveland Pl, 4th Fl, Denver, CO 80202. 8AM-5PM. **303-640-5161**, Fax: 303-640-4730 Access civil by ✉✋💻

County Court - Criminal Division *Misdemeanor* www.courts.state.co.us/district/02nd/02dist.htm 1437 Bannock St, Rm 111A, Denver, CO 80202. 8AM-5PM. **720-865-7820**. ✉✋💻

Probate Court www.courts.state.co.us/district/02nd/02dist.htm 1437 Bannock, Rm 230, Denver, CO 80202. 8:30AM-4PM. **720-865-8310**, Fax: 720-865-8576.

Dolores County

22nd District & County Courts *Felony, Misdemeanor, Civil, Eviction, Small Claims, Probate* PO Box 511, Dove Creek, CO 81324. 8AM-5PM M, T, TH; 8AM-N Fri. **970-677-2258**. Office is closed Wednesdays. Access ☎✉✋💻

Douglas County

Douglas County Combined Court *Felony, Misdemeanor, Civil, Eviction, Small Claims, Probate* www.courts.state.co.us/district/18th/18dist.htm 4000 Justice Way, #2009, Castle Rock, CO 80104. 8:30AM-N; 1:15PM-4PM. **303-663-7200**. ✉✋💻

Eagle County

Eagle Combined Court *Felony, Misdemeanor, Civil, Eviction, Small Claims, Probate* PO Box 597, Eagle, CO 81631. 8AM-12:00-1-4PM. **970-328-6373**, Fax: 970-328-6328. **Fax**✉✋💻

Elbert County

Elbert District & County Courts *Felony, Misd., Civil, Eviction, Small Claims, Probate* www.courts.state.co.us/district/18th/18dist.htm PO Box 232, Kiowa, CO 80117. 8AM-4PM. **303-621-2131**. ✉✋💻

El Paso County

El Paso Combined Court *Felony, Misdemeanor, Civil Actions, Probate* www.gofourth.org PO Box 2980, Colorado Springs, CO 80901-2980. 8AM-5PM (closed at noon 1 hr). **719-448-7599**, Fax: 719-448-7685. Records for the County and District Courts are combined. **Fax**✉✋💻

Fremont County

District & County Courts *Felony, Misd., Civil, Eviction, Small Claims, Probate, Tarffic* www.courts.state.co.us/district/11th/dist11.htm 136 Justice Center Rd, Rm 103, Canon City, CO 81212. 8AM-5PM. **719-269-0100**, Fax: 719-269-0134. ✉**Fax**✋💻

Garfield County

9th District & County Courts *Felony, Misd., Civil, Eviction, Small Claims, Probate* www.courts.state.co.us/district/09th/dist09.htm 109 8th St, #104, Glenwood Springs, CO 81601. 8AM-5PM. **970-945-5075**, Fax: 970-945-8756. This court handles cases in the county for the area east of New Castle. ✉✋💻

County Court - Rifle *Misd., Civil Actions Under $15,000, Eviction, Small Claims* www.courts.state.co.us/district/09th/dist09.htm 110 E 18th St, Rifle, CO 81650. 8AM-5PM. **970-625-5100**, Fax: 970-625-1125. This court handles cases in the county for the area from New Castle to the west. ☎**Fax**✉✋💻

Gilpin County

1st District & County Courts *Felony, Misdemeanor, Civil, Eviction, Small Claims, Probate* 2960 Dory Hill Rd, #200, Golden, CO 80403-8768. 8AM-5PM. **303-582-5323**, Fax: 303-582-3112. ✉✋💻

Grand County

14th District & County Courts *Felony, Misdemeanor, Civil, Eviction, Small Claims, Probate* PO Box 192, Hot Sulphur Springs, CO 80451. 8AM-4PM. **970-725-3357**. ☎✉✋💻

Gunnison County

7th District & County Courts *Felony, Misd., Civil, Eviction, Small Claims, Probate* www.courts.state.co.us/district/07th/dist07.htm 200 E Virginia Ave, Gunnison, CO 81230. 8:30AM-4:30PM M-Th; 8:30AM-3PM F. **970-641-3500**, Fax: 970-641-6876. ✉✋💻

Hinsdale County

7th District & County Courts *Felony, Misd., Civil, Eviction, Small Claims, Probate* www.courts.state.co.us/district/07th/dist07.htm PO Box 245, Lake City,

CO 81235. 8:30-N M,W,F (Jun-Aug); 8:30AM-N T,F (Sept-May). **970-944-2227**, Fax: 970-944-2289. ☎Fax⊠🖐️💻

Huerfano County
3rd District & County Courts *Felony, Misd., Civil, Eviction, Small Claims, Probate* www.courts.state.co.us/district/03rd/03dist.htm 401 Main St, #304, Walsenburg, CO 81089. 8AM-4PM. **719-738-1040**, Fax: 719-738-1267. ⊠🖐️💻

Jackson County
8th District & County Courts *Felony, Misd., Civil, Eviction, Small Claims, Probate* www.courts.state.co.us/district/08th/08dist.htm PO Box 308, Walden, CO 80480. 9AM-1PM. **970-723-4363**. ⊠🖐️💻

Jefferson County
1st District & County Courts *Felony, Misdemeanor, Civil, Eviction, Small Claims, Probate, Traffic* 100 Jefferson County Pky, Golden, CO 80401-6002. 8AM-4PM. **303-271-6267**, Fax: 303-271-6188. ⊠🖐️💻

Kiowa County
15th District & County Courts *Felony, Misd., Civil, Eviction, Small Claims, Probate* www.courts.state.co.us/district/15th/15dist.html PO Box 353, Eads, CO 81036. 9AM-4PM. **719-438-5558**, Fax: 719-438-5300. ☎Fax⊠🖐️💻

Kit Carson County
Kit Carson Combined Court *Felony, Misd., Civil, Eviction, Small Claims, Probate* www.courts.state.co.us/district/13th/13dist.htm 251 16th St, #301, Burlington, CO 80807. 8AM-4PM. **719-346-5524**. ⊠🖐️💻

Lake County
Lake County Combined Courts *Felony, Misdemeanor, Civil, Eviction, Small Claims, Probate* PO Box 55, Leadville, CO 80461. 8AM-N, 1-4PM. **719-486-0535**. ⊠🖐️💻

La Plata County
La Plata Combined Courts *Felony, Misdemeanor, Civil, Small Claims, Probate* 1060 E 2nd Ave, Durango, CO 81301. 8AM-4PM. **970-247-2304**, Fax: 970-247-4348 Cri; 259-0258 Civ. Fax for civil section is 970-259-0258. ⊠🖐️💻

Larimer County
8th District Court *Felony, Civil Actions Over $10,000, Probate* www.courts.state.co.us/district/08th/08dist.htm 201 La Porte Ave, #100, Ft Collins, CO 80521. 8AM-4PM. **970-498-6100**, Fax: 970-498-6110. ⊠🖐️💻

County Court *Misd., Civil Actions Under $15,000, Eviction, Small Claims* www.courts.state.co.us/district/08th/08dist.htm 201 La Porte Ave, #100, Ft Collins, CO 80521. 8AM-4PM. **970-498-6100**, Fax: 970-498-6110. ⊠🖐️💻

Las Animas County
3rd District Court *Felony, Misdemeanor, Civil, Eviction, Small Claims, Probate* www.courts.state.co.us/district/03rd/03dist.htm 200 E 1st St, Rm 304, Trinidad, CO 81082. 8AM-5PM. **719-846-3316/2221**, Fax: 719-846-9367. ⊠🖐️💻

Lincoln County
18th District & County Courts *Felony, Misd., Civil, Eviction, Small Claims, Probate* www.courts.state.co.us/district/18th/18dist.htm PO Box 128, Hugo, CO 80821. 8AM-5PM. **719-743-2455**. ☎⊠🖐️💻

Logan County
13th District Court *Felony, Civil Over $10,000, Probate* www.courts.state.co.us/district/13th/13dist.htm 110 N Riverview Rd, Rm 205, Sterling, CO 80751. 8AM-4PM. **970-522-6565**, Fax: 970-522-6566. ⊠🖐️💻

County Court *Misd., Civil Actions Under $15,000, Eviction, Small Claims* www.courts.state.co.us/district/counties.htm 110 N Riverview Rd, Rm 210, Sterling, CO 80751. 8AM-4PM. **970-522-1572**, Fax: 970-526-5359. Fax number will change in late 2003. 🖐️💻

Mesa County
Mesa County Combined Court *Felony, Civil Actions Over $10,000, Probate* Mesa County District Court PO Box 20000-5030, Grand Junction, CO 81502. 8AM-4PM. **970-257-3625**. ⊠🖐️💻

Mineral County
12th District & County Courts *Felony, Misdemeanor, Civil, Eviction, Small Claims, Probate* PO Box 427, Creede, CO 81130. 8AM-12:00-1-3PM. **719-658-2575**. ⊠🖐️💻

Moffat County
Moffat County Combined Court *Felony, Misdemeanor, Civil, Eviction, Small Claims, Probate* 221 W Victory Wy, #300, Craig, CO 81625. 8AM-4PM. **970-824-8254**. ⊠🖐️💻

Montezuma County
22nd District Court *Felony, Civil Actions Over $15,000, Probate* www.courts.state.co.us/district/22nd/22distindex.htm 109 W Main St, #210, Cortez, CO 81321. 8AM-4PM. **970-565-1111**. ⊠🖐️💻

County Court *Misd., Civil Actions Under $15,000, Eviction, Small Claims* www.courts.state.co.us/district/22nd/22distindex.htm 601 N Mildred Rd, Cortez, CO 81321. 8AM-4PM. **970-565-7580**. ⊠🖐️💻

Montrose County
7th District & County Courts *Felony, Misdemeanor, Civil, Eviction, Small Claims, Probate* www.courts.state.co.us 1200 N Grand Ave, #A, Montrose, CO 81401-3164. 9AM-4PM. **970-252-4300; 242-4309**, Fax: 970-252-4309. ⊠🖐️💻Fax

Morgan County
13th District Court *Felony, Civil Actions Over $10,000, Probate* www.courts.state.co.us/district/13th/13dist.htm PO Box 130, Ft Morgan, CO 80701. 8AM-4PM. **970-542-3435**, Fax: 970-542-3436. Fax⊠🖐️💻

County Court *Misd., Civil Actions Under $15,000, Eviction, Small Claims* www.courts.state.co.us/district/13th/13dist.htm PO Box 695, Ft Morgan, CO 80701. 8AM-3PM. **970-542-3414**, Fax: 970-542-3416. ⊠🖐️💻

Otero County
Otero County Combined Courts *Felony, Civil, Probate* www.courts.state.co.us/district/16th/16dist.htm Courthouse, Rm 207 13 W 3rd St, La Junta, CO 81050. 8AM-5PM. **719-384-4951**, Fax: 719-384-4991. Although combined, these courts have separate offices and record databases. ⊠🖐️💻

Ouray County
7th District & County Courts *Felony, Misd., Civil, Eviction, Small Claims, Probate* www.courts.state.co.us/district/07th/dist07.htm PO Box 643, Ouray, CO

81427. 8:30AM-N, 1-4PM M-TH; Closed Fri. **970-325-4405**, Fax: 970-325-7364. ✉✋💻

Park County

Park County Combined Courts *Felony, Misd., Civil, Eviction, Small Claims, Probate* www.courts.state.co.us/district/11th/dist11.htm PO Box 190, Fairplay, CO 80440. 8AM-5PM. **719-836-2940**, Fax: 719-836-2892. ✉✋💻

Phillips County

13th District & County Courts *Felony, Misd., Civil, Eviction, Small Claims, Probate* www.courts.state.co.us/district/13th/13dist.htm 221 S Interocean, Holyoke, CO 80734. 8AM-1PM. **970-854-3279**, Fax: 970-854-3179. ☎Fax✉✋

Pitkin County

9th District & County Courts *Felony, Misd., Civil, Eviction, Small Claims, Probate* www.courts.state.co.us/district/09th/dist09.htm 506 E Main St, #300, Aspen, CO 81611. 8AM-N, 1-5PM. **925-7635**, Fax: 970-925-6349. ✉Fax✋💻

Prowers County

15th District Court *Felony, Civil Actions Over $10,000, Probate* www.courts.state.co.us/district/15th/15dist.htm 301 S Main St, #300, Lamar, CO 81052-2834. 8AM-5PM. **719-336-7424**, Fax: 719-336-9757. Access Fax✉✋💻

County Court *Misd., Civil Actions Under $15,000, Eviction, Small Claims* www.courts.state.co.us/district/15th/15dist.htm 301 S Main St, #100, Lamar, CO 81052-2634. 8AM-12:00-1-5PM. **719-336-7416**, Fax: 719-336-4145. ✉✋💻Fax

Pueblo County

Combined Courts *Felony, Misdemeanor, Civil, Eviction, Small Claims, Probate* 320 W 10th St, Pueblo, CO 81003. 8AM-5PM. **719-583-7000**, Fax: 719-583-7126.

Civil phone: 719-583-7026, Probate: 719-583-7030. ✉✋💻

Rio Blanco County

9th District & County Courts *Felony, Misd., Civil, Eviction, Small Claims, Probate* www.courts.state.co.us/district/09th/dist09.htm 555 Main St, Rm 303, PO Box 1150, Meeker, CO 81641. 8AM-N, 1-5PM. **970-878-5622**. ☎✉✋💻

Rio Grande County

12th District & County Courts *Felony, Misdemeanor, Civil, Eviction, Small Claims, Probate* 6th & Cherry, PO Box 427, Del Norte, CO 81132. 8AM-N, 1-4PM. **719-657-3394**. ✉✋💻

Routt County

Routt Combined Courts *Felony, Misdemeanor, Civil, Eviction, Small Claims, Probate* PO Box 773117, Steamboat Springs, CO 80477. 8AM12:00-1-4PM. **970-879-5020**, Fax: 970-879-3531. ✉✋💻

Saguache County

12th District & County Courts *Felony, Misdemeanor, Civil, Eviction, Small Claims, Probate* PO Box 164, Saguache, CO 81149. 8AM-N, 1-5PM. **719-655-2522**, Fax: 719-655-2522. ✉✋💻

San Juan County

6th District & County Courts *Felony, Misdemeanor, Civil, Eviction, Small Claims, Probate* PO Box 900, Silverton, CO 81433. 8AM-4PM T & TH, 8AM-N Wed. **970-387-5790**. ✉✋💻

San Miguel County

7th District & County Courts *Felony, Misd., Civil, Eviction, Small Claims, Probate* www.7thjudicialdistrictco.org PO Box 919, Telluride, CO 81435. 9AM-N, 1-4PM. **970-728-3891**, Fax: 970-728-6216. ☎✉✋💻

Sedgwick County

13th District & County Courts *Felony, Misd., Civil, Eviction, Small Claims,*

Probate www.courts.state.co.us/district/13th/13dist.htm 3rd & Pine, Julesburg, CO 80737. 8AM-1PM. **970-474-3627**, Fax: 970-474-2026. Fax✉✋💻

Summit County

Summit Combined Courts *Felony, Misdemeanor, Civil, Eviction, Small Claims, Probate* www.courts.state.co.us PO Box 185, Breckenridge, CO 80424. 8AM-N, 1-4PM. **970-453-2241 District; 970-453-2272 County**. District Court uses PO Box 269. ✋💻

Teller County

Teller Combined Courts *Felony, Misd., Civil, Eviction, Small Claims, Probate* www.tellercountycourts.com PO Box 997, Cripple Creek, CO 80813. 9AM-N; 1PM-4PM. **719-689-2574**. ✉✋💻

Washington County

Washington County Combined Court *Felony, Misd., Civil, Eviction, Small Claims, Probate* www.courts.state.co.us/district/13th/13dist.htm PO Box 455 (26861 Hwy 34), Akron, CO 80720. 8AM-N, 1-5PM. **970-345-2756**, Fax: 970-345-2829. ☎✉✋💻

Weld County

19th District & County Courts *Felony, Misdemeanor, Civil, Eviction, Small Claims, Probate* PO Box 2038, Greeley, CO 80632. 8AM-4PM closed at noon for 1 hour. **970-351-7300**, Fax: 970-336-7245. Probate/water offices can be faxed at 970-3469136 ✉✋💻

Yuma County

13th District & County Courts *Felony, Misd., Civil, Eviction, Small Claims, Probate* www.courts.state.co.us/district/13th/13dist.htm PO Box 347, Wray, CO 80758. 8AM-4PM. **970-332-4118**, Fax: 970-332-4119. ✉✋💻

Key: Symbols refer to criminal records access unless otherwise noted. phone-☎ mail-✉ fax-**Fax** in person-✋ online-💻 email-**Email**

Connecticut

State Court Administration: Chief Court Administrator, 231 Capitol Av, Hartford, CT, 06106; 860-757-2100, Fax: 860-757-2130. www.jud.state.ct.us

Court Structure: The Superior Court is the sole court of original jurisdiction for all causes of action, except for matters over which the probate courts have jurisdiction as provided by statute. The state is divided into 15 Judicial Districts, 20 Geographic Area Courts, and 14 Juvenile Districts. The Superior Court - comprised primarily of the Judicial District Courts and the Geographical Area Courts - has five divisions: Criminal, Civil, Family, Juvenile, and Administrative Appeals. When not combined, the Judicial District Courts handle felony and civil cases while the Geographic Area Courts handle misdemeanors (some handle small claims.)

Divorce Records are maintained by the Chief Clerk at the Judicial District Courts.

Probate Courts: Probate is handled by city Probate Courts, which we have listed, and are not part of the state court system. Information request requirements are consistent across the state; requesters must provide full name of decedent, year and place of death, and SASE. There is no search fee; the certification fee is $5.00 for 1st 2 pages and $2.00 for each additional page; and, the copy fee is $1.00 per page.

Online Access: The Judicial Branch provides access to civil, small claims and/or family court records via the Internet, located online at www.jud2.state.ct.us (click on "Party Name Inquiry"). The site contains party name search, assignment lists, and calendars. Also, questions about the fuller commercial system available through Judicial Information Systems should be directed to the CT JIS Office at 860-282-6500. There is currently no online access to criminal records; however, criminal and motor vehicle data is available for purchase in database format.

Additional Information: Mail requests to perform criminal searches should be made to the Department of Public Safety, 1111 Country Club Rd, PO Box 2794, Middletown, CT 06457, 860-685-8480. The search fee is $25.00.

The State Record Center in Enfield, CT is the repository for criminal and some civil records. Case records are sent to the Record Center from 3 months to 5 years after disposition by the courts. These records are then maintained 10 years for misdemeanors and 20+ years for felonies. If certain that the record is at the Record Center, it is quicker to direct the request there rather than to the original court. Only written requests accepted. Search requirements: full defendant name, docket #, disposition date, court action. Fee is $5.00 for each docket. Direct Requests to: Conn. Record Center, 111 Phoenix Ave, Enfield CT 06082, 860-741-3714.

Fairfield County

Danbury Judicial District Court *Felony, Civil Actions, Divorce, Eviction, Small Claims* 146 White St, Danbury, CT 06810. 9AM-5PM. **203-207-8600**. ⌧ ✍

Bridgeport Judicial District Court *Felony, Civil Actions, Divorce* 1061 Main St, Attn: criminal or civil, Bridgeport, CT 06604. 9AM-5PM. **203-579-6527**. ⌧ ✍

Stamford-Norwalk Judicial District Court *Felony, Misdemeanors, Civil Actions, Divorce* 123 Hoyt St, Stamford, CT 06905. 9AM-5PM. Civil: 203-965-5307, Crim: 203-965-5208. ⌧✍

Geographical Area Court #2 *Misdemeanor, Eviction, Small Claims* 172 Golden Hill St, Bridgeport, CT 06604. 9AM-4PM. Civil: 203-579-6527, Crim: 203-579-6560. Serving the towns of Bridgeport, Easton, Fairfield, Monroe, Stratford, Trumbull. ✍

Geographical Area Court #3 *Misdemeanor, Eviction, Small Claims* 146 White St, Danbury, CT 06810. 9AM-5PM. **203-207-8600**. Serving the towns of Bethel, Brookfield, Danbury, New Fairfield, Newtown, Redding, Ridgefield and Sherman. ✍

Geographical Area Court #20 *Misdemeanor, Eviction, Small Claims* 17 Belden Ave, Norwalk, CT 06850. 9AM-5PM. **203-846-3237**, Civil: 203-846-4206, Crim: 203-846-3237. Serving the towns of New Canaan, Norwalk, Weston, Westport and Wilton. ✍

Hartford County

Hartford Judicial District Court - Civil *Civil Actions, Divorce* www.jud.state.ct.us 95 Washington St, Hartford, CT 06106. 9AM-5PM. **860-548-2700**, Fax: 860-548-2711 Access civil records by⌧🖳✍.

New Britain Judicial District Court *Felony, Civil Actions, Small Claims, Divorce* 20 Franklin Square, New Britain, CT 06051. 9AM-5PM. Civil: 860-515-5180, Crim: 860-515-5080. ☎⌧✍

Hartford Judicial District Court - Criminal *Felony* 101 LaFayette St, Hartford, CT 06106. 9AM-5PM. **860-566-**

1630. Hartford Judicial shares phone line and address with Geo. Court #14. ⌧✍

Geographical Area Court #17 *Misdemeanor, Eviction, Small Claims* www.jud2.state.ct.us 131 N Main St, Bristol, CT 06010. 9AM-5PM. **860-582-8111**. Serving the towns of Bristol, Burlington, Plainville, Plymouth and Southington. ✍⌧

Geographic Area Court #15 *Misdemeanor, Eviction, Small Claims* 20 Franklin Square, New Britain, CT 06051. 9AM-5PM. Civil: 860-515-5180, Crim: 860-515-5080. Serving the towns of Berlin, New Britain, Newington, Rocky Hill and Wethersfield. Access by ⌧✍

Geographical Area Court #13 *Misdemeanor* 111 Phoenix, Enfield, CT 06082. 9AM-5PM. **860-741-3727**. Eviction cases are handled by Hartford Housing, 860-756-7920. Serving the towns of East Granby, East Windsor, Enfield, Granby, Simsbury, Suffield, Windsor and Windsor Locks. ✍⌧

Geographical Area Court #12 *Misdemeanor, Eviction, Small Claims*

Key: Symbols refer to criminal records access unless otherwise noted. phone-☎ mail-⌧ fax-**Fax** in person-✍ online-🖳 email-**Email**

410 Center St, Manchester, CT 06040. 9AM-5PM; Phone Hours: 9AM-4PM. **860-647-1091**. Serving towns of East Hartford, Glastonbury, Manchester, Marlborough, South Windsor. Evictions are handled by a special Housing Court, 18 Trinity, Hartford, 860-566-8550. ✉ 👆

Geographical Area Court #14 *Misdemeanor* 101 LaFayette St, Hartford, CT 06106. 9AM-5PM. **860-566-1630**. Serving the towns of Avon, Bloomfield, Canton, Farmington, Hartford and West Hartford. ✉ 👆

Litchfield County

Litchfield Judicial District Court *Felony, Civil Actions, Divorce* PO Box 247, Litchfield, CT 06759. 9AM-5PM. **860-567-0885**, Fax: 860-567-4779. **Fax** ✉ 👆

Geographical Area Court #18 *Misdemeanor, Eviction, Small Claims* 80 Doyle Rd (PO Box 667), Bantam, CT 06750. 9AM-5PM. **860-567-3942**. Serving Barkhamsted, Bethlehem, Bridgewater, Canaan, Colebrook, Cornwall, Goshen, Hartland, Harwinton, Kent, Litchfield, Morris, New Hartford, New Milford, Norfolk, N Canaan, Roxbury, Salisbury, Sharon, Thomaston, Torrington, Warren, Wash & Winchester ✉ 👆

Middlesex County

Middlesex District Court - Criminal & GA Court #9 *Felony, Misdemeanor* 1 Court St, 1st Fl, Middletown, CT 06457-3348. 9AM-5PM. **860-343-6445**. Serving the towns of Chester, Clinton, Cromwell, Deep River, Durham, East Haddam, East Hampton, Essex, Haddam, Killingworth, Middlefield, Middletown, Old Saybrook, Portland and Westbrook. Access by ✉ 👆

Middlesex Judicial District Court - Civil *Civil Actions, Divorce, Eviction, Small Claims* 1 Court St, 2nd Fl, Middletown, CT 06457-3374. 9AM-5PM. **860-343-6400**, Fax: 860-343-6423 Access civil records by✉ 💻 👆.

New Haven County

Ansonia-Milford Judicial District Court *Felony, Civil Actions, Divorce* 14 W River St (PO Box 210), Milford, CT 06460. 9AM-4PM. **203-877-4293**. ✉ 👆

Waterbury Judicial District Court *Civil Actions, Small Claims, Divorce* 300

Grand St, Waterbury, CT 06702. 9AM-5PM. **203-591-3300**, Fax: 203-591-3325. Civil phone: Small claims: 203-591-3320, Crim: 203-236-8100. Address mail requests for Misdemeanor criminal searches to 400 Grand St. (Geographical Area Court #4). Access civil records by**Fax**✉ 💻 👆.

Meriden Judicial District Court *Civil Actions, Divorce, Eviction, Housing Small Claims* 54 W Main St, Rm 128, Meriden, CT 06451. 9AM-4PM. **203-238-6666** Access civil records by✉ 💻 👆.

New Haven Judicial District Court *Felony, Civil Actions, Family, Divorce, Small Claims* www.jud.state.ct.us/directory/directory/location/newhaven.htm 235 Church St, New Haven, CT 06510. 9AM-5PM. **203-503-6800**, Fax: 203-789-6424. ✉ 👆

Geographical Area Court #5 *Misdemeanor, Eviction, Small Claims* 106 Elizabeth St, Derby, CT 06418. 9AM-5PM. **203-735-7438**, Civil: 203-735-9654, Crim: 203-735-7438. Serving the towns of Ansonia, Beacon Falls, Derby, Orange, Oxford, Seymour and Shelton. ✉ 👆

Geographical Area Court #23 *Misdemeanor, Eviction* 121 Elm St, New Haven, CT 06510. 9AM-5PM. **203-789-7461**, Fax: 203-789-7492. Civil phone: 203-503-6800. Small claims is located at 235 Church St, Clerk's Office, New Haven, CT 06510, 203-503-6800. Towns of Bethany, Branford, East Haven, Guilford, Madison, New Haven, North Branford and Woodbridge. ✉ 👆

Geographical Area Court #7 *Misdemeanor, Small Claims* 54 W Main St, Meriden, CT 06451. 9AM-5PM. Fax: 203-238-6016. Criminal phone: 203-238-6130. Serving the towns of Cheshire, Hamden, Meriden, North Haven and Wallingford. ☎ ✉ 👆

Geographical Area Court #4 *Felony, Misdemeanor, Traffic* www.jud.state.ct.us 400 Grand St, Waterbury, CT 06702. 9AM-5PM. **203-236-8100**, Fax: 203-236-8099. Towns of Middlebury, Naugatuck, Prospect, Southbury, Waterbury, Watertown, Wolcott, Woodbury.☎ ✉ 👆

Geographical Area Court #22 *Misdemeanor, Eviction, Housing Small Claims* 14 W River St, Milford, CT 06460. 1-2:30PM, 4-5PM. 203-874-0674 (Small Claims), Civil: 203-877-4293,

Crim: 203-874-1116. Serving the towns of Milford and West Haven. ✉ 👆

New London County

New London Judicial District Court *Felony, Civil Actions, Divorce* 70 Huntington St, New London, CT 06320. 9AM-5PM. **860-443-5363**. ✉ 👆

Norwich Judicial District Court *Civil Actions, Divorce* www.jud.state.ct.us/ 1 Courthouse Sq, Norwich, CT 06360. 9AM-5PM. **860-887-3515**, Fax: 860-887-8643 by☎ ✉**Fax**💻 👆

Geographical Area Court #10 *Misdemeanor, Eviction, Small Claims* www.jud.state.ct.us 112 Broad St, New London, CT 06320. 9AM-5PM. **860-443-8343**, Civil: 860-443-8346. Serving the towns of East Lyme, Groton, Ledyard, Lyme, New London, N Stonington, Old Lyme, Stonington and Waterford. ✉ 👆

Geographical Area Court #21 *Misdemeanor, Eviction, Small Claims* www.jud.state.ct.us 1 Courthouse Sq, Norwich, CT 06360. 1-2:30PM, 4-5PM. Civil: 860-887-3515, Crim: 860-889-7338. Serving the towns of Bozrah, Colchester, Franklin, Griswold, Lebanon, Lisbon, Montville, Norwich, Preston, Salem, Sprague and Voluntown. 👆

Tolland County

Tolland Judicial District Court - Civil *Civil Actions, Divorce* 69 Brooklyn St, Rockville, CT 06066. 9AM-5PM. **860-896-4920** by✉ 💻 👆

Tolland Judicial District Court - Criminal *Felony* 20 Park St, Vernon, CT 06066. 9AM-5PM. **860-870-3200**. The address can use either Rockville or Vernon, but postal service will sometimes return mail addressed to Rockville. 👆

Geographical Area Court #19 *Misdemeanor* www.jud2.state.ct.us 20 Park St PO Box 980, Rockville, CT 06066-0980. 9AM-4PM. **860-870-3200**. Serving the towns of Andover, Bolton, Columbia, Coventry, Ellington, Hebron, Mansfield, Somers, Stafford, Tolland, Union, Vernon and Willington. ✉ 👆

Windham County

Windham Judicial District Court *Civil Actions, Divorce* 155 Church St, Putnam, CT 06260. 9AM-5PM. **860-928-7749**,

Key: Symbols refer to criminal records access unless otherwise noted. phone-☎ mail-✉ fax-**Fax** in person-👆 online-💻 email-**Email**

Fax: 860-928-7076 Access civil records by ☎ ✉ 🖥 ✋.

Geographical Area Court #11 *Felony, Misdemeanor, Eviction, Small Claims*

120 School St, #110, Danielson, CT 06239-3024. 9AM-5PM. **860-779-8480**, Fax: 860-779-8488. Serving the towns of Ashford, Brooklyn, Canterbury, Chaplin, Eastford, Hampton, Killingly, Plainfield,

Pomfret, Putnam, Scotland, Sterling, Thompson, Windham and Woodstock. ☎ ✉ ✋

Delaware

State Court Administration: Administrative Office of the Courts, 820 N French, 11th Fl, Wilmington, DE, 19801; 302-255-0090, Fax: 302-255-2217. http://courts.state.de.us

Court Structure: The Superior Court, the State's court of general jurisdiction, has original jurisdiction over criminal and civil cases except equity cases. The Court has exclusive jurisdiction over felonies and almost all drug offenses. The Court of Common Pleas has jurisdiction in civil cases where the amount in controversy, exclusive of interest, does not exceed $50,000. In criminal cases, the Court of Common Pleas handles all misdemeanors occurring in the State except certain drug-related offenses and traffic offenses. The Court of Chancery has jurisdiction to hear all matters relating to equity. The litigation in this tribunal deals largely with corporate issues, trusts, estates, other fiduciary matters, disputes involving the purchase of land and questions of title to real estate as well as commercial and contractual matters. The Justice of the Peace Court, the initial entry level into the court system for most citizens, has jurisdiction over civil cases in which the disputed amount is less than $15,000. In criminal cases, the Justice of the Peace Court hears certain misdemeanors and most motor vehicle cases (excluding felonies) and the Justices of the Peace may act as committing magistrates for all crimes.

Online Access: Chancery, Superior, Common Pleas and Supreme Court opinions and orders are available free online at http://courts.st ate.de.us/opinions. Supreme, Superior and Common Pleas Court calendars are free at http://courts.state.de.us/calendars. Chancery and Supreme Court filings are available at http://www.virtualdocket.com. Registration and fees required.

Additional Information: Effective 1/15/95, the civil case limit of the Justice of the Peace Courts increased from $5,000 to $15,000; the Courts of Common Pleas' limit went from $15,000 to $50,000.

Criminal histories are available with a signed release from the offender at the Delaware State Police Headquarters, Criminal Records Section in Dover DE. For information on criminal history retrieval requirements, call 302-739-5880.

Kent County

Superior Court *Felony, Misd, Civil Over $50,000*   http://courts.state.de.us/superior Office of Prothonotary, 38 The Green, Dover, DE 19901. 8AM-4:30PM. **302-739-3184**, Fax: 302-739-6717. Court refers records request to State Agency- 302-739-5961 ✋

Court of Common Pleas *Misdemeanor, Civil Actions Under $50,000*   38 The Green, Dover, DE 19901. 8AM-4:30PM. **302-739-4618**, Fax 302-739-4501. ✉ ✋

Chancery Court *Civil, Probate* http://courts.state.de.us/chancery   38 The Green, Dover, DE 19901. 8:30AM-4:30PM. **302-736-2242**, Fax: 302-736-2240, Probate: 302-744-2330 Access civil records by ✋

Dover Justice of the Peace #16 *Civil Actions Under $15,000, Eviction, Small Claims* http://courts.state.de.us/jpcourt 480 Bank Ln, Dover, DE 19904. 8AM-4PM. **302-739-4316**, Fax: 302-739-6797 Access civil records by ✉ ✋

Harrington Justice of the Peace #6 *Misdemeanor* http://courts.state.de.us/jp court 35 Cams Fortune Way, Harrington, DE 19952. 8AM-4PM. **302-422-5922**, Fax: 302-422-1527. ✋ ✉

Dover Justice of the Peace #7 *Misdemeanor* 480 Bank Ln, Dover, DE 19903. Open 24 hours. **302-739-4554**, Fax: 302-739-6797.

Smyrna Justice of the Peace #8 *Misdemeanor* 100 Monrovia Ave, Smyrna, DE 19977. 8AM-4PM. **302-653-7083**, Fax: 302-653-2888.

New Castle County

Superior Court *Felony, Misdemeanor, Civil Actions Over $50,000* http://courts.state.de.us/superior Office of the Prothonotary 500 N King St, #500, Wilmington, DE 19801. 8:30AM-5PM. **302-255-0800**, Fax: 302-255-2264/66. ✋

Chancery Court *Civil, Probate* http://courts.state.de.us/chancery   500 N King St, #1551, Wilmington, DE 19801. 8:30AM-5PM. **302-255-0544**, Fax: 302-

255-2213, Probate: 302-571-7545 Access civil records by ☎ Fax ✉ ✋

Court of Common Pleas *Misdemeanor, Civil Under $50,000*   500 N King St, Wilmington, DE 19801-3704. 8:30AM-4:30PM. **302-255-0900**, Fax: 302-255-2243. Fax for civil is 302-255-2245. ☎ Fax ✉ ✋

Wilmington Justice of the Peace #13 *Civil Under $15,000, Eviction, Small Claims*   1010 Concord Ave Concord Professional Ctr, Wilmington, DE 19802. 8AM-4PM. **302-577-2550**, Fax: 302-577-2526 Access civil records by ✋

Middletown Justice #9 *Civil Under $15,000, Misdemeanor, Eviction, Small Claims* 757 N Broad St, Middletown, DE 19709. 8AM-4PM M T TH F, Noon-8PM W. **302-378-5221**, Fax: 302-378-5220. Due to a court fire, criminal cases 7/24/2000 to 5/1/2001 were heard at New Castle JP Court 11, 323-4450. Civil cases were heard at Prices Corner JP Court 12, 995-8646. Now, all new cases are back at Middletown. ✋

Prices Corner Justice of the Peace #12
Civil Under $15,000, Eviction, Small Claims http://courts.state.de.us/jpcourt 212 Greenbank Rd, Wilmington, DE 19808. 8AM-4PM. **302-995-8646**, Fax: 302-995-8642 Access civil records by✉✋

Wilmington Justice of the Peace #15
Misdemeanor http://courts.state.de.us/jp court 130 Hickman Rd, #13, Claymont, DE 19703. 8AM-4PM. **302-798-5327**, Fax: 302-798-4508. Effective 06/01/99, the court assumed DUI cases. This court was formally located at 716 Philadelphia Pike in Wilmington. Access by ✋✉

Prices Corner Justice of the Peace #10
Misdemeanor http://courts.state.de.us/jp court 210 Greenbank Rd, Wilmington, DE 19808. 8AM-11PM. **302-995-8640**, Fax: 302-995-8642. Access by ✋✉

New Castle Justice of the Peace #11
Misdemeanor 61 Christiana Rd, New Castle, DE 19720. Open 24 hours. **302-323-4450**, Fax: 302-323-4452. ✋✉

Wilmington Justice of the Peace #20
Misdemeanor Public Safety Bldg 300 N Walnut St, Wilmington, DE 19801. 8AM-midnight. **302-577-7234**, Fax: 302-577-7237. Court now also maintains the case records from the former JP Court #18. ✋

Sussex County

Superior Court *Felony, Misd., Civil Actions* http://courts.state.de.us/superior PO Box 756 (The Circle), Georgetown, DE 19947. 8AM-4:30PM. Fax: 302-856-5739. Civil phone: 302-856-5742, Crim: 302-856-5741. ✋

Chancery Court *Civil, Probate* http://courts.state.de.us/chancery 34 The Circle PO Box 424, Georgetown, DE 19947. 8:30AM-4:30PM. **302-856-5775**, Probate: 302-855-7875 Access civil records by☎✉✋

Court of Common Pleas *Misdemeanor, Civil Actions Under $50,000* http://courts.state.de.us/commonpleas PO Box 426, Georgetown, DE 19947. 8:30AM-4:30PM. **302-856-5333**, Fax: 302-856-5056. ☎Fax✉✋

Seaford Justice of the Peace #19 *Civil Actions Under $15,000, Eviction, Small Claims* 408 Stein Hwy, Seaford, DE 19973. 8AM-4PM. **302-629-5433**, Fax: 302-628-6517 Access civil records by✋✉.

Georgetown Justice of the Peace #17
Civil Under $15,000, Eviction, Small Claims 23730 Shortly Rd, Georgetown, DE 19947. 8AM-4PM. **302-856-1447**, Fax: 302-856-4654 by✉✋

Justice of the Peace #6 *Misdemeanor* 35 Cams Fortune Way, Harrington, DE 19952-1790. 8AM-4PM. **302-422-5922**, Fax: 302-422-1527. Some old civil cases also located here. ✉✋

Seaford Justice of the Peace #4
Misdemeanor court 408 Stein Hwy, Seaford, DE 19973. 8:00 am - Midnight. **302-628-2036**, Fax 302-528-2049. ✉✋

Millsboro Justice of the Peace #1
Misdemeanor 553 E DuPont Hwy, Millsboro, DE 19966. 8AM-4PM. **302-934-7268**, Fax: 302-934-1414. ✋✉

Rehoboth Beach Justice of the Peace #2
Misdemeanor 31 Rte 24, Rehoboth Beach, DE 19971-9738. 8AM-Midnight. **302-645-6163**, Fax 302-645-8842. ✉✋

Georgetown Justice of the Peace #3
Misdemeanor 17 Shortly Rd, Georgetown, DE 19947. 24 hours daily. **302-856-1445**, Fax: 302-856-5844. ✉✋

District of Columbia

State Court Administration: Executive Office, 500 Indiana Av NW, Room 1500, Washington, DC, 20001; 202-879-1700, Fax: 202-879-4829. www.dcsc.gov

Court Structure: The Superior Court in DC is divided into 17 divisions, 4 of which are shown in this book: Criminal, Civil, Landlord and Tenant, and Tax-Probate. The Tax-Probate Division of the Superior Court handles probate. Eviction is part of the court's Landlord and Tenant Branch (202-879-4879).

Online Access: The Superior Court and Court of Appeals offer access to opinions at www.dcbar.org.

Superior Court - Criminal Division *Felony, Misdemeanor* www.dcsc.gov 500 Indiana Ave NW, Rm 4001, Washington, DC 20001. 8:30AM-5PM. **202-879-1373**, Fax: 202-879-0146. ✉Fax✋

Superior Court - Civil Division *Civil Actions, Small Claims* www.dcbar.org/dcsc/ 500 Indiana Ave NW, JM 170, Washington, DC 20001. 8:30AM-5PM M-F; 9AM-N S. **202-879-1133**, Fax: 202-879-8335. Criminal phone: 202-879-1373. Small Claims is a separate branch that handles claims of $5,000 or less. Access civil records by☎✉✋💻

Superior Court - Landlord & Tenant Branch *Eviction* www.dcsc.gov 500 Indiana Ave NW, Rm JM 255, Washington, DC 20001. 8:30AM-5PM M-F; 9AM-N Sat; 6:30-8PM Wed evenings. **202-879-4879**. This information applies to the Landlord & Tenant Branch only. Access civil records by✋✉.

Superior Court - Probate Division *Probate* 500 Indiana Ave NW, Washington, DC 20001. 9AM-4PM. **202-879-1499**, Fax: 202-393-5849/879-1452(auditing).

Key: Symbols refer to criminal records access unless otherwise noted. phone-☎ mail-✉ fax-**Fax** in person-✋ online-💻 email-**Email**

Florida

State Court Administration: Office of State Courts Administrator, Supreme Court Bldg, 500 S Duval, Tallahassee, FL, 32399-1900; 850-922-5082, Fax: 850-488-0156. www.flcourts.org/

Court Structure: All counties have combined Circuit and County Courts. The Circuit Court is the court of general jurisdiction.

Online Access: 53 Clerk of Courts/Recorders give access to index data at www.myflorida.com, a government sponsored website. Supreme Court dockets are available online at http://jweb.flcourts.org/pls/docket/ds_docket_search. There is no statewide, online computer system for external access available for the Circuit and County Courts. The Florida Legislature mandated that court documents must be imaged and available for inspection over a publicly available website. In response to concerns of identity theft and fraud, the Florida Legislature recently passed new laws concerning privacy of public documents on public websites. These laws now make it possible for certain of these documents viewed on the Clerk websites to be either redacted of sensitive information or in some cases removed completely. The Clerk of the Circuit Court cannot place an image or copy of the following documents on a publicly available Internet website for general public display: Military discharges; Death certificates; Court files, records or papers relating to Family Law, Juvenile Law or Probate Law cases.

Additional Information: All courts have one address and switchboard; however, the divisions within the court(s) are completely separate. Requesters should specify which court and which division --e.g., Circuit Civil, County Civil, etc. -- the request is directed to, even though some counties will automatically check both with one request.

Fees are set by statute and are as follows as of July 1, 2004: Search Fee - $1.50 per name per year; Certification Fee - $1.50 per document plus copy fee; Copy Fee - $1.00 per page; some county copy fees may vary.

Alachua County

Circuit & County Courts *Felony, Misdemeanor, Civil, Eviction, Small Claims, Probate* www.alachuaclerk.org PO Box 600 201 E University Ave, Gainesville, FL 32602. 8:15AM-5PM. **352-374-3636**, Fax: 352-381-0144-felony, 338-3207-civil. Civil phone: 352-374-3636, Crim: 352-374-3681 (felony). Misdeamenor records: 352-337-6250. Fax number for ancient (older) records is 352-337-6158. **Fax**✉️✋

Baker County

Circuit & County Courts - Civil *Civil, Eviction, Small Claims, Probate* http://bakercountyfl.org/clerk/ 339 E Macclenny Ave, Macclenny, FL 32063. 8:30AM-5PM. **904-259-0202, 904-259-0209 (Circuit civ)**, Fax: 904-259-4176. Civil phone: 904-259-0208 (Cty), Probate: 904-259-0209 ✉️✋🖥️

Circuit & County Courts - Criminal *Felony, Misd.* http://bakercountyfl.org/clerk/ 339 E Macclenny Ave, Macclenny, FL 32063. 8:30AM-5PM. **904-259-0206**, Fax: 904-259-4176. County Court Misdemeanor phone nubmer is 904-259-0204. ✉️✋🖥️

Bay County

Circuit Court - Civil *Civil Actions Over $15,000, Probate* www.baycoclerk.com PO Box 2269, Panama City, FL 32402. 8AM-4:30PM. Fax: 850-747-5188. Civil phone: 850-747-5715, Crim: 850-747-5123, Probate: 850-747-5118 Access civil records by ☎️**Fax**✉️✋🖥️

Circuit Court - Criminal *Felony* www.baycoclerk.com PO Box 2269, Panama City, FL 32402. 8AM-4:30PM. **850-747-5125**, Fax: 850-747-5188. **Fax**✉️✋🖥️

County Court - Civil *Civil Actions Under $15,000, Eviction, Small Claims* www.baycoclerk.com PO Box 2269, Panama City, FL 32402. 8AM-4:30PM. **850-747-5114**, Fax: 850-747-5188 Access civil records by ☎️**Fax**✉️✋🖥️

County Court - Misdemeanor *Misdemeanor* www.baycoclerk.com PO Box 2269, Panama City, FL 32402. 8AM-4:30PM. **850-747-5146**, Fax: 850-747-5188. ☎️**Fax**✉️✋🖥️

Bradford County

Circuit Court *Felony, Civil Actions Over $15,000, Probate* http://circuit8.org PO Drawer B, Starke, FL 32091. 8AM-5PM. **904-964-6280**, Fax: 904-964-4454. ☎️✉️✋🖥️

County Court *Misdemeanor, Civil Actions Under $15,000, Eviction, Small Claims* www.bradford-co-fla.org/ PO Drawer B, Starke, FL 32091. 8AM-5PM. **904-964-6280**, Fax: 904-964-4454. ✉️**Fax**✋

Brevard County

Circuit Court - Civil *Civil, Eviction, Small Claims, Probate* www.brevardclerk.us PO Box 2767 Offical Records Copy Desk, Titusville, FL 32781-2767. 8AM-5PM. **321-264-5245**, Fax: 321-264-5246 Access civil records by ☎️**Fax**✉️✋🖥️.

County Court - Misdemeanor *Misdemeanor* www.brevardclerk.us/ PO Box 2767, 700 S Park Ave, Bldg B, Titusville, FL 32781. 8AM-4:30PM. **321-637-5445**, Fax: 321-264-5246. ☎️**Fax**✉️🖥️✋

Circuit Court - Felony *Felony* www.brevardclerk.us PO Box H 700 S Park Ave, Titusville, FL 32781-0239. 8AM-5PM. **321-264-5245**, Fax: 321-264-5345. ☎️**Fax**✉️🖥️✋

Broward County

Circuit & County Courts *Felony, Misdemeanor, Civil, Eviction, Small Claims, Probate* www.browardclerk.org 201 SE 6th St, Ft Lauderdale, FL 33301. 9AM-4PM. **954-712-7899**, Fax: 954-831-7166. Civil phone: 954-831-5740, Crim: 954-831-5680, Probate: 954-831-7154. ☎️**Fax**✉️🖥️✋✉️

Calhoun County

Circuit & County Court *Felony, Misdemeanor, Civil, Eviction, Small Claims, Probate* www.calhounclerk.com

Key: Symbols refer to criminal records access unless otherwise noted. phone-☎️ mail-✉️ fax-**Fax** in person-✋ online-🖥️ email-**Email**

20859 E Central Ave #130, 425 E Central, Blountstown, FL 32424. 8AM-4PM. **850-674-4545**, Fax: 850-674-5553. Criminal phone: 850-674-8764. Access ☎ ✉ ✋

Charlotte County

Circuit & County Courts - Civil Div. *Civil, Eviction, Small Claims, Probate* http://co.charlotte.fl.us/clrkinfo/clerk_default .htm PO Box 511687, Punta Gorda, FL 33951-1687. 8AM-5PM. **941-637-2279**, Fax: 941-637-2116 Access civil records by ✉ ✋ 💻

Circuit & County Courts - Criminal Division *Felony, Misdemeanor* http://co.charlotte.fl.us/clrkinfo/clerk_default .htm PO Box 511687, Punta Gorda, FL 33951-1687. 8AM-5PM. **941-637-2269**, Fax: 941-637-2159. ☎ ✉ ✋ 💻

Citrus County

Circuit Court *Felony, Civil Actions Over $15,000, Probate* www.clerk.citrus.fl.us 110 N Apopka, Rm 101, Inverness, FL 34450-4299. 8AM-5PM. **352-341-6400**, Fax: 352-341-6413. Marriage license data is found online at the web site. ☎ Fax ✉ ✋ 💻

County Court *Misdemeanor, Civil Actions Under $15,000, Eviction, Small Claims* www.clerk.citrus.fl.us 110 N Apopka, Rm 101, Inverness, FL 34450. 8AM-5PM. **352-341-6400**, Fax: 352-341-6413. ☎ Fax ✉ ✋ 💻

Clay County

Circuit Court *Felony, Civil Actions Over $15,000, Probate* http://clerk.co.clay.fl.us PO Box 698, Green Cove Springs, FL 32043. 8:30AM-4:30PM. **904-284-6302**, Fax: 904-284-6390. ✉ ✋

County Court *Misdemeanor, Civil Actions Under $15,000, Eviction, Small Claims* http://clerk.co.clay.fl.us PO Box 698, Green Cove Springs, FL 32043. 8:30AM-4:30PM. **904-284-6316**, Fax: 904-284-6390. ✉ ✋ 💻

Collier County

Circuit Court *Felony, Civil Actions Over $15,000, Probate* www.clerk.collier.fl.us PO Box 413044, Naples, FL 34101-3044. 8AM-5PM. **239-732-2646**, Crim: 239-732-2648. ✉ 💻 ✋

County Court *Misdemeanor, Civil Actions Under $15,000, Eviction, Small Claims* www.clerk.collier.fl.us PO Box

413044, Naples, FL 34101-3044. 8AM-5PM. Fax: 239-774-8020. Civil phone: 239-732-2646, Crim: 239-732-2648. ✉ 💻 ✋

Columbia County

Circuit & County Courts *Felony, Misdemeanor, Circuit/County, Civil, Eviction, Small Claims, Probate* www.columbiaclerk.com PO Drawer 2069, Lake City, FL 32056. 8AM-5PM. **386-758-1342**, Civil phone: 386-758-1036, Crim: 386-758-1164. Access records: ✋

Dade County

Better known as Miami-Dade County.

Circuit & County Courts - Civil *Civil, Eviction, Small Claims, Probate* www.miami-dadeclerk.com/dadecoc 73 W Flagler St, #242, Miami, FL 33130. 9AM-4PM. **305-275-1155**, Fax: 305-349-7410 Civil. County Court hears civil actions up to $15,000. Access civil records by ☎ Fax ✉ 💻 ✋.

Circuit & County Courts - Criminal *Felony, Misdemeanor* www.miami-dadeclerk.com/dadecoc/ 1351 NW 12th St, #9000, Miami, FL 33125. 9AM-4PM. **305-275-1155**, Fax: 305-548-5526. Criminal phone: 305-548-5527. Although located in the same building, the records of the felony and misdemeanor courts are not co-mingled. Search Circuit Court for felonies; County for misdememanors. ☎ Fax ✉ 💻 ✋

De Soto County

Circuit & County Courts *Felony, Misdemeanor, Civil, Eviction, Small Claims, Probate* http://12circuit.state.fl.us 115 E Oak St, Arcadia, FL 34266. 8AM-5PM. **863-993-4876**, Fax: 863-993-4669. Civil phone: 863-993-4880, Probate: 863-993-4880. County Court & Evictions 863-993-4880. ☎ Fax ✉ ✋

Dixie County

Circuit & County Courts *Felony, Misdemeanor, Civil, Eviction, Small Claims, Probate* PO Drawer 1206, Cross City, FL 32628-1206. 9AM-5PM. **352-498-1200**, Fax: 352-498-1201. ✉ ✋

Duval County

Circuit & County Courts - Civil Division *Civil, Eviction, Small Claims, Probate* www.duval.fl.us.landata.com/ 330 E Bay St, Jacksonville, FL 32202. 8:30AM-4:30PM. **904-630-2038**, Fax:

904-630-7506 Access civil records by Fax ✉ 💻 ✋.

Circuit & County Courts - Criminal Division *Felony, Misdemeanor* www.duval.fl.us.landata.com/ 330 E Bay St, Rm M101, Jacksonville, FL 32202. 8AM-5PM. **904-630-2065**, Fax: 904-630-7505. ✉ Fax 💻 ✋

Escambia County

Circuit & County Courts - Civil Division *Civil, Eviction, Small Claims, Probate* www.clerk.co.escambia.fl.us 190 Governmental Ctr, Pensacola, FL 32501. 8AM-5PM. **850-595-4170**, Civil: 850-595-4130 (Circ Ct. Civil), Probate: 850-595-4300. Mail address is PO Box 333, Pensacola FL 32591-0333. Access civil records by ☎ Fax ✉ ✋ 💻

Circuit & County Courts - Criminal Division *Felony, Misdemeanor* www.clerk.co.escambia.fl.us 190 Governmental Ctr, Pensacola, FL 32501. 8AM-5PM. **850-595-4150**, Fax: 850-595-4198. Criminal phone: 850-595-4185 County. Misdemeanor records: 850-595-4185. Fax ✉ 💻

Flagler County

Circuit & County Courts *Felony, Misdemeanor, Civil, Eviction, Small Claims, Probate* http://clerk.co.flagler.fl.us PO Box 787, Bunnell, FL 32110. 8:30AM-4:30PM. Fax: 386-437-7454 crim; 586-2116 civil. Civil phone: 386-437-7430, Crim: 386-437-7419. ☎ Fax ✉ ✋ 📧

Franklin County

Circuit & County Courts *Felony, Misdemeanor, Civil, Eviction, Small Claims, Probate* www.franklinclerk.com/ 33 Market St, #203, Apalachicola, FL 32320. 8:30AM-4:30PM. **850-653-8862**, Fax: 850-653-2261. ✉ ✋ 💻

Gadsden County

Circuit & County Courts - Criminal Division *Felony, Misdemeanor* www.co.leon.fl.us/court/court.htm 24 N Adams, Quincy, FL 32351. 8:30AM-5PM. **850-875-8610**, Fax: 850-875-7265, Requests may be sent to PO Box 1649, ZIP is 32353 Fax ✉ ✋

Circuit & County Courts - Civil Division *Civil, Eviction, Small Claims, Probate* www.clerk.co.gadsden.fl.us PO Box 1649, Quincy, FL 32353. 8:30AM-

5PM. **850-875-8621**, Fax: 850-875-8612 prob:850-875-8622. ☎**Fax**✉💻**Email**👆

Gilchrist County
Circuit & County Courts *Felony, Misd., Civil, Eviction, Small Claims, Probate* www.co.gilchrist.fl.us/cophone/ PO Box 37, Trenton, FL 32693. 8:30AM-5PM. **352-463-3170**, Fax: 352-463-3166. ✉👆

Glades County
Circuit & County Courts *Felony, Misdemeanor, Civil, Eviction, Small Claims, Probate* PO Box 10, Moore Haven, FL 33471. 8AM-5PM. **863-946-6011**, Fax: 863-946-0560. ✉**Fax**👆

Gulf County
Circuit & County Courts *Felony, Misdemeanor, Civil, Eviction, Small Claims, Probate* www.gulfclerk.com 1000 Cecil Costin Blvd, Port St Joe, FL 32456. 9AM-5PM. **850-229-6112**, Fax: 850-229-6174. **Fax**✉👆

Hamilton County
Circuit & County Courts *Felony, Misdemeanor, Civil, Eviction, Small Claims, Probate* 207 NE 1st St, #106, Jasper, FL 32052. 8:30AM-4:30PM. **386-792-1288**, Fax: 386-792-3524. ✉👆

Hardee County
Circuit & County Courts *Felony, Misdemeanor, Civil, Eviction, Small Claims, Probate* www.jud10.org PO Drawer 1749, Wauchula, FL 33873-1749. 8AM-5PM. **863-773-4174**, Fax: 863-773-4422. ✉👆

Hendry County
Circuit & County Courts *Felony, Misdemeanor, Civil, Eviction, Small Claims, Probate* PO Box 1760, LaBelle, FL 33975-1760. 8:30AM-5PM. **863-675-5369**, Fax: 863-612-4748. Criminal phone: 863-675-5214. Access by ✉👆

Hernando County
Circuit & County Courts *Felony, Misd., Civil, Eviction, Small Claims, Probate* www.clerk.co.hernando.fl.us 20 N Main St, Brooksville, FL 34601. 8AM-5PM. **352-540-6377**, Fax: 352-754-4247. Civil phone: 352-540-6377, Crim: 352-540-6444, Probate: 352-540-6366. ✉💻👆

Highlands County
Circuit & County Courts *Felony, Misd., Civil, Eviction, Small Claims, Probate* www.clerk.co.highlands.fl.us 590 S Commerce Ave, Sebring, FL 33870-3867. 8AM-5PM. Fax: 863-402-6575. Civil phone: 863-402-6591, Crim: 863-402-6597. ✉👆

Hillsborough County
Circuit & County Courts *Felony, Misdemeanor, Civil, Eviction, Small Claims, Probate* www.hillsclerk.com 419 Pierce St, Tampa, FL 33602. 8AM-5PM. **813-276-8100**, Fax: 813-272-7707. Civil phone: x7803, Crim: x7802. **Fax**✉💻👆

Holmes County
Circuit & County Courts *Felony, Misdemeanor, Civil, Eviction, Small Claims, Probate* PO Box 397, Bonifay, FL 32425. 8AM-4PM. **850-547-1100**, Fax: 850-547-6630. ✉👆

Indian River County
Circuit & County Courts *Felony, Misdemeanor, Civil, Eviction, Small Claims, Probate* www.clerk.indian-river.org PO Box 1028, Vero Beach, FL 32961. 8:30AM-5PM. **772-770-5185**, Fax: 772-770-5008. ✉👆💻

Jackson County
Circuit & County Courts *Felony, Misdemeanor, Civil, Eviction, Small Claims, Probate* www.jacksonclerk.com PO Box 510, Marianna, FL 32447. 8AM-4:30PM. **850-482-9552**, Fax: 850-482-7849. **Fax**✉👆

Jefferson County
Circuit & County Courts *Felony, Misd., Civil, Eviction, Small Claims, Probate* www.myjeffersoncounty.com Jefferson County Courthouse, Rm 10, Monticello, FL 32344. 8AM-5PM. **850-342-0218**, Fax: 850-342-0222. **Fax**✉👆

Lafayette County
Circuit & County Courts *Felony, Misdemeanor, Civil, Eviction, Small Claims, Probate* PO Box 88, Mayo, FL 32066. 8AM-5PM. **386-294-1600**, Fax: 386-294-4231. ☎✉**Fax**👆

Lake County
Circuit & County Courts *Felony, Misd., Civil, Eviction, Small Claims, Probate* www.lakecountyclerk.org/default1.asp 550 W Main St, or PO Box 7800, Tavares, FL 32778. 8:30AM-5PM. **352-742-4100**, Fax: 352-742-4166. Civil phone: 352-742-4145, Crim: 352-742-4126 (Felony) 352-742-4128 (Misdemeanor), Probate: 352-742-4122. **Fax**✉👆

Lee County
Circuit & County Courts *Felony, Misdemeanor, Civil, Eviction, Small Claims, Probate, Traffic* www.leeclerk.org PO Box 2469, Ft Myers, FL 33902. 7:45AM-5PM. **239-335-2283**. ✉💻👆

Leon County
Circuit & County Courts *Felony, Misdemeanor, Civil, Eviction, Small Claims, Probate* www.clerk.leon.fl.us PO Box 726, Tallahassee, FL 32302. 8:30AM-5PM. **850-577-4000**, Civil: 850-577-4170, Crim: 850-577-4070, Probate: 850-577-4180. ✉💻👆

Levy County
Circuit & County Courts *Felony, Misdemeanor, Civil, Eviction, Small Claims, Probate* www.levyclerk.com PO Box 610, Bronson, FL 32621. 8AM-5PM. **352-486-5100**, Civil: 352-486-5277, Crim: 352-486-5272, Probate: 352-486-5459. ✉👆

Liberty County
Circuit & County Courts *Felony, Misdemeanor, Civil, Eviction, Small Claims, Probate* www.libertyclerk.com PO Box 399, Bristol, FL 32321. 8AM-5PM. **850-643-2215**, Fax: 850-643-2866. ✉👆

Madison County
Circuit & County Courts *Felony, Misdemeanor, Civil, Eviction, Small Claims, Probate* PO Box 237, Madison, FL 32341. 8AM-5PM. **850-973-1500**, Fax: 850-973-2059. ☎✉👆

Manatee County
Circuit & County Courts *Felony, Misdemeanor, Civil, Eviction, Small Claims, Probate* www.manateeclerk.com PO Box 25400, Bradenton, FL 34206. 8:30AM-5PM. **941-749-1800**, Fax: 941-741-4082. ☎**Fax**✉💻👆**Email**

Marion County
Circuit & County Courts *Felony, Misd., Civil, Eviction, Small Claims, Probate* www.marioncountyclerk.org PO Box 1030, Ocala, FL 34478. 8AM-5PM. **352-620-3892 (cty civ)**, Fax: 352-620-3300 (civ); 840-5668 (crim). Civil phone: 352-620-3891 (Circ), Crim: 352-620-3861, Probate: 352-620-3874. **Fax**✉👆

Martin County

Circuit & County Courts *Felony, Misd., Civil, Eviction, Small Claims, Probate* http://clerk-web.martin.fl.us/ClerkWeb/ PO Box 9016, Stuart, FL 34995. 8AM-5PM. **772-288-5576**, Fax: 772-288-5724; 288-5991 (civil). ☎**Fax**✉✋

Monroe County

Circuit & County Courts *Felony, Misdemeanor, Civil, Eviction, Small Claims, Probate* www.co.monroe.fl.us 500 Whitehead St, Key West, FL 33040. 8:30AM-5PM. **305-294-4641**, Fax: 305-295-3623. Civil phone: 305-292-3310, Crim: 305-292-3390. ✉**Fax**✋🖥

Nassau County

Circuit & County Courts *Felony, Misdemeanor, Civil, Eviction, Small Claims, Probate* www.nassauclerk.com PO Box 456, (76347 Veterans Way), Fernandina Beach, FL 32035. 8:30AM-5PM. Fax: 904-321-5723 civ; 491-3649 crim. Civil phone: 904-548-4600, Crim: 904-548-4607, Probate: 904-548-4600. ☎**Fax**✉✋

Okaloosa County

Circuit & County Courts *Felony, Misdemeanor, Civil, Eviction, Small Claims, Probate* www.clerkofcourts.cc 1250 N Eglin Pky, Shalimar, FL 32579. 8AM-5PM. **850-651-7200**, Fax: 850-651-7230. ✉🖥✋

Okeechobee County

Circuit & County Courts *Felony, Misdemeanor, Civil, Eviction, Small Claims, Probate* 304 NW 2nd St, Rm 101, Okeechobee, FL 34972. 8:30AM-5PM. **863-763-2131**. Access by ✉✋

Orange County

Circuit & County Courts *Felony, Misdemeanor, Civil, Eviction, Small Claims, Probate* http://orangeclerk.ocfl.net PO Box 4994, (425 N Orange Ave), Orlando, FL 32801-1544. 8AM-5PM. **407-836-2060**. Mail requests should use room numbers; civil circuit-310; civil county-350; crim circuit-210; crim county-250. ✉🖥**Email**

County Court #3 *Misdemeanor, Civil Actions Under $15,000, Eviction, Small Claims* http://orangeclerk.ocfl.net Clerk of Courts 475 W Story Rd, Ocoee, FL 34761. 8-5PM. **407-667-6240**. ✉🖥✋

County Court - NE Orange Division *Misdemeanor, Civil Actions Under $15,000, Eviction, Small Claims* http://orangeclerk.ocfl.net 450 N Lakemont Ave, Winter Park, FL 32792. 7:30AM-5:30PM. **407-671-1116**. ☎✉🖥✋

County Court - Apopka Branch *Misdemeanor, Civil Actions Under $15,000, Eviction, Small Claims* http://orangeclerk.ocfl.net 1111 N Rock Springs Rd, Apopka, FL 32712. 7:30AM-5:30PM. **407-654-1030**. Records maintained at Orlando office. ✉🖥✋

Osceola County

Circuit Court - Civil *Civil Actions Over $5,000, Probate* www.ninja9.org/ 2 Courthouse Sq, Kissimmee, FL 34741. 8:30AM-5PM. **407-343-3500**, Probate: 407-343-3506 ✉✋🖥

Circuit & County Courts - Criminal Division *Felony, Misdemeanor* www.osceolaclerk.com 2 Courthouse Square, Kissimmee, FL 34741. 8:30AM-5PM. **407-343-3543/3555**. ✉✋🖥

County Court - Civil *Eviction, Small Claims* www.osceolaclerk.com 2 Courthouse Sq, #2000, Kissimmee, FL 34741. 8:30AM-5PM. **407-343-3500** Access civil records by ✉✋🖥

Palm Beach County

Circuit Court - Civil Division *Civil* www.pbcountyclerk.com PO Box 4667, West Palm Beach, FL 33402. 8AM-5PM. **561-355-2986**, Fax: 561-355-4643 Access civil records by ☎✉🖥✋.

Circuit & County Courts - Criminal Division *Felony, Misdemeanor* www.pbcountyclerk.com 205 N Dixie Hwy, West Palm Beach, FL 33401. 8AM-5PM. **561-355-2519**, Fax: 561-355-3802. Faxes can only be received by state agencies. ☎**Fax**✉🖥✋

County Court - Civil Division *Eviction, Small Claims* www.pbcountyclerk.com 205 N Dixie Hwy, West Palm Beach, FL 33402. 8AM-5PM. **561-355-2500**, Fax: 561-355-4643 ☎✉🖥✋

Circuit Court - Probate Division *Probate* www.pbcountyclerk.com PO Box 4238, West Palm Beach, FL 33402. 8AM-5PM. **561-355-2900**. Online access to 15th judicial circuit records is available at http://web3172.co.palm-beach.fl.us.

Registration and password required. Access civil records by ✉✋🖥

Pasco County

Circuit & County Courts - Civil Division *Civil, Eviction, Small Claims, Probate* www.pascoclerk.com/ 38053 Live Oak Ave, Dade City, FL 33523. 8:30AM-5PM. **352-521-4482** Access civil records by ✉🖥✋

Circuit & County Courts - Criminal Division *Felony, Misdemeanor* www.jud6.org 38053 Live Oak Ave, Dade City, FL 33523-3894. 8:30AM-5PM. **352-521-4504**. ✉🖥✋

Pinellas County

Circuit & County Courts - Civil Division *Civil, Eviction, Small Claims, Probate* www.jud6.org 315 Court St, Rm170, Clearwater, FL 33756. 8AM-5PM. **727-464-3267**, Fax: 727-464-4070 Access civil records by**Fax**✉🖥✋.

Criminal Justice Center *Felony* www.jud6.org Circuit Criminal Court Records 14250 49th St N, Clearwater, FL 34622. 8AM-5PM. **727-464-6793**, Fax: 727-464-6233. **Fax**✉🖥✋

County Court - Criminal Division *Misdemeanor* www.jud6.org 14250 49th St N, Clearwater, FL 34622-2831. 8AM-5PM. **727-464-7000**, Fax: 727-464-7040. ✉🖥✋

Polk County

Circuit Court - Civil Division *Civil Actions Over $15,000, Probate* www.polk-county.net/clerk/clerk.html PO Box 9000, Drawer CC2, Bartow, FL 33831-9000. 8AM-5PM. **863-534-4488**, Fax: 863-534-7707, Probate: 863-534-4478 Access civil records ☎✉🖥✋

Circuit & County Courts - Felony Division *Felony* www.polk-county.net/clerk/clerk.html PO Box 9000, Drawer CC9, Bartow, FL 33830. 8AM-5PM. **863-534-4000**, Fax: 863-534-4137. ☎✉✋

Circuit & County Courts - Misdemeanor Division *Misdemeanor,* www.polk-county.net/clerk/clerk.html PO Box 9000, Drawer CC10, Bartow, FL 33831-9000. 8AM-5PM. **863-534-4446**, Fax: 863-534-4137. ✉✋

County Court - Civil Division *Civil Actions Under $15,000, Eviction, Small*

Key: Symbols refer to criminal records access unless otherwise noted. phone-☎ mail-✉ fax-**Fax** in person-✋ online-🖥 email-**Email**

Claims www.polkcountyclerk.net/ PO Box 9000, Drawer CC12, Bartow, FL 33830-9000. 8AM-5PM. **863-534-4556 (County Court)**, Fax: 863-534-4045 (County Court) by☎⊠🖳✋

Putnam County

Circuit & County Courts - Civil Division *Civil, Eviction, Small Claims, Probate* PO Box 758, Palatka, FL 32178. 8:30AM-5PM. **386-329-0361**, Fax: 386-329-0888 Access civil records by⊠**Fax**✋🖃

Circuit & County Courts - Criminal Division *Felony, Misdemeanor* PO Box 758, Palatka, FL 32178. 8:30AM-5PM. **386-329-0257**, Fax: 386-329-0888. ⊠**Fax**✋🖃

St. Johns County

Circuit & County Courts - Civil Division *Civil, Eviction, Small Claims, Probate* www.co.st-johns.fl.us PO Drawer 300, St Augustine, FL 32085-0300. 8AM-5PM. **904-819-3600**, Fax: 904-819-3661 Probate: 904-819-3654. Access civil records by**Fax**⊠🖳✋.

Circuit & County Courts - Criminal Division *Felony, Misdemeanor* www.co.st-johns.fl.us PO Drawer 300, St Augustine, FL 32085-0300. 8AM-5PM. **904-819-3600**, Fax: 904-819-3666. Civil phone: 904-819-3651, Crim: 904-819-3615. **Fax**⊠🖳✋

St. Lucie County

Circuit & County Courts - Civil Division *Civil, Eviction, Small Claims, Probate* www.slcclerkofcourt.com PO Drawer 700, Ft Pierce, FL 34954. 8AM-5PM. **772-462-2758 (Circuit)**, Fax: 772-462-1998 (Circ.); 772-785-5884 (Cty). Civil phone: 772-785-5880 (County). Small claims phone is 772-785-5880; Small Claims and County Civil files and microfiche located at Courthouse Annex, 250 NW County Club Dr, Pt St. Lucie, FL 34986. Access civil records by⊠✋🖳

Circuit & County Courts - Criminal Division *Felony, Misdemeanor* www.martin.fl.us/GOVT/co/schack PO Drawer 700, Ft Pierce, FL 34954. 8AM-5PM. **772-462-6900**, Fax: 772-462-2833. **Fax**⊠✋🖳

Santa Rosa County

Circuit & County Courts - Civil Division *Civil, Eviction, Small Claims, Probate* www.santarosaclerk.com/ PO Box 472, Milton, FL 32572. 8AM-4:30PM. **850-623-0135** Access civil records by**Fax**⊠✋🖳

Circuit & County Courts - Criminal Division *Felony, Misd.* www.co.santa-rosa.fl.us/santa_rosa/clerk/index.html PO Box 472, Milton, FL 32572. 8AM-4:30PM. **850-623-0135**, Fax: 850-626-5705. Criminal phone: 850-983-1011. Misdemeanor phone number is 850-623-0135 x1007 or x2140; fax 850-626-7849. ⊠✋🖳

Sarasota County

Circuit & County Courts - Civil *Civil, Eviction, Small Claims, Probate* www.sarasotaclerk.com/ PO Box 3079, Sarasota, FL 34230. 8:30AM-5PM. **941-861-7400** by⊠🖳✋.

Circuit & County Courts - Criminal *Felony, Misd.* www.sarasotaclerk.com PO Box 3079, Sarasota, FL 34230. 8:30AM-5PM. **941-861-7400**. ⊠🖳✋

Seminole County

Circuit & County Courts - Civil Division *Civil, Eviction, Small Claims, Probate* www.18thcircuit.state.fl.us PO Box 8099, Sanford, FL 32772. 8AM-4:30PM. **407-665-4330**, Fax: 407-330-7193. Civil phone: 407-665-4366, Probate: 407-665-4374. Access civil records by⊠✋🖳

Circuit & County Courts - Criminal Division *Felony, Misdemeanor* www.seminoleclerk.org 301 N Park Ave, Sanford, FL 32771. 8AM-4:30PM. **407-665-4356 (Felony) 4377 (Misd)**, Fax: 407-330-7193. ⊠✋

Sumter County

Circuit & County Courts - Civil Division *Civil, Eviction, Small Claims, Probate* 209 N Florida St, Bushnell, FL 33513. 8:30AM-5PM. **352-793-0211**, Fax: 352-568-6608 Access civil records by**Fax**⊠✋🖳

Circuit & County Courts - Criminal Division *Felony, Misdemeanor* 209 N Florida St, Bushnell, FL 33513. 8:30AM-5PM. **352-793-0211**, Fax: 352-568-6608. ⊠✋

Suwannee County

Circuit & County Courts *Felony, Misd., Civil, Eviction, Small Claims, Probate* www.suwclerk.org/index2.html 200 S Ohio Ave, Live Oak, FL 32060. 8:30AM-5PM.

386-362-0500, Fax: 386-362-0567. ⊠✋🖳

Taylor County

Circuit & County Courts *Felony, Misdemeanor, Civil, Eviction, Small Claims, Probate* PO Box 620, Perry, FL 32348. 8AM-5PM. **850-838-3506**, Fax: 850-838-3549. ⊠✋

Union County

Circuit & County Courts *Felony, Misdemeanor, Civil, Eviction, Small Claims, Probate* http://circuit8.org Courthouse, Rm 103, Lake Butler, FL 32054. 8AM-5PM. **386-496-3711**, Fax: 386-496-1718. **Fax**⊠✋🖳

Volusia County

Circuit & County Courts - Civil Division *Civil, Eviction, Small Claims, Probate* www.clerk.org PO Box 6043, De Land, FL 32721. 8AM-4:30PM. **386-736-5915**, Fax: 386-822-5711 Access civil records by**Fax**⊠🖳✋.

Circuit & County Courts - Criminal Division *Felony, Misdemeanor* www.clerk.org PO Box 6043, De Land, FL 32721-6043. 8AM-4:30PM. **386-736-5915**, Fax: 386-740-5175. ⊠🖳✋

Wakulla County

Circuit & County Courts *Felony, Misdemeanor, Civil, Eviction, Small Claims, Probate* www.wakullaclerk.com/ 3056 Crawfordville Hwy, Crawfordville, FL 32327. 8AM-5PM. **850-926-0905**, Fax: 850-926-0938 (Civil); 926-0936 (Crim). Civil phone: 850-926-0323, Crim: 850-926-0359. Felony/Misdemeanor court: 850-926-0324. **Fax**⊠✋

Walton County

Circuit & County Courts *Felony, Misd., Civil, Eviction, Small Claims, Probate* www.co.walton.fl.us/clerk/ PO Box 1260, De Funiak Springs, FL 32435. 8AM-4:30PM. **850-892-8115**, Fax: 850-892-7551. **Fax**⊠🖳✋

Washington County

Circuit & County Courts *Felony, Misdemeanor, Civil, Eviction, Small Claims, Probate* PO Box 647, Chipley, FL 32428-0647. 8AM-4PM. **850-638-6285**, Fax: 850-638-6297. ☎**Fax**⊠✋

Georgia

State Court Administration: Court Administrator, 244 Washington St SW, #300, Atlanta, GA, 30334; 404-656-5171, Fax: 404-651-6449. http://www.georgiacourts.org

Court Structure: Georgia's Superior Courts are arranged in 49 circuits of general jurisdiction, and these assume the role of a State Court if the county does not have one. The 69 State Courts, like Superior Courts, can conduct jury trials, but are limited jurisdiction. Each county has a Probate, a Juvenile, and a Magistrate Court; the latter has jurisdiction over civil actions under $15,000, also one type of misdemeanor related to passing bad checks. Magistrate Courts also issue arrest warrants and set bond on all felonies. Probate courts can, in certain cases, issue search and arrest warrants, and hear miscellaneous misdemeanors.

Online Access: A few county courts offer Internet access to court records, but there is no online access available statewide, although one is being planned. Supreme Court docket information and opinions are available from the web. A certified copy of a Supreme Court Opinion can be purchased online for $5.00 at www2.state.ga.us/Courts/Supreme/main_pp.html.

Additional Information: In most Georgia counties, the courts will not perform criminal record searches, and, in many cases, will not do civil record searches. An in-person search or the use of a record retriever is required.

The Georgia Crime Information Center is the felony criminal history state repository.

Appling County

Superior & State Court *Felony, Misdemeanor, Civil* PO Box 269 38 S Main St, Baxley, GA 31513. 8AM-5PM. **912-367-8126**, Fax: 912-367-8180. 🖐

Probate Court 36 S Main St, #B Appling County Courthouse, Baxley, GA 31513. 8:30AM-5PM. **912-367-8114**, Fax: 912-367-8166.

Atkinson County

Superior Court *Felony, Misdemeanor, Civil* PO Box 6 South Main, Courthouse Square, Pearson, GA 31642. 8AM-5PM. **912-422-3343**, Fax: 912-422-7025. 🖐

Probate Court PO Box 855, Pearson, GA 31642. 8AM-5PM. **912-422-3552**, Fax: 912-422-7842.

Bacon County

Superior Court *Felony, Misdemeanor, Civil* PO Box 376, Alma, GA 31510. 9AM-5PM. **912-632-4915**. ✉🖐

Probate Court PO Box 389, Alma, GA 31510. 9AM-5PM. **912-632-7661**, Fax: 912-632-7662.

Baker County

Superior Court *Felony, Misd., Civil* PO Box 10 Governmental Bldg, Newton, GA 39870. 9AM-5PM. **229-734-3004**, Fax: 229-734-7770. 🖐

Probate Court https://www.gaprobate.org/counties/baker/index.html PO Box 548, Newton, GA 39870. 9AM-5PM M-W & F; 9AM-N Th. **229-734-3007**, Fax: 229-734-8822.

Baldwin County

Superior & State Court *Felony, Misdemeanor, Civil* PO Drawer 987, Milledgeville, GA 31059-0987. 8:30AM-5PM. **478-445-4007**, Fax: 478-445-1404. 🖐

Probate Court https://www.gaprobate.org/counties/baldwin/index.html 121 N Wilkinson St, #109, Milledgeville, GA 31061. 8:30AM-5PM. **478-445-4807**, Fax: 478-445-5178.

Banks County

Superior Court *Felony, Misd., Civil* PO Box 337 144 Yorah Homer Rd, Homer, GA 30547. 8:00AM-5PM. **706-677-6240**, Fax: 706-677-6294. 🖐

Probate Court https://www.gaprobate.org/counties/banks/index.html 144 Yonah Homer Rd, Homer, GA 30547. 8AM-5PM. **706-677-6250**, Fax: 706-677-2337.

Barrow County

Superior Court *Felony, Misdemeanor, Civil* PO Box 1280, Winder, GA 30680. 8AM-5PM. **770-307-3035**, Fax: 770-867-4800. 🖐

Probate Court https://www.gaprobate.org/counties/barrow/index.html Barrow County Courthouse, 30 N Broad St, Winder, GA 30680. 8AM-5PM. **770-307-3045**, Fax: 770-307-4470.

Bartow County

Superior Court *Felony, Misd., Civil* 135 W Cherokee, #233, Cartersville, GA 30120. 8AM-5PM. **770-387-5025**, Fax: 770-387-5611. Access 🖐

Probate Court https://www.gaprobate.org/counties/bartow/index.html 135 W Cherokee, #243A, Cartersville, GA 30120. 8AM-5PM. **770-387-5075**, Fax: 770-387-5074.

Ben Hill County

Superior Court *Felony, Misdemeanor, Civil* PO Box 1104 115 S Sheridan, Fitzgerald, GA 31750. 8:30AM-4:30PM. **229-426-5135**, Fax: 229-426-5487. 🖐

Probate Court 111 S Sheridan St, Fitzgerald, GA 31750. 8:30AM-4:30PM. **229-426-5137**, Fax: 229-426-5486.

Berrien County

Superior Court *Felony, Misdemeanor, Civil* 101 E Marion Ave, #3, Nashville, GA 31639. 8AM-4:30PM. **229-686-5506**. ✉🖐

Probate Court https://www.gaprobate.org/counties/berrien/index.html 101 E Marion Ave, #2, Nashville, GA 31639. 8AM-4:30-M-FRI. **229-686-5213**, Fax: 229-686-9495.

Bibb County

Superior Court *Felony, Civil* PO Box 1015 601 Mulberry St, Rm 216, Macon, GA 31202. 8:30AM-5PM. **478-621-6527**. ✉🖐

Key: Symbols refer to criminal records access unless otherwise noted. phone-☎ mail-✉ fax-**Fax** in person-🖐 online-💻 email-**Email**

State Court *Misdemeanor, Civil* www.co.bibb.ga.us PO Box 5086, Macon, GA 31213-7199. 8AM-5PM. **478-621-6676**, Fax: 478-621-6326. Court calendar can be found online. The website will have access to court record indexes in the near future. ✉🖐

Probate Court www.co.bibb.ga.us/probate 207 Bibb County Courthouse PO Box 6518, Macon, GA 31208-6518. 8AM-5PM. **478-621-6494**, Fax: 478-621-6686.

Bleckley County

Superior Court *Felony, Misdemeanor, Civil* 306 SE 2nd St, Cochran, GA 31014. 8:30AM-5PM. **478-934-6671**, Fax: 478-934-3205. 🖐

Probate Court https://www.gaprobate.org/counties/bleckley/index.html 306 SE 2nd St, Cochran, GA 31014. 8:30AM-5PM. **478-934-3204**, Fax: 478-934-3205.

Brantley County

Superior Court *Felony, Misdemeanor, Civil* PO Box 1067 117 Brantley St, Nahunta, GA 31553. 8AM-5PM. **912-462-5635**, Fax: 912-462-6247. 🖐

Probate Court PO Box 207, Nahunta, GA 31553. 8AM-5PM. **912-462-5192**, Fax: 912-462-8360.

Brooks County

Superior Court *Felony, Misd, Civil* http://www2.state.ga.us/courts/superior/dca/dca2sohp.htm PO Box 630, Quitman, GA 31643. 8AM-5PM. **229-263-4747/5150**, Fax: 229-263-5050. 🖐

Probate Court PO Box 665, Quitman, GA 31643. 8AM-5PM. **229-263-5567**, Fax: 229-263-5058.

Bryan County

Superior & State Court *Felony, Misdemeanor, Civil* PO Box 670, Pembroke, GA 31321. 8AM-5PM. **912-653-3872**, Fax: 912-653-3870. ✉🖐

Probate Court www.georgiacourts.org/probate/bryan PO Box 418, Pembroke, GA 31321. 8:30AM-12, 1-5PM. **912-653-3856**, Fax: 912-653-3845.

Bulloch County

Superior & State Court *Felony, Misdemeanor, Civil* Judicial Annex Bldg 20 Siebald St, Statesboro, GA 30458. 8:00AM-5PM. **912-764-9009**, Fax: 912-764-5953. 🖐Fax✉

Probate Court https://www.gaprobate.org/counties/bulloch/index.html PO Box 1005, Statesboro, GA 30459. 8:00AM-5PM. **912-489-8749**, Fax: 912-764-8740.

Burke County

Superior & State Court *Felony, Misdemeanor, Civil* PO Box 803 111 E 6th St, Rm 107, Waynesboro, GA 30830. 9AM-5PM. **706-554-2279**, Fax: 706-554-7887. 🖐

Probate Court https://www.gaprobate.org/counties/burke/index.html PO Box 322, Waynesboro, GA 30830. 9AM-5PM. **706-554-3000**, Fax: 706-554-6693.

Butts County

Superior Court *Felony, Misdemeanor, Civil* PO Box 320 26 3rd St, Jackson, GA 30233. 8AM-5PM. **770-775-8215**. 🖐Fax✉

Probate Court, *Traffic* https://www.gaprobate.org/counties/butts/index.html 25 3rd St, #7, Jackson, GA 30233. 8AM-5PM. **770-775-8204**, Fax: 770-775-8004.

Calhoun County

Superior Court *Felony, Misdemeanor, Civil* PO Box 69, Morgan, GA 39866. 8AM-5PM. **229-849-2715**, Fax: 229-849-0072. 🖐

Camden County

Superior Court *Felony, Misdemeanor, Civil* PO Box 550 210 E 4th St, Woodbine, GA 31569. 9AM-5PM. **912-576-5624**. 🖐

Probate Court, *Misdemeanor Drug* PO Box 818, Woodbine, GA 31569. 9AM-5PM. **912-576-3785**, Fax: 912-576-5484.

Candler County

Superior & State Court *Felony, Misdemeanor, Civil* PO Drawer 830, Metter, GA 30439. 8:30AM-5PM. **912-685-5257**, Fax: 912-685-2946. ✉🖐

Probate Court https://www.gaprobate.org/counties/candler/index.html Courthouse Square, Metter, GA 30439. 8:30AM-5PM. **912-685-2357**, Fax: 912-685-5130.

Carroll County

Superior & State Court *Felony, Misd., Civil* PO Box 1620, Carrollton, GA 30117. 8AM-5PM. **770-214-3125**, Fax: 770-830-5988. Civil phone: 770-830-5835 Ext 2245&2246, Crim: 770-830-5835 Ext 2247&2239. ✉🖐

Probate https://www.gaprobate.org/counties/carroll/index.html Carroll County Courthouse 311 Newnan St, Rm 204, Carrollton, GA 30117. 8AM-5PM. **770-830-5840**, Fax: 770-830-5995.

Catoosa County

Superior Court *Felony, Misdemeanor, Civil,* 875 Lafayette St, Ringgold, GA 30736. 8:30AM-5PM. **706-935-4231**. 🖐

Probate Court 875 Lafayette St, Justice Bldg, Ringgold, GA 30736. 9AM-5PM. **706-935-3511**, Fax: 706-935-3519.

Charlton County

Superior Court *Felony, Misdemeanor, Civil* Courthouse PO Box 760, Folkston, GA 31537. 8:30AM-5PM. **912-496-2354**. 🖐

Probate Court https://www.gaprobate.org/counties/charlton/index.html 100 S 3rd St, Folkston, GA 31537. 8AM-5PM. **912-496-2230**, Fax: 912-496-1156.

Chatham County

Superior Court *Felony, Civil* www.chathamcourts.org PO Box 10227, Savannah, GA 31412-0427. 8AM-5PM. **912-652-7197**, Fax: 912-652-7380. Civil phone: 912-652-7200, Crim: 912-652-7209. ✉🖐

State Court *Misdemeanor, Civil* www.statecourt.org/ County Courthouse, 133 Montgomery St, Savannah, GA 31401. 8AM-5PM. **912-652-7224**, Fax: 912-652-7229. ✉Fax🖐

Probate Court www.chathamcourts.org 133 Montgomery St, Rm 509, Savannah, GA 31401. 8AM-5PM. **912-652-7264**, Fax: 912-652-7262.

Chattahoochee County

Superior & Magistrate Court *Felony, Misdemeanor, Civil, Eviction, Small Claims* PO Box 120, Cusseta, GA 31805. 8AM-5PM. **706-989-3424**, Fax: 706-989-0396. Magistrate Court is 706-989-3643. 🖐

Probate Court PO Box 119, Cusseta, GA 31805. 8AM-N, 1-5PM. **706-989-3603**, Fax: 706-989-2015.

Chattooga County

Superior & State Court *Felony, Misdemeanor, Civil, Eviction, Small Claims* PO Box 159, Summerville, GA 30747. 8:30AM-5PM. **706-857-0706**. 🖐

Probate Court https://www.gaprobate.org/counties/chattooga/index.html PO Box 467 10035 Commerce St, Summerville, GA 30747. 8:30AM-N, 1-5PM. **706-857-0709**, Fax: 706-857-0877.

Cherokee County

Superior & State Court *Felony, Misdemeanor, Civil* 90 North St, #G170, Canton, GA 30114. 8AM-5PM. **678-493-6501**. 🖐

Probate Court https://www.gaprobate.org/counties/cherokee/index.html 90 North St, Rm 340, Canton, GA 30114. 8AM-5PM. **678-493-6160**, Fax: 678-493-6170.

Clarke County

Superior & State Court *Felony, Misd., Civil* http://athensclarke.allclerks.us PO Box 1805, Athens, GA 30603. 8AM-5PM. **706-613-3190**. Located at 325 E Washington, Rm 450, 30601. 🖐

Probate Court 325 E Washington St, #215, Athens, GA 30601. 8AM-5PM. **706-613-3320**, Fax: 706-613-3323.

Clay County

Superior Court *Felony, Misdemeanor, Civil, Eviction* PO Box 550, Ft Gaines, GA 39851. 8AM-4:30PM. **229-768-2631**, Fax: 229-768-3047. 🖐

Probate Court PO Box 448, 210 S Washington, Ft Gaines, GA 39851. 8AM-4:30PM. **229-768-2445**, Fax: 229-768-2710.

Clayton County

Superior Court *Felony, Civil* www.co.clayton.ga.us/superior_court/clerk_of_courts 9151 Tara Blvd, #ICL19, Jonesboro, GA 30236-4912. 8AM-5PM. **770-477-3405**. ✉🖐

State Court *Misdemeanor* www.co.clayton.ga.us/state_court/clerk_of_courts/ 9151 Tara Blvd, #1CL181, Jonesboro, GA 30236. 8AM-5PM. **770-477-3388**. 🖐

Probate Court www.co.clayton.ga.us/probate_court/ 121 S McDonough St, Annex 3, Jonesboro, GA 30236-3694. 8AM-4:30PM **770-477-3299**, Fax:770-477-3306

Clinch County

Superior & State Court *Felony, Misdemeanor, Civil* PO Box 433, Homerville, GA 31634. 8AM-5PM. **912-487-5854**, Fax: 912-489-3083. ✉🖐

Probate Court PO Box 364, Homerville, GA 31634. 9AM-12:00,1-5PM. **912-487-5523**, Fax: 912-487-3083.

Cobb County

Superior Court *Felony, Misdemeanor, Civil* www.cobbgasupctclk.com/index.htm PO Box 3370, Marietta, GA 30061. 8AM-5PM. **770-528-1300**, Fax: 770-528-1382. ✉💻🖐

State Court - Civil & Criminal Divisions *Misdemeanor, Civil, Eviction* www.cobbstatecourtclerk.com 12 E Park Square, Marietta, GA 30090-9630. 8AM-5PM. Civil: 770-528-1203, Crim: 770-528-1262. 🖐

Probate Court https://www.gaprobate.org/counties/cobb/index.html 32 Waddell St, Marietta, GA 30060. 8AM-4:30PM. **770-528-1990**, Fax: 770-528-1996.

Coffee County

Superior & State Court *Felony, Misdemeanor, Civil* 101 S Peterson Ave, Douglas, GA 31533. 8:30AM-5PM. **912-384-2865**. 🖐

Probate Court, *Civil* https://www.gaprobate.org/counties/coffee/index.html 101 S Peterson Ave, Douglas, GA 31533. 8:30AM-5PM. **912-384-5213**, Fax: 912-384-0291.

Colquitt County

Superior & State Court *Felony, Misd., Civil* http://www2.state.ga.us/courts/superior/dca/dca2sohp.htm PO Box 2827, Moultrie, GA 31776. 8AM-5PM. **229-616-7420**, Civil: 229-616-7066 Sup; 616-7420 state, Crim: 229-616-7423 Sup; 616-7064 state. 🖐

Probate Court https://www.gaprobate.org/counties/colquitt/index.html PO Box 264 Rm 108 Colquitt County Govt Bldg, Moultrie, GA 31776-0264. 8AM-5PM. **229-616-7415**, Fax: 229-616-7489.

Columbia County

Superior Court *Felony, Misdemeanor, Civil* PO Box 2930, Evans, GA 30809. 8AM-5PM. **706-312-7139**, Fax: 706-312-7152. Located at 640 Ronald Reagan Dr in Evans. 🖐

Probate Court PO Box 525, Appling, GA 30802. 8AM-4:30PM. **706-541-1254**, Fax: 706-541-4001.

Cook County

Superior Court *Felony, Misdemeanor, Civil* 212 N Hutchinson Ave, Adel, GA 31620. 8:30AM-4:30PM. **229-896-7717**. ✉🖐

Probate Court, *Misdemeanor Traffic* 212 N Hutchinson Ave, Adel, GA 31620. 8:30AM-5PM. **229-896-3941**, Fax: 229-896-6083.

Coweta County

Superior Court *Felony, Civil* PO Box 943 200 Court Square, Newnan, GA 30264. 8AM-5PM. **770-254-2693/2695**, Fax: 770-254-3700. 🖐

State Court *Misdemeanor, Civil* www.coweta.ga.us/Resources/stateclk.html 9A E Broad St, Newnan, GA 30263. 8AM-5PM. **770-254-2699**. 🖐✉

Probate Court https://www.gaprobate.org/counties/coweta/index.html 22 E Broad St, Newnan, GA 30263. 8AM-5PM. **770-254-2640**, Fax: 770-254-2648.

Crawford County

Superior Court *Felony, Misdemeanor, Civil* PO Box 1037, Roberta, GA 31058. 9AM-5PM. **478-836-3328**. 🖐✉

Probate Court https://www.gaprobate.org/counties/crawford/index.html PO Box 1028, Roberta, GA 31078. 9AM-5PM. **478-836-3313**, Fax: 478-836-4111.

Crisp County

Superior & Juvenile Court *Felony, Misdemeanor, Civil Actions Over $15,000* PO Box 747, Cordele, GA 31010-0747. 8:30AM-5PM. **229-276-2616**. ✉🖐

Probate Court https://www.gaprobate.org/counties/crisp/index.html 210 S 7th St, Rm 103, Cordele, GA 31015. 9AM-5PM. **229-276-2621**, Fax: 229-273-9184.

Dade County

Superior Court *Felony, Misdemeanor, Civil, Eviction, Small Claims* www.gsccca.org/clerks/ PO Box 417, Trenton, GA 30752. 8:30AM-5PM. **706-657-4778**; Sm Claims 706-657-4113, ✉**Fax**🖐

Probate Court https://www.gaprobate.org/counties/dade/index.html PO Box 605, Trenton, GA 30752. 8:30AM-12:00,1-5PM. **706-657-4414**, Fax: 706-657-4305.

Dawson County

Superior Court *Felony, Misdemeanor, Civil* 25 Tucker Ave, #106, Dawsonville, GA 30534. 8AM-5PM. **706-344-3510**, Fax: 706-344-3511. ☒**Fax**👋

Probate Court https://www.gaprobate.org/counties/dawson/index.html 25 Tucker Ave, #102, Dawsonville, GA 30534. 8AM-5PM, closed for noon hour. **706-344-3580**, Fax: 706-265-6155.

Decatur County

Superior & State Court *Felony, Misdemeanor, Civil* PO Box 336, Bainbridge, GA 39818. 8AM-5PM. **229-248-3025**. 👋

Probate Court https://www.gaprobate.org/counties/decatur/index.html PO Box 234, Bainbridge, GA 39818. 9AM-5PM. **229-248-3016**, Fax: 229-248-3858.

De Kalb County

Superior Court *Felony, Misd., Civil* www.co.dekalb.ga.us/superior/index.htm 556 N McDonough St, Decatur, GA 30030. 7:30AM-6PM. **404-371-2836**, Fax: 404-371-2635. 👋💻

State Court *Misdemeanor, Civil* www.dekalbstatecourt.net 556 N McDonough St, Decatur, GA 30030. 8:30AM-5PM. **404-371-2261**, Fax: 404-371-3064. 👋💻☒

Probate Court www.co.dekalb.ga.us/probate 103 County Courthouse 556 N McDonough St, Rm 1100, Decatur, GA 30030. 8:30AM-4:00PM. **404-371-2718**, Fax: 404-371-7055.

Dodge County

Superior Court *Felony, Misdemeanor, Civil* PO Drawer 4276 5401 Anson Ave, Eastman, GA 31023. 9AM-5PM. **478-374-2871**. 👋

Probate Court PO Box 514, Eastman, GA 31023. 9AM-N, 1-5PM. **478-374-3775**, Fax: 478-374-9197.

Dooly County

Superior Court *Felony, Misdemeanor, Civil* PO Box 326, Vienna, GA 31092-0326. 8:30AM-5PM. **229-268-4234**, Fax: 229-268-1427. 👋

Probate Court PO Box 304, Vienna, GA 31092. 8AM-5PM M,T,Th,F; 8:30AM-N W & Sat or by appointment. **229-268-4217**, Fax: 229-268-6142.

Dougherty County

Superior & State Court *Felony, Misd., Civil* www.albany.ga.us/doco/court_system.htm PO Box 1827, Albany, GA 31702. 8:30AM-5PM. **229-431-2198**. 💻👋

Probate Court https://www.gaprobate.org/counties/dougherty/index.html PO Box 1827 225 Pine Ave, #123, Albany, GA 31702. 8:30AM-5PM. **229-431-2102**, Fax: 229-434-2694. Search the probate court index at www.dougherty.ga.us.

Douglas County

Superior Court *Felony, Misdemeanor, Civil* Douglas County Courthouse 8700 Hospital Dr, Douglasville, GA 30134. 8AM-5PM. **770-920-7252**. Access by 👋

Probate Court 8700 Hospital Dr, Douglasville, GA 30134. 8AM-5PM. **770-920-7249**, Fax: 770-920-7381.

Early County

Superior & State Court *Felony, Misdemeanor, Civil* PO Box 849, Blakely, GA 39823. 8AM-5PM. **229-723-3033**, Fax: 229-723-4411. Access by 👋

Echols County

Superior Court *Felony, Misd., Civil* http://www2.state.ga.us/courts/superior/dca/dca2sohp.htm PO Box 213, Statenville, GA 31648. 8AM-N, 1-4:30PM. **229-559-5642**, Fax: 229-559-5792. Access by 👋

Effingham County

Superior Court *Felony, Misdemeanor, Civil* PO Box 387, Springfield, GA 31329. 8:30AM-5PM. **912-754-2146**. ☒👋

Probate Court https://www.gaprobate.org/counties/effingham/index.html 901 Pine St PO Box 387, Springfield, GA 31329. 8:30AM-5PM. **912-754-2112**, Fax: 912-754-3894.

Elbert County

Superior & State Court *Felony, Misdemeanor, Civil* PO Box 619, Elberton, GA 30635. 8AM-5PM. **706-283-2005**, Fax: 706-213-7286. ☒👋

Probate Court Elbert County Courthouse, Elberton, GA 30635. 8AM-5PM. **706-283-2016**, Fax: 706-283-9668.

Emanuel County

Superior & State Court *Felony, Misdemeanor, Civil* PO Box 627,

Swainsboro, GA 30401. 8AM-5PM. **478-237-8911**, Fax: 478-237-3570. 👋

Probate Court PO Box 70, Swainsboro, GA 30401. 8AM-5PM. **478-237-7091**, Fax: 478-237-2633.

Evans County

Superior & State Court *Felony, Misdemeanor, Civil* PO Box 845, Claxton, GA 30417. 8AM-5PM. **912-739-3868**, Fax: 912-739-2504. Access by 👋

Probate Court https://www.gaprobate.org/counties/effingham/index.html 123 W Main St, PO Box 852, Claxton, GA 30417. 8AM-5PM. **912-739-4080**, Fax: 912-739-4077.

Fannin County

Superior Court *Felony, Misd., Civil* http://9thjudicialdistrict-ga.org/dca9apphp.shtml PO Box 1300 420 W Main St, Blue Ridge, GA 30513. 9AM-5PM. **706-632-2039**. 👋

Probate Court 420 W Main St #2, Blue Ridge, GA 30513. 8AM-5PM. **706-632-3011**, Fax: 706-632-7167.

Fayette County

Superior Court *Felony, Misdemeanor, Civil* www.admin.co.fayette.ga.us PO Box 130, Fayetteville, GA 30214. 8AM-5PM. **770-716-4290**, Civil: 770-716-4294, Crim: 770-716-4293. 👋

Probate Court https://www.gaprobate.org/counties/fayette/index.html 1 Center Dr., Fayetteville, GA 30214. 8AM-5PM. **770-716-4220**, Fax: 770-716-4854.

Floyd County

Superior Court *Felony, Misdemeanor, Civil* www.floydsuperiorcourt.org PO Box 1110 #3 Government Plaza, #101, Rome, GA 30163. 8AM-5PM. **706-291-5190**, Fax: 706-233-0035. 👋

Probate Court 3 Government Plaza, #201 County Administrative Offices, Rome, GA 30162. 8AM-5:00PM. **706-291-5136/8**, Fax: 706-291-5189.

Forsyth County

Superior & State Court *Felony, Misdemeanor, Civil, Eviction, Small Claims* www.forsythco.com 100 Courthouse Square, Rm 010, Cumming, GA 30040. 8:30AM-5PM. **770-781-2120**, Fax: 770-886-2858. 👋

Probate Court County Courthouse Annex, Rm 101 112 W Maple St,

Cumming, GA 30130. 8:30AM-5PM. **770-781-2140**, Fax: 770-886-2839.

Franklin County

Superior Court *Felony, Misdemeanor, Civil* PO Box 70, Carnesville, GA 30521. 8AM-5PM. **706-384-2514**. Access by 🖐

Probate Court https://www.gaprobate.org/counties/franklin/index.html PO Box 207 9592 Lavonia Rd, Carnesville, GA 30521. 8AM-5PM. **706-384-2403**, Fax: 706-384-2636.

Fulton County

Superior Court *Civil* www.fcclk.org 136 Pryor St SW, Rm C-155 Superior Court Clerk, Atlanta, GA 30303. 8:30AM-5PM. Fax: 404-302-8416. Civil phone: 404-730-5344 Access civil records by 🖐 🖥.

Superior Court *Felony, Misdemeanor, Eviction* www.fcclk.org 136 Pryor St SW, Rm C-515, Atlanta, GA 30303. 8:30AM-5PM. **404-730-5770**, Fax: 404-893-2773. Criminal phone: 404-730-5248. 🖐

State Court *Misdemeanor, Civil* www.fultonstatecourt.com TG100 Justice Center Twr 185 Central Ave SW, Atlanta, GA 30303. 8:30AM-5PM. **404-730-5000**, Fax: 404-730-8141 Civil; 335-3521 Criminal Fax. 🖐

Probate Court https://www.gaprobate.org/counties/fulton/index.html 136 Pryor St, # 230, Atlanta, GA 30303. 8:30AM-5PM. **404-730-4640**, Fax: 404-730-8283.

Gilmer County

Superior Court *Felony, Misd., Civil* http://9thjudicialdistrict-ga.org/dca9apphp.shtml #1 Westside Square, Ellijay, GA 30540. 8:30AM-5PM. **706-635-4462**, Fax: 706-635-1462. 🖐

Probate Court https://www.gaprobate.org/counties/gilmer/index.html 51 Sand St., Ellijay, GA 30540. 8:30AM-5PM. **706-635-4763**, Fax: 706-635-4761.

Glascock County

Superior Court *Felony, Misdemeanor, Civil* PO Box 231 62 E Main St, Gibson, GA 30810. Mon, tue, Thu, Fri 8am-5pm; Wed 8am-12pm. **706-598-2084**, Fax: 706-598-2577. 🖐

Probate Court PO Box 277, Gibson, GA 30810. 8AM-N, 1-5PM-M.T,Th,Fri; 8am-12:00-W. **706-598-3241**, Fax: 706-598-2471.

Glynn County

Superior Court *Felony, Civil* PO Box 1355, Brunswick, GA 31521. 8AM-5PM. **912-554-7272**, Fax: 912-267-5625. ☎Fax✉🖐

State Court *Misdemeanor, Civil* 701 "H" St, #104, Brunswick, GA 31520. 9AM-5PM. **912-554-7325**, Fax: 912-261-3849. 🖐

Probate Court, *Civil, Small Claims* https://www.gaprobate.org/counties/glynn/index.html 701 H St, Box 302, Brunswick, GA 31520. 8:30AM-5PM. **912-554-7231**, Fax: 912-466-8001.

Gordon County

Superior Court *Felony, Misdemeanor, Civil* 100 Wall St, #102, Calhoun, GA 30701. 8:30AM-5PM. **706-629-9533**, Fax: 706-629-2139. ✉🖐

Probate Court https://www.gaprobate.org/counties/gordon/index.html PO Box 669, Calhoun, GA 30703. 8:30AM-5PM. **706-629-7314**, Fax: 706-629-4698.

Grady County

Superior Court *Felony, Misdemeanor, Civil* 250 N Broad St, Box 8, Cairo, GA 39828. 8AM-5PM. **229-377-2912**. 🖐

Probate Court Courthouse, 250 N Broad St, #1 Box 1, Cairo, GA 39828. 8AM-5PM. **229-377-4621**, Fax: 229-378-8052.

Greene County

Superior & Juvenile Court *Felony, Misdemeanor, Civil, Eviction, Small Claims* 113 N Main St, #109, Greensboro, GA 30642. 8AM-5PM. **706-453-3340**, Fax: 706-453-9179. 🖐

Gwinnett County

Superior & State Court *Felony, Misd., Civil, Eviction, Small Claims* www.gwinnettcourts.com/courts/Supcourt.htm PO Box 880 (75 Langley Dr), Lawrenceville, GA 30046. 8AM-5PM. **770-822-8100**. 🖥🖐

Probate Court www.gwinnettcourts.com/courts/Procourt.htm 75 Langley Dr Justice & Admin Ctr, Lawrenceville, GA 30045. 8:AM-4:30PM. **770-822-8250**, Fax: 770-822-8274. Search records by name for free at website; click on "Data Search."

Habersham County

Superior & State Court *Felony, Misd., Civil* www.co.habersham.ga.us 555

Monroe St, Unit 35, Clarkesville, GA 30523. 8AM-5PM. **706-754-2923**. ✉🖐

Probate Habersham County Courthouse PO Box 625, Clarkesville, GA 30523. 8AM-5PM. **706-754-2013**, Fax: 706-754-5093.

Hall County

Superior & State Court *Felony, Misdemeanor, Civil* PO Box 1336, Gainesville, GA 30503. 8AM-5PM. **770-531-7025**, Fax: 770-531-7070; 536-0702 real estate. 🖐

Probate www.hallcounty.org/clerk.asp Hall County Courthouse, Rm 123 225 Green St, Gainesville, GA 30501. 8AM-4:30PM. **770-531-6923**, Fax: 770-531-4946.

Hancock County

Superior Court *Felony, Misdemeanor, Civil* PO Box 451 Courthouse Square, Sparta, GA 31087. 9AM-5PM. **706-444-6644**, Fax: 706-444-6221. ✉🖐

Probate Court https://www.gaprobate.org/counties/hancock/index.html 601 Courthouse Square, Sparta, GA 31087. 8AM-5PM. **706-444-5343**, Fax: 706-444-8024.

Haralson County

Superior Court *Felony, Misdemeanor, Civil* Drawer 849 4485 Georgia Hwy 120, Buchanan, GA 30113. 8:30AM-5PM. **770-646-2005**, Fax: 770-646-2035, Access by ✉🖐

Probate Court https://www.gaprobate.org/counties/haralson/index.html PO Box 620, Buchanan, GA 30113. 8:30AM-5PM. **770-646-2008**, Fax: 770-646-3419.

Harris County

Superior Court *Felony, Misdemeanor, Civil* PO Box 528, Hamilton, GA 31811. 8AM-5PM. **706-628-4944**, Fax: 706-628-7039. 🖐

Probate Court PO Box 569, Hamilton, GA 31811. 8AM-5PM (No longer close at noon). **706-628-5038**, Fax: 706-628-7322.

Hart County

Superior Court *Felony, Misdemeanor, Civil* PO Box 386, Hartwell, GA 30643. 8:30AM-5PM. **706-376-7189**, Fax: 706-376-1277. 🖐

Probate Court https://www.gaprobate.org/counties/hart/index.html PO Box 1159,

Hartwell, GA 30643. 8:30AM-5PM. **706-376-2565**, Fax: 706-376-9032.

Heard County

Superior Court *Felony, Misdemeanor, Civil* PO Box 249, Franklin, GA 30217. 8:30AM-5PM. **706-675-3301**. 🖐

Probate Court https://www.gaprobate.org/counties/heard/index.html PO Box 478, Franklin, GA 30217. 8:30AM-5PM. **706-675-3353**, Fax: 706-675-0819.

Henry County

Superior Court *Felony, Misdemeanor, Civil* One Courthouse Square, McDonough, GA 30253. 8AM-5PM. **770-954-2121**. 🖐

Probate Court https://www.gaprobate.org/counties/henry/index.html 99 Sims St., McDonough, GA 30253. 8AM-4:45PM. **770-954-2303**, Fax: 770-954-2308.

Houston County

Superior Court *Felony, Misdemeanor, Civil* www.houstoncountyga.org 201 Perry Pky, Perry, GA 31069. 8:30AM-5PM. **478-218-4720**, Fax: 478-218-4745. Civil phone: 478-218-4740, Crim: 478-218-4730. Fax✉🖐

State Court *Misdemeanor, Civil* www.houstoncountyga.com 202 Carl Vinson Pky, Warner Robins, GA 31088. 8AM-5PM. **478-542-2105**, Fax: 478-542-2077. County recorder's office offers free online access to liens at the website. 🖐

Probate Court www.houstoncountyga.org/probate_court.htm PO Box 1801 201 N Perry Pky, Perry, GA 31069. 8AM-4PM. **478-218-4710**, Fax: 478-218-4715.

Irwin County

Superior Court *Felony, Misdemeanor, Civil* 113 N Irwin Ave, Ocilla, GA 31774. 8AM-5PM. **229-468-5356**. ☎✉🖐

Probate Court https://www.gaprobate.org/counties/irwin/index.html 202 S Irwin Ave., Ocilla, GA 31774. 8:00-12:00 - 1:00-5:00. **229-468-5138**, Fax: 229-468-5702.

Jackson County

Superior & State Court *Felony, Misdemeanor, Civil* PO Box 7, Jefferson, GA 30549. 8AM-5PM. **706-367-6360**, Fax: 706-367-2468. Criminal phone: 707-367-6369. 🖐

Probate Court https://www.gaprobate.org/counties/jackson/index.html 500 Jackson Pky, Jefferson, GA 30549. 8:AM-5PM. **706-367-6366**, Fax: 706-367-7211.

Jasper County

Superior Court *Felony, Misdemeanor, Civil* 126 W Green St, #110, Monticello, GA 31064. 8AM-5PM. **706-468-4901**, Fax: 706-468-4946. 🖐

Probate Court https://www.gaprobate.org/counties/jasper/index.html Jasper County Courthouse 126 W Green St, #111, Monticello, GA 31064. 8AM-4:30PM. **706-468-4903**, Fax: 706-468-4926.

Jeff Davis County

Superior & State Court *Felony, Misdemeanor, Civil* PO Box 429, Hazlehurst, GA 31539. 8AM-5PM. **912-375-6615**, Fax: 912-375-6637. Fax✉🖐

Probate Court PO Box 446, Hazlehurst, GA 31539. 9AM-5PM. **912-375-6626**, Fax: 912-375-6629.

Jefferson County

Superior & State Court *Felony, Misdemeanor, Civil* PO Box 151, Louisville, GA 30434. 8AM-5PM. **478-625-7922**, Fax: 478-625-4037. 🖐

Probate Court https://www.gaprobate.org/counties/jefferson/index.html PO Box 307, Louisville, GA 30434. 8AM-5PM. **478-625-3258**, Fax: 478-625-0245.

Jenkins County

Superior & State Court *Felony, Misdemeanor, Civil* PO Box 659, Millen, GA 30442. 8:30AM-5PM. **478-982-4683**, Fax: 478-982-1274. 🖐

Probate Court https://www.gaprobate.org/counties/jenkins/index.html PO Box 904 611 E Winthrope Ave, Millen, GA 30442. 8:30AM-5PM. **478-982-5581**, Fax: 478-982-2829.

Johnson County

Superior & Magistrate Court *Felony, Misdemeanor, Civil, Eviction, Small Claims* PO Box 321, Wrightsville, GA 31096. 9AM-5PM. **478-864-3484**, Fax: 478-864-1343. 🖐

Probate Court PO Box 264, Wrightsville, GA 31096. 9AM-5PM. **478-864-3316**, Fax: 478-864-0528.

Jones County

Superior Court *Felony, Misdemeanor, Civil* PO Box 39 110 S Jefferson St,

Gray, GA 31032. 8:30AM-4:30PM. **478-986-6671/6674**. 🖐

Lamar County

Superior Court *Felony, Misdemeanor, Civil* 326 Thomaston St, Box 7, Barnesville, GA 30204. 8AM-5PM. **770-358-5145**, Fax: 770-358-5814. 🖐

Probate Court 326 Thomaston St, Barnesville, GA 30204. 8AM-5PM. **770-358-5155**, Fax: 770-358-5348.

Lanier County

Superior Court *Felony, Misdemeanor, Civil* County Courthouse 100 Main St, Lakeland, GA 31635. 8AM-N, 1-5PM. **229-482-3594**, Fax: 229-482-8333. 🖐

Probate Court https://www.gaprobate.org/counties/lanier/index.html County Courthouse 100 Main St, Lakeland, GA 31635. 8AM-N, 1-5PM. **229-482-3668**, Fax: 229-482-8333.

Laurens County

Superior & Magistrate Court *Felony, Misdemeanor, Civil, Eviction, Small Claims* PO Box 2028, Dublin, GA 31040. 8:30AM-5:30PM. **478-272-3210**, Fax: 478-275-2595. 🖐

Probate Court https://www.gaprobate.org/counties/laurens/index.html PO Box 2098 County Courthouse, Rm 108, Dublin, GA 31040. 8:30AM-5:30PM. **478-272-2566**, Fax: 478-277-2932.

Lee County

Superior Court *Felony, Misdemeanor, Civil* PO Box 597, Leesburg, GA 31763. 8AM-5PM. **229-759-6018**. Access ✉🖐

Probate Court, *Traffic* PO Box 592, Leesburg, GA 31763. 8AM-5PM. **229-759-6005**, Fax: 229-759-3345.

Liberty County

Superior & State Court *Felony, Misdemeanor, Civil* www.libertyco.com PO Box 50, Hinesville, GA 31313-0050. 8AM-5PM. **912-876-3625**, Fax: 912-876-7394. Civil phone: 912-876-7276, Crim: 912-876-7289. ✉🖐

Probate Court PO Box 28, Hinesville, GA 31310. 8AM-5PM. **912-876-3635**, Fax: 912-876-3589.

Lincoln County

Superior Court *Felony, Misdemeanor, Civil* PO Box 340, Lincolnton, GA 30817. 9AM-5PM. **706-359-5505**. 🖐

Long County

Superior & State Court *Felony, Misdemeanor, Civil* PO Box 458, Ludowici, GA 31316. 8:30AM-5PM. **912-545-2123**, Fax: 912-545-2020. ✉️**Fax**🖐️

Lowndes County

Superior & State Court *Felony, Misd., Civil* http://www2.state.ga.us/courts/superior/dca/dca2sohp.htm PO Box 1349, Valdosta, GA 31603. 8AM-5PM. **229-333-5127**. 🖐️

Probate Court www.lowndescounty.com/ PO Box 72, Valdosta, GA 31603. 8AM-5PM. **229-333-5103**, Fax: 229-333-7646.

Lumpkin County

Superior, Juvenile & Magistrate Court *Felony, Misdemeanor, Civil, Eviction, Small Claims* 99 Courthouse Hill, #D, Dahlonega, GA 30533-0541. 8AM-5PM. **706-864-3736**, Fax: 706-864-5298. For Magistrate Court criminal records info, call 706-864-7760. 🖐️

Probate Court 99 Courthouse Hill, #C, Dahlonega, GA 30533. 8AM-5PM. **706-864-3847**, Fax: 706-864-9271.

McDuffie County

Superior Court *Felony, Misdemeanor, Civil* PO Box 158 337 Main St, Rm 101, Thomson, GA 30824. 8AM-5PM. **706-595-2134**. 🖐️

Probate Court PO Box 2028, Thomson, GA 30824. 8AM-5PM. **706-595-2124**, Fax: 706-597-2644.

McIntosh County

Superior & State Court *Felony, Misdemeanor, Civil* PO Box 1661, Darien, GA 31305. 8AM-4:30PM. **912-437-6641**, Fax: 912-437-6673. 🖐️

Probate Court www.darientel.net/~pcourt/ PO Box 453, Darien, GA 31305. 8AM-5PM. **912-437-6636**, Fax: 912-437-6635.

Macon County

Superior Court *Felony, Misdemeanor, Civil* PO Box 337, Oglethorpe, GA 31068. 8AM-5PM. **478-472-7661**. 🖐️

Probate Court https://www.gaprobate.org/counties/macon/index.html PO Box 216 100 Sumter St, Oglethorpe, GA 31068. 8AM-N, 1-5PM. **478-472-7685**, Fax: 478-472-5643.

Madison County

Superior Court *Felony, Misdemeanor, Civil* PO Box 247, Danielsville, GA 30633. 8AM-5PM. **706-795-3352**, Fax: 706-795-2209. 🖐️

Probate Court PO Box 207, Danielsville, GA 30633. 8AM-5PM. **706-795-6365**, Fax: 706-795-5933.

Marion County

Superior Court *Felony, Misdemeanor, Civil* PO Box 41, Buena Vista, GA 31803. 8:30AM-5PM. **229-649-7321**, Fax: 229-649-7931. 🖐️

Meriwether County

Superior Court *Felony, Misdemeanor, Civil* PO Box 160, Greenville, GA 30222. 8:30AM-5PM. **706-672-4416**, Fax: 706-672-9465. 🖐️

Probate Court PO Box 608, Greenville, GA 30222. 8:30AM-5PM. **706-672-4952**, Fax 706-672-6660, probate 706-672-1817

Miller County

Superior & State Court *Felony, Misdemeanor, Civil* PO Box 66, Colquitt, GA 39837. 8-5PM. **229-758-4102**. 🖐️

Mitchell County

Superior & State Court *Felony, Misdemeanor, Civil* PO Box 427, Camilla, GA 31730. 8:30AM-5PM. **229-336-2022**. 🖐️

Probate Court https://www.gaprobate.org/counties/mitchell/index.html PO Box 229, Camilla, GA 31730. 8:30AM-5PM. **229-336-2016**, Fax: 229-336-2354.

Monroe County

Superior Court *Felony, Misdemeanor, Civil* PO Box 450, Forsyth, GA 31029. 8AM-5PM. **478-994-7022**, Fax: 478-994-7053. ✉️🖐️

Probate Court PO Box 187, Forsyth, GA 31029. 8AM-5:00PM. **478-994-7036**, Fax: 478-994-7054.

Montgomery County

Superior Court *Felony, Misdemeanor, Civil* PO Box 311, Mt Vernon, GA 30445. 8AM-5PM. **912-583-4401**. 🖐️

Probate Court https://www.gaprobate.org/counties/montgomery/index.html PO Box 444 400 Railroad Ave, Mt Vernon, GA 30445. 9AM-5PM. **912-583-2681**, Fax: 912-583-4343.

Morgan County

Superior Court *Felony, Misdemeanor, Civil* PO Box 130 149 E Jefferson St, Madison, GA 30650. 9AM-5PM. **706-342-3605**. 🖐️

Probate Court PO Box 857, Madison, GA 30650. 9AM-5PM. **706-343-6500**, Fax: 706-343-6465. This court also has Misdemeanor and Traffic cases.

Murray County

Superior Court *Felony, Misdemeanor, Civil* PO Box 1000, Chatsworth, GA 30705. 8:30AM-5PM. **706-695-2932**. 🖐️

Probate Court https://www.gaprobate.org/counties/murray/index.html 115 Fort St, Chatsworth, GA 30705. 8:30AM-5PM. **706-695-3812**, Fax: 706-517-1340.

Muscogee County

Superior & State Court *Felony, Misdemeanor, Civil* PO Box 2145, Columbus, GA 31902. 8:30AM-5PM. **706-653-4351**, Fax 706-653-4359. ✉️🖐️

Probate Court PO Box 1340, Columbus, GA 31902. 8:30AM-4PM. **706-653-4333**.

Newton County

Superior Court *Felony, Misdemeanor, Civil, Probate* 1132 Usher St, Covington, GA 30014. 8AM-5PM. **770-784-2035**, Fax: 770-385-8930, Probate: 770-784-2045. Probate in Rm 148. ✉️🖐️

Oconee County

Superior & Magistrate Courts *Felony, Misdemeanor, Civil, Eviction, Small Claims* PO Box 1099, Watkinsville, GA 30677. 8AM-5PM. **706-769-3940**, Fax: 706-769-3948. 🖐️

Probate Court www.oconeecounty.net PO Box 54, Watkinsville, GA 30677. 8-5PM. **706-769-3936**, Fax: 706-769-3934.

Oglethorpe County

Superior Court *Felony, Misdemeanor, Civil* www.gsccca.org/Clerks/default.asp PO Box 68, Lexington, GA 30648. 8-5. **706-743-5731**, Fax: 706-743-5335. 🖐️

Probate Court https://www.gaprobate.org/counties/oglethorpe/index.html PO Box 70 111 W Main St, Lexington, GA 30648. 7:30AM-5PM. **706-743-5350**, Fax: 706-743-3514.

Key: Symbols refer to criminal records access unless otherwise noted. phone-☎️ mail-✉️ fax-**Fax** in person-🖐️ online-🖥️ email-**Email**

Paulding County

Superior Court *Felony, Misdemeanor, Civil* 11 Courthouse Square, Rm G2, Dallas, GA 30132. 8AM-5PM. **770-443-7527**, Civil phone: 770-443-7529, Crim: 770-505-6582. 🖑

Probate Court https://www.gaprobate.org/counties/paulding/index.html 25 Courthouse Sq. Annex, Rm 102, Dallas, GA 30132. 8AM-5PM. **770-443-7541**, Fax: 770-443-7631.

Peach County

Superior Court *Felony, Misdemeanor, Civil* PO Box 389, Ft Valley, GA 31030. 8:30AM-5PM. **478-825-5331**. 📫🖑

Probate Court PO Box 327, Ft Valley, GA 31030. 8AM-5PM. **478-825-2313**, Fax: 478-825-2678.

Pickens County

Superior Court *Felony, Misd., Civil* http://9thjudicialdistrict-ga.org/dca9apphp.shtml 52 N Main St, #102, Jasper, GA 30143. 8AM-5PM. **706-253-8763**. 🖑

Probate Court https://www.gaprobate.org/counties/pickens/index.html 50 N Main St, #203, Jasper, GA 30143. 8AM-N, 1-5PM. **706-253-8756**, Fax: 706-253-8760.

Pierce County

Superior & State Court *Felony, Misdemeanor, Civil* PO Box 588 312 Nichols St, Blackshear, GA 31516. 9AM-5PM. **912-449-2020**. 🖑

Probate Court PO Box 406 312 Nichols St, Blackshear, GA 31516. 9AM-5PM. **912-449-2029**, Fax: 912-449-1417.

Pike County

Superior Court *Felony, Misdemeanor, Civil* PO Box 10, Zebulon, GA 30295. 8AM-5PM. **770-567-2000**. Access by 🖑

Probate Court PO Box 324, Zebulon, GA 30295. 8:30AM--12:00-1PM-5PM. **770-567-8734**, Fax: 770-567-2019.

Polk County

Superior Court *Felony, Misdemeanor, Civil* PO Box 948 100 Proir St, Rm 106, Cedartown, GA 30125. 9AM-5PM. **770-749-2114**, Fax: 770-749-2148. 📫🖑

Probate Court www.polkcountygeorgia.us/courts.html Polk County Courthouse. Rm 102, Cedartown, GA 30125. 9AM-4:45PM. **770-749-2128/2129**, Fax: 770-749-2150.

Pulaski County

Superior Court *Felony, Misdemeanor, Civil* PO Box 60, Hawkinsville, GA 31036. 8AM-5PM. **478-783-1911**, Fax: 478-892-3308. 🖑

Probate Court Pulaski County Courthouse PO Box 156, Hawkinsville, GA 31036. 8AM-5PM. **478-783-2061**, Fax: 478-783-9219.

Putnam County

Superior & State Court *Felony, Misdemeanor, Civil* County Courthouse, Eatonton, GA 31024. 8AM-5PM. **706-485-4501**, Fax: 706-485-2875. 🖑

Probate Court https://www.gaprobate.org/counties/putnam/index.html County Courthouse 100 S Jefferson Ave, Eatonton, GA 31024. 8AM-5PM. **706-485-5476/9761**, Fax: 706-485-2515.

Quitman County

Superior Court *Felony, Misdemeanor, Civil* PO Box 307, Georgetown, GA 39854. 8AM-N, 1-5. **229-334-2578**. 🖑

Rabun County

Superior Court *Felony, Misdemeanor, Civil* 25 Courthouse Sq, #105, Clayton, GA 30525. 8:30AM-5PM. **706-782-3615**, Fax: 706-782-1391. 📫🖑

Probate Court www.rabuncountygov.com/contactus.htm 25 Courthouse Sq, #215, Clayton, GA 30525. 8:30AM-5:00PM. **706-782-3614**, Fax: 706-782-9278.

Randolph County

Superior Court *Felony, Misdemeanor, Civil* PO Box 98, Cuthbert, GA 39840. 8AM-5PM. **229-732-2216**, Fax: 229-732-5881. 🖑

Probate Court PO Box 424, Cuthbert, GA 39840. 8AM-5PM. **229-732-2671**, Fax: 229-732-5781.

Richmond County

Superior Court *Felony, Mids., Civil* www.augustaga.gov/departments/clerk_sup/default.htm 530 Greene St, Augusta, GA 30911. 8:30AM-5PM. **706-821-2460**, Fax: 706-821-2448. 📫🖑🖥

State Court *Misdemeanor, Civil* www.augustaga.gov/ 401 Walton Way, #218A, Augusta, GA 30911. 8:30AM-5PM. **706-821-1233**. 🖑

Civil & Magistrate Court *Civil Actions Under $45,000, Eviction, Small Claims*

530 Greene St, Rm 705, Augusta, GA 30911. 8:30AM-5PM. **706-821-2370**, Fax: 706-821-2381. The Magistrate Court does have some misdemeanor records related to violations of city ordinances. Access civil records by ☎📫🖑

Probate Court 530 Greene St, Rm 401, Augusta, GA 30911. 8:30AM-5PM. **706-821-2434**, Fax: 706-821-2442.

Rockdale County

Superior Court *Felony, Civil* PO Box 937 922 Court St, Conyers, GA 30012. 8AM-4:45PM. **770-929-4021**. 🖑

State Court *Misdemeanor, Civil* PO Box 938, Conyers, GA 30012. 8AM-4:45PM. **770-929-4019**. 🖑

Probate Court https://www.gaprobate.org/counties/rockdale/index.html 922 Court St NE, Rm 107, Conyers, GA 30012. 8:30AM-4:30PM. **770-929-4058**, Fax: 770-918-6463.

Schley County

Superior Court *Felony, Misdemeanor, Civil* www.gsccca.org/clerks/ PO Box 7 14 S Broad St., Ellaville, GA 31806. 8AM-N,1-5PM. **229-937-5581**, Fax: 229-937-5588. 🖑

Probate Court https://www.gaprobate.org/counties/schley/index.html PO Box 385, Ellaville, GA 31806. 8:30AM-N, 1-5PM. **229-937-2905**, Fax: 229-937-5588.

Screven County

Superior Court *Felony, Misdemeanor, Civil* PO Box 156 216 Mims Rd, Sylvania, GA 30467. 8:30AM-5PM. **912-564-2614**, Fax: 912-564-2622. 🖑

State Court *Misdemeanor, Civil* PO Box 156, Sylvania, GA 30467. 8:00AM-5PM. **912-564-2614**, Fax: 912-564-2622. 🖑

Probate Court 216 Mims Rd, #107, Sylvania, GA 30467. 8AM-5PM. **912-564-2783**, Fax: 912-564-9139.

Seminole County

Superior Court *Felony, Misdemeanor, Civil* PO Box 672 Main St, Donalsonville, GA 39845. 8:30AM-5PM. **229-524-2525**, Fax: 229-524-8883. Fax📫🖑

Spalding County

Superior Court *Felony, Misdemeanor, Civil* PO Box 1046, Griffin, GA 30224.

8AM-5PM. Civil: 770-467-4746, Crim: 770-467-4745. ✉🖑

State Court *Misdemeanor, Civil, Probate* PO Box 1046, Griffin, GA 30224. 8AM-5PM. **770-467-4745**, Civil: 770-467-4746, Crim: 770-467-4745. ✉🖑

Probate Court https://www.gaprobate.org /counties/spalding/index.html 132 E Solomon St, Griffin, GA 30223. 8AM-5PM. **770-467-4340**, Fax: 770-467-4243.

Stephens County

Superior Court *Felony, Misdemeanor, Civil* 205 Alexander St N, #202, Toccoa, GA 30577. 8AM-5PM. **706-886-9496**, Fax: 706-886-5710. 🖑

State Court *Misdemeanor, Civil* 205 N Alexander St, Rm 202 County Government Bldg, Toccoa, GA 30577. 8AM-5PM. **706-886-3598/9496**. 🖑

Probate Court 205 N Alexander #108, Toccoa, GA 30577. 8AM-5PM, closed for lunch. **706-886-2828**, Fax: 706-886-2631.

Stewart County

Superior Court *Felony, Misdemeanor, Civil* PO Box 910 Main St, Lumpkin, GA 31815. 8AM-4:30PM. **229-838-6220**. 🖑

Probate Court https://www.gaprobate.org /counties/stewart/index.html PO Box 876, Lumpkin, GA 31815. 8AM-N, 1-4:30PM. **229-838-4394**, Fax: 229-838-9084.

Sumter County

State Court *Misdemeanor, Civil* PO Box 333, Americus, GA 31709. 9AM-5PM. **229-928-4537**. 🖑

Probate Court PO Box 246, Americus, GA 31709. 8AM-5PM. **229-928-4551**, Fax: 229-928-4622.

Talbot County

Superior Court *Felony, Misdemeanor, Civil* PO Box 325, Talbotton, GA 31827. 9AM-5PM. **706-665-3239**, Fax: 706-665-8637. 🖑

Taliaferro County

Superior Court *Felony, Misdemeanor, Civil* PO Box 182, Crawfordville, GA 30631. 9AM-5PM. **706-456-2123**. 🖑

Tattnall County

Superior & State Court *Felony, Misdemeanor, Civil* PO Box 39,

Reidsville, GA 30453. 8AM-5PM. **912-557-6716**, Fax: 912-557-4861. 🖑

Probate Court PO Box 699, Reidsville, GA 30453. 8:30AM-5PM. **912-557-6719**, Fax: 912-557-3976.

Taylor County

Superior Court *Felony, Misdemeanor, Civil* PO Box 248 Courthouse Square, Butler, GA 31006. 8AM-5PM. **478-862-5594**, Fax: 478-862-5334. Access by 🖑

Telfair County

Superior Court *Felony, Misdemeanor, Civil* Courthouse 128 Oak St, #2, McRae, GA 31055. 8:30AM-4:30PM. **229-868-6525**, Fax: 229-868-7956. ☎🖑

Probate Court 128 E Oak St, #1, McRae, GA 31055. 8:30AM-N, 1-4:30PM. **229-868-6038**, Fax: 229-868-7620.

Terrell County

Superior Court *Felony, Misdemeanor, Civil* PO Box 189 513 S Main St, Dawson, GA 39842. 8:30AM-5PM. **229-995-2631**. 🖑

Probate Court https://www.gaprobate.or g/counties/terrell/index.html PO Box 67, Dawson, GA 39842. **229-995-5515**, Fax: 229-995-4301.

Thomas County

Superior & State Court *Felony, Misd., Civil* www.thomascoclerkofcourt.org PO Box 1995, Thomasville, GA 31799. 8-5. **229-225-4108**, Fax: 229-225-4110. 🖑

Probate Court PO Box 1582, Thomasville, GA 31799. 8AM-5PM. **229-225-4116**, Fax: 229-227-1698.

Tift County

Superior & State Court *Felony, Misdemeanor, Civil* PO Box 354, Tifton, GA 31793. 8AM-5PM. **229-386-7810**. Call 229-786-7815 to reach the Superior Court. 🖑

Probate Court PO Box 792 225 Tift Ave, Rm 117, Tifton, GA 31793. 9AM-5PM. **229-386-7936, 229-386-7914**, Fax: 229-386-7926.

Toombs County

Superior & State Court *Felony, Misdemeanor, Civil* PO Drawer 530, Lyons, GA 30436. 8:30AM-5PM. **912-526-3501**, Fax: 912-526-1015. 🖑

Probate Court Toombs County Courthouse PO Box 1370, Lyons, GA 30436. 8:30AM-5PM. **912-526-8696**, Fax: 912-526-1008.

Towns County

Superior Court *Felony, Misdemeanor, Civil* 48 River St, #E, Hiawassee, GA 30546. 8:30-4:30PM. **706-896-2130**. 🖑

Treutlen County

Superior & State Court *Felony, Misdemeanor, Civil* PO Box 356, Soperton, GA 30457. 8AM-5PM. **912-529-4215**, Probate: 912-529-3342. ✉🖑

Troup County

Superior & State Court *Felony, Misdemeanor, Civil* 900 Dallas St., LaGrange, GA 30240. 8AM-5PM. **706-883-1740**. 🖑

Probate Court www.georgiacourts.org/co unties/troup/ 900 Dallis St County Admin. Bldg., LaGrange, GA 30240. 8AM-5PM. **706-883-1690**, Fax: 706-812-7933.

Turner County

Superior Court *Felony, Misdemeanor, Civil* PO Box 106 219 E College Ave, Ashburn, GA 31714. 8AM-5PM. **229-567-2011**, Fax: 229-567-0450. 🖑

Probate Court PO Box 2506, Ashburn, GA 31714. 8AM-5PM. **229-567-2151**, Fax: 229-567-0358.

Twiggs County

Superior Court *Felony, Misdemeanor, Civil* PO Box 243, Jeffersonville, GA 31044. 8AM-5PM. **478-945-3350**. 🖑

Probate Court, *Misdemeanor Traffic* PO Box 186, Jeffersonville, GA 31044. 9AM-5PM. **478-945-3390/3252**, Fax: 478-945-6070.

Union County

Superior Court *Felony, Misdemeanor, Civil* 114 Courthouse St, #5, Blairsville, GA 30512. 8AM-5PM. **706-439-6022**, Fax: 706-439-6026. 🖑

Probate Court 114 Courthouse St, #8, Blairsville, GA 30512. 8-4:30PM. **706-439-6005**, Fax: 706-439-6009.

Upson County

Superior Court *Felony, Misdemeanor, Civil* PO Box 469, Thomaston, GA

30286. 8AM-5PM. **706-647-7835**, Fax: 706-647-8999. ✉🖐

Probate Court PO Box 906, Thomaston, GA 30286. 8AM-5PM. **706-647-7015**, Fax: 706-646-3341.

Walker County

Superior & State Court *Felony, Misdemeanor, Civil* PO Box 448, LaFayette, GA 30728. 8AM-5PM. **706-638-1772**. 🖐

Probate Court www.walkercounty.org PO Box 436, LaFayette, GA 30728. 8AM-5PM. **706-638-2852**, Fax: 706-638-2869.

Walton County

Superior Court *Felony, Misdemeanor, Civil* PO Box 745, Monroe, GA 30655. 8:30AM-5PM. **770-267-1307**, Fax: 770-267-1441. 🖐

Probate Court https://www.gaprobate.org/counties/walton/index.html PO Box 629, Monroe, GA 30655. 8:30AM-5PM. **770-267-1345, 267-1387**, Fax: 770-267-1417. Also has traffic and misdemeanor records.

Ware County

Superior & State Court *Felony, Misdemeanor, Civil* PO Box 776, Waycross, GA 31502. 9AM-5PM. **912-287-4340**. 🖐

Probate Court Ware County Courthouse, #123 800 Church St, Waycross, GA 31501. 9AM-5PM. **912-287-4315/6**, Fax: 912-287-4317, Probate: 912-287-4316.

Warren County

Superior Court *Felony, Misdemeanor, Civil* PO Box 227 100 Main St, Warrenton, GA 30828. 8AM-5PM. **706-465-2262**, Fax: 706-465-0232. ✉🖐

Probate Court PO Box 364, Warrenton, GA 30828. 8AM-4:30PM. **706-465-2227**, Fax: 706-465-1300.

Washington County

Superior & State Court *Felony, Misdemeanor, Civil* PO Box 231, Sandersville, GA 31082. 9AM-5PM. **478-552-3186**. ✉🖐

Probate Court PO Box 669, Sandersville, GA 31082. 9AM-N, 1-5PM. **478-552-3304**, Fax: 478-552-7424.

Wayne County

Superior & State Court *Felony, Misdemeanor, Civil* PO Box 920, Jesup, GA 31598. 8:30AM-5PM. **912-427-5930**, Fax: 912-427-5939. 🖐

Probate Court 174 N Brunswick St, Jesup, GA 31598. 8:30AM-5PM. **912-427-5940**, Fax: 912-427-5944.

Webster County

Superior Court *Felony, Misdemeanor, Civil* PO Box 117, Preston, GA 31824. 8AM-4:30PM. **229-828-3525**. 🖐

Wheeler County

Superior Court *Felony, Misdemeanor, Civil* PO Box 38, Alamo, GA 30411. 8AM-4PM. **912-568-7137**. Access by 🖐

White County

Superior Court *Felony, Misdemeanor, Civil* 59 S Main St, #B, Cleveland, GA 30528. 8:30AM-5PM. **706-865-2613**, Fax: 706-865-7749. 🖐

Probate Court, *Misd.* 59 S Main St, #H, Cleveland, GA 30528. 8:30AM-5PM. **706-865-4141**, Fax: 706-865-1324.

Whitfield County

Superior Court *Felony, Misd., Civil* PO Box 868 300 W Crawford St, Dalton, GA 30722. 8AM-5PM. **706-275-7450**, Fax: 706-275-7462. 🖐

Probate Court 301 Crawford St, Dalton, GA 30720. 8AM-4:45PM. **706-275-7400**, Fax: 706-281-1735.

Wilcox County

Superior & Magistrate Courts *Felony, Misdemeanor, Civil, Eviction, Small Claims* 103 N Broad St, Abbeville, GA 31001. 9AM-5PM. **229-467-2442**, Fax: 229-467-2886. ✉🖐

Probate Court 103 N Broad St, Abbeville, GA 31001. 9AM-5PM. **229-467-2220**, Fax: 229-467-2000.

Wilkes County

Superior Court *Felony, Misdemeanor, Civil* 23 E Court St, Rm 205, Washington, GA 30673. 9AM-5PM. **706-678-2423**. 🖐

Probate Court https://www.gaprobate.org/counties/wilkes/index.html 23 E Court St, Rm 422, Washington, GA 30673. 8:30AM-5PM. **706-678-2523**, Fax: 706-678-4854.

Wilkinson County

Superior Court *Felony, Misdemeanor, Civil* PO Box 250, Irwinton, GA 31042. 8AM-5PM. **478-946-2221**, Fax: 478-946-1497. 🖐

Worth County

Superior & State Court *Felony, Misdemeanor, Civil, Small Claims* 201 N Main St, Rm 13, Sylvester, GA 31791. 8AM-5PM. **229-776-8205**, Fax: 229-776-8237. 🖐

Probate Court https://www.gaprobate.org/counties/worth/index.html 201 N Main St, Rm 12, Sylvester, GA 31791. 8AM-5PM. **229-776-8207**, Fax: 229-776-1540.

Hawaii

State Court Administration: Administrative Director of Courts, Judicial Branch, 417 S King St, Honolulu, HI, 96813; 808-539-4900, Fax: 808-539-4855. www.courts.state.hi.us

Court Structure: Hawaii's trial level is comprised of Circuit Courts (with Family Courts) and District Courts. These trial courts function in four judicial circuits: First (Oahu), Second (Maui/Molokai/Lanai), Third (Hawaii County), and Fifth (Kauai/Niihau). The Fourth Circuit was merged with the Third in 1943.

Circuit Courts are general jurisdiction and handle all jury trials, felony cases, and civil cases over $20,000, also probate and guardianship. The District Court handles criminal cases punishable by a fine and/or less then 1-yr imprisonment and some civil cases up to $20,000, also landlord/tenant and DUI cases.

Online Access: Free online access to all Circuit Court and family court records, and civil records from the District courts is available at the website www.courts.state.hi.us (click on "Search Court Records"). Search by name or case number. These records are not considered "official" for FCRA compliant searches. Most courts have access back to mid 1980's. Also, opinions from the Appellate Court are available from the home page url.

Additional Information: Most Hawaii state courts offer a public access terminal to search records at the courthouse. Civil cases down to $5000 minimum are found at the Circuit Court if a jury is involved.

Hawaii County

3rd Circuit Court Legal Documents Section *Felony, Misdemeanor, Civil Over $5,000, Probate* www.courts.state.hi.us PO Box 1007, Hilo, HI 96721-1007. 7:45AM-4:30PM. **808-961-7404**, Fax: 808-961-7416. ✉Fax🖐💻

District Court *Misdemeanor, Civil Actions Under $20,000, Eviction, Small Claims* www.courts.state.hi.us/index.jsp PO Box 4879, Hilo, HI 96720. 7:45AM-4:30PM. **808-961-7470**, Fax: 808-961-7447. ☎Fax✉🖐💻

Honolulu County

1st Circuit Court *Felony, Civil Actions Over $5,000, Probate, Family* www.courts.state.hi.us/index.jsp Legal Documents Branch 777 Punchbowl St, 1st Fl, Honolulu, HI 96813. 7:45AM-4:30PM. **808-539-4300**, Fax: 808-539-4314. ✉🖐💻

District Court - Civil Division *Civil Actions Under $20,000, Eviction, Small Claims* www.courts.state.hi.us/index.jsp 1111 Alakea St, 3rd Fl, Honolulu, HI 96813. 7:45AM-4:30PM. **808-538-5151**, Fax: 808-538-5444 Access civil records by ☎✉🖐💻

District Court - Criminal Division *Misdemeanor* www.courts.state.hi.us/index.jsp 1111 Alakea St, 3rd Fl, Judicial Services, Honolulu, HI 96813. 8AM-4:15PM. **808-538-5100**, Fax: 808-538-5111. Fax✉🖐💻

Kauai County

5th Circuit Court *Felony, Misdemeanor, Civil Actions Over $20,000, Probate* www.courts.state.hi.us 3059 Umi St Rm, #101, Lihue, HI 96766. 7:45AM-4:30PM. **808-246-3300**, Fax: 808-246-3310. ✉🖐💻

District Court 5th Circuit - Criminal *Misdemeanor* www.courts.state.hi.us/index.jsp 3059 Umi St, Rm 111, Lihue, HI 96766. 7:45AM-4:30PM. **808-246-3330**, Fax: 808-246-3309. ☎Fax✉🖐💻

District Court 5th Circuit - Civil *Civil Actions Under $20,000, Eviction, Small Claims* www.courts.state.hi.us/index.jsp 4357 Rice St, #101, Lihue, HI 96766. 7:45AM-4:30PM. **808-246-3301**, Fax: 808-241-7103 Access civil records by ☎Fax✉🖐💻

Maui County

2nd Circuit Court *Felony, Misdemeanor, Civil Actions Over $5,000, Probate* www.courts.state.hi.us 2145 Main St, #106, Wailuku, HI 96793. 7:45AM-4:30PM. **808-244-2929**, Fax: 808-244-2932. Also covers the counties of Lanai and Molokai. ✉🖐💻

Wailuku District Court *Misdemeanor, Civil Actions Under $20,000, Eviction, Small Claims* www.courts.state.hi.us 2145 Main St, #137, Wailuku, HI 96793. 7:45AM-4:30PM. **808-244-2800**, Fax: 808-244-2849. ✉🖐💻

Molokai District Court *Misdemeanor, Civil Actions Under $20,000, Eviction, Small Claims* www.courts.state.hi.us PO Box 284, Kaunakakai, HI 96748. 7:45AM-4:30PM. **808-553-5451**, Fax: 808-553-3374. 🖐💻

Lanai District Court *Misdemeanor, Civil Actions Under $20,000, Eviction, Small Claims* www.courts.state.hi.us/index.jsp PO Box 631376, Lanai City, HI 96763. 7:45-4:30PM. **808-565-6447**. ✉🖐💻

Idaho

State Court Administration: Administrative Director of Courts, Supreme Court Building, PO Box 83720, 451 W State St, Boise, ID, 83720; 208-334-2246, Fax: 208-334-2146. http://www.isc.idaho.gov/

Court Structure: District judges hear felony criminal cases and civil actions if the amount involved is more than $10,000, and appeals of decisions of the Magistrate Division. The Magistrate Division hears probate matters, divorce proceedings, juvenile proceedings, initial felony proceedings through the preliminary hearing, criminal misdemeanors, infractions, civil cases when the amount in dispute does not exceed $10,000, and cases in Small Claims Court, established for disputes of $4,000 or less.

Online Access: Although appellate and supreme court opinions are available from the web, there is no statewide computer system offering external access. ISTARS is a statewide intra-court/intra-agency system run and managed by the State Supreme Court. All counties are on ISTARS, and all courts provide public access terminals on-site. For tribal court information, visit www.isc.idaho.gov/tribalmn.htm.

Key: Symbols refer to criminal records access unless otherwise noted. phone-☎ mail-✉ fax-Fax in person-🖐 online-💻 email-**Email**

Additional Information: A statewide court administrative rule states that record custodians do not have a duty to "compile or summarize information contained in a record, nor ... to create new records for the requesting party." Under this rule, some courts will not perform searches.

Many courts require a signed release for employment record searches.

The following fees are mandated statewide: Search Fee - none; Certification Fee - $1.00 per document plus copy fee; Copy Fee - $1.00 per page. Not all jurisdictions currently follow these guidelines. Some counties charge $5.00 or $6.00 to do a search. A detailed description of the court rules regarding access to records may be found in Idaho Court Administrative Rule 32.

Ada County

District & Magistrate Courts *Civil, Eviction, Small Claims, Probate* http://www2.state.id.us/fourthjudicial 200 W Front, Rm 1155, Boise, ID 83702-5931. 8:30-5PM. **208-287-6900**. ✉ ☝

Ada County Criminal Court *Felony, Misd.,* http://www2.state.id.us/fourthjudicial 200 W Front St, Rm 1190, Boise, ID 83702-5931. 8AM-5PM. **208-287-6900**, Crim: Ext 2. ✉ ☝

Adams County

District & Magistrate Courts *Felony, Misdemeanor, Civil, Eviction, Small Claims, Probate* PO Box 48, Council, ID 83612. 8AM-5PM. **208-253-4561/4233**, Fax: 208-253-4880. **Fax**✉ ☝

Bannock County

District & Magistrate Courts *Felony, Misd., Civil, Eviction, Small Claims, Probate* www.co.bannock.id.us/clkcrt1.htm 624 E Center, Rm 220, Pocatello, ID 83201. 8AM-5PM. **208-236-7351**, Fax: 208-236-7013. Civil phone: 208-236-7350, Crim: 208-236-7352, Probate: 208-236-7351. Misdemeanors: 208-236-7272. **Fax**✉ ☝

Bear Lake County

District & Magistrate Courts *Felony, Misdemeanor, Civil, Eviction, Small Claims, Probate* PO Box 190, Paris, ID 83261. 8:30AM-5PM. **208-945-2208**, Fax: 208-945-2780. **Fax**✉ ☝

Benewah County

District & Magistrate Courts *Felony, Misdemeanor, Civil, Eviction, Small Claims, Probate* Courthouse 701 College Ave, St Maries, ID 83861. 9AM-5PM. **208-245-3241**, Fax: 208-245-3046. ✉**Fax**☝

Bingham County

District & Magistrate Courts *Felony, Misdemeanor, Civil, Eviction, Small Claims, Probate* 501 N Maple St, #402, Blackfoot, ID 83221-1700. 8AM-N, 1-5PM. **208-785-8040 X3124 (Dist) X3121**

(Magis), Fax: 208-785-8057 (Dist) 208-782-3167 (Magist). Civil phone: X3123 or X3124, Crim: X3118, X3117 or X3122, Probate: X3123 or X3124. Small Claims X3120. ☎**Fax**✉ ☝

Blaine County

District & Magistrate Courts *Felony, Misdemeanor, Civil, Eviction, Small Claims, Probate* 201 2nd Ave S, #106, Hailey, ID 83333. 9AM-5PM. **208-788-5548**, Fax: 208-788-5527. The Magistrate Court (Misdemeanor, Small Claims, Eviction, Probate) is in #106; Magistrate Court phone is 208-788-5525; fax 208-788-5527. ☝

Boise County

District & Magistrate Courts *Felony, Misdemeanor, Civil, Eviction, Small Claims, Probate* PO Box 126, Idaho City, ID 83631. 8AM-5PM. **208-392-4452**, Fax: 208-392-6712. ☝

Bonner County

District & Magistrate Courts *Felony, Misdemeanor, Civil, Eviction, Small Claims, Probate* 215 S 1st Ave Bonner Courthouse, Sandpoint, ID 83864. 9-5PM. **208-265-1432**, Fax: 208-265-1447. ☝

Bonneville County

District & Magistrate Courts *Felony, Misdemeanor, Civil, Eviction, Small Claims, Probate* www.co.bonneville.id.us 605 N Capital, Idaho Falls, ID 83402. 8AM-5PM. **208-529-1350**, Fax: 208-529-1300. ☝

Boundary County

District & Magistrate Courts *Felony, Misdemeanor, Civil, Eviction, Small Claims, Probate* www.boundary-idaho.com Boundary County Courthouse PO Box 419, Bonners Ferry, ID 83805. 9AM-5PM. **208-267-5504**, Fax: 208-267-7814. ☝

Butte County

District & Magistrate Courts *Felony, Misdemeanor, Civil, Eviction, Small Claims, Probate* 326 W Grand Ave,

Arco, ID 83213. 9AM-N; 1PM-5PM. **208-527-8259**, Fax: 208-527-3448. ☎**Fax**✉ ☝

Camas County

District & Magistrate Courts *Felony, Misdemeanor, Civil, Eviction, Small Claims, Probate* PO Box 430, Fairfield, ID 83327. 8:30AM-N, 1-5PM. **208-764-2238**, Fax: 208-764-2349. ✉ ☝

Canyon County

District & Magistrate Courts *Felony, Misd., Civil, Eviction, Small Claims, Probate* www.the3rdjudicialdistrict.com 1115 Albany, Caldwell, ID 83605. 8:30AM-5PM. Civil: 208-454-7570, Crim: 208-454-7571. Small claims: 208-454-7577 ☝

Caribou County

District & Magistrate Courts *Felony, Misdemeanor, Civil, Eviction, Small Claims, Probate* 159 S Main, Soda Springs, ID 83276. 9AM-5PM. **208-547-4342**, Fax: 208-547-4759. ☎**Fax**✉ ☝

Cassia County

District & Magistrate Courts *Felony, Misd., Civil, Eviction, Small Claims, Probate* www.cassiacounty.org/judicial/default.htm 1459 Overland, Burley, ID 83318. 8:30AM-5PM. **208-878-7351 Magistrate; 878-4367 Dist**, Fax: 208-878-1003. **Fax**✉ ☝

Clark County

District & Magistrate Courts *Felony, Misdemeanor, Civil, Eviction, Small Claims, Probate* PO Box 205, DuBois, ID 83423. 9AM-5PM. **208-374-5402**, Fax: 208-374-5609. ☝

Clearwater County

District & Magistrate Courts *Felony, Misdemeanor, Civil, Eviction, Small Claims, Probate* PO Box 586, Orofino, ID 83544. 8AM-5PM. **208-476-5596**, Fax: 208-476-5159. ☎**Fax**✉ ☝

Key: Symbols refer to criminal records access unless otherwise noted. phone-☎ mail-✉ fax-**Fax** in person-☝ online-💻 email-**Email**

Custer County

District & Magistrate Courts *Felony, Misdemeanor, Civil, Eviction, Small Claims, Probate* PO Box 385, Challis, ID 83226. 8AM-5PM. **208-879-2359**, Fax: 208-879-6412. ☎✉🖐

Elmore County

District & Magistrate Courts *Felony, Misdemeanor, Civil, Eviction, Small Claims, Probate* 150 S 4th E, #5, Mountain Home, ID 83647. 9-5PM. **208-587-2133 x208**, Fax: 208-587-2134. 🖐

Franklin County

District & Magistrate Courts *Felony, Misdemeanor, Civil, Eviction, Small Claims, Probate* 39 W Oneida, Preston, ID 83263. 9AM-5PM. **208-852-0877**, Fax: 208-852-2926. ☎Fax✉🖐

Fremont County

District & Magistrate Courts *Felony, Misdemeanor, Civil, Eviction, Small Claims, Probate* 151 W 1st N, St Anthony, ID 83445. 9AM-5PM. **208-624-7401**, Fax: 208-624-4607. Fax✉🖐

Gem County

District & Magistrate Courts *Felony, Misd., Civil, Eviction, Small Claims, Probate* www.co.gem.id.us/judicial/default.htm 415 E Main St, Emmett, ID 83617. 8AM-5PM. **208-365-4561-District Court. 208-365-4221-Magistrate Court**, Fax: 208-365-6172. ✉🖐

Gooding County

District & Magistrate Courts *Felony, Misdemeanor, Civil, Eviction, Small Claims, Probate* PO Box 27, Gooding, ID 83330. 8AM-5PM. Fax: 208-934-4408. Civil phone: 208-934-4261, Crim: 208-934-4861. Magistrate Court: 208-934-4261. Magistrate Court address is PO Box 477. Only felony reocrds are available at District Court. 🖐

Idaho County

District & Magistrate Courts *Felony, Misd., Civil, Eviction, Small Claims, Probate* 320 W Main, Grangeville, ID 83530. 8:30AM-5PM. **208-983-2776**, Fax: 208-983-2376. ☎Fax✉🖐

Jefferson County

District & Magistrate Courts *Felony, Misdemeanor, Civil, Eviction, Small Claims, Probate* PO Box 71, Rigby, ID 83442. 9AM-5PM. **208-745-7736**, Fax: 208-745-6636. 🖐

Jerome County

District & Magistrate Courts *Felony, Misdemeanor, Civil, Eviction, Small Claims, Probate* 300 N Lincoln St, Jerome, ID 83338. 8:30AM-5PM. **208-324-8811**, Fax: 208-324-2719. Fax✉🖐

Kootenai County

District & Magistrate Court *Felony, Misd., Civil, Eviction, Small Claims, Probate* www.co.kootenai.id.us/departments/districtcourt/ 324 W Garden Ave (PO Box 9000), Coeur d'Alene, ID 83816-9000. 9AM-5PM. **208-446-1180**, Fax: 208-446-1188. Civil phone: 208-446-1160, Crim: 208-446-1170. ✉🖐

Latah County

District & Magistrate Courts *Felony, Misdemeanor, Civil, Eviction, Small Claims, Probate* PO Box 8068, Moscow, ID 83843. 8:30AM-5PM M-W, 8AM-5PM TH,F. **208-883-2255**, Fax: 208-883-2259. ☎Fax✉🖐

Lemhi County

District & Magistrate Courts *Felony, Misdemeanor, Civil, Eviction, Small Claims, Probate* 206 Courthouse Dr, Salmon, ID 83467. 8AM-5PM. **208-756-2815**, Fax: 208-756-8424. Civil phone: x225, Crim: x225, Probate: x242. ☎Fax✉🖐

Lewis County

District & Magistrate Courts *Felony, Misdemeanor, Civil, Eviction, Small Claims, Probate* 510 Oak St (PO Box 39), Nezperce, ID 83543. 9AM-5PM. **208-937-2251**, Fax: 208-937-9233. ☎Fax✉🖐

Lincoln County

District & Magistrate Courts *Felony, Misdemeanor, Civil, Eviction, Small Claims, Probate* Drawer A, Shoshone, ID 83352. 8:30AM-5PM. **208-886-2173**, Fax: 208-886-2458. 🖐✉Fax

Madison County

District & Magistrate Courts *Felony, Misdemeanor, Civil, Eviction, Small Claims, Probate* PO Box 389, Rexburg, ID 83440. 9AM-5PM. **208-356-9383**, Fax: 208-356-5425. 🖐

Minidoka County

District & Magistrate Courts *Felony, Misdemeanor, Civil, Eviction, Small Claims, Probate* PO Box 368, Rupert, ID 83350. 8:30AM-5PM. **208-436-9041 (Dist)** 436-7186 **(Magis)**, Fax: 208-436-5857. Fax✉🖐

Nez Perce County

District & Magistrate Court *Felony, Misd., Civil, Eviction, Small Claims, Probate* www.co.nezperce.id.us/clerk/clerk.htm PO Box 896 (1230 Main St), Lewiston, ID 83501. 8AM-5PM. **208-799-3040**, Fax: 208-799-3058. ☎Fax✉🖐

Oneida County

District & Magistrate Courts *Felony, Misdemeanor, Civil, Eviction, Small Claims, Probate* 10 Court St, Malad City, ID 83252. 9AM-5PM. **208-766-4285 X111,112,114,105**, Fax: 208-766-2990. ☎Fax✉🖐

Owyhee County

District & Magistrate Courts-I *Felony, Misd., Civil, Eviction, Small Claims, Probate* http://owyheecounty.net/court/Index.htm Courthouse, PO Box 128, Murphy, ID 83650. 8:30AM-5PM. **208-495-2806**, Fax 208-495-1226. Fax✉🖐

Homedale Magistrate Court *Misdemeanor, Civil Under $10,000, Eviction, Small Claims* http://owyheecounty.net/court/index.htm 31 W Wyoming, Homedale, ID 83628-3402. 8:30-5PM. **208-337-4540**, Fax 208-337-3035. ✉🖐

Payette County

District & Magistrate Courts *Felony, Misdemeanor, Civil, Eviction, Small Claims, Probate* 1130 3rd Ave N, #104, Payette, ID 83661. 9AM-5PM. **208-642-6000 (Dist),** 642-6010(Magis), Fax: 208-642-6011. Rm 104 - District Court; Rm 106 - Magistrate Court. Access Fax✉🖐

Power County

District & Magistrate Courts *Felony, Misdemeanor, Civil, Eviction, Small Claims, Probate* 543 Bannock Ave, American Falls, ID 83211. 9AM-5PM. **208-226-7611 (Dist),** 226-7618 **(Magist)**, Fax: 208-226-7612. ☎Fax✉🖐

Shoshone County

District & Magistrate Courts *Felony, Misdemeanor, Civil, Eviction, Small Claims, Probate* 700 Bank St, Wallace,

ID 83873. 9AM-5PM. **208-752-1266**, Fax: 208-753-0921. ☎ ✉ 🖐

Teton County

District & Magistrate Courts *Felony, Misdemeanor, Civil, Eviction, Small Claims, Probate* 89 N Main, #5, Driggs, ID 83422. 9AM-5PM. **208-354-2239**, Fax: 208-354-8496. Address and telephone given above are for District Court. Magistrate Court phone: 208-354-2239. ☎ **Fax** ✉ 🖐

Twin Falls County

District & Magistrate Courts *Felony, Misdemeanor, Civil, Eviction, Small Claims, Probate* www.co.twin-falls.id.us/5thdistrict PO Box 126, Twin Falls, ID 83303-0126. 8AM-5PM. **208-736-4013**, Fax: 208-736-4155. 🖐

Valley County

District & Magistrate Courts-I *Felony, Misdemeanor, Civil, Eviction, Small Claims, Probate* PO Box 1350, Cascade, ID 83611. 8AM-5PM. **208-382-7178**, Fax: 208-382-7184. A Courthouse Annex in McCall handles Misdemeanors, Small Claims & Juvenile. However, the McCall Court does not do checks and forwards its closed cases to Cascade. ☎ Fax ✉ 🖐

Washington County

District & Magistrate Courts *Felony, Misd., Civil, Eviction, Small Claims, Probate* www.the3rdjudicialdistrict.com PO Box 670, Weiser, ID 83672. 8:30AM-5PM. **208-414-2092**, Fax: 208-414-3925. This court will only perform searches for probate records, and these requests must be in writing. 🖐

Illinois

State Court Administration: Administrative Office of Courts, 222 N LaSalle 13th Floor, Chicago, IL, 60601; 312-793-3250, Fax: 312-793-1335. http://www.state.il.us/court/

Court Structure: Illinois is divided into 22 judicial circuits; 3 are single county: Cook, Du Page (18th Circuit) and Will (12th Circuit). The other 19 circuits consist of 2 or more contiguous counties. The Circuit Court of Cook County is the largest unified court system in the world. Its 2300-person staff handles 2.4 million cases each year. The civil part of the various Circuit Courts in Cook County is divided as follows: under $30,000 are "civil cases" and over $30,000 are "civil law division cases."

Probate is handled by the Circuit Court in all counties.

Online Access: The web page offers access to supreme and appellate opinions. While there is no statewide public online system available, a number of Illinois Circuit Courts offer online access. A vendor, Judici.com, offers free searching for a growing number of counties. The Judici.com home page also offers a commercial subscription service for multi-county searching.

Additional Information: The search fee is set by statute and has three levels based on the county population. The higher the population, the larger the fee. In most courts, both civil and criminal data is on computer from the same starting date. In most Illinois courts the search fee is charged on a per name per year basis.

Adams County

Circuit Court *Felony, Misdemeanor, Civil, Eviction, Small Claims, Probate* www.co.adams.il.us 521 Vermont St, Quincy, IL 62301. 8:15AM-4:30PM. **217-277-2100**, Fax: 217-277-2116. ☎ ✉ **Fax** 🖐 🖥 **Email**

Alexander County

Circuit Court *Felony, Misdemeanor, Civil, Eviction, Small Claims, Probate* 2000 Washington Ave, Cairo, IL 62914. 8AM-N-1-4PM. **618-734-0107**, Fax: 618-734-7003. **Fax** ✉ 🖐

Bond County

Circuit Court *Felony, Misdemeanor, Civil, Small Claims, Probate* www.johnkking.com 200 W College Ave, Greenville, IL 62246. 8AM-4:30PM. **618-664-3208**, Fax: 618-664-2257. ✉ 🖐

Boone County

Circuit Court *Felony, Misdemeanor, Civil, Eviction, Small Claims, Probate* 601 N Main, #303, Belvidere, IL 61008. 8:30AM-5PM. **815-544-0371**. ✉ 🖐

Brown County

Circuit Court *Felony, Misdemeanor, Civil, Eviction, Small Claims, Probate* Brown County Courthouse 200 Court St, Rm 5, Mt Sterling, IL 62353. 8:30AM-4:30PM. **217-773-2713**. **Fax** ✉ 🖐

Bureau County

Circuit Court *Felony, Misdemeanor, Civil, Eviction, Small Claims, Probate* www.bccirclk.gov 702 S Main, Princeton, IL 61356. 8AM-4PM. **815-872-2001**, Fax: 815-872-0027. ✉ 🖐 🖥

Calhoun County

Circuit Court *Felony, Misdemeanor, Civil, Eviction, Small Claims, Probate* PO Box 486, Hardin, IL 62047. 8:30AM-4:30PM. **618-576-2451**, Fax: 618-576-9541. **Fax** ✉ 🖐

Carroll County

Circuit Court *Felony, Misdemeanor, Civil, Eviction, Small Claims, Probate* 301 N Main St PO Box 32, Mt Carroll, IL 61053. 8:30AM-4:30PM. **815-244-0230**, Fax: 815-244-3869. ✉ 🖐 🖥

Cass County

Circuit Court *Felony, Misdemeanor, Civil, Eviction, Small Claims, Probate* PO Box 203, Virginia, IL 62691. 8:30-4:30PM. **217-452-7225**. ✉ **Fax** 🖐

Champaign County

Circuit Court *Felony, Misdemeanor, Civil, Eviction, Small Claims, Probate* www.cccircuitclerk.com 101 E Main, Urbana, IL 61801. 8:30AM-4:30PM. Fax: 217-384-3879. Civil phone: 217-384-3725, Crim: 217-384-3727. ⊠🖳✋

Christian County

Circuit Court *Felony, Misdemeanor, Civil, Eviction, Small Claims, Probate* PO Box 617, Taylorville, IL 62568. 8AM-4PM. **217-824-4966**, Fax: 217-824-5030. ☎⊠✋

Clark County

Circuit Court *Felony, Misdemeanor, Civil, Eviction, Small Claims, Probate* PO Box 187, Marshall, IL 62441. 8AM-4PM. **217-826-2811**, Crim: 217-826-2811. ⊠✋

Clay County

Circuit Court *Felony, Misdemeanor, Civil, Eviction, Small Claims, Probate* PO Box 100, Louisville, IL 62858. 8AM-4PM. **618-665-3523**, Fax: 618-665-3543. Fax⊠✋

Clinton County

Circuit Court *Felony, Misdemeanor, Civil, Eviction, Small Claims, Probate* County Courthouse PO Box 407, Carlyle, IL 62231. 8AM-4PM. **618-594-2464**. ⊠✋

Coles County

Circuit Court *Felony, Misdemeanor, Civil, Eviction, Small Claims, Probate* PO Box 48, Charleston, IL 61920. 8:30AM-4:30PM. **217-348-0516**. Fax⊠✋🖳

Cook County

Cases are heard in six district courts within the county. Each court has a central index. Eventually all case files are maintained at District 1.

Circuit Court - Criminal Division *Felony* www.cookcountyclerkofcourt.org 2650 S California Ave, Chicago, IL 60608. 8:30AM-4:30PM. **773-869-3140 Admin**, Fax: 773-869-4444. Criminal phone: 773-869-3677. Cases are heard in six district courts within the county and each court has a central index. This location houses criminal records only. ⊠✋

Circuit Court - Chicago District 1 *Misdemeanor, Civil Action Under $100,000, Eviction, Small Claims, Probate* www.cookcountyclerkofcourt.org 50 W Washington, Rm 601, Chicago, IL 60602. 8:30AM-4:30PM. **312-603-5030**, Fax: 312-603-3659 (crim). Civil phone: 312-603-5145, Crim: 312-603-4641, Probate: 312-603-6441. Probate is a separate division at this same address, Rm 1202. ☎⊠🖳✋

Maywood District 4 *Felony, Civil Action Under $100,000, Eviction, Small Claims* www.cookcountyclerkofcourt.org 1500 S Maybrook Dr, Rm 236, Maywood, IL 60153-2410. 8:30AM-4:30PM. **708-865-4937**, Civil phone: 708-865-4973, Crim: 708-865-5517. Bellwood, Berkeley, Berwyn, Broadview, Brookfield, Cicero, Elmwood Park, Forest Park, Franklin Park, Hillside, La Grange Park, Maywood, Melrose Park, Northlake, North Riverside, Oak Park, River Forest, River Grove, Riverside, Stone Park, Westchester. 🖳✋

Rolling Meadows District 3 *Felony, Civil Under $100,000, Eviction, Small Claims* www.cookcountyclerkofcourt.org 2121 Euclid Ave, Rolling Meadows, IL 60008-1566. 8:30AM-4:30PM. **847-818-3000**, Civil: 847-818-2300, Crim: 847-818-2928. Arlington Hgts, Barrington, Bartlett, Bensonville, Buffalo Grove, Elgin, Elk Grove Village, Hanover Pk, Harwood Hgts, Inverness, Mt. Prospect, Norridge, Palatine, Prospect Hgts, Rolling Meadows, Roselle, Rosemont, Schaumburg, Schiller Pk, Wheeling. 🖳✋

Bridgeview District 5 *Felony, Civil Action Under $100,000, Eviction, Small Claims* www.cookcountyclerkofcourt.org 10220 S 76th Ave, Rm 121 Bridgeview Court Bldg, Bridgeview, IL 60453. 8:30-4:30PM. Civil: 708-974-6500, Crim: 708-974-6422. Alsip, Bridgeview, Burbank, Countryside, Evergreen Pk, Forest View, Hickory Hills, Hinsdale, Hodgkins, Hometown, Justice, Lagrange, Lemont, Lyons, McCook, Oak Lawn, Orland Hills, Palos Park, Stickney, Summit, West Haven, Willow Springs, Worth. 🖳✋

Markham District 6 *Felony, Misdemeanor, Civil Action Under $30,000, Eviction, Small Claims, Traffic* www.cookcountyclerkofcourt.org 16501 S Kedzie Pkwy Rm119, Markham, IL 60426-5509. 8:30AM-4:30PM. **708-210-4262**, Civil: 708-210-4227, Crim: 708-

210-4588. Blue Is, Burnham, Calumet, Chicago Hgts, Crestwood, Crete, Dixmoor, Dolton, Flossmoor, Glenwood, Harvey, Hazelcrest, Homewood, Lansing, Lynwood, Markham, Matteson, Midlothian, Oak Forest, Posen, Riverdale, Robbins, Sauk Village, Tinley Pk. ⊠🖳✋

Skokie District 2 *Misdemeanor, Civil Action Under $100,000, Eviction, Small Claims* www.cookcountyclerkofcourt.org Skokie Court Bldg, Rm 136 5600 Old Orchard Rd, Skokie, IL 60076-1023. 8:30AM-4:30PM. **847-470-7250**. Deerfield, Des Plaines, Evanston, Glencoe, Glenview, Golf, Kenilworth, Lincolnwood, Morton Grove, Niles, Northbrook, Northfield, Park Ridge, Prospect Heights, Skokie, Wilmette, Winnetka. ⊠🖳✋

Crawford County

Circuit Court *Felony, Misdemeanor, Civil, Eviction, Small Claims, Probate* PO Box 655, Robinson, IL 62454-0655. 8AM-4PM. **618-544-3512**, Fax: 618-546-5628. Fax⊠✋

Cumberland County

Circuit Court *Felony, Misdemeanor, Civil, Eviction, Small Claims, Probate* PO Box 145, Toledo, IL 62468. 8AM-4PM. **217-849-3601**, Fax: 217-849-2655. ☎Fax⊠✋

De Kalb County

Circuit Court *Felony, Misdemeanor, Civil, Eviction, Small Claims, Probate* www.co.kane.il.us/judicial/ 133 W State St, Sycamore, IL 60178. 8:30AM-4:30PM. Fax: 815-895-7140. Civil phone: 815-895-7131, Crim: 815-895-7138. ⊠✋🖳

De Witt County

Circuit Court *Felony, Misdemeanor, Civil, Eviction, Small Claims, Probate* 201 Washington St, Clinton, IL 61727. 8:30AM-4:30PM. **217-935-2195**, Fax: 217-935-3310. ⊠Fax✋

Douglas County

Circuit Court *Felony, Misdemeanor, Civil, Eviction, Small Claims, Probate* PO Box 50, Tuscola, IL 61953. 8:30AM-4:30PM. **217-253-2352**, Crim: 217-253-2353 -Traffic. ⊠✋

Key: Symbols refer to criminal records access unless otherwise noted.   phone-☎   mail-⊠   fax-**Fax**   in person-✋   online-🖳   email-**Email**

Du Page County

Circuit Court *Felony, Misdemeanor, Civil, Eviction, Small Claims, Probate* www.co.dupage.il.us/courtclerk/ 505 N County Farm Rd, Wheaton, IL 60187. 8:30AM-4:30PM. **630-407-8700**, Fax: 630-682-7082. Civil phone: 630-682-7100, Crim: 630-682-7080/630-407-8600. ⊠ ⍦

Edgar County

Circuit Court *Felony, Misdemeanor, Civil, Eviction, Small Claims, Probate* County Courthouse 115 W Court, Paris, IL 61944. 8AM-4PM. **217-466-7447**. ⍦

Edwards County

Circuit Court *Felony, Misdemeanor, Civil, Eviction, Small Claims, Probate* County Courthouse, Albion, IL 62806. 8AM-4PM. **618-445-2016**, Fax: 618-445-4943. ⊠ ⍦

Effingham County

Circuit Court *Felony, Misdemeanor, Civil, Small Claims, Probate* 100 E Jefferson PO Box 586, Effingham, IL 62401. 8AM-4PM. **217-342-4065**, Fax: 217-342-6183. ⊠ ⍦

Fayette County

Circuit Court *Felony, Misdemeanor, Civil, Eviction, Small Claims, Probate* 221 S 7th St, Vandalia, IL 62471. 8AM-4PM. **618-283-5009**. ☎ ⊠ Fax ⍦

Ford County

Circuit Court *Felony, Misdemeanor, Civil, Eviction, Small Claims, Probate* 200 W State St, Paxton, IL 60957. 8:30AM-4:30PM. **217-379-2641**, Fax: 217-379-3445. ⊠ Fax ⍦

Franklin County

Circuit Court *Felony, Misdemeanor, Civil, Small Claims, Probate, Entry and Detainer, Traffic* County Courthouse PO Box 485, Benton, IL 62812. 8AM-4PM. Civil: 618-439-2011. Traffic 618-438-6731 ⊠ ⍦

Fulton County

Circuit Court *Felony, Misdemeanor, Civil, Eviction, Small Claims, Probate* PO Box 152, Lewistown, IL 61542. 8AM-4PM. **309-547-3041**, Fax: 309-547-3674. ⊠ ⍦

Gallatin County

Circuit Court *Felony, Misdemeanor, Civil, Eviction, Small Claims, Probate* County Courthouse PO Box 249, Shawneetown, IL 62984. 8AM-N, 1-4PM. **618-269-3140**, Fax: 618-269-4324. Fax ⊠ ⍦

Greene County

Circuit Court *Felony, Misdemeanor, Civil, Eviction, Small Claims, Probate* 519 N Main, County Courthouse, Carrollton, IL 62016. 8AM-4PM. **217-942-3421**, Fax: 217-942-5431. ☎ Fax ⊠ ⍦

Grundy County

Circuit Court *Felony, Misdemeanor, Civil, Eviction, Small Claims, Probate* PO Box 707, Morris, IL 60450. 8AM-4:30PM. **815-941-3256**, Fax: 815-941-3265. ⊠ ⍦

Hamilton County

Circuit Court *Felony, Misdemeanor, Civil, Eviction, Small Claims, Probate* County Courthouse, McLeansboro, IL 62859. 8AM-4:30PM. **618-643-3224**, Fax: 618-643-3455. ⊠ ⍦

Hancock County

Circuit Court *Felony, Misdemeanor, Civil, Eviction, Small Claims, Probate* PO Box 189 500 Main St, #8, Carthage, IL 62321. 8AM-4PM. **217-357-2616**, Fax: 217-357-2231. ☎ Fax ⊠ ⍦

Hardin County

Circuit Court *Felony, Misdemeanor, Civil, Eviction, Small Claims, Probate* PO Box 308 County Courthouse, Main & Market Sts, Elizabethtown, IL 62931. 8AM-4PM. **618-287-2735**, Fax: 618-287-2713. ⊠ Fax ⍦

Henderson County

Circuit Court *Felony, Misdemeanor, Civil, Eviction, Small Claims, Probate* www.9thjudicial.org/ County Courthouse PO Box 546, Oquawka, IL 61469. 8AM-4PM. **309-867-3121**, Fax: 309-867-3207. ☎ ⊠ ⍦

Henry County

Circuit Court *Felony, Misdemeanor, Civil, Eviction, Small Claims, Probate* PO Box 9 Henry County Courthouse, Cambridge, IL 61238. 8AM-4:30PM. **309-937-3572**. ⊠ ⍦ 🖥

Iroquois County

Circuit Court *Felony, Misdemeanor, Civil, Eviction, Small Claims, Probate* 550 S 10th St, Watseka, IL 60970. 8:30AM-4:30PM. **815-432-6950 (6952 Traff) (6991 Ch Supp)**, Fax: 815-432-6953. Access criminal records. Fax ⊠ ⍦

Jackson County

Circuit Court *Felony, Misdemeanor, Civil, Eviction, Small Claims, Probate* www.circuitclerk.co.jackson.il.us PO Drawer 730 County Courthouse, 1001 Walnut, Murphysboro, IL 62966. 8AM-4PM. **618-687-7300**. ⊠ ⍦ 🖥

Jasper County

Circuit Court *Felony, Misdemeanor, Civil, Eviction, Small Claims, Probate* 100 W Jourdan St, Newton, IL 62448. 8AM-4PM. **618-783-2524**. Access ⊠ ⍦

Jefferson County

Circuit Court *Felony, Misdemeanor, Civil, Eviction, Small Claims, Probate* PO Box 1266, Mt Vernon, IL 62864. 8AM-5PM. **618-244-8008**, Fax: 618-244-8029. ☎ Fax ⊠ ⍦

Jersey County

Circuit Court *Felony, Misdemeanor, Civil, Eviction, Small Claims, Probate* 201 W Pearl St, Jerseyville, IL 62052. 8:30AM-4:30PM. **618-498-5571**, Fax: 618-498-6128. Fax ⊠ ⍦

Jo Daviess County

Circuit Court *Felony, Misdemeanor, Civil, Eviction, Small Claims, Probate* 330 N Bench St, Galena, IL 61036. 8AM-4PM. **815-777-2295/0037**. ⊠ ⍦ 🖥

Johnson County

Circuit Court *Felony, Misdemeanor, Civil, Eviction, Small Claims, Probate* PO Box 517, Vienna, IL 62995. 8AM-4PM. **618-658-4751**, Fax: 618-658-2908. ⊠ ⍦

Kane County

Circuit Court *Felony, Misdemeanor, Civil, Eviction, Small Claims, Probate* www.cic.co.kane.il.us/ PO Box 112, Geneva, IL 60134. 8:30AM-4:30PM. **630-232-3413**, Fax: 630-208-2172. Civil phone: 630-208-3323, Crim: 630-208-3319. ☎ Fax ⊠ ⍦ 🖥

Kankakee County

Circuit Court *Felony, Misdemeanor, Civil, Eviction, Small Claims, Probate* 450 E Court St, County Courthouse, Kankakee, IL 60901. 8:30AM-4:30PM. **815-937-2905**, Fax 815-939-8830. ✉️🖐️

Kendall County

Circuit Court *Felony, Misdemeanor, Civil, Eviction, Small Claims, Probate* PO Drawer M 807 W John St, Yorkville, IL 60560. 8AM-4:30PM. **630-553-4183**, Civil phone: 630-553-4183, Crim: 630-553-4184. Traffic/DUI: 630-553-4185. ✉️🖐️🖥️

Knox County

Circuit Court *Felony, Misdemeanor, Civil, Eviction, Small Claims, Probate* County Courthouse, Galesburg, IL 61401. 8:30AM-4:30PM. **309-345-3817**, Fax: 309-345-0098. **Fax**✉️🖐️

Lake County

Circuit Court *Felony, Misdemeanor, Civil, Eviction, Small Claims, Probate* www.19thcircuitcourt.state.il.us 18 N County St, Waukegan, IL 60085. 8:30AM-5PM. **847-377-3600 (Admin.)**, Civil: 847-377-3209, Crim: 847-377-3211. by✉️🖐️

La Salle County

Circuit Court - Civil Division *Civil, Eviction, Small Claims, Probate* PO Box 617 111 W Madison St, Ottawa, IL 61350-0617. 8AM-4:30PM. Fax: 815-433-9198. Civil phone: 815-434-8671, Crim: 815-434-8271 Access civil records by✉️**Fax**🖥️🖐️.

Circuit Court - Criminal Div. *Felony, Misdemeanor* www.lasallecounty.com 707 Etna Rd, #141, Ottawa, IL 61360. 8AM-4:30PM. **815-434-8271**, Fax: 815-434-8299. Civil phone: 815-434-8671. 🖐️

Lawrence County

Circuit Court *Felony, Misdemeanor, Civil, Eviction, Small Claims, Probate* County Courthouse 1100 State St, Lawrenceville, IL 62439. 8AM-4PM. **618-943-2815**, Fax 618-943-5205. ✉️🖐️

Lee County

Circuit Court *Felony, Misdemeanor, Civil, Eviction, Small Claims, Probate* 309 S Galena, #320, Dixon, IL 61021. 8:30-4:30PM. **815-284-5234**. ✉️🖐️🖥️

Livingston County

Circuit Court *Felony, Misdemeanor, Civil, Eviction, Small Claims, Probate* 112 W Madison St, Pontiac, IL 61764. 8AM-4:30PM. **815-844-2602**. ✉️🖐️

Logan County

Circuit Court *Felony, Misdemeanor, Civil, Eviction, Small Claims, Probate* www.co.logan.il.us/circuit_clerk/ County Courthouse PO Box 158, Lincoln, IL 62656. 8:30AM-4:30PM. **217-732-2376**, Fax: 217-732-1231; 732-1232 civ.fax. Civil phone: 217-735-1163. ✉️**Fax**🖐️🖥️

McDonough County

Circuit Court *Felony, Misdemeanor, Civil, Eviction, Small Claims, Probate* County Courthouse #1 Courthouse Sq, Macomb, IL 61455. 8AM-4PM. **309-837-4889**, Fax: 309-833-4493. ☎️**Fax**✉️🖐️

McHenry County

Circuit Court *Felony, Misdemeanor, Civil, Eviction, Small Claims, Probate* www.mchenrycircuitclerk.org 2200 N Seminary Ave, Woodstock, IL 60098. 8AM-4:30PM. **815-334-4307**, Fax: 815-338-8583. ☎️**Fax**✉️🖥️🖐️

McLean County

Circuit Court *Felony, Misdemeanor, Civil, Eviction, Small Claims, Probate* www.mcleancountyil.gov/ Attn: Clerk PO Box 2420, Bloomington, IL 61702-2420. 8:30AM-4:30PM. **309-888-5301**, Civil: 309-888-5341, Crim: 309-888-5321. ✉️🖐️🖥️

Macon County

Circuit Court *Felony, Misdemeanor, Civil, Eviction, Small Claims, Probate* www.court.co.macon.il.us 253 E Wood St, Decatur, IL 62523. 8AM-4:30PM. Fax: 217-424-1350. Civil phone: 217-424-1454, Crim: 217-421-0272, Probate: 217-424-1455. **Fax**✉️🖥️🖐️

Macoupin County

Circuit Court *Felony, Misdemeanor, Civil, Eviction, Small Claims, Probate* PO Box 197, Carlinville, IL 62626. 8:30AM-4:30PM. **217-854-3211**, Fax: 217-854-7361. ✉️🖐️

Madison County

Circuit Court *Felony, Misdemeanor, Civil, Eviction, Small Claims, Probate* www.co.madison.il.us 155 N Main St, Edwardsville, IL 62025. 8:30AM-4:30PM. **618-692-6240**, Fax: 618-692-0676. ✉️🖐️🖥️

Marion County

Circuit Court *Felony, Misdemeanor, Civil, Eviction, Small Claims, Probate* PO Box 130 100 E Main, Salem, IL 62881. 8AM-4PM. **618-548-3856**, Fax: 618-548-2358. 🖐️

Marshall County

Circuit Court *Felony, Misdemeanor, Civil, Eviction, Small Claims, Probate* PO Box 328, Lacon, IL 61540-0328. 8:30AM-N, 1-4:30PM. **309-246-6435**, Fax: 309-246-2173. Access by ✉️🖐️

Mason County

Circuit Court *Felony, Misdemeanor, Civil, Eviction, Small Claims, Probate* www.masoncountyil.org/ 125 N Plum, Havana, IL 62644. 8AM-4PM. **309-543-6619**, Fax: 309-543-4214. ✉️🖐️

Massac County

Circuit Court *Felony, Misdemeanor, Civil, Eviction, Small Claims, Probate* PO Box 152 Courthhouse Square, Metropolis, IL 62960. 8AM-N, 1-4PM. **618-524-9359**, Fax 618-524-4850. ✉️🖐️

Menard County

Circuit Court *Felony, Misdemeanor, Civil, Eviction, Small Claims, Probate* PO Box 466, Petersburg, IL 62675. 8:30AM-4:30PM. **217-632-2615**. ✉️🖐️

Mercer County

Circuit Court *Felony, Misdemeanor, Civil, Eviction, Small Claims, Probate* www.mercercountyil.org PO Box 175, Aledo, IL 61231. 8-4PM. **309-582-7122**, Fax: 309-582-7121. ☎️**Fax**✉️🖐️🖥️

Monroe County

Circuit Court *Felony, Misdemeanor, Civil, Eviction, Small Claims, Probate* 100 S Main St, Waterloo, IL 62298. 8AM-4:30PM. **618-939-8681**, Fax: 618-939-1929. Civil phone: x274, Crim: x273, Probate: x274. ☎️**Fax**✉️🖐️

Montgomery County

Circuit Court *Felony, Misdemeanor, Civil, Eviction, Small Claims, Probate* www.courts.montgomery.k12.il.us County Courthouse, PO Box C, Hillsboro, IL 62049. 8-4PM. **217-532-9546**. ✉️🖥️🖐️

Key: Symbols refer to criminal records access unless otherwise noted. phone-☎️ mail-✉️ fax-**Fax** in person-🖐️ online-🖥️ email-**Email**

Morgan County

Circuit Court *Felony, Misdemeanor, Civil, Eviction, Small Claims, Probate* 300 W State St, Jacksonville, IL 62650. 8:30AM-4:30PM. **217-243-5419**, Fax: 217-243-2009. ✉🖑

Moultrie County

Circuit Court *Felony, Misdemeanor, Civil, Eviction, Small Claims, Probate* www.circuit-clerk.moultrie.il.us 10 S Main, #7 Moultrie County Courthouse, Sullivan, IL 61951. 8:30AM-4:30PM. **217-728-4622**. ✉🖑

Ogle County

Circuit Court *Felony, Misdemeanor, Civil, Eviction, Small Claims, Probate* www.oglecounty.org/marty/circuitclerk.html PO Box 337, Oregon, IL 61061. 8:30AM-4:30PM. **815-732-1130**, Civil: 815-732-1130, Crim: 815-732-1140. ✉💻🖑

Peoria County

Circuit Court *Felony, Misdemeanor, Civil, Eviction, Small Claims, Probate* 324 Main St, Peoria, IL 61602. 8:30AM-5PM. **309-672-6953**, Fax: 309-677-6228. ☎✉🖑

Perry County

Circuit Court *Felony, Misdemeanor, Civil, Eviction, Small Claims, Probate* PO Box 219, Pinckneyville, IL 62274. 8AM-4PM. **618-357-6726**. Access ✉🖑

Piatt County

Circuit Court *Felony, Misdemeanor, Civil, Eviction, Small Claims, Probate* www.chittendensuperiorcourt.com/ PO Box 288, Monticello, IL 61856. 8:30AM-4:30PM. **217-762-4966**, Fax: 217-762-8394. ☎Fax✉🖑

Pike County

Circuit Court *Felony, Misdemeanor, Civil, Eviction, Small Claims, Probate* Pike County Courthouse 100 E Washington St, Pittsfield, IL 62363. 8:30AM-4:30PM. **217-285-6612**, Fax: 217-285-4726. ✉🖑💻

Pope County

Circuit Court *Felony, Misdemeanor, Civil, Eviction, Small Claims, Probate* PO Box 438, Golconda, IL 62938. 8AM-4PM. **618-683-3941**, Fax: 618-683-3018. ☎Fax✉🖑

Pulaski County

Circuit Court *Felony, Misdemeanor, Civil, Eviction, Small Claims, Probate* PO Box 88 500 Illinois Ave, Rm C, Mound City, IL 62963. 8AM-4PM. **618-748-9300**, Fax: 618-748-9329. ✉🖑

Putnam County

Circuit Court *Felony, Misdemeanor, Civil, Eviction, Small Claims, Probate* 120 N 4th St, Hennepin, IL 61327. 9AM-4PM. **815-925-7016**, Fax: 815-925-7492. ✉🖑

Randolph County

Circuit Court *Felony, Misdemeanor, Civil, Eviction, Small Claims, Probate* County Courthouse, Rm 302, Chester, IL 62233. 8AM-4PM. **618-826-5000 X194**, Fax: 618-826-3761. ✉🖑

Richland County

Circuit Court *Felony, Misdemeanor, Civil, Eviction, Small Claims, Probate* 103 W Main, #21, Olney, IL 62450. 8AM-4PM. **618-392-2151**, Fax: 618-392-5041. ✉🖑

Rock Island County

Circuit Court *Felony, Misdemeanor, Civil, Eviction, Small Claims, Probate* www.co.rock-island.il.us/Government/CircuitClk/CircuitClk.html PO Box 5230 (210 15th St), Rock Island, IL 61204-5230. 8AM-4:30PM. **309-786-4451**, Fax: 309-786-3029. ✉💻🖑

St. Clair County

Circuit Court *Felony, Misdemeanor, Civil, Eviction, Small Claims, Probate* 10 Public Square, Belleville, IL 62220-1623. 8AM-4PM. **618-277-6832**, Crim: Extension #4 for felony. Access by ✉🖑

Saline County

Circuit Court *Felony, Misdemeanor, Civil, Eviction, Small Claims, Probate* County Courthouse, Harrisburg, IL 62946. 8AM-4PM. **618-253-5096**, Fax: 618-252-3904. Fax✉🖑

Sangamon County

Circuit Court *Felony, Misdemeanor, Civil, Eviction, Small Claims, Probate* www.co.sangamon.il.us/court/ 200 S 9th St, Rm 405, Springfield, IL 62701. 8:30AM-4:30PM. **217-753-6674**, Fax: 217-753-6665. Fax✉🖑💻

Schuyler County

Circuit Court *Felony, Misdemeanor, Civil, Eviction, Small Claims, Probate* PO Box 80, Rushville, IL 62681. 8AM-4PM. **217-322-4633**, Fax: 217-322-6164. ✉🖑

Scott County

Circuit Court *Felony, Misdemeanor, Civil, Eviction, Small Claims, Probate* 35 E Market St, Winchester, IL 62694. 8AM-N, 1-4PM. **217-742-5217**, Fax: 217-742-5853. ✉🖑

Shelby County

Circuit Court *Felony, Misdemeanor, Civil, Eviction, Small Claims, Probate* County Courthouse PO Box 469, Shelbyville, IL 62565. 8AM-4PM. **217-774-4212**, Fax: 217-774-4109. Fax✉🖑

Stark County

Circuit Court *Felony, Misdemeanor, Civil, Eviction, Small Claims, Probate* 130 W Main St, Toulon, IL 61483. 8:30AM-4:30PM. **309-286-5941**. ✉🖑

Stephenson County

Circuit Court *Felony, Misdemeanor, Civil, Eviction, Small Claims, Probate* www.judici.com PO Box 785, Freeport, IL 61032. 8:30AM-4:30PM. **815-235-8266**. ✉🖑💻

Tazewell County

Circuit Court *Felony, Misdemeanor, Civil, Small Claims, Probate* Courthouse, 4th & Court Sts, Pekin, IL 61554. 8:30AM-5PM. **309-477-2214**. ✉🖑

Union County

Circuit Court *Felony, Misdemeanor, Civil, Eviction, Small Claims, Probate* Union County Courthouse 309 W Market, Rm 101, Jonesboro, IL 62952. 8AM-N,1-4PM. **618-833-5913**, Fax: 618-833-5223. Fax✉🖑💻

Vermilion County

Circuit Court *Felony, Misdemeanor, Civil, Eviction, Small Claims, Probate* 7 N Vermilion, Danville, IL 61832. 8:30AM-4:30PM. **217-554-7700**, Fax: 217-554-7728. ☎✉🖑💻

Wabash County

Circuit Court *Felony, Misdemeanor, Civil, Eviction, Small Claims, Probate* PO Box 997, 401 Market St, Mt Carmel,

IL 62863. 8AM-5PM. **618-262-5362**, Fax: 618-263-4441. ✉ ✋

Warren County

Circuit Court *Felony, Misdemeanor, Civil, Eviction, Small Claims, Probate* 100 W Broadway, Monmouth, IL 61462. 8AM-4:30PM. **309-734-5179**. ✉ ✋

Washington County

Circuit Court *Felony, Misdemeanor, Civil, Eviction, Small Claims, Probate* 101 E St Louis St, Nashville, IL 62263. 8AM-4PM. **618-327-4800 X305**, Fax: 618-327-3583. ✉ ✋

Wayne County

Circuit Court *Felony, Misdemeanor, Civil, Small Claims, Probate* County Courthouse 307 E Main St, Fairfield, IL 62837. 8AM-4:30PM. **618-842-7684**, Fax: 618-842-2556. ✉**Fax** ✋

White County

Circuit Court *Felony, Misdemeanor, Civil, Small Claims, Probate* PO Box 310 301 E Main, County Courthouse, Carmi, IL 62821. 8AM-4PM. **618-382-2321 x4**, Fax: 618-382-2322. Access by **Fax**✉ ✋

Whiteside County

Circuit Court *Felony, Misdemeanor, Civil, Eviction, Small Claims, Probate* 200 E Knox St, Morrison, IL 61270-2698. 8:30AM-4:30PM. **815-772-5188**, Fax: 815-772-5187. ☎**Fax**✉ ✋ 💻

Will County

Circuit Court *Felony, Misdemeanor, Civil, Eviction, Small Claims, Probate* www.willcountycircuitcourt.com 14 W Jefferson St, #212, Joliet, IL 60432. 8:30AM-4:30PM. **815-727-8592**, Fax: 815-727-8896. **Fax**✉ ✋ 💻

Williamson County

Circuit Court *Felony, Misdemeanor, Civil, Eviction, Small Claims, Probate* 200 W Jefferson St, Marion, IL 62959. 8AM-4PM. **618-997-1301 X153**. ✉ ✋

Winnebago County

Circuit Court *Felony, Misdemeanor, Civil, Eviction, Small Claims, Probate* www.cc.co.winnebago.il.us 400 W State St, Rockford, IL 61101. 8AM-5PM. **815-978-3031 (records)**, Fax: 815-987-3012. Civil phone: 815-987-2510, Crim: 815-987-3079/3175. Criminal records Rm 108. Civil in Rm 104. ☎ ✉ ✋ 💻

Woodford County

Circuit Court *Felony, Misdemeanor, Civil, Eviction, Small Claims, Probate* County Courthouse PO Box 284, 115 N Main, #201, Eureka, IL 61530. 8AM-5PM. **309-467-3312**. Access by ✉ ✋

Indiana

State Court Administration: State Court Administrator, 115 W Washington St, #1080, Indianapolis, IN, 46204; 317-232-2542, Fax: 317-232-6856. www.in.gov/judiciary

Court Structure: There are 92 judicial circuits with Circuit Courts or Combined Circuit and Superior Courts. In addition, there are 48 City Courts and 25 Town Courts. County Courts are gradually being restructured into divisions of the Superior Courts. Note that Small Claims in Marion County are heard at the township and records are maintained at that level. The phone number for the township offices are indicated in Marion County.

Online Access: There is no statewide trial court records service available. However, the website above gives free access to an index of docket information for Supreme, Appeals, and Tax Court cases.

Additional Information: The Circuit Court Clerk/County Clerk in every county is the same individual and is responsible for keeping all county judicial records. However, it is recommended that, when requesting a record, the request indicate which court heard the case (Circuit, Superior, or County). Many courts are no longer performing searches, especially criminal searches, based on a 7/8/96 statement by the State Board of Accounts.

Adams County

Circuit & Superior Court *Felony, Misdemeanor, Civil, Eviction, Small Claims, Probate* 112 S 2nd St, Decatur, IN 46733. 8AM-4:30PM. **260-724-5309**, Fax: 260-724-5313. ✋

Allen County

Circuit & Superior Court *Felony, Misdemeanor, Civil, Eviction, Small Claims, Probate* www.co.allen.in.us 715 S Calhoun St, Rm 200, Courthouse, Ft Wayne, IN 46802. 8AM-4:30PM. **260-449-7245**. ✋

Bartholomew County

Circuit & Superior Court *Felony, Misd., Civil, Eviction, Small Claims, Probate* www.bartholomewco.com/ PO Box 924, Columbus, IN 47202-0924. 8AM-5PM. **812-379-1600**, Fax: 812-379-1675. **Fax**✉ ✋ 💻

Benton County

Circuit Court *Felony, Misdemeanor, Civil, Eviction, Small Claims, Probate* www.bentoncounty.org 706 E 5th St, #37, Fowler, IN 47944-1556. 8:30AM-4PM. **765-884-0930** Fax765-884-0322✉ ✋**Fax**

Blackford County

Circuit & Superior Court *Felony, Misdemeanor, Civil, Eviction, Small Claims, Probate* 110 W Washington St, Hartford City, IN 47348. 8AM-4PM. **765-348-1130**. ✉ ✋

Boone County

Circuit & Superior Court I & II *Felony, Misd., Civil, Eviction, Small Claims, Probate* www.bccn.boone.in.us/bccn/Boone_Clerk.html Rm 212, Courthouse Sq, Lebanon, IN 46052. 7AM-4PM. **765-482-3510**. ✉ ✋

Key: Symbols refer to criminal records access unless otherwise noted.   phone-☎   mail-✉   fax-**Fax**   in person-✋   online-💻   email-**Email**

Brown County

Circuit Court *Felony, Misdemeanor, Civil, Eviction, Small Claims, Probate* Box 85, Nashville, IN 47448. 8AM-4PM. **812-988-5510**, Fax: 812-988-5515. ✍

Carroll County

Circuit & Superior Court *Felony, Misdemeanor, Civil, Eviction, Small Claims, Probate* Courthouse, 101 W Main, Delphi, IN 46923. 8AM-5PM M,T,Th,F; 8AM-N Wed. **765-564-4485**, Fax: 765-564-1835. ✍

Cass County

Circuit & Superior Court *Felony, Misdemeanor, Civil, Eviction, Small Claims, Probate* 200 Court Park, Logansport, IN 46947. 8AM-4PM. **574-753-7730**. ✉ ✍

Clark County

Circuit, Superior & County Court *Felony, Misd., Civil, Eviction, Small Claims, Probate* www.clarkprosecutor.org/html/courts/courts.htm 501 E Court, Rm 137, Jeffersonville, IN 47130. 8:30AM-4:30 M-F, 8:30-N Sat. **812-285-6244**. ✍

Clay County

Circuit & Superior Court *Felony, Misdemeanor, Civil, Eviction, Small Claims, Probate* 609 E National Ave, #213, Brazil, IN 47834. 8AM-4PM. **812-448-9024**. ✉ ✍

Clinton County

Circuit & Superior Court *Felony, Misdemeanor, Civil, Eviction, Small Claims, Probate* 265 Courthouse Square, Frankfort, IN 46041. 8AM-4PM M-TH,8AM-5PM F; 8/AM-12PM Thur. **765-659-6335**. ✍ 🖳

Crawford County

Circuit Court *Felony, Misdemeanor, Civil, Eviction, Small Claims, Probate* Box 375, English, IN 47118. 8AM-4PM M,F; 8AM-6PM T-Th. **812-338-2565**, Fax: 812-338-2507. **Fax**✉ ✍

Daviess County

Circuit & Superior Court *Felony, Misdemeanor, Civil, Eviction, Small Claims, Probate* PO Box 739, Washington, IN 47501. 8AM-4PM. **812-254-8664**, Fax: 812-254-8698. Civil phone: 812-254-8664, Crim: 812-254-8669, Probate: 812-254-8664. ✉ ✍ 🖳

Dearborn County

Circuit & Superior Court *Felony, Misd., Civil, Eviction, Small Claims, Probate* www.dearborncounty.org/datafiles/judges.html Courthouse 215 W High St, Lawrenceburg, IN 47025. 8:30AM-4:30PM. **812-537-8867**, Fax: 812-532-2021. ✍

Decatur County

Circuit & Superior Court *Felony, Misd., Civil, Eviction, Small Claims, Probate* www.decaturcounty.in.gov 150 Courthouse Square, #244, Greensburg, IN 47240. 8AM-4PM, 8AM-5PM F. **812-663-8223/8642**, Fax: 812-663-8642. ✉ ✍

DeKalb County

Circuit & Superior Court *Felony, Misdemeanor, Civil, Eviction, Small Claims, Probate* PO Box 230, Auburn, IN 46706. 8:30AM-4:30PM. **219-925-0912**, Fax: 219-925-5126. ✍

Delaware County

Circuit Court *Felony, Misdemeanor, Civil, Small Claims, Probate* www.dcclerk.org Box 1089, Muncie, IN 47308. 8:30AM-4:30PM. **765-747-7726**, Fax: 765-747-7768. ✍ 🖳

Dubois County

Circuit & Superior Court *Felony, Misdemeanor, Civil, Eviction, Small Claims, Probate* 1 Courthouse Square, Jasper, IN 47546. 8AM-4PM. **812-481-7070/7035/7020**, Fax: 812-481-7030. ✍

Elkhart County

Goshen Circuit & Superior Courts 3, 4 *Felony, Misd., Civil, Eviction, Small Claims, Probate* www.elkhartcountyindiana.com/administrative/clerk.html Courthouse, 101 N Main St, Goshen, IN 46526. 8AM-5PM M, 8AM-4PM T-F. **574-535-6431**, Fax: 574-535-6471. Includes Circuit Court (Rm 204) and Superior Court 3 (Rm 205, 535-6438) and 4 (Rm 105, 535-6403). Access by ✍ 🖳

Elkhart Superior Courts 1, 2, 5, 6 *Felony, Misd., Civil, Eviction, Small Claims, Probate* www.elkhartcountyindiana.com/administrative/clerk.html 315 S 2nd St, Elkhart, IN 46516. 8AM-4PM T-F, 8AM-5PM M. **574-523-2233/2305/2007**, Fax: 574-523-2323. ✍ 🖳

Fayette County

Circuit & Superior Court *Felony, Misdemeanor, Civil, Eviction, Small* Claims, Probate www.co.fayette.in.us PO Box 607, Connersville, IN 47331-0607. 8:30AM-4PM (5PM on Wed). **765-825-1813**. ✍

Floyd County

Circuit, Superior & County Court *Felony, Misdemeanor, Civil, Eviction, Small Claims, Probate* Box 1056, City County Bldg, New Albany, IN 47150. 8AM-4PM. **812-948-5414**, Fax: 812-948-4711. ✉ ✍

Fountain County

Circuit Court *Felony, Misdemeanor, Civil, Eviction, Small Claims, Probate* Box 183, Covington, IN 47932. 8AM-4PM. **765-793-2192**, Fax: 765-793-5002. ✉ ✍

Franklin County

Circuit Court *Felony, Misdemeanor, Civil, Eviction, Small Claims, Probate* 459 Main, Brookville, IN 47012. 8:30AM-4PM. **765-647-5111**, Fax: 765-647-3224. ✍

Fulton County

Circuit Court *Felony, Misdemeanor, Civil, Eviction, Small Claims, Probate* 815 Main St, PO Box 524, Rochester, IN 46975. 8AM-4PM M-TH, 8AM-5PM F. **574-223-2911**, Fax 574-223-8304. ✉ ✍

Gibson County

Circuit & Superior Court *Felony, Misdemeanor, Civil, Eviction, Small Claims, Probate* Courthouse PO Box 630, Princeton, IN 47670. 8AM-4PM. **812-386-6474**, Fax: 812-386-5025. ✍

Grant County

Circuit & Superior Court *Felony, Misdemeanor, Civil, Eviction, Small Claims, Probate* www.grantcounty.net Courthouse 101 E 4th St, Marion, IN 46952. 8AM-4PM. **765-668-8121**, Fax: 765-668-6541. ✍

Greene County

Circuit & Superior Court *Felony, Misdemeanor, Civil, Eviction, Small Claims, Probate* PO Box 229, Bloomfield, IN 47424. 8AM-4PM. **812-384-8532**, Fax: 812-384-8458. ✍

Hamilton County

Circuit & Superior Court *Felony, Misdemeanor, Civil, Eviction, Small Claims, Probate* www.co.hamilton.in.us One Hamilton County Square, #106,

Noblesville, IN 46060-2233. 8AM-4:30PM. **317-776-9629**, Fax: 317-776-9727. ✋

Hancock County

Circuit & Superior Court *Felony, Misdemeanor, Civil, Eviction, Small Claims, Probate* 9 E Main St, Rm 201, Greenfield, IN 46140. 8AM-4PM. **317-477-1109**, Fax: 317-462-1163. ✋

Harrison County

Circuit Court *Civil, Eviction, Probate* 300 N Capitol, Corydon, IN 47112. 8AM-4:30PM. **812-738-4289**. ✉✋

Superior Court *Felony, Misdemeanor, Small Claims* 1445 Gardner Ln, #3126, Corydon, IN 47112. 8AM-4:30PM. **812-738-8149**, Fax: 812-738-2459. ✋

Hendricks County

Circuit & Superior Court *Felony, Misdemeanor, Civil, Eviction, Small Claims, Probate* PO Box 599, Danville, IN 46122. 8AM-4PM. **317-745-9231**, Fax: 317-745-9306. ✋

Henry County

Circuit & Superior Courts I & II *Felony, Misdemeanor, Civil, Eviction, Small Claims, Probate* PO Box B, New Castle, IN 47362. 8AM-4PM. **765-529-6401**. ✋

Howard County

Circuit & Superior Court *Felony, Misd., Civil, Eviction, Small Claims, Probate* http://co.howard.in.us/clerk1 PO Box 9004, Kokomo, IN 46904. 8AM-4PM. **765-456-2204**, Fax: 765-456-2267. Civil phone: 765-456-2000, Crim: 765-456-2000. Small Claims 765-456-2204. ✋🖥

Huntington County

Circuit & Superior Court *Felony, Misdemeanor, Civil, Eviction, Small Claims, Probate* PO Box 228, Huntington, IN 46750. 8AM-4:30PM. **260-358-4817**, Fax: 260-358-4880. ✋

Jackson County

Circuit Court *Felony, Misdemeanor, Civil, Eviction, Small Claims, Probate* PO Box 318, Brownstown, IN 47220. 8AM-4:30PM. **812-358-6117**, Fax: 812-358-6187. Will not perform searches for private companies. ✋

Superior Court *Felony, Misdemeanor, Civil, Eviction, Small Claims* PO Box 788, Seymour, IN 47274. 8AM-4:30PM. **812-522-9676**, Fax: 812-523-6065. ✋

Jasper County

Circuit Court *Felony, Misdemeanor, Civil, Eviction, Small Claims, Probate* 115 W Washington, Rensselaer, IN 47978. 8AM-4PM. **219-866-4941**, Civil: 219-866-4926, Crim: 219-866-4926, Probate: 218-866-4929. ✉✋

Superior Court *Felony, Misdemeanor, Civil, Eviction, Small Claims* 115 W Washington St, Rensselaer, IN 47978. 8AM-4PM. **219-866-4922**, Civil: 219-866-4922, Crim: 21-866-4922, Probate: 219-866-4912. ✉✋

Jay County

Circuit & Superior Court *Felony, Misdemeanor, Civil, Eviction, Small Claims, Probate* www.co.jay.in.us Courthouse, Portland, IN 47371. 8:30AM-4:30PM. **260-726-4951**. ✉✋🖥

Jefferson County

Circuit & Superior Court *Felony, Misdemeanor, Civil, Eviction, Small Claims, Probate* Courthouse, 300 E Main St, Rm 203, Madison, IN 47250. 8AM-4PM. **812-265-8923**, Fax: 812-265-8950. ✋

Jennings County

Circuit Court *Felony, Misdemeanor, Civil, Eviction, Small Claims, Probate* Courthouse PO Box 385, Vernon, IN 47282. 8AM-4PM. **812-352-3070**. ✋

Johnson County

Circuit & Superior Court *Felony, Misd., Civil, Eviction, Small Claims, Probate* Courthouse, PO Box 368, Franklin, IN 46131. 8AM-4:30PM. **317-736-3708**, Fax: 317-736-3749. Civil phone: 317-736-3708, Crim: 317-736-3986, Probate: 317-736-3913. ☎Fax✉✋🖥

Knox County

Circuit & Superior Court *Felony, Misd., Civil, Eviction, Small Claims, Probate* 101 N 7th St, Vincennes, IN 47591. 8AM-4PM. **812-885-2521**. ✉✋

Kosciusko County

Circuit & Superior Court *Felony, Misdemeanor, Civil, Eviction, Small Claims, Probate* 121 N Lake, Warsaw, IN 46580. 8AM-4:30PM. **574-372-2331**,

Fax: 574-372-2338. Civil phone: 574-372-2331, Crim: 574-372-2457 (1st), 372-2453 (2nd & 3rd). **Fax**✋

LaGrange County

Circuit & Superior Court *Felony, Misdemeanor, Civil, Eviction, Small Claims, Probate* 105 N Detroit St, Courthouse, LaGrange, IN 46761. 8AM-4PM M-TH, 8AM-5PM F. **260-463-3442**, Fax: 260-463-2187. ☎✉✋

Lake County

Circuit & Superior Court *Felony, Misd., Civil, Eviction, Small Claims, Probate* www.lakecountyin.org/index.jsp 2293 N Main St, Courthouse, Crown Point, IN 46307. 8:30AM-4PM. **219-755-3460**, Fax: 219-755-3520. ✉✋

La Porte County

Circuit & Superior Court *Felony, Misdemeanor, Civil, Eviction, Probate* 813 Lincolnway, La Porte, IN 46350. 8:00AM-4PM. **219-326-6808**, Fax: 219-326-6626. ✋

Lawrence County

Circuit, Superior & County Court *Felony, Misdemeanor, Civil, Eviction, Small Claims, Probate* 31 Courthouse 916 15th St, Rm 31, Bedford, IN 47421. 8:30AM-4:30PM. **812-275-7543**, Fax: 812-277-2024. Superior Court I is located at 1410 I St, 812-275-3124. Superior Court II is located at 1420 I St, 812-275-4161. All small claims are filed in Superior II. ✋

Madison County

Circuit, Superior & County Court *Felony, Misd., Civil, Eviction, Small Claims, Probate* http://madisoncty.com/courts/index.html PO Box 1277, Anderson, IN 46015-1277. 8AM-4PM. **765-641-9443**, Fax: 765-640-4203. ✋

Marion County

Circuit & Superior Court *Felony, Misdemeanor, Civil, Probate* www.indygov.org/clerk 200 E Washington St, Indianapolis, IN 46204. 8AM-4:30PM. **317-327-4740**, Civil phone: 317-327-4733, Crim: 317-327-4733. The Municipal Court of Marion County, once separate, is now part of Superior Court. All records now merged. ✉🖥✋

Marshall County

Circuit & Superior Court 1 & 2 *Felony, Misdemeanor, Civil, Eviction, Small Claims, Probate* 211 W Madison St, Plymouth, IN 46563. 8AM-4PM. **574-936-8922**, Fax: 574-936-8893. ✋🖥

Martin County

Circuit Court *Felony, Misdemeanor, Civil, Eviction, Small Claims, Probate* PO Box 120 (111 Main St), Shoals, IN 47581. 8AM-4PM. **812-247-3651**, Fax: 812-247-2791. ✉**Fax**✋

Miami County

Circuit & Superior Court *Felony, Misdemeanor, Civil, Eviction, Small Claims, Probate* PO Box 184, Peru, IN 46970. 8AM-4PM. **765-472-3901**, Fax: 765-472-1778. **Fax**✉✋🖥

Monroe County

Circuit Court *Felony, Misdemeanor, Civil, Eviction, Small Claims, Probate* www.co.monroe.in.us/ PO Box 547, Bloomington, IN 47402. 8AM-4PM. **812-349-2614**, Fax: 812-349-2610. ✉**Fax**✋🖥

Montgomery County

Circuit, Superior & County Court *Felony, Misdemeanor, Civil, Eviction, Small Claims, Probate* www.montgomeryco.net/ PO Box 768, Crawfordsville, IN 47933. 8:30AM-4:30PM. **765-364-6430**, Fax: 765-364-6355. ✉**Fax**✋🖥

Morgan County

Circuit & Superior Court *Felony, Misdemeanor, Civil, Eviction, Small Claims, Probate* PO Box 1556, Martinsville, IN 46151. 8AM-4PM. **765-342-1025**, Fax: 765-342-1111. ✋

Newton County

Circuit & Superior Court *Felony, Misd., Civil, Eviction, Small Claims, Probate* PO Box 49, Kentland, IN 47951. 8AM-4PM. **219-474-6081**. ✉✋

Noble County

Circuit, Superior I & Superior II Court *Felony, Misdemeanor, Civil, Eviction, Small Claims, Probate* 101 N Orange St, Albion, IN 46701. 8AM-4PM. **260-636-2736**, Fax: 260-636-4000. **Fax**✉✋

Ohio County

Circuit & Superior Court *Felony, Misdemeanor, Civil, Eviction, Small Claims, Probate* PO Box 185, Rising Sun, IN 47040. 9AM-4PM M,T,Th,F 9AM-N Sat. **812-438-2610**, Fax: 812-438-1215. ✋

Orange County

Circuit & County Court *Felony, Civil, Eviction, Small Claims, Probate* Courthouse, Court St, Paoli, IN 47454. 8AM-4PM. **812-723-2649**, Fax: 812-723-0239. ✉**Fax**✋

Superior Court *Felony (Class D), Misdemeanor* 205 E Main St, Paoli, IN 47454. 8AM-N, 1-4. **812-723-7134**. ✋

Owen County

Circuit Court *Felony, Misdemeanor, Civil, Eviction, Small Claims, Probate* PO Box 146, Courthouse, Spencer, IN 47460. 8AM-4PM. **812-829-5015**, Fax: 812-829-5147. ✋

Parke County

Circuit Court *Felony, Misdemeanor, Civil, Eviction, Small Claims, Probate* 116 W High St, Rm 204, Rockville, IN 47872. 8AM-4PM. **765-569-5132**. ✋

Perry County

Circuit Court *Felony, Misd., Civil, Eviction, Small Claims, Probate* 2219 Payne St, #219, Courthouse, Tell City, IN 47586. 8AM-4PM. **812-547-3741**. ✋

Pike County

Circuit Court *Felony, Misd., Civil, Eviction, Small Claims, Probate* PO Box 407, Petersburg, IN 47567. 8AM-4PM. **812-354-6025**, Fax 812-354-3552. ✉✋

Porter County

Circuit Court *Felony, Misdemeanor, Civil, Eviction, Small Claims, Probate* www.porterco.org/ Records Division, Courthouse 16 E Lincolnway, Rm 217, Valparaiso, IN 46383-5659. 8:30AM-4:30PM. **219-465-3453**, Fax: 219-465-3592. ✉✋

Superior Court *Misdemeanor, Civil, Small Claims, Probate* 3560 Willow Creek Dr, Portage, IN 46368. 8:30AM-4:30PM. **219-759-2501**. ✉✋

Posey County

Circuit & Superior Court *Felony, Misd., Civil, Eviction, Small Claims, Probate*
http://members.sigecom.net/pcc/ PO Box 606 300 Main St, Mount Vernon, IN 47620-0606. 8AM-4PM. **812-838-1306**, Fax: 812-838-1307. ✋

Pulaski County

Circuit & Superior Court *Felony, Misdemeanor, Civil, Eviction, Small Claims, Probate* 112 E Main, Rm 230, Winamac, IN 46996. 8AM-4PM. **574-946-3313**, Fax: 574-946-4953. ✋

Putnam County

Circuit & Superior Court *Felony, Misdemeanor, Civil, Eviction, Small Claims, Probate* PO Box 546, Greencastle, IN 46135. 8AM-4PM. **765-653-2648**. ✋🖥

Randolph County

Circuit & Superior Court *Felony, Misdemeanor, Civil, Eviction, Small Claims, Probate* PO Box 230 Courthouse, Winchester, IN 47394-0230. 8AM-4PM. **765-584-7070 X231**, Fax: 765-584-2958. **Fax**✉✋🖥

Ripley County

Circuit Court *Felony, Misdemeanor, Civil, Eviction, Small Claims, Probate* PO Box 177, Versailles, IN 47042. 8AM-4PM. **812-689-6115**. ✉✋

Rush County

Circuit & Superior Court *Felony, Misdemeanor, Civil, Eviction, Small Claims, Probate* PO Box 429, Rushville, IN 46173. 8AM-4PM. **765-932-2086**, Fax: 765-932-4165. ✋

St. Joseph County

Circuit & Superior Court *Felony, Misdemeanor, Civil, Eviction, Small Claims, Probate* 101 S Main St, South Bend, IN 46601. 8AM-4:30PM. **574-235-9635**, Fax: 574-235-9838. ✋

Scott County

Circuit & Superior Court *Felony, Misdemeanor, Civil, Eviction, Small Claims, Probate* 1 E McClain Ave, #120, Scottsburg, IN 47170. 8:30AM-4:30PM. **812-752-8420**, Fax: 812-752-5459. ✋

Shelby County

Circuit & Superior Court *Felony, Misdemeanor, Civil, Eviction, Small Claims, Probate* 407 S Harrison St, Rm 206, Shelbyville, IN 46176. 8AM-4PM. **317-392-6320**. ✋

Spencer County

Circuit Court *Felony, Misdemeanor, Civil, Eviction, Small Claims, Probate* PO Box 12, Rockport, IN 47635. 8-4PM. **812-649-6027**, Fax: 812-649-6030. 🖐

Starke County

Circuit Court *Felony, Misdemeanor, Civil, Eviction, Small Claims, Probate* Courthouse 53 E Washington St, Knox, IN 46534. 8:30-4PM. **574-772-9128**. 🖐

Steuben County

Circuit & Superior Court *Felony, Misdemeanor, Civil, Eviction, Small Claims, Probate* Courthouse, 55 S Public Square, Angola, IN 46703. 8AM-4:30PM. **260-668-1000 X2240**. 🖐

Sullivan County

Circuit & Superior Court *Felony, Misdemeanor, Civil, Eviction, Small Claims, Probate* Courthouse, Rm 304 PO Box 370, Sullivan, IN 47882-0370. 8AM-4PM. **812-268-4657**. 🖐💻

Switzerland County

Circuit & Superior Court *Felony, Misdemeanor, Civil, Eviction, Small Claims, Probate* Courthouse 212 W Main St, Vevay, IN 47043. 8-3:30PM M-W & F; 8AM-N Th. **812-427-3175**, Fax: 812-427-2017. 🖐

Tippecanoe County

Circuit, Superior & County Court *Felony, Misdemeanor, Civil, Eviction, Small Claims, Probate* www.county.tippecanoe.in.us PO Box 1665, Lafayette, IN 47902. 8AM-4:30PM. **765-423-9326**, Fax: 765-423-9194. 🖐✉💻

Tipton County

Circuit Court *Felony, Misdemeanor, Civil, Eviction, Small Claims, Probate* Tipton County Courthouse, Tipton, IN 46072. 8AM-4PM M-Th, 8AM-5PM F. **765-675-2791**, Fax: 765-675-7797. 🖐

Union County

Circuit Court *Felony, Misdemeanor, Civil, Eviction, Small Claims, Probate* 26 W Union St, Liberty, IN 47353. 8-4PM. **765-458-6121**, Fax: 765-458-5263. 🖐

Vanderburgh County

Circuit & Superior Court *Felony, Misd., Civil, Eviction, Small Claims, Probate* www.vanderburghgov.org/vander/countyclerk/index.htm PO Box 3356 (Civic Ctr Courts Bldg - Rm 216), Evansville, IN 47732-3356. 8AM-5PM. **812-435-5160**, Fax: 812-435-5849. Civil phone: 812-435-5722, Crim: 812-435-5169, Probate: 812-435-5377. 🖐

Vermillion County

Circuit Court *Felony, Misdemeanor, Civil, Eviction, Small Claims, Probate* PO Box 10, Newport, IN 47966-0010. 8AM-4PM. **765-492-3500**. 🖐

Vigo County

Circuit Court *Felony, Misd., Civil, Eviction, Small Claims, Probate* http://vigocountyin.com 2nd Fl, Courthouse PO Box 8449, Terre Haute, IN 47807-8449. 8AM-4PM. **812-462-3211**. 🖐💻

Wabash County

Circuit & Superior Court *Felony, Misdemeanor, Civil, Eviction, Small Claims, Probate* 69 W Hill St, Wabash, IN 46992. 8AM-4PM. **260-563-0661 X230**, Fax: 260-569-1352. 🖐💻

Warren County

Circuit Court *Felony, Misdemeanor, Civil, Eviction, Small Claims, Probate* 125 N Monroe, #11, Williamsport, IN 47993. 8AM-4PM. **765-762-3510**, Fax: 765-762-7251. 🖐

Warrick County

Circuit & Superior Court *Felony, Misdemeanor, Civil, Eviction, Small Claims, Probate* One County Square, #200, Boonville, IN 47601. 8AM-4PM. **812-897-6160**. 🖐

Washington County

Circuit & Superior Court *Felony, Misdemeanor, Civil, Small Claims, Probate* Courthouse 99 Public Sq, #102, Salem, IN 47167. 8:30AM-4PM M-Th, 8:30AM-6PM F. **812-883-1634/5748**, Fax: 812-883-8108. Will only return calls to toll-free numbers. 🖐

Wayne County

Circuit & Superior Court *Felony, Misd., Civil, Eviction, Small Claims, Probate* www.co.wayne.in.us/courts Courthouse 301 E Main St, Richmond, IN 47374. 8:30AM-5PM M; 8:30AM-4:30PM T-F. **765-973-9200**, Fax: 765-973-9490. ✉**Fax**🖐💻

Wells County

Circuit & Superior Court *Civil, Probate* 102 W Market, Rm 201, Bluffton, IN 46714. 8AM-4:30PM. **260-824-6479**. 🖐

White County

Circuit Court *Civil, Probate* PO Box 350 110 N Main, Monticello, IN 47960. 8AM-4PM. **574-583-7032**, Fax: 574-583-1532 Access civil records by🖐

Superior Court *Felony, Misdemeanor, Eviction, Small Claims* PO Box 1005 110 N Main, Monticello, IN 47960. 8-4PM. **574-583-9520**, Fax: 574-583-2437. 🖐

Whitley County

Circuit & Superior Court *Felony, Misd., Civil, Eviction, Small Claims, Probate* 101 W Van Buren, Rm 10, Columbia City, IN 46725. 8AM-4:30PM. **260-248-3102**, Fax: 260-248-3137. 🖐

Key: Symbols refer to criminal records access unless otherwise noted. phone-☎ mail-✉ fax-**Fax** in person-🖐 online-💻 email-**Email**

Iowa

State Court Administration: State Court Administrator, Judicial Branch Bldg, 1111 East Court Ave, Des Moines, IA, 50319; 515-281-5241, Fax: 515-242-0014. www.judicial.state.ia.us

Court Structure: The District Court is the court of general jurisdiction. Effective 7/1/95, the Small Claims limit increased to $4000 from $3000.

Vital records were moved from courts to the County Recorder's office in each county.

Online Access: Criminal, civil, probate, traffic and appellate information is now available from all 99 counties in Iowa at http://www.judicial.state.ia.us/online_records/. The Iowa Courts online site is providing basic case information for no charge; a more extensive fee portion will be available in the near future. Name searches are available on a statewide or specific county basis. While this is an excellent site with much information, there is one important consideration to keep in mind: although records are updated daily, the historical records offered are not from the same starting date on a county-by-county basis. Also, from the home page one may access supreme and apppellate court opinions.

Additional Information: In most courts, the Certification Fee is $10.00 plus copy fee. Copy Fee is $.50 per page. Most courts do not do searches and recommend either in person searches or use of a record retriever.

Courts that accept written search requests usually require an SASE.

Most courts have a public access terminal for access to that court's records.

Adair County

5th District Court *Felony, Misdemeanor, Civil, Eviction, Small Claims, Probate* PO Box L, Greenfield, IA 50849. 8AM-4:30PM. **641-743-2445**, Fax: 641-743-2974. 🖐🖥

Adams County

5th District Court *Felony, Misdemeanor, Civil, Eviction, Small Claims, Probate* Courthouse PO Box 484, Corning, IA 50841. 8AM-4:30PM. **641-322-4711**, Fax: 641-322-4523. 🖐🖥

Allamakee County

1st District Court *Felony, Misdemeanor, Civil, Eviction, Small Claims, Probate* www.iowacourtsonline.org PO Box 248, Waukon, IA 52172. 8AM-4:30PM Monday - Friday. **563-568-6351**. 🖐🖥

Appanoose County

8th District Court *Felony, Misdemeanor, Civil, Eviction, Small Claims, Probate* PO Box 400, Centerville, IA 52544. 8AM-4:30 PM. **641-856-6101**, Fax: 641-856-2282. 🖐🖥

Audubon County

4th District Court *Felony, Misdemeanor, Civil, Eviction, Small Claims, Probate* 318 Leroy St, #6, Audubon, IA 50025. 8AM-4:30PM. **712-563-4275**, Fax: 712-563-4276. 🖐🖥

Benton County

6th District Court *Felony, Misdemeanor, Civil, Eviction, Small Claims, Probate* www.iowacourtsonline.org PO Box 719, Vinton, IA 52349. 8AM-4:30PM. **319-472-2766**, Fax: 319-472-2747. 🖐🖥

Black Hawk County

1st District Court *Felony, Misdemeanor, Civil, Eviction, Small Claims, Probate* 316 E 5th St, Waterloo, IA 50703. 8AM-4:30PM. **319-833-3331**. Access by 🖐🖥

Boone County

2nd District Court *Felony, Misdemeanor, Civil, Eviction, Small Claims, Probate* 201 State St, Boone, IA 50036. 8AM-4:30PM. **515-433-0561**, Fax: 515-433-0563. Access by 🖐🖥

Bremer County

2nd District Court *Felony, Misdemeanor, Civil, Eviction, Small Claims, Probate* www.co.bremer.ia.us/ PO Box 328, Waverly, IA 50677. 8AM-4:30PM. **319-352-5661**, Fax: 319-352-1054. 🖥

Buchanan County

1st District Court *Felony, Misdemeanor, Civil, Eviction, Small Claims, Probate* PO Box 259, Independence, IA 50644. 8AM-4:30PM. **319-334-2196**, Fax: 319-334-7455. ✉🖐🖥

Buena Vista County

3rd District Court *Felony, Misdemeanor, Civil, Eviction, Small Claims, Probate* PO Box 1186, Storm Lake, IA 50588. 8AM-4:30PM. **712-749-2546**, Fax: 712-749-2700. 🖐🖥

Butler County

2nd District Court *Felony, Misdemeanor, Civil, Eviction, Small Claims, Probate* PO Box 307, Allison, IA 50602. 9AM-3:30PM. **319-267-2487**, Fax: 319-267-2488. 🖐🖥

Calhoun County

2nd District Court *Felony, Misdemeanor, Civil, Eviction, Small Claims, Probate* Box 273, Rockwell City, IA 50579. 8AM-4:30PM. **712-297-8122**, Fax: 712-297-5082. 🖐🖥

Carroll County

2nd District Court *Felony, Misdemeanor, Civil, Eviction, Small Claims, Probate* PO Box 867, Carroll, IA 51401. 8AM-4:30PM. **712-792-4327**, Fax: 712-792-4328. 🖐🖥

Cass County

4th District Court *Felony, Misdemeanor, Civil, Eviction, Small Claims, Probate* 5 W 7th St, Courthouse, Atlantic, IA 50022. 8AM-4:30PM. **712-243-2105**. 🖐🖥

Key: Symbols refer to criminal records access unless otherwise noted. phone-☎ mail-✉ fax-**Fax** in person-🖐 online-🖥 email-**Email**

Cedar County

7th District Court *Felony, Misdemeanor, Civil, Eviction, Small Claims, Probate* 400 Cedar St Attn: Cedar County Clerk of Court, Tipton, IA 52772. 8AM-4:30PM. **563-886-2101**. ✋🖳

Cerro Gordo County

2nd District Court *Felony, Misdemeanor, Civil, Eviction, Small Claims, Probate* 220 W Washington, Mason City, IA 50401. 8AM-4:30PM. **641-424-6431**. ✋🖳

Cherokee County

3rd District Court *Felony, Misdemeanor, Civil, Eviction, Small Claims, Probate* Courthouse Drawer F, Cherokee, IA 51012. 8AM-4:30PM. **712-225-6744**, Fax: 712-225-6749. ✋🖳

Chickasaw County

1st District Court *Felony, Misdemeanor, Civil, Eviction, Small Claims, Probate* County Courthouse 8 E Prospect, New Hampton, IA 50659. 8AM-4:30PM. **641-394-2106**, Fax: 641-394-5106. ✋🖳.

Clarke County

5th District Court *Felony, Misdemeanor, Civil, Eviction, Small Claims, Probate* 100 S Main St Clarke County Courthouse, Osceola, IA 50213. 8AM-4:30PM. **641-342-6096**, Fax: 641-342-2463. ✋🖳

Clay County

3rd District Court *Felony, Misdemeanor, Civil, Eviction, Small Claims, Probate* Courthouse, 215 W 4th St, Spencer, IA 51301. 8 -4:30 PM. **712-262-4335**. ✋🖳

Clayton County

1st District Court *Felony, Misdemeanor, Civil, Eviction, Small Claims, Probate* PO Box 418 Clayton County Courthouse, Elkader, IA 52043. 8AM-4:30PM. **563-245-2204**, Fax: 563-245-2825. ✋🖳

Clinton County

7th District Court *Felony, Misdemeanor, Civil, Eviction, Small Claims, Probate* Courthouse (PO Box 2957), Clinton, IA 52733. 8AM-4:30PM. **563-243-6213**, Fax: 563-243-3655. ✋🖳

Crawford County

3rd District Court *Felony, Misdemeanor, Civil, Eviction, Small Claims, Probate* 1202 Broadway, Denison, IA 51442.

8AM-4:30. **712-263-2242**, Fax: 712-263-5753. ✋🖳

Dallas County

5th District Court *Felony, Misdemeanor, Civil, Eviction, Small Claims, Probate* 801 Court St, Adel, IA 50003. 8AM-4:30PM. **515-993-5816**, Fax: 515-993-6991. ✋✉🖳

Davis County

8th District Court *Felony, Misdemeanor, Civil, Eviction, Small Claims, Probate* Davis County Courthouse, Bloomfield, IA 52537. 8AM4:30PM. **641-664-2011**, Fax: 641-664-2041. ✋🖳

Decatur County

5th District Court *Felony, Misdemeanor, Civil, Eviction, Small Claims, Probate* 207 N Main St, Leon, IA 50144. 8AM-4:30PM. **641-446-4331**, Fax: 641-446-3759. ✋🖳

Delaware County

District Court *Felony, Misdemeanor, Civil, Eviction, Small Claims, Probate* Delaware County Courthouse PO Box 527, Manchester, IA 52057. 8AM-4:30PM. **563-927-4942**, Fax: 563-927-3074. ✋🖳

Des Moines County

8th District Court *Felony, Misdemeanor, Civil, Eviction, Small Claims, Probate* www.judicial.state.ia.us/district/d8.asp 513 Main St PO Box 158, Burlington, IA 52601. 8AM-4:30PM. **319-753-8262/8262**, Fax: 319-753-8253. City of Des Moines is not located here; see Polk county. ✋🖳

Dickinson County

3rd District Court *Felony, Misdemeanor, Civil, Eviction, Small Claims, Probate* PO Drawer O-N, Spirit Lake, IA 51360. 8AM-4:30PM. **712-336-1138**, Fax: 712-336-4005. ✋🖳

Dubuque County

1st District Court *Felony, Misdemeanor, Civil, Eviction, Small Claims, Probate* 720 Central, Dubuque, IA 52001. 8AM-4:30PM. **563-589-4418**. Access by ✋🖳

Emmet County

3rd District Court *Felony, Misdemeanor, Civil, Eviction, Small Claims, Probate* Emmet County 609 1st Ave N,

Estherville, IA 51334. 8AM-4:30PM. **712-362-3325**. ✋🖳

Fayette County

Fayette County District Court *Felony, Misdemeanor, Civil, Eviction, Small Claims, Probate, Traffic* PO Box 458, West Union, IA 52175. 8AM-N, 4:30PM. **563-422-5694**, Fax: 563-422-3137. ✋🖳

Floyd County

2nd District Court *Felony, Misd., Civil, Eviction, Small Claims, Probate* http//www.iowacourtsonline.org 101 S Main St, Charles City, IA 50616. 8AM-4:30PM. **641-228-7777**, Fax: 641-228-7772. ✋🖳

Franklin County

2nd Judicial District Court *Felony, Misdemeanor, Civil, Eviction, Small Claims, Probate* 12 1st Ave NW PO Box 28, Hampton, IA 50441. 8AM-4PM. **641-456-5626**, Fax: 641-456-5628. ✋🖳

Fremont County

4th District Court *Felony, Misdemeanor, Civil, Eviction, Small Claims, Probate* www.co.fremont.ia.us/ PO Box 549, Sidney, IA 51652. 8:00AM-4:30PM. **712-374-2232**, Fax: 712-374-3330. ✋🖳

Greene County

2nd District Court *Felony, Misdemeanor, Civil, Eviction, Small Claims, Probate* Greene County Courthouse 114 N Chestnut, Jefferson, IA 50129. 8AM-4:30PM. **515-386-2516**. ✋🖳

Grundy County

1st District Court *Felony, Misdemeanor, Civil, Eviction, Small Claims, Probate* www.grundycounty.org/clerkofcourt/index.asp Grundy County Courthouse 706 G Ave, Grundy Center, IA 50638. 8AM-4:30PM. **319-824-5229**, Fax: 319-824-3447. ✋🖳

Guthrie County

5th District Court *Felony, Misdemeanor, Civil, Eviction, Small Claims, Probate* Courthouse 200 N 5th St, Guthrie Center, IA 50115. 8AM-4:30PM. **641-747-3415**. ✋🖳

Hamilton County

2nd District Court *Felony, Misd., Civil, Eviction, Small Claims, Probate*

Courthouse, PO Box 845, Webster City, IA 50595. 8:30AM-4:30PM. **515-832-9600**. Access by 👋🖥️

Hancock County

2nd District Court *Felony, Misdemeanor, Civil, Eviction, Small Claims, Probate* 855 State St, Garner, IA 50438. 9AM-3:30PM. **641-923-2532**, Fax: 641-923-3521. Access by 👋🖥️

Hardin County

2nd District Court *Felony, Misdemeanor, Civil, Eviction, Small Claims, Probate* Courthouse PO Box 495, Eldora, IA 50627. 9AM-3:30PM. **641-858-2328**, Fax: 641-858-2320. 👋🖥️

Harrison County

District Court *Felony, Misdemeanor, Civil, Eviction, Small Claims, Probate* Court House, Logan, IA 51546. 8:30AM-3:30PM. **712-644-2665**. 👋🖥️

Henry County

8th District Court *Felony, Misdemeanor, Civil, Eviction, Small Claims, Probate* Clerk of Court PO Box 176, Mount Pleasant, IA 52641. 8AM-4:30PM. Fax: 319-385-4144. Civil phone: 319-385-2632, Crim: 319-385-3150/4203. 👋🖥️

Howard County

1st District Court *Felony, Misdemeanor, Civil, Eviction, Small Claims, Probate* www.judicial.state.ia.us/district/d1.asp Courthouse 137 N Elm St, Cresco, IA 52136. 8-4:30PM. **563-547-2661**. 👋🖥️

Humboldt County

2nd District Court *Felony, Misdemeanor, Civil, Eviction, Small Claims, Probate* PO Box 100, Dakota City, IA 50529. 8AM-4:30PM. **515-332-1806**, Fax: 515-332-7100. 👋🖥️

Ida County

3rd District Court *Felony, Misdemeanor, Civil, Eviction, Small Claims, Probate* Courthouse 401 Moorehead St, Ida Grove, IA 51445. 8AM-4:30PM T, TH, F. **712-364-2628**, Fax: 712-364-2699. 👋🖥️

Iowa County

6th District Court *Felony, Misdemeanor, Civil, Eviction, Small Claims, Probate* PO Box 266, Marengo, IA 52301. 8AM-4:30PM. **319-642-3914**. ✉️👋🖥️

Jackson County

7th District Court *Felony, Misdemeanor, Civil, Eviction, Small Claims, Probate* 201 W Platt, Maquoketa, IA 52060. 8AM-4:30PM. **563-652-4946**, Fax: 563-652-2708. 👋🖥️

Jasper County

5th District Court *Felony, Misdemeanor, Civil, Eviction, Small Claims, Probate* www.judicial.state.ia.us/decisions/district/d5.asp 101 1st St N, Rm 104, Newton, IA 50208. 8AM-4:30PM. **641-792-3255**, Fax: 641-792-2818. Civil phone: 641-792-3255, Crim: 641-792-9161. 👋🖥️

Jefferson County

8th District Court *Felony, Misdemeanor, Civil, Eviction, Small Claims, Probate* PO Box 984, Fairfield, IA 52556. 8AM-4:30PM. **641-472-3454**, Fax: 641-472-9472. 👋🖥️

Johnson County

6th District Court *Felony, Misdemeanor, Civil, Eviction, Small Claims, Probate* PO Box 2510, Iowa City, IA 52244. 8AM-4:30PM. **319-356-6060**. 👋🖥️

Jones County

6th District Court *Felony, Misdemeanor, Civil, Eviction, Small Claims, Probate* PO Box 19 Attn: Clerk of District Court, Anamosa, IA 52205. 8AM-4:30PM. **319-462-4341**. 👋🖥️

Keokuk County

8th District Court *Felony, Misdemeanor, Civil, Eviction, Small Claims, Probate* 101 S Main, Courthouse, Sigourney, IA 52591. 8AM-4:30PM. **641-622-2210**, Fax: 641-622-2171. Access by 👋🖥️

Kossuth County

3rd District Court *Felony, Misdemeanor, Civil, Eviction, Small Claims, Probate* Kossuth County Courthouse 114 W State St, Algona, IA 50511. 8AM-4:30PM. **515-295-3240**. 👋🖥️

Lee County

8th District Court *Felony, Misdemeanor, Civil, Eviction, Small Claims, Probate* PO Box 1443, Ft Madison, IA 52627. 8AM-4:30PM. **319-372-3523**. 👋🖥️

Linn County

District Court *Felony, Misdemeanor, Civil, Eviction, Small Claims, Probate* Linn County Courthouse PO Box 1468,

Cedar Rapids, IA 52406-1468. 8AM-4:30PM. **319-398-3411**, Fax: 319-398-3449. 👋🖥️

Louisa County

8th District Court *Felony, Misdemeanor, Civil, Eviction, Small Claims, Probate* PO Box 268, Wapello, IA 52653. 8AM-4:30PM. **319-523-4541**, Fax: 319-523-4542. 👋🖥️

Lucas County

5th District Court *Felony, Misdemeanor, Civil, Eviction, Small Claims, Probate* Courthouse, 916 Braden, Chariton, IA 50049. 8AM-4:30PM. **641-774-4421**, Fax: 641-774-8669. Access 👋🖥️

Lyon County

3rd District Court *Felony, Misdemeanor, Civil, Eviction, Small Claims, Probate* Courthouse, Rock Rapids, IA 51246. 8AM-4:30PM. **712-472-2623**, Fax: 712-472-2422. 👋🖥️

Madison County

5th District Court *Felony, Misdemeanor, Civil, Eviction, Small Claims, Probate* PO Box 152, Winterset, IA 50273. 8AM-4:30PM. **515-462-4451**, Fax: 515-462-9825. 👋🖥️

Mahaska County

8th District Court *Felony, Misdemeanor, Civil, Eviction, Small Claims, Probate* Courthouse 106 S 1st St, Oskaloosa, IA 52577. 8AM-4:30PM. **641-673-7786**, Fax: 641-672-1256. Access by 👋🖥️

Marion County

5th District Court *Felony, Misdemeanor, Civil, Eviction, Small Claims, Probate* PO Box 497, Knoxville, IA 50138. 8AM-4:30PM. **641-828-2207**, Fax: 641-828-7580. 👋🖥️

Marshall County

2nd District Court *Felony, Misd., Civil, Eviction, Small Claims, Probate* Courthouse 17 E Main St, Marshalltown, IA 50158. 8AM-4:30PM. **641-754-1603**, Fax: 641-754-1600. 👋🖥️

Mills County

4th District Court *Felony, Misdemeanor, Civil, Eviction, Small Claims, Probate* 418 Sharp St, Courthouse, Glenwood, IA 51534. 8AM-4:30PM. **712-527-4880**, Fax: 712-527-4936. Access by 👋🖥️

Mitchell County

2nd District Court *Felony, Misdemeanor, Civil, Eviction, Small Claims, Probate* 508 State St, Osage, IA 50461. 9AM-3:30PM. **641-732-3726**, Fax: 641-732-3728. Access by 🖐️ 🖥️

Monona County

3rd District Court *Felony, Misdemeanor, Civil, Eviction, Small Claims, Probate* www.iowacourtsonline.org 610 Iowa Ave Attn: Clerk of Court, Onawa, IA 51040. 8AM-4:30PM. **712-423-2491**. 🖐️ 🖥️

Monroe County

8th District Court *Felony, Misdemeanor, Civil, Eviction, Small Claims, Probate* Courthouse, 10 Benton Ave E, Albia, IA 52531. 8AM-4:30PM. **641-932-5212**, Fax: 641-932-3245. Access by 🖐️ 🖥️

Montgomery County

4th District Court *Felony, Misdemeanor, Civil, Eviction, Small Claims, Probate* PO Box 469, Red Oak, IA 51566. 8:30AM-4:30PM. **712-623-4986**. 🖐️ 🖥️

Muscatine County

7th District Court *Felony, Misdemeanor, Civil, Eviction, Small Claims, Probate* PO Box 8010, Courthouse, Muscatine, IA 52761. 8AM-4:30PM. **563-263-6511**, Fax: 563-264-3622. Criminal phone: 563-263-2447. 🖐️ 🖥️

O'Brien County

3rd District Court *Felony, Misdemeanor, Civil, Eviction, Small Claims, Probate* Courthouse, Criminal Records, Primghar, IA 51245. 8AM-4:30PM. **712-757-3255**, Fax: 712-757-2965. Access by 🖐️ 🖥️

Osceola County

3rd District Court *Felony, Misdemeanor, Civil, Eviction, Small Claims, Probate* Courthouse, Criminal Records, Sibley, IA 51249. 8AM-4:30PM (may be closed Monday & Wednesday). **712-754-3595**, Fax: 712-754-2480. Access by 🖐️ 🖥️

Page County

4th District Court *Felony, Misdemeanor, Civil, Eviction, Small Claims, Probate* 112 E Main, Box 263, Clarinda, IA 51632. 8AM-4:30PM. **712-542-3214**, Fax: 712-542-5460. Access by 🖐️ 🖥️

Palo Alto County

3rd District Court *Felony, Misdemeanor, Civil, Eviction, Small Claims, Probate* PO Box 387, Emmetsburg, IA 50536. 8AM-4:30PM. **712-852-3603**. 🖐️ 🖥️

Plymouth County

3rd Judicial District *Felony, Misdemeanor, Civil, Eviction, Small Claims, Probate* Plymouth County Clerk of District Court Courthouse 215 4th Ave SE, Le Mars, IA 51031. 8AM-4:30PM. **712-546-4215**. 🖐️ 🖥️

Pocahontas County

2nd District Court *Felony, Misdemeanor, Civil, Eviction, Small Claims, Probate* Courthouse 99 Court Square, Pocahontas, IA 50574. 9AM-3:30PM. **712-335-4208**, Fax: 712-335-5045. 🖐️ 🖥️

Polk County

District Court *Felony, Misdemeanor, Civil, Eviction, Small Claims, Probate* www.judicial.state.ia.us 500 Mulberry St, Rm 201, Des Moines, IA 50309. 8AM-4:30PM. **515-286-3772**, Fax: 515-286-3172 (Civil) 323-5250 (Criminal). 📧 🖐️ 🖥️

Pottawattamie County

4th District Court *Felony, Misdemeanor, Civil, Eviction, Small Claims, Probate* 227 S 6th St, Council Bluffs, IA 51501. 8:30AM-4:30PM. **712-328-5604**. 🖐️ 🖥️

Poweshiek County

8th District Court *Felony, Misdemeanor, Civil, Eviction, Small Claims, Probate* PO Box 218, Montezuma, IA 50171. 8AM-4:30PM. **641-623-5644**, Fax: 641-623-5320. 🖐️ 🖥️

Ringgold County

5th District Court *Felony, Misdemeanor, Civil, Small Claims, Probate, Traffic* 109 W Madison (PO Box 523), Mount Ayr, IA 50854. 8AM-4:30PM. **641-464-3234**, Fax: 641-464-2478. Access by 🖐️ 🖥️

Sac County

2nd District Court *Felony, Misd., Civil, Eviction, Small Claims, Probate* www.iowacourtsonline.org PO Box 368, Sac City, IA 50583. 8AM-4:30PM. **712-662-7791**, Fax: 712-662-7978. 🖐️ 🖥️

Scott County

7th District Court *Felony, Misdemeanor, Civil, Eviction, Small Claims, Probate* courtsonline org 416 W 4th St, Davenport, IA 52801. 8AM-4:30PM. **563-326-8786**. 🖐️ 🖥️

Shelby County

4th District Court *Felony, Misdemeanor, Civil, Eviction, Small Claims, Probate* www.shco.org PO Box 431, Harlan, IA 51537. 8:30AM-3:30PM. **712-755-5543**, Fax: 712-755-2667. The court will not perform name searches. Access by 🖐️ 🖥️

Sioux County

3rd District Court *Felony, Misdemeanor, Civil, Eviction, Small Claims, Probate* PO Box 47, Courthouse, Orange City, IA 51041. 8AM-4:30PM. **712-737-2286**, Fax: 712-737-8908. 🖐️ 🖥️

Story County

2nd District Court *Felony, Misdemeanor, Civil, Probate* PO Box 408 1315 S B Ave, Nevada, IA 50201. 8AM-4:30PM. **515-382-7410**, Probate: 515-382-7420. Also has a branch in Ames that handles minor misdemeanors, traffic, and small claims. 🖐️ 🖥️

Ames Associate District Court *Misdemeanor (Minor), Small Claims, Eviction* PO Box 748 515 Clark St, Ames, IA 50010. 8AM-4:30PM. **515-239-5140**. A branch of the District Court in Nevada. 🖐️ 🖥️

Tama County

6th Judicial District Court *Felony, Misdemeanor, Civil, Eviction, Small Claims, Probate* PO Box 306, Toledo, IA 52342. 8AM-4:30PM. **641-484-3721**, Fax: 641-484-6403. 🖐️ 🖥️

Taylor County

5th District Court *Felony, Misdemeanor, Civil, Eviction, Small Claims, Probate* Courthouse, Bedford, IA 50833. 8AM-4:30PM. **712-523-2095**, Fax: 712-523-2936. 🖐️ 🖥️

Union County

5th District Court *Felony, Misdemeanor, Civil, Eviction, Small Claims, Probate* Courthouse, Creston, IA 50801. 8AM-4:30PM. **641-782-7315**, Fax: 641-782-8241. 🖐️ 📧 🖥️

Key: Symbols refer to criminal records access unless otherwise noted. phone-☎ mail-✉ fax-**Fax** in person-🖐️ online-🖥️ email-**Email**

Van Buren County

8th District Court *Felony, Misdemeanor, Civil, Eviction, Small Claims, Probate* Courthouse Criminal Records, Keosauqua, IA 52565. 8AM-4:30PM. **319-293-3108**, Fax: 319-293-3811.

Wapello County

8th District Court *Felony, Misdemeanor, Civil, Eviction, Small Claims, Probate* 101 W 4th, Ottumwa, IA 52501. 8AM-3:30PM. **641-683-0060**, Fax: 641-683-0064. SSNs not available to public.

Warren County

5th District Court *Felony, Misdemeanor, Civil, Eviction, Small Claims, Probate* PO Box 379, Indianola, IA 50125. 8AM-4:30PM. **515-961-1033**, Fax: 515-961-1071. Civil phone: 515-961-1027, Crim: 961-1033, Probate 515-961-1037.

Washington County

8th District Court *Felony, Misdemeanor, Civil, Eviction, Small Claims, Probate* PO Box 391, Washington, IA 52353. 8AM-4:30PM. **319-653-7741**, Fax: 319-653-7787.

Wayne County

5th District Court *Felony, Misdemeanor, Civil, Eviction, Small Claims, Probate* PO Box 424, Corydon, IA 50060. 8AM-4:30PM. **641-872-2264**, Fax: 641-872-2431.

Webster County

2nd District Court *Felony, Misdemeanor, Civil, Eviction, Small Claims, Probate* 701 Central Ave, Courthouse, Ft Dodge, IA 50501. 8AM-4:30PM. **515-576-7115**. Access by

Winnebago County

2nd District Court *Felony, Misd., Civil, Eviction, Small Claims, Probate* www.iowacourtsonline.org 126 S Clark Box 468, Forest City, IA 50436. 9AM-3:30PM. **641-585-4520**, Fax: 641-585-2615.

Winneshiek County

1st District Court *Felony, Misdemeanor, Civil, Eviction, Small Claims, Probate* 201 W Main St, Decorah, IA 52101. 8AM-4:30PM. **563-382-2469**, Fax: 563-382-0603.

Woodbury County

3rd District Court *Felony, Civil, Eviction, Probate* Woodbury County Courthouse 620 Douglas, Rm 101, Sioux City, IA 51101-1248. 8AM-4:30PM. **712-279-6611**, Fax: 712-279-6021.

Associate District Court *Misdemeanor, Civil, Eviction, Small Claims* 407 7th St County Clerk at Law Enforcement Ctr, Sioux City, IA 51101. 8AM-4:30PM. **712-279-6624**.

Worth County

2nd District Court *Felony, Misd., Civil, Eviction, Small Claims, Probate* 1000 Central Ave, Northwood, IA 50459. 9AM-3:30PM. **641-324-2840**, Fax: 641-324-2360. Case # required for documents; will fax back results.

Wright County

2nd District Court *Felony, Misdemeanor, Civil, Eviction, Small Claims, Probate* PO Box 306, Clarion, IA 50525. 9AM-3:30PM. **515-532-3113**, Fax: 515-532-2343. Access by

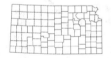

Kansas

State Court Administration: Judicial Administrator, Kansas Judicial Center, 301 SW 10th St, Topeka, KS, 66612; 785-296-4873, Fax: 785-296-7076. www.kscourts.org

Court Structure: The District Court is the court of general jurisdiction. There are 110 courts in 31 districts in 105 counties.

Online Access: Commercial online access is available for District Court Records in 4 counties - Johnson, Sedgwick, Shawnee, and Wyandotte - through Access Kansas, part of the Information Network of Kansas (INK) Services. Franklin and Finney counties may be available late in 2004. A user can access INK through their Internet site at www.accesskansas.org or via a dial-up system. The INK subscription fee is $75.00, and the annual renewal fee is $60.00. There is no per minute connect charge but there is a transaction fee. Other information from INK includes Drivers License, Title, Registration, Lien, and UCC searches. For additional information or a registration packet, call 800-4-KANSAS (800-452-6727).

The Kansas Appellate Courts offer free online access to case information at www.kscourts.org.

Additional Information: Five counties - Cowley, Crawford, Labette, Montgomery and Neosho - have two hearing locations, but only one record center, which is the location included here. Many Kansas courts do not do criminal record searches and will refer any criminal requests to the Kansas Bureau of Investigation. The Kansas Legislature's Administrative Order 156 (Fall, 2000) allows Courts to charge up to $12.00 per hour for search services, though courts may set their own search fees, if any.

Allen County

District Court *Felony, Misdemeanor, Civil, Eviction, Small Claims, Probate* PO Box 630 1 N Washington St, Iola, KS 66749. 8AM-5PM. **620-365-1425**, Fax: 620-365-1429. **Fax**✉

Anderson County

District Court *Felony, Misd., Civil, Eviction, Small Claims, Probate* www.kscourts.org/dstcts/4dstct.htm PO Box 305, Garnett, KS 66032. 8AM-N, N-4PM. **785-448-6886**, Fax: 785-448-3230. **Fax**✉

Atchison County

District Court *Felony, Misdemeanor, Civil, Eviction, Small Claims, Probate* PO Box 408, Atchison, KS 66002. 8-5. **913-367-7400**, Fax: 913-367-1171.

Key: Symbols refer to criminal records access unless otherwise noted. phone-☎ mail-✉ fax-**Fax** in person-🖐 online-💻 email-**Email**

Barber County

District Court *Felony, Misdemeanor, Civil, Eviction, Small Claims, Probate* 118 E Washington, Medicine Lodge, KS 67104. 8AM-N,1-5PM. **620-886-5639**, Fax: 620-886-5854. ✋

Barton County

District Court *Felony, Misdemeanor, Civil, Eviction, Small Claims, Probate* 1400 Main, Rm 306, Great Bend, KS 67530. 8AM-5PM. **620-793-1856**, Fax: 620-793-1860. Fax✉✋

Bourbon County

District Court *Felony, Misdemeanor, Civil, Eviction, Small Claims, Probate* PO Box 868, Ft Scott, KS 66701. 8:30AM-4:30PM. **620-223-0780**, Fax: 620-223-5303. ✋

Brown County

District Court *Felony, Misdemeanor, Civil, Eviction, Small Claims, Probate* PO Box 417, Hiawatha, KS 66434. 8AM-5PM. **785-742-7481**, Fax: 785-742-3506. ☎Fax✉✋

Butler County

District Court *Felony, Misdemeanor, Civil, Eviction, Small Claims, Probate* 201 W Pine, #101, El Dorado, KS 67042. 8AM-5PM. **316-322-4370**, Fax: 316-321-9486. ✋Fax

Chase County

District Court *Felony, Misdemeanor, Civil, Eviction, Small Claims, Probate* PO Box 529, Cottonwood Falls, KS 66845. 8AM-5PM. **620-273-6319**, Fax: 620-273-6890. ✋

Chautauqua County

District Court *Felony, Misdemeanor, Civil, Eviction, Small Claims, Probate* www.14thjudicialdistrict-ks.org/ 215 N Chautauqua, PO Box 306, Sedan, KS 67361. 8:30AM-4:30PM. **620-725-5870**, Fax: 620-725-3027. ✉✋

Cherokee County

District Court *Felony, Misdemeanor, Civil, Eviction, Small Claims, Probate* PO Box 189, Columbus, KS 66725. 8AM-5PM. **620-429-3880**, Fax: 620-429-1130. ✉Fax✋

Cheyenne County

District Court *Felony, Misdemeanor, Civil, Eviction, Small Claims, Probate* PO Box 646, St Francis, KS 67756. 8AM-N,1-5PM. **785-332-8850**, Fax: 785-332-8851. Fax✉✋

Clark County

District Court *Felony, Misdemeanor, Civil, Eviction, Small Claims, Probate* www.kscourts.org/dstcts/16dstct.htm PO Box 790, Ashland, KS 67831. 8AM-5PM. **620-635-2753**, Fax: 620-635-2155. ✉Fax✋

Clay County

District Court *Felony, Misdemeanor, Civil, Eviction, Small Claims, Probate* www.co.riley.ks.us/districtcourt/ PO Box 203, Clay Center, KS 67432. 8AM-5PM. **785-632-3443**, Fax 785-632-2651. ✉✋

Cloud County

District Court *Felony, Misdemeanor, Civil, Eviction, Small Claims, Probate* www.kscourts.org/dstcts/12dstct.htm 811 Washington, Concordia, KS 66901. 8:00AM-5PM. **785-243-8124**, Fax: 785-243-8188. Fax✉✋

Coffey County

District Court *Felony, Misdemeanor, Civil, Eviction, Small Claims, Probate* www.kscourts.org/dstcts/4dstct.htm PO Box 330, Burlington, KS 66839. 8AM-4PM. **620-364-8628**, Fax: 620-364-8535. ✉Fax✋Email

Comanche County

District Court *Felony, Misdemeanor, Civil, Eviction, Small Claims, Probate* www.kscourts.org/dstcts/16dstct.htm PO Box 722, Coldwater, KS 67029. 8-5PM. **620-582-2182**, Fax: 620-582-2603. ✋

Cowley County

Winfield District Court *Felony, Misdemeanor, Civil, Eviction, Small Claims, Probate* PO Box 472, Winfield, KS 67156. 8AM-N,1-4PM. **620-221-5470**, Fax: 620-221-1097. This court covers northern part of county. Fax✉✋

Arkansas City District Court *Felony, Misdemeanor, Civil, Eviction, Small Claims, Probate* PO Box 1152, Arkansas City, KS 67005. 8AM-N,1-4PM. **620-441-4520**, Fax: 620-442-7213. This court covers the southern county. All felony records are kept at Winfield. ✉✋

Crawford County

Records back to 8/92 can be searched at both courts. For cases prior to 8/92, search both courts separately.

Girard District Court *Felony, Misdemeanor, Civil, Probate* PO Box 69, Girard, KS 66743. 8AM-5PM. **620-724-6211**, Fax: 620-724-4987. ☎Fax✋

Pittsburg District Court *Misd., Civil, Eviction, Small Claims, Probate* 602 N Locust, Pittsburg, KS 66762. 8AM-5PM. **620-231-0391**, Fax 620-231-0316. ✋✉

Decatur County

District Court *Felony, Misdemeanor, Civil, Eviction, Small Claims, Probate* PO Box 89, Oberlin, KS 67749. 8-5PM. **785-475-8107**, Fax: 785-475-8170. ✋

Dickinson County

District Court *Felony, Misdemeanor, Civil, Eviction, Small Claims, Probate* PO Box 127, Abilene, KS 67410. 9AM-5PM. **785-263-3142**, Fax: 785-263-4407. ✉Fax✋Email

Doniphan County

District Court *Felony, Misdemeanor, Civil, Eviction, Small Claims, Probate* PO Box 295, Troy, KS 66087. 8AM-5PM. **785-985-3582**, Fax: 785-985-2402. ☎Fax✉✋

Douglas County

District Court *Felony, Misd., Civil, Eviction, Small Claims, Probate* www.douglas-county.com/District_Court/dc.asp 111 E 11th St, Rm 144, Lawrence, KS 66044-2966. 8-4PM. **785-832-5256**, Fax: 785-832-5174. ☎Fax✉✋💻

Edwards County

District Court *Felony, Misdemeanor, Civil, Eviction, Small Claims, Probate* www.kscourts.org/dstcts/24dstct.htm PO Box 232, Kinsley, KS 67547. 8AM-5PM. **620-659-2442**, Fax: 620-659-2998. ✋

Elk County

District Court *Felony, Misdemeanor, Civil, Eviction, Small Claims, Probate* PO Box 306, Howard, KS 67349. 8AM-4:30PM. **620-374-2370**, Fax: 620-374-3531. ✉✋

Key: Symbols refer to criminal records access unless otherwise noted. phone-☎ mail-✉ fax-Fax in person-✋ online-💻 email-Email

Ellis County

District Court *Felony, Misdemeanor, Civil, Eviction, Small Claims, Probate* www.23rdjudicial.org PO Box 8, Hays, KS 67601. 8AM-5PM. **785-628-9415**, Fax: 785-628-8415. 🖐

Ellsworth County

District Court *Felony, Misdemeanor, Civil, Eviction, Small Claims, Probate* 210 N Kansas, Ellsworth, KS 67439-3118. 8AM-5PM. **785-472-3832**, Fax: 785-472-5712. ☎Fax☒🖐

Finney County

District Court *Felony, Misdemeanor, Civil, Eviction, Small Claims, Probate* PO Box 798, Garden City, KS 67846. 8AM-4:30PM. Fax: 620-271-6140. Civil phone: 620-271-6121, Crim: 620-271-6132. 🖐

Ford County

District Court *Felony, Misdemeanor, Civil, Eviction, Small Claims, Probate* www.kscourts.org/dstcts/16dstct.htm 101 W Spruce, Dodge City, KS 67801. 8AM-5PM. **620-227-4609**, Fax: 620-227-6799. Civil phone: 620-227-4610, Crim: 620-227-4608. Fax☒🖐

Franklin County

District Court *Felony, Misdemeanor, Civil, Eviction, Small Claims, Probate* www.kscourts.org/dstcts/4dstct.htm POBox 637 (301 S Main), Ottawa, KS 66067. 8AM-12, 1PM-4PM. **785-242-6000**, Fax: 785-242-5970. 🖐🖥

Geary County

District Court *Felony, Misdemeanor, Civil, Eviction, Small Claims, Probate* PO Box 1147, Junction City, KS 66441. 8AM-5PM. **785-762-5221**, Fax: 785-762-4420. ☒🖐Email

Gove County

District Court *Felony, Misdemeanor, Civil, Eviction, Small Claims, Probate* PO Box 97, Gove, KS 67736. 8AM-N, 1-5PM. **785-938-2310**, Fax: 785-938-2312. Fax☒🖐

Graham County

District Court *Felony, Misdemeanor, Civil, Eviction, Small Claims, Probate* 410 N Pomeroy, Hill City, KS 67642. 8AM-5PM. **785-421-3458**, Fax: 785-421-5463. ☒🖐

Grant County

District Court *Felony, Misdemeanor, Civil, Eviction, Small Claims, Probate* 108 S Glenn, Ulysses, KS 67880. 8:30AM-5PM. **620-356-1526**, Fax: 620-353-2131. 🖐☒

Gray County

District Court *Felony, Misdemeanor, Civil, Eviction, Small Claims, Probate* www.kscourts.org/dstcts/16dstct.htm PO Box 487, Cimarron, KS 67835. 8AM-5PM. **620-855-3812**, Fax: 620-855-7037. Fax☒🖐

Greeley County

District Court *Felony, Misdemeanor, Civil, Eviction, Small Claims, Probate* PO Box 516, Tribune, KS 67879. 8AM-N, 1-5PM. **620-376-4292**. Access by ☒🖐

Greenwood County

District Court *Felony, Misd., Civil, Eviction, Small Claims, Probate* 311 N Main, Eureka, KS 67045. 8AM-5PM. **620-583-8153**, Fax 620-583-6818. ☒🖐

Hamilton County

District Court *Felony, Misd., Civil, Eviction, Small Claims, Probate* PO Box 745, Syracuse, KS 67878. 8AM-5PM. **620-384-5159**, Fax: 620-384-7806. 🖐

Harper County

District Court *Felony, Misdemeanor, Civil, Eviction, Small Claims, Probate* PO Box 467, Anthony, KS 67003. 8AM-N, 1-5PM. **620-842-3721**, Fax: 620-842-6025. 🖐

Harvey County

District Court *Felony, Misdemeanor, Civil, Eviction, Small Claims, Probate* PO Box 665, Newton, KS 67114-0665. 9AM-5PM. **316-284-6890**, Fax: 316-283-4601. Civil phone: 316-284-6894, Crim: 316-284-6896. ☒Fax🖐

Haskell County

District Court *Felony, Misdemeanor, Civil, Eviction, Small Claims, Probate* PO Box 146, Sublette, KS 67877. 8AM-5PM. **620-675-2671**, Fax: 620-675-8599. ☎☒Fax🖐

Hodgeman County

District Court *Felony, Misd., Civil, Eviction, Small Claims, Probate* www.kscourts.org/dstcts/24dstct.htm PO Box 187,

Jetmore, KS 67854. 8:30-5PM. **620-357-6522**, Fax: 620-357-6216. 🖐

Jackson County

District Court *Felony, Misdemeanor, Civil, Eviction, Small Claims, Probate* 400 New York Ave, #311, Holton, KS 66436. 8AM-4:30PM. **785-364-2191**, Fax: 785-364-3804. 🖐

Jefferson County

District Court *Felony, Misdemeanor, Civil, Eviction, Small Claims, Probate* PO Box 327, Oskaloosa, KS 66066. 8AM-4:30PM. **785-863-2461**, Fax: 785-863-2369. 🖐

Jewell County

District Court *Felony, Misdemeanor, Civil, Eviction, Small Claims, Probate* www.kscourts.org/dstcts/12dstct.htm 307 N Commercial, Mankato, KS 66956. 8AM-5PM. **785-378-4030**, Fax: 785-378-4035. ☎Fax☒🖐

Johnson County

District Court *Felony, Misdemeanor, Civil, Eviction, Small Claims, Probate* www.jocoks.com/countyclerk/ 100 N Kansas, Olathe, KS 66061. 8:30AM-4PM. **913-715-3500**, Fax: 913-715-3481. Civil phone: 913-715-3400, Crim: 913-715-3460. Search requests should be made to the Records Center, phone 913-715-3480. Fax☒🖐

Kearny County

District Court *Felony, Misdemeanor, Civil, Eviction, Small Claims, Probate* PO Box 64, Lakin, KS 67860. 8AM-N,1-5PM. **620-355-6481**, Fax: 620-355-7462. ☒🖐

Kingman County

District Court *Felony, Misdemeanor, Civil, Eviction, Small Claims, Probate* PO Box 495 (130 N Spruce St), Kingman, KS 67068. 8AM-N, 1-5PM. **620-532-5151**, Fax: 620-532-2952. ☒Fax🖐

Kiowa County

District Court *Felony, Misdemeanor, Civil, Eviction, Small Claims, Probate* www.kscourts.org/dstcts/16dstct.htm 211 E Florida, Greensburg, KS 67054. 8AM-5PM. **620-723-3317**, Fax: 620-723-2970. Fax☒🖐

Labette County

District Court *Felony, Misdemeanor, Civil, Eviction, Small Claims, Probate*

Courthouse 501 Merchant, 3rd Fl, Oswego, KS 67356. 8AM-5PM. **620-795-4533 X 245 (620-421-4120 Parsons)**, Fax: 620-795-3056 (316-421-3633 Parsons). 🖑

District Court *Felony, Misd., Civil, Eviction, Small Claims, Probate* 201 S Central, Parsons, KS 67357. 8AM-5PM. **620-421-4120**, Fax 620-421-3633. ✉🖑

Lane County

District Court *Felony, Misdemeanor, Civil, Eviction, Small Claims, Probate* www.kscourts.org/dstcts/24dstct.htm PO Box 188, Dighton, KS 67839. 8AM-5PM. **620-397-2805**, Fax 620-397-5526. ✉🖑

Leavenworth County

District Court *Felony, Misdemeanor, Civil, Eviction, Small Claims, Probate* 601 S 3rd St, Leavenworth, KS 66048. 8AM-5PM. **913-684-0700**, Fax: 913-684-0492. Civil phone: 913-684-0701, Crim: 913-684-0704. ✉🖑

Lincoln County

District Court *Felony, Misdemeanor, Civil, Eviction, Small Claims, Probate* www.kscourts.org/dstcts/12dstct.htm 216 E Lincoln Ave, Lincoln, KS 67455. 8AM-12, 1-5PM. **785-524-4057**, Fax: 785-524-3204. 🖑

Linn County

District Court *Felony, Misdemeanor, Civil, Eviction, Small Claims, Probate* PO Box 350 318 Chestnut St., Mound City, KS 66056-0350. 8AM-4:30PM. **913-795-2660**, Fax: 913-795-2004. 🖑

Logan County

District Court *Felony, Misdemeanor, Civil, Eviction, Small Claims, Probate* 710 W 2nd St, Oakley, KS 67748-1233. 8:30AM-N, 1-5PM. **785-672-3654**, Fax: 785-672-3517. 🖑

Lyon County

District Court *Felony, Misdemeanor, Civil, Eviction, Small Claims, Probate* www.lyoncounty.org/MV2Base.asp?VarCN =115 430 Commercial St, Emporia, KS 66801. 8AM-4PM. **620-341-3281**, Fax: 620-341-3497. Fax✉🖑

McPherson County

District Court *Felony, Misdemeanor, Civil, Eviction, Small Claims, Probate* PO Box 1106, McPherson, KS 67460.

8AM-5PM. **620-241-3422**, Fax: 620-241-1372. ✉🖑

Marion County

District Court *Felony, Misdemeanor, Civil, Eviction, Small Claims, Probate* PO Box 298, Marion, KS 66861. 8AM-5PM; 9AM-5PM (open to public). **620-382-2104**, Fax: 620-382-2259. 🖑

Marshall County

District Court *Felony, Misdemeanor, Civil, Eviction, Small Claims, Probate* PO Box 86, 1201 Broadway, Office #5, Marysville, KS 66508. 8AM-5PM; Search hours: 8:30AM-4:30PM. **785-562-5301**, Fax: 785-562-2458. Records are located in old historical courthouse located next door at 1207 Broadway. Fax✉🖑

Meade County

Meade County Dist. Ct. *Felony, Misd., Civil, Eviction, Small Claims, Probate* www.kscourts.org/dstcts/16dstct.htm PO Box 623, Meade, KS 67864. 8AM-5PM. **620-873-8750**, Fax: 620-873-8759. 🖑

Miami County

District Court *Felony, Misdemeanor, Civil, Eviction, Small Claims, Probate* PO Box 187, Paola, KS 66071. 8AM-4:30PM. **913-294-3326**, Fax: 913-294-2535. 🖑

Mitchell County

District Court *Felony, Misdemeanor, Civil, Eviction, Small Claims, Probate* www.kscourts.org/dstcts/12dstct.htm 115 S Hersey, Beloit, KS 67420. 8AM-5PM. **785-738-3753**, Fax: 785-738-4101. ✉🖑

Montgomery County

Independence District Court *Felony, Misdemeanor, Civil, Eviction, Small Claims, Probate* 300 E Main St, #201, Independence, KS 67301. 8AM-5PM. **620-330-1070**, Fax: 620-331-6120. Fax✉🖑

Coffeyville District Court *Civil, Eviction, Small Claims, Probate* 102 W 7th St, #A, Coffeyville, KS 67337. 8AM-5PM. **620-251-1060**, Fax: 620-251-2734. This court covers civil cases for the southern part of the county, although cases can be filed in either court. It is recommended to search both courts. Access civil records by Fax✉🖑

Morris County

District Court *Felony, Misdemeanor, Civil, Eviction, Small Claims, Probate* County Courthouse, Council Grove, KS 66846. 8AM-5PM. **620-767-6838**, Fax: 620-767-6488. Fax✉🖑

Morton County

District Court *Felony, Misdemeanor, Civil, Eviction, Small Claims, Probate* PO Box 825, Elkhart, KS 67950. 8AM-N, 1-5PM. **620-697-2563**, Fax: 620-697-4289. 🖑

Nemaha County

District Court *Felony, Misdemeanor, Civil, Eviction, Small Claims, Probate* PO Box 213, Seneca, KS 66538. 8AM-5PM. **785-336-2146**, Fax: 785-336-6450. ☎✉🖑

Neosho County

Erie District Court *Felony, Misdemeanor, Civil, Eviction, Small Claims, Probate* Neosho County Courthouse, PO Box 19, Erie, KS 66733. 8AM-N, 1-4:30PM. **620-244-3831**, Fax: 620-244-3830. Criminal phone: 620-431-5700. This is the main court for the county. ✉🖑

Chanute District Court *Felony, Misdemeanor, Civil, Eviction, Small Claims* 102 S Lincoln, PO Box 889, Chanute, KS 66720. 8AM-5PM. **620-431-5700**, Fax: 620-431-5710. This is a branch court of Erie. 🖑

Ness County

District Court *Felony, Misd., Civil, Eviction, Small Claims, Probate* PO Box 445, Ness City, KS 67560. 8AM-5PM. **785-798-3693**, Fax: 785-798-3348. 🖑

Norton County

District Court *Felony, Misdemeanor, Civil, Eviction, Small Claims, Probate* PO Box 70, Norton, KS 67654. 8AM-5PM. **785-877-5720**, Fax: 785-877-5722. ✉🖑

Osage County

District Court *Felony, Misdemeanor, Civil, Eviction, Small Claims, Probate* www.kscourts.org/dstcts/4dstct.htm PO Box 549, Lyndon, KS 66451. 8AM-N,1-4PM. **785-828-4514**, Fax: 785-828-4704. 🖑💻

Key: Symbols refer to criminal records access unless otherwise noted. phone-☎ mail-✉ fax-Fax in person-🖑 online-💻 email-**Email**

Osborne County

District Court *Felony, Misdemeanor, Civil, Eviction, Small Claims, Probate* 423 W Main PO Box 160, Osborne, KS 67473. 8AM-5PM. **785-346-5911**, Fax: 785-246-5992. ✋Fax✉

Ottawa County

District Court *Felony, Misdemeanor, Civil, Eviction, Small Claims, Probate* 307 N Concord, Minneapolis, KS 67467. 8AM-12:00-1-5PM. **785-392-2917**, Fax: 785-392-3626. ✋

Pawnee County

District Court *Felony, Misdemeanor, Civil, Eviction, Small Claims, Probate* www.kscourts.org/dstcts/24dstct.htm PO Box 270, Larned, KS 67550. 8AM-5PM. **620-285-6937**, Fax: 620-285-3665. Fax✉ ✋

Phillips County

District Court *Felony, Misdemeanor, Civil, Eviction, Small Claims, Probate* PO Box 564, Phillipsburg, KS 67661. 8AM-5PM. **785-543-6830**, Fax: 785-543-6832. ✋✉

Pottawatomie County

District Court *Felony, Misdemeanor, Civil, Eviction, Small Claims, Probate* PO Box 129, Westmoreland, KS 66549. 8AM-4:30PM. **785-457-3392**, Fax: 785-457-2107. ✋

Pratt County

District Court *Felony, Misdemeanor, Civil, Eviction, Small Claims, Probate* www.prattcounty.org PO Box 984, Pratt, KS 67124. 8AM-N, 1-5PM. **620-672-4100**, Fax: 620-672-2902. ✉Fax✋

Rawlins County

District Court *Felony, Misd., Civil, Eviction, Small Claims, Probate* 607 Main, #F, Atwood, KS 67730. 9-5PM. **785-626-3465**, Fax: 785-626-3350. ✋

Reno County

District Court *Felony, Misdemeanor, Civil, Eviction, Small Claims, Probate* 206 W 1st, Hutchinson, KS 67501. 8AM-N, 1-5PM. **620-694-2956**, Fax: 620-694-2958. ✉✋

Republic County

District Court *Felony, Misdemeanor, Civil, Eviction, Small Claims, Probate* www.kscourts.org/dstcts/12dstct.htm PO Box 8, Belleville, KS 66935. 8AM-5PM. **785-527-7234**, Fax: 785-527-5029. ✋

Rice County

District Court *Felony, Misdemeanor, Civil, Eviction, Small Claims, Probate* 101 W Commercial, Lyons, KS 67554. 8:00AM-5PM. **620-257-2383**, Fax: 620-257-3826. Fax✉✋

Riley County

District Court *Felony, Misdemeanor, Civil, Eviction, Small Claims, Probate* www.co.riley.ks.us/districtcourt/ PO Box 158, Manhattan, KS 66505-0158. 8:30AM-5PM. **785-537-6364**. ✋

Rooks County

District Court *Felony, Misdemeanor, Civil, Eviction, Small Claims, Probate* 115 N Walnut PO Box 532, Stockton, KS 67669. 8AM-5PM. **785-425-6718**, Fax: 785-425-6568. ✉✋

Rush County

District Court *Felony, Misdemeanor, Civil, Eviction, Small Claims, Probate* www.kscourts.org/dstcts/24dstct.htm PO Box 387, La Crosse, KS 67548. 8-5PM. **785-222-2718**, Fax: 785-222-2748. ✋

Russell County

District Court *Felony, Misdemeanor, Civil, Eviction, Small Claims, Probate* PO Box 876, Russell, KS 67665. 8AM-5PM. **785-483-5641**, Fax: 785-483-2448. Fax✉✋

Saline County

District Court *Felony, Misdemeanor, Civil, Eviction, Small Claims, Probate* PO Box 1760, Salina, KS 67402-1760. 8:30AM-4PM. **785-309-5831**, Fax: 785-309-5845. ✉✋

Scott County

District Court *Felony, Misdemeanor, Civil, Eviction, Small Claims, Probate* 303 Court, Scott City, KS 67871. 8AM-N, 1-5PM. **620-872-7208**. ✋

Sedgwick County

District Court *Felony, Misdemeanor, Civil, Eviction, Small Claims, Probate* http://distrct18.state.ks.us/ 525 N Main, Wichita, KS 67203. 8AM-4PM. **316-383-7302**, Fax: 316-660-5780. Civil phone: 316-660-5719, Crim: 316-660-5719, Probate: 316-660-5721. Phone numbers above are for records department; direct numbers for the divisions are: criminal-316-660-5720 (fax-660-5777); civil-316-660-5690 (fax-660-5775). Fax✉🖥✋

Seward County

District Court *Felony, Misd., Civil, Eviction, Small Claims, Probate* 415 N Washington, #103, Liberal, KS 67901. 8:30AM-5PM. **620-626-3234**, Fax: 620-626-3302. Civil phone: 620-626-3391, Crim: 620-626-3234, Probate: 620-626-3232. Court will do searches on occasion. Small Claims Court: 620-626-3232. ✋

Shawnee County

District Court *Felony, Misdemeanor, Civil, Eviction, Small Claims, Probate* www.shawneecourt.org 200 E 7th Rm 209, Topeka, KS 66603. 8AM-5PM. **785-233-8200 X4327**, Fax: 785-291-4911. Civil phone: x5158, Crim: x5157, Probate: x4358. Fax✉✋🖥

Sheridan County

District Court *Felony, Misdemeanor, Civil, Eviction, Small Claims, Probate* PO Box 753, Hoxie, KS 67740. 8AM-N, 1PM-5PM. **785-675-3451**, Fax: 785-675-2256. ☎Fax✉✋

Sherman County

District Court *Felony, Misdemeanor, Civil, Eviction, Small Claims, Probate* 813 Broadway, Rm 201, Goodland, KS 67735. 8:30AM-5PM. **785-899-4850**, Fax: 785-899-4858. ✋

Smith County

District Court *Felony, Misdemeanor, Civil, Eviction, Small Claims, Probate* PO Box 273, Smith Center, KS 66967. 8AM-5PM. **785-282-5140/41**, Fax: 785-282-5145. ✋

Stafford County

District Court *Felony, Misdemeanor, Civil, Eviction, Small Claims, Probate* www.staffordcounty.org PO Box 365, St John, KS 67576. 8AM-5PM. **620-549-3295**, Fax: 620-549-3298. Access by ✋

Stanton County

District Court *Felony, Misdemeanor, Civil, Eviction, Small Claims, Probate* PO Box 913, Johnson, KS 67855. 8AM-5PM. **620-492-2180**, Fax: 620-492-6410. ☎Fax✉✋

Stevens County

District Court *Felony, Misdemeanor, Civil, Eviction, Small Claims, Probate* 200 E 6th, Hugoton, KS 67951. 8AM-

5PM Closed noon-1PM. **620-544-2484**, Fax: 620-544-2528. 🖐

Sumner County

District Court *Felony, Misdemeanor, Civil, Eviction, Small Claims, Probate* PO Box 399 Sumner County Courthouse, Wellington, KS 67152. 8AM-N, 1-5PM. **620-326-5936**, Fax: 620-326-5365. Court will not perform searches for "employment purposes" nor lien searches. Summit requests on their request form. ✉️**Fax**🖐

Thomas County

District Court *Felony, Misdemeanor, Civil, Eviction, Small Claims, Probate* PO Box 805, Colby, KS 67701. 8:30AM-5PM. **785-462-4540**, Fax: 785-462-2291. **Fax**✉️🖐

Trego County

District Court *Felony, Misdemeanor, Civil, Eviction, Small Claims, Probate* 216 N Main, Wakeeney, KS 67672. 8:30AM-5PM. **785-743-2148**, Fax: 785-743-2726. ✉️🖐

Wabaunsee County

District Court *Felony, Misdemeanor, Civil, Eviction, Small Claims, Probate* Courthouse, PO Box 278, Alma, KS 66401. 8AM-4:30PM. **785-765-2406**, Fax: 785-765-2487. 🖐

Wallace County

District Court *Felony, Misdemeanor, Civil, Eviction, Small Claims, Probate* PO Box 8, Sharon Springs, KS 67758. 8AM-N,1-5PM. **785-852-4289**, Fax: 785-852-4271. 🖐

Washington County

District Court *Felony, Misdemeanor, Civil, Eviction, Small Claims, Probate* www.kscourts.org/dstcts/12dstct.htm Courthouse, 214 C St, Washington, KS 66968. 8AM-N,1-5PM. **785-325-2381**, Fax: 785-325-2557. **Fax**✉️🖐

Wichita County

District Court *Felony, Misdemeanor, Civil, Eviction, Small Claims, Probate* 206 S 4th St PO Box 968, Leoti, KS 67861. 8AM-5PM. **620-375-4454**, Fax: 620-375-2999. This court is not in Wichita, KS. Wichita City is in Sedgwick County. 🖐

Wilson County

District Court *Felony, Misdemeanor, Civil, Eviction, Small Claims, Probate* PO Box 246, Fredonia, KS 66736. 8:30AM-5PM. **620-378-4533**, Fax: 620-378-4531. **Fax**✉️🖐

Woodson County

District Court *Felony, Misdemeanor, Civil, Eviction, Small Claims, Probate* PO Box 228, Yates Center, KS 66783. 8AM-N,1-5PM. **620-625-8610**, Fax: 620-625-8674. 🖐

Wyandotte County

District Court *Felony, Misdemeanor, Civil, Eviction, Small Claims, Probate* 710 N 7th St, Kansas City, KS 66101. 8AM-5PM. Civil: 913-573-2901, Crim: 913-573-2905. Crminal fax: 913-573-8177, civil fax: 813-573-4134. 🖥️🖐

Kentucky

State Court Administration: Administrative Office of Courts, 100 Mill Creek Park, Frankfort, KY, 40601; 502-573-1682, Fax: 502-573-1669. http://www.kycourts.net

Court Structure: The Circuit Court is the court of general jurisdiction and the District Court is the limited jurisdiction court. Most of Kentucky's counties combined the courts into one location and records are co-mingled. Circuit courts have jurisdiction over cases involving capital offenses and felonies, divorces, adoptions, terminations of parental rights, land dispute title problems and contested probates of will. Juvenile matters, city and county ordinances, misdemeanors, traffic offenses, probate of wills, felony preliminary hearings, and civil cases involving $4,000 or less are heard in District Court. Ninety percent of all Kentuckians involved in court proceedings appear in District Court.

Probate Courts: Probate is handled by the Circuit Court if contested and by the District Court if uncontested.

Online Access: There are statewide, online computer systems called SUSTAIN and KyCourts available for internal judicial/state agency use only, and KY Bar attorneys may register to use the KCOJ court records data at http://courtnetpublic.kycourts.net. No courts offer online access to records. However, you may search daily court calendars by county for free at http://dockets.kycourts.net. Also, you may search online for open dockets (limited) of the supreme court at http://162.114.20.136/dockets.

Additional Information: Until 1978, county judges handled all cases; therefore, in many cases, District and Circuit Court records go back only to 1978. Records prior to that time are archived.

Many courts refer requests for criminal searches to the Administrative Office of Courts (AOC - 502-573-2350 or 800-928-6381) due to lack of personnel for searching at the court level. AOC maintains records on an internal system called COURTNET, which contains information on opening, closing, proceedings, disposition, and parties to including individual defendants. Felony convictions are accessible back to 1978, and Misdemeanors back five years. The required Release Form is available from the AOC at the numbers above. A check or money order for the search fee of $10.00 per requested individual ($5.00 fee if non-profit or if you are the individual) is payable to the State Treasurer of Kentucky. A SASE and a second postage-attached envelope must accompany the request.

Key: Symbols refer to criminal records access unless otherwise noted. phone-📞 mail-✉️ fax-**Fax** in person-🖐 online-🖥️ email-**Email**

Adair County

Circuit & District Court *Felony, Misdemeanor, Civil, Eviction, Small Claims, Probate* 500 Public Square, #6, Columbia, KY 42728. 8AM-4PM. **270-384-2626**, Fax: 270-384-4299. ✉️ ✍️

Allen County

Circuit & District Court *Felony, Misdemeanor, Civil, Eviction, Small Claims, Probate* Box 477, Scottsville, KY 42164. 8-4:30PM. **270-237-3561**. ✍️

Anderson County

Circuit Court *Felony, Civil Actions Over $4,000* Courthouse 151 S Main St, Lawrenceburg, KY 40342. 8:30AM-5PM. **502-839-3508**. ✍️

District Court *Misd., Civil Actions Under $4,000, Eviction, Small Claims, Probate* 151 S Main, Lawrenceburg, KY 40342. 8:30AM-N, 1--5PM M-TH, 8:30AM-6PM F. **502-839-5445**.

Ballard County

Circuit & District Court *Felony, Misdemeanor, Civil, Eviction, Small Claims, Probate* Box 265, Wickliffe, KY 42087. 8AM-4PM. **270-335-5123**, Fax: 270-335-3849. ✍️

Barren County

Circuit & District Court *Felony, Misdemeanor, Civil, Eviction, Small Claims, Probate* PO Box 1359, Glasgow, KY 42142-1359. 8AM-4:30PM. **270-651-3763**, Fax: 270-651-6203. Access by ✍️

Bath County

Circuit & District Court *Felony, Misdemeanor, Civil, Eviction, Small Claims, Probate* Box 558, Owingsville, KY 40360. 8AM-4PM. **606-674-2186 X6821**, Fax: 606-674-3996. ✍️

Bell County

Circuit & District Court *Felony, Misdemeanor, Civil, Eviction, Small Claims, Probate* Box 307, Pineville, KY 40977. 8:30AM-4PM. **606-337-2942/9900**, Fax: 606-337-8850. ✍️

Boone County

Circuit & District Court *Felony, Misdemeanor, Civil, Eviction, Small Claims, Probate* 6025 Rogers Ln, #141, Burlington, KY 41005. 8:30AM-4:30PM. **859-334-2286**, Fax: 859-334-3650. Civil

phone: 859-334-2287 District, Crim: 859-334-3536 District. ✍️

Bourbon County

Circuit & District Court *Felony, Misdemeanor, Civil, Eviction, Small Claims, Probate* Box 740, Paris, KY 40361. 8:30AM-4:30PM M-TH, 8:30AM-6PM F. **859-987-2624**, Fax: 859-987-6049. ✍️

Boyd County

Circuit & District Court *Felony, Misdemeanor, Civil, Eviction, Small Claims, Probate* Box 694, Catlettsburg, KY 41129-0694. 8:30AM-4PM. **606-739-4131**, Fax: 606-739-6330. Access by ✍️

Boyle County

Circuit Court *Felony, Civil Actions Over $4,000* Courthouse, 321 Main St, Danville, KY 40422. 8AM-5PM. **859-239-7442**, Fax: 859-239-7000. ✍️

District Court *Misdemeanor, Civil Actions Under $4,000, Eviction, Small Claims, Probate* Courthouse, 3rd Fl, Danville, KY 40422. 8AM-4:30PM. **859-239-7362**, Fax: 859-239-7807. Civil phone: 859-239-7394. Access ✉️**Fax**✍️

Bracken County

Circuit & District Court *Felony, Misdemeanor, Civil, Eviction, Small Claims, Probate* PO Box 205, Brooksville, KY 41004-0205. 8AM-4:30PM M,T,TH,F, 8:30AM-N W & Sat. **606-735-3328**, Fax: 606-735-3900. ✍️

Breathitt County

Circuit & District Court *Felony, Misdemeanor, Civil, Eviction, Small Claims, Probate* 1137 Main St, Jackson, KY 41339. 8AM-4PM M,T,TH,F; 8AM-N W; 9AM-N Sat. **606-666-5768**, Fax: 606-666-4893. ✉️ ✍️

Breckinridge County

Circuit & District Court *Felony, Misdemeanor, Civil, Eviction, Small Claims, Probate* Box 111, Hardinsburg, KY 40143. 8AM-4PM. **270-756-2239**, Fax: 270-756-1129. ✍️

Bullitt County

Circuit & District Court *Felony, Misdemeanor, Civil, Eviction, Small Claims, Probate* Box 746, Shephardsville, KY 40165. 8AM-4PM. **502-543-7104**, Fax: 502-543-7158. ✍️

Butler County

Circuit & District Court *Felony, Misdemeanor, Civil, Eviction, Small Claims, Probate* Box 625, Morgantown, KY 42261. 8AM-4:30PM M-F; 9AM-N Sat. **270-526-5631**. ✉️ ✍️

Caldwell County

Circuit & District Court *Felony, Misdemeanor, Civil, Eviction, Small Claims, Probate* 105 W Court Sq, Princeton, KY 42445. 8AM-4PM. **270-365-6884**, Fax: 270-365-9171. ✍️

Calloway County

Circuit & District Court *Felony, Misdemeanor, Civil, Eviction, Small Claims, Probate* 312 N 4th St, Murray, KY 42071. 8AM-4:30PM. **270-753-2714**, Fax: 270-759-9822. Circuit court civil/criminal phone- 270-753-2773. ✍️

Campbell County

Circuit Court *Felony, Civil Over $4,000* www.kycourts.net/clerks/campbellclerk.shtm 330 York St Rm 8, Newport, KY 41071. 8:30AM-4PM. **859-292-6314**. ✍️

District Court *Misdemeanor, Civil Under $4,000, Eviction, Small Claims, Probate* www.kycourts.net/clerks/campbellclerk.shtm 600 Columbia St, Newport, KY 41071-1816. 8:30AM-4PM. **859-292-6305**, Fax: 859-292-6593. ✍️

Carlisle County

Circuit & District Court *Felony, Misdemeanor, Civil, Eviction, Small Claims, Probate* Box 337, Bardwell, KY 42023. 8AM-4PM. **270-628-5425**, Fax: 270-628-5456. ☎️**Fax**✉️✍️

Carroll County

Circuit & District Court *Felony, Misdemeanor, Civil, Eviction, Small Claims, Probate* 802 Clay St, Carrollton, KY 41008. 8AM-4:30PM. **502-732-4305**, Fax: 502-732-8138. ✍️

Carter County

Circuit Court *Felony, Civil Actions Over $4,000* 100 E Main St, Grayson, KY 41143. 8:30AM-4PM M-F; 9AM-N Sat. **606-474-5191**, Fax: 606-474-8826. ✍️

District Court *Misdemeanor, Civil Actions Under $4,000, Eviction, Small Claims, Probate* Courthouse, Rm 203 300 W Main, Grayson, KY 41143. 8AM-4PM. **606-474-6572**, Fax: 606-474-8584. ✍️

Key: Symbols refer to criminal records access unless otherwise noted. phone-☎️ mail-✉️ fax-**Fax** in person-✍️ online-🖥️ email-**Email**

Casey County

Circuit & District Court *Felony, Misdemeanor, Civil, Eviction, Small Claims, Probate* PO Box 147, Liberty, KY 42539. 8AM-4:30PM M, Tu & F, 8AM-4PM W-Th, 8AM-N Sat. **606-787-6510**. 🖐

Christian County

Circuit & District Court *Felony, Misdemeanor, Civil, Eviction, Small Claims, Probate* Christian County Justice Ctr 100 Justice Way, Hopkinsville, KY 42240. 8AM-4:30PM. **270-889-6539**, Fax: 270-889-6564. 🖐

Clark County

Circuit Court *Felony, Civil Actions Over $4,000* Box 687, Winchester, KY 40392. 8AM-4PM. **859-737-7264**. Access by 🖐

District Court *Misdemeanor, Civil Actions Under $4,000, Eviction, Small Claims, Probate* PO Box 687, Winchester, KY 40392-0687. 8AM-4PM. **859-737-7141**, Fax 859-737-7005. ✉🖐

Clay County

Circuit & District Court *Felony, Misdemeanor, Civil, Eviction, Small Claims, Probate* 79 Highway 80, #3, Manchester, KY 40962. 7:30AM-4:30PM. **606-598-3663**, Fax: 606-598-4047. 🖐

Clinton County

Circuit & District Court *Felony, Misdemeanor, Civil, Eviction, Small Claims, Probate* Courthouse 2nd Fl 100 S Cross St, Albany, KY 42602. 8AM-4:30PM M-F; 8AM-N Sat. **606-387-6424**, Fax: 606-387-8154. ☎✉🖐

Crittenden County

Circuit & District Court *Felony, Misdemeanor, Civil, Eviction, Small Claims, Probate, Traffic* 107 S Main, Marion, KY 42064. 8AM-4:30PM. **270-965-4200 (and) 270-965-4046**. 🖐

Cumberland County

Circuit & District Court *Felony, Misd., Civil, Eviction, Small Claims, Probate* Box 395, Burkesville, KY 42717. 8AM-4PM. **270-864-2611**. ✉Fax🖐

Daviess County

Circuit & District Court *Felony, Misdemeanor, Civil, Eviction, Small Claims, Probate* Box 277 (100 E Second St), Owensboro, KY 42302. 8AM-4PM. **270-687-7330 (Circuit Crim)**, Civil: 270-687-7220 (Circuit Civil); 270-687-7205 (District Civil), Crim: 270-687-7330 (Circuit Crim); 270-687-7200 (District Crim), Probate: 270-687-7207. 🖐

Edmonson County

Circuit & District Court *Felony, Misdemeanor, Civil, Eviction, Small Claims, Probate* Box 739 110 Cross Main St., Brownsville, KY 42210. 8AM-4:30PM M-W,F; 8AM-N Th,S. **270-597-2584**, Fax: 270-597-2884. Access by 🖐

Elliott County

Circuit & District Court *Felony, Misdemeanor, Civil, Eviction, Small Claims, Probate* Box 788, Sandy Hook, KY 41171. 8AM-4PM M-F; 9AM-N Sat. **606-738-5238**, Fax: 606-738-6962. 🖐

Estill County

Circuit & District Court *Felony, Misdemeanor, Civil, Eviction, Small Claims, Probate* 130 Main St, Rm 207, Irvine, KY 40336. 8AM-4PM. **606-723-3970**, Fax: 606-723-1158. ☎Fax✉🖐

Fayette County

Circuit Court - Criminal & Civil Divisions *Felony, Civil Over $4,000* www.kycourts.net/Courts/FayetteCourtsNS.shtm 120 N Limestone, Lexington, KY 40507. 8:30AM-4:30PM. Fax: 859-246-2146. Civil phone: 859-246-2141, Crim: 859-246-2224. ✉🖐

District Court - Criminal & Civil *Misdemeanor, Civil Actions Under $4,000, Eviction, Small Claims, Probate* www.kycourts.net/Courts/FayetteCourtsNS.shtm 150 N Limestone #D112, Lexington, KY 40507. 8AM-4PM. Civil: 859-246-2240, Crim: 859-246-2228. 🖐

Fleming County

Circuit & District Court *Felony, Misdemeanor, Civil, Eviction, Small Claims, Probate* Courthouse 100 Court Square, Flemingsburg, KY 41041. 8AM-4:30PM. **606-845-7011**, Fax: 606-849-2400. 🖐

Floyd County

Circuit Court *Felony, Civil Actions Over $4,000* 127 S Lake Dr, Prestonsburg, KY 41653-3368. 8AM-4PM. **606-886-3090**, Fax: 606-886-9075. Civil phone: 606-886-2124, Crim: 606-886-9114. ✉🖐

District Court *Misdemeanor, Small Claims, Probate* 127 S Lake Dr, Prestonsburg, KY 41653. 8AM-4PM. **606-886-9114**. Probate: 606-886-2124. Small claims: 606-886-2124. ☎✉🖐

Franklin County

Circuit Court *Felony, Civil Over $4,000* www.kycourts.net/Counties/Franklin.asp?County=Franklin Box 678 (214 St Clair St), Frankfort, KY 40602. 8AM-4:30PM. **502-564-8380**, Fax: 502-564-8188. Criminal phone: 502-573-2350/Adm. Criminal records located at; 100 Mill Creek Park, Frankfort KY 40601- walkin 7am-3pm or drive thru 7am -10pm Access by 🖐✉

District Court *Misdemeanor, Civil Actions Under $4,000, Eviction, Small Claims, Probate* Box 678, Frankfort, KY 40601. 8AM-4:30PM. **502-564-7013**, Fax: 502-564-8188. 🖐

Fulton County

Circuit & District Court *Felony, Misdemeanor, Civil, Eviction, Small Claims, Probate* Box 198, Hickman, KY 42050. 8AM-4PM. **270-236-3944**, Fax: 270-236-3729. 6 days of the court docket information can be found at www.kycourts.com. 🖐

Gallatin County

Circuit Court *Felony, Civil Actions Over $4,000* Box 256 (100 Main St), Warsaw, KY 41095. 8AM-4:30PM M,T,Th,F; Closed W. **859-567-5241**. Access ✉🖐

District Court *Misdemeanor, Civil Actions Under $4,000, Eviction, Small Claims, Probate* Box 256, Warsaw, KY 41095. 8AM-4:30PM T,Th,F; 8AM-6PM M; 8AM-N Sat. **859-567-2388**, Probate: 859-567-2388 x1. Access by ✉🖐

Garrard County

Circuit & District Court *Felony, Misdemeanor, Civil, Eviction, Small Claims, Probate* 7 Public Square Courthouse Annex, Lancaster, KY 40444. 8AM-4PM M,T,TH,F, 8AM-N Wed & Sat. **859-792-6032**, Fax: 859-792-6414. Circuit Clerk phone 859-792-2961. 🖐

Grant County

Circuit & District Court *Felony, Misdemeanor, Civil, Eviction, Small Claims, Probate* Courthouse 101 N Main, Williamstown, KY 41097. 8AM-

---

Key: Symbols refer to criminal records access unless otherwise noted. phone-☎ mail-✉ fax-**Fax** in person-🖐 online-🖥 email-**Email**

4PM. **859-824-4467 (Circuit) 859-823-5251 (District).** 🖑

Graves County

Circuit & District Court *Felony, Misd., Civil, Eviction, Small Claims, Probate* Courthouse 100 E Broadway, Mayfield, KY 42066. 8AM-4:30PM. **270-247-1733,** Fax: 270-247-7358. 🖑

Grayson County

Circuit & District Court *Felony, Misdemeanor, Civil, Eviction, Small Claims, Probate* 125 E White Oak, Leitchfield, KY 42754. 8AM-5PM. **270-259-3040,** Fax: 270-259-9866. ✉🖑

Green County

Circuit & District Court *Felony, Misdemeanor, Civil, Eviction, Small Claims, Probate* 203 W Court St, Greensburg, KY 42743. 8AM-4PM M-W, F; 8AM-12:30PM Sat. **270-932-5631,** Fax: 270-932-6468. **Fax**✉🖑

Greenup County

Circuit & District Court *Felony, Misdemeanor, Civil, Eviction, Small Claims, Probate* Courthouse Annex 301 Main St, Greenup, KY 41144. 9AM-4:30PM. **606-473-9869,** Fax: 606-473-7388. 🖑

Hancock County

Circuit & District Court *Felony, Misdemeanor, Civil, Eviction, Small Claims, Probate* Courthouse PO Box 250, Hawesville, KY 42348. 8AM-4PM M,T,W,F; 8AM-5:30PM Th. **270-927-8144,** Fax: 270-927-8629. Access by 🖑

Hardin County

Circuit & District Court *Felony, Misdemeanor, Civil, Eviction, Small Claims, Probate* Hardin County Justice Ctr 120 E Dixie Ave, Elizabethtown, KY 42701. 8AM-4:30PM;. **270-766-5000,** Fax: 270-766-5243. 🖑

Radcliff District Court *Probate, Eviction* 220 Freedom Way, Radcliff, KY 40160. 8:30AM-12, 12:00-4PM. **270-351-1299/4799,** Fax: 270-351-1301.

Harlan County

Circuit & District Court *Felony, Misdemeanor, Civil, Eviction, Small Claims, Probate* Box 190, Harlan, KY 40831. 8AM-4:30PM. **606-573-2680.** 🖑

Harrison County

Circuit & District Court *Felony, Misdemeanor, Civil, Eviction, Small Claims, Probate* 115 Court St #1, Cynthiana, KY 41031. 8:30AM-4:30PM M-F, 9AM-12PM Sat. **859-234-1914,** Fax: 859-234-6787. 🖑

Hart County

Circuit & District Court *Felony, Misdemeanor, Civil, Eviction, Small Claims, Probate* Box 248, Munfordville, KY 42765. 8-4PM. **270-524-5181.** 🖑

Henderson County

Circuit & District Court *Felony, Civil Actions Over $4,000* PO Box 675, Henderson, KY 42420. 8AM-6PM M; 8AM-4:30PM T-F. **270-826-2405/1566,** Fax: 270-831-2710 (District). 🖑

Henry County

Circuit & District Court *Felony, Misd., Civil, Eviction, Small Claims, Probate* PO Box 359 (30 Main St), New Castle, KY 40050. 8AM-4:30PM. **502-845-7551,** Fax: 502-845-2969. 🖑

Hickman County

Circuit & District Court *Felony, Misdemeanor, Civil, Eviction, Small Claims, Probate* 109 S Washington St, Clinton, KY 42031. 8AM-4PM. **270-653-3901,** Fax: 270-653-3989. ✉🖑

Hopkins County

Circuit & District Court *Felony, Misd., Civil, Eviction, Small Claims, Probate* Courthouse 30 S Main St, Madisonville, KY 42431. 7:30AM-4PM. **270-824-7502,** Fax: 270-824-7032. 🖑

Jackson County

Circuit Court *Felony, Civil Actions Over $4,000* PO Box 84, McKee, KY 40447. 8AM-4PM M-F 8AM-N Sat. **606-287-7783,** Fax: 606-287-3277. **Fax**✉🖑

District Court *Misdemeanor, Civil Actions Under $4,000, Eviction, Small Claims, Probate* PO Box 84, McKee, KY 40447. 8AM-4PM M-F; 8AM-N Sat. **606-287-8651,** Fax: 606-287-3277. **Fax**✉🖑

Jefferson County

Circuit & District Court *Felony, Misdemeanor, Civil, Eviction, Small Claims, Probate* Hall of Justice 600 W Jefferson St, Louisville, KY 40202. **502-595-3064,** Fax: 502-595-4629. Civil phone: 502-595-3015, Crim: 502-595-3042. ✉🖑

Jessamine County

Circuit Court *Felony, Civil Actions Over $4,000* 107 N Main St, Nicholasville, KY 40356. 8AM-4:30PM M-W, F; 8AM-12PM TH. **859-885-4531.** ✉🖑

District Court *Misdemeanor, Civil Actions Under $4,000, Eviction, Small Claims, Probate* 107 N Main St, Nicholasville, KY 40356. 8AM-4:30PM M-W; 8AM-N TH; 8AM-4:30PM F. **859-887-1005,** Fax: 859-887-0425. ✉🖑

Johnson County

Circuit & District Court *Felony, Misdemeanor, Civil, Eviction, Small Claims, Probate* Box 1405, Paintsville, KY 41240. 8AM-4:30PM; 8:30AM-N Sat Driver's license only. **606-789-5181,** Fax: 606-789-4192. 🖑

Kenton County

Circuit Court *Felony, Civil Actions Over $4,000* www.aoc.state.ky.us/kenton 230 Madison Ave (PO Box 669), Covington, KY 41011. 8AM-5PM. **859-292-6521,** Fax: 859-292-6611. 🖑

District Court *Misdemeanor, Civil Under $4,000, Eviction, Small Claims, Probate* www.aoc.state.ky.us/kenton 230 Madison Ave, 3rd Fl, Covington, KY 41011. 7-5. **859-292-6523,** Fax: 859-292-6611. 🖑

Knott County

Circuit & District Court *Felony, Misdemeanor, Civil, Eviction, Small Claims, Probate* PO Box 1317, Hindman, KY 41822. 8AM-4PM; 8AM-N Sat. **606-785-5021.** ☎**Fax**✉🖑

Knox County

Circuit & District Court *Felony, Misdemeanor, Civil, Eviction, Small Claims, Probate* PO Box 760 (401 Court Sq #202, Barbourville, KY 40906. 8AM-4:30PM M-F; 8:30AM-N Sat. **606-546-3075 (Circuit) 546-3232 (Dist),** Fax: 606-546-7949. 🖑

Larue County

Circuit & District Court *Felony, Misdemeanor, Civil, Eviction, Small Claims, Probate* Courthouse Annex PO Box 191 (209 W High St), Hodgenville, KY 42748. 8AM-4PM. **270-358-3421,** Fax: 270-358-3731. 🖑

Laurel County

Circuit & District Court *Felony, Misdemeanor, Civil, Eviction, Small Claims, Probate* Box 1798, London, KY 40743-1798. 8AM-4:30PM. **606-864-2863**, Fax: 606-864-8264. Access by 🖐

Lawrence County

Circuit & District Court *Felony, Misdemeanor, Civil, Eviction, Small Claims, Probate* Courthouse PO Box 212, Louisa, KY 41230. 8:30AM-4:30PM M-F, 8:30AM-N Sat. **606-638-4215**, Fax: 606-638-0264. ✉🖐

Lee County

Circuit & District Court *Felony, Misdemeanor, Civil, Eviction, Small Claims, Probate* Box E, Beattyville, KY 41311. 8AM-4PM M-F; 8:30AM-11:30AM Sat. **606-464-8400**, Fax: 606-464-0144. 🖐

Leslie County

Circuit & District Court *Felony, Misdemeanor, Civil, Eviction, Small Claims, Probate* Box 1750, Hyden, KY 41749. 8AM-4PM M-gaF; 8AM-N Sat. **606-672-2505**, Fax: 606-672-5128. 🖐

Letcher County

Circuit & District Court *Felony, Misdemeanor, Civil, Eviction, Small Claims, Probate* 156 W Main St, #201, Whitesburg, KY 41858. 8:30AM-4PM M-F; 8:30AM-12PM first Sat of month. **606-633-7559/8810**, Fax: 606-633-5864. 🖐

Lewis County

Circuit & District Court *Felony, Misdemeanor, Civil, Eviction, Small Claims, Probate* PO Box 70, Vanceburg, KY 41179. 8AM-4:30PM M,T,Th,F 8:30-N W,Sat. **606-796-3053**, Fax: 606-796-3030. ✉🖐

Lincoln County

Circuit & District Court *Felony, Misdemeanor, Civil, Eviction, Small Claims, Probate* 101 E Main, Stanford, KY 40484. 8AM-4PM; 9AM-12PM Sat. **606-365-2535**, Fax: 606-365-3389. 🖐

Livingston County

Circuit & District Court *Felony, Misdemeanor, Civil, Eviction, Small Claims, Probate* PO Box 160, Smithland, KY 42081. 8AM-6PM M 8AM-4PM T-F. **270-928-2172**. 🖐

Logan County

Circuit Court *Felony, Civil Actions Over $4,000* Box 420 (W 4th St), Russellville, KY 42276-0420. 8AM-4:30PM M-Th; 8AM-5PM F. **270-726-2424**, Fax: 270-726-7893. 🖐

District Court *Misdemeanor, Civil Actions Under $4,000, Eviction, Small Claims, Probate* Box 420, Russellville, KY 42276. 8AM-4:30PM. **270-726-3107**, Fax: 270-726-7893. 🖐

Lyon County

Circuit & District Court *Felony, Misdemeanor, Civil, Eviction, Small Claims, Probate* Box 565, Eddyville, KY 42038. 8AM-4PM. **270-388-7231**. This court also handles domestic violence, traffic, and juvenile cases. 🖐

McCracken County

Circuit Court *Felony, Civil Actions Over $4,000* Box 1455 (301 S 6th St), Paducah, KY 42002-1455. 8:30AM-4:30PM M, 8:30AM-4:30PM T-F. **270-575-7280**. Visitors may only search from 2PM-4PM on Thursday. Access by 🖐

District Court *Misdemeanor, Civil Actions Under $4,000, Eviction, Small Claims, Probate* Box 1436, Paducah, KY 42002. 8:30-4:30PM. **270-575-7270**. 🖐

McCreary County

Circuit & District Court *Felony, Misdemeanor, Civil, Eviction, Small Claims, Probate* Box 40, Whitley City, KY 42653. 8:30AM-4:30PM. **606-376-5041**, Fax: 606-376-8844. Access by 🖐

McLean County

Circuit & District Court *Felony, Misdemeanor, Civil, Eviction, Small Claims, Probate* Box 145 (210 E Main St), Calhoun, KY 42327. 8AM-4:30PM M-F; open till 6PM F. **270-273-3966**, Fax: 270-273-5918. 🖐

Madison County

Circuit Court *Felony, Civil Over $4,000* www.kycourts.net/Circuit/Circuit_Intro.shtm PO Box 813 (101 W Main St) Madison County Courthouse, Richmond, KY 40476. 8AM-4PM. **859-624-4793**. 🖐

District Court *Misdemeanor, Civil Actions Under $4,000, Eviction, Small Claims, Probate* Madison Hall of Justice 351 W Main St, Richmond, KY 40475.

8AM-4PM. **859-624-4722**, Fax: 859-624-4746. 🖐

Magoffin County

Circuit & District Court *Felony, Misdemeanor, Civil, Eviction, Small Claims, Probate* Box 147, Salyersville, KY 41465. 8AM-4PM. **606-349-2215**, Fax: 606-349-2209. Fax✉🖐

Marion County

Circuit & District Court *Felony, Misdemeanor, Civil, Eviction, Small Claims, Probate* 120 W Main St, #6, Lebanon, KY 40033. 8:30AM-4:30PM M-F; 8:30AM-N Sat. **270-692-2681**. 🖐

Marshall County

Circuit & District Court *Felony, Misd., Civil, Eviction, Small Claims, Probate* 80 Judicial Dr, Unit #101, Benton, KY 42025. 8-4:30PM. **270-527-3883/1721**, Fax: 270-527-5865. ☎Fax✉🖐

Martin County

Circuit & District Court *Felony, Misd., Civil, Eviction, Small Claims, Probate* Box 430, Inez, KY 41224. 8AM-4PM except 1st & 3rd Th 8AM-7PM. **606-298-3508**, Fax: 606-298-4202. 🖐

Mason County

Circuit Court *Felony, Civil Actions Over $4,000* 100 W 3rd St, Maysville, KY 41056. 8:30AM-4:30PM. **606-564-4340**, Fax: 606-564-0932. 🖐

District Court *Misdemeanor, Civil Actions Under $4000, Eviction, Small Claims, Probate* 100 W 3rd St, Maysville, KY 41056. 8:30AM-4:30PM. **606-564-4011**, Fax: 606-564-0932. 🖐

Meade County

Circuit & District Court *Felony, Misdemeanor, Civil, Eviction, Small Claims, Probate* Courthouse 516 Fairway Dr, Brandenburg, KY 40108. 8AM-4:30AM except Thurs. 8AM-6:30PM. **270-422-4961**, Fax: 270-422-2147. This court asks all record requests go to the AOC in Frankfort. 🖐

Menifee County

Circuit & District Court *Felony, Misdemeanor, Civil, Eviction, Small Claims, Probate* Box 172, Frenchburg, KY 40322. 8:30AM-4PM. **606-768-2461**, Fax: 606-768-2462. 🖐

Key: Symbols refer to criminal records access unless otherwise noted. phone-☎ mail-✉ fax-**Fax** in person-🖐 online-💻 email-**Email**

Mercer County

Circuit & District Court *Felony, Misdemeanor, Civil, Eviction, Small Claims, Probate* Courthouse, 224 Main St S, Harrodsburg, KY 40330-1696. 8AM-4:30PM. **859-734-6306**, Fax: 859-734-9159. Civil phone: 859-734-6305, Crim: 859-734-6307, Probate: 859-734-6305. Circuit Civil & Crim: 859-734-6306 🖑

Metcalfe County

Circuit & District Court *Felony, Misdemeanor, Civil, Eviction, Small Claims, Probate* Box 485, Edmonton, KY 42129. 8AM-4PM. **270-432-3663**, Fax: 270-432-4437. ☎Fax⊠🖑

Monroe County

Circuit & District Court *Felony, Misdemeanor, Civil, Eviction, Small Claims, Probate* 200 N Main St #B, Tompkinsville, KY 42167. 8AM-4PM. **270-487-5480**, Fax: 270-487-0068. 🖑

Montgomery County

Circuit & District Court *Felony, Misdemeanor, Civil, Eviction, Small Claims, Probate* Courthouse, One Court St (PO Box 327), Mt Sterling, KY 40353. 8:30AM-4PM. **859-498-5966**, Fax: 859-498-9341. 🖑

Morgan County

Circuit & District Court *Felony, Misdemeanor, Civil, Eviction, Small Claims, Probate* Box 85, West Liberty, KY 41472. 8AM-4PM. **606-743-3763**, Fax: 606-743-2633. ⊠🖑

Muhlenberg County

Circuit Court *Felony, Civil Actions Over $4,000* Box 776 (109 E Main St), Greenville, KY 42345. 8AM-4PM. **270-338-4850 (Felony)**, Fax: 270-338-0177. Direct mail felony record requests to state AOC in Frankfort. 🖑

District Court *Misdemeanor, Civil Actions Under $4,000, Eviction, Small Claims, Probate* Box 776, Greenville, KY 42345. 8AM-4PM. **270-338-0995**, Fax: 270-338-0177. 🖑

Nelson County

Circuit & District Court *Felony, Misdemeanor, Civil, Eviction, Small Claims, Probate* Box 845, Bardstown, KY 40004. 8:30AM-4:30PM. **502-348-3648**. ⊠🖑

Nicholas County

Circuit & District Court *Felony, Misdemeanor, Civil, Eviction, Small Claims, Probate* PO Box 109, Carlisle, KY 40311. 8:30AM-4:30PM. **859-289-2336**, Fax: 859-289-6141. Fax⊠

Ohio County

Circuit & District Court *Felony, Misdemeanor, Civil, Eviction, Small Claims, Probate* PO Box 67 (130 E Washington, #300), Hartford, KY 42347. 8:30AM-4:30PM. **270-298-3671**, Fax: 270-298-9565. 🖑

Oldham County

Circuit & District Court *Felony, Misd., Civil, Eviction, Small Claims, Probate* 100 W Main St, La Grange, KY 40031. 8AM-4PM. **502-222-9837**, Fax: 502-222-3047. Direct criminal record requests to state AOC in Frankfort. 🖑

Owen County

Circuit & District Court *Felony, Misdemeanor, Civil, Eviction, Small Claims, Probate* Box 473, Owenton, KY 40359. 8AM-4PM. **502-484-2232**, Fax: 502-484-0625. Fax⊠🖑

Owsley County

Circuit & District Court *Felony, Misd., Civil, Eviction, Small Claims, Probate* Box 130 (N Court St), Booneville, KY 41314. 8AM-4PM M-F, 8AM-N Sat. **606-593-6226**, Fax: 606-593-6343. 🖑

Pendleton County

Circuit & District Court *Felony, Misd., Civil, Eviction, Small Claims, Probate* PO Box 69 (223 Main St.), Falmouth, KY 41040. 8AM-4PM. **859-654-3347**. 🖑

Perry County

Circuit Court *Felony, Civil Actions Over $4,000* Box 7433, Hazard, KY 41701. 8AM-4PM. **606-435-6000**, Fax: 606-435-6143. 🖑

District Court *Misdemeanor, Civil Actions Under $4,000, Eviction, Small Claims, Probate* PO Box 7433, Hazard, KY 41702. 8-4PM. **606-435-6002**. 🖑

Pike County

Circuit & District Court *Felony, Misdemeanor, Civil, Eviction, Small Claims, Probate* PO Box 1002, Pikeville, KY 41502. 8AM-4:30PM. **606-433-7557**, Fax: 606-433-7044. 🖑

Powell County

Circuit & District Court *Felony, Misd., Civil, Eviction, Small Claims, Probate* Box 578, Stanton, KY 40380. 8AM-4PM M,T,W,F, 8AM-N Th & Sat. **606-663-4141**, Fax: 606-663-2710. 🖑

Pulaski County

Circuit & District Court *Felony, Misdemeanor, Civil, Eviction, Small Claims, Probate* Box 664 100 N Maine, Courthouse Sq 3rd Fl, Somerset, KY 42502. 8AM-4:30PM M-F, 8AM-N Sat. **606-677-4029**, Fax: 606-677-4002. 🖑

Robertson County

Circuit & District Court *Felony, Misdemeanor, Civil, Eviction, Small Claims, Probate* PO Box 63 211 Court St, Mt Olivet, KY 41064. 8:30AM-4:30PM. **606-724-5993**, Fax: 606-724-5721. 🖑

Rockcastle County

Circuit & District Court *Felony, Misdemeanor, Civil, Eviction, Small Claims, Probate* Courthouse Annex, 1st Fl 205 E Main St., Rm 102, Mt Vernon, KY 40456. 8-4PM M-W & F; 8AM-6PM Th; 8:30AM-N Sat. **606-256-2581**. 🖑

Rowan County

Circuit & District Court *Felony, Misdemeanor, Civil, Eviction, Small Claims, Probate* www.kycourts.net 627 E Main, Morehead, KY 40351-1398. 8:30AM-4:30PM M-F 8:30AM-N SAT. **606-784-4574**, Fax: 606-784-1899. 🖑

Russell County

Circuit & District Court *Felony, Misd., Civil, Eviction, Small Claims, Probate* 410 Monument Square, #203, Jamestown, KY 42629. 7:30AM-5PM. **270-343-2185**, Fax: 270-343-5808. 🖑

Scott County

Circuit & District Court *Felony, Misdemeanor, Civil, Eviction, Small Claims, Probate* 119 N Hamilton, Georgetown, KY 40324. 8:30-4:30PM. **502-863-0474**. ⊠🖑

Shelby County

Circuit & District Court *Felony, Misdemeanor, Civil, Eviction, Small Claims, Probate* 501 Main St, Shelbyville, KY 40065. 8:30AM-4:30PM. **502-633-1287**, Fax: 502-633-0146 (633-6421 Dist Ct fax). Civil phone: 502-633-4736 (Dist Ct). 🖑

Simpson County

Circuit & District Court *Felony, Misdemeanor, Civil, Eviction, Small Claims, Probate* www.dockets.kycourts.net Box 261, Franklin, KY 42135-0261. 8AM-4PM. **270-586-8910/4241**, Fax: 270-586-0265. 🖐

Spencer County

Circuit & District Court *Felony, Misdemeanor, Civil, Eviction, Small Claims, Probate* Box 282, Taylorsville, KY 40071. 7:45AM-4PM. **502-477-3220**, Fax: 502-477-9368. ✉🖐

Taylor County

Circuit & District Court *Felony, Misdemeanor, Civil, Eviction, Small Claims, Probate* 203 N Court Courthouse, Campbellsville, KY 42718. 8AM-4:30PM. **270-465-6686**, Fax: 270-789-4356. 🖐

Todd County

Circuit & District Court *Felony, Misd., Civil, Eviction, Small Claims, Probate* Box 337 (202 E. Washington St), Elkton, KY 42220. 8AM-4:30PM. **270-265-5631**, Fax: 270-265-2122. 🖐

Trigg County

Circuit & District Court *Felony, Misdemeanor, Civil, Eviction, Small Claims, Probate* Box 673, Cadiz, KY 42211. 8AM-4PM. **270-522-6270**. District Court phone- 270-522-7070. 🖐

Trimble County

Circuit & District Court *Felony, Misdemeanor, Civil, Eviction, Small Claims, Probate* Box 248, Bedford, KY 40006. 8AM-4:30PM M,T,Th,F 8AM-N Sat. **502-255-3213, 502-255-3525 (District)**, Fax: 502-255-4953. 🖐

Union County

Circuit & District Court *Felony, Misdemeanor, Civil, Eviction, Small Claims, Probate* Box 59, Morganfield, KY 42437. 8AM-4PM. **270-389-0800/0804**, Fax: 270-389-9887. No searches performed on Thursday. 🖐

Warren County

Circuit & District Court *Felony, Misd., Civil, Eviction, Small Claims, Probate* 1001 Center St #102, Bowling Green, KY 42101-2184. 8:AM-4:30PM. **270-746-7400**, Fax: 270-746-7501. 🖐

Washington County

Circuit & District Court *Felony, Misd., Civil, Eviction, Small Claims, Probate* PO Box 346, Springfield, KY 40069. 8AM-4:30PM; 8:30-12 on Sat. **859-336-3761**, Fax: 859-336-9824. 🖐

Wayne County

Circuit & District Court *Felony, Misdemeanor, Civil, Eviction, Small Claims, Probate* 109 N Main St, Monticello, KY 42633-1458. 8AM-4:15PM M-F; 8:30AM-N Sat. **606-348-5841**, Fax: 606-348-4225. ✉🖐

Webster County

Circuit & District Court *Felony, Misdemeanor, Civil, Eviction, Small Claims, Probate* Box 290 (25 US Hiway 41A South), Dixon, KY 42409. 8AM-4PM. **270-639-9160**, Fax: 270-639-6757. **Fax**✉🖐

Whitley County

Williamsburg Circuit & District Court *Felony, Misdemeanor, Civil, Eviction, Small Claims, Probate* Box 329, Williamsburg, KY 40769. 8AM-4PM. **606-549-2973**. Circuit court: 606-549-2973. District court: 606-549-5162. 🖐

Corbin Circuit & District Court *Felony, Misdemeanor, Civil, Eviction, Small Claims, Probate* 805 S Main St #10, Corbin, KY 40701. 8AM-4PM. **606-523-1085**, Fax: 606-523-2049. Access by 🖐

Wolfe County

Circuit & District Court *Felony, Misd., Civil, Eviction, Small Claims, Probate* www.kycourts.net/clerks/wolfeclerk.shtm Box 296, Campton, KY 41301. 8:30AM-4:30PM. **606-668-3736**, Fax: 606-668-3198. ✉🖐

Woodford County

Circuit & District Court *Felony, Misdemeanor, Civil, Eviction, Small Claims, Probate* 130 Court St, Versailles, KY 40383. 8AM-4PM M-Th; 8AM-6PM F. **859-873-3711**, Fax: 859-879-8531. 🖐

Louisiana

State Court Administration: Judicial Administrator, Judicial Council of the Supreme Court, 400 Royal Street, Suite 1190, New Orleans, LA, 70130; 504-310-2550, Fax: 504-310-2587. www.lasc.org

Court Structure: The trial court of general jurisdiction in Louisiana is the district court. A District Court Clerk in each Parish holds all the records for that Parish. Each Parish has its own clerk and courthouse. City courts are courts of record and generally exercise concurrent jurisdiction with the district court in civil cases where the amount in controversy does not exceed $15,000. In criminal matters, they generally have jurisdiction over ordinance violations and misdemeanor violations of state law. City judges also handle a large number of traffic cases. Parish courts exercise jurisdiction in civil cases worth up to $10,000 and criminal cases punishable by fines of $1,000 or less, or imprisonment of six months or less. Cases are appealable from the parish courts directly to the courts of appeal.

A municipality may have a Mayor's Court; the mayor may hold trials, but nothing over $30.00, and there are no records.

Online Access: The online computer system named CMIS is operating and development is continuing. It is for internal use only; there is no plan to permit online public access. A number of Parishes that do offer a means of remote online access to the public. Also, search opinions from the state Supreme Court at www.lasc.org/opinion_search.asp. Online records go back to 1995.

Key: Symbols refer to criminal records access unless otherwise noted. phone-☎ mail-✉ fax-**Fax** in person-🖐 online-🖥 email-**Email**

Acadia Parish

15th District Court *Felony, Misd., Civil, Probate* www.acadiaparishclerk.com PO Box 922, Crowley, LA 70527. 8:30AM-4:30PM. **337-788-8881**, Fax: 337-788-1048. ☎Fax✉ ⍦

Allen Parish

33rd District Court *Felony, Misdemeanor, Civil, Probate* PO Box 248, Oberlin, LA 70655. 8AM-4:30PM. **337-639-4351**, Fax 337-639-2030. ✉⍦

Ascension Parish

23rd District Court *Felony, Misd., Civil, Probate* www.eatel.net/~apcc/Clerk_of_Court/indexx.html PO Box 192, Donaldsonville, LA 70346. 8:30AM-4:30PM. **225-473-9866**, civ fax: 225-473-8641; crim fax: 473-9287 Fax✉⍦

Assumption Parish

23rd District Court *Felony, Misdemeanor, Civil, Probate* PO Box 249, Napoleonville, LA 70390. 8:30AM-4:30PM. **985-369-6653**, Fax: 985-369-2032. Fax✉⍦

Avoyelles Parish

12th District Court *Felony, Misdemeanor, Civil, Probate* PO Box 219, Marksville, LA 71351. 8:30AM-4:30PM. **318-253-7523**. ✉⍦

Beauregard Parish

36th District Court *Felony, Misd., Civil, Probate* PO Box 100, DeRidder, LA 70634. 8AM-4:30PM. **337-463-8595**, Fax: 337-462-3916. ✉⍦

Bienville Parish

2nd District Court *Felony, Misd., Civil, Probate* www.bienvilleparish.org/clerk 100 Courthouse Dr, Rm 100, Arcadia, LA 71001. 8:30AM-4:30PM. **318-263-2123**, Fax: 318-263-7426. Fax✉⍦

Caddo Parish

1st District Court *Felony, Misdemeanor, Civil, Probate* www.caddoclerk.com 501 Texas St, Rm 103, Shreveport, LA 71101-5408. 8:30AM-5PM. **318-226-6786**, Fax: 318-677-5371. Civil phone: 318-226-6778, Crim: 318-226-6786. ✉⍦💻

Shreveport City Court *Civil Actions Under $15,000, Small Claims* 1244 Texas, Shreveport, LA 71101. 8AM-5PM. **318-673-5800** Access civil records by✉⍦

Calcasieu Parish

14th District Court *Felony, Misdemeanor, Civil, Probate* www.calclerkofcourt.com PO Box 1030, Lake Charles, LA 70602. 8:30AM-4:30PM. **337-437-3550**, Fax: 337-437-3350/3833. ✉⍦

Lake Charles City Court *Civil Actions Under $25,000, Small Claims* www.lakecharlescitycourt.com/ PO Box 1664, Lake Charles, LA 70602. 8:30AM-4PM. **337-491-1564** Access civil records by✉⍦

Caldwell Parish

37th District Court *Felony, Misdemeanor, Civil, Probate* PO Box 1327, Columbia, LA 71418. 8AM-4:30PM. **318-649-2272**, Fax: 318-649-2037. All record requests must be in writing. ✉⍦

Cameron Parish

38th District Court *Felony, Misdemeanor, Civil, Probate* PO Box 549, Cameron, LA 70631. 8:30AM-4:30PM. **337-775-5316**, Fax: 337-775-7172. Fax✉⍦

Catahoula Parish

7th District Court *Felony, Misdemeanor, Civil, Probate* PO Box 654, Harrisonburg, LA 71340. 8AM-4:30PM. **318-744-5497**, Fax 318-744-5488. ✉⍦

Claiborne Parish

2nd District Court *Felony, Misdemeanor, Civil, Probate* PO Box 330, Homer, LA 71040. 8:30AM-4:30PM. **318-927-9601**, Fax 318-927-2345. ✉⍦

Concordia Parish

7th District Court *Felony, Misdemeanor, Civil, Probate* www.concordiaclerk.org/ PO Box 790, Vidalia, LA 71373. 8:30AM-4:30PM. **318-336-4204**, Fax: 318-336-8777. ✉⍦

De Soto Parish

11th District Court *Felony, Misdemeanor, Civil, Probate* PO Box 1206, Mansfield, LA 71052. 8AM-4:30PM. **318-872-3110**, Fax: 318-872-4202. Crim phone: 318-872-3181. ✉⍦

Bossier Parish

26th District Court *Felony, Misdemeanor, Civil, Probate* www.bossierclerk.com PO Box 430, Benton, LA 71006. 8:30AM-4:30PM.

318-965-2336, Fax: 318-965-2713. ✉💻⍦

East Baton Rouge Parish

19th District Court *Felony, Misdemeanor, Civil, Probate* www.ebrclerkofcourt.org/ PO Box 1991, Baton Rouge, LA 70821. 7:30AM-5:30PM. **225-389-3950**, Fax: 225-389-3392. Criminal phone: 225-389-3964. ✉💻⍦

Baton Rouge City Court *Civil Actions Under $20,000, Small Claims, Criminal Traffic* www.brgov.com/dept/citycourt 233 St Louis St, Baton Rouge, LA 70802. 8AM-5PM. **225-389-5279**, Fax: 225-389-5260. Civil phone: 225-389-3017, Crim: 225-389-5294 Access civil records by✉⍦Fax💻

East Carroll Parish

6th District Court *Felony, Misdemeanor, Civil, Probate* 400 1st St, Lake Providence, LA 71254. 8:30AM-4:30PM. **318-559-2399**. ✉⍦

East Feliciana Parish

20th District Court *Felony, Misdemeanor, Civil, Probate* www.eastfelicianaclerk.com/court.html PO Box 599, Clinton, LA 70722. 8:30AM-4:30PM. **225-683-5145**, Fax: 225-683-3556. Fax✉⍦

Evangeline Parish

13th District Court *Felony, Misdemeanor, Civil, Probate* PO Drawer 347, Ville Platte, LA 70586. 8AM-4:30PM. **337-363-5671**, Fax: 337-363-5780. Fax✉⍦

Franklin Parish

5th District Court *Felony, Misdemeanor, Civil, Probate* PO Box 1564, Winnsboro, LA 71295. 8:30AM-4:30PM. **318-435-5133**, Fax: 318-435-5134. Access ✉⍦

Grant Parish

35th District Court *Felony, Misdemeanor, Civil, Probate* PO Box 263, Colfax, LA 71417. 8:30AM-4:30PM. **318-627-3246**, Fax: 318-627-3201. ☎ Fax✉⍦

Iberia Parish

16th District Court *Felony, Misdemeanor, Civil, Probate* PO Drawer 12010, New Iberia, LA 70562-2010. 8:30AM-4:30PM. **337-365-7282**, Fax: 337-365-0737. ⍦

Key: Symbols refer to criminal records access unless otherwise noted. phone-☎ mail-✉ fax-Fax in person-⍦ online-💻 email-Email

Iberville Parish

18th District Court *Felony, Misdemeanor, Civil, Probate* PO Box 423, Plaquemine, LA 70764. 8:30AM-4:30PM. **225-687-5160**, Fax: 225-687-5260. ✉ ✋

Jackson Parish

2nd District Court *Felony, Misdemeanor, Civil, Probate* PO Drawer 730, Jonesboro, LA 71251. 8:30AM-4:30PM. **318-259-2424**, Fax: 318-395-0386. ☎ ✉ ✋

Jefferson Parish

24th District Court *Felony, Misdemeanor, Civil, Probate* www.jpclerkofcourt.us/ PO Box 10, Gretna, LA 70053. 8:30AM-4:30PM. Fax: 504-364-3797. Civil phone: 504-364-2611, Crim: 504-364-2992. ✉ 💻 ✋

Jefferson Davis Parish

31st District Court *Felony, Misdemeanor, Civil, Probate* PO Box 799, Jennings, LA 70546. 8:30AM-4:30PM. **337-824-8340**, Fax: 337-824-1354. ✉ ✋

Lafayette Parish

15th District Court *Felony, Misdemeanor, Civil, Probate* www.lafayetteparishclerk.com PO Box 2009 c/o Clerk of Court, Lafayette, LA 70502. 8:30AM-4:30PM. **337-291-6400**, Fax: 337-291-6392. Access ☎ Fax ✉ ✋

Lafourche Parish

17th District Court *Felony, Misdemeanor, Civil, Probate* PO Box 818, Thibodaux, LA 70302. 8:30AM-4:30PM. **985-447-4841**, Fax: 985-447-5800. Fax ✉ ✋

La Salle Parish

28th District Court *Felony, Misdemeanor, Civil, Probate* PO Box 1316, Jena, LA 71342. 8:30AM-4:30PM. **318-992-2158**, Fax: 318-992-2157. ☎ Fax ✉ ✋

Lincoln Parish

3rd District Court *Felony, Misdemeanor, Civil, Probate* PO Box 924, Ruston, LA 71273-0924. 8:30AM-4:30PM. **318-251-5130**, Fax: 318-255-6004. Access ✉ ✋

Livingston Parish

21st District Court *Felony, Misdemeanor, Civil, Probate* PO Box 1150, Livingston, LA 70754. 8AM-4:30PM. **225-686-2216**. ✋ ✉

Madison Parish

6th District Court *Felony, Misdemeanor, Civil, Probate* PO Box 1710, Tallulah, LA 71282. 8:30AM-4:30PM. **318-574-0655**, Fax: 318-574-3961. ☎ ✉ ✋ Fax

Morehouse Parish

4th District Court *Felony, Misdemeanor, Civil, Probate* PO Box 1543, Bastrop, LA 71221. 8:30AM-4:30PM. **318-281-3343**, Fax: 318-281-3775. ☎ Fax ✉ ✋

Natchitoches Parish

10th District Court *Felony, Misdemeanor, Civil, Probate, Small Claims* PO Box 476, Natchitoches, LA 71458. 8:30AM-4:30PM. **318-352-8152**, Fax: 318-352-9321. ☎ ✉ ✋

Orleans Parish

Criminal District Court *Felony, Misdemeanor* 2700 Tulane Ave, Rm 115, New Orleans, LA 70119. 8:15AM-3PM. **504-827-3546**, Fax: 504-827-3385. ✉ Fax ✋

Civil District Court *Civil, Probate, Domestic Relations* www.orleanscdc.gov 421 Loyola Ave, Rm 402 Attn: Clerk of Civil Dist. Ct., New Orleans, LA 70112. 8AM-6PM. **504-592-9100**, Fax: 504-592-9128 Access civil records by ☎ ✉ 💻 ✋

New Orleans City Court *Civil Actions Under $20,000, Small Claims* www.orleanscdc.gov/ 421 Loyola Ave, Rm 201, New Orleans, LA 70112. 8:30AM-4PM. **504-592-9155**, Fax: 504-592-9281 Access civil records ✉ 💻 ✋

Ouachita Parish

4th District Court *Felony, Misdemeanor, Civil, Probate* PO Box 1862, Monroe, LA 71210-1862. 8:30AM-5PM. **318-327-1444**, Fax: 318-327-1462. Fax ✉ ✋

Plaquemines Parish

25th District Court *Felony, Misdemeanor, Civil, Probate* PO Box 40, (301 Maine St), Belle Chasse, LA 70037. 8:30AM-4:30PM. **504-392-4969**. ✋

Pointe Coupee Parish

18th District Court *Felony, Misdemeanor, Civil, Probate* PO Box 86, New Roads, LA 70760. 8:30AM-4:30PM. **225-638-9596**, Fax: 225-638-9590. ✋

Rapides Parish

9th District Court *Felony, Misdemeanor, Civil, Probate* www.rapidesclerk.org PO Box 952, Alexandria, LA 71309. 8:30AM-4:30PM. **318-473-8153**, Fax: 318-473-4667. ✉ ✋

Red River Parish

39th District Court *Felony, Misdemeanor, Civil, Probate* PO Box 485, Coushatta, LA 71019. 8:30AM-4:30PM. **318-932-6741**. ✉ ✋

Richland Parish

5th District Court *Felony, Misdemeanor, Civil, Probate* PO Box 119, Rayville, LA 71269. 8:30AM-4:30PM. **318-728-4171**. ✉ ✋

Sabine Parish

11th District Court *Felony, Misdemeanor, Civil, Probate* Sabine Clerk of Court PO Box 419, Many, LA 71449. 8AM-4:30PM. **318-256-6223**, Fax: 318-256-9037. Fax ✉ ✋

St. Bernard Parish

34th District Court *Felony, Misdemeanor, Civil, Probate* PO Box 1746, Chalmette, LA 70044. 8:30AM-4:30PM. **504-271-3434**. Access by ✉ ✋

St. Charles Parish

29th District Court *Felony, Misdemeanor, Civil, Probate* PO Box 424, Hahnville, LA 70057. 8:30AM-4:30PM. **985-783-6632**, Fax: 985-783-2005. ✉ ✋

St. Helena Parish

21st District Court *Felony, Misdemeanor, Civil, Probate* PO Box 308, Greensburg, LA 70441. 8:30AM-4:30PM. **225-222-4514**. ✉ ✋

St. James Parish

23rd District Court *Felony, Misdemeanor, Civil, Probate* PO Box 63, Convent, LA 70723. 8AM-4:30PM. **225-562-7496**, Fax: 504-562-2383. ✉ ✋

Key: Symbols refer to criminal records access unless otherwise noted.   phone-☎   mail-✉   fax-Fax   in person-✋   online-💻   email-Email

St. John the Baptist Parish

40th District Court *Felony, Misd., Civil, Probate* www.stjohnclerk.org PO Box 280, Edgard, LA 70049. 8:30AM-4:30PM. **985-497-3331**, Fax: 985-497-3972. ✉️**Fax**👋

St. Landry Parish

27th District Court *Felony, Misd., Civil, Probate* www.stlandry.org PO Box 750 Courtthouse, Opelousas, LA 70570. 8AM-4:30PM. **337-942-5606**, Fax: 337-948-1653. ✉️**Fax**👋

St. Martin Parish

16th District Court *Felony, Misd., Civil, Probate* PO Box 308, St. Martinville, LA 70582. 8:30AM-4:30PM. **337-394-2210**, Fax: 337-394-7772. 👋

St. Mary Parish

16th Judicial District Court *Felony, Misd., Civil, Probate* PO Box 1231, Franklin, LA 70538. 8:30-4:30PM. **337-828-4100 X200**, Fax: 337-828-2509. 👋

St. Tammany Parish

22nd District Court *Felony, Misdemeanor, Civil, Probate* www.stpgov.org/othergov/clerk/index.html PO Box 1090, Covington, LA 70434. 8:30-4:30PM. **985-809-8700**. ✉️👋💻

Tangipahoa Parish

21st District Court *Felony, Misd., Civil, Probate* www.tangiclerk.org PO Box 667, Amite, LA 70422. 8:30AM-4:30PM. **985-**748-4146, Fax: 985-748-6503; civ is 748-6746; crim is 747-3387. ✉️👋

Tensas Parish

6th District Court *Felony, Misdemeanor, Civil, Probate* PO Box 78 201 Courthouse Sq, St. Joseph, LA 71366. 8:30AM-4:30PM. **318-766-3921**. 👋

Terrebonne Parish

32nd District Court *Felony, Misdemeanor, Civil, Probate* PO Box 1569, Houma, LA 70361. 8:30AM-4:30PM. **985-868-5660**. Access by ✉️👋

Union Parish

3rd District Court *Felony, Misd., Civil, Probate* Courthouse Bldg 100 E Bayou #105, Farmerville, LA 71241. 8:30AM-4:30PM. **318-368-3055**, Fax: 318-368-3861. ✉️**Fax**👋

Vermilion Parish

15th District Court *Felony, Misdemeanor, Civil, Probate* 100 N. State St, #101, Abbeville, LA 70511-0790. 8:30AM-4:30PM. **337-898-1992**, Fax: 337-898-0404. Access ☎️**Fax**✉️👋

Vernon Parish

30th District Court *Felony, Misd., Civil, Probate* PO Box 40, Leesville, LA 71496. 8AM-4:30PM. **337-238-1384**, Fax: 337-238-9902. ✉️👋

Washington Parish

22nd District Court *Felony, Misdemeanor, Civil, Probate* PO Box 607, Franklinton, LA 70438. 8AM-4:30PM. **985-839-4663/7821**. ✉️👋

Webster Parish

26th District Court *Felony, Misd, Civil, Probate* PO Box 370, Minden, LA 71058-0370. 8:30AM-4:30PM. **318-371-0366**, Fax: 318-371-0226. **Fax**✉️👋

West Baton Rouge Parish

18th District Court *Felony, Misdemeanor, Civil, Probate* PO Box 107, Port Allen, LA 70767. 8:30AM-4:30PM. **225-383-0378**. Access ☎️✉️👋

West Carroll Parish

5th District Court *Felony, Misdemeanor, Civil, Probate* PO Box 1078, Oak Grove, LA 71263. 8:30AM-4:30PM. **318-428-3281**. ✉️👋

West Feliciana Parish

20th District Court *Felony, Misdemeanor, Civil, Probate* PO Box 1843, St Francisville, LA 70775. 8:30AM-4:30PM. **225-635-3794**, Fax: 225-635-3770. ✉️👋

Winn Parish

8th District Court *Felony, Misdemeanor, Civil, Probate* 100 Main St, #103, Winnfield, LA 71483. 8AM-4:30PM. **318-628-3515**, Fax 318-628-3527. ✉️👋

Maine

State Court Administration: State Court Administrator, PO Box 4820, Portland, ME, 04112; 207-822-0792, Fax: 207-822-0781. http://www.state.me.us/courts

Court Structure: One Superior Court, the court of general jurisdiction is located in each of Maine's sixteen counties, except for Aroostook County, which has two Superior Courts. Both Superior and District Courts handle misdemeanor and felony cases, with jury trials being held in Superior Court only. The District Court hears both civil and criminal and always sits without a jury. Within the District Court is the Family Division, which hears all divorce and family matters, including child support and paternity cases. The District Court also hears child protection cases, and serves as Maine's juvenile court. Actions for protection from abuse or harassment, mental health, small claims cases and money judgments are filed in the District Court. Traffic violations are processed primarily through a centralized Violations Bureau, part of the District Court system. Prior to year 2001, District Courts accepted civil cases involving claims less than $30,000. Now, District Courts have jurisdiction concurrent with that of the Superior Court for all civil actions except cases vested in the Superior Court by statute.

Probate Courts: Probate Courts are part of the county court system, not the state system. Even though the Probate Court may be housed with other state courts, it is on a different phone system and calls may not be transferred.

Key: Symbols refer to criminal records access unless otherwise noted.   phone-☎️   mail-✉️   fax-**Fax**   in person-👋   online-💻   email-**Email**

Online Access: The website offers access to Maine Supreme Court opinions and administrative orders, but not all documents are available online. Also, the site offers online access to trial court schedules by region and case type. Some county level courts are online through a private vendor.

Additional Information: Per administrative order, Maine Superior and District courts increased their search fees effective September 1st, 2003 as follows: 1) $15.00 for a search-previously, most courts charged $0 for a search; 2) copy fee 1st page is $2.00, $1.00 each additional; 3) If mail requests do not include a self-addressed stamped envelope, then add an additional $5.00. As we go to press, it is not yet clear if additional fees will be charged for certification. Also, there is some confusion at the courts regarding if the $15.00 fee is for a "combined" search of both civil and criminal, or if one fee for civil and one fee for crimianl. Most mail requests of a name search for full criminal history record information are returned to the sender, referring them to the State Bureau of Investigation. Mail requests that make a specific inquiry related to an identified case are responded to in writing.

Androscoggin County

Androscoggin Superior Court *Felony, Misdemeanor, Civil Actions* PO Box 3660, Auburn, ME 04212-3660. 8AM-4:30PM. **207-783-5450**. Access by ✉ ✋

North Androscoggin District Court 11 *Misd., Civil Actions, Eviction, Small Claims* 2 Main St, Livermore Falls, ME 04254. 8AM-4PM T-Th. **207-897-3800**. ✉ ✋

Lewiston District Court - South 8 *Misd., Civil Actions, Eviction, Small Claims* PO Box 1345 71 Lisbon St, Lewiston, ME 04243-1345. 8AM-4PM. Civil: 207-795-4801, Crim: 207-795-4800. ✉ ✋

Probate Court 2 Turner St, Auburn, ME 04210. 8:30AM-5PM. **207-782-0281**, Fax: 207-782-1135.

Aroostook County

Caribou Superior Court *Felony, Misdemeanor, Civil Actions* 144 Sweden St, #101, Caribou, ME 04736. 8AM-4PM. **207-498-8125**. ✉ ✋

Fort Kent District Court - District 1 *Misdemeanor, Civil Actions, Eviction, Small Claims* Division of Western Aroostook PO Box 473, Fort Kent, ME 04743. 8-4PM. **207-834-5003**. ☎ ✉ ✋

District Court 2 *Misdemeanor, Civil Actions, Eviction, Small Claims* PO Box 794 (27 Riverside Dr), Presque Isle, ME 04769. 8AM-4PM. **207-764-2055**. ✉ ✋

Caribou District Court - East 1 *Misdemeanor, Civil Actions, Eviction, Small Claims* 144 Sweden St, Caribou, ME 04736. 8-4PM. **207-493-3144**. ✉ ✋

Houlton District Court - South 2 *Misdemeanor, Civil Actions, Eviction, Small Claims* PO Box 457, Houlton, ME 04730. 8AM-4PM. **207-532-2147**. ✉ ✋

Madawaska District Court - West *Misdemeanor, Civil Actions, Eviction, Small Claims* PO Box 127 645 E Main St, Madawaska, ME 04756. 8AM-4PM M,T,F. **207-728-4700**. Access ☎ ✉ ✋

Probate Court 26 Court St #103, Houlton, ME 04730. 8AM-4:30PM. **207-532-1502**.

Cumberland County

Superior Court - Civil *Civil Actions* 142 Federal St, Portland, ME 04101. 8AM-4:30PM. **207-822-4105**, Civil: 207-822-4105, Crim: 207-822-4113. Access civil records by ✋

Superior Court - Criminal *Felony, Misdemeanor* 142 Federal St, Portland, ME 04101. 8-4:30PM. **207-822-4113**. ✋

Portland District Court - South 9 *Civil Civil Actions, Eviction, Small Claims* PO Box 412 205 Newbury St, Portland, ME 04112. 8AM-4:30PM. **207-822-4200**. Also see Sagadahoc Dist. Court, which handles cases from eastern Cumberland County. Also, Brighton Dist Court which handles cases from western Cumberland County. Access civil records by ✋

Portland District Court - South 9 Criminal *Misdemeanor* PO Box 412, Portland, ME 04112. 8AM-4:30PM. **207-822-4204**. ✋ ✉

Bridgton District Court - North 9 *Misdemeanor, Civil Actions, Eviction, Small Claims* 2 Chase Common, Bridgton, ME 04009. 8AM-4PM. **207-647-3535**. ☎ ✉ ✋

Probate Ct www.cumberlandcounty.org PO Box 15277, Portland, ME 04101-4196. 8:30AM-4:30PM. **207-871-8382**, Fax: 207-791-2658.

Franklin County

Superior Court *Felony, Misd., Civil Actions* 140 Main St, Farmington, ME 04938. 8AM-4PM. **207-778-3346**. ✉ ✋

Franklin District Court 12 *Misdemeanor, Civil Actions, Eviction, Small Claims* 129 Main St, Farmington, ME 04938. 8-4PM. **207-778-8200**. ✉ ✋

Probate Court County Courthouse 140 Main St, Farmington, ME 04938. 8:30AM-4PM. **207-778-5888**, Fax: 207-778-5899.

Hancock County

Superior Court *Felony, Misdemeanor, Civil Actions* 50 State St, Ellsworth, ME 04605-1926. 8-4PM. **207-667-7176**. ✋

Bar Harbor District Court - South 5 *Misd., Civil Actions, Eviction, Small Claims* 93 Cottage St, Bar Harbor, ME 04609. 8AM-4PM. **207-288-3082**. ✉ ✋

Ellsworth District Court - Central 5 *Misdemeanor, Civil Actions, Eviction, Small Claims* 50 State St #2, Ellsworth, ME 04605. 8-4PM. **207-667-7141**. ✉ ✋

Probate Court 50 State St, #6, Ellsworth, ME 04605. 8:30AM-4PM. **207-667-8434**, Fax: 207-667-5316, Probate: 667-9098.

Kennebec County

Superior Court *Felony, Misdemeanor, Civil Actions* 95 State St, Clerk of Court, Augusta, ME 04330. 8AM-4PM. **207-624-5800**. ✋

Maine District Court 7 *Misdemeanor, Civil Actions, Eviction, Small Claims* Division of Southern Kennebec 145 State St, Augusta, ME 04330-7495. 8AM-4PM. **207-287-8075**. ✉ ✋

Waterville District Court - District 7 *Misdemeanor, Civil Actions, Eviction, Small Claims* 18 Colby St PO Box 397, Waterville, ME 04903. 8AM-4PM. **207-873-2103**. ✉ ✋

Probate Ct www.datamaine.com/probate 95 State St, Augusta, ME 04330. 8AM-4PM. **207-622-7558 or 207-622-7559**, Fax: 207-621-1639.

Key: Symbols refer to criminal records access unless otherwise noted. phone-☎ mail-✉ fax-**Fax** in person-✋ online-💻 email-**Email**

Knox County

Superior Court *Felony, Misd., Civil Actions* 62 Union St, Rockland, ME 04841. 8AM-4PM. **207-594-2576.** ✉️ 🖐️

District Court 6 *Misd., Civil Actions, Eviction, Small Claims* 62 Union St, Rockland, ME 04841. 8AM-4PM. **207-596-2240.** 🖐️ ✉️

Probate http://knoxcounty.midcoast.com 62 Union St, Rockland, ME 04841. 8AM-4PM. **207-594-0427,** Fax: 207-594-0443.

Lincoln County

Lincoln County Superior Court *Felony, Misdemeanor, Civil Actions* www.co.lincoln.me.us High St PO Box 249, Wiscasset, ME 04578. 8AM-4PM. **207-882-7517,** Fax:207-882-7741. ✉️ 🖐️

District Court 6 *Misdemeanor, Civil Actions, Eviction, Small Claims* www.co.lincoln.me.us 32 High St PO Box 249, Wiscasset, ME 04578. 8AM-4PM. **207-882-6363,** Fax 207-882-5980. ✉️ 🖐️

Probate Ct www.co.lincoln.me.us/dep.html 32 High St PO Box 249, Wiscasset, ME 04578. 8AM-4PM. **207-882-7392,** Fax: 207-882-4324.

Oxford County

Superior Court *Felony, Misd., Civil Actions* Courthouse, 26 Western Ave, PO Box 179, South Paris, ME 04281-0179. 8AM-4PM. **207-743-8936.** ✉️ 🖐️

South Paris District Court - South 11 *Misd., Civil Actions, Eviction, Small Claims* 26 Western Ave, South Paris, ME 04281. 8AM-4PM. **207-743-8942.** ✉️ 🖐️

Rumford District Court - Div. of North Oxford *Misdemeanor, Civil Actions, Eviction, Small Claims* Municipal Bldg 145 Congress St, Rumford, ME 04276. 8AM-4PM. **207-364-7171.** ✉️ 🖐️

Probate Court www.oxfordcounty.org/pro bate.htm 26 Western Ave, PO Box 179, South Paris, ME 04281. 8AM-4PM. **207-743-6671,** Fax: 207-743-2656.

Penobscot County

Superior Court *Felony, Misdemeanor, Civil Actions* 97 Hammond St, Bangor, ME 04401. 8AM-4:30PM. **207-561-2300.** No charge for a single search. ✉️ 🖐️

Millinocket District Court - North 13 *Misdemeanor, Civil Actions, Eviction, Small Claims* 207 Penobscot Ave, Millinocket, ME 04462. 8AM-4PM. **207-723-4786.** ✉️ 🖐️

Bangor District Court *Misdemeanor, Civil Actions , Eviction, Small Claims* 73 Hammond St, Bangor, ME 04401. 8AM-4PM. **207-941-3040.** Access by ✉️ 🖐️

Newport District Court - West 3 *Misdemeanor, Civil Actions, Eviction, Small Claims* 12 Water St, Newport, ME 04953. 8AM-4PM. **207-368-5778.** ✉️ 🖐️

Central District Court - Central 13 *Misdemeanor, Civil Actions, Eviction, Small Claims* 66 Maine St, Lincoln, ME 04457. 8AM-4PM. **207-794-8512.** 🖐️

Probate Court 97 Hammond St, Bangor, ME 04401-4996. 8AM-4:30PM. **207-942-8769,** Fax: 207-941-8499.

Piscataquis County

Superior Court *Felony, Misdemeanor, Civil Actions* 159 E Main St, Dover-Foxcroft, ME 04426. 8AM-4PM. **207-564-8419,** Fax: 207-564-3363. ✉️ 🖐️

District Court 13 *Misdemeanor, Civil Actions, Eviction, Small Claims* 163 E Main St, Dover-Foxcroft, ME 04426. 8AM-4PM. **207-564-2240.** ✉️ 🖐️

Probate Court 159 E Main St, Dover-Foxcroft, ME 04426. 8:30AM-4PM. **207-564-2431,** Fax: 207-564-2431.

Sagadahoc County

Superior Court *Felony, Misdemeanor, Civil Actions* 752 High St, PO Box 246, Bath, ME 04530. 8AM-4:30PM. **207-443-9733.** ✉️ 🖐️

West Bath District Court 6 *Misd., Civil Actions, Eviction, Small Claims* 147 New Meadows Rd, West Bath, ME 04530. 8AM-4PM. **207-442-0200.** Also handles eastern Cumberland County. 🖐️

Probate Court 752 High St, Bath, ME 04530. 8:30AM-4:30PM. **207-443-8218,** Fax: 207-443-8217.

Somerset County

Superior Court *Felony, Misd., Civil Actions* PO Box 725, Skowhegan, ME 04976. 8AM-4PM. **207-474-5161,** Access by 🖐️

District Court 12 *Misdemeanor, Civil Actions, Eviction, Small Claims* PO Box 525 47 Court St, Skowhegan, ME 04976. 8AM-4PM. **207-474-9518.** ✉️ 🖐️

Probate 41 Court St, Skowhegan, ME 04976. 8:30AM-4:30PM. **207-474-3322.**

Waldo County

Superior Court *Felony, Misdemeanor, Civil Actions* 137 Church St, PO Box 188, Belfast, ME 04915. 8AM-4PM. **207-338-1940.** ✉️ 🖐️

District Court 5 *Misdemeanor, Civil Actions, Eviction, Small Claims* PO Box 382, 103 Church St, Belfast, ME 04915. 8AM-4PM. **207-338-3107.** ✉️ 🖐️

Probate Court 39A Spring St PO Box 323, Belfast, ME 04915-0323. 8AM-4PM. **207-338-2780/2963,** Fax: 207-338-2360.

Washington County

Superior Court *Felony, Misdemeanor, Civil* Clerk of Court, PO Box 526, Machias, ME 04654. 8AM-4PM. **207-255-3326.** ✉️ 🖐️

Calais District Court - North 4 *Misd., Civil Actions, Eviction, Small Claims* PO Box 929, Calais, ME 04619. 8AM-4PM. **207-454-2055; TTY# 207-454-0085.** 🖐️

Maine District Court 4 *Misdemeanor, Civil Actions, Eviction, Small Claims* 47 Court St PO Box 297, Machias, ME 04654. 8AM-4PM. **207-255-3044.** ✉️ 🖐️

Probate Court PO Box 297, Machias, ME 04654. 8AM-4PM. **207-255-6591.**

York County

Superior Court *Felony, Misdemeanor, Civil Actions* Clerk of Court, PO Box 160, Alfred, ME 04002. 8AM-4:30PM. **207-324-5122.** ✉️ 🖐️

York District Court - South 10 *Misdemeanor, Civil Actions, Eviction, Small Claims* PO Box 770 Chase's Pond Rd, York, ME 03909-0770. 8AM-4PM. **207-363-1230.** ✉️ 🖐️

Biddeford District Court - East 10 *Misdemeanor, Civil Actions, Eviction, Small Claims* 25 Adams St, Biddeford, ME 04005. 8-4PM. **207-283-1147.** ✉️ 🖐️

Springvale District Court - West 10 *Misdemeanor, Civil Actions, Eviction, Small Claims* 447 Main St, Springvale, ME 04083. 8-4PM. **207-459-1400.** ✉️ 🖐️

Probate Court PO Box 399, 45 Kennebunk Rd, Alfred, ME 04002. 8:30AM-4:30PM. **207-324-1577,** Fax: 207-324-0163.

Key: Symbols refer to criminal records access unless otherwise noted. phone-☎️ mail-✉️ fax-**Fax** in person-🖐️ online-💻 email-**Email**

Maryland

State Court Administration (All County District Courts including Baltimore City Court); Court Administrator, Administrative Office of the Courts, 361 Rowe Blvd, Courts of Appeal Building, Annapolis, MD, 21401; 410-260-1400, Fax: 410-974-2169. www.courts.state.md.us

Court Structure: The Circuit Court is the highest court of record. There is a Circuit Court with an elected clerk in each county of Maryland and Baltimore City. The jurisdiction of the District Court includes all landlord-tenant cases, replevin actions, motor vehicle violations, misdemeanors and certain felonies. In civil cases the District Court has exclusive jurisdiction in claims for amounts up to $5,000, and concurrent jurisdiction with the circuit courts in claims for amounts above $5,000 but less than $25,000. The jurisdiction of the court in criminal cases is concurrent with the Circuit Court for offenses in which the penalty may be confinement for three years or more or a fine of $2,500 or more; or offenses which are felonies.

Probate Courts: The Circuit Court handles Probate in Montgomery and Harford counties. In other counties, probate is handled by the Register of Wills. Probate is a county, not a court, function.

Online Access: An online computer system -- see www.courts.state.md.us/dialup.html -- called the Judicial Information System (JIS) or (SJIS) provides dial-up access to civil and criminal case information from the following:

> 1. All District Courts - All civil and all misdemeanors 2. All Circuit Courts Civil - All civil records are online through JIS.

> 3. Circuit Courts Criminal - Three courts are on JIS - Anne Arundel, Carroll county, and Baltimore City Court

Inquiries may be made to: the District Court traffic system for case information data, calendar information data, court schedule data, or officer schedule data; the District Court criminal system for case information data or calendar caseload data; the District Court civil system for case information data, attorney name and address data; the land records system for land and plat records. There is an annual $50.00 for JIS dial-up access, which must be included with the application. For additional information or to receive a registration packet, write or call Judicial Information Systems, Security Administrator, 2661 Riva Rd., Suite 900, Annapolis, MD 21401, 410-260-1031, or visit the website above.

Additional Information: In most circuit courts, copies are $.50 per page and certification is $5.00. In most district courts, copies are $.25 per page and certification is $5.00.

Allegany County

4th Judicial Circuit Court *Felony, Misdemeanor, Civil Actions Over $25,000* 30 Washington St, Cumberland, MD 21502. 8AM-4:30PM. **301-777-5922**, Fax: 301-777-2100.

District Court *Misdemeanor, Civil Actions Under $25,000, Eviction, Small Claims* 3 Pershing St, 2nd Fl, Cumberland, MD 21502. 8:30AM-4:30PM. **301-777-2105**. Access ✉️🖥️✋

Register of Wills www.registers.state.md.us/county/al/html/allegany.html 59 Prospect Sq. 1st Fl, Cumberland, MD 21502. 8AM-4:30PM. **301-724-3760, 888-724-0148 in MD**, Fax: 301-724-1249.

Anne Arundel County

5th Judicial Circuit Court *Felony, Misdemeanor, Civil Actions Over $25,000* Box 71 (7 Church St), Annapolis, MD 21404-0071. 8:30AM-4:30PM (Phone hours-11AM-3:30pm). **410-222-1397**, Civil: 410-222-1431. Access by 🖥️✋

District Court *Misdemeanor, Civil Actions Under $25,000, Eviction, Small Claims* 251 Rowe Blvd, #141, Annapolis, MD 21401. 8:30AM-4:30PM. **410-260-1370**. ✉️🖥️✋

Register of Wills www.registers.state.md.us/county/aa/html/annearundel.html PO Box 2368 7 1/2 Circuit Courthouse-Church Circle #403, Annapolis, MD 21404-2368. 8:30AM-4:30PM. **410-222-1430, 800-679-6665 in MD**, Fax: 410-222-1467. Wills only; no genealogy searches.

Baltimore City

8th Judicial Circuit Court - Civil Division *Civil Actions Over $25,000* www.baltocts.state.md.us/ 111 N Calvert, Rm 409, Baltimore, MD 21202. 8:30AM-4:30PM. **410-396-5188**, Civil: 410-369-3045 Access civil records ☎️✉️🖥️✋

8th Judicial Circuit Court - Criminal Division *Felony, Misdemeanor* 110 N Calvert Rm 200, Baltimore, MD 21202. 8:30AM-4:30PM. **410-333-3750**. 🖥️✋

District Court - Civil Division *Civil Actions Under $25,000, Eviction, Small Claims* 501 E Fayette St, Baltimore, MD 21202. 8:30AM-4:30PM. **410-878-8900** Access civil records by ✉️🖥️✋.

District Court - Criminal Division *Misdemeanor* 5800 Wabash Ave, Baltimore, MD 21215. 8:30AM-4:30PM. **410-878-8000**. ✉️🖥️✋

Register of Wills www.registers.state.md.us/city/bc/html/baltimorecity.html Courthouse East, 111 N Calvert St, Rm 352, Baltimore, MD 21202. 8AM-4:30PM. **410-752-5131, 888-876-0035 in MD**, Fax: 410-752-3494.

Baltimore County

3rd Judicial Circuit Court *Felony, Civil Actions Over $25,000* 401 Bosley Ave, 2nd Fl, Towson, MD 21204. 8:30AM-4:30PM. **410-887-2601**. Access by ✋

District Court *Misdemeanor, Civil Actions Under $25,000, Eviction, Small Claims* 120 E Chesapeake Ave, Towson, MD 21286-5307. 8:30AM-4:30PM. **410-512-2000**, Crim: 410-512-2101. 🖥️✋

Key: Symbols refer to criminal records access unless otherwise noted. phone-☎️ mail-✉️ fax-**Fax** in person-✋ online-🖥️ email-**Email**

Register of Wills *Probate* www.registers.state.md.us/county/ba/html/baltimore.html 401 Bosley Ave, Mail Stop 3507, Towson, MD 21204-4403. 8AM-4:30PM. **410-887-6685, 888-642-5387 in MD**, Fax: 410-583-2517.

Calvert County

7th Judicial Circuit Court *Felony, Misdemeanor, Civil Actions Over $25,000* www.courts.state.md.us/clerks/calvert 175 Main St Courthouse, Prince Frederick, MD 20678. 8:30AM-4:30PM. **410-535-1660**. 🖐

District Court *Misdemeanor, Civil Actions Under $25,000, Eviction, Small Claims* 200 Duke St Rm 2200, Prince Frederick, MD 20678. 8:30AM-4:30PM. **410-535-8800**. 🖐🖥

Register of Wills www.registers.state.md.us/county/cv/html/calvert.html Courthouse, 175 Main St, Prince Frederick, MD 20678. 8:30AM-4:30PM. **410-535-0121, 888-374-0015 in MD**, Fax: 410-414-3952.

Caroline County

2nd Judicial Circuit Court *Felony, Misdemeanor, Civil Actions Over $25,000* Box 458, Denton, MD 21629. 8:30AM-4:30PM. **410-479-1811**, Fax: 410-479-1142. Misdemeanor case records held at District Court until appealed, then stored at Circuit Court. 🖐

District Court *Misdemeanor, Civil Actions Under $25,000, Eviction, Small Claims* 207 S 3rd St, Denton, MD 21629. 8:30AM-4:30PM. **410-819-4600**, Fax: 410-479-5808. 🖐🖐

Register of Wills www.registers.state.md.us/county/ca/html/caroline.html County Courthouse, 109 Market St, Rm 119 PO Box 416, Denton, MD 21629. 8AM-4:30PM. **410-479-0717, 888-786-0019 in MD**, Fax: 410-479-4983.

Carroll County

5th Judicial Circuit Court *Felony, Misdemeanor, Civil Actions Over $25,000* 55 N Court St, Westminster, MD 21157. 8:30AM-4:30PM. **410-386-2026**, Fax: 410-876-0822. Civil phone: 410-386-2326, Crim: 410-386-2025. 🖥🖐

District Court *Misdemeanor, Civil Actions Under $25,000, Eviction, Small Claims* 101 N Court St, Westminster, MD 21157. 8:30-4:30. **410-871-3500**. 🖥🖐

Register of Wills www.registers.state.md.us/county/cr/html/carroll.html 55 N Court St, Rm 104, Westminster, MD 21157. 8:30AM-4:30PM. **410-848-2586, 888-876-0034 in MD**, Fax: 410-876-0657.

Cecil County

2nd Judicial Circuit Court *Felony, Misdemeanor, Civil Actions Over $25,000* 129 E Main St, Rm 108, Elkton, MD 21921. 8:30AM-4:30PM. **410-996-5325**, Fax: 410-392-6032. Civil phone: 410-996-5369. 🖐

District Court *Misd., Civil Actions Under $25,000, Eviction, Small Claims* 170 E Main St, Elkton, MD 21921. 8:30AM-4:30PM. **410-996-2700**. 🖥🖐

Register of Wills *Probate* www.registers.state.md.us/county/ce/html/cecil.html County Courthouse, #101 PO Box 468, Elkton, MD 21922-0468. 8:30AM-4:30PM. **410-398-2737, 888-398-0301 in MD**, Fax: 410-996-1039.

Charles County

Circuit Court for Charles County *Felony, Misd., Civil Actions Over $2,500* www.courts.state.md.us/clerks/charles/ PO Box 970, La Plata, MD 20646. 8:30AM-4:30PM. **301-932-3201x223**. 🖐

District Court *Misdemeanor, Civil Actions Under $25,000, Eviction, Small Claims* PO Box 3070, La Plata, MD 20646. 8:30AM-4:30PM. **301-932-3300**, Civil phone: 301-932-3290, Crim: 301-932-3295. 🖥🖐

Register of Wills www.registers.state.md.us/county/ch/html/charles.html Box 3080 (Courthouse, 200 E Charles St), La Plata, MD 20646. 8:30AM-4:30PM. **301-932-3345, 888-256-0054 in MD**, Fax: 301-932-3349.

Dorchester County

1st Judicial Circuit Court *Felony, Misdemeanor, Civil Actions Over $25,000* Box 150, Cambridge, MD 21613. 8:30AM-4:30PM. **410-228-0481**. 🖐

District Court *Misd., Civil Actions Under $25,000, Eviction, Small Claims* 310 Gay St, Cambridge, MD 21613. 8:30AM-4:30PM. **410-901-1420**. 🖥🖐

Register of Wills www.registers.state.md.us/county/do/html/dorchester.html 206 High St, Cambridge, MD 21613. 8AM-4:30PM; Public hours 8:30AM-4:30PM. **410-228-4181, 888-242-6257 in MD**, Fax: 410-228-4988.

Frederick County

6th Judicial Circuit Court *Felony, Misdemeanor, Civil Actions Over $25,000* 100 W Patrick St, Frederick, MD 21701. 8:30AM-4:30PM. **301-694-1970**. 🖐

District Court *Misdemeanor, Civil Actions Under $25,000, Eviction, Small Claims* 100 W Patrick St, Frederick, MD 21701. 8:30-4:30. **301-694-2000**. 🖥🖐

Register of Wills www.registers.state.md.us/county/fr/html/frederick.html 100 W Patrick St, Frederick, MD 21701. 8AM-4:30PM. **301-663-3722, 888-258-0526**, Fax: 301-846-0744.

Garrett County

4th Judicial Circuit Court *Felony, Misdemeanor, Civil Actions Over $25,000* PO Box 447, Oakland, MD 21550. 8:30AM-4:30PM. **301-334-1937**, Fax: 301-334-5017. Civil phone: 301-334-1944, Crim: 301-334-1943. ✉🖐

District Court *Misd., Civil Actions Under $25,000, Eviction, Small Claims* www.courts.state.md.us/district/dcgarrett.html 205 S 3rd St, Oakland, MD 21550. 8:30AM-4:30PM. **301-334-8020**. 🖥🖐

Register of Wills www.registers.state.md.us/county/ga/html/garrett.html Courthouse, 313 E Alder St, Rm 103, Oakland, MD 21550. 8AM-4:30PM. **301-334-1999, 888-334-2203 in MD**, Fax: 301-334-1984.

Harford County

3rd Judicial Circuit *Felony, Misdemeanor, Civil Actions Over $25,000* www.courts.state.md.us/harford.html 20 W Courtland St, Bel Air, MD 21014. 8:30AM-4:30PM. Civil phone: 410-638-3430, Crim: 410-638-3042. 🖐

District Court *Misdemeanor, Civil Actions Under $25,000, Eviction, Small Claims* 2 S Bond St, Bel Air, MD 21014. 8:30-4:30PM. **410-836-4545**. ✉🖥🖐

Register of Wills www.registers.state.md.us/county/ha/html/harford.html 20 W Courtland St, Rm 304 Court House, Bel Air, MD 21014. 8:30AM-4:30PM. **410-638-3275, 888-258-0525 in MD**, Fax: 410-893-3177.

Howard County

5th Judicial Circuit Court *Felony, Misdemeanor, Civil Actions Over $25,000* 8360 Court Ave, Ellicott City, MD 21043. 8:30AM-4:30PM. **410-313-2111**. 🖐

District Court *Misdemeanor, Civil Actions Under $25,000, Eviction, Small Claims* 3451 Courthouse Dr, Ellicott City, MD 21043. 8:30AM-4:30PM. **410-480-7700.** ✉️🖥️👋

Register of Wills www.registers.state.md.us/county/ho/html/howard.html 8360 Court Ave, Ellicott City, MD 21043. 8:30AM-4:30PM. **410-313-2133, 888-848-0136 in MD,** Fax: 410-313-3409.

Kent County

2nd Judicial Circuit Court *Felony, Misdemeanor, Civil Actions Over $25,000* www.courts.state.md.us/clerks/kent/records.html 103 N Cross St Courthouse, Chestertown, MD 21620. 8:30AM-4:30PM. **410-778-7460,** Fax: 410-778-7412. 👋

District Court *Misdemeanor, Civil Actions Under $25,000, Eviction, Small Claims* 103 N Cross St, Chestertown, MD 21620. 8:30AM-4:30PM. **410-810-3362,** Fax: 410-810-3361. 🖥️👋

Register of Wills www.registers.state.md.us/county/ke/html/kent.html 103 N Cross St, Chestertown, MD 21620. 8AM-4:30PM. **410-778-7466, 888-778-0179 in MD,** Fax: 410-778-2466, Probate: 410-778-7465 & 410-778-7463.

Montgomery County

6th Judicial Circuit Court *Felony, Misdemeanor, Civil Actions Over $25,000* www.montgomerycountymd.gov/mc/judicial/ 50 Maryland Ave, Rockville, MD 20850. 8:30AM-4:30PM. **240-777-9466.** ☎️✉️**Fax**👋

District Court *Misdemeanor, Civil Actions Under $25,000, Eviction, Small Claims* 8552 Second Ave, Silver Spring, MD 20910. 8:30AM-4:30PM. **301-563-8500.** ✉️🖥️👋

Rockville District Court *Misdemeanor, Civil Actions Under $25,000, Eviction, Small Claims* 27 Courthouse Square, Rockville, MD 20850. 8:30AM-4:30PM. Civil phone: 301-279-1500, Crim: 301-279-1565. ✉️🖥️👋

Register of Wills www.registers.state.md.us/county/mo/html/montgomery.html Judicial Ctr, 50 Maryland Ave, #322, Rockville, MD 20850. 8:30AM-4:30PM. **240-777-9600,** Fax: 240-777-9602.

Prince George's County

7th Judicial Circuit Court *Felony, Misdemeanor, Civil Actions Over $25,000* 14735 Main St, Upper Marlboro, MD 20772. 8:30AM-4:30PM. Civil: 301-952-3240, Crim: 301-952-3344. Access by 👋

District Court *Misdemeanor, Civil Actions Under $25,000, Eviction, Small Claims* 14735 Main St, Rm 173B, Upper Marlboro, MD 20772. 8:30AM-4:30PM. **301-952-4080.** ✉️🖥️👋

Register of Wills www.registers.state.md.us/county/pg/html/princegeorges.html PO Box 1729, Upper Marlboro, MD 20773. 8:30AM-4:30PM (3:30 is paperwork cutoff time). **301-952-3250, 888-464-4219 in MD,** Fax: 301-952-4489.

Queen Anne's County

2nd Judicial Circuit Court *Felony, Misdemeanor, Civil Actions Over $25,000* Courthouse 100 Courthouse Sq, Centreville, MD 21617. 8:30AM-4:30PM. **410-758-1773.** Misdemeanor case records held at Dist. Court until appealed, then stored at Circuit Court. Access records 👋

District Court *Misdemeanor, Civil Actions Under $25,000, Eviction, Small Claims* 120 Broadway, Centreville, MD 21617. 8:30AM-4:30PM. **410-819-4000.** 🖥️👋

Register of Wills www.registers.state.md.us/county/qa/html/queenannes.html Liberty Bldg, 107 N Liberty St #220 PO Box 59, Centreville, MD 21617. 8AM-4:30PM. **410-758-0585, 888-758-0010 in MD,** Fax: 410-758-4408.

St. Mary's County

7th Judicial Circuit Court *Felony, Misdemeanor, Civil Actions Over $25,000* PO Box 676, Leonardtown, MD 20650. 8:30AM-4:30PM. **301-475-4567.** 👋

District Court *Misdemeanor, Civil Actions Under $25,000, Eviction, Small Claims* Carter State Office Bldg 23110 Leonard Hall Dr, PO Box 653, Leonardtown, MD 20650. 8:30AM-4:30PM. **301-475-4530.** Access by 🖥️👋

Register of Wills *Probate* www.registers.state.md.us/county/sm/html/stmarys.html 41605 Court House Drive, Leonardtown, MD 20650. 8:30AM-4:30PM. **301-475-5566, 888-475-4821 in MD,** Fax: 301-475-4968.

Somerset County

1st Judicial Circuit Court *Felony, Misdemeanor, Civil Actions Over $25,000* PO Box 99, Princess Anne, MD 21853. 8:30AM-4:30PM. **410-651-1555,** Fax: 410-651-1048. 👋

District Court *Misdemeanor, Civil Actions Under $25,000, Eviction, Small Claims* 12155 Elm St #C, Princess Anne, MD 21853-1358. 8:30AM-4:30PM. **410-845-4700.** Misdemeanor cases go to Circuit Court if preliminary hearing waived. Records held at court where trial heard. 🖥️👋

Register of Wills www.registers.state.md.us/county/so/html/somerset.html 30512 Prince William St, Princess Anne, MD 21853. 8:30AM-4:30PM. **410-651-1696,** 888-758-0039 in MD, Fax: 410-651-3873.

Talbot County

Circuit Court *Felony, Misdemeanor, Civil Actions Over $25,000* www.courts.state.md.us/clerks/talbot/index.html PO Box 723, Easton, MD 21601. 8:30AM-4:30PM. **410-822-2611,** Fax: 410-820-8168. 👋

District Court *Misdemeanor, Civil Actions Under $25,000, Eviction, Small Claims* 108 W Dover St, Easton, MD 21601. 8:30AM-4:30PM. **410-819-5850.** 🖥️👋

Register of Wills www.registers.state.md.us/county/ta/html/talbot.html Courthouse, 11 N Washington St, Easton, MD 21601. 8AM-4:30PM. **410-770-6700, 888-822-0039 in MD,** Fax: 410-822-5452.

Washington County

Washington County Circuit Court *Felony, Misdemeanor, Civil Actions Over $25,000* Box 229, Hagerstown, MD 21741. 8:30AM-4:30PM. **301-733-8660,** Fax: 301-791-1151. Civil phone: 301-790-4972, Crim: 301-790-7941. 👋

District Court *Misdemeanor, Civil Actions Under $25,000, Eviction, Small Claims* 36 W Antietam St, Hagerstown, MD 21740. 8:30AM-4:30PM. **240-420-4600.** 🖥️👋

Register of Wills www.registers.state.md.us/county/wa/html/washington.html 95 W Washington, Hagerstown, MD 21740. 8:00AM-4:30PM. **301-739-3612, 888-739-0013 in MD,** Fax: 301-733-8636.

Key: Symbols refer to criminal records access unless otherwise noted. phone-☎️ mail-✉️ fax-**Fax** in person-👋 online-🖥️ email-**Email**

Wicomico County

1st Judicial Circuit Court *Felony, Misdemeanor, Civil Actions Over $25,000* PO Box 198, Salisbury, MD 21803-0198. 8:30AM-4:30PM. **410-543-6551,** Fax: 410-546-8590. ☎ ✉ ✋

District Court *Misdemeanor, Civil Actions Under $25,000, Eviction, Small Claims* 201 Baptist St, Salisbury, MD 21801. 8:30-4:30. **410-543-6600.** 🖥 ✋

Register of Wills www.registers.state.md.us/county/wi/html/wicomico.html 101 N Division St, Rm 102, Salisbury, MD 21801. 8:30AM-4:30PM. **410-543-6635, 888-786-0018 in MD,** Fax: 410-334-3440.

Worcester County

1st Judicial Circuit Court *Felony, Misdemeanor, Civil Actions Over $25,000* Box 40, Snow Hill, MD 21863. 8:30AM-4:30PM. Civil: 410-632-5501, Crim: 410-632-5502. ✋

District Court *Misdemeanor, Civil Actions Under $25,000, Eviction, Small Claims* 301 Commerce St, Snow Hill, MD 21863-1007. 8:30AM-4:30PM. **410-219-7830,** Fax: 410-219-7840. 🖥 ✋

Register of Wills www.registers.state.md.us/county/wo/html/worcester.html Courthouse, 1 W Market St, Rm 102, Snow Hill, MD 21863-1074. 8AM-4:30PM. **410-632-1529, 888-256-0047 in MD,** Fax: 410-632-5600.

Massachusetts

State Court Administration: Chief Justice for Administration and Management, 2 Center Plaza, Room 540, Boston, MA, 02108; 617-742-8575, Fax: 617-742-0968. www.state.ma.us/courts/admin/index.html

Court Structure: The various court sections are called "Departments." While Superior Courts and District Courts have concurrent jurisdiction in civil cases, the practice is to assign cases less than $25,000 to District Court and those over $25,000 to Superior.

In addition to misdemeanors, the District Courts and Boston Municipal Courts have jurisdiction over certain minor felonies.

Eviction cases may be filed at a county District Court or at the regional "Housing Court." A case may be moved from a District Court to a Housing Court, but never the reverse. They also hear misdemeanor "Code Violation" cases and prelims for these. There are five Housing Court Regions - Boston (Suffolk County), Worcester (County), Southeast (Plymouth and Bristol Counties), Northeast (Essex County), and Western (Berkshire, Franklin, Hampden and Hampshire Counties). The Southeast Housing Court has three branches - Brockton, Fall River, and New Bedford.

Probate Courts: There are more than 20 Probate and Family Court locations in MA - one per county plus two each in Bristol, plus a Middlesex satellite in Cambridge and Lawrence.

Online Access: Online access to records on the statewide Trial Courts Information Center website is available to attorneys and law firms at www.ma-trialcourts.org/tcic/welcome.jsp. Contact Peter Nylin by email at nylin_p@jud.state.ma.us. Site is updated daily.

Additional Information: In July 2003, the state mandated that the certification fee be $2.50 and the copy fee be $1.00 per page for all Superior and District Courts.

Barnstable County

Superior Court *Felony, Civil Actions Over $25,000* 3195 Main St PO Box 425, Barnstable, MA 02630. 8:30AM-4:30PM. **508-375-6684.** Their public access terminal is connected to the statewide Superior Court system. Access records ✋

Barnstable District Court *Felony, Misdemeanor, Civil, Eviction, Small Claims* Route 6A, PO Box 427, Barnstable, MA 02630. 8:30AM-4:30PM. **508-375-6600.** Includes Barnstable, Yarmouth, and Sandwich. ☎ ✉ ✋

Orleans District Court *Felony, Misdemeanor, Civil, Eviction, Small Claims* 237 Rock Harbor Rd, Orleans, MA 02653. 8:30AM-4:30PM. **508-255-4700.** Includes Brewster, Chatham, Dennis, Eastham, Orleans, Truro, Wellfleet, Harwich, Provincetown. ✋

Falmouth District Court *Felony, Misdemeanor, Civil, Eviction, Small Claims* 161 Jones Rd, Falmouth, MA 02540. 8:30AM-4:30PM. **508-495-1500,** Fax: 505-495-0992. Includes Falmouth, Mashpee, and Bourne. Access by ☎ ✋

Probate & Family Court *Probate* PO Box 346, Barnstable, MA 02630. 8AM-4PM. **508-375-6600,** Fax: 508-362-3662.

Berkshire County

Superior Court *Felony, Civil Actions Over $25,000* 76 East St, Pittsfield, MA 01201. 8:30AM-4:30PM. **413-499-7487,** Fax: 413-442-9190. ✉ ✋

Pittsfield District Court #27 *Felony, Misdemeanor, Civil, Eviction, Small Claims* 24 Wendell Ave, Pittsfield, MA 01201. 8:30AM-4:30PM. **413-442-5468,** Fax: 413-499-7327. Includes Becket,

Dalton, Hancock, Hinsdale, Lanesborough, Lenox, Peru, Pittsfield, Richmond, Washington and Windsor. This court exercises concurrent jurisdiction over Hancock and Windsor with the North Berkshire Divisions. ☎ ✉ ✋

South Berkshire District Court *Felony, Misdemeanor, Civil, Eviction, Small Claims* 9 Gilmore Ave, Great Barrington, MA 01230. 8:30AM-4:30PM. **413-528-3520,** Fax: 413-528-0757. Includes Alford, Becket, Egremont, Great Barrington, Lee, Lenox, Monterey, Mt. Washington, New Marlborough, Otis, Sandisfield, Sheffield, Stockbridge, Tyringham, and West Stockbridge. Shares jurisdiction of Becket and Lenox with Pittsfield Dist. Court. **Fax** ✉ ✋

North Berkshire District Court #28 *Felony, Misd., Civil, Eviction, Small Claims* City Hall - 10 Main St, North Adams, MA 01247. 8AM-4:30PM. **413-663-5339**, Fax: 413-664-7209. Handles cases for Adams, Chesire, Clarksburg, Florida, Hancock, New Ashford, North Adams, Savoy, Williamstown, and Windsor. Exercises concurrent jurisdiction over Hancock and Windsor with the Pittsfield Division. Includes cases from closed Court #30. **Fax**☒ ᵕ

Probate & Family Court *Probate* 44 Bank Row, Pittsfield, MA 01201. 8:30AM-4PM. **413-442-6941**, Fax: 413-443-3430.

Bristol County

Superior Court - Taunton *Felony, Civil Actions Over $25,000* 9 Court St, Taunton, MA 02780. 8AM-4:30PM. **508-823-6588 X1**. ☒ ᵕ

Taunton District Court *Felony, Misdemeanor, Civil, Eviction, Small Claims* 15 Court St, Taunton, MA 02780. 8:30AM-4:30PM. **508-824-4032**, Fax: 508-824-2282. Includes Berkley, Dighton, Easton, Raynham, Rehoboth, Seekonk, and Taunton. ☎☒ ᵕ

Attleboro District Court 34 *Felony, Misd., Civil, Eviction, Small Claims* Courthouse, 88 N Main St, Attleboro, MA 02703. 8AM-4:30PM. **508-222-5900**, Fax: 508-223-3916 crim; 508-222-4869 civ. Includes Attleboro, Mansfield, North Attleboro, and Norton. ☎☒ ᵕ

New Bedford District Court 33 *Felony, Misd., Civil, Eviction, Small Claims* 75 N 6th St, New Bedford, MA 02740. 8:30AM-4PM. **508-999-9700**. Includes Acushnet, Dartmouth, Fairhaven, Freetown, New Bedford, and Westport. ☒ ᵕ **Fax**

Fall River District Court *Felony, Misdemeanor, Civil, Eviction, Small Claims* 45 Rock St, Fall River, MA 02720. 8AM-4:30PM. **508-679-8161**, Fax: 508-675-5477. Includes Fall River, Freetown, Somerset, Swansea, and Westport. ☒ ᵕ**Fax**

Taunton Probate & Family Court *Probate* 11 Court St PO Box 567, Taunton, MA 02780. 9AM-4PM. **508-824-4004**, Fax: 508-821-4630.

New Bedford Probate & Family Court *Probate* 505 Pleasant St, New Bedford,

MA 02740. 8AM-4:30PM. **508-999-5249**, Fax: 508-999-1269.

Dukes County

Superior Court *Felony, Civil Actions Over $25,000* PO Box 1267, Edgartown, MA 02539. 8AM-4PM. **508-627-4668**. ☒ ᵕ

Edgartown District Court *Felony, Misdemeanor, Civil, Eviction, Small Claims* PO Box 1284 Courthouse, 81 Main St, Edgartown, MA 02539-1284. 8:30AM-4:30PM. **508-627-3751/4622**. Includes Edgartown, Oak Bluffs, Tisbury, West Tisbury, Aquinnah, Gosnold, and Elizabeth Islands. ᵕ

Probate & Family Court *Probate* PO Box 237 Rm 104, 1st Fl, Edgartown, MA 02539. 10AM-3PM. **508-627-4703**, Fax: 508-627-7664.

Essex County

Civil case records locations: Session A in Salem, Session B in Newburyport and Session C & D in Lawrence. All finished Superior Court criminal files are in Salem.

Superior Court - Salem *Felony, Session A Civil Actions Over $25,000* 34 Federal St, Salem, MA 01970. 8:00AM-4:30PM. **978-744-5500**, Fax: 978-741-0691 (civ); 978-825-9989 (crim). Civil phone: X223, Crim: X343. ᵕ

Superior Court - Lawrence *Session C & D Civil Actions Over $25,000* 43 Appleton Way, Lawrence, MA 01840. 8AM-4:30PM. **978-687-7463**. Index cards are found in the Salem office (records prior to 1985). Access civil records by ᵕ

Superior Court - Newburyport *Felony, Session B Civil Actions Over $25,000* 145 High St, Newburyport, MA 01950. 8AM-4:30PM. **978-462-4474**. Access by ᵕ

Peabody District Court 86 *Felony, Misdemeanor, Civil, Eviction, Small Claims* One Lowell St, Peabody, MA 01960. 8:30AM-4:30PM. **978-532-3100**. Includes Lynnfield and Peabody. ᵕ

Salem District Court 36 *Felony, Misdemeanor, Civil, Eviction, Small Claims* 65 Washington St, Salem, MA 01970. 8:30AM-4:30PM. **978-744-1167**. Includes Beverly, Danvers, Manchester by the Sea, Middleton, and Salem. ᵕ

Lynn District Court *Felony, Misdemeanor, Civil, Eviction, Small Claims* 580 Essex St, Lynn, MA 01901.

8AM-4:30PM. **781-598-5200**. Includes Lynn, Marblehead, Nahant, Saugus, and Swampscott. ☒ ᵕ

Gloucester District Court *Felony, Misd., Civil, Eviction, Small Claims* 197 Main St, Gloucester, MA 01930. 8:30AM-4:30PM. **978-283-2620**. Includes Essex, Gloucester, and Rockport. ☒ ᵕ

Lawrence District Court *Felony, Misd., Civil, Eviction, Small Claims* 2 Appleton St., Lawrence, MA 01840. 8AM-4:30PM. **978-687-7184**, Civil: 978-689-2810. Includes Andover, Lawrence, Methuen, and North Andover. ☒ ᵕ

Newburyport District Court 22 *Felony, Misdemeanor, Civil, Eviction, Small Claims* 188 State St, Newburyport, MA 01950. 8:30AM-4:30PM. **978-462-2652**. Includes Amesbury, Merrimac, Newbury, Newburyport, Rowley, Salisbury, and West Newbury. ☒ ᵕ

Haverhill District Court *Felony, Misdemeanor, Civil, Eviction, Small Claims* PO Box 1389, Haverhill, MA 01831. 8:30AM-4:30PM. **978-373-4151**, Fax: 978-521-6886. Includes Boxford, Bradford, Georgetown, Groveland, and Haverhill. ☎**Fax**☒ ᵕ

Ipswich District Court *Felony, Misdemeanor, Civil, Eviction, Small Claims* 30 S Main St, PO Box 246, Ipswich, MA 01938. 8:30AM-4:30PM. **978-356-2681**, Fax: 978-356-4396. Includes Hamilton, Ipswich, Topsfield, and Wenham. ᵕ

Probate & Family Court 36 Federal St, Salem, MA 01970. 8:00AM-4:30PM. **978-744-1020**, Fax: 978-741-2957.

Franklin County

Superior Court *Felony, Civil Actions Over $25,000* PO Box 1573, Greenfield, MA 01302. 8:30AM-4:30PM. **413-774-5535**, Fax: 413-774-4770. **Fax**ᵕ

Orange District Court #42 *Felony, Misd., Civil, Eviction, Small Claims* One Court Square, Orange, MA 01364. 8:30AM-4:30PM. **978-544-8277**, Fax: 978-544-5204. Includes Athol, Erving, New Salem, Orange, Warwick, and Wendell, Shutesbury, Leverett. ☎☒ ᵕ

Greenfield District Court *Felony, Misdemeanor, Civil, Eviction, Small Claims* 425 Main St, Greenfield, MA 01301. 8:30AM-4:30PM. **413-774-5533**,

Fax: 413-774-5328. Includes Ashfield, Bernardston, Buckland, Charlemont, Colrain, Conway, Deerfield, Gill, Greenfield, Hawley, Leath, Leverett, Leyden, Monroe, Montague, Northfield, Rowe, Shelburne, Shutesbury, Sunderland, and Whately. 🖑

Probate & Family Court *Probate* www.fcpfc.com PO Box 590, Greenfield, MA 01302. 8AM-4:30PM. **413-774-7011**, Fax: 413-774-3829.

Hampden County

Superior Court *Felony, Civil Actions Over $25,000* 50 State St, PO Box 559, Springfield, MA 01102-0559. 8:30AM-4:30PM. **413-735-6016**, Fax: 413-737-1611. 🖑

Holyoke District Court *Felony, Misdemeanor, Civil, Eviction, Small Claims* 20 Court Sq, Holyoke, MA 01041-5075. 9AM-3:00PM. **413-538-9710**, Fax: 413-533-7165. **Fax**🖂🖑

Palmer District Court *Felony, Misdemeanor, Civil, Eviction, Small Claims* 235 Sykes St, Palmer, MA 01069. 8:30AM-4:30PM. **413-283-8916**, Fax: 413-283-6775. Includes Ludlow, Monson, Wilbraham, Palmer, Wales, Brimfield, Holland, and Hampden. Access by 🖑

Springfield District Court *Felony, Misdemeanor, Civil, Eviction, Small Claims* 50 State St, Springfield, MA 01103. 8:00AM-4:30PM. **413-748-7613**, Fax: 413-747-4841. Civil phone: 413-748-8659, Crim: 413-748-7982. Includes Agawam, East Longmeadow, Longmeadow, Springfield, and West Springfield. 🖑

Westfield District Court *Felony, Misdemeanor, Civil, Eviction, Small Claims* 224 Elm St, Westfield, MA 01085. 8AM-4PM. **413-568-8946**, Fax: 413-568-4863. Includes Blandford, Chester, Granville, Montgomery, Russell, Southwick, Tolland, and Westfield. 🖑

Chicopee District Court #20 *Felony, Misdemeanor, Civil, Eviction, Small Claims* 30 Church St, Chicopee, MA 01020. 8:30AM-4:30PM. **413-598-0099**, Fax: 413-598-8176. 🖑

Probate & Family Court *Probate* 50 State St, Springfield, MA 01103-0559. 8AM-4:25PM. **413-748-7746**, Fax: 413-781-5605.

Hampshire County

Superior Court *Felony, Civil Actions Over $25,000* PO Box 1119, Northampton, MA 01061. 9AM-4PM. **413-584-5810 x331**, Fax: 413-586-8217, 🖂**Fax**🖑

Northampton District Court *Felony, Misdemeanor, Civil, Eviction, Small Claims* Courthouse, 15 Gothic St, Northampton, MA 01060. 8:30AM-4:30PM. **413-584-7776**, Fax: 413-584-9479. Civil phone: 413-584-7400, Crim: 413-584-7400. Includes Chesterfield, Cummington, Easthampton, Goshen, Hatfield, Huntington, Middlefield, Northampton, Plainfield, Southampton, Westhampton, Williamsburg, and Worthington. **Fax**🖂🖑

Ware District Court *Felony, Misd., Civil, Eviction, Small Claims* PO Box 300, Ware, MA 01082. 8AM-4:00PM. **413-967-3301**, Fax: 413-967-7986. Includes Amherst, Belchertown, Granby, Hadley, South Hadley, Pelham, Ware, all the MDC Quabbin Reservoir and Watershed Area. **Fax**🖂🖑

Probate & Family Court *Probate* 33 King St #3, Northampton, MA 01060. 8:30AM-4:30PM. **413-586-8500**, Fax: 413-584-1132.

Middlesex County

Superior Court - East Cambridge *Felony, Civil Actions Over $25,000* 40 Thorndike St Edward J Sullivan Courthouse, East Cambridge, MA 02141. 8:30AM-4:30PM. **617-494-4010**. 🖂🖑

Superior Court - Lowell *Felony, Civil Actions Over $25,000* 360 Gorham St, Lowell, MA 01852. 8:30AM-4:30PM. **978-453-0201**. 🖂🖑

Natick District Court *Felony, Misdemeanor, Civil, Eviction, Small Claims* 117 E Central, Natick, MA 01760. 8:30AM-4:30PM. **508-653-4332**. Includes Natick and Sherborn. 🖑

Framingham District Court *Felony, Misd., Civil, Eviction, Small Claims* 600 Concord St (PO Box 1669), Framingham, MA 01701. 8:30AM-4:30PM. **508-875-7461**. Includes Ashland, Framingham, Holliston, Hopkinton, Sudbury, and Wayland. 🖂🖑**Fax**

Concord District Court 47 *Felony, Misdemeanor, Civil, Eviction, Small Claims* 305 Walden St, Concord, MA 01742. 8:30AM-4:30PM. **978-369-0500**.

Includes Concord, Carlisle, Lincoln, Lexington, Bedford, Acton, Maynard, and Stow. 🖂🖑

Cambridge District Court 52 *Felony, Misdemeanor, Civil, Eviction, Small Claims* PO Box 338, East Cambridge, MA 02141. 8:30AM-4:30PM. **617-494-4095**, Civil: 617-494-4095 X502, Crim: 617-494-4095 X501. Includes Cambridge, Arlington, and Belmont. 🖑🖂

Woburn District Court 53 *Felony, Misdemeanor, Civil, Eviction, Small Claims* 30 Pleasant St, Woburn, MA 01801. 8:30AM-4:30PM. **781-935-4000**. Includes Burlington, North Reading, Reading, Stoneham, Wilmington, Winchester, and Woburn. 🖂🖑

Waltham District Court 51 *Felony, Misdemeanor, Civil, Eviction, Small Claims* 38 Linden St, Waltham, MA 02154. 8:30AM-4:30PM. **781-894-4500**. Includes Waltham, Watertown, and Weston. 🖂🖑

Newton District Court *Felony, Misd., Civil, Eviction, Small Claims* www.state.ma.us/courts/courtsandjudges/courts/newtondistrictmain.html 1309 Washington, West Newton, MA 02141. 8:30AM-1PM; 2-4:30PM. **617-494-0102**. ☎🖂🖑

Marlborough District Court 21 *Felony, Misd., Civil, Eviction, Small Claims* 45 Williams St, Marlborough, MA 01752. 8AM-4:30PM. **508-485-3700**. Includes Marlborough and Hudson. ☎🖂🖑

Malden District Court *Felony, Misd., Civil, Eviction, Small Claims* 89 Summer St., Malden, MA 02148. 8:30AM-4:30PM. **781-322-7500**. Includes Malden, Melrose, Everett, and Wakefield. 🖑

Lowell District Court *Felony, Misdemeanor, Civil, Eviction, Small Claims* 41 Hurd St, Lowell, MA 01852. 8:30AM-4:30PM. **978-459-4101**, Civil: x235, Crim: X204. Includes Billerica, Chelmsford, Dracut, Lowell, Tewksbury, and Tyngsboro. 🖂🖑

Ayer District Court *Felony, Misdemeanor, Civil, Eviction, Small Claims* 25 E Main St, Ayer, MA 01432. 8:30AM-4:30PM. **978-772-2100**, Fax: 978-772-5345. Includes Ayer, Ashby, Boxborough, Dunstable, Groton, Littleton, Pepperell, Shirley, Townsend, Westford and Devens Regional Enterprise Zone. 🖂🖑

Key: Symbols refer to criminal records access unless otherwise noted. phone-☎ mail-🖂 fax-**Fax** in person-🖑 online-🖳 email-**Email**

Somerville District Court *Felony, Misdemeanor, Civil, Eviction, Small Claims* 175 Fellsway, Somerville, MA 02145. 8:30AM-4:30PM. **617-666-8000**. Includes Medford and Somerville. 🖐

Probate & Family Court 208 Cambridge St PO Box 410480, East Cambridge, MA 02141-0005. 8AM-4:30PM. **617-768-5800**, Fax: 617-225-0781.

Nantucket County

Superior Court *Felony, Civil Actions Over $25,000* PO Box 967, Nantucket, MA 02554. 8:30AM-4PM. **508-228-2559**, Fax: 508-228-3725. ☎**Fax**✉🖐

Nantucket District Court *Felony, Misdemeanor, Civil, Eviction, Small Claims* 16 Broad St PO Box 1800, Nantucket, MA 02554. 8AM-4PM. **508-228-0460**. 🖐

Probate & Family Court PO Box 1116, Nantucket, MA 02554. 8:30AM-4PM. **508-228-2669**, Fax: 508-228-3662.

Norfolk County

Superior Court *Felony, Civil Actions Over $25,000* 650 High St, Dedham, MA 02026. 8:30AM-4:30PM. **781-326-1600**, Fax: 781-326-3871(Civ); 781-320-9726 (Crim. fax). Civil phone: ext 1, Crim phone: ext 2. ✉🖐

Wrentham District Court *Felony, Misdemeanor, Civil, Eviction, Small Claims* 60 East St, Wrentham, MA 02093. 8:30AM-4:30PM. **508-384-3106**, Fax: 508-384-5052. Includes Foxborough, Franklin, Medway, Millis, Norfolk, Plainville, Walpole, and Wrentham. 🖐

Stoughton District Court *Felony, Misdemeanor, Civil, Eviction, Small Claims* 1288 Central St, Stoughton, MA 02072. 8:30AM-4:30PM. **781-344-2131**. Includes Avon, Canton, Sharon, and Stoughton. ✉🖐

Brookline District Court *Felony, Misdemeanor, Civil, Eviction, Small Claims* 360 Washington St, Brookline, MA 02445. 8:30AM-4:30PM. **617-232-4660**, Fax: 617-739-0734. Access ✉

Dedham District Court *Felony, Misdemeanor, Civil, Eviction, Small Claims* 631 High St, Dedham, MA 02026. 8:15AM-4:30PM. **781-329-4777**. Includes Dedham, Dover, Medfield, Needham, Norwood, Wellesley, and Westwood. 🖐

Quincy District Court *Felony, Misdemeanor, Civil, Eviction, Small Claims* One Dennis Ryan Parkway, Quincy, MA 02169. 8:30AM-4:30PM. **617-471-1650**. Includes Braintree, Cohasset, Holbrook, Quincy, Randolph, and Weymouth, Quincy. Access by 🖐

Probate & Family Court 35 Shawmut Rd, Canton, MA 02021. 8:15AM-4:30PM. **781-830-1200**, Fax: 781-830-4310 (Reg) 781-830-4320 (Probation) 781-730-4355 (Trial). Due to health concerns, Probate was moved from the old location on High St in Dedham in 2003. Should remain at this new Canton location until 2008.

Plymouth County

Superior Court - Brockton *Felony, Civil Actions Over $25,000* 72 Belmont St, Brockton, MA 02401. 8:30AM-4:30PM. **508-583-8250**. 🖐

Superior Court - Plymouth *Felony, Civil Actions Over $25,000* Plymouth Superior Court Court St, Plymouth, MA 02360. 8:30AM-4:30PM. **508-747-6911**. 🖐(some search exceptions)

Wareham District Court *Felony, Misd., Civil, Eviction, Small Claims* 2200 Cranberry Hwy, Junction Routes 28 & 58, West Wareham, MA 02576. 8AM-4:30PM. **508-295-8300**, Fax: 508-291-6376. Includes Carver, Lakeville, Marion, Mattpoinsett, Middleboro, Rochester, and Wareham. ☎✉🖐

Plymouth 3rd District Court *Felony, Misd., Civil, Eviction, Small Claims* Courthouse, S Russell St, Plymouth, MA 02360. 8:30AM-4:30PM. **508-747-0500**. Includes Duxbury, Halifax, Hanson, Kingston, Marshfield, Pembroke, Plymouth, and Plympton. ✉🖐

Hingham District Court *Felony, Misdemeanor, Civil, Eviction, Small Claims* 28 George Washington Blvd, Hingham, MA 02043. 8:30AM-4:30PM. **781-749-7000**, Fax: 781-740-8390. Includes Hanover, Hingham, Hull, Norwell, Rockland, and Scituate. ✉🖐

Brockton District Court *Felony, Misdemeanor, Civil, Eviction, Small Claims* PO Box 7610 (215 Main St.), Brockton, MA 02303-7610. 8:30AM-4:30PM. **508-587-8000**. Includes Abington, Bridgewater, Brockton, East

Bridgewater, West Bridgewater, and Whitman. ✉🖐

Probate & Family Court 11 Russell PO Box 3640, Plymouth, MA 02361. 8:30AM-4:30PM. **508-747-6204**, Fax: 508-746-6846.

Suffolk County

Superior Court - Civil *Civil* 90 Devonshire St, Rm 807 Copy Dept, Boston, MA 02109. 8:30AM-5PM. **617-788-7677** Access civil records by✉🖐

Superior Court - Criminal *Felony* 90 Devonshire St #607, USPO & Courthouse, Boston, MA 02109. 8:30-5. **617-788-8160**, Fax 617-788-7798. ✉🖐

Roxbury District Court *Felony, Misdemeanor, Civil, Eviction, Small Claims* 85 Warren St, Roxbury, MA 02119. 8:30AM-4:30PM. **617-427-7000**, Fax: 617-442-0615. Access ☎**Fax**✉🖐

East Boston District Court *Misd., Civil Actions Under $25,000, Eviction, Small Claims* 37 Meridian St, East Boston, MA 02128. 8:30AM-4:30PM. **617-569-7550**, Fax: 617-561-4988. Includes East Boston and Winthrop. 🖐

Boston Municipal Court *Misdemeanor, Civil, Small Claims* Civil Clerk's Office 90 Devonshire St, Boston, MA 02109. 8:30AM-4:30PM. **617-788-8412**. ✉🖐

South Boston District Court *Felony, Misdemeanor, Civil, Eviction, Small Claims* 535 E Broadway, South Boston, MA 02127. 8:30AM-4:30PM. **617-268-9292/9293**, Fax: 617-268-7321. 🖐

Charlestown District Court *Felony, Misdemeanor, Civil, Eviction, Small Claims* 3 City Square, Charlestown, MA 02129. 8:30AM-4:30PM. **617-242-5400**, Fax: 617-242-1677. **Fax**✉🖐

Brighton District Court *Felony, Misdemeanor, Civil, Eviction, Small Claims* 52 Academy Hill Rd, Brighton, MA 02135. 8:30AM-4:30PM. **617-782-6521**, Fax: 617-254-2127. Includes Allston and Brighton. Access ☎✉🖐

Chelsea District Court *Felony, Misdemeanor, Civil, Eviction, Small Claims* 120 Broadway, Chelsea, MA 02150-2606. 8:30AM-4:30PM. **617-660-9200**. Includes Chelsea and Revere. ☎✉🖐

Key: Symbols refer to criminal records access unless otherwise noted. phone-☎ mail-✉ fax-**Fax** in person-🖐 online-💻 email-**Email**

Dorchester District Court *Felony, Misd., Civil, Eviction, Small Claims* 510 Washington St, Dorchester, MA 02124. 8:30AM-4:30PM. **617-288-9500**. ✉️ 👋

West Roxbury District Court *Felony, Misdemeanor, Civil, Eviction, Small Claims* Courthouse, 445 Arborway, Jamaica Plain, MA 02130. 8:30AM-4:30PM. **617-971-1200**. Includes West Roxbury, Jamaica Plain, Hyde Park, Roslindale, Parts of Mission Hill, and Mattapan sections of Boston. 👋

Probate & Family Court *Probate* 24 New Chardon St PO Box 9667, Boston, MA 02114-4703. 8:30AM-4:30PM. **617-788-8300**, Fax: 617-788-8962.

Worcester County

Superior Court *Felony, Civil Actions Over $25,000* 2 Main St Rm 21, Worcester, MA 01608. 8AM-4:30PM. **508-770-1899**. ✉️ 👋

East Brookfield District Court *Felony, Misdemeanor, Civil, Eviction, Small Claims* 544 E Main St, East Brookfield, MA 01515-1701. 8:30AM-4:30PM. **508-885-6305/6306**, Fax: 508-885-7623. Includes Brookfield, East Brookfield, Hardwick, Leicester, New Braintree, North Brookfield, Spencer, Warren, and West Brookfield. ✉️ 👋

Clinton District Court *Felony, Misd., Civil, Eviction, Small Claims* 300 Boylston St, Clinton, MA 01510. 8:30AM-4:30PM. **978-368-7811**, Fax: 978-368-7827. Includes Berlin, Bolton,

Boylston, Clinton, Harvard, Lancaster, Sterling, and West Boylston. ✉️ 👋

Winchendon District Court *Felony, Misdemeanor, Civil, Eviction, Small Claims* 80 Central St, Winchendon, MA 01475. 8:30AM-4:30PM. **978-297-0156**, Fax: 978-297-0161. Includes Ashburnham, Winchendon, Phillipston, Royalston, and Templeton. ☎️ ✉️ 👋

Uxbridge District Court *Felony, Misdemeanor, Civil, Eviction, Small Claims* 261 S Main St, Uxbridge, MA 01569. 8:30AM-4:30PM. **508-278-2454**, Fax: 508-278-2929. Includes Blackstone, Douglas, Millville, Northbridge, Sutton, and Uxbridge. ✉️ 👋

Milford District Court *Felony, Misdemeanor, Civil, Eviction, Small Claims* PO Box 370, Milford, MA 01757. 8:30AM-4:30PM. **508-473-1260**. Includes Mendon, Upton, Hopedale, and Milford in Worcester County; also includes Bellingham in Norfolk County. 👋

Leominster District Court *Felony, Misdemeanor, Civil, Eviction, Small Claims* 25 School St, Leominster, MA 01453. 8:30AM-4:30PM. **978-537-3722**, Fax: 978-537-3970. Includes Princeton and Leominster. ☎️ ✉️ 👋

Gardner District Court *Felony, Misd., Civil, Small Claims* 108 Matthews St, Gardner, MA 01440-0040. 8:30AM-4:30PM. **978-632-2373**, Fax: 978-630-3902. Includes Gardner, Hubbardston, Petersham, Westminster. ☎️ Fax ✉️ 👋

Fitchburg District Court 16 *Felony, Misdemeanor, Civil, Eviction, Small Claims* 100 Elm St, Fitchburg, MA 01420. 8:30AM-4:30PM. **978-345-2111**, Fax: 978-342-2461. Includes Fitchburg and Lunenburg. 👋

Dudley District Court 64 *Felony, Misdemeanor, Civil, Eviction, Small Claims* PO Box 100, Dudley, MA 01571. 8AM-4:30PM. **508-943-7123**, Fax: 508-949-0015. Includes Charlton, Dudley, Oxford, Southbridge, Sturbridge, and Webster. ☎️ Fax ✉️ 👋

Worcester District Court *Felony, Misdemeanor, Civil, Eviction, Small Claims* 50 Harvard St, Worcester, MA 01608. 8AM-4:30PM. **508-757-8350**, Fax: 508-797-0716. Includes Auburn, Millbury, and Worcester. Access ✉️ 👋

Westborough District Court *Felony, Misd., Civil, Eviction, Small Claims* 175 Milk St, Westborough, MA 01581. 8AM-4:30PM. **508-366-8266**, Fax: 508-366-8268. Includes Grafton, Northborough, Shrewsbury, Southborough, and Westborough. ✉️ 👋

Probate & Family Court 2 Main St, Worcester, MA 01608. 8:30AM-4:00PM. **508-770-0825 x217**, Fax: 508-752-6138.

Michigan

State Court Administration: State Court Administrator, PO Box 30048 (925 W Ottawa St), Lansing, MI, 48909; 517-373-0130, Fax: 517-373-2112. http://courts.michigan.gov

Court Structure: The Circuit Court is the court of general jurisdiction. District, Municipal and probate Courts are limited jurisdiction.

There is a Court of Claims in Lansing that is a function of the 30th Circuit Court with jurisdiction over claims against the state of Michigan. A Recorder's Court in Detroit was abolished as of October 1, 1997.

As of January 1, 1998, the Family Division of the Circuit Court was created. Domestic relations actions and juvenile cases, including criminal and abuse/neglect, formerly adjudicated in the Probate Court, were transferred to the Family Division of the Circuit Court. Mental health and estate cases continue to be handled by the Probate Courts.

Six counties (Barry, Berrien, Iron, Isabella, Lake, and Washtenaw) and the 46th Circuit Court are participating in a "Demonstration" pilot project designed to streamline court services and consolidate case management. These courts may refer to themselves as County Trial Courts.

Online Access: There is a wide range of online computerization of the judicial system from "none" to "fairly complete," but there is no statewide court records network. Some Michigan courts provide public access terminals in clerk's offices, and some courts are

Key: Symbols refer to criminal records access unless otherwise noted. phone-☎️ mail-✉️ fax-Fax in person-👋 online-💻 email-Email developing off-site electronic filing and searching capability. A few offer remote online to the public. The Criminal Justice Information Center (CJIC), the repository for MI criminal record info, offers online access. Results are available in seconds; fee is $10.00 per name. Go to www.michigan.gov/ichat or call 517-322-5546. Subscribe to email updates of appellate opinions at http://courtofappeals.mijud.net/resources/subscribe.htm. There is no fee.

Additional Information: Court records are considered public unless spcifically made non-public by statute, court rules, caseload, or court order. Courts will, however, affirm that cases exist and provide case numbers.

Some courts will not perform criminal searches. Rather, they refer requests to the State Police.

Costs, search requirements, and procedures vary widely because each jurisdiction may create its own administrative orders.

Alcona County

23rd Circuit Court *Felony, Civil Actions Over $25,000* PO Box 308, Harrisville, MI 48740. 8:30AM-N, 1-4:30PM. **989-724-6807**, Fax: 989-724-5838. 📞✉🖐

81st District Court *Misdemeanor, Civil Actions Under $25,000, Eviction, Small Claims* PO Box 385, Harrisville, MI 48740. 8:30AM-4:30PM. **989-724-5313**, Fax: 989-724-5397. Fax✉🖐

Probate Court PO Box 328, Harrisville, MI 48740. 8:30AM-4:30PM. **989-724-6880**, Fax: 989-724-6196.

Alger County

11th Circuit Court *Felony, Civil Actions Over $25,000* 101 Court St, PO Box 538, Munising, MI 49862. 8AM-4PM. **906-387-2076**, Fax: 906-387-2156. 📞✉🖐

93rd District Court *Misdemeanor, Civil Actions Under $25,000, Eviction, Small Claims* PO Box 186, Munising, MI 49862. 8AM-4PM. **906-387-3879**, Fax: 906-387-2688. Fax✉🖐

Probate Court 101 Court St, Munising, MI 49862. 8AM-N, 1-4PM. **906-387-2080**, Fax: 906-387-4134.

Allegan County

48th Circuit Court *Felony, Civil Actions Over $25,000* 113 Chestnut St, Allegan, MI 49010. 8AM-5PM. **269-673-0300**, Fax: 269-673-0298. ✉🖐

57th District Court *Misdemeanor, Civil Under $25,000, Eviction, Small Claims* www.allegancounty.org/districtct/index.htm 113 Chestnut St, Allegan, MI 49010. 8:30-4:30PM. **269-673-0400**, Civil: 269-673-0355, Crim:269-673-0400. ✉🖐

Probate Court 2243 33rd St, Allegan, MI 49010. 8AM-5PM. **269-673-0250**, Fax: 269-673-5875.

Alpena County

26th Circuit Court *Felony, Civil Actions Over $25,000* 720 W Chisholm #2,

Alpena, MI 49707. 8:30AM-4:30PM. **989-354-9520**, Fax: 989-356-9644. Fax✉🖐

88th District Court *Misdemeanor, Civil Actions Under $25,000, Eviction, Small Claims* 719 W Chisholm #3, Alpena, MI 49707. 8:30AM-4:30PM. **989-354-9678**, Fax: 989-354-9678. Fax✉🖐

Probate Court 719 W Chisholm St, Alpena, MI 49707. 8:30AM-4:30PM. **989-354-9650**, Fax: 989-354-9782.

Antrim County

13th Circuit Court *Felony, Civil Actions Over $25,000* PO Box 520, Bellaire, MI 49615. 8:30AM-5PM. **231-533-6353**, Fax: 231-533-6935. Fax✉🖐

86th District Court *Misdemeanor, Civil Actions Under $25,000, Eviction, Small Claims* PO Box 597, Bellaire, MI 49615. 8AM-4:30PM. **231-533-6441**, Fax: 231-533-6322. Fax✉🖐

Probate Court 205 Cayuga St PO Box 130, Bellaire, MI 49615. 8:30AM-12:00, 12:30-4:30PM. **231-533-6681**, Fax: 231-533-6600.

Arenac County

23rd Circuit Court *Felony, Civil Actions Over $25,000* 120 N Grove St PO Box 747, Standish, MI 48658. 8:30AM-5PM. **989-846-9186**, Fax: 989-846-9199. ✉🖐

81st District Court *Misdemeanor, Civil Actions Under $25,000, Eviction, Small Claims* PO Box 129, Standish, MI 48658. 8:30AM-5PM. **989-846-9538**, Fax: 989-846-2008. 📞Fax✉🖐

Probate Court 120 N Grove PO Box 666, Standish, MI 48658. 8:30AM-5PM. **989-846-6941**, Fax: 989-846-6757.

Baraga County

12th Circuit Court *Felony, Civil Actions Over $25,000* 16 N 3rd St, L'Anse, MI

49946. 8:30AM-4:30PM. **906-524-6183**, Fax: 906-524-6186. 📞✉🖐

97th District Court *Misdemeanor, Civil Actions Under $25,000, Eviction, Small Claims* 16 N 3rd St, L'Anse, MI 49946. 8:30AM-N,1-4:30PM. **906-524-6109**, Fax: 906-524-7017. ✉🖐

Probate County Courthouse 16 N 3rd St, L'Anse, MI 49946. 8:30AM-N, 1-4:30PM. **906-524-6390**, Fax: 906-524-6186.

Barry County

5th Circuit Court *Felony, Civil Actions Over $25,000* www.barrycounty.org 220 W State St, Hastings, MI 49058. 8AM-5PM. **269-945-1285**, Fax: 269-945-0209. Fax✉🖐

56B District Court *Misdemeanor, Civil Actions Under $25,000, Eviction, Small Claims* 206 W Court St #202, Hastings, MI 49058. 8AM-5PM. **269-945-1404**, Fax: 269-948-3314. 📞Fax✉🖐

Probate Court www.barrycounty.org/Departments/Probate.htm 206 W Court St, #302, Hastings, MI 49058. 8AM-5PM. **269-945-1390**, Fax: 269-948-3322.

Bay County

18th Circuit Court *Felony, Civil Actions Over $25,000* http://baycountycourt.com 1230 Washington Ave #725, Bay City, MI 48708-5737. 8AM-5PM. **989-895-4265**, Fax: 989-895-4099. 📞Fax✉🖐

74th District Court *Misdemeanor, Civil Actions Under $25,000, Eviction, Small Claims* www.baycountycourts.com/ 1230 Washington Ave, Bay City, MI 48708. 8AM-5PM. **989-895-4232**, Fax: 989-895-4233. Civil phone: 989-895-4203, Crim: 989-895-4229. Current docket data is available on the website; in the future, case info will also. 🖐

Probate Court 1230 Washington, #715, Bay City, MI 48708. 8AM-5PM. **989-895-4205**, Fax: 989-895-4194. Access the courts' calendar of scheduled cases free at

www.baycountycourts.com/bcc/home.nsf/
public/court_calendar.htm.

Benzie County

19th Circuit Court *Felony, Civil Actions Over $25,000* PO Box 377, Beulah, MI 49617. 8AM-5PM. **231-882-9671 & 800-315-3593,** Fax: 231-882-5941. **☎Fax**⊠☝

85th District Court *Misdemeanor, Civil Actions Under $25,000, Eviction, Small Claims* PO Box 377, Beulah, MI 49617. 9AM-5PM. **231-882-0019**, Fax: 231-882-0022. **Fax**⊠☝

Probate Court 448 Court Pl, County Gov't Ctr. PO Box 377, Beulah, MI 49617. 8:30AM-N, 1-5PM. **231-882-9675**, Fax: 231-882-5987.

Berrien County

2nd Circuit Court *Felony, Civil Actions Over $25,000* www.berriencounty.org/ 811 Port St, St Joseph, MI 49085. 8:30AM-5PM. **269-983-7111 X8368**, Fax: 269-982-8642. ⊠☝

5th District Court - Trial Court Criminal Division *Misdemeanor, Civil Actions Under $25,000, Eviction, Small Claims* www.berriencounty.org Attn: Records 811 Port St, St Joseph, MI 49085. 8:30AM-5PM. **269-983-7111**, Fax: 269-982-8643. ⊠☝

Probate Court 811 Port St., St Joseph, MI 49085. 8:30AM-5PM. **269-983-7111 X8365**, Fax: 269-982-8644.

Branch County

15th Circuit Court *Felony, Civil Actions Over $25,000* www.co.branch.mi.us 31 Division St, Coldwater, MI 49036. 9AM-5PM. **517-279-4306**, Fax: 517-278-5627. ⊠☝

3A District Court *Misdemeanor, Civil Actions Under $25,000, Eviction, Small Claims* www.branchcountycourts.com 31 Division St., Coldwater, MI 49036. 8AM-5PM. **517-279-4308**, Fax: 517-279-4333. Civil phone: 517-279-4331, Crim: 517-279-4329. Small Claims is 279-4330 and Traffic is 279-4328. ⊠☝

Probate Court 31 Division St., Coldwater, MI 49036. 8AM-N, 1-5PM. **517-279-4318**, Fax: 517-279-0516.

Calhoun County

37th Circuit Court *Felony, Civil Over $25,000* www.calhouncountymi.gov/Depar
tments/CircuitCourt/OverviewCircuitCourt.h
tm 161 E Michigan Ave, Battle Creek, MI 49014-4066. 8AM-N, 1-5PM. **269-969-6518, 269-969-6530.** ☝

10th District Court *Misdemeanor, Civil Under $25,000, Eviction, Small Claims* www.calhouncountymi.gov/Departments/Di
strictCourt/OverviewDistrictCourt.htm 161 E Michigan Ave, Battle Creek, MI 49014. 8:00AM-4PM. **269-969-6666**, Fax: 269-969-6663. Civil phone: 269-969-6683, Crim: 269-969-6678. The 10th District Court Marshall Branch's records and administration is now housed here. Fax⊠☝

Probate www.calhouncountymi.gov/Depart
ments/ProbateCourt/OverviewProbateCourt.
htm Justice Ctr, 161 E Michigan Ave, Battle Creek, MI 49014. 8AM-5PM, F 9-5PM. **269-969-6794**, Fax: 269-969-6797.

Cass County

43rd Circuit Court *Felony, Civil Actions Over $25,000* 120 N Broadway File Room; 60296 M-62, #10, Cassopolis, MI 49031. 8AM-5PM. **269-445-4416**, Fax: 269-445-4406. Civil phone: 269-445-4453. Fax⊠☝

4th District Court *Misdemeanor, Civil Actions Under $25,000, Eviction, Small Claims* 60296 M 62 #10, Cassopolis, MI 49031-8716. 8AM-5PM. **269-445-4424**, Fax: 269-445-4486. ☎⊠☝

Probate Court 60296 - M62, Cassopolis, MI 49031. 8AM-N, 1-5PM. **269-445-4454**, Fax: 269-445-4453.

Charlevoix County

33rd Circuit Court *Felony, Civil Over $25,000* www.charlevoixcounty.org/clerk
.asp 203 Antrim St, Charlevoix, MI 49720. 9AM-5PM. **231-547-7200**, Fax: 231-547-7217. ⊠**Fax**☝

90th District Court *Misdemeanor, Civil Actions Under $25,000, Eviction, Small Claims* 301 State St, Court Bldg, Charlevoix, MI 49720. 9AM-5PM. **231-547-7227**, Fax: 231-547-7253. Civil phone: 231-547-7254. Access ⊠**Fax**☝

Probate Court 301 State St, County Bldg, Charlevoix, MI 49720. 9AM-5PM. **231-547-7214; 547-7215,** Fax: 231-547-7256. Shares the same judge with Emmet County Probate Court.

Cheboygan County

53rd Circuit Court *Felony, Civil Actions Over $25,000* PO Box 70, Cheboygan,
MI 49721. 8:30AM-5PM. **231-627-8808.** ☎⊠☝

89th District Court *Misdemeanor, Civil Actions Under $25,000, Eviction, Small Claims* www.89thdistrictcourt.org/ PO Box 70, Cheboygan, MI 49721. 8:30AM-4PM. **231-627-8809**, Fax: 231-627-8444. **☎Fax**⊠☝

Probate 870 S Main St PO Box 70, Cheboygan, MI 49721. 8:30AM-4:30PM. **231-627-8823**, Fax: 231-627-8868.

Chippewa County

50th Circuit Court *Felony, Civil Actions Over $25,000* 319 Court St, Sault Ste Marie, MI 49783. 8AM-5PM. **906-635-6300**, Fax: 906-635-6851. ⊠☝

91st District Court *Misdemeanor, Civil Actions Under $25,000, Eviction, Small Claims* 325 Court St, Sault Ste Marie, MI 49783. 9AM-4:30PM. **906-635-6320**, Fax: 906-635-7605. Call before faxing for instructions. ⊠**Fax**☝

Probate Court 319 Court St., Sault Ste Marie, MI 49783. 9AM-5PM. **906-635-6314**, Fax: 906-635-6852.

Clare County

55th Circuit Court *Felony, Civil Actions Over $25,000* 225 W Main St, PO Box 438, Harrison, MI 48625. 8AM-4:30PM. **989-539-7131**, Fax 989-539-6616. ⊠☝

80th District Court *Misdemeanor, Civil Actions Under $25,000, Eviction, Small Claims* 225 W. Main St, Harrison, MI 48625. 8AM-4:30PM. **989-539-7173**, Fax: 989-539-4036. ⊠**Fax**☝

Probate Court 225 W. Main St. PO Box 96, Harrison, MI 48625. 8AM-4:30PM. **989-539-7109**. This is combined with Gladwin County Probate Court.

Clinton County

29th Circuit Court *Felony, Civil Actions Over $25,000* www.clinton-county.org PO Box 69, St Johns, MI 48879-0069. 8AM-5PM. **989-224-5140**, Fax: 989-227-6421. ⊠☝

65th District Court *Misdemeanor, Civil Actions Under $25,000, Eviction, Small Claims* 100 E State St, #3400, St Johns, MI 48879-1571. 8AM-5PM. **989-224-5150**, Fax: 989-224-5154. Access by ☝

Probate Court www.clinton-county.org 100 E State St #4300, St Johns, MI 48879. 8AM-5PM. **989-224-5190**, Fax: 989-224-5102.

Key: Symbols refer to criminal records access unless otherwise noted. phone-☎ mail-⊠ fax-**Fax** in person-☝ online-💻 email-**Email**

Crawford County

46th Circuit Court *Felony, Civil Actions Over $25,000* www.Circuit46.org 200 W Michigan Ave, Grayling, MI 49738. 8:30AM-3:30PM. **989-348-2841**, Fax: 989-344-3223. ✉🖐🖥☎Fax

46th Circuit Trial Court - District Division *Misdemeanor, Civil Actions Under $25,000, Eviction, Small Claims* www.Circuit46.org 200 W Michigan Ave, Grayling, MI 49738. 8AM-4:30PM. **989-348-2841 X242**, Fax: 989-344-3290. ☎✉Fax🖐🖥

Probate Court www.Circuit46.org 200 W Michigan Ave, Grayling, MI 49738. 8:00AM-4:30PM. **989-344-3237**, Fax: 989-344-3277. Search cases by name free at www.circuit46.org/Cases/cases.html.

Delta County

47th Circuit Court *Felony, Civil Actions Over $25,000* 310 Ludington St, Escanaba, MI 49829. 8AM-4PM. **906-789-5105**, Fax: 906-789-5196. ✉🖐

94th District Court *Misdemeanor, Civil Actions Under $25,000, Eviction, Small Claims* 310 Ludington St., Escanaba, MI 49829. 8AM-4PM. Fax: 906-789-5198. Civil phone: 906-789-5106, Crim: 906-789-5108. ✉🖐

Probate Court 310 Ludington St., Escanaba, MI 49829. 8AM-N, 1-4PM. **906-789-5112**, Fax: 906-789-5140.

Dickinson County

41st Circuit Court *Felony, Civil Actions Over $25,000* PO Box 609, Iron Mountain, MI 49801. 8AM-4:30PM. **906-774-0988**, Fax: 906-774-4660. ✉🖐

95 B District Court *Misdemeanor, Civil Actions Under $25,000, Eviction, Small Claims* County Courthouse PO Box 609, Iron Mountain, MI 49801. 8AM-4:30PM. **906-774-0506**, Fax: 906-774-8560. May require a signed release for certain records. ✉Fax🖐

Probate Court PO Box 609, Iron Mountain, MI 49801. 8AM-4:30PM. **906-774-1555**, Fax: 906-774-1561.

Eaton County

56th Circuit Court *Felony, Civil Over $25,000* www.eatoncountycourts.org/courts.html 1045 Independence Blvd, Charlotte, MI 48813. 8AM-5PM. 517-

543-7500 **X396**, Fax: 517-543-4475. Fax✉🖐

56A District Court *Misdemeanor, Civil Under $25,000, Eviction, Small Claims* www.eatoncountycourts.org/courts.html 1045 Independence Blvd, Charlotte, MI 48813. 8AM-5PM. **517-543-7500**, Fax: 517-541-1469. Civil phone: x281, Crim: x283. 🖐

Probate Court www.eatoncountycourts.org/courts.html 1045 Independence Blvd Probate Court, Charlotte, MI 48813. 8AM-5PM. **517-543-7500 X234**.

Emmet County

57th Circuit Court *Felony, Civil Actions Over $25,000* www.co.emmet.mi.us/ 200 Division St, Petoskey, MI 49770. 8-5PM. **231-348-1744**, Fax 231-348-0602. ✉🖐

90th District Court *Misdemeanor, Civil Actions Under $25,000, Eviction, Small Claims* 200 Division St., Petoskey, MI 49770. 8AM-5PM. **231-348-1750**, Fax: 231-348-0616. Civil phone: 231-348-1753, Crim: 231-348-1752. Fax✉🖐

Probate Court 200 Division St., Petoskey, MI 49770. 8AM-5PM. **231-348-1707**, Fax: 231-348-0672. Shares the same judge with Charlevoix County Probate Court.

Genesee County

7th Circuit Court *Felony, Civil Actions Over $25,000, and domestic (i.e. Divorce, Support, Custody)* www.co.genesee.mi.us 900 S Saginaw, Flint, MI 48502. 8AM-5PM. **810-257-3220**. Cases files could be located at one of seven lower courts in the county. The Clerk's index will indicate the exact location. Probate court is located in a separate office at the same address. ✉🖐🖥

67th District Court *Misdemeanor, Civil Actions Under $25,000, Eviction, Small Claims* www.co.genesee.mi.us 630 S Saginaw, Flint, MI 48502. 8AM-4PM. **810-257-3170**. Cases files can be located at any one of 7 lower courts in the county. The Clerk's index will indicate the exact location. ✉🖐

Probate Court 900 S Saginaw St #502, Flint, MI 48502. 8AM-4PM. **810-257-3528**, Fax: 810-257-2713.

Gladwin County

55th Circuit Court *Felony, Civil Actions Over $25,000* 401 W Cedar, Gladwin, MI

48624. 8:30AM-4:30PM. **989-426-7351**, Fax: 989-426-6917. Fax✉🖐

80th District Court *Misdemeanor, Civil Actions Under $25,000, Eviction, Small Claims* 401 W Cedar, Gladwin, MI 48624. 8:30AM-4:30PM. **989-426-9207**, Fax: 989-246-0894. ✉Fax🖐

Probate Court 401 W Cedar, Gladwin, MI 48624. 8:30AM-4:30PM. **989-426-7451**, Fax: 989-426-6936. Is combined with Clare County Probate Court.

Gogebic County

32nd Circuit Court *Felony, Civil Over $25,000* www.gogebic.org/circuit.htm 200 N Moore St, Bessemer, MI 49911. 8:30AM-4:30PM. **906-663-4518**, Fax: 906-663-4660. ✉🖐

98th District Court *Misdemeanor, Civil Actions Under $25,000, Eviction, Small Claims* 200 N Moore St, Bessemer, MI 49911. 8:30AM-4:30PM. **906-663-4611**, Fax: 906-667-1102. ✉🖐

Probate 200 N Moore St., Bessemer, MI 49911. 8:30AM-N, 1-4:30PM. **906-667-0421**, Fax: 906-663-4660.

Grand Traverse County

13th Circuit Court *Felony, Civil Actions Over $25,000* 328 Washington St, Traverse City, MI 49684. 8AM-5PM. **231-922-4710**. ☎✉🖐

86th District Court *Misdemeanor, Civil Actions Under $25,000, Eviction, Small Claims* 328 Washington St., Traverse City, MI 49684. 8AM-5PM. **231-922-4580**, Fax: 231-922-4454. ☎✉🖐

Probate Court 400 Boardman Av, Traverse City, MI 49684. 8AM-5PM. **231-922-6862**, Fax: 231-922-4458.

Gratiot County

29th Circuit Court *Felony, Civil Actions Over $25,000* 214 E Center St, Ithaca, MI 48847. 8:00AM-N, 1:00PM-4:30PM. **989-875-5215**. ✉🖐

65-B District Court *Misdemeanor, Civil Actions Under $25,000, Eviction, Small Claims* 245 E Newark St, Ithaca, MI 48847. 8AM-4:30PM. **989-875-5240**, Fax: 989-875-5290. 🖐

Probate 214 E Center St PO Box 217, Ithaca, MI 48847. 8AM-N, 1PM-4:30PM. **989-875-5231**, Fax: 989-875-5331.

Key: Symbols refer to criminal records access unless otherwise noted.   phone-☎   mail-✉   fax-Fax   in person-🖐   online-🖥   email-Email

Hillsdale County

1st Circuit Court *Felony, Civil Actions Over $25,000* 29 N Howell, Hillsdale, MI 49242. 8:30AM-5PM. **517-437-3391**, Fax: 517-437-3392. ✉🖐

2nd District Court *Misdemeanor, Civil Actions Under $25,000, Eviction, Small Claims* 49 N Howell, Hillsdale, MI 49242. 8AM-4:30PM; 8AM-5PM Traffic. **517-437-7329**, Fax: 517-437-2908. ☎✉🖐

Probate Court 29 N Howell, Hillsdale, MI 49242. 8:30AM-N, 1-5PM. **517-437-4643**, Fax: 517-437-4148.

Houghton County

12th Circuit Court *Felony, Civil Actions Over $25,000* 401 E Houghton Ave, Houghton, MI 49931. 8AM-4:30PM. **906-482-5420**. ✉🖐

97th District Court *Misdemeanor, Civil Actions Under $25,000, Eviction, Small Claims* 401 E Houghton Ave., Houghton, MI 49931. 8AM-4:30PM. **906-482-4980**, Fax: 906-482-5270. ✉**Fax**🖐

Probate Court 401 E. Houghton Ave., Houghton, MI 49931. 8AM-4:30PM. **906-482-3120**, Fax: 906-487-5964.

Huron County

52nd Circuit Court *Felony, Civil Actions Over $25,000* 250 E Huron Ave, Bad Axe, MI 48413. 8:30AM-5PM. **989-269-9942**, Fax: 989-269-6160. ☎✉🖐

73B District Court *Misdemeanor, Civil Actions Under $25,000, Eviction, Small Claims* 250 E Huron Ave., Bad Axe, MI 48413. 8:30AM-5PM. **989-269-9987**, Fax: 989-269-6167. ☎**Fax**✉🖐

Probate Court 250 E. Huron Ave., Bad Axe, MI 48413. 8:30AM-N, 1-5PM. **989-269-9944**, Fax: 989-269-0004.

Ingham County

30th Circuit Court *Felony, Civil Over $25,000* www.ingham.org/cc/circuit.htm 313 W. Kalamazoo (PO Box 40771), Lansing, MI 48933. 9:00AM-5:00PM. **517-483-6500**, Fax 517-483-6501. ✉🖐

54 A District Court *Misdemeanor, Civil Actions Under $25,000, Eviction, Small Claims* 124 W Michigan Ave, Lansing, MI 48933. 8AM-4:30PM. **517-483-4433**, Fax: 517-483-4108. Civil phone: 517-483-4426, Crim: 517-483-4445. This court covers the City of Lansing. 🖐

54 B District Court *Misdemeanor, Civil Actions Under $25,000, Eviction, Small Claims* http://cityofeastlansing.com 101 Linden, East Lansing, MI 48823. 8AM-4:30PM. **517-351-7000**, Fax: 517-351-3371. Civil phone: 517-351-1730, Crim: 517-336-8630. This court covers the City of East Lansing. ✉🖐

55th District Court *Misdemeanor, Civil Actions Under $25,000, Eviction, Small Claims* 700 Buhl St., Mason, MI 48854. 8:30AM-5PM. **517-676-8400**. This court covers all of Ingham County except for Lansing and East Lansing. ✉🖐

Lansing Probate Court 313 W Kalamazoo, Lansing, MI 48933. 8AM-N, 1-5PM. **517-483-6300**, Fax: 517-483-6150. The probate court located in Mason was closed; all their records reside here.

Ionia County

8th Circuit Court *Felony, Civil Over $25,000* www.ioniacounty.org/Circuit/Circuit-Home.asp 100 Main, Ionia, MI 48846. 8:30AM-5PM. **616-527-5322**, Fax: 616-527-8201. ☎**Fax**✉🖐

64 A District Court *Misdemeanor, Civil Under $25,000, Eviction, Small Claims* www.ioniacounty.org/district/home1.asp 101 W Main, Ionia, MI 48846. 7:45AM-5:30PM. **616-527-5346**, Fax: 616-527-5343. **Fax**✉🖐

Probate Court www.ioniacounty.org/Probate/Probate_home.asp 100 Main, Ionia, MI 48846. 8:30AM-5PM. **616-527-5326**, Fax: 616-527-5321.

Iosco County

23rd Circuit Court *Felony, Civil Actions Over $25,000* www.iosco.net/ PO Box 838, Tawas City, MI 48764. 9AM-5PM. **989-362-3497**, Fax: 989-984-1012. ☎✉🖐

81st District Court *Misdemeanor, Civil Actions Under $25,000, Eviction, Small Claims* PO Box 388, Tawas City, MI 48764. 8:30AM-5PM. **989-362-4441**, Fax: 989-984-1021. ✉🖐

Probate Court PO Box 421, Tawas City, MI 48764. 8AM-5PM. **989-984-1037**, Fax: 989-984-1035.

Iron County

41st Circuit Court *Felony, Civil Actions Over $25,000* 2 South 6th St #9, Crystal Falls, MI 49920. 8AM- 1200-12:30-4PM. **906-875-3221**, Fax: 906-875-6675. **Fax**✉🖐

95 B District Court *Misdemeanor, Civil Actions Under $25,000, Eviction, Small Claims* 2 S 6th St., Crystal Falls, MI 49920. 8AM-4PM. **906-875-0619**, Fax: 906-875-6775. ✉🖐

Probate www.iron.org 2 S 6th St, #10, Crystal Falls, MI 49920. 8AM-N, 12:30-4PM. **906-875-0659**, Fax: 906-875-0656.

Isabella County

21st Circuit Court *Felony, Civil Actions Over $25,000* 200 N Main St, Mount Pleasant, MI 48858. 8AM-4:30PM. **989-772-0911 X259**. ✉🖐

76th District Court *Misdemeanor, Civil Actions Under $25,000, Eviction, Small Claims* www.isabellacounty.org/trial.html 300 N Main St., Mount Pleasant, MI 48858. 8AM-4:30PM. **989-772-0911 X490**, Fax: 989-779-8022. ✉🖐

Probate Court www.isabellacounty.org 300 N Main St, Mount Pleasant, MI 48858. 8AM-4:30PM. **989-772-0911 x316 (or x276)**, Fax: 989-779-8022.

Jackson County

4th Circuit Court *Felony, Civil Actions Over $25,000* www.co.jackson.mi.us 312 S Jackson St, Jackson, MI 49201. 8AM-5PM. **517-788-4268**. ☎✉🖐

12th District Court *Misdemeanor, Civil Actions Under $25,000, Eviction, Small Claims* www.d12.com 312 S Jackson St., Jackson, MI 49201. 7AM-6PM. **517-788-4260**, Fax: 517-788-4262. **Fax**✉🖐

Probate Court 312 S Jackson St, 1st Fl, Jackson, MI 49201. 8AM-5PM. **517-788-4290**, Fax: 517-788-4291.

Kalamazoo County

9th Circuit Court *Felony, Civil Over $25,000* www.kalcounty.com/courts/index.htm 227 W Michigan Ave, Kalamazoo, MI 49007. 8-5PM. **269-383-8837**. ✉🖐

8th District Court - South *Misdemeanor, Civil Actions Under $25,000, Eviction, Small Claims* 7810 Shaver Rd., Portage, MI 49002. 8AM-5PM. **269-383-6460**, Fax: 269-321-3645. This court covers Kalamazoo County South of N Ave. (Kilgore Rd). ✉🖐

8th District Court - Crosstown *Civil Actions Under $25,000, Eviction, Small Claims* 150 E Crosstown Parkway, Kalamazoo, MI 49001. 8AM-5PM. **269-384-8020**, Fax: 269-383-8899. This court covers City of Kalamazoo. Access civil records by **Fax**☒🖐

8th District Court - North *Misdemeanor* 227 W Michigan St., Kalamazoo, MI 49007. 8AM-5PM. **269-384-8171**, Fax: 269-384-8047. Court covers Kalamazoo County. **Fax**☒🖐

Probate Court 150 E Crosstown Parkway, Kalamazoo, MI 49001. 9AM-N, 1-5PM T; 8AM-N, 1-5PM M,W-F. **269-383-8666/8933**, Fax: 269-383-8685.

Kalkaska County

46th Circuit Court *Felony, Civil Actions Over $25,000* www.Circuit46.org PO Box 10, Kalkaska, MI 49646. 9AM-5PM. **231-258-3300**. ☒🖐💻

46th Circuit Trial Court - District Court *Misdemeanor, Civil Actions Under $25,000, Eviction, Small Claims* www.Circuit46.org 605 N Birch St., Kalkaska, MI 49646. 8-4:30PM. **231-258-9031**, Fax 231-258-2424. ☎☒🖐💻

Circuit Trial Court - Probate Division *Probate* www.Circuit46.org 605 N Birch, Kalkaska, MI 49646. 8AM-4:30PM. **231-258-3330ext.2**, Fax: 231-258-3329. Search cases by name free at www.circuit46.org/Cases/cases.html.

Kent County

17th Circuit Court *Felony, Civil Over $25,000* www.accesskent.com/government /courts/17cc_index.htm 180 Ottawa Ave NW, #2400, Grand Rapids, MI 49503. 8AM-5PM. **616-632-5480**, Fax: 616-632-5458. ☒🖐

59th District Court - Walker *Misd., Civil Actions Under $25,000, Eviction, Small Claims* 4343 Remembrance Rd NW, Walker, MI 49544. 8AM--5PM. **616-453-5765**, Fax 616-791-6851. ☒🖐

62 B District Court - Kentwood *Misdemeanor, Civil Actions Under $25,000, Eviction, Small Claims* 4740 Walma Ave, Kentwood, MI 49512. 8AM-5PM. **616-698-9310**, Fax: 616-698-8199. ☒🖐

59th District Court - Grandville *Misdemeanor, Civil Actions Under $25,000, Eviction, Small Claims* 3181 Wilson Ave SW, Grandville, MI 49418. 8:30AM--5PM. **616-538-9660**, Fax: 616-538-5144. ☒🖐

61st District Court - Grand Rapids *Misdemeanor, Civil Actions Under $25,000, Eviction, Small Claims* www.grcourt.org 180 Ottawa Ave NW #1400 Kent County Courthouse, Grand Rapids, MI 49503. 7:45AM-4:45PM. **616-632-5525**, Fax: 616-632-5582. ☒🖐💻

62 A District Court - Wyoming *Misdemeanor, Civil Actions Under $25,000, Eviction, Small Claims* www.ci.wyoming.mi.us/courts.htm 2650 De Hoop Ave SW, Wyoming, MI 49509. 8AM-5PM. **616-530-7385**, Fax: 616-249-3419. Civil phone: 616-530-7386, Crim: 616-257-9814. ☒**Fax**🖐

63rd District Court - 1st Division *Misdemeanor, Civil Actions Under $25,000, Eviction, Small Claims* 105 Maple St, Rockford, MI 49341. 8AM-5PM. **616-866-1576**, Fax: 616-866-3080. ☒🖐**Fax**

Probate Court 180 Ottawa Ave NW #2500, Grand Rapids, MI 49503. 8:30AM-4:30PM. **616-632-5440**, Fax: 616-632-5430.

Keweenaw County

12th Circuit Court *Felony, Civil Actions Over $25,000* 5095 4th St., Eagle River, MI 49950-9744. 9AM-4PM. **906-337-2229**, Fax: 906-337-2795. ☒🖐

97th District Court *Misdemeanor, Civil Actions Under $25,000, Eviction, Small Claims* 5095 4th St., Eagle River, MI 49950. 9AM-4PM. **906-337-2229**, Fax: 906-337-2795. **Fax**☒🖐

Probate HC1 Box 607, Courthouse, Eagle River, MI 49950. 9AM-4PM. **906-337-1927**, Fax: 906-337-2795.

Lake County

Lake County Trial Court *Felony, Misdemeanor, Civil Actions, Eviction, Small Claims, Probate* 800 10th St, #300, Baldwin, MI 49304. 8AM-N, 1-5PM. **231-745-4614**. ☒🖐

Lake County Trial Court *Probate, Probate* 800 10th St, #300, Baldwin, MI 49304-7970. 8:30AM-5PM. **231-745-4614**, Fax: 231-745-6232.

Lapeer County

40th Circuit Court *Felony, Civil Actions Over $25,000* 255 Clay St, Lapeer, MI 48446. 8AM-5PM. **810-667-0358**. ☒🖐

71 A District Court *Misdemeanor, Civil Actions Under $25,000, Eviction, Small Claims* 255 Clay St., Lapeer, MI 48446. 8AM-5PM. **810-667-0314**. ☒🖐

Probate Court 255 Clay St., Lapeer, MI 48446. 8AM-5PM. **810-667-0261**, Fax: 810-667-0271.

Leelanau County

13th Circuit Court *Felony, Civil Actions Over $25,000* PO Box 467, Leland, MI 49654. 9AM-5PM. **231-256-9824**, Fax: 231-256-8295. ☒**Fax**🖐

86th District Court *Misdemeanor, Civil Under $25,000, Eviction, Small Claims* www.co.leelanau.mi.us/government0254.asp PO Box 486, Leland, MI 49654. 8AM-4PM. **231-256-8250**, Fax: 231-256-8275. ☎**Fax**☒🖐

Family Court *Probate* PO Box 595, Leland, MI 49654. 9AM-5PM. **231-256-9803**, Fax: 231-256-9845.

Lenawee County

39th Circuit Court *Felony, Civil Actions Over $25,000* 425 N Main St, Adrian, MI 49221. 8-4:30PM. **517-264-4597**. ☒🖐

2A District Court *Misdemeanor, Civil Actions Under $25,000, Eviction, Small Claims* 425 N Main St., Adrian, MI 49221. 8AM-4:30PM. **517-264-4673 & 264-4668**, Fax: 517-264-4665 Probation; 264-4681. 🖐

Probate Court 425 N Main St., Adrian, MI 49221. 8AM-4:30PM. **517-264-4614**, Fax: 517-264-4616.

Livingston County

44th Circuit Court *Felony, Civil Actions Over $25,000* www.co.livingston.mi.us/ 204 S Highlander Way #4, Howell, MI 48843. 8AM-5PM. **517-546-9816**. Juvenile records: 517-546-1500. ☒🖐

53 B District Court *Misdemeanor, Civil Actions Under $25,000, Eviction, Small Claims* http://co.livingston.mi.us/DistrictC ourt/brighton.htm 224 N1st St, Brighton, MI 48116. 8AM-5PM. **810-229-6615**, Fax: 810-229-1770. ☒🖐**Fax**

53 A District Court *Misdemeanor, Civil Under $25,000, Eviction, Small Claims* http://co.livingston.mi.us/DistrictCourt 204 S Highlander Way #1, Howell, MI 48843. 8AM-5PM. **517-548-1000**, Fax: 517-548-9445. Civil phone: 517-548-1000 x369, Crim: 517-548-1000 x279. 🖐

Probate www.co.livingston.mi.us/probatec our 204 Highlander Way #2, Howell, MI 48843. 8AM-5PM. **517-546-3750**, Fax: 517-552-2510.

Luce County

11th Circuit Court *Felony, Civil Actions Over $25,000* 407 W Harrie, Newberry, MI 49868. 8AM-4PM. **906-293-5521**, Fax: 906-293-0050. ✉🖐

92nd District Court *Misdemeanor, Civil Actions Under $25,000, Eviction, Small Claims* 407 W Harrie, Newberry, MI 49868. 8AM-4PM. **906-293-5531**, Fax: 906-293-3581. ☎**Fax**✉🖐

Probate Court 407 W. Harrie, Newberry, MI 49868. 8AM-N, 1-4PM. **906-293-5601**, Fax: 906-293-3581. This is a combined court with Mackinac County Probate Court.

Mackinac County

11th Circuit Court *Felony, Civil Actions Over $25,000* 100 S Marley St, Rm 10, St Ignace, MI 49781. 8:30AM-4:30PM. **906-643-7300**, Fax: 906-643-7302. ✉🖐

92nd District Court *Misdemeanor, Civil Actions Under $25,000, Eviction, Small Claims* 100 S Marley, Rm 55, St Ignace, MI 49781. 8:30AM-4:30PM. **906-643-7321**, Fax: 906-643-7302. ✉🖐

Probate Court 100 S Marley St Rm. 15, St Ignace, MI 49781. 8:30AM-N, 1-4:30PM. **906-643-7303**, Fax: 906-643-8861. This is a combined court with Luce County Probate Court.

Macomb County

16th Circuit Court *Felony, Civil Over $25,000* www.macombcountymi.gov/CIR CUITCOURT/index.htm 40 N Main St, Mount Clemens, MI 48043. 8AM-4:30PM. **586-469-5120**. Access by ✉🖐

42nd District Court Division 2 *Misdemeanor, Civil Actions Under $25,000, Eviction, Small Claims* www.macombcountymi.gov/ 43565 Elizabeth St., Mount Clemens, MI 48043. 8:30AM-5PM. **586-725-9500**, Fax: 586-469-5516. Civil phone: 586-493-0567, Crim: 586-469-5046. Includes City of New Baltimore, Village of New Haven, and townships of Lenox and Chesterfield. This court was formerly located in New Baltimore. ✉🖐

42nd District Court Division 1 *Misdemeanor, Civil Actions Under*

$25,000, Eviction, Small Claims www.macombcountymi.gov/ 14713 Thirty-three Mile Rd., PO Box 6, Romeo, MI 48065. 8:30AM-4:45PM. **586-752-9679**, Fax: 586-469-5515. ✉🖐

41 B District Court - Clinton TWP *Misdemeanor, Civil Actions Under $25,000, Eviction, Small Claims* 40700 Romeo Plank Rd, Clinton Township, MI 48038-2951. 8:30AM-4:30PM. **586-286-8010**, Fax: 586-228-2555. ✉🖐

37th District Court - Warren & Center Line *Misdemeanor, Civil Actions Under $25,000, Eviction, Small Claims* 8300 Common Rd., Warren, MI 48093. 8:30AM-4:30PM. **586-574-4900**, Fax: 586-574-4932. ✉🖐**Fax**

39th District Court - Roseville & Fraser *Misd., Civil Actions Under $25,000, Eviction, Small Claims* 29733 Gratiot Ave, Roseville, MI 48066. 8AM-4:30PM. **586-773-2010**, Fax 586-445-5070. ✉🖐

40th District Court - St. Clair Shores *Misdemeanor, Civil Actions Under $25,000, Eviction, Small Claims* 27701 Jefferson, St. Clair Shores, MI 48081. 8:30AM-4:30PM. **586-445-5281**, Fax: 586-445-4003. Civil phone: 586-445-5282, Crim: 586-445-5281. ✉🖐**Fax**

41 A District Court - Sterling Heights *Misdemeanor, Civil Actions Under $25,000, Eviction, Small Claims* 40111 Dodge Park, Sterling Heights, MI 48313. 8:30AM-4:30PM. **586-446-2500**, Civil phone: 586-446-2535, Crim: 586-446-2550. ✉🖐

41 A District Court - Shelby *Misd., Civil Actions Under $25,000, Eviction, Small Claims* 51660 Van Dyke, Shelby Township, MI 48316. 8AM-12:00, 1-4:30PM. **586-739-7325**, Fax: 586-726-4555; 997-6172 (Civil). ✉🖐

41 B District Court - Mt Clemens *Civil Actions Under $25,000, Eviction, Small Claims* 1 Crocker Blvd, Mount Clemens, MI 48043. 8AM-4:30PM. **586-469-6870**, Fax: 586-469-5037 Access civil records by✉**Fax**🖐

Probate www.macombcountymi.gov 21850 Dumham, Mount Clemens, MI 48043-1075. 8:30AM-5PM. **586-469-5290**, Fax: 586-783-0971.

Manistee County

19th Circuit Court *Felony, Civil Actions Over $25,000* 415 3rd St, Manistee, MI

49660. 8:30AM-5PM. **231-723-3331**, Fax: 231-723-1492. ✉🖐

85th District Court *Misdemeanor, Civil Actions Under $25,000, Eviction, Small Claims* 415 3rd St, Manistee, MI 49660. 8:30AM-5PM. **231-723-5010**, Fax: 231-723-1491. **Fax**✉🖐

Probate Court 415 3rd St, Manistee, MI 49660. 8:30AM-N, 1-5PM. **231-723-3261**, Fax: 231-398-3558.

Marquette County

25th Circuit Court *Felony, Civil Actions Over $25,000* 234 W Baraga, Marquette, MI 49855. 8AM-5PM. **906-225-8330**, Fax: 906-228-1572. ✉🖐

96th District Court *Misdemeanor, Civil Actions Under $25,000, Eviction, Small Claims* County Courthouse, Marquette, MI 49855. 8:00AM-5PM. **906-225-8235**, Fax: 906-225-8255. **Fax**✉🖐

Probate Court 234 W Baraga, Marquette, MI 49855. 8AM-5PM. **906-225-8300**, Fax: 906-225-8293/228-1533.

Mason County

51st Circuit Court *Felony, Civil Actions Over $25,000* 304 E Ludington Ave, Ludington, MI 49431. 9AM-5PM. **231-845-1445**, Fax: 231-843-1972. ☎✉🖐

79th District Court *Misdemeanor, Civil Actions Under $25,000, Eviction, Small Claims* County Court 304 E.Ludington Ave., Ludington, MI 49431. 9AM-5PM. **231-843-4130**, Fax: 231-845-9076. 🖐

Probate Court 304 E Ludington Ave, Ludington, MI 49431. 9AM-N, 1-5PM. **231-843-8666**, Fax: 231-843-1972.

Mecosta County

49th Circuit Court *Felony, Civil Over $25,000* www.co.mecosta.mi.us/circuit.asp 400 Elm, Big Rapids, MI 49307. 8:30AM-5PM. **231-592-0783**, Fax: 231-592-0193. **Fax**✉🖐

77th District Court *Misdemeanor, Civil Actions Under $25,000, Eviction, Small Claims* 400 Elm, Big Rapids, MI 49307. 8:30AM-4:30PM. **231-592-0799**, Fax: 231-796-2180. Civil phone: 231-592-0799, Crim: 231-592-0190. ✉🖐

Probate Court 400 Elm St PO Box 820, Big Rapids, MI 49307. 8:30AM-5PM. **231-592-0135**, Fax: 231-592-0191. Shares the same judge with Osceola County Probate Court.

Menominee County

41st Circuit Court *Felony, Civil Actions Over $25,000* 839 10th Ave, Menominee, MI 49858. 8AM-4:30PM. **906-863-9968**, Fax: 906-863-8839. ✉🖑

95 A District Court *Misdemeanor, Civil Actions Under $25,000, Eviction, Small Claims* 839 10th Ave, Menominee, MI 49858. 8AM-4:30PM. **906-863-8532**, Fax: 906-863-2023. **Fax**✉🖑

Probate Court, *Juvenile* 839 10th Ave., Menominee, MI 49858. 8AM-4:30PM. **906-863-2634**, Fax: 906-863-9904.

Midland County

42nd Circuit Court *Felony, Civil Over $25,000* www.midlandcounty.org/circuitcourt/index.htm Courthouse, 301 W Main St, Midland, MI 48640. 8AM-5PM. **989-832-6735**, Fax: 989-832-6610. ☎✉🖑

75th District Court - Civil Division *Civil Actions Under $25,000, Eviction, Small Claims* 301 W Main St, Midland, MI 48640. 8:30AM-4:30PM. **989-832-6701**. Small Claims can be reached at 989-832-6717. Access civil records by✉🖑

75th District Court - Criminal Division *Misdemeanor* 301 W Main St, Midland, MI 48640-5183. 8:30AM-5PM. **989-832-6702 (6714-traffic)**. ✉🖑

Probate www.midlandcounty.org 301 W Main St, Midland, MI 48640. 8AM-5PM. **989-832-6880**, Fax: 989-832-6607.

Missaukee County

28th Circuit Court *Felony, Civil Over $25,000* www.missaukee.org/court.htm? PO Box 800, Lake City, MI 49651. 9AM-5PM. **231-839-4967**, Fax: 231-839-3684. ☎**Fax**✉🖑

84th District Court *Misdemeanor, Civil Actions Under $25,000, Eviction, Small Claims* PO Box 800, Lake City, MI 49651. 9AM-5PM. **231-839-4590**. ✉🖑

Probate Court PO Box 800, Lake City, MI 49651. 9AM-N, 1-5PM. **231-839-2266**, Fax: 231-839-5856. ✉

Monroe County

38th Circuit Court *Felony, Civil Over $25,000* www.co.monroe.mi.us/Courts/index.html 106 E 1st St, Monroe, MI 48161. 8:30AM-5PM. **734-240-7020**, Fax: 734-240-7045. ✉🖑

1st District Court *Misdemeanor, Civil Under $25,000, Eviction, Small Claims* www.co.monroe.mi.us/DistrictCourt/index.html 106 E 1st St, Monroe, MI 48161. 8AM-4:45 PM. **734-240-7075**, Fax: 734-240-7098. ✉🖑

Probate www.co.monroe.mi.us/Courts/index.html 106 E 1st St, Monroe, MI 48161. 8AM-N, 1-5PM. **734-240-7346**.

Montcalm County

8th Circuit Court *Felony, Civil Actions Over $25,000* www.montcalm.org/ 639 N.State St., Stanton, MI 48888. 8AM-5PM. **989-831-3520**, Fax: 989-831-3525. Closes for lunch hour. ✉🖑**Fax**

64 B District Court *Misdemeanor, Civil Actions Under $25,000, Eviction, Small Claims* 617 N State Rd #D, Stanton, MI 48888. 8AM-5PM. **989-831-7450**, Fax: 989-831-7452. ✉🖑**Fax**

Probate Court 625 N State St. PO Box 309, Stanton, MI 48888. 8AM-5PM. **989-831-7316**, Fax: 989-831-7314.

Montmorency County

26th Circuit Court *Felony, Civil Actions Over $25,000* PO Box 789, Atlanta, MI 49709. 8:30AM-N, 1-4:30PM. **989-785-8022**, Fax: 989-785-8023. ✉🖑

88th District Court *Misdemeanor, Civil Actions Under $25,000, Eviction, Small Claims* County Courthouse PO Box 789, Atlanta, MI 49709. 8:30AM-N, 1-4:30PM. **989-785-8035**, Fax: 989-785-8036. ✉**Fax**🖑

Probate PO Box 789, Atlanta, MI 49709-0789. **989-785-8064**, Fax: 989-785-8065.

Muskegon County

14th Circuit Court *Felony, Civil Actions Over $25,000* County Bldg, 6th Fl 990 Terrace St, Muskegon, MI 49442. 8AM-5PM. **231-724-6251**, Fax: 231-724-6695. ☎✉**Fax**🖑

60th District Court *Misdemeanor, Civil Under $25,000, Eviction, Small Claims* www.co.muskegon.mi.us/60thdistrict/ 990 Terrace, 1st Fl, Muskegon, MI 49442. 8:30AM-4:45PM. **231-724-6250**, Fax: 231-724-3489. ✉🖑

Probate Court 990 Terrace St, 5th Fl, Muskegon, MI 49442. 8AM-5PM. **231-724-6241**, Fax: 231-724-6232.

Newaygo County

27th Circuit Court *Felony, Civil Actions Over $25,000* PO Box 885, White Cloud, MI 49349-0885. 8AM-N; 1-5PM. **231-689-7269**, Fax: 231-689-7007. ✉**Fax**🖑

78th District Court *Misdemeanor, Civil Actions Under $25,000, Eviction, Small Claims* 1092 Newell St, White Cloud, MI 49349. 8AM-N, 1-5PM. **231-689-7257**, Fax: 231-689-7258. **Fax**✉🖑

Probate PO Box 885 (1092 Newell St.), White Cloud, MI 49349. 8AM-N, 1-5PM. **231-689-7270**, Fax: 231-689-7276.

Oakland County

6th Circuit Court *Felony, Civil Actions Over $25,000* www.co.oakland.mi.us/ 1200 N Telegraph Rd, Pontiac, MI 48341. 8:30AM-4:30PM. **248-858-0581**. ✉🖑

52nd District Court - Division 2 *Misdemeanor, Civil Actions Under $25,000, Eviction, Small Claims* 5850 Lorac, Clarkston, MI 48346. 8:30AM-4:30PM. Fax: 248-625-5602. Civil phone: 248-625-4994, Crim: 248-625-4888. Court covers Springfield, Holly, Groveland, Brandon, Independence, Clarkston & Ortonville and townships of Whie Lake and Rose. ☎**Fax**✉🖑

45 A District Court - Berkley *Misdemeanor, Civil Actions Under $25,000, Eviction, Small Claims* 3338 Coolidge, Berkley, MI 48072. 8:30AM-4:45PM. **248-544-3300**, Fax: 248-546-2416. ✉🖑

46th District Court *Misdemeanor, Civil Actions Under $25,000, Eviction, Small Claims* www.cityofsouthfield.com/46court/ 26000 Evergreen Rd, Southfield, MI 48076. 8AM-4:30PM (counter). **248-796-5800**, Civil: 248-796-5870, Crim: 248-796-5880. ✉🖑

47th District Court - Farmington, Farmington Hills *Misdemeanor, Civil Actions Under $25,000, Eviction, Small Claims* 31605 W 11 Mile Rd, Farmington Hills, MI 48336. 8:30AM-4:30PM; 'til 6:30PM 3rd Tues each month. **248-871-2900**. 🖑

48th District Court *Misdemeanor, Civil Actions Under $25,000, Eviction, Small Claims* 4280 Telegraph Rd, Bloomfield Hills, MI 48302. 8:30AM-4:30PM. **248-647-1141**, Fax: 248-647-8955. ☎✉🖑

52nd District Court - Division 1 *Misdemeanor, Civil Actions Under $25,000, Eviction, Small Claims* www.52-1districtcourt.com 48150 Grand River, Novi, MI 48374. 8:30AM-4:30PM. Civil: 248-305-6080, Crim: 248-305-6460. ☎✉👋

51st District Court - Waterford *Misdemeanor, Civil Actions Under $25,000, Eviction, Small Claims* 5100 Civic Center Dr, Waterford, MI 48329. 8:30AM-4:45PM. **248-674-4655**. ✉👋

52nd District Court - Division 4 (Troy, Clawson) *Misdemeanor, Civil Actions Under $25,000, Eviction, Small Claims* 520 W Big Beaver Rd, Troy, MI 48084. 8:15AM-4:15PM. **248-528-0400**, Fax: 248-528-3588. **Fax**✉👋

52nd District Court - Division 3 *Misdemeanor, Civil Actions Under $25,000, Eviction, Small Claims* www.co.oakland.mi.us/courts/ 700 Barclay Circle, Rochester Hills, MI 48307. 8:30AM-4:30PM. **248-853-5553**, Fax: 248-853-3277. ☎**Fax**✉👋

45 B District Court *Misdemeanor, Civil Actions Under $25,000, Eviction, Small Claims* 13600 Oak Park Blvd, Oak Park, MI 48237. 9AM-5PM. **248-691-7440**, Fax: 248-691-7158. Court covers Huntington Woods, Oak Park, Pleasant Ridge, and Royal Oak Township. ✉👋

44th District Court - Royal Oak *Misdemeanor, Civil Actions Under $25,000, Eviction, Small Claims* www.ci.royal-oak.mi.us/ 400 E Eleven Mile Rd, Box 20, Royal Oak, MI 48068. 8AM-4:30PM. **248-246-3600**, Fax: 248-246-3601. ✉👋

43rd District Court *Misdemeanor, Civil Actions Under $25,000, Eviction, Small Claims* 43 E Nine Mile Rd, Hazel Park, MI 48030. 8:30AM-4:30PM. **248-547-3034**, Fax: 248-546-4088. ✉👋

50th District Court - Pontiac Civil Division *Civil Actions Under $25,000, Eviction, Small Claims* 70 N Saganaw, Pontiac, MI 48342. 8:30AM-4:30PM. **248-758-3820**, Fax: 248-758-3888. Criminal phone: 248-758-3820 Access civil records by✉👋 - best via **Fax**

50th District Court - Pontiac Criminal Division *Misdemeanor* 70 N Saganaw, Pontiac, MI 48342. 8:30AM-4:30PM. **248-758-3820**, Fax: 248-758-3888. ✉**Fax**👋

Probate Court 1200 N Telegraph Rd 1st Fl, Oakland County Complex, East Wing, Pontiac, MI 48341. 8AM-5PM. **248-858-0260**, Fax: 248-452-2016.

Oceana County

27th Circuit Court *Felony, Civil Actions Over $25,000* 100 State St, #M-34, Hart, MI 49420. 9-5PM. **231-873-3977**. ✉👋

79th District Court *Misdemeanor, Civil Actions Under $25,000, Eviction, Small Claims* PO Box 471, Hart, MI 49420. 8AM-5PM. **231-873-4530**, Fax: 231-873-1861. ✉👋

Probate Court County Bldg 100 S State St, #M-10, Hart, MI 49420. 9AM-N, 1-5PM. **231-873-3666**, Fax: 231-873-1943.

Ogemaw County

34th Circuit Court *Felony, Civil Actions Over $25,000* 806 W Houghton, West Branch, MI 48661. 8:30AM-4:30PM. **989-345-0215**, Fax: 989-345-7223. ☎**Fax**✉👋

82nd District Court *Misdemeanor, Civil Actions Under $25,000, Eviction, Small Claims* PO Box 365, West Branch, MI 48661. 8:30AM-4:30PM. **989-345-5040**, Fax: 989-345-5910. **Fax**✉👋

Probate Court County Courthouse, Rm 203 806 W Houghton Ave, West Branch, MI 48661. 8:30AM-N, 1-4:30PM. **989-345-0145**, Fax: 989-345-5901.

Ontonagon County

32nd Circuit Court *Felony, Civil Actions Over $25,000* 725 Greenland Rd, Ontonagon, MI 49953. 8:30AM-4:30PM. **906-884-2806**, Fax: 906-884-6796. ✉**Fax**👋

98th District Court *Misdemeanor, Civil Actions Under $25,000, Eviction, Small Claims* 725 Greenland Rd, Ontonagon, MI 49953. 8:30AM-4:30PM. **906-884-2865**, Fax: 906-884-2916. ✉👋

Probate Court 725 Greenland Rd, Ontonagon, MI 49953. 8:30AM-4:30PM. **906-884-4117**, Fax: 906-884-2916.

Osceola County

49th Circuit Court *Felony, Civil Actions Over $25,000* 301 W Upton, Reed City, MI 49677. 9AM-5PM. **231-832-6103**, Fax: 231-832-6149. ☎**Fax**✉👋

77th District Court *Misdemeanor, Civil Actions Under $25,000, Eviction, Small Claims* 410 W Upton, Reed City, MI 49677. 8:30AM-4:30PM. **231-832-6155**, Fax: 231-832-9190. ☎✉**Fax**👋

Probate Court 410 W Upton, Reed City, MI 49677. 8:30AM-N, 1-4:30PM. **231-832-6124**, Fax: 231-832-6181. Shares the same judge with Mecosta County Probate.

Oscoda County

23rd Circuit Court *Felony, Civil Actions Over $25,000* PO Box 399 311 Morenci Ave, Mio, MI 48647. 8:30AM-4:30PM. **989-826-1110**, Fax 989-826-1136. ✉👋

81st District Court *Misdemeanor, Civil Actions Under $25,000, Eviction, Small Claims* PO Box 625, Mio, MI 48647. 8:30AM-4:30PM. **989-826-1106**. ✉👋

Probate Court PO Box 399, Mio, MI 48647. 8:30AM-N, 1-4:30PM. **989-826-1107**, Fax: 989-826-1158.

Otsego County

46th Circuit Court *Felony, Civil Actions Over $25,000* www.Circuit46.org 225 Main St, Gaylord, MI 49735. 8AM-4:30PM. **989-732-7500(Clerk)**, Fax: 989-731-7519. ☎✉👋💻

46th Circuit Trial Court - District Court *Misdemeanor, Civil Actions Under $25,000, Eviction, Small Claims* www.circuit46.org 800 Livingston Blvd, #1C, Gaylord, MI 49735. 8AM-4:30PM. **989-732-6486**, Fax: 989-732-5130. ✉👋💻

Probate Court www.Circuit46.org 800 Livingston Blvd, #1C, Gaylord, MI 49735. 8AM-4:30PM. **989-731-0204**, **989-731-0201**, Fax: 989-731-5130. Search cases by name free at www.circuit46.org/Cases/cases.html.

Ottawa County

20th Circuit Court *Felony, Civil Actions Over $25,000* www.co.ottawa.mi.us/Courts /courts.htm 414 Washington Ave, Grand Haven, MI 49417. 8AM-5PM. **616-846-8136**, Fax: 616-846-8138. ✉👋

58th District Court - Holland *Misdemeanor, Civil Actions Under $25,000, Eviction, Small Claims* www.co.ottawa.mi.us/Courts/courts.htm 57 W 8th St, Holland, MI 49423. 8AM-5PM. **616-392-6991**, Fax 616-392-5013. ✉👋

58th District Court - Hudsonville *Misdemeanor, Civil Actions Under $25,000, Eviction, Small Claims* www.co.ottawa.mi.us/Courts/courts.htm 3100 Port Sheldon, Hudsonville, MI

49426. 8AM-N; 1-5PM. **616-662-3100 x2**, Fax: 616-669-2950. ✉✋

58th District Court - Grand Haven *Misdemeanor, Civil Actions Under $25,000, Eviction, Small Claims* www.co.ottawa.mi.us/Courts/courts.htm 414 Washington Ave, Grand Haven, MI 49417. 8AM-5PM. **616-846-8280**, Fax: 616-846-8291. Civil phone: 616-846-8289, Crim: 616-846-8127, Probate: 616-846-8281. ✉**Fax**✋

Probate Court www.co.ottawa.mi.us/Courts/Probate/probate.htm 12120 Fillmore St, West Olive, MI 49460. 8AM-5PM. **616-786-4110**, Fax: 616-738-4624.

Presque Isle County

53rd Circuit Court *Felony, Civil Actions Over $25,000* PO Box 110, Rogers City, MI 49779. 8:30AM-4:30PM. **989-734-3288**, Fax: 989-734-7635. ☎**Fax**✉✋

89th District Court *Misdemeanor, Civil Actions Under $25,000, Eviction, Small Claims* PO Box 110, Rogers City, MI 49779. 8:30AM-4:30PM. **989-734-2411**, Fax: 989-734-3400. ✉✋

Probate 151 Huron Ave PO Box 110, Rogers City, MI 49779. 8:30AM-4:30PM. **989-734-3268**, Fax: 989-734-4420.

Roscommon County

34th Circuit Court *Felony, Civil Actions Over $25,000* 500 Lake St #1 Attn: County Clerk Reg of Deeds, Roscommon, MI 48653. 8:30AM-4:30PM. **989-275-1902**, Fax: 989-275-0602. **Fax**✉✋

83rd District Court *Misdemeanor, Civil Actions Under $25,000, Eviction, Small Claims* 500 Lake St, Roscommon, MI 48653. 8:30AM-4:30PM. **989-275-5312**, Fax: 989-275-6033. ☎**Fax**✉✋

Probate Court PO Box 607 500 Lake St. Rm. 132, Roscommon, MI 48653. 8:30AM-4:30PM. **989-275-5221**, Fax: 989-275-8537.

Saginaw County

10th Circuit Court *Felony, Civil Over $25,000* www.saginawcounty.com/clerk/court/index.html 111 S Michigan Ave, Saginaw, MI 48602. 8AM-5:00PM. **989-790-5541**, Fax: 989-790-5248, Probate: 989-790-5233. ✉✋

70th District Court - Civil Division *Civil Actions Under $25,000, Eviction, Small Claims* 111 S Michigan Ave, Saginaw,

MI 48602. 8AM-4:45PM. **989-790-5380**, Fax: 989-790-5562 Access civil records by✉✋

70th District Court - Criminal Division *Misdemeanor* www.saginawcounty.com/DistrictCourt 111 S Michigan Ave, Saginaw, MI 48602. 8AM-4:45PM. **989-790-5385**, Fax: 989-790-5589. **Fax**✉✋

Probate/Family Court *Probate* 111 S Michigan St, Saginaw, MI 48602. 8AM-5PM. **989-790-5320**, Fax: 989-790-5328.

St. Clair County

31st Circuit Court *Felony, Civil Over $25,000* www.stclaircounty.org/index.asp 201 McMorran Blvd, Port Huron, MI 48060. 8AM-4:30PM. **810-985-2200**, Fax: 810-985-4796. ✉**Fax**✋

St. Clair County

72nd District Court *Misdemeanor, Civil Actions Under $25,000, Eviction, Small Claims* 201 McMorran Blvd, Rm 2900, Port Huron, MI 48060. 8AM-4:30PM M-Thl; 9AM-4:30PM. Civil: 810-985-2077, crim: 810-985-2072. Access records ✋

Probate 201 McMorran Blvd Rm 2600, Port Huron, MI 48060. 8AM-4:30PM. **810-985-2066**, Fax: 810-985-2179.

St. Joseph County

45th Circuit Court *Felony, Civil Over $25,000* www.stjosephcountymi.org/ccircuit.htm PO Box 189, Centreville, MI 49032. 9AM-5PM. **269-467-5531**, Fax: 269-467-5628. by-✉✋

3-B District Court *Misdemeanor, Civil Actions Under $25,000, Eviction, Small Claims* PO Box 67, Centreville, MI 49032. 8-5PM. **269-467-5627**. **Fax**✉✋

Probate Court www.stjosephcountymi.org/cprobate.htm PO Box 190, Centreville, MI 49032. 8AM-5PM. **269-467-5538**, Fax: 269-467-5560.

Sanilac County

24th Circuit Court *Felony, Civil Actions Over $25,000* www.sanilaccounty.net/ 60 W Sanilac, Rm 203, Sandusky, MI 48471. 8AM-4:30PM. **810-648-3212 x8227**, Fax: 810-648-5466. ✉✋

73rd District Court *Misdemeanor, Civil Actions Under $25,000, Eviction, Small Claims* 60 W Sanilac, Sandusky, MI 48471. 8AM-4:30PM. **810-648-3250**. ✉✋

Probate Court 60 W Sanilac Ave. Rm 106, Sandusky, MI 48471-1096. 8AM-N, 1-4:30. **810-648-3221**, Fax 810-648-2900.

Schoolcraft County

11th Circuit Court *Felony, Civil Actions Over $25,000* 300 Walnut St, Rm 164, Manistique, MI 49854. 8AM-4PM. **906-341-3618**. Access records-☎**Fax**✉✋

93rd District Court *Misdemeanor, Civil Actions Under $25,000, Eviction, Small Claims* 300 Walnut St, Rm 135, Manistique, MI 49854. 8AM-4PM. **906-341-3630**, Fax: 906-341-8006. ✉✋

Probate Court 300 Walnut St, Rm 129, Manistique, MI 49854. 8AM-N, 1-4PM. **906-341-3641**, Fax: 906-341-3627.

Shiawassee County

35th Circuit Court *Felony, Civil Actions Over $25,000* 208 N Shiawassee St, Corunna, MI 48817. 8AM-5PM. **989-743-2262**, Fax: 989-743-2241. ☎**Fax**✉✋

66th District Court *Misdemeanor, Civil Actions Under $25,000, Eviction, Small Claims* 110 E Mack St, Corunna, MI 48817. 8AM-5PM. **989-743-2395**, Fax: 989-743-2469. ☎**Fax**✉✋

Probate Court 110 E Mack St, Corunna, MI 48817. 8AM-5PM. **989-743-2211**, Fax: 989-743-2349.

Tuscola County

54th Circuit Court *Felony, Civil Actions Over $25,000* www.tuscolacounty.org 440 N State St, Caro, MI 48723. 8AM-N, 1-3:30PM. **989-672-3780**, Fax: 989-672-4266. Civil phone: 989-672-3775, crim: 989-672-3776, ✉✋

71 B District Court *Misdemeanor, Civil Actions Under $25,000, Eviction, Small Claims* 440 N State St., Caro, MI 48723. 8AM-4:30PM. **989-672-3800**, Fax: 989-673-0451. ☎✉✋

Probate Court 440 N State St, Caro, MI 48723. 8AM-N, 1-4:30PM. **989-672-3850**, Fax: 989-672-2057.

Van Buren County

36th Circuit Court *Felony, Civil Actions Over $25,000* 212 Paw Paw St #101, Paw Paw, MI 49079. 8:30AM-5PM. **269-657-8218**. ✉✋

7th District Court - West Division *Misdemeanor, Civil Actions Under $25,000, Eviction, Small Claims* 1007 E

Wells, PO Box 311, South Haven, MI 49090. 8:30AM-4:30PM. **269-637-5258**, Fax: 269-637-9169. ✉🖐

7th District Court *Misdemeanor, Civil Actions Under $25,000, Eviction, Small Claims* 212 Paw Paw St, Paw Paw, MI 49079. 9AM-4:30PM. **269-657-8222**, Fax: 269-657-8223. ✉🖐

Probate Court 212 Paw Paw St, #220, Paw Paw, MI 49079. 8:30AM-5PM. **269-657-8225**, Fax: 269-657-7573.

Washtenaw County

22nd Circuit Court *Felony, Civil Over $25,000* www.e.washtenaworg/depts/courts/index.htm PO Box 8645, Ann Arbor, MI 48107-8645. 8:30AM-4:30PM. **734-222-3001**. ✉🖐

14th District Court A-2 *Misdemeanor, Civil Actions Under $25,000, Eviction, Small Claims* 415 W Michigan Ave, Ypsilanti, MI 48197. 8AM-4:30PM. **734-484-6690**, Fax: 734-484-6697. ✉🖐

14A-1 District Court *Misdemeanor, Civil Under $25,000, Eviction, Small Claims* www.co.washtenaw.mi.us/depts/courts/index.htm 4133 Washtenaw, Ann Arbor, MI 48107-8645. 8AM-4:30PM. **734-973-4545**, Fax: 734-973-4693. ✉🖐

14th District Court A-3 *Misdemeanor, Civil Actions Under $25,000, Eviction, Small Claims* 122 S Main St, Chelsea, MI 48118. 8AM-4:30PM. **734-475-8606**, Fax: 734-475-0460. 🖐

14th District Court B - Civil Division *Civil Actions Under $25,000, Eviction, Small Claims* 7200 S Huron River Dr, Ypsilanti, MI 48197. 8AM-5PM. **734-483-5300**, Fax: 734-483-3630. Access civil records-✉🖐

14th District Court B - Criminal Division *Misdemeanor* 7200 S Huron River Dr, Ypsilanti, MI 48197. 8-5PM. **734-483-1333**, Fax 734-483-3630. ✉🖐

15th District Court - Civil Division *Civil Actions Under $25,000, Eviction, Small Claims* www.co.washtenaw.mi.us/depts/courts/index.htm 101 E Huron, Box 8650, Ann Arbor, MI 48107. 8:30AM-4:30PM. **734-222-3389**, Fax: 734-222-3335. Criminal phone: 734-222-3380 (crim traffic). Access civil records-📞**Fax**✉🖐

15th District Court - Criminal Division *Misdemeanor, Traffic* www.co.washtenaw.mi.us/depts/courts/index.htm 101 E Huron, Box 8650, Ann Arbor, MI 48107-

8650. 8AM-4:30PM. **734-222-3380**, Fax: 734-222-3335. Civil phone: 734-222-3389. ✉**Fax**🖐

Probate www.co.washtenaw.mi.us/depts/courts/index.htm PO Box 8645, Ann Arbor, MI 48107. 8:30AM-4:30PM. **734-994-2474 ext 2**, Fax: 734-222-3019.

Wayne County

3rd Circuit Court *Civil Actions Over $25,000* www.3rdcc.org 201 Coleman A Young Municipal Ctr, Detroit, MI 48226. 8AM-4:30PM. **313-224-5530**. Access civil records-📞✉🖐

Frank Murphy Hall of Justice *Felony* 1441 St Antoine, Detroit, MI 48226. 8AM-4:30PM. **313-224-2500**, Fax: 313-224-2786. ✉🖐

36th District Court *Felony, Misd., Civil Under $25,000, Eviction, Small Claims Under $3000* www.36thdistrictcourt.org/criminal-faq.html 421 Madison, Detroit, MI 48226. 8AM-4:30PM. Civil: 313-965-6098, crim: 313-965-5029. Small Claims phone number is 313-965-5972. 📞🖐

20th District Court *Misdemeanor, Civil Actions Under $25,000, Eviction, Small Claims* 6045 Fenton, Dearborn Heights, MI 48127. 9AM-5PM. **313-277-7480**, Fax: 313-277-7141. ✉🖐

19th District Court *Misdemeanor, Civil Actions Under $25,000, Eviction, Small Claims* www.cityofdearborn.org 16077 Michigan Ave, Dearborn, MI 48126. 8AM-4:30PM. **313-943-2056**, Fax: 313-943-3071. **Fax**✉🖐

16th District Court *Misdemeanor, Civil Actions Under $25,000, Eviction, Small Claims* 15140 Farmington Rd, Livonia, MI 48154-5498. 8:30AM-4:30PM. **734-466-2500**; 466-2550 Probation, Civil: X3541, Crim: X3452. 🖐

17th District Court *Misdemeanor, Civil Actions Under $25,000, Eviction, Small Claims* 15111 Beech-Daly Rd, Redford, MI 48239. 8:30AM-4:15PM. **313-387-2790**, Fax: 313-538-3468. ✉🖐

29th District Court *Misdemeanor, Civil Actions Under $25,000, Eviction, Small Claims* 34808 Sims Ave, Wayne, MI 48184. 8AM-4:30PM. **734-722-5220**, Fax: 734-722-7003. 📞✉🖐

35th District Court *Misdemeanor, Civil Infractions, Civil Actions Under $25,000, Eviction, Small Claims* www.35thdistrictcourt.org 660 Plymouth

Rd, Plymouth, MI 48170. 8:30AM-4:25PM. **734-459-4740**, Fax: 734-454-9303. ✉🖐

34th District Court *Misdemeanor, Civil Actions Under $25,000, Eviction, Small Claims* 11131 S Wayne Rd, Romulus, MI 48174. 8:30AM-4PM. **734-941-4462**, Fax: 734-941-7530. ✉🖐

33rd District Court *Misdemeanor, Civil Actions Under $25,000, Eviction, Small Claims* 19000 Van Horn Rd, Woodhaven, MI 48183. 8:30AM-4:30PM. **734-671-0201**, Fax: 734-671-0307. Civil phone: 734-671-0225, crim: 734-671-0201. ✉**Fax**🖐

32 A District Court *Misdemeanor, Civil Actions Under $25,000, Small Claims* 19617 Harper Ave, Harper Woods, MI 48225. 8:30AM-4:30PM. **313-343-2590**, Fax: 313-343-2594. Civil phone: 313-343-2592. 📞**Fax**✉🖐

18th District Court *Misdemeanor, Civil Actions Under $25,000, Eviction, Small Claims* www.18thdistrictcourt.com 36675 Ford Rd, Westland, MI 48185. 8:30AM-4PM M,F; 8:30AM-5:30PM T,W; 8:30AM-5:30PM Th. **734-595-8720**, Fax: 734-595-0160. 📞✉🖐

30th District Court *Misdemeanor, Civil Actions Under $25,000, Eviction, Small Claims* 12050 Wood Ward Ave, Highland Park, MI 48203. 8AM-4:30PM. **313-252-0300**, Fax 313-865-1115. ✉🖐

21st District Court *Misdemeanor, Civil Actions Under $25,000, Eviction, Small Claims* 6000 Middlebelt Rd, Garden City, MI 48135. 8:30AM-4:30PM. **734-525-8805**, Fax: 734-421-4797. ✉🖐

28th District Court *Misdemeanor, Civil Actions Under $25,000, Eviction, Small Claims* www.28thdistrictcourt.com/ 14720 Reaume Parkway, Southgate, MI 48195. 8:30AM-4:30PM. **734-258-3068**, Fax: 734-246-1405. Civil phone: 734-258-3068, crim: 734-258-3068. 🖐

24th District Court - Allen Park & Melvindale *Misdemeanor, Civil Actions Under $25,000, Eviction, Small Claims* www.24thdiscourt.org 6515 Roosevelt, Allen Park, MI 48101-2524. 8:30AM-4:30PM. **313-928-0535**, Fax: 313-928-1860. Civil phone: 313-928-1899. **Fax**✉🖐

22nd District Court *Misdemeanor, Civil Actions Under $25,000, Eviction, Small Claims* 27331 S River Park Dr, Inkster,

MI 48141. 8:30AM-4:30PM. **313-277-8200**, Fax: 313-277-8221. ✉✋

31st District Court *Misdemeanor, Civil Actions Under $25,000, Eviction, Small Claims* 3401 Evaline Ave, Hamtramck, MI 48212. 8AM-4PM. **313-876-7710**, Fax: 313-876-7724. ✉✋

23rd District Court *Misdemeanor, Civil Actions Under $25,000, Eviction, Small Claims* 23511 Goddard Rd, Taylor, MI 48180. 8:15AM-4:45PM. **734-374-1334**, Fax: 734-374-1303. Civil phone: 734-374-1328. ✉✋

25th District Court *Misdemeanor, Civil Actions Under $25,000, Eviction, Small Claims* 1475 Cleophus, Lincoln Park, MI 48146. 9AM-4:30PM. **313-382-8603**, Fax: 313-382-9361. Civil phone: 313-382-9317, crim: 313-382-8600. ✉☎✋

26-1 District Court *Misdemeanor, Civil Actions Under $25,000, Eviction, Small Claims* 10600 W Jefferson, River Rouge, MI 48218. 8:30AM-4:30PM. **313-842-7819**, Fax: 313-842-5923. ✉✋

26-2 District Court *Misdemeanor, Civil Actions Under $25,000, Eviction, Small Claims* 3869 W Jefferson, Ecorse, MI 48229. 9AM-4PM. **313-386-7900**, Fax: 313-928-5956. ✉Fax✋

27th District Court *Misdemeanor, Civil Actions Under $25,000, Eviction, Small Claims* 2015 Biddle Ave, Wyandotte, MI 48192. 8:30AM-4:30PM. **734-324-4475**, Fax: 734-324-4472. The 27-2 District Court in Riverview was closed as of 12/31/03. All of their records are now at this court. ✉✋

Probate Court 1307 Coleman A Young Muni. Ctr 13th Fl, 2 Woodward Ave, Detroit, MI 48226. 8AM-4:30PM. **313-224-5706**, www.probatewayneco.org Search online at http://public.wcpc.us/pa/

Wexford County

28th Circuit Court *Felony, Civil Actions Over $25,000* PO Box 490, Cadillac, MI 49601. 8:30-5PM. **231-779-9450**. ✉✋

84th District Court *Misdemeanor, Civil Actions Under $25,000, Eviction, Small Claims* 437 E Division St, Cadillac, MI 49601. 8:30AM-5PM. **231-779-9515**, Fax: 231-779-5396. ✉Fax✋

Probate Court 437 E Division, Cadillac, MI 49601. 8:30AM-5PM. **231-779-9510**, Fax: 231-779-9485.

Minnesota

State Court Administration: State Court Adminstrator, 135 Minn. Judicial Center, 25 Constitution Ave, St Paul, MN, 55155; 651-296-2474, Fax: 651-297-5636. www.courts.state.mn.us

Court Structure: There are 97 District Courts comprising 10 judicial districts. Effective July 1, 1996, the limit for small claims was raised from $5000 to $7500.

Online Access: Appellate and Supreme Court opinions are available from the website. There is an online system in place that allows internal and external access, but only for government personnel.

Additional Information: Statewide certification and copy fees are as follows: Certification Fee: $10.00 per document, Copy Fee: $5.00 per document (not per page). Most courts take personal checks.

An exact name is required to search, e.g., a request for "Robert Smith" will not result in finding "Bob Smith." The requester must request both names and pay two search and copy fees.

When a search is permitted by "plaintiff or defendant," most jurisdictions stated that a case is indexed by only the 1st plaintiff or defendant, and a 2nd or 3rd party would not be sufficient to search.

The 3rd, 5th, 8th and 10th Judicial Districts no longer will perform criminal record searches for the public.

Aitkin County

9th Judicial District Court *Felony, Misdemeanor, Civil, Eviction, Small Claims, Probate* 209 Second St NW, Aitkin, MN 56431. 8AM-4:30PM. **218-927-7350**, Fax: 218-927-4535. ✉✋

Anoka County

10th Judicial District Court *Felony, Misdemeanor, Civil, Eviction, Small Claims, Probate* 325 E Main St, Anoka, MN 55303. 8AM-4:30PM. **763-323-5966**, Fax: 763-323-6013. Criminal phone: 763-422-7385. ✋

Becker County

7th Judicial District Court *Felony, Misdemeanor, Civil, Eviction, Small Claims, Probate* PO Box 787, Detroit Lakes, MN 56502. 8AM-4:30PM. **218-846-7305**, Fax: 218-847-7620. ✋

Beltrami County

District Court *Felony, Misdemeanor, Civil, Eviction, Small Claims, Probate* 619 Beltrami Ave NW, #10, Bemidji, MN 56601-3068. 8AM-4:30PM. **218-759-4531**, Fax: 218-759-4209. Civil phone: 218-759-4128, crim: 281-759-4125. ✋

Benton County

7th Judicial District Court *Felony, Misdemeanor, Civil, Eviction, Small Claims, Probate, Family* 615 Highway 23 PO Box 189, Foley, MN 56329-0189. 8AM-4:30PM. **320-968-5205**, Fax: 320-968-5353. ✋

Big Stone County

Big Stone District Court *Felony, Misdemeanor, Civil, Eviction, Small*

Claims, Probate 20 SE 2nd St, Ortonville, MN 56278. 8AM-4:30PM. **320-839-2536**, Fax: 320-839-2537. ✍

Blue Earth County

5th Judicial District Court *Felony, Misdemeanor, Civil, Eviction, Small Claims, Probate* www.co.blue-earth.mn.us/dept/courts.php3 204 S 5th St, Mankato, MN 56001. 8AM-4:30PM. **507-389-8841**, Fax: 507-389-8437. ✍

Brown County

5th Judicial District Court *Felony, Misdemeanor, Civil, Eviction, Small Claims, Probate* PO Box 248, New Ulm, MN 56073-0248. 8AM-5PM. **507-233-6670**, Fax: 507-359-9562. ✋

Carlton County

6th Judicial District Court *Felony, Misd., Civil, Eviction, Small Claims, Probate* www.courts.state.mn.us/districts/sixth/index.html PO Box 190 (301 Walnut St), Carlton, MN 55718. 8AM-4PM. **218-384-4281**, Fax: 218-384-9182. Civil phone: 218-384-9139, crim: 218-384-9109, Probate: 218-384-9113. ✍

Carver County

1st Judicial District Court *Misd., Civil, Eviction, Small Claims, Probate* www.co.carver.mn.us/depts.htm 604 E 4th St Box 4, Chaska, MN 55318-2183. 8AM-4:30PM. **952-361-1420**, Fax: 952-361-1491. ✉ ✍

Cass County

9th Judicial District Court *Felony, Misdemeanor, Civil, Eviction, Small Claims, Probate* 300 Minnesota Ave, PO Box 3000, Walker, MN 56484. 8AM-4:30PM. **218-547-7200**, Fax: 218-547-1904. ✍

Chippewa County

8th Judicial District Court *Felony, Misdemeanor, Civil, Eviction, Small Claims, Probate* Chippewa County Court Administor 629 N 11th St, Montevideo, MN 56265. 8AM-4:30PM. **320-269-7774**, Fax: 320-269-7733. ✍

Chisago County

10th Judicial District Court *Felony, Misdemeanor, Civil, Eviction, Small Claims, Probate* 313 N Main St, Rm 358, Center City, MN 55012. 8AM-4:30PM. **651-213-0485**, Fax: 651-213-0359. ✍

Clay County

7th Judicial District Court *Felony, Misdemeanor, Civil, Eviction, Small Claims, Probate* www.co.clay.mn.us/Depts/CourtAdm/CourtAdm.htm PO Box 280 c/o County Court Administration, Moorhead, MN 56561. 8AM-4:30PM. **218-299-5065**, Fax: 218-299-7307. ✍

Clearwater County

9th Judicial District Court *Felony, Misdemeanor, Civil, Eviction, Small Claims, Probate* 213 Main Ave North, Bagley, MN 56621. 8AM-4:30PM. **218-694-6177**, Fax: 218-694-6213. ✍

Cook County

6th Judicial District Court *Felony, Misdemeanor, Civil, Eviction, Small Claims, Probate, Juvenile, Traffic* www.6courts.com 411 W 2nd St, Grand Marais, MN 55604-2307. 8AM-4PM. **218-387-3610**, Fax: 218-387-3007. ✍

Cottonwood County

5th Judicial District Court *Felony, Misdemeanor, Civil, Eviction, Small Claims, Probate* PO Box 97, Windom, MN 56101. 8AM-4:30PM. **507-831-4551**, Fax: 507-831-1425. ✉**Fax**✍

Crow Wing County

District Court *Felony, Misdemeanor, Civil, Eviction, Small Claims, Probate* 326 Laurel St, Brainerd, MN 56401. 8AM-5PM. **218-824-1310**, Fax: 218-824-1311. ✍

Dakota County

1st Judicial District Court - Division 3 *Felony, Misdemeanor, Civil, Eviction, Small Claims, Probate* www.co.dakota.mn.us/courts 1 Mendota Rd West, #140, West St Paul, MN 55118-4767. 8AM-4:30PM. **651-554-6200**, Fax: 651-554-6226. Formerly located at 125 3rd Ave North, S. St. Paul. ✍

District Court *Felony, Misdemeanor, Civil, Eviction, Small Claims, Probate* www.co.dakota.mn.us/courts Judicial Center 1560 Hwy 55, Hastings, MN 55033. 8AM-4:30PM. **651-438-8100**, Fax: 651-438-8162. ✍

1st Judicial District Court - Apple Valley *Misdemeanor, Civil, Eviction, Small Claims,* www.co.dakota.mn.us/courts 14955 Galaxie Ave, Apple Valley, MN 55124. 8AM-4:30PM. **952-891-7256**,

Fax: 952-891-7285. Civil phone: 952-891-7244, crim: 952-891-7239. ✍

Dodge County

3rd Judicial District Court *Felony, Misd., Civil, Eviction, Small Claims, Probate* www.courts.state.mn.us/districts/third/counties/dodge.htm 22 Sixth St E, Dept. 12, Mantorville, MN 55955. 8AM-4:30PM. **507-635-6260**, Fax: 507-635-6271. ✍

Douglas County

7th Judicial District Court *Felony, Misdemeanor, Civil, Eviction, Small Claims, Probate* 305 8th Ave West, Alexandria, MN 56308. 8AM-4:30PM. **320-762-3882**, Fax: 320-762-8863. ✍

Faribault County

5th Judicial District Court *Felony, Misdemeanor, Civil, Eviction, Small Claims, Probate* PO Box 130, Blue Earth, MN 56013. 8AM-4:30PM. **507-526-6273**, Fax: 507-526-3054. ✍

Fillmore County

3rd Judicial District Court *Felony, Misd., Civil, Eviction, Small Claims, Probate* www.courts.state.mn.us/districts/third/ 101 Fillmore St PO Box 436, Preston, MN 55965. 8AM-4:30PM. **507-765-4483**, Fax: 507-765-4571. ✍

Freeborn County

3rd Judicial District Court *Felony, Misd., Civil, Eviction, Small Claims, Probate* www.courts.state.mn.us/districts/third/ 411 S Broadway, Albert Lea, MN 56007. 8AM-5PM. **507-377-5153**, Fax: 507-377-5260. ✍

Goodhue County

1st Judicial District Court *Felony, Misdemeanor, Civil, Eviction, Small Claims, Probate* 454 W 6th St, Red Wing, MN 55066. 8AM-4:30PM. **651-267-4800**, Fax: 651-267-4989. ✍

Grant County

8th Judicial District Court *Felony, Misdemeanor, Civil, Eviction, Small Claims, Probate* PO Box 1007 (10 2nd St NE), Elbow Lake, MN 56531. 8AM-4PM. **218-685-4825**. ✍

Hennepin County

4th Judicial Dist. Court - Div. 1 *Civil* www.courts.state.mn.us/districts/fourth/ 1251 C Government Ctr, 300 S 6th St, Minneapolis, MN 55487. 8AM-4:30PM.

612-348-3164, Fax: 612-348-2131. Civil phone: 612-348-3170. Access civil records-Fax ⊠ ✍

4th Judicial District Court - Division 1 Criminal *Felony, Misdemeanor* www.courts.state.mn.us/districts/fourth/ 300 S 6th St, Minneapolis, MN 55487. 8AM-4:30PM. **612-348-2612**, Fax: 612-348-6099. Fax ⊠ ✍

4th Judicial District Court - Division 3 Ridgedale *Misd., Eviction, Small Claims* www.courts.state.mn.us/districts/fourth/ 12601 Ridgedale Dr, Minnetonka, MN 55305. 8AM-4:30PM. **952-541-7000**, Fax: 952-541-6297. ⊠ ✍

4th Judicial District Court - Division 4 Southdale *Misdemeanor* www.courts.state .mn.us/districts/fourth/ 7009 York Ave South, Edina, MN 55435. 8AM-4:30PM. **952-830-4877**, Fax 952-830-4993. ⊠ ✍

4th Judicial District Court - Division 2 Brookdale *Misdemeanor* www.courts.stat e.mn.us/districts/fourth/ 6125 Shingle Creek Parkway, Brooklyn Center, MN 55430. 8AM-4:30PM. **763-569-2799**, Fax: 763-569-3697. ⊠ ✍

4th Judicial Dist. Court - Div. 1 *Probate* www.courts.state.mn.us/districts/fourth/ C400 Government Ctr, 300 S 6th St, Minneapolis, MN 55487. 7AM-5PM. **612-348-3244**, Fax: 612-348-2130.

Houston County

3rd Judicial District Court *Felony, Misdemeanor, Civil, Eviction, Small Claims, Probate* www.courts.state.mn.us/districts/third/ 304 S Marshall, Rm 204, Caledonia, MN 55921. 8AM-4:30PM. **507-725-5806**, Fax: 507-725-5550. Criminal phone: 507-725-5828. ✍

Hubbard County

9th Judicial District Court *Felony, Misdemeanor, Civil, Eviction, Small Claims, Probate* 301 Court St, Park Rapids, MN 56470. 8AM-4:30PM. **218-732-3573**, Fax: 218-732-0137. ⊠ ✍

Isanti County

10th Judicial District Court *Felony, Misdemeanor, Civil, Eviction, Small Claims, Probate* 555 18th Ave SW, Cambridge, MN 55008-9386. 8AM-4:30PM. **763-689-2292**, Fax: 763-689-8340. ✍

Itasca County

9th Judicial District Court *Felony, Misd., Civil, Eviction, Small Claims, Probate* www.co.itasca.mn.us/Court/Gov_cou.htm 123 4th St NE, Grand Rapids, MN 55744-2600. 8AM-4PM. **218-327-2870**, Fax: 218-327-2897. ⊠ ✍

Jackson County

5th Judicial District Court *Felony, Misdemeanor, Civil, Eviction, Small Claims, Probate* PO Box 177, Jackson, MN 56143. 8:30AM-4:30PM. **507-847-4400**, Fax: 507-847-5433. Fax ⊠ ✍

Kanabec County

10th Judicial District Court *Felony, Misdemeanor, Civil, Eviction, Small Claims, Probate* 18 N Vine #318, Mora, MN 55051-1385. 8AM-4:30PM. **320-679-6400**, Fax: 320-679-6411. ✍

Kandiyohi County

8th Judicial District Court *Felony, Misdemeanor, Civil, Eviction, Small Claims, Probate* 505 Becker Ave SW, Willmar, MN 56201. 8:30AM-4:30PM. **320-231-6206**, Fax: 320-231-6276. ✍

Kittson County

9th Judicial District Court *Felony, Misdemeanor, Civil, Eviction, Small Claims, Probate* 410 Fifth St S, #204, Hallock, MN 56728. 8:00AM-4:30PM. **218-843-3632**, Fax: 218-843-3634. ✍

Koochiching County

9th Judicial District Court *Felony, Misd, Civil, Eviction, Small Claims, Probate* www.courts.state.mn.us/districts/ninth/ Court House 715 4th St, International Falls, MN 56649. 8AM-4PM. **218-283-1160**, Fax: 218-283-1162. ✍

Lac qui Parle County

8th Judicial District Court *Felony, Misd, Civil, Eviction, Small Claims, Probate* www.courts.state.mn.us/districts/eighth/dist08.htm PO Box 36 (600 6th St), Madison, MN 56256. 8:30AM-4:30PM. **320-598-3536**, Fax: 320-598-3915. ✍

Lake County

6th Judicial District Court *Felony, Misdemeanor, Civil, Eviction, Small Claims, Probate* www.6courts.com 601 3rd Ave, Two Harbors, MN 55616. 8AM-4:30PM. **218-834-8330**, Fax: 218-834-8397. ✍

Lake of the Woods County

9th Judicial District Court *Felony, Misdemeanor, Civil, Eviction, Small Claims, Probate* PO Box 808, Baudette, MN 56623. 7:30AM-4PM. **218-634-1451/1388**, Fax 218-634-9444. Fax ⊠ ✍

Le Sueur County

1st Judicial District Court *Felony, Misdemeanor, Civil, Eviction, Small Claims, Probate* 88 S Park Ave, Le Center, MN 56057. 8AM-4:30PM. **507-357-2251**, Fax: 507-357-6433. ✍

Lincoln County

5th Judicial District Court *Felony, Misdemeanor, Civil, Eviction, Small Claims, Probate* PO Box 15, Ivanhoe, MN 56142-0015. 8AM-N,12:30-4:30PM. **507-694-1355 or 507-694-1505**, Fax: 507-694-1717. ✍

Lyon County

5th Judicial District Court *Felony, Misdemeanor, Civil, Eviction, Small Claims, Probate* 607 W Main, Marshall, MN 56258. 8:30AM-4:30PM. **507-537-6734**, Fax: 507-537-6150. ✍

McLeod County

1st Judicial District Court *Felony, Misd, Civil, Eviction, Small Claims, Probate* www.co.mcleod.mn.us/mcleodco.cfm?pageID=14&sub=yes 830 E 11th, Glencoe, MN 55336. 8AM-4:30PM. **320-864-5551**, Fax: 320-864-5905. ✍

Mahnomen County

9th Judicial District Court *Felony, Misdemeanor, Civil, Eviction, Small Claims, Probate* PO Box 459, Mahnomen, MN 56557. 8AM-4:30PM. **218-935-2251**, Fax: 218-935-2851. ✍

Marshall County

9th Judicial District Court *Felony, Misdemeanor, Civil, Eviction, Small Claims, Probate* 208 E Colvin, Warren, MN 56762. 8AM-4:30PM. **218-745-4921**, Fax: 218-745-4343. ⊠ ✍

Martin County

5th Judicial District Court *Felony, Misdemeanor, Civil, Eviction, Small Claims, Probate* 201 Lake Ave, Rm 304 Martin County Court Administration, Fairmont, MN 56031. 8AM-5PM. **507-238-3205**, Fax: 507-238-1913. ✍

Key: Symbols refer to criminal records access unless otherwise noted. phone-☎ mail-⊠ fax-Fax in person-✍ online-🖳 email-**Email**

Meeker County

8th Judicial District Court *Felony, Misdemeanor, Civil, Eviction, Small Claims, Probate* 325 N Sibley, Litchfield, MN 55355. 8AM-4:30PM. **320-693-5230**, Fax: 320-693-5254.

Mille Lacs County

7th Judicial District Court *Felony, Misdemeanor, Civil, Eviction, Small Claims, Probate* Courthouse 635 2nd St SE, Milaca, MN 56353. 8AM-4:30PM. **320-983-8313**, Fax 320-983-8384. **Fax**

Morrison County

7th Judicial District Court *Felony, Misdemeanor, Civil, Eviction, Small Claims, Probate* 213 SE 1st Ave, Little Falls, MN 56345. 8AM-4:30PM. **320-.32-0325**, Fax: 320-632-0340 Probate: 320-632-0327.

Mower County

Mower County District Court *Felony, Misdemeanor, Civil, Eviction, Small Claims, Probate* www.co.mower.mn.us/administrator.html 201 1st St NE, Austin, MN 55912. 8AM-5PM. **507-437-9465**, Fax: 507-434-2702.

Murray County

5th Judicial District Court *Felony, Misdemeanor, Civil, Eviction, Small Claims, Probate* PO Box 57, Slayton, MN 56172-0057. 8AM-5PM. **507-836-6163**, Fax: 507-836-6019.

Nicollet County

5th Judicial District Court *Felony, Misdemeanor, Civil, Eviction, Small Claims, Probate* PO Box 496, St Peter, MN 56082. 8AM-5PM. **507-931-6800**, Fax: 507-931-4278. Civil phone: 507-934-0386, crim: 507-934-0388, Probate: 507-934-0380.

Nobles County

5th Judicial District Court *Felony, Misdemeanor, Civil, Eviction, Small Claims, Probate* PO Box 547, Worthington, MN 56187. 8AM-4:30PM. **507-372-8263**, Fax: 507-372-4994.

Norman County

9th Judicial District Court *Felony, Misdemeanor, Civil, Eviction, Small Claims, Probate* 16 3rd Ave E, Ada, MN 56510-0146. 8AM-4:30PM. **218-784-5458**, Fax: 218-784-3110.

Olmsted County

Olmsted County District Court *Felony, Misdemeanor, Civil, Eviction, Small Claims, Probate.* www.courts.state.mn.us/districts/third/counties/olmsted.htm 151 4th St SE, Rochester, MN 55904. 8AM-5PM., Fax: 507-285-8996. Civil phone: 507-285-8108, crim: 507-285-8201.

Otter Tail County

Otter Tail County District Court *Felony, Misdemeanor, Civil, Eviction, Small Claims, Probate* PO Box 417, Fergus Falls, MN 56538-0417. 8-5PM. **218-998-8420**, Fax: 218-998-8438.

Pennington County

9th Judicial District Court *Felony, Misdemeanor, Civil, Eviction, Small Claims, Probate* PO Box 619, Thief River Falls, MN 56701. 8AM-4:30PM. **218-681-7023**, Fax 218-681-0907. ✉

Pine County

10th Judicial District Court *Felony, Misd., Civil, Eviction, Small Claims, Probate* 315 Main St S., Pine City, MN 55063. 8AM-4:30PM. **320-629-5634**.

Pipestone County

5th Judicial District Court *Felony, Misdemeanor, Civil, Eviction, Small Claims, Probate* 416 S Hiawatha Ave (PO Box 337), Pipestone, MN 56164. 8:30AM-4:30PM. **507-825-6730**, Fax: 507-825-6733.

Polk County

9th Judicial District Court *Felony, Misdemeanor, Civil, Eviction, Small Claims, Probate* Court Administrator 612 N Broadway #301, Crookston, MN 56716. 8AM-4:30PM. **218-281-2332**, Fax: 218-281-2204. Child protection and child service cases are available as of 7/1/2002. ✉

Pope County

8th Judicial District Court *Felony, Misd, Civil, Eviction, Small Claims, Probate* www.courts.state.mn.us/districts/eighth/default.htm 130 E Minnesota Ave, Glenwood, MN 56334. 8AM-4:30PM. **320-634-5222**, Fax: 320-634-5527.

Ramsey County

2nd Judicial District Court *Felony, Misdemeanor, Civil, Probate* www.ramsey.courts.state.mn.us 15 W Kellogg, Rm 1700, St Paul, MN 55102. 8AM-4:30PM. Fax: 651-266-8263 civil; 266-8172 crim. Civil phone: 651-266-8253, crim: 651-266-8180.

2nd Judicial District Court - Maplewood Area *Misdemeanor* www.ramsey.courts.state.mn.us 2785 White Bear Ave, Maplewood, MN 55109. 8AM-4:30PM. **651-777-9111**, Fax: 651-777-3970. This court holds the records for the closed New Brighton Court.

Red Lake County

9th Judicial District Court *Felony, Misdemeanor, Civil, Eviction, Small Claims, Probate* PO Box 339, Red Lake Falls, MN 56750. 8AM-4:30PM. **218-253-4281**, Fax: 218-253-4287.

Redwood County

5th Judicial District Court *Felony, Misdemeanor, Civil, Eviction, Small Claims, Probate* PO Box 130, Redwood Falls, MN 56283. 8AM-4:30PM. **507-637-4020**, Fax: 507-637-4021.

Renville County

8th Judicial District Court *Felony, Misdemeanor, Civil, Eviction, Small Claims, Probate* 500 E DePue Ave, 3rd level, Olivia, MN 56277. 8AM-4:30PM. **320-523-3680**, Fax: 320-523-3689.

Rice County

3rd Judicial District Court *Felony, Misdemeanor, Civil, Eviction, Small Claims, Probate* www.courts.state.mn.us/districts/third/ 218 NW 3rd St, Faribault, MN 55021. 8AM-4:30PM. **507-332-6107**, Fax: 507-332-6199.

Rock County

5th Judicial District Court *Felony, Misdemeanor, Civil, Eviction, Small Claims, Probate* PO Box 745, Luverne, MN 56156. 8AM-5PM. **507-283-5020**, Fax: 507-283-5017. ✉

Roseau County

9th Judicial District Court *Felony, Misdemeanor, Civil, Eviction, Small Claims, Probate* 606 5th Ave SW Rm 20, Roseau, MN 56751. 8AM-4:30PM. **218-463-2541**, Fax: 218-463-1889. ✉

St. Louis County

All three St Louis County courts can access computer records for the county and direct you to the appropriate court to get the physical file.

Key: Symbols refer to criminal records access unless otherwise noted. phone-☎ mail-✉ fax-**Fax** in person-✍ online-💻 email-**Email**

6th Judicial District Court *Felony, Misdemeanor, Civil, Eviction, Small Claims, Probate* www.6courts.com 100 N 5th Ave W, Rm 320, Duluth, MN 55802-1294. 8AM-4:30PM. **218-726-2460**, Fax: 218-726-2473. Civil phone: 218-726-2430, Crim: 218-726-2460, Probate: 218-726-2521. ✋

6th Judicial District Court - Hibbing Branch *Felony, Misdemeanor, Civil, Eviction, Small Claims, Probate* www.courts.state.mn.us/districts/sixth/index.html 1810 12th Ave East, Hibbing, MN 55746. 8AM-4:30PM. **218-262-0105**, Fax: 218-262-0219. ✉️✋

6th Judicial District Court - Virginia Branch *Felony, Misd., Civil, Eviction, Small Claims, Probate* www.6courts.com 300 S 5th Ave, Virginia, MN 55792. 8AM-4:30PM. **218-749-7106**, Fax: 218-749-7109. ✋

Scott County

1st Judicial District Court *Felony, Misd., Civil, Eviction, Small Claims, Probate* Scott County Justice Ctr 200 Fourth Ave W, Shakopee, MN 55379. 8AM-4:30PM. **952-496-8200**, Fax: 952-496-8211. ✋

Sherburne County

10th Judicial District Court *Felony, Misdemeanor, Civil, Eviction, Small Claims, Probate* Sherburne County Government Ctr 13880 Hwy #10, Elk River, MN 55330-4608. 8AM-5PM. **763-241-2800**, Fax: 763-241-2816. ✋

Sibley County

1st Judicial District Court *Felony, Misdemeanor, Civil, Eviction, Small Claims, Probate* PO Box 867, Gaylord, MN 55334. 8AM-4:30PM. **507-237-4051**, Fax: 507-237-4062. ✉️✋

Stearns County

Stearns County District Court *Felony, Misdemeanor, Civil, Small Claims, Eviction, Probate, Traffic* www.co.stearns.mn.us/departments/other/court/index.htm 725 Courthouse Square, St Cloud, MN 56303. 8AM-4:30PM. **320-656-3620**, Fax: 320-656-6335. ✋

Steele County

3rd Judicial District Court *Felony, Misd., Civil, Eviction, Small Claims, Probate* www.courts.state.mn.us/districts/third/ PO Box 487 (111 E Main St), Owatonna, MN 55060. 8AM-4:30PM. **507-444-7700**, Fax: 507-444-7491. ✋

Stevens County

8th Judicial District Court *Felony, Misd, Civil, Eviction, Small Claims, Probate* PO Box 530, Morris, MN 56267. 8AM-4:30PM (8AM-4PM Summer hours). **320-589-7287**, Fax: 320-589-7288. ✋

Swift County

8th Judicial District Court *Felony, Misdemeanor, Civil, Eviction, Small Claims, Probate* PO Box 110, Benson, MN 56215. 8AM-4:30PM. **320-843-2744**, Fax: 320-843-4124. ✋

Todd County

7th Judicial District Court *Felony, Misdemeanor, Civil, Eviction, Small Claims, Probate* 221 1st Ave South, Long Prairie, MN 56347. 8AM-4:30PM. **320-732-7800**, Fax: 320-732-2506. ✋✉️

Traverse County

8th Judicial District Court *Felony, Misdemeanor, Civil, Eviction, Small Claims, Probate* 702 2nd Ave N PO Box 867, Wheaton, MN 56296. 8AM-N, 12:30-4:30PM. **320-563-4343**, Fax: 320-563-4311. ✋

Wabasha County

3rd Judicial District Court *Felony, Misdemeanor, Civil, Eviction, Small Claims, Probate* www.courts.state.mn.us/districts/third/counties/wabasha.htm 625 Jefferson Ave, Wabasha, MN 55981. 8AM-4PM. **651-565-3012**, Fax: 651-565-3160. Civil phone: 651-565-3012/3087/3051, crim: 651-565-3010/3524/3070. ✋

Wadena County

7th Judicial District Court *Felony, Misdemeanor, Civil, Eviction, Small Claims, Probate* County Courthouse 415 S Jefferson St, Wadena, MN 56482. 8AM-4:30PM. **218-631-7634**, Fax: 218-631-7635. ✋

Waseca County

3rd Judicial District Court *Felony, Misdemeanor, Civil, Eviction, Small Claims, Probate* www.courts.state.mn.us/districts/third/ 307 N State St, Waseca, MN 56093. 8AM-4:30PM. **507-835-0540**, Fax: 507-835-0633. ✋

Washington County

10th Judicial District Court *Felony, Misdemeanor, Civil, Eviction, Small Claims, Probate* www.co.washington.mn.us/crtadmn.htm 14949 62nd St North PO Box 3802, Stillwater, MN 55082-3802. 7:30AM-5PM. **651-430-6263**, Fax: 651-430-6300. ✋

Watonwan County

5th Judicial District Court *Felony, Misdemeanor, Civil, Eviction, Small Claims, Probate* PO Box 518 710 2nd Ave.South, St James, MN 56081. 8AM-5PM. **507-375-1236**, Fax: 507-375-5010. Civil phone: 507-375-1235, crim: 507-375-1237, Probate: 507-375-1234. ✋✉️

Wilkin County

8th Judicial District Court *Felony, Misdemeanor, Civil, Eviction, Small Claims, Probate* PO Box 219, Breckenridge, MN 56520. 8AM-4:30PM. **218-643-7172**, Fax: 218-643-7167. ✋

Winona County

3rd Judicial District Court *Felony, Misdemeanor, Civil, Eviction, Small Claims, Probate* www.courts.state.mn.us/districts/third/counties/winona.htm 171 W 3rd St, Winona, MN 55987. 8-4:30PM. **507-457-6386**, Fax: 507-457-6392. ✋

Wright County

10th Judicial District Court *Felony, Misd., Civil, Eviction, Small Claims, Probate* www.courts.state.mn.us/home/ 10 NW 2nd St, Rm 201, Buffalo, MN 55313-1192. 8AM-4:30PM. **763-682-7549**, Fax: 763-682-7300. ✋

Yellow Medicine County

8th Judicial District Court *Felony, Misdemeanor, Civil, Eviction, Small Claims, Probate* 415 9th Ave, Granite Falls, MN 56241. 8AM-4PM. **320-564-3325**, Fax: 320-564-4435. ✋

Key: Symbols refer to criminal records access unless otherwise noted.   phone-☎   mail-✉️   fax-**Fax**   in person-✋   online-🖥️   email-**Email**

Mississippi

State Court Administration: Court Administrator, Supreme Court, Box 117, Surpeme Ct. (450 High St), Jackson, MS, 39205; 601-359-3697, Fax: 601-359-2443. www.mssc.state.ms.us

Court Structure: The court of general jurisdiction is the Circuit Court with 70 courts in 22 districts. Justice Courts were first created in 1984, replacing the Justice of the Peace. Prior to 1984, records were kept separately by each Justice of the Peace, so the location of such records today is often unknown. Probate is handled by the Chancery Courts, as are property matters.

Criminal Courts: The Administrative Office of Courts offers a statewide search via fax requesting with a 24 hour turnaround time.There is a $25.00 start-up fee and a $5.00 per name search fee. Call 601-354-7449 or fax 601-354-7459 for details.

Online Access: A statewide online computer system is in use internally for court personnel. There are plans underway to make this system available to the public, however this has been put on hold. The website offers searching of the MS Supreme Court and Court of Appeals Decisions, including dockets of the trial courts.

Additional Information: A number of Mississippi counties have two Circuit Court Districts. A search of either court in such a county will include the index from the other court.

Full name is a search requirement for all courts. DOB and SSN are very helpful for differentiating between like-named individuals.

Adams County

Circuit & County Court *Felony, Misdemeanor, Civil Actions Over $2,500* PO Box 1224 115 S Wall, Natchez, MS 39121. 8AM-5PM. **601-446-6326**, Fax: 601-445-7955. ⊠**Fax**✥

Chancery Court *Probate* PO Box 1006, Natchez, MS 39121. 8AM-5PM. **601-446-6684**, Fax: 601-445-7913.

Alcorn County

Circuit Court *Felony, Civil Actions Over $2,500* PO Box 430 Attn: Circuit Clerk, Corinth, MS 38835. 8AM-5PM. **662-286-7740**, Fax: 662-286-7767. ⊠**Fax**✥

Chancery Court *Probate* PO Box 69, Corinth, MS 38835-0069. 8AM-5PM. **662-286-7702**, Fax: 662-286-7706.

Amite County

Circuit Court *Felony, Civil Actions Over $2,500* PO Box 312, Liberty, MS 39645. 8AM-5PM. **601-657-8932**, Fax: 601-657-1082. **Fax**⊠✥

Chancery Court *Probate* PO Box 680, Liberty, MS 39645. 8AM-5PM. **601-657-8022**, Fax: 601-657-8288.

Attala County

Circuit Court *Felony, Civil Actions Over $2,500* Courthouse, Kosciusko, MS 39090. 8AM-5PM. **662-289-1471**, Fax: 662-289-7666. **Fax**⊠✥

Chancery Court *Probate* 230 W. Washington, Kosciusko, MS 39090. 8-5. **662-289-2921**, Fax: 662-289-7662.

Benton County

Circuit Court *Felony, Civil Actions Over $2,500* PO Box 262, Ashland, MS 38603. 8AM-5PM. **662-224-6310**, Fax: 662-224-6312. ⊠✥

Chancery Court *Probate* PO Box 218, Ashland, MS 38603. 8AM-5PM. **662-224-6300**, Fax: 662-224-6303.

Bolivar County

Circuit & County Court - 1st District *Felony, Misdemeanor, Civil* PO Box 205, Rosedale, MS 38769. 8AM-5PM. **662-759-6521**. ⊠✥

Circuit & County Court - 2nd District *Felony, Misdemeanor, Civil* PO Box 670, Cleveland, MS 38732. 8AM-5PM. **662-843-2061**, Fax: 662-846-2943. ⊠✥

Rosedale Chancery Court *Probate* PO Box 238, Rosedale, MS 38769. 8AM-N, 1-5. **662-759-3762**, Fax: 662-759-3467.

Cleveland Chancery Court *Probate* PO Box 789, Cleveland, MS 38732. 8AM-5PM. **662-843-2071**, Fax: 662-846-2940.

Calhoun County

Circuit Court *Felony, Civil Actions Over $2,500* PO Box 25, Pittsboro, MS 38951. 8AM-5PM. **662-412-3101**, Fax: 662-412-3103. ⊠✥

Chancery Court *Probate* PO Box 8, Pittsboro, MS 38951. 8AM-5PM. **662-412-3117**, Fax: 662-412-3128.

Carroll County

Circuit Court *Felony, Civil Actions Over $2,500* PO Box 6, Vaiden, MS 39176. 8AM-5PM. **662-464-5476**, Fax: 662-464-5407. ⊠✥

Chancery Court *Probate* PO Box 60, Carrollton, MS 38917. 8AM-12; 1-5PM. **662-237-9274**, Fax: 662-237-9642.

Chickasaw County

Circuit Court - 2nd District *Felony, Civil Actions Over $2,500* Courthouse 234 W Main St Rm #203, Okolona, MS 38860. 8AM-5PM. **662-447-2838**, Fax: 662-447-5024. **Fax**⊠✥

Circuit Court - 1st District *Felony, Civil Actions Over $2,500* 1 Pinson Sq, Rm 2, Houston, MS 38851. 8AM-5PM. **662-456-2331**, Fax: 662-456-4831. **Fax**⊠✥

Chancery Court *Probate* 234 W Main, Rm 201, Okolona, MS 38860-1438. 8AM-N; 1-5PM. **662-447-2092**, Fax: 662-447-5024.

Chancery Court *Probate* Courthouse Bldg, 1 Pinson Square, Houston, MS 38851. 8AM-5PM. **662-456-2513**, Fax: 662-456-5295.

Choctaw County

Circuit Court *Felony, Civil Actions Over $2,500* PO Box 34, Ackerman, MS 39735. 8AM-5PM. **662-285-6245**, Fax: 662-285-2196. ⊠✥

Chancery Court *Probate* PO Box 250, Ackerman, MS 39735. 8AM-5PM. **662-285-6329**, Fax: 662-285-3444.

Claiborne County

Circuit Court *Felony, Civil Actions Over $2,500* PO Box 549, Port Gibson, MS 39150. 8AM-5PM. **601-437-5841**, Fax: 601-437-4543. ✉ 🖐

Chancery Court *Probate, Small Claims* PO Box 449, Port Gibson, MS 39150. 8-5. **601-437-4992**, Fax: 601-437-3137.

Clarke County

Circuit Court *Felony, Civil Actions* PO Box 216, Quitman, MS 39355. 8AM-5PM. **601-776-3111**, Fax: 601-776-1001. **Fax**✉ 🖐

Chancery Court *Probate* PO Box 689, Quitman, MS 39355. 8AM-5PM. **601-776-2126**, Fax: 601-776-2756.

Clay County

Circuit Court *Felony, Civil Actions Over $2,500* PO Box 364, West Point, MS 39773. 8AM-5PM. **662-494-3384**, Fax: 662-495-2057. ✉ 🖐

Chancery Court *Probate* PO Box 815, West Point, MS 39773. 8AM-5PM. **662-494-3124**, Fax: 662-492-4059.

Coahoma County

Circuit & County Court *Felony, Civil* PO Box 849, Clarksdale, MS 38614-0849. 8AM-5PM. **662-624-3014**, Fax: 662-624-3075. **Fax**✉ 🖐

Chancery Court *Probate* PO Box 98, Clarksdale, MS 38614. 8AM-5PM. **662-624-3000**, Fax: 662-624-3040.

Copiah County

Circuit Court *Felony, Civil Actions Over $2,500* PO Box 467, Hazlehurst, MS 39083. 8AM-5PM. **601-894-1241**, Fax: 601-894-3026. Also, use 601-894-3301 for the 22nd Circuit Court District. **Fax**✉ 🖐

Chancery Court *Probate* 122 S Lowe St, Hazlehurst, MS 39083. 8AM-5PM. **601-894-3021**, Fax: 601-894-4081.

Covington County

Circuit Court *Felony, Civil Actions Over $2,500* PO Box 667, Collins, MS 39428. 8AM-5PM. **601-765-6506**, Fax: 601-765-5012. **Fax**✉ 🖐

Chancery Court *Probate* PO Box 1679, Collins, MS 39428. 8AM-5PM. **601-765-4242**, Fax: 601-765-5016.

De Soto County

Circuit & County Court *Felony, Misdemeanor, Civil* www.desotoms.com 2535 Hwy 51 South, Hernando, MS 38632. 8AM-5PM. **662-429-1325**. ✉ 🖐

Chancery Court, Rm 100 *Probate* 2535 Hwy 51 South (PO Box 949), Hernando, MS 38632. 8AM-5PM. **662-429-1320**, Fax: 662-449-1420.

Forrest County

Circuit & County Court *Felony, Misdemeanor, Civil* PO Box 992, Hattiesburg, MS 39403. 8AM-5PM. **601-582-3213**, Fax: 601-545-6065. ✉ 🖐

Chancery Court *Probate* PO Box 951, Hattiesburg, MS 39403. 8AM-5PM. **601-545-6040**, Fax: 601-545-6043.

Franklin County

Circuit Court *Felony, Civil Actions Over $2,500* PO Box 267, Meadville, MS 39653. 8AM-5PM. **601-384-2320**, Fax: 601-384-8244. **Fax**✉ 🖐

Chancery Court *Probate* PO Box 297, Meadville, MS 39653. 8AM-5PM. **601-384-2330**, Fax: 601-384-5864.

George County

Circuit Court *Felony, Civil Actions Over $2,500* 355 Cox St, #C, Lucedale, MS 39452. 8AM-5PM M-F, 9AM-12PM Sat. **601-947-4881**, Fax: 601-947-8804. **Fax**✉ 🖐

Chancery Court *Probate* 355 Cox St, #A, Lucedale, MS 39452. 8AM-5PM. **601-947-4801**, Fax: 601-947-1300.

Greene County

Circuit Court *Felony, Civil Actions Over $2,500* PO Box 310, Leakesville, MS 39451. 8AM-5PM **601-394-2379**, Fax: 601-394-2334. ☎**Fax**✉ 🖐

Chancery Court *Probate* PO Box 610, Leakesville, MS 39451. 8AM-5PM. **601-394-2377**, Fax: 601-394-4445.

Grenada County

Circuit Court *Felony, Civil Actions Over $2,500* PO Box 1517, Grenada, MS 38902-1517. 8AM-5PM. **662-226-1941**, Fax: 662-227-2865. 🖐

Chancery Court *Probate* PO Box 1208, Grenada, MS 38902. 8AM-5PM. **662-226-1821**, Fax: 662-227-2860.

Hancock County

Circuit Court *Felony, Civil Actions Over $2,500* PO Box 249 152 Main St, Bay St. Louis, MS 39520. 8AM-5PM. **228-467-5265**, Fax: 228-467-2779 Probate: 228-467-5404. ✉ 🖐

Chancery Court *Probate* PO Box 550, Bay St. Louis, MS 39520. 8AM-5PM. **228-467-5404**, Fax: 228-467-3159.

Harrison County

Circuit Court - 1st District *Felony, Civil Actions Over $75,000* PO Box 998, Gulfport, MS 39502. 8AM-5PM. **228-865-4147**, Fax: 228-865-4009. ✉ 🖐

Circuit Court - 2nd District *Felony, Civil Actions Over $75,000* PO Box 235, Biloxi, MS 39533. 8AM-5PM. **228-435-8258**, Fax: 228-435-8277. **Fax**✉ 🖐

County Court - 1st District *Misdemeanor, Civil Actions Under $75,000* PO Box 998, Gulfport, MS 39502. 8AM-5PM. **228-865-4097**, Fax: 228-865-4099. Criminal phone: 228-865-4145. ✉ 🖐

County Court - 1st District *Misdemeanor, Civil Actions Under $200,000* PO Box 998, Gulfport, MS 39502. 8AM-5PM. **228-435-8294/8232**, Fax: 228-435-8277. **Fax**✉ 🖐

Biloxi Chancery Court *Probate* http://co.harrison.ms.us/departments/chanclerk/court.asp PO Box 544, Biloxi, MS 39533. 8AM-5PM. **228-435-8228**, Fax: 228-435-8281. Search Chancery dockets free at http://co.harrison.ms.us/dockets/.

Gulfport Chancery Court *Probate* http://co.harrison.ms.us/departments/chanclerk/court.asp PO Drawer CC, Gulfport, MS 39502. 8AM-N, 1-5PM. **228-865-4092, 865-4095**, Fax: 228-865-1646/865-4054. Search Chancery Court dockets for free at http://co.harrison.ms.us/dockets/.

Hinds County

Circuit & County Court - 1st District *Felony, Misdemeanor, Civil* www.co.hinds.ms.us/pgs/index.asp PO Box 327, Jackson, MS 39205. 8AM-5PM. **601-968-6628**. ✉ 🖐

Circuit & County Court - 2nd District *Felony, Misdemeanor, Civil* PO Box 999, Raymond, MS 39154. 8AM-N, 1-5PM. **601-857-8038**. ✉ 🖐

Raymond Chancery Court *Probate* PO Box 88, Raymond, MS 39154. 8AM-5PM. **601-857-8055**, Fax: 601-857-4953.

Jackson Chancery Court *Probate* PO Box 686, Jackson, MS 39205. 8AM-5PM. **601-968-6540**, Fax: 601-973-5554.

Holmes County

Circuit Court *Felony, Civil Actions Over $2,500* PO Box 718, Lexington, MS 39095. 8AM-5PM. **662-834-2476**, Fax: 662-834-3870. Fax⊠🖐

Chancery Court *Probate* PO Box 239, Lexington, MS 39095. 8AM-5PM. **662-834-2508**, Fax: 662-834-3020.

Humphreys County

Circuit Court *Felony, Civil Actions Over $2,500* PO Box 696, Belzoni, MS 39038. 8AM-5PM. **662-247-3065**, Fax: 662-247-3906. Fax⊠🖐

Chancery Court *Probate* PO Box 547, Belzoni, MS 39038. 8AM-N, 1-5PM. **662-247-1740**, Fax: 662-247-0101.

Issaquena County

Circuit Court *Felony, Civil Actions Over $2,500* PO Box 27, Mayersville, MS 39113. 8AM-12:00, 1-5PM. **662-873-2761**, Fax: 662-873-2061. ⊠🖐

Chancery Court *Probate* PO Box 27, Mayersville, MS 39113. 8AM-12:00,1-5PM. **662-873-2761**, Fax: 662-873-2061.

Itawamba County

Circuit Court *Felony, Civil Actions Over $2,500* 201 W Main, Fulton, MS 38843. 8AM-5PM. **662-862-3511**, Fax: 662-862-4006. ☎Fax⊠🖐

Chancery Court *Probate* 201 W Main, Fulton, MS 38843. 8-5 M-F; 8AM-N Sat. **662-862-3421**, Fax: 662-862-3421.

Jackson County

Circuit Court *Felony, Civil* www.co.jackson.ms.us/ PO Box 998, Pascagoula, MS 39568-0998. 8AM-5PM. **228-769-3025**, Fax: 228-769-3180. ⊠🖐💻

County Court *Misdemeanor, Civil over $25,000* www.co.jackson.ms.us/ PO Box 998 (3104 Magnolia St), Pascagoula, MS 39568. 8AM-5PM. **228-769-3181**. ⊠🖐

Chancery Court *Probate* www.co.jackson.ms.us/ PO Box 998, Pascagoula, MS 39568. 8AM-5PM. **228-769-3124, 769-3124**, Fax: 228-769-3397.

Access to Chancery Court monthly dockets are available at www.co.jackson.ms.us/DS/ChanceryDockets.html.

Jasper County

Circuit Court - 2nd District *Felony, Civil Actions Over $2,500* PO Box 447, Bay Springs, MS 39422. 8AM-5PM. **601-764-2245**, Fax: 601-764-3078. ⊠🖐fax.

Circuit Court - 1st District *Felony, Civil Actions Over $2,500* PO Box 58, Paulding, MS 39348. 8AM-5PM. **601-727-4941**, Fax: 601-727-4475. Fax⊠🖐

Bay Springs Chancery Court *Probate* PO Box 1047, Bay Springs, MS 39422. 8-5. **601-764-3368**, Fax: 601-764-3999.

Paulding Chancery Court *Probate* PO Box 38, Paulding, MS 39348. 8AM-5PM. **601-727-4941**, Fax: 601-727-4475.

Jefferson County

Circuit Court *Felony, Civil Actions Over $2,500* PO Box 305, Fayette, MS 39069. 8AM-5PM. **601-786-3422**, Fax: 601-786-9676. ☎⊠🖐

Chancery Court *Probate* PO Box 145, Fayette, MS 39069. 8AM-5PM. **601-786-3021**, Fax: 601-786-6009.

Jefferson Davis County

Circuit Court *Felony, Civil Actions Over $2,500* PO Box 1082, Prentiss, MS 39474. 8AM-5PM. **601-792-4231**, Fax: 601-792-4957. ☎Fax⊠🖐

Chancery Court *Probate* PO Box 1137, Prentiss, MS 39474. 8AM-5PM. **601-792-4204**, Fax: 601-792-2894.

Jones County

Circuit & County Court - 2nd District *Felony, Misdemeanor, Civil* PO Box 1336, Laurel, MS 39441. 8AM-5PM. **601-425-2556**. ⊠🖐

Circuit & County Court - 1st District *Felony, Misdemeanor, Civil* 101 N. Court St., #B, Ellisville, MS 39437. 8AM-5PM. **601-477-8538**. ⊠Fax🖐

Ellisville Chancery Court *Probate* 101 N Court St. #D PO Box 248, Ellisville, MS 39437. 8AM-N, 1-5PM. **601-477-3307**, Fax: 601-477-1240.

Laurel Chancery Court *Probate* www.chancery19thms.com PO Box 1468, Laurel, MS 39441. 8AM-5PM. **601-428-0527**, Fax: 601-428-3610 Probate: 602-428-3182.

Kemper County

Circuit Court *Felony, Civil Actions Over $2,500* PO Box 130, De Kalb, MS 39328. 8AM-5PM. **601-743-2224**, Fax: 601-743-4173. Fax⊠

Chancery Court *Probate* PO Box 188, De Kalb, MS 39328. 8AM-5PM. **601-743-2460**, Fax: 601-743-2789.

Lafayette County

Circuit Court *Felony, Civil Actions Over $2,500* LaFayette County Courthouse One Couerthouse Sq, #201, Oxford, MS 38655. 8AM-5PM. **662-234-4951**, Fax: 662-236-0238. ⊠🖐

Chancery Court *Probate* PO Box 1240, Oxford, MS 38655. 8AM-5PM. **662-234-2131**, Fax: 662-234-5038.

Lamar County

Circuit Court *Felony, Civil Actions Over $2,500* PO Box 369, Purvis, MS 39475. 8AM-5PM. **601-794-8504**, Fax: 601-794-3905. ⊠🖐

Chancery Court *Probate* PO Box 247, Purvis, MS 39475. 8AM-5PM. **601-794-8504**, Fax: 601-794-3903.

Lauderdale County

Circuit & County Court *Felony, Civil Actions Over $2,500* PO Box 1005, Meridian, MS 39302-1005. 8AM-5PM. **601-482-9738**, Fax: 601-484-3970. County Court can be reached at 601-482-9715. ⊠Fax🖐

Chancery Court *Probate* PO Box 1587, Meridian, MS 39302. 8AM-5PM. **601-482-9701**, Fax: 601-486-4921.

Lawrence County

Circuit Court *Felony, Civil Actions Over $2,500* PO Box 1249, Monticello, MS 39654. 8AM-5PM. **601-587-4791**, Fax: 601-587-0750. ☎Fax⊠🖐

Chancery Court *Probate* 517 Broad St, Courthouse Sq PO Box 821, Monticello, MS 39654. 8AM-5PM. **601-587-7162**, Fax: 601-587-0767.

Leake County

Circuit Court *Felony, Civil Actions Over $2,500* PO Box 67, Carthage, MS 39051. 8AM-5PM. **601-267-8357**, Fax: 601-267-8889. ⊠🖐

Chancery Court www.co.leake.ms.us/ PO Box 72, Carthage, MS 39051. 8AM-5PM. **601-267-7371/72**, Fax: 601-267-6137.

Lee County

Circuit & County Court *Felony, Civil Actions Over $2,500* Circuit Court - PO Box 762 County Court - PO Box 736, Tupelo, MS 38802. 8AM-5PM. **662-841-9022/9023(Circuit)** , **-9730 (County)**, Fax: 662-680-6079. ⊠ 🖐

Chancery Court *Probate* PO Box 7127, Tupelo, MS 38802. 8AM-5PM. **662-841-9100**, Fax: 662-680-6091.

Leflore County

Circuit & County Court *Felony, Civil Actions Over $2,500* PO Box 1953, Greenwood, MS 38935-1953. 8AM-5PM. **662-453-1435**, Fax: 662-455-1278. **Fax**⊠ 🖐

Chancery Court *Probate* PO Box 250, Greenwood, MS 38935-0250. 8AM-5PM. **662-453-1041; 453-1432 (court admin)**, Fax: 662-455-7959/7965.

Lincoln County

Circuit Court *Felony, Civil Actions Over $2,500* PO Box 357, Brookhaven, MS 39602. 8AM-5PM. **601-835-3435**, Fax: 601-835-3482. **Fax**⊠ 🖐

Lincoln Chancery Court *Probate* www.15thchancerydistrictms.org PO Box 555, Brookhaven, MS 39602. 8AM-5PM. **601-835-3412**, Fax: 601-835-3423.

Lowndes County

Circuit & County Court *Felony, Civil* PO Box 31, Columbus, MS 39703. 8AM-5PM. **662-329-5900**. ⊠ 🖐

Chancery Court *Probate* PO Box 684, Columbus, MS 39703. 8AM-5PM. **662-329-5800**.

Madison County

Circuit & County Court *Felony, Civil* PO Box 1626, Canton, MS 39046. 8AM-5PM. **601-859-4365**, Fax: 601-859-8555. ⊠ 🖐

Chancery Court *Probate* PO Box 404, Canton, MS 39046. 8AM-5PM. **601-859-1177**, Fax: 601-859-0795.

Marion County

Circuit Court *Felony, Civil Actions Over $2,500* 250 Broad St, #1, Columbia, MS 39429. 8AM-5PM. **601-736-8246**. ⊠ 🖐 fax.

Chancery Court *Probate* 250 Broad St, #2, Columbia, MS 39429. 8AM-5PM.

601-444-0205, Fax: 601-444-0206. Civil phone: 601-736-2691.

Marshall County

Circuit Court *Felony, Civil Actions Over $2,500* PO Box 459, Holly Springs, MS 38635. 8AM-5PM. **662-252-3434**, Fax: 662-252-5951. ⊠ 🖐 fax.

Chancery Court *Probate* PO Box 219, Holly Springs, MS 38635. 8AM-5PM. **662-252-4431**, Fax: 662-252-0004.

Monroe County

Circuit Court *Felony, Civil Actions Over $2,500* PO Box 843, Aberdeen, MS 39730. 8AM-5PM. **662-369-8695**, Fax: 662-369-3684. 🖐

Chancery Court *Probate* PO Box 578, Aberdeen, MS 39730. 8AM-5PM. **662-369-8143**, Fax: 662-369-7928.

Montgomery County

Circuit Court *Felony, Civil Actions Over $2,500* PO Box 765, Winona, MS 38967. 8AM-5PM. **662-283-4161**, Fax: 662-283-3363. ⊠ 🖐

Chancery Court *Probate* PO Box 71, Winona, MS 38967. 8AM-5PM. **662-283-2333**, Fax: 662-283-2233.

Neshoba County

Circuit Court *Felony, Civil Actions Over $2,500* 401 E Beacon St #110, Philadelphia, MS 39350. 8AM-5PM. **601-656-4781**, Fax: 601-650-3997. ⊠ 🖐

Chancery Court *Probate* 401 Beacon St #107, Philadelphia, MS 39350. 8AM-5PM. **601-656-3581**, Fax: 601-656-5915.

Newton County

Circuit Court *Felony, Civil Actions Over $2,500* PO Box 447, Decatur, MS 39327. 8AM-5PM. **601-635-2368**, Fax: 601-635-3210. ⊠ 🖐

Chancery Clerk Office *Probate* PO Box 68, Decatur, MS 39327. 8AM-5PM. **601-635-2367**, Fax: 601-635-3479. Civil phone: 601-635-3370.

Noxubee County

Circuit Court *Felony, Civil Actions Over $2,500* PO Box 431, Macon, MS 39341. 8AM-5PM. **662-726-5737**, Fax: 662-726-6041. ⊠**Fax**🖐

Chancery Court *Probate* PO Box 147, Macon, MS 39341. 8AM-5PM. **662-726-4243**, Fax: 662-726-2272.

Oktibbeha County

Circuit Court *Felony, Civil Actions Over $2,500* Courthouse 101 E Main, Starkville, MS 39759. 8AM-5PM. **662-323-1356**. ⊠**Fax**🖐

Chancery Court *Probate* Courthouse, 101 E Main, Starkville, MS 39759. 8AM-5PM. **662-323-5834**, Fax: 662-338-1064.

Panola County

Circuit Court - 1st District *Felony, Civil Actions Over $2,500* PO Box 130, Sardis, MS 38666. 8AM-5PM. **662-487-2073**, Fax: 662-487-3595. **Fax**⊠ 🖐

Circuit Court - 2nd District *Felony, Civil Actions Over $2,500* PO Box 346, Batesville, MS 38606. 8AM-5PM. **662-563-6210**, Fax: 662-563-8233. **Fax**⊠ 🖐

Panola County Chancery Clerk *Probate* 151 Public Square, Batesville, MS 38606. 8AM-5PM. **662-563-6205**, Fax: 662-563-6277.

Sardis Chancery Court *Probate* PO Box 130, Sardis, MS 38666. 8AM-N, 1-5PM. **662-487-2070**, Fax: 662-487-3595.

Pearl River County

Circuit Court *Felony, All Civil Actions* Courthouse, Poplarville, MS 39470. 8AM-5PM. **601-403-2300**, Fax: 601-403-2327. Civil phone: ext 324, crim: ext 323. ⊠**Fax**🖐

Chancery Court *Probate* PO Box 431, Poplarville, MS 39470. 8AM-5PM. **601-403-2300**, Fax: 601-403-2317.

Perry County

Circuit Court *Felony, Civil Actions Over $2,500* PO Box 198, New Augusta, MS 39462. 8AM-5PM. **601-964-8663**, Fax: 601-964-8740. ⊠**Fax**🖐

Chancery Court *Probate* PO Box 198, New Augusta, MS 39462. 8AM-5PM. **601-964-8398**, Fax: 601-964-8746.

Pike County

Circuit & County Court *Felony, Civil* PO Drawer 31, Magnolia, MS 39652. 8AM-5PM. **601-783-2581**, Fax: 601-783-6322. **Fax**⊠ 🖐

Chancery Court *Probate, Civil* PO Box 309, Magnolia, MS 39652. 8AM-5PM. **601-783-3362**, Fax: 601-783-5982.

Key: Symbols refer to criminal records access unless otherwise noted. phone-☎ mail-⊠ fax-**Fax** in person-🖐 online-💻 email-**Email**

Pontotoc County

Circuit Court *Felony, Civil Actions Over $2,500* PO Box 428, Pontotoc, MS 38863. 8AM-5PM. **662-489-3908**. ✉ 🖐

Chancery Court *Probate* 11 E Washington PO Box 209, Pontotoc, MS 38863. 8AM-5PM. **662-489-3900**, Fax: 662-489-3940.

Prentiss County

Circuit Court *Felony, Civil Actions Over $2,500* PO Box 727 101 N Main St, Booneville, MS 38829. 8AM-5PM. **662-728-4611**, Fax: 662-728-2006. Fax✉🖐

Chancery Court *Probate* PO Box 477, Booneville, MS 38829. 8AM-5PM. **662-728-8151**, Fax: 662-728-2007.

Quitman County

Circuit Court *Felony, Civil Actions Over $2,500* Courthouse 230 Chestnut St, Marks, MS 38646. 8AM-5PM. **662-326-8003**, Fax: 662-326-8004. Fax✉🖐

Chancery Court *Probate* 230 Chestnut St, Marks, MS 38646. 8AM-N, 1-5PM. **662-326-2661**, Fax: 662-326-8004.

Rankin County

Circuit & County Court *Felony, Misd., Civil* www.rankincounty.org PO Drawer 1599, Brandon, MS 39043. 8AM-5PM. **601-825-1466**. ✉🖐

Chancery Court *Probate, Civil* www.rankincounty.org 203 Town Sq PO Box 700, Brandon, MS 39042. 8AM-5PM. **601-825-1649**, Fax: 601-824-2450.

Scott County

Circuit Court *Felony, Civil Actions Over $2,500* PO Box 371, Forest, MS 39074. 8AM-5PM. **601-469-3601**. ✉🖐

Chancery Court *Probate* 100 Main St PO Box 630, Forest, MS 39074. 8AM-5PM. **601-469-1922, 601-469-1927**, Fax: 601-469-5180.

Sharkey County

Circuit Court *Felony, Civil Actions Over $2,500* PO Box 218 (400 Locust St), Rolling Fork, MS 39159. 8AM-N, 1-5PM. **662-873-2766**, Fax: 662-873-6045. Fax✉🖐

Chancery Court *Probate* 120 Locust St PO Box 218, Rolling Fork, MS 39159. 8AM-N,1-5PM. **662-873-2755**, Fax: 662-873-6045.

Simpson County

Circuit Court *Felony, Civil Actions Over $2,500* PO Box 307, Mendenhall, MS 39114. 8AM-5PM. **601-847-2474**, Fax: 601-847-4011. Fax✉🖐

Chancery Court *Probate* Chancery Bldg PO Box 367, Mendenhall, MS 39114. 8-5PM. **601-847-2626**, Fax: 601-847-7016.

Smith County

Circuit Court *Felony, Civil Actions Over $2,500* PO Box 517, Raleigh, MS 39153. 8AM-5PM. **601-782-4751**, Fax: 601-782-4007. ✉🖐

Chancery Court *Probate* 123 Main St PO Box 39, Raleigh, MS 39153. 8AM-5PM. **601-782-9811**, Fax: 601-782-4690.

Stone County

Circuit Court *Felony, Civil Actions Over $2,500* Courthouse, 323 Cavers Ave, Wiggins, MS 39577. 8AM-5PM. **601-928-5246**, Fax: 601-928-5248. Fax✉🖐

Chancery Court *Probate* 323 E Cavers PO Drawer 7, Wiggins, MS 39577. 8AM-5PM. **601-928-5266**, Fax: 601-928-6464.

Sunflower County

Circuit Court *Felony, Civil Actions Over $2,500* PO Box 569, Indianola, MS 38751. 8AM-5PM. **662-887-1252**, Fax: 662-887-7077. ✉🖐

Chancery Court *Probate* 200 Main St PO Box 988, Indianola, MS 38751. 8AM-5PM. **662-887-4703**, Fax: 662-887-7054.

Tallahatchie County

Charleston Circuit Court *Felony, Civil Actions Over $2,500* PO Box 86, Charleston, MS 38921. 8AM-5PM. **662-647-8758**, Fax: 662-647-8490 Probate: 662-647-5551. ✉🖐

Chancery Court *Probate* PO Box 180, Sumner, MS 38957. 8AM-N, 1-5PM. **662-375-8731**, Fax: 662-375-7252.

Chancery Court *Probate* #1 Main St PO Box 350, Charleston, MS 38921. 8AM-5PM. **662-647-5551**, Fax: 662-647-8490.

Tate County

Circuit Court *Felony, Civil Actions Over $2,500* 201 Ward St, Senatobia, MS 38668. 8AM-5PM. **662-562-5211**, Fax: 662-562-7486. ✉🖐

Chancery Court *Probate* 201 Ward St, Senatobia, MS 38668. 8AM-5PM. **662-562-5661**, Fax: 662-560-6205.

Tippah County

Circuit Court *Felony, Civil Actions Over $2,500* Courthouse, Ripley, MS 38663. 8AM-5PM. **662-837-7370**, Fax: 662-837-1030. ☎Fax✉🖐

Chancery Court *Probate* PO Box 99, Ripley, MS 38663. 8AM-5PM. **662-837-7374**, Fax: 662-837-7148 Probate: 662-837-3607.

Tishomingo County

Circuit Court *Felony, Civil Actions Over $2,500* 1008 Battleground Dr, Iuka, MS 38852. 8AM-5PM. **662-423-7026**, Fax: 662-423-1667. ✉🖐

Chancery Court *Probate* 1008 Battleground Dr, Iuka, MS 38852. 8AM-5PM. **662-423-7010**, Fax: 662-423-7005.

Tunica County

Circuit Court *Felony, Civil Actions Over $2,500* PO Box 184, Tunica, MS 38676. 8AM-5PM. **662-363-2842**. ✉🖐

Chancery Court *Probate* PO Box 217, Tunica, MS 38676. 8AM-N, 1-5PM. **662-363-2451**, Fax: 662-357-5934.

Union County

Circuit Court *Felony, Civil Actions Over $2,500* PO Box 298, New Albany, MS 38652. 8AM-5PM. **662-534-1910**, Fax: 662-534-2059. Fax✉🖐

Chancery Court *Probate* PO Box 847, New Albany, MS 38652. 8AM-5PM. **662-534-1900**, Fax: 662-534-1907.

Walthall County

Circuit Court *Felony, Civil Actions Over $2,500* 200 Ball Ave, Tylertown, MS 39667. 8AM-N; 1-5PM. **601-876-5677**, Fax: 601-876-4077. ✉🖐

Chancery Court *Probate* PO Box 351, Tylertown, MS 39667. 8AM-5PM. **601-876-3553**, Fax: 601-876-6026.

Warren County

Circuit & County Court *Felony, Misdemeanor, Civil* PO Box 351, Vicksburg, MS 39181. 8AM-5PM. **601-636-3961**. ✉🖐

Chancery Court *Probate* PO Box 351, Vicksburg, MS 39181. 8AM-5PM. **601-636-4415**, Fax: 601-630-8016.

Washington County

Circuit & County Court *Felony, Misdemeanor, Civil* PO Box 1276,

Greenville, MS 38702. 8AM-5PM. **662-378-2747**, Fax: 662-334-2698. Fax ☒ ⚕

Chancery Court *Probate* PO Box 309, Greenville, MS 38702-0309. 8AM-5PM. **662-332-1595**, Fax: 662-334-2725.

Wayne County

Circuit Court *Felony, Civil Actions Over $2,500* PO Box 428, Waynesboro, MS 39367. 8AM-5PM. **601-735-1171**, Fax: 601-735-6261. Fax ☒ ⚕

Chancery Court *Probate* Courthouse, 609 Azalea Dr, Waynesboro, MS 39367. 8-5. **601-735-2873**, Fax: 601-735-6224.

Webster County

Circuit Court *Felony, Civil Actions Over $2,500* PO Box 308, Walthall, MS 39771. 8AM-5PM. **662-258-6287**, Fax: 662-258-7686. Fax ☒ ⚕

Chancery Court *Probate* PO Box 398, Walthall, MS 39771. 8AM-5PM. **662-258-4131**, Fax: 662-258-6657.

Wilkinson County

Circuit Court *Felony, Civil Actions Over $2,500* PO Box 327, Woodville, MS 39669. 8:00AM-5:00PM. **601-888-6697**, Fax: 601-888-6984. ☒ ⚕

Chancery Court *Probate* PO Box 516, Woodville, MS 39669. 8AM-5PM. **601-888-4381**, Fax: 601-888-6776.

Winston County

Circuit Court *Felony, Civil Actions Over $2,500* PO Drawer 785, Louisville, MS 39339. 8AM-5PM. **662-773-3581**, Fax: 662-773-7192. You may email requests to kim@winstoncounty.org. Fax ☒ ⚕ Email

Chancery Court *Probate* PO Drawer 69, Louisville, MS 39339. 8AM-5PM. **662-773-3631**, Fax: 662-773-8814.

Yalobusha County

Coffeeville Circuit Court *Felony, Civil Actions Over $2,500* PO Box 260, Coffeeville, MS 38922. 8AM-5PM. **662-675-8187**, Fax: 662-675-8004. ☎ Fax ☒ ⚕

Water Valley Circuit Court *Felony, Civil Actions Over $2,500* PO Box 1431, Water Valley, MS 38965. 8AM-5PM. **662-473-1341**, Fax: 662-473-5020. Fax ☒ ⚕

Chancery Court *Probate* PO Box 260, Coffeeville, MS 38922. 8-N, 1-5PM. **662-675-2716**, Fax 662-675-8004/473-3622.

Chancery Court *Probate* PO Box 664, Water Valley, MS 38965. 8AM-5PM. **662-473-2091**, Fax: 662-473-3622.

Yazoo County

Circuit & County Court *Felony, Misdemeanor, Civil* PO Box 108, Yazoo City, MS 39194. 8AM-5PM. **662-746-1872**. ☒ ⚕

Chancery Court *Probate* PO Box 68, Yazoo City, MS 39194. 8AM-5PM. **662-746-2661**, Fax: 662-746-3893.

Missouri

State Court Administration: State Court Administrator, 2112 Industrial Dr., PO Box 104480, Jefferson City, MO, 65109; 573-751-4377, Fax: 573-751-5540. www.osca.state.mo.us

Court Structure: The Circuit Court is the court of general jurisdiction. There are 45 circuits comprised of 114 county circuit courts and one independent city court. There are also Associate Circuit Courts with limited jurisdiction and some counties have Combined Courts, a growing trend. Municipal Courts only have jurisdiction over traffic and ordinance violations.

Online Access: Casenet, a limited but growing online system, is available at www.courts.mo.gov/casenet. The system includes 75 counties (with more projected) as well as the Eastern, Western, and Southern Appellate Courts, the Supreme Court, and Fine Collection Center. Cases can be searched case number, filing date, or litigant name. One may search supreme and appellate court opinions at the home page.

Additional Information: Starting in 2004, many circuit and associate courts no longer accept mail or fax requests to perform criminal record searches. Instead, the court instructs you to forward your mail criminal search request to the MO State Highway Patrol Criminal Records Division, PO Box 563, Jefferson City, MO 65102. 573-526-6288 (instructions) or 573-526-6153 (voice); Fax 573-751-9382. $5.00 check or money order required for search. Note that most courts participate in the MO CaseNet online system where record searches can be perfomed for free on the Internet.

While the Missouri State Statutes set the Civil Case limit at $25,000 for the Associate Courts, and over $25,000 for the Circuit Courts, a great many Missouri County Courts have adopted their own Local Court Rules regarding civil cases and the monetary limits. Presumably, Local Court's Rules are setup to allow the county to choose which court - Circuit or Associate - to send a case. This may depend on the court's case load, but generally, the cases are assigned more by "the nature of the case" and less by the monetary amount involved. Often, Local Court Rules are found where both the Circuit and the Associate Court are located in the same building, or share the same offices and perhaps the same phones. A solution for court record searches is to use this source to find a telephone number of a County's Court Clerk, and call to determine the court location of the case.

Adair County

Circuit Court *Felony, Misdemeanor, Civil Actions Over $25,000* PO Box 690, Kirksville, MO 63501. 8AM-5PM. **660-665-2552**, Fax: 660-665-3420. ⚕

Associate Circuit Court *Misdemeanor, Civil Actions Under $25,000, Eviction,* *Small Claims, Probate* Courthouse, Kirksville, MO 63501. 8AM-5PM. **660-665-3877**, Fax: 660-785-3222. (probable in person only).

Andrew County

Circuit Court *Felony, Civil Actions Over $45,000* PO Box 208 Division I, Savannah, MO 64485. 8AM-5PM. **816-324-4221**, Fax: 816-324-5667. 🖐️🖥️

Associate Circuit Court *Misdemeanor, Civil Actions Under $45,000, Eviction, Small Claims, Probate* PO Box 49, Savannah, MO 64485. 8AM-5PM. **816-324-3921**, Fax: 816-324-3191. ✉️🖐️🖥️

Atchison County

Circuit Court *Felony, Misdemeanor, Civil Actions Over $25,000* PO Box 280, Rock Port, MO 64482. 8:30AM-4:30PM. **660-744-2707**, Fax: 660-744-5705. 🖐️

Associate Division *Misdemeanor, Civil Actions Under $25,000, Eviction, Small Claims, Probate, Traffic* PO Box 187, Rock Port, MO 64482. 8AM-4:30PM. **660-744-2700**, Fax: 660-744-6100. 🖐️

Audrain County

Circuit Court *Felony, Misdemeanor, Civil Actions Over $25,000* www.audrain-county.org Courthouse, 101 N Jefferson, Mexico, MO 65265. 8AM-5PM. Fax: 573-581-3237. Civil phone: 573-473-5842, crim: 573-473-5840. 🖐️🖥️

Associate Circuit Court Div II *Misdemeanor, Civil Actions Under $25,000, Eviction, Small Claims, Probate* Courthouse, 101 N Jefferson, Rm 205, Mexico, MO 65265. 8AM-5PM. **573-473-5850**, Fax: 573-581-3364 Probate: 573-473-5854. ✉️🖐️🖥️

Barry County

Circuit Court *Felony, Misdemeanor, Civil Actions Over $25,000* 102 West St #1 Barry County Courthouse, Cassville, MO 65625. 8-4PM. **417-847-2361**. 🖐️

Associate Circuit Court *Misdemeanor, Civil Actions Under $25,000, Eviction, Small Claims, Probate* 102 West St #2 Judicial Center, Cassville, MO 65625. 7:30AM-4PM. Civil phone: 417-847-2127, crim: 417-847-6557. ✉️🖐️

Barton County

Circuit & Associate Court *Felony, Misdemeanor, Civil, Eviction, Small Claims, Probate* Courthouse, 1007 Broadway, Lamar, MO 64759. 8AM-4:30PM. **417-682-2444**, Fax: 417-682-2960. ✉️🖥️🖐️

Bates County

Circuit Court *Felony, Misdemeanor, Civil Actions Over $25,000* http://tacnet.missouri.org/~court27/ Bates County Courthouse, Butler, MO 64730. 8AM-4:30PM. **660-679-5171**, Fax: 660-679-4446. Fax✉️🖐️🖥️

Associate Circuit Court *Misdemeanor, Civil Actions Under $25,000, Eviction, Small Claims, Probate* Courthouse, Butler, MO 64730. 8:30AM-4PM. **660-679-3311**. ✉️🖥️

Benton County

Circuit & Associate Court *Felony, Misdemeanor, Civil Actions, Eviction, Small Claims, Probate* www.positech.net/~dcourt PO Box 37, Warsaw, MO 65355. 8AM-4:30PM. **660-438-7712**, Fax: 660-438-5755. Associate court clerk: 660-438-6231. 🖐️🖥️

Bollinger County

Circuit Court *Felony, Misdemeanor, Civil Actions Over $25,000* PO Box 949, Marble Hill, MO 63764. 8-4PM. **573-238-1900 Ext 6**, Fax: 573-238-2773. 🖐️🖥️

Associate Circuit Court *Misd., Civil Actions Under $25,000, Eviction, Small Claims, Probate* PO Box 1040, Marble Hill, MO 63764-1040. 8AM-4PM. **573-238-1900 ext 4**, Fax 573-238-4511. 🖐️🖥️

Boone County

Circuit and Associate Court *Felony, Misdemeanor, Civil, Eviction, Small Claims, Probate* 705 E Walnut, Columbia, MO 65201. 8AM-5PM. **573-886-4000**, Fax: 573-886-4044 Probate: 573-886-4090. 🖥️🖐️

Buchanan County

Circuit & Associate Court *Felony, Misdemeanor, Civil, Eviction, Small Claims* 411 Jules St Rm 331, St Joseph, MO 64501. 8AM-5PM. **816-271-1462**, Fax: 816-271-1538. 🖐️🖥️

Probate Court Buchanan County Courthouse 411 Jules St, Rm 333, St Joseph, MO 64501. 8AM-5PM. **816-271-1477**, Fax: 816-271-1538.

Butler County

Circuit Court *Felony, Misdemeanor, Civil Actions Over $25,000* Courthouse, Poplar Bluff, MO 63901. 7:30AM-4PM. **573-686-8082**, Fax: 573-686-8094. 🖐️

Associate Circuit Court *Misdemeanor, Civil Actions Under $25,000, Eviction, Small Claims, Probate* Courthouse, Poplar Bluff, MO 63901. 7:30AM-4PM. **573-686-8087**, Fax: 573-686-8093 Probate: 573-686-8073. Probate records are in a separate office. Fax✉️🖐️

Caldwell County

Circuit and Associate Court *Felony, Misdemeanor, Civil, Eviction, Small Claims, Probate* PO Box 68, Kingston, MO 64650. 7:30AM-4:30PM. **816-586-2581**, Fax: 816-586-2333. ☎️✉️🖐️

Callaway County

Circuit & Associate Court *Felony, Misdemeanor, Civil Actions, Eviction, Small Claims, Probate* 10 E 5th St, Fulton, MO 65251. 8AM-5PM. **573-642-0780**, Fax: 573-642-0700. 🖐️🖥️

Camden County

Circuit Court *Felony, Misd., Civil Over $25,000* www.camdenmo.org 1 Court Circle, #8, Camdenton, MO 65020. 8:30AM-4:30PM. **573-346-4440**, Fax: 573-346-5422. 🖐️

Associate Circuit Court *Misdemeanor, Civil Under $25,000, Eviction, Small Claims, Probate* www.camdenmo.org 1 Court Circle #8, Camdenton, MO 65020. 8:00AM-5:00PM. **573-346-4440**, Fax: 573-346-5422. Civil phone: X261, crim: X305. 🖐️

Cape Girardeau County

Circuit & Associate Circuit Court - Civil Division *Civil* 44 N Lorimier PO Box 2047, Cape Girardeau, MO 63702. 8AM-4:30PM. **573-335-8253**, Fax: 573-331-2565. Access civil records-✉️🖐️🖥️

Circuit Court - Criminal Division I & II *Felony, Misdemeanor* 100 Court St, Jackson, MO 63755. 8AM-4:30PM. **573-243-8446** (misdemeanors), Fax: 573-204-2405. Criminal phone: 573-243-1755 (felo.). ✉️🖐️🖥️

Carroll County

Circuit Court *Felony, Misd, Civil Actions Over $25,000* PO Box 245, Carrollton, MO 64633. 8:30AM-4:30PM. **660-542-1466**, Fax: 660-542-1444. Fax✉️🖐️🖥️

Associate Circuit Court *Misdemeanor, Civil Actions Under $25,000, Eviction, Small Claims, Probate* Courthouse 8 S Main, #1, Carrollton, MO 64633.

8:30AM-4:30PM. **660-542-1818**, Fax: 660-542-1877. 🖐️🖥️

Carter County

Circuit Court *Felony, Misdemeanor, Civil Actions Over $20,000* PO Box 578, Van Buren, MO 63965. 8AM-4PM. **573-323-4513**, Fax: 573-323-4885. 🖐️🖥️

Associate Circuit Court *Misdemeanor, Civil Actions Under $20,000, Eviction, Small Claims, Probate* PO Box 328, Van Buren, MO 63965. 8-4PM. **573-323-4344**, Fax: 573-323-8914. ☎️Fax✉️🖐️🖥️

Cass County

Circuit Court *Felony, Misdemeanor, Civil Actions Over $25,000* 102 E Wall, Harrisonville, MO 64701. 8AM-5:00PM. **816-380-8230**, Fax: 816-380-8225. Civil phone: 816-380-8235/8240, Felony court: 816-380-8229. Misdemeanor Court: 816-380-8226. ☎️✉️🖐️

Associate Circuit Court *Misdemeanor, Civil Actions Under $25,000, Eviction, Small Claims, Felony* 2501 W Well St, Harrisonville, MO 64701. 8AM-4:30PM. **816-380-8200**, Fax 816-380-8195. ✉️🖐️

Probate Court 2501 W. Wall St, Harrisonville, MO 64701. 8AM-4:30PM. **816-380-8217**, Fax: 816-380-8215.

Cedar County

Circuit & Associate Court *Felony, Misd., Civil Actions, Eviction, Small Claims, Probate* PO Box 665, Stockton, MO 65785. 8AM-4:30PM. **417-276-6700**, Fax: 417-276-5001. Fax✉️🖐️🖥️

Chariton County

Circuit Court *Felony, Misdemeanor, Civil Actions Over $25,000* PO Box 112, Keytesville, MO 65261. 8:30AM-4:30PM. **660-288-3602**, Fax: 660-288-3763. Fax✉️🖐️🖥️

Associate Circuit Court *Misdemeanor, Civil Actions Under $25,000, Eviction, Small Claims, Probate* 306 S Cherry, Keytesville, MO 65261. 8AM-4:30PM. **660-288-3271**, Fax: 660-288-1511. ☎️Fax✉️🖐️

Christian County

Circuit Court *Felony, Misdemeanor, Civil Actions Over $45,000* www.geocities.com/circuit38/ PO Box 278, Ozark, MO 65721. 8AM-4:30PM. **417-**

581-6372, Fax: 417-581-0391 Probate: 417-581-4523. ✉️🖐️🖥️

Associate Circuit Court - Civil Division 1 *Civil Actions Under $45,000, Eviction, Small Claims* 110 W Elm St, Rm 203, Ozark, MO 65721. 8AM-4:30PM. **417-581-2425**. ☎️✉️🖐️🖥️

Associate Circuit Court - Criminal Division 2 *Misdemeanor, Probate* 110 W Elm St, Rm 105, Ozark, MO 65721. 8AM-4:30PM. **417-581-4523**, Fax: 417-581-1443. Court will not perform name searches and asks searchers to contact the MSHP at 573-526-6288. 🖐️🖥️

Clark County

Circuit Court *Felony, Misd., Civil Over $45,000* 111 E Court, #2, Kahoka, MO 63445. 8AM-4PM. **660-727-3292**, Fax: 660-727-1051. ☎️Fax✉️🖐️🖥️

Associate Circuit Court *Misdemeanor, Civil Actions Under $45,000, Eviction, Small Claims, Probate* 113 W Court, Kahoka, MO 63445. 8AM-4PM. **660-727-3628**, Fax: 660-727-2544. ✉️Fax🖐️

Clay County

Circuit Court *Felony, Misdemeanor, Civil Actions Over $25,000* www.circuit7.net/ PO Box 218, Liberty, MO 64069-0218. 8AM-5PM. **816-792-7706**, Fax: 816-792-7778. 🖐️🖥️

Associate Circuit Court *Misdemeanor, Civil Actions Under $25,000, Eviction, Small Claims, Probate* www.circuit7.net PO Box 218, Liberty, MO 64069-0218. 8AM-5PM. **816-792-7706**, Fax: 816-792-7778. ✉️🖐️🖥️

Clinton County

Circuit Court *Felony, Misdemeanor, Civil Actions Over $25,000* PO Box 275, Plattsburg, MO 64477. 8AM-5PM. **816-539-3731**, Fax: 816-539-3893. 🖐️

Associate Circuit Court *Misdemeanor, Civil Actions Under $45,000, Eviction, Small Claims, Probate* PO Box 383, Plattsburg, MO 64477. 8AM-4:30PM. **816-539-3755**, Fax: 816-539-3439 Probate: 816-539-3298. Fax✉️🖐️

Cole County

Circuit & Associate Court *Felony, Misdemeanor, Civil Actions, Eviction, Small Claims, Probate* PO Box 1870, Jefferson City, MO 65102-1870. 7:30AM-4:30PM. Fax: 573-635-0796. Civil phone:

573-634-9151, crim phone: 573-634-9171. 🖐️🖥️Fax✉️

Cooper County

Circuit Court *Felony, Misdemeanor, Civil Actions Over $25,000* 200 Main St, Rm 26, Boonville, MO 65233. 8:30AM-5:00PM. **660-882-2232**, Fax: 660-882-2043. ✉️🖐️🖥️

Associate Circuit Court *Misdemeanor, Civil Actions Under $25,000, Eviction, Small Claims, Probate* 200 Main, Rm 31, Boonville, MO 65233. 8:30AM-5PM. **660-882-5604**, Fax: 660-882-8747. ✉️🖐️

Crawford County

Circuit Court *Felony, Misdemeanor, Civil Actions Over $25,000* PO Box 177, Steelville, MO 65565. 8AM-4:30PM. **573-775-2866**, Fax: 573-775-2452. ✉️🖐️🖥️

Associate Circuit Court *Misdemeanor, Civil Actions Under $25,000, Eviction, Small Claims, Probate* PO Box B.C., Steelville, MO 65565. 8AM-5PM. **573-775-2149**, Fax: 573-775-4010. Court will look up specific case file is case number given. 🖥️

Dade County

Circuit & Associate Court *Felony, Misdemeanor, Civil Actions, Eviction, Small Claims, Probate* Courthouse, Greenfield, MO 65661. 8AM-4PM. **417-637-2271**, Fax: 417-637-5055. ✉️🖐️🖥️

Dallas County

Circuit Court *Felony, Misdemeanor, Civil Actions Over $25,000.* www.positech.net/~dcourt PO Box 373 108 S Maple St, Buffalo, MO 65622. 7:30AM-4PM. **417-345-2243**, Fax: 417-345-5539. 🖐️🖥️

Associate Circuit Court *Misdemeanor, Civil Actions Under $45,000, Eviction, Small Claims, Probate* PO Box 1150, Buffalo, MO 65622. 8AM-N, 1-4PM. **417-345-7641**, Fax: 417-345-5358. ☎️🖐️🖥️

Daviess County

Circuit Court *Felony, Misdemeanor, Civil Actions Over $45,000* PO Box 337, Gallatin, MO 64640. 8AM-4:30PM. **660-663-2932**, Fax: 660-663-3876. ☎️Fax✉️🖐️

Key: Symbols refer to criminal records access unless otherwise noted. phone-☎️ mail-✉️ fax-**Fax** in person-🖐️ online-🖥️ email-**Email**

Associate Division Circuit Court *Misdemeanor, Civil Actions Under $45,000, Eviction, Small Claims, Probate* Courthouse PO Box 233, 102 N Main St #6, Gallatin, MO 64640. 8AM-4:30PM. **660-663-2532**. Probate: 660-663-2532. Probate records unavailable before 1890 due to Courthouse fire. ✉ ✋

De Kalb County

Circuit Court *Felony, Civil Actions Over $45,000* PO Box 248, Maysville, MO 64469. 8:30AM-4:30PM. **816-449-2602**, Fax: 816-449-2440. ✋

Associate Circuit Court *Misdemeanor, Civil Actions Under $45,000, Eviction, Small Claims, Probate* PO Box 248, Maysville, MO 64469. 8:30AM-4:30PM. **816-449-5400**, Fax: 816-449-2440. Probate: 816-449-5400. Court will not do name searches. ✋

Dent County

Circuit Court *Felony, Misdemeanor, Civil Actions Over $25,000* 112 E 5th St, Salem, MO 65560. 8AM-4:30PM. **573-729-3931**, Fax: 573-729-9414. ✋ 💻

Associate Circuit Court *Misdemeanor, Civil Actions Under $25,000, Eviction, Small Claims, Probate* 112 E 5th St, Salem, MO 65560. 8AM-4:30PM. **573-729-3134**, Fax: 573-729-5172. Probate: 573-729-3134. Small Claims and Probate fax is 573-729-5172. ✉ **Fax** ✋ 💻

Douglas County

Circuit Court *Felony, Misdemeanor, Civil Actions Over $25,000* PO Box 249, Ava, MO 65608. 8AM-4:30PM. **417-683-4713**, Fax: 417-683-2794. ☎ ✉ ✋

Associate Circuit Court *Misdemeanor, Civil Actions Under $25,000, Eviction, Small Claims, Probate* PO Box 276 203 SE 2nd St, Ava, MO 65608. 8AM-4:30PM. **417-683-2114**, Fax: 417-683-3121. ✋

Dunklin County

Circuit Court Division I *Felony, Misdemeanor, Civil Actions Over $25,000* PO Box 567, Kennett, MO 63857. 8:30AM-4:30PM. **573-888-2456**, Fax: 573-888-0319. ✋ 💻

Associate Circuit Court *Felony, Misdemeanor, Civil Actions Under $25,000, Eviction, Small Claims, Probate* Courthouse Rm 103, Kennett, MO 63857. 8AM-4:30PM. **573-888-3378**, Fax: 573-

888-0754 Probate: 573-888-3272. Probate address is Rm #202. ✋ 💻

Franklin County

Circuit Court *Felony, Civil Actions Over $25,000* 300 E Main St, Rm 301, Union, MO 63084. 8AM-4:30PM. **636-583-6303**. ✉ 💻 ✋

Associate Circuit Court *Misdemeanor, Civil Actions Under $25,000, Eviction, Small Claims, Probate* 120 S Church Sreet, #B, Union, MO 63084. 8AM-4:30PM. **636-583-6326**. 💻 ✋

Gasconade County

Circuit Court *Felony, Misdemeanor, Civil Actions Over $25,000* 119 E 1st St, Rm 6, Hermann, MO 65041-1182. 8AM-4:30PM. **573-486-2632**, Fax: 573-486-5812. ✋ 💻

Associate Circuit Court *Misdemeanor, Civil Actions Under $25,000, Eviction, Small Claims, Probate* 119 E. 1st St. Rm 3, Hermann, MO 65041. 8AM-4:30PM. **573-486-2321**, Fax: 573-486-5812. 💻 ✋

Gentry County

Circuit Court *Felony, Misdemeanor, Civil Actions Over $25,000* PO Box 27, Albany, MO 64402. 8AM-4:30PM. **660-726-3618**, Fax: 660-726-4102. ✉ ✋

Associate Circuit Court *Misdemeanor, Civil Actions Under $25,000, Eviction, Small Claims, Probate* 200 W Clay St, Albany, MO 64402. 8AM-4:30PM. **660-726-3411**, Fax: 660-726-4102. ✋ ✉ fax.

Greene County

Circuit Court *Felony, Civil Actions Over $25,000* www.greenecountymo.org 1010 Booneville, Springfield, MO 65802. 8AM-5AM. **417-868-4074**, Fax: 417-868-4168. ✉ ✋ 💻

Associate Circuit Court *Misdemeanor, Civil Under $25,000, Eviction, Small Claim, Probate* www.greenecountymo.org 1010 N Boonville, Springfield, MO 65802. 8AM-5PM. **417-868-4110**, Probate: 417-868-4027. Probate is a separate court at the same address. ✉ ✋ 💻

Grundy County

Circuit Court *Felony, Misdemeanor, Civil Actions Over $25,000* Courthouse 700 Main St, PO Box 196, Trenton, MO 64683. 8:30AM-4:30PM. **660-359-6605**, Fax: 660-359-6604. Access records ✋ 💻

Associate Circuit Court *Misdemeanor, Civil Actions Under $25,000, Eviction, Small Claims, Probate* PO Box 26 7th and Main Sts., Trenton, MO 64683. 8AM-4:30PM. **660-359-6606/6909**. ✋ 💻

Harrison County

Circuit & Associate Court *Felony, Misdemeanor, Civil Actions, Eviction, Small Claims, Probate* PO Box 189, Bethany, MO 64424. 8AM-4:30PM. **660-425-6425/6432**, Fax 660-425-6390. ✋ 💻

Henry County

Circuit & Associate Court *Felony, Misdemeanor, Civil, Small Claims* http://tacnet.missouri.org/~court27 PO Box 487, Clinton, MO 64735. 8AM-4:30PM. **660-885-7232**, Fax: 660-885-8247. ✋ 💻

Hickory County

Circuit Court *Felony, Misdemeanor, Civil Actions Over $45,000* www.positech.net/~dcourt PO Box 101, Hermitage, MO 65668. 8AM-4:30PM. **417-745-6421**, Fax: 417-745-6670. ✉ ✋ 💻

Associate Circuit Court *Misdemeanor, Civil Under $45,000, Eviction, Small Claims, Probate* www.positech.net/~dcourt PO Box 75 Courthouse Square, Hermitage, MO 65668. 8AM-N; 12:30PM-4:30PM. **417-745-6822**, Fax: 417-745-6670. ✉ ✋ 💻

Holt County

Circuit Court *Felony, Misdemeanor, Civil Actions Over $25,000* PO Box 318, Oregon, MO 64473. 8AM-4:30PM. **660-446-3301**, Fax: 660-446-3328. **Fax** ✉ ✋

Associate Circuit Court *Misdemeanor, Civil Actions Under $25,000, Eviction, Small Claims, Probate* PO Box 173, Oregon, MO 64473. 8:30AM-4:30PM. **660-446-3380**. ✋

Howard County

Circuit Court *Felony, Civil Actions Over $30,000* 1 Courthouse Square, Fayette, MO 65248. 8:30AM-4:30PM. **660-248-2194**, Fax: 660-248-1075. ✋ 💻

Associate Circuit Court *Misdemeanor, Civil Actions Under $45,000, Eviction, Small Claims, Probate* PO Box 370, Fayette, MO 65248. 8:30AM-4:30PM. **660-248-3326**, Fax: 660-248-1075. Probate: 660-248-3326. ✋ 💻

Key: Symbols refer to criminal records access unless otherwise noted. phone- ☎ mail-✉ fax-**Fax** in person- ✋ online- 💻 email-**Email**

Howell County

Circuit Court *Felony, Misdemeanor, Civil Actions Over $25,000* PO Box 967, West Plains, MO 65775. 8AM-4:30PM. **417-256-3741**, Fax: 417-256-4650. 🖐️💻

Associate Circuit Court *Misd., Civil Actions Under $45,000, Eviction, Small Claims, Probate* 222 Courthouse, West Plains, MO 65775. 8AM-4:30PM. **417-256-4050**, Fax: 417-256-5826. ✉️🖐️💻

Iron County

Circuit Court *Felony, Civil Actions Over $25,000* PO Box 24, Ironton, MO 63650. 8AM-4PM. **573-546-2811**, Fax: 573-546-2166. 🖐️💻

Associate Circuit Court *Misd., Civil Actions Under $25,000, Eviction, Small Claims, Probate* PO Box 325, Ironton, MO 63650. 8:30AM-4PM. **573-546-2511**, Fax: 573-546-6006. **Fax**✉️🖐️💻

Jackson County

Independence Circuit Court - Civil Annex *Civil, Eviction, Small Claims, Probate* 308 W Kansas #310, Independence, MO 64050. 8AM-5PM. **816-881-3943**, Fax: 816-881-3681 Probate: 816-881-4552. Direct mail criminal record searches to #310; civil to #204. This court is on the same computer system as Kansas City for civil cases, but files maintained separately. Access civil records-🖐️💻

Circuit Court - Civil Division *Civil, Eviction, Small Claims, Probate* www.16thcircuit.org 415 E 12th, 3rd Fl, Kansas City, MO 64106. 8AM-5PM. **816-881-3926; 881-3522**, Fax: 816-881-4327 Probate: 816-881-3755. Has combined computer system with the Independence civil court. Access civil records-💻🖐️

Circuit Court - Criminal Division *Felony, Misd.* www.16thcircuit.org 1315 Locust, 2nd Fl, Kansas City, MO 64106. 8AM-5PM. **816-881-4350**, Fax: 816-881-3420. Court will only pull file copies if a case number is given. 💻🖐️

Jasper County

Each of the 4 courts in the county must be searched for an accurate overall search.

Joplin Circuit Court *Felony, Misd., Civil Actions Over $45,000* Courthouse, 3rd Fl 601 S Pearl, Joplin, MO 64801. 8:00AM-N, 1-5:00PM. **417-625-4310**. Although the Joplin Circuit and Associate Circuit

courts merged, the records are only comingled from 07/00 forward. 🖐️💻

Carthage Circuit Court *Felony, Misdemeanor, Civil Actions, Eviction, Small Claims, Probate* www.osca.state.mo.us/circuits/index.nsf Courthouse, Rm 303 302 S. Main St, Carthage, MO 64836. 8:00AM-5:00PM. **417-358-0441**, Fax: 417-358-0461. Carthage Circuit and Associate Circuit courts merged, but records are only comingled from 07/00 forward. ✉️🖐️💻

Joplin Associate Circuit Court *Misdemeanor, Civil Actions Under $45,000, Eviction, Small Claims, Probate* Courthouse, 2nd Fl 601 S Pearl, Joplin, MO 64801. 8AM-N, 1-5PM. **417-625-4316**, Fax: 417-625-4340. ✉️**Fax**🖐️💻

Carthage Associate Circuit Court *Misdemeanor, Civil Actions Under $45,000, Eviction, Small Claims, Probate* Courthouse, Rm 304 302 S. Main St, Carthage, MO 64836. 8:30AM-N, 1-4:30PM. **417-358-0450**, Fax: 417-358-0460. 🖐️💻

Mercer County

Associate Circuit Court *Misdemeanor, Civil Actions Under $45,000, Eviction, Small Claims, Probate* Courthouse Rm 304 302 S Main St, Carthage, MO 64836. 8:30AM-4:30PM. **417-358-0450**, Fax: 417-358-0460. 🖐️💻

Jefferson County

Circuit & Associate Court - Civil Division *Civil Actions, Eviction, Small Claims, Probate* PO Box 100, Hillsboro, MO 63050. 8AM-5PM. **636-797-5443**, Fax: 636-797-5073. Access civil records- 📞**Fax**✉️🖐️

Circuit & Associate Court - Criminal Division *Felony, Misdemeanor* PO Box 100, Hillsboro, MO 63050. 8AM-4:30PM. **636-797-5370**, Fax: 636-797-5073. ✉️**Fax**🖐️

Johnson County

Circuit Court *Felony, Civil Actions Over $25,000* Johnson County Justice Ctr 101 W Market, Warrensburg, MO 64093. 8AM-4:30PM. **660-422-7413**, Fax: 660-422-7417. 🖐️✉️

Associate Circuit Court *Misdemeanor, Civil Actions Under $45,000, Eviction, Small Claims* Johnson County Courthouse 300 N Holden #304,

Warrensburg, MO 64093. 8AM-4:30PM. **660-422-7410**. ✉️🖐️

Knox County

Circuit Court *Felony, Misdemeanor, Civil Actions Over $25,000* PO Box 116, Edina, MO 63537. 8:30AM-N, 1-4PM. **660-397-2305**, Fax 660-397-3331. ✉️🖐️

Associate Circuit Court *Misdemeanor, Civil Actions Under $25,000, Eviction, Small Claims, Probate* PO Box 126, Edina, MO 63537. 8:30AM-4PM. **660-397-3146**, Fax: 660-397-3331. ✉️🖐️

Laclede County

Circuit & Associate Court *Felony, Misdemeanor, Civil. Eviction, Small Claims, Probate* 200 N Adams St, Lebanon, MO 65536. 8AM-4PM. **417-532-2471, 532-9196**, Fax: 417-532-3683. 📞**Fax**✉️🖐️

Lafayette County

Circuit & Associate Court *Felony, Misdemeanor, Civil Actions, Eviction, Small Claims, Probate* PO Box 10, Lexington, MO 64067. 8AM-4:30PM. **660-259-6101**, Fax: 660-259-6148 Probate: 660-259-2324. Circuit and Associate courts combined as of 9/2004; telephone numbers may change. 🖐️💻

Lawrence County

Circuit Court *Felony, Civil Actions Over $25,000* One Courthouse Square #201, Mt Vernon, MO 65712. 8AM-4:30PM. **417-466-2471**. ✉️🖐️

Associate Circuit Court *Misdemeanor, Civil Actions Under $45,000, Eviction, Small Claims, Probate* 1 Courthouse Sq, #102, Mt Vernon, MO 65712. 8:30AM-5PM. **417-466-2463**, Probate: 417-466-2105. ✉️🖐️

Lewis County

Circuit & Associate Court *Felony, Misd, Civil Actions, Eviction, Small Claims, Probate* PO Box 97, Monticello, MO 63457. 8AM-N,1-4:30PM. **573-767-5232**, Fax: 573-767-5342. 🖐️

Lincoln County

Circuit & Associate Court *Felony, Misdemeanor, Civil Actions, Eviction, Small Claims, Probate* Lincoln County Justice Ctr 45 Business park Dr, Troy, MO 63379. 8:00AM-4:30PM. **636-528-6300**. 🖐️💻

Linn County

Circuit & Associate Court *Felony, Misdemeanor, Civil Actions, Eviction, Small Claims, Probate* PO Box 84 108 S High St, Linneus, MO 64653-0084. 8AM-N, 1-4:30PM. **660-895-5212**, Fax: 660-895-5277. Fax✉🖑🖥

Consolidated Circuit Court *Misdemeanor, Civil Actions Under $25,000, Eviction, Small Claims, Probate* Box 84, Linneus, MO 64653. 8AM-4:30PM. **660-895-5212**, Fax: 660-895-5277. ☎✉🖑🖥

Livingston County

Circuit Court *Felony, Civil Actions Over $25,000* 700 Webster St, Chillicothe, MO 64601. 8:00AM-5:00PM. **660-646-1718**, Fax: 660-646-2734. 🖑

Associate Circuit Court *Misdemeanor, Civil Actions Under $25,000, Eviction, Small Claims, Probate* Livingston County Courthouse, #8, Chillicothe, MO 64601. Public hours: 8:30AM-4:30PM; Office hours: 8AM-5PM. **660-646-3103**, Fax: 660-646-8014. ☎Fax✉🖑

McDonald County

Circuit & Associate Court *Felony, Misdemeanor, Civil, Small Claims, Probate* PO Box 157, Pineville, MO 64856. 8AM-4:30PM. **417-223-7515**, Fax: 417-223-4125. Fax✉🖑🖥

Macon County

Circuit Court *Felony, Misdemeanor, Civil Actions Over $25,000* PO Box 382, Macon, MO 63552. 8:AM-5PM. **660-385-4631**, Fax: 660-385-4235. Civil phone: 660-385-4631, crim phone: 660-385-4631. Fax✉🖑🖥

Associate Circuit Court *Misdemeanor, Civil Actions Under $25,000, Eviction, Small Claims, Probate* PO Box 491, Macon, MO 63552. 8AM-4:30PM. **660-385-3531**, Fax: 660-385-3132. 🖑🖥

Madison County

Circuit Court *Felony, Misdemeanor, Civil Actions Over $25,000* PO Box 470, Fredericktown, MO 63645-0470. 8-5PM. **573-783-2102**, Fax: 573-783-2715. 🖑🖥

Associate Circuit Court *Misdemeanor, Civil Actions Under $25,000, Small Claims, Probate, Traffic* PO Box 521, Fredericktown, MO 63645. 8AM-5PM. **573-783-3105**, Fax: 573-783-5920. ☎Fax✉🖑🖥

Maries County

Circuit Court *Felony, Misdemeanor, Civil Actions Over $25,000* PO Box 213, Vienna, MO 65582. 8AM-4PM. **573-422-3338**, Fax: 573-422-3976. Fax✉

Associate Circuit Court *Misdemeanor, Civil Actions Under $25,000, Eviction, Small Claims, Probate* PO Box 490, Vienna, MO 65582. 8AM-4PM. **573-422-3303**, Fax: 573-422-3976. Most civil cases are directed to the Circuit Court regardless of limit. 🖑

Marion County

Circuit Court Division 2 *Felony, Misdemeanor, Civil Actions Over $45,000* 906 Broadway, Rm 105, Hannibal, MO 63401. 8:30AM-N, 1-5PM. **573-221-0198**, Fax: 573-221-9328. Jurisdiction is Twps of Miller and Mason only. 🖑

Circuit Court Division 1 *Felony, Civil Actions Over $25,000* PO Box 392, 100 S Main St, Palmyra, MO 63461. 8:30AM-N, 1-5PM. **573-769-2550**, Fax: 573-769-6012. 🖑

Palmyra Associate Circuit Court *Misdemeanor, Civil Actions Under $45,000, Eviction, Small Claims, Probate* PO Box 449 100 S. Main St, Palmyra, MO 63461. 8AM-N, 1-5PM. **573-769-2318**, Fax: 573-769-4558. 🖑

Hannibal Associate Circuit Court *Misdemeanor, Civil Actions Under $45,000, Eviction, Small Claims, Probate* 906 Broadway, Hannibal, MO 63401. 8AM-5PM. **573-221-0288**, Fax: 573-221-0945. 🖑

Mercer County

Circuit Court *Felony, Misdemeanor, Civil Actions Over $45,000* Courthouse 802 E Main, Princeton, MO 64673. 8:30AM-N, 1-4:30PM. **660-748-4335**, Fax: 660-748-4339. Access records-🖑🖥

Associate Circuit Court *Misdemeanor, Civil Actions Under $45,000, Eviction, Small Claims, Probate* Mercer County Courthouse 802 E Main St, Princeton, MO 64673. 8:30AM-4:30PM. **660-748-4232**, Fax: 660-748-4292. 🖑🖥

Miller County

Circuit Court *Felony, Misdemeanor, Civil Actions Over $25,000* PO Box 11, Tuscumbia, MO 65082. 8AM-4:30PM. **573-369-1980**. ☎Fax✉🖑

Associate Circuit Court *Misdemeanor, Civil Actions Under $25,000, Eviction, Small Claims, Probate* Miller County Courthouse Annex, Tuscumbia, MO 65082. 8AM-4PM. **573-369-1970**. ✉🖑

Mississippi County

Circuit & Associate Court *Felony, Misdemeanor, Civil, Small Claims, Eviction, Probate* PO Box 369, Charleston, MO 63834. 8AM-5PM. **573-683-2146 x1**, Fax: 573-683-7696. 🖑🖥

Moniteau County

Circuit Court *Felony, Misdemeanor, Civil Actions Over $25,000, Small Claims* 200 E Main, California, MO 65018. 8AM-4:30PM. **573-796-2071**. Access records🖑

Associate Circuit Court *Misdemeanor, Civil Actions Under $45,000, Eviction, Small Claims, Probate* 200 E Main, California, MO 65018. 8AM-4:30PM. **573-796-4671**. The court will not do probate record searches. 🖑

Monroe County

Circuit Court *Felony, Misdemeanor, Civil Actions Over $45,000* PO Box 227, Paris, MO 65275. 8AM-4:30PM. **660-327-5204**, Fax: 660-327-5781. ✉🖑

Associate Circuit Court *Misdemeanor, Civil Actions Under $45,000, Eviction, Small Claims, Probate* 300 N Main, Courthouse, Paris, MO 65275. 8AM-N, 1-4:30PM. **660-327-5220**, Fax: 660-327-5651. ✉🖑

Montgomery County

Circuit Court *Felony, Misdemeanor, Civil Actions Over $25,000* 211 E 3rd, Montgomery City, MO 63361. 8AM-4:30PM. **573-564-3341**, Fax: 573-564-3914. 🖥🖑

Associate Circuit Court *Misdemeanor, Civil Actions Under $25,000, Eviction, Small Claims, Probate* 211 E 3rd St, Montgomery City, MO 63361. 8:00AM-4:30PM. **573-564-3348**. 🖥🖑

Morgan County

Circuit Court *Felony, Civil Actions Over $25,000* 211 E Newton, Versailles, MO 65084. 8AM-5PM. **573-378-4413**, Fax: 573-378-5356. Access records-☎✉🖑

Associate Circuit Court *Misdemeanor, Civil Actions Under $25,000, Eviction, Small Claims, Probate* 211 E Newton St, Versailles, MO 65084. 8:30AM-5PM.

573-378-4235, Fax: 573-378-6847. Criminal phone: 573-378-4060. ☎ ✉ 👆

New Madrid County

Circuit Court *Felony, Misd., Civil Actions Over $25,000* County Courthouse 450 Main St, New Madrid, MO 63869. 8AM-4:30PM. **573-748-2228**. 👆💻

Associate Circuit Court *Misdemeanor, Civil Actions Under $25,000, Eviction, Small Claims, Probate* County Courthouse, New Madrid, MO 63869. 8AM-5PM. **573-748-5556**, Fax: 573-748-5409. ✉ 👆💻

Newton County

Circuit and Associate Court *Felony, Misdemeanor, Civil Actions, Eviction, Small Claims, Probate* PO Box 130, Neosho, MO 64850. 8AM-5PM. **417-451-8257**, Fax: 417-451-8298 Civ. Civil phone: 417-451-8257, crim: 417-451-8214, Probate: 417-451-8232. Probate is separate at 101 S Wood #204. 👆💻

Nodaway County

Circuit Court *Felony, Misd., Civil Over $25,000* 305 N Main St #206, Maryville, MO 64468. 8AM-4:30PM. **660-582-5431**, Fax: 660-582-5499. 👆

Associate Circuit Court *Misd., Civil Under $45,000, Eviction, Small Claims, Probate* 303 N Market, Courthouse Annex, Maryville, MO 64468. 8AM-N; 1-4:30PM. **660-582-2531**, Fax: 660-582-2047. Probate: 660-582-4221. 👆

Oregon County

Circuit Court *Felony, Misdemeanor, Civil Actions Over $45,000* PO Box 406, Alton, MO 65606. 8-4PM. **417-778-7460**, Fax: 417-778-7206. ☎ Fax ✉ 👆💻

Associate Circuit Court *Misdemeanor, Civil Actions Under $45,000, Eviction, Small Claims, Probate* PO Box 211, Alton, MO 65606. 8:00AM-4:00PM. **417-778-7461**, Fax: 417-778-6209. ✉ 👆💻

Osage County

Circuit Court *Felony, Misdemeanor, Civil Actions Over $25,000* PO Box 825, Linn, MO 65051. 8AM-4:30PM. **573-897-3114**. ☎ ✉ Fax 👆💻

Associate Circuit Court *Misdemeanor, Civil Actions Under $25,000, Eviction, Small Claims, Probate* PO Box 470, Linn, MO 65051. 8AM-4:30PM. **573-897-2136**, Fax: 573-897-4741. ☎ ✉ 👆💻

Ozark County

Circuit Court *Felony, Misdemeanor, Civil Actions Over $25,000* PO Box 36, Gainesville, MO 65655. 8AM-N, 12:30-4:30PM. **417-679-4232**, Fax: 417-679-4554. 👆

Associate Circuit Court *Misdemeanor, Civil Actions Under $25,000, Eviction, Small Claims, Probate* PO Box 278, Gainesville, MO 65655. 8AM-4:30PM. **417-679-4611**, Fax: 417-679-2099. 👆

Pemiscot County

Circuit Court, Division I *Felony, Misdemeanor, Civil Actions Over $45,000* County Courthouse PO Box 34, Caruthersville, MO 63830. 7:30AM-4:30PM. **573-333-0182**. 👆💻

Associate Circuit Court *Misdemeanor, Civil Actions Under $45,000, Eviction, Small Claims, Probate* County Courthouse PO Drawer 228, Caruthersville, MO 63830. 7:30AM-4:30PM. **573-333-2784**. ✉ 👆

Perry County

Circuit Court *Felony, Misdemeanor, Civil Actions Over $25,000* 15 W Saint Maries St #2, Perryville, MO 63775-1399. 8AM-5PM. **573-547-6581**, Fax: 573-547-9323. Fax ✉ 👆💻

Associate Circuit Court *Misd., Civil Under $25,000, Eviction, Small Claims, Probate* 15 W Ste Marie, #2, Perryville, MO 63775-1399. 8AM-5PM. **573-547-7861**, Fax: 573-547-9323. ✉ 👆💻

Pettis County

Circuit Court *Felony, Misdemeanor, Civil Actions Over $45,000* PO Box 804, Sedalia, MO 65302-0804. 8AM-5PM. **660-826-0617**, Fax: 660-826-4520. Also see Associate Circuit Court for add'l civil actions over $45,000. ☎ Fax ✉ 👆💻

Associate Circuit Court *Misdemeanor, Civil Actions Under $45,000, Eviction, Small Claims, Probate* 415 S Ohio, Sedalia, MO 65301. 8:30AM-5PM. **660-826-4699**, Fax: 660-827-8613. Civil actions over $45,000 may also be filed here. ☎ Fax ✉ 👆💻

Probate Court 415 S. Ohio, Sedalia, MO 65301. 8:30AM-5PM. **660-826-0368**,

Fax: 660-827-8637. Probate records free at http://casenet.osca.state.mo.us/casenet/.

Phelps County

Circuit & Associate Court *Felony, Misdemeanor, Civil, Small Claims, Eviction, Probate* 200 N Main St, Rolla, MO 65401. 8AM-5PM. **573-364-1891 X200**, Fax: 573-364-1419. Civil phone: 573-364-1891 X214, crim: 573-364-1891 X202, Probate: 573-364-1891 X251. 👆

Pike County

Circuit Court *Felony, Misdemeanor, Civil Actions Over $25,000* 115 W Main, Bowling Green, MO 63334. 8AM-4:30PM. **573-324-3112**. 👆💻

Associate Circuit Court *Misdemeanor, Civil Actions Under $25,000, Eviction, Small Claims, Probate* 115 W Main, Bowling Green, MO 63334. 8AM-4:30PM. **573-324-5582**, Fax: 573-324-6297. 👆💻

Platte County

Circuit Court *Felony, Misd., Civil Actions Over $25,000* 415 Third St #5, Platte City, MO 64079. 8AM-5PM. **816-858-2232**, Fax: 816-858-3392. ✉ 💻 👆

Associate Circuit Court *Misdemeanor, Civil Actions Under $25,000, Eviction, Small Claims* 415 Third St #5, Platte City, MO 64079. 8AM-5PM. **816-858-2232**, Fax: 816-858-3392. ✉ 💻 👆

Probate Court 415 Third St, #95, Platte City, MO 64079. 8AM-5PM. **816-858-3438**, Fax: 816-858-3392 Probate: 816-858-3440. Can search by name or case # at http://casenet.osca.state.mo.us/casenet/.

Polk County

Circuit & Associate Court *Felony, Misdemeanor, Civil, Eviction, Small Claims, Probate* www.positech.net/~dcourt 102 E Broadway, Rm 14, Bolivar, MO 65613. 8AM-5PM. **417-326-4912**, Fax: 417-326-4194. 👆💻

Pulaski County

Circuit & Associate Circuit Courts *Felony, Misdemeanor, Civil, Eviction, Small Claims* 301 Historic Rt 66 E, #202, Waynesville, MO 65583. 8AM-4:30PM. **573-774-4755**, Fax: 573-774-6967. 👆

Probate Court 301 Historic 66 East, #316, Waynesville, MO 65583. **573-774-4784**, Fax: 573-774-6673.

Key: Symbols refer to criminal records access unless otherwise noted. phone-☎ mail-✉ fax-**Fax** in person-👆 online-💻 email-**Email**

Putnam County

Circuit Court *Felony, Misdemeanor, Civil Actions Over $45,000* Courthouse Rm 202, Unionville, MO 63565. 8AM-12; 1PM-5PM. **660-947-2071**, Fax: 660-947-2320. ✉✋🖥

Associate Circuit Court *Misd., Civil Actions Under $45,000, Eviction, Small Claims, Probate* Courthouse Rm 101, Unionville, MO 63565. 9AM-5PM. **660-947-2117**, Fax: 660-947-7348. ✉✋🖥

Ralls County

Circuit Court *Felony, Misdemeanor, Civil Actions Over $25,000* PO Box 444, New London, MO 63459. 8:30AM-4:30PM. **573-985-5633**. ✉✋

Associate Circuit Court *Misdemeanor, Civil Actions Under $25,000, Eviction, Small Claims, Probate* PO Box 466 311 S Main, New London, MO 63459. 8:00AM-4:30PM. **573-985-5641**, Fax: 573-985-3446. ☎✉Fax✋

Randolph County

Circuit & Associate Court *Felony, Misdemeanor, Civil Actions, Eviction, Small Claims, Probate* 223 N Williams, Moberly, MO 65270. 8AM-4:30PM. **660-263-4474**, Fax: 660-263-5966 Crim; 263-1007 civil. Fax✉✋🖥

Ray County

Circuit Court *Felony, Misdemeanor, Civil Actions Over $25,000* www.osca.state.mo.us/circuits/index.nsf/County+/+Ray PO Box 594, Richmond, MO 64085. 8AM-4PM. **816-776-3377**, Fax: 816-776-6016. ✋🖥

Associate Circuit Court *Misdemeanor, Civil Actions Under $25,000, Eviction, Small Claims, Probate* Ray County Courthouse 100 W Main St, Richmond, MO 64085-1710. 8AM-4PM. **816-776-2335**, Fax: 816-776-2185. Fax✉✋🖥

Reynolds County

Circuit Court *Felony, Civil Actions Over $45,000* PO Box 76, Centerville, MO 63633. 8AM-4PM. **573-648-2494 X34**, Fax: 573-648-2503. ☎✉✋🖥

Associate Circuit Court *Misdemeanor, Civil Actions Under $45,000, Eviction, Small Claims, Probate* PO Box 39, Centerville, MO 63633. 8AM-4PM. **573-648-2494 X31**, Fax: 573-648-2503 Probate: x35. ✋🖥

Ripley County

Circuit Court *Felony, Misdemeanor, Civil Actions Over $25,000* Courthouse, Doniphan, MO 63935. 8AM-4PM. **573-996-2818**, Fax: 573-996-7826. Fax✉✋

Associate Circuit Court *Misdemeanor, Civil Actions Under $25,000, Eviction, Small Claims, Probate* 100 Court Sq, Courthouse, Doniphan, MO 63935. 8AM-4PM. **573-996-2013**, Fax: 573-996-5014. ✋

St. Charles County

Circuit & Associate Court *Felony, Misdemeanor, Civil Actions, Eviction, Small Claims, Probate* 300 N 2nd St, St. Charles, MO 63301. 8:30AM-5PM. **636-949-7900 x3098**, Fax: 636-949-7390. Criminal phone: 636-949-7380, Probate: 636-949-7900 x3086. Traffic Court: 636-949-7385. 🖥✋

St. Clair County

Circuit & Associate Circuit Courts *Felony, Misdemeanor, Civil, Eviction, Small Claims, Probate* PO Box 493, Osceola, MO 64776. 8AM-4:30PM. **417-646-2226**, Fax: 417-646-2401. ✉✋🖥

Ste. Genevieve County

Circuit Court *Felony, Misd., Civil Actions Over $25,000* 55 S 3rd, Rm 23, Ste Genevieve, MO 63670. 8AM-5PM. **573-883-2705**, Fax: 573-883-9351. ✋🖥

Associate Circuit Court *Misdemeanor, Civil Actions Under $45,000, Eviction, Small Claims, Probate* 55 S 3rd St, Ste Genevieve, MO 63670. 8AM-5PM. **573-883-2265**, Fax: 573-883-9351. ✋🖥

St. Francois County

Circuit Court - Division I & II *Felony, Civil Over $25,000* www.sfcgov.org 1 N Washington, Rm 303, Farmington, MO 63640. 8AM-5PM. **573-756-4551**, Fax: 573-756-3733. ✋🖥

Associate Circuit Court *Misdemeanor, Civil Actions Under $25,000, Eviction, Small Claims, Probate* County Courthouse, 2nd Fl 1 N Washington, Rm 202, Farmington, MO 63640. 8AM-5PM. **573-756-5755**, Fax: 573-756-8173. ✋🖥

St. Louis County

Separate listing for St. Louis City.

Circuit Court of St. Louis County *Felony, Misdemeanor, Civil Actions* www.stlouisco.com/circuitcourt 7900

Carondelet, Clayton, MO 63105-1766. 8AM-5PM. **314-615-8029**, Fax: 314-615-8739. ☎Fax✉✋

Associate Circuit - Civil Division *Civil Actions Under $25,000, Eviction, Small Claims, Probate* 7900 Carondelet, Clayton, MO 63105. 8AM-5PM. **314-615-8090**, Fax: 314-615-2689 Probate: 314-615-2629. Small claims: 314-615-8091. Access civil records-☎✉✋

Associate Circuit Court - Criminal Div. *Misdm'r* www.stlouisco.com/circuitcourt 7900 Carondolet Av, Clayton, MO 63105. 8AM-5PM. **314-615-2675**, Fax: 314-615-2689. ☎✉Fax✋

St. Louis City

Circuit & Associate Circuit Courts - Civil *Civil, Eviction, Small Claims, Probate* www.stlcitycircuitcourt.com 10 N Tucker, Civil Courts Bldg, St Louis, MO 63101. 8:00AM-5:00PM. **314-622-4405**, Fax: 314-622-4537 Probate: 314-622-4300. Small Claims: 314-622-3788. Probate is located on the 10th Fl. Access civil records-✉🖥✋

City of St Louis Circuit Court - Criminal *Felony, Misdemeanor* www.stlcitycircuitcourt.com/PDF/Telephone List/TeleDirectory.pdf 1114 Market St, 2nd Fl, Carnahan Courthouse Attention: Case Records/File Section, St Louis, MO 63101. 9AM-4PM. **314-622-4773 (gen info)**, Fax: 314-613-7486 (crim) Crim: 314-622-4485 or 4486 (felony), 314-622-4548 (misd.). Court clerk's admin. office located 10 N Tucker. ✋✉Fax🖥

Saline County

Circuit Court *Felony, Misd., Civil Actions Over $25,000* PO Box 597 101 E Main St #205, Marshall, MO 65340. 8:00AM-4:30PM. **660-886-2300**. ✋🖥

Associate Circuit Court *Misdemeanor, Civil Actions Under $25,000, Eviction, Small Claims* PO Box 751, Marshall, MO 65340. 8AM-4:30PM. **660-886-6988**, Fax: 660-886-2919. Probate: 660-886-8808. ☎✉✋🖥

Schuyler County

Circuit Court *Felony, Misdemeanor, Civil Actions Over $45,000* PO Box 186, Lancaster, MO 63548. 8AM-4PM. **660-457-3784**, Fax: 660-457-3016. Misdemeanor and probate phone is 660-457-3755. ✉✋🖥

Key: Symbols refer to criminal records access unless otherwise noted. phone-☎ mail-✉ fax-Fax in person-✋ online-🖥 email-Email

Associate Circuit Court *Misdemeanor, Civil Actions Under $45,000, Eviction, Small Claims, Probate* Box 158, Lancaster, MO 63548. 8:00AM-4PM. **660-457-3755**, Fax: 660-457-3016. ✉Fax👆💻

Scotland County

Circuit Court *Felony, Civil Actions Over $25,000* 117 S Market St #106, Memphis, MO 63555. 8AM-4PM. **660-465-8605**, Fax: 660-465-8673. ✉👆💻

Associate Circuit Court *Misdemeanor, Civil Actions Under $25,000, Eviction, Small Claims, Probate* Courthouse, Rm 102 117 S Market, Memphis, MO 63555. 8AM-4:30PM. **660-465-2404**, Fax: 660-465-8673. ☎✉👆💻

Scott County

Circuit Court *Felony, Misdemeanor, Civil Actions Over $25,000* PO Box 277, Benton, MO 63736. 8:00AM-5PM. **573-545-3596**, Fax: 573-545-3597. 👆💻

Associate Circuit Court *Misdemeanor, Civil Actions Under $45,000, Eviction, Small Claims, Probate* PO Box 249, Benton, MO 63736. 8AM-N, 1-5PM. **573-545-3576**, Fax: 573-545-4231. ✉👆💻

Shannon County

Circuit Court *Felony, Misdemeanor, Civil Actions Over $45,000* PO Box 148, Eminence, MO 65466. 8AM-4:30PM. **573-226-3315**, Fax: 573-226-5321. ✉👆💻

Associate Circuit Court *Misdemeanor, Civil Actions Under $45,000, Eviction, Small Claims, Probate* PO Box 845, Eminence, MO 65466-0845. 8AM-4:30PM. **573-226-5515**, Fax: 573-226-3239. ✉Fax👆💻

Shelby County

Circuit Court *Felony, Misd., Civil Over $45,000* PO Box 176, Shelbyville, MO 63469. 8AM-4:30PM. **573-633-2151**, Fax: 573-633-1004. ✉Fax👆

Associate Circuit Court *Misdemeanor, Civil Actions Under $25,000, Eviction, Small Claims, Probate* PO Box 206, Shelbyville, MO 63469. 8AM-4:30PM. **573-633-2151**, Fax: 573-633-2142. ☎Fax✉👆

Stoddard County

Circuit Court *Felony, Misdemeanor, Civil Actions Over $25,000* PO Box 30, Bloomfield, MO 63825. 8:30AM-4:30PM. **573-568-4640**, Fax: 573-568-2271. ✉👆💻

Associate Division III & Probate *Civil Actions Under $25,000, Eviction, Small Claims, Probate* PO Box 518, Bloomfield, MO 63825. 7:30AM-4PM. **573-568-4640 x3**, Fax: 573-568-3229. Access civil records-☎Fax✉👆💻

Associate Circuit Court - Criminal Division II *Misdemeanor* PO Box 218, Bloomfield, MO 63825. 8:30AM-4:30PM. **573-568-4640 x2**, Fax: 573-568-2299. 👆💻

Stone County

Circuit Court *Felony, Misdemeanor, Civil Actions Over $25,000* PO Box 18, Galena, MO 65656. 7:30AM-N; 12:30PM-4:00PM. **417-357-6114; 417-357-6115 child support**, Fax: 417-357-6163. ☎Fax✉👆

Circuit Court - Division II & III *Misdemeanor, Civil Actions, Eviction, Small Claims, Probate* www.stoneco-mo.us PO Box 186, Galena, MO 65656. 7:30AM-4PM. **417-357-6511**, Fax: 417-357-6163. No collar limit on civil actions; prior to 2001, the civil action maximum limit was $25,000. ☎Fax✉👆

Sullivan County

Circuit & Associate Court *Felony, Misdemeanor, Civil Actions, Eviction, Small Claims, Probate* Courthouse, 109 N Main, Milan, MO 63556-1358. 9:00AM-4:30PM. **660-265-4717 (Circ,); 660-265-3303 (Assoc. Ct)**, Fax: 660-265-5071. 👆💻

Taney County

Circuit Court *Felony, Civil Actions Over $25,000* PO Box 335, Forsyth, MO 65653. 8AM-5PM. **417-546-7230**, Fax: 417-546-6133. ✉👆💻

Associate Circuit Court - Division I *Felony, Misd., Probate* PO Box 129, Forsyth, MO 65653. 8AM-5PM. **417-546-7212**, Fax: 417-546-4513. ✉👆💻

Associate Circuit Court - Division II *Civil Actions Under $25,000, Eviction, Small Claims* PO Box 1030, Forsyth, MO 65653. 8AM-5PM. **417-546-7206**, Fax:

417-546-5821. Access civil records by-✉👆💻

Texas County

Circuit Court *Felony, Misd., Civil Over $25,000* 210 N Grand, Houston, MO 65483. 8:30-N; 12:30PM-4:30PM. **417-967-3742**, Fax: 417-967-4220. 👆

Associate Circuit Court *Misdemeanor, Civil Actions Under $25,000, Eviction, Small Claims, Probate* County Courthouse 210 N Grand, #302, Houston, MO 65483. 8AM-N; 1-5PM. **417-967-3663**, Fax: 417-967-4128. ☎Fax✉👆

Vernon County

Circuit & Associate Court *Felony, Misdemeanor, Civil Actions, Eviction, Small Claims, Probate* Courthouse, 3rd Fl 100 W Cherry St, Nevada, MO 64772. 8AM-4:30PM. **417-448-2525/2550**, Fax: 417-448-2512. 👆💻

Warren County

Circuit Court *Felony, Misdemeanor, Civil Actions Over $25,000* 104 W Main, Warrenton, MO 63383. 8AM-4:30PM. **636-456-3363**, Fax: 636-456-8573. 💻👆

Associate Circuit Court *Misdemeanor, Civil Actions Under $25,000, Eviction, Small Claims, Probate* Warren County Courthouse 104 W Main, Warrenton, MO 63383. 8:30AM-4:30PM. **636-456-3375**, Fax: 636-456-2422. ☎Fax✉💻👆

Washington County

Circuit Court *Felony, Misdemeanor, Civil Actions Over $45,000* PO Box 216, Potosi, MO 63664. 8AM-5PM. **573-438-4171**, Fax: 573-438-7900. ✉👆💻

Associate Circuit Court *Misd., Civil Under $45,000, Eviction, Small Claims, Probate* 102 N Missouri St, Potosi, MO 63664. 8AM-5PM. **573-438-3691**, Fax: 573-438-7900. ☎Fax✉👆💻

Wayne County

Circuit Court *Felony, Misd., Civil Over $45,000* PO Box 78, Greenville, MO 63944. 8:30AM-4:30PM. **573-224-3014**, Fax: 573-224-3015. ✉👆💻

Div. III Circuit Court *Misdemeanor, Civil Actions Under $45,000, Eviction, Small Claims, Probate* PO Box 47, Greenville, MO 63944. 8:30AM-4:30PM. **573-224-3052**, Fax: 573-224-3225. ☎Fax✉👆💻

Key: Symbols refer to criminal records access unless otherwise noted. phone-☎ mail-✉ fax-**Fax** in person-👆 online-💻 email-**Email**

Webster County

Circuit Court *Felony, Civil Actions Over $25,000* PO Box 529, Marshfield, MO 65706. 8AM-5PM. **417-859-2006**, Fax: 417-468-3786 (Circuit). 🖐️💻

Associate Circuit Court *Misdemeanor, Civil Under $25,000, Eviction, Small Claims, Probate* Courthouse, Marshfield, MO 65706. 8AM-5PM. **417-859-2041**, Fax: 417-859-6265. Probate: 417-859-2041. ✉️🖐️💻

Worth County

Circuit Court *Felony, Misd., Civil Actions Over $45,000* PO Box 340, Grant City, MO 64456. 8:30AM-4:30PM. **660-564-2210**, Fax: 660-564-2432. ✉️🖐️

Associate Circuit Court *Misdemeanor, Civil Actions Under $45,000, Eviction, Small Claims, Probate* PO Box 428, Grant City, MO 64456. 9AM-4:30PM. **660-564-2152**, Fax: 660-564-2432. ✉️🖐️

Wright County

Circuit Court *Felony, Misdemeanor, Civil Actions Over $25,000* PO Box 39, Hartville, MO 65667. 8AM-4:30PM. **417-741-7121**, Fax: 417-741-7504. ✉️🖐️

Associate Circuit Court *Misdemeanor, Civil Actions Under $25,000, Eviction, Small Claims, Probate* PO Box 58, Hartville, MO 65667. 8AM-4:30PM. **417-741-6450**, Fax: 417-741-7120. ☎️Fax✉️🖐️

Montana

State Court Administration: Court Administrator, Justice Building, 215 N Sanders, Room 315 (PO Box 203002), Helena, MT, 59620; 406-444-2621, Fax: 406-444-0834.

Court Structure: The District Courts have no maximum amount for civil judgment cases. Most District Courts handle civil over $7,000; there are exceptions that handle a civil minimum as low as $5,000. Limited Jurisdiction Courts, which are also known as Justice Courts, may handle civil actions up to $7,000. The Small Claims limit is $3,000.

Many Montana Justices of the Peace maintain case record indexes on their personal PCs, which does speed the retrieval process.

Online Access: Supreme Courts Opinions, Orders, and recently Filed Briefs may be found at www.lawlibrary.state.mt.us/dscgi/ds.py/View/Collection-36. Federal District court records are also available here. A few individual county courts offer online access.

Beaverhead County

District Court *Felony, Civil Actions Over $7,000, Eviction, Probate* Beaverhead County Courthouse 2 S Pacific St, Dillon, MT 59725. 8AM-5PM. **406-683-3725**, Fax: 406-683-3728. Fax✉️🖐️

Big Horn County

District Court *Felony, Civil Actions Over $7,000, Probate* 121 W 3rd St, Rm 221 PO Box 908, Hardin, MT 59034. 8AM-5PM. **406-665-9750**, Fax: 406-665-9755. Fax✉️🖐️

Blaine County

District Court *Felony, Civil Actions Over $5,000, Eviction, Probate* PO Box 969, Chinook, MT 59523. 8AM-5PM. **406-357-3230**, Fax: 406-357-3109. Fax✉️🖐️

Broadwater County

District Court *Felony, Civil Actions Over $7,000, Probate* 515 Broadway, Townsend, MT 59644. 8AM-N, 1-5PM. **406-266-9236**, Fax: 406-266-4720. Fax✉️🖐️

Carbon County

District Court *Felony, Civil Actions, Probate* PO Box 948, Red Lodge, MT 59068. 8AM-5PM. **406-446-1225**, Fax: 406-446-1911. Fax✉️🖐️

Carter County

District Court *Felony, Civil Actions Over $5,000, Eviction, Probate* PO Box 322, Ekalaka, MT 59324. 8AM-5PM. **406-775-8714**, Fax: 406-775-8730. ☎️Fax✉️🖐️

Cascade County

District Court *Felony, Civil Actions Over $7,000, Probate* County Courthouse 415 2nd Ave North, Great Falls, MT 59401. 8AM-5PM. **406-454-6780**. ✉️🖐️

Chouteau County

District Court *Felony, Civil Actions Over $5,000, Eviction, Probate* PO Box 459, Ft Benton, MT 59442. 8AM-5PM. **406-622-5024**, Fax: 406-622-3028. Fax✉️🖐️

Custer County

District Court *Felony, Civil Actions Over $5,000, Eviction, Probate* 1010 Main, Miles City, MT 59301-3419. 8AM-5PM. **406-874-3326**, Fax 406-874-3451. ✉️🖐️

Daniels County

District Court *Felony, Civil Actions Over $5,000, Probate* PO Box 67, Scobey, MT 59263. 8AM-5PM. **406-487-2651**, Fax: 406-487-5432. Access records-✉️🖐️fax.

Dawson County

District Court *Felony, Civil Actions Over $5,000, Eviction, Probate* www.dawsoncountymontana.com/clerk_of_court.htm 207 W Bell, Glendive, MT 59330. 8AM-5PM. **406-377-3967**, Fax: 406-377-7280. ✉️🖐️

Deer Lodge County

District Court *Felony, Civil Actions Over $5,000, Eviction, Probate* 800 S Main, Anaconda, MT 59711. 8AM-5PM. **406-563-4041**, Fax: 406-563-4077. ✉️🖐️

Fallon County

District Court *Felony, Civil Actions Over $5,000, Eviction, Probate* PO Box 1521, Baker, MT 59313. 8AM-5PM. **406-778-7114**, Fax: 406-778-2815. ✉️🖐️

Key: Symbols refer to criminal records access unless otherwise noted. phone-☎️ mail-✉️ fax-**Fax** in person-🖐️ online-💻 email-**Email**

Fergus County

District Court *Felony, Civil Actions Over $7,000, Eviction, Probate* www.co.fergus.mt.us PO Box 1074 (712 W Main), Lewistown, MT 59457. 8AM-5PM. **406-538-5026**, Fax: 406-538-6076. ☎Fax✉👋

Flathead County

District Court *Felony, Civil Over $5,000, Probate* www.co.flathead.mt.us/clkcrt/index.html 800 S Main (920 S. Main, 3rd Fl), Kalispell, MT 59901. 8AM-5PM. **406-758-5660**. ✉👋

Gallatin County

Clerk of District Court *Felony, Civil Actions Over $7,000, Probate* 615 S 16th, Rm 302, Bozeman, MT 59715. 8-5PM. **406-582-2165**, Fax 406-582-2176. ✉👋

Garfield County

District Court *Felony, Civil Actions Over $5,000, Eviction, Probate* PO Box 8, Jordan, MT 59337. 8AM-5PM. **406-557-6254**, Fax: 406-557-2625. ☎✉👋

Glacier County

District Court *Civil Actions, Probate* 512 E Main St, Cut Bank, MT 59427. 8AM-5PM. **406-873-5063 X36**, Fax: 406-873-5627. Fax✉👋

Golden Valley County

District Court *Felony, Civil Actions Over $5,000, Eviction, Probate* PO Box 10, Ryegate, MT 59074. 8AM-5PM. **406-568-2231**, Fax: 406-568-2231. Fax✉👋

Granite County

District Court *Felony, Civil Actions Over $7,000, Eviction, Probate* PO Box 399, Philipsburg, MT 59858-0399. 8AM-N, 1-5PM. **406-859-3712**, Fax: 406-859-3817. ☎Fax✉👋

Hill County

District Court *Felony, Civil Over $5,000, Eviction, Probate* http://co.hill.mt.us Hill County Courthouse, Havre, MT 59501. 8AM-5PM. **406-265-5481 X224**, Fax: 406-265-3693. Access records-Fax✉👋

Jefferson County

District Court *Felony, Civil Actions Over $7,000, Eviction, Probate* PO Box H, Boulder, MT 59632. 8AM-N, 1-5PM. **406-225-4041 & 4042**, Fax: 406-225-4044. ✉Fax👋

Judith Basin County

District Court *Felony, Civil Actions Over $5,000, Probate* PO Box 307, Stanford, MT 59479. 8AM-5PM. **406-566-2277 X113**, Fax: 406-566-2211. ☎✉👋

Lake County

District Court *Felony, Civil Actions Over $7,000, Probate* Clerk of District Court Office 106 4th Ave E, Polson, MT 59860. 8AM-5PM. **406-883-7254**, Fax: 406-883-7343. ☎Fax✉👋

Lewis and Clark County

District Court *Felony, Civil Actions Over $5,000, Eviction, Probate, Small Claims* www.co.lewis-clark.mt.us 228 Broadway PO Box 158, Helena, MT 59624. 8AM-5PM. **406-447-8216**, Fax: 406-447-8275. Fax✉🖥👋

Liberty County

District Court *Felony, Civil Actions Over $5,000, Eviction, Probate* PO Box 549, Chester, MT 59522. 8AM-5PM. **406-759-5615**, Fax: 406-759-5996. ☎✉👋fax.

Lincoln County

District Court *Felony, Civil Actions Over $7,000, Probate* 512 California Ave, Libby, MT 59923. 8AM-5PM. **406-293-7781**, Fax: 406-293-9816. ✉👋

McCone County

District Court *Felony, Civil Actions Over $5,000, Eviction, Probate* PO Box 199, Circle, MT 59215. 8AM-5PM. **406-485-3410**, Fax: 406-485-3410. ✉👋

Madison County

District Court *Felony, Civil Actions Over $5,000, Eviction, Probate* PO Box 185, Virginia City, MT 59755. 8AM-5PM. **406-843-4230**, Fax: 406-843-5207. Fax✉👋

Meagher County

District Court *Felony, Civil Actions Over $5,000, Eviction, Probate* PO Box 443, White Sulphur Springs, MT 59645. 8AM-5PM. **406-547-3612 Ext110**, Fax: 406-547-3836. Access records- ☎✉Fax👋

Mineral County

District Court *Felony, Civil Actions Over $5,000, Probate* PO Box 129, Superior, MT 59872. 8AM-N,1-5PM. **406-822-3538**, Fax: 406-822-3579. Fax✉👋

Missoula County

District Court *Felony, Civil Actions Over $7,000, Probate* 200 W Broadway, Missoula, MT 59802. 8AM-5PM. **406-258-4780**, Fax: 406-258-4899. Fax✉👋

Musselshell County

District Court *Felony, Civil Actions Over $5,000, Eviction, Probate* 506 Main St, Roundup, MT 59072. 8AM-5PM. **406-323-1413**, Fax: 406-323-1710. ✉👋

Park County

District Court *Felony, Civil Actions Over $7,000, Eviction, Probate* PO Box 437, Livingston, MT 59047. 8AM-5PM. **406-222-4125**, Fax: 406-222-4128. Fax✉👋

Petroleum County

District Court *Felony, Civil Actions Over $5,000, Eviction, Probate* PO Box 226, Winnett, MT 59087. 8AM-5PM. **406-429-5311**, Fax: 406-429-6328. ☎✉👋

Phillips County

District Court *Felony, Civil Actions Over $5,000, Eviction, Probate* PO Box 530, Malta, MT 59538. 8AM-5PM. **406-654-1023**, Fax: 406-654-1023. ✉👋

Pondera County

District Court *Felony, Civil Actions Over $5,000, Eviction, Probate* 20 Fourth Ave SW, Conrad, MT 59425. 8AM-5PM. **406-271-4026**, Fax: 406-271-4081. Fax✉👋

Powder River County

District Court *Felony, Civil Actions Over $5,000, Probate* PO Box 239, Broadus, MT 59317. 8AM-N, 1-5PM. **406-436-2320**, Fax: 406-436-2325. Fax✉👋

Powell County

District Court *Felony, Civil Actions Over $5,000, Eviction, Probate* 409 Missouri Ave, Deer Lodge, MT 59722. 8AM-5PM. **406-846-3680 X234/235**, Fax: 406-846-2784. ✉👋

Prairie County

District Court *Felony, Civil Actions Over $5,000, Eviction, Probate* PO Box 125, Terry, MT 59349. 8AM-N; 1PM-5PM. **406-635-5575**. ✉👋

Ravalli County

District Court *Felony, Civil Actions Over $7,000, Probate* http://co.ravalli.mt.us/ Ravalli County Courthouse 205 Bedford

#D, Hamilton, MT 59840. 8AM-5PM. **406-375-6214**, Fax 406-375-6327. ✉✋

Richland County

District Court *Felony, Civil Actions Over $5,000, Eviction, Probate* 201 W Main, Sidney, MT 59270. 8AM-5PM. **406-433-1709**, Fax: 406-433-6945. ☎Fax✉✋

Roosevelt County

District Court *Felony, Civil Actions Over $5,000, Eviction, Probate* County Courthouse 400 2nd Ave S, Wolf Point, MT 59201. 8AM-5PM. **406-653-6266**, Fax: 406-653-6203. Fax✉✋

Rosebud County

District Court *Felony, Civil Actions Over $5,000, Eviction, Probate* PO Box 48, Forsyth, MT 59327. 8AM-5PM. **406-356-7322**, Fax: 406-356-7551. ✉✋

Sanders County

District Court *Felony, Civil Actions Over $7,000, Eviction, Probate* PO Box 519, Thompson Falls, MT 59873. 8AM-5PM. **406-827-6962**, Fax 406-827-0094. ✉✋

Sheridan County

District Court *Felony, Civil Actions Over $5,000, Eviction, Probate* www.co.sheridan.mt.us/ 100 W Laurel, Plentywood, MT 59254. 8AM-N, 1-5PM. **406-765-3404**, Fax: 406-765-2602. ☎✉✋

Silver Bow County

District Court *Felony, Civil Actions Over $5,000, Probate* 155 W Granite St, Butte, MT 59701. 8AM-5PM. **406-497-6350**, Fax: 406-497-6358. Fax✉✋

Stillwater County

District Court *Felony, Civil Actions Over $5,000, Eviction, Probate* PO Box 367, Columbus, MT 59019. 8AM-5PM. **406-322-8030**, Fax: 406-322-8048. ☎✉✋

Sweet Grass County

District Court *Felony, Civil Actions Over $5,000, Eviction, Probate* PO Box 698, Big Timber, MT 59011. 8AM-N, 1-5PM. **406-932-5154**, Fax: 406-932-5433. ☎✉✋

Teton County

District Court *Felony, Civil Actions Over $5,000, Eviction, Probate* PO Box 487, Choteau, MT 59422. 8AM-5PM. **406-466-2909**, Fax: 406-466-2910. ☎✉✋

Toole County

District Court *Felony, Civil Actions Over $5,000, Eviction, Probate* PO Box 850, Shelby, MT 59474. 8AM-5PM. **406-424-8330**, Fax: 406-424-8331. ☎Fax✉✋

Treasure County

District Court *Felony, Civil Actions Over $5,000, Eviction, Probate* PO Box 392, Hysham, MT 59038. 8AM-5PM. **406-342-5547**, Fax: 406-342-5445. Fax✉✋

Valley County

Clerk of District Court *Felony, Civil Actions Over $5,000, Eviction, Probate* 501 Court Sq #6, Glasgow, MT 59230. 8AM-5PM. **406-228-6268**, Fax: 406-228-6212. Fax✉✋

Wheatland County

District Court *Felony, Civil Actions Over $5,000, Eviction, Probate* Box 227, Harlowton, MT 59036. 8AM-5PM. **406-632-4893**, Fax: 406-632-4873. ✉✋

Wibaux County

District Court *Felony, Civil Actions Over $5,000, Eviction, Probate* PO Box 292, Wibaux, MT 59353. 8AM-5PM, Closed 12-1. **406-796-2484**, Fax: 406-796-2484. ☎Fax✉✋

Yellowstone County

District Court *Felony, Civil Over $7,000, Probate* www.co.yellowstone.mt.us/clerk_court/ PO Box 35030 (217 N 27 St), Billings, MT 59107. 8AM-5PM. **406-256-2862**, Fax: 406-256-2995. Civil phone: 406-256-2851, crim: 406-256-2860, Probate: 406-256-2865. ✉✋

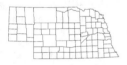

Nebraska

State Court Administration: Court Administrator, PO Box 98910, Lincoln, NE, 68509-8910; 402-471-2643, Fax: 402-471-2197. http://court.nol.org/AOC/index.html

Court Structure: The District Court is the court of general jurisdiction. The minimum on civil judgment matters for District Courts is $15,000, however, the State raised the County Court limit on civil matters from $15,000 to $45,000 as of Sept. 1, 2001. As it is less expensive to file civil cases in County Court than in District Court, civil cases in the $15,000 to $45,000 range are more likely to be found in County Court, if after Sept. 1, 2001. Consequently, some District Courts have raised their civil minimum to $45,000.

The number of judicial districts went from 21 to the current 12 in July 1992. County Courts have juvenile jurisdiction in all but 3 counties. Douglas, Lancaster, and Sarpy counties have separate Juvenile Courts.

Probate Courts: Probate is handled by County Courts. Many have records on microfiche back to the mid/late 1800s.

Online Access: An online access subscription service is available for NE District and County courts, except Douglas County District Court. Case details, all party listings, payments and actions taken for criminal, civil, probate, juvenile, and traffic is available. Users must be registered with Nebrask@ Online, there is a start-up fee. The fee is $.60 per record or a flat rate of $300.00 per month. Go to www.nebraska.gov/faqs/justice for more info and how far back records go per county. Supreme Court opinions are available from http://court.nol.org/opinions/. Also, Douglas, Lancaster, and Sarpy county courts offer internet access with registration and password required.

Key: Symbols refer to criminal records access unless otherwise noted. phone-☎ mail-✉ fax-**Fax** in person-✋ online-💻 email-**Email**

Additional Nebraska Courts Information: Most Nebraska courts require the public to do their own in-person searches and will not respond to written search requests. The State Attorney General has recommended that courts not perform searches because of the time involved and concerns over possible legal liability.

Adams County

County Court *Misdemeanor, Civil Actions Under $45,000, Eviction, Small Claims, Probate* PO Box 95, Hastings, NE 68902-0095. 8AM-5PM. **402-461-7143**, Fax: 402-461-7144. 🖐️💻

District Court *Felony, Civil Actions Over $15,000* http://adamscounty.org/courts/district PO Box 9, Hastings, NE 68902. 8:30AM-5PM. **402-461-7264**, Fax: 402-461-7269. 🖐️💻

Antelope County

District Court *Felony, Civil Actions Over $15,000* PO Box 45, Neligh, NE 68756. 8:30AM-5PM. **402-887-4508**, Fax: 402-887-4870. 🖐️💻

Antelope County Court *Misdemeanor, Civil Actions Under $45,000, Eviction, Small Claims, Probate* 501 Main, Neligh, NE 68756. 8:30AM-5PM. **402-887-4650**, Fax: 402-887-4160. Access records-🖐️💻

Arthur County

District & County Court *Felony, Misdemeanor, Civil, Eviction, Small Claims, Probate* PO Box 126 205 Fir St., Arthur, NE 69121. 8AM-4PM. **308-764-2203**, Fax: 308-764-2216. 📞Fax📩🖐️

Banner County

District Court *Felony, Civil Actions Over $15,000* PO Box 67, Harrisburg, NE 69345. 8AM-5PM. **308-436-5265**, Fax: 308-436-4180. Fax📩🖐️💻

Banner County Court *Misdemeanor, Civil Actions Under $45,000, Eviction, Small Claims, Probate* PO Box 67, Harrisburg, NE 69345. 1-5PM. **308-436-5268**. Probate: 308-436-5268. 🖐️💻📩

Blaine County

District Court *Felony, Civil Actions Over $15,000* www.nol.org/home/DC8/ Lincoln Ave, Box 136, Brewster, NE 68821. 8AM-4PM. **308-547-2222 Ext 201**, Fax: 308-547-2228 Fax📩🖐️💻

Blaine County Court *Misdemeanor, Civil Actions Under $45,000, Eviction, Small Claims, Probate* Lincoln Ave, Box 123, Brewster, NE 68821. 8AM-4PM.

308-547-2222 ext 202, Probate: Ext 202. Fax: 308-547-2228. 📞Fax📩🖐️💻

Boone County

District Court *Felony, Civil Actions Over $45,000* 222 Fourth St, Albion, NE 68620. 8:30AM-5PM. **402-395-2057**, Fax: 402-395-6592. 📞Fax📩🖐️💻

Boone County Court *Misdemeanor, Civil Actions Under $45,000, Eviction, Small Claims, Probate* 222 S 4th St, Albion, NE 68620. 8AM-5PM. **402-395-6184**, Fax: 402-395-6592. Fax📩🖐️💻

Box Butte County

District Court *Felony, Civil Actions Over $15,000* 515 Box Butte #300, Alliance, NE 69301. 9AM-4PM. **308-762-6293**, Fax: 308-762-5700. Access records-🖐️💻

Box Butte County Court *Misdemeanor, Civil Actions Under $45,000, Eviction, Small Claims, Probate* PO Box 613, Alliance, NE 69301. 8:30AM-5PM. **308-762-6800**, Fax: 308-762-2650. 🖐️💻

Boyd County

District Court *Felony, Civil Actions Over $15,000* PO Box 26, Butte, NE 68722. 8:15AM-4PM. **402-775-2391**, Fax: 402-775-2146. 📩Fax🖐️💻

Boyd County Court *Misdemeanor, Civil Actions Under $45,000, Eviction, Small Claims, Probate* PO Box 396, Butte, NE 68722. 8AM-5PM W,Th. **402-775-2211**, Fax: 402-775-2146. Probate: 402-775-2211. 🖐️💻

Brown County

District Court *Felony, Civil Actions Over $15,000* 148 W Fourth St, Ainsworth, NE 69210. 8AM-5PM. **402-387-2705**, Fax: 402-387-0918. Fax📩🖐️💻

Brown County Court *Misdemeanor, Civil Actions Under $45,000, Eviction, Small Claims, Probate* 148 W Fourth St, Ainsworth, NE 69210. 8AM-5PM. **402-387-2864**, Fax: 402-387-0918. 📞Fax📩🖐️💻

Buffalo County

District Court *Felony, Civil Actions Over $15,000* PO Box 520, Kearney, NE

68848. 8AM-5PM. **308-236-1246**, Fax: 308-233-3693. 🖐️💻

Buffalo County Court *Misdemeanor, Civil Actions Under $45,000, Eviction, Small Claims, Probate* PO Box 520, Kearney, NE 68848. 8AM-5PM. **308-236-1228**, Fax: 308-236-1243. 🖐️💻

Burt County

District Court *Felony, Civil Actions Over $15,000* 111 N 13th St, Tekamah, NE 68061. 8AM-4:30PM. **402-374-2905**, Fax: 402-374-2906. 📩🖐️💻

Burt County Court *Misdemeanor, Civil Actions Under $45,000, Eviction, Small Claims, Probate* 111 N 13th St, PO Box 87, Tekamah, NE 68061. 8AM-4:30PM. **402-374-2950**, Fax: 402-374-2951. 🖐️💻

Butler County

District Court *Felony, Civil Actions Over $15,000* 451 5th St, David City, NE 68632-1666. 8:30AM-5PM. **402-367-7460**, Fax: 402-367-3249. 📩🖐️💻

Butler County Court *Misdemeanor, Civil Actions Under $45,000, Eviction, Small Claims, Probate* 451 5th St, David City, NE 68632-1666. 8AM-N, 1-5PM. **402-367-7480**, Fax: 402-367-3249. 🖐️💻

Cass County

District Court *Felony, Civil Actions Over $45,000* Cass County Courthouse 346 Main St, Plattsmouth, NE 68048. 8-5PM. **402-296-9339**, Fax: 402-296-9345. 🖐️💻

Cass County Court *Misdemeanor, Civil Actions Under $45,000, Eviction, Small Claims, Probate* Cass County Courthouse 346 Main St Rm 301, Plattsmouth, NE 68048. 8-5PM. **402-296-9339**, Fax: 402-296-9345. Probate: 402-296-9334. 🖐️💻

Cedar County

District Court *Felony, Civil Actions Over $45,000* PO Box 796, Hartington, NE 68739-0796. 8AM-5PM. **402-254-6957**, Fax: 402-254-6954. Access records-🖐️💻

Cedar County Court *Misdemeanor, Civil Actions Under $45,000, Eviction, Small Claims, Probate* P O Box 695, Hartington, NE 68739. 8AM-5PM. **402-254-7441**, Fax: 402-254-6954. 🖐️💻

Key: Symbols refer to criminal records access unless otherwise noted. phone-📞 mail-📩 fax-**Fax** in person-🖐️ online-💻 email-**Email**

Chase County

District Court *Felony, Civil Actions Over $15,000* PO Box 1299, Imperial, NE 69033. 8AM-4PM. **308-882-5266**, Fax: 308-882-5390. ☎Fax✉🖐💻

Chase County Court *Misdemeanor, Civil Actions Under $45,000, Eviction, Small Claims, Probate* PO Box 1299, Imperial, NE 69033. 8:00AM-4:00PM. **308-882-4690**, Fax: 308-882-5679. ✉🖐💻

Cherry County

District Court *Felony, Civil Actions Over $45,000* 365 N Main St, Valentine, NE 69201. 8:30AM-4:30PM. **402-376-1840**, Fax: 402-376-3830. Access records-🖐💻

Cherry County Court *Misdemeanor, Civil Actions Under $45,000, Eviction, Small Claims, Probate* 365 N Main St, Valentine, NE 69201. 8AM-5PM. **402-376-2590**, Fax: 402-376-5942. 🖐💻

Cheyenne County

District Court *Felony, Civil Actions Over $15,000* PO Box 217, Sidney, NE 69162. 8AM-N,1-5PM. **308-254-2814**, Fax: 308-254-7832. 🖐💻

Cheyenne County Court *Misdemeanor, Civil Actions Under $45,000, Eviction, Small Claims, Probate* 1000 10th Ave, Sidney, NE 69162. 8AM-5PM. **308-254-2929**, Fax: 308-254-4641 permission to use required. ✉🖐💻

Clay County

District Court *Felony, Civil Actions Over $15,000* Clerk of The District Court 111 W Fairfield St, Clay Center, NE 68933. 8:30AM-5PM. **402-762-3595**, Fax: 402-762-3604. 🖐💻

Clay County Court *Misdemeanor, Civil Actions Under $45,000, Eviction, Small Claims, Probate, Traffic, Juvenile* 111 W Fairfield St, Clay Center, NE 68933. 8:30AM-5PM. **402-762-3651**, Fax: 402-762-3250. 🖐💻

Colfax County

District Court *Felony, Civil Actions Over $15,000* www.colfaxcounty.ne.gov 411 E 11th St, Schuyler, NE 68661. 8:30AM-4:30PM. **402-352-8506**, Fax: 402-352-8550. 🖐💻

Colfax County Court *Misdemeanor, Civil Actions Under $45,000, Eviction, Small Claims, Probate* 411 E 11th St Box 191, Schuyler, NE 68661. 8AM-4:30PM. **402-352-8511**, Fax: 402-352-8535. 🖐💻

Cuming County

District Court *Felony, Civil Actions Over $15,000* 200 S Lincoln, Rm 200, West Point, NE 68788. 8:30AM-4:30PM. **402-372-6004**, Fax: 402-372-6017. Fax🖐💻

Cuming County Court *Misdemeanor, Civil Actions Under $45,000, Eviction, Small Claims, Probate* 200 S Lincoln, Rm 103, West Point, NE 68788. 8:30AM-4:30PM. **402-372-6003**, Fax: 402-372-6030. Probate: 402-372-6003. 🖐💻

Custer County

District Court *Felony, Civil Actions Over $15,000* 431 S 10th Ave, Broken Bow, NE 68822. 9AM-5PM. **308-872-2121**, Fax: 308-872-5826. ☎Fax✉🖐💻

Custer County Court *Misdemeanor, Civil Actions Under $45,000, Eviction, Small Claims, Probate* 431 S 10th Ave, Broken Bow, NE 68822. 8AM-12 1-5PM. **308-872-5761**, Fax: 308-872-6052. 🖐💻

Dakota County

District Court *Felony, Civil Actions Over $15,000* PO Box 66, Dakota City, NE 68731. 8AM-4:30PM. **402-987-2115**, Fax: 402-987-2117. Fax✉🖐💻

Dakota County Court *Misdemeanor, Civil Actions Under $45,000, Eviction, Small Claims, Probate* PO Box 385, Dakota City, NE 68731. 8AM-4:30PM. **402-987-2145**, Fax: 402-987-2185. Fax✉🖐💻.

Dawes County

District Court *Felony, Civil Actions Over $15,000* PO Box 630, Chadron, NE 69337. 8:30AM-4:30PM. **308-432-0109**, Fax: 308-432-0110. 🖐💻

Dawes County Court *Misdemeanor, Civil Actions Under $45,000, Eviction, Small Claims, Probate* PO Box 806, Chadron, NE 69337. 7:30AM-4:30PM. **308-432-0116**, Fax: 308-432-0118. 🖐💻

Dawson County

District Court *Felony, Civil Actions Over $15,000* www.dawsoncountyne.net PO Box 429, Lexington, NE 68850. 8-5PM. **308-324-4261**, Fax: 308-324-3374. 🖐💻

Dawson County Court *Misdemeanor, Civil Actions Under $45,000, Eviction, Small Claims, Probate* 700 N Washington St, Lexington, NE 68850. 8AM-5PM. **308-324-5606**, Fax: 308-324-5607. Court personnel will only search records if specific case # given. 🖐💻

Deuel County

District Court *Felony, Civil Actions Over $15,000* PO Box 327, Chappell, NE 69129. 8AM-4PM. **308-874-3308/2818**, Fax: 308-874-3472. ☎Fax✉🖐💻

Deuel County Court *Misdemeanor, Civil Actions Under $45,000, Eviction, Small Claims, Probate* PO Box 514, Chappell, NE 69129. 8AM-4PM. **308-874-2909**, Fax: 308-874-3472. ✉🖐💻

Dixon County

District Court *Felony, Civil Actions Over $15,000* PO Box 395, Ponca, NE 68770. 8AM-N, 1-5PM. **402-755-2881**, Fax: 402-755-2632. 🖐💻

Dixon County Court *Misdemeanor, Civil Actions Under $45,000, Eviction, Small Claims, Probate* PO Box 497, Ponca, NE 68770. 8AM-4:30PM. **402-755-2355**, Fax: 402-755-2632. Access records-🖐💻

Dodge County

District Court *Felony, Civil Actions Over $15,000* PO Box 1237, Fremont, NE 68026. 8:30AM-4:30PM. **402-727-2780**, Fax: 402-727-2773. Access records-🖐💻

Dodge County Court *Misdemeanor, Civil Actions Under $45,000, Eviction, Small Claims, Probate* 428 N Broad St, Fremont, NE 68025. 8AM-5PM. **402-727-2755**, Fax: 402-727-2762. 🖐💻

Douglas County

District Court *Felony, Civil Actions Over $15,000* www.co.douglas.ne.us 1701 Farnam Hall of Justice, Rm 300, Omaha, NE 68183. 8AM-4:30PM. **402-444-7018**, Fax: 402-444-1757. ✉🖐💻

Douglas County Court *Misdemeanor, Civil Under $45,000, Eviction, Small Claims, Probate* www.co.douglas.ne.us 1819 Farnam, #F03, Omaha, NE 68183. 8AM-4:30PM. Fax: 402-444-2325. Civil phone: 402-444-5424, crim: 402-444-5387. 🖐💻

Dundy County

District Court *Felony, Civil Actions Over $15,000* PO Box 506, Benkelman, NE 69021. 8AM-4PM. **308-423-2058**. 🖐💻

Dundy County Court *Misdemeanor, Civil Actions Under $45,000, Eviction, Small Claims, Probate* PO Box 378, Benkelman, NE 69021. 8AM-4PM. **308-423-2374.** 🖐️💻

Fillmore County

District Court *Felony, Civil Actions Over $15,000* www.fillmorecounty.org PO Box 147, Geneva, NE 68361-0147. 8AM-N, 1-5PM. **402-759-3811,** Fax: 402-759-4440. ☎Fax✉️🖐️💻

Fillmore County Court *Misdemeanor, Civil Actions Under $45,000, Eviction, Small Claims, Probate* PO Box 66, Geneva, NE 68361. 8AM-5PM. **402-759-3514,** Fax: 402-759-4440. Fax✉️🖐️💻

Franklin County

District Court *Felony, Civil Actions Over $15,000* PO Box 146, Franklin, NE 68939. 8:30AM-4:30PM. **308-425-6202,** Fax: 308-425-6093. Access records-🖐️💻

Franklin County Court *Misdemeanor, Civil Actions Under $45,000, Eviction, Small Claims, Probate* PO Box 174, Franklin, NE 68939. 8:30AM-4:30PM. **308-425-6288,** Fax: 308-425-6289. Court personnel not permitted to do record searches. 🖐️💻

Frontier County

District Court *Felony, Civil Actions Over $15,000* PO Box 40, Stockville, NE 69042. 9AM-4:30PM. **308-367-8641,** Fax: 308-367-8730. ✉️🖐️💻

Frontier County Court *Misdemeanor, Civil Actions Under $45,000, Eviction, Small Claims, Probate* PO Box 38, Stockville, NE 69042. 9AM-4:30PM. **308-367-8629,** Fax: 308-367-8730. Fax✉️🖐️💻

Furnas County

District Court *Felony, Civil Actions Over $15,000* PO Box 413, Beaver City, NE 68926. 10AM-N, 1-3PM. **308-268-4015,** Fax: 308-268-3205. ✉️🖐️💻

Furnas County Court *Misdemeanor, Civil Actions Under $45,000, Eviction, Small Claims, Probate* 912 R St (PO Box 373), Beaver City, NE 68926. 8AM-4PM. **308-268-4025.** 🖐️💻

Gage County

District Court *Felony, Civil Actions Over $45,000* 612 Grant St, #11, Beatrice, NE 68310-2946. 8AM-5PM. **402-223-1332,** Fax: 402-223-1313. ✉️Fax🖐️💻

Gage County Court *Misdemeanor, Civil Actions Under $45,000, Eviction, Small Claims, Probate* 612 Grant St, #17, Beatrice, NE 68310-2946. 8AM-5PM. Civil: 402-223-1328, crim: 402-223-1325, Probate: 402-223-1327. ✉️🖐️💻

Garden County

District Court *Felony, Civil Actions Over $15,000* PO Box 486, Oshkosh, NE 69154. 8AM-4PM. **308-772-3924,** Fax: 308-772-0124. Fax✉️🖐️💻

Garden County Court *Misdemeanor, Civil Actions Under $45,000, Eviction, Small Claims, Probate* PO Box 465, Oshkosh, NE 69154. 8AM-4PM. **308-772-3696.** 🖐️💻

Garfield County

District Court *Felony, Civil Actions Over $15,000* PO Box 218, Burwell, NE 68823. 9AM-5PM. **308-346-4161.** ✉️🖐️

Garfield County Court *Misdemeanor, Civil Actions Under $45,000, Eviction, Small Claims, Probate* PO Box 431, Burwell, NE 68823. 9AM-4PM. **308-346-4123,** Fax: 308-346-5064. ✉️🖐️💻

Gosper County

District Court *Felony, Civil Actions Over $15,000* www.co.gosper.ne.us/court.html PO Box 136, Elwood, NE 68937. 8:30AM-4:30PM. **308-785-2611.** 🖐️💻

Gosper County Court *Misdemeanor, Civil Actions Under $45,000, Eviction, Small Claims, Probate* PO Box 55, Elwood, NE 68937. 8:30AM-4:30PM. **308-785-2531,** Fax: 308-785-2300 (call before faxing). 🖐️💻

Grant County

District Court *Felony, Civil Actions Over $15,000* PO Box 139, Hyannis, NE 69350. 8AM-4PM. **308-458-2488,** Fax: 308-458-2780. Fax✉️🖐️💻

Grant County Court *Misdemeanor, Civil Actions Under $45,000, Eviction, Small Claims, Probate* PO Box 97, Hyannis, NE 69350. 11AM-4PM only on 2nd Tues of month. **308-458-2433,** Fax: 308-327-5623. Civil phone: 308-327-2692. This court will not do record searches by name, etc. but will send and certify copies of specific records. 🖐️💻

Greeley County

District Court *Felony, Civil Actions Over $15,000* PO Box 287, Greeley, NE 68842. 8AM-N; 1PM-4PM. **308-428-3625,** Fax: 308-428-3022. ✉️🖐️💻

Greeley County Court *Misdemeanor, Civil Actions Under $45,000, Eviction, Small Claims, Probate* PO Box 302, Greeley, NE 68842. 8AM-5PM. **308-428-2705,** Fax: 308-428-6500. 🖐️💻

Hall County

District Court *Felony, Civil Actions Over $15,000* 111 W First St, Box 1926, Grand Island, NE 68802. 8AM-5PM. **308-385-5144,** Fax: 308-385-5110. ✉️🖐️💻

Hall County Court *Misdemeanor, Civil Actions Under $45,000, Eviction, Small Claims, Probate* 111 W 1st #1, Grand Island, NE 68801. 8AM-5PM. **308-385-5135.** 🖐️💻

Hamilton County

District Court *Felony, Civil Actions Over $15,000* PO Box 201, Aurora, NE 68818-0201. 8AM-5PM. **402-694-3533,** Fax: 402-694-2250. 🖐️💻

Hamilton County Court *Misdemeanor, Civil Actions Under $45,000, Eviction, Small Claims, Probate* PO Box 323, Aurora, NE 68818. 8AM-5PM. **402-694-6188,** Fax: 402-694-2250. Will not do name searches, but will provide specific documents. 🖐️💻

Harlan County

District Court *Felony, Civil Actions Over $15,000* PO Box 698, Alma, NE 68920. 8:30AM-4:30PM. **308-928-2173,** Fax: 308-928-2079. ☎✉️🖐️💻

Harlan County Court *Misdemeanor, Civil Actions Under $45,000, Eviction, Small Claims, Probate* PO Box 379, Alma, NE 68920. 8:30AM-4:30PM. **308-928-2179,** Fax: 308-928-2170. 🖐️💻

Hayes County

District Court *Felony, Civil Actions Over $15,000* PO Box 370, Hayes Center, NE 69032. 8AM-4PM. **308-286-3413,** Fax: 308-286-3208. Fax✉️🖐️💻

Hayes County Court *Misdemeanor, Civil Actions Under $45,000, Eviction, Small Claims, Probate* PO Box 370, Hayes Center, NE 69032. 9AM-N, 1-4PM

Tuesday (Clerk's hours). **308-286-3315**.
☎✉✋💻

Hitchcock County

District Court *Felony, Civil Actions Over $15,000* www.co.hitchcock.ne.us/court.html PO Box 248, Trenton, NE 69044. 8:30AM-4PM. **308-334-5646**, Fax: 308-334-5398. ☎Fax✉✋💻

Hitchcock County Court *Misdemeanor, Civil Actions Under $45,000, Eviction, Small Claims, Probate* PO Box 248, Trenton, NE 69044. 8:30AM-4PM. **308-334-5383**. ☎✉✋💻

Holt County

District Court *Felony, Civil Actions Over $15,000* PO Box 755, O'Neill, NE 68763. 8AM-4:30PM. **402-336-2840**, Fax: 402-336-3601. ☎Fax✉✋💻

Holt County Court *Misdemeanor, Civil Actions Under $45,000, Eviction, Small Claims, Probate* 204 N 4th St, O'Neill, NE 68763. 8AM-4:30PM. **402-336-1662**, Fax: 402-336-1663. Access records-✋💻

Hooker County

District Court *Felony, Civil Actions Over $15,000* PO Box 184, Mullen, NE 69152. 8:30AM-N, 1-4:30PM. **308-546-2244**, Fax: 308-546-2490. ✋💻

Hooker County Court *Misdemeanor, Civil Actions Under $45,000, Eviction, Small Claims, Probate* PO Box 184, Mullen, NE 69152. 8:30AM-4:30PM. **308-546-2249**, Fax: 308-546-2490 (Sheriff). Fax✉✋💻

Howard County

District Court *Felony, Civil Actions Over $15,000* PO Box 25, St Paul, NE 68873. 8AM-5PM. **308-754-4343**, Fax: 308-754-4125. ✋💻

Howard County Court *Misdemeanor, Civil Actions Under $45,000, Eviction, Small Claims, Probate* 612 Indian St #6, St Paul, NE 68873. 8AM-N; 1PM-4PM. **308-754-4192**. ✋💻

Jefferson County

District Court *Felony, Civil Actions Over $15,000* County Courthouse 411 Fourth St, Fairbury, NE 68352. 9AM-5PM. **402-729-2019**, Fax: 402-729-6596. ✋💻

Jefferson County Court *Misdemeanor, Civil Actions Under $45,000, Eviction, Small Claims, Probate* 411 Fourth St, Fairbury, NE 68352. 8AM-N, 1-5PM. **402-729-2312**. Court will not perform name searches for the public. ✋💻

Johnson County

District Court *Felony, Civil Actions Over $15,000* PO Box 416, Tecumseh, NE 68450. 8AM-N, 1-4:30PM. **402-335-6301**, Fax: 402-335-6311. ✋💻

Johnson County Court *Misdemeanor, Civil Actions Under $45,000, Eviction, Small Claims, Probate* PO Box 285, Tecumseh, NE 68450. 8AM-4:30PM. **402-335-6313**, Fax: 402-335-6314. ✋

Kearney County

District Court *Felony, Civil Actions Over $15,000* PO Box 208, Minden, NE 68959. 8:30AM-5PM. **308-832-1742**, Fax: 308-832-0636. Access records-✋💻

Kearney County Court *Misdemeanor, Civil Actions Under $45,000, Eviction, Small Claims, Probate* PO Box 377, Minden, NE 68959. 8AM-5PM. **308-832-2719**, Fax: 308-832-0636. ✋💻✉

Keith County

District Court *Felony, Civil Actions Over $15,000* PO Box 686, Ogallala, NE 69153. 8AM-4PM. **308-284-3849**, Fax: 308-284-3978. Fax✉✋💻

Keith County Court *Misdemeanor, Civil Actions Under $45,000, Eviction, Small Claims, Probate* PO Box 358, Ogallala, NE 69153. 8AM-5PM. **308-284-3693**, Fax: 308-284-6825. Access records-✋💻

Keya Paha County

District Court *Felony, Civil Actions Over $15,000* www.co.keya-paha.ne.us PO Box 349, Springview, NE 68778. 8AM-5PM. **402-497-3791**, Fax: 402-497-3799. Fax✉✋💻

Keya Paha County Court *Misdemeanor, Civil Actions Under $45,000, Eviction, Small Claims, Probate* PO Box 275, Springview, NE 68778. 8AM-4PM every 2nd Friday of each month. **402-497-3021**, Probate: 402-684-3601. ✋💻

Kimball County

District Court *Felony, Civil Actions Over $15,000* 114 E 3rd St, Kimball, NE 69145. 8AM-5PM M-Th, 8AM-4PM F. **308-235-3591**, Fax: 308-235-3654. ✋💻

Kimball County Court *Misdemeanor, Civil Actions Under $45,000, Small*

Claims, Probate 114 E 3rd St, Kimball, NE 69145. 8-5PM. **308-235-2831**. ✋💻

Knox County

District Court *Felony, Civil Actions Over $45,000* PO Box 126, Center, NE 68724. 8:30AM-4:30PM. **402-288-5606**, Fax: 402-288-5609. ✋💻

Knox County Court *Misdemeanor, Civil Actions Under $45,000, Eviction, Small Claims, Probate* PO Box 125, Center, NE 68724. 8:30AM-4:30PM. **402-288-5607**, Fax: 402-288-5609. Access records-✋💻

Lancaster County

District Court *Felony, Civil Actions Over $15,000* www.ci.lincoln.ne.us/cnty/discrt/index.htm 575 S Tenth St, Lincoln, NE 68508-2810. 8AM-4:30PM. **402-441-7328**, Fax: 402-441-6190. ✉✋💻

Lancaster County Court *Misdemeanor, Civil Actions Under $45,000, Eviction, Small Claims, Probate* 575 S 10th, Lincoln, NE 68508. 8AM-4:30PM. **402-441-7291**. ✋💻

Lincoln County

District Court *Felony, Civil Actions Over $15,000* www.seda-cog.org/snyder/ical/calendar.asp PO Box 1616 301 N Jeffers 3rd Fl, North Platte, NE 69103-1616. 8-5PM. **308-534-4350 X301 & X303**. ✋💻

Lincoln County Court *Misdemeanor, Civil Actions Under $45,000, Eviction, Small Claims, Probate* PO Box 519, North Platte, NE 69103. 8AM-5PM. **308-534-4350**, Fax: 308-534-3525. ✋💻

Logan County

District Court *Felony, Civil Actions Over $15,000* PO Box 8, Stapleton, NE 69163. 8:30AM-N; 1-4:30PM M-TH; 8:30AM-N; 1-4PM F. **308-636-2311**. ✉✋💻

Logan County Court *Misdemeanor, Civil Actions Under $45,000, Eviction, Small Claims, Probate* PO Box 8, Stapleton, NE 69163. 8AM-N, 1-4PM Wed. **308-636-2677**. Fax✉✋💻

Loup County

District Court *Felony, Civil Actions Over $15,000* PO Box 146, Taylor, NE 68879. 8:30AM-4:30PM M-Th, 8:30AM-N F. **308-942-6035**, Fax: 308-942-6015. ✋💻

Loup County Court *Misdemeanor, Civil Actions Under $45,000, Eviction, Small Claims, Probate* PO Box 146, Taylor, NE

68879. 8:30AM-4:30 M-Th, 8:30AM-N F. **308-942-6035**, Fax: 308-942-3103. ✋🖥

McPherson County

District Court *Felony, Civil Actions Over $15,000* PO Box 122, Tryon, NE 69167. 8:30AM-4:30PM. **308-587-2363**, Fax: 308-587-2363 (Call first). Fax✉✋🖥

McPherson County Court *Misdm'r, Civil Actions Under $45,000, Eviction, Small Claims, Probate* PO Box 122, Tryon, NE 69167. 8:30AM-N, 1-4:30PM Tu; 8:30AM-N, Th. **308-587-2363**, Fax: 308-587-2363 (Call first). Fax✉✋🖥

Madison County

District Court *Felony, Civil Actions Over $45,000* PO Box 249, Madison, NE 68748. 8AM-5PM. **402-454-3311 X140**, Fax: 402-454-6528. Access records-✋🖥

Madison County Court *Misdemeanor, Civil Actions Under $45,000, Eviction, Small Claims, Probate* PO Box 230, Madison, NE 68748. 8:30AM-5PM. **402-454-3311**, Fax: 402-454-3438. Civil phone: ext 142, crim: ext 181, Probate: ext 165. ✉✋🖥

Merrick County

District Court *Felony, Civil Actions Over $15,000* PO Box 27, Central City, NE 68826. 8AM-5PM. **308-946-2461**, Fax: 308-946-3692. ✋🖥

Merrick County Court *Misdemeanor, Civil Actions Under $45,000, Eviction, Small Claims, Probate* County Courthouse, PO Box 27, Central City, NE 68826. 8AM-5PM. **308-946-2812**. ✋🖥

Morrill County

District Court *Felony, Civil Actions Over $15,000* PO Box 824, Bridgeport, NE 69336. 8AM-N, 1-4:30PM. **308-262-1261**, Fax: 308-262-1799. ✋🖥

Morrill County Court *Misdemeanor, Civil Actions Under $45,000, Eviction, Small Claims, Probate* PO Box 418, Bridgeport, NE 69336. 8AM-4:30PM. **308-262-0812**. ✋🖥

Nance County

District Court *Felony, Civil Actions Over $15,000* PO Box 338, Fullerton, NE 68638. 8AM-5PM. **308-536-2365**, Fax: 308-536-2742. ✋

Nance County Court *Misdemeanor, Civil Actions Under $45,000, Eviction, Small Claims, Probate* PO Box 837, Fullerton, NE 68638. 8AM-5PM. **308-536-2675**, Fax: 308-536-2742. ✉✋🖥

Nemaha County

District Court *Felony, Civil Actions Over $15,000* 1824 N St, Auburn, NE 68305. 8AM-5PM. **402-274-3616**, Fax: 402-274-4478. ✋✉

Nemaha County Court *Misdemeanor, Civil Actions Under $45,000, Eviction, Small Claims, Probate* 1824 N St, Auburn, NE 68305. 8AM-N, 1-5PM. **402-274-3008**, Fax: 402-274-4605. ✋🖥

Nuckolls County

District Court *Felony, Civil Actions Over $15,000* PO Box 362, Nelson, NE 68961. 8:30AM-4:30PM. **402-225-4341**, Fax: 402-225-2373. The Court's search services not available to employers using employment agencies. ✋🖥

Nuckolls County Court *Misdemeanor, Civil Actions Under $45,000, Eviction, Small Claims, Probate* PO Box 372, Nelson, NE 68961. 8AM-4:30PM. **402-225-2371**, Fax: 402-225-2373. Mail access limited to short searches.

Otoe County

District Court *Felony, Dissolutions, Civil Actions Over $15,000* 1021 Central Ave, Rm 209 PO Box 726, Nebraska City, NE 68410. 8AM-5PM doors close at 4:30PM. **402-873-9550**. ✋🖥

Otoe County Court *Misdemeanor, Civil Actions Under $45,000, Eviction, Small Claims, Probate* 1021 Central Ave, Rm 109 PO Box 487, Nebraska City, NE 68410-0487. 8AM-5PM. **402-873-9575**, Fax: 402-873-9030. Fax✉✋🖥

Pawnee County

District Court *Felony, Civil Actions Over $15,000* PO Box 431, Pawnee City, NE 68420. 8AM-4PM. **402-852-2963**. ☎✉✋🖥

Pawnee County Court *Misdemeanor, Civil Actions Under $45,000, Eviction, Small Claims, Probate* PO Box 471, Pawnee City, NE 68420. 8AM-4:30PM. **402-852-2388**, Fax: 402-852-2388. Probate requests accepted by ✉. Access to all other records-✋🖥

Perkins County

District Court *Felony, Civil Actions Over $15,000* PO Box 156, Grant, NE 69140. 8AM-4PM. **308-352-4643**, Fax: 308-352-2455. Fax✉✋🖥

Perkins County Court *Misdemeanor, Civil Actions Under $45,000, Eviction, Small Claims, Probate* PO Box 222, Grant, NE 69140. 8-4PM. **308-352-4415**, Fax: 308-352-4700. ☎Fax✉✋🖥

Phelps County

District Court *Felony, Civil Actions Over $45,000* PO Box 462, Holdrege, NE 68949. 9AM-5PM. **308-995-2281**. ✋🖥

Phelps County Court *Misdemeanor, Civil Actions Under $45,000, Eviction, Small Claims, Probate* PO Box 255, Holdrege, NE 68949. 8AM-12:00, 1-5PM. **308-995-6561**, Fax: 308-995-6562. ✋🖥

Pierce County

District Court *Felony, Civil Actions Over $15,000* 111 W Court St, Rm 12, Pierce, NE 68767. 8:30 AM-4:30PM. **402-329-4335**, Fax: 402-329-6412. ✋🖥

Pierce County Court *Misdemeanor, Civil Actions Under $45,000, Eviction, Small Claims, Probate* 111 W Court St, Rm 11, Pierce, NE 68767. 8:30AM-4:30PM. **402-329-6245**, Fax: 402-329-6412. ✋🖥

Platte County

District Court *Felony, Civil Actions Over $15,000* PO Box 1188, Columbus, NE 68602-1188. 8:30AM-5PM. **402-563-4906**, Fax: 402-562-6718. ✋🖥

Platte County Court *Misdemeanor, Civil Actions Under $45,000, Eviction, Small Claims, Probate* PO Box 538, Columbus, NE 68602-0538. 8AM-5PM. **402-563-4905**, Fax: 402-562-8158. ✋🖥

Polk County

District Court *Felony, Civil Actions Over $15,000* PO Box 447, Osceola, NE 68651. 8AM-N,1-5PM. **402-747-3487**, Fax: 402-747-8299. Access records-✋🖥

Polk County Court *Misdemeanor, Civil Actions Under $45,000, Eviction, Small Claims, Probate* PO Box 506, Osceola, NE 68651. 8AM-5PM. **402-747-5371**, Fax: 402-747-2656. Access records-✋🖥

Key: Symbols refer to criminal records access unless otherwise noted. phone-☎ mail-✉ fax-**Fax** in person-✋ online-🖥 email-**Email**

Red Willow County

District Court *Felony, Civil Actions Over $15,000* 520 Norris Ave (PO Box 847), McCook, NE 69001. 8AM-4PM. **308-345-4583**, Fax: 308-345-7907. ✉✋💻

Red Willow County Court *Misdemeanor, Civil Actions Under $45,000, Eviction, Small Claims, Probate* 502 Norris Ave (PO Box 199), McCook, NE 69001. 8AM-4PM. **308-345-1904**, Fax: 308-345-1904. ✉**Fax**✋💻

Richardson County

District Court *Felony, Civil Actions Over $15,000* 1700 Stone St, Falls City, NE 68355. 8:30AM-5PM. **402-245-2023**, Fax: 402-245-3725. Access records-✋💻

Richardson County Court *Misdemeanor, Civil Actions Under $45,000, Eviction, Small Claims, Probate* 1700 Stone St Rm 205, Falls City, NE 68355. 8AM-5PM. **402-245-2812**, Fax: 402-245-3352. ✋💻

Rock County

District Court *Felony, Civil Actions Over $15,000* PO Box 367, Bassett, NE 68714. 9AM-5PM. **402-684-3933**, Fax: 402-684-2741. ☎**Fax**✉✋💻

Rock County Court *Misdemeanor, Civil Actions Under $45,000, Eviction, Small Claims, Probate* PO Box 249, Bassett, NE 68714. 8AM-5PM. **402-684-3601**, Fax: 402-684-2741. Access records-✋💻

Saline County

District Court *Felony, Civil Actions Over $15,000* PO Box 865, Wilber, NE 68465. 8AM-N, 1-5PM. **402-821-3179**, Fax: 402-821-2132. ✉✋💻

Saline County Court *Misdemeanor, Civil Actions Under $45,000, Eviction, Small Claims, Probate* PO Box 865, Wilber, NE 68465. 8AM-N; 1PM-5PM. **402-821-2131**, Fax: 402-821-2132. **Fax**✉✋💻

Sarpy County

District Court *Felony, Civil Actions Over $50,000* 1210 Golden Gate Dr, #3141, Papillion, NE 68046. 8-4:45PM. **402-593-2267**, Fax: 402-593-4403. ☎✉✋💻

Sarpy County Court *Misdemeanor, Civil Actions Under $50,000, Eviction, Small Claims, Probate* www.sarpy.com/ 1210 Golden Gate Dr, #3142, Papillion, NE 68046. 8-4:45PM. **402-593-5775**. ✋💻

Saunders County

District Court *Felony, Civil Actions Over $15,000* County Courthouse 433 N Chestnut, Wahoo, NE 68066. 8AM-5PM. **402-443-8113**, Fax: 402-443-8170. ✋💻

Saunders County Court *Misdemeanor, Civil Actions Under $45,000, Eviction, Small Claims, Probate* 433 N Chestnut, Wahoo, NE 68066. 8AM-5PM. **402-443-8119**, Fax: 402-443-8121. ✋💻

Scotts Bluff County

District Court *Felony, Civil Actions Over $15,000* 1725 10th St, PO Box 47, Gering, NE 69341-0047. 8AM-4:30PM. **308-436-6641**, Fax: 308-436-6759. ✋💻

Scotts Bluff County Court *Misdemeanor, Civil Actions Under $45,000, Eviction, Small Claims, Probate* 1725 10th St, Gering, NE 69341. 8AM-5PM. **308-436-6648**. Access records✋💻

Seward County

District Court *Felony, Civil Actions Over $15,000* PO Box 36, Seward, NE 68434. 8AM-5PM. **402-643-4895**. ✋💻

Seward County Court *Misdemeanor, Civil Actions Under $45,000, Eviction, Small Claims, Probate* PO Box 37, Seward, NE 68434. 8AM-5PM. **402-643-3341**, Fax: 402-643-2950. ✋💻

Sheridan County

District Court *Felony, Civil Actions Over $10,000* PO Box 581, Rushville, NE 69360. 8:30AM-4:30PM. **308-327-5654**, Fax: 308-327-5618. ✉**Fax**✋💻

Sheridan County Court *Misdemeanor, Civil Actions Under $45,000, Eviction, Small Claims, Probate* PO Box 430, Rushville, NE 69360. 8AM-4:30PM. **308-327-2692**, Fax: 308-327-5623. **Fax**✉✋💻

Sherman County

District Court *Felony, Civil Actions Over $15,000* 630 O St PO Box 456, Loup City, NE 68853. 8:30AM-4:30PM. **308-745-1513 x103**, Fax: 308-745-0297. ✉✋💻

Sherman County Court *Misdemeanor, Civil Actions Under $45,000, Eviction, Small Claims, Probate* 630 O St PO Box 55, Loup City, NE 68853. 8:30AM-4:30PM. **308-745-1513 x102**, Fax: 308-745-1510. **Fax**✉✋💻

Sioux County

District Court *Felony, Civil Actions Over $15,000* PO Box 158, Harrison, NE 69346. 8AM-4:30PM. **308-668-2443**, Fax: 308-668-2443. ✉✋💻

Sioux County Court *Misdemeanor, Civil Actions Under $45,000, Eviction, Small Claims, Probate* PO Box 158, Harrison, NE 69346. 8AM-4:30. **308-668-2443**, Fax: same. ☎**Fax**✉✋💻

Stanton County

District Court *Felony, Civil Actions Over $15,000* PO Box 347, Stanton, NE 68779. 8:30AM-4:30PM. **402-439-2222**, Fax: 402-439-2200. **Fax**✉✋💻

Stanton County Court *Misdemeanor, Civil Actions Under $45,000, Eviction, Small Claims, Probate* 804 Ivy St, PO Box 536, Stanton, NE 68779. 8:30AM-4:30PM. **402-439-2221**, Fax: 402-439-2229. Probate: 402-439-2221. ✋💻

Thayer County

District Court *Felony, Civil Actions Over $15,000* PO Box 297, Hebron, NE 68370. 8AM-N, 1:00PM-4:30PM. **402-768-6116**, Fax 402-768-6128. **Fax**✉✋💻

Thayer County Court *Misdemeanor, Civil Actions Under $45,000, Eviction, Small Claims, Probate* PO Box 94, Hebron, NE 68370. 8AM-4:30PM. **402-768-6325**, Fax: 402-768-7232. ✉✋💻

Thomas County

District Court *Felony, Civil Actions Over $15,000* PO Box 226, Thedford, NE 69166. 8AM-N, 1-4PM. **308-645-2261**, Fax 308-645-2623. **Fax**✉✋💻

Thomas County Court *Misdemeanor, Civil Actions Under $45,000, Eviction, Small Claims, Probate* PO Box 233, Thedford, NE 69166. 8AM-N, 1-4PM. **308-645-2266**, Fax: 308-645-2623. **Fax**✉✋💻

Thurston County

District Court *Felony, Civil Actions Over $15,000* PO Box 216, Pender, NE 68047. 8:30AM-5PM. **402-385-3318**, Fax: 402-385-2762. ✋💻

Thurston County Court *Misdemeanor, Civil Actions Under $45,000, Eviction, Small Claims, Probate* County Courthouse, PO Box 129, Pender, NE 68047. 8:30AM-N,1-5PM. **402-385-3136**, Fax: 402-385-3143. Access records-✋💻

Valley County

District Court *Felony, Civil Actions Over $15,000* 125 S 15th St, Ord, NE 68862. 8AM-5PM. **308-728-3700**, Fax: 308-728-7725. **Fax**✉ 🖐 🖵

Valley County Court *Misdemeanor, Civil Actions Under $45,000, Eviction, Small Claims, Probate* 125 S 15th St, Ord, NE 68862. 8AM-5PM. **308-728-3831**, Fax: 308-728-7725. ☎**Fax**✉ 🖐 🖵

Washington County

District Court *Felony, Civil Actions Over $15,000* PO Box 431, Blair, NE 68008. 8AM-N; 1PM-4:30PM. **402-426-6899**, Fax: 402-426-6898. Access records-🖐 🖵

Washington County Court *Misdemeanor, Civil Actions Under $45,000, Eviction, Small Claims, Probate* 1555 Colfax St, Blair, NE 68008. 8AM-4:30PM. **402-426-6833**, Fax: 402-426-6840. 🖐 🖵

Wayne County

District Court *Felony, Civil Actions Over $15,000* http://county.waynene.org/court_system/ 510 Pearl St, Wayne, NE 68787. 8:30AM-5PM. **402-375-2260**. 🖐 🖵

Wayne County Court *Misdemeanor, Civil Actions Under $45,000, Eviction, Small Claims, Probate* 510 Pearl St, Wayne, NE 68787. 8AM-5PM. **402-375-1622**, Fax: 402-375-1622. 🖐 🖵

Webster County

District Court *Felony, Civil Actions Over $15,000* 621 N Cedar, Red Cloud, NE 68970. 8:30AM-4:30PM. **402-746-2716**, Fax: 402-746-2710. Access records-🖐 🖵

Webster County Court *Misdemeanor, Civil Actions Under $45,000, Eviction, Small Claims, Probate* 621 N Cedar, Red Cloud, NE 68970. 8:30AM-4:30PM. **402-746-2777**, Fax: 402-746-2771. 🖐 🖵

Wheeler County

District Court *Felony, Civil Actions Over $15,000* PO Box 127, Bartlett, NE 68622. 9AM-N, 1-5PM. **308-654-3235**, Fax: 308-654-3470. 🖐 🖵

Wheeler County Court *Misdemeanor, Civil Actions Under $45,000, Eviction, Small Claims, Probate* PO Box 127, Bartlett, NE 68622. 10AM-3PM 1st & 2nd Mon & every Th. **308-654-3376**, Fax: 308-654-3442. ✉ 🖐 🖵

York County

District Court *Felony, Civil Actions Over $15,000* 510 Lincoln Ave, York, NE 68467. 8:30AM-5PM. **402-362-4038**, Fax: 402-362-2577. The SSN does not show up in the computer index, but will show in case files. Access records-🖐 🖵

York County Court *Misdemeanor, Civil Actions Under $45,000, Eviction, Small Claims, Probate* 510 Lincoln Ave, York, NE 68467. 8AM-5PM. **402-362-4925**, Fax: 402-362-2577. Access records-🖐 🖵

Nevada

State Court Administration: Supreme Court of Nevada, Administrative Office of the Courts, Capitol Complex, 201 S Carson St, Carson City, NV, 89701; 775-684-1700, Fax: 775-684-1723. http://www.nvsupremecourt.us/aoc/aoc.html

Court Structure: There are 17 District Courts are the courts of general jurisdiction and are within 9 judicial districts. Their minimum civil limit raises from $7,500 to $10,000 on Jan 1, 2005. The Justice Courts are named for the township of jurisdiction. Note that, due to their small populations, some townships no longer have Justice Courts. The Justice Courts handle misdemeanor crime and traffic matters, small claims disputes, evictions, and other civil matters less than $7,500 (increases to $10,000 on Jan 1, 2005). The justices of the peace also preside over felony and gross misdemeanor arraignments and conduct preliminary hearings to determine if sufficient evidence exists to hold criminals for trial at District Court.

Probate is handled by the District Courts.

Online Access: Some Nevada Courts have internal online computer systems, but only Clark and Washoe counties offer online access to the public. A statewide court automation system is being implemented. The Supreme Court website gives access to opinions.

Additional Information: Many Nevada Justice Courts are small and have very few records. Their hours of operation vary widely and contact is difficult. It is recommended that requesters call ahead for information prior to submitting a written request or attempting an in-person retrieval.

Carson City

1st Judicial District Court *Felony, Gross Misdemeanor, Civil Actions Over $7,500, Probate* 885 E Musser St, #3031, Carson City, NV 89701-4775. 9AM-5PM. **775-887-2082**, Fax: 775-887-2177. ✉ 🖐

Justice & Municipal Court *Minor Misdemeanor, Civil Actions Under $7,500, Eviction, Small Claims* 885 E Musser St, #2007, Carson City, NV 89701-4775. 8:30AM-5PM. **775-887-2121**, Fax: 775-887-2297. ✉ 🖐

Churchill County

3rd Judicial District Court *Felony, Gross Misdemeanor, Civil Over $7,500, Probate* www.churchillcounty.org/dcourt/ 73 N Maine St, #B, Fallon, NV 89406. 8AM-N, 1-5PM. **775-423-6080**, Fax: 775-423-8578. **Fax**✉ 🖐

New River Justice Court *Misdemeanor, Civil Under $7,500, Eviction, Small Claims* www.churchillcounty.org/jcourt/ 71 N Maine St, Fallon, NV 89406. 8AM-5PM. **775-423-2845**, Fax: 775-423-0472. ✉**Fax** 🖐

Key: Symbols refer to criminal records access unless otherwise noted. phone-☎ mail-✉ fax-**Fax** in person-🖐 online-🖵 email-**Email**

Clark County

8th Judicial District Court *Felony, Gross Misdemeanor, Civil Over $7,500, Probate* www.co.clark.nv.us/district_court/courthome.htm 200 S 3rd (PO Box 551601), Las Vegas, NV 89155. 8-5PM. **702-455-3156**, Fax 702-455-4929. ✉☝

Bunkerville Justice Court *Misdemeanor, Civil Actions Under $7,500, Eviction, Small Claims* 190 W Virgin St, Bunkerville, NV 89007. 7-4:30PM M-Th. **702-346-5711**, Fax 702-346-7212. ✉☝

Goodsprings Township Jean Justice Court *Misdemeanor, Civil Actions Under $7,500, Eviction, Small Claims* 1 Main St (PO Box 19155), Jean, NV 89019. 7AM-4PM M-Th. **702-874-1405**, Fax: 702-874-1612. ☎Fax✉☝

Boulder Township Justice Court *Misdemeanor, Civil Actions Under $7,500, Eviction, Small Claims* 505 Ave G, Boulder City, NV 89005. 7:30AM-4:30PM M-TH. **702-455-8000**, Fax: 702-455-8003. Fax✉☝

Mesquite Township Justice Court *Felony, Misdemeanor, Civil Actions Under $7,500, Eviction, Small Claims* 500 Hillside Dr, Mesquite, NV 89027-3116. 7AM-4PM. **702-346-5298**, Fax: 702-346-7319. ☎Fax✉☝

North Las Vegas Township Justice *Misdemeanor, Civil Actions Under $7,500, Eviction, Small Claims* 2428 N Martin L King Blvd, N Las Vegas, NV 89032-3700. 7:15AM-5:45PM. **702-455-7802**, Fax: 702-455-7831. Civil phone: 702-455-7801. Judge must approve all search requests. ☎✉☝

Henderson Township Justice *Misdemeanor, Civil Actions Under $7,500, Eviction, Small Claims* www.co.clark.nv.us/justicecourt_hd/general_information.htm 243 Water St, Henderson, NV 89015. 7AM-5:30PM M-Th. Fax: 702-455-7935. Civil phone: 702-455-7978, crim: 702-455-7929. Traffic: 702-455-7980. ✉☝

Laughlin Township Justice Court *Misdemeanor, Civil Actions Under $7,000, Eviction, Small Claims* 101 Civic Way, #2, Laughlin, NV 89029. 8AM-4:30PM (T-Fri). **702-298-4622**, Fax: 702-298-7508. Fax✉☝

Moapa Township Justice Court *Misd., Civil Actions Under $7,500, Eviction, Small Claims* www.co.clark.nv.us/ 1340 E Com Hwy, PO Box 280, Moapa, NV 89025. 8AM-5PM M-Th. **702-864-2333**, Fax: 702-864-2585. Fax✉☝

Moapa Valley Township Justice Court *Misdemeanor, Civil Actions Under $7,500, Eviction, Small Claims* 320 N Moapa Valley Blvd PO Box 337, Overton, NV 89040. 6:30-4:30PM M-Th. **702-397-2840**, Fax 702-397-2842. ✉☝

Las Vegas Township Justice *Misd., Civil Actions $7,500, Eviction, Small Claims* www.co.clark.nv.us/justicecourt_lv/welcome.htm PO Box 552511 (200 S 3rd, 2nd Fl) Las Vegas, NV 89155-2511. 8AM-5PM. **702-455-4435**, Fax: 702-455-4529. ☎Fax✉☝

Searchlight Township Justice *Misd., Civil Actions Under $7,500, Eviction, Small Claims* PO Box 815, Searchlight, NV 89046. 7AM-5:30PM M-Th. **702-297-1252**, Fax: 702-297-1022. Fax✉☝

Douglas County

9th Judicial District Court *Felony, Gross Misdemeanors, Civil Over $7,500, Probate* http://cltr.co.douglas.nv.us/CourtClerk/courtideas/courtclerkhome.htm PO Box 218, Minden, NV 89423. 8AM-5PM. **775-782-9820**, Fax: 775-782-9954. ✉☝

East Fork Justice Court *Misdemeanor, Civil Actions Under $7,500, Eviction, Small Claims* PO Box 218, Minden, NV 89423. 8AM-5PM. **775-782-9955**, Fax: 775-782-9947. ✉☝

Tahoe Justice Court *Misdemeanor, Civil Actions Under $7,500, Eviction, Small Claims* PO Box 7169, Stateline, NV 89449. 9AM-5PM. **775-586-7200**, Fax: 775-586-7203. ☎✉☝

Elko County

4th Judicial District Court *Felony, Gross Misdemeanor, Civil Actions Over $7,500, Probate* 571 Idaho St, 3rd Fl, Elko, NV 89801. 9AM-5PM. **775-753-4600**, Fax: 775-753-4610. ☎✉☝

Elko Justice Court *Misdemeanor, Civil Actions Under $7,500, Eviction, Small Claims* PO Box 176, Elko, NV 89803. 9AM-N, 1-5PM. **775-738-8403**, Fax: 775-738-8416. ✉☝

Carlin Justice Court *Misdemeanor, Civil Actions Under $7,500, Eviction, Small Claims* PO Box 789, Carlin, NV 89822. 8AM-5PM. **775-754-6321**, Fax: 775-754-6893. ✉☝

Eastline Justice Court *Misdemeanor, Civil Actions Under $7,500, Eviction, Small Claims* PO Box 2300, West Wendover, NV 89883. 9AM-5PM. **775-664-2305**, Fax: 775-664-2979. ✉☝

Jackpot Justice Court *Misdemeanor, Civil Actions Under $7,500, Eviction, Small Claims* PO Box 229, Jackpot, NV 89825. 9AM-N, 1-5PM. **775-755-2456**, Fax: 775-755-9455. Fax✉☝

Wells Justice Municipal Court *Misd., Civil Actions Under $7,500, Eviction, Small Claims* PO Box 297, Wells, NV 89835. 9AM-N,1-5PM. **775-752-3726**, Fax 775-752-3363. ✉☝

Esmeralda County

5th Judicial District Court *Felony, Gross Misdemeanor, Civil Actions Over $7,500, Probate* PO Box 547, Goldfield, NV 89013. 8-5PM; Closed lunch. **775-485-6309**, Fax: 775-485-6376. Fax✉☝

Esmeralda Justice Court *Misdemeanor, Civil Actions Under $7,500, Eviction, Small Claims* PO Box 370, Goldfield, NV 89013. 8AM-5PM. **775-485-6359**, Fax: 775-485-3462. ☎Fax✉☝

Eureka County

7th Judicial District Court *Felony, Gross Misdemeanor, Civil Actions Over $7,500, Probate* PO Box 677, Eureka, NV 89316. 8AM-N, 1-5PM. **775-237-5262**, Fax: 775-237-6015. ☎Fax✉☝

Beowawe Justice Court *Misdemeanor, Civil Actions Under $7,500, Eviction, Small Claims* PO Box 211338, Crescent Valley, NV 89821. 8AM-N, 1-5PM. **775-468-0244**, Fax: 775-468-0323. ✉☝

Eureka Justice Court *Misdemeanor, Civil Actions Under $7,500, Eviction, Small Claims* PO Box 496, Eureka, NV 89316. 8AM-N,1-5PM. **775-237-5540**, Fax: 775-237-6016. ☎✉☝

Humboldt County

6th Judicial District Court *Felony, Gross Misd., Civil Actions Over $7,500, Probate* 50 W 5th St, Winnemucca, NV 89445. 8AM-5PM. **775-623-6343**, Fax: 775-623-6309. ☎Fax✉☝

Union Justice Court *Misdemeanor, Civil Under $7,500, Eviction, Small Claims* www.humboldt-county-nv.net/justice/ PO Box 1218, Winnemucca, NV 89446. 8AM-5PM. **775-623-6377**, Fax: 775-623-6439. Fax✉☝

Lander County

6th Judicial District Court *Felony, Gross Misdemeanor, Civil Actions Over $7,500, Probate* 315 S Humboldt, Battle Mountain, NV 89820. 8-5PM. **775-635-5738**, Fax: 775-635-5761. ☎Fax✉👋

Argenta Justice Court *Misd., Civil Under $10,000, Eviction, Small Claims* 315 S Humboldt, Battle Mountain, NV 89820. 7:30AM-6PM. **775-635-5151**, Fax: 775-635-0604. ☎Fax✉👋

Austin Justice Court *Misdemeanor, Civil Actions Under $7,500, Eviction, Small Claims* PO Box 100, Austin, NV 89310. 8AM-4PM M, 8AM-N T-Th. **775-964-2380**, Fax: 775-964-2327. ☎✉Fax👋

Lincoln County

7th Judicial District Court *Felony, Gross Misdemeanor, Civil Actions Over $7,500, Probate* PO Box 90, Pioche, NV 89043. 9AM-5PM. **775-962-5390**, Fax: 702-962-5180. ✉👋

Meadow Valley Justice Court *Misdemeanor, Civil Actions Under $7,500, Eviction, Small Claims* PO Box 36, Pioche, NV 89043. 9-5PM. **775-962-5140**, Fax: 775-962-5559. ☎Fax✉👋

Pahranagat Valley Justice Court *Misdemeanor, Civil Actions Under $7,500, Eviction, Small Claims* PO Box 449, Alamo, NV 89001. 9AM-5PM. **775-725-3357**, Fax: 775-725-3566. Fax✉👋

Lyon County

3rd Judicial District Court *Felony, Gross Misd., Civil Actions Over $7,500, Probate* 27 S Main St (PO Box 816), Yerington, NV 89447. 8AM-5PM. **775-463-6503**, Fax: 775-463-6575. ☎✉👋

Dayton Township Justice Court *Misd., Civil Actions Under $7,500, Eviction, Small Claims* 235 Main St, Dayton, NV 89403. 8AM-5PM. **775-246-6233**, Fax: 775-246-6203. ☎Fax✉👋

Smith Valley Justice Court *Misdemeanor, Civil Actions Under $7500.00, Eviction, Small Claims* PO Box 141, Smith, NV 89430. 8AM-N Tues & Fri or by appointment. **775-465-2313**, Fax: 775-465-2153. ☎✉👋

Fernley Justice Court *Misdemeanor, Civil Actions Under $7,500, Eviction, Small Claims* 565 E Main St, Fernley,

NV 89408. 8AM-5PM. **775-575-3355**, Fax: 775-575-3359. ☎✉👋

Mason Valley Justice Court *Misd., Civil Actions Under $7,500, Eviction, Small Claims* 30 Nevin Way, Yerington, NV 89447. 8AM-5PM. **775-463-6639**, Fax: 775-463-6638. ☎✉👋

Mineral County

5th Judicial District Court *Felony, Gross Misd., Civil Actions Over $7,500, Probate* PO Box 1450, Hawthorne, NV 89415. 8AM-5PM. **775-945-2446**, Fax: 775-945-0706. ☎Fax✉👋

Hawthorne Justice Court *Misd., Civil Under $7,500, Eviction, Small Claims* PO Box 1660, Hawthorne, NV 89415. 8AM-5PM. **775-945-3859**, Fax: 775-945-0700. This court holds records from **Schurz Justice Court.** ☎✉👋fax.

Nye County

5th Judicial District Court *Felony, Gross Misdemeanor, Civil Over $7,500, Probate* PO Box 1031, Tonopah, NV 89049. 8AM-5PM. **775-482-8131**, Fax: 775-482-8133. ☎Fax✉👋

Tonopah Justice Court *Misd., Civil Under $7,500, Eviction, Small Claims* PO Box 1151, Tonopah, NV 89049. 8AM-N, 1-5PM. **775-482-8155**. ☎✉👋

Beatty Justice Court *Misdemeanor, Civil Actions Up to $7,500, Eviction, Small Claims* PO Box 805, Beatty, NV 89003. 8AM-5PM. **775-553-2951**, Fax: 775-553-2136. ☎✉👋

Pershing County

6th Judicial District Court *Felony, Civil Actions Over $7,500, Probate* PO Box 820, Lovelock, NV 89419. 9AM-5PM. **775-273-2410**, Fax: 775-273-2434. ☎Fax If 3 names or less- ✉👋

Lake Township Justice Court *Misd., Civil Actions Under $7,500, Eviction, Small Claims* PO Box 8, Lovelock, NV 89419. 8AM-5PM. **775-273-2753**, Fax: 775-273-0416. ☎✉👋

Storey County

1st Judicial District Court *Felony, Gross Misdemeanor, Civil Actions Over $7,500, Probate* PO Drawer D, Virginia City, NV 89440. 9AM-5PM. **775-847-0969**, Fax: 775-847-0921. ☎✉Fax👋

Virginia City Justice Court *Misd., Civil Actions Under $7,500, Eviction, Small Claims* PO Box 674, Virginia City, NV 89440. 9AM-5PM. **775-847-0962**, Fax: 775-847-0915. ☎✉👋

Washoe County

2nd Judicial District Court *Felony, Gross Misd., Civil Over $7,500, Probate* www.washoecourts.com/ PO Box 30083, Reno, NV 89520. 8AM-5PM. **775-328-3110**, Fax: 775-328-3515. ☎💻✉👋

Incline Village Justice Court *Misdemeanor, Civil Actions Under $7,500, Eviction, Small Claims* 865 Tahoe Blvd, #301, Incline Village, NV 89451. 9AM-5PM. **775-832-4100**, Fax: 775-832-4162. ✉👋

Verdi Justice Court *Misdemeanor, Civil Actions Under $7,500, Eviction, Small Claims* PO Box 740, Verdi, NV 89439. 8AM-4PM. **775-345-0173**, Fax: 775-345-0633. All record requests must be in writing. ✉👋

Wadsworth Justice Court *Misdemeanor, Civil Actions Under $7,500, Eviction, Small Claims* PO Box 68, Wadsworth, NV 89442. 8AM-5PM T,W,TH only. **775-575-4585**, Fax: 775-575-0253. ✉👋

Sparks Justice Court *Misdemeanor, Civil Actions Under $7,500, Eviction, Small Claims* http://207.228.25.168/sjc/ 630 Greenbrae Dr, Sparks, NV 89431. 8AM-5PM. **775-352-3003**. ☎✉👋

Reno Justice Court *Misdemeanor, Civil Actions Under $7,500, Eviction, Small Claims* http://207.228.25.162/rjc/ PO Box 30083, Reno, NV 89520. 8AM-5PM. **775-325-6501**, Fax: 775-325-6510 crim (civil fax: 775-325-6715). Criminal phone: 775-325-6500. ✉👋

White Pine County

Ely Justice Court *Misdemeanor, Civil Actions Under $7,500, Eviction, Small Claims* 801 Clark St, #6, Ely, NV 89301. 9AM-5PM. **775-289-2678**, Fax: 775-289-3392. ☎Fax✉👋

Lund Justice Court *Misdemeanor, Civil Actions Under $7,500, Eviction, Small Claims* PO Box 87, Lund, NV 89317. 10AM-2:30PM M,W,F. **775-238-5400**, Fax: 775-238-5400. ✉👋

Key: Symbols refer to criminal records access unless otherwise noted. phone-☎ mail-✉ fax-Fax in person-👋 online-💻 email-Email

New Hampshire

State Court Administration: Administrative Office of the Courts, Supreme Court Bldg, 2 Noble Dr, Concord, NH, 03301; 603-271-2521, Fax: 603-271-3977. www.state.nh.us/courts/home.htm

Court Structure: The Superior Court is the court of General Jurisdiction. Felony cases include Class A misdemeanors.

The District Court upper civil limit was increased to $25,000 from $10,000 on 1/1/93. Filing a civil case in the monetary "overlap" area between the Superior Court minimum and the District Court maximum is at the discretion of the filer.

The municipal courts have been closed as the judges retire. The caseload and records are absorbed by the nearest District Court.

Online Access: While there is no statewide access available for trial court records, the web page has a lot of useful information, including opinions and directives form the Supreme Court, Superior Courts, and District Courts. Click on Search. Probate Court website is www.state.nh.us/courts/probate.htm

Additional Information: Important Notice - Fee Changes Pending

Fees for searching, copies, and certification are set by the New Hampshire Supreme Court. Effective September 10, 2004, the New Hampshire Supreme Court directed all New Hampshire District Courts to immediately enact a most dramatic fee increase (as much as 2500%) for a record search.The new fee structure is as follows: Record research fee: $25.00 per name; Certificate of Judgment $10.00; certification fee $5.00; copy fee $.50 per page; computer screen printout $.50 per page. Previously, the fee structure was as follows: Computer search - $10.00 for up to 10 names in one request; $25.00 for 10 or more names in one request; $25.00 per hour for search time beyond one hour.As we go to press, only one court has made the switchover (Keene District Court in Chesire County). It is uncertain if and when the other District Court Clerks will institute this fee increase. As a result, we are leaving the current fee sturcture in place in the text of this book, and advising readers of possible increases. We also advise to call the District Court before mailing search requests.

Belknap County

Superior Court *Felony, Civil Over $1,500* 64 Court St, Laconia, NH 03246. 8AM-4:30PM. **603-524-3570.** ☎ ✉ ✍

Laconia District Court *Misdemeanor, Civil Actions Under $25,000, Eviction, Small Claims* 26 Academy St PO Box 1010, Laconia, NH 03247. 8AM-4PM. **603-524-4128.** Includes City of Laconia and the towns of Meredith, New Hampton, Gilford, Belmont, Alton, Gilmanton, Center Harbor, and Barnstead. ✉ ✍

Probate Court 64 Court St PO Box 1343, Laconia, NH 03247-1343. 8AM-4PM. **603-524-0903.**

Carroll County

Superior Court *Felony, Civil Actions Over $1,500* 96 Water Village Rd -box 3, Ossipee, NH 03864-7267. 8AM-4PM. **603-539-2201.** ✉ ✍

Northern Carroll County District Court *Misdemeanor, Civil Actions Under $25,000, Eviction, Small Claims* PO Box 940, Conway, NH 03818. 8AM-4PM. **603-356-7710.** Includes Towns of Conway, Bartlett, Jackson, Eaton, Chatham, Hart's Location, Albany, Madison and the unincorporated places of Hale's Location, Cutt's Grant, Hadley's

Purchase, and portions of Livermore and Waterville. ✉ ✍

Southern Carroll County District Court *Misdemeanor, Civil Actions Under $25,000, Eviction, Small Claims* 96 Water Village Rd #2, Ossipee, NH 03864. 8AM-4PM. **603-539-4561.** The former Wolfeboro District Court has been combined with this court. Includes Towns of Ossipee, Tamworth, Freedom, Effingham, Wakefield, Wolfeboro, Brookfield, Tuftonboro, Moultonborough, and Sandwich. ✉ ✍

Probate Court 96 Water Village Rd., Ossipee, NH 03864. 8:AM-4:00PM. **603-539-4123**, Fax: 603-539-4761.

Cheshire County

Superior Court *Felony, Civil Actions Over $1,500, Family law* 12 Court St, Keene, NH 03431. 8AM-4PM. **603-352-6902.** ✉ ✍

Jaffrey-Peterborough District Court *Misdemeanor, Civil Actions Under $25,000, Eviction, Small Claims* 84 Peterborough St PO Box 39, Jaffrey, NH 03452-0039. 8AM-4PM. **603-532-8698.** Includes towns of Peterborough, Hancock, Greenville, Greenfield, New Ipswich, Temple, Sharon, Jaffrey, Dublin, Fitzwilliam, and Rindge. ✉ ✍

Keene District Court *Misdemeanor, Civil Under $25,000, Eviction, Small Claims* PO Box 364, Keene, NH 03431. 8AM-4PM. **603-352-2559.** Includes city of Keene and the towns of Stoddard, Westmoreland, Surry, Gilsum, Sullivan, Nelson, Roxbury, Marlow, Swanzey, Marlborough, Winchester, Richmond, Hinsdale, Harrisville, Walpole, Alstead, Troy, and Chesterfield. ✉ ✍

Probate Court 12 Court St, Keene, NH 03431. 8AM-4:30PM. **603-357-7786.**

Coos County

Superior Court *Felony, Civil Actions Over $1,500* 55 School St #301, Lancaster, NH 03584. 8AM-4PM. **603-788-4900.** ✉ ✍

Berlin District Court *Misdemeanor, Civil Actions Under $25,000, Eviction, Small Claims* 220 Main St, Berlin, NH 03570. 8AM-4PM. **603-752-3160.** Includes towns of Berlin, Dummer, and Milan and the unincorporated places of Cambridge and Success. ✉ ✍

Gorham District Court *Misdemeanor, Civil Actions Under $25,000, Eviction, Small Claims* PO Box 176, Gorham, NH 03581. 8AM-4PM. **603-466-2454.** Includes towns of Gorham, Shelburne, and Randolph and the unincorporated places of Bean's Purchase, Martin's Location, Green's Grant, Pinkham's Grant, Sargent's Purchase, Thompson & Meserve's Purchase and Low & Burbank's Grant. Access records-✉🖐

Colebrook District Court *Misdemeanor, Civil Actions Under $25,000, Eviction, Small Claims* PO Box 5 - 10 Bridge St, Colebrook, NH 03576. 8AM-N,1-4PM. **603-237-4229**. Includes towns of Colebrook, Pittsburg, Clarksville, Wentworth's Location, Errol, Millsfield, Columbia, Stewartstown, Stratford, and unincorp. Dix's Grant, Atkinson & Gilmanton Academy Grant, Second College, Grant, Dixville, Erving's Location, and Odell. ✉🖐

Lancaster District Court *Misdemeanor, Civil Actions Under $25,000, Eviction, Small Claims* 55 School St, #201, Lancaster, NH 03584. 8:30AM-4PM. **603-788-4485**. Includes Lancaster, Whitefield, Northumberland, Stark, Jefferson, Carroll, Kilkenny, Bean's Grant, Chandler's Purchase and Crawford's Purchase. ✉🖐

Probate Court 55 School St #104, Lancaster, NH 03584. 8AM-4PM. **603-788-2001**.

Grafton County

Superior Court *Felony, Civil Actions Over $1,500* 3785 Dartmouth College Hwy, North Haverhill, NH 03774. 8AM-4:30PM. **603-787-6961**. ✉🖐

Littleton District Court *Misdemeanor, Civil Actions Under $25,000, Eviction, Small Claims* 134 Main St, Littleton, NH 03561. 8AM-4PM. **603-444-7750**. Includes towns of Littleton, Monroe, Lyman, Lisbon, Franconia, Bethlehem, Sugar Hill, and Easton. ✉🖐

Plymouth District Court *Misd., Civil Under $25,000, Eviction, Small Claims* 26 Green St, Plymouth, NH 03264. 8AM-4PM. **603-536-3326**. Includes towns of Plymouth, Bristol, Dorchester, Groton, Wentworth, Rumney, Ellsworth, Thornton, Campton, Ashland, Hebron, Holderness, Bridgewater, Alexandria, Lincoln, Woodstock, and portions of Livermore and Waterville. ✉🖐

Haverhill District Court *Misdemeanor, Civil Actions Under $25,000, Eviction, Small Claims* Grafton County Courthouse 3785 Dartmouth College Highway - Box 10, North Haverhill, NH 03774. 8:00AM-4:30PM. **603-787-6626**. Includes towns of

Haverhill, Bath, Landaff, Benton, Piermont, and Warren. ✉🖐

Lebanon District Court *Misdemeanor, Civil Actions Under $25,000, Eviction, Small Claims* 38 Centerra Parkway, Lebanon, NH 03766. 8AM-4PM. **603-643-3555**. Includes towns of Lebanon, Enfield, Canaan, Grafton, Orange, Hanover, Orford, and Lyme. ✉🖐

Probate Court 3785 Dartmouth College Hwy, Box 3, North Haverhill, NH 03774-4936. 8AM-4PM. **603-787-6931**.

Hillsborough County

Superior Court - Southern District *Felony, Civil Actions Over $1,500* 30 Spring St, Nashua, NH 03061. 8AM-4PM. **603-883-6461**. ✉🖐

Superior Court - North District *Felony, Civil Actions Over $1,500* 300 Chestnut St Rm 127, Manchester, NH 03101. 8:30AM-4PM. **603-669-7410**. ✉🖐

Manchester District Court *Misdemeanor, Civil Actions Under $25,000, Eviction, Small Claims* PO Box 456, Manchester, NH 03105. 8AM-4PM. **603-624-6510**. Includes city of Manchester. ✉

Nashua District Court *Misdemeanor, Civil Actions Under $25,000, Eviction, Small Claims* PO Box 310, Nashua, NH 03061-0310. 8AM-4PM. **603-880-3333**. Includes city of Nashua and the towns of Hudson and Hollis. ✉🖐

Hillsborough District Court *Misdemeanor, Civil Actions Under $25,000, Eviction, Small Claims* PO Box 763, Hillsborough, NH 03244. 8AM-4PM. **603-464-5811**. Includes towns of Hillsborough, Deering, Windsor, Antrim, and Bennington. ✉🖐

Goffstown District Court *Misdemeanor, Civil Actions Under $25,000, Eviction, Small Claims* PO Box 129, Goffstown, NH 03045. 8AM-4PM. **603-497-2597**. Includes towns of Goffstown, Weare, New Boston, and Francestown. ✉🖐

Merrimack District Court *Misd., Civil Actions Under $25,000, Eviction, Small Claims* PO Box 324, Merrimack, NH 03054-0324. 8AM-4PM. **603-424-9916**. Includes towns of Merrimack, Litchfield, and Bedford. ✉🖐

Milford District Court *Misdemeanor, Civil Actions Under $25,000, Eviction, Small Claims* 180 Elm St, Milford, NH 03055-4735. 8AM-4PM. **603-673-2900**. Includes towns of Milford, Brookline, Amherst, Mason, Wilton, Lyndeborough, and Mont Vernon. Access records-✉🖐

Probate Court PO Box P, Nashua, NH 03061-6015. 8AM-4PM. **603-882-1231**, Fax: 603-882-1620.

Merrimack County

Superior Court *Felony, Civil Actions Over $1,500* PO Box 2880, Concord, NH 03302-2880. 8AM-4PM. **603-225-5501**. ☎✉🖐

New London District Court *Misdemeanor, Civil Actions Under $25,000, Eviction, Small Claims* PO Box 1966, New London, NH 03257. 8:30AM-4PM. **603-526-6519**. Includes towns of New London, Wilmot, Newbury, and Sutton. ✉🖐

Concord District Court *Misd., Civil Under $25,000, Eviction, Small Claims* 32 Clinton St, PO Box 3420, Concord, NH 03302-3420. 8AM-4PM. **603-271-6400**. The former Pittsfield District Court combined with this court. Includes city of Concord, and the towns of Loudon, Canterbury, Dunbarton, Bow, Hopkinton, Pittsfield, Chichester, and Epsom. ✉🖐

Franklin District Court *Misdemeanor, Civil Actions Under $25,000, Eviction, Small Claims* 7 Hancock Terrace, Franklin, NH 03235. 8AM-4PM. **603-934-3290**. Includes city of Franklin and the towns of Northfield, Danbury, Andover, Boscawen, Salisbury, Hill, Webster, Sanbornton, and Tilton. ✉🖐

Henniker District Court *Misdemeanor, Civil Actions Under $25,000, Eviction, Small Claims* 2 Depot St, Henniker, NH 03242. 8AM-4PM. **603-428-3214**. Includes towns of Henniker, Warner, and Bradford. ✉🖐

Hooksett District Court *Misdemeanor, Civil Actions Under $25,000, Eviction, Small Claims* 101 Merrimack, Hooksett, NH 03106. 8AM-4PM. **603-485-9901**. Includes towns of Allenstown, Pembroke, and Hooksett. ✉🖐

Probate Court 163 N Main St, Concord, NH 03301. 8AM-4:30PM July-Aug.: 8-4. **603-224-9589**, Fax: 603-225-0179.

Rockingham County

Superior Court *Felony, Civil Actions Over $1,500* PO Box 1258, Kingston, NH 03848-1258. 8-4PM. **603-642-5256.** 🖐

Salem District Court *Misdemeanor, Civil Actions Under $25,000, Eviction, Small Claims* 35 Geremonty Dr, Salem, NH 03079. 8AM-4PM. **603-893-4483.** Includes towns of Salem, Windham, and Pelham. ✉🖐

Portsmouth District Court *Misd., Civil Under $25,000, Eviction, Small Claims* 111 Parrott Ave, Portsmouth, NH 03801. 8-4PM. **603-431-2192.** Includes city of Portsmouth and the towns of Newington, Greenland, Rye, and New Castle. ✉🖐

Exeter District Court *Misdemeanor, Civil Actions Under $25,000, Eviction, Small Claims* PO Box 394, Exeter, NH 03833. 8AM-4PM. **603-772-2931.** Includes towns of Exeter, Newmarket, Stratham, Newfields, Fremont, East Kingston, Kensington, Epping, and Brentwood. ✉🖐

Hampton District Court *Misdemeanor, Civil Actions Under $25,000, Eviction, Small Claims* PO Box 10, Hampton, NH 03843-0010. 8AM-4PM. **603-926-8117.** Includes towns of Hampton, Hampton Falls, North Hampton, South Hampton, and Seabrook. ✉🖐

Plaistow District Court *Misdemeanor, Civil Actions Under $25,000, Eviction, Small Claims* 14 Elm St (PO Box 129), Plaistow, NH 03865. 8AM-4PM. **603-382-4651,** Fax: 603-382-4952. Includes towns of Plaistow, Hampstead, Kingston, Newton, Atkinson, and Danville. ✉🖐

Derry District Court *Misdemeanor, Civil Actions Under $25,000, Eviction, Small Claims* 10 Manning St, Derry, NH 03038. 8AM-4PM. **603-434-4676.** Includes towns of Derry, Londonderry, Chester, and Sandown. ☎✉🖐

Auburn District Court *Misdemeanor, Civil Actions Under $25,000, Eviction, Small Claims* 5 Priscilla Lane, Auburn, NH 03032. 8AM-4PM. Civil: 603-624-2265, crim: 603-624-2084. Includes towns of Auburn, Candia, Deerfield, Northwood, Nottingham, Raymond. ✉🖐

Probate Court PO Box 789, Kingston, NH 03848. 8AM-4PM. **603-642-7117.**

Strafford County

Superior Court *Felony, Civil Over $1,500* PO Box 799, Dover, NH 03821-0799. 8:30-4PM. **603-742-3065.** ✉🖐

Rochester District Court *Misd., Civil Under $25,000, Eviction, Small Claims* 76 N Main St, Rochester, NH 03867. 8AM-4PM. **603-332-3516.** Includes city of Rochester and the towns of Barrington, Milton, New Durham, Farmington, Strafford, and Middleton. ✉🖐

Durham District Court *Misd., Civil Under $25,000, Eviction, Small Claims* 1 Main St, Durham, NH 03824. 8:30AM-4PM. **603-868-2323.** Includes towns of Durham, Lee, and Madbury. ✉🖐

Dover District Court *Misdemeanor, Civil Under $20,000, Eviction, Small Claims* 25 St Thomas St, Dover, NH 03820. 8AM-4PM. **603-742-7202,** Fax: 603-742-5956. Note: Includes City of Dover, Somersworth, and Rollinsford. ✉🖐

Probate Court PO Box 799, Dover, NH 03821-0799. 8-4:30PM. **603-742-2550.**

Sullivan County

Superior Court *Felony, Civil Over $1,500* 22 Main St, Newport, NH 03773. 8AM-4:00PM. **603-863-3450.** ✉🖐

Claremont District Court *Misdemeanor, Civil Actions Under $25,000, Eviction, Small Claims* PO Box 313, Claremont, NH 03743. 8AM-4PM. **603-542-6064.** Includes city of Claremont and the towns of Cornish, Unity, Charlestown, Acworth, Langdon, and Plainfield. ☎✉🖐

Newport District Court *Misdemeanor, Civil Actions Under $25,000, Eviction, Small Claims* 55 Main St, Newport, NH 03773. 8AM-4PM. **603-863-1832.** Includes towns of Newport, Grantham, Croydon, Springfield, Sunapee, Goshen, Lempster, Washington. ✉🖐

Probate Court PO Box 417, Newport, NH 03773. 8AM-4PM. **603-863-3150.**

New Jersey

State Court Administration (All County Superior Courts and Special Civil Parts): Administrative Office of the Courts, RJH Justice Complex, Courts Bldg 7th Floor, CN 037, Trenton, NJ, 08625; 609-984-0275, Fax: 609-984-6968. http://www.judiciary.state.nj.us/admin.htm

Court Structure: Each Superior Court has 2 divisions; one for the Civil Division and another for the Criminal Division. Search requests should be addressed separately to each division.

Civil cases in which the amounts in controversy exceeds $15,000 are heard in the Civil Division of Superior Court. Cases in which the amounts in controversy are between $3,000 and $15,000 are heard in the Special Civil Part of the Civil Division. Those in which the amounts in controversy are less than $3,000 also are heard in the Special Civil Part and are known as small claims cases. Probate is handled by Surrogates.

Criminal Courts: Criminal searches may be done in person at the court on their public access terminal, but the Superior court now directs non-in person searches to the New Jersey State Police Records and ID Section at 609-882-2000, x2991 or x2918, which are fingerprint-based searches. For information on purchase of statewide public access criminal records databases, call 609-292-4681.

Online Access: The Judiciary's civil motion calendar is searchable online at http://www.judiciary.state.nj.us/calendars.htm. The database includes all Superior Court Motion Calendars for the Civil Division (Law-Civil Part, Special CivilPart and Chancery-General Equity), and proceeding information for a six-week period (two weeks prior to the current date and four weeks following).

Key: Symbols refer to criminal records access unless otherwise noted. phone-☎ mail-✉ fax-**Fax** in person-🖐 online-🖥 email-**Email**

The state has 3 computerized case management systems - ACMS, AMIS, and FACTS - which are not open to the general public:

ACMS (Automated Case Management System) contains data on all active civil cases statewide from the Law Division-Civil Part, Chancery Division-Equity Part, the Special Civil Part statewide, and the Appellate Division.

AMIS (Archival Management Information System) contains closed civil case information. Records go back to the late 1980s.

FACTS (Family Automated Case Tracking System) contains information on dissolutions from all counties.

The fee is $1.00 per minute of use, and a $500 collateral account is required. For further information or an Inquiry System Guidebook containing hardware and software requirements and an enrollment form, write to: Superior Court Clerk's Office, Electronic Access Program, 25 Market St, CN971, Trenton NJ 08625, FAX 609-292-6564, or call 609-292-4987.

Another useful site giving decisions is maintained by the Rutgers Law School, go to http://lawlibrary.rutgers.edu/search.shtml.

Additional Information: Starting in 2004, Superior Courts have the option of directing civil case inquiries to the main NJ Superior Court, PO Box 971, Trenton, NJ 08625, Attn: Judgment Unit; telephone 609-292-4804. The Judgement unit will not accept fax requests, but will do a phone search; there is also a public access terminal for case lookups at their office at the Justice Complex, 25 Market St, Trenton.

Note: Cape May County offices are located in the city of Cape May Court House, and not City of Cape May.

Atlantic County

Superior Court - Criminal Div. *Felony* www.judiciary.state.nj.us/atlantic/index.htm Criminal Courthouse 5909 Main St, Mays Landing, NJ 08330. 8:30AM-4:30PM. **609-625-7000**, Fax: 609-645-5875. Criminal phone: 609-909-8140.

Superior Court - Civil Division *Civil Actions Over $15,000, Probate* www.judiciary.state.nj.us/atlantic/index.htm 5905 Main St, Mays Landing, NJ 08330. 8:30AM-4:30PM. **609-625-7000 X3370**, Fax: 609-645-5875. Records location is 1201 Bacharach Blvd. Access civil records-

Superior Court Special Civil Part *Civil Under $15,000, Eviction, Small Claims* www.judiciary.state.nj.us/atlantic/index.htm 1201 Bacharach Blvd., Atlantic City, NJ 08401. 8:30AM-4:30PM. **609-345-6700 X3347**, Fax: 609-343-2326. Access civil records- in person fax.

Bergen County

Superior Court - Crim. Division *Felony* www.judiciary.state.nj.us/bergen/index.htm 10 Main St, Rm 134, Justice Ctr, Hackensack, NJ 07601. 8:30AM-4:30PM. **201-527-2445**, Fax: 201-342-9083.

Superior Court - Civil Division *Civil Actions Over $15,000, Probate* www.judiciary.state.nj.us/bergen/index.htm 10 Main St. Rm 119, Justice Ctr, Hackensack, NJ 07601. 8:30AM-4:30PM. **201-527-2700 ext 2**, Fax: 201-752-4031. Access civil records-

Superior Court Special Civil Part *Civil Under $15,000, Eviction, Small Claims* www.judiciary.state.nj.us/bergen/index.htm 10 Main St. Rm 430, Justice Ctr,

Hackensack, NJ 07601. 8:30AM-4:30PM. **201-527-2700 ext 2**. Access civil records-

Burlington County

Superior Court - Crim. Division *Felony* www.judiciary.state.nj.us/burlington/index.htm 49 Rancocas Rd, Mount Holly, NJ 08060. 8AM-5PM. **609-518-2568**.

Superior Court - Civil Division *Civil Actions Over $15,000, Probate* www.judiciary.state.nj.us/burlington/index.htm 49 Rancocas Rd, Mount Holly, NJ 08060. 8AM-5PM. **609-518-2622**. Access civil records-

Superior Court Special Civil Part *Civil Under $15,000, Eviction, Small Claims* www.judiciary.state.nj.us/burlington/index.htm 49 Rancocas Rd., Mount Holly, NJ 08060. 8AM-5PM. **609-518-2865**, Fax: 609-518-2872. Access civil records- Fax

Camden County

Superior Court - Crim. Division *Felony* www.judiciary.state.nj.us/camden/index.htm Hall of Justice 101 S 5th St, Camden, NJ 08103. 8AM-4PM. **856-379-2200**, Fax: 856-379-2255. Criminal phone: x3343. Fax

Superior Court - Civil Division *Civil Actions Over $15,000, Probate* www.judiciary.state.nj.us/camden/index.htm Hall of Justice, 101 S 5th St, Camden, NJ 08103. 8:30AM-4:30PM. **856-379-2200**, Fax: 856-379-2255. Criminal phone: x3343. Access civil records-

Superior Court Special Civil Part *Civil Under $15,000, Eviction, Small Claims* www.judiciary.state.nj.us/camden/index.htm

Hall of Justice Complex, 101 S. 5th St., Camden, NJ 08103. 8:30AM-4:30PM. **856-379-2202**. Access records-

Cape May County

Superior Court - Crim. Division *Felony* www.judiciary.state.nj.us/atlantic/index.htm 9 N Main St, Superior Court, Cape May Court House, NJ 08210. 8:30-4:30PM. **609-463-6550**, Fax: 609-463-6458.

Superior Court - Civil Division *Civil Over $15,000, Probate* www.judiciary.state.nj.us/atlantic/index.htm Civil/Equity Division-Law DN-203, 9 N Main St, Cape May Court House, NJ 08210. 8:30AM-4:30PM. **609-463-6506**, Fax: 609-463-6465. Access civil records-

Superior Court Special Civil Part *Civil Under $15,000, Eviction, Small Claims* www.judiciary.state.nj.us/atlantic/index.htm DN-203, 9 N. Main St, Cape May Court House, NJ 08210. 8:30AM-4:30PM. **609-463-6502**, Fax: 609-463-6465. Access civil records-

Cumberland County

Superior Court - Crim. Division *Felony* www.judiciary.state.nj.us/gloucester/cum/index.htm PO Box 757 Courthouse, Broad/Fayette Strs, Bridgeton, NJ 08302. 8:30AM-4:30PM. **856-453-4300**, Fax: 856-451-7152.

Superior Court - Civil Division *Civil Actions Over $15,000, Probate* www.judiciary.state.nj.us/gloucester/cum/index.htm PO Box 757, Bridgeton, NJ 08302. 8:30AM-4:30PM. **856-453-4330**, Fax: 856-451-7152. Criminal phone: 856-453-4300. Access civil records-

Superior Court Special Civil Part *Civil Under $15,000, Eviction, Small Claims* www.judiciary.state.nj.us/gloucester/cum/index.htm PO Box 10, Bridgeton, NJ 08302. 8:30AM-4:30PM. **856-453-4350**. Access civil records-☎ ✉ 🖥 🖑

Essex County

Superior Court - Crim. Division *Felony* www.judiciary.state.nj.us/essex/index.htm 50 W Market St, Rm 100s Essex County Court Bldg,, Newark, NJ 07102-1681. 8:30AM-4:30PM. **973-693-5965, 973-693-5700 (switchboard)**. ✉ 🖑

Superior Court - Civil Division *Civil Actions Over $15,000, Probate* www.judiciary.state.nj.us/essex/index.htm 465 Dr. Martin Luther King Blvd, Newark, NJ 07102-1681. 8:30AM-4:30PM. **973-693-6460**. Access civil records- 🖥 🖑

Superior Court Special Civil Part *Civil Under $15,000, Eviction, Small Claims* www.judiciary.state.nj.us/essex/index.htm 465 Martin Luther King Blvd, Newark, NJ 07102. 8:30AM-4:30PM. **973-693-6494; 693-6460**, Fax: 973-621-5914. Access civil records- ✉ 🖥 🖑

Gloucester County

Superior Court - Crim. Division *Felony* www.judiciary.state.nj.us/gloucester/glo/index.htm PO Box 187 (1 N Broad St), Woodbury, NJ 08096. 8:30AM-4:30 PM. **856-853-3531**. ✉ 🖑

Superior Court - Civil Division *Civil Actions Over $15,000, Probate* www.judiciary.state.nj.us/gloucester/glo/index.htm 1 N Broad St, Woodbury, NJ 08096. 8:30AM-4:30 PM. **856-853-3250**. Access civil records- ✉ 🖥 🖑

Superior Court Special Civil Part *Civil Under $15,000, Eviction, Small Claims* www.judiciary.state.nj.us/gloucester/glo/index.htm Old Courthouse, 1 N Broad St., Woodbury, NJ 08096. 8:30AM-4:30PM. **856-853-3392**, Fax: 856-853-3416. Access civil records- ✉ 🖥 🖑

Hudson County

Superior Court - Crim. Division *Felony* www.judiciary.state.nj.us/hudson/index.htm 595 Newark Ave, Jersey City, NJ 07306. 8:30AM-4:30PM. **201-795-6704**, Fax: 201-217-5210. ✉ 🖑

Superior Court - Civil Division *Civil Actions Over $15,000, Probate* www.judiciary.state.nj.us/hudson/index.htm

583 Newark Ave, Jersey City, NJ 07306. 8:30AM-4:30PM. **201-271-5162; 201-217-5163 (Records Rm)**. Access civil records-✉ 🖑

Superior Court Special Civil Part *Civil Under $15,000, Eviction, Small Claims* www.judiciary.state.nj.us/hudson/index.htm 595 Newark Ave, Jersey City, NJ 07306. 8:30AM-4:30PM. **201-795-6680**. Access civil records-🖥 🖑

Hunterdon County

Superior Court - Crim. Division *Felony* www.judiciary.state.nj.us/somerset/index.htm 65 Park Ave, Flemington, NJ 08822. 8:30AM-4:30PM. **908-237-5840**, Fax: 908-237-5841. Access records-**Fax** ✉ 🖑

Superior Court - Civil Division *Civil Actions Over $15,000, Probate* www.judiciary.state.nj.us/somerset/index.htm Hunterdon County Justice Ctr 65 Park Ave, Flemington, NJ 08822. 8:30AM-4:30PM. **908-237-5820**, Probate: 908-788-1156. Probate records are indexed separately and are located on the 2nd Fl Surrogate/Probate office. Access civil records-✉ 🖥 🖑 ☎

Superior Court Special Civil Part *Civil Under $15,000, Eviction, Small Claims* www.judiciary.state.nj.us/somerset/index.htm Hunterdon County Justice Ctr 65 Park Ave, 2nd Fl, Flemington, NJ 08822. 8:30AM-4:30PM. **908-237-5820**. Access civil records-☎ ✉ 🖥 🖑

Mercer County

Superior Court - Crim. Division *Felony* www.judiciary.state.nj.us/mercer/index.htm 209 S. Broad PO Box 8068, Trenton, NJ 08650-0068. 8:30AM-4:30PM; Search Hours: 9-3:30. **609-571-4000 ext 4**. 🖑

Superior Court - Civil Division *Civil Actions Over $15,000, Probate* www.judiciary.state.nj.us/mercer/index.htm 175 S Broad PO Box 8068, Trenton, NJ 08650-0068. 8:30AM-4:30PM. **609-571-4490**, Fax: 609-571-4473. Access civil records-**Fax** ✉ 🖥 🖑

Superior Court Special Civil Part *Civil Under $15,000, Eviction, Small Claims* www.judiciary.state.nj.us/mercer/index.htm Box 8068, Trenton, NJ 08650. 8:30AM-4:30PM. **609-571-4490 ext 1**, Fax: 609-571-4489. Access civil records-✉ 🖥 🖑

Middlesex County

Superior Court - Crim. Division *Felony* www.judiciary.state.nj.us/middlesex/index.ht

m PO Box 964 (1 JFK Sq), New Brunswick, NJ 08903. 8:30AM-4:30PM. **732-981-3128**. ✉ 🖑

Superior Court - Civil Division *Civil Actions Over $15,000, Probate* www.judiciary.state.nj.us/middlesex/index.htm PO Box 2633 1 JFK Sq, 2nd Fl Tower, New Brunswick, NJ 08903. 8:30AM-4:30PM. **732-981-2464**, Probate: 732-745-3055. Access civil records-✉ 🖥 🖑

Superior Court Special Civil Part *Civil Under $15,000, Eviction, Small Claims* www.judiciary.state.nj.us/middlesex/index.htm PO Box 1146 (1 JKF Sq, 3rd Fl Tower), New Brunswick, NJ 08903. 8:30AM-4:30PM. **732-981-2044**. Access civil records-✉ 🖥 🖑

Monmouth County

Superior Court - Crim. Division *Felony* www.judiciary.state.nj.us/monmouth/index.htm 71 Monument Park, Rm 149, 1st Flr, E Wing PO Box 1271, Freehold, NJ 07728-1271. 8:30-4:30PM. **732-677-4300**. 🖑

Superior Court - Civil Division *Civil Over $15,000* www.judiciary.state.nj.us/monmouth/index.htm PO Box 1255 71 Monument Pk, Freehold, NJ 07728-1255. 8:30AM-4:30PM. **732-677-4268**. Access civil records-✉ 🖥 🖑

Superior Court Special Civil Part *Civil Under $15,000, Eviction, Small Claims* www.judiciary.state.nj.us/monmouth/index.htm Courthouse, 71 Monument Pk. PO Box 1270, Freehold, NJ 07728. 8:30AM-4:30PM. **732-677-4223**. Access civil records-✉ 🖥 🖑

Morris County

Superior Court - Crim. Division *Felony* www.judiciary.state.nj.us/morris/index.htm PO Box 910 (Washington St), Morristown, NJ 07960-0910. 8:30AM-4:30PM. **973-656-4115**, Fax: 973-656-4123. Criminal phone: 973-656-4169. **Fax** ✉ 🖑

Superior Court - Civil Division *Civil Actions Over $15,000, Probate* www.judiciary.state.nj.us/morris/index.htm PO Box 910 (Washington St), Morristown, NJ 07963-0910. 8:30AM-4:30PM. **973-656-4115**, Fax: 973-656-4123. Access civil records- 🖥 🖑

Superior Court Special Civil Part *Civil Under $15,000, Eviction, Small Claims* www.judiciary.state.nj.us/morris/index.htm PO Box 910 (Court St), Morristown, NJ

07963-0910. 8:30AM-4:30PM. **973-656-4125**. Access civil records-✉️🖥️🤚

Ocean County

Superior Court - Crim. Division *Felony*
www.judiciary.state.nj.us/ocean/index.htm
PO Box 2191 (120 Hooper Ave) Justice Complex, Rm 220, Toms River, NJ 08754-2191. 8:30AM-4:30PM. **732-929-2009**. ✉️🤚

Superior Court - Civil Division *Civil Actions Over $15,000, Probate* www.judiciary.state.nj.us/ocean/index.htm 118 Washington #121, Toms River, NJ 08754. 8:30AM-4:30PM. **732-929-2035**. Access civil records-🖥️🤚

Superior Court Special Civil Part *Civil Under $15,000, Eviction, Small Claims* www.judiciary.state.nj.us/ocean/index.htm 118 Washington St, Toms River, NJ 08754. 8:30AM-4:30PM. **732-929-2016**, Fax: 732-506-5398. Access records-🖥️🤚

Passaic County

Superior Court - Crim. Division *Felony* www.judiciary.state.nj.us/passaic/index.htm 77 Hamilton St. 2nd Fl, Paterson, NJ 07505-2108. 8:30AM-4:30PM. **973-247-8403**, Fax: 973-247-8401. ✉️🤚

Superior Court - Civil Division *Civil Actions Over $15,000, Probate* www.judiciary.state.nj.us/passaic/index.htm 77 Hamilton St, Ist Fl, Paterson, NJ 07505-2108. 8:30AM-4:30PM. **973-247-8215**, Probate: 973-881-4760. Probate is located on the 2nd Fl with General Equity Div. Access civil records-☎️✉️🖥️🤚

Superior Court Special Civil Part *Civil Under $15,000, Eviction, Small Claims* www.judiciary.state.nj.us/passaic/index.htm 71 Hamilton St. Old Courthouse, 2nd Fl, Paterson, NJ 07505. 8:30AM-4:30PM. **973-247-8238**. Access records-✉️🖥️🤚

Salem County

Superior Court - Crim. Division *Felony* www.judiciary.state.nj.us/gloucester/sal/index.htm PO Box 78 (92 Market St), Salem, NJ 08079-1913. 8:30AM-4:30PM. **856-935-7510**. 🤚

Superior Court - Civil Division *Civil Actions Over $15,000, Probate*

www.judiciary.state.nj.us/gloucester/sal/index.htm PO Box 29 (92 Market St), Salem, NJ 08079-1913. 8:30AM-4:30PM. **856-935-7510 X8214**, Fax: 856-935-6551 Probate: 856-935-7510 X8322. Probate located at the County Surrogate's office at this 92 Market St address in Salem. Access civil records-🤚🖥️

Superior Court Special Civil Part *Civil Under $15,000, Eviction, Small Claims* www.judiciary.state.nj.us/gloucester/sal/index.htm PO Box 29 (92 Market St), Salem, NJ 08079. 8:30AM-4:30PM. **856-935-7510 x8214**, Fax: 856-935-6551. Access civil records-☎️**Fax**✉️🖥️🤚

Somerset County

Superior Court - Crim. Division *Felony* www.judiciary.state.nj.us/somerset/index.htm PO Box 3000 (20 N Bridge St, 2nd Fl), Somerville, NJ 08876-1262. 8:30AM-4:30PM. **908-231-7600**. ☎️**Fax**✉️🤚

Superior Court - Civil Division *Civil, Probate* www.judiciary.state.nj.us/somerset/index.htm Somerset Cty Courthouse, Civil Division PO Box 3000 (Bridge & Main St), Somerville, NJ 08876-1262. 8:30AM-4:30PM. **908-231-7054**. Access civil records-☎️✉️🖥️🤚

Superior Court Special Civil Part *Civil Under $15,000, Eviction, Small Claims* www.judiciary.state.nj.us/somerset/index.htm Somerset County Courthouse, Bridge and Main St PO Box 3000, Somerville, NJ 08876-1262. 8:30AM-4:30PM. **908-231-7014/7015**. Access civil records-✉️🖥️🤚

Sussex County

Superior Court - Crim. Division *Felony* www.judiciary.state.nj.us/morris/index.htm 43-47 High St, Sussex Judicial Ctr, Newton, NJ 07860. 8:30AM-4:30PM. **973-579-0696**. 🤚

Superior Court - Civil Division *Civil Over $15,000, Probate* www.judiciary.state.nj.us/morris/index.htm 43-47 High St, Sussex Judicial Ctr, Newton, NJ 07860. 8:30AM-4:30PM. **973-579-0914/0915**. Access civil records-☎️✉️🖥️🤚

Superior Court Special Civil Part *Civil Under $15,000, Eviction, Small Claims* www.judiciary.state.nj.us/morris/index.htm

43-47 High St., Newton, NJ 07860. 8:30AM-4:30PM. **973-579-0918**, Fax: 973-579-0736. Access civil records-☎️**Fax**✉️🖥️🤚

Union County

Superior Court - Crim. Division *Felony* www.judiciary.state.nj.us/union/index.htm County Courthouse - Tower Bldg 5th Fl, Elizabeth, NJ 07207. 8:30AM-4:30PM. Fax: 908-659-3391 Crim. Civil phone: 908-659-3844, crim: 908-659-3376, Probate: 908-527-4280. 🤚

Superior Court - Civil Division *Civil Actions Over $15,000* www.judiciary.state.nj.us/union/index.htm 2 Broad St, Elizabeth, NJ 07207. 8:30AM-4:30PM. **908-659-4176**, Fax: 908-659-4185. Access civil records-☎️✉️🖥️🤚

Superior Court Special Civil Part *Civil Under $15,000, Eviction, Small Claims* www.judiciary.state.nj.us/union/index.htm 2 Broad St, Elizabeth, NJ 07207. 8:30AM-4:30PM. **908-659-3637/8**. Access civil records-☎️✉️🖥️🤚

Warren County

Warren County Superior Court *Felony* www.judiciary.state.nj.us/somerset/index.htm Criminal Case Management Division PO Box 900, Belvidere, NJ 07823. 8:30AM-4:30PM. **908-475-6990**, Fax: 908-475-6982. Civil phone: 908-475-6140, crim: 908-475-6990, Probate: 908-475-6223. Access records-☎️✉️**Fax**🤚

Superior Court - Civil Division *Civil Actions Over $15,000, Probate* www.judiciary.state.nj.us/somerset/index.htm PO Box 900 (314 2nd St), Belvidere, NJ 07823. 8:30AM-4:30PM. **908-475-6140**. Access civil records-✉️🖥️🤚

Superior Court Special Civil Part *Civil Under $15,000, Eviction, Small Claims* www.judiciary.state.nj.us/somerset/index.htm PO Box 900 (314 2nd St), Belvidere, NJ 07823. 8:30AM-4:30PM. **908-475-6140**. Access civil records-✉️🖥️🤚

Key: Symbols refer to criminal records access unless otherwise noted. phone-☎️ mail-✉️ fax-**Fax** in person-🤚 online-🖥️ email-**Email**

New Mexico

State Court Administration (All County District & Magistrate Courts): Administrative Office of the Courts, Supreme Court Building, Rm 25 (237 Don Gaspar), Santa Fe, NM, 87501; 505-827-4800, Fax: 505-827-7549. http://www.nmcourts.com

Court Structure: The 30 District Courts in 13 districts are the courts of general jurisdiction. The Magistrate Courts handle civil cases up to $10,000, and are refered to as Small Claims. Also, the Bernalillo Metropolitan Court has jurisdiction in cases up to $10,000. Municipal Courts handle petty misdemeanors, DWI/DUI, traffic violations and other municipal ordinance violations.

Probate Courts: County Clerks handle "informal" (uncontested) probate cases, and the District Courts handle "formal" (contested) probate cases.

Online Access: The www.nmcourts.com website offers free access to District and Magistrate Court case information. In general, records are available from June, 1997 forward.

A commercial online service is available for the Metropolitan Court of Bernalillo County. There is a $35.00 set up fee, a connect time fee based on usage. The system is available 24 hours a day. Call 505-345-6555 for more information.

Also, a statewide search is available from the DPS at http://www.osogrande.com/online-services.html. The fee is $10.00. You must set up an account and receive a password. When a record is found, a signed release from the subject must be presented (faxed) to DPS in order to receive the detail page. For more information visit the website mentioned or call 505-345-6555.

Additional Information: There are some "shared" courts in New Mexico, with one county handling cases arising in another. Records are held at the location(s) indicated in the text.

All magistrate courts and the Bernalillo Metropolitan Court have public access terminals to access civil records only.

Bernalillo County

2nd Judicial District Court *Felony, Civil* www.cabq.gov/cjnet/dst2alb PO Box 488, Albuquerque, NM 87103. 8AM-5PM. **505-841-7425 (Administration),** Fax: 505-841-7446. Civil phone: 505-841-7451, crim: 505-841-7542, ✉️💻✋

Metropolitan Court *Misdemeanor, Civil Actions Under $10,000, Eviction, Small Claims* www.metrocourt.state.nm.us 401 Lomas NW, Albuquerque, NM 87102. 8AM-5PM. **505-841-8151/841-8160,** Fax: 505-222-4800. Records phone is 505-841-8240 ☎️**Fax**✉️💻✋

County Clerk *Probate* www.bernco.gov/live/departments.asp?dept=2317 #1 Civic Plaza NW, 6th Fl, Albuquerque, NM 87102. 8AM-4:30PM. **505-768-4247,** Fax: 505-768-5180.

Catron County

7th Judicial District Court *Felony, Civil* PO Drawer 1129, Socorro, NM 87801. 8AM-4PM. **505-835-0050,** Fax: 505-838-5217. This court is also responsible for Socorro County. ☎️**Fax**✉️💻✋

Quemado Magistrate Court *Misd., Civil Actions Under $10,000, Eviction, Small Claims* PO Box 283, Quemado, NM 87829. 8AM-5PM. **505-773-4604,** Fax: 505-773-4688. ✉️**Fax**✋

Reserve Magistrate Court *Misd., Civil Actions Under $10,000, Eviction, Small Claims* PO Box 447, Reserve, NM 87830. 8AM-5PM. **505-533-6474,** Fax: 505-533-6623. ✉️**Fax**💻✋

County Clerk *Probate* PO Box I, Socorro, NM 87801. 8AM-5PM. **505-835-0423,** Fax: 505-835-1043. Local Probate Judge-505-533-6247, PO Box 663, Reserve NM, 87830 by appointment.

Chaves County

5th Judicial District Court *Felony, Civil* www.fifthdistrictcourt.com Box 1776, Roswell, NM 88202. 8AM-N,1-5PM. **505-622-2212,** Fax: 505-624-9510. 💻✋

Magistrate Court *Misdemeanor, Civil Actions Under $10,000, Eviction, Small Claims* www.nmcourts.com 200 E 4th St, Roswell, NM 88201. 8AM-4PM M, T, TH, F; 9AM-4PM W. **505-624-6088,** Fax: 505-624-6092. 💻✋

County Clerk *Probate* Box 580, Roswell, NM 88202. 7AM-5PM. **505-624-6614,** Fax: 505-624-6523.

Cibola County

13th Judicial District Court *Felony, Civil, Probate* Box 758, Grants, NM 87020. 8AM-5PM. **505-287-8831,** Fax: 505-285-5755. **Fax**✉️💻✋

Magistrate Court *Misdemeanor, Civil Actions Under $10,000, Eviction, Small Claims* 515 W High, Grants, NM 87020. 8AM-4PM. **505-285-4605. Fax**✋💻

County Clerk *Probate* 515 W. High St PO Box 190, Grants, NM 87020. 8AM-5PM. **505-285-2535/285-2540,** Fax: 505-285-2562.

Colfax County

8th Judicial District Court *Felony, Civil* Box 160, Raton, NM 87740. 8AM-4PM. **505-445-5585,** Fax: 505-445-2626. ☎️✉️💻✋

Cimarron Magistrate Court *Misd., Civil Actions Under $10,000, Eviction, Small Claims* PO Drawer 367, Highway 21, Cimarron, NM 87714. 8:30AM-3PM Weds only. **505-376-2634,** Fax: 505-376-9108. On days when this court is not in session, you may call the Springer Magistrate Ct. 505-483-2417. ✋✉️💻

Springer Magistrate Court *Misd., Civil Actions Under $10,000, Eviction, Small Claims* 300 Colbert Ave. PO Box 760, Springer, NM 87747. 8AM-4PM. **505-483-2417,** Fax: 505-483-0127. 💻✋

Raton Magistrate Court *Misdemeanor, Civil Actions Under $10,000, Eviction, Small Claims* PO Box 68, Raton, NM 87740. 8AM-5PM. **505-445-2220,** Fax: 505-445-8966. ☎️✉️**Fax**✋💻

County Clerk *Probate* PO Box 159, Raton, NM 87740. 8AM-5PM. **505-445-5551**, Fax: 505-445-4031.

Curry County

9th Judicial District Court *Felony, Civil* www.nmcourts9thjdc.com/ Curry County Courthouse 700 N Main, #11, Clovis, NM 88101. 8AM-4PM. **505-762-9148**, Fax: 505-763-5160. 🖳✋

Magistrate Court *Misdemeanor, Civil Actions Under $10,000, Eviction, Small Claims* 221 Pile, Clovis, NM 88101. 8AM-4PM. **505-762-3766**, Fax: 505-769-1437. ☎✉**Fax**🖳✋

De Baca County

10th Judicial District Court *Felony, Civil* Box 910, Ft. Sumner, NM 88119. 8AM-4:30PM. **505-355-2896**, Fax: 505-355-2899. ☎✉🖳✋

Magistrate Court *Misdemeanor, Civil Actions Under $10,000, Eviction, Small Claims* Box 24, Ft Sumner, NM 88119. 8AM-5PM. **505-355-7371**, Fax: 505-355-7149. ✋✉🖳

County Clerk *Probate* 514 Ave C PO Box 347, Ft. Sumner, NM 88119. 8AM-N, 1-4:30PM. **505-355-2601**, Fax: 505-355-2441.

Dona Ana County

3rd Judicial District Court *Felony, Civil* www.thirddistrictcourt.com/ 201 W Picacho, #A, Las Cruces, NM 88005. 8AM-N, 1-5PM. **505-523-8200**, Fax: 505-523-8290. ✉🖳✋

Hatch Magistrate Court *Misdemeanor, Civil Actions Under $10,000, Eviction, Small Claims* PO Box 896, Hatch, NM 87937. 8:30AM-4PM Monday. **505-267-5202**, Fax: 505-267-5088. Note that this court is only open on Mondays. ✉✋🖳

Las Cruces Magistrate Court *Misd., Civil Actions Under $10,000, Eviction, Small Claims* 151 N Church, Las Cruces, NM 88001. 8AM-4PM. **505-524-2814**, Fax: 505-525-2951. ✋✉🖳

Anthony Magistrate Court *Misd., Civil Actions Under $10,000, Eviction, Small Claims* PO Box 1259, Anthony, NM 88021. 8AM-N, 1-5PM. **505-233-3147**. 🖳✉✋

County Clerk *Probate* c/o Third Judicial District 201 W Picacho #A, Los Cruces,

NM 88005. 8AM-5PM. **505-523-8200**, Fax: 505-523-8290.

Eddy County

5th Judicial District Court *Felony, Civil* www.fifthdistrictcourt.com 102 N Canal St #240, Carlsbad, NM 88220. 8-N, 1-5PM. **505-885-4740**, Fax: 505-887-7095. ✋🖳

Carlsbad Magistrate Court *Misd., Civil Actions Under $10,000, Eviction, Small Claims* 1949 S Canal St, Carlsbad, NM 88220. 8AM-4PM. **505-885-3218**, Fax: 505-887-3460. 🖳✉✋

Artesia Magistrate Court *Misd., Civil Actions Under $10,000, Eviction, Small Claims* www.nmcourts.com 109 N 15th St, Artesia, NM 88210. 8AM-4PM. **505-746-2481**, Fax: 505-746-6763. This court also handles preliminary felonies, traffic, and DUI cases. ☎✉🖳

County Clerk *Probate* Eddy County Probate Judge 101 W. Green #312, Carlsbad, NM 88220. 8AM-5PM. **505-885-3383**, Fax: 505-234-1793.

Grant County

6th Judicial District Court *Felony, Civil* Box 2339, Silver City, NM 88062. 8AM-5PM. **505-538-3250**, Fax: 505-388-5439. **Fax**✉🖳✋

Silver City Magistrate Court *Misd., Civil Actions Under $10,000, Eviction, Small Claims* www.nmcourts.com 1620 E Pine St, Silver City, NM 88061. 8AM-5PM. **505-538-3811**, Fax: 505-538-8079. ✉**Fax**✋🖳

Bayard Magistrate Court *Misdemeanor, Civil Actions Under $10,000, Eviction, Small Claims* PO Box 125, Bayard, NM 88023. 8AM-5PM. **505-537-3042**, Fax: 505-537-7365. ✉**Fax**✋🖳

County Clerk *Probate* Box 898, Silver City, NM 88061. 8AM-5PM. **505-574-0042**, Fax: 505-574-0076. 🖳access.

Guadalupe County

4th Judicial District Court *Felony, Civil* 420 Parker Ave #5 Guadalupe County Courthouse, Santa Rosa, NM 88435. 8AM-N; 1PM-5PM. **505-472-3888**, Fax: 505-472-4451. 🖳✋

Vaughn Magistrate Court *Misd., Civil Actions Under $10,000, Eviction, Small Claims* c/o Santa Rosa Justice Court 603 Parker Av, Santa Rosa, NM 88435. 8AM-4PM. **505-584-2345**. The Vaughn court is

only open the 2nd Wednesday of the month. It is located at 8th & Calle De Carill, Vaughn, NM 88353. Most records are at Santa Rosa (phone # given here). ✉✋🖳

Santa Rosa Magistrate Court *Misdemeanor, Civil Actions Under $10,000, Eviction, Small Claims* 603 Parker Ave, Santa Rosa, NM 88435. 8AM-4PM. **505-472-3237**. 🖳✉✋

County Clerk *Probate* 420 Parker Ave, Courthouse, Santa Rosa, NM 88435. 8-5. **505-472-3791**, Fax: 505-472-4791.

Harding County

10th Judicial District Court *Felony, Civil* Box 1002, Mosquero, NM 87733. 9AM-3PM M-W,F. **505-673-2252**, Fax: 505-673-2252. ☎**Fax**✉🖳✋

Magistrate Court *Misdemeanor, Civil Actions Under $10,000, Eviction, Small Claims* Box 9, Roy, NM 87743. 8AM-4PM. **505-485-2549**, Fax: 505-485-2407. ✉☎✋

County Clerk *Probate* County Clerk, Box 1002, Mosquero, NM 87733. 8AM-4PM. **505-673-2301**, Fax: 505-673-2922.

Hidalgo County

6th Judicial District Court *Felony, Civil* PO Box 608, Lordsburg, NM 88045. 8AM-N, 1-5PM. **505-542-3411**, Fax: 505-542-3481. ☎**Fax**✉🖳✋

Magistrate Court *Misdemeanor, Civil Under $10,000, Eviction, Small Claims* www.nmcourts.com 420 Wabash Ave, Lordsburg, NM 88045. 8AM-5PM. **505-542-3582**. ✉✋fax.

County Clerk *Probate* 300 S Shakespeare, Lordsburg, NM 88045. 8-5. **505-542-9213**, Fax: 505-542-3193.

Lea County

Jal Magistrate Court *Misdemeanor, Civil Actions Under $10,000, Eviction, Small Claims* PO Box 507, Jal, NM 88252. 8-4pm T,Th. **505-395-2740**, Fax: 505-395-2595. Access records-✉✋🖳

Tatum Magistrate Court *Misdemeanor, Civil Actions Under $10,000, Eviction, Small Claims* PO Box 918, Tatum, NM 88267. 8AM-4PM. **505-398-5300**, Fax: 505-398-5310. ☎✉**Fax**✋🖳

Eunice Magistrate Court *Misdemeanor, Civil Actions Under $10,000, Eviction,*

Small Claims PO Box 240, Eunice, NM 88231. 8AM-4PM M,W,F. **505-394-3368**, Fax: 505-394-3335. 🖳✉✋

Hobbs Magistrate Court *Misd, Civil Under $10,000, Eviction, Small Claims* www.nmcourts.com 2110 N Alto Dr, Hobbs, NM 88240-3455. 8AM-4PM. **505-397-3621**, Fax: 505-393-9121. 🖳✉✋

Lovington Magistrate Court *Misd., Civil Actions Under $10,000, Eviction, Small Claims* www.nmcourts.com 100 W Central, #D, Lovington, NM 88260. 8AM-4PM. **505-396-6677**, Fax: 505-396-6163. ☎Fax✉✋🖳

County Clerk *Probate* www.leacounty-nm.org Box 1507, Lovington, NM 88260. 8-5. **505-396-8619**, Fax: 505-396-3293.

5th Judicial District Court *Felony, Civil* www.fifthdistrictcourt.com 100 N. Main, #6-C, Lovington, NM 88260. 8AM-5PM. **505-396-8571**, Fax: 505-396-2428. Fax✉🖳✋

Lincoln County

12th Judicial District Court *Felony, Civil* www.12thdistrict.com Box 725, Carrizozo, NM 88301. 8AM-5PM. **505-648-2432**, Fax: 505-648-2581. 🖳✋

Ruidoso Magistrate Court *Misd., Civil Actions Under $10,000, Eviction, Small Claims* 301 W Highway 70 #2, Ruidoso, NM 88345. 8AM-4PM. **505-378-7022**, Fax: 505-378-8508. 🖳✉✋

Carrizozo Magistrate Court *Misd., Civil Actions Under $10,000, Eviction, Small Claims* 310 11th St, Carrizozo, NM 88301. 8AM-12:00, 1-4PM. **505-648-2380**, Civil: 505-378-7022. Fax✋✉🖳

County Clerk *Probate* PO Box 338, Carrizozo, NM 88301. 8AM-5PM. **505-648-2394**, Fax: 505-648-2576. This court will do searches.

Los Alamos County

Magistrate Court *Misdemeanor, Civil Actions Under $10,000, Eviction, Small Claims* 1319 Trinity Dr, Los Alamos, NM 87544. 8AM-4PM. **505-662-2727**, Fax: 505-661-6258. 🖳✋

County Clerk-Probate *Probate* PO Box 30, Los Alamos, NM 87544. 7:30AM-5PM. **505-662-8010**, Fax: 505-662-8008.

Luna County

6th Judicial District Court *Felony, Civil* www.nmcourts.com County Courthouse,

Rm 40, Deming, NM 88030. 8-4PM. **505-546-9611**, Fax: 505-546-0971. ✉🖳✋

Magistrate Court *Misd., Civil Actions Under $10,000, Eviction, Small Claims* www.nmcourts.com 912 S Silver St, Deming, NM 88030. 8-N, 1-5PM. **505-546-9321**, Fax: 505-546-4896. ✉✋🖳

County Clerk *Probate* PO Box 1838, Deming, NM 88031. 8AM-5PM. **505-546-0491**, Fax: 505-546-4708. There can be some probate cases (those in dispute) at the District Court level.

McKinley County

11th Judicial District Court *Felony, Civil* 201 W. Hill, Rm 4, Gallup, NM 87301. 8AM-N, 1-5PM. **505-863-6816**, Fax: 505-722-8401. ☎✉🖳✋

Magistrate Court *Misdemeanor, Civil Actions Under $10,000, Eviction, Small Claims* 285 Boardman Dr, Gallup, NM 87301. 8AM-4PM. **505-722-6636**, Fax: 505-863-3510. 🖳✋

County Clerk *Probate* PO Box 1268, Gallup, NM 87305. 8AM-5PM. **505-863-6866**, Fax: 505-863-1419.

Thoreau Magistrate Court *Misd., Civil Actions Under $10,000, Eviction, Small Claims* 39 First St, Thoreau, NM 87323. 8:30AM-4PM Every Other Friday. **505-862-7871**, Fax: 505-862-8606. This court is open only every other Friday. ✉✋🖳

Mora County

4th Judicial District Court *Felony, Civil* PO Box 1540, Las Vegas, NM 87701. 8AM-N, 1-4PM. **505-425-7281**, Fax: 505-425-6307. 🖳✋fax.

Magistrate Court *Misdemeanor, Civil Actions Under $10,000, Eviction, Small Claims* 1927 7th St, Las Vegas, NM 87701-4957. 8AM-4PM (closed for lunch). **505-425-5204**. 🖳✋

Probate Court PO Box 360, Mora, NM 87732. 8AM-5PM. **505-387-5014**.

Otero County

12th Judicial District Court *Felony, Civil* www.12thdistrict.net 1000 New York Ave, Rm 209, Alamogordo, NM 88310-6940. 8AM-5PM. **505-437-7310**, Fax: 505-434-8886. 🖳✉✋

Magistrate Court *Misd., Civil Actions Under $10,000, Eviction, Small Claims* 263 Robert H Bradley Dr, Alamogordo,

NM 88310-8288. 8AM-4PM. **505-437-9000 x256**, Fax: 505-439-1365. 🖳✉✋

County Clerk *Probate* 1000 New York Ave, Rm 108, Alamogordo, NM 88310-6932. 7:30AM-6PM. **505-437-4942**, Fax: 505-443-2922.

Quay County

10th Judicial District Court *Felony, Civil* Box 1067, Tucumcari, NM 88401. 8AM-5PM. **505-461-2764**, Fax: 505-461-4498. ☎Fax✉✋

Tucumcari Magistrate Court *Misd., Civil Actions Under $10,000, Eviction, Small Claims* PO Box 1301, Tucumcari, NM 88401. 8AM-4PM. **505-461-1700**, Fax: 505-461-4522. San Jon Magistrate Court (closed) records are here. 🖳✋

County Clerk *Probate* 300 S 3rd St PO Box 1225, Tucumcari, NM 88401. 8AM-5PM. **505-461-0510**, Fax: 505-461-0513.

Rio Arriba County

Rio Arriba Magistrate Court - Division 1 *Misdemeanor, Civil Actions Under $10,000, Eviction, Small Claims* PO Box 538 (1332 Hiway 17), Chama, NM 87520. 8AM-N, 1-5PM. **505-756-2278**, Fax: 505-756-2477. ✉Fax✋🖳

Rio Arriba Magistrate Court - Division 2 *Misdemeanor, Civil Actions Under $10,000, Eviction, Small Claims* 410 Paseo de Onate, Espanola, NM 87532. 8AM-4PM. **505-753-2532**, Fax: 505-753-4802. ✉✋🖳

County Clerk *Probate* PO Box 158, Tierra Amarilla, NM 87575. 8AM-5PM. **505-588-7724**, Fax: 505-588-7418.

Roosevelt County

9th Judicial District Court *Felony, Civil* 109 W 1st St, #207, Portales, NM 88130. 8AM-4PM. **505-356-4463**, Fax: 505-359-2140. 🖳✋

Magistrate Court *Misdemeanor, Civil Actions Under $10,000, Eviction, Small Claims, Felonies* www.nmcourts.com 42427 US Hwy 70, Portales, NM 88130. 8AM-4PM. **505-356-8569**, Fax: 505-359-6883. ☎✉Fax✋🖳

County Clerk *Probate* Roosevelt County Courthouse 109 W 1st, Portales, NM 88130. 8AM-5PM. **505-356-8562**, Fax: 505-356-3560.

Key: Symbols refer to criminal records access unless otherwise noted. **phone-☎ mail-✉ fax-Fax in person-✋ online-🖳 email-Email**

Sandoval County

13th Judicial District Court *Felony, Civil* 100 Avenida De Justicia, Bernalillo, NM 87004. 8AM-N, 1-5PM. **505-867-2376**. Fax ⊠ 🖥 ✋

Bernalillo Magistrate Court *Misd., Civil Actions Under $10,000, Eviction, Small Claims* PO Box 818, Bernalillo, NM 87004. 8AM-4PM. **505-867-5202 X2-6**, Fax: 505-867-0970. 🖥 ⊠ ✋

Cuba Magistrate Court *Misdemeanor, Civil Actions Under $10,000, Eviction, Small Claims* PO Box 1497, Cuba, NM 87013. 8AM-N, 1-5PM. **505-289-3519**, Fax: 505-289-3013. 🖥 ✋

Probate Court PO Box 40, Bernalillo, NM 87004. 8-5. **505-867-7572**, Fax: 505-867-9365. Civil phone: 505-867-7645.

San Juan County

11th Judicial Dist. Court *Felony, Civil* www.eleventhdistrictcourt.state.nm.us/ 103 S Oliver, Aztec, NM 87410. 8AM-N, 1-5PM. **505-334-6151**, Fax: 505-334-1940. 🖥 ✋ ⊠fax.

Aztec Magistrate Court *Misdemeanor, Civil Actions Under $10,000, Eviction, Small Claims* 200 Gossett, Aztec, NM 87410. 8AM-4PM. **505-334-9479**, Fax: 505-334-2178. 🖥 ✋

Farmington Magistrate Court *Misd., Civil Actions Under $10,000, Eviction, Small Claims* www.nmcourts.com 950 W Apache St, Farmington, NM 87401. 8AM-4PM. **505-326-4338**, Fax: 505-325-2618. 🖥 ✋

County Clerk *Probate* PO Box 550, Aztec, NM 87410. 7AM-5:30PM. **505-334-9471**, Fax: 505-334-3635.

San Miguel County

4th Judicial District Court *Felony, Civil, Probate* PO Box 1540, Las Vegas, NM 87701. 8AM-N, 1-5PM. **505-425-7281**, Fax: 505-454-8611. Also handles cases for Mora County. 🖥 ✋

Magistrate Court *Misdemeanor, Civil Actions Under $10,000, Eviction, Small Claims* 1927 7th St, Las Vegas, NM 87701-4957. 8AM-4PM. **505-425-5204**, Fax: 505-425-0422. Access records- 🖥 ✋

County Clerk *Probate* San Miguel County Clerk 500 W National Ave, #113, Las Vegas, NM 87701. 8AM-N, 1-5PM. **505-425-9331**, Fax: 505-454-1799.

Santa Fe County

First Judicial District Court *Felony, Civil* http://firstdistrictcourt.com Box 2268, Santa Fe, NM 87504. 8AM-4PM. **505-476-0189**, Fax: 505-827-5055. Because this court also handles the counties of Los Alamos and Rio Arriba, you must indicate which county you are searching. ☎ ⊠ 🖥 ✋

Santa Fe Magistrate Court *Misd., Civil Actions Under $10,000, Eviction, Small Claims* 2056 Galisteo St, Santa Fe, NM 87505. 8AM-4PM. **505-984-9914**, Fax: 505-986-5866. Also, the clerk for the **Pojaoque Magistrate Court** may be contacted here. Fax ⊠ ✋ 🖥

County Clerk *Probate* Box 276, Santa Fe, NM 87504-0276. 8AM-5PM. **505-986-6279**, Fax: 505-986-6362.

Sierra County

7th Judicial District Court *Felony, Civil* PO Box 3009, Truth or Consequences, NM 87901. 8AM-4PM. **505-894-7167**, Fax: 505-894-7168. Fax ⊠ 🖥 ✋

Magistrate Court *Misdemeanor, Civil Actions Under $10,000, Eviction, Small Claims* 155 W Barton, Truth or Consequences, NM 87901. 8AM-4PM. **505-894-3051**, Fax: 505-894-0476. 🖥 ✋

County Clerk *Probate* 100 N Date St, Truth or Consequences, NM 87901. 8AM-5PM. **505-894-2840**, Fax: 505-894-2516 Probate: 505-894-4416.

Socorro County

Magistrate Court *Misdemeanor, Civil Actions Under $10,000, Eviction, Small Claims* 102 Winkler St, Socorro, NM 87801. 8AM-4PM. **505-835-2500**, Fax: 505-838-0428. Access records- ⊠ ✋ 🖥

County Clerk *Probate* 200 Church St, Socorro, NM 87801. 8AM-5PM. **505-835-0423**, Fax: 505-835-1043.

Taos County

8th Judicial District Court *Felony, Civil* 105 Albright St, #H, Taos, NM 87571. 8AM-4PM. **505-758-3173**, Fax: 505-751-1281. ✋ 🖥

Taos Magistrate Court *Misdemeanor, Civil Actions Under $10,000, Eviction, Small Claims* 920 Salazar Rd, #B, Taos, NM 87571. 8AM-4PM. **505-758-4030**, Fax: 505-751-0983. 🖥 ✋

Questa Magistrate Court

Questa Magistrate Court *Misd., Civil Actions Under $10,000, Eviction, Small Claims* www.nmcourts.com PO Box 586, Questa, NM 87556. 8AM-N,1-4PM. **505-586-0761**, Fax: 505-586-0428. 🖥 ⊠ ✋

County Clerk *Probate* 105 Albright, #E, Taos, NM 87551. 8AM-N;1-5PM. **505-758-8266**, Fax: 505-751-3391/737-6390.

Torrance County

7th Judicial District Court *Felony, Civil* www.nmcourts.com County Courthouse PO Box 78, Estancia, NM 87016. 8AM-4PM. **505-384-2974**, Fax: 505-384-2229. ⊠ 🖥 ✋

Moriarty Magistrate Court *MIsd., Civil Actions Under $10,000, Eviction, Small Claims* PO Box 2027, Moriarty, NM 87035. 8AM-4PM. **505-832-4476**, Fax: 505-832-1563. 🖥 ⊠ ✋

Estancia Magistrate Court *Misd., Civil Under $10,000, Eviction, Small Claims* Neil Mertz Judicial Complex PO Box 274, Estancia, NM 87016. 8-4PM. **505-384-2926**, Fax 505-384-3157. ⊠Fax ✋ 🖥

County Clerk *Probate* PO Box 767, Estancia, NM 87016. 8AM-5PM. **505-384-2221/1226**, Fax: 505-384-4080.

Union County

8th Judicial District Court *Felony, Civil* Box 310, Clayton, NM 88415. 8AM-N, 1-5PM. **505-374-9577**, Fax: 505-374-2089. ⊠ 🖥 ✋

Magistrate Court *Misdemeanor, Civil Actions Under $10,000, Eviction, Small Claims* www.nmcourts.com/ 836 Main St, Clayton, NM 88415. 8AM-N, 12:30-4:30PM. **505-374-9472**, Fax: 505-374-9368. 🖥 ⊠ ✋

County Clerk *Probate* PO Box 430, Clayton, NM 88415. 9AM-N, 1-5PM. **505-374-9491**, Fax: 505-374-2763.

Valencia County

13th Judicial District Court *Felony, Civil* Box 1089, Los Lunas, NM 87031. 8AM-5PM. **505-865-4291**, Fax: 505-865-8801. ⊠ 🖥 ✋

Belen Magistrate Court *Misdemeanor, Civil Actions Under $10,000, Eviction, Small Claims* 901 W Castillo, Belen, NM 87002. 8AM-4PM. **505-864-7509**, Fax: 505-864-9532. Access records- 🖥 ⊠ ✋

Key: Symbols refer to criminal records access unless otherwise noted. phone- ☎ mail- ⊠ fax- Fax in person- ✋ online- 🖥 email- Email

Los Lunas Magistrate Court *Misd.,* *Civil Actions Under $10,000, Eviction,* *Small Claims* 1206 Main St, Los Lunas, NM 87031. 8AM-4PM. **505-865-4637,** Fax: 505-865-0639. 🖥✉🖑   **County Clerk** *Probate*   www.co.valen cia.nm.us/Clerk.htm PO Box 969, Los Lunas, NM 87031. 8AM-4:30PM. **505-866-2073,** Fax: 505-866-2023.

New York

State Court Administration: Office of Court Administration, 25 Beaver St, New York, NY, 10004; 212-428-2100, Fax: . www.courts.state.ny.us

Court Structure: "Supreme and County Courts" are the highest trial courts in the state, equivalent to Circuit or District Courts in other states. New York's Supreme and County Courts may be administered together or separately; when separate, there is a clerk for each. Supreme and/or County Courts are not appeals courts. Supreme Courts handle civil cases (usually civil cases over $25,000 but there are many exceptions). County Courts handle felony cases, and in many counties, these County Courts also handle misdemeanors. City Courts handle misdemeanors and lower-value civil cases, small claims, and eviction cases. Not all counties have City Courts, thus cases there fall to the Supreme and County Courts respectively, or, in a many counties, to the small Town and Village Courts, which can number in the dozens within a county.

The staff at NY Superior, County, and City Courts are NY state employees. However, in some counties (usually smaller NY counties), the clerk for Supreme and County Courts may also be the County Clerk - these duo-role clerks are employed partly by the county, and partly by the state, which creates a question of whose directives and rules do they follow in regard to court record search procedures. More below.Records for Supreme and County Courts are maintained by the County Clerks, who are county employees. There are exceptions. In New York City - with its five boroughs - the courts records are administered directly by the state OCA (Office of Court Administration). Also, there are a small number of upstate counties where the Supreme Court OR County Court records are maintained by their court clerk (state employee), and only an index list of cases and defendants is provided to the County Clerk (county employee). Now you will find separate entries for County Clerk among the court profiles of NY counties. While the County Clerks are not courts, they do hold court records and the methods for searching at the County Clerk office are far different from searching at the Courts themselves. 1. In counties where the County Clerk and the Chief Court Clerk are one in the same, you will find only the standard Supreme & County Court listing. 2. In other counties - where the Supreme and County Courts direct all searches to the County Clerk - you will find the information for searching at the County Clerk office. 3. Because they are in different locations or maintain separate case indexes, the Supreme Court and the County Court may appear as separate entries in the profiles.

In some NY counties, the address for the County Clerk is the same as for the Supreme and County Courts. Exceptions are noted in the court profiles, and a separate profile is provided that lists the County Clerk and the County rules for a countywide record search. Note also that, due to limitations in the receiving of records from the Chief Court Clerks, the County Clerk may only be able to do a civil record search, or, rarely, only a criminal record search. Each county is going to be different.City Courts - While all City Courts are administered by state employees, there are a few City Courts that will do a city-only record check despite the edict to state employees that they must direct record searches to the OCA for the statewide record check. Records from City Courts do not go to the County Clerk. Records from City Courts go directly to the OCA.In at least 20 New York Counties, misdemeanor records are only available at city, town, or village courts. This is also true of small claims and eviction records. Town and Village Courts are be listed at the end of each county section.

Now you have an overview of the confusing array of NY courts. You may conclude that an accurate search for misdemeanor records is nearly impossible as there are over 1200 Town and Village Courts in New York which may or may not be accurately reporting their case records.

Criminal Courts: July 14th, 2003, per Section 14 of Assembly Bill A02106, the NY Office of Court Administration (OCA) of the NY Unified Court System expanded its criminal record history search. What was formerly a single county search from one of thirteen counties in the New York City area suddenly became a statewide, all-counties inclusive search. The New York State Office of Court Administration-OCA (address below) has mandated that all criminal record requests made to the Supreme Court Clerk (or made to the County Court Clerk or City Court Clerk) be forwarded to the OCA office for processing. The OCA does not wish to have its clerks performing county only searches. OCA will perform an electronic search for criminal history information from a database of criminal case records from all boroughs and all counties including Supreme Courts, County Courts, and City Courts. At press time, it is not clear that all City Courts submit all misdemeanors to this database. The search fee, payable by check, is $52.00 per name. The search is available by mail or in-person (6 to 24-hour turnaround time), or high volume requesters may order online with email return (same day if ordered by 2:30 pm). Direct mail and in person requests to: Office of Court Administration (OCA) , Criminal History Search, 25 Beaver St, 8th Floor, NY, NY 10004.

Many Counties Still Offer a Countywide Criminal Record Search-

---

Key: Symbols refer to criminal records access unless otherwise noted. phone-☎ mail-✉ fax-**Fax** in person-🖑 online-🖥 email-**Email**

Each county has at least one Chief Court Clerk (sometimes called the Chief Clerk of the Court) who is an employee of the State Unified Court System. Remember, there are two courts - Supreme and County - so there may be a Chief Clerk at each, and each may act independently of the other. So, 1. Chief Court Clerk duties may coincide with the county Supreme Court, which is the general jurisdiction court, AND the County Court - OR 2. they may have separate Chief Clerks. Usually, it is smaller NY counties that combine the roles.In counties outside of NYC, as cases are closed, the general rule is that the files are given to the County Clerk who is responsible for the public record. Each county has a County Clerk employed by the county (and in rare instances, the clerk may be both the state's Chief Court Clerk and the County's County Clerk). State edicts aside, the reality is that either type of clerk may sell county criminal and/or civil records. The County Clerk can because they are not state employees, and the Chief Court Clerk can - though they are told not to and seldom do - because it just makes life easier for everyone.

It is the Chief Court Clerks, who are state employees, who are forbidden by the state edict to sell their records even though those same records are shared and maintained by the County Clerk who, more often than not, does sell them for a handsome profit. Conversely, when the Chief Clerk follows the state's directive, the funds generated from the $52.00 statewide searches goes directly to the OCA. Until the July 14th, 2003 OCA mandate, nearly all of the County Clerks permitted the public to perform their own searches of the criminal records, usually via an index found in books or public access terminal. Also, some County Clerks performed record searches for a fee. Prior to 07/14/03, a County Clerk's office either: 1) used the Chief Court Clerk's computer/database to sell the record for the old $16.00 fee, and turned the money over to the Chief Court Clerk, or 2) performed the search using their own index and charged a fee of $5.00 per name for each 2 years searched, $16.00 for 7 years, or some other similar fee.

Public Access Terminals- The County Clerks, since they already handle real estate, judgments, and lien records, can also provide access to these records AND civil records (received from the Supreme Court Clerk) on their public access terminals. You will find, however, there are far, far fewer County Clerks who offer access to criminal records on the county-owned public access terminals.

City Courts- The City Courts throughout the state do not provide public access terminals. However, plans are to add public access terminals at City Courts, but there is no promise on that nor is there a set timetable for plugging the public in.

Supreme Courts- Since most Supreme Court Clerks are well aware that their civil records are accessible on the County Clerk office (and in most cases on the County Clerk's public access terminals), the Supreme Court clerks do not provide public access terminals patched into their own Supreme Court computer systems.

County Courts- You will find that rarely does a County Court provide public access terminals where you can view their criminal records. It is also rare to find County Court criminal records on the County Clerk's public access terminal. In some counties, the County Court provides the County Clerk with only a paper record of criminal indexes. (In the court profiles, you will find a public access terminal is indicated, but it may not indicate if or if not criminal records are available.)

OCA Unaware of County Clerk Search Procedures-

What helped to contribute to the intrigue of "who gets the money for doing the search" is that the OCA administrators entrusted with instituting the policy changes (in July, 2003) literally had no idea about the County Clerks' searches. They did not realize that most County Clerks permit the public to search the county index and that a number of County Clerks perform record searching for a fee from a non-OCA database, i.e. the county clerk database.

The bottom line is that in many counties the OCA mandate will NOT affect what the County Clerks do regarding criminal or civil record searches. Although the OCA has asked the County Clerks to stop performing searches from their County Clerk indexes, OCA technically has no control over the County Clerks and their indices. Thus, many of the County Clerks who either permitted the public to do their own record searching or who performed the $5.00 (or higher) record search from their database will continue to do so. The July, 2003 OCA edict does not impede these services. This is a real benefit to the users of criminal records who wish to have only a county search, and also to the hands-on record retrievers who will be able to continue to perform in-person searches at the County Clerk offices outside of New York City. In fact, it has been found that more and more County Clerks are offering to perform countywide searches for you, and ignoring the profitless (for the clerk office) and exorbitant (for the public) $52.00 OCA statewide record search. Please note that nearly all the City Courts no longer do criminal record searchs and send misdemeanor record requesters to the OCA for the $52.00 statewide record search.

An Evolving Situation-

As of press time, we have indicated the counties where the County Clerks (and a limited number of Supreme and County Court Clerks) continue to provide countywide criminal record searches. We have also indicated when the County Clerk or Chief Clerk instructs criminal record searches to contact OCA. This information is subject to change, and does.

Probate Courts: Probate is handled by Surrogate Courts. Surrogate Courts may also hear Domestic Relations cases in some counties.

Online Access: The OCA offers online access to approved requesters for criminal records. Requesters receive information back via email. Call OCA for details on how to set up an account. Search fee is $52.00 per record, highest statewide record fee in the U.S.

Open Civil Supreme Court case information is available for all 62 New York counties through the court system's website - http://e.courts.state.ny.us. Decisions are available for many Supreme Court Civil Cases in Broome, Kings, Nassau, New York, Queens, and Suffolk Counties. Select decisions from New York Supreme Criminal Court and other criminal courts are also available. The information is also available at all courts.

Also, you may search for future court dates for defendants in these 21 criminal courts: Bronx Criminal Court, Bronx Supreme Court, Dutchess County Court, Buffalo City Court, Erie County Court, Kings Criminal Court, Kings Supreme Court, Nassau

Key: Symbols refer to criminal records access unless otherwise noted. phone-☎ mail-✉ fax-Fax in person-✋ online-💻 email-Email

County Court, Nassau District Court, New York Criminal Court, New York Supreme Court, Orange County Court, Putnam County, Queens Criminal Court, Queens Supreme Court, Richmond Criminal Court, Richmond Supreme Court, Rockland County Court, Suffolk County Court, Suffolk District Court, Westchester County Court.

Additional Information: In all but a few NY counties, the Supreme and County Court records are maintained in some format in the County Clerk's office, which (with the exception of New York City and its boroughs) may index civil cases by defendant, whereas the courts themselves maintain only a plaintiff index. And, while most criminal courts in the state are indexed by defendant and plaintiff, many New York City courts are indexed by plaintiff only.

Almost all County Courts (felony records) will provide a Certificate of Disposition. This Certificate is a certified document from the court that indicates the disposition of a case. The fee for a Certificate of Disposition is either $5.00 or $6.00, depending upon the county. To obtain a Certificate of Disposition, you must prepay, you must include the name and an exact as possible date (either the disposition date or the arrest date - this requirement varies from county to county), or provide the case number. Some counties also ask for a signed release (this and other details will be noted in the individual court profiles).

Albany County

County Clerk *Felony, Civil* www.albanycounty.com/clerk Courthouse, Rm 128, 16 Eagle St, Albany, NY 12207. 9AM-5PM (4:30 cut-off time). **518-487-5118**, Fax: 518-487-5099. Countywide record search requests. ✉ ✋ ▭

Albany City Court - Civil Part *Civil Under $15,000, Eviction, Small Claims* City Hall, Rm 209, Albany, NY 12207. 8:30AM-5PM. **518-434-5115**, Fax: 518-434-5034. Access civil records-✉ ✋

Albany City Court - Misdemeanors *Misdemeanor* Morton & Broad St, Albany, NY 12202. 8AM-4PM. **518-462-6714**, Fax: 518-447-8778. ✉ ✋

Cohoes City Court *Misd., Civil Actions Under $15,000, Eviction, Small Claims* PO Box 678 97 Mohawk St, Cohoes, NY 12047-0678. 8AM-4PM. **518-233-2133**. Access records- (use statewide search)

Watervliet City Court *Misdemeanor, Civil Actions Under $15,000, Eviction, Small Claims* 2 15th St, Watervliet, NY 12189. 8AM-3PM. **518-270-3803**, Fax: 518-270-3812. ✉ ✋

Surrogate Court *Probate* Courthouse, 16 Eagle St, Albany, NY 12207. 9AM-5PM. **518-487-5393**, Fax: 518-487-5087.

Allegany County

County Clerk *Civil* 7 Court St, Belmont, NY 14813. 9AM-5PM; 8:30AM-4PM Summer hours. **585-268-9270**, Fax: 585-269-9659. Felony records in Allegany County are managed by the County-Court Clerk who directs search requests to OCA for statewide search. Access civil records here-☎ ✉ ✋ ▭

Surrogate Court *Probate* Courthouse, 7 Court St, Belmont, NY 14813. 9AM-5PM Sept-May; 8:30AM-4PM June-Aug. **585-268-5815**, Fax: 585-268-7090.

Bronx Borough

Supreme Court - Civil Division *Civil Over $25,000* www.courts.state.ny.us/courts/12jd/ 851 Grand Concourse Mezzanine, Rm 118, Bronx, NY 10451. 9AM-5PM. **718-590-3647 Clerk**, Fax: 718-590-8122. Access civil records-✋ ▭

Supreme Court - Criminal Division *Felony* www.courts.state.ny.us/courts/12jd/ 851 Grand Concourse, Rm 123, Bronx, NY 10451. 9AM-5PM. **718-590-3803**, Fax: 718-590-3708. Civil phone: 718-590-3722, crim: 718-590-2854. ✉ ✋

Supreme Court - Criminal Div. - Misdemeanors www.courts.state.ny.us/courts/12jd/ Central Clerk's Office 215 W 161st St, Bronx, NY 10451. 9AM-1PM, 2-5PM. **718-590-2853**. ✉ ✋

Civil Court of the City of New York - Bronx Branch *Civil Actions Under $25,000, Eviction, Small Claims* www.courts.state.ny.us/courts/12jd/ 851 Grand Concourse Window 6, Basement, Bronx, NY 10451. 9AM-5PM. **718-590-3601, 718-590-3597 records room**. Access civil records-☎ ✋

Surrogate Court *Probate* 851 Grand Concourse, Bronx, NY 10451. 9AM-5PM. **718-590-4515**, Fax: 718-537-5158.

Broome County

County Clerk *Felony, Civil* PO Box 2062 Broome County Clerk, County Office Bldg, Binghamton, NY 13902. 8AM-5PM; 7:30AM-4PM June-August. **607-778-2255**, Fax: 607-778-2243. Countywide record search requests. Fax ✉ ✋

Binghamton City Court *Misdemeanor, Civil Actions Under $15,000, Eviction, Small Claims* Governmental Plaza, Binghamton, NY 13901. 9AM-5PM. **607-772-7006**, Fax: 607-772-7041. ✉ ✋

Surrogate Court *Probate* PO Box 1766, Binghamton, NY 13902. 9AM-5PM, Summer 8AM-4PM **607-778-2111**, Fax: 607-778-2308.

Cattaraugus County

County Clerk *Felony, Civil* 303 Court St, Little Valley, NY 14755. 9AM-5PM. **716-938-9111 x2297**, Fax: 716-938-2387. Countywide record search request. ✉ ✋

Olean City Court *Misdemeanor, Civil Actions Under $15,000, Eviction, Small Claims* PO Box 631 101 E State St, Olean, NY 14760. 8:30AM-N, 1-5PM. **716-376-5620**, Fax: 716-376-5623. Access records- (use statewide search).

Salamanca City Court *Misdemeanor, Civil Actions Under $15,000, Eviction, Small Claims* Municipal Center 225 Wildwood Ave, Salamanca, NY 14779. 8AM-4PM. **716-945-4153**. ✉ ✋

Surrogate Court *Probate* 303 Court St, Little Valley, NY 14755. 9AM-5PM. **716-938-9111**, Fax: 716-938-6983. Public can search, but fee if court searches for them.

Cayuga County

County Clerk *Felony, Misdemeanor, Civil* 160 Genesee St Attn: County Clerk, Auburn, NY 13021. 9AM-5PM Sept-June; 8AM-4PM July-Aug. **315-253-1271**, Fax: 315-253-1653. With a specific case number, you can search countywide at County Clerk office. The County Clerk will not do a criminal record name search. Access records- (use statewide search)

Auburn City Court *Misdemeanor, Civil Actions Under $15,000, Eviction, Small Claims* 157 Genesee St, Auburn, NY 13021-3434. 8AM-4PM. **315-253-1570**, Fax: 315-253-1085. Access records- (use statewide search)

Surrogate Court *Probate* www.courts.state.ny.us/www/jd7/cayuga_surrogate.htm Courthouse, 152 Genesee St,

Auburn, NY 13021-3471. 8:30AM-4:30PM; Summer hours 8AM-4:00PM. **315-255-4316**, Fax: 315-255-4322.

Chautauqua County

County Clerk *Felony, Civil* www.co.chautauqua.ny.us/clerk/clerkframe. htm Courthouse PO Box 170, Mayville, NY 14757. 9AM-5PM/Summer 8:30AM-4:30PM. **716-753-4331**, Fax: 716-753-4293. 🖐. Non in-person felony record requests are managed by the Supreme Court clerk who directs searches to OCA for $52.00 statewide search.

Supreme & County Court - Civil *Civil* www.co.chautauqua.ny.us/clerk/clerkframe. htm PO Box 170 1 N Erie St, Mayville, NY 14757. 9AM-5PM/Summer 8:30AM-4:30PM. **716-753-4331**, Fax: 716-753-4293. Access civil records- ✉ 🖐

Jamestown City Court *Misdemeanor, Civil Actions Under $15,000, Eviction, Small Claims* City Hall, Jamestown, NY 14701. 8:30AM-5PM. **716-483-7561/7562**, Fax: 716-483-7519. Access records- (use statewide search)

Dunkirk City Court *Misdemeanor, Civil Actions Under $15,000, Eviction, Small Claims* City Hall 342 Central Ave, Dunkirk, NY 14048. 9AM-5PM. **716-366-2055**, Fax: 716-366-3622. Access records- (use statewide search).

Surrogate Court *Probate* Gerace Office Bldg (3 N Erie St) PO Box C, Mayville, NY 14757. 9AM-5PM; July-Sept. 3: 8:30AM-4:30PM. **716-753-4339**, Fax: 716-753-4600.

Chemung County

Supreme & County Court - Criminal *Felony* PO Box 588 Hazlett Bldg, 6th Fl, Elmira, NY 14902-0588. 9AM-5PM. **607-737-2084**. See County Clerk for Supreme court civil case records. ✉ 🖐

County Clerk *Civil Actions* www.chemungcounty.com PO Box 588 210 Lake St, Elmira, NY 14901. 8:30AM-4:30PM. **607-737-2920**, Fax: 607-737-2897. Access civil records- ✉ **Fax** 🖐 💻

Elmira City Court *Misdemeanor, Civil Actions Under $15,000, Eviction, Small Claims* 317 E Church St, Elmira, NY 14901. 8AM-4PM. **607-737-5681**, Fax: 607-737-5820. Access records- (use statewide search).

Surrogate Court *Probate* 224 Lake St, Elmira, NY 14902. 9AM-5PM; 8:30-4:30

July-Sept. 3. **607-737-2946/2819**, Fax: 607-737-2874.

Chenango County

County Clerk *Felony, Civil* County Office Bldg, 1st Fl 5 Court St, Norwich, NY 13815-1676. 8:30AM-5PM. **607-337-1450**. Countywide record search requests. ✉ 🖐

Norwich City Court *Misdemeanor, Civil Actions Under $15,000, Eviction, Small Claims* 1 Court Plaza, Norwich, NY 13815. 8:30AM-4:30PM. **607-334-1224**, Fax: 607-334-8494. 🖐

Surrogate Court *Probate* County Office Bldg 5 Court St, Norwich, NY 13815. 9AM-5PM, Summer-8:30-4:30PM. **607-337-1822/1827**, Fax: 607-337-1834.

Clinton County

County Clerk *Civil* County Gov't Ctr 137 Margaret St, 1st Fl, Plattsburgh, NY 12901. 8AM-5PM. **518-565-4701**. The County Clerk does not have a separate index of criminal records; see the Supreme and County Court. Online access to current/pending civil cases is at http://e.courts.state.ny.us. Access civil records- 🖐 💻

Supreme and County Court *Civil, Felony* County Gov't Ctr 137 Margaret St, 1st Fl, Plattsburgh, NY 12901. 9AM-N, 1-5PM. **518-565-4715**. Fax: 518-565-4708. The County-Court directs criminal search requestrs to the OCA for statewide record check, but civil records are with the County Clerk, see above. Online access to current/pending civil cases is at http://e.courts.state.ny.us. Access civil records- 🖐 💻

Plattsburg City Court *Misdemeanor, Civil Actions Under $15,000, Eviction, Small Claims* 24 US Oval, Plattsburgh, NY 12903. 8AM-4PM. **518-563-7870**, Fax: 518-563-3124. Access records- (use statewide search).

Surrogate Court *Probate* 137 Margaret St, #315, Plattsburgh, NY 12901-2933. 8-5PM. **518-565-4630**, Fax: 518-565-4769.

Columbia County

County Clerk *Felony, Civil* 560 Warren St, Hudson, NY 12534. 9AM-5PM. **518-828-3339**, Fax: 518-828-5299. Countywide record search requests. ✉ 🖐

Hudson City Court *Misd., Civil Actions Under $15,000, Eviction, Small Claims*

www.nycourts.gov/courts/3jd/ 429 Warren St, Hudson, NY 12534. 8AM-3:45PM. **518-828-3100**, Fax: 518-828-3628. Access records- use statewide search.

Surrogate Court *Probate* Courthouse, 401 Union St, Hudson, NY 12534. 9AM-5PM. **518-828-0414**, Fax: 518-828-1603.

Cortland County

County Clerk *Felony, Civil* 46 Greenbush St, #101, Cortland, NY 13045. 8:30PM-4:30PM. **607-753-5021**. County-wide record search requests. ✉ 🖐

Cortland City Court *Misdemeanor, Civil Actions Under $15,000, Eviction, Small Claims* 25 Court St, Cortland, NY 13045. 8:30AM-4:30PM. **607-753-1811**, Fax: 607-753-9932. ✉ 🖐

Surrogate Court *Probate* 46 Greenbush St, #301, Cortland, NY 13045. 9AM-5PM; July-Sept 8:30AM-4:30PM. **607-753-5355**, Fax: 607-756-3409.

Delaware County

County Clerk *Felony, Civil* 3 Court St, Delhi, NY 13753. 8:30AM-5PM. **607-746-2123**, Fax: 607-746-6924. County-wide record search requests. ✉ 🖐

Surrogate Court *Probate* 3 Court St, Delhi, NY 13753. 9AM-5PM; July-Sept 3: 9AM-4:30PM. **607-746-2126**, Fax: 607-746-3253.

Dutchess County

County Clerk *Felony, Civil* www.dutchessny.gov/dcclerk.htm 22 Market St, Poughkeepsie, NY 12601-3203. 9AM-5PM. **845-486-2139 (records); 486-2120 (main)**. Countywide record search requests. ✉ 🖐

Beacon City Court *Misdemeanor, Civil Actions Under $15,000, Eviction, Small Claims* One Municipal Plaza, #2, Beacon, NY 12508. 8AM-4PM. **845-838-5030**, Fax: 845-838-5041. Access records- (use statewide search).

Poughkeepsie City Court *Misdemeanor, Civil Actions Under $15,000, Eviction, Small Claims* Civic Center Plaza PO Box 300, Poughkeepsie, NY 12602. 8-4PM. **845-451-4091**, Fax: 845-485-6795. 🖐

Surrogate Court *Probate* 10 Market St, Poughkeepsie, NY 12601. 9AM-5PM. **845-486-2235**, Fax: 845-486-2234.

Key: Symbols refer to criminal records access unless otherwise noted. phone- ☎ mail- ✉ fax- **Fax** in person- 🖐 online- 💻 email- **Email**

Erie County

County Clerk *Felony, Civil* www.erie.gov/depts/government/clerk/civil criminal.phtml 25 Delaware Ave, 1st Fl, Buffalo, NY 14202. 9AM-5PM; usually closed 1 hour for lunch but time varies. Fax: 716-858-6550. Civil phone: 716-858-7766, crim: 716-858-7877. Countywide record search requests. 🖐

Lackawanna City Court *Misdemeanor, Civil Actions Under $15,000, Eviction, Small Claims* 714 Ridge Rd, Rm 225, Lackawanna, NY 14218. 8:30AM-4:30PM. **716-827-6486**, Fax: 716-825-1874. Civil phone: 716-827-6661, crim: 716-827-6487. Access records- (use statewide search).

Buffalo City Court *Misdemeanor, Civil Actions Under $15,000, Eviction, Small Claims* 50 Delaware Ave, Buffalo, NY 14202. 9AM-5PM. **716-845-2689**, Fax: 716-847-8257. Civil phone: 716-845-2662, crim: 716-845-2661. 🖐

Tonawanda City Court *Misdemeanor, Civil Actions Under $15,000, Eviction, Small Claims, Criminal* 200 Niagara St, Tonawanda, NY 14150. 9AM-4PM. **716-693-3484**, Fax: 716-693-1612. 🖂 🖐

Surrogate Court *Probate* 92 Franklin St, Buffalo, NY 14202. 9AM-5PM. **716-854-2560**, Fax: 716-853-3741.

Essex County

County Clerk *Civil, Felony* PO Box 247 7559 Court St, Essex County Government Ctr, Elizabethtown, NY 12932. 8AM-5PM. Fax: 518-873-3548. Civil phone: 518-873-3600, 518-873-3601. County Clerk will not do criminal record searches for County-Court criminal records; clerk will only do civil record searches. You may search criminal books in person, otherwise use statewide search for felony court records.

Surrogate Court *Probate* 7559 Court St PO Box 505, Elizabethtown, NY 12932. 9-5PM. **518-873-3384** Fax 518-873-3731.

Franklin County

County Clerk *Felony, Civil* 355 W Main St Attn: County Clerk, Malone, NY 12953-1817. 9AM-5PM; 8AM-4PM Summer hours. **518-481-1681**. Felony records are managed by the County-Court clerk who directs search requests to OCA for a $52.00 statewide search. However, criminal records are accessible in person here on the public access terminal. 🖐

Supreme & County Court *Felony, Civil* 355 W Main St Court Clerk, Malone, NY 12953-1817. 9AM-5PM; 8AM-4PM Summer hours. **518-481-1748**, crim: 518-481-1749. Supreme court directs criminal search requests to the OCA for a $52.00 statewide record check. Search civil records at County Clerk, see separate listing. Access to current/pending Supreme Court civil cases is available at http://e.courts.state.ny.us/. 🖂 🖐

Surrogate Court *Probate* 355 W Main St, Malone, NY 12953-1817. 8AM-5PM, June-Aug 8:00AM-4PM. **518-481-1736 & 1737**, Fax: 518-483-7583.

Fulton County

Supreme & County Court *Felony, Civil* 223 W Main St County Bldg, Johnstown, NY 12095. 9AM-5PM. **518-736-5539 (court) 518-736-5555 (county clerk)**. Hamilton County Supreme Court cases are heard here. Supreme court clerk directs criminal search requests to the OCA for a $52.00 statewide record check, however the County Clerk office (same location) may permit in person criminal record search requests. Access records- 🖐

Gloversville City Court *Misdemeanor, Civil Actions Under $15,000, Eviction, Small Claims* City Hall, Frontage Rd, Gloversville, NY 12078. 8AM-4PM. **518-773-4527**, Fax: 518-773-4599. Access records- (use statewide search).

Surrogate Court *Probate* 223 W Main St, Johnstown, NY 12095. 9AM-5PM (8AM-4PM July-August). **518-736-5685**, Fax: 518-762-6372.

Genesee County

County Clerk *Felony, Civil* PO Box 379 (15 Main St) Attn: County Clerk, Batavia, NY 14021-0379. 8:30AM-5PM. **585-344-2550 x2243**, Fax: 585-344-8551. Countywide criminal search requests. Fax🖂 🖐

Batavia City Court *Misdemeanor, Civil Actions Under $15,000, Eviction, Small Claims* Genesee County Courts Facility 1 W Main St, Batavia, NY 14020. 9AM-5PM. **585-344-2550 X2416, 2417, 2418**, Fax: 585-344-8556. 🖂 🖐

Surrogate Court *Probate* 1 W Main St, Batavia, NY 14020. 9AM-5PM; June-Sept 3 8:30-4:30. **585-344-2550 ext 2237**, Fax: 585-344-8517. $25.00 search fee.

Greene County

Supreme & County Court *Felony, Civil* Courthouse, County Clerk 320 Main St, Catskill, NY 12414. 9AM-5PM; 8:30AM-4:30PM Summer hours. **518-943-2050 x71 (county clerk)**, 518-943-2230 (court clerk), Fax: 518-943-2146. Search requests processed by the County Clerk. Fax🖂 🖐

Surrogate Court *Probate* Courthouse, 320 Main St, Catskill, NY 12414. 9AM-5PM. **518-943-2484**, Fax: 518-943-1864.

Hamilton County

Supreme Court *Civil* Hamilton County Clerk PO Box 204, Rte 8, Lake Pleasant, NY 12108. 8:30AM-4:30PM. **518-548-7111 (Hamilton county clerk) 518-736-5539 (Fulton court clerk)**. Supreme court (civil cases) in Hamilton County are heard in Fulton County. Civil records eventually returned to Hamilton County Clerk once the case is completed in Fulton. Original filings made in Hamilton, but subsequent filings usually made at Fulton. Access civil records-🖂 Fax🕿 🖐 🖳

County Clerk & County Court *Felony, Civil* Hamilton County Clerk PO Box 204, Rte 8, Lake Pleasant, NY 12108. 8:30AM-4:30PM. **518-548-7111**. Countywide record search requests. Civil cases are heard in Fulton County (518-736-5539, Patricia, for info). Once closed, civil case records are returned to Hamilton County clerk. 🖂 🖐

Surrogate Court *Probate* PO Box 780 White Birch Lane, Indian Lake, NY 12842. 8:30AM-4:30PM. **518-648-5411**, Fax: 518-648-6286. Court is located in Hamilton County Ofc. Bldg.

Herkimer County

County Clerk *Felony, Civil* 109 Mary St Herkimer County Office Bldg, Herkimer, NY 13350-1993. 9AM-5PM Sept-May; 8:30AM-4PM June-Aug. **315-867-1133**, Fax: 315-867-1349. Countywide record search requests. 🖂 🖐

Little Falls City Court *Misdemeanor, Civil Actions Under $15,000, Eviction, Small Claims* 659 E Main St, Little Falls, NY 13365. 8:30AM-4:30PM. **315-823-1690**, Fax: 315-823-1623. 🖂 🖐

Surrogate Court *Probate* 301 N Washington St, #5550, Herkimer, NY 13350. 9AM-5PM Sept-May; 8:30AM-4PM June-Aug. **315-867-1170**.

Key: Symbols refer to criminal records access unless otherwise noted. phone-🕿 mail-🖂 fax-**Fax** in person-🖐 online-🖳 email-**Email**

Jefferson County

Supreme & County Court *Felony, Civil* www.co.jefferson.ny.us/Jefflive.nsf/cclerk Jefferson County Clerk's Office-Court Records 175 Arsenal St, County Bldg, Watertown, NY 13601-3783. 9AM-5PM; 8:30AM-4PM July-Aug hours. **315-785-3200 County Clerk**, Fax: 315-785-5145 Countywide record search requests are processed by the County Clerk. ✉️ 🖐️

Watertown City Court *Misdemeanor, Civil Actions Under $15,000, Eviction, Small Claims* 245 Washington St Municipal Bldg, Watertown, NY 13601. 8:30AM4:30PM. **315-785-7785**, Fax: 315-785-7818. Access records- (use statewide search).

Surrogate Court *Probate* County Court Complex 163 Arsenal St, 3rd Fl, Watertown, NY 13601-2562. 9AM-4:30PM Sept-May; 8:30AM-4PM June-Aug. **315-785-3019**, Fax: 315-785-5194.

Kings Borough

Supreme Court - Civil Division *Civil Over $25,000* www.courts.state.ny.us/courts/2jd/kings.shtml#sup 360 Adams St, Brooklyn, NY 11201. 9AM-3PM. **718-643-5894**, Fax: 718-643-8187. Access civil records- 🖐️ 🖥️

Civil Court of the City of New York - Kings Branch *Civil Actions Under $25,000, Eviction, Small Claims* www.courts.state.ny.us/courts/2jd/kings.shtml#sup 141 Livingston St, Brooklyn, NY 11201. 9AM-5PM. **718-643-5069/643-8133 Clerk**. Access civil records- 🖐️

Surrogate Court *Probate* www.couts.state.ny.us/courtguides/Guide_24.pdf 2 Johnson St, Brooklyn, NY 11201. 9AM-5PM. **718-643-5262**, Fax: 718-643-6237.

Lewis County

Supreme & County Court *Felony, Civil* Courthouse, County Clerk PO Box 232, Lowville, NY 13367. 8:30AM-4:30PM. **315-376-5333 (County); 315-376-5380 (Supreme)**, Fax: 315-376-3768. Countywide search requests. ✉️ 🖐️

Surrogate Court *Probate* Courthouse, 7660 State St, Lowville, NY 13367. 8:30AM-4:30PM, June-Aug 8:30-4PM. **315-376-5344**, Fax: 315-376-4145.

Livingston County

County Clerk *Felony, Civil* 6 Court St, Rm 201, Geneseo, NY 14454. 8:30AM-

4:30PM Oct-May; 8AM-4PM June-Sept. **585-243-7010**, Fax: 585-243-7928. Countywide search requests made to the County Court Clerk. ☎️✉️**Fax**🖐️

Surrogate Court *Probate* 2 Court St, Geneseo, NY 14454. 9AM-5PM. **585-243-7095**, Fax: 585-243-7583.

Madison County

County Clerk *Felony, Civil* County Office Bldg PO Box 668, Wampsville, NY 13163. 9AM-5PM. **315-366-2261**, Fax: 315-366-2615. Countywide search requests. ✉️ 🖐️

Oneida City Court *Misdemeanor, Civil Actions Under $15,000, Eviction, Small Claims* 109 N Main St, Oneida, NY 13421. 8:30AM-4:30PM. **315-363-1310**, Fax: 315-363-3230. Access records- (use statewide search).

Surrogate Court *Probate* PO Box 607, Wampsville, NY 13163. 9AM-5PM. **315-366-2392**, Fax: 315-366-2539.

Monroe County

County Clerk *Felony, Civil* www.clerk.co.monroe.ny.us County Office Bldg, County Clerk Office 39 Main St W, Rochester, NY 14614. 9AM-5PM. **585-428-5151**, Fax: 716-428-4698. Countywide search requests. **Fax**✉️🖥️🖐️

Rochester City Court - Civil *Civil Actions Under $15,000, Eviction, Small Claims* 99 Exchange Blvd Hall of Justice, Rm 6, Rochester, NY 14614. 9AM-5PM. **585-428-2444**, Fax: 585-428-2588. Access civil records- 🖐️

Rochester City Court - Criminal *Misdemeanor* 150 S Plymouth, Rm 123 Public Safety Bldg, Rochester, NY 14614. 9AM-5PM. **585-428-2447**, Fax: 585-428-2732. 🖐️

Surrogate Court *Probate* Hall of Justice, Rm 541 99 Exchange Blvd, Rochester, NY 14614. 9AM-5PM. **585-428-5200**, Fax: 585-428-2650.

Montgomery County

County Clerk *Felony, Misdemeanor, Civil* PO Box 1500 64 E Broadway, County Office Bldg, Fonda, NY 12068. 9AM-5PM; 8:30AM-4PM (civil). **518-853-8113**. Countywide record search requests. 🖐️

Amsterdam City Court *Misdemeanor, Civil Actions Under $15,000, Eviction,*

Small Claims Public Safety Bldg, Rm 208 One Guy Park Ave Ext, Amsterdam, NY 12010. 8AM-4PM. **518-842-9510**, Fax: 518-843-8474. ✉️🖐️

Surrogate Court *Probate* 58 Broadway PO Box 1500, Fonda, NY 12068. 9AM-5PM. **518-853-8108**, Fax: 518-853-8230.

Nassau County

County Clerk *Felony, Civil Actions Over $15,000* www.co.nassau.ny.us/clerk/ 240 Old Country Rd, Mineola, NY 11501. 9AM-5PM. **516-571-2272**. Holds records for the Supreme Court and for the County Court. As a rule, this office directs search requests to the OCA for the $52.00 statewide search, however, the records dept. can perform in person searches.

County Court *Felony* www.co.nassau.ny.us/clerk/ 262 Old Country Rd, Mineola, NY 11501. 9AM-5PM. **516-571-2800**, Fax: 516-571-2160. 🖐️

District Court - 3rd District *Misd., Civil Actions Under $15,000, Eviction, Small Claims* 435 Middle Neck Rd, Great Neck, NY 11023. 9AM-5PM. **516-571-8400/8401**, Fax: 516-571-8403. Court has records only for its district. Records include Town of North Hempstead violations. Access civil records- 🖐️

District Court - 1st & 2nd Districts *Misdemeanor, Civil Actions Under $15,000, Eviction, Small Claims* 99 Main St, Hempstead, NY 11550. 9AM-5PM. **516-572-2355**. Civil: 516-572-2266. Records for 2nd District are separate prior to 1980. 1st District handles Misdemeanor case records. Access records- (use statewide search).

Long Beach City Court *Misdemeanor, Civil Actions Under $15,000, Eviction, Small Claims* 1 W Chester St, Long Beach, NY 11561. 9AM-5PM. **516-431-1000**, Fax: 516-889-3511. Access records- (use statewide search).

Glen Cove City Court *Misdemeanor, Civil Actions Under $15,000, Eviction, Small Claims* 13 Glen St, Glen Cove, NY 11542-2704. 9AM-5PM. **516-676-0109**, Fax: 516-676-1570. Access records- (use statewide search).

Surrogate Court *Probate* 262 Old Country Rd, Mineola, NY 11501. 9AM-5PM. **516-571-2082**, Fax: 516-571-3864.

New York - Manhattan

Supreme Court - Civil Division *Civil Actions* www.nycourts.gov/supctmanh/ County Clerk, 60 Centre St, Rm 103, New York, NY 10007. 9AM-3PM. **212-374-4704/374-8339**. Record search requests are managed by the County Clerk office; information here is for that County Clerk office. Access civil records- ✉ ✍ 🖥

Supreme Court - Criminal Division *Felony, Misdemeanor* 100 Centre St, Rm 1000, New York, NY 10013. 9AM-5PM. **212-374-4985**, crim: 212-374-4190. The Court will only process mail or in person requests for specific documents or papers related to felony cases. ✉ ✍

Civil Court of the City of New York *Civil Actions Under $25,000, Eviction, Small Claims* 111 Centre St, New York, NY 10013. 9AM-5PM. **212-374-4646**, Fax: 212-374-5709. Access civil records- ✉ ✍ ☎

Surrogate Court *Probate* www.courts.state.ny.us/courts/nyc/surrogates/index.shtml 31 Chambers St, New York City, NY 10007. 9-5PM. **212-374-8233, 374-8232**.

Niagara County

County Clerk *Felony, Civil Actions Over $25,000* 175 Hawley St, Lockport, NY 14094. 9AM-5PM; 8:30AM-4:30PM Summer Hours. **716-439-7030**, Fax: 716-439-7066. County Clerk maintains records for the Supreme Court (Civil) and the County Court (criminal). ✉ **Fax** ✍

Niagara Falls City Court *Misdemeanor, Civil Actions Under $15,000, Eviction, Small Claims* PO Box 1586, Niagara Falls, NY 14302-2725. 8:30AM-4:30PM. **716-278-9800**, Fax: 716-278-9809. Civil phone: 716-278-9860, crim: 716-278-9800. ✉ ✍

Lockport City Court *Misdemeanor, Civil Actions Under $15,000, Eviction, Small Claims* Municipal Bldg, One Locks Plaza, Lockport, NY 14094. 8AM-4:30PM. Fax: 716-439-6684. Civil phone: 716-439-6660, crim: 716-439-6671. Access records- (use statewide search).

North Tonawanda City Court *Misdemeanor, Civil Actions Under $15,000, Eviction, Small Claims* City Hall, North Tonawanda, NY 14120-5446. 8AM-5PM. **716-693-1010**, Fax: 716-743-1754. ✉ ✍

Surrogate Court *Probate* Niagara's County Courthouse 175 Hawley St, Lockport, NY 14094. 9AM-5PM. **716-439-7130/7131**, Fax: 716-439-7319.

Oneida County

County Clerk *Felony, Civil* 800 Park Ave, Utica, NY 13501. 8:30AM-5PM, 8:30AM-4:30PM Summer hours. Fax: 315-798-6440. Civil phone: 315-798-5776, crim: 315-798-5797. Search requests made to the County Clerk. ✉ **Fax** ✍

Sherrill City Court *Misdemeanor, Civil Actions Under $15,000, Eviction, Small Claims* 373 Sherrill Rd, Sherrill, NY 13461. 8AM-4PM. **315-363-0996**, Fax: 315-363-1176. ✉ ✍

Rome City Court *Misdemeanor, Civil Actions Under $15,000, Eviction, Small Claims* 100 W Court St, Rome, NY 13440. 8:30AM-4:30PM; 8:30AM-4PM Summer Hours. **315-337-6440**, Fax: 315-338-0343. ✍

Utica City Court *Misdemeanor, Civil Actions Under $15,000, Eviction, Small Claims* 411 Oriskany St W, Utica, NY 13502. 8:30AM-4:30PM. Fax: 315-724-0762 (criminal)/792-8038 (civil). Civil phone: 315-724-8157, crim: 315-724-8227. Access records- (use statewide search).

Surrogate Court *Probate* Oneida County Office Bldg 8th Fl 800 Park Ave, Utica, NY 13501. 8:30AM-4:30PM Sept-May; 8:30AM-4PM June-Aug. **315-797-923**, Fax: 315-797-9237.

Onondaga County

County Clerk *Felony, Civil* 401 Montgomery St, Rm 200, Syracuse, NY 13202. 8AM-5PM. **315-435-8200**. Civil: 315-435-2234, crim: 315-435-2236. Countywide record search requests. All requests must be in writing. ✉ ✍

Syracuse City Court *Misdemeanor, Civil Actions Under $15,000, Eviction, Small Claims* 505 State St, Rm 130, Syracuse, NY 13202-2179. 9AM-4PM. **315-671-2773**, Fax: 315-671-2742 Civil; 671-2744 criminal. Civil phone: 315-671-2782, crim: 315-671-2760. Small claims phone is 315-671-2784; their fax is 315-671-2741 ☎ **Fax** ✉ ✍

Surrogate Court *Probate* http://surrogate5th.courts.state.ny.us/public/ Onondaga Courthouse, Rm 209 401 Montgomery St,

Syracuse, NY 13202. 9AM-5PM. **315-671-2100**, Fax: 315-671-1162.

Ontario County

County Clerk *Felony, Civil* 20 Ontario St Municipal Bldg, Canandaigua, NY 14424. 8:30AM-5PM. Fax: 585-393-2951. Civil phone: 585-396-4205, crim: 585-393-2953. All criminal record search requests made to the Supreme Court Clerk are forwarded to the OCA for processing (see Introduction). However, criminal search requests made to the County Court Clerk are processed here by- **Fax** ✉ ✍

Geneva City Court *Misdemeanor, Civil Actions Under $15,000, Eviction, Small Claims* 255 Exchange St, Geneva, NY 14456. 8AM-4PM. **315-789-6560**, Fax: 315-781-2802. Access records- (use statewide search).

Canandaigua City Court *Misdemeanor, Civil Actions Under $15,000, Eviction, Small Claims* 2 N Main St, Canandaigua, NY 14424-1448. 8AM-4PM. **585-396-5011**, Fax: 585-396-5012. Access records- (use statewide search).

Surrogate Court *Probate* 27 N Main St, Canandaigua, NY 14424-1447. 9AM-5PM. **585-396-4055**, Fax: 585-396-4576.

Orange County

County Clerk *Felony, Civil* 255 Main St, Goshen, NY 10924. 9AM-5PM. **845-291-3080**, Fax: 845-291-2691. Search requests made to the County Clerk. **Fax** ✉ ✍

Port Jervis City Court *Misdemeanor, Civil Actions Under $15,000, Eviction, Small Claims* 14-18 Hammond St, Port Jervis, NY 12771-2495. 9AM-5PM. **845-858-4034**, Fax: 845-858-9883. ✉ ✍

Newburgh City Court *Misdemeanor, Civil Actions Up to $15,000, Eviction, Small Claims* 57 Broadway, Newburgh, NY 12550. 8AM-4PM. **845-565-3208**, Civil: 845-565-3074, crim: 845-565-3208. Access records- (use statewide search).

Middletown City Court *Misdemeanor, Civil Actions Under $15,000, Eviction, Small Claims* 2 James St, Middletown, NY 10940. 8:30AM-4PM. **845-346-4050**, Fax: 845-343-5737. Access records- (use statewide search).

Surrogate Court *Probate* 30 Park Pl Surrogate's Courthouse, Goshen, NY 10924. 9AM-5PM; Vault closes at 4PM. **845-291-2193**, Fax: 845-291-2196.

Orleans County

Supreme and County Court *Felony, Civil* Courthouse, 3 S Main, Albion, NY 14411-9998. 9AM-5PM; 8:30AM-4PM Summer hours. **585-589-4457**, Fax: 585-589-0632. The court directs felony search requests to the OCA statewide record search. Access civil records through the County Clerk, see below. Access to current/pending Supreme Court civil cases is at http://e.courts.state.ny.us/. 👋

County Clerk *Civil* Courthouse, Attn: County Clerk 3 S Main, Albion, NY 14411-9998. 9AM-5PM; 8:30AM-4PM Summer hours. **585-589-5334**, Fax: 585-589-0181. 👋 ✉

Surrogate Court *Probate* 3 S Main St, Albion, NY 14411. 9AM-5PM. **585-589-4457**, Fax: 585-589-0632.

Oswego County

County Clerk *Felony, Civil* 46 E Bridge St, Oswego, NY 13126. 9AM-5PM. **315-349-8616**, Fax: 315-349-8692. Countywide search requests. ✉ 👋

Oswego City Court *Misdemeanor, Civil Actions Under $15,000, Eviction, Small Claims* Conway Municipal Bldg 20 W Oneida St, Oswego, NY 13126. 8:30AM-5PM. **315-343-0415**, Fax: 315-343-0531. Access records- (use statewide search).

Fulton City Court *Misdemeanor, Civil Actions Under $15,000, Eviction, Small Claims* 141 S 1st St, Fulton, NY 13069. 8:30AM-4:30PMSummer 8:30AM-4PM. **315-593-8400**, Fax: 315-592-3415. Access records- (use statewide search).

Surrogate Court *Probate* Courthouse, 25 E Oneida St, Oswego, NY 13126. 9AM-5PM Sept-May; 8:30AM-3:30 PM June-Aug. **315-349-3295**.

Otsego County

County Clerk *Felony, Civil* 197 Main St Public Office Bldg, Cooperstown, NY 13326. 9AM-5PM; 8AM-5PM Summer hours. **607-547-4276**. Countywide record search requests. ✉ 👋

Oneonta City Court *Misdemeanor, Civil Actions Under $15,000, Eviction, Small Claims* 81 Main St, Oneonta, NY 13820. 8AM-4PM. **607-432-4480**, Fax: 607-432-2328. Access records- (use statewide search).

Surrogate Court *Probate* Surrogate's Office 197 Main St, Cooperstown, NY 13326. 9AM-5PM. **607-547-4338**, Fax: 607-547-7566.

Putnam County

County Clerk *Felony, Civil* 40 Gleneida Ave County Clerk Office, Carmel, NY 10512. 9AM-5PM; 8AM-4PM Summer hours. **845-225-3641 X307**, Fax: 845-228-0231. Search online for future court appearances at http://e.courts.state.ny.us. Direct criminal search requests to the County-Court Clerk. ✉ 👋

Surrogate's Court *Probate* Historic Courthouse 44 Gleneida Ave, Carmel, NY 10512. 9AM-5PM. **845-225-3641 X295**, Fax: 845-228-5761.

Queens Borough

Supreme Court - Civil Division *Civil Actions Over $25,000* www.courts.state.ny.us/courts/11jd/index.shtml 88-11 Sutphin Blvd, #106, Jamaica, NY 11435. 9AM-5PM, no cashier transactions after 4:45PM. **718-298-1000**, Fax: 718-520-2204. Access civil records- ✉ 👋 🖥

Supreme Court - Criminal Div. *Felony, Misd.* www.courts.state.ny.us/11jd/queens/ 125-01 Queens Blvd, Kew Gardens, NY 11415. 9:30AM-4:30PM. **718-520-3542**. Access records- (use statewide search).

Civil Court of the City of New York - Queens Branch *Civil Actions Under $25,000, Eviction, Small Claims* 89-17 Sutphin Blvd, Jamaica, NY 11435. 9AM-5PM. **718-262-7100**. Civil: 212-791-6000. Housing court information: 212-791-6070. Access civil records- 👋

Surrogate Court *Probate* www.courts.state.ny.us/11jd/queens/contact_us.htm 88-11 Sutphin Blvd, Jamaica, NY 11435. 9AM-5PM. **718-298-0500**.

Rensselaer County

County Clerk *Felony, Civil* www.rensco.com 105 3rd St, Troy, NY 12180. 8:30AM-5PM. **518-270-4080**, Fax: 518-271-7998. Countywide record search requests. ✉ 👋

Troy City Court *Misdemeanor* 51 State St, 2nd Fl, Troy, NY 12180. 9AM-3:30PM. **518-271-1602**, Fax: 518-274-2816. ✉ 👋

Rensselaer City Court *Misdemeanor, Civil Actions Under $15,000, Eviction, Small Claims* City Hall, Rensselaer, NY 12144. 8AM-3:30PM. **518-462-6751**, Fax: 518-462-3307. ✉ 👋

Surrogate Court *Probate* County Courthouse 80 2nd St, Troy, NY 12180. 9-5. **518-270-3724**, Fax: 518-272-5452.

Richmond Borough

Supreme Court - Civil Division *Civil Actions Over $25,000* 130 Stuyvesant Pl, c/o Richmond County Clerk, Staten Island, NY 10301. 9AM-5PM. **718-390-5389 Court Desk**, Civil: 718-390-5352. Access civil records- 👋

Supreme Court - Criminal Division *Felony, Misdemeanor* 18 Richmond Terrace, Rm 110, Staten Island, NY 10301. 9AM-5PM, Closed 1-2PM. **718-390-2739**. ✉ 👋

Civil Court of the City of New York - Richmond Branch *Civil Actions Under $25,000, Eviction, Small Claims* 927 Castleton Ave, Staten Island, NY 10310. 9AM-4:30PM. **718-390-5417/5419**. Access civil records- ✉ 👋

Surrogate Court *Probate* 18 Richmond Terrace, Rm 201, Staten Island, NY 10301. 9AM-5PM. **718-390-5400**, Fax: 718-390-8741.

Rockland County

County Clerk *Felony, Civil* www.rocklandcountyclerk.com 1 S Main St, #100, New City, NY 10956. 7AM-6:30PM M-TH, 7AM-5:30PM F. **845-638-5070**, Civil: x4, Crim: x3. Countywide record search requests. Misdemeanor records maintained by city, town, village courts, but this clerk may have a misdemeanor record if you provide the index number. ✉ 🖥 👋

Surrogate Court *Probate* 15 Main St, #270, New City, NY 10956. 9AM-5PM. **845-638-5330**, Fax: 845-638-5632.

St. Lawrence County

Supreme & County Court *Felony, Civil* 48 Court St, Canton, NY 13617-1169. 8:30AM-4:30PM (Thurs. til 7PM). **315-379-2237 (couty clerk); 315-379-2219 (Court Clerk)**, Fax: 315-379-2302. Direct all search requests to the County Clerk office; information given here is for that County Clerk office. **Fax** ✉ 👋

Ogdensburg City Court *Misdemeanor, Civil Actions Under $15,000, Eviction, Small Claims* 330 Ford St, Ogdensburg, NY 13669. 8AM-4PM. **315-393-3941**, Fax: 315-393-6839. Access records- (use statewide search).

Surrogate Court *Probate* 48 Court St Surrogate Bldg, Canton, NY 13617. 9AM-5PM Sept-June; 8AM-4PM July-Aug. **315-379-2217/9427**.

Key: Symbols refer to criminal records access unless otherwise noted. phone-☎ mail-✉ fax-**Fax** in person-👋 online-🖥 email-**Email**

Saratoga County

County Clerk *Civil* 40 McMaster St, Ballston Spa, NY 12020. 9AM-5PM. **518-885-2213 X4410**, Fax: 518-884-4726. The county clerk does not have a seperate index of criminal records; see the Supreme and County Court. Access civil records-✉ 🖐 🖥

Supreme & County Court *Felony, Civil* 30 McMaster St, Ballston Spa, NY 12020. 9AM-5PM. **518-885-2213 X2224**. See County Clerk for Supreme court civil case records. Access to current/pending Supreme Court civil cases is available at http://e.courts.state.ny.us/. Misdemeanor records are maintained by city, town and village courts. ✉ 🖐

Saratoga Springs City Court *Misdemeanor, Civil Actions Under $15,000, Eviction, Small Claims* City Hall 474 Broadway, Saratoga Springs, NY 12866. 8AM-4PM. **518-581-1797**. Access records- (use statewide search).

Mechanicville City Court *Misdemeanor, Civil Actions Under $15,000, Eviction, Small Claims* 36 N Main St, Mechanicville, NY 12118. 8AM-4PM. **518-664-9876**, Fax: 518-664-8606. Access records- (use statewide search).

Surrogate Court *Probate* 30 McMaster St, Bldg 3, Ballston Spa, NY 12020. 9-5PM. **518-884-4722**, Fax: 518-884-4774.

Schenectady County

Supreme & County Court *Felony, Civil* 612 State St, Schenectady, NY 12305. 9AM-5PM. **518-388-4322**, Fax: 518-388-4520. Direct civil record requests to County Clerk, see below. Access to current/pending civil cases is available at http://e.courts.state.ny.us/. ✉ 🖐

County Clerk *Civil* 620 State St, Attn: County Clerk, Schenectady, NY 12305. 9AM-5PM. **518-388-4222**, Fax: 518-388-4224. For felony records see the County-Court clerk at the Supreme/County Court above. Access civil records-✉ 🖐 🖥

Schenectady City Court - Criminal *Misdemeanor* 531 Liberty St, Schenectady, NY 12305. 8AM-4PM. **518-382-5239**, Fax: 518-382-5241. Access records- (use statewide search).

Schenectady City Court - Civil *Civil Actions Under $15,000, Eviction, Small Claims* Jay St, City Hall, #215, Schenectady, NY 12305. 8AM-4PM. **518-382-5077**, Fax: 518-382-5080. Access civil records-✉ 🖐

Surrogate Court *Probate* 612 State St Judicial Bldg, Schenectady, NY 12305. 9-5PM. **518-388-4293**, Fax: 518-377-6378.

Schoharie County

Supreme & County Court *Felony, Civil, Misdemeanor, Eviction, Small Claims* PO Box 549 284 Main St, Attn: County Clerk, Schoharie, NY 12157. 8:30AM-5PM. **518-295-8316 (County Clerk); 518-295-8342 (Supreme)**, Fax: 518-295-8338. Direct search requests to the County Clerk who processes the requests. Fax✉ 🖐

Surrogate Court *Probate* Courthouse, 290 Main St PO Box 669, Schoharie, NY 12157. 9AM-5PM. **518-295-8387**.

Schuyler County

County Clerk *Felony, Civil* Courthouse 105 9th St, #8, Watkins Glen, NY 14891. 9AM-5PM. **607-535-8133**. Countywide record search requests. ☎ ✉ 🖐

Surrogate's Court *Probate* County Courthouse 105 9th St, Watkins Glen, NY 14891. 9AM-5PM. **607-535-7144**, Fax: 607-535-4918.

Seneca County

County Clerk *Felony, Civil* 1 DiPronio Dr, County Office Bldg Attn: Seneca County Clerk, Waterloo, NY 13165-1396. 8:30AM-5PM. **315-539-1771**, Fax: 315-539-3789. Countywide record search requests. ✉ 🖐

Surrogate Court *Probate* 48 W Williams St, Waterloo, NY 13165. 9AM-5PM. **315-539-7531**, Fax: 315-539-3267.

Steuben County

Supreme & County Court *Felony, Civil* 3 E Pulteney Sq - County Clerk, Bath, NY 14810. 8:30AM-5PM. **607-776-9631 x3210 (County clerk); x3200 (Court Clerks)**, Fax: 607-776-2812. Direct all search requests to the County Clerk office; information given here is for that County Clerk office. Fax✉ 🖐

Hornell City Court *Misdemeanor, Civil Under $15,000, Eviction, Small Claims* www.nycourts.gov/courts/7jd/hornell/index.s html PO Box 627 (82 Main St), Hornell, NY 14843-0627. 8AM-3:30PM. **607-324-7531**, Fax: 607-324-6325. Access records- (use statewide search).

Corning City Court *Misdemeanor, Civil Actions Under $15,000, Eviction, Small Claims* 12 Civic Center Plaza, Corning, NY 14830-2884. 8AM-4PM. **607-936-**

4111, Fax: 607-936-0519. Access records- (use statewide search).

Surrogate Court *Probate* 3 E Pulteney Sq, Bath, NY 14810-1598. 9AM-5PM. **607-776-7126**, Fax: 607-776-4987.

Suffolk County

Supreme & County Court - Main *Felony, Civil* www.courts.state.ny.us/cour ts/10jd/suffolk/supreme.shtml 310 Centre Dr Attn: Court Actions, Riverhead, NY 11901. 9AM-5PM. **631-852-3793, 631-852-1462** county, Civil: 631-852-3793, crim: 631-852-2016. ✉ 🖐

1st District Court - Criminal *Misd.* http://courts.state.ny.us/courts/10jd/suffolk/di st/ 400 Carleton Ave, Central Islip, NY 11722. 9AM-5PM. **631-853-7500** (all county District Courts). 🖐

4th District Court *Misdemeanor, Civil Under $15,000, Eviction, Small Claims* http://courts.state.ny.us/courts/10jd/suffolk/ North County Complex C158, Hauppauge, NY 11787. 9AM-5PM. Civil: 631-853-5400, crim: 631-853-5357. Access records- (use statewide search).

3rd District Court *Misdemeanor, Civil Under $15,000, Eviction, Small Claims* http://courts.state.ny.us/courts/10jd/suffolk/ 1850 New York Ave, Huntington Station, NY 11746. 9AM-1PM, 2-4:30PM. **631-854-4545**. 🖐

Suffolk District Courts 1 & 5 - Civil *Civil Under $15,000, Eviction, Small Claims* http://courts.state.ny.us/courts/10 jd/suffolk/ 3105-1 Veterans Memorial Hwy, Ronkonkoma, NY 11779-7614. 9AM-5PM. **631-854-9676 (1st); 9673 (5th)**. Access civil records-✉ 🖐

2nd District Court *Misdemeanor, Civil Under $15,000, Eviction, Small Claims* http://courts.state.ny.us/courts/10jd/suffolk/ 375 Cormac Rd, Deer Park, NY 11702. 9AM-1PM, 2-5PM. **631-854-1950**. Access records- (use statewide search).

6th District Court *Misdemeanor, Civil Under $15,000, Eviction, Small Claims* http://courts.state.ny.us/courts/10jd/suffolk/ 150 W Main St, Patchogue, NY 11772. 9AM-5PM. **631-854-1440**. Criminal searches must be done at the OCA. The misdemeanor records here cover only Brookhaven Town Ordinance violations. Access records- (use statewide search).

Surrogate Court *Probate* 320 Centre Dr, Riverhead, NY 11901. 9AM-5PM. **631-852-1745**, Fax: 631-852-1777.

Sullivan County

Supreme & County Court *Felony, Civil, Misdemeanor* County Courthouse 414 Broadway, Monticello, NY 12701. 9AM-5PM. **845-794-4066**. Civil records and criminal record index are maintained at County Clerk's office, see separate listing. However, actual felony records located here at County-Court Clerk office. ✉ ✋

County Clerk *Felony, Civil* 100 North St Sullivan Gov't Ctr, Monticello, NY 12701. 9AM-5PM. **845-794-3000 x5012**. Countywide record search requests. ✋

Surrogate Court *Probate* County Government Ctr 100 North St, Monticello, NY 12701. 9AM-5PM. **845-794-3000 X3450/3451**, Fax: 845-794-0310.

Tioga County

Court Clerk *Civil, Felony* PO Box 307 16 Court St, Owego, NY 13827. 9AM-5PM. **607-687-8660**, Fax: 607-687-8686. Countywide civil record search requests. County clerk has only a paper index list of felony proceedings. Felony records are managed by the County-Court Clerk, see below. Access civil records-✋ 💻

Supreme & County Court *Felony* PO Box 307 16 Court St, Owego, NY 13827. 8:30AM-4:30PM. **607-687-0544**, Fax: 607-687-3240. For civil records, see County Clerk. Also, access to current/pending Supreme Court civil cases is available at http://e.courts.state.ny.us/. Access criminal records by-✋ or use statewide search.

Surrogate Court *Probate* PO Box 10 20 Court St, Owego, NY 13827. 9AM-5PM. **607-687-1303**, Fax: 607-687-3240. Court located in the County Court Annex Bldg.

Tompkins County

Supreme & County Court *Felony, Civil* Tomkins County Clerk 320 N Tioga St, Ithaca, NY 14850. 9AM-5PM (Court Clerks have Summer hours-8:30AM-4:30PM). **607-274-5431 (County Clerk); 607-272-0466 (Count Clerks)**, Fax: 607-274-5445. Direct all search requests to the County Clerk office; information given here is for that County Clerk office. **Fax**✉ ✋

Ithaca City Court *Misdemeanor, Civil Actions Under $15,000, Eviction, Small Claims* www.nycourts.gov/ithaca/city 118 E Clinton St, Ithaca, NY 14850. 8AM-

4PM. **607-273-2263**. Access records- (use statewide search).

Surrogate Court *Probate* 320 N Tioga St, Ithaca, NY 14850. 9AM-5PM. **607-277-0622**, Fax: 607-256-2572.

Ulster County

County Clerk *Felony, Civil* www.co.ulster.ny.us PO Box 1800 244 Fair St, Kingston, NY 12401. 9AM-4:45PM. **845-340-3288 (Clerk); 845-340-3770 (Switchboard)**, Fax: 845-340-3299. Countywide record search requests. ☎✉ ✋

Kingston City Court *Misdemeanor, Civil Actions Under $15,000, Eviction, Small Claims* One Garraghan Dr, Kingston, NY 12401. 8:30AM-4PM. **845-338-2974**. Access records- (use statewide search).

Surrogate Court *Probate* PO Box 1800 240 Fair St, Kingston, NY 12402. 9AM-5PM. **845-340-3348**, Fax: 845-340-3352.

Warren County

County Clerk *Civil, Felony* 1340 State Route 9 Attn: County Clerk, Lake George, NY 12845. 9AM-5PM. **518-761-6420/6426**. Countywide civil record search requests. ✋

Supreme & County Court *Felony* 1340 State Rte 9, Lake George, NY 12845. 9AM-4:30. **518-761-6430/6431**. Direct civil searches to County Clerk only, see separate entry. Also, a criminal record disposition index is maintained at County Clerk's office but actual felony records are located here at Supreme & County Court County-Court Clerk office. ✉ ✋

Glens Falls City Court *Misdemeanor, Civil Actions Under $15,000, Eviction, Small Claims* 42 Ridge St, Glens Falls, NY 12801. 8:30AM-4:30PM. **518-798-4714**, Fax: 518-798-0137. Access records- (use statewide search).

Surrogate Court *Probate* 1340 State Rte 9 County Municipal Ctr, Lake George, NY 12845. 9-5PM. **518-761-6514/6515/6512**, Fax: 518-761-6465 x6511.

Washington County

County Clerk *Civil* 383 Broadway, Bldg A, Fort Edward, NY 12828. 8:30AM-4:30PM. **518-746-2170**, Fax: 518-746-2166. Access civil records-✉ ✋ 💻

Supreme & County Court *Felony, Civil* 383 Broadway, Fort Edward, NY 12828. 8:30AM-4:30PM. Civil: 518-746-2520,

crim: 518-746-2521. Misdemeanor records at city, town, village courts. ✋

Surrogate Court *Probate* 383 Broadway, Fort Edward, NY 12828. 8:30AM-4:30PM. **518-746-2546**, Fax: 518-746-2547.

Wayne County

Supreme & County Court *Felony, Civil, Eviction, Small Claims* 9 Pearl St PO Box 608, Lyons, NY 14489-0608. 9AM-5PM. **315-946-7470**, Fax: 315-946-5978. Direct all search requests to the County Clerk office; clerk info given here. **Fax**✉ ✋

Surrogate Court *Probate* 54 Broad St, #106 Hall of Justice, Lyons, NY 14489. 9-4PM. **315-946-5430**, Fax: 315-946-5433.

Westchester County

County Clerk *Felony, Civil* www.westchesterclerk.com and www.courts.state.ny.us/courts/9jd/Westchester/supreme county.shtml 110 Dr Martin L King Blvd Rm 330, White Plains, NY 10601. 8AM-4:45PM. **914-995-3070**, Fax: 914-995-3172. Record search requests made to the County Clerk. ✉ ✋

Mt Vernon City Court *Misdemeanor, Civil Actions Under $15,000, Eviction, Small Claims* Municipal Bldg Roosevelt Square, Mt Vernon, NY 10550-2019. 8:30AM-4:30PM (payments to 3:30PM only). **914-665-2400**, Fax: 914-699-1230. Criminal phone: 914-665-2409. Small claims: 665-2404; Landlord/Tenant: 665-2402; Traffic: 665-2405. ✋

White Plains City Court *Misdemeanor, Civil Actions Under $15,000, Eviction, Small Claims* 77 S Lexington Ave, White Plains, NY 10601. 8:30AM-4:30PM. Fax: 914-422-6058. Civil phone: 914-422-6050, crim: 914-422-6075. ✉ ✋

Rye City Court *Misdemeanor, Civil Actions Under $15,000, Eviction, Small Claims* 21 McCullough Pl, Rye, NY 10580. 8:30AM-4:30PM. **914-967-1599**, Fax: 914-967-3308. ✉ ✋

New Rochelle City Court *Misdemeanor, Civil Under $15,000, Small Claims* www.courts.state.ny.us/courts/9jd/Westchester/NewRochelle.shtml 475 North Ave, New Rochelle, NY 10801. 9AM-5PM. Fax: 914-654-0344. Civil phone: 914-654-2299, crim: 914-654-2311. Access records- (use statewide search).

Key: Symbols refer to criminal records access unless otherwise noted. phone-☎ mail-✉ fax-**Fax** in person-✋ online-💻 email-**Email**

Peekskill City Court *Misdemeanor, Civil Actions Under $15,000, Eviction, Small Claims* 2 Nelson Ave, Peekskill, NY 10566. 9AM-5PM. **914-737-3405**. Access records- (use statewide search).

Yonkers City Court *Misdemeanor, Civil Actions Under $15,000, Eviction, Small Claims* 100 S Broadway, Yonkers, NY 10701. 9AM-3:30PM. Fax: 914-377-6966. Civil phone: 914-377-6376, crim: 914-377-6352. ✉ 👋

Surrogate Court *Probate* 140 Grand St, 8th Fl, White Plains, NY 10601. 9AM-5PM. **914-995-3712**, Fax: 914-995-3728.

Wyoming County

Supreme & County Court *Felony, Civil* 143 N Main St, #104, Warsaw, NY 14569. 9AM-5PM. **585-786-8810 county clerk, 585-786-2253 (court clerks)**, Fax: 585-786-3703 (county clerk), 585-786-2818. Direct all search requests to the County Clerk office; information given here is for that County Clerk office. ☎Fax✉ 👋 Supreme and County Court office is at 147 Main St.

Surrogate Court *Probate* 147 N Main St, Warsaw, NY 14569. 9AM-5PM. **585-786-3148**, Fax: 585-786-3800.

Yates County

County Clerk *Felony, Civil* 417 Liberty St, #1107, Penn Yan, NY 14527. 9AM-5PM; 8:30AM-4:30PM. **315-536-5120**, Fax: 315-536-5545. Countywide record search requests. ✉Fax👋

Surrogate Court *Probate* 415 Liberty St, Penn Yan, NY 14527. 9AM-5PM. **315-536-5130**, Fax: 315-536-5190.

North Carolina

State Court Administration: Administrative Office of the Courts, Justice Bldg, PO Box 2448 (2 E Morgan St), Raleigh, NC, 27602; 919-733-7107, Fax: 919-715-5779. http://www.nccourts.org/Courts/

Court Structure: The Superior Court is the court of general jurisdiction, the District Court is limited. The counties combine the courts, thus searching is done through one court, not two, within the county. Small claims court ($4000 or less) is part of the District Court Division.

Probate Courts: Probate is handled by County Clerks.

Online Access: There is no statewide online access; web access to civil and criminal dockets available at some individual courts.

Access active District/Superior Court criminal calendars on a county or statewide basis at http://www1.aoc.state.nc.us/www/calendars.html. Historical information is not available.

Also, civil court calendars are now available online at http://www1.aoc.state.nc.us/www/calendars/Civil.html for 43 Counties.

Also, appellate and supreme court opinions are available www.aoc.state.nc.us/www/public/html/opinions.htm.

Additional Information: Many courts recommend that civil searches be done in person or by a retriever and that only criminal searches be requested in writing (for a $10.00 search fee, which is certified in most jurisdictions). Many courts have archived their records prior to 1968 in the Raleigh State Archives, 919-733-5722. A list of companies offering NC criminal records online is at www.nccourts.org/Citizens/GoToCourt/Default.asp?topic=1.

You may locate information on the courts at www.nccourts.org. Search civil and criminal court calendars at www1.aoc.state.nc.us/www/calendars.html.

Alamance County

Superior-District Court - Criminal *Felony, Misdemeanor* 212 W Elm St, #105, Graham, NC 27253. 8AM-5PM. **336-438-1001**. ✉ 👋

Superior-District Court - Civil *Civil, Eviction, Small Claims, Probate* 1 Court Square, Graham, NC 27253. 8AM-5PM. **336-438-1002**, Civil: 336-438-1013, crim: 336-438-1001, Probate: 336-438-1008. Access civil records- 👋

Alexander County

Superior-District Court *Felony, Misd., Civil, Eviction, Small Claims, Probate*

PO Box 100, Taylorsville, NC 28681. 8AM-5PM. **828-632-2215**, Fax: 828-632-3550. ✉ 👋

Alleghany County

Superior-District Court *Felony, Misdemeanor, Civil, Eviction, Small Claims, Probate* PO Box 61, Sparta, NC 28675. 8AM-5PM. **336-372-8949**, Fax: 336-372-4899. Fax✉ 👋

Anson County

Superior-District Court *Felony, Misd., Civil, Eviction, Small Claims, Probate* PO Box 1064 (114 N Greene St), Wadesboro, NC 28170. 8AM-5PM. **704-694-2314**, Fax: 704-695-1161. ✉ 👋

Ashe County

Superior-District Court *Felony, Misd., Civil, Eviction, Small Claims, Probate* 150 Government Circle #3100, Jefferson, NC 28640-9378. 8AM-5PM. **336-246-5641**, Fax: 336-246-4276. ✉ 👋

Avery County

Superior-District Court *Felony, Misdemeanor, Civil, Eviction, Small Claims, Probate* PO Box 115, Newland, NC 28657. 8AM-4:30PM. **828-733-2900**, Fax: 828-733-8410. ✉ 👋

Beaufort County

Superior-District Court *Felony, Misd., Civil, Eviction, Small Claims, Probate* PO Box 1403, Washington, NC 27889.

Key: Symbols refer to criminal records access unless otherwise noted. phone-☎ mail-✉ fax-Fax in person-👋 online-🖥 email-Email

8:30AM-5:30PM. **252-946-5184**, Civil: 252-974-7817. ✉ ✋

Bertie County

Superior-District Court *Felony, Misdemeanor, Civil, Eviction, Small Claims, Probate* PO Box 370, Windsor, NC 27983. 8AM-5PM. **252-794-3039**, Fax: 252-794-2482. ✉ ✋

Bladen County

Superior-District Court *Felony, Misdemeanor, Civil, Eviction, Small Claims, Probate* PO Box 2619, Elizabethtown, NC 28337. 8:30AM-5PM. Civil: 910-862-2143, crim: 910-862-2818, Probate: 910-862-4911. ✉ ✋

Brunswick County

Superior-District Court *Felony, Misd., Civil, Eviction, Small Claims, Probate* 310 Goverment Ctr Dr.,unit 1, Bolivia, NC 28422. 8:30AM-5:00PM. **910-253-8502**, Fax: 910-253-7652. ✉ ✋

Buncombe County

Superior-District Court *Felony, Misd., Civil, Eviction, Small Claims, Probate* 60 Court Plaza, Asheville, NC 28801-3519. 8:30AM-5PM. **828-232-2605**, Fax: 828-251-6257. Civil phone: 828-232-2636, crim: 828-232-2652, Probate: 828-232-2694. ✉Fax ✋

Burke County

Superior-District Court *Felony, Misdemeanor, Civil, Eviction, Small Claims, Probate* PO Box 796, Morganton, NC 28680. 8AM-5PM. **828-432-2800**, Fax: 828-438-5460. Civil phone: 828-432-2805. ✉ ✋

Cabarrus County

Superior-District Court *Felony, Misdemeanor, Civil, Eviction, Small Claims, Probate* PO Box 70, Concord, NC 28026-0070. 8:30AM-5PM. **704-786-4137 (Estates & Special Proceed)**, Civil: 704-786-4201, crim: 704-786-4138 (Superior); 786-4211 (Dist.). ✉ ✋

Caldwell County

Superior-District Court *Felony, Misdemeanor, Civil, Eviction, Small Claims, Probate* PO Box 1376, Lenoir, NC 28645. 8AM-5PM. **828-757-1373**, Fax: 828-757-1479. ✉ ✋

Camden County

Superior-District Court *Felony, Misdemeanor, Civil, Eviction, Small Claims, Probate* PO Box 219, Camden, NC 27921. 8AM-5PM. **252-331-4871**, Fax: 252-331-4827. Civil phone: 252-331-4871 ext 272 (District & Superior), crim: 252-331-4871 ext 270 (Superior) ext 269 (District), Probate: 252-331-4871 ext 273. Small Claims ext 268. ✉Fax ✋

Carteret County

Superior-District Court - Carteret County *Felony, Misdemeanor, Civil, Eviction, Small Claims, Probate* Courthouse Square, Beaufort, NC 28516. 8AM-5PM. **252-728-8500**, Fax: 252-728-6502. ✉Fax ✋

Caswell County

Superior-District Court *Felony, Misd., Civil, Eviction, Small Claims, Probate* PO Drawer 790, Yanceyville, NC 27379. 8:30AM-5PM. **336-694-4171**, Fax: 336-694-7338. ✉ ✋

Catawba County

Superior-District Court *Felony, Misd., Civil, Eviction, Small Claims, Probate* www.co.catawba.nc.us/state/clerk/clerklst.htm PO Box 790, Newton, NC 28658. 8AM-5PM. **828-466-6100**, Civil: 828-466-6104, crim: 828-466-6106, Probate: 828-466-6103. ✉ ✋

Chatham County

Superior-District Court *Felony, Misdemeanor, Civil, Eviction, Small Claims, Probate* PO Box 369, Pittsboro, NC 27312. 8AM-5PM. **919-542-3240**, Fax: 919-542-1402. Access records- ✉ ✋

Cherokee County

Superior-District Court *Felony, Misdemeanor, Civil, Eviction, Small Claims, Probate* 75 Peachtree St, Rm 201, Murphy, NC 28906. 8AM-5PM. **828-837-2522**, Fax: 828-837-8178. ✉ ✋

Chowan County

Superior-District Court *Felony, Misdemeanor, Civil, Eviction, Small Claims, Probate* N.C. Courier Box 106319 PO Box 588, Edenton, NC 27932. 9AM-5PM. **252-482-2323**, Fax: 252-482-2190. ✉ ✋

Clay County

Superior-District Court *Felony, Misdemeanor, Civil, Eviction, Small Claims, Probate* PO Box 506, Hayesville, NC 28904. 8AM-5PM. **828-389-8334**, Fax: 828-389-3329. Fax ✉ ✋

Cleveland County

Superior-District Court *Felony, Misdemeanor, Civil, Eviction, Small Claims, Probate* 100 Justice Pl, Shelby, NC 28150. 8AM-5PM. **704-484-4862**, Fax: 704-480-5487. Fax ✉ ✋

Columbus County

Superior-District Court *Felony, Misdemeanor, Civil, Eviction, Small Claims, Probate* PO Box 1587, Whiteville, NC 28472. 8AM-5PM. Fax: 910-641-3027. Civil phone: 910-641-3000, crim: 910-641-3020, Probate: 910-641-3010. ✉Fax ✋

Craven County

Superior-District Court *Felony, Misd., Civil, Eviction, Small Claims, Probate* PO Box 1187, New Bern, NC 28563. 8AM-5PM. **252-514-4774**, Fax: 252-514-4891. Civil phone: 252-514-4860, crim: 352-514-4777. ✉ ✋

Cumberland County

Superior-District Court *Felony, Misdemeanor, Civil, Eviction, Small Claims, Probate* PO Box 363, Fayetteville, NC 28302. 8:30AM-5PM. **910-678-2902**, Civil: 910-678-2909, crim: 910-678-2906. ✉ ✋

Currituck County

Superior-District Court *Felony, Misdemeanor, Civil, Eviction, Small Claims, Probate* PO Box 175, Currituck, NC 27929. 8AM-5PM. **252-232-2010**, Fax: 252-232-3722. ✋

Dare County

Superior-District Court *Felony, Misdemeanor, Civil, Eviction, Small Claims, Probate* PO Box 1849, Manteo, NC 27954. 8:30AM-5PM. **252-475-9100**, Fax: 252-473-1620. Access records- ✉ ✋

Davidson County

Superior-District Court *Felony, Misd., Civil, Eviction, Small Claims, Probate* PO Box 1064, Lexington, NC 27293-1064. 8AM-5PM. **336-249-0351**, Fax: 336-249-6951. ✉ ✋

Davie County

Superior-District Court *Felony, Misdemeanor, Civil, Eviction, Small Claims, Probate* 140 S Main St, Mocksville, NC 27028. 8:30AM-5PM. Fax: 336-751-4720. Civil phone: 336-751-3507, crim: 336-751-3508. ✉✋

Duplin County

Superior-District Court *Felony, Misdemeanor, Civil, Eviction, Small Claims, Probate* PO Box 189, Kenansville, NC 28349. 8AM-5PM. Fax: 910-296-2310. Civil phone: 910-296-1686, crim: 910-296-2306. ✉✋

Durham County

Superior-District Court *Felony, Misdemeanor, Civil, Eviction, Small Claims, Probate* 201 E Main St, Durham, NC 27702. 8:30AM-5PM. Civil: 919-564-7050, crim: 919-564-7270. ✉✋

Edgecombe County

Superior-District Court *Felony, Misdemeanor, Civil, Eviction, Small Claims, Probate* PO Drawer 9, Tarboro, NC 27886. 8AM-5PM. Fax: 252-823-1278. Civil phone: 252-823-6161, crim: 252-823-2056. ✉✋

Forsyth County

Superior-District Court *Felony, Misd., Civil, Eviction, Small Claims, Probate* PO Box 20099, Winston Salem, NC 27120-0099. 8AM-5PM. **336-761-2250**, Fax: 336-761-2018. Civil phone: 336-761-2340, crim: 336-761-2366. ✉✋

Franklin County

Superior-District Court *Felony, Misd., Civil, Eviction, Small Claims, Probate* 102 S Main St, Louisburg, NC 27549. 8:30AM-5PM. **919-496-5104**, Fax: 919-496-0407. ✉✋

Gaston County

Superior-District Court *Felony, Misdemeanor, Civil, Eviction, Small Claims, Probate* Gaston County Court House 325 N Marietta St. #1004, Gastonia, NC 28052-2331. 8:30AM-5PM. **704-852-3100**. ✉✋

Gates County

Superior-District Court *Felony, Misd., Civil, Eviction, Small Claims, Probate* PO Box 31, Gatesville, NC 27938. 8AM-5PM. **252-357-1365**, Fax: 252-357-1047. Access records-✉✋

Graham County

Superior-District Court *Felony, Misdemeanor, Civil, Eviction, Small Claims, Probate* PO Box 1179, Robbinsville, NC 28771. 8AM-5PM. **828-479-7986**, Fax: 828-479-6417. Civil phone: X7974, crim: X7975. ✉✋

Granville County

Superior-District Court *Felony, Misdemeanor, Civil, Eviction, Small Claims, Probate* Courthouse, 101 Main St, Oxford, NC 27565. **919-693-2649**, Fax: 919-693-8944. Civil phone: Ext 1, crim: Ext 2. ✉✋

Greene County

Superior-District Court *Felony, Misd., Civil, Eviction, Small Claims, Probate* PO Box 675, Snow Hill, NC 28580. 8AM-5PM. **252-747-3505**. ✉✋

Guilford County

Superior-District Court *Felony, Misd., Civil, Eviction, Small Claims, Probate* 201 S Eugene, PO Box 3008, Greensboro, NC 27402. 8AM-5PM. Civil: 336-574-4305, crim: 336-574-4307. ✉✋

Halifax County

Superior-District Court *Felony, Misdemeanor, Civil, Eviction, Small Claims, Probate* PO Box 66, Halifax, NC 27839. 8:30AM-5PM. **252-583-5061**, Fax: 252-583-1005. Access records-✉✋

Harnett County

Superior-District Court *Felony, Misdemeanor, Civil, Eviction, Small Claims, Probate* 301 W Cornelius Blvd, Lillington, NC 27546. 8:30AM-5PM. **910-814-4600**, Fax: 910-893-3683. Civil phone: 910-814-4602, crim: 910-814-4601, Probate: 910-814-4603. ✉✋

Haywood County

Superior-District Court *Felony, Misdemeanor, Civil, Eviction, Small Claims, Probate* 215 N. Main, Waynesville, NC 28786. 8AM-5PM. **828-456-3540**, Fax: 828-456-4937. Criminal phone: 828-452-2578. ✉✋

Henderson County

Superior-District Court *Felony, Misdemeanor, Civil, Eviction, Small Claims, Probate* PO Box 965, Hendersonville, NC 28793. 8:30AM-5PM. Civil: 828-697-4851, crim: 828-697-4859. ✉✋

Hertford County

Superior-District Court *Felony, Misdemeanor, Civil, Eviction, Small Claims, Probate* PO Box 86, Winton, NC 27986. 8AM-5PM. **252-358-7845**, Fax: 252-358-0793. ✉✋

Hoke County

Superior-District Court *Felony, Misdemeanor, Civil, Eviction, Small Claims, Probate* PO Drawer 1569, Raeford, NC 28376. 8:30AM-5PM. **910-875-3728**, Fax: 910-904-1708. ✉✋

Hyde County

Superior-District Court *Felony, Misdemeanor, Civil, Eviction, Small Claims, Probate* PO Box 337, Swanquarter, NC 27885. 8:00AM-5:00PM. **252-926-4101**, Fax: 252-926-1002. ☎✉✋

Iredell County

Superior-District Court *Felony, Misd., Civil, Eviction, Small Claims, Probate* PO Box 186, Statesville, NC 28687. 8:30AM-5PM. Fax: 704-878-3261. Civil phone: 704-878-4306, crim: 704-878-4204, Probate: 704-878-4311. ✉✋

Jackson County

Superior-District Court *Felony, Misdemeanor, Civil, Eviction, Small Claims, Probate* 401 Grindstaff Cove Rd, Sylva, NC 28779. 8:30AM-5PM. **828-586-7512**, Fax: 828-586-9009. ✉✋

Johnston County

Superior-District Court *Felony, Misdemeanor, Civil, Eviction, Small Claims, Probate* PO Box 297, Smithfield, NC 27577. 8AM-5PM. **919-934-3192**, Fax: 919-934-5857. ✉✋

Jones County

Superior-District Court *Felony, Misdemeanor, Civil, Eviction, Small Claims, Probate* PO Box 280, Trenton, NC 28585. 8AM-5PM. **252-448-7351**, Fax: 252-448-1607. ✉✋

Lee County

Superior-District Court *Felony, Misdemeanor, Civil, Eviction, Small Claims, Probate* PO Box 4209, Sanford, NC 27331. 8AM-5PM. **919-708-4400**, Fax: 919-775-3483. Civil phone: 919-708-4402, crim: 919-708-4407, Probate: 919-708-4417. ✉✋

Key: Symbols refer to criminal records access unless otherwise noted. phone-☎ mail-✉ fax-**Fax** in person-✋ online-🖳 email-**Email**

Lenoir County

Superior-District Court *Felony, Misd., Civil, Eviction, Small Claims, Probate* www.nccourts.org/County/Lenoir/Default.as p PO Box 68, Kinston, NC 28502-0068. 8AM-5PM. **252-527-6231**, Fax: 252-527-9154. ✉👋

Lincoln County

Superior-District Court *Felony, Misd., Civil, Eviction, Small Claims, Probate* PO Box 8, Lincolnton, NC 28093. 8:30AM-5PM. Fax: 704-736-8718. Civil phone: 704-736-8563, crim: 704-736-8561, Probate: 704-736-8565. ✉👋

McDowell County

Superior-District Court *Felony, Misd., Civil, Eviction, Small Claims, Probate* 21 S Main St, Marion, NC 28752. 8:30AM-5PM. **828-652-7717 x201**, Fax: 828-659-2641. Civil phone: 828-652-7717 x208, crim: 828-652-7717 x228. ✉👋

Macon County

Superior-District Court *Felony, Misdemeanor, Civil, Eviction, Small Claims, Probate* PO Box 288, Franklin, NC 28744. 8:30AM-5PM. **828-349-2000**, Fax: 828-369-2515. ✉👋

Madison County

Superior-District Court *Felony, Misdemeanor, Civil, Eviction, Small Claims, Probate* PO Box 217, Marshall, NC 28753. 8AM-5PM. **828-649-2531**, Fax: 828-649-2829. ✉👋

Martin County

Superior-District Court *Felony, Misdemeanor, Civil, Eviction, Small Claims, Probate* PO Box 807, Williamston, NC 27892. 8AM-5PM. **252-792-2515**, Fax: 252-792-6668. ✉👋

Mecklenburg County

Superior-District Court *Felony, Misd., Civil, Eviction, Small Claims, Probate* 800 E 4th St PO Box 37971, Charlotte, NC 28237. 8AM-5PM. Civil: 704-347-7814, crim: 704-347-7809. ✉👋

Mitchell County

Superior-District Court *Felony, Misdemeanor, Civil, Eviction, Small Claims, Probate* www.clerkofcourt.org PO Box 402, Bakersville, NC 28705. 8:30AM-5PM. **828-688-2161**, Fax: 828-688-2168. ✉👋

Montgomery County

Superior-District Court *Felony, Misdemeanor, Civil, Eviction, Small Claims, Probate* PO Box 527, Troy, NC 27371. 8:30AM-5PM. **910-576-4211**, Fax: 910-576-5020. ☎Fax✉👋

Moore County

Superior-District Court *Felony, Misdemeanor, Civil, Eviction, Small Claims, Probate* PO Box 936, Carthage, NC 28327. 8AM-5PM. **910-947-2396**, Fax: 910-947-1444. ✉👋

Nash County

Superior-District Court *Felony, Misdemeanor, Civil, Eviction, Small Claims, Probate* PO Box 759, Nashville, NC 27856. 8AM-5PM. Fax: 252-459-6050. Civil phone: 252-459-4081, crim: 252-459-4085. ✉👋

New Hanover County

Superior-District Court *Felony, Misdemeanor, Civil, Eviction, Small Claims, Probate* PO Box 2023, Wilmington, NC 28402. 8AM-5PM. **910-341-1111**, Fax: 910-251-2676. Criminal phone: 910-341-1302. ✉👋

Northampton County

Superior-District Court *Felony, Misdemeanor, Civil, Eviction, Small Claims, Probate* PO Box 217, Jackson, NC 27845. 8:30AM-5PM. **252-534-1631**, Fax: 252-534-1308. ✉👋

Onslow County

Superior-District Court *Felony, Misd., Civil, Eviction, Small Claims, Probate* 625 Court St, Jacksonville, NC 28540. 8AM-5PM. **910-455-4458**. ✉👋

Orange County

Superior-District Court *Felony, Misdemeanor, Civil, Eviction, Small Claims, Probate* 106 E Margaret Lane, Hillsborough, NC 27278. 8AM-5PM. Fax: 919-644-3043. Civil phone: 919-245-2210, crim: 919-245-2200, Probate: 919-245-2214. ✉👋

Pamlico County

Superior-District Court *Felony, Misd., Civil, Eviction, Small Claims, Probate* PO Box 38, Bayboro, NC 28515. 8AM-5PM. Fax: 252-745-6018. Civil phone: 252-745-6000, crim: 252-745-6001, Probate: 252-745-6002. ✉👋

Pasquotank County

Superior-District Court *Felony, Misdemeanor, Civil, Eviction, Small Claims, Probate* PO Box 449, Elizabeth City, NC 27907-0449. 8AM-5PM. **252-331-4751**. ✉👋

Pender County

Superior-District Court *Felony, Misdemeanor, Civil, Eviction, Small Claims, Probate* PO Box 310, Burgaw, NC 28425. 8:30AM-5PM. **910-259-1229**, Fax: 910-259-1292. Fax✉👋

Perquimans County

Superior-District Court *Felony, Misdemeanor, Civil, Eviction, Small Claims, Probate* PO Box 33, Hertford, NC 27944. 8AM-5PM. **252-426-1505**, Fax: 252-426-1901. Access records-✉👋

Person County

Superior-District Court *Felony, Misdemeanor, Civil, Eviction, Small Claims, Probate* 105 S Main St, Roxboro, NC 27573. 8:30AM-5PM. Fax: 336-597-0568. Civil phone: 336-597-0554, crim: 336-597-0556. ✉👋

Pitt County

Superior - District Court *Felony, Misd., Civil, Eviction, Small Claims, Probate* PO Box 6067, Greenville, NC 27835. 8AM-5PM. **252-695-7100**, Fax: 252-695-7376. Civil phone: 252-695-7150, crim: 252-695-7117. ✉👋

Polk County

Superior-District Court *Felony, Misdemeanor, Civil, Eviction, Small Claims, Probate* PO Box 38, Columbus, NC 28722. 8AM-5PM. **828-894-8231**, Fax: 828-894-5752. Access records-✉👋

Randolph County

Superior-District Court *Felony, Misd., Civil, Eviction, Small Claims, Probate* 176 E Salisbury St #201, Asheboro, NC 27203. 8AM-5PM. **336-328-3000**, Fax: 336-328-3131. Civil phone: 336-328-3004, crim: 336-328-3005. ✉👋

Richmond County

Superior-District Court *Felony, Misdemeanor, Civil, Eviction, Small Claims, Probate* 114 E Franklin St #103, Rockingham, NC 28379. 8AM-5PM. Fax: 910-997-9126. Civil phone: 910-997-9102, crim: 910-997-9101. ✉👋

Key: Symbols refer to criminal records access unless otherwise noted. phone-☎ mail-✉ fax-Fax in person-👋 online-💻 email-Email

Robeson County
Superior-District Court *Felony, Misd., Civil, Eviction, Small Claims, Probate* PO Box 1084, Lumberton, NC 28359. 8:15AM-5:15PM. **910-737-5035**, Fax: 910-618-5598. Civil phone: 910-671-3372, crim: 910-671-3395. ✉✋

Rockingham County
Superior-District Court *Felony, Misd., Civil, Eviction, Small Claims, Probate* PO Box 127, Wentworth, NC 27375. 8AM-5PM. **336-342-8700**, Civil: 336-342-8722, crim: 336-342-8706, Probate: 336-342-8703. ✉✋

Rowan County
Superior-District Court *Felony, Misdemeanor, Civil, Eviction, Small Claims, Probate* PO Box 4599, 210 N Main St, Salisbury, NC 28144. 8AM-5PM. **704-639-7505**, Probate: 704-639-7680. Crim District: 704-639-6766; Superior Court: 704-639-7676. ✉✋

Rutherford County
Superior-District Court *Felony, Misdemeanor, Civil, Eviction, Small Claims, Probate* PO Box 630, Rutherfordton, NC 28139. 8:30AM-5PM. Fax: 828-286-4322. Civil phone: 828-286-9136, crim: 828-286-3243. ✉✋

Sampson County
Superior-District Court *Felony, Misd., Civil, Eviction, Small Claims, Probate* www.sampsoncountyclerkofcourt.org Courthouse, Clinton, NC 28328. 8AM-5PM. **910-592-5191**, Fax: 910-592-5502. Civil phone: 910-592-5192, crim: 910-592-6981. ☎✉✋

Scotland County
Superior-District Court *Felony, Misd., Civil, Eviction, Small Claims, Probate* PO Box 769, Laurinburg, NC 28353. 8:30AM-5PM. **910-277-3240**, Civil: 910-277-3265, crim: 910-277-3250, Probate: 910-277-3260. Small claims phone is 910-277-3244. ✉✋

Stanly County
Superior-District Court *Felony, Misdemeanor, Civil, Eviction, Small Claims, Probate* PO Box 668, Albemarle, NC 28002-0668. 8:30AM-5PM. **704-982-2161**, Fax: 704-982-8107. ✉✋

Stokes County
Superior-District Court *Felony, Misdemeanor, Civil, Eviction, Small Claims, Probate* PO Box 250, Danbury, NC 27016. 8AM-5PM. **336-593-9173**, Fax: 336-593-5459. Access records-✉✋

Surry County
Superior-District Court *Felony, Misdemeanor, Civil, Eviction, Small Claims, Probate* PO Box 345, Dobson, NC 27017. 8AM-5PM. **336-386-3700**, Fax: 336-386-9879. Access records-✉✋

Swain County
Superior-District Court *Felony, Misd., Civil, Eviction, Small Claims, Probate* Clerk of Superior Court PO Box 1397, Bryson City, NC 28713. 8:30AM-5PM. **828-488-2288**, Fax: 828-488-9360. ✋

Transylvania County
Superior-District Court *Felony, Misdemeanor, Civil, Eviction, Small Claims, Probate* 12 E Main St, Brevard, NC 28712. 8AM-5PM. **828-884-3120**, Fax: 828-883-2161. Access records-✉✋

Tyrrell County
Superior-District Court *Felony, Misdemeanor, Civil, Eviction, Small Claims, Probate* PO Box 406, Columbia, NC 27925. 8:30AM-5PM. **252-796-6281**, Fax: 252-796-0008. Access records-✉✋

Union County
Superior-District Court *Felony, Misdemeanor, Civil, Eviction, Small Claims, Probate* PO Box 5038, Monroe, NC 28111. 8AM-5PM. **704-283-4313**, Fax: 704-289-2444. Access records-✉✋

Vance County
Superior-District Court *Felony, Misd., Civil, Eviction, Small Claims, Probate* 156 Church St. #101, Henderson, NC 27536. 8AM-5PM. **252-738-9000**. ✉✋

Wake County
Superior-District Court *Felony, Misd., Civil, Eviction, Small Claims, Probate* http://web.co.wake.nc.us/courts PO Box 351, Raleigh, NC 27602. 8:30AM-5:00PM. **919-755-4105**, Civil: 919-755-4108, crim: 919-755-4112. ✉✋

Warren County
Superior-District Court *Felony, Misd., Civil, Eviction, Small Claims, Probate*
PO Box 709, Warrenton, NC 27589. 8:30AM-5PM. **252-257-3261**, Fax: 252-257-5529. Access records-✉✋

Washington County
Superior-District Court *Felony, Misdemeanor, Civil, Eviction, Small Claims, Probate* PO Box 901, Plymouth, NC 27962. 8AM-5PM. **252-793-3013**, Fax: 252-793-1081. Access records-✉✋

Watauga County
Superior-District Court *Felony, Misdemeanor, Civil, Eviction, Small Claims, Probate* Courthouse #13 842 W King St, Boone, NC 28607-3525. 8AM-5PM. **828-265-5364**, Fax: 828-262-5753. Civil phone: 828-265-5432, crim: 828-265-5430, Probate: 828-265-5443. ✉✋

Wayne County
Superior-District Court *Felony, Misdemeanor, Civil, Eviction, Small Claims, Probate* PO Box 267, Goldsboro, NC 27530. 8AM-5PM. **919-731-7921**, Fax: 919-731-2037. Civil phone: 919-731-7919, crim: 919-731-7910. ✉✋

Wilkes County
Superior-District Court *Felony, Misd., Civil, Eviction, Small Claims, Probate* 500 Courthouse Drive, #1115, Wilkesboro, NC 28697. 8AM-5PM. Fax: 336-667-1985. Civil phone: 336-667-1201, crim: 336-667-5266. ✉✋

Wilson County
Superior-District Court *Felony, Misdemeanor, Civil, Eviction, Small Claims, Probate* PO Box 1608, Wilson, NC 27894. 9AM-5PM. **252-291-7500**, Fax: 252-291-8049-Crim 291-8635-civil. Civil phone: 252-291-7502, Probate: 252-291-7502. ✉Fax✋

Yadkin County
Superior-District Court *Felony, Misdemeanor, Civil, Eviction, Small Claims, Probate* PO Box 95, Yadkinville, NC 27055. 8AM-5PM. **336-679-8838**, Fax: 336-679-4378. Access records-✉✋

Yancey County
Superior-District Court *Felony, Misd., Civil, Eviction, Small Claims, Probate* 110 Town Square, Burnsville, NC 28714. 8:30AM-5PM. **828-682-2122**, Fax: 828-682-6296. ✉✋

Key: Symbols refer to criminal records access unless otherwise noted. phone-☎ mail-✉ fax-Fax in person-✋ online-💻 email-Email

North Dakota

State Court Administration: State Court Administrator, North Dakota Judiciary, 600 E Blvd, 1st Floor Judicial Wing, Dept. 180, Bismarck, ND, 58505-0530; 701-328-4216, Fax: 701-328-2092. www.ndcourts.com

Court Structure: In 1995, the County Courts merged with the District Courts statewide. County court records are maintained by the 53 District Court Clerks in the seven judicial districts. We recommend stating "include all County Court cases" in search requests. There are 76 Municipal Courts that handle traffic cases.

Online Access: A statewide computer system for internal purposes is in operation in most counties. You may now search North Dakota Supreme Court dockets and opinions at www.ndcourts.com. Search by docket number, party name, or anything else that may appear in the text. Records are from 1991 forward. Email notification of new opinions is also available.

Additional Information: In Summer, 1997, the standard search fee in District Courts increased to $10.00 per name, and the certification fee increased to $10.00 per document. Copy fees remain at $.50 per page, but many courts charge only $.25.

Adams County

Southwest Judicial District Court *Felony, Misdemeanor, Civil, Eviction, Small Claims, Probate* 602 Adams Ave, PO Box 469, Hettinger, ND 58639. 8:30AM-5PM. **701-567-2460**, Fax: 701-567-2910. Search requests must be in writing. **Fax**⊠♨

Barnes County

Southeast Judicial District Court *Felony, Misdemeanor, Civil, Eviction, Small Claims, Probate* PO Box 774, Valley City, ND 58072. 8AM-5PM. **701-845-8512**, Fax: 701-845-1341. **Fax**⊠♨

Benson County

Northeast Judicial District Court *Felony, Misdemeanor, Civil, Eviction, Small Claims, Probate* PO Box 213, Minnewaukan, ND 58351. 8:30AM-4:30PM. **701-473-5345**, Fax: 701-473-5571. **Fax**⊠♨

Billings County

Southwest Judicial District Court *Felony, Misdemeanor, Civil, Eviction, Small Claims, Probate* PO Box 138, Medora, ND 58645. 9AM-N, 1-5PM. **701-623-4492**, Fax: 701-623-4896. **Fax**⊠♨

Bottineau County

Northeast Judicial District Court *Felony, Misdemeanor, Civil, Eviction, Small Claims, Probate* 314 W 5th St, Bottineau, ND 58318. 8:30AM-5PM. **701-228-3983**, Fax: 701-228-2336. **Fax**⊠♨

Bowman County

Southwest Judicial District Court *Felony, Misd., Civil, Eviction, Small Claims, Probate* PO Box 379, Bowman, ND 58623. 8:00AM-N, 1-4:30PM. **701-523-3450**, Fax: 701-523-5443. ⊠♨

Burke County

Northwest Judicial District Court *Felony, Misd., Civil, Eviction, Small Claims, Probate* PO Box 219, Bowbells, ND 58721. 8:30AM-N, 1-5 PM. **701-377-2718**, Fax: 701-377-2020. ⊠♨

Burleigh County

South Central Judicial District Court *Felony, Misdemeanor, Civil, Eviction, Small Claims, Probate* PO Box 1055, Bismarck, ND 58502. 8AM-5PM. **701-222-6690**, Fax: 701-221-3756. Criminal phone: Fax: 701-222-6758. ⊠♨

Cass County

East Central Judicial District Court *Felony, Misdemeanor, Civil, Eviction, Small Claims, Probate* PO Box 2806, Fargo, ND 58108. 8AM-5PM. Fax: 701-241-5636. Civil phone: 701-241-5645, crim: 701-241-5660, Probate: 701-241-5655. ⊠**Fax**♨

Cavalier County

Northeast Judicial District Court *Felony, Misd., Civil, Eviction, Small Claims, Probate* 901 Third St, Langdon, ND 58249. 8:30AM-4:30PM. **701-256-2124**, Fax: 701-256-2124. **Fax**⊠♨

Dickey County

Southeast Judicial District Court *Felony, Misd., Civil, Eviction, Small Claims, Probate* Clerk of Court PO Box 336, Ellendale, ND 58436. 9-N, 1-5PM. **701-349-3249x4**, fax 701-349-3560⊠♨

Divide County

Northwest Judicial District Court *Felony, Misd., Civil, Eviction, Small Claims, Probate* PO Box 68, Crosby, ND 58730. 8:30AM-N, 1-5PM. **701-965-6831**, Fax: 701-965-6943. **Fax**⊠♨

Dunn County

District Court *Felony, Misdemeanor, Civil, Small Claims, Probate* PO Box 136, Manning, ND 58642-0136. 8AM-N,12:30-4:30PM. **701-573-4447**, Fax: 701-573-4444. **Fax**⊠♨

Eddy County

Southeast Judicial District Court *Felony, Misdemeanor, Civil, Eviction, Small Claims, Probate* 524 Central Ave, New Rockford, ND 58356. 8AM-4PM. **701-947-2813 x2013**, Fax: 701-947-2067. **Fax**⊠♨

Emmons County

South Central Judicial District Court *Felony, Misd., Civil, Eviction, Small Claims, Probate* PO Box 905, Linton, ND 58552. 8:30AM-N, 1-5PM. **701-254-4812**, Fax: 701-254-4012. **Fax**⊠♨

Foster County

Southeast Judicial District Court *Felony, Misd., Civil, Eviction, Small Claims, Probate* PO Box 257, Carrington, ND 58421. 8:30AM-4:30PM. **701-652-1001**, Fax: 701-652-2173. ⊠♨

Golden Valley County

Southwest Judicial District Court *Felony, Misdemeanor, Civil, Eviction, Small Claims, Probate* PO Box 9, Beach,

ND 58621-0009. 8AM-N, 1-4PM. **701-872-3713**, Fax: 701-872-4383. **Fax**☒ ✍

Grand Forks County

Northeast Central Judicial District Court *Felony, Misdemeanor, Civil, Eviction, Small Claims, Probate* PO Box 5939, Grand Forks, ND 58206-5939. 8AM-5PM. **701-780-8214**, Fax: 701-780-8217. ☒ ✍

Grant County

South Central Judicial District Court *Felony, Misdemeanor, Civil, Eviction, Small Claims, Probate* PO Box 258, Carson, ND 58529. 8AM-N, 12:30-4PM. **701-622-3615**, Fax: 701-622-3717. **Fax**☒ ✍

Griggs County

Southeast Judicial District Court *Felony, Misdemeanor, Civil, Eviction, Small Claims, Probate* PO Box 326, Cooperstown, ND 58425. 8AM-N, 1-4:30PM. **701-797-2772**, Fax: 701-797-3587. **Fax**☒ ✍

Hettinger County

Southwest Judicial District Court *Felony, Misd., Civil, Eviction, Small Claims, Probate* PO Box 668, Mott, ND 58646. 8AM-N, 1-4:30PM. **701-824-2645**, Fax: 701-824-2717. **Fax**☒ ✍

Kidder County

District Court *Felony, Misd., Civil, Eviction, Small Claims, Probate* PO Box 66, Steele, ND 58482. 9AM-5PM. **701-475-2632**, Fax: 701-475-2202. ☒ ✍

La Moure County

Southeast Judicial District Court *Felony, Misd., Civil, Eviction, Small Claims, Probate* PO Box 128, LaMoure, ND 58458. 9AM-N, 1-5PM. **701-883-5193**, Fax: 701-883-4240. **Fax**☒ ✍

Logan County

South Central Judicial District Court *Felony, Misd., Civil, Eviction, Small Claims, Probate* PO Box 6, Napoleon, ND 58561. 8:30AM-4:30PM. **701-754-2751**, Fax: 701-754-2270. **Fax**☒ ✍

McHenry County

Northeast Judicial District Court *Felony, Misdemeanor, Civil, Eviction, Small Claims, Probate* PO Box 117, Towner, ND 58788. 8AM-4:30PM. **701-537-5729**, Fax: 701-537-5969. **Fax**☒ ✍

McIntosh County

South Central Judicial District Court *Felony, Misdemeanor, Civil, Eviction, Small Claims, Probate* PO Box 179, Ashley, ND 58413. 8AM-4:30PM. **701-288-3450**, Fax: 701-288-3671. **Fax**☒

McKenzie County

Northwest Judicial District Court *Felony, Misd., Civil, Eviction, Small Claims, Probate* PO Box 524, Watford City, ND 58854. 8:30AM-N, 1-5PM. **701-444-3452**, Fax: 701-444-3916. ☒ ✍

McLean County

South Central Judicial District Court *Felony, Misdemeanor, Civil, Eviction, Small Claims, Probate* PO Box 1108, Washburn, ND 58577. 8AM-N, 12:30-4:30PM. **701-462-8541**, Fax: 701-462-8212. ☒ ✍

Mercer County

District Court *Felony, Misd., Civil, Eviction, Small Claims, Probate* PO Box 39, Stanton, ND 58571. 8AM-4PM. **701-745-3262**, Fax: 701-745-3710. **Fax**☒ ✍

Morton County

South Central Judicial District Court *Felony, Misdemeanor, Civil, Eviction, Small Claims, Probate* 210 2nd Ave NW, Mandan, ND 58554. 8AM-5PM. **701-667-3358**, crim: 701-667-3355. ☒ ✍

Mountrail County

Northwest Judicial District Court *Felony, Misd., Civil, Eviction, Small Claims, Probate* PO Box 69, Stanley, ND 58784. 8:30AM-4:30PM. **701-628-2915**, Fax: 701-628-2276. ☒ ✍

Nelson County

Northeast Central Judicial District Court *Felony, Misdemeanor, Civil, Eviction, Small Claims, Probate* Nelson County Recorder-Clerk of Court 210 B Ave W, #203, Lakota, ND 58344-7410. 8:30AM-N; 1PM-4:30PM. **701-247-2462**, Fax: 701-247-2412. **Fax**☒ ✍ **Email**

Oliver County

South Central Judicial District Court *Felony, Misdemeanor, Civil, Eviction, Small Claims, Probate* Box 125, Center, ND 58530. 8AM-4PM. **701-794-8777**, Fax: 701-794-3476. **Fax**☒ ✍

Pembina County

Pembina County District Court *Felony, Misdemeanor, Civil, Eviction, Small Claims, Probate* 301 Dakota St West #6, Cavalier, ND 58220-4100. 8:30AM-5PM. **701-265-4275**, Fax: 701-265-4876. **Fax**☒ ✍

Pierce County

Northeast Judicial District Court *Felony, Misdemeanor, Civil, Eviction, Small Claims, Probate* 240 SE 2nd St, Rugby, ND 58368. 9AM-5PM. **701-776-6161**, Fax: 701-776-5707. **Fax**☒ ✍

Ramsey County

District Court *Felony, Misdemeanor, Civil, Eviction, Small Claims, Probate* 524 4th Ave #4, Devils Lake, ND 58301. 8AM-N; 1:00PM-5:00PM. **701-662-1309**, Fax: 701-662-1303. **Fax**☒ ✍

Ransom County

Southeast Judicial District Court *Felony, Misd., Civil, Eviction, Small Claims, Probate* PO Box 626, Lisbon, ND 58054. 8:30AM-5PM. **701-683-5823 X120**, Fax: 701-683-5826. Criminal phone: 701-683-5823 x142. **Fax**☒ ✍

Renville County

Northeast Judicial District Court *Felony, Misdemeanor, Civil, Eviction, Small Claims, Probate* PO Box 68, Mohall, ND 58761. 9AM-4:30PM. **701-756-6398**, Fax: 701-756-6398. **Fax**☒ ✍

Richland County

Southeast Judicial District Court *Felony, Misd., Civil, Eviction, Small Claims, Probate* 418 2nd Ave North, Wahpeton, ND 58074. 8AM-5PM. **701-671-1524**, Fax: 701-671-1512. ☒**Fax** ✍

Rolette County

Northeast Judicial District Court *Felony, Misdemeanor, Civil, Eviction, Small Claims, Probate* PO Box 460, Rolla, ND 58367. 8:30AM-4:30PM. **701-477-3816**, Fax: 701-477-5770. **Fax**☒ ✍

Sargent County

Southeast Judicial District Court *Felony, Misdemeanor, Civil, Eviction, Small Claims, Probate* PO Box 176 (355 Main St), Forman, ND 58032. 9AM-N, 12:30-4:30PM. **701-724-6241 X115**, Fax: 701-724-6244. **Fax**☒ ✍

Sheridan County

South Central Judicial District Court *Felony, Misd., Civil, Eviction, Small Claims, Probate* PO Box 409, McClusky, ND 58463. 9AM-N, 1-5PM. **701-363-2207**, Fax: 701-363-2953. ✉✍

Sioux County

South Central Judicial District Court *Felony, Misdemeanor, Civil, Eviction, Small Claims, Probate* Box L, Fort Yates, ND 58538. 9AM-4:30PM. **701-854-3853**, Fax: 701-854-3854. Access records-✉✍

Slope County

Southwest Judicial District Court *Felony, Misdemeanor, Civil, Eviction, Small Claims, Probate* PO Box JJ, Amidon, ND 58620. 8:00AM-N; 1:00PM-5:00PM. **701-879-6275**, Fax: 701-879-6278. **Fax**✉✍

Stark County

District Court *Felony, Misd., Civil, Eviction, Small Claims, Probate* 51 Third St #106, Dickinson, ND 58602. 7AM-5PM. **701-227-3184**, Fax: 701-227-3185. Civil phone: 701-227-3182, crim: 701-227-3180, Probate: 701-227-3181. ✉✍

Steele County

East Central Judicial District Court *Felony, Misd., Civil, Eviction, Small Claims, Probate* PO Box 296, Finley, ND 58230. 8AM-N; 1-4:30PM. **701-524-2152**, Fax: 701-524-1325. ✉✍

Stutsman County

Southeast Judicial District Court *Felony, Misdemeanor, Civil, Eviction, Small Claims, Probate* 511 2nd Ave SE, Jamestown, ND 58401. 8AM-5PM. **701-252-9042**, Fax: 701-251-1006. ✉**Fax**✍

Towner County

Northeast Judicial District Court *Felony, Misd., Civil, Eviction, Small Claims, Probate* Box 517, Cando, ND 58324. 8:30AM-N; 1-5. **701-968-4340 Ext 3**, Fax: 701-968-4344. **Fax**✉✍

Traill County

East Central Judicial District Court *Felony, Misdemeanor, Civil, Eviction, Small Claims, Probate* PO Box 805, Hillsboro, ND 58045. 8AM-4:30PM. **701-636-4454**, Fax: 701-636-5124. ☎**Fax**✉✍

Walsh County

Northeast Judicial District Court *Felony, Misdemeanor, Civil, Eviction, Small Claims, Probate* 600 Cooper Ave, Grafton, ND 58237. 8:30AM-5PM. **701-352-0350**, Fax: 701-352-4466. ✉✍

Ward County

Northwest Judicial District Court *Felony, Misd., Civil, Eviction, Small Claims, Probate* PO Box 5005, Minot, ND 58702-5005. 8AM-4:30PM. **701-857-6460**, Fax: 701-857-6468. ✉✍

Wells County

Southeast Judicial District Court *Felony, Misd., Civil, Eviction, Small Claims, Probate* PO Box 155, Fessenden, ND 58438. 8AM-4:30PM. **701-547-3840**, Fax: 701-547-3719. ✉✍

Williams County

Northwest Judicial District Court *Felony, Misdemeanor, Civil, Eviction, Small Claims, Probate* PO Box 2047, Williston, ND 58802. 8AM-5PM. **701-774-4374**, Fax: 701-774-4379. ✉✍

Ohio

State Court Administration: Administrative Director, Supreme Court of Ohio, 30 E Broad St, 3rd Fl, Columbus, OH, 43266-0419; 614-466-2653, Fax: 614-752-8736. www.sconet.state.oh.us

Court Structure: The Court of Common Pleas is the general jurisdiction court and County Courts have limited jurisdiction. Effective July 1, 1997, the dollar limits for civil cases in County and Municipal Courts were raised as follows: County Court - from $3,000 to $15,000; Municipal Court - from $10,000 to $15,000. In addition the small claims limit was raised from $2,000 to $3,000.

Effective in 2001, Ohio Common Pleas Courts may name their own civil action limits, though most of these courts have yet to make changes. In effect, these Common Pleas courts may take any civil cases. However, civil maximum limits for Ohio's County Courts and Municipal Courts remains the same: $15,000.

Probate Courts: Probate courts are separate from the Court of Common Pleas, but Probate Court phone numbers are given with that court in each county.

Online Access: There is no statewide computer system, but a number of Circuits and Municipal courts offer online access. Appellate and Supreme Court case opinions and annoucements are available at the web page.

Adams County

Common Pleas Court *Felony, Civil Actions Over $3,000, Probate* 110 W Main, Rm 207, West Union, OH 45693. 8:30AM-4PM. **937-544-2344**, Fax: 937-544-8271 Probate: 937-544-2368. ✉✍

County Court *Misdemeanor, Civil Actions Under $15,000, Small Claims* 110 W Main, Rm 25, West Union, OH 45693. 8AM-4PM. **937-544-2011**, Fax: 937-544-8911. ✉✍

Allen County

Common Pleas Court *Felony, Civil Actions Over $15,000, Probate* PO Box 1243 301 N Main, Lima, OH 45802. 8AM-4:30PM. **419-228-3700**, Fax: 419-222-8427. Probate is a separate court. ✍

Key: Symbols refer to criminal records access unless otherwise noted. phone-☎ mail-✉ fax-**Fax** in person-✍ online-🖥 email-**Email**

Lima Municipal Court *Misdemeanor, Civil Actions Under $15,000, Eviction, Small Claims* www.limamunicipalcourt.org 109 N Union St (PO Box 1529), Lima, OH 45802. 8AM-5PM. **419-221-5275**, Fax: 419-998-5526. Civil phone: 419-221-5250. ☎Fax✉ ✋Email🖳

Ashland County

Common Pleas Court *Felony, Civil Actions Over $10,000, Probate* www.ashlandcounty.org/clerkofcourts 142 W 2nd St, Ashland, OH 44805. 8AM-4PM. **419-282-4242**, Fax: 419-282-4240 Probate: 419-282-4284. Probate court is a separate court at the same address. ✋🖳

Ashland Municipal Court *Misdemeanor, Civil Actions Under $15,000, Eviction, Small Claims* www.ashland-ohio.com 1209 E Main St, Ashland, OH 44805. 8AM-5PM. **419-289-8137x**, Fax: 419-289-8545. ☎✉Fax✋

Ashtabula County

Common Pleas Court *Felony, Civil Actions Over $10,000, Probate* 25 W Jefferson St, Jefferson, OH 44047. 8AM-4:30PM. **440-576-3637**, Fax: 440-576-2819 Probate: 440-576-3451. Probate is a separate office at the same location. Probate fax is 440-576-3633. ✋🖳

County Court Western Division *Misdemeanor, Civil Actions Under $15,000, Small Claims* 117 W Main St, Geneva, OH 44041. 8-4:30PM. **440-466-1184**, Fax: 440-466-7171. ✋✉Fax🖳

County Court Eastern Division *Misdemeanor, Civil Actions Under $15,000, Eviction, Small Claims* www.co.ashtabula.oh.us/ 25 W Jefferson St, Jefferson, OH 44047. 8AM-4:30PM. **440-576-3617**. ✉Fax✋🖳

Ashtabula Municipal Court *Misdemeanor, Civil Actions Under $15,000, Eviction, Small Claims* www.ashtabulamunicipalcourt.com 110 W 44th St, Ashtabula, OH 44004. 8AM-4:30PM. **440-992-7110**, Fax: 440-998-5786. 440-992-7109 directory. ✋🖳

Athens County

Common Pleas Court *Felony, Civil Actions Over $10,000, Probate* www.athenscountycpcourt.org PO Box 290, Athens, OH 45701-0290. 8AM-4PM. **740-592-3242**, Probate: 740-592-3251. ✋🖳

Athens Municipal Court *Misdemeanor, Civil Actions Under $15,000, Eviction, Small Claims* City Hall, 8 E Washington St, Athens, OH 45701. 8AM-4PM. **740-592-3328**, Fax: 740-592-3331. ✉✋

Auglaize County

Common Pleas Court *Felony, Civil Actions Over $10,000, Probate* PO Box 409, Wapakoneta, OH 45895. 8AM-4:30PM. **419-738-4219 or 419-738-4280**, Fax: 419-738-7953 Probate: 419-738-7710. Fax✋

Auglaize County Municipal Court *Misd., Civil Actions Under $15,000, Eviction, Small Claims* PO Box 409, Wapakoneta, OH 45895. 8AM-4:30PM. **419-738-2923**, Civil: 419-738-2917. ✋

Belmont County

Common Pleas Court *Felony, Civil Actions Over $3,000, Probate* Belmont County Clerk of Courts Main St, Courthouse, St Clairsville, OH 43950. 8:30AM-4:30PM. **740-695-2121**, Civil: 740-695-2169, Probate: 740-695-2121 X202. ✉✋

County Court Eastern Division *Misdemeanor, Civil Actions Under $15,000, Small Claims* 400 W 26th St, Bellaire, OH 43906. 8AM-4PM. **740-676-4490**. ✉✋

County Court Western Division *Misdemeanor, Civil Actions Under $15,000, Small Claims* 147 W Main St, St Clairsville, OH 43950. 8AM-4PM. **740-695-2875**, Fax: 740-695-7285. Fax✉✋

County Court Northern Division *Misd., Civil Actions Under $15,000, Small Claims* PO Box 40, Martins Ferry, OH 43935. 8AM-4PM. **740-633-3147**, Fax: 740-633-6631. ✉Fax✋

Brown County

Common Pleas Court *Felony, Civil Actions Over $3,000, Probate* 101 S Main, Georgetown, OH 45121. 7:30AM-4:30PM. **937-378-3100**, Probate: 937-378-6549. ✋

County Municipal Court *Misdemeanor, Civil Actions Under $15,000, Eviction, Small Claims* www.browncountycourt.org 770 Mount Orab Pike, Georgetown, OH 45121. 7:30AM-4:30PM M-F; 9AM-N S. **937-378-6358**, Fax: 937-378-2462. ✉✋🖳

Butler County

Common Pleas Court *Felony, Civil Actions Over $3,000, Probate* www.butlercountyclerk.org 315 High St, General Division Government Services Ctr, 3rd Fl, Hamilton, OH 45011. 8:30AM-4:30PM. **513-887-3287**, Fax: 513-887-3089 Probate: 513-887-3294. Service Center: 513-887-3288. 🖳✋

Hamilton Municipal Court *Misdemeanor, Civil Under $15,000, Small Claims* www.hamiltonmunicipalcourt.org 345 High St, #2, Hamilton, OH 45011. 8AM-5PM. **513-785-7300**, Fax: 513-785-7315. ☎✋🖳

County Court Area #2 *Misdemeanor, Civil Actions Under $15,000, Small Claims* Butler County Courthouse 101 High St, 1st Fl, Hamilton, OH 45011. 8AM-5PM. **513-887-3459**. ☎✋✉

County Court Area #3 *Misd., Civil Actions Under $15,000, Small Claims* 9113 Cincinnati, Dayton Rd, West Chester, OH 45069. 8:AM-5PM. **513-867-5070**, Fax: 513-777-0558. ✉✋

County Court Area #1 *Misdemeanor, Civil Actions Under $15,000, Small Claims* 118 W High, Oxford, OH 45056. 8:30AM-5PM. **513-523-4748**, Fax: 513-523-4737. ✉✋☎

Carroll County

Common Pleas Court *Felony, Civil Actions Over $15,000, Probate* PO Box 367, Carrollton, OH 44615. 8AM-4PM. **330-627-4886**, Fax: 330-627-6737 Probate: 330-627-2323. Probate Court address is 119 Public Sq, Courthouse, Carrollton, OH. ✋

County Court *Misdemeanor, Civil Actions Under $15,000, Small Claims, Evictions* 119 S Lisbon St, #301, Carrollton, OH 44615. 8AM-4PM. **330-627-5049**, Fax: 330-627-3662. ✋

Champaign County

Common Pleas Court *Felony, Civil Actions Over $10,000, Probate* 200 N Main St, Urbana, OH 43078. 8AM-4PM. **937-653-2746**, Probate: 937-652-2108. Probate is separate court at phone number given. ☎✉✋

Champaign County Municipal Court *Misdemeanor, Civil Actions Under $15,000, Eviction, Small Claims* PO Box 85, Urbana, OH 43078. 8AM-4PM. **937-653-7376**. ✉✋

Clark County

Common Pleas Court *Felony, Civil Actions Over $10,000, Probate* www.co.clark.oh.us 101 N Limestone St, Springfield, OH 45502. 8AM-4:30PM. **937-328-2458; 937-328-4648 (Domestic)**, Fax: 937-328-2436 Probate: 937-328-2434. Probate Court and records are at the same address, separate office. 🖑💻

Clark County Municipal Court *Misdemeanor, Civil Actions Under $15,000, Eviction, Small Claims* www.clerkofcourts.municipal.co.clark.oh.us 50 E Columbia St, Springfield, OH 45502. 8AM-5PM. **937-328-3700**, Civil: 937-328-3715, crim: 937-328-3726. ✉🖑💻

Clermont County

Common Pleas Court *Felony, Civil Actions Over $10,000, Probate* 270 Main St, Batavia, OH 45103. 8:30AM-4:30PM. **513-732-7130**, Fax: 513-732-7050 Probate: 513-732-7243. Probate court at 76 S Riverside Dr, Batavia 45103 🖑💻

Clermont County Municipal Court *Misd., Civil Under $15,000, Eviction, Small Claims* www.clermontclerk.org 289 Main St Civil Court: 66 S Riverside Rd, Batavia, OH 45103. 8AM-5PM. Civil: 513-732-7292, crim: 513-732-7290. ✉🖑💻

Clinton County

Common Pleas Court *Felony, Civil Actions Over $15,000, Probate* 46 S South St, Wilmington, OH 45177. 7:30AM-4:30PM. **937-382-2316**, Fax: 937-383-3455 Probate: 937-382-2280. Probate fax is 937-383-1158; hours are 8AM-4:30PM. ✉🖑

Clinton County Municipal Court *Misdemeanor, Civil Actions Under $15,000, Eviction, Small Claims* 69 N South St PO Box 71, Wilmington, OH 45177. 8AM-4PM. **937-382-8985**, Fax: 937-383-0130. Access records-**Fax**✉🖑

Columbiana County

Common Pleas Court *Felony, Civil Over $15,000, Probate* www.ccclerk.org 105 S Market St, Lisbon, OH 44432. 8AM-4PM. **330-424-7777**, Fax: 330-424-3960. 🖑💻

Municipal Court Northwest Area *Misdemeanor, Civil Actions Under $15,000, Small Claims* www.ccclerk.org 130 Penn Ave, Salem, OH 44460. 8AM-4PM. **330-332-0297**. ✉🖑💻

Municipal Court Eastern Area *Misdemeanor, Civil Under $15,000, Small Claims* www.ccclerk.org/the_courts.htm 31 N Market St, East Palestine, OH 44413. 8AM-4PM. **330-426-3774**, Fax: 330-426-6328. 🖑💻

Municipal Court Southwest Area *Misd., Civil Under $15,000, Small Claims* www.ccclerk.org/the_courts.htm 41 N Park Ave, Lisbon, OH 44432. 8AM-4PM. **330-424-5326**, Fax: 330-424-6658. 🖑💻

East Liverpool Municipal Court *Misdemeanor, Civil Actions Under $15,000, Eviction, Small Claims* www.eastliverpool.com/court.html 126 W 6th St, East Liverpool, OH 43920. 8AM-4PM. **330-385-5151**, Fax: 330-385-1566. ☎**Fax**✉🖑💻

Coshocton County

Common Pleas Court *Felony, Civil Over $10,000, Probate* 318 Main St, Coshocton, OH 43812. 8AM-4PM. **740-622-1456**, Probate: 740-622-1837. ✉🖑

Coshocton Municipal Court *Misd., Civil Actions Under $15,000, Eviction, Small Claims* www.coshoctonmunicipalcourt.com 760 Chesnut St, Coshocton, OH 43812. 8-4:30PM M-W F; 8-N TH. **740-622-2871**, Fax: 740-623-5928. ☎**Fax**✉🖑💻

Crawford County

Common Pleas Court *Felony, Civil Actions Over $3,000, Probate* www.crawford-co.org/Clerk/default.html 112 E Mansfield St, #204, Bucyrus, OH 44820. 8:30AM-4:30PM. **419-562-2766**, Fax: 419-562-8011 Probate: 419-562-8891. ✉🖑💻

Crawford County Municipal Court *Misdemeanor, Civil Actions Under $15,000, Eviction, Small Claims* PO Box 550, Bucyrus, OH 44820. 8:30AM-4:30PM. **419-562-2731**, Fax: 419-562-7064. ✉🖑

Crawford County Municipal Court Eastern Division *Misdemeanor, Civil Actions Under $15,000, Eviction, Small Claims* 301 Harding Way E, Galion, OH 44833. 8AM-5PM. **419-468-6819**, Fax: 419-468-6828. ✉🖑

Cuyahoga County

Common Pleas Court - General Div. *Felony, Civil Over $10,000, Probate* www.cuyahoga.oh.us/common/default.htm 1200 Ontario St, Cleveland, OH 44113. 8:30AM-4:30PM. **216-443-8560**, Fax: 216-443-5424. Civil phone: 216-443-7966, crim: 216-443-7985, Probate: 216-443-8764. Probate is a separate division with separate records and personnel. 🖑

Cleveland Municipal Court - Civil Division *Civil Under $15,000, Eviction, Small Claims* http://clevelandmunicipalcourt.org/home.html 1200 Ontario St, Cleveland, OH 44113. 8AM-3:50PM. **216-664-4870**, Fax: 216-664-4065. Court plans to have online records access. Access civil records-**Fax**✉🖑

Cleveland Municipal Court - Criminal Division *Misdemeanor* http://clevelandmunicipalcourt.org/home.html 1200 Ontario St, Cleveland, OH 44113. 8AM-3:50PM. **216-664-3268**. Court plans to have online records access. 🖑

Lyndhurst Municipal Court *Misdemeanor, Civil Actions Under $15,000, Eviction, Small Claims* 5301 Mayfield Rd, Lyndhurst, OH 44124. 8:30AM-5PM M-TH; -4PM F. **440-461-6500**, Fax: 440-442-1910. ✉🖑

Cleveland Heights Municipal Court *Misdemeanor, Civil Actions Under $15,000, Eviction, Small Claims* www.clevelandheightscourt.com 40 Severance Cir, Cleveland Heights, OH 44118. 8AM-5PM. **216-291-4901**, Fax: 216-291-2459. 💻🖑

Berea Municipal Court *Misdemeanor, Civil Actions Under $15,000, Eviction, Small Claims* www.bereamunicourt.org 11 Berea Commons, Berea, OH 44017. 8AM-4:30PM. Fax: 440-891-3387-civ; 440-234-2768-crim/traffic. Civil phone: 440-826-5860, crim: 440-826-5862. **Fax**✉🖑💻

Shaker Heights Municipal Court *Misdemeanor, Civil Actions Under $15,000, Eviction, Small Claims* www.shakerheightscourt.org 3355 Lee Rd, Shaker Heights, OH 44120. 8:30AM-4:30PM. **216-491-1300**, Fax: 216-491-1314. Criminal Clerk open to 6:30PM on Mondays. ☎**Fax**✉🖑

Garfield Heights Municipal Court *Misdemeanor, Civil Actions Under*

$15,000, Eviction, Small Claims www.ghmc.org 5555 Turney Rd, Garfield Heights, OH 44125. 8:30AM-4:30PM. **216-475-1900**. ☎ ✉ ✋ 💻

Parma Municipal Court *Misdemeanor, Civil Actions Under $15,000, Eviction, Small Claims* 5555 Powers Blvd, Parma, OH 44125. 8:30AM-4:30PM. **440-887-7400**, Fax: 440-887-7485. ☎**Fax**✉✋

Euclid Municipal Court *Misdemeanor, Civil Actions Under $15,000, Eviction, Small Claims* 555 E 222 St, Euclid, OH 44123-2099. 8:30AM-4:30PM. **216-289-2888**, Fax: 216-289-8254. ✉✋

Lakewood Municipal Court *Misd., Civil Actions Under $15,000, Eviction, Small Claims* www.lakewoodcourtoh.com 12650 Detroit Ave, Lakewood, OH 44107. 8AM-5PM. **216-529-6700**, Fax: 216-529-7687. **Fax**✉✋💻

South Euclid Municipal Court *Misd., Civil Actions Under $15,000, Eviction, Small Claims* 1349 S Green Rd, South Euclid, OH 44121. 8:30AM-5PM. **216-381-2880**, Fax: 216-381-1195. ✉✋

Bedford Municipal Court *Misdemeanor, Civil Actions Under $15,000, Eviction, Small Claims* www.bedfordmuni.org/ 165 Center Rd, Bedford, OH 44146. 8:30AM-4:30PM. **440-232-3420**, Fax: 440-232-2510. **Fax**✉✋💻

East Cleveland Municipal Court *Misd., Civil Actions Under $15,000, Eviction, Small Claims* 14340 Euclid Ave, East Cleveland, OH 44112. 8:30AM-4:30PM. **216-681-2021/2022**. ✉✋

Rocky River Municipal Court *Misdemeanor, Civil Actions Under $15,000, Eviction, Small Claims* www.rrcourt.net/ 21012 Hilliard Blvd, Rocky River, OH 44116. 8:30AM-4:30PM. **440-333-0066**, Fax: 440-356-5613. ☎**Fax**✉✋💻

Darke County

Common Pleas Court *Felony, Civil Over $15,000, Probate* Courthouse, Greenville, OH 45331. 8:30AM-4:30PM. **937-547-7335**, Fax: 937-547-7305 Probate: 937-547-7345. Probate is a separate court located at 300 Garst Ave. ✉✋

County Court *Misdemeanor, Civil Actions Under $15,000, Small Claims* Courthouse, Greenville, OH 45331-1990. 8:30AM-4:30PM. **937-547-7340**, Fax: 937-547-7378. ✉✋

Defiance County

Common Pleas Court *Felony, Civil Actions Over $10,000, Probate* PO Box 716, Defiance, OH 43512. 8:30AM-4:30PM. **419-782-1936**, Probate: 419-782-4181. ☎✋

Defiance Municipal Court *Misd., Civil Actions Under $15,000, Eviction, Small Claims* 324 Perry St, Defiance, OH 43512. 8AM-5PM. **419-782-5756**, Fax: 419-782-2018. Civil phone: 419-782-4092. ✉✋

Delaware County

Common Pleas Court *Felony, Civil Actions Over $15,000, Probate* www.delawarecountyclerk.org 91 N Sandusky, Delaware, OH 43015. 8:30AM-4:30PM. **740-833-2500**, Fax: 740-833-2499 Probate: 740-833-2680. Probate Court is separate and located at 88 N Sandusky St; Probate hours are 8:30AM-4:30PM. Access records-✉✋

Delaware Municipal Court *Misdemeanor, Civil Actions Under $15,000, Eviction, Small Claims* www.municipalcourt.org 70 N Union St, Delaware, OH 43015. 8AM-4:30PM. **740-548-6707**, Fax: 740-368-1583. Civil phone: 740-368-1550, crim: 740-368-1555. ☎✉✋💻

Erie County

Common Pleas Court *Felony, Civil Actions Over $10,000, Probate* 323 Columbus Ave, 1st Fl, Sandusky, OH 44870. 8AM-4PM M-Th/8AM-5PM F. **419-627-7705**, Fax: 419-627-6873 Probate: 419-627-7759. ✋

Erie County Court *Misd., Civil Under $15,000, Small Claims* 150 W Mason Rd, Milan, OH 44846. 8AM-4PM. **419-499-4689**, Fax: 419-499-3300. ✉✋

Sandusky Municipal Court *Misdemeanor, Civil Actions Under $15,000, Eviction, Small Claims* 222 Meigs St, Sandusky, OH 44870. 7AM-4PM. **419-627-5926**, Fax: 419-627-5950. Civil phone: 419-627-5914, crim: 419-627-5975. Access records-☎**Fax**✉✋

Vermilion Municipal Court *Misdemeanor, Civil Actions Under $15,000, Eviction, Small Claims* www.vermilionmunicipalcourt.org 687 Decatur St, Vermilion, OH 44089. 8AM-4PM. **440-967-6543**, Fax: 440-967-1467. **Fax**✉✋💻

Fairfield County

Common Pleas Court *Felony, Civil Actions Over $10,000, Probate* www.fairfieldcountyclerk.com/ 224 E Main, Clerk's Office, Lancaster, OH 43130-0370. 8AM-4PM. **740-687-7030**, Probate: 740-687-7093. Probate Court is separate from this court but at same address. ✋💻

Fairfield County Municipal Court *Misdemeanor, Civil Actions Under $15,000, Eviction, Small Claims* www.fairfieldcountymunicipalcourt.org/ PO Box 2390, Lancaster, OH 43130. 8AM-4PM. **740-687-6621**. ✉✋💻

Fayette County

Common Pleas Court *Felony, Civil Actions Over $10,000, Probate* 110 E Court St, Washington Court House, OH 43160. 9AM-4PM. **740-335-6371**, Probate: 740-335-0640. Probate is a separate court. ✉✋

Municipal Court *Misdemeanor, Civil Actions Under $15,000, Eviction, Small Claims* Washington Courthouse 119 N Main St, Washington Court House, OH 43160. 8AM-4PM. **740-636-2350**, Fax: 740-636-2359. ✉✋

Franklin County

Common Pleas Court *Felony, Civil Over $15,000* www.franklincountyclerk.com 369 S High St, Columbus, OH 43215-6311. 8AM-5PM. **614-462-3600**, Fax: 614-462-4325 Civil (614-462-6661 Crim.). Civil phone: 614-462-3621, crim phone: 614-462-3650, Probate: 614-462-3894. ✉✋

Franklin County Municipal Court - Civil Division *Civil Actions Under $15,000, Eviction, Small Claims* www.fcmcclerk.com 375 S High St, 3rd Fl, Columbus, OH 43215. 8AM-5PM. **614-645-7220**, Fax: 614-645-6919 (for filings only). Civil phone: 614-645-8161. Access civil records-☎**Fax**✉💻✋

Franklin County Municipal Court - Criminal Division *Misdemeanor* www.fcmcclerk.com 375 S High St, 2nd Fl, Columbus, OH 43215. Open 24 hours a day. **614-645-8186**. ✉💻✋

Probate Court 373 S High St, 22nd Fl, Columbus, OH 43215-6311. 8AM-5PM. **614-462-3894**, Fax: 740-393-6832. Search online at www.co.franklin.oh.us/probate/ProbateSearch.html. 💻

Fulton County

Common Pleas Court *Felony, Civil Actions Over $3,000, Probate* 210 S Fulton, Wauseon, OH 43567. 8:30AM-4:30PM. **419-337-9230**, Probate: 419-337-9242. ✋

County Court Western District *Misd., Civil Actions Under $15,000, Small Claims* 224 S Fulton St, Wauseon, OH 43567. 8:30AM-4:30PM. **419-337-9212**, Fax: 419-337-9286. ✉✋

County Court Eastern District *Misdemeanor, Civil Under $15,000, Small Claims* www.fultoncountyoh.com/courts.htm 204 S Main St, Swanton, OH 43558. 8:30AM-4:30PM. **419-826-5636**, Fax: 419-825-3324. ✉✋

Gallia County

Common Pleas Court - Gallia County Courthouse *Felony, Civil Actions Over $10,000, Probate* 18 Locust St, Rm 1290, Gallipolis, OH 45631-1290. 8AM-4PM. **740-446-4612 x223**, Fax: 740-441-2094 Probate: 740-446-4612 x240. ✋

Gallipolis Municipal Court *Misd., Civil Actions Under $15,000, Eviction, Small Claims* 518 2nd Ave, Gallipolis, OH 45631. 7:30AM-5PM. **740-446-9400**, Fax: 740-441-2070. ☎✉✋

Geauga County

Common Pleas Court *Felony, Civil Actions Over $10,000, Probate* www.co.geauga.oh.us 100 Short Court, Chardon, OH 44024. 8AM-4:30PM. **440-285-2222 X2380**, Fax: 440-286-2127 Probate: 440-285-2222 X2000. ✋💻

Chardon Municipal Court *Misd., Civil Under $15,000, Eviction, Small Claims* www.co.geauga.oh.us/departments/muni_court.htm 111 Water St, Chardon, OH 44024. 8AM-4:30PM. **440-286-2670/2684**, Fax: 440-286-2679. ✉✋

Greene County

Common Pleas Court *Felony, Civil Actions Over $10,000, Probate* www.co.greene.oh.us/clerk.htm 45 N Detroit St (PO Box 156), Xenia, OH 45385. 8AM-4:30PM. **937-562-5290**, Fax: 937-562-5309 Probate: 937-376-5280. ✋💻

Fairborn Municipal Court *Misd., Civil Actions Under $20,000, Eviction, Small Claims* http://ci.fairborn.oh.us/Court/municipal_court.htm 44 W Hebble Ave, Fairborn, OH 45324. 7:30AM-4:30PM. Fax: 937-879-4422. Civil phone: 937-754-3044, crim: 937-754-3040. ✉✋💻

Xenia Municipal Court *Misdemeanor, Civil Actions Under $15,000, Eviction, Small Claims* http://xmcwa.ci.xenia.oh.us 101 N Detroit, Xenia, OH 45385. 8AM-4:30PM. **937-376-7294; 376-7297 (Civil Clerk)**, Fax: 937-376-7288. **Fax**✉✋💻

Guernsey County

Common Pleas Court *Felony, Civil Actions Over $10,000, Probate* www.guernseycountycpcourt.org/ 801 E Wheeling Ave D-300, Cambridge, OH 43725. 8:30AM-4PM. **740-432-9230**, Fax: 740-432-7807 Probate: 740-432-9262. Probate is a separate division with separate records and personnel. 💻✋

Cambridge Municipal Court *Misd., Civil Actions Under $15,000, Eviction, Small Claims* 134 Southgate Pky, Cambridge, OH 43725. 8:30AM-4:30PM. **740-439-5585**, Fax: 740-439-5666. Civil phone: x240, crim: x226. ✉✋fax.

Hamilton County

Common Pleas Court *Felony, Civil Actions Over $10,000, Probate* www.courtclerk.org 1000 Main St, Rm 315, Cincinnati, OH 45202. 8AM-4PM. Civil phone: 513-946-5635, crim: 513-946-5671, Probate: 513-946-3580. Probate is separate court. ✉💻✋

Hamilton County Municipal Court - Civil *Civil Under $15,000, Eviction, Small Claims* www.courtclerk.org 1000 Main St, Rm 115, Cincinnati, OH 45202. 8AM-4PM. **513-946-5700**, Fax: 513-946-5710. Criminal phone: 513-946-6029. Access civil records-**Fax**✉💻✋

Hamilton County Municipal Court - Criminal *Misd.* www.courtclerk.org 1000 Sycamore St #111, Cincinnati, OH 45202. 8AM-4PM. **513-946-6029/6040**. ✋💻

Hancock County

Common Pleas Court *Felony, Civil Actions Over $10,000, Probate* www.co.hancock.oh.us/commonpleas/ 300 S Main St, Findlay, OH 45840. 8:30AM-4:30PM. **419-424-7037/7008**, Probate: 419-424-7079. Access records-✉✋💻

Findlay Municipal Court *Misdemeanor, Civil Under $15,000, Eviction, Small Claims* PO Box 826, Findlay, OH 45839.

8AM-5PM; 8AM-7PM Tuesday only. Fax: 419-424-7803. Civil phone: 419-424-7143, crim: 419-424-7141. ✉✋

Hardin County

Common Pleas Court *Felony, Civil Actions Over $10,000* Courthouse, #310, Kenton, OH 43326. 8:30AM-4PM. **419-674-2278**, Fax: 419-674-2273 Probate: 419-674-2230. ✉**Fax**✋

Hardin County Municipal Court *Misdemeanor, Civil Under $15,000, Eviction, Small Claims* PO Box 250, Kenton, OH 43326. 8:30AM-4PM. **419-674-4362**, Fax: 419-674-4096. ✉✋

Harrison County

Common Pleas Court *Felony, Civil Actions Over $3,000, Probate* 100 W Market, Cadiz, OH 43907. 8:30AM-4:30PM. **740-942-8500**, Fax: 740-942-3006 Probate: 740-942-8868. ✋

Harrison County Court *Misdemeanor, Civil Actions Under $15,000, Small Claims* Courthouse 100 W Market St, Cadiz, OH 43907. 8:00AM-4:30PM. **740-942-8865**, Fax: 740-942-3541. ✋

Henry County

Common Pleas Court *Felony, Civil Actions Over $10,000, Probate* PO Box 70, Napoleon, OH 43545. 8:30AM-4:30PM. **419-592-5926**, Fax: 419-592-0803 Probate: 419-592-7771. Probate Court's address is PO Box 70; probate fax is 419-592-7000. **Fax**✉✋

Napoleon Municipal Court *Misd., Civil Actions Under $15,000, Eviction, Small Claims* PO Box 502, Napoleon, OH 43545. 8AM-5PM. **419-592-2851**, Fax: 419-592-1805. ☎**Fax**✉✋

Highland County

Common Pleas Court *Felony, Civil Actions Over $10,000, Probate* PO Box 821, Hillsboro, OH 45133. 8AM-4:30PM. **937-393-9957**, Fax: 937-393-9878 Probate: 937-393-9981. Probate is a separate court. Access records-✉**Fax**✋

Hillsboro County Municipal Court *Misdemeanor, Civil Actions Under $15,000, Eviction, Small Claims* 130 Homestead Ave, Hillsboro, OH 45133. 7AM-3:30PM M,T,Th,F; 7AM-N W. **937-393-3022**, Fax: 937-393-0517. ☎**Fax**✉✋

Key: Symbols refer to criminal records access unless otherwise noted. phone-☎ mail-✉ fax-**Fax** in person-✋ online-💻 email-**Email**

Hocking County

Common Pleas Court *Felony, Civil Actions Over $10,000* PO Box 108, Logan, OH 43138. 8:30AM-4PM. **740-385-2616**, Fax: 740-385-1822 Probate: 740-385-3022. Probate is a separate court at the number given. ☎Fax⊠⍟

Hocking County Municipal Court *Misdemeanor, Civil Actions Under $15,000, Eviction, Small Claims* www.Hocking County Municipal Court PO Box 950, Logan, OH 43138-1278. 8:30AM-4PM. **740-385-2250**, Fax: 740-385-3826. ⊠⍟fax.

Holmes County

Common Pleas Court *Felony, Civil Actions Over $10,000, Probate* 1 E Jackson St, #306, Millersburg, OH 44654. 8:30AM-4:30PM. **330-674-1876**, Fax: 330-674-0289 Probate: 330-674-5881. Juvenile and probate court at #201. Fax⊠⍟

County Court *Misdemeanor, Civil Actions Under $15,000, Small Claims* 1 E Jackson St, #101, Millersburg, OH 44654. 8:30AM-4:30PM. **330-674-4901**, Fax: 330-674-5514. ☎Fax⊠⍟

Huron County

Common Pleas Court *Felony, Civil Actions Over $10,000, Probate* www.huroncountyclerk.com 2 E Main St, Norwalk, OH 44857. 8AM-4:30PM. **419-668-5113**, Probate: 419-668-4383. Probate is separate court. ⍟🖥

Norwalk Municipal Court *Misd., Civil Actions Under $15,000, Eviction, Small Claims* www.norwalkmunicourt.com 45 N Linwood, Norwalk, OH 44857. 8:30AM-4:30PM. **419-663-6750**, Fax: 419-663-6749. Fax⊠⍟

Bellevue Municipal Court *Misdemeanor, Civil Actions Under $15,000, Eviction, Small Claims* 3000 Seneca Industrial Pky, Bellevue, OH 44811. 8:30AM-4:30PM. **419-483-5880**, Fax: 419-484-8060. ☎⊠⍟

Jackson County

Common Pleas Court *Felony, Civil Actions Over $10,000, Probate* 226 Main St, Jackson, OH 45640. 8AM-4PM. **740-286-2006**, Fax: 740-286-4061 Probate: 740-286-1401. Access records-⊠Fax⍟

Jackson County Municipal Court *Misdemeanor, Civil Actions Under* $15,000, Eviction, Small Claims 350 Portsmouth St, #101, Jackson, OH 45640-1764. 8AM-4PM. **740-286-2718**, Fax: 740-286-0679. ⍟

Jefferson County

Common Pleas Court *Felony, Civil Actions Over $500, Probate* 301 Market St (PO Box 1326), Steubenville, OH 43952. 8:30AM-4:30PM. **740-283-8583**. Probate is at PO Box 649 and can be reached at 740-283-8653. ⊠⍟

County Court #1 *Misdemeanor, Civil Actions Under $15,000, Small Claims* www.uov.net/jeffcodp/court1.htm 1007 Franklin Ave, Toronto, OH 43964. 8AM-4PM. **740-537-2020**. ⊠⍟

County Court #2 *Misdemeanor, Civil Actions Under $15,000, Small Claims* www.uov.net/jeffcodp/court1.htm PO Box 2207, Wintersville, OH 43953. 8AM-4PM. **740-264-7644**. ⊠⍟

County Court #3 *Misdemeanor, Civil Actions Under $15,000, Small Claims* www.uov.net/jeffcodp/court1.htm PO Box 495, Dillonvale, OH 43917. 8AM-4PM. **740-769-2903**. ⊠⍟

Steubenville Municipal Court *Misd., Civil Under $15,000, Eviction, Small Claims* www.uov.net/jeffcodp/court1.htm 123 S 3rd St, Steubenville, OH 43952. 8:30AM-4PM. **740-283-6020**, Fax: 740-283-6167. ⊠⍟

Knox County

Common Pleas Court *Felony, Civil Over $10,000* www.knoxcountyclerk.org Knox County Clerk of Courts 117 E High St, #201, Mt Vernon, OH 43050. 8AM-4PM. **740-393-6788**, Probate: 740-393-6798. Probate is a separate office located at 111 E High St. 🖥⍟

Mount Vernon Municipal Court *Misdemeanor, Civil Actions Under $15,000, Eviction, Small Claims* www.mountvernonmunicipalcourt.org 5 N Gay St, Mount Vernon, OH 43050. 8AM-4PM. **740-393-9510**, Fax: 740-393-5349. ☎Fax⊠⍟🖥

Probate Ct 111 E High St, Mt Vernon, OH 43050. 8AM-4PM, 8AM-6PM Tues. **740-393-6796**, Fax: 740-393-6832.

Lake County

Common Pleas Court *Felony, Civil Actions Over $10,000, Probate* www.lakecountyohio.org PO Box 490, Painesville, OH 44077. 8-4:30PM. **440-350-2626**, Probate: 440-350-2624. ⍟🖥

Mentor Municipal Court *Misdemeanor, Civil Actions Under $15,000, Eviction, Small Claims* 8500 Civic Center Blvd, Mentor, OH 44060-2418. 8AM-4PM daily except Wed 8AM-6PM. Fax: 440-974-5742. Civil phone: 440-974-5744, crim: 440-974-5745. Access records-⍟

Painesville Municipal Court *Misd., Civil Under $15,000, Eviction, Small Claims* www.painesvillemunicipalcourt.org/ 7 Richmond St (PO Box 601), Painesville, OH 44077. 8AM-4:30PM. **440-392-5900**, Fax: 440-352-0028. Fax⊠⍟

Willoughby Municipal Court *Misd., Civil Actions Under $15,000, Eviction, Small Claims* www.willoughbycourt.com One Public Square, Willoughby, OH 44094-7888. 7:30AM-4:30 PM (till 7:30 on Mon). **440-953-4150**, Fax: 440-953-4149. Civil phone: 440-953-4170. Court serves these communites: Eastlake, Kirtland, Kirtland Hills, Lakeland Community College, Lakeline, Timberlake, Waite Hill, Wickliffe, Willoughby, Willoughby Hills, and Willowick. ⊠⍟

Lawrence County

Common Pleas Court *Felony, Civil Actions* www.lawrencecountyclkofcrt.org Clerk of the Courts PO Box 208, Ironton, OH 45638. 8:30AM-4PM. **740-533-4355/4329**, Fax: 740-533-4383 Probate: 740-533-4340. Probate is a separate court at Veterans Square in Ironton. ⍟🖥

Lawrence County Municipal Court *Misdemeanor, Civil Actions Under $15,000, Eviction, Small Claims* PO Box 126, Chesapeake, OH 45619. 8:30AM-4PM. **740-867-3128/3127**, Fax: 740-867-3547. ☎Fax⊠⍟

Ironton Municipal Court *Misdemeanor, Civil Actions Under $15,000, Eviction, Small Claims* PO Box 237, Ironton, OH 45638. 8:30AM-4PM. **740-532-3062**, Fax: 740-533-6088. Access records-⊠⍟

Licking County

Common Pleas Court *Felony, Civil Actions Over $15,000, Probate* www.lcounty.com/clerkofcourts/ PO Box 4370, Newark, OH 43058-4370. 8AM-4:30PM. **740-349-6171**, Fax: 740-349-6945 Probate: 740-349-6141. Probate court has a separate clerk at the same address. ⍟🖥

Licking County Municipal Court
Misdemeanor, Civil Actions Under $15,000, Eviction, Small Claims www.newarkohio.net/municipal/index.html 40 W Main St, Newark, OH 43055. 8AM-4:30PM. Civil: 740-349-6631, crim: 740-349-6627. ☎Fax✉🖐💻

Logan County

Common Pleas Court *Felony, Civil Over $10,000* www.co.logan.oh.us/clerkofcourts/ 101 S Main St, Rm 18, Bellefontaine, OH 43311-2097. 8:30AM-4:30PM. **937-599-7260.** 🖐

Bellefontaine Municipal Court *Misdemeanor, Civil Actions Under $15,000, Eviction, Small Claims* 226 W Columbus Ave, Bellefontaine, OH 43311. 8AM-4:30PM. **937-599-6127.** 🖐Fax✉

Lorain County

Common Pleas Court *Felony, Civil Actions Over $10,000, Probate* www.loraincounty.com/clerk 225 Court St., Elyria, OH 44035. 8AM-4:30PM. **440-329-5536,** Fax: 440-329-5404 Probate: 440-329-5175. 💻🖐

Lorain Municipal Court *Misd., Civil Actions Under $15,000, Eviction, Small Claims* www.lorainmunicourt.org 200 W Erie Ave, Lorain, OH 44052. 8:30AM-4:30PM. **440-204-2140,** Fax: 440-204-2146. 💻🖐

Elyria Municipal Court *Misdemeanor, Civil Actions Under $15,000, Eviction, Small Claims* www.elyriamunicourt.org 328 Broad St (PO Box 1498), Elyria, OH 44036. 8AM-4:30PM. **440-323-5743,** Fax: 440-323-0785-Civil, 440-323-8095-Criminal Crim: 440-323-1328. Fax✉🖐

Vermilion Municipal Ct *Misdemeanor, Civil Under $15,000, Eviction, Small Claims* www.vermilionmunicipalcourt.org 687 Decatour St, Vermilion, OH 44089-1152. 8AM-4PM. **440-967-6543,** Fax: 440-967-1467. Fax✉🖐💻

Oberlin Municipal Court *Misd., Civil Under $15,000, Eviction, Small Claims* 85 S Main St, Oberlin, OH 44074. 8-4PM. **440-775-1751,** Fax: 440-775-0619. 🖐

Avon Lake Municipal Court *Misd., Civil Actions Under $15,000, Eviction, Small Claims* 32855 Walker Rd, Avon Lake, OH 44012. 8:30AM-4:30PM. **440-930-4103.** ☎✉🖐

Lucas County

Common Pleas Court *Felony, Civil Actions Over $10,000, Probate* www.co.lucas.oh.us/clerk 700 Adams, Courthouse, Toledo, OH 43624. 8AM-4:45PM. **419-213-4483 & 4484,** Fax: 419-213-4487 Probate: 419-213-4775. Search Probate records separately; probate hours are 8:30-4:30. Fax✉🖐💻

Toledo Municipal Court *Misdemeanor, Civil Actions Under $15,000, Eviction, Small Claims* www.tmc-clerk.com 555 N Erie St, Toledo, OH 43624-1391. 8AM-4:30PM civil; 6AM-6PM M-F, 6-11:30AM Sat crim & traffic. **419-245-1926 (Small Claims),** Fax: 419-245-1801. Civil phone: 419-245-1927, crim: 419-936-3650. A second web site is at www.toledomunicipalcourt.org. ✉Fax🖐Email💻

Oregon Municipal Court *Misdemeanor, Civil Under $15,000, Eviction, Small Claims, Traffic* www.ci.oregon.oh.us/ctydpt/court/court.htm 5330 Seaman Rd, Oregon, OH 43616. 8:30AM-4:30PM. Fax: 419-698-7013. Civil phone: 419-698-7008, crim: 419-698-7173. ☎Fax✉🖐

Sylvania Municipal Court *Misd., Civil Actions Under $15,000, Eviction, Small Claims* www.sylvaniacourt.com 6700 Monroe St, Sylvania, OH 43560-1995. 7:30AM-4PM. **419-885-8975,** Fax: 419-885-8987. Civil phone: 419-885-8985, crim: 419-885-8975. Fax✉🖐💻

Maumee Municipal Ct *Misdemeanor, Civil Under $15,000, Eviction, Small Claims* www.maumee.org/city/municipalclerk.htm 400 Conant St, Maumee, OH 43537-3397. 8AM-4:30PM. Fax: 419-897-7129. Civil phone: 419-897-7145, crim: 419-897-7136. ☎Fax✉🖐💻

Madison County

Madison County Municipal Court *Misdemeanor, Civil Actions Under $15,000, Eviction, Small Claims* Main & High St, PO Box 646, London, OH 43140. 8AM-4PM. **740-852-1669,** Fax: 740-852-0812. ☎Fax✉🖐

Common Pleas Court *Felony, Civil Actions Over $10,000, Probate* PO Box 557, London, OH 43140. 8AM-4PM. **740-852-9776,** Fax: 740-845-1778 Probate: 740-852-0756. 🖐

Mahoning County

Common Pleas Court *Felony, Civil Actions Over $15,000, Probate* 120 Market St, Youngstown, OH 44503. 8-4PM. **330-740-2103,** Fax: 330-740-2105 Probate: 330-740-2312. ☎Fax✉🖐

County Court #2 *Misdemeanor, Civil Actions Under $15,000, Small Claims* 127 Boardman Canfield Rd, Boardman, OH 44512. 8:30AM-4PM. **330-726-5546,** Fax: 330-740-2035. ✉Fax🖐

County Court #3 *Misdemeanor, Civil Actions Under $15,000, Small Claims* 605 E Ohio Ave, Sebring, OH 44672. 8:30AM-4PM. **330-938-9873,** Fax: 330-938-6518. ✉🖐

County Court #4 *Misdemeanor, Civil Actions Under $15,000, Small Claims* 6000 Mahoning Ave, Youngstown, OH 44515-2288. 8:30AM-4PM. **330-740-2001,** Fax: 330-740-2036. Fax✉🖐

County Court #5 *Misdemeanor, Civil Actions Under $15,000, Small Claims* 72 N Broad St, Canfield, OH 44406. 8:30AM-4PM. **330-533-3643,** Fax: 330-740-2034. Fax✉🖐

Youngstown Municipal Court - Criminal Records *Misdemeanor* 26 S Phelps St, Youngstown, OH 44503. 8AM-4PM. **330-742-8860,** Fax: 330-742-8786. Fax✉🖐

Youngstown Municipal Court - Civil Records *Civil Actions Under $15,000, Eviction, Small Claims* PO Box 6047, Youngstown, OH 44501-6047. 8AM-4PM. **330-742-8863,** Fax: 330-742-8786. Access civil records-☎Fax✉🖐

Campbell Municipal Court *Misd., Civil Actions Under $15,000, Eviction, Small Claims* 351 Tenney Ave, Campbell, OH 44405. 8AM-4PM. **330-755-2165,** Fax: 330-750-3058. Fax✉🖐

Struthers Municipal Court *Misd., Civil Actions Under $15,000, Eviction, Small Claims* 6 Elm St, Struthers, OH 44471. 8AM-4PM; Public access only on Tuesday and Thursday. **330-755-1800,** Fax: 330-755-2790. ✉🖐

Marion County

Common Pleas Court *Felony, Civil Actions Over $10,000* 100 N Main St, Marion, OH 43301-1823. 8:30AM-

4:30PM. **740-223-4270**, Fax: 740-223-4279 Probate: 740-232-4260. ✉✋

Marion Municipal Court *Misdemeanor, Civil Actions Under $15,000, Eviction, Small Claims* 233 W Center St, Marion, OH 43302-0326. 8:30AM-4:30PM. **740-387-0439**, Fax: 740-382-5274. Civil phone: 740-383-5515, crim: 740-382-4031. ✉✋

Medina County

Common Pleas Court *Felony, Civil Actions Over $10,000, Probate* www.medinacommonpleas.com 93 Public Square, Medina, OH 44256. 8AM-4:30PM. **330-725-9720**, Fax: 330-764-8454 Probate: 330-725-9703. ✉✋💻

Wadsworth Municipal Court *Misdemeanor, Civil Actions Under $15,000, Eviction, Small Claims* www.wadsworthmunicipalcourt.com/main.htm 120 Maple St, Wadsworth, OH 44281-1825. 8AM-4PM. **330-335-1596**, Fax: 330-335-2723. Covers Villages of Gloria Glens, Lodi, Seville, Westfield Center; Townships of: Guilford, Harrisville, Homer, Sharon, Wadsworth, and Westfield. **Fax**✉✋

Medina Municipal Court *Misdemeanor, Civil Under $15,000, Eviction, Small Claims* www.medinamunicipalcourt.org 135 N Elmwood, Medina, OH 44256. 8AM-4:30PM. **330-723-3287**, Fax: 330-225-1108. ✉💻✋

Meigs County

Common Pleas Court *Felony, Civil Actions Over $3,000, Probate* PO Box 151, Pomeroy, OH 45769. 8:30AM-4:30PM. **740-992-5290**, Fax: 740-992-4429 Probate: 740-992-3096. Probate fax is 740-992-6727. ✋

Meigs County Court *Misdemeanor, Civil Actions Under $15,000, Small Claims* 2nd St Courthouse, Pomeroy, OH 45769. 8:30AM-4:30PM. **740-992-2279**, Fax: 740-992-4570. ✋

Mercer County

Common Pleas Court *Felony, Civil Over $10,000, Probate* 101 N Main St, Rm 205 PO Box 28, Celina, OH 45822. 8:30AM-4PM. **419-586-6461**, Fax: 419-586-5826 Probate: 419-586-2418. ✋

Celina Municipal Court *Misdemeanor, Civil Actions Under $15,000, Eviction, Small Claims* PO Box 362, Celina, OH

45822. 8AM-5PM. **419-586-6491**, Fax: 419-586-4735. **Fax**✉✋

Miami County

Common Pleas Court & Court of Appeals *Felony, Civil Over $10,000, Probate* www.onthesquare.com/muni/index.htm Safety Bldg, 201 W Main St, 3rd Fl, Troy, OH 45373. 8AM-4PM. **937-440-6010**, Fax: 937-440-6011 Probate: 937-440-6050. Probate is a separate division on the 2nd Fl. **Fax**✉✋

Miami County Municipal Court *Misdemeanor, Civil Actions Under $15,000, Eviction, Small Claims* www.co.miami.oh.us/muni/index.htm 201 W Main St, Troy, OH 45373. 8AM-4PM. **937-440-3910**, Fax: 937-440-3911. Civil phone: 937-440-3918, crim: 937-440-3910. ✉✋💻

Monroe County

Common Pleas Court *Felony, Civil Over $3,000, Probate* 101 N Main St, Rm 26, Woodsfield, OH 43793. 8:30AM-4:30PM. **740-472-0761**, Fax: 740-472-2549 Probate: 740-472-1654. ✉**Fax**✋

County Court *Misd., Civil Actions Under $15,000, Small Claims* 101 N Main St, Rm 35, Woodsfield, OH 43793. 9AM-4:30PM. **740-472-5181**. ☎✉✋

Montgomery County

Common Pleas Court *Felony, Civil Actions Over $10,000, Probate* www.clerk.co.montgomery.oh.us 41 N Perry St, Dayton, OH 45422. 8:30AM-4:30PM. **937-225-4512**, Fax: 937-496-7389/7220. Criminal phone: 937-225-4536, Probate: 937-225-4640. ✋💻

County Court - Area 2 *Misdemeanor, Civil Under $15,000, Small Claims under $3,000.* http://countycourt.dynip.com/ 6111 Taylorsville Rd, Huber Heights, OH 45424. 9AM-4PM. **937-496-7231**, Fax: 937-496-7236. ☎**Fax**✉✋💻**Email**

County Court - Area 1 *Misdemeanor, Civil Actions Under $15,000, Small Claims* www.clerk.co.montgomery.oh.us/ 195 S Clayton Rd, New Lebanon, OH 45345-9601. 8AM-4PM; (12PM-7PM, M); (9-4PM, F). **937-687-9099**, Fax: 937-687-7119. ✉✋💻

Dayton Municipal Court - Civil Division *Civil Under $15,000, Eviction, Small Claims* www.daytonmunicipalcourt.org 301 W 3rd St, PO Box 968, Dayton, OH 45402-0968. 8AM-4:30PM. **937-333-**

4471, Fax: 937-333-4468. Access civil records-☎✉✋online.

Dayton Municipal Court - Criminal Division *Misdemeanor* www.daytonmunicipalcourt.org 301 W 3rd St, Rm 331, Dayton, OH 45402. 8AM-4:30PM. **937-333-4315**, Fax: 937-333-4490. ✋💻

Miamisburg Municipal Court *Misd., Civil Actions Under $15,000, Eviction, Small Claims* 10 N 1st St, Miamisburg, OH 45342. 8AM-4PM. **937-866-2203**, Fax: 937-866-0135. ✉✋

Vandalia Municipal Court *Misd., Civil Actions Under $15,000, Eviction, Small Claims* www.vandaliacourt.com/ PO Box 429 Justice Center, 2nd Fl, Vandalia, OH 45377. 8AM-4PM. **937-898-3996**, Fax: 937-898-6648. **Fax**✉✋💻

Kettering Municipal Court *Misd., Civil Actions Under $15,000, Eviction, Small Claims* www.ketteringcourt.org 3600 Shroyer Rd, Kettering, OH 45429. 8:30AM-4:30PM. **937-296-2461**, Fax: 937-534-7017. ☎✉✋

Oakwood Municipal Court *Misd., Civil Actions Under $15,000, Eviction, Small Claims* 30 Park Ave, Dayton, OH 45419. 8:30AM-4PM. **937-293-3058**, Fax: 937-297-2939. ✋✉

Morgan County

Common Pleas Court *Felony, Civil Actions Over $3,000, Probate* 19 E Main St, McConnelsville, OH 43756. 8AM-4PM M-Th; 8AM-5PM F. **740-962-4752**, Fax: 740-962-4589 Probate: 740-962-2861. Above number is for Clerk. The Common Pleas Court can be reached at 740-962-3371. ✉✋

Morgan County Court *Misdemeanor, Civil Actions Under $15,000, Small Claims* 37 E Main St, McConnelsville, OH 43756. 8AM-4PM. **740-962-4031**, Fax: 740-962-2895. **Fax**✉✋

Morrow County

Common Pleas Court *Felony, Civil Over $3,000, Probate* 48 E High St, Mount Gilead, OH 43338. 8AM-4:30PM. **419-947-2085**, Fax: 419-947-5421 Probate: 419-947-5575. ☎**Fax**✉✋

Municiapl Court *Misd., Civil Actions Under $15,000, Small Claims* 48 E High St, Mount Gilead, OH 43338. 7:30AM-5PM. **419-947-5045**, Fax: 419-947-9161. ✉✋

Key: Symbols refer to criminal records access unless otherwise noted. phone-☎ mail-✉ fax-**Fax** in person-✋ online-💻 email-**Email**

Muskingum County

Common Pleas Court *Felony, Civil Actions, Probate* 401 Main St, Zanesville, OH 43701. 8:30AM-4:30PM. **740-455-7104**, Probate: 740-455-7113. As of 1/1/2001, there is no dollar limit on civil actions; prior, the civil action minimum was $15,000. ✉ 🖐

County Court *Misdemeanor, Civil Actions Under $15,000, Small Claims* www.muskingumcountycourt.org 27 N 5th St, Zanesville, OH 43701. 8AM-4PM. **740-455-7138**, Fax: 740-455-7157. **Fax**✉ 🖐 🖥

Zanesville Municipal Court *Misd., Civil Actions Under $15,000, Eviction, Small Claims* PO Box 566, Zanesville, OH 43702. 9AM-4:30PM. **740-454-3269**, Fax: 740-455-0739. ✉ 🖐fax.

Noble County

Common Pleas Court *Felony, Civil Actions Over $3,000* 350 Courthouse, Caldwell, OH 43724. 8-11:30AM,12:30-4PM M-W; 8-11:30AM, 12:30-6PM F. **740-732-4408**, Fax: 740-732-0100 Probate: 740-732-5047. Probate is a separate office at 270 Courthouse, in Caldwell. ☎**Fax**✉ 🖐

Noble County Court *Misdemeanor, Civil Actions Under $15,000, Small Claims* 100 Courthouse, Caldwell, OH 43724. 8:30AM-4PM M-W,F; 8:30-N Th. **740-732-5795**, Fax: 740-732-1435. **Fax**✉ 🖐

Ottawa County

Common Pleas Court *Felony, Civil Actions Over $10,000, Probate* www.ottawacocpcourt.com 315 Madison St, 3rd Fl, Port Clinton, OH 43452. 8:30AM-4:30PM. **419-734-6755 (Gen'l Division)**, Probate: 419-734-6830. Probate is a separate court at 315 Madison St., Rm 306. 🖐

Ottawa County Municipal Court *Misdemeanor, Civil Actions Under $15,000, Eviction, Small Claims* www.ottawacountymunicipalcourt.com/ 1860 E Perry St, Port Clinton, OH 43452. 8:30AM-4:30PM. **419-734-4143**, Fax: 419-732-2862. 🖐 🖥

Paulding County

Common Pleas Court *Felony, Civil Actions Over $3,000, Probate* 115 N Williams St, Rm 104, Paulding, OH 45879. 8AM-4PM. **419-399-8210**, Fax:

419-399-8248 Probate: 419-339-8256. **Fax**✉ 🖐

County Court *Misdemeanor, Civil Actions Under $15,000, Small Claims* www.pauldingcountycourt.com 201 E Carolina St, #2, Paulding, OH 45879. 8AM-4PM. **419-399-2792**, Fax: 419-399-3421. **Fax**✉ 🖐

Perry County

Common Pleas Court *Felony, Civil Actions Over $3,000, Probate* www.lawrencecountyclkofcrt.org PO Box 67, New Lexington, OH 43764. 8AM-4PM. **740-342-1022**, Fax: 740-342-5527 Probate: 740-342-1493. 🖐

Perry County Court *Misdemeanor, Civil Actions Under $15,000, Small Claims* PO Box 207, New Lexington, OH 43764-0207. 8:30AM-4:30PM M,W,F. **740-342-3156**, Fax: 740-342-2188. 🖐

Pickaway County

Common Pleas Court *Felony, Civil Actions Over $10,000, Probate* www.pickawaycountycpcourt.org/ County Courthouse 207 Court St, PO Box 270, Circleville, OH 43113. 8AM-4PM. **740-474-5231**, Probate: 740-474-3950. ✉ 🖐 🖥

Circleville Municipal Court *Misdemeanor, Civil Actions Under $15,000, Eviction, Small Claims* www.circlevillecourt.com/ PO Box 128, Circleville, OH 43113. 8AM-4PM. **740-474-3171**, Fax: 740-477-8291. ☎**Fax**✉ 🖐 🖥

Pike County

Common Pleas Court *Felony, Civil Actions Over $15,000, Probate* 100 E 2nd St, 2nd Fl, Waverly, OH 45690. 8:30AM-4PM. **740-947-2715**, Fax: 740-947-1729 Probate: 740-947-2560. Probate is a separate court at 230 Waverly Plaza, #600. 🖐

Pike County Court *Misdemeanor, Civil Actions Under $15,000, Small Claims* 230 Waverly Plaza, #900, Waverly, OH 45690. 8:30AM-4PM. Crim: 740-947-4003. ☎**Fax**✉ 🖐

Portage County

Common Pleas Court *Felony, Civil Actions Over $10,000, Probate* PO Box 1035, Ravenna, OH 44266. 8AM-4PM. **330-297-3644**, Fax: 330-297-4554. Civil

phone: 330-297-3644, crim: 330-297-3640, Probate: 330-297-3870. Probate Court address is 203 W Main, Ravenna, OH 44266-0936. 🖐 🖥

Portage Municipal Court - Kent Branch *Misdemeanor, Civil Actions Under $15,000, Eviction, Small Claims* www.co.portage.oh.us/ 214 S Water, Kent, OH 44240. 8AM-4PM. **330-678-9170**, Fax: 330-677-9944. Civil phone: 330-678-9170, crim: 330-678-9100. 🖐 🖥

Portage County Municipal Court *Misdemeanor, Civil Actions Under $15,000, Eviction, Small Claims* www.co.portage.oh.us/ PO Box 958, Ravenna, OH 44266. 8AM-4PM. Fax: 330-297-3526 (civ); 297-5867 (crim). Civil phone: 330-297-3635, crim: 330-297-3639. ✉ 🖐 🖥

Preble County

Common Pleas Court *Felony, Civil, Probate* 101 E Main, 3rd Fl, Eaton, OH 45320. 8AM-4:30PM. **937-456-8160; 456-8165 (common pleas)**, Fax: 937-456-9548 Probate: 937-456-8138. Probate office is separate from this court. ✉ 🖐

Eaton Municipal Court *Misdemeanor, Civil Under $15,000, Eviction, Small Claims* www.eatonmunicipalcourt.com PO Box 65 (101 E Main St), Eaton, OH 45320. 8AM-N, 1-4:30PM. **937-456-4941/6204**, Fax: 937-456-4685. ✉ 🖐 🖥

Putnam County

Common Pleas Court *Felony, Civil Actions Over $10,000, Probate* 245 E Main, Rm 301, Ottawa, OH 45875. 8:30AM-4:30PM. **419-523-3110**, Fax: 419-523-5284 Probate: 419-523-3012. Probate is a separate court. **Fax**✉ 🖐

Putnam County Court *Misdemeanor, Civil Actions Under $10,000, Small Claims* 245 E Main, Rm 303, Ottawa, OH 45875. 8:30AM-4:30PM. **419-523-3110**, Fax: 419-523-5284. ✉ 🖐

Richland County

Common Pleas Court *Felony, Civil Actions Over $10,000, Probate* www.richlandcountyoh.us/coc.htm 50 Park Ave E, 2nd Fl PO Box 127, Mansfield, OH 44901. 8AM-4PM. **419-774-5549**, Probate: 419-755-5583. 🖐 ✉

Mansfield Municipal Court *Misd., Civil Actions Under $15,000, Eviction, Small Claims* PO Box 1228, Mansfield, OH

Key: Symbols refer to criminal records access unless otherwise noted. phone-☎ mail-✉ fax-**Fax** in person-🖐 online-🖥 email-**Email**

44901. 8AM-4PM. **419-755-9617**, Fax: 419-755-9647. ☎**Fax**✉✋💻

Ross County

Common Pleas Court *Felony, Civil Actions Over $10,000, Probate* www.co.ross.oh.us/ County Courthouse 2 N Paint St, #A, Chillicothe, OH 45601. 8AM-4PM. **740-702-3010**, Fax: 740-702-3018 Probate: 740-774-1179. ✋💻

Chillicothe Municipal Court *Misdemeanor, Civil Actions Under $15,000, Eviction, Small Claims* www.chillicothemunicipalcourt.org 26 S Paint St, Chillicothe, OH 45601. 7:30AM-4:30PM. **740-773-3515**, Fax: 740-774-1101. ✉✋💻

Sandusky County

Common Pleas Court *Felony, Civil Actions Over $3,000, Probate* 100 N Park Ave, #320, Fremont, OH 43420. 8AM-4:30PM. **419-334-6161/6163**, Fax: 419-334-6164 Probate: 419-334-6217. ✋

County Court #2 *Misdemeanor, Civil Actions Under $15,000, Small Claims* www.sandusky-county.org/ 215 W Main St, Woodville, OH 43469. 8AM-4:30PM. **419-849-3961**, Fax: 419-849-3932. ☎**Fax**✉✋

County Court #1 *Misdemeanor, Civil Actions Under $15,000, Small Claims* www.co.sandusky.oh.us/ 847 E McPherson Hwy (PO Box 267), Clyde, OH 43410. 8AM-4:30PM. **419-547-0915**, Fax: 419-547-9198. Access records-☎**Fax**✉✋

Fremont Municipal Court *Misd., Civil Actions Under $15,000, Eviction, Small Claims* PO Box 886, Fremont, OH 43420-0071. 8AM-4:30PM. **419-332-1579**, Fax: 419-332-1570. **Fax**✉✋

Scioto County

Common Pleas Court *Felony, Civil Actions Over $15,000, Probate* www.sciotocountycpcourt.org 602 7th St, Rm 205, Portsmouth, OH 45662. 8AM-4:30PM. **740-355-8226**, Fax: 740-354-2057 Probate: 740-355-8243. Probate is a separate office at the same address in Rm 201. ✋💻

Portsmouth Municipal Court *Misdemeanor, Civil Actions Under $15,000, Eviction, Small Claims* www.portsmouth-municipal-court.com 728 2nd St, Portsmouth, OH 45662. 8AM-4PM. **740-354-3283**, Fax: 740-353-6645. ✉✋💻

Seneca County

Common Pleas Court *Felony, Civil Actions Over $10,000, Probate* 117 E Market, Tiffin, OH 44883. 8:30AM-4:30PM. **419-447-0671**, Fax: 419-443-7919 Probate: 419-447-3121. ☎**Fax**✉✋

Fostoria Municipal Court *Misdemeanor, Civil Actions Under $15,000, Eviction, Small Claims* PO Box 985, Fostoria, OH 44830. 8:30AM-5PM, W; 8:30AM-N. **419-435-8139**, Fax: 419-435-1150. ☎**Fax**✉✋

Tiffin Municipal Court *Misdemeanor, Civil Actions Under $15,000, Eviction, Small Claims* PO Box 694, Tiffin, OH 44883. 8:30AM-4:30PM. **419-448-5412**, Fax: 419-448-5419. Civil phone: 419-448-5418, crim: 419-448-5411. **Fax**✉✋

Shelby County

Common Pleas Court *Felony, Civil Actions Over $10,000, Probate* http://co.shelby.oh.us/commonpleas/ PO Box 809, Sidney, OH 45365. 8AM-4PM. **937-498-7221**, Fax: 937-498-4840. ✉✋

Sidney Municipal Court *Misdemeanor, Civil Actions Under $15,000, Eviction, Small Claims* www.sidneyoh.com 201 W Poplar, Sidney, OH 45365. 8AM-4:30PM. **937-498-0011**, Fax: 937-498-8179. Send mail requests to the address above; phone and in person searches are made at the court at 110 W Court St. ☎**Fax**✉✋

Stark County

Alliance Municipal Court *Misdemeanor, Civil Under $15,000, Eviction, Small Claims* www.starkcountyjis.org/alliance/ 470 E Market St, Rm 16, Alliance, OH 44601. 8:30AM-4:30PM. **330-823-6600**, Fax: 330-829-2231. Includes Alliance, Lexington, Marlboro, Washington, Paris, Uniontown, Minerva, Limaville, and Roberstville. **Fax**✉✋💻

Common Pleas Court - Civil Division *Civil Actions Over $15,000* www.starkclerk.org PO Box 21160, Canton, OH 44701. 8:30AM-4:30PM. **330-451-7795**, Fax: 330-451-7853. Access civil records-☎**Fax**✉✋💻

Common Pleas Court - Criminal Division *Felony* www.starkclerk.org PO Box 21160, Canton, OH 44701-1160. 8:30AM-4:30PM. **330-451-7929**, Fax: 330-451-7853. Access records-✉✋💻

Canton Municipal Court

Canton Municipal Court *Misdemeanor, Civil Actions Under $15,000, Eviction, Small Claims* www.cantoncourt.org 218 Cleveland Ave SW PO Box 24218, Canton, OH 44702-4218. 8AM-4:30PM. **330-489-3203**, Fax: 330-489-3075 (civil) 489-3372 (criminal). Includes Canton, North Canton, Louisville, Lake, Plain, Nimishillen, Osnaburg, Pike, Sandy, Hartville, East Canton, Myers Lake, East Sparta, Waynesburg, and Magnolia. ☎**Fax**✉✋💻

Massillon Municipal Court *Misd., Civil Under $15,000, Eviction, Small Claims* www.massilloncourt.org/ Two James Duncan Plaza, Massillon, OH 44646-6690. 8:30AM-4:30PM. **330-830-2591**, Fax: 330-830-3648. Civil phone: 330-830-1731, crim: 330-830-1732. Includes Massillon, Canal Fulton, Bethlehem, Jackson, Lawrence, Perry, Sugarcreek, Tuscarawas, Beach City, Brewster, Hills and Dales, Navarre, and Wilmot. **Fax**✉✋💻

Summit County

Common Pleas Court *Felony, Civil Actions Over $10,000, Probate* www.cpclerk.co.summit.oh.us 209 S High St, Akron, OH 44308. 9:30AM-4:15PM. **330-643-2201 (Divorce)**, Fax: 330-643-7772. Civil phone: 330-643-2217, crim: 330-643-2282, Probate: 330-643-2350. For faster service, mail requests to Clerk at 53 University Ave, Akron 44308. Probate is a separate court. ✉✋💻

Cuyahoga Falls Municipal Court *Misd., Civil Under $15,000, Eviction, Small Claims* www.cfmunicourt.com 2310 2nd St, Cuyahoga Falls, OH 44221. 8AM-8PM (Criminal), 8AM-4:30PM (Civil). **330-971-8110**, Fax: 330-971-8114. Civil phone: 330-971-8108, crim: 330-971-8109. ☎✉✋💻

Akron Municipal Court *Misdemeanor, Civil Actions Under $15,000, Eviction, Small Claims* http://courts.ci.akron.oh.us 217 S High St, Rm 837, Akron, OH 44308. 8AM-4:30PM. Fax: 330-375-2427. Civil phone: 330-375-2920, crim: 330-375-2570. Access records-✉✋💻

Barberton Municipal Court *Misd., Civil Under $15,000, Eviction, Small Claims* www.cityofbarberton.com/clerkofcourts Municipal Bldg 576 W Park Ave, Barberton, OH 44203-2584. 8AM-5PM (civ); Crim/traffic to 8PM. **330-753-2261**, Fax: 330-848-6779. ☎**Fax**✉✋💻

Key: Symbols refer to criminal records access unless otherwise noted. phone-☎ mail-✉ fax-**Fax** in person-✋ online-💻 email-**Email**

Trumbull County

Common Pleas Court *Felony, Civil Actions Over $10,000, Probate* www.clerk.co.trumbull.oh.us 161 High St, Warren, OH 44481. 8:30AM-4:30PM. **330-675-2557**, Probate: 330-675-2521. ✉🖐💻

Trumbull County Court Central *Misd., Civil Actions Under $15,000, Eviction, Small Claims* 180 N Mecca St, Cortland, OH 44410. 8AM-4PM. **330-637-5023**, Fax: 330-637-5021. ☎**Fax**✉🖐

Trumbull County Court East *Misdemeanor, Civil Under $15,000, Eviction, Small Claims* 7130 Brookwood Dr, Brookfield, OH 44403. 8:30AM-4:30PM. **330-448-1726**, Fax: 330-448-6310. ☎**Fax**✉🖐

Niles Municipal Court *Misd., Civil Under $15,000, Eviction, Small Claims* www.nilesmunicourt.org 15 E State St, Niles, OH 44446-5051. 8AM-4PM. **330-652-5863**, Fax: 330-544-9025. **Fax**✉🖐

Newton Falls Municipal Court *Misdemeanor, Civil Actions Under $15,000, Eviction, Small Claims* 19 N Canal St, Newton Falls, OH 44444-1302. 7:30AM-4:00PM. **330-872-0302**, Fax: 330-872-3899. **Fax**✉🖐

Girard Municipal Court *Misdemeanor, Civil Actions Under $15,000, Eviction, Small Claims* City Hall 100 N Market St, #A, Girard, OH 44420-2559. 8AM-4PM. Fax: 330-545-7045. Civil phone: 330-545-3177, crim: 330-545-0069. traffic records: 330-545-3049. **Fax**✉🖐

Warren Municipal Court *Misdemeanor, Civil Actions Under $15,000, Eviction, Small Claims* 141 South St SE (PO Box 1550), Warren, OH 44482. 8AM-4:30PM. **330-841-2525**, Fax: 330-841-2760. Civil phone: 330-841-2525 x112-115, crim: 330-841-2525 x105-110. **Fax**✉🖐

Tuscarawas County

Common Pleas Court *Felony, Civil Actions Over $15,000, Probate* www.co.tuscarawas.oh.us 125 E High (PO Box 628), New Philadelphia, OH 44663. 8AM-4:30PM. **330-365-3243**, Fax: 330-343-4682 Probate: 330-365-3266. Probate is a separate court at 101 E High Ave. 🖐💻

County Court *Misdemeanor, Civil Actions Under $15,000, Small Claims* 220 E 3rd, Uhrichsville, OH 44683. 8AM-4:30PM. **740-922-4795**, Fax: 740-922-7020. Probation office: 740-922-3653 & 922-4360. **Fax**✉🖐

New Philadelphia Municipal Court *Misdemeanor, Civil Actions Under $15,000, Eviction, Small Claims* www.npmunicipalcourt.org/ 166 E High Ave, New Philadelphia, OH 44663. 8AM-4:30PM. **330-343-6797**, Fax: 330-364-6885. Civil phone: 330-231-6797, crim: 330-234-6797. The New Philadelphia Municipal Court has territorial jurisdiction within the municipal corporations of New Philadelphia and Dover, and villages of Baltic, Bolivar, Midvale, Mineral City, Roswell, Stonecreek, Strasburg, Sugarcreek, Zoar. 🖐

Union County

Common Pleas Court *Felony, Civil Actions Over $10,000, Probate* www.co.union.oh.us/Clerk_of_Courts/clerk_of_courts.html County Courthouse, Clerk of Courts 215 W 5th, 2nd Fl, Marysville, OH 43040. 8:30AM-4PM. **937-645-3006**, Fax: 937-645-3162. Civil phone: 937-645-3145, crim: 937-645-3140, Probate: 937-645-3029. Probate is located at the same address, separate office. Probate fax: 937-645-3160. 🖐💻

Marysville Municipal Court *Misd., Civil Under $15,000, Eviction, Small Claims* City Hall Bldg 125 E 6th St, Marysville, OH 43040. 8AM-4PM. **937-644-9102**, Fax: 937-644-1228. ☎**Fax**✉🖐

Van Wert County

Common Pleas Court *Felony, Civil Actions, Probate* www.vwcommonpleas.org 305 Courthouse 121 E Main St, Van Wert, OH 45891. 8AM-4PM. **419-238-6935**, Fax: 419-238-2874; Clerk- 238-4760 Probate: 419-238-0027. Probate records are at 108 Main St., Van Wert. 🖐

Van Wert Municipal Court *Misdemeanor, Civil Actions Under $15,000, Eviction, Small Claims* http://vanwert.org/gov/court/index.htm 124 S Market, Van Wert, OH 45891. 8AM-4PM. **419-238-5767**. ✉🖐

Vinton County

Common Pleas Court *Felony, Civil Actions Over $3,000, Probate* County Courthouse 100 E Main St, McArthur, OH 45651. 8:30AM-4PM. **740-596-3001**, Fax: 740-596-9611 Probate: 740-596-3438. 🖐

Vinton County Court *Misdemeanor, Civil Actions Under $15,000, Small Claims$3,000.* County Courthouse, McArthur, OH 45651. 8:30AM-4PM. **740-596-5000**, Fax: 740-596-9721. ☎✉🖐

Warren County

Common Pleas Court *Felony, Civil Actions Over $3,000, Probate* www.co.warren.oh.us/clerkofcourt/ PO Box 238, Lebanon, OH 45036. 8:30AM-4:30PM. **513-695-1120**, Fax: 513-695-2965 Probate: 513-695-1180. ✉🖐💻

County Court *Misdemeanor, Civil Under $15,000, Small Claims under $3000* www.co.warren.oh.us/countycourt 550 Justice Dr, Lebanon, OH 45036. 8AM-4:30PM. **513-695-1370**. ☎✉🖐

Mason Municipal Court *Misdemeanor, Civil Under $15,000, Eviction, Small Claims* www.masonmunicipalcourt.org 5950 S Mason Montgomery Rd, Mason, OH 45040-3712. 7:30AM-4PM. **513-398-7901**, Fax: 513-459-8085. ☎**Fax**✉🖐💻

Lebanon Muncipal Court *Misdemeanor, Civil Actions, Eviction, Small Claims* www.ci.lebanon.oh.us/departments/courts/courts.htm City Bldg, 50 S Broadway, Lebanon, OH 45036-1777. 8AM-4PM. **513-932-3060**, Fax: 513-933-7212. **Fax**✉🖐

Franklin Municipal Court *Misdemeanor, Civil Actions Under $15,000, Eviction, Small Claims* 1 Benjamin Franklin Way, Franklin, OH 45005. 8:30AM-5PM. **937-746-2858**, Fax: 937-743-7751. ☎✉🖐

Washington County

Common Pleas Court *Felony, Civil Actions Over $10,000, Probate* www.washingtongov.org 205 Putnam St, Marietta, OH 45750. 8AM-4:15PM. **740-373-6623**, Probate: 740-373-6623. 🖐

Marietta Municipal Court *Misdemeanor, Civil Actions Under $15,000, Eviction, Small Claims* www.mariettacourt.com 301 Putnam (PO Box 615), Marietta, OH 45750. 8AM-5PM. **740-373-4474**, Fax: 740-373-2547. ✉🖐💻

Key: Symbols refer to criminal records access unless otherwise noted. phone-☎ mail-✉ fax-**Fax** in person-🖐 online-💻 email-**Email**

Wayne County

Common Pleas Court *Felony, Civil Actions Over $15,000, Probate* http://waynecountyclerkofcourts.org PO Box 507, Wooster, OH 44691. 8AM-4:30PM. **330-287-5590**, Fax: 330-287-5416 Probate: 330-287-5575. Probate is a separate court. ✉ ✋

Wayne County Municipal Court Clerk *Misdemeanor, Civil Actions Under $15,000, Eviction, Small Claims* 215 N Grant St, Wooster, OH 44691-4817. 8AM-4:30PM. **330-287-5650**, Fax: 330-263-4043. Access records-✋

Williams County

Common Pleas Court *Felony, Civil Actions Over $10,000, Probate* 1 Courthouse Sq Clerk of Court of Common Pleas, Bryan, OH 43506. 8:30AM-4:30PM. **419-636-1551**, Fax: 419-636-7877 Probate: 419-636-1548. Probate Court is at the same address. ✉ ✋

Bryan Municipal Court *Misdemeanor, Civil Actions Under $15,000, Eviction, Small Claims* 1399 E High, PO Box 546, Bryan, OH 43506. 8:30AM-4:30PM. **419-636-6939**, Fax: 419-636-3417. **Fax** ✉ ✋

Wood County

Common Pleas Court *Felony, Civil Actions Over $10,000, Probate* Courthouse Sq, Bowling Green, OH 43402. 8:30AM-4:30PM. **419-354-9280**, Fax: 419-354-9241 Probate: 419-354-9230. Probate record searching is separate. **Fax** ✉ ✋

Bowling Green Municipal Court *Misdemeanor, Civil Actions Under $15,000, Eviction, Small Claims* www.bgcourt.org PO Box 326, Bowling Green, OH 43402. 8:30AM-4:30PM. **419-352-5263**, Fax: 419-352-9407. ☎**Fax** ✉ ✋ 🖥

Perrysburg Municipal Court *Misdemeanor, Civil Actions Under $15,000, Eviction, Small Claims* www.perrysburgcourt.com/ 300 Walnut St, Perrysburg, OH 43551. 8AM-4:30PM (8AM-7PM Tues.). **419-872-7900**, Fax: 419-872-7905. ☎**Fax** ✉ 🖥 ✋

Wyandot County

Common Pleas Court *Felony, Civil Actions Over $10,000, Probate* www.co.wyandot.oh.us/clerk/index.html 109 S Sandusky Ave, Rm 31, Upper Sandusky, OH 43351. 8:30AM-4:30PM. **419-294-1432**, Fax: 419-294-6414 Probate: 419-294-2302. **Fax** ✉ ✋ ☎

Upper Sandusky Municipal Court *Misdemeanor, Civil Actions Under $15,000, Eviction, Small Claims* 119 N 7th St, Upper Sandusky, OH 43351. 8AM-4:30PM. **419-294-3809**, Fax: 419-09-0474. ✉ ✋

Oklahoma

State Court Administration: Administrative Director of Courts, 1915 N Stiles #305, Oklahoma City, OK, 73105; 405-521-2450, Fax: 405-521-6815. www.oscn.net

Court Structure: There are 82 District Courts in 26 judicial districts. Cities with populations in excess of 200,000 (Oklahoma City and Tulsa) have municipal criminal courts of record. Cities with less than 200,000 do not have such courts.

The small claims limit was raised from $3000 to $4500 in 1998.

Online Access: Free Internet access is available for District Courts in 12 counties and all Appellate courts at www.oscn.net. Both civil and criminal docket information is available for the counties invoved. Also, one can search the Oklahoma Supreme Court Network by single cite or multiple cite (no name searches) from the www.oscn.net Internet site .

Case information is available in bulk form for downloading to computer. For information, call the Administrative Director of Courts, 405-521-2450.

Also, the Oklahoma District Court Records free website at www.odcr.com offers searching from over 30 District Courts. More counties are being added as they are readied; they hope to eventually feature all OK District Courts. Please note many of the county records in this system do not go back 7 years.

Adair County

15th Judicial District Court *Felony, Misdemeanor, Civil, Eviction, Small Claims, Probate* PO Box 426 (220 W Division), Stilwell, OK 74960. 8AM-4:30PM. **918-696-7633**. ☎**Fax** ✉ ✋

Alfalfa County

4th Judicial District Court *Felony, Misdemeanor, Civil, Eviction, Small Claims, Probate* County Courthouse 300 S Grand, Cherokee, OK 73728. 8:30AM-4:30PM. **580-596-3523**. ✉ ✋

Atoka County

25th Judicial District Court *Felony, Misdemeanor, Civil, Eviction, Small Claims, Probate* 200 E Court St, Atoka, OK 74525. 8:30AM-4:30PM. **580-889-3565**. ✉ ✋

Beaver County

1st Judicial District Court *Felony, Misdemeanor, Civil, Eviction, Small Claims, Probate* PO Box 237 (111 W 2nd), Beaver, OK 73932. 9AM-N, 1-5PM. **580-625-3191**. ✉ ✋

Beckham County

2nd Judicial District Court *Felony, Misd., Civil, Eviction, Small Claims, Probate* PO Box 520 (302 E Main St), Sayre, OK 73662. 9AM-5PM. **580-928-3330**, Fax: 580-928-9278. **Fax** ✉ ✋ 🖥

Blaine County

4th Judicial District Court *Felony, Misdemeanor, Civil, Eviction, Small Claims, Probate* 212 N Weigle St, Watonga, OK 73772. 8AM-4PM. **580-623-5970**. ✉ ✋ 🖥

Key: Symbols refer to criminal records access unless otherwise noted. phone-☎ mail-✉ fax-**Fax** in person-✋ online-🖥 email-**Email**

Bryan County

19th Judicial District Court *Felony, Misdemeanor, Civil, Eviction, Small Claims, Probate* Courthouse 3rd Fl 402 W Evergreen St, Durant, OK 74701. 8:00AM-12:00PM,1:00PM-5:00PM. **580-924-1446.** ✉✋💻

Caddo County

6th Judicial District Court *Felony, Misdemeanor, Civil, Eviction, Small Claims, Probate* PO Box 10 (201 W Oklahoma Ave), Anadarko, OK 73005. 8:30AM-4:30PM. **405-247-3393.** ✉✋

Canadian County

26th Judicial District Court *Felony, Misdemeanor, Civil, Eviction, Small Claims, Probate* PO Box 730 (301 N Choctaw St), El Reno, OK 73036. 8AM-4:30PM. **405-262-1070.** Use ext 168 for civil; 165 for criminal; 170 for probate. ✉💻✋

Carter County

20th Judicial District Court *Felony, Misdemeanor, Civil, Eviction, Small Claims, Probate* www.brightok.net/carter county/CarterCountyCourtClerk.html PO Box 37 (First & B Southwest) Court Clerk, Ardmore, OK 73402. 8AM-N, 1-5PM. **580-223-5253.** ✉✋

Cherokee County

15th Judicial District Court *Felony, Misdemeanor, Civil, Eviction, Small Claims, Probate* 213 W Delaware, Rm 302, Tahlequah, OK 74464. 8AM-4:30PM. **918-456-0691**, Fax: 918-458-6587. ☎✉✋💻

Choctaw County

17th Judicial District Court *Felony, Misdemeanor, Civil, Eviction, Small Claims, Probate* 300 E Duke, Hugo, OK 74743. 8AM-4PM. **580-326-7554 & 7555.** ☎Fax✉✋

Cimarron County

1st Judicial District Court *Felony, Misdemeanor, Civil, Eviction, Small Claims, Probate* PO Box 788, Boise City, OK 73933. 9AM-N,1-5PM. **580-544-2221.** ☎✉✋

Cleveland County

21st Judicial District Court - Civil Branch *Civil, Eviction, Small Claims, Probate* 200 S Peters, Norman, OK 73069. 8AM-5PM. **405-321-6402.** Access civil records-✉💻✋

21st Judicial District Court - Criminal *Felony, Misdemeanor* 200 S Peters, Norman, OK 73069. 8AM-5PM. **405-321-6402.** ✉💻✋

Coal County

25th Judicial District Court *Felony, Misd., Civil, Eviction, Small Claims, Probate* 4 N Main St, Coalgate, OK 74538. 8AM-4PM. **580-927-2281.** ✋✉

Comanche County

5th Judicial District Court *Felony, Misdemeanor, Civil, Eviction, Small Claims, Probate* 315 SW 5th St, Rm 504, Lawton, OK 73501-4390. 8AM-5PM. **580-355-4017.** Traffic and marriage licenses also handled here. ✉💻✋

Cotton County

5th Judicial District Court *Felony, Misdemeanor, Civil, Eviction, Small Claims, Probate* 301 N Broadway, Walters, OK 73572. 8AM-4PM. **580-875-3029.** ✉✋💻

Craig County

12th Judicial District Court *Felony, Misdemeanor, Civil, Eviction, Small Claims, Probate* 301 W Canadian, Vinita, OK 74301. 8:30AM-4:30PM. **918-256-6451.** ✉✋💻

Creek County

All three courts should be searched. There is not overall countywide database.

24th Judicial District Court *Felony, Misdemeanor, Civil, Eviction, Small Claims, Probate* 222 E Dewey Ave, #201, Sapulpa, OK 74066. 8AM-5PM. **918-227-2525**, Fax: 918-227-5030. ✋💻

24th Judicial District Court *Felony, Misdemeanor, Civil, Eviction, Small Claims, Probate* PO Box 1055, Bristow, OK 74010. 8AM-5PM. **918-367-5537**, Fax: 918-367-5505. ✋✉💻

24th Judicial District Court *Felony, Misdemeanor, Civil, Eviction, Small Claims, Probate* 222 E Dewey Ave, #201, Drumright, OK 74030. 8AM-5PM. **918-352-2575.** ✋

Custer County

2nd Judicial District Court *Felony, Misdemeanor, Civil, Eviction, Small*

Claims, Probate PO Box D (3rd & B St), Arapaho, OK 73620. 8AM-4PM. **580-323-3233**, Fax: 580-331-1121. ✉✋💻

Delaware County

13th Judicial District Court *Felony, Misdemeanor, Civil, Eviction, Small Claims, Probate* Box 407 (Whitehead & Krause St), Jay, OK 74346. 8AM-4:30PM. **918-253-4420.** ✉✋💻

Dewey County

4th Judicial District Court *Felony, Misd., Civil, Small Claims, Probate* Box 278 (Broadway & Ruble), Taloga, OK 73667. 8AM-4PM. **580-328-5521.** ✉✋

Ellis County

2nd Judicial District Court *Felony, Misd., Civil, Eviction, Small Claims, Probate* Box 217 ((100 S Washington St), Arnett, OK 73832. 8:30AM-4:30PM. **580-885-7255.** ☎✉✋💻

Garfield County

4th Judicial District Court *Felony, Misdemeanor, Civil, Eviction, Small Claims, Probate* 114 W Broadway, Enid, OK 73701-4024. 8AM-4:30PM. **580-237-0232.** 💻✋

Garvin County

21st Judicial District Court *Felony, Misd., Civil, Eviction, Small Claims, Probate* PO Box 239 (201 W Grant), Pauls Valley, OK 73075. 8:30AM-4:30PM. **405-238-5596.** ✉✋💻

Grady County

6th Judicial District Court *Felony, Misdemeanor, Civil, Eviction, Small Claims, Probate* PO Box 605 (4th & Choctaw Ave), Chickasha, OK 73023. 8AM-4:30PM. **405-224-7446.** ✋

Grant County

4th Judicial District Court *Felony, Misdemeanor, Civil, Eviction, Small Claims, Probate* 112 E Guthrie, Medford, OK 73759. 8AM-4:30PM. **580-395-2828.** ✉✋💻

Greer County

2nd Judicial District Court *Felony, Misdemeanor, Civil, Eviction, Small Claims, Probate* PO Box 216 (Courthouse Sq), Mangum, OK 73554. 9AM-5PM. **580-782-3665.** ✉✋

Key: Symbols refer to criminal records access unless otherwise noted. phone-☎ mail-✉ fax-**Fax** in person-✋ online-💻 email-**Email**

Harmon County

3rd Judicial District Court *Felony, Misdemeanor, Civil, Eviction, Small Claims, Probate* 114 W Hollis, Hollis, OK 73550. 8AM-5PM. **580-688-3617**, Fax: 580-688-2900. ☒Fax☝

Harper County

1st Judicial District Court *Felony, Misdemeanor, Civil, Eviction, Small Claims, Probate* Box 347 (311 SE 1st St), Buffalo, OK 73834. 8AM-4PM. **580-735-2010**. ☒☝

Haskell County

16th Judicial District Court *Felony, Misdemeanor, Civil, Eviction, Small Claims, Probate* 202 E Main, Stigler, OK 74462. 8AM-4:30PM. **918-967-3323**, Fax: 918-967-2819. ☎Fax☒☝🖥

Hughes County

22nd Judicial District Court *Felony, Misdemeanor, Civil, Eviction, Small Claims, Probate* 200 N Broadway Box 32, Holdenville, OK 74848. 8AM-4:30PM. **405-379-3384**. ☒☝🖥

Jackson County

3rd Judicial District Court *Felony, Misdemeanor, Civil, Eviction, Small Claims, Probate* PO Box 616 (101 N Main, Rm 303) Jackson County Courthouse, Altus, OK 73522. 8AM-4PM. **580-482-0448**. ☒☝

Jefferson County

5th Judicial District Court *Felony, Misdemeanor, Civil, Eviction, Small Claims, Probate* 220 N Main, Rm 302, Waurika, OK 73573. 8AM-4PM. **580-228-2961**, Fax: 580-228-2185. ☒☝

Johnston County

20th Judicial District Court *Felony, Misdemeanor, Civil, Eviction, Small Claims, Probate* 403 W Main, #201, Tishomingo, OK 73460. 8:30AM-4:30PM. **580-371-3281**. ☒☝

Kay County

8th Judicial District Court *Felony, Misdemeanor, Civil, Eviction, Small Claims, Probate* www.courthouse.kay.ok.us/home.html Box 428, Newkirk, OK 74647. 8:00AM-4:30PM. **580-362-3350**. This courthouse holds the closed case files for the satelite courts in Ponca City (580-762-2148) and Blackwell (580-363-2080). ☎☒☝🖥

Kingfisher County

4th Judicial District Court *Felony, Misdemeanor, Civil, Eviction, Small Claims, Probate* Box 328 (101 S Main St), Kingfisher, OK 73750. 8:00AM-4:30PM. **405-375-3813**. ☒☝🖥

Kiowa County

3rd Judicial District Court *Felony, Misdemeanor, Civil, Eviction, Small Claims, Probate* Box 854 (316 S Main St), Hobart, OK 73651. 9AM-5PM. **580-726-5125**. ☎☒☝

Latimer County

16th Judicial District Court *Felony, Misdemeanor, Civil, Eviction, Small Claims, Probate* 109 N Central, Rm 200, Wilburton, OK 74578. 8AM-4:30PM. **918-465-2011**. ☒☝

Le Flore County

16th Judicial District Court *Felony, Misdemeanor, Civil, Eviction, Small Claims, Probate* PO Box 688 (110 Front St), Poteau, OK 74953. 8AM-4:30PM. **918-647-3181**. ☒☝

Lincoln County

23rd Judicial District Court *Felony, Misd., Civil, Eviction, Small Claims, Probate* PO Box 307 (811 Manvel Ave), Chandler, OK 74834. 8:30AM-4:30PM. **405-258-1309**. ☒☝🖥

Logan County

9th Judicial District Court *Felony, Misdemeanor, Civil, Eviction, Small Claims, Probate* 301 E Harrison, Rm 201, Guthrie, OK 73044. 8:30AM-4:30PM. **405-282-0123**. ☒☝🖥

Love County

20th Judicial District Court *Felony, Misdemeanor, Civil, Eviction, Small Claims, Probate* 405 W Main, Marietta, OK 73448. 8AM-4:30PM. **580-276-2235**. ☒☝

McClain County

21st Judicial District Court *Felony, Misdemeanor, Civil, Eviction, Small Claims, Probate* 121 N 2nd, Rm 231, Purcell, OK 73080. 8AM-4:30PM. **405-527-3221**. ☒☝🖥

McCurtain County

17th Judicial District Court *Felony, Misdemeanor, Civil, Eviction, Small Claims, Probate* Box 1378 (108 N Central Ave), Idabel, OK 74745. 8AM-4PM. **580-286-3693**, Fax: 580-286-7095. ☒☝🖥

McIntosh County

18th Judicial District Court *Felony, Misdemeanor, Civil, Eviction, Small Claims, Probate* Box 426 (110 N 1st St), Eufaula, OK 74432. 8AM-4PM. **918-689-2282**. ☒☝

Major County

4th Judicial District Court *Felony, Misdemeanor, Civil, Small Claims, Probate* 500 E Broadway, Fairview, OK 73737. 8:30AM-4:30PM. **580-227-4690**. ☎Fax☒☝

Marshall County

20th Judicial District Court *Felony, Misdemeanor, Civil, Eviction, Small Claims, Probate* Box 58, Madill, OK 73446. 8:30AM-5PM. **580-795-3278 X240**. ☒☝

Mayes County

12th Judicial District Court *Felony, Misd., Civil, Eviction, Small Claims, Probate* Box 867 (1st & Adair), Pryor, OK 74362. 9AM-5PM. Civil: 918-825-2185, crim: 918-825-0133. ☎☒☝🖥

Murray County

20th Judicial District Court *Felony, Misd., Civil, Eviction, Small Claims, Probate* Box 578 (10th & Wyandotte St), Sulphur, OK 73086. 8AM-4:30PM, closed for lunch. **580-622-3223**. ☒☝

Muskogee County

15th Judicial District Court *Felony, Misdemeanor, Civil, Eviction, Small Claims, Probate* Box 1350 (200 State St), Muskogee, OK 74402. 8AM-4:30PM. **918-682-7873**. Access records-☒☝🖥

Noble County

8th Judicial District Court *Felony, Misdemeanor, Civil, Eviction, Small Claims, Probate* 300 Courthouse Dr, Box 14, Perry, OK 73077. 8AM-4:30PM. **580-336-5187**. ☒☝🖥

Nowata County

11th Judicial District Court *Felony, Misdemeanor, Civil, Eviction, Small Claims, Probate* 229 N Maple, Nowata, OK 74048. 8AM-4:30PM. **918-273-0127**. ☒☝

Okfuskee County

24th Judicial District Court *Felony, Misdemeanor, Civil, Eviction, Small Claims, Probate* Box 30 (3rd & Atlanta St), Okemah, OK 74859. 8:30AM-4:30PM. **918-623-0525**, Fax: 918-623-2687. ✉ ✋

Oklahoma County

District Court *Felony, Misdemeanor, Civil, Eviction, Small Claims, Probate* 320 Robert S Kerr St, Rm 409, Oklahoma City, OK 73102. 8AM-5PM. **405-713-1705**, Civil: 405-713-1725, crim: 405-713-1713, Probate: 405-713-1725. Small claims: 405-713-1738. ✉ 💻 ✋

Okmulgee County

You must search both courts in this county, records are not co-mingled.

24th Judicial District Court - Henryetta Branch *Felony, Misdemeanor, Civil, Eviction, Small Claims, Probate* 115 S 4th, Henryetta, OK 74437. 8:30AM-4:30PM. **918-652-7142**, Fax: 918-650-0287. ☎(Limited) ✉ ✋

24th Judicial District Court - Okmulgee Branch *Felony, Misdemeanor, Civil, Eviction, Small Claims, Probate* 314 W 7th, Okmulgee, OK 74447. 8AM-4:30PM. **918-756-3042**. Access records-☎ ✉ ✋

Osage County

10th Judicial District Court *Felony, Misd., Civil, Eviction, Small Claims, Probate, Divorce* County Courthouse 600 Grandview, Pawhuska, OK 74056. 9AM-5PM. **918-287-4104**. ✉ ✋ 💻

Ottawa County

13th Judicial District Court *Felony, Misdemeanor, Civil, Eviction, Small Claims, Probate* 102 E Central Ave, #300, Miami, OK 74354. 9:00AM-5:00PM. **918-542-2801**. ✉ ✋ 💻

Pawnee County

14th Judicial District Court *Felony, Misdemeanor, Civil, Eviction, Small Claims, Probate* Courthouse, 500 Harrison St, Pawnee, OK 74058. 8AM-4:30PM. **918-762-2547**. ✉ ✋ 💻

Payne County

9th Judicial District Court *Felony, Misdemeanor, Civil, Eviction, Small Claims, Probate* 606 S Husband, Rm 308, Stillwater, OK 74074. 8AM-5PM. **405-372-4774**. ✉ 💻 ✋

Pittsburg County

18th Judicial District Court *Felony, Misdemeanor, Civil, Eviction, Small Claims, Probate* Box 460 (115 E Carl Albert Pky), McAlester, OK 74502. 8AM-5PM. **918-423-4859**. ✉ ✋

Pontotoc County

22nd Judicial District Court *Felony, Misdemeanor, Civil, Eviction, Small Claims, Probate* Box 427 (120 W 13th), Ada, OK 74820. 8AM-N; 1-5PM. **580-332-5763**. ✉ ✋

Pottawatomie County

23rd Judicial District Court *Felony, Misdemeanor, Civil, Eviction, Small Claims, Probate* 325 N Broadway, Shawnee, OK 74801. 8:30AM-N, 1-5 PM. **405-273-3624**. Access records-✉ ✋ 💻

Pushmataha County

17th Judicial District Court *Felony, Misdemeanor, Civil, Eviction, Small Claims, Probate* Pushmataha County Courthouse 302 SW B, Antlers, OK 74523. 8AM-4:30PM. **580-298-2274**. ✉ ✋ 💻

Roger Mills County

2nd Judicial District Court *Felony, Misdemeanor, Civil, Eviction, Small Claims, Probate* Box 409 (LL Males Blvd & Broadway), Cheyenne, OK 73628. 8AM-4:30PM. **580-497-3361**. ☎ ✉ Fax ✋ 💻

Rogers County

12th Judicial District Court *Felony, Misdemeanor, Civil, Eviction, Small Claims, Probate* Box 839 (219 S Missouri), Claremore, OK 74018. 8AM-4:30PM. **918-341-5711**. ☎ ✉ 💻 ✋

Seminole County

22nd Judicial District Court - Wewoka Branch *Felony, Misd., Civil, Eviction, Small Claims, Probate* Box 130 (120 S Wewoka Ave), Wewoka, OK 74884. 8AM-4PM. **405-257-6236**. ✉ ✋ 💻

22nd Judicial District Court - Seminole Branch *Civil, Small Claims, Probate* Box 1320, (401 Main St), Seminole, OK 74868. 8AM-N, 1-4PM. **405-382-3424**. Criminal records are now maintained at Seminole County Court Clerk, PO Box 130, Wewoka, OK, 405-257-6236. Access civil records-☎ ✉ ✋

Sequoyah County

15th Judicial District Court *Felony, Misdemeanor, Civil, Eviction, Small Claims, Probate* 120 E Chickasaw, Sallisaw, OK 74955. 8AM-4PM. **918-775-4411**. ☎ ✉ ✋

Stephens County

5th Judicial District Court *Felony, Misdemeanor, Civil, Eviction, Small Claims, Probate* 101 S 11th St, Rm 301, Duncan, OK 73533. 8:30AM-4:30PM. **580-470-2000**. ✉ ✋

Texas County

1st Judicial District Court *Felony, Misdemeanor, Civil, Eviction, Small Claims, Probate* Box 1081 (319 N Main St), Guymon, OK 73942. 9AM-5PM. **580-338-3003**. ✉ ✋ 💻

Tillman County

3rd Judicial District Court *Felony, Misdemeanor, Civil, Eviction, Small Claims, Probate* Box 116 (Main & Gladstone), Frederick, OK 73542. 8AM-4PM. **580-335-3023**. ✉ ✋

Tulsa County

14th Judicial District Court *Felony, Misdemeanor, Civil, Eviction, Small Claims, Probate* 500 S Denver Ave, Tulsa, OK 74103-3832. 8:30AM-5PM. **918-596-5000**. Access records-✉ 💻 ✋

Wagoner County

15th Judicial District Court *Felony, Misd., Civil, Eviction, Small Claims, Probate* Box 249 (302 E Cherokee St), Wagoner, OK 74477. 8:00AM-4:30PM. **918-485-4508**. ✉ ✋ 💻

Washington County

11th Judicial District Court *Felony, Misd., Civil, Eviction, Small Claims, Probate* 420 S Johnstone, Rm 212, Bartlesville, OK 74003. 8AM-5PM. **918-337-2880**, Fax: 918-337-2898. Criminal phone: 918-337-2870. Fax ✉ ✋

Washita County

2nd Judicial District Court *Felony, Misdemeanor, Civil, Small Claims, Probate* Box 397 (111 E Main St), Cordell, OK 73632. 8AM-4PM. **580-832-3836**. ✉ ✋ 💻

Key: Symbols refer to criminal records access unless otherwise noted. phone-☎ mail-✉ fax-**Fax** in person-✋ online-💻 email-**Email**

Woods County

4th Judicial District Court *Felony, Misdemeanor, Civil, Eviction, Small Claims, Probate* Box 924 (407 Government St), Alva, OK 73717. 9AM-5PM. **580-327-3119**. ✉️✋

Woodward County

4th Judicial District Court *Felony, Misdemeanor, Civil, Eviction, Small Claims, Probate* 1600 Main St, Woodward, OK 73801. 9AM-5PM. **580-256-3413**. ✉️✋

Oregon

State Court Administration (All Circuit Courts): Court Administrator, Supreme Court Building, 1163 State St, Salem, OR, 97301-2563; 503-986-5500, Fax: 503-986-5503. www.ojd.state.or.us

Court Structure: Effective January 15, 1998, the District and Circuit Courts were combined into "Circuit Courts." At the same time, three new judicial districts were created by splitting existing ones.

Probate Courts: Probate is handled by the Circuit Court except in 6 counties (Gilliam, Grant, Harney, Malheur, Sherman, and Wheeler) where Probate in handled by County Courts.

Online Access: Online computer access is available through the Oregon Judicial Information Network (OJIN). OJIN Online includes almost all cases filed in the Oregon state courts. Generally, the OJIN database contains criminal, civil, small claims, probate, and some but not all juvenile records. However, it does not contain any records from municipal nor county courts. There is a one-time setup fee of $295.00, plus a monthly usage charge (minimum $10.00) based on transaction type, type of job, shift, and number of units/pages (which averages $10-13 per hour). For further information and/or a registration packet, write to: Oregon Judicial System, Information Systems Division, ATTN: Technical Support, 1163 State Street, Salem OR 97310, or call 800-858-9658, or visit www.ojd.state.or.us/ojin.

Additional Information: Many Oregon courts indicated that in person searches would markedly improve request turnaround time as court offices are understaffed or spread very thin. Most Circuit Courts that have records on computer do have a public access terminal that will speed up in-person or retriever searches. Most records offices close from Noon to 1PM Oregon time for lunch. No staff is available during that period.

Baker County

Circuit Court *Felony, Misdemeanor, Civil, Probate* www.ojd.state.or.us/baker 1995 3rd St, #220, Baker City, OR 97814. 8AM-N, 1-5PM. **541-523-6305**, Fax: 541-523-9738. ☎️**Fax**✉️✋

Benton County

Circuit Court *Felony, Misdemeanor, Civil, Eviction, Small Claims, Probate* www.ojd.state.or.us/benton Box 1870 (120 NW 4th St), Corvallis, OR 97339. 8AM-N, 1-5PM. **541-766-6828**, Fax: 541-766-6028. ☎️✉️💻✋

Clackamas County

Circuit Court *Felony, Misdemeanor, Civil, Eviction, Small Claims, Probate* 807 Main St, Oregon City, OR 97045. 10AM-5PM. **503-655-8447**, crim: 503-655-8643. Records management: 503-650-3036. Access records-✉️💻✋

Clatsop County

Circuit Court *Felony, Misdemeanor, Civil, Eviction, Small Claims, Probate* www.ojd.state.or.us/clt/index.html Box 835, Astoria, OR 97103. 8AM-N, 1-5PM. **503-325-8583**, Fax: 503-325-9300. Civil phone: 503-325-8555. ☎️✉️💻✋

Columbia County

Circuit Court *Felony, Misdemeanor, Civil, Eviction, Small Claims, Probate* Columbia County Courthouse 230 Strand St, St. Helens, OR 97051. 8AM-5PM. **503-397-2327**, Fax: 503-397-3226. ✉️**Fax**💻✋

Coos County

Circuit Court *Felony, Misdemeanor, Civil, Eviction, Small Claims, Probate* http://cooscurrycourts.org Courthouse, Coquille, OR 97423. 8AM-N,1-5PM. **541-396-3121**, Fax: 541-396-3456. Civil phone: X401, crim: X402. Eviction, Small Claims and Probate records are available at 541-756-2020 ext 556. Circuit Court Annex at 1975 McPherson, North Bend, OR 97459. ☎️✉️💻✋

Crook County

Circuit Court *Felony, Misdemeanor, Civil, Eviction, Small Claims, Probate* Crook County Courthouse 300 NE 3rd St, Prineville, OR 97754. 8AM-5PM. **541-447-6541**. ☎️✉️✋💻

Curry County

Circuit Court *Felony, Misdemeanor, Civil, Eviction, Small Claims, Probate* www.cooscurrycourts.org Box 810, Gold Beach, OR 97444. 8-12 MTWF; 8-12 &1:30-5 Th. **541-247-4511**. ☎️✉️💻✋

Deschutes County

Deschutes County Courts *Felony, Misd., Civil, Eviction, Small Claims, Probate* www.deschutescircuitcourt.org 1100 NW Bond, Bend, OR 97701. 8AM-5PM. **541-388-5300**, Civil phone: X209, crim: X210, Probate: X208. ☎️✉️💻✋

Douglas County

Circuit Court *Felony, Misdemeanor, Civil, Eviction, Small Claims, Probate* www.ojd.state.or.us/douglas 1036 SE

Douglas, Roseburg, OR 97470. 8AM-N, 1-5PM. **541-957-2471**, Fax: 541-957-2462. ☎✉🖥✋

Gilliam County

Circuit Court *Felony, Misd., Civil* http://seventhdistrict.ojd.state.or.us/ Box 622, Condon, OR 97823. 1-5. **541-384-3572**, Fax 541-384-2166. ☎✉🖥✋

County Court *Probate* 221 S Oregon PO Box 427, Condon, OR 97823. 8:30AM-N, 1-5PM **541-384-2311**, Fax 541-384-2166

Grant County

Circuit Court *Felony, Misdemeanor, Civil* www.ojd.state.or.us/grant Box 159 (205 S Humbolt St), Canyon City, OR 97820. 8AM-N, 1-5PM. **541-575-1438**, Fax: 541-575-2165. ✉🖥✋

County Court *Probate* 201 Humbolt St, #290, Canyon City, OR 97820-6186. 8-5. **541-575-1675**, Fax: 541-575-2248.

Harney County

Circuit Court *Felony, Misdemeanor, Civil* www.ojd.state.or.us/harney 450 N Buena Vista, Burns, OR 97720. 8AM-12PM; 1PM-5PM. **541-573-5207**, Fax: 541-573-5715. ☎Fax✉🖥✋

County Court *Probate* 450 N Buena Vista Ave, Burns, OR 97720-1518. 8:30AM-N, 1-5PM. **541-573-6641**, Fax: 541-573-8370.

Hood River County

Circuit Court *Felony, Misdemeanor, Civil, Eviction, Small Claims, Probate* http://seventhdistrict.ojd.state.or.us/ 309 State St, Hood River, OR 97031. 8AM-N, 1-5PM. **541-386-1862**, Fax: 541-386-3465. ☎Fax✉🖥✋

Jackson County

Circuit Court *Felony, Misdemeanor, Civil Actions, Eviction, Small Claims, Probate* http://jackson-court.ojd.state.or.us/ 100 S Oakdale, Medford, OR 97501. 8:30AM-5PM. **541-776-7171**, Fax: 541-776-7057. ✉🖥✋

Jefferson County

Circuit Court *Felony, Misdemeanor, Civil, Eviction, Small Claims, Probate* 75 SE C St, #G, Madras, OR 97741-1750. 8AM-5PM. **541-475-3317**, Fax: 541-475-3421. ✉🖥✋

Josephine County

Circuit Court *Felony, Misdemeanor, Civil, Eviction, Small Claims, Probate* Josephine County Courthouse, Rm 254 500 NW 6th St, Grants Pass, OR 97526. 8AM-4PM. **541-476-2309**, Fax: 541-471-2079. Fax✉🖥✋

Klamath County

Circuit Court *Felony, Misdemeanor, Civil, Eviction, Small Claims, Probate* http://klamath-court.ojd.state.or.us 316 Main St, Klamath Falls, OR 97601. 8AM-5PM. **541-883-5503**, Fax: 541-882-6109. Civil phone: x222, crim: x232. ✉Fax🖥✋

Lake County

Circuit Court *Felony, Misdemeanor, Civil, Eviction, Small Claims, Probate* 513 Center St, Lakeview, OR 97630. 8AM-N, 1-5PM. **541-947-6051**, Fax: 541-947-3724. ✉🖥✋

Lane County

Circuit Court *Felony, Misdemeanor, Civil, Eviction, Small Claims, Probate* 125 E 8th Ave, Eugene, OR 97401. 8AM-5PM. **541-682-4020**. 🖥✋

Lincoln County

Lincoln County Courts *Felony, Misd., Civil, Eviction, Small Claims, Probate* www.ojd.state.or.us/lincoln PO Box 100, Newport, OR 97365. 8AM-N, 1-5PM. **541-265-4236**, Fax: 541-265-7561. ✉🖥✋

Linn County

Circuit Court *Felony, Misdemeanor, Civil, Eviction, Small Claims, Probate* www.ojd.state.or.us/linn-circuit PO Box 1749, Albany, OR 97321. 8AM-5PM. Civil phone: 541-967-3845, crim: 541-967-3841. ✉🖥✋

Malheur County

Circuit Court *Felony, Misdemeanor, Civil, Eviction, Small Claims* www.ojd.state.or.us/malheur 251 B St W, Vale, OR 97918. 8AM-5PM. **541-473-5171**, Fax: 541-473-2213. ✉🖥✋

County Court *Probate* 251 B St West #4, Vale, OR 97918. 8:30AM-N, 1-5:00PM. **541-473-5123**, Fax: 541-473-5523. Civil phone: 541-473-5151.

Marion County

Circuit Court *Felony, Misdemeanor, Civil, Eviction, Small Claims, Probate* http://marion-court.ojd.state.or.us PO Box 12869 (100 High St NE), Salem, OR 97309. 8AM-5PM. **503-588-5101**, Fax: 503-373-4360. Access records-✉🖥✋

Morrow County

Circuit Court *Felony, Misdemeanor, Civil, Eviction, Small Claims, Probate* www.ojd.state.or.us/morrow PO Box 609, Heppner, OR 97836. 8AM-N, 1-5PM. **541-676-5264**, Fax: 541-676-9902. ☎Fax✉🖥✋

Multnomah County

Circuit Court *Felony, Misdemeanor, Civil Actions Over $10,000, Probate* 1021 SW 4th Ave, Rm 131, Portland, OR 97204. 8AM-4:30PM (Tele: 8:30-11AM; 1-3:30PM). **503-988-3003**. ✉🖥✋

Circuit Court - Civil Division *Civil Actions, Eviction, Small Claims* www.ojd.state.or.us/multnomah 1021 SW 4th Ave, Rm 210, Portland, OR 97204. 8:30AM-5PM (Tele: 8:30-5). **503-988-3022**. Access civil records-☎✉🖥✋

Polk County

Circuit Court *Felony, Misdemeanor, Civil, Eviction, Small Claims, Probate* www.ojd.state.or.us/plk/index.htm Polk County Courthouse, Rm 301 850 Main St, Dallas, OR 97338. 8AM-5PM. **503-623-3154**, Civil: 503-623-3154, crim: 503-831-1778. Fax criminal: 503-831-1779; civil fax: 503-623-6614. ☎Fax✉🖥✋

Sherman County

Circuit Court *Felony, Misdemeanor, Civil* PO Box 402, Moro, OR 97039. 1-5PM. **541-565-3650**. ☎✉🖥✋

County Court *Probate* PO Box 365, Moro, OR 97039. 8AM-5PM. **541-565-3606**, Fax: 541-565-3312.

Tillamook County

Circuit Court *Felony, Misdemeanor, Civil, Eviction, Small Claims, Probate* 201 Laurel Ave, Tillamook, OR 97141. 8AM-N; 1PM-5PM. **503-842-8014**, Fax: 503-842-2597. ✉Fax🖥✋

Umatilla County

Circuit Court *Felony, Misdemeanor, Civil, Eviction, Small Claims, Probate* www.ojd.state.or.us/umatilla PO Box 1307,

Pendleton, OR 97801. 8AM-N; 1PM-5PM. **541-278-0341**, Fax: 541-276-9030. ☒🖳✋

Union County

Circuit Court *Felony, Misdemeanor, Civil, Eviction, Small Claims, Probate* www.ojd.state.or.us/union 1008 K Ave, La Grande, OR 97850. 8AM-N, 1-5PM. **541-962-9500**, Fax: 541-963-0444. ☒🖳✋

Wallowa County

Circuit Court *Felony, Misdemeanor, Civil, Eviction, Small Claims, Probate* www.ojd.state.or.us/wallowa 101 S River St, Rm 204, Enterprise, OR 97828. 8AM-N; 1PM-5PM. **541-426-4991**, Fax: 541-426-4992. ☎☒🖳✋

Wasco County

Circuit Court *Felony, Misdemeanor, Civil, Eviction, Small Claims, Probate* http://seventhdistrict.ojd.state.or.us/html/wasco.html PO Box 1400, The Dalles, OR 97058-1400. 8AM-N,1-5PM. **541-296-3154**, Fax: 541-506-2711. Civil phone: 541-506-2704, crim: 541-506-2708, Probate: 541-506-2704. ☎Fax☒🖳✋

Washington County

Circuit Court *Felony, Misdemeanor, Civil, Eviction, Small Claims, Probate* 150 N 1st, Hillsboro, OR 97124. 8-11:30AM, 12:30-3PM. **503-846-8888 x2302 (civ) x6060 (crim)**, Fax: 503-846-6087. ☎☒🖳✋

Wheeler County

Circuit Court *Felony, Misdemeanor, Civil* http://seventhdistrict.ojd.state.or.us/ PO Box 308, Fossil, OR 97830. 8:30AM-11:30AM. **541-763-2541**, Fax: 541-763-2026. ☎☒🖳✋

County Court *Probate* PO Box 327 (701 Adams, Rm 204), Fossil, OR 97830. 8:30AM-4PM. **541-763-2400**, Fax: 541-763-2026. Probate index available remotely online on the statewide OJIN system, 800-858-9658 for info.

Yamhill County

Circuit Court *Felony, Misdemeanor, Civil, Eviction, Small Claims, Probate* http://yamhill-court.ojd.state.or.us/ 535 NE 5th, McMinnville, OR 97128. 9AM-N, 1-5PM. **503-434-7530**, Fax: 503-472-5805. ☒🖳✋

Pennsylvania

State Court Administration: Administrative Office of Pennsylvania Courts, PO Box 719, Mechanicsburg, PA, 17055; 717-795-2000, Fax: 717-795-2050. www.courts.state.pa.us

Court Structure: The Courts of Common Pleas are the general trial courts, with jurisdiction over both civil and criminal matters and appellate jurisdiction over matters disposed of by the special courts. The civil records clerk of the Court of Common Pleas is called the Prothonotary.

Small claims cases are, usually, handled by the District Justice Courts. These courts, which are designated as "special courts," also handle civil cases up to $8,000. However, all small claims and civil actions are recorded through the Prothonotary Section (civil) of the Court of Common Pleas, which then holds the records. It is not necessary to check with each District Court, but rather to check with the Prothonotary for the county.

Probate Courts: Probate is handled by the Register of Wills.

Online Access: The state's 556 District Justice Courts are served by a statewide, automated case management system; online access to the case management system is not available.

Common Pleas criminal docket information if available from 20 counties by name or docket number for free at http://ujsportal.pacourts.us. Click on "E-Services." Name search under "Other Criteria." This site also provides access to appellate case information. Also, search Appellate Court dockets at http://pacmsdocketsheet.aopc.org.

The Infocon County Access System provides direct dial-up access to court record information for 16 counties - Armstrong, Bedford, Blair, Butler, Clarion, Clinton, Erie, Franklin, Huntingdon, Juaniata, Lawrence, Mercer, Mifflin, Pike, Potter and Susquehanna. Set up entails a $50.00 base set-up fee plus $25.00 per county. The monthly usage fee minimum is $25.00, plus time charges. For Information, call Infocon at 814-472-6066.

Additional Information: Fees vary widely among jurisdictions. Many courts will not conduct searches due to a lack of personnel or, if they do search, turnaround time may be excessively lengthy. Many courts have public access terminals for in-person searches.

Adams County

Court of Common Pleas - Civil *Civil, Eviction* 111-117 Baltimore St, Gettysburg, PA 17325. 8AM-4:30PM. **717-334-6781 X285**, Fax: 717-334-0532. Access civil records-✋

Court of Common Pleas - Criminal *Felony, Misdemeanor* 111-117 Baltimore

St, Gettysburg, PA 17325. 8AM-4:30PM. **717-337-9806**; Fax:717-334-9333. ☒✋

Register of Wills *Probate* 111-117 Baltimore St Rm 102, Gettysburg, PA 17325. 8AM-4:30PM. **717-337-9826**, Fax: 717-334-1758.

Allegheny County

Court of Common Pleas - Civil *Civil* www.county.allegheny.pa.us City County Bldg, 414 Grant St 1st Fl, Pittsburgh, PA 15219. 8:30AM-4:30PM. **412-350-4200**. Access civil records-☒✋🖳

Court of Common Pleas - Criminal *Felony, Misdemeanor* www.county.alle

Key: Symbols refer to criminal records access unless otherwise noted. phone-☎ mail-☒ fax-**Fax** in person-✋ online-🖳 email-**Email**

gheny.pa.us/cofc/index.asp 220 Courthouse 436 Grant St, Pittsburgh, PA 15219. 8:30AM-4:30PM. **412-350-5322**, Fax: 412-350-6154. Pittsburgh Magistrate Court phone: 412-255-2700. ✉🖐️🖥️

Register of Wills *Probate* www.county.allegheny.pa.us/regwills/index.asp 414 Grant St, City County Bldg, PIttsburgh, PA 15219. 8:30AM-4:30PM. **412-350-4183**, Fax: 412-350-3028.

Armstrong County

Court of Common Pleas - Civil *Civil, Eviction* www.geocities.com/acprothonotary 500 E Market St, Kittanning, PA 16201. 8-4:30PM. **724-548-3251**, Fax: 724-548-3236. Access civil records-🖥️🖐️

Court of Common Pleas - Criminal *Felony, Misdemeanor* www.geocities.com/acprothonotary 500 Market St, Kittanning, PA 16201. 8AM-4:30PM. **724-548-3252**. Access records-✉🖥️🖐️

Register of Wills *Probate* 500 Market St Armstrong County Courthouse, Kittanning, PA 16201. 8AM-4:30PM. **724-548-3256 X220**, Fax: 724-548-3236. Access by subscription at www.ic-access.com, 814-472-6066.

Beaver County

Court of Common Pleas - Civil *Civil, Eviction* www.co.beaver.pa.us/prothonotary/ Beaver County Courthouse, 810 3rd St, Beaver, PA 15009. 8:30AM-4:30PM. **724-728-5700**. Access civil records-🖐️✉

Court of Common Pleas - Criminal *Felony, Misdm'r* www.co.beaver.pa.us/ Beaver County Courthouse 810 3rd St, Beaver, PA 15009. 8:30AM-4:30PM. **724-728-5700**, Fax: 724-728-8853. Fax✉🖐️🖥️

Register of Wills *Probate* Beaver County Courthouse 810 3rd St, Beaver, PA 15009. 8:30AM-4:30PM. **724-728-5700 X11265, X11274**, Fax: 724-728-9810.

Bedford County

Court of Common Pleas - Criminal/Civil *Felony, Misdemeanor, Civil, Eviction* Bedford County Courthouse, Bedford, PA 15522. 8:30AM-4:30PM. **814-623-4833**, Fax: 814-623-4831. Access records-✉🖥️🖐️

Register of Wills *Probate* 200 S Juliana St, Bedford, PA 15522. 8:30AM-4:30PM. **814-623-4836**, Fax: 814-624-0488.

Access by subscription at www.ic-access.com, 814-472-6066.

Berks County

Court of Common Pleas - Civil *Civil, Eviction* 2nd Fl, 633 Court St, Reading, PA 19601. 8AM-4PM. **610-478-6970**, Fax: 610-478-6969. Access civil records-✉🖐️🖥️

Court of Common Pleas - Criminal *Felony, Misdemeanor* 4th Fl, 633 Court St, Reading, PA 19601. 8AM-5PM. **610-478-6550**, Fax: 610-478-6593. ✉🖐️

Register of Wills *Probate* www.berksregofwills.com 633 Court St, 2nd Fl, Reading, PA 19601. 8AM-5PM. **610-478-6600**, Fax: 610-478-6251. Search free at website; includes records for both the county and the City of Reading.

Blair County

Court of Common Pleas - Criminal/Civil *Felony, Misd., Civil, Eviction* 423 Allegheny St, #144, Hollidaysburg, PA 16648. 8AM-4PM. **814-693-3080**, crim: 814-693-3084. ✉🖥️🖐️

Register of Wills *Probate* 423 Allegheny, #145, Hollidaysburg, PA 16648-2022. 8AM-4PM. **814-693-3095**, Fax: 814-693-3093. Access by subscription at www.ic-access.com, 814-472-6066.

Bradford County

Court of Common Pleas - Criminal/Civil *Felony, Misdemeanor, Civil, Eviction* Courthouse, 301 Main St, Towanda, PA 18848. 9AM-5PM. **570-265-1705**, Fax: 570-265-1735. ✉🖐️

Register of Wills *Probate* 301 Main St., Towanda, PA 18848. 9AM-5PM. **570-265-1702**, Fax: 570-265-1721.

Bucks County

Court of Common Pleas - Civil *Civil, Eviction* www.buckscounty.org/courts/ 55 E Court St, Doylestown, PA 18901. 8:15AM-4:15PM. **215-348-6191**. Access civil records-🖥️🖐️

Court of Common Pleas - Crim. *Felony, Misd* www.buckscounty.org/courts/ Bucks County Courthouse, 55 E Court St, Doylestown, PA 18901. 8AM-4:30PM. **215-348-6389**, Fax: 215-348-6740. ✉🖥️🖐️

Register of Wills *Probate* www.buckscounty.org Bucks County

Courthouse 55 E Court St., Doylestown, PA 18901. 8AM-4:30PM. **215-348-6265**, Fax: 215-348-6156. For a limited time, access is free at www.buckscounty.org/departments/public_access.

Butler County

Court of Common Pleas - Civil *Civil, Eviction* Butler County Courthouse, PO Box 1208, Butler, PA 16001-1208. 8:30AM-4:30PM. **724-284-5214**. Access civil records-☎✉🖥️🖐️

Court of Common Pleas - Crim. *Felony, Misd'r* www.co.butler.pa.us/CoC.htm PO Box 1208 Butler County Courthouse, 124 W Diamond St, Butler, PA 16003-1208. 8:30AM-4:30PM. **724-284-5233**, Fax: 724-284-5244. Civil phone: 724-284-5214. ✉🖥️🖐️

Register of Wills *Probate* Butler County Courthouse, PO Box 1208, Butler, PA 16003-1208. 8:30AM-4:30PM. **724-284-5348**, Fax: 724-284-5278. Access by subscription at www.ic-access.com, 814-472-6066.

Cambria County

Court of Common Pleas - Civil *Civil, Eviction* 200 S Center St, Ebensburg, PA 15931. 9AM-4PM. **814-472-1636**, Fax: 814-472-5632. Access civil -☎✉**Fax**🖐️

Court of Common Pleas - Criminal *Felony, Misdemeanor* Cambria County Courthouse, S Center St, Ebensburg, PA 15931. 9-4PM. **814-472-1540**. ✉🖐️🖥️

Register of Wills *Probate* www.co.cambria.pa.us 200 S Center St, Ebensburg, PA 15931. 9AM-4PM. **814-472-5440 X1440**, Fax: 814-472-0762 Probate: 814-472-1438.

Cameron County

Court of Common Pleas - Civil *Civil, Eviction* Cameron County Courthouse, 20 E 5th St, Emporium, PA 15834. 8:30AM-4PM. **814-486-9329**, Fax: 814-468-0464. Access civil records-☎**Fax**✉🖐️

Court of Common Pleas - Criminal *Felony, Misdemeanor* 20 E 5th St, Emporium, PA 15834. 8:30AM-4PM. **814-486-9330**, Fax: 814-486-0464. ☎**Fax**✉🖐️🖥️

Register of Wills *Probate* Cameron County Courthouse, E 5th St, Emporium, PA 15834. 8:30AM-4PM. **814-486-3355**, Fax: 814-486-0464.

Key: Symbols refer to criminal records access unless otherwise noted. phone-☎ mail-✉ fax-**Fax** in person-🖐️ online-🖥️ email-**Email**

Carbon County

Court of Common Pleas - Civil *Civil, Eviction* www.carboncourts.com/ PO Box 130, Courthouse, Jim Thorpe, PA 18229. 8:30AM-4:30PM. **570-325-2481**, Fax: 570-325-8047. Access civil records-🖐🖳

Court of Common Pleas - Crim. *Felony, Misd.* www.carboncourts.com County Courthouse, Jim Thorpe, PA 18229. 8:30AM-4PM. **570-325-3637**, Fax: 570-325-5705. ☎✉🖐🖳

Register of Wills *Probate* PO Box 286, Jim Thorpe, PA 18229. 8:30AM-4:30PM. **570-325-2261**, Fax: 570-325-5098. Docket information is free online at www.carboncourts.com/pubacc.htm. Registration required.

Centre County

Court of Common Pleas - Criminal/Civil *Felony, Misd., Civil, Eviction* www.co.centre.pa.us/courts.htm Centre County Courthouse, Bellefonte, PA 16823. 8:30AM-5PM. **814-355-6796**. ✉🖐

Register of Wills *Probate* www.co.centre.pa.us/courts.htm Willowbank Office Bldg 414 Holmes Ave, #2, Bellefonte, PA 16823. 8:30AM-5PM. **814-355-6724, 355-6760**, Fax: 814-355-8685.

Chester County

Court of Common Pleas - Civil *Civil, Eviction* www.chesco.org 2 N High St, #130, West Chester, PA 19380. 8:30AM-4:30PM. **610-344-6300**, crim: 610-344-6135. Access civil records-🖳🖐

Court of Common Pleas - Criminal *Felony, Misdemeanor* www.chesco.org 2 N High St, #160, West Chester, PA 19380. 8:30AM-4:30PM. **610-344-6135**. ✉🖳🖐

Register of Wills *Probate* 2 N High St, #109, West Chester, PA 19380-3073. 8:30AM-4:30PM. **610-344-6335**, Fax: 610-344-6218. Internet access to probate records requires a sign-up and payment. Sign-up/logon at http://epin.chesco.org.

Clarion County

Court of Common Pleas - Civil *Civil, Eviction* Clarion County Courthouse, 421 Main St, Clarion, PA 16214. 8:30AM-4:30PM. **814-226-1119**, Fax: 814-227-2501. Access civil recs-☎Fax✉🖳🖐

Court of Common Pleas - Criminal *Felony, Misdemeanor* Clarion County

Courthouse, Main St, Clarion, PA 16214. 8AM-4:30PM. **814-226-1119**, Fax: 814-227-2501. ☎Fax✉🖳🖐

Register of Wills *Probate* County Courthouse 421 Main St, Clarion, PA 16214. 8:30AM-4:30PM. **814-226-4000 X2500**, Fax: 814-226-1117. Access by subscription at www.ic-access.com, 814-472-6066.

Clearfield County

Court of Common Pleas - Criminal/Civil *Felony, Misdemeanor, Civil, Eviction* www.clearfieldco.org PO Box 549 (1 N 2nd St), Clearfield, PA 16830. 8:30AM-4PM. **814-765-2641**, Fax: 814-765-7659. Civil phone: ext. 5988, crim: ext. 5980. ✉🖐

Register of Wills & Clerk of Orphans Court *Probate* PO Box 361, Clearfield, PA 16830. 8:30AM-4PM. **814-765-2641 X1350/1**, Fax: 814-765-6089.

Clinton County

Court of Common Pleas - Criminal/Civil *Felony, Misd., Civil, Eviction* www.clintoncountypa.com/courts.htm 230 E Water St, Lock Haven, PA 17745. 8AM-5PM M, T, Th, F; 8AM-12:30PM Wed. **570-893-4007**. 🖳🖐

Register of Wills *Probate* www.clintoncountypa.com PO Box 943, Lock Haven, PA 17745. 8:30AM-5PM M,T,Th,F; 8AM-12:30PM Wed. **570-893-4010**, Fax: 570-893-4273. Access by subscription at www.ic-access.com, 814-472-6066.

Columbia County

Court of Common Pleas - Criminal/Civil *Felony, Misd., Civil, Eviction* http://columbiapa.org/county/courts/index.html PO Box 380, Bloomsburg, PA 17815. 8AM-4:30PM. **570-389-5614**. Opinons for civil and criminal cases are listed at the website. ✉🖐

Register of Wills *Probate* 35 W Main St PO Box 380, Bloomsburg, PA 17815. 8AM-4:30PM. **570-389-5635/32**, Fax: 570-389-5636.

Crawford County

Court of Common Pleas - Civil *Civil, Eviction* Crawford County Courthouse 903 Diamond Pk, Meadville, PA 16335. 8:30AM-4:30PM. **814-333-7324**, crim: 814-333-7442. Access civil records-✉🖐

Court of Common Pleas - Crim *Felony, Misdemeanor* http://co.crawford.pa.us/cler

k_of_courts/clerk_of_courts_home.htm Crawford County Courthouse 903 Diamond Pk, Meadville, PA 16335. 8:30AM-4:30PM. **814-333-7442**, Fax: 814-337-7349. Access records-✉🖐🖳

Register of Wills *Probate* 903 Diamond Pk, Meadville, PA 16335. 8:30AM-4:30PM. **814-373-2537, 814-333-7338**, Fax: 814-337-5296.

Cumberland County

Court of Common Pleas - Civil *Civil, Eviction* www.ccpa.net Cumberland County Courthouse, Rm 100 One Courthouse Square, Carlisle, PA 17013-3387. 8AM-4:30PM. **717-240-6195**, Fax: 717-240-6573. Access civil records-🖐

Court of Common Pleas - Criminal *Felony, Misdemeanor* www.ccpa.net Cumberland County Courthouse, East Wing 1 Courthouse Sq, Carlisle, PA 17013-3387. 8AM-4:30PM. **717-240-6250**, Fax: 717-240-6571. ✉🖐🖳

Register of Wills *Probate* County Courthouse, Rm 102 1 Courthouse Sq, Carlisle, PA 17013. 8AM-4:30PM. **717-240-6345**, Fax: 717-240-7797.

Dauphin County

Court of Common Pleas - Civil *Civil, Eviction* http://dsf.pacounties.org/dauphin/site/default.asp PO Box 945, Harrisburg, PA 17108. 8AM-4:30PM. **717-780-6520**. Access civil records-☎✉🖐

Court of Common Pleas - Crim. *Felony, Misdemeanor* http://dsf.pacounties.org/dauphin/site/default.asp Front & Market St, Harrisburg, PA 17101. 8:AM-4:30PM. **717-255-2692**. ✉🖐

Register of Wills *Probate* Front & Market Sts, Rm 103, Harrisburg, PA 17101. 8AM-4:30PM. **717-780-6500**, Fax: 717-780-6474.

Delaware County

Court of Common Pleas - Criminal/Civil *Felony, Misd., Civil, Eviction* www.co.delaware.pa.us 201 W Front St, Media, PA 19063. 8:30AM-4:30PM. **610-891-4370**, Fax: 610-891-7257. ✉🖐

Register of Wills *Probate* Delaware County Courthouse 201 W Front St, Media, PA 19063. 8:30AM-4:30PM. **610-891-4400**, Fax: 610-891-4812.

Elk County

Court of Common Pleas - Criminal/Civil *Felony, Misd., Civil,*

Eviction www.co.elk.pa.us/Courthouse.htm PO Box 237, Ridgway, PA 15853. 8:30AM-4PM. **814-776-5344**, Fax: 814-776-5303. ☎**Fax**✉✍🖳

Register of Wills *Probate* PO Box 314, Ridgway, PA 15853. 8:30AM-4PM. **814-776-5349**, Fax: 814-776-5382.

Erie County

Court of Common Pleas - Civil *Civil, Eviction* www.eriecounty.biz Erie County Courthouse, 140 W 6th St, Erie, PA 16501. 8:30AM-4:30PM. **814-451-6250**, crim: 814-451-6221. Access civil records-✉🖳✍

Court of Common Pleas - Crim. *Felony, Misdemeanor* www.eriecountygov.org/defa ult.aspx?id=courts County Courthouse, 140 W 6th St, Erie, PA 16501. 8:30AM-4:30PM. **814-451-6229**, Fax: 814-451-6420. ✉🖳✍

Register of Wills *Probate* Erie County Courthouse 140 W 6th St, Erie, PA 16501. 8:30AM-4:30PM. **814-451-6260**, Fax: 814-451-7010. Access by subscription at www.ic-access.com, 814-472-6066.

Fayette County

Court of Common Pleas - Civil *Civil, Eviction* 61 E Main St, Uniontown, PA 15401. 8-4:30PM. **724-430-1272**, Fax: 724-430-4555. Access civil records-✉✍

Court of Common Pleas - Criminal *Felony, Misdemeanor* 61 E Main St, Uniontown, PA 15401. 8AM-4:30PM. **724-430-1253**, Fax: 724-438-8410. **Fax**✉✍🖳

Register of Wills *Probate* 61 E Main St, Uniontown, PA 15401. 8AM-4:30PM. **724-430-1206**, Fax: 724-430-1275.

Forest County

Court of Common Pleas *Felony, Misdemeanor, Civil, Eviction, Probate* http://users.penn.com/~wrncourt/ 526 Elm St, #2 Forest County Courthouse, Tionesta, PA 16353. 9AM-4PM. **814-755-3526**, Fax: 814-755-8837. Computerized records includes the Register of Wills. ✉**Fax**✍🖳

Franklin County

Court of Common Pleas - Civil *Civil, Eviction* 157 Lincoln Way E, Chambersburg, PA 17201. 8:30AM-

4:30PM. **717-261-3858**, Fax: 717-264-6772. Access civil records-✍🖳

Court of Common Pleas - Criminal *Felony, Misdemeanor* 157 Lincoln Way E, Chambersburg, PA 17201. 8:30AM-4:30PM. **717-261-3805**, Fax: 717-261-3896. ✉✍

Register of Wills *Probate* 157 Lincoln Way E, Chambersburg, PA 17201. 8:30AM-4:30PM. **717-261-3872**, Fax: 717-263-5717. Access by subscription at www.ic-access.com, 814-472-6066.

Fulton County

Court of Common Pleas - Criminal/Civil *Felony, Misdemeanor, Civil, Eviction* Fulton County Courthouse 201 N 2nd St, McConnellsburg, PA 17233. 8:30AM-4:30PM. **717-485-4212**, Fax: 717-485-5568 Attn: Court of Common Pleas. ✉✍

Register of Wills *Probate* 201 N 2nd St, McConnellsburg, PA 17233. 8:30-4:30. **717-485-4212**, Fax: 717-485-5568.

Greene County

Court of Common Pleas - Civil *Civil, Eviction* Greene County Courthouse Rm 105, Waynesburg, PA 15370. 8:30AM-4:30PM. **724-852-5289**. Access civil records-✉✍

Court of Common Pleas - Criminal *Felony, Misdemeanor* Greene County Courthouse 10 E High St, Waynesburg, PA 15370. 8:30AM-4:30PM. **724-852-5281**, Fax: 724-852-5316. ✉✍free.

Register of Wills *Probate* Greene County Courthouse 10 E High St, Waynesburg, PA 15370. 8:30AM-4PM. **724-852-5283**.

Huntingdon County

Court of Common Pleas - Criminal/Civil *Felony, Misdemeanor, Civil, Eviction* PO Box 39, Courthouse, Huntingdon, PA 16652. 8:30AM-4:30PM. **814-643-1610**, Fax: 814-643-4172. ✍🖳

Register of Wills *Probate* Courthouse 223 Penn St, Huntingdon, PA 16652. 8:30AM-4:30PM. **814-643-2740**. Access by subscription at www.ic-access.com, 814-472-6066.

Indiana County

Court of Common Pleas - Criminal/Civil *Felony, Misd., Civil, Eviction* County Courthouse, 825 Philadelphia St,

Indiana, PA 15701. 8AM-4PM. **724-465-3855/3858**, Fax: 724-465-3968. ✉✍🖳

Register of Wills *Probate* County Courthouse, 825 Philadelphia St, Indiana, PA 15701. 8AM-4:30PM. **724-465-3860**, Fax: 724-465-3863.

Jefferson County

Court of Common Pleas - Criminal/Civil *Felony, Misdemeanor, Civil, Eviction* Courthouse, 200 Main St, Brookville, PA 15825. 8:30AM-4:30PM. **814-849-1606 X225**, Fax: 814-849-1625. ✉✍🖳

Register of Wills *Probate* Jefferson County Courthouse, 200 Main St, Brookville, PA 15825. 8:30AM-4:30PM. **814-849-1610**, Fax: 814-849-1677.

Juniata County

Court of Common Pleas - Criminal/Civil *Felony, Misd., Civil, Eviction* Juniata County Courthouse, Mifflintown, PA 17059. 8AM-4:30PM. **717-436-7715**, Fax: 717-436-7734. ☎✉✍

Register of Wills *Probate* Juniata County Courthouse PO Box 68, Mifflintown, PA 17059. 8AM-4:30PM, 8AM-12PM Wed (June-Sept). **717-436-7709**, Fax: 717-436-7756. Access by subscription at www.ic-access.com, 814-472-6066.

Lackawanna County

Court of Common Pleas - Civil *Civil, Eviction* Clerk of Judicial Records 200 N Washington Ave, Scranton, PA 18503-1551. 9AM-4PM. **570-963-6724**, Civil phone: 717-963-6723. Access civil records-✍

Court of Common Pleas - Criminal *Felony, Misdemeanor* Lackawanna County Courthouse, Scranton, PA 18503. 9AM-4PM. **570-963-6759**, Fax: 570-963-6459. ✉**Fax**✍

Register of Wills *Probate* Courthouse 200 N Washington Ave, Scranton, PA 18503. 9AM-4PM. **570-963-6702**, Fax: 570-963-6377.

Lancaster County

Court of Common Pleas - Civil *Civil, Eviction* www.co.lancaster.pa.us/courts/sit e/default.asp 50 N Duke St, PO Box 83480, Lancaster, PA 17608-3480. 8:30AM-5PM. **717-299-8282**, Fax: 717-293-7210. Access civil records-🖳✍

Court of Common Pleas - Crim. *Felony, Misdemeanor* www.co.lancaster.pa.us/cour

Key: Symbols refer to criminal records access unless otherwise noted. phone-☎ mail-✉ fax-**Fax** in person-✍ online-🖳 email-**Email**

ts/site/default.asp Clerk of Courts 50 N Duke St, Lancaster, PA 17602. 8:30AM-5PM. **717-299-8275.** ✉🖐

Register of Wills *Probate* 50 N Duke St., Lancaster, PA 17602. 8:30AM-4:30PM. **717-299-8243**, Fax: 717-295-5914.

Lawrence County
Court of Common Pleas - Criminal/ Civil *Felony, Misdemeanor, Civil, Eviction* www.co.lawrence.pa.us 430 Court St, New Castle, PA 16101-3593. 8AM-4PM. **724-656-2143**, Fax: 724-656-1988. Civil phone: 724-656-1960, crim: 724-656-2188. **Fax**✉💻🖐

Register of Wills *Probate* 430 Court St, New Castle, PA 16101-3593. 8AM-4PM. **724-656-2128/2159**, Fax: 724-656-1966. Access by subscription at www.ic-access.com, 814-472-6066.

Lebanon County
Court of Common Pleas - Civil *Civil, Eviction* Municipal Bldg, Rm 104 400 S 8th St, Lebanon, PA 17042. 8:30AM-4:30PM. **717-274-2801 X2120.** Access civil records-✉🖐

Court of Common Pleas - Criminal *Felony, Misd.* Municipal Bldg, Rm 102, 400 S 8th St, Lebanon, PA 17042. 8:30-4:30PM. **717-274-2801 x2118.** ☎✉🖐

Register of Wills *Probate* Municipal Bldg, Rm 105, 400 S 8th St, Lebanon, PA 17042. 8:30AM-4:30PM. **717-274-2801 X2215**, Fax: 717-274-8094 Probate: Ext 2217 & 2218.

Lehigh County
Access to the county online system requires monthly usage fee. Search by name or case number. Includes Wills. Call Lehigh Cty Computer Svcs Dept at 610-782-3286 for info.

Court of Common Pleas - Civil *Civil, Eviction* www.lccpa.org 455 W Hamilton St, Allentown, PA 18101-1614. 8:30AM-4:30PM. **610-782-3148**, Fax: 610-770-3840. Civil phone: 610-782-3148, crim: 610-782-3077. Access civil -✉💻🖐

Court of Common Pleas - Criminal *Felony, Misdemeanor* www.lccpa.org Clerk of Courts 455 W Hamilton St, Allentown, PA 18101-1614. 8:30AM-4:30PM. **610-782-3077**, Fax: 610-770-6797. Civil phone: 610-782-3148, crim: 610-782-3077. Access records-✉💻🖐

Register of Wills *Probate* 455 W Hamilton, Allentown, PA 18101-1614.

8AM-4PM. **610-782-3170**, Fax: 610-782-3932. 💻

Luzerne County
Court of Common Pleas - Civil *Civil, Eviction* 200 N River St, Wilkes Barre, PA 18711-1001. 9AM-4:30PM. **570-825-1745**, Fax: 570-825-1757. Access civil records-☎✉🖐

Court of Common Pleas - Criminal *Felony, Misd.* 200 N River St, Wilkes Barre, PA 18711. 8AM-4:30PM. **570-825-1585**, Fax: 570-825-1843. **Fax**✉🖐

Register of Wills *Probate* 200 N River St, Wilkes Barre, PA 18711. 9AM-4:30PM. **570-825-1672, 570-825-1500 X670**, Fax: 570-826-0869.

Lycoming County
Court of Common Pleas - Criminal/ Civil *Felony, Misdemeanor, Civil, Eviction* 48 W 3rd St, Williamsport, PA 17701. 8:30AM-5PM. **570-327-2251**, Fax: 570-327-2505. ✉🖐💻

Register of Wills *Probate* Lycoming Co Courthouse, 48 W 3rd St, Williamsport, PA 17701. 8:30AM-5PM. **570-327-2263, 327-2258**, Fax: 570-327-6790.

McKean County
Court of Common Pleas - Criminal/Civil *Felony, Misdemeanor, Civil, Eviction* PO Box 273, Smethport, PA 16749. 8:30AM-4:30PM. **814-887-3270**, Fax: 814-887-3219. ✉💻

Register of Wills *Probate* PO Box 202, Smethport, PA 16749-0202. 8:30-4:30. **814-887-3263**, Fax: 814-887-2242.

Mercer County
Court of Common Pleas - Civil *Civil, Eviction* 105 Mercer County Courthouse, Mercer, PA 16137. 8:30AM-4:30PM. **724-662-3800**. Access civil records-🖐💻

Court of Common Pleas - Crim. *Felony, Misdemeanor* www.mcc.co.mercer.pa.us/LOCRULES.htm 112 Mercer County Courthouse, Mercer, PA 16137. 8:30AM-4:30PM. **724-662-3800 X2248.** ✉🖐

Register of Wills *Probate* 112 Mercer County Courthouse, Mercer, PA 16137. 8:30AM-4:30PM. **724-662-3800 X2248**, Fax: 724-662-1604.

Mifflin County
Court of Common Pleas - Criminal/ Civil *Felony, Misdemeanor, Civil, Eviction* www.co.mifflin.pa.us 20 N

Wayne St, Lewistown, PA 17044. 8AM-4:30PM. **717-248-8146**, Fax: 717-248-5275. 🖐💻

Register of Wills *Probate* 20 N Wayne St., Lewistown, PA 17044. 8AM-4:30PM. **717-242-1449**, Fax: 717-248-2503. Access by subscription at www.ic-access.com, 814-472-6066.

Monroe County
Court of Common Pleas - Civil *Civil, Eviction* Monroe County Courthouse - Prothonotary 7th & Monroe St, Stroudsburg, PA 18360. 8:30AM-4:30PM. **570-517-3988**, Fax: 570-420-3582. Passport info 570-517-3370. Access civil records-✉🖐

Court of Common Pleas - Criminal *Felony, Misd.* \County Courthouse, Rm 312, Stroudsburg, PA 18360-2190. 8:30AM-4:30PM. **570-517-3385.** ✉🖐

Register of Wills *Probate* Monroe County Courthouse, Stroudsburg, PA 18360. 8:30AM-4:30PM. **570-517-3359**, Fax: 570-420-3537. Access wills records online at www.landex.com/remote/. Fee. Wills go back to 11/1836.

Montgomery County
Court of Common Pleas - Civil *Civil, Eviction* www.montcopa.org PO Box 311 Airy & Swede St, Norristown, PA 19404-0311. 8:30AM-4:15PM. **610-278-3360**, Fax: 610-278-5994. Access civil records-✉💻🖐

Court of Common Pleas - Criminal *Felony, Misdemeanor* PO Box 311 Airy & Swede St, Norristown, PA 19404-0311. 8:30AM-4:15PM. **610-278-3346**, Fax: 610-278-5183. Access records-✉💻🖐

Register of Wills *Probate* Airy & Swede St PO Box 311, Norristown, PA 19404. 8:30AM-4:15PM. **610-278-3400**, Fax: 610-278-3240. Search probate cases at www.montcopa.org/mway/index.html.

Montour County
Court of Common Pleas - Criminal/ Civil *Felony, Misdemeanor, Civil, Eviction* Montour County Courthouse, 29 Mill St, Danville, PA 17821. 9AM-4PM. **570-271-3010**, Fax: 570-271-3089. ☎**Fax**✉🖐💻

Register of Wills *Probate* 29 Mill St, Danville, PA 17821. 9AM-4PM. **570-271-3012**, Fax: 570-271-3071. Access by subscription at www.ic-access.com, 814-472-6066.

Northampton County

Court of Common Pleas - Civil *Civil, Eviction* www.nccpa.org Gov't Center, 669 Washington St, Rm 207, Easton, PA 18042-7498. 8:30AM-4:30PM. **610-559-3060**. Access civil records-📠

Court of Common Pleas - Criminal *Felony, Misdemeanor* www.nccpa.org 669 Washington St, Easton, PA 18042-7494. 8:30AM-4:30PM. **610-559-3000 X3046**, Fax: 610-252-4391. ✉ 📠

Register of Wills *Probate* Governnment Ctr, 669 Washington St, Easton, PA 18042. 8:30AM-4:30PM. **610-559-3094**, Fax: 610-559-3735.

Northumberland County

Court of Common Pleas - Civil *Civil, Eviction* County Courthouse 201 Market St, Rm #7, Sunbury, PA 17801-3468. 9AM-5PM M; 9AM-4:30PM T-F. **570-988-4151**. Access civil records-📞 ✉ 📠

Court of Common Pleas - Crim. *Felony, Misd.* County Courthouse, 201 Market St, Rm 7, Sunbury, PA 17801-3468. 9AM-5PM M; 9AM-4:30PM T-F. **570-988-4148**, Civil: 570-988-4151. ✉ 📠

Register of Wills *Probate* 201 Market St County Courthouse, Sunbury, PA 17801. 9AM-4:30PM. **570-988-4143 and 570-988-4140**, Fax: 570-988-4141.

Perry County

Court of Common Pleas - Criminal/Civil *Felony, Misd., Civil, Eviction* PO Box 223, (1 Courthouse Sq), New Bloomfield, PA 17068. 8AM-4PM. **717-582-2131**, Civil: 717-582-2131 X2240, crim: 717-582-2131 X2241. 📞📠✉📠

Register of Wills *Probate* PO Box 223, New Bloomfield, PA 17068. 8AM-4PM. **717-582-2131**, Fax: 717-582-5149.

Philadelphia County

Court of Common Pleas - Civil *Civil* http://courts.phila.gov/ First Judicial District of PA Rm 284, City Hall, Philadelphia, PA 19107. 9AM-5PM. **215-686-6656**, Fax: 215-567-7380. Access civil records-✉ 💻 📠

Clerk of Quarter Session *Felony, Misd.* http://courts.phila.gov/ 1301 Filbert St, #310, Philadelphia, PA 19107. 8AM-5PM. **215-683-7700 X01 & X02**. ✉📠

Municipal Court *Felony, Misdemeanor, Civil Actions Under $10,000, Eviction* http://fjd.phila.gov 34 S 11th St, 5th Fl, Philadelphia, PA 19107. 9AM-5PM. **215-686-7000**, Fax: 215-569-9254. Court has jurisdiction over certain criminal offenses with jail terms up to five years. ✉ 📠

Register of Wills *Probate* City Hall, Rm 180, Philadelphia, PA 19107. 8:30AM-4:30PM. **215-686-6250/6282**, Fax: 215-686-6293.

Pike County

Court of Common Pleas - Civil *Felony, Misdemeanor, Civil, Eviction* 412 Broad St, Milford, PA 18337. 8:30AM-4:30PM. **570-296-7231**. 📞✉💻📠

Register of Wills *Probate* 506 Broad St, Milford, PA 18337. 8:30AM-4:30PM. **570-296-3508**, Fax: 570-296-3514. Access by subscription at www.ic-access.com, 814-472-6066.

Potter County

Court of Common Pleas - Civil *Felony, Misdemeanor, Civil, Eviction* 1 E 2nd St, Rm 23, Coudersport, PA 16915. 8:30AM-4:30PM. **814-274-9740**, Fax: 814-274-3361. 📞📠✉📠💻

Register of Wills *Probate* 1 E 2nd St, Courthouse, Rm 20, Coudersport, PA 16915. 8:30AM-4:30PM. **814-274-8370**. Access by subscription at www.ic-access.com, 814-472-6066.

Schuylkill County

Court of Common Pleas - Civil *Civil, Eviction* www.co.schuylkill.pa.us/ 401 N 2nd St, Pottsville, PA 17901-2528. 8:30AM-4:30PM. **570-628-1270**, Fax: 570-628-1261. Access civil records-✉ 📠

Court of Common Pleas - Crim. *Felony, Misdemeanor* www.co.schuylkill.pa.us/ 410 N 2nd St, Pottsville, PA 17901. 8:30AM-4:30PM. **570-622-5570 X1141**, Fax: 570-628-1143. Civil phone: 570-628-1270. 📠✉📠

Register of Wills *Probate* Courthouse 401 N 2nd St, Pottsville, PA 17901-2520. 8:30AM-4:30PM. **570-628-1377**, Fax: 570-628-1384.

Snyder County

Court of Common Pleas - Criminal/Civil *Felony, Misd., Civil, Eviction* www.seda-cog.org/snyder/ical/calendar.asp Snyder County Courthouse, PO Box 217, Middleburg, PA 17842. 8:30AM-4PM. **570-837-4202**. ✉📠

Register of Wills *Probate* www.seda-cog.org/snyder/ical/calendar.asp County Courthouse, 9 W Market St PO Box 217, Middleburg, PA 17842. 8:30AM-4PM. **570-837-4224**, Fax: 570-837-4299.

Somerset County

Court of Common Pleas - Civil *Civil, Eviction* www.co.somerset.pa.us 111 E Union St, #190, Somerset, PA 15501. 8:30AM-4PM. **814-445-1428**, Fax: 814-444-9270. Access civil -📞**Fax**✉📠

Court of Common Pleas - Criminal *Felony, Misd.* www.co.somerset.pa.us 111 E Union St, #180, Somerset, PA 15501. 8:30AM-4PM. **814-445-1435**, Civil: 814-445-1428. 📞✉📠

Register of Wills *Probate* 111 E Union St, #170, Somerset, PA 15501-0586. 8:30AM-4PM. **814-445-1548**, Fax: 814-445-7991.

Sullivan County

Court of Common Pleas - Criminal/Civil *Felony, Misd., Civil, Eviction, Probate* Main St, Laporte, PA 18626. 8:30-4PM. **570-946-7351**, Probate: 570-946-7351. Includes Register of Wills. 📠

Susquehanna County

Court of Common Pleas - Civil *Civil, Eviction* Susquehanna Courthouse PO Box 218, Montrose, PA 18801. 9AM-4:30PM. **570-278-4600 X120**. Access civil records-✉ 📠 💻

Court of Common Pleas - Criminal *Felony, Misdemeanor* PO Box 218 Susquehanna Courthouse, 11 Maple St, Montrose, PA 18801. 8:30AM-4:30PM. **570-278-4600 x321, x320, x323**, Fax: 570-278-4191. ✉ 📠 💻

Register of Wills *Probate* Susquehanna County Courthouse PO Box 218, Montrose, PA 18801. 8:30AM-4:30PM. **570-278-4600 X113**, Fax: 570-278-2963.

Tioga County

Court of Common Pleas - Criminal/Civil *Felony, Misd., Civil, Eviction* 116 Main St, Wellsboro, PA 16901. 9AM-4:30PM. **570-724-9281**. ✉📠

Register of Wills *Probate* 116 Main St, Wellsboro, PA 16901. 9AM-4:30PM. **570-724-9260**. Access wills records online at www.landex.com/remote/. Fee. Images and wills go back to 2/1999.

Union County

Court of Common Pleas - Criminal/Civil *Felony, Misdemeanor, Civil, Eviction* www.unionco.org 103 S 2nd St, Lewisburg, PA 17837. 8:30AM-4:30PM. **570-524-8751.** ☎ ✉ ✍ 🖥

Register of Wills *Probate* 103 S 2nd St, Lewisburg, PA 17837-1996. 8:30AM-4:30PM. **570-524-8761.** Search wills online at www.courthouseonline.com/WillsSearch.asp?State=PA&County=Union&Abbrev=Un&Office=RW

Venango County

Court of Common Pleas - Criminal/Civil *Felony, Misdemeanor, Civil, Eviction* www.co.venango.pa.us Venango County Courthouse 1168 Liberty St, Franklin, PA 16323. 8:30AM-4:30PM. **814-432-9577**, Fax: 814-432-9579. ✉ ✍ 🖥

Register of Wills/ Recorder *Probate* 1168 Liberty St, Franklin, PA 16323. 8:30AM-4:30PM. **814-432-9534**, Fax: 814-432-9569 Probate: 814-432-9539.

Warren County

Court of Common Pleas - Criminal/Civil *Felony, Misdemeanor, Civil, Eviction* http://users.penn.com/~wrncourt 4th & Market St, Warren, PA 16365. 8:30AM-4:30PM. **814-728-3440**, Fax: 814-728-3459. **Fax**✉ ✍ 🖥

Register of Wills *Probate* Courthouse, 204 4th Ave, Warren, PA 16365.

8:30AM-4:30PM. **814-728-3430**, Fax: 814-728-3476.

Washington County

Court of Common Pleas - Civil *Civil, Eviction* www.co.washington.pa.us 1 S Main St, #1001, Washington, PA 15301. 9AM-4:30PM. **724-228-6770**. Access civil records-✍

Court of Common Pleas - Criminal *Felony, Misd.* Courthouse, #1005 1 S Main St, Washington, PA 15301. 9AM-4:30PM. **724-228-6787**, Fax: 724-228-6890. Civil phone: 724-228-6770. ✉ ✍

Register of Wills *Probate* Courthouse, 1 S Main St, #1002, Washington, PA 15301. 9AM-4:30PM. **724-228-6775**, Fax: 724-250-4820.

Wayne County

Court of Common Pleas - Criminal/Civil *Felony, Misdemeanor, Civil, Eviction* 925 Court St, Honesdale, PA 18431. 8:30AM-4:30PM. **570-253-5970 X200**, Fax: 570-253-0687. ✍

Register of Wills *Probate* www.co-wayne-pa-us.org 925 Court St, Honesdale, PA 18431. 8:30AM-4:30PM. **570-253-5970 X212**, Probate: ext. 213.

Westmoreland County

Court of Common Pleas - Civil *Civil, Eviction* Courthouse Sq, Rm 501 PO Box 1630, Greensburg, PA 15601-1168. 8:30AM-4PM. **724-830-3502**, Fax: 724-830-3517. Access civil records-🖥 ✍

Court of Common Pleas - Crim. *Felony, Misd.* Criminal Division, 203 Courthouse Square, Greensburg, PA 15601-1168.

8:30AM-4PM. **724-830-3734**, Fax: 724-830-3472/850-3979. **Fax**✉ 🖥 ✍

Register of Wills *Probate* 2 N Main St, #301, Greensburg, PA 15601. 8:30AM-4PM. **724-830-3177**, Fax: 724-850-3976.

Wyoming County

Court of Common Pleas - Criminal/Civil *Felony, Misd., Civil, Eviction* County Courthouse, Tunkhannock, PA 18657. 8:30AM-4PM. **570-836-3200 X232-234**, Fax: 570-836-4781. ✍

Register of Wills *Probate* Wyoming County Courthouse 1 Courthouse Sq, Tunkhannock, PA 18657. 8:30AM-4PM. **570-836-3200 X2235**, Fax: 570-996-5053.

York County

Court of Common Pleas - Civil *Civil* www.york-county.org/departments/courts/crtfl.htm York County Courthouse, 45 N George St, York, PA 17401. 8:30AM-4:30PM. **717-771-9611**, crim: 717-771-9612. Access civil records-🖥 ✍ ✉

Court of Common Pleas - Crim. *Felony, Misdemeanor* www.york-county.org/departments/courts/crtfl.htm 45 N George St York County Courthouse, York, PA 17401. 8:30AM-4:30PM. **717-771-9612**, Fax: 717-771-9096. **Fax**✉ ✍ ✍

Register of Wills *Probate* York County Courthouse 28 E Market St, York, PA 17401. 8:00AM-4:30PM. **717-771-9263**, Fax: 717-771-4678. Access wills records online at www.landex.com/remote/. Fee. Images and wills go back to 2/1999.

Rhode Island

State Court Administration: Court Administrator, Supreme Court, 250 Benefit St, Providence, RI, 02903; 401-222-3272, Fax: 401-222-3599. www.courts.state.ri.us

Court Structure: Rhode Island has five counties, but only four Superior/District Court Locations (2nd-Newport, 3rd-Kent, 4th-Washignton, and 6th-Providence/Bristol Districts). Bristol and Providence counties are completely merged at the Providence location. Civil claims between $5000 and $10,000 may be filed in either Superior or District Court at the discretion of the filer.

Probate Courts: Probate is handled by the Town Clerk at the 39 cities and towns across Rhode Island.

Online Access: The Rhode Island Judiciary offers free Internet access to court criminal records statewide at http://courtconnect.courts.state.ri.us. A word of caution, this website is provided as an informational service only and should not be relied upon as an official record of the court.

The Superior (civil, family) and Appellate courts are online internally for court personnel only.

Key: Symbols refer to criminal records access unless otherwise noted. phone-☎ mail-✉ fax-**Fax** in person-✍ online-🖥 email-**Email**

Bristol County

Superior & District Courts *Probate Only* c/o Bristol Town Hall 10 Court St, Bristol, RI 02809. 8:30-4PM. **401-253-7000**. Do not send criminal or civil (except probate) record requests here. All civil and criminal cases are handled by the Providence County courts.

Probate Courts: Bristol Town Hall 401-253-7000 x21, Barrington Town 401-247-1900 x4, Warren Town 401-245-7340.

Kent County

Superior Court *Felony, Civil Actions Over $10,000* www.courts.state.ri.us 222 Quaker Ln, Warwick, RI 02886. 8:30AM-4:00PM. **401-822-1311**. 🖑 🖵

3rd Division District Court *Misdemeanor, Civil Actions Under $10,000, Eviction, Small Claims* 222 Quaker Ln, Warwick, RI 02886-0107. 8:30AM-4:30PM. **401-822-1771**. 🖑 🖵

Probate Courts: East Greenwich Town Hall 401-886-8607; West Greenwich Town Hall 401-392-3800; Warwick City Hall 401-738-2000 (x6213); Coventry Town Hall 401-822-9174; West Warwick Town Hall 401-822-9201.

Newport County

Superior Court *Felony, Civil Actions Over $10,000* Florence K Murray Judicial Complex 45 Washington Sq, Newport, RI 02840. 8:30AM-4:30PM (July and August till 4PM). **401-841-8330**, Fax: 401-846-1673. ✉Fax🖑🖵

2nd District Court *Misdemeanor, Civil Actions Under $10,000, Eviction, Small Claims* 45 Washington Square, Newport, RI 02840. 8:30AM-4:30PM (4PM-summer months). **401-841-8350**. 🖑 🖵

Probate Courts: Tiverton Town Hall 401-625-6700; Newport City Hall 401-846-9600; Little Compton Town Hall 401-635-4400; Middletown Town 401-847-0009; Portsmouth Town 401-683-2101; Jamestown Town 401-423-7200.

Providence County

Providence/Bristol Superior Court *Felony, Civil Actions Over $10,000* www.courts.state.ri.us 250 Benefit St, Providence, RI 02903. 8:30AM-4PM. **401-222-3250**. All civil and criminal cases handled by the Providence County court & Bristol County court. 🖑 🖵

6th Division District Court *Misd., Civil Actions Under $10,000, Eviction, Small Claims* 1 Dorrance Plaza, 2nd Fl, Providence, RI 02903. 8:30AM-4PM. **401-458-5400**. ✉☎🖑🖵

Probate Courts: Pawtucket City Hall 401-728-0500 x259 or x223; North Smithfield Town Hall 401-767-2200 x216, North Providence Town Hall 401-232-0900; East Providence City Hall 401-435-7500; Glocester Town Hall 401-568-6206; Lincoln Town Hall 401-333-8450, 333-8451; Johnston Town Hall 401-553-8830; Foster Town Hall 401-392-9200; Cumberland Town Hall 401-728-2400; Scituate Town Hall 401-647-2822; Smithfield Town Hall 401-233-1000 X111; Cranston City Hall 401-461-1000 X3197; Woonsocket City Hall 401-762-6400, Probate: 401-767-9248; Central Falls City Hall 401-727-7400; Burrillville Town Hall 401-568-4300 x114 or x110; Providence City Hall 401-421-7740.

Washington County

Superior Court *Felony, Civil Actions Over $10,000* 4800 Towerhill Rd, Wakefield, RI 02879. 8:30AM-4:30PM (Sept-June) 8:30AM-4PM (July & Aug). **401-782-4121**. ✉🖑🖵

4th District Court *Misd., Civil Actions Under $10,000, Eviction, Small Claims* 4800 Towerhill Rd, Wakefield, RI 02879. 8:30AM-4:30PM. **401-782-4131**. 🖑🖵

Probate Courts: Exeter Town Hall 401-294-3891 (295-7500); Charlestown Town Hall 401-364-1200; Hopkinton Town Hall 401-377-7777; South Kingstown Town Hall 401-789-9331;New Shoreham Town Hall 401-466-3200; North Kingstown Town Hall 401-294-3331; Richmond Town Hall 401-539-2497; Westerly Town Hall 401-348-2500; Narragansett Town Hall 401-789-1044 X621.

South Carolina

State Court Administration: Court Administration, 1015 Sumter St, 2nd Floor, Columbia, SC, 29201; 803-734-1800, Fax: 803-734-1355. http://www.sccourts.org/

Court Structure: The 46 SC counties are divided among sixteen judicial circuits. The circuit courts are in operation at the county level and consist of a court of general sessions (criminal) and a court of common pleas (civil). A family court is also in operation at the county level. The over 300 Magistrate and Municipal Courts (often referred to as "Summary Courts") only handle misdemeanor cases involving a $500.00 fine and/or 30 days or less jail time.

The maximum civil claim monetary amount for the Magistrate Courts increased from $2,500 to $5,000 as of January 1, 1996. In 2001, this civil limit was raised to $7,500.

Online Access: Appellate and Supreme Court opinions are available from the website. There is no access to statewide trial court records, but several counties offer online access.

Additional Information: If requesting a record in writing, it is recommended that the words "request that General Session, Common Pleas, and Family Court records be searched" be included in the request.

Most South Carolina courts will not conduct searches. However, if a name and case number are provided, many will pull and copy the record. Search fees vary widely as they are set by each county individually.

Key: Symbols refer to criminal records access unless otherwise noted. phone-☎ mail-✉ fax-Fax in person-🖑 online-🖵 email-**Email**

Abbeville County

Circuit Court *Felony, Misdemeanor, Civil Actions Over $7,500* PO Box 99 103 Court Sq, Rm 102, Abbeville, SC 29620. 8AM-5PM. **864-366-5074**, Fax: 864-459-9188.

Probate Court PO Box 70, Abbeville, SC 29620. 9AM-5PM. **864-459-4626**, Fax: 864-459-4023.

Aiken County

Circuit Court *Felony, Misdemeanor, Civil Actions Over $7,500* PO Box 583, Aiken, SC 29802. 8:30AM-5PM. **803-642-1715**.

Probate Court PO Box 1576 (109 Park Ave), Aiken, SC 29802. 8:30AM-5PM. **803-642-2000**, Fax: 803-642-2007.

Allendale County

Circuit Court *Felony, Misdemeanor, Civil Actions Over $7,500* PO Box 126 611 A W Mulberry St, Allendale, SC 29810. 9AM-5PM. **803-584-2737**, Fax: 803-584-7058. Access records-📞✉ 👋

Probate Court PO Box 603, Courthouse Complex, Allendale, SC 29810. 9AM-5PM. **803-584-3157**, Fax: 803-584-7053.

Anderson County

Circuit Court *Felony, Misdemeanor, Civil Actions Over $7,500* PO Box 8002, Anderson, SC 29622. 8:30AM-5PM. **864-260-4053**, Fax: 864-260-4715. 👋💻

Probate Court PO Box 8002, Anderson, SC 29622. 8:30AM-5PM. **864-260-4049**, Fax: 864-260-4811. Access to the county probate court, marriage, and guardian/conservatorship records is free at http://acpass.andersoncountysc.org/Probate_Main.htm

Bamberg County

Circuit Court *Felony, Misdemeanor, Civil Actions Over $7,500* PO Box 150, Bamberg, SC 29003. 9AM-5PM. **803-245-3025**, Fax: 803-245-3088. ✉👋fax.

Probate Court PO Box 180, Bamberg, SC 29003. 9AM-5PM. **803-245-3008**, Fax: 803-245-3008.

Barnwell County

Circuit Court *Felony, Misdemeanor, Civil Actions Over $7,500* PO Box 723, Barnwell, SC 29812. 9AM-5PM. **803-541-1020**, Fax: 803-541-1025. Records location is; 141 Main St, Barnwell, SC, 29812. 👋

Probate Court Rm 108, County Courthouse, Barnwell, SC 29812. 9AM-5PM. **803-541-1032**, Fax: 803-541-1012.

Beaufort County

Circuit Court *Felony, Misdemeanor, Civil Actions Over $7,500* www.bcgov.org/Clerk_Court/clerk_court.htm PO Drawer 1128 (128 Ribaut Rd, Rm 208), Beaufort, SC 29901. 8AM-5PM. **843-470-5218**, Fax: 843-470-5248. 👋

Probate Court PO Box 1083, Beaufort, SC 29901-1083. 8AM-5PM. **843-470-5319**, Fax: 843-470-5324.

Berkeley County

Circuit Court *Felony, Misdemeanor, Civil Actions Over $7,500* PO Box 219, Moncks Corner, SC 29461. 9AM-5PM. **843-719-4400**. 👋

Probate Court 300 B California Ave, Moncks Corner, SC 29461. 9AM-5PM. **843-719-4519**, Fax: 843-719-4527.

Calhoun County

Circuit Court *Felony, Misdemeanor, Civil Actions Over $7,500* PO Box 709, St Matthews, SC 29135-0709. 9AM-5PM. **803-874-3524**, Fax: 803-874-1942. 👋

Probate Court 902 Huff Dr., St Matthews, SC 29135. 9AM-5PM. **803-874-3514**, Fax: 803-874-1942.

Charleston County

Circuit Court *Felony, Misdemeanor, Civil Actions Over $7,500* http://www3.charlestoncounty.org 100 Broad St, #106, Charleston, SC 29401-2210. 8:30AM-5PM. **843-958-5000**, Fax: 843-958-5020. ✉💻👋

Charleston Magistrate Court *Civil Actions Under $7,500, Misd., Eviction, Small Claims* www.charlestoncounty.org 4045 Bridgeview Dr PO Box 60037, Charleston, SC 29419. 8:30AM-4:30PM. **843-202-6600**, Fax: 843-202-6620. Criminal phone: 843-554-2462. 👋💻-other requests for background checks are forwarded to Sheriff's Office (843-202-6610).

Probate Court 84 Broad St., North Charleston, SC 29401-2284. 8:30AM-5PM. **843-958-5030**, Fax: 843-958-5044. Access Estate and Wills records free at http://www3.charlestoncounty.org/connect/LU_GROUP_2?ref=Conserv

Cherokee County

Circuit Court *Felony, Misdemeanor, Civil Actions Over $7,500* PO Drawer 2289, Gaffney, SC 29342. 8:30AM-5PM. **864-487-2571**, Fax: 864-487-2754. Civil phone: 864-487-2533. 👋

Probate Court 1434 N Limestone St, Peachtree Ctr, Gaffney, SC 29340. 9AM-4:30. **864-487-2583**, Fax: 864-902-8426.

Chester County

Circuit Court *Felony, Misdemeanor, Civil Actions Over $7,500* PO Drawer 580, Chester, SC 29706. 8:30AM-5PM. **803-385-2605**, Fax: 803-581-7975. 👋

Probate Court PO Drawer 580, Chester, SC 29706. 8:30AM-5PM. **803-385-2604**, Fax: 803-581-5180. Records go back to late 1780s.

Chesterfield County

Circuit Court *Felony, Misd., Civil Actions Over $7,500* PO Box 529, Chesterfield, SC 29709. 8:30-5PM. **843-623-2574**, Fax: 843-623-6944. ✉👋

Probate Court County Courthouse, 200 W Main St, Chesterfield, SC 29709. 8:30AM-5PM. **843-623-2376**, Fax: 843-623-9886.

Clarendon County

Circuit Court *Felony, Misdemeanor, Civil Actions Over $7,500* PO Box 136, Manning, SC 29102. 8:30AM-5PM. **803-435-4444**, Civil: 803-435-4443, crim: 803-435-4210x309. Access records-✉👋

Probate Court PO Box 307, Manning, SC 29102. 8:30AM-5PM. **803-435-8774**, Fax: 803-435-8698.

Colleton County

Circuit Court *Felony, Misdemeanor, Civil Actions Over $7,500* www.colletoncounty.org/legalcourt/index.html PO Box 620, Walterboro, SC 29488. 8:00AM-5PM. **843-549-5791**, Fax: 843-549-2875. Access records-📞Fax✉👋

Probate Court PO Box 1036, Walterboro, SC 29488-0031. 8:00AM-5PM. **843-549-7216**, Fax: 843-549-5571.

Darlington County

Circuit Court *Felony, Misd., Civil Actions Over $7,500* PO Box 1177, Darlington, SC 29540. 8:30-5PM. **843-398-4339**, Fax: 843-398-4172. 👋✉fax.

Probate Court #1 Public Sq, Courthouse, Rm 208, Darlington, SC 29532. 8:30AM-5PM. **843-398-4310**, Fax: 843-398-4076.

Dillon County

Circuit Court *Felony, Misdemeanor, Civil Actions Over $7,500* PO Drawer

1220, Dillon, SC 29536. 8:30AM-5PM. **843-774-1425**. ✉ 🖐

Probate Court PO Box 189, Dillon, SC 29536. 8:30AM-5PM. **843-774-1423**, Fax: 843-841-3732.

Dorchester County

Circuit Court *Felony, Misdemeanor, Civil Actions Over $7,500* 101 Ridge St, St George, SC 29477. 8:30AM-5PM. **843-563-0160**, Fax: 843-563-0178. Civil phone: 843-563-0113. Access records-🖐

Dorchester County Court *Civil Actions Under $7,500, Eviction, Small Claims* 101 Ridge St, St George, SC 29477. 8AM-5PM. Fax: 843-563-0123. Civil phone: 843-563-0164, crim: 843-563-0130. Access civil records-✉

Probate Court 101 Ridge St, County Courthouse, St George, SC 29477. 8:30AM-5PM. **843-563-0105**, Fax: 843-563-0245.

Edgefield County

Circuit Court *Felony, Misdemeanor, Civil Actions Over $7,500* PO Box 34, Edgefield, SC 29824. 8:30AM-5PM. **803-637-4082**, Fax: 803-637-4117. ✉ 🖐

Probate Court 124 Courthouse Square, Edgefield, SC 29824. 8:30AM-5PM. **803-637-4076**, Fax: 803-637-7157.

Fairfield County

Circuit Court *Felony, Misdemeanor, Civil Actions Over $7,500* PO Drawer 299, Winnsboro, SC 29180. 9AM-5PM. **803-712-6526**. 🖐

Probate Court PO Box 385, Winnsboro, SC 29180. 9AM-5PM. **803-712-6519**, Fax: 803-712-6939.

Florence County

Circuit Court *Felony, Misdemeanor, Civil Actions Over $7,500* www.florenceco.org/index.html Drawer E, City County Complex (180 N Irby St), Florence, SC 29501. 8:30AM-5PM. **843-665-3031**. 🖥 🖐

Probate Court 180 N Irby, MSC-L, Florence, SC 29501. 8:30AM-5PM. **843-665-3085**, Fax: 843-665-3068.

Georgetown County

Circuit Court *Felony, Misdemeanor, Civil Actions Over $7,500* PO Box 421270, Georgetown, SC 29442. 8:30AM-5PM. **843-546-3215**, Fax: 843-546-3281. Civil phone: 843-545-3041, crim: 843-545-3053. Access records-🖐

Probate Court PO Box 421270, Georgetown, SC 29442. 8:30AM-5PM. **843-545-3274**, Fax: 843-545-3292.

Greenville County

Circuit Court *Felony, Misd., Civil Over $7,500* www.greenvillecounty.org 305 E North St, Rm 227, Greenville, SC 29601. 8:30AM-5PM. **864-467-8551**, Fax: 864-467-8513. 🖐

Probate Court www.greenvillecounty.org/probate/index.htm 301 University Ridge, #1200, Greenville, SC 29601. 8:30AM-5PM. **864-467-7170**, Fax: 864-467-7198.

Greenwood County

Circuit Court *Felony, Misdemeanor, Civil Actions Over $7,500* Courthouse, Rm 114 528 Monument St, Greenwood, SC 29646. 8:30AM-5PM. **864-942-8547**, Fax: 864-942-8693. Access records-✉ 🖐

Probate Court PO Box 1210, Greenwood, SC 29648. 8:30AM-5PM. **864-942-8625**, Fax: 864-942-8620.

Hampton County

Circuit Court *Felony, Civil Actions Over $7,500* www.hcroster.com/ PO Box 7, Hampton, SC 29924. 8AM-5PM. **803-943-7510**. 🖐

Probate Court PO Box 601, Hampton, SC 29924. 8AM-5PM. **803-943-7512**, Fax: 803-943-7596, 803-943-7540.

Horry County

Circuit Court *Felony, Misdemeanor, Civil Actions Over $7,500* PO Box 677, Conway, SC 29526. 8AM-5PM. **843-915-5080**, Fax: 843-915-6018. ☎ ✉ 🖐

Probate Court www.horrycounty.org/ PO Box 288, Conway, SC 29528. 8AM-5PM. **843-915-5370**, Fax: 843-915-6370/71.

Jasper County

Circuit Court *Felony, Misdemeanor, Civil Actions Over $7,500* PO Box 248, Ridgeland, SC 29936. 8:30AM-5PM. **843-726-7710**. 🖐

Probate Court PO Box 1028, Ridgeland, SC 29936. 9AM-5PM. **843-726-7719**, Fax: 843-726-5137.

Kershaw County

Circuit Court *Felony, Misdemeanor, Civil Actions Over $7,500* County Courthouse, Rm 313 PO Box 1557, Camden, SC 29020. 8:30-5PM. **803-425-1500 x5623**, Fax: 803-425-1505. ✉ 🖐

Probate Court 1121 Broad St, Rm 302, Camden, SC 29020. 8:30AM-5PM. **803-425-1500 x5351**, Fax: 803-425-7673.

Lancaster County

Circuit Court *Felony, Misdemeanor, Civil Actions Over $7,500* PO Box 1809, Lancaster, SC 29721. 8:30AM-5PM. **803-285-1581**, Fax: 803-416-9388. 🖐

Probate Court www.lancastercountysc.net/ProbateCourt/ PO Box 1809, Lancaster, SC 29721. 8:30AM-5PM. **803-283-3379**, Fax: 803-283-3370.

Laurens County

Circuit Court *Felony, Misdemeanor, Civil Actions Over $7,500* PO Box 287, Laurens, SC 29360. 9AM-5PM. **864-984-3538**, Fax: 864-984-7023. ✉ 🖐

Probate Court PO Box 194 (100 Hillcrest Sq #A), Laurens, SC 29360. 9AM-5PM. **864-984-7315**, Fax: 864-984-3779 Probate: 864-984-7731.

Lee County

Circuit Court *Felony, Misdemeanor, Civil Actions Over $7,500* PO Box 387, Bishopville, SC 29010. 9AM-5PM. **803-484-5341**, Fax: 803-484-1632. ✉ 🖐

Probate Court PO Box 24, Bishopville, SC 29010. 9AM-5PM. **803-484-5341 X338, X339, X361**, Fax: 803-484-6881.

Lexington County

Circuit Court *Felony, Misd., Civil Over $7,500* Lexington County Courthouse, Rm 107 205 E Main St, Lexington, SC 29072. 8AM-5PM. **803-359-8212**, Fax: 803-359-8314. Civil phone: 803-359-8252, crim: 803-359-8553. **Fax** ✉ 🖐

Probate Court County Courthouse, Rm 110 139 E Main St, Lexington, SC 29072-3488. 8AM-5PM. **803-359-8324**, Fax: 803-359-8199.

McCormick County

Circuit Court *Felony, Misdemeanor, Civil Actions Over $7,500* 133 S Mine St, McCormick, SC 29835. 9AM-5PM. **864-465-2195**, Fax: 864-465-0071 . 🖐

Probate Court 133 S Mine St, #101, McCormick, SC 29835. 9AM-5PM. **864-465-2630**, Fax: 864-465-0071.

Marion County

Circuit Court *Felony, Misdemeanor, Civil Actions Over $7,500* PO Box 295, Marion, SC 29571. 8:30AM-5PM. **843-423-8240**. 🖐

Key: Symbols refer to criminal records access unless otherwise noted. phone-☎ mail-✉ fax-**Fax** in person-🖐 online-🖥 email-**Email**

Probate Court PO Box 583, Marion, SC 29571. 8:30AM-5PM. **843-423-8244**, Fax: 843-431-5026.

Marlboro County

Circuit Court *Felony, Misd., Civil Actions Over $7,500* PO Drawer 996, Bennettsville, SC 29512. 8:30AM-5PM. **843-479-5613**, Fax 843-479-5640. ✉ ✋

Marlboro County Summary Court *Civil Under $7,500, Eviction, Small Claims* PO Box 418, Bennettsville, SC 29512. 8:30-4:30PM. **843-479-5620/5621**, Fax: 843-479-5646. Access civil records-✉

Probate Court PO Box 455, Bennettsville, SC 29512. 8:30AM-5PM. **843-479-5610**, Fax: 843-479-5668.

Newberry County

Circuit Court *Felony, Misd., Civil Over $7,500* www.newberrycounty.net PO Box 278, Newberry, SC 29108. 8:30AM-5PM. **803-321-2110**, Fax: 803-321-2111. ✋

Probate Court www.newberrycounty.net/ PO Box 442, Newberry, SC 29108. 8:30-5PM. **803-321-2118**, Fax: 803-321-2119.

Oconee County

Circuit Court *Felony, Misdemeanor, Civil Actions Over $7,500* PO Box 678, Walhalla, SC 29691. 8:30AM-5PM. **864-638-4280**, Fax: 864-638-4282. ✋

County Summary Court *Civil Actions Under $7,500, Eviction, Small Claims* 208 Booker Dr, Walhalla, SC 29691. 8:30AM-5PM. **864-638-4127**, Fax: 864-638-4229. Access civil records-✉

Probate Court PO Box 471, Walhalla, SC 29691. 8:30AM-5PM. **864-638-4275**, Fax: 864-638-4278.

Orangeburg County

Circuit Court *Felony, Misdemeanor, Civil Actions Over $7,500* PO Box 9000, Orangeburg, SC 29116. 8:30AM-5PM. **803-533-6260**, Fax: 803-534-3848. ✋

Probate Court PO Drawer 9000, Orangeburg, SC 29116-9000. 8:30AM-5PM. **803-533-6280**, Fax: 803-533-6279.

Pickens County

Circuit Court *Felony, Misd., Civil Over $7,500* www.co.pickens.sc.us/ PO Box 215, Pickens, SC 29671. 8:30AM-5PM. **864-898-5857**, Fax: 864-898-5863. ✋

Probate Court 222 McDaniel Ave, #B-16, Pickens, SC 29671. 8:00AM-5PM. **864-898-5903**, Fax: 864-898-5924.

Richland County

Circuit Court *Felony, Misd., Civil Over $7,500* PO Box 2766, Columbia, SC 29202. 8:30-5PM. **803-576-1999**, Fax: 803-748-5039 civ; 576-1925 crim. ✋

Probate Court www.richlandonline.com/probate.htm PO Box 192 (1701 Main St, #207), Columbia, SC 29202. 8:30AM-5PM. **803-576-1961**, Fax: 803-576-1993.

Saluda County

Circuit Court *Felony, Misdemeanor, Civil Actions Over $7,500* County Courthouse 100 E Church St, #6, Saluda, SC 29138. 8:30AM-5PM. **864-445-3303/2168**, Fax: 864-445-3772. ✋

Probate Court 100 E Church St, Saluda, SC 29138. 8:30AM-5PM. **864-445-7110**, Fax: 864-445-9726.

Spartanburg County

Circuit Court *Felony, Misdemeanor, Civil Over $7,500* www.spartanburgcounty.org/govt/depts/coc/index.htm County Courthouse 180 Magnolia St, Spartanburg, SC 29306. 8:30AM-5PM. **864-596-2591**, Fax: 864-596-2239. ✋

Probate Court 180 Magnolia St, Rm 302, Spartanburg, SC 29306-2392. 8:30AM-5PM. **864-596-2556**, Fax: 864-596-2011.

Sumter County

Circuit Court *Felony, Misd., Civil Over $7,500* www.sumtercountysc.org 141 N Main, Sumter, SC 29150. 8:30AM-5PM. **803-436-2227**, Fax: 803-436-2223. Civil phone: 803-436-2231, crim: 803-436-2264/65. ✉✋

Probate Court 141 N Main, Rm 111, Sumter, SC 29150. 8:30AM-5PM. **803-436-2166**, Fax: 803-436-2407.

Union County

Circuit Court *Felony, Misd., Civil Over $7500* www.countyofunion.com/Clerk.html PO Box 703 (210 W Main St), Union, SC 29379. 9AM-5PM. **864-429-1630**, Fax: 864-429-1715. Court will mail or fax case documents w/ case number. ✋

Probate Court PO Box 447, Union, SC 29379. 9AM-5PM. **864-429-1625**, Fax: 864-427-1198.

Williamsburg County

Circuit Court *Felony, Misd., Civil Actions Over $7,500* 125 W Main St, Kingstree, SC 29556. 8:30AM-5PM. **843-355-9321 X552**, Fax: 843-354-7821. ✋

Probate Court PO Box 1005, Kingstree, SC 29556. 8:00AM-5PM. **843-355-9321 x558**, Fax: 843-355-9305.

York County

Circuit Court *Felony, Misdemeanor, Civil Actions Over $7,500* PO Box 649, York, SC 29745. 8AM-5PM. **803-684-8506**. Civil: 803-684-8507, crim: 803-628-3036. Fax ✉ ✋

Probate Court PO Box 219, York, SC 29745. 8AM-5PM. **803-684-8513 X8630**, Fax: 803-684-8536.

South Dakota

State Court Administration: State Court Administrator, State Capitol Building, 500 E Capitol Av, Pierre, SD, 57501; 605-773-3474, Fax: 605-773-5627. www.sdjudicial.com

Court Structure: The state re-aligned their circuits from 8 to 7 effective June, 2000.

South Dakota has a statewide criminal record search database, administered by the State Court Administrator's Office in Pierre. All criminal record information from July 1, 1989 forward, statewide, is contained in the database. To facilitate quicker access for the public, the state has designated 10 county record centers to process all mail or ongoing commercial accounts' criminal record requests. All mail requests are forwarded to, and commercial account requests are assigned to one of 10 specific county court clerks for processing a statewide search. For quicker service on mail requests, use Hanson or Miner counties. Note that walk-in requesters seeking a single or minimum of requests may still obtain a record from their local county court. Five counties (Buffalo,

Key: Symbols refer to criminal records access unless otherwise noted. phone-☎ mail-✉ fax-**Fax** in person-✋ online-🖥 email-**Email**

Campbell, Dewey, McPherson, and Ziebach) do not have computer terminals in-house. The criminal records from these counties are entered into the database by court personnel from another location.

The fee is $15.00 per record. State authorized commercial accounts may order and receive records by fax, there is an additional $5.00 fee unless a non-toll free line is used.

Requesters who wish to set up a commercial account are directed to contact Jill Gusso at the Court Administrator's Office in Pierre

Online Access: There is no statewide online access computer system currently available. Larger courts are being placed on computer systems at a rate of 4 to 5 courts per year. Access is intended for internal use only. Smaller courts place their information on computer cards that are later sent to Pierre for input by the state office.

Additional Information: Most South Dakota courts do not allow the public to perform searches, but rather require the court clerk to do them for a fee of $15.00 per name (increased from $5.00 as of July 1, 1997). A special Record Search Request Form must be used. Searches will be returned with a disclaimer stating that the clerk is not responsible for the completeness of the search. Clerks are not required to respond to telephone or Fax requests. Many courts are not open all day so they prefer written requests.

Aurora County

Circuit Court *Felony, Misdemeanor, Civil, Eviction, Small Claims, Probate* PO Box 366 401 N Main St, Plankinton, SD 57368-0366. 8AM-N, 1-5PM. **605-942-7165**, Fax: 605-942-7170. Fax✉🖐

Beadle County

Circuit Court *Felony, Misdemeanor, Civil, Eviction, Small Claims, Probate* PO Box 1358, Huron, SD 57350-1358. 8AM-5PM. **605-353-7165**, Fax: 605-353-0118. ✉🖐

Bennett County

Circuit Court *Felony, Misd., Civil, Eviction, Small Claims, Probate* PO Box 281, Martin, SD 57551-0281. 8-4:30PM. **605-685-6969**, Fax 605-685-1075. ✉🖐

Bon Homme County

Circuit Court *Felony, Misd., Civil, Eviction, Small Claims, Probate* PO Box 6, Tyndall, SD 57066. 8AM-4:30PM. **605-589-4215**, Fax 605-589-4245. ✉🖐

Brookings County

Circuit Court *Felony, Misd., Civil, Eviction, Small Claims, Probate* 314 6th Ave, Brookings, SD 57006. 8AM-5PM. **605-688-4200**, Fax 605-688-4952. ✉🖐

Brown County

Circuit Court *Felony, Misd., Civil, Eviction, Small Claims, Probate* 101 1st Ave SE, Aberdeen, SD 57401. 8-5. **605-626-2451**, Fax: 605-626-2491. ✉🖐

Brule County

Circuit Court *Felony, Misdemeanor, Civil, Eviction, Small Claims, Probate* 300 S Courtland, #111, Chamberlain, SD 57325-1599. 8AM-N, 1-5PM. **605-734-4580**, Fax: 605-734-4582. Fax✉🖐

Buffalo County

Circuit Court *Felony, Misdemeanor, Civil, Eviction, Small Claims, Probate* PO Box 148, Gann Valley, SD 57341. 9AM-N. **605-293-3234**, Fax: 605-293-3240. Only records prior to 2000 are at Gann Valley. Records after 2000 at the Brule Circuit Ct. Clerk, 300 S Courtland, #111, Chamberlin, SD 57325, 605-734-4586. Records -605-734-4580 ✉🖐

Butte County

Circuit Court *Felony, Misdemeanor, Civil, Eviction, Small Claims, Probate* PO Box 250, Belle Fourche, SD 57717-0250. 8AM-N, 1-5PM. **605-892-2516**, Fax: 605-892-2836. ✉🖐

Campbell County

Circuit Court *Felony, Misd., Civil, Small Claims, Probate* PO Box 146, Mound City, SD 57646. 8AM-N T-W-F. **605-955-3536**, Fax: 605-955-3308. ✉🖐

Charles Mix County

Circuit Court *Felony, Misdemeanor, Civil, Eviction, Small Claims, Probate* PO Box 640, Lake Andes, SD 57356. 8AM-4:30PM. **605-487-7511**, Fax: 605-487-7547. Fax✉🖐

Clark County

Circuit Court *Felony, Misdemeanor, Civil, Eviction, Small Claims, Probate* PO Box 294, Clark, SD 57225. 8AM-N, 1-5PM. **605-532-5851**. ✉🖐

Clay County

Circuit Court *Felony, Misdemeanor, Civil, Eviction, Small Claims, Probate* PO Box 377, Vermillion, SD 57069.

8AM-5PM. **605-677-6755/6**, Fax: 605-677-8885. ✉🖐

Codington County

Circuit Court *Felony, Misdemeanor, Civil, Eviction, Small Claims, Probate* PO Box 1054, Watertown, SD 57201. 8AM-5PM. **605-882-5095**. ✉🖐

Corson County

Circuit Court *Felony, Misdemeanor, Civil, Eviction, Small Claims, Probate* PO Box 175, McIntosh, SD 57641. 9:30AM-2:30PM. **605-273-4201**, Fax: 605-273-4597. ✉🖐

Custer County

Circuit Court *Felony, Misdemeanor, Civil, Eviction, Small Claims, Probate* 420 Mt Rushmore Rd, Custer, SD 57730. 8AM-5PM. **605-673-4816**, Fax: 605-673-3416. ✉🖐

Davison County

Circuit Court *Felony, Misd., Civil, Eviction, Small Claims, Probate* PO Box 927, Mitchell, SD 57301. 8AM-5PM. **605-995-8105**, Fax 605-995-8105. ✉🖐

Day County

Circuit Court *Felony, Misdemeanor, Civil, Small Claims, Probate* 711 W 1st St, Webster, SD 57274. 8AM-5PM. **605-345-3771**, Fax: 605-345-3818. ✉🖐

Deuel County

Circuit Court *Felony, Misdemeanor, Civil, Eviction, Small Claims, Probate* PO Box 308, Clear Lake, SD 57226. 8AM-5PM. **605-874-2120**. ✉🖐

Dewey County

Circuit Court *Felony, Misdemeanor, Civil, Eviction, Small Claims, Probate*

Key: Symbols refer to criminal records access unless otherwise noted. phone-☎ mail-✉ fax-Fax in person-🖐 online-💻 email-Email

PO Box 96, Timber Lake, SD 57656. 9:30-N, 1-2:30PM. **605-865-3566**. ✉ ✋

Douglas County

Circuit Court *Felony, Misdemeanor, Civil, Eviction, Small Claims, Probate* PO Box 36, Armour, SD 57313. 8:30AM-1:30PM M-Th. **605-724-2585**. **Fax**✉ ✋

Edmunds County

Circuit Court *Felony, Misdemeanor, Civil, Eviction, Small Claims, Probate* PO Box 384, Ipswich, SD 57451. 8AM-N, 1-5PM. **605-426-6671**, Fax: 605-426-6323. **Fax**✉ ✋

Fall River County

Circuit Court *Felony, Misdemeanor, Civil, Eviction, Small Claims, Probate* 906 N River St, Hot Springs, SD 57747. 8AM-5PM. **605-745-5131**. Also handles cases for Shannon County. ✉ ✋

Faulk County

Circuit Court *Felony, Misdemeanor, Civil, Eviction, Small Claims, Probate* PO Box 357, Faulkton, SD 57438. 1:00PM-5:00PM. **605-598-6223**, Fax: 605-598-6252. ✉ ✋

Grant County

Circuit Court *Felony, Misdemeanor, Civil, Eviction, Small Claims, Probate* PO Box 509, Milbank, SD 57252. 8AM-N, 1-5PM. **605-432-5482**. ✉ ✋

Gregory County

Circuit Court *Felony, Misdemeanor, Civil, Eviction, Small Claims, Probate* PO Box 430, Burke, SD 57523. 8AM-N, 1-5PM. **605-775-2665**. ✉ ✋

Haakon County

Circuit Court *Felony, Misdemeanor, Civil, Eviction, Small Claims, Probate* PO Box 70, Philip, SD 57567. 8AM-N. **605-859-2627**. ✉ ✋

Hamlin County

Circuit Court *Felony, Misdemeanor, Civil, Eviction, Small Claims, Probate* PO Box 256, Hayti, SD 57241. 8:30AM-N, 12:30-4:30PM. **605-783-3751**, Fax: 605-783-2157. ✉ ✋

Hand County

Circuit Court *Felony, Misdemeanor, Civil, Small Claims, Probate* PO Box 122, Miller, SD 57362. 8AM-5PM. **605-853-3337**, Fax: 605-853-3779. **Fax**✉ ✋

Hanson County

Circuit Court *Felony, Misdemeanor, Civil, Small Claims, Probate* PO Box 127, Alexandria, SD 57311. 8AM-5PM; Closed from 12:00-1:00. **605-239-4446**, Fax: 605-239-9446. ✉ ✋

Harding County

Circuit Court *Felony, Misdemeanor, Civil, Eviction, Small Claims, Probate* PO Box 534, Buffalo, SD 57720. 9:30AM-N, 1-2:30PM. **605-375-3351**. This court is the designated search center of Harding and Pennington County criminal records. For eviction information this court says to contact Harding County Sheriff, PO Box 207, Buffalo SD 57720. **Fax**✉ ✋

Hughes County

Circuit Court *Felony, Misdemeanor, Civil, Eviction, Small Claims, Probate* 104 E Capital, Pierre, SD 57501. 8AM-5PM. **605-773-3713**. ✉ ✋

Hutchinson County

Circuit Court *Felony, Misdemeanor, Civil, Eviction, Small Claims, Probate* 140 Euclid, Rm 36, Olivet, SD 57052-2103. 8AM-N, 1-5PM. **605-387-4215**, Fax: 605-387-4208. **Fax**✉ ✋

Hyde County

Circuit Court *Felony, Misdemeanor, Civil, Eviction, Small Claims, Probate* PO Box 306, Highmore, SD 57345. 8AM-12PM. **605-852-2512**, Fax: 605-852-2767. **Fax**✉ ✋

Jackson County

Circuit Court *Felony, Misdemeanor, Civil, Eviction, Small Claims, Probate* PO Box 128, Kadoka, SD 57543. 8AM-N, 1-5PM. **605-837-2122**. ✉ ✋

Jerauld County

Circuit Court *Felony, Misdemeanor, Civil, Eviction, Small Claims, Probate* PO Box 435, Wessington Springs, SD 57382. 8AM-5PM. **605-539-1202**, Fax: 605-539-1203. ✉ ✋

Jones County

Circuit Court *Felony, Misdemeanor, Civil, Eviction, Small Claims, Probate* PO Box 448, Murdo, SD 57559. 8AM-N, 1-5PM. **605-669-2361**, Fax: 605-669-2641. Criminal cases and records at Potter County. ✉ ✋

Kingsbury County

Circuit Court *Felony, Misdemeanor, Civil, Eviction, Small Claims, Probate* PO Box 176, De Smet, SD 57231-0176. 8AM-N, 1-5PM. **605-854-3811**, Fax: 605-854-9080. ✉ ✋

Lake County

Circuit Court *Felony, Misdemeanor, Civil, Eviction, Small Claims, Probate* 200 E Center St, Madison, SD 57042. 8AM-N, 1-5PM. **605-256-5644**. ✉ ✋

Lawrence County

Circuit Court *Felony, Misdemeanor, Civil, Eviction, Small Claims, Probate* PO Box 626, Deadwood, SD 57732. 8AM-5PM. **605-578-2040**. **Fax**✉ ✋

Lincoln County

Circuit Court *Felony, Misdemeanor, Civil, Eviction, Small Claims, Probate* Clerk of Courts 100 E 5th St, Canton, SD 57013. 8AM-5PM. **605-987-5891**. ✉ ✋

Lyman County

Circuit Court *Felony, Misdemeanor, Civil, Eviction, Small Claims, Probate* PO Box 235, Kennebec, SD 57544. 8AM-5PM. **605-869-2277**. ✉ ✋

McCook County

Circuit Court *Felony, Misdemeanor, Civil, Eviction, Small Claims, Probate* PO Box 504, Salem, SD 57058. 8AM-12:30, 1-4:30PM. **605-425-2781**, Fax: 605-425-3144. ✉ ✋

McPherson County

Circuit Court *Felony, Misd., Civil, Eviction, Small Claims, Probate* PO Box 248, Leola, SD 57456. 8AM-N. **605-439-3361**, Fax: 605-439-3394. ✉ ✋

Marshall County

Circuit Court *Felony, Misdemeanor, Civil, Eviction, Small Claims, Probate* PO Box 130, Britton, SD 57430. 8AM-N, 1-5PM M-TH. **605-448-5213**. ☎ ✉ ✋

Meade County

Circuit Court *Felony, Misdemeanor, Civil, Eviction, Small Claims, Probate* PO Box 939, Sturgis, SD 57785. 8AM-N, 1-5PM. **605-347-4411**, Fax: 605-347-3526. ✉ ✋

Mellette County

Circuit Court *Felony, Misdemeanor, Civil, Eviction, Small Claims, Probate*

PO Box 257, White River, SD 57579. 8AM-N. **605-259-3230**, Fax: 605-259-3194. ✉ ✋

Miner County

Circuit Court *Felony, Misdemeanor, Civil, Eviction, Small Claims, Probate* PO Box 265, Howard, SD 57349. 8AM-N; 1-5PM. **605-772-4612**, Fax: 605-772-4412. **Fax**✉ ✋

Minnehaha County

Circuit Court *Felony, Misdemeanor, Civil, Eviction, Small Claims, Probate* 425 N Dakota Ave, Sioux Falls, SD 57104. 8AM-5PM. **605-367-5900**, Fax: 605-367-5916. ✉ ✋

Moody County

Circuit Court *Felony, Misdemeanor, Civil, Eviction, Small Claims, Probate* 101 E Pipestone, Flandreau, SD 57028. 8AM-5PM. **605-997-3181**, Fax: 605-997-3861. ✉ ✋

Pennington County

Circuit Court *Felony, Misdemeanor, Civil, Eviction, Small Claims, Probate* PO Box 230, Rapid City, SD 57709. 8AM-5PM. **605-394-2575**. Direct all record search requests to Harding County, PO Box 534, Buffalo SD 57720; phone 605-375-3351. None at this location.

Perkins County

Circuit Court *Felony, Misdemeanor, Civil, Eviction, Small Claims, Probate* PO Box 426, Bison, SD 57620-0426. 8AM-N, 1-5PM. **605-244-5626**, Fax: 605-244-7110. **Fax**✉ ✋

Potter County

Circuit Court *Felony, Misdemeanor, Civil, Eviction, Small Claims, Probate* 201 S Exene, Gettysburg, SD 57442. 8AM-N, 1-5PM. **605-765-9472**, Fax: 605-765-9670. **Fax**✉ ✋

Roberts County

Circuit Court *Felony, Misdemeanor, Civil, Eviction, Small Claims, Probate* 411 2nd Ave E, Sisseton, SD 57262. 8AM-5PM. **605-698-3395**, Fax: 605-698-7894. ✉ ✋

Sanborn County

Circuit Court *Felony, Misdemeanor, Civil, Eviction, Small Claims, Probate* PO Box 56, Woonsocket, SD 57385. 8AM-5PM. **605-796-4515**, Fax: 605-796-4502. **Fax**✉ ✋

Shannon County

Circuit Court *Felony, Misdemeanor, Civil, Eviction, Small Claims, Probate* 906 N River St, Hot Springs, SD 57747. 8AM-5PM. **605-745-5131**. Also handles cases for Fall River County. ✉ ✋

Spink County

Circuit Court *Felony, Misdemeanor, Civil, Eviction, Small Claims, Probate* 210 E 7th Ave, Redfield, SD 57469. 8AM-5PM. **605-472-4535**, Fax: 605-472-4352. ☎**Fax**✉ ✋

Stanley County

Circuit Court *Felony, Misdemeanor, Civil, Eviction, Small Claims, Probate* PO Box 758, Fort Pierre, SD 57532. 8AM-5PM. **605-223-7735**, Fax: 605-223-7738. **Fax**✉ ✋

Sully County

Circuit Court *Felony, Misdemeanor, Civil, Eviction, Small Claims, Probate* PO Box 188, Onida, SD 57564. 8AM-N. **605-258-2535**, Fax: 605-258-2270. ✉ ✋

Todd County

Circuit Court *Felony, Misdemeanor, Civil, Eviction, Small Claims, Probate* 200 E 3rd St PO Box 311, Winner, SD

57580. 8AM-5PM. **605-842-2266**, Fax: 605-842-2267. ✉ ✋

Tripp County

Circuit Court *Felony, Misdemeanor, Civil, Eviction, Small Claims, Probate* PO Box 311 200 E 3rd St, Winner, SD 57580. 8AM-5PM. **605-842-2266**, Fax: 605-842-2267. ✉ ✋

Turner County

Circuit Court *Felony, Misdemeanor, Civil, Eviction, Small Claims, Probate* PO Box 446, Parker, SD 57053. 8AM-5PM. **605-297-3115**, Fax: 605-297-2115. ✉ ✋

Union County

Circuit Court *Felony, Misdemeanor, Civil, Eviction, Small Claims, Probate* PO Box 757, Elk Point, SD 57025. 8:30AM-5PM. **605-356-2132**, Fax: 605-356-3687. **Fax**✉ ✋

Walworth County

Circuit Court *Felony, Misdemeanor, Civil, Eviction, Small Claims, Probate* PO Box 328, Selby, SD 57472. 8AM-5PM. **605-649-7311**, Fax: 605-649-7624. ✉ ✋

Yankton County

Circuit Court *Felony, Misdemeanor, Civil, Small Claims (and Eviction), Probate* Clerk of Courts PO Box 155, Yankton, SD 57078. 8AM-5PM. **605-668-3080**, Fax: 605-668-5411. ✉ ✋

Ziebach County

Circuit Court *Felony, Misdemeanor, Civil, Eviction, Small Claims, Probate* PO Box 306, Dupree, SD 57623. 9:30AM-N, 1-2:30PM. **605-365-5159**. ✉ ✋

Key: Symbols refer to criminal records access unless otherwise noted. phone-☎ mail-✉ fax-**Fax** in person-✋ online-💻 email-**Email**

Tennessee

State Court Administration: Administrative Office of the Courts, 511 Union St (Nashville City Center) #600, Nashville, TN, 37219; 615-741-2687, Fax: 615-741-6285. www.tsc.state.tn.us

Court Structure: Criminal cases are handled by the Circuit Courts and General Sessions Courts. All General Sessions Courts have raised the maximum civil case limit to $15,000 from $10,000. Generally, misdemeanor cases are heard by General Sessions, but in Circuit Court if connected to a felony. Chancery Courts, in addition to handling probate, also hear certain types of equitable civil cases. Combined courts vary by county, and the counties of Davidson, Hamilton, Knox, and Shelby have separate Criminal Courts.

Probate Courts: Probate is handled in the Chancery or County Courts, except in Shelby and Davidson Counties where it is handled by the Probate Court.

Online Access: The Administrative Office of Courts provides access to Appellate Court opinions at the website www.tsc.state.tn.us. Several counties offer online access to court records.

Anderson County

7th District Circuit & General Sessions Court *Felony, Misdemeanor, Civil, Eviction, Small Claims* 100 N Main St, Clinton, TN 37716. 8AM-4:30PM. **865-457-5400**, Fax: 865-259-2345. 🖐

Chancery Court *Civil, Probate* Anderson County Courthouse PO Box 501, Clinton, TN 37717. 8:30AM-4:30PM. **865-457-5400**, Fax: 865-457-6267 Probate: 865-457-6207. Access civil records- ☎ ✉ 🖐

Bedford County

17th District Circuit & General Sessions Court *Felony, Misdemeanor, Civil, Eviction, Small Claims* 1 Public Sq, #200, Shelbyville, TN 37160. 8AM-4PM. **931-684-3223**. 🖐

Chancery Court *Civil, Probate* Chancery Court, 1 Public Sq, #302, Shelbyville, TN 37160. 8AM-4PM M-Th, 8AM-5PM Fri. **931-684-1672**. Access civil records- 🖐

Benton County

24th District Circuit & General Sessions Court *Felony, Misdemeanor, Civil, Eviction, Small Claims* 1 E Court Sq, Rm 207, Camden, TN 38320. 8AM-4PM M-Th; 8AM-5PM F. **731-584-6711**, Fax: 731-584-2081. 🖐

Chancery Court *Civil, Probate* 1 E Court Sq, Courthouse Rm 206, Camden, TN 38320. 8AM-4PM M-Th; 8AM-5PM F. **731-584-4435**, Fax: 731-584-1407. Access civil records- 🖐

Bledsoe County

12th District Circuit & General Sessions Court *Felony, Misdemeanor, Civil, Eviction, Small Claims* PO Box 455, Pikeville, TN 37367. 8AM-4PM. **423-447-6488**, Fax: 423-447-2534. 🖐

Chancery Court *Civil, Probate* PO Box 389, Pikeville, TN 37367. 8AM-4PM M,T,W,F; 8AM-N Sat. **423-447-2484**, Fax: 423-447-6856. Access civil records- **Fax** ✉ 🖐

Blount County

5th District General Sessions Court *Misdemeanor, Civil, Eviction, Small Claims* www.blounttn.org/circuit/ 926 E Lamar Alexander Pky, Maryville, TN 37804-6201. 8AM-4:30PM. **865-273-5450**, Fax: 865-273-5411. ✉ 🖐

Circuit Court *Felony, Misdemeanor, Civil* 926 E Lamar Alexander Pky 1st Fl, Maryville, TN 37804. 8AM-4:30PM. **865-273-5400**, Fax: 865-273-5411. ✉ 🖐

County Clerk *Probate* 345 Court St, Old Courthouse, Maryville, TN 37804. 8AM-4:30. **865-273-5800**, Fax: 865-273-5815.

Bradley County

10th District Circuit & General Sessions Court *Felony, Misdemeanor, Civil, Eviction, Small Claims* Courthouse, Rm 205 155 N Ocoee St, Cleveland, TN 37311-5068. 8:30AM-4:30PM M-Th, 8:30AM-5PM Fri. **423-476-0692**, Fax: 423-476-0488. ✉ 🖐

Chancery Court *Civil, Probate* 55 N Ocoee St, Rm 203, Cleveland, TN 37311. 8:30AM-4:30PM M-Th, 8:30-5PM Fri. **423-476-0526**. Access civil records- ☎ 🖐

Campbell County

8th District Circuit & General Sessions Court *Felony, Misdemeanor, Civil, Eviction, Small Claims* PO Box 26, Jacksboro, TN 37757. 8AM-4:30PM. **423-562-2624**. ✉ 🖐

Chancery Court *Civil, Probate* PO Box 182 (570 Main St, #110), Jacksboro, TN 37757. 8AM-4:30PM. **423-562-3496**. Access civil records- 🖐 ✉

Cannon County

16th District Circuit & General Sessions Court *Felony, Misdemeanor, Civil, Eviction, Small Claims* County Courthouse Public Sq, Woodbury, TN 37190. 8AM-4PM M T TH F; 8AM-N W. **615-563-4461**, Fax 615-563-6391. 🖐

County Court *Probate* County Courthouse Public Square, Woodbury, TN 37190. 8AM-4PM M T TH F; 8AM-N S. **615-563-4278/5936**, Fax: 615-563-1289.

Carroll County

24th District Circuit & General Sessions Court *Felony, Misdemeanor, Civil, Eviction, Small Claims* 99 Court Sq, #103, Huntingdon, TN 38344. 8AM-4PM. Civil: 731-986-1929 (Circuit), 731-986-1926 (Gen Sess). Access records- 🖐

Chancery Court *Civil, Probate* 99 Court Sq, #105, Huntingdon, TN 38344. 8AM-4PM. **731-986-1920**. Access civil records- ✉ 🖐

Carter County

1st District Circuit & General Sessions Court *Felony, Misdemeanor, Civil, Eviction, Small Claims* Carter County Justice Ctr 900 E Elk Ave, Elizabethton,

TN 37643. 8AM-5PM. **423-542-1835**, Fax: 423-542-3742. Civil phone: 423-542-1825. ✋

County Court *Probate* 801 E Elk Ave., Elizabethton, TN 37643. 8AM-4:30PM. **423-542-1814**, Fax: 423-547-1502.

Cheatham County

23rd District Circuit Court *Felony, Civil Actions over $15,000, Misdemeanors* 100 Public Sq, Rm 225, Ashland City, TN 37015. 8AM-4PM. **615-792-3272**, Fax: 615-792-3203. Circuit Court is Rm 225, General Sessions Rm 223 (615-792-4866); each court must be searched separately. Circuit court handles felony, civil actions over $15,000, some misdemeanors. ✉ ✋

General Sessions *Misdemeanor, Civil under $15,000, Eviction, Small Claims* 100 Public Sq, Rm 223, Ashland City, TN 37015. 8AM-4PM. **615-792-4866**, Fax: 615-792-3203. ✉ ✋

Chancery Court *Civil, Probate* Clerk & Master, #106, Ashland City, TN 37015. 8AM-4PM. **615-792-4620**. Access civil records- ✋

Chester County

26th District Circuit & General Sessions Court *Felony, Misd., Civil, Eviction, Small Claims* PO Box 133, Henderson, TN 38340. 8AM-4PM. **731-989-2454**, Fax: 731-989-9184. ✉ ✋

Chancery Court *Civil, Probate* Clerk & Master, PO Box 262, Henderson, TN 38340. 8AM-4PM. **731-989-7171**, Fax: 731-989-7176. Access civil records- ✉ ✋

Claiborne County

8th District Criminal, Circuit & General Sessions Court *Felony, Misd., Civil, Eviction, Small Claims* 1740 Main St, #201, Tazewell, TN 37879. 8:30AM-4PM M-F, 9AM-N Sat. **423-626-8181**, Fax: 423-626-5631. ✉ Fax ✋

Chancery Court *Civil, Probate* PO Box 180, Tazewell, TN 37879. 8:30AM-N, 1-4PM. **423-626-3284**, Fax: 423-626-3604. Access civil records- ✉ ✋

Clay County

13th District Circuit & General Sessions Court *Felony, Misdemeanor, Civil, Eviction, Small Claims* PO Box

749, Celina, TN 38551. 8AM-5PM. **931-243-2557**. ✋

Chancery Court *Civil, Probate* PO Box 332, Celina, TN 38551. 8AM-4PM M T TH F; 8AM-N W. **931-243-3145**. Access civil records- ✉ ✋

Cocke County

4th District Circuit Court *Felony, Misdemeanor, Civil Actions Over $15,000* 111 Court Ave, Rm 201, Newport, TN 37821. 8:30AM-5PM. **423-623-6124**, Fax: 423-625-3889. Access records- ✉ ✋

General Sessions Court *Misdemeanor, Civil Actions Under $15,000, Eviction, Small Claims* 111 Court Ave, Newport, TN 37821. 8AM-4PM. **423-623-8619**, Fax: 423-623-9808. ☎ ✉ ✋

Chancery Court *Civil, Probate* Courthouse Annex 360 E Main St, #103, Newport, TN 37821. 8AM-4:30PM. **423-623-3321**, Fax: 423-625-3642. Criminal phone: 423-623-6124. Access civil records- ☎ ✉ ✋

Coffee County

14th District Circuit & General Sessions Court *Felony, Misdemeanor, Civil, Eviction, Small Claims* PO Box 629, Manchester, TN 37349. 8AM-4:30PM. **931-723-5110**. ✉ ✋

Chancery Court *Civil, Probate* 300 Hillsboro Blvd, Rm 102, Manchester, TN 37355. 8AM-4:30. **931-723-5132**, crim: 931-723-5110. Access civil records- ✉ ✋

Crockett County

Circuit & General Sessions Court *Felony, Misdemeanor, Civil, Eviction, Small Claims* 1 S Bell St, #6, Courthouse, Alamo, TN 38001. 8AM-4PM. **731-696-5462**, Fax: 731-696-2605. ✉ Fax ✋

Chancery Court *Civil, Probate* 1 S Bell St, #5, Alamo, TN 38001. 8AM-4PM. **731-696-5458**, Fax: 731-696-3028. Access civil records- ✉ ✋

Cumberland County

13th District Circuit & General Sessions Court *Felony, Misdemeanor, Civil, Eviction, Small Claims* 2 N Main St, #302, Crossville, TN 38555. 8AM-4PM. **931-484-6647 General Sess;** Circuit 931-484-5852, Fax: 931-456-5013. ✋

Chancery Court *Civil, Probate* 2 N Main St, #101, Crossville, TN 38555-4583. 8AM-4PM. **931-484-4731**, crim: 931-484-5852. Access civil records- ✉ ✋

Davidson County

20th District Criminal Court *Felony, Misd.* www.nashville.org/ccrt/ Metro Courthouse, Rm 309 601 Mainstream Dr., Nashville, TN 37201. 8AM-4PM. **615-862-5601**, Fax: 615-862-5676. ✉ 🖳 ✋

Circuit Court *Civil* www.nashville.gov/circuit 506 Metro Courthouse, Nashville, TN 37201. 8AM-4:30PM. **615-862-5181**. Physical address is 523 Mainstream Dr, #200, Nashville. Access civil records- ✉ ✋

General Sessions Court *Civil Actions Under $15,000, Eviction, Small Claims* www.nashville.gov/circuit/sessions/ 501 Great Circle Rd., Nashville, TN 37228. 8AM-4:30PM. **615-862-5195**, Fax: 615-862-5924. Access civil records- ✉ ✋

Probate Court 105 Metro Courthouse, Nashville, TN 37201. 8AM-4:30. **615-862-5980**, Fax: 615-862-5987.

Decatur County

24th District Circuit & General Sessions Court *Felony, Misdemeanor, Civil, Eviction, Small Claims* PO Box 488, Decaturville, TN 38329. 8AM-4PM M T TH F; 8AM-N W & S. **731-852-3125**, Fax: 731-852-2130. ✋

Chancery Court *Civil, Probate* Clerk & Master, Decaturville, TN 38329. 9M-4PM M T TH F; 9AM-N W. **731-852-3422**, Fax 731-852-2130. access civil records ✋

De Kalb County

13th District Circuit & General Sessions Court *Felony, Misdemeanor, Civil, Eviction, Small Claims* 1 Public Sq, Rm 303, Smithville, TN 37166. 8AM-4:30PM M,T,W,Th; 8AM-5PM Fri. **615-597-5711**. ✋

Chancery Court *Civil, Probate* 1 Public Square, Rm 302, Smithville, TN 37166. 8AM-4PM. **615-597-4360**. ✋

Dickson County

23rd District Circuit Court *Felony, Misdemeanor, Civil Actions Over $15,000* Court Square, PO Box 70, Charlotte, TN 37036. 8AM-4PM. **615-789-7010**, Fax: 615-789-7018. ☎ Fax ✉ ✋

Key: Symbols refer to criminal records access unless otherwise noted. phone-☎ mail-✉ fax-Fax in person-✋ online-🖳 email-Email

General Sessions *Civil Actions Under $15,000, Eviction, Small Claims* PO Box 217, Charlotte, TN 37036. 8AM-4PM. **615-789-5414**, Fax: 615-789-3456. Access civil records-☎ ✉ ✋

County Court *Probate* Court Square 4000 Hwy 48 N, #1, Charlotte, TN 37036. 8AM-4PM. **615-789-0250**.

Dyer County

29th District Circuit & General Sessions Court *Felony, Misdemeanor, Civil, Eviction, Small Claims* PO Box 1360, Dyersburg, TN 38025. 8:30AM-4:30PM. **731-286-7809**, Fax: 731-288-7728. ✉ ✋

Chancery Court *Civil, Probate* PO Box 1360, Dyersburg, TN 38024. 8:30AM-4:30PM. **731-286-7818**, Fax: 731-288-7706. Access civil records-✉ ✋

Fayette County

25th District Circuit & General Sessions Court *Felony, Misdemeanor, Civil, Eviction, Small Claims* PO Box 670, Somerville, TN 38068. 9AM-5PM. **901-465-5205**, Fax: 901-465-5215. ✋

Chancery Court *Civil, Probate* PO Drawer 220, Somerville, TN 38068. 9AM-5PM. **901-465-5220**, Fax: 901-465-5217. Access civil records-✋

Fentress County

8th District Circuit & General Sessions Court *Felony, Misdemeanor, Civil, Eviction, Small Claims* PO Box 699, Jamestown, TN 38556. 8AM-4PM M-F; 8AM-N Sat. **931-879-7919**, Fax: 931-879-3014. ✉ ✋fax.

Chancery Court *Civil, Probate* PO Box 66, Jamestown, TN 38556. 9AM-5PM M T TH F; 9AM-N W. **931-879-8615**, Fax: 931-879-4236. Access civil records-✉ ✋

Franklin County

12th District Circuit Court & General Sessions *Felony, Misdemeanor, Civil, Eviction, Small Claims* 1 S Jefferson St, Winchester, TN 37398. 8AM-4:30PM. **931-967-2923**, Fax 931-962-1479. ✉ ✋

County Court *Probate* 1 S Jefferson St, Winchester, TN 37398. 8AM-4:30PM. **931-962-1485**, Fax: 931-962-3394.

Gibson County

28th District Circuit & General Sessions Court *Felony, Misdemeanor, Civil, Eviction, Small Claims* 295 N College PO Box 147, Trenton, TN 38382. 8AM-4:30PM. **731-855-7615**, Fax: 731-855-7676. **Fax**✉ ✋

Chancery Court *Civil, Probate* Clerk & Master PO Box 290, Trenton, TN 38382. 8AM-4:30PM. **731-855-7639**, Fax: 731-855-7655. Access civil records-✋

Giles County

22nd District Circuit & General Sessions Court *Felony, Misd., Civil, Eviction, Small Claims* PO Box 678, Pulaski, TN 38478. 8AM-4PM. **931-363-5311**, Fax: 931-424-4790. ☎ ✉ **Fax** ✋

County Court *Probate* PO Box 678, Pulaski, TN 38478. 8AM-4PM. **931-363-1509**, Fax: 931-424-4795.

Grainger County

4th District Circuit & General Sessions Court *Felony, Misd., Civil, Eviction, Small Claims* PO Box 157, Rutledge, TN 37861. 8:30-4:30PM. **865-828-3605**. ✋

Chancery Court *Civil, Probate* Clerk & Master PO Box 160, Rutledge, TN 37861. 8:30AM-4:30PM M,T,Th,F, 8:30AM-N Wed. **865-828-4436**, Fax: 865-828-8714. Access civil records-☎ **Fax** ✉ ✋

Greene County

3rd District Circuit & General Sessions Court *Felony, Misdemeanor, Civil, Eviction, Small Claims* 101 S Main, Geene County Courthouse, Greeneville, TN 37743. 8AM-4:30PM. **423-798-1760**, Fax: 423-798-1763. ✋

County Court *Probate* 204 N Cutler St, #200 Courthouse Annex, Greeneville, TN 37745. 8AM-4:30PM. **423-798-1708**, 798-1709, Fax: 423-798-1822.

Grundy County

12th District Circuit & General Sessions Court *Felony, Misdemeanor, Civil, Eviction, Small Claims* PO Box 161, Altamont, TN 37301. 8AM-4PM M-Th; 8AM-5PM F. **931-692-3368**, Fax: 931-692-2414. Access records-✉ **Fax** ✋

Chancery Court *Civil, Probate* PO Box 174, Altamont, TN 37301. 8AM-4PM M-Th; 8AM-5pm F. **931-692-3455**, Fax: 931-692-4125. access civil recs-☎ ✉ ✋

Hamblen County

3rd District Circuit & General Sessions Court *Felony, Misdemeanor, Civil, Eviction, Small Claims* 510 Allison St, Morristown, TN 37814. 8AM-4PM M-Th, 8AM-5PM Fri, 9-11:30AM Sat. **423-586-5640**, Fax: 423-585-2764. ✉ ✋

Chancery Court *Civil* 511 W 2nd North St, Morristown, TN 37814. 8AM-4PM M-Th; 8AM-4:30PM F. **423-586-9112**, Fax: 423-318-2510. **Fax**✉ ✋

Hamilton County

11th Dist. General Sessions Court *Civil Under $15,000, Eviction, Small Claims* www.hamiltontn.gov/courts/sessions/default.htm Civil Division, 600 Market St, Rm 111, Chattanooga, TN 37402. 8AM-4PM. **423-209-7630**, Fax: 423-209-7631. Access civil records-☎ ✉ ✋ 🖥

11th District Civil Court *Civil Actions Over $15,000* www.hamiltontn.gov/courts/ Rm 500, Courthouse 625 Georgia Ave, Chattanooga, TN 37402. 8AM-4PM. **423-209-6700**, Fax: 423-209-6701. Access civil records-☎ **Fax** ✉ ✋ 🖥

11th District Criminal Court *Felony, Misdemeanor* www.hamiltontn.gov/courts/ 600 Market St, Rm 102, Chattanooga, TN 37402. 8AM-4PM. **423-209-7500**, Fax: 423-209-7501. Access records-✉ ✋ 🖥

Chancery Court *Civil, Probate* www.hamiltontn.gov/Courts/ClerkMaster/default.htm Chancery Court, Clerk & Master 201 E 7th St, Rm 300, Chattanooga, TN 37402. 8-4. **423-209-6600**, Fax: 423-209-6601. Access civil records-☎ ✉ ✋ 🖥

Hancock County

3rd District Circuit & General Sessions Court *Felony, Misdemeanor, Civil, Eviction, Small Claims* PO Box 347, Sneedville, TN 37869. 8-4PM, W S 8-12. **423-733-2954**, Fax 423-733-2119. ✉ ✋

Chancery Court *Civil, Probate* PO Box 277, Sneedville, TN 37869. 8AM-4PM. **423-733-4524**, Fax: 423-733-2762. Access civil records-✉ ✋

Hardeman County

25th District Circuit & General Sessions Court *Felony, Misdemeanor, Civil, Eviction, Small Claims* Courthouse, 100 N Main, Bolivar, TN 38008. 8:30AM-4:30PM M-Th, 8AM-5PM Fri. **731-658-6524**, Fax: 731-658-4584. ✋

Chancery Court *Civil, Probate* PO Box 45, Bolivar, TN 38008. 8:30AM-4:30PM M-TH, 8:30AM-5PM F. **731-658-3142**, Fax: 731-658-4580. Access civil records-☎ ✉ **Fax** ✋

Hardin County

24th District Circuit & General Sessions Court *Felony, Misdemeanor, Civil, Eviction, Small Claims* 601 Main St, Savannah, TN 38372. 8AM-4:30PM M T TH F; 8AM-N W. **731-925-3583**, Fax: 731-926-2955.

County Court *Probate* 601 Main St, Savannah, TN 38372. 8AM-4:30PM M T TH F; 8AM-12PM W & S. **731-925-3921**, Fax: 731-926-4313.

Hawkins County

3rd District Circuit & General Sessions Court *Felony, Misdemeanor, Civil, Eviction, Small Claims* 100 E Main St, Rogersville, TN 37857. 8AM-4PM. **423-272-3397**, Fax: 423-272-9646.

Chancery Court *Civil, Probate* PO Box 908, Rogersville, TN 37857. 8AM-4PM. **423-272-8150**. Access civil records-

Haywood County

28th District Circuit & General Sessions Court *Felony, Misdemeanor, Civil, Eviction, Small Claims* 1 N Washington Ave, Brownsville, TN 38012. 8:30AM-5PM. **731-772-1112**, Fax: 731-772-8139. Access records-☎ ✉ **Fax**

Chancery Court *Civil, Probate* 1 N Washington PO Box 356, Brownsville, TN 38012. 8:30AM-5PM. **731-772-0122**, Fax 731-772-7802. access civil records

Henderson County

26th District Circuit & General Sessions Court *Felony, Misdemeanor, Civil, Eviction, Small Claims* 17 Monroe Ave, #9, Henderson County Courthouse, Lexington, TN 38351. 8AM-4:30PM M T TH F. **731-968-2031**, Fax: 731-967-9441 (criminal). ✉

Chancery Court *Civil, Probate* 17 Monroe, Rm 2, 2nd Fl, Lexington, TN 38351. 8AM-4:30PM. **731-968-2801**, Fax: 731-967-5380. Access civil records-☎ ✉ **Fax**

Henry County

24th District Circuit & General Sessions Court *Felony, Misdemeanor, Civil, Eviction, Small Claims* PO Box 429, Paris, TN 38242. 8AM-4:30PM. **731-642-0461**, Fax: 731-642-1244. **Fax** ✉

County Court *Probate* PO Box 24, Paris, TN 38242. 8AM-4:30PM. **731-642-2412**, Fax: 731-644-0947.

Hickman County

21st District Circuit & General Sessions Court *Felony, Misdemeanor, Civil, Eviction, Small Claims* 104 College Ave, #204, Centerville, TN 37033. 8-4. **931-729-2211**, Fax: 931-729-6141. ✉ **Fax**

Chancery Court *Civil, Probate* 104 College Ave, #202, Centerville, TN 37033. 8AM-4PM. **931-729-2522**, Fax: 931-729-3726. Access civil records- ✉

Houston County

23rd District Circuit & General Sessions Court *Felony, Misdemeanor, Civil, Eviction, Small Claims* PO Box 403, Erin, TN 37061. 8AM-4:30PM. **931-289-4673**, Fax: 931-289-5182.

Chancery Court *Civil, Probate* PO Box 332, Erin, TN 37061. 8AM-4PM. **931-289-3870**, Fax: 931-289-5679. Access civil records- ✉

Humphreys County

23rd District Circuit & General Sessions Court *Felony, Misdemeanor, Civil, Eviction, Small Claims* Rm 106, Waverly, TN 37185. 8-4:30PM. **931-296-2461**, Fax: 931-296-1651. ☎ **Fax** ✉

County Court *Probate* Clerk, Rm 2 Courthouse Annex, Waverly, TN 37185. 8AM-4:30PM. **931-296-7671, 931-296-6503**, Fax: 931-296-0823.

Jackson County

15th District Circuit & General Sessions Court *Felony, Misdemeanor, Civil, Eviction, Small Claims* PO Box 205, Gainesboro, TN 38562. 8AM-4PM M T TH F; 8AM-3PM W; 8AM-N S. **931-268-9314**, Fax: 931-268-4555. **Fax** ✉

Chancery Court *Probate* PO Box 733, Gainesboro, TN 38562-0733. 8AM-4PM M T TH F; 8AM-3PM W. **931-268-9516**, Fax: 931-268-9512.

Jefferson County

4th District Circuit & General Sessions Court *Felony, Misdemeanor, Civil, Eviction, Small Claims* PO Box 671, Dandridge, TN 37725. 8AM-4PM. **865-397-2786**, Fax: 865-397-4894. ✉

County Court *Probate* PO Box 710, Dandridge, TN 37725. 8AM-4PM M-F,

8AM-11PM Sat. **865-397-2935**, Fax: 865-397-3839.

Johnson County

1st District Circuit & General Sessions Court *Felony, Misd., Civil, Eviction, Small Claims* PO Box 73, Mountain City, TN 37683. 8:30AM-5PM. **423-727-9012**, Fax: 423-727-7047. ☎ ✉

Chancery Court *Civil, Probate* PO Box 196, Mountain City, TN 37683. 8:30AM-12:00,1-5PM. **423-727-7853**, Fax: 423-727-7047. Access civil records- ✉

Knox County

Circuit Court *Civil Actions Over $15,000* www.knoxcounty.org 400 Main Ave, Rm M-30 PO Box 379, Knoxville, TN 37901. 8AM-5PM; 4:30 PM Fri. **865-215-2400**, Fax: 865-215-4251. Access civil records-☎ **Fax** ✉

6th District Criminal Court *Felony, Misdemeanor* www.knoxcounty.org 400 Main Ave, Rm 149, Knoxville, TN 37902. 8AM-4:30PM. **865-215-2492**, Fax: 865-215-4291. **Fax** ✉

General Sessions Court *Civil Actions Under $15,000, Eviction, Small Claims* www.knoxcounty.org 300 Main Ave, Rm 318 PO Box 379, Knoxville, TN 37901. 8AM-4:30PM. **865-215-2518**. Access civil records- ✉

Chancery Court *Civil, Probate* www.knoxcounty.org 400 Main Ave, Rm 215, Knoxville, TN 37902. 8AM-4:30PM. **865-215-2555 (Chancery)**, Fax: 865-215-2920. Criminal phone: 865-215-2492, Probate: 865-215-2389. Access civil records-☎ **Fax** ✉

Lake County

29th District Circuit & General Sessions Court *Felony, Misd., Civil, Eviction, Small Claims* 229 Church St, PO Box 11, Tiptonville, TN 38079. 8-4. **731-253-7137**, Fax: 731-253-8930.

Chancery Court *Probate* 229 Church Lake County Courthouse Box 12, Tiptonville, TN 38079. 9AM-4PM. **731-253-8926**. Access civil records- ✉

Lauderdale County

25th District Circuit Court *Felony, Misdemeanor, Civil Actions Over $15,000* Lauderdale County Justice Ctr 675 Hwy 51 S, PO Box 509, Ripley, TN 38063.

8AM-4:30PM. **731-635-0101**, Fax: 731-221-8663. ✉🖐

General Sessions Court *Civil Actions Under $15,000, Eviction, Small Claims* PO Box 509, Ripley, TN 38063. 8AM-4:30PM (till noon on Wed). **731-635-2572**, Fax: 731-221-8663. Access civil records-✉🖐

County Court *Probate* Courthouse, 100 Court Sq, Ripley, TN 38063. 8AM-4:30PM M T TH F; 8AM-N W. **731-635-2561**, Fax: 731-635-9682.

Lawrence County

22nd District Circuit & General Sessions Court *Felony, Misd., Civil, Eviction, Small Claims* NBU #12, 240 W Gaines, Lawrenceburg, TN 38464. 8-4:30. **931-762-4398**, Fax: 931-766-4471. 🖐

County Clerk *Probate* 240 W Gaines St, NBU #2, Lawrenceburg, TN 38464. 8AM-4:30PM. **931-762-7700; ext 116**, Fax: 931-766-4146. Leon Clanton Ext 177 Access civil records-🖐

Lewis County

21st District Circuit & General Sessions Court *Felony, Misdemeanor, Civil, Eviction, Small Claims* Courthouse, 110 Park Ave N Rm 201, Hohenwald, TN 38462. 8AM-4:30PM. **931-796-3724**, Fax: 931-796-6021. 🖐

Chancery Court *Civil, Probate* Lewis County Courthouse 110 Park Ave N, Rm 208, Hohenwald, TN 38462. 8AM-4:30PM. **931-796-3734**, Fax: 931-796-6017. Access civil records-🖐

Lincoln County

17th District Circuit & General Sessions Court *Felony, Misdemeanor, Civil, Eviction, Small Claims* 112 Main Ave S, Rm 203, Fayetteville, TN 37334. 8AM-4PM. **931-433-2334**, Fax: 931-438-1577. ☎Fax✉🖐

Chancery Court *Civil, Probate* 112 Main Ave, Rm B109, Fayetteville, TN 37334. 8AM-4PM. **931-433-1482**, Fax: 931-433-9313. Access civil records-🖐

Loudon County

9th District Criminal & Circuit Court *Felony, Misdemeanor, Civil* www.loudoncounty.com/ccc.htm PO Box 280, Loudon, TN 37774. 8-4:30PM. **865-458-2042**, Fax: 865-458-2043. ☎Fax✉🖐

General Sessions Court *Misd., Eviction, Small Claims* www.loudoncounty.com/ccc.htm 12680 Hwy 11 W, #3, Lenoir City, TN 37771, 423-986-3505; Fax: 865-458-2043. ☎Fax✉🖐

County Court *Probate* 101 Mulberry St, #200, Loudon, TN 37774. 8AM-4:30PM. **865-458-2726**, Fax: 865-458-9891.

McMinn County

10th District Circuit & General Sessions Court *Felony, Misdemeanor, Civil, Eviction, Small Claims, Probate* PO Box 506, Athens, TN 37303. 8:30AM-4PM. **423-745-1923**, Fax: 423-744-1642. ☎Fax✉🖐

McNairy County

25th District Circuit & General Sessions Court *Felony, Misdemeanor, Civil, Eviction, Small Claims* 300 Industrial Dr, Selmer, TN 38375. 8AM-4:30PM M-F; 8AM-N Sat. **731-645-1015**, Fax: 731-645-1003. ✉🖐

Chancery Court *Civil, Probate* Chancery Court, Clerk & Master Courthouse, Rm 205, Selmer, TN 38375. 8AM-4PM M,T,Th,F; Closed W. **731-645-5446**, Fax: 731-646-1165. Access civil records-🖐

Macon County

15th District Circuit & General Sessions Court *Felony, Misdemeanor, Civil, Eviction, Small Claims, Probate* Court Clerk 904 Hwy 52 Bypass, Lafayette, TN 37083. 8AM-4:30PM M-TH; 8AM-5PM F. **615-666-2354**, Fax: 615-666-3001 Probate 615-666-2000. 🖐

Madison County

26th District Circuit Court *Felony, Misdemeanor, Civil Actions Over $15,000* www.co.madison.tn.us 515 S Liberty St, Jackson, TN 38301. 8AM-4PM. **731-423-6035 x1049**. Misdemeanor cases here are usually accompanied by felonies. 🖐

General Sessions Court *Misdemeanor, Civil Actions Under $15,000, Eviction, Small Claims* 515 S Liberty St, Jackson, TN 38301. 8AM-4PM. Civil: 731-423-6018, crim: 731-423-6128. 🖐

Probate Division - General Sessions Division II *Probate* 110 Irby St, #102, Jackson, TN 38302. 8:30-12, 1-4:30PM. **731-988-3025**, Fax: 731-988-3807.

Marion County

12th District Circuit & General Sessions Court *Felony, Misdemeanor, Civil, Eviction, Small Claims* PO Box 789, Courthouse Sq, Jasper, TN 37347. 8AM-4PM. **423-942-2134**, Fax: 423-942-4160. ☎✉🖐

Chancery Court *Civil, Probate* PO Box 789, Jasper, TN 37347. 8AM-4PM. **423-942-2601**, Fax: 423-942-0291. Access civil records-✉🖐

Marshall County

17th District Circuit & General Sessions Court *Felony, Misdemeanor, Civil, Eviction, Small Claims* Courthouse, Lewisburg, TN 37091. 8AM-4PM. **931-359-0536**, Fax: 931-359-0543. 🖐

Chancery Court *Probate* 201 Marshall County Courthouse, Lewisburg, TN 37091. 8AM-4PM. **931-359-2181**, Fax: 931-359-0524. Probate is handled by the Clerk & Master.

Maury County

Circuit & General Sessions Court *Felony, Misdemeanor, Civil, Eviction, Small Claims* Maury County Courthouse 41 Public Square, Columbia, TN 38401. 8AM-4PM. **931-381-3690**, Fax: 931-381-3985. Criminal phone: 931-375-1100. 🖐

Probate Court Maury County Courthouse, Clerk & Masters Office 41 Public Square, Columbia, TN 38401. 8AM-4PM. **931-381-3690 x515**, Fax: 931-308-5614.

Meigs County

9th District Circuit & General Sessions Court *Felony, Misdemeanor, Civil, Eviction, Small Claims* PO Box 205, Decatur, TN 37322. 8:30AM-4:30PM till noon on Wed. **423-334-5821**, Fax: 423-334-4819. 🖐

Chancery Court *Civil, Probate* PO Box 5, Decatur, TN 37322. 8AM-5PM M T TH F; 8:30AM-N W. **423-334-5243**. Access civil records-🖐

Monroe County

10th District Circuit 1 Courts *Felony, Misdemeanor, Civil over $10,000* 105 College St, Madisonville, TN 37354. 8AM-4:30PM. **423-442-2396**, Fax: 423-442-9538. ✉🖐

General Sessions Court *Civil under $15,000, Eviction, Small Claims* 300 Tellico St, Madisonville, TN 37354.

8AM-4:30PM. **423-442-9537**, Fax: 423-420-9091. Access civil records-✉ ✋

Chancery Court *Civil, Probate* 105 College St, #2, Madisonville, TN 37354. 8:30AM-4:30PM (4PM on W). **423-442-2644**, Fax: 423-420-0048 Probate: 423-442-4573. Access civil records-✉ ✋

Montgomery County

Montgomery County Circuit & General Sessions Court *Felony, Misdemeanor, Civil, Evictions, Small Claims* 2 Millennium Plaza, #115, Clarksville, TN 37040. 8AM-4:30PM. **931-648-5700**, Fax: 931-648-5731. Access records-✉ ✋

Chancery Court *Civil, Probate* Chancery Court, Clerk & Master County Court Center, 2 Millenium Plaza, #101, Clarksville, TN 37040. 8AM-4:15PM. **931-648-5703**. Access civil records-✋

Moore County

17th District Circuit & General Sessions Court *Felony, Misdemeanor, Civil, Eviction, Small Claims* Courthouse, PO Box 206, Lynchburg, TN 37352. 8AM-4:30PM MTWF; 8AM-N Sat. **931-759-7208**, Fax: 931-759-5673. ✉ ✋

Chancery Court *Civil, Probate* PO Box 206, Lynchburg, TN 37352. 8AM-4:30PM M-W,F; 8AM-N Sat. **931-759-7028**, Fax: 931-759-5610. Access civil records-✋

Morgan County

9th District Circuit & General Sessions Court *Felony, Misd., Civil, Eviction, Small Claims* PO Box 163, Wartburg, TN 37887. 8AM-4PM. **423-346-3503**. ✋

Chancery Court *Civil, Probate* PO Box 789, Wartburg, TN 37887. 8AM-4PM. **423-346-3881**. Access civil recs-☎ ✉ ✋

Obion County

27th District Circuit Court *Felony, Misdemeanor, Civil Actions Over $10,000* 7 Bill Burnett Cir, Union City, TN 38261. 8:30AM-4:30PM. **731-885-1372**, Fax: 731-885-7515. ✉ ✋

General Sessions Court *Civil Actions Under $15,000, Eviction, Small Claims* 9 Bill Burnett Cir, Union City, TN 38281-0236. 8:30AM-4:30PM. **731-885-1811**, Fax: 731-885-7515. civil records-✉ ✋

Chancery Court *Civil, Probate* PO Box 187, Union City, TN 38281. 8:30AM-

4:30PM. **731-885-2562**, Fax: 731-885-7515. Access civil records-☎ ✉ ✋

Overton County

13th District Circuit & General Sessions Court *Felony, Misdemeanor, Civil, Eviction, Small Claims* Overton County Courthouse 100 Joan Tom Poindexter Dr, Livingston, TN 38570. 8AM-4:30PM M T Th F, 8AM-N W & S. **931-823-2312**, Fax 931-823-9728. ✉ ✋

County Court *Probate* Courthouse Annex, University St PO Box 127, Livingston, TN 38570. 8AM-4PM. **931-823-2536**, Fax: 931-823-7631.

Perry County

21st District Circuit & General Sessions Court *Felony, Misdemeanor, Civil, Eviction, Small Claims* PO Box 91, Linden, TN 37096. 8AM-4PM. **931-589-2218**, Fax: 931-589-2350. ✉ ✋ ☎

Chancery Court *Civil, Probate* PO Box 251, Linden, TN 37096. 8AM-4PM. **931-589-2217**, Fax: 931-589-2350. Access civil records-✋

Pickett County

13th District Circuit & General Sessions Court *Felony, Misdemeanor, Civil, Eviction, Small Claims* PO Box 188, Byrdstown, TN 38549. 8AM-4PM. **931-864-3958**, Fax 931-864-6885. ✉ ✋

County Court *Probate* PO Box 5, Courthoue Square, Byrdstown, TN 38549. 8AM-4PM M T Th F, 8-11AM W & S. **931-864-3879**, Fax: 931-864-7087.

Polk County

10th District Circuit & General Sessions Court *Felony, Misdemeanor, Civil, Eviction, Small Claims* PO Box 256, Benton, TN 37307. 8:30AM-4:30PM. **423-338-4524**, Fax: 423-338-8611. ✉ ✋

Chancery Court *Civil, Probate* PO Drawer L, Benton, TN 37307. 8:30AM-4:30PM. **423-338-4522**, Fax: 423-338-4553. Access civil records-✉ ✋

Putnam County

13th District Circuit & General Sessions Court *Felony, Misdemeanor, Civil, Eviction, Small Claims* www.dockets.putnamco.org 421 E Spring St, 1C-49A, Cookeville, TN 38501. 8AM-

4PM. **931-528-1508**. Current docket are at the website. ✋

Probate & Juvenile Court *Probate, Juvenile* PO Box 220, Cookeville, TN 38503-0220. 8AM-4:00PM. **931-526-7106**, Fax: 931-372-8201.

Rhea County

12th District Circuit & General Sessions Court *Felony, Misdemeanor, Civil, Eviction, Small Claims, Probate* 1475 Market St, Rm 200, Dayton, TN 37321. 8AM-4:30PM. **423-775-7805**, Fax: 423-775-7895. Civil phone: 423-775-7805, crim: 423-775-7818, Probate: 423-775-7806. Probate at Rhea County Clerk and Master's Office. Fax- 423-775-4046. ✉**Fax** ✋

Roane County

9th District Circuit & General Sessions Court *Felony, Misdemeanor, Civil, Eviction, Small Claims* PO Box 73, Kingston, TN 37763. 8:30AM-6PM Mon; 8:30AM-4:30PM T-F. **865-376-2390**, Fax: 865-717-4141. General Sessions: 865-376-5584, their records are separate from Circuit Court. ✉**Fax** ✋

Chancery Court *Civil, Probate* PO Box 402, Kingston, TN 37763. 8:30AM-6PM M, 8:30AM-4:30PM T-F. **865-376-2487**, Fax: 865-376-1228. Access civil records-☎ ✉ ✋

Robertson County

19th District Circuit Court *Felony, Misdemeanor* County Courthouse, Rm 200, Springfield, TN 37172. 8AM-4:30PM. **615-384-7864**, Fax: 615-384-0246. ☎**Fax**✉ ✋

General Sessions Court *Misdemeanor, Civil Actions under $15,000, Eviction, Small Claims, Traffic* 529 S Brown St., Springfield, TN 37172-2941. 8AM-4:30PM. **615-382-2324**, Fax: 615-382-3113. **Fax**✉ ✋

Chancery Court *Civil, Probate* 501 Main St - 101 Robertson County Courthouse, Springfield, TN 37172. 8AM-4:30PM. **615-384-5650**. Access civil records-✉ ✋

Rutherford County

16th District Circuit Court *Felony, Misdemeanor, Civil Actions Over $15,000* Judicial Bldg, Rm 201, Murfreesboro, TN 37130. 8AM-4:15PM. Fax: 615-217-

7118. Civil phone: 615-898-7820, crim: 615-898-7812. 🖐

General Sessions Court *Civil Actions Under $15,000, Eviction, Small Claims* Judicial Bldg, Rm 101, Murfreesboro, TN 37130. 8AM-4:15PM. **615-898-7831**, Fax 615-898-7835. Access civil records-🖐

County Court *Probate* 319 N Maple St, Murfreesboro, TN 37130. 8AM-4PM M-Th; 8AM-5PM F. **615-898-7798**, Fax: 615-898-7830.

Scott County

8th District Circuit & General Sessions Court *Felony, Misdemeanor, Civil, Eviction, Small Claims, Probate* PO Box 330, Huntsville, TN 37756. 8AM-4:30PM. **423-663-2440**, Fax: 423-663-2595. ☎🖂🖐

Sequatchie County

12th District Circuit & General Sessions Court *Felony, Misd., Civil, Eviction, Small Claims* PO Box 551, Dunlap, TN 37327. 8AM-4PM. **423-949-2618**, Fax: 423-949-2902. ☎**Fax**🖂🖐

Chancery Court *Civil, Probate* PO Box 1651, Dunlap, TN 37327. 8AM-4PM. **423-949-3670**, Fax: 423-949-2579. Access civil records-**Fax**🖂🖐

Sevier County

General Sessions Court *Misdemeanor, Civil Actions Under $25,000, Eviction, Small Claims* 125 Court Ave, #107E, Sevierville, TN 37862. 8AM-4:30PM M-TH, 8AM-6PM F. **865-453-6116**, Fax: 865-774-3842. Civil phone: 865-429-5671, crim: 865-453-6116. **Fax**🖂🖐

4th District Circuit Court *Felony, Misdemeanor, Civil Actions over $15,000* 125 Court Ave, #204E, Sevierville, TN 37862. 8AM-4:30PM M-TH, 8AM-6PM F. **865-453-5536**, Fax: 865-774-9792. Crim phone: 865-774-3731. **Fax**🖂🖐

County Court *Probate* 125 Court Ave, #202, Sevierville, TN 37862. 8-4:30PM. **865-453-5502**, Fax: 865-453-6830.

Shelby County

Circuit Court *Civil Actions Over $25,000* www.circuitcourt.co.shelby.tn.us/ 140 Adams Ave, Rm 224, Memphis, TN 38103. 8AM-4:30PM. **901-545-4006**, Fax: 901-545-3952. A second office is located at 942 Mt. Moriah, phone 901-685-9992. civil records-**Fax**🖂🖐🖥

30th District Criminal Court *Felony* www.co.shelby.tn.us/county_gov/court_clerks/criminal_court/index.html Office of the Criminal Court 201 Poplar, Rm 4-01, Memphis, TN 38103. 8AM-4:30PM. **901-545-5001**, Fax: 901-545-3679. **Fax**🖂🖐🖥

General Sessions - Civil *Civil Actions Under $25,000, Eviction, Small Claims* http://generalsessionscourt.co.shelby.tn.us 140 Adams, Rm 106, Memphis, TN 38103. 8AM-4:30PM. **901-576-4031**, Fax: 901-545-4515. East Divison office is at 942-A Mt. Moriah Rd., 901-685-9992, fax 901-685-9856. civil records-🖐🖥

Chancery Court *Civil Actions Under $25,000, Equity Cases (also, lower Circuit Court Civil issues)* www.co.shelby.tn.us/county_gov/court_clerks/chancery_court/index.htm 140 Adams, Rm 308, Memphis, TN 38103. 8AM-4:30PM. **901-545-4002**, Fax: 901-545-3309. Access civil records-🖂**Fax**🖐🖥

General Sessions - Crim *Misdemeanor* http://generalsessionscourt.co.shelby.tn.us 201 Poplar, Rm 81, Memphis, TN 38103. 8AM-4:30PM. **901-545-5100**, Fax: 901-545-3655. 🖂🖐🖥

Probate www.probate.co.shelby.tn.us 140 Adams, Rm 124, Memphis, TN 38103. 8AM-4:30PM. **901-545-4040**, Fax: 901-545-4746. Probate court records are free at www.probatedata.co.shelby.tn.us.

Smith County

15th District Circuit & General Sessions Court *Felony, Misdemeanor, Civil, Eviction, Small Claims* 211 Main St, Carthage, TN 37030. 8AM-4PM. **615-735-0500 (Gen Sess.)**; **615-735-8260 (Circuit)**, Fax: 615-735-8261. ☎🖂🖐

Chancery Court *Civil, Probate* 211 N Main St, Carthage, TN 37030. 8AM-4PM. **615-735-2092**, Fax: 615-735-8261. Access civil records-**Fax**🖂🖐

Stewart County

23rd District Circuit & General Sessions Court *Felony, Misdemeanor, Civil, Eviction, Small Claims* PO Box 193, Dover, TN 37058. 8AM-4:30PM. **931-232-7042**, Fax 931-232-3111. 🖂🖐

Chancery Court *Civil, Probate* PO Box 102, Dover, TN 37058. 8AM-4:30PM. **931-232-5665**, Fax: 931-232-3111. Access civil records-🖂🖐

Sullivan County

Kingsport Circuit Court - Civil Division *Civil Actions Over $15,000* 225 W Center St, Kingsport, TN 37660. 8AM-5PM. **423-224-1724**. civil records-☎🖂🖐

Bristol Circuit Court - Civil Division *Civil* www.bridgeweb.org/ Courthouse, Rm 131 801 Anderson St, Bristol, TN 37620. 8AM-5PM. **423-989-4354**. Access civil records-🖐

2nd District Circuit Court *Felony, Misdemeanor* 140 Blockville ByPass, PO Box 585, Blountville, TN 37617. 8AM-5PM. **423-323-5158**. 🖐

Kingsport General Sessions *Misd., Civil Actions Under $15,000, Eviction, Small Claims* 200 Shelby St, Kingsport, TN 37660. 8AM-5PM. **423-224-1711**. Access records-🖐

Chancery Court *Civil, Probate* PO Box 327, Blountville, TN 37617. 8AM-5PM. **423-323-6483**, Fax: 423-279-3280. Access civil records- 🖂🖐

Bristol General Sessions Court *Misd., Civil Under $15,000, Eviction, Small Claims* www.bridgeweb.org/docketts.htm Courthouse 801 Anderson St, Rm 131, Bristol, TN 37620. 8AM-5PM. **423-989-4352**. 🖐

Sumner County

18th District Circuit & General Sessions Court *Felony, Misdemeanor, Civil, Eviction, Small Claims* Public Sq, PO Box 549, Gallatin, TN 37066. 8AM-4:30PM. **615-452-4367**, Fax: 615-451-6027. 🖐

Chancery Court *Civil, Probate* Rm 300, Sumner County Courthouse, Gallatin, TN 37066. 8AM-4:30PM. **615-452-4282**, Fax: 615-451-6031. Access civil records-☎**Fax**🖂🖐

Tipton County

25th District Circuit & General Sessions Court *Felony, Misdemeanor, Civil, Eviction, Small Claims* 1801 S College, Rm 102, Covington, TN 38019. 8AM-5PM. **901-475-3310**. 🖂🖐

Chancery Court *Civil, Probate* Tipton County Justice Ctr 1801 S College, #110, Covington, TN 38019. 8AM-5PM. **901-476-0209**, Fax: 901-476-0246. Access civil records-☎**Fax**🖂🖐

Key: Symbols refer to criminal records access unless otherwise noted. phone-☎ mail-🖂 fax-**Fax** in person-🖐 online-🖥 email-**Email**

Trousdale County

15th District Circuit & General Sessions Court *Felony, Misdemeanor, Civil, Eviction, Small Claims* 200 E Main St, Rm 5, Hartsville, TN 37074. 8AM-4:30PM. **615-374-3411**, Fax: 615-374-1100. 🖐

Chancery Court *Civil, Probate* Courthouse Rm 1 200 E Main St, Hartsville, TN 37074. 8AM-4:30PM. **615-374-2996**, Fax: 615-374-1100. Access civil records-🖐

Unicoi County

1st District Circuit & General Sessions Court *Felony, Misdemeanor, Civil, Eviction, Small Claims* PO Box 2000, Erwin, TN 37650. 9AM-5PM. **423-743-3541**. ✉🖐

Probate Court PO Box 340, Erwin, TN 37650. 9AM-5PM M-F, 9AM-N Sat. **423-743-3381**, Fax: 423-743-5430.

Union County

8th District Circuit & General Sessions Court *Felony, Misdemeanor, Civil, Eviction, Small Claims* 901 E Main St, #220, Maynardville, TN 37807. 8AM-4PM Mon-Fri; 8AM-N Sat. **865-992-5493**. ✉🖐

Chancery Court *Civil, Probate* 901 Main St, #215, Maynardville, TN 37807-3510. 8AM-4PM (6PM F). **865-992-5942**. Access civil records-☎ ✉🖐

Van Buren County

31st District Circuit & General Sessions Court *Felony, Misdemeanor, Civil, Eviction, Small Claims* PO Box 126, Spencer, TN 38585. 8AM-5PM. **931-946-2153**, Fax: 931-946-7572. ✉🖐

County Court *Probate* PO Box 153, Spencer, TN 38585. 8AM-4PM M-TH; 8AM-5PM F. **931-946-7175**, Fax: 931-946-7572.

Warren County

31st District Circuit & General Sessions Court *Felony, Misdemeanor, Civil,* *Eviction, Small Claims* 111 Court Sq, PO Box 639, McMinnville, TN 37111. 8AM-4:30PM M-TH; 8AM-5PM F. **931-473-2373**, Fax: 931-473-3726. ✉🖐

Chancery Court *Civil, Probate* PO Box 639, McMinnville, TN 37111. 8AM-4:30PM M-TH, 8AM-5PM F. **931-473-2364**, Fax: 931-473-3232. Access civil records-✉🖐

Washington County

1st District Circuit & General Sessions Court *Felony, Misdemeanor, Civil, Eviction, Small Claims* PO Box 356, Jonesborough, TN 37659. 8AM-5PM. **423-753-1611**, Fax: 423-753-1809. 🖐 Access to all public records is available in Johnson County.

Johnson City Law Court - Civil *Civil Actions Over $15,000* 101 E Market St, Johnson City, TN 37604. 8AM-5PM. **423-461-1475**, Fax: 423-926-4862. Access civil records-✉🖐

General Sessions *Civil Actions Under $15,000, Eviction, Small Claims* 101 E Market St, Johnson City, TN 37604. 8AM-5PM. **423-461-1412**, Fax: 423-926-4862. Access civil records-✉🖐

Probate Court PO Box 218, Jonesborough, TN 37659. 8AM-5PM. **423-753-1623**, Fax: 423-753-4716.

Wayne County

22nd District Circuit & General Sessions Court *Felony, Misdemeanor, Civil, Eviction, Small Claims* PO Box 869, Waynesboro, TN 38485. 8AM-4PM M T TH F; 8AM-N W & S. **931-722-5519**, Fax: 931-722-5994. ☎✉🖐

Chancery Court *Civil, Probate* PO Box 101, Waynesboro, TN 38485. 8AM-4PM. **931-722-5517**, Fax: 931-722-5517. Access civil records-✉🖐

Weakley County

27th District Circuit & General Sessions Court *Felony, Misdemeanor, Civil, Eviction, Small Claims* PO Box 28,

Dresden, TN 38225. 8AM-4:30PM. **731-364-3455**, Fax: 731-364-6765. 🖐

Chancery Court *Civil, Probate* PO Box 197, Dresden, TN 38225. 8AM-4:30PM. **731-364-3454**, Fax: 731-364-5247. Court will not do searches for geneaology. Access civil records-✉🖐

White County

13th District Circuit & General Sessions Court *Felony, Misdemeanor, Civil, Eviction, Small Claims* 111 Depot St, #1, Sparta, TN 38583. 8AM-5PM. **931-836-3205**, Fax: 931-836-3526. 🖐

Chancery Court *Civil, Probate* White County Courthouse Rm 303, Sparta, TN 38583. 8AM-4PMn. **931-836-3787**. Access civil records-☎🖐

Williamson County

21st District Circuit & General Sessions Court *Felony, Misdemeanor, Civil, Eviction, Small Claims* 135 4th Ave, Rm 203, Franklin, TN 37064. 8AM-4:30PM. **615-790-5454**, Fax: 615-790-5411. ✉🖐

Chancery Court *Civil, Probate* Clerk & Master PO Box 1666, Franklin, TN 37064. 8AM-4:30PM. **615-790-5428**, Fax: 615-790-5626. Access civil records-☎✉🖐

Wilson County

15th District Circuit & General Sessions Court *Felony, Misdemeanor, Civil, Eviction, Small Claims* PO Box 518, Lebanon, TN 37088-0518. 8AM-4PM M-Th, 8AM-5PM F. **615-444-2042**, Fax: 615-449-3420. 🖐

Probate Court PO Box 950, Lebanon, TN 37088-0950. 8AM-4:30PM M-Th, 8AM-5PM Fri. **615-443-2627**, Fax: 615-443-2628 Probate: 615-444-2835. Probate is now Clerk & Master.

Key: Symbols refer to criminal records access unless otherwise noted.   phone-☎   mail-✉   fax-Fax   in person-🖐   online-💻   email-Email

Texas

State Court Administration: Office of Court Administration, PO Box 12066, Austin, TX, 78711; 512-463-1625, Fax: 512-463-1648. www.courts.state.tx.us

Court Structure: The legal court structure for Texas is explained extensively in the "Texas Judicial Annual Report." Generally, Texas District Courts have general civil jurisdiction and exclusive felony jurisdiction, along with typical variations such as contested probate and divorce. As of 01/15/04, four additional District Courts were implemented. The County Court structure consists of two forms of courts - "Constitutional" and "at Law. " The Constitutional upper claim limit is $100,000 while the At Law upper limit is $5,000. For civil matters up to $5000, we recommend searchers start at the Constitutional County Court as they, generally, offer a shorter waiting time for cases in urban areas. In some counties the District Court or County Court handles evictions.District Courts handle felonies. County Courts handle misdemeanors and general civil cases.We have indicated when a record search is automatically combined for two courts, for example a District and County court or both county courts.

Probate Courts: Probate is handled in Probate Court in the 10 largest counties and in District Courts or County Courts at Law elsewhere. However, the County Clerk is responsible for the records in every county.

Online Access: Appellate court case information is searchable for free on the Internet from the website of each appellate court, reached from the website mentioned above. Court of Criminal Appeals opinions are found at www.cca.courts.state.tx.us. A number of local county courts offer online access to their records, but there is no statewide system of local level court records.

Anderson County

District Court *Felony, Civil* www.co.anderson.tx.us PO Box 1159, Palestine, TX 75802-1159. 8AM-N, 1-5PM. **903-723-7412**. The court also holds family Cases. ✉ 🖐

County Court *Misdemeanor, Civil, Probate* 500 N Church, Palestine, TX 75801. 8AM-5PM. **903-723-7432**. ✉ 🖐

Andrews County

District Court *Felony, Civil* PO Box 328, Andrews, TX 79714. 8AM-5PM. **432-524-1417**. ✉ 🖐

County Court *Misdemeanor, Civil, Probate* PO Box 727, Andrews, TX 79714. 8-5PM. **432-524-1426**. ☎✉ 🖐

Angelina County

District Court *Felony, Civil* PO Box 908, Lufkin, TX 75902. 8AM-5PM. **936-634-4312**, Fax: 936-634-5915. ✉ 🖐

County Court *Misdemeanor, Civil, Probate* www.angelinacounty.net PO Box 908 (215 E Lufkin Ave), Lufkin, TX 75902. 8AM-5PM. **936-634-8339**, Fax: 936-634-8460. ✉ 🖐

Aransas County

District Court *Felony, Civil* 301 N Live Oak, Rockport, TX 78382. 8AM-5PM. **361-790-0128**, Fax 361-790-5211. ✉ 🖐

County Court *Misdemeanor, Civil, Probate* 301 N Live Oak, Rockport, TX 78382. 8AM-4:30PM. **361-790-0122**.

✉no fax, because we require the $5.00 search fee before we do the search, (if court does the search), 🖐

Archer County

District Court *Felony, Civil* PO Box 815, Archer City, TX 76351. 8:30AM-5PM. **940-574-4615**. ✉ 🖐

County Court *Misdemeanor, Civil, Probate* PO Box 427, Archer City, TX 76351. 8:30AM-5PM. **940-574-4302**. ☎✉ 🖐

Armstrong County

District & County Court *Felony, Misdemeanor, Civil, Probate* PO Box 309 100 Trice St., Claude, TX 79019. 8AM-N, 1-5PM. **806-226-2081**, Fax: 806-226-5301. ✉ 🖐

Atascosa County

District Court *Felony, Civil* Courthouse Circle, #4-B, Jourdanton, TX 78026. 8AM-N, 1-5PM. **830-769-3011**. ✉ 🖐

County Court *Misdemeanor, Civil, Probate* #1 Courthouse Cirlce, #102, Jourdanton, TX 78026. 8AM-5PM. **830-767-2511**. 🖐

Austin County

District Court *Felony, Civil Actions* www.austincounty.com/dclerk.html 1 E Main, Bellville, TX 77418-1598. 8AM-N, 1-5PM. **979-865-5911 x121**. The District

website is www.cvtv.net/~tx155district/. ✉ 🖐

County Court at Law *Misdemeanor, Civil, Probate* 1 E Main, Bellville, TX 77418. 8AM-5PM. **979-865-5911**, Fax: 979-865-0336. ✉ 🖐

Bailey County

District Court *Felony, Civil* 300 S 1st St, Muleshoe, TX 79347. 8AM-5PM. **806-272-3165**, Fax: 806-272-3124. ☎✉ 🖐 🖥

County Court *Misdemeanor, Civil, Probate* 300 S 1st St, Muleshoe, TX 79347. 8:30AM-N, 1-5PM. **806-272-3044**, Fax: 806-272-3538. ✉ 🖐 🖥

Bandera County

District Court *Felony, Civil, Probate* www.banderacounty.org/departments/district_clerk.htm PO Box 2688 (500 Main St), Bandera, TX 78003. 7:30AM-4:30PM. **830-796-4606**, Fax: 830-796-8499. Fax✉ 🖐 🖥

County Court *Misdemeanor, Civil, Eviction, Probate* PO Box 823 (500 Main St), Bandera, TX 78003. 8AM-4:30PM. **830-796-3332**, Fax: 830-796-8323. Fax✉ 🖐

Bastrop County

District Court *Felony, Civil* PO Box 770, Bastrop, TX 78602. 8AM-5PM. **512-332-7244**, Fax: 512-332-7249. ✉ 🖐 fax.

County Court *Misdemeanor, Probate* PO Box 577, Bastrop, TX 78602. 8-5. **512-332-7234.** ☎ ✉ ✋

Baylor County

District & County Court *Felony, Misdemeanor, Civil, Probate* PO Box 689, Seymour, TX 76380. 8:30AM-5PM. **940-889-3322.** ☎ ✉ ✋

Bee County

District Court *Felony, Civil* PO Box 666, Beeville, TX 78104-0666. 8AM-5PM. **361-362-3242**, Fax: 361-362-3282. ✉ ✋ 🖥

County Court *Misdemeanor, Civil, Probate* 105 W Corpus Christi St , Rm 103, Beeville, TX 78102. 8AM-N, 1-5PM. **361-362-3245**, Fax: 361-362-3247. ☎**Fax**✉ ✋

Bell County

District Court *Felony, Civil* www.bellcountytx.com/districtclerk/index.htm 104 S Main St, PO Box 909, Belton, TX 76513. 8AM-5PM. **254-933-5197**, Fax: 254-933-5199. Civil phone: 254-933-5195, crim: 254-933-5957. ✉ ✋

County Court *Misdemeanor, Civil, Probate* Bell County Clerk's Office PO Box 480, Belton, TX 76513. 8AM-5PM. **254-933-5165**, Fax: 254-933-5176. Civil phone: 254-933-5174, crim: 254-933-5170. ✉ ✋

Bexar County

District Court - Central Records *Felony, Civil* www.co.bexar.tx.us/dclerk 100 Dolorosa, County Courthouse Chief Court Clerk/Records, San Antonio, TX 78205. 8AM-5PM. **210-335-2113**, Civil: 210-335-2661, crim: 210-335-2591. There is a separate court clerk for civil and criminal, though records are centralized. ✉**Fax**🖥 ✋

County Court - Civil Central Filing Department *Civil* 100 Dolorosa, San Antonio, TX 78205-3083. 8AM-5PM. **210-335-2231**, crim: 210-335-2238. There are twelve hearing locations where open cases are held. Closed cases are forwarded here. Access civil records-✉ ✋

County Court - Criminal *Misdemeanor* www.co.bexar.tx.us/dclerk 300 Dolorosa, #4101, San Antonio, TX 78205. 8AM-5PM. **210-335-2238**, Civil: 210-335-2231, crim: 210-335-2238. ✉ 🖥 ✋

Probate Court #2 www.co.bexar.tx.us/pcourt/probatecourts.htm 100 Dolorosa St, Rm 108, San Antonio, TX 78205. 8AM-5PM. **210-335-2241**.

Blanco County

District Court *Felony, Civil, Probate* www.courts.state.tx.us/district/33rd/index.htm PO Box 382, Johnson City, TX 78636. 8AM-4:30PM. **830-868-0973**, Fax: 830-868-2084. ✉ ✋

County Court *Misdemeanor, Civil, Probate* PO Box 65, Johnson City, TX 78636. 8-4:30PM. **830-868-7357**. ✉ ✋

Borden County

District & County Court *Felony, Misdemeanor, Civil, Probate* PO Box 124, Gail, TX 79738. 8AM-5PM. **806-756-4312**. ✉ ✋

Bosque County

District Court *Felony, Civil* Main & Morgan St, PO Box 674, Meridian, TX 76665. 8AM-5PM. **254-435-2334**. ✉ ✋

County Court *Misdemeanor, Civil, Probate* PO Box 617, Meridian, TX 76665. 8AM-5PM. **254-435-2201**, Fax: 254-435-2152. ✉ ✋

Bowie County

District & County Court at Law *Felony, Misdemeanor, Civil, Probate* www.co.bowie.tx.us/ 710 James Bowie Dr, PO Box 248, New Boston, TX 75570. 8AM-5PM. **903-628-6750**, Probate: 903-628-6740. Probate records are at this address in County Clerk's office. ✉ ✋

Brazoria County

District Court *Felony, Civil* www.brazoria-county.com/dclerk/ 111 E Locus, #500, Angleton, TX 77515-4678. 8AM-5PM. **979-864-1316**. ☎ ✉ ✋

County Court *Misdemeanor, Civil* 111 E Locust, #200, Angleton, TX 77515. 8AM-5PM. Fax: 979-848-1031 (civil); -1020 (Crim.). Civil phone: 979-864-1385, crim: 979-864-1380. Access records-**Fax**✉ ✋

Probate Court 111 E Locust, #200, Angleton, TX 77515. 8AM-5PM. **979-864-1367**, Fax: 979-864-1031.

Brazos County

District Court *Felony, Civil* www.co.brazos.tx.us/disclerk 300 E 26th St, #216 (PO Box 2208), Bryan, TX 77806. 8AM-5PM. **979-361-4230**, Fax: 979-361-0197. ✉ ✋

County Court *Misdemeanor, Civil under $500, Probate* 300 E 26th St, #120, Bryan, TX 77803. 8AM-5PM. **979-361-4128**. County Clerk holds misdemeanor records prior to 1986 only. Newer cases filed at District Clerks Office. ✉ ✋

Brewster County

District Court *Felony, Civil* PO Box 1024, Alpine, TX 79831. 9AM-12, 1-5PM. **432-837-6216**, Fax: 432-837-6217. ☎**Fax**✉ ✋

County Court *Misdemeanor, Civil, Probate* PO Box 119 (201 W Ave. E), Alpine, TX 79831. 9AM-5PM. **432-837-3366**, Fax: 432-837-6217. ✉**Fax**✋

Briscoe County

District & County Court *Felony, Misdemeanor, Civil, Probate* PO Box 555, Silverton, TX 79257. 8AM-5PM. **806-823-2134**, Fax: 806-823-2359. **Fax**✉ ✋

Brooks County

District Court *Felony, Civil* www.brooks-county.com PO Box 534, Falfurrias, TX 78355. 8AM-5PM. **361-325-5604**, Fax: 361-325-5679. ☎**Fax**✉ 🖥 ✋

County Court *Misdemeanor, Civil, Probate* PO Box 427, Falfurrias, TX 78355. 8AM-5PM. **361-325-5604 X245,246,248.** ☎**Fax**✉ ✋

Brown County

District Court *Felony, Civil* 200 S Broadway, Brownwood, TX 76801. 8AM-5PM. **325-646-5514**. ✉ ✋ ☎

County Court *Misd., Civil, Probate* 200 S Broadway, Brownwood, TX 76801. 8:30AM-5PM. **325-643-2594**. ✉ ✋

Burleson County

District Court *Felony, Civil* 100 W Buck, #303, Caldwell, TX 77836. 8AM-12, 1-5PM. **979-567-2336**. ✉ ✋

County Court *Misdemeanor, Civil, Probate* 100 W Buck, #203, Caldwell, TX 77836. 8AM-5PM. **979-567-2329**, Fax: 979-567-2376. ✉**Fax**✋

Key: Symbols refer to criminal records access unless otherwise noted. phone-☎ mail-✉ fax-**Fax** in person-✋ online-🖥 email-**Email**

Burnet County

District Court *Felony, Civil* www.courts.state.tx.us/district/33rd/index.ht m 1701 E Polk St, #90, Burnet, TX 78611. 8AM-5PM. **512-756-5450**. ✉ ✍

County Court *Misdemeanor, Civil, Probate* 220 S Pierce, Burnet, TX 78611. 8AM-5PM. **512-756-5403**, Fax: 512-756-5410. **Fax**✉✍

Caldwell County

District Court *Felony, Civil* 201 E San Antonio St, Lockhart, TX 78644. 8:30AM-N, 1-5PM. **512-398-1806**. ☎**Fax**✉✍

County Court *Misd., Civil, Probate* PO Box 906, Lockhart, TX 78644. 8:30AM-N, 1-5PM. **512-398-1804**. ✉✍

Calhoun County

District Court *Felony, Civil* PO Box 658 (c/o District Clerk), Port Lavaca, TX 77979. 8AM-5PM. **361-553-8698**. ✉✍

County Court *Misdemeanor, Civil, Probate* 211 S Ann, Port Lavaca, TX 77979. 8AM-5PM. **361-553-4411**, Fax: 361-553-4420. ☎✉✍

Callahan County

District Court *Felony, Civil* 100 W 4th St, #300, Baird, TX 79504-5396. 8AM-5PM. **325-854-1800**. ✉✍

County Court *Misdemeanor, Civil, Probate* 100 W 4th St, #104, Baird, TX 79504-5300. 8AM-5PM. **325-854-1217**, Fax: 325-854-1227. ☎**Fax**✉✍

Cameron County

District Court *Felony, Civil* 974 E Harrison St, Brownsville, TX 78520. 8Am-5PM. **956-544-0839**. ✉✍🖵

County Court No. 1, 2 & 3 *Misd., Civil, Probate* www.co.cameron.tx.us/ PO Box 2178, Brownsville, TX 78522-2178. 8AM-5PM. Fax: 956-544-0894. Civil phone: 956-544-0867, crim: 956-544-0848, Probate: 956-544-0867. ✉✍

Camp County

District Court *Felony, Civil* 126 Church St, Rm 203, Pittsburg, TX 75686. 8-5PM. **903-856-3221**, Fax 903-856-0560. ✉✍

County Court *Misdemeanor, Civil, Probate* 126 Church St, Rm 102, Pittsburg, TX 75686. 8AM-N, 1-5PM.
903-856-2731, Fax: 903-856-2309. **Fax**✉✍

Carson County

District & County Court *Felony, Misdemeanor, Civil, Probate* PO Box 487, Panhandle, TX 79068. 8AM-N, 1-5PM. **806-537-3623**, Fax: 806-537-3623. ✉**Fax**✍

Cass County

District Court *Felony, Civil* PO Box 510, Linden, TX 75563. 8AM-5PM. **903-756-7514**. ✉✍

County Court *Misdemeanor, Probate* PO Box 449, Linden, TX 75563. 8AM-5PM. **903-756-5071**. ✍

Castro County

District & County Court *Felony, Misd., Civil, Probate* www.242ndcourt.com 100 E Bedford, Rm 101, Dimmitt, TX 79027. 8AM-5PM. **806-647-3338**. ✉✍

Chambers County

District Clerk *Felony, Civil* Drawer NN, Anahuac, TX 77514. 8AM-N, 1-5PM. **409-267-8276**. ✉✍

County Court *Misdemeanor, Civil, Probate* www.co.chambers.tx.us PO Box 728, Anahuac, TX 77514. 8AM-5PM. **409-267-8315**, Fax 409-267-4453. ✍

Cherokee County

District Court *Felony, Civil* Drawer C, Rusk, TX 75785. 8AM-N, 1-5PM. **903-683-6908** clerk; civil 903-683-5945/5883, crim: 903-683-4533. ✉**Fax**✍

County Court *Misdemeanor, Civil, Probate* Cherokee County Clerk, PO Box 420, Rusk, TX 75785. 8AM-5PM. **903-683-2350**, Fax: 903-683-5931. ✍

Childress County

District & County Court *Felony, Misdemeanor, Civil, Probate* Courthouse, Box 4, Childress, TX 79201. 8:30AM-N, 1-5PM. **940-937-6143**, Fax: 940-937-3479. ✉✍

Clay County

District Clerk *Felony, Civil* PO Box 568, Henrietta, TX 76365. 8AM-N, 1-5PM. **940-538-4561**, Fax 940-538-4431. ✍

County Court *Misdemeanor, Civil, Probate* PO Box 548, Henrietta, TX 76365. 8AM-5PM. **940-538-4631**. ✉✍

Cochran County

District & County Court *Felony, Misdemeanor, Civil, Probate* County Courthouse, Rm 102, Morton, TX 79346. 8AM-5PM. **806-266-5450**, Fax: 806-266-9027. **Fax**✉✍

Coke County

District & County Court *Felony, Misdemeanor, Civil, Probate* PO Box 150, Robert Lee, TX 76945. 8AM-5PM. **325-453-2631**, Fax 325-453-2650. ✉✍

Coleman County

District Court *Felony, Civil* PO Box 512, Coleman, TX 76834. 8AM-4:30PM. **325-625-2568**. ✉✍

County Court *Misdemeanor, Civil, Probate* PO Box 591, Coleman, TX 76834. 8AM-5PM. **325-625-2889**. ✉✍

Collin County

District Clerk *Felony, Civil* www.co.collin.tx.us/district_courts/index.jsp PO Box 578, McKinney, TX 75070. 8AM-4:30PM. Civil: 972-548-4320, crim: 972-548-4430. ✉**Fax**🖵✍

County Court At Law *Misd., Civil, Probate* www.co.collin.tx.us/county_cour t_law/index.jsp 1800 N Graves, #110, McKinney, TX 75069. 8AM-4:30PM. **972-548-6420**, Fax: 972-548-6433 Probate: 972-548-6465. Probate is in #115; Probate fax: 972-548-6468. ✉🖵✍

Collingsworth County

District & County Court *Felony, Misdemeanor, Civil, Probate* County Courthouse, Rm 3 800 W Ave, Box 10, Wellington, TX 79095. 9AM-5PM. **806-447-2408**, Fax: 806-447-5418. ✉✍

Colorado County

District Court *Felony, Civil* County Courthouse, Rm 210E 400 Spring St, Columbus, TX 78934. 8AM-N, 1-5PM. **979-732-2536**. ✉✍

County Court *Misdemeanor, Civil, Probate* PO Box 68 County Courthouse, Columbus, TX 78934. 8AM-5PM. **979-732-2155**, Fax: 979-732-8852. ✉✍

Comal County

District Court *Felony, Civil* 150 N Seguin, #304, New Braunfels, TX 78130-5161. 8AM-4:30PM. **830-620-5574**, Fax: 830-608-2006. **Fax**✉✍🖵

Key: Symbols refer to criminal records access unless otherwise noted. phone-☎ mail-✉ fax-**Fax** in person-✍ online-🖵 email-**Email**

County Court at Law *Misdemeanor, Civil, Probate* 100 Main Plaza, #303, New Braunfels, TX 78130. 8AM-4:30PM. Fax: 830-608-2021. Civil phone: 830-620-5586, crim: 830-620-5582, Probate: 830-620-5539. Access records- ☎Fax⊠ 👆

Comanche County

District Court *Felony, Civil* County Courthouse Box 206, Comanche, TX 76442. 8:30AM-N, 1-5PM. **325-356-2342**, Fax: 325-356-2150. ⊠ 👆

County Court *Misd., Civil, Probate* County Courthouse, Comanche, TX 76442. 8:30-5PM. **325-356-2655**. ⊠ 👆

Concho County

District & County Court *Felony, Misdemeanor, Civil, Probate* PO Box 98, Paint Rock, TX 76866. 8:30AM-5PM. **325-732-4322**, Fax 325-732-2040. ⊠ 👆

Cooke County

District Court *Felony, Civil* County Courthouse, 100 S Dixon, Gainesville, TX 76240. 8AM-5PM. **940-668-5450**, Fax: 940-668-5476. ⊠ 👆

County Court *Misdemeanor, Civil, Probate* County Courthouse, Gainesville, TX 76240. 8-5PM. **940-668-5422**. ⊠ 👆

Coryell County

District Court *Felony, Civil* PO Box 4, Gatesville, TX 76528. 8AM-5PM. **254-865-5911**, Fax: 254-865-5064. Fax⊠ 👆

County Court *Misdemeanor, Civil, Probate* PO Box 237, Gatesville, TX 76528. 8AM-N, 1-5PM. **254-865-5016**, Fax: 254-865-8631. ⊠ 👆

Cottle County

District & County Court *Felony, Misdemeanor, Civil, Probate* PO Box 717, Paducah, TX 79248. 9AM-N, 1-5PM. **806-492-3823**. ⊠ 👆

Crane County

District & County Court *Felony, Misdemeanor, Civil, Probate* PO Box 578, Crane, TX 79731. 9AM-12 1-5PM. **432-558-3581**. ⊠ 👆

Crockett County

District & County Court *Felony, Misdemeanor, Civil, Probate* PO Drawer C, Ozona, TX 76943. 8AM-5PM. **325-392-2022**. ⊠ 👆

Crosby County

District Court *Felony, Civil* 201 W Aspen St, #207, Crosbyton, TX 79322-2500. 8AM-N, 1-5PM. **806-675-2071**, Fax: 806-675-2433. ☎Fax⊠ 👆

County Court *Misdemeanor, Civil, Probate* 201 W Aspen St, #102, Crosbyton, TX 79322-2500. 8AM-N, 1:00PM-5PM. **806-675-2334**. ⊠ 👆

Culberson County

District & County Court *Felony, Misdemeanor, Civil, Probate* PO Box 158, Van Horn, TX 79855. 8AM-N; 1PM-5PM. **432-283-2058**. ☎⊠Fax 👆

Dallam County

District & County Court *Felony, Misdemeanor, Civil, Probate* PO Box 1352, Dalhart, TX 79022. 9AM-5PM. **806-244-4751**, Fax: 806-249-2252. Fax⊠ 👆

Dallas County

www.dallascounty.org

District Court - Criminal *Felony* 133 N Industrial Blvd, LB12 Attn: District Clerk, Dallas, TX 75207-4313. 8AM-4:30PM. **214-653-5950**, Fax: 214-653-5986. ⊠💻 👆

District Court - Civil 600 Commerce St, Dallas, TX 75202-4606. 8AM-6PM. **214-653-7421**. Access civil records- ⊠💻 👆

County Court - Misdemeanor 133 N Industrial Blvd, #LB43, Dallas, TX 75207-4313. 8AM-4PM. **214-653-5740**. ⊠💻 👆

County Court - Civil 509 W Main, 3rd Fl, Dallas, TX 75202. 8AM-4:30PM. **214-653-7131**, Civil: 214-653-7441, crim: 214-653-5740. No civil claims limit as of 05/23/97 in Dallas County. Access civil records- ☎⊠💻 👆

Probate Court #3 509 Main St Records Bldg, 2nd Fl, Dallas, TX 75202. 8AM-4:30PM. **214-653-7243**. The remote access system for civil and criminal records in this county also includes probate records. Also, name search free at www.dallascounty.org/applications/english/record-search/intro.html; there is a fee for documents.

Dawson County

District Court *Felony, Civil* Drawer 1268, Lamesa, TX 79331. 8:30AM-5PM. **806-872-7373**, Fax 806-872-9513. ⊠ 👆

County Court *Misdemeanor, Civil, Probate* Drawer 1268, Lamesa, TX 79331. 8:30AM-1200-15PM. **806-872-3778**, Fax: 806-872-2473. ⊠ 👆

Deaf Smith County

District Court *Felony, Civil* 235 E 3rd St, Rm 304, Hereford, TX 79045. 8AM-5PM. **806-364-3901**, Fax: 806-363-7007. Fax⊠ 👆

County Court *Misdemeanor, Civil, Probate* Deaf Smith Courthouse 235 E 3rd, Rm 203, Hereford, TX 79045. 8AM-5PM. **806-363-7077**. ⊠ 👆

Delta County

District & County Court *Felony, Misdemeanor, Civil, Probate* PO Box 455, Cooper, TX 75432. 8AM-5PM. **903-395-4400 x223**, Fax: 903-395-2178. ☎⊠ 👆

Denton County

District Court *Felony, Civil* http://dentoncounty.com/dept/main.asp?Dept=26 PO Box 2146, Denton, TX 76202. 8AM-4:30PM. **940-349-2200**, Fax: 940-349-2201. Civil phone: 940-349-2205, crim: 940-349-2210. ⊠Fax💻 👆

County Court *Misdm'r, Civil, Probate* http://dentoncounty.com/dept/main.asp?Dept=17 Attn: County Clerk PO Box 2187, Denton, TX 76202-2187. 8AM-5PM. **940-349-2012**, Civil: 940-349-2016, crim: 940-349-2013, Probate: 940-349-2036. ⊠ 👆💻

De Witt County

County Court *Misdemeanor, Probate* 307 N Gonzales, Cuero, TX 77954. 8AM-5PM. **361-275-3724**, Fax: 361-275-8994. ⊠ 👆

District Court *Felony, Civil* PO Box 845, Cuero, TX 77954. 8AM-5PM. **361-275-2221**. ⊠ 👆

Dickens County

District & County Court *Felony, Misd., Civil, Probate* PO Box 120, Dickens, TX 79229. 8AM-5PM. **806-623-5531**, Fax: 806-623-5319. ⊠Fax☎ 👆

Key: Symbols refer to criminal records access unless otherwise noted. phone-☎ mail-⊠ fax-Fax in person-👆 online-💻 email-Email

Dimmit County

District Court *Felony, Civil* 303 S 5th, Carrizo Springs, TX 78834. 8AM-N; 1PM-5PM. **830-876-2323 #244**, Fax: 830-876-5036. ✉ ⍟

County Court *Misdemeanor, Civil, Probate* 103 N 5th, Carrizo Springs, TX 78834. 8AM-5PM. **830-876-2323 x232**, Fax: 830-876-4205. ☎**Fax**✉⍟

Donley County

District & County Court *Felony, Misd., Civil, Probate* PO Drawer U, Clarendon, TX 79226. 8AM-N, 1-5PM. **806-874-3436**, Fax: 806-874-5146. ✉ ⍟

Duval County

District Court *Felony, Civil* PO Drawer 428, San Diego, TX 78384. 8AM-5PM. **361-279-3322 X239**. ☎✉⍟

County Court *Misdemeanor, Civil, Probate* PO Box 248, San Diego, TX 78384. 8AM-N, 1-5PM. **361-279-3322**. ✉⍟

Eastland County

District Court *Felony, Civil* 100 W Main St, #206, Eastland, TX 76448. 8AM-5PM. **254-629-2664**, Fax: 254-629-6070. ☎**Fax**✉⍟

County Court *Misdemeanor, Probate* PO Box 110, Eastland, TX 76448. 8AM-5PM. **254-629-1583**. No civil records after 1977; criminal and probate records only thereafter. ✉⍟

Ector County

District Court *Felony, Civil* County Courthouse 300 N Grant, Rm 301, Odessa, TX 79761. 8AM-5PM. **432-498-4290**, Fax: 432-498-4292. ☎✉⍟

County Court *Misdemeanor, Civil, Probate* PO Box 707, Odessa, TX 79760. 8AM-4:30PM. **432-498-4130**. ✉⍟

Edwards County

District & County Court *Felony, Misdemeanor, Civil, Probate* PO Box 184, Rocksprings, TX 78880. 8AM-N, 1-5PM. **830-683-2235**, Fax: 830-683-5376. ☎**Fax**✉⍟

Ellis County

District Court *Felony, Civil* 305 E Franklin, Waxahachie, TX 75165. 8AM-5PM. **972-825-5091**. ✉⍟

County Court *Misdemeanor, Civil, Probate* www.co.ellis.tx.us/ PO Box 250, Waxahachie, TX 75168. 8AM-4:30PM. **972-923-5070**. ✉⍟

El Paso County

District Court *Felony, Civil* www.co.el-paso.tx.us/districtclerk/ 500 E San Antonio, Rm 103, El Paso, TX 79901. 8AM-4:45PM. **915-546-2021**, Civil: 915-834-8256, crim: 915-834-8255. ✉⍟🖳

County Court *Misdemeanor, Civil* www.co.el-paso.tx.us 500 E San Antonio St, Rm 105, El Paso, TX 79901. 8AM-4:45PM. **915-546-2072**. ☎✉**Fax**⍟🖳

Probate Court 500 E San Antonio, Rm 703, El Paso, TX 79901. 8AM-12:00,1-5PM. **915-546-2161**, Fax: 915-533-4448. Access records at www.idocket.com; Records go back to 12/31/1986.

Erath County

District Court *Felony, Civil* 112 W College, Courthouse Annex, Stephenville, TX 76401. 8AM-5PM. **254-965-1486**, Fax: 254-965-7156. District Court Phone # is 254-965-1485; Fax is 254--965-4287 ✉**Fax**⍟

County Court *Misdemeanor, Civil, Probate* Erath County Courthouse, Stephenville, TX 76401. 8AM-4PM. **254-965-1482**. ✉⍟

Falls County

District Court *Felony, Civil* 3rd Fl, NW Corner 125 Bridge St, Rm 301, Marlin, TX 76661. 8AM-N, 1-4:30PM. **254-883-1419**. Mail requests to PO Box 229. In care of the District Clerk. ✉⍟

County Court *Misdemeanor, Civil, Probate* PO Box 458, Marlin, TX 76661. 8AM-5PM. **254-883-1408**. ☎✉⍟

Fannin County

District Court *Felony, Civil* Fannin County Courthouse, #201, Bonham, TX 75418. 8AM-N, 1-5PM. **903-583-7459**, Fax: 903-640-1826. **Fax**✉⍟

County Court *Misdemeanor, Civil, Probate* County Courthouse 101 E Sam Rayburn, #102, Bonham, TX 75418. 8AM-5PM. **903-583-7486**, Fax: 903-583-7811. Civil phone: 903-640-2008, crim: 903-583-7488, Probate: 903-640-2008. ☎✉⍟

Fayette County

District Court *Felony, Civil* www.cvtv.net/~tx155district/ Fayette County Courthouse 151 N Washington, La Grange, TX 78945. 8AM-5PM. **979-968-3548**, Fax: 979-968-2618. ✉⍟

County Court *Misdemeanor, Civil, Probate* PO Box 59, La Grange, TX 78945. 8-5PM. **979-968-3251**. ☎✉⍟

Fisher County

32nd District Court *Felony, Civil* PO Box 88, Roby, TX 79543. 8AM-5PM. **325-776-2279**, Fax: 325-776-3253. ✉**Fax**⍟

County Court *Misdemeanor, Civil, Probate* Box 368, Roby, TX 79543-0368. 8AM-N, 1-5PM. **325-776-2401**. ✉⍟

Floyd County

District Court *Felony, Civil* PO Box 67, Floydada, TX 79235. 8:30AM-N, 1-4:45PM. **806-983-4923**. ✉⍟

County Court *Misdemeanor, Civil, Probate* Courthouse, Rm 101 Main St, Floydada, TX 79235. 8:30AM-N, 1-5PM. **806-983-4900**. Access records-☎✉⍟

Foard County

District & County Court *Felony, Misdemeanor, Civil, Probate* PO Box 539, Crowell, TX 79227. 9AM-4:30PM. **940-684-1365**. ✉⍟

Fort Bend County

District Court *Felony, Civil* 301 Jackson, Richmond, TX 77469. 8AM-5PM. **281-341-4515**, Fax: 281-341-4519. Civil phone: 281-341-4562, crim: 281-341-4542. Physical court location is 401 Jackson. ✉🖳⍟

County Court *Misdemeanor, Civil, Probate, Juvenile* www.co.fort-bend.tx.us Attn: Clerk 301 Jackson St, #101, Richmond, TX 77469. 8AM-4PM. **281-341-8685**, Fax: 281-341-4520. ✉🖳⍟

Franklin County

District Court *Felony, Civil* PO Box 750, Mount Vernon, TX 75457. 8AM-5PM. **903-537-4786**. ✉⍟

County Court *Misdemeanor, Civil, Probate* PO Box 68, Mount Vernon, TX 75457. 8AM-5PM. **903-537-4252 ext 6**, Fax: 903-537-4252. ✉**Fax**⍟

Freestone County

District Court *Felony, Civil* PO Box 722, Fairfield, TX 75840. 8AM-5PM. **903-389-2534**. ☎ ✉ ⚓

County Court *Misdemeanor, Civil, Probate* PO Box 1010, Fairfield, TX 75840. 8AM-5PM. **903-389-2635**. ✉ ⚓

Frio County

District Court *Felony, Civil* 500 E San Antonio, Box 8, Pearsall, TX 78061. 8AM-5PM. **830-334-8073**, Fax: 830-334-0047. ✉ ⚓

County Court *Misdemeanor, Civil, Probate* 500 E San Antonio St, #6, Pearsall, TX 78061. 8AM-5PM. **830-334-2214**, Fax: 830-334-0021. **Fax** ✉ ⚓

Gaines County

District Court *Felony, Civil* 101 S Main, Rm 213, Seminole, TX 79360. 8AM-N, 1-5PM. **432-758-4013**, Fax: 432-758-4036. ☎ ✉ ⚓

County Court *Misdemeanor, Civil, Probate* 101 S Main, Rm 107, Seminole, TX 79360. 8-5PM. **432-758-4003**. ✉ ⚓

Galveston County

District Court *Felony, Civil* www.co.galveston.tx.us/District_Courts/default.htm 722 Moody St, Rm 404, Galveston, TX 77550. 8AM-5PM. **409-766-2424**, Fax: 409-766-2292. **Fax** ✉ ⚓

County Court *Misd., Civil, Probate* www.co.galveston.tx.us/County_Courts/ PO Box 2450, Galveston, TX 77553-2450. 8AM-5PM. **409-766-2200**, Civil: 409-766-2203, crim: 409-770-5112, Probate: 409-766-2202. ✉ ⚓

Garza County

District & County Court *Felony, Misdemeanor, Civil, Probate* PO Box 366, Post, TX 79356. 8AM-N,1-5PM. **806-495-4430**, Fax 806-495-4431. ✉ ⚓

Gillespie County

District Court *Felony, Civil* 101 W Main, Rm 204, Fredericksburg, TX 78624. Public hours 8AM-5PM. **830-997-6517**. ✉ ⚓

County Court *Misdemeanor, Civil, Probate* 101 W Main, #13, Fredericksburg, TX 78624. 8AM-4PM. **830-997-6515**, Fax 830-997-9958. ✉ ⚓

Glasscock County

District & County Court *Felony, Misdemeanor, Civil, Probate* PO Box 190 117 E Currie, Garden City, TX 79739. 8AM-4PM. **432-354-2371**. ✉ ⚓

Goliad County

District & County Court *Felony, Misdemeanor, Civil, Probate* PO Box 50 (127 N Courthouse Sq), Goliad, TX 77963. 8AM-5PM, closed 1 hour at noon. **361-645-3294**, Fax 361-645-3858. ✉ ⚓

Gonzales County

District Court *Felony, Civil* PO Box 34, Gonzales, TX 78629-0034. 8AM-N 1-5PM. **830-672-2326**, Fax: 830-672-9313. ☎ **Fax** ✉ ⚓

County Court *Misdemeanor, Civil, Probate* PO Box 77, Gonzales, TX 78629. 8AM-5PM. **830-672-2801**, Fax: 830-672-2636. ✉ ⚓

Gray County

District Court *Felony, Civil* PO Box 1139, Pampa, TX 79066-1139. 8:30AM-5PM. **806-669-8010**, Fax: 806-669-8053. **Fax** ✉ ⚓

County & Probate Court *Misdemeanor, Civil, Probate* PO Box 1902, Pampa, TX 79066-1902. 8:30AM-5PM. **806-669-8004**, Fax: 806-669-8054. ☎ **Fax** ✉ ⚓

Grayson County

District Court *Felony, Civil, Family* www.co.grayson.tx.us 200 S Crockett, Rm 120-A, Sherman, TX 75090. 8AM-5PM. **903-813-4352**. ✉ ⚓

County Court *Misdemeanor, Civil, Probate* www.co.grayson.tx.us 200 S Crockett, Sherman, TX 75090. 8AM-5PM. **903-813-4336**, Fax: 903-892-8300. Civil phone: 903-813-4335, Probate: 903-813-4241. ✉ ⚓ 🖥

Gregg County

District Court *Felony, Civil* www.co.gregg.tx.us/government/courts.asp PO Box 711, Longview, TX 75606. 8AM-5PM. **903-237-2663**. ☎ **Fax** ✉ ⚓ 🖥

County Court *Misd., Civil, Probate* www.co.gregg.tx.us/government/commissionersCourt/county_judge.asp 101 E Methvin, #200, Longview, TX 75606. 8AM-5PM. **903-236-8430**. ✉ ⚓ 🖥

Grimes County

District Court *Felony, Civil* PO Box 234, Anderson, TX 77830. 8AM-4:45PM. **936-873-2111/2606**, Fax: 936-873-2415. ☎ **Fax** ✉ ⚓

County Court *Misdemeanor, Civil, Probate* PO Box 209, Anderson, TX 77830. 8AM-4:45PM. **936-873-2606 X251**. ✉ ⚓

Guadalupe County

District Court *Felony, Civil* www.co.guadalupe.tx.us/ 101 E Court St, Seguin, TX 78155. 8AM-5PM. **830-303-4188**, Fax: 830-379-1943. Will look up case info if case number is known. ⚓ 🖥

County Court *Misdemeanor, Civil, Probate* 101 E Court St, Seguin, TX 78155. 8AM-4:30PM. **830-303-4188 X266,234,232**, Fax 830-372-1206. ✉ ⚓

Hale County

District Court *Felony, Civil* www.242ndcourt.com/ 500 Broadway, #200, Plainview, TX 79072-8050. 8AM-N; 1-5PM. **806-291-5226**, Fax: 806-291-5206. ☎ **Fax** ✉ ⚓

County Court *Misdemeanor, Civil, Probate* 500 Broadway, #140, Plainview, TX 79072-8030. 8AM-N, 1-5PM. **806-291-5261**, Fax: 806-291-9810. ✉ **Fax** ⚓

Hall County

District & County Court *Felony, Misdemeanor, Civil, Probate* County Courthouse 512 Main St, #8, Memphis, TX 79245. 8:30AM-N; 1-5PM. **806-259-2627**, Fax: 806-259-5078. ☎ ✉ ⚓

Hamilton County

District Court *Felony, Civil* County Courthouse, Hamilton, TX 76531. 8AM-5PM M-Th; 8AM-4:30PM F. **254-386-3417**, Fax: 254-386-8610. **Fax** ✉ ⚓

County Court *Misdemeanor, Civil, Probate* County Courthouse, Hamilton, TX 76531. 8AM-5PM. **254-386-3518**, Fax: 254-386-8727. ✉ **Fax** ⚓

Hansford County

District & County Court *Felony, Misdemeanor, Civil, Probate* PO Box 397, Spearman, TX 79081. 8:00AM-5PM. **806-659-4110**, Fax: 806-659-4168. ☎ **Fax** ✉ ⚓

Key: Symbols refer to criminal records access unless otherwise noted. phone-☎ mail-✉ fax-**Fax** in person-⚓ online-🖥 email-**Email**

Hardeman County

District & County Court *Felony, Misdemeanor, Civil, Probate* PO Box 30, Quanah, TX 79252. 8:30AM-5PM. **940-663-2901**. ✉✋

Hardin County

District Court *Felony, Civil* PO Box 2997 300 Monroe, Kountze, TX 77625. 8AM-4PM. **409-246-5150**. ✉✋

County Court *Misdemeanor, Civil, Probate* PO Box 38, Kountze, TX 77625. 8AM-5PM. **409-246-5185**. ✉✋☎

Harris County

District Court *Felony, Misd., Civil Over $100,000* www.hcdistrictclerk.com District Clerk PO Box 4651, Houston, TX 77210-4651. 8AM-6PM. **713-755-5734**, Fax: 713-755-5480 (civil). Civil phone: 713-755-5711 x2, crim: 713-755-7801. Phone and mail requests are managed by a private company at 888-545-5577. 💻✋ (or ☎✉ via the private company).

County Court *Civil Under $100,000* www.cclerk.hctx.net PO Box 1525 Civil Courts Bldg, 301 Fannin, Rm 101, Houston, TX 77251-1525. 8AM-4:30PM. **713-755-6421**. The Information Department (for record information) telephone is 713-755-6405, located at County Admin Bldg, 1001 Preston, 4th Fl. Small claims and evictions are handled by county Justice of Peace Courts; usually there are two per precinct. Access civil records-☎✉💻✋

Probate Court 1115 Congress, 6th Fl, Houston, TX 77002. 8AM-4:30PM. **713-755-6425**, Fax: 713-755-5468. Probate dockets available through the Harris County online system. Call 713-755-7815 for info. Dockets are free at www.cclerk.hctx.net/coolice/default.asp?Category=ProbateCourt&Service=pc_inquiry.

Harrison County

71st District Court *Felony, Civil* www.co.harrison.tx.us PO Box 1119, Marshall, TX 75671-1119. 8AM-5PM. **903-935-8409**. ✉✋

County Court *Misdemeanor, Civil, Probate* PO Box 1365, Marshall, TX 75671. 8AM-5PM. **903-935-8403**. ✉✋

Hartley County

District & County Court *Felony, Misdemeanor, Civil, Probate* PO Box Q,

Channing, TX 79018. 8:30AM-N, 1-5PM. **806-235-3582**, Fax 806-235-2316. ✉✋

Haskell County

District Court *Felony, Civil* PO Box 27, Haskell, TX 79521. 8:30AM-N, 1-5PM M-Th; 8:30AM-4:30PM F. **940-864-2030**. ✉✋

County Court *Misdemeanor, Civil, Probate* PO Box 725, Haskell, TX 79521. 8AM-N, 1-5. **940-864-2451**. **Fax**✉✋

Hays County

www.co.hays.tx.us
District Court *Felony, Civil* 110 E Martin Luther King, #123, San Marcos, TX 78666. 8AM-5PM. **512-393-7660**, Fax: 512-393-7674. ☎✉✋💻

County Court *Misdemeanor, Civil, Probate* Justice Center 110 E Martin L King Dr, San Marcos, TX 78666. 8AM-5PM. **512-393-7738**, Fax: 512-393-7735. Civil phone: 512-393-7739, crim: 512-393-7738, Probate: 512-393-7734. ✉✋💻

Hemphill County

District & County Court *Felony, Misdemeanor, Civil, Probate* PO Box 867, Canadian, TX 79014. 8AM-5PM. **806-323-6212**. ☎✉✋

Henderson County

District Court *Felony, Civil* District Clerk Henderson County 100 E Tyler, Rm 203, Athens, TX 75751. 8AM-5PM. **903-675-6115**. ✉✋

County Court *Misd., Civil, Probate* PO Box 632, Athens, TX 75751. 8AM-5PM. **903-675-6140**, Fax: 903-675-6105. Civil phone: 903-675-6144, crim: 903-677-7205, Probate: 903-677-7206. ✉**Fax**✋

Hidalgo County

District Court *Felony, Civil* 100 N Closner, Box 87, Edinburg, TX 78540. 8AM-5PM. **956-318-2200**. ✉✋💻

County Court *Misdemeanor, Civil, Probate* PO Box 58, Edinburg, TX 78540. 7:30AM-5:00PM. **956-318-2100**. ✉✋💻

Hill County

District Court *Felony, Misdmeanor, Civil* PO Box 634, Hillsboro, TX 76645. 8AM-5PM. **254-582-4023**. ✉✋

County Court *Probate* PO Box 398, Hillsboro, TX 76645. 8AM-5PM. **254-582-4012**, Fax: 254-582-4003 Probate: 254-582-4030.

Hockley County

District Court *Felony, Civil* 802 Houston St, #316, Levelland, TX 79336. 9AM-5PM. **806-894-8527**, Fax: 806-894-3891. ☎✉✋

County Court *Misdemeanor, Civil, Probate* County Courthouse 802 Houston St, #213, Levelland, TX 79336. 9AM-5PM. **806-894-3185**. ✉✋

Hood County

District Court *Felony, Civil* County Courthouse 100 E Pearl, #21, Granbury, TX 76048. 8AM-5PM. **817-579-3236**, Fax: 817-579-3239. ✉✋

County Court *Misdemeanor, Civil, Probate* PO Box 339, Granbury, TX 76048. 8AM-5PM. **817-579-3222**, Fax: 817-579-3227. ✉✋

Hopkins County

District Court *Felony, Civil* 118 Church St, Sulphur Springs, TX 75483. 8AM-5PM. **903-438-4081**, Civil: 903-438-4084, crim: 903-438-4083. ✉✋

County Court *Misd., Civil, Probate* www.hopkinscountytx.org/departments.htm PO Box 288, Sulphur Springs, TX 75483. 8AM-5PM. **903-438-4074**, Fax: 903-438-4110. Probate: 903-438-4078. Probate Court at 411 College St. ✉✋

Houston County

District Court *Felony, Civil* County Courthouse 401 E Houston, PO Box 1186, Crockett, TX 75835. 8AM-4:30PM. **936-544-3255 x222**, Fax: 936-544-9523. **Fax**✉✋

County Court *Misdemeanor, Civil, Probate* PO Box 370, Crockett, TX 75835. 8AM-4:30. **936-544-3255**, Fax: 936-544-1954. ✉✋

Howard County

District Court *Felony, Civil* PO Box 2138, Big Spring, TX 79721. 8AM-5PM. **432-264-2223**, Fax 432-264-2256. ✉✋

County Court *Misdemeanor, Civil, Probate* PO Box 1468, Big Spring, TX 79721. 8AM-5PM. **432-264-2213**, Fax: 432-264-2215. Access records-☎✉✋

Hudspeth County

District & County Court *Felony, Misdemeanor, Civil, Probate* PO Drawer 58, Sierra Blanca, TX 79851. 8AM-5PM. **915-369-2301**, Fax: 915-369-3005. ☎Fax✉🖐

Hunt County

District Court *Felony, Civil* Court Clerk PO Box 1437, Greenville, TX 75403. 8AM-5PM. **903-408-4172**. ✉🖐

County Court *Misd., Civil, Probate* PO Box 1316, Greenville, TX 75403-1316. 8AM-5PM. **903-408-4130**. ✉🖐

Hutchinson County

District Court *Felony, Civil* PO Box 580, Stinnett, TX 79083. 9AM-5PM. **806-878-4017**, Fax: 806-878-4042. ✉🖐

County Court *Misdemeanor, Civil, Probate* PO Box 1186 Hutchinson County Clerk, Stinnett, TX 79083. 9AM-5PM. **806-878-4002**. ✉🖐

Irion County

District & County Court *Felony, Misdemeanor, Civil, Probate* PO Box 736, Mertzon, TX 76941-0736. 8AM-5PM. **325-835-2421**, Fax: 325-835-2008. ✉Fax🖐

Jack County

District Court *Felony, Civil* 100 Main, County Courthouse, Jacksboro, TX 76458. 8AM-5PM. **940-567-2141**, Fax: 940-567-2696. ✉🖐

County Court *Misdemeanor, Civil, Probate* 100 Main, Jacksboro, TX 76458. 8AM-5PM. **940-567-2111**. ☎✉🖐

Jackson County

District Court *Felony, Civil* 115 W Main, Rm 203, Edna, TX 77957. 8AM-5PM. **361-782-3812**. ✉🖐

County Court *Misdemeanor, Civil, Probate* 115 W Main, Rm 101, Edna, TX 77957. 8AM-5PM. **361-782-3563**. 🖐

Jasper County

District Court *Felony, Civil* County Courthouse, #202 PO Box 2088, Jasper, TX 75951. 8-4:30. **409-384-2721**. ✉🖐

County Court *Misdemeanor, Civil, Probate* Rm 103, Courthouse, Main at Lamar PO Box 2070, Jasper, TX 75951.

8AM-4:30PM. **409-384-2632**, Fax: 409-384-7198. Access records-☎✉Fax🖐

Jeff Davis County

District & County Court *Felony, Misdemeanor, Civil, Probate* PO Box 398, Fort Davis, TX 79734. 9AM-N, 1-5PM. **432-426-3251**, Fax: 432-426-3760. ✉🖐fax.

Jefferson County

District Court *Felony, Civil* www.co.jefferson.tx.us PO Box 3707 Pearl St Courthouse, Beaumont, TX 77704. 8AM-5PM. **409-835-8580**, Fax: 409-835-8527. ✉💻🖐

County Court *Misd., Civil, Probate* http://jeffersontxclerk.hartintercivic.com/ PO Box 1151, Beaumont, TX 77704. 8AM-5PM. **409-835-8479**, Fax: 409-839-2394 Probate: 409-835-8483. Search probate records back to 1988 free at http://jeffersontxclerk.hartic.com/search.asp?cabinet=probate. ✉🖐💻

Jim Hogg County

District & County Court *Felony, Misdemeanor, Civil, Probate* PO Box 878, Hebbronville, TX 78361. 9AM-5PM. **361-527-4031**, Fax: 361-527-5843. 🖐

Jim Wells County

79th District Court *Felony, Civil* PO Drawer 2219, Alice, TX 78333. 8AM-N, 1-5PM. **361-668-5717**. ✉🖐

County Court *Misdemeanor, Civil, Probate* PO Box 1459 200 N Almond, Alice, TX 78333. 8:00AM-N, 1-5PM. **361-668-5702**. Access records-☎✉🖐

Johnson County

District Court *Felony, Civil* PO Box 495, Cleburne, TX 76033-0495. 8AM-5PM. **817-556-6839**, Fax: 817-556-6120. Fax✉🖐

County Court *Misdemeanor, Civil, Probate* www.johnsoncountytx.org/ Rm 104 PO Box 662, Cleburne, TX 76033-0662. 8AM-N, 1-4:30PM. **817-556-6300**, Civil: 817-556-6870, crim: 817-556-6319, Probate: 817-556-6322. ✉🖐

Jones County

District Court *Felony, Misdemeanor, Civil* PO Box 308, Anson, TX 79501. 8AM-5PM. **325-823-3731**, Fax: 325-823-4200. ✉🖐

Karnes County

District Court *Felony, Civil* County Courthouse 101 N Panna Maria Ave, Karnes City, TX 78118-2930. 8AM-N, 1-5PM. **830-780-2562**, Fax: 830-780-3227. ✉🖐

County Court *Misdemeanor, Civil, Probate* 101 N Panna Maria Ave, #9 Courthouse, Karnes City, TX 78118-2929. 8AM-5PM. **830-780-3938**, Fax: 830-780-4576. ✉🖐

Kaufman County

District Court *Felony, Civil* County Courthouse, 100 W Mulberry St, Kaufman, TX 75142. 8AM-5PM. **972-932-4331 X214**. ✉🖐

County Court *Misdemeanor, Civil, Probate* http:www.kaufmancounty.net County Courthouse, Kaufman, TX 75142. 8-4:30PM. **972-932-4331 x220**. ✉🖐

Kendall County

District Court *Felony, Civil* 201 E. San Antonio, #201, Boerne, TX 78006. 8AM-N, 1-5PM. **830-249-9343**. ✉🖐

County Court *Misdemeanor, Probate* 201 E San Antonio, #127, Boerne, TX 78006. 8AM-5PM. **830-249-9343**, Fax: 830-249-3472. ✉🖐

Kenedy County

District & County Court *Felony, Misdemeanor, Civil, Probate* PO Box 227, Sarita, TX 78385. 8:30AM-N, 1PM-4:30PM. **361-294-5220**, Fax: 361-294-5218. ☎✉🖐

Kent County

District & County Court *Felony, Misdemeanor, Civil, Probate* PO Box 9, Jayton, TX 79528. 8:30AM-N, 1-5PM. **806-237-3881**, Fax 806-237-2632. ✉🖐

Kerr County

District Court *Felony, Civil* 700 Main, County Courthouse, Kerrville, TX 78028. 8AM-5PM. **830-792-2281**. ✉🖐

County Court & County Court at Law *Misd., Civil, Probate* www.kerrcounty.org/ 700 Main St, #122, Kerrville, TX 78028-5389. 8AM-5PM. **830-792-2262**, Fax: 830-792-2274 Probate: 830-792-2298. ☎✉Fax🖐

Kimble County

District & County Court *Felony, Misdemeanor, Civil, Probate* 501 Main St, Junction, TX 76849. 8AM-N, 1-5PM. **325-446-3353**, Fax 325-446-2986. ✉ 🖐

King County

District & County Court *Felony, Misdemeanor, Civil, Probate* PO Box 135, Guthrie, TX 79236. 9AM-N, 1-5PM. **806-596-4412**, Fax: 806-596-4664. Civil phone: 806-596-4412, crim: 806-596-4412, Probate: 806-596-4412. ✉ 🖐

Kinney County

District & County Court *Felony, Misdemeanor, Civil, Probate* PO Drawer 9, Brackettville, TX 78832. 8AM-5PM. **830-563-2521**, Fax: 830-563-2644. ☎ Fax ✉ 🖐

Kleberg County

District & County Court at Law *Felony, Civil* PO Box 312, Kingsville, TX 78364-0312. 8AM-N, 1-5 PM. **361-595-8561**, Fax: 361-595-8525. ☎ Fax ✉ 🖐 💻

County Court - Criminal *Misdemeanor, Probate* PO Box 1327, Kingsville, TX 78364. 8AM-N; 1-5PM. **361-595-8548**. Court also handles civil cases dealing with occupational licenses & bond forfeitures. ☎ ✉ 🖐

Knox County

District & County Court *Felony, Misdemeanor, Civil, Probate* PO Box 196, Benjamin, TX 79505. 8AM-N, 1-5PM. **940-459-2441**. ✉ 🖐

Lamar County

District Court *Felony, Civil* www.co.lamar.tx.us/ 119 N Main, Rm 306, Paris, TX 75460. 8AM-5PM. **903-737-2427**. ✉ 🖐 💻

County Court *Misdemeanor, Civil, Probate* www.co.lamar.tx.us 119 N Main, Paris, TX 75460. 8AM-5PM. **903-737-2420**. ☎ Fax ✉ 🖐 💻

Lamb County

District Court *Felony, Civil* 100 6th, Rm 212, Courthouse, Littlefield, TX 79339. 8AM-N, 1-5PM. **806-385-4222**. ✉ 🖐

County Court *Misdemeanor, Civil, Probate* County Courthouse, Rm 103 Box 3, Littlefield, TX 79339-3366. 8:30AM-12:00, 1-5PM. **806-385-4222 X214**, Fax: 806-385-6485. ✉ 🖐

Lampasas County

District Court *Felony, Civil* PO Box 327, Lampasas, TX 76550. 8AM-5PM. **512-556-8271 X240**, Fax: 512-556-9463. ✉ 🖐

County Court *Misdemeanor, Civil, Probate* PO Box 347, Lampasas, TX 76550. 8AM-5PM. **512-556-8271 X37**. ✉ 🖐

La Salle County

District Court *Felony, Civil* PO Box 340, Cotulla, TX 78014. 8AM-5PM. **830-879-4434**. ✉ 🖐

District & County Courts *Misdemeanor, Civil, Probate* PO Box 340, Cotulla, TX 78014. 8AM-5PM. **830-879-4432**, Fax: 830-879-2933. ✉ 🖐

Lavaca County

District Court *Felony, Civil* PO Box 306, Hallettsville, TX 77964. 8AM-N, 1-5PM. **361-798-2351**. ✉ 🖐

County Court *Misdemeanor, Civil, Probate* PO Box 326, Hallettsville, TX 77964. 8AM-5PM. **361-798-3612**. ✉ 🖐

Lee County

District Court *Felony, Civil* PO Box 176, Giddings, TX 78942. 8AM-N, 1-5PM. **979-542-2947**, Fax: 979-542-2444. ✉ 🖐

County Court *Misdemeanor, Civil, Probate* PO Box 419, Giddings, TX 78942. 8AM-5PM. **979-542-3684**, Fax: 979-542-2623. ✉ 🖐

Leon County

District Court *Felony, Civil* PO Box 39 139 E Main St, Centerville, TX 75833. 8AM-5PM. **903-536-2227**. ✉ 🖐

County Court *Misdemeanor, Civil, Probate* PO Box 98, Centerville, TX 75833. 8AM-5PM. **903-536-2352**. ✉ 🖐

Liberty County

District Court *Felony, Civil* 1923 Sam Houston, Rm 303, Liberty, TX 77575. 8AM-N, 1-5PM. **936-336-4600**. ✉ 🖐

County Court *Misdemeanor, Civil, Probate* PO Box 369, Liberty, TX 77575. 8AM-5PM. **936-336-4670**. ✉ 🖐

Limestone County

District Court *Felony, Civil* PO Box 230, Groesbeck, TX 76642. 8AM-5PM.

254-729-3206, Fax: 254-729-2960. ☎ Fax ✉ 🖐

County Court *Misdemeanor, Civil, Probate* PO Box 350, Groesbeck, TX 76642. 8AM-5PM. **254-729-5504**, Fax: 254-729-2951. ✉ 🖐

Lipscomb County

District & County Court *Felony, Misdemeanor, Civil, Probate* PO Box 70, Lipscomb, TX 79056. 8:30AM-N, 1-5PM. **806-862-3091**, Fax: 806-862-3004. Fax ✉ 🖐

Live Oak County

District Court *Felony, Civil* PO Drawer 440, George West, TX 78022. 8AM-5PM. **361-449-2733 X105**. ☎ Fax ✉ 🖐

County Court *Misd., Civil, Probate* PO Box 280, George West, TX 78022. 8AM-5PM. **361-449-2733 X3**, Civil: X103, crim: X129, Probate: X103. ✉ 🖐

Llano County

District Clerk *Felony, Civil* www.courts.state.tx.us/district/33rd/index.htm PO Box 877, Llano, TX 78643-0877. 8AM-4:30PM. **325-247-5036**, Fax: 325-248-0492. ✉ 🖐

County Court *Misdemeanor, Civil, Probate* PO Box 40, Llano, TX 78643-0040. 8-4:30. **325-247-4455**. ☎ ✉ 🖐

Loving County

District & County Court *Felony, Misdemeanor, Civil, Probate* PO Box 194, Mentone, TX 79754. 9AM-N, 1-5PM. **432-377-2441**, Fax: 432-377-2701. ☎ Fax ✉ 🖐

Lubbock County

District Court *Felony, Civil* www.co.lubbock.tx.us/DClerk/d_clerk.htm PO Box 10536 (904 Broadway #105), Lubbock, TX 79408-3536. 8AM-5PM. **806-775-1623**, Fax: 806-775-1382 Fax ✉ 🖐

County Courts *Misd., Civil, Probate* www.co.lubbock.tx.us/CCourt/c_courts.htm Courthouse, Rm 207 PO Box 10536, Lubbock, TX 79408. 8:30AM-5PM. Civil: 806-775-1051, crim: 806-775-1044, Probate: 806-775-1048. ✉ 🖐

Lynn County

District Court *Felony, Civil* PO Box 939, Tahoka, TX 79373. 8:30AM-5PM.

806-561-4274, Fax: 806-561-4151. Fax✉✋

County Court *Misdemeanor, Civil, Probate* PO Box 937, Tahoka, TX 79373. 8:30AM-5PM. **806-561-4750**, Fax: 806-561-4988. ✉✋

McCulloch County

District Court *Felony, Civil* County Courthouse, Rm 205, Brady, TX 76825. 8:30AM-5PM. **325-597-0733**, Fax: 325-597-0606. ✉Fax✋🖳

County Court *Misdemeanor, Civil, Probate* County Courthouse, Brady, TX 76825. 8AM-12:00, 1-5PM. **325-597-0733**. ✉✋🖳

McLennan County

District Court *Felony, Civil* www.co.mclennan.tx.us/ PO Box 2451, Waco, TX 76703. 8AM-5PM. Fax: 254-757-5060. Civil phone: 254-757-5057, crim: 254-757-5054. ✉✋

County Clerk's Office *Misdemeanor, Civil, Probate* PO Box 1727, Waco, TX 76703. 8AM-5PM. **254-757-5185**, Fax: 254-757-5146. Civil phone: 254-757-5189, crim: 254-757-5140, Probate: 254-757-5186. ✉✋

McMullen County

District & County Court *Felony, Misdemeanor, Civil, Probate* PO Box 235, Tilden, TX 78072. 8AM-4PM. **361-274-3215**, Fax: 361-274-3858. ✉✋

Madison County

District Court *Felony, Civil* 101 W Main, Rm 226, Madisonville, TX 77864. 8AM-N, 1-5PM. **936-348-9203**. ✉✋

County Court *Misd., Civil, Probate* www.co.madison.tx.us/coclerk.html 101 W Main, Rm 102, Madisonville, TX 77864. 8AM-4:30PM. **936-348-2638**, Fax: 936-348-5858. ✉✋

Marion County

District Court *Felony, Civil* PO Box 628, Jefferson, TX 75657. 8AM-5PM. **903-665-2441/2013**. ✉✋

County Court *Misdemeanor, Probate* PO Box 763, Jefferson, TX 75657. 8AM-N, 1-5PM. **903-665-3971**. ☎✉✋

Martin County

District & County Court *Felony, Misdemeanor, Civil, Probate* PO Box 906, Stanton, TX 79782. 8AM-N, 1-5PM. **432-756-3412**, Fax 432-607-2212. ✉✋

Mason County

District & County Court *Felony, Misdemeanor, Civil, Probate* PO Box 702, Mason, TX 76856. 8AM-N, 1-4PM. **325-347-5253**, Fax 325-347-6868. ✉✋

Matagorda County

District Court *Felony, Civil* www.co.matagorda.tx.us/ 1700 7th St, Rm 307, Bay City, TX 77414-5092. 8AM-N, 1-5PM. **979-244-7621**. ✉✋

County Court *Misdemeanor, Civil, Probate* 1700 7th St, Rm 202, Bay City, TX 77414-5094. 8AM-5PM. **979-244-7680**, Fax: 979-244-7688. ✉✋

Maverick County

District Court *Felony, Civil* 500 Quarry St, #5, Eagle Pass, TX 78853. 8AM-5PM. **830-773-2629**. ✉✋

County Court *Misdemeanor, Civil, Probate* 500 Quarry St, #2, Eagle Pass, TX 78853. 8AM-5PM. **830-773-2829**, Civil: X228, crim: X228, Probate: X228. ✉✋

Medina County

District Court *Felony, Civil* County Courthouse, Rm 209, Hondo, TX 78861. 8AM-5PM. **830-741-6070**. ✉✋

County Court at Law *Misdemeanor, Civil, Probate* 1100 16th St, Rm 203, Hondo, TX 78861. 8AM-N, 1-5PM. **830-741-6040**. ☎✉✋

Menard County

District & County Court *Felony, Misdemeanor, Civil, Probate* PO Box 1038, Menard, TX 76859. 8AM-N, 1-5PM. **325-396-4682**, Fax: 325-396-2047. ✉✋

Midland County

District Court *Felony, Civil* www.co.midland.tx.us/DC/default.asp 200 W Wall, #301, Midland, TX 79701. 8AM-5PM. **432-688-4500**. ✉✋🖳

County Court *Misdemeanor, Civil, Probate* PO Box 211, Midland, TX 79702. 8AM-5PM. **432-688-4402**, Fax: 432-688-8973. Access records-✉✋🖳

Milam County

District Court *Felony, Civil* PO Box 999, Cameron, TX 76520. 8AM-5PM. **254-697-7052**. ✉✋

County Court *Misdemeanor, Civil, Probate* 107 W Main St, Cameron, TX 76520. 8AM-5PM. **254-697-7049**, Fax: 254-697-7055. ✉✋

Mills County

District & County Court *Felony, Misdemeanor, Civil, Probate* PO Box 646, Goldthwaite, TX 76844. 8AM-N, 1-5PM. **325-648-2711**, Fax: 325-648-3251. ✉Fax✋

Mitchell County

District Court *Felony, Civil* County Courthouse, Colorado City, TX 79512. 9AM-4PM. **325-728-5918**. ✉✋

County Court *Misdemeanor, Civil, Probate* 349 Oak St, Rm 103, Colorado City, TX 79512. 8AM-N, 1-5PM. **325-728-3481**, Fax: 325-728-5322. ✉✋

Montague County

District Clerk *Felony, Civil* PO Box 155, Montague, TX 76251. 8AM-5PM. **940-894-2571**. ✉✋

County Court *Misdemeanor, Civil, Probate* PO Box 77, Montague, TX 76251. 8AM-5PM. **940-894-2461**. ✉✋

Montgomery County

District Court *Felony, Civil* www.co.montgomery.tx.us/dcourts/index.shtml PO Box 2985, Conroe, TX 77305. 8AM-4PM M-T,Th-F; 8AM-4:30PM W. **936-539-7855**. ✉✋

County Court *Misdemeanor, Civil, Probate* www.co.montgomery.tx.us PO Box 959, Conroe, TX 77305. 8AM-5PM. **936-539-7885**, Fax 936-760-6990. ✉✋

Moore County

District Court *Felony, Civil* 715 Dumas Ave, #109, Dumas, TX 79029. 8:30AM-5PM. **806-935-4218**, Fax: 806-935-6325. ✉✋

County Court *Misdemeanor, Civil, Probate* 715 Dumas Ave, Rm 105, Dumas, TX 79029. 8:30AM-5PM. **806-**

935-6164/2009, Fax: 806-935-9004. ⊠**Fax**👆

Morris County

District Court *Felony, Civil* 500 Broadnax, Daingerfield, TX 75638. 8AM-5PM. **903-645-2321.** ⊠👆

County Court *Misdemeanor, Probate* 500 Broadnax, Daingerfield, TX 75638. 8AM-5PM. **903-645-3911.** ⊠👆

Motley County

District & County Court *Felony, Misdemeanor, Civil, Probate* PO Box 660, Matador, TX 79244. 9AM-N, 1-5PM. **806-347-2621**, Fax: 806-347-2220. ⊠**Fax**👆

Nacogdoches County

District Court *Felony, Civil* 101 W Main, #215, Nacogdoches, TX 75961. 8AM-5PM. **936-560-7730**, Fax: 936-560-7839. ⊠👆

County Court *Misdemeanor, Civil, Probate* www.co.nacogdoches.tx.us/ County Clerk 101 W Main, Rm 205, Nacogdoches, TX 75961. 8AM-5PM. **936-560-7733**. The County Clerk is the Clerk for County Court at Law, except for Juvenile, Family Law, including Divorce & Adoption (for these cases see the District Clerk). ⊠👆

Navarro County

District Court *Felony, Civil* www.navarrocounty.org/ PO Box 1439, Corsicana, TX 75151. 8AM-5PM. **903-654-3040**, Fax: 903-654-3088. ☎**Fax**⊠👆🖥

County Court *Misdemeanor, Civil, Probate* PO Box 423, Corsicana, TX 75151. 8AM-4:45. **903-654-3035**. ⊠👆

Newton County

District Court *Felony, Civil* PO Box 535, Newton, TX 75966. 8AM-4:30PM. **409-379-3951.** ⊠👆

County Court *Misdemeanor, Civil, Probate* PO Box 484, Newton, TX 75966. 8AM-4:30PM. **409-379-5341**, Fax: 409-379-9049. ⊠👆

Nolan County

District Court *Felony, Civil* 100 E 3rd, #200A, Sweetwater, TX 79556. 8:30AM-N, 1-5PM. **325-235-2111.** ⊠👆

County Court *Misdemeanor, Civil, Probate* 100 E 3rd St, #108, Sweetwater, TX 79556-4546. 8:30AM-N, 1-5PM. **325-235-2462.** ⊠👆

Nueces County

District & County Court *Felony, Misdemeanor, Civil, Probate* www.co.nueces.tx.us/districtclerk/ PO Box 2987, Corpus Christi, TX 78403-2987. 8AM-5PM. **361-888-0450**, Fax: 361-888-0571. Criminal phone: 361-888-0495. Records are combined at this location. ⊠👆🖥

Ochiltree County

District Court *Felony, Civil* 511 S Main, Perryton, TX 79070. 8:30AM-5PM. **806-435-8054**, Fax: 806-435-8058. **Fax**⊠👆

County Court *Misdemeanor, Civil, Probate* 511 S Main St, Perryton, TX 79070. 8:30AM-N, 1-5PM. **806-435-8039**, Fax: 806-435-2081. **Fax**⊠👆

Oldham County

District & County Court *Felony, Misdemeanor, Civil, Probate* PO Box 360, Vega, TX 79092. 8:30AM-N, 1-5PM. **806-267-2667.** ⊠👆

Orange County

District Court *Felony, Civil* PO Box 427, Orange, TX 77630. 8AM-5PM. **409-883-7740.** ⊠👆fax.

County Court *Misd., Civil, Probate* www.co.orange.tx.us 123 S 6th St, Orange, TX 77630. 8AM-5PM. **409-882-7055**, Fax 409-882-7812. ☎**Fax**⊠👆

Palo Pinto County

District Court *Felony, Civil* PO Box 189, Palo Pinto, TX 76484-0189. 8AM-4:30PM. **940-659-1279.** ⊠👆

County Court *Misdemeanor, Civil, Probate* PO Box 219, Palo Pinto, TX 76484. 8:30AM-4:30PM. **940-659-1277**, Fax: 940-659-2590. ⊠👆

Panola County

District Court *Felony, Civil* County Courthouse, Rm 227, Carthage, TX 75633. 8AM-5PM. **903-693-0306**, Fax: 903-693-6914. ⊠👆

County Court *Misdemeanor, Civil, Probate* County Courthouse, Rm 201, Carthage, TX 75633. 8AM-5PM. **903-693-0302.** ⊠👆fax.

Parker County

District Court *Felony, Civil* www.parkercountytx.com 117 Ft. Worth Ave (PO Box 2050), Weatherford, TX 76086. 8AM-5PM. **817-599-6591**, Fax: 817-598-6131. Civil phone: 817-598-6114, crim: 817-598-6194 or x6200/x6214. Starting 9/03 County Court at Law cases filed with District Clerk. All civil cases filed with District Court. ⊠👆🖥

County Court *Misdemeanor* Parker County Clerk - Court Division PO Box 819, Weatherford, TX 76086-0819. 8AM-N, 1-4PM. **817-594-1632.** As of 9/1/03 county court cases are filed with District Clerk. 11/04 new County Court At Law #2 (a second county court location) will begin taking cases. All civil cases will be filed with District Clerk. ☎⊠👆

Probate Court 1112 Santa Fe Dr PO Box 819, Weatherford, TX 76086. 8AM-5PM. **817-594-7461.**

Parmer County

District Court *Felony, Civil* PO Box 195, Farwell, TX 79325-0195. 8:30AM-N, 1-5PM. **806-481-3419**, Fax: 806-481-9416. **Fax**⊠👆🖥

County Court *Misdemeanor, Civil, Probate* PO Box 356, Farwell, TX 79325. 8:30AM-N; 1-5PM **806-481-3691.** ⊠👆

Pecos County

District Court *Felony, Civil* 400 S Nelson, Fort Stockton, TX 79735. 8AM-5PM. **432-336-3503**, Fax: 432-336-6437. **Fax**⊠👆

County Court *Misdemeanor, Civil, Probate* 103 W Callaghan, Fort Stockton, TX 79735. 8AM-5PM. **432-336-7555**, Fax: 432-336-7557. ⊠👆

Polk County

District Court *Felony, Civil* 101 W Church, #205, Livingston, TX 77351. 8AM-5PM. **936-327-6814.** ⊠👆

County Court *Misdemeanor, Civil, Probate* PO Drawer 2119, Livingston, TX 77351. 8AM-5PM. **936-327-6804**, Fax: 936-327-6874. Criminal phone: 936-327-6805. ⊠👆

Potter County

District Court *Felony, Civil* www.co.potter.tx.us/districtclerk PO Box

9570, Amarillo, TX 79105-9570. 7:30-5:30PM. **806-379-2300**. Fax✉️💻✋

County Court & County Courts at Law 1 & 2 *Misdemeanor, Civil, Probate* www.co.potter.tx.us/countyclerk/index.html PO Box 9638, Amarillo, TX 79105. 8AM-5PM. **806-379-2285**, Fax: 806-379-2296. Limited civil records filed here, most with the District Clerk. ✉️✋

Presidio County
District & County Court *Felony, Misdemeanor, Civil, Probate* PO Box 789, Marfa, TX 79843. 8AM-N, 1-4PM. **432-729-4812**, Fax 432-729-4313. ✉️✋

Rains County
District & County Court *Felony, Misdemeanor, Civil, Probate* PO Box 187, Emory, TX 75440. 8AM-5PM. **903-474-9999**, Fax: 903-474-9390. Fax District Court criminal: 903-473-0163. ✉️Fax✋

Randall County
District Courts *Felony, Civil* www.randallcounty.org PO Box 1096, Canyon, TX 79015. 8AM-5PM. **806-468-5600**, Fax: 806-468-5604. Fax✉️💻✋

County Court *Misd., Civil, Probate* www.randallcounty.org/cclerk/default.htm PO Box 660, Canyon, TX 79015. 8-5PM. **806-468-5505**. 📞✉️Fax✋💻Email

Reagan County
District & County Court *Felony, Misdemeanor, Civil, Probate* PO Box 100, Big Lake, TX 76932. 8:30AM-5PM. **325-884-2442**, Fax 325-884-1503. ✉️✋

Real County
District & County Court *Felony, Misdemeanor, Civil, Probate* PO Box 750, Leakey, TX 78873. 8AM-5PM. **830-232-5202**, Fax: 830-232-6888. ✋

Red River County
District Court *Felony, Civil* 400 N Walnut, Clarksville, TX 75426. 8:30AM-N, 1-5PM. **903-427-3761**, Fax: 903-427-1201. ✉️✋

County Court *Misdemeanor, Probate* 200 N Walnut, Clarksville, TX 75426. 8:30AM-5PM. **903-427-2401**. ✉️✋

Reeves County
District Court *Felony, Civil* PO Box 848, Pecos, TX 79772. 8AM-N, 1-5PM. **432-445-2714**, Fax 432-445-7455. ✉️✋

County Court *Misdemeanor, Civil, Probate* PO Box 867, Pecos, TX 79772. 8AM-5PM. **432-445-5467**. Probate records handled by County Clerk. ✉️✋

Refugio County
District Court *Felony, Civil* PO Box 736, Refugio, TX 78377. 8AM-N, 1-5PM. **361-526-2721**. ✉️✋

County Court *Misdemeanor, Civil, Probate* PO Box 704, Refugio, TX 78377. 8AM-5PM. **361-526-2233**. ✉️✋

Roberts County
District & County Court *Felony, Misdemeanor, Civil, Probate* PO Box 477, Miami, TX 79059. 8AM-N, 1-5PM. **806-868-2341**. ✉️✋

Robertson County
District Court *Felony, Civil* www.robertsoncountycourthouse.com/ PO Box 250, Franklin, TX 77856. 8AM-5PM. **979-828-3636**. ✉️✋

County Court *Misdemeanor, Civil, Probate* PO Box 1029, Franklin, TX 77856. 8-5PM. **979-828-4130**. ✉️Fax✋

Rockwall County
District Court *Felony, Civil* www.rockwallcountytexas.com 1101 Ridge Rd, #209, Rockwall, TX 75087. 8AM-5PM. **972-882-0260**, Fax: 972-882-0268. ✉️✋

County Court *Misdemeanor, Civil, Probate* www.rockwallcountytexas.com/ 1101 Ridge Rd, #101, Rockwall, TX 75087. 8AM-5PM. **972-882-0220**, Fax: 972-882-0229. 📞✉️✋💻

Runnels County
District Court *Felony, Civil* PO Box 166, Ballinger, TX 76821. 8:30AM-5PM. **325-365-2638**, Fax: 325-365-9229. 📞Fax✉️✋

County Court *Misdemeanor, Civil, Probate* PO Box 189, Ballinger, TX 76821. 8:30AM-N, 1-5PM. **325-365-2720**, Fax: 325-365-3408. 📞✉️✋

Rusk County
District Court *Felony, Civil* PO Box 1687, Henderson, TX 75653. 8AM-5PM. **903-657-0353**, Fax 903-657-1914. ✉️✋

County Court at Law *Misdemeanor, Civil, Probate* PO Box 758, Henderson, TX 75653-. 8AM-5PM. **903-657-0330**, Fax: 903-657-0300. ✉️✋

Sabine County
District Court *Felony, Civil* PO Box 850, Hemphill, TX 75948. 8AM-4:00PM. **409-787-2912**. ✉️✋

County Court *Misdemeanor, Probate* PO Drawer 580, Hemphill, TX 75948-0580. 8AM-4PM. **409-787-2889**. ✉️✋

San Augustine County
District Court *Felony, Civil* County Courthouse, Rm 202, San Augustine, TX 75972. 8AM-4:15PM. **936-275-2231**, Fax: 936-275-2389. 📞✉️✋

County Court *Misd., Probate* 100 W Columbia, Rm 106, San Augustine, TX 75972. 8AM-4:30PM. **936-275-2452**, Fax 936-275-9579. 📞✉️✋

San Jacinto County
District Court *Felony, Civil* 1 State Hwy 150, Rm 4, Coldspring, TX 77331. 8AM-N, 1-5PM. **936-653-2909**. ✉️✋

County Court *Misdemeanor, Civil, Probate* www.co.san-jacinto.tx.us 1 State Hwy 150, Rm 2, Coldspring, TX 77331. 8AM-4:30PM. **936-653-2324**. ✉️✋

San Patricio County
District Court *Felony, Civil* PO Box 1084, Sinton, TX 78387. 8AM-5PM. **361-364-6225**. ✉️✋

County Court *Misdemeanor, Civil, Probate* PO Box 578, Sinton, TX 78387. 8AM-5PM. **361-364-6290**, Fax: 361-364-6112. 📞✉️✋

San Saba County
District & County Court *Felony, Misdemeanor, Civil, Probate* www.courts.state.tx.us/district/33rd/index.htm County Courthouse 500 E Wallace, #202, San Saba, TX 76877. 8AM-N, 1-4:30PM. **325-372-3375**. ✉️✋

Schleicher County

District & County Court *Felony, Misd., Civil, Probate* PO Drawer 580, Eldorado, TX 76936. 9AM-N, 1-5PM. **325-853-2833**, Fax: 325-853-2768. ✉ ✋

Scurry County

132nd District Court *Felony, Civil* 1806 25th St, #402, Snyder, TX 79549. 8AM-5PM. **325-573-5641**. ✉ ✋

County Court *Misdemeanor, Civil, Probate* County Courthouse 1806 25th St, #300, Snyder, TX 79549. 8:30AM-5PM. **325-573-5332**. ✉ ✋

Shackelford County

District & County Court *Felony, Misdemeanor, Civil, Probate* PO Box 247, Albany, TX 76430. 8:30AM-5PM. **325-762-2232**. ✉ ✋

Shelby County

District Court *Felony, Civil* PO Drawer 1953, Center, TX 75935. 8AM-4:30PM. **936-598-4164**. ✉ ✋

County Court *Misdemeanor, Civil, Probate* PO Box 1987, Center, TX 75935. 8AM-4:30PM. **936-598-6361**, Fax: 936-598-3701. ✉ ✋

Sherman County

District & County Court *Felony, Misdemeanor, Civil, Probate* PO Box 270, Stratford, TX 79084. 8AM-N, 1-5PM. **806-366-2371**, Fax: 806-366-5670. ✉ ✋

Smith County

District Court *Felony, Civil* www.smith-county.com/dc_desc.htm PO Box 1077, Tyler, TX 75710. 8AM-5PM. **903-535-0666**, Fax: 903-535-0683. ✉ ✋

County Court at Law *Misdemeanor, Civil, Probate* PO Box 1018 200 E Ferguson, #300, Tyler, TX 75710. 8AM-5PM. **903-535-0630**, Fax: 903-535-0684. Civil phone: 903-535-0636/37/38, crim: 903-535-0645/46/47, Probate: 903-535-0634. There are three Courts at Law at this location. ✉ ✋

Somervell County

District & County Court *Felony, Misdemeanor, Civil, Probate* PO Box 1098, Glen Rose, TX 76043. 8AM-5PM. **254-897-4427**, Fax: 254-897-3233. Evictions are handled by Justice of the Peace, POB 237, Glen Rose, TX 76043, 254-897-2120. ✉ ✋

Starr County

District & County Court *Felony, Misdemeanor, Civil, Probate* Starr County Courthouse, Rm 304, Rio Grande City, TX 78582. 8AM-5PM. **956-487-8482 (Dist)** 487-8485 **(County)**, Fax: 956-487-8493. Handles civil county court cases. ☎ **Fax** ✉ ✋

County Court *Misdemeanor, Probate* Starr County Courthouse, Rm 201, Rio Grande City, TX 78582. 8AM-5PM. **956-487-8032**, Fax: 956-487-8674. See District & County Court for civil county court cases. ✉ ✋ 🖥

Stephens County

District Court *Felony, Civil, Misd.* 200 W Walker, Breckenridge, TX 76424. 8:30AM-5PM. **254-559-3151**, Fax: 254-559-8127. **Fax** ✉ ✋

County Clerk *Probate* 200 W Walker, Breckenridge, TX 76424. 8:30AM-5PM. **254-559-3700**. **Fax** ✉ ✋

Sterling County

District & County Court *Felony, Misdemeanor, Civil, Probate* PO Box 55, Sterling City, TX 76951. 8:30AM-4PM M-Th; -1:30PM F. **325-378-5191**. ✉ ✋

Stonewall County

District & County Court *Felony, Misdemeanor, Civil, Probate* PO Drawer P, Aspermont, TX 79502. 8AM-N, 1-4:30PM. **940-989-2272**. ☎ ✉ ✋

Sutton County

District & County Court *Felony, Misdemeanor, Civil, Probate* 300 E Oak, #3, Sonora, TX 76950. 8:30AM-4:30PM. **325-387-3815**. ✉ ✋

Swisher County

District & County Court *Felony, Misd., Civil, Probate* www.242ndcourt.com/ County Courthouse, 119 S Maxwell, Tulia, TX 79088. 8AM-5PM. **806-995-4396**, Fax: 806-995-4121. ✉ **Fax** ✋ **Email**

Tarrant County

District Court *Felony, Civil* www.tarrantcounty.com 401 W Belknap Tarrant County District Clerk's Office, Fort Worth, TX 76196-0402. 8AM-5PM. **817-884-1574** (884-1265 Family Div.), Civil: 817-884-1240, crim: 817-884-1342. ✉ 🖥 ✋

County Court - Criminal *Misdemeanor* www.tarrantcounty.com 401 W Belknap Tarrant County District Clerk's Office, Fort Worth, TX 76196-0402. 7:30AM-4:30PM. **817-884-1195**, Fax: 817-884-3295. Small Claims, Evictions, and low-level civil cases handled by JP/Municipal Courts. ✉ 🖥 ✋

Probate Court http://cc.co.tarrant.tx.us County Courthouse, 100 W Weatherford St Probate Court #1 Rm 260A, Fort Worth, TX 76196. 8AM-4:30PM. **817-884-1200**, Fax: 817-884-3178 Probate: 817-884-1254. Search probate records at http://cc.co.tarrant.tx.us/CCPublicAccess/ASP/Probate/ProbatePublicBrowse.asp?tc_countyclerkNav=|

Taylor County

District Court *Felony, Civil* 300 Oak St, Abilene, TX 79602. 8AM-N, 1-5PM. **325-674-1316**. ✉ ✋

County Court *Misdemeanor, Civil, Probate* www.taylorcountytexas.org PO Box 5497, Abilene, TX 79608. 8AM-5PM. **325-674-1202**, Fax: 325-674-1279. ✉ ✋

Terrell County

District & County Court *Felony, Misdemeanor, Civil, Probate* PO Drawer 410, Sanderson, TX 79848. 9AM-N, 1-5PM. **432-345-2391**, Fax: 432-345-2653. ✉ ✋

Terry County

District Court *Felony, Civil* 500 W Main, Rm 209E, Brownfield, TX 79316. 8:30AM-5PM. **806-637-4202**. ✉ ✋

County Court *Misdemeanor, Civil, Probate* 500 W Main, Rm 105, Brownfield, TX 79316-4398. 8:30AM-5PM. **806-637-8551**, Fax: 806-637-4874. ✉ ✋

Throckmorton County

District & County Court *Felony, Misdemeanor, Civil, Probate* PO Box 309, Throckmorton, TX 76483. 8AM-N, 1-4:30PM M-Th; 8AM-N Friday. **940-849-2501**. ✉ ✋

Titus County

District Court *Felony, Civil* 105 W 1st St PO Box 492, Mount Pleasant, TX

Key: Symbols refer to criminal records access unless otherwise noted. phone-☎ mail-✉ fax-**Fax** in person-✋ online-🖥 email-**Email**

75455. 8AM-5PM. **903-577-6721**, Fax: 903-577-6719. ☎ ✉ 👋

County Court *Misdemeanor, Civil, Probate* 100 W 1st St, #204, Mount Pleasant, TX 75455. 8AM-5PM. **903-577-6796**, Fax: 903-577-6793. ✉ 👋

Tom Green County

District Court *Felony, Civil* www.co.tom-green.tx.us/distclrk/ County Courthouse 112 W Beauregard, San Angelo, TX 76903. 8AM-5PM. **325-659-6579**, Fax: 325-659-3241. ✉ 👋 💻

County Court *Misdemeanor, Civil, Probate* http://justice.co.tom-green.tx.us 124 W Beauregard, San Angelo, TX 76903. 8AM-4:30PM. **325-659-6555**. ✉ 👋 💻

Travis County

District Court *Felony, Civil* www.co.travis.tx.us/ PO Box 1748, Austin, TX 78767. 8AM-5PM. Fax: 512-854-9549 Civil; 512-854-4566 Crim. Civil phone: 512-854-9457, crim phone: 512-854-9420. ☎ ✉ 👋

County Court *Misdemeanor, Civil, Probate* www.co.travis.tx.us PO Box 1748, Austin, TX 78767-1748. 8AM-5PM. Fax: 512-854-4220. Civil phone: 512-854-9090, crim: 512-854-9440, Probate: 512-854-9595. Records include appeals from the Travis County JP Courts. ☎ ✉ 👋

Trinity County

District Court *Felony, Civil* PO Box 548, Groveton, TX 75845. 8AM-5PM. **936-642-1118**. ✉ 👋

County Court *Misdemeanor, Civil, Probate* PO Box 456, Groveton, TX 75845. 8AM-5PM. **936-642-1208**, Fax: 936-642-3004. ✉ 👋

Tyler County

District Court *Felony, Civil* 203 Courthouse 100 W Bluff, Woodville, TX 75979. 8AM-N, 1-4:30PM. **409-283-2162**. ✉ 👋

County Court *Misdemeanor, Civil, Probate* County Courthouse, Rm 110 100 W Bluff, Woodville, TX 75979. 8AM-4:30PM. **409-283-2281**, Fax: 409-283-6305. ✉ 👋

Upshur County

District Court *Felony, Misd., Civil, Probate* www.countyofupshur.com PO Box 950, Gilmer, TX 75644. 8AM-5PM. **903-680-8283**, Fax 903-843-3540. ✉ 👋

County Court *Misdemeanor, Civil, Probate* PO Box 730, Gilmer, TX 75644. 8AM-5PM. **903-680-8126**, Fax: 903-843-5492. ✉ 👋

Upton County

District & County Court *Felony, Misd., Civil, Probate* www.co.upton.tx.us/ PO Box 465, Rankin, TX 79778. 8AM-5PM. **432-693-2861**, Fax: 432-693-2129. **Fax** ✉ 👋

Uvalde County

District Court *Felony, Civil* County Courthouse, #15, Uvalde, TX 78801. 8AM-5PM. **830-278-3918**. ☎ ✉ 👋

County Clerk *Misdemeanor, Civil, Probate* PO Box 284, Uvalde, TX 78802. 8AM-5PM. **830-278-6614**. ✉ 👋

Val Verde County

District Court *Felony, Civil* PO Box 1544, Del Rio, TX 78841. 8AM-4:30PM. **830-774-7538**, Civil: 830-774-7538, crim: 830-774-7539. ✉ 👋

County Court *Misd., Civil, Probate* PO Box 1267, Del Rio, TX 78841-1267. 8AM-4:30PM. **830-774-7564**. ✉ 👋

Van Zandt County

District Court *Felony, Civil* 121 E Dallas St, Rm 302, Canton, TX 75103. 8AM-5PM. **903-567-6576**, Fax: 903-567-1283. ✉ **Fax** 👋

County Court *Misdemeanor, Civil, Probate* 121 E Dallas St, #202, Canton, TX 75103. 8AM-5PM. **903-567-6503**, Fax: 903-567-6722. ✉ 👋

Victoria County

District Court *Felony, Civil* PO Box 2238, Victoria, TX 77902. 8AM-5PM. **361-575-0581**, Fax: 361-572-5682. ✉ 👋 💻

County Court *Misdemeanor, Civil, Probate* 115 N Bridge, Rm 103, Victoria, TX 77901. 8AM-5PM. **361-575-1478**, Fax: 361-575-6276. ☎ **Fax** ✉ 👋 💻

Walker County

District Court *Felony, Civil* 1100 University Ave, Rm 301, Huntsville, TX 77340. 8AM-N, 1-5PM. **936-436-4972**. ✉ 👋

County Court *Misdemeanor, Civil, Probate* PO Box 210, Huntsville, TX 77342-0210. 8AM-4:45PM. **936-436-4922**, Fax: 936-436-4928. Criminal fax # 936-436-4962. ✉ 👋

Waller County

District Court *Felony, Civil* www.cvtv.net/~tx155district/ 836 Austin St, Rm 318, Hempstead, TX 77445. 8AM-N, 1-5PM. **979-826-7735**. ✉ 👋

County Court *Misdemeanor, Civil, Probate* 836 Austin St, Rm 217, Hempstead, TX 77445. 8AM-N, 1-5PM. **979-826-7711**. ✉ 👋

Ward County

District Court *Felony, Civil* PO Box 440, Monahans, TX 79756. 8AM-N-1-5PM. **432-943-2751**, Fax: 432-943-3810. ✉ 👋

County Court *Misdemeanor, Civil, Probate* County Courthouse, Monahans, TX 79756. 8AM-5PM. **432-943-3294**, Fax: 432-943-6054. ✉ 👋

Washington County

District Court *Felony, Civil* 100 E Main, #304, Brenham, TX 77833-3753. 8AM-5PM. **979-277-6200**. ✉ 👋

County Court *Misdemeanor, Civil, Probate* 100 E Main, #102, Brenham, TX 77833. 8AM-5PM. **979-277-6200**, Fax: 979-277-6278. ✉ 👋

Webb County

District Court *Felony, Civil* www.webbcounty.com PO Box 667, Laredo, TX 78042-0667. 8AM-5PM. **956-523-4268**, Fax: 956-523-5063. ✉ **Fax** 👋 💻

County Court *Misdemeanor, Civil Under $5,000, Probate* 1110 Victoria, #201, Laredo, TX 78040. 8AM-5PM. **956-523-4266**, Fax: 956-523-5035. Civil phone: 956-523-4262, crim: 956-523-4261, Probate: 956-523-4257. ✉ 👋 💻

Wharton County

District Court *Felony, Civil* PO Drawer 391, Wharton, TX 77488. 8AM-5PM.

979-532-5542, Fax: 979-532-1299. ⊠**Fax**🖑

County Court *Misdemeanor, Civil, Probate* PO Box 69, Wharton, TX 77488. 8AM-5PM. **979-532-2381.** ⊠🖑

Wheeler County

District Court *Felony, Civil* PO Box 528, Wheeler, TX 79096. 8AM-5PM. **806-826-5931,** Fax: 806-826-5503. ☎⊠🖑

County Court *Misdemeanor, Civil, Probate* PO Box 465, Wheeler, TX 79096. 8AM-5PM. **806-826-5544,** Fax: 806-826-3282. ⊠🖑

Wichita County

District Court *Felony, Civil* PO Box 718, Wichita Falls, TX 76307. 8AM-5PM. **940-766-8190.** ☎⊠🖑

County Court *Misdemeanor, Probate* PO Box 1679, Wichita Falls, TX 76307. 8AM-5PM. **940-766-8160,** Fax: 940-716-8554. Criminal phone: 940-766-8173, Probate: 940-766-8172. ☎⊠🖑

Wilbarger County

District Court *Felony, Civil* 1700 Wilbarger, Rm 33, Vernon, TX 76384. 8AM-5PM. **940-553-3411,** Fax: 940-553-2316. ⊠🖑

County Court *Misdemeanor, Civil, Probate* 1700 Wilbarger, Rm 15, Vernon, TX 76384. 8AM-5. **940-552-5486.** ⊠🖑

Willacy County

District Court *Felony, Civil* County Courthouse, Raymondville, TX 78580. 8AM-5PM. **956-689-2532,** Fax: 956-689-5713. ⊠🖑

County Court *Misd., Civil, Probate* 540 W Hidalgo, Raymondville, TX 78580. 8AM-N, 1-5PM. **956-689-2710.** ⊠🖑

Williamson County

District Court *Felony, Civil* www.williamson-county.org PO Box 24, Georgetown, TX 78627. 8AM-5PM. **512-943-1212,** Fax: 512-943-1222. ⊠🖑

County Court *Misd., Civil, Probate* 405 MLK St, Box 14, Georgetown, TX 78626. 8AM-5PM. Fax: 512-943-1154 (civil). Civil phone: 512-943-1140, crim: 512-943-1150, prob: 512-943-1140. ⊠🖑🖥

Wilson County

District Court *Felony, Civil* PO Box 812, Floresville, TX 78114. 8AM-N, 1-4:30PM. **830-393-7322,** Fax: 830-393-7319. Request must be in writing if court personnel are to do search. **Fax**⊠🖑

County Court *Misdemeanor, Civil, Probate* PO Box 27, Floresville, TX 78114. 8-5. **830-393-7308.** ☎⊠**Fax**🖑

Winkler County

District Court *Felony, Civil* PO Box 1065, Kermit, TX 79745. 8AM-5PM. **432-586-3359.** ⊠🖑

County Court *Misdemeanor, Civil, Probate* PO Box 1007, Kermit, TX 79745. 8AM-5PM. **432-586-3401.** ⊠🖑

Wise County

District Court *Felony, Civil* PO Box 308, Decatur, TX 76234. 8AM-5PM. **940-627-5535,** Fax: 940-627-0705. ⊠🖑

County Court at Law *Misdemeanor, Civil, Probate* PO Box 359, Decatur, TX 76234. 8AM-5PM. **940-627-3351,** Fax: 940-627-2138. ⊠🖑

Wood County

District Court *Felony, Civil* www.co.wood.tx.us/dclerk.html PO Box 1707, Quitman, TX 75783. 8AM-5PM. **903-763-2361,** Fax: 903-763-1511. ⊠**Fax**🖑

County Court *Misdemeanor, Civil, Probate* PO Box 1796, Quitman, TX 75783. 8AM-5PM. **903-763-2711,** Fax: 903-763-5641. ⊠🖑

Yoakum County

District Court *Felony, Civil* PO Box 899, Plains, TX 79355. 8AM-5PM. **806-456-7453,** Fax: 806-456-8767. **Fax**⊠🖑

County Court *Misdemeanor, Civil, Probate* PO Box 309, Plains, TX 79355. 8AM-5PM. **806-456-2721,** Fax: 806-456-6175 (County Judge Office). ⊠🖑

Young County

District Court *Felony, Civil* 516 4th St, Rm 201, Courthouse, Graham, TX 76450. 8:30AM-N, 1-5PM. **940-549-0029,** Fax: 940-549-4874. ☎**Fax**⊠🖑

County Court *Misdemeanor, Civil, Probate* 516 4th St, Rm 104, Graham, TX 76450. 8:30AM-N, 1-5PM. **940-549-8432,** Fax: 940-521-0305. ⊠🖑

Zapata County

District Court *Felony, Civil* PO Box 788, Clerk's Office, Zapata, TX 78076. 8AM-N, 1-5PM. **956-765-9930,** Fax: 956-765-9931. **Fax**⊠🖑

County Court *Misdemeanor, Civil, Probate* PO Box 789, Zapata, TX 78076. 8AM-N, 1-5PM. **956-765-9915,** Fax: 956-765-9933. ⊠🖑

Zavala County

District Court *Felony, Civil* PO Box 704, Crystal City, TX 78839. 8AM-N, 1-5PM. **830-374-3456.** ☎⊠🖑

County Court *Misd., Civil, Probate* Zavala County Courthouse 200 E Uvalde, Crystal City, TX 78839. 8AM-5PM. **830-374-2331,** Fax: 830-374-5955. ⊠🖑

Utah

State Court Administration (All District Courts): Court Administrator, PO Box 140241 (450 S State St), Salt Lake City, UT, 84114; 801-578-3800, Fax: 801-578-3859. http://www.utcourts.gov

Court Structure: 41 District Courts are arranged in eight judicial districts. Branch courts in larger counties, such as Salt Lake, which were formerly Circuit Courts and elevated to District Courts have full jurisdiction over felony as well as misdemeanor cases. Justice Courts are established by counties and municipalities and have the authority to deal with class B and C misdemeanors, violations of ordinances, small claims, and infractions committed within their territorial jurisdiction. The Justice Court shares

Key: Symbols refer to criminal records access unless otherwise noted. phone-☎ mail-⊠ fax-**Fax** in person-🖑 online-🖥 email-**Email**

jurisdiction with the Juvenile Court over minors 16 or 17 years old, who are charged with certain traffic offenses. Automobile homicide, alcohol or drug related traffic offenses, reckless driving, fleeing an officer, and driving on a suspended license are excepted. Those charges are handled through Juvenile Court.

Online Access: Case information from all Utah District Court locations is available through XChange. Fees include $25.00 registration and $30.00 per month which includes 200 searches. Each additional minute is billed at $.20. Records go back to at least 1998 for all District Courts. Information about XChange and the subscription agreement can be found at www.utcourts.gov/records/xchange or call 801-238-7877.

One may search for supreme or appellate opinions at the website.

Additional Information: You may submit record requests by mail to at the address listed above or fax 801-578-3859. Fees for faxed or mailed search requests is $21.00 per hpur with no charge for the first 15 minutes. The copy fee is $.25 per page.

Utah Code Rule 4-202.08 sets fees for county record searches at the same rate mentioned above. But, at the county level, there is a wide variance of per hour charges statewide. The standard hourly search fee depends on which office person does the search; the basic clerk is $15.00. Yet, many courts still report their search fee as $10.00 per hour, many without the first 15 minutes free.

Salt Lake, Ogden, Provo and Orem District Courts have automated information phone lines that provide court appearance look-up, outstanding fine balance look-up, and judgment/divorce decree lookup. Use these numbers:

Salt Lake District Court - 801-238-7830   Provo & Orem District Court - 801-429-1000

Ogden & Roy District Court - 801-395-1111

Beaver County

5th Judicial District Court *Felony, Misdemeanor, Civil, Eviction, Probate* PO Box 1683, Beaver, UT 84713. 8AM-5PM. **435-438-5309**, Fax: 435-438-5395. Fax✉✋💻

Box Elder County

1st District Court *Felony, Misdemeanor, Civil, Eviction, Small Claims, Probate* 43 N Main PO Box 873, Brigham City, UT 84302. 8AM-5PM. **435-734-4600**, Fax: 435-734-4610. Fax✉💻✋

Cache County

1st District Court *Felony, Misdemeanor, Civil, Eviction, Small Claims, Probate* 135 N 100 W, Logan, UT 84321. 8AM-5PM. **435-750-1300**, Fax: 435-750-1355. ☎✉💻✋

Carbon County

7th District Court *Felony, Misd., Civil, Eviction, Small Claims, Probate* 149 E 100 S, Price, UT 84501. 8AM-5PM. **435-636-3400**, fax 435-637-7349. ☎✉💻✋

Daggett County

8th District Court *Felony, Misd., Civil, Eviction, Probate* PO Box 219, Manila, UT 84046. 8AM-N, 1-5PM. **435-784-3154**, Fax: 435-784-3335. Fax✉✋💻

Davis County

2nd District Court *Felony, Civil, Probate* PO Box 769, Farmington, UT 84025. 8AM-5PM. **801-447-3800**, Fax: 801-447-3881. ☎✉💻✋

2nd District Court - Bountiful Department *Felony, Misdemeanor, Civil, Eviction, Small Claims, Probate* 805 S Main, Bountiful, UT 84010. 8AM-5PM. Fax: 801-397-7010. Civil phone: 801-397-7004, crim: 801-397-7008. Small Claims: 397-7002. ☎✉💻✋

2nd District Court - Layton Department *Felony, Misdemeanor, Civil, Eviction, Small Claims, Probate* 425 Wasatch Dr, Layton, UT 84041. 8AM-5PM. **801-444-4300**. ✉💻✋

Duchesne County

8th District Court *Felony, Misdemeanor, Civil, Eviction, Small Claims, Probate* PO Box 990, Duchesne, UT 84021. 8AM-5PM. **435-738-2753**, Fax: 435-738-2754. ☎✉Fax💻✋

8th District Court - Roosevelt Department *Felony, Misdemeanor, Civil, Eviction, Probate* PO Box 1286, Roosevelt, UT 84066. 8AM-5PM. **435-722-0235**, Fax: 435-722-0236. ✉💻✋

Emery County

7th District Court *Felony, Misdemeanor, Civil, Eviction, Probate* PO Box 635, Castle Dale, UT 84513. 8AM-5PM. **435-381-2619**, Fax: 435-381-5625. Phone for hearing impaired is 800-992-0172. ☎Fax✉✋💻

Garfield County

6th District Court *Felony, Misdemeanor, Civil, Eviction, Small Claims, Probate* PO Box 77, Panguitch, UT 84759. 9AM-5PM. **435-676-8826 X104**, Fax: 435-676-8239. Fax✉✋💻

Grand County

7th District Court *Felony, Misdemeanor, Civil, Eviction, Probate* 125 E Center, Moab, UT 84532. 8AM-5PM. **435-259-1349**, Fax: 435-259-4081. ☎✉💻✋

Iron County

5th District Court *Felony, Misdemeanor, Civil, Eviction, Small Claims, Probate* 40 N 100 E, Cedar City, UT 84720. 8AM-5PM. **435-867-3250**, Fax: 435-867-3212. Hearing location also in Parawon, but records held here. ✉☎💻✋

Juab County

4th District Court *Felony, Misd., Civil, Eviction, Probate* 160 N. Main PO Box 249, Nephi, UT 84648. 8AM-5PM. **435-623-0901**, fax 435-623-0922. ☎✉💻✋

Kane County

6th District Court *Felony, Misdemeanor, Civil, Eviction, Small Claims, Probate* 76 N Main, Kanab, UT 84741. 8AM-5PM. **435-644-2458**, Fax: 435-644-2052. ☎Fax✉✋💻

Millard County

4th District Court *Felony, Misdemeanor, Civil, Eviction, Small Claims, Probate* 765 S Hwy 99, #6, Fillmore, UT 84631. 8AM-5PM. **435-743-6223**, Fax: 435-743-6923. ☎✉💻✋

Key: Symbols refer to criminal records access unless otherwise noted. phone-☎ mail-✉ fax-Fax in person-✋ online-💻 email-Email

Morgan County

2nd District Court *Felony, Misdemeanor, Civil, Eviction, Small Claims, Probate* PO Box 886, Morgan, UT 84050. 8AM-5PM. **801-845-4020**, Fax: 801-829-6176. ☎Fax✉🖥✋

Piute County

6th District Court *Felony, Misdemeanor, Civil, Eviction, Small Claims, Probate* PO Box 99, Junction, UT 84740. 9AM-N, 1-5PM. **435-577-2840**, Fax: 435-577-2433. ✉✋🖥

Rich County

1st District Court *Felony, Misd., Civil, Eviction, Probate* PO Box 218, Randolph, UT 84064. 9-5PM. **435-793-2415**, F-435-793-2410. ☎Fax✋🖥🖥

Salt Lake County

3rd District Court - Salt Lake Dept. *Felony, Misd., Civil, Eviction, Small Claims, Probate* 450 S State St, Salt Lake City, UT 84111. 8AM-5PM. **801-238-7300**, Fax: 801-238-7396. ✉🖥✋

3rd District Court - West Valley Department *Felony, Misdemeanor, Civil, Eviction* 3636 S Constitution Blvd, West Valley, UT 84119. 8AM-5PM. **801-982-2400**, Fax: 801-967-9857. ✉🖥✋

3rd District Court - Sandy Department *Felony, Misdemeanor, Civil, Eviction, Small Claims* 210 W 10,000 S, Sandy, UT 84070-3282. 8AM-5PM. **801-565-5714**, Fax: 801-565-5703. ☎✉🖥✋

San Juan County

7th District Court *Felony, Misd., Civil, Eviction, Probate* PO Box 68, Monticello, UT 84535. 8AM-5PM. **435-587-2122**, F- 435-587-2372. ✉Fax🖥✋

Sanpete County

6th District Court *Felony, Misdemeanor, Civil, Eviction, Small Claims, Probate* 160 N Main, Manti, UT 84642. 8AM-5PM. **435-835-2121**, Fax: 435-835-2135. ☎Fax✉✋🖥

Sevier County

6th District Court *Felony, Misd., Civil, Eviction, Probate* 895 E 300 N, Richfield, UT 84701-2345. 8AM-5PM. **435-896-2700**, Fax: 435-896-8047. Fax✉🖥✋

Summit County

3rd District Court *Felony, Misdemeanor, Civil, Small Claims, Evictions, Probate* 6300 N Silver Creek, Park City, UT 84098. **435-615-4300**. ✉🖥✋

3rd District Court *Probate* PO Box 128, 60 N Main, Coalville, UT 84017. 8AM-5PM. **435-336-3205**, Fax: 435-336-3061. The courts is open 2 to 3 days a week.

Tooele County

3rd District Court *Felony, Misdemeanor, Civil, Eviction, Small Claims, Probate* 47 S Main, Tooele, UT 84074. 8AM-5PM. **435-843-3210**, Fax: 435-882-8524. Fax✉✋

Uintah County

8th District Court *Felony, Misdemeanor, Civil, Eviction, Probate* 920 E Hwy 40, Vernal, UT 84078. 8AM-5PM. **435-781-9300**, Fax: 435-789-0564. ✉🖥✋

Utah County

4th District Court *Felony, Misdemeanor, Civil, Eviction, Small Claims, Probate* www.utcourts.gov/ 125 N 100 W, Provo, UT 84601. 8AM-5PM. **801-429-1000**, Fax: 801-429-1033. Civil phone: 1-801-429-1172, crim: 1-801-429-1171, Probate: 1-801-429-1172. ☎✉Fax✋

4th District Court - Spanish Forks Dept. *Felony, Misd., Civil, Eviction, Small Claims* 40 S Main St, Spanish Forks, UT 84660. 8-5PM. **801-798-8674**, Fax: 801-798-1377. ☎Fax✉🖥✋

4th District Court - Orem Department *Misdemeanor, Civil, Eviction, Small Claims* 97 E Center, Orem, UT 84057. 8AM-5PM. **801-764-5865/5864**, Fax: 801-226-5244. ✉🖥✋

4th District Court - American Fork Department *Misdemeanor, Civil, Eviction, Small Claims* 75 E 80 N, #202 PO Box 986, American Fork, UT 84003-0986. 8AM-5PM. **801-756-9654**, Fax: 801-763-0153. ✉🖥✋

Wasatch County

4th District Court *Felony, Misdemeanor, Civil, Eviction, Probate* 1361 S Hwy 40 PO Box 730, Heber City, UT 84032. 8AM-5PM. **435-654-4676**, Fax: 435-654-5281. Small claims handled by two Justice Courts. Heber City Justice Court: 435-654-1662, Wasatch County Justice Court: 435-654-2679. ☎Fax✉🖥✋

Washington County

5th District Court *Felony, Misdemeanor, Civil, Eviction, Small Claims, Probate* 220 N 200 E, St. George, UT 84770. 8AM-5PM. Fax: 435-986-5723. Civil phone: 435-986-5701, crim: 435-986-5700. ✉🖥✋fax.

Wayne County

6th District Court *Felony, Misdemeanor, Civil, Eviction, Small Claims, Probate* PO Box 189, Loa, UT 84747. 9AM-5PM. **435-836-2731**, Fax: 435-836-2479. ☎✉Fax✋🖥

Weber County

2nd District Court *Felony, Misd., Civil, Eviction, Small Claims, Probate* 2525 Grant Ave, Ogden, UT 84401. 8AM-5PM. **801-395-1060**, Civil: 801-395-1091, crim: 801-395-1102, Probate: 801-395-1173. Until 12/02, a Disctrict Court was in Roy; it is now a Justice Court. ☎✉🖥✋

Vermont

State Court Administration: Administrative Office of Courts, Court Administrator, 109 State St, Montpelier, VT, 05609-0701; 802-828-3278, Fax: 802-828-3457. www.vermontjudiciary.org

Court Structure: As of September, 1996, all small claims came under the jurisdiction of Superior Court, the court of general jurisdiction. All counties have a diversion program in which first offenders go through a process that includes a letter of apology, community service, etc. and, after 2 years, the record is expunged. These records are never released.

Probate Courts: There is one Probate Court per county except in the four southern counties (Bennington, Rutland, Windsor, and Windham) which have two each.

Online Access: Court calendars for all Superior, District, and Family courts are shown at the website above. Supreme Court opinions are available also from the website. In addition, Supreme Court opinions are maintained by the Vermont Department of Libraries at http://dol.state.vt.us. There is no statewide system of local court records.

Additional Vermont Court Information: There are statewide search, certification and copy fees, as follows: Search fee - $10.00 per name; Certification Fee - $5.00 per document plus copy fee; Copy Fee - $.25 per page with a $1.00 minimum.

Addison County

Superior Court *Civil, Eviction, Small Claims* 7 Mahady Ct, Middlebury, VT 05753. 8:30AM-4:30PM. **802-388-7741**. Access civil records-⊠ ✋

District Court *Felony, Misdemeanor* 7 Mahady Ct, Middlebury, VT 05753. 8AM-4:30PM. **802-388-4237**. ⊠ ✋

Probate Court 7 Mahady Ct, Middlebury, VT 05753. 8AM-4:30PM. **802-388-2612**.

Bennington County

Superior Court *Civil, Eviction, Small Claims* 207 South St PO Box 4157, Bennington, VT 05201. 8AM-4:30PM. **802-447-2700**, Fax: 802-447-2703. Criminal phone: 802-447-2727. Access civil records-☎ ⊠ ✋

District Court *Felony, Misdemeanor* 200 Veterans Memorial Dr, #13, Bennington, VT 05201. 7:45AM-4:30PM. **802-447-2727**, Fax: 802-447-2750. ⊠ ✋

Probate Court - Manchester District PO Box 446, Manchester, VT 05254. 8AM-N, 1-4:20PM. **802-362-1410**.

Probate Court - Bennington District 207 South St PO Box 65, Bennington, VT 05201. 8:30AM-N, 1:00-4:30pm. **802-447-2705**, Fax: 802-447-2703 (Attn: Probate Court).

Caledonia County

Superior Court *Civil, Eviction, Small Claims* 1126 Main St, #1, St Johnsbury,

VT 05819. 8AM-4:30PM. **802-748-6600**, Fax 802-748-6603. access civil-☎ ⊠ ✋

District Court *Felony, Misdemeanor* 1126 Main St, #1, St Johnsbury, VT 05819. 8AM-4:30PM. **802-748-6600**, Fax: 802-748-6603. Fax⊠ ✋

Probate Court 1126 Main St PO Box 406, St Johnsbury, VT 05819. 8-4:30PM. **802-748-6605**, Fax: 802-748-6603.

Chittenden County

Superior Court *Civil, Eviction, Small Claims* www.chittendensuperiorcourt.com/ 175 Main St (PO Box 187), Burlington, VT 05402. 8AM-4:30PM. **802-863-3467**. Access civil records-☎ ⊠ ✋ 💻 🖥

District Court *Felony, Misdemeanor* 32 Cherry St, #300, Burlington, VT 05401. 8AM-4:30PM. **802-651-1800**. ⊠ ✋

Probate Court PO Box 511, Burlington, VT 05402. 8AM-4:30PM. **802-651-1518**.

Essex County

District & Superior Court *Felony, Misdemeanor, Civil, Eviction, Small Claims* www.state.vt.us/courts Box 75, Guildhall, VT 05905. 8AM-4:30PM. **802-676-3910**, Fax: 802-676-3463. ⊠ ✋

Probate Court PO Box 426, Island Pond, VT 05846. 8:30AM-N, 1-3:30PM. **802-723-4770**, Fax: 802-723-4770.

Franklin County

Superior Court *Civil, Eviction, Small Claims* Box 808, Church St, St Albans,

VT 05478. 8AM-4:30PM. **802-524-3863**, Fax: 802-524-7996. Access civil-⊠ ✋

District Court *Felony, Misdemeanor* 36 Lake St, St Albans, VT 05478. 8AM-4:30PM. **802-524-7997**, Fax: 802-524-7946. ⊠ ✋

Franklin Probate Court 17 Church St, Albans, VT 05478. 8AM-N, 1-4:30PM. **802-524-4112**.

Grand Isle County

District & Superior Court *Felony, Misdemeanor, Civil, Eviction, Small Claims* PO Box 7, North Hero, VT 05474. 8AM-4:30PM. **802-372-8350**, Fax: 802-372-3221. ☎ Fax⊠ ✋

Probate Court PO Box 7, North Hero, VT 05474. 8AM-4:30PM. **802-372-8350**, Fax: 802-372-3221.

Lamoille County

Superior Court *Civil, Eviction, Small Claims* Box 490, Hyde Park, VT 05655. 8AM-12:00, 12:30-4:30PM. **802-888-2207**. Access civil records-⊠ ✋

District Court *Felony, Misd.* PO Box 489, Hyde Park, VT 05655-0489. 8AM-4:30PM. **802-888-3887**, Fax: 802-888-2591. Civil phone: 802-888-2207. ⊠ ✋

Probate Court PO Box 102, Hyde Park, VT 05655-0102. 8AM-N, 12:30-4:30PM. **802-888-3306**, Fax: 802-888-0669.

Orange County

District & Superior Court *Felony, Misdemeanor, Civil, Eviction, Small*

Key: Symbols refer to criminal records access unless otherwise noted. phone-☎ mail-⊠ fax-**Fax** in person-✋ online-🖥 email-**Email**

Claims 5 Court St, Chelsea, VT 05038-9746. 8AM-4:30PM. **802-685-4610**, Fax: 802-685-3246. ☎**Fax**✉ ⁕

Probate Court 5 Court St, Chelsea, VT 05038-9746. 8AM-N, 1-4:30PM. **802-685-4610**, Fax: 802-685-3246. Bradford and Randolph Districts were consolidated into this one probate court June 1, 1994.

Orleans County

Superior Court *Civil, Eviction, Small Claims* 247 Main St, #1, Newport, VT 05855-1203. 8AM-4:30PM. **802-334-3344**, Fax: 802-334-3385. Access civil records-☎**Fax**✉ ⁕

District Court *Felony, Misdemeanor* 217 Main St, #4, Newport, VT 05855. 8AM-4:30PM. **802-334-3325**. ✉

Probate Court 247 Main St, Newport, VT 05855. 8AM-N, 1-4:30PM. **802-334-3366**, Fax: 802-334-3385.

Rutland County

Superior Court *Civil, Eviction, Small Claims* 83 Center St, Rutland, VT 05701. 8AM-4:30PM. **802-775-4394**. Access civil records-✉ ⁕

District Court *Felony, Misdemeanor* 92 State St, Rutland, VT 05701-2886. 8AM-4:30PM. **802-786-5880**. ☎✉ ⁕

Probate Court - Rutland District 83 Center St, Rutland, VT 05701. 8-4:30PM. **802-775-0114**, Fax: 802-775-1671.

Probate Court - Fair Haven District 3 N Park Pl, Fair Haven, VT 05743. 8AM-4PM. **802-265-3380**, Fax: 802-265-3380.

Washington County

Superior Court *Civil, Eviction, Small Claims* #828-5551 65 State St, Montpelier, VT 05602-3594. 8AM-4:30PM. **802-828-2091**. Access civil records-☎✉ ⁕

District Court *Felony, Misdemeanor* 255 N Main, Barre, VT 05641. 8AM-4:30PM. **802-479-4252**. ✉ ⁕

Probate Court 10 Elm St, #2, Montpelier, VT 05602. 8AM-N, 1-4:30PM M-Th; 8AM-N, 1-4PM F. **802-828-3405**.

Windham County

Superior Court *Civil, Eviction, Small Claims* Box 207, Newfane, VT 05345. 9AM-4PM. **802-365-7979**, Fax: 802-365-4360. Access civil records-☎**Fax**✉ ⁕

District Court *Felony, Misd., Civil Suspension* www.vermontjudiciary.org/courts/district/index.htm#Windham 30 Putney Rd, #2, Brattleboro, VT 05301.

8AM-4:30PM. **802-257-2800**, Fax: 802-257-2853. ✉ ⁕

Probate Court - Westminster District PO Box 47 39 Square, Bellows Falls, VT 05101-0047. 8AM-N,1-4:30PM. **802-463-3019**, Fax: 802-463-0144.

Probate Court - Marlboro District PO Box 523, Brattleboro, VT 05302. 8AM-N, 1-4:30PM. **802-257-2898**.

Windsor County

Superior Court *Civil, Eviction, Small Claims* Box 458, Woodstock, VT 05091. 8AM-4:30PM. **802-457-2121**, Fax: 802-457-3446. Access civil records-☎✉ ⁕

District Court *Felony, Misdemeanor* Windsor Circuit Unit 1 82 Railroad Row, White River Junction, VT 05001-1962. 8AM-4:30PM. **802-295-8865**, Fax: 802-295-8897. ✉ ⁕

Probate Court - Windsor District PO Box 402, Rte 106, Cota Fuel Bldg, North Springfield, VT 05150. 8AM-N, 1-4:30PM. **802-886-2284**.

Probate Court - Hartford District PO Box 275, Woodstock, VT 05091. 8AM-N, 1-4:30PM. **802-457-1503**, Fax: 802-457-3446.

Virginia

State Court Administration (All Circuit & District Courts, Court of Appeals, and Supreme Court): Executive Secretary, Administrative Office of Courts, 100 N 9th St 3rd Fl, Supreme Court Bldg, Richmond, VA, 23219; 804-786-6455, Fax: 804-786-4542. www.courts.state.va.us

Court Structure: The Circuit Courts in 31 districts are the courts of general jurisdiction. There are 123 District Courts of limited jurisdiction. Please note that a district can comprise a county or a city. Records of civil action from $3000 to $15,000 can be at either the Circuit or District Court as either can have jurisdiction. It is necessary to check both record locations as there is no concurrent database nor index.

Online Access: There are 3 available systems. None are statewide; each county must be searched separately. Cases from 132 General District Courts may be searched free at http://208.210.219.132/courtinfo/vadistrict/select.jsp?court=. You can search records from over 90 Circuit courts at http://208.210.219.132/courtinfo/vacircuit/select.jsp?court=. While these systems do not include DOBs, SSNs and Addresses, another access system known as LOPAS does. There are no fees to use LOPAS, but access is granted on a request-by-request basis. All courts except Fairfax County and Alexandria City Circuit Courts are on LOPAS. Anyone wishing to establish an account or receive information on LOPAS must contact the Supreme Court of Virginia, 100 N 9th St, Richmond VA 23219 or by phone at 804-786-6455 or fax at 804-786-4542. This is a difficult sign to get on as it is an old dial-up system with 20 phone lines serving requesters.

The www.courts.state.va.us site offers access to Supreme Court and Appellate opinions.

Additional Information: In many jurisdictions, the certification fee is $2.00 per document plus copy fee. Copy fee is $.50 per page.

Key: Symbols refer to criminal records access unless otherwise noted. phone-☎ mail-✉ fax-**Fax** in person-⁕ online-🖥 email-**Email**

Accomack County

2nd Circuit Court *Felony, Civil Actions Over $15,000, Probate* PO Box 126, Accomac, VA 23301. 9-5PM. **757-787-5776**, Fax: 757-787-1849. **Fax**⊠🖥🖐

2A General District Court *Misd., Civil Actions Under $15,000, Eviction, Small Claims* PO Box 276, Accomac, VA 23301. 8:30AM-4:30PM. **757-787-0923**. ☎⊠🖥🖐

Albemarle County

16th Circuit & District Court *Felony, Misdemeanor, Civil, Eviction, Probate* 501 E Jefferson St, Charlottesville, VA 22902. 8:30AM-4:30PM. **434-972-4085**, Fax: 434-972-4071. ⊠🖥🖐

Alleghany County

25th Circuit Court *Felony, Civil Over $15,000, Probate* www.alleghanycountyclerk.com PO Box 670, Covington, VA 24426. 8:30AM-5PM M-F; 9AM-N Sat. **540-965-1730**, Fax: 540-965-1732. 🖥🖐

25th General District Court *Misdemeanor, Civil Actions Under $15,000, Eviction, Small Claims* PO Box 139, Covington, VA 24426. 9AM-5PM. **540-965-1720**, Fax: 540-965-1722. 🖥🖐

Amelia County

11th Circuit Court *Felony, Civil Over $15,000, Probate* www.governdata.com/amelia.htm PO Box 237 (1 E Main St, B-5), Amelia, VA 23068. 8:30AM-4:30PM. **804-561-2128**. Will search on telephone request if not busy. ⊠🖥🖐

11th General District Court *Misdemeanor, Civil Actions Under $15,000, Eviction, Small Claims* PO Box 24, Amelia, VA 23002. 8:30AM-4:30PM. **804-561-2456**, Fax: 804-561-6956. 🖥🖐

Amherst County

24th Circuit Court *Felony, Civil Actions Over $15,000, Probate* PO Box 462, Amherst, VA 24521. 8AM-5PM. **434-946-9321**, Fax: 434-946-9323. 🖥🖐

24th General District Court *Misdemeanor, Civil Actions Under $15,000, Eviction, Small Claims* PO Box 513, Amherst, VA 24521. 8AM-4PM. **434-946-9351**, Fax: 434-946-9359. Has handled misdemeanor cases since 1985. ⊠🖥🖐

Appomattox County

10th Circuit Court *Felony, Civil Actions Over $15,000, Probate* PO Box 672 125 Court St, Appomattox, VA 24522. 8:30AM-4:30PM. **434-352-5275**, Fax: 434-352-2781. 🖥🖐

10th General District Court *Misdemeanor, Civil Actions Under $15,000, Eviction, Small Claims* PO Box 187 121 Court St, Appomattox, VA 24522. 8:30AM-4:30PM. **434-352-5540**, Fax: 434-352-0717. **Fax**⊠🖥🖐

Arlington County

17th Circuit Court *Felony, Civil Actions Over $15,000, Probate* http://158.59.15.115/arlington/ 1425 N Courthouse Rd, Arlington, VA 22201. 8AM-4PM. **703-228-7010**. 🖐

17th General District Court *Misd., Civil Actions Under $15,000, Eviction, Small Claims* 1425 N Courthouse Rd, Rm 2500, Arlington, VA 22201. 8AM-4PM. **703-228-7900**, Civil: 703-228-4485. Phone access limited to 4 requests. ☎⊠🖥🖐

Augusta County

25th Circuit Court *Felony, Civil Actions Over $15,000, Probate* PO Box 689, Staunton, VA 24402-0689. 8AM-5PM. **540-245-5321**, Fax: 540-245-5318. Court prefers that searches be done in person. Mail access is limited; they will only search back to 1987. Phone available for very short search only. Access - ☎⊠🖐

25th General District Court *Misdemeanor, Civil Actions Under $15,000, Eviction, Small Claims* 6 E Johnson St, 2nd Fl, Staunton, VA 24401. 8:30AM-4:30PM. **540-245-5300**, Fax: 540-245-5365. ⊠🖥🖐

Bath County

25th Circuit Court *Felony, Civil Actions Over $15,000, Probate* PO Box 180, Warm Springs, VA 24484. 8:30AM-4:30PM. **540-839-7226**, Fax: 540-839-7248. 🖥🖐

25th General District Court *Misdemeanor, Civil Actions Under $15,000, Eviction, Small Claims* PO Box 96, Warm Springs, VA 24484. 8:30AM-4:30PM. **540-839-7242**, Fax: 540-839-7248. **Fax**⊠🖥🖐

Bedford County

County Circuit Court *Felony, Civil Actions Over $15,000, Probate* 123 E Main St, #201, Bedford, VA 24523. 8:30AM-5PM. **540-586-7632**, Fax: 540-586-6197. 🖥🖐

24th General District Court *Misd., Civil Actions Under $15,000, Eviction, Small Claims, Traffic* 123 E Main St, #202, Bedford, VA 24523. 8AM-4PM. **540-586-7637**, Fax: 540-586-7684. 🖥🖐

Bland County

27th Circuit Court *Felony, Civil Over $15,000, Probate* PO Box 295, Bland, VA 24315. 8AM-6PM. **276-688-4562**, Fax: 276-688-4562. ☎**Fax**⊠🖥🖐

27th General District Court *Misd., Civil Actions Under $15,000, Eviction, Small Claims* PO Box 157, Bland, VA 24315. 8AM-5PM. **276-688-4433**, Fax: 276-688-4789. ☎**Fax**⊠🖥🖐

Botetourt County

25th Circuit Court *Felony, Civil Actions Over $15,000, Probate* PO Box 219, Fincastle, VA 24090. 8:30AM-4:30PM. **540-473-8274**, Fax: 540-473-8209. ⊠🖥🖐

25th General District Court *Misd., Civil Actions Under $15,000, Eviction, Small Claims* PO Box 858, Fincastle, VA 24090-0858. 8AM-4PM. **540-473-8244**, Fax: 540-473-8344. ⊠🖥🖐

Brunswick County

6th Circuit Court *Felony, Civil, Probate* 216 N Main St, Lawrenceville, VA 23868. 8:30AM-5PM. **434-848-2215**, Fax: 434-848-4307. 🖐🖥

6th General District Court *Misdemeanor, Civil Actions Under $15,000, Eviction, Small Claims* 202 Main St, Lawrenceville, VA 23868-0066. 8:30AM-4:30PM. **434-848-2315**, Fax: 434-848-2550. Access records-⊠🖐🖥

Buchanan County

29th Circuit Court *Felony, Misd., Civil Actions Over $15,000, Probate* PO Box 929, Grundy, VA 24614. 8:30AM-5PM. **276-935-6567**. 🖥🖐

29th Judicial District Court *Civil Actions Under $15,000, Eviction, Small Claims* PO Box 654, Grundy, VA 24614.

Key: Symbols refer to criminal records access unless otherwise noted. phone-☎ mail-⊠ fax-**Fax** in person-🖐 online-🖥 email-**Email**

8AM-4PM. **276-935-6526**, Fax: 276-935-5479. Access civil -**Fax**✉✋☎🖥

Buckingham County

10th Circuit Court *Felony, Civil Actions Over $15,000, Probate* Rte 60, PO Box 107, Buckingham, VA 23921. 8:30AM-4:30PM. **434-969-4734**, Fax: 434-969-2043. ✋🖥

Buckingham General District Court *Misdemeanor, Civil Actions Under $15,000, Eviction, Small Claims* PO Box 127, Buckingham, VA 23921. 8:30AM-4:30PM. **434-969-4755**, Fax: 434-969-1762. ✉🖥✋fax.

Campbell County

24th Circuit Court *Felony, Civil Actions Over $15,000, Probate* 732 Village Hwy PO Box 7, Rustburg, VA 24588. 8:30AM-4:30PM. **434-592-9517**. ✉🖥✋

24th General District Court *Misdemeanor, Civil Actions Under $15,000, Eviction, Small Claims* 1st Fl New Courthouse Bldg, PO Box 97, Rustburg, VA 24588. 8AM-4PM. **434-332-9546**, Fax: 434-332-9694. 🖥✋✉

Caroline County

15th Circuit Court *Felony, Civil Actions Over $15,000, Probate* Main St & Courthouse Ln, PO Box 309, Bowling Green, VA 22427-0309. 8:30AM-4PM. **804-633-5800**. 🖥✋

15th General District Court *Misd., Civil Actions Under $15,000, Eviction, Small Claims* PO Box 511, Bowling Green, VA 22427. 8AM-4PM. **804-633-5720**, Fax: 804-633-3033. ✉🖥✋

Carroll County

27th Circuit Court *Felony, Civil Actions Over $15,000, Probate* PO Box 218, Hillsville, VA 24343. 8AM-5PM. **276-728-3117**. 🖥✋

Carroll Combined District Court *Misdemeanor, Civil Actions Under $15,000, Eviction, Small Claims* PO Box 698, Hillsville, VA 24343. 8AM-4:30PM. **276-728-7751**, Fax: 276-728-2582. ✋🖥

Charles City County

9th Circuit Court *Felony, Civil Actions Over $15,000, Probate* 10700 Courthouse Rd, PO Box 86, Charles City, VA 23030-0086. 8:30AM-4:30PM. **804-829-9212**, Fax: 804-829-5647. ✉🖥✋

9th General District Court *Misdemeanor, Civil Actions Under $15,000, Eviction, Small Claims* Charles City Courthouse PO Box 57, Charles City, VA 23030. 8:30AM-4PM. **804-829-9224**, Fax: 804-829-5109. ✉🖥✋

Charlotte County

10th Circuit Court *Felony, Civil Actions Over $15,000, Probate* PO Box 38, Charlotte Courthouse, VA 23923. 8:30AM-4:30PM. **434-542-5147**. ✋

Charlotte General District Court *Misdemeanor, Civil Actions Under $15,000, Eviction, Small Claims* PO Box 127, Charlotte Courthouse, VA 23923. 8:30AM-4:30PM. **434-542-5600**, Fax: 434-542-5902. 🖥✋

Chesterfield County

12th Circuit Court *Felony, Civil Over $15,000, Probate* www.co.chesterfield.va.us/JusticeAdministration/CircuitCourtClerk/clerhome.asp 9500 Courthouse Rd, PO Box 125, Chesterfield, VA 23832. 8:30AM-5PM. **804-748-1241**, Fax: 804-796-5625. ✉✋ The probate clerk will not search their court records.

12th General District Court *Misdemeanor, Civil Actions Under $15,000, Eviction, Small Claims* www.courts.state.va.us/courts/gd/Chesterfield/home.html PO Box 144, Chesterfield, VA 23832. 8AM-4PM. **804-748-1231**, Fax: 804-748-1757. ✉🖥✋

Clarke County

26th Circuit Court *Felony, Civil Actions Over $15,000, Probate* PO Box 189, Berryville, VA 22611. 9AM-5PM. **540-955-5116**, Fax: 540-955-0284. 🖥✋

General District Court *Misdemeanor, Civil Actions Under $15,000, Eviction, Small Claims* www.co.clarke.va.us 104 N Church St (PO Box 612), Berryville, VA 22611. 8:30AM-4:30PM. **540-955-5128**, Fax: 540-955-1195. 🖥✋

Craig County

25th Circuit Court *Felony, Civil Actions Over $15,000, Probate* PO Box 185, New Castle, VA 24127-0185. 9AM-5PM. **540-864-6141**. 🖥✋

25th General District Court *Misdemeanor, Civil Actions Under $15,000, Eviction, Small Claims* Craig County General District Court PO Box 232, New Castle, VA 24127. 8:15AM-4:45PM. **540-864-5989**. ✉🖥✋

Culpeper County

16th Circuit Court *Felony, Civil Actions Over $15,000, Probate* 135 W Cameron St, Culpeper, VA 22701-3097. 8:30AM-4:30PM. **540-727-3438**. ✋

16th General District Court *Misdemeanor, Civil Actions Under $15,000, Eviction, Small Claims* 135 W Cameron St, Culpeper, VA 22701. 8:30AM-4:30PM. **540-727-3417**, Fax: 540-727-3474. ✉🖥✋

Cumberland County

10th Circuit Court *Felony, Civil Actions Over $15,000, Probate* PO Box 8, Cumberland, VA 23040. 8:30AM-4:30PM. **804-492-4442**. 🖥✋

10th General District Court *Misdemeanor, Civil Actions Under $15,000, Eviction, Small Claims* PO Box 24, Cumberland, VA 23040. 8:30AM-4:30PM. **804-492-4848**, Fax: 804-492-9455. ☎**Fax**✉🖥✋

Dickenson County

29th Circuit Court *Felony, Civil Actions Over $15,000, Probate* PO Box 190, Clintwood, VA 24228. 8:30AM-4:30PM. **276-926-1616**, Fax: 276-926-6465. ✉🖥✋

29th General District Court *Misd., Civil Actions Under $15,000, Eviction, Small Claims* PO Box 128, Clintwood, VA 24228. 8:30AM-4:30PM. **276-926-1630**, Fax: 276-926-4815. ☎✉✋

Dinwiddie County

11th Circuit Court *Felony, Civil Actions Over $15,000, Probate* PO Box 63, Dinwiddie, VA 23841. 8:30AM-4:30PM. **804-469-4540**. ✉🖥✋

11th General District Court *Misdemeanor, Civil Actions Under $15,000, Eviction, Small Claims,Traffic* PO Box 280, Dinwiddie, VA 23841. 8:30AM-4:30PM. **804-469-4533**, Fax: 804-469-5383. ✉🖥✋

Essex County

15th Circuit Court *Felony, Civil Actions Over $15,000, Probate* PO Box 445 305 Prince St, Tappahannock, VA 22560. 8:30AM-5PM. **804-443-3541**. ✋

Key: Symbols refer to criminal records access unless otherwise noted. phone-☎ mail-✉ fax-**Fax** in person-✋ online-🖥 email-**Email**

15th General District Court *Misdemeanor, Civil Actions Under $15,000, Eviction, Small Claims* PO Box 66, Tappahannock, VA 22560. 8AM-12:30PM, 1-4:30PM. **804-443-3744**, Fax: 804-443-4122. 🖳🤚

Fairfax County

19th Circuit Court *Felony, Civil Over $15,000, Probate* www.fairfaxcounty.gov/courts/circuit 4110 Chain Bridge Rd, Fairfax, VA 22030. 8AM-4PM. Civil: 703-691-7320 x311, crim: 246-2228. 🤚

19th General District Court *Misd., Civil under $15,000, Eviction, Small Claims* www.fairfaxcounty.gov/living/legal/ 4110 Chain Bridge Rd, Fairfax, VA 22030. 8AM-4PM. **703-246-2153**, Fax: 703-591-2349. Civil phone: 703-246-3012, crim: 703-691-7320. Traffic Division: 703-246-3764. ☎🤚🖳

Fauquier County

Circuit Court *Felony, Civil Actions Over $15,000, Probate* www.fauquiercounty.gov/government/departments/circuitcourt 40 Culpeper St, Warrenton, VA 20186-3298. 8AM-4:30PM. **540-347-8610**, Civil: 540-347-8601, crim: 540-347-8605, Probate: 540-347-8606. Chancery court: 540-347-8607. 🖳🤚

20th General District Court *Misd., Civil Actions Under $15,000, Eviction, Small Claims* 6 Court St, Warrenton, VA 20186. 8:30AM-4:30PM. Fax: 540-347-5756. Civil phone: 540-347-8676, crim: 540-347-8624. 🖳🤚

Floyd County

27th Circuit Court *Felony, Civil Actions Over $15,000, Probate* 100 E Main St, #200, Floyd, VA 24091. 8:30AM-4:30PM, 8:30-N Sat. **540-745-9330**. 🖳🤚

27th General District Court *Misd., Civil Actions Under $15,000, Eviction, Small Claims* 100 E Main St, Floyd, VA 24091-2101. 8AM-4:30PM. **540-745-9327**, Fax: 540-745-9329. 🖳🤚

Fluvanna County

16th Circuit Court *Felony, Civil Actions Over $15,000, Probate* PO Box 550, Palmyra, VA 22963. 8:AM-4:30PM. **434-591-1970**, Fax: 434-591-1971. ✉🤚🖳

16th General District Court *Misd., Civil Actions Under $15,000, Eviction, Small Claims* Fluvanna County Courthouse PO Box 417, Palmyra, VA 22963. 8:30AM-4:30PM. **434-591-1980**, Fax: 434-591-1981 press 4. 🖳🤚

Franklin County

22nd Judicial Circuit Court *Felony, Civil Actions Over $15,000, Probate* www.courts.state.va.us/courts/circuit/Franklin/home.html PO Box 567 275 S Main St, #212, Rocky Mount, VA 24151. 8:30AM-5PM. **540-483-3065**, Fax: 540-483-3042. Note that Franklin City is not the same as Franklin County. Only Franklin County records are here. 🤚🖳

22nd General District Court *Misdemeanor, Civil Actions Under $15,000, Eviction, Small Claims* www.courts.state.va.us/courts/combined/Franklin_City/home.html PO Box 569 275 S Main St, #111, Rocky Mount, VA 24151. 8:30AM-4:30PM. **540-483-3060**, Fax: 540-483-3036. 🖳🤚

Frederick County

Circuit Court *Felony, Misdemeanor, Civil, Probate* www.winfredclerk.com 5 N Kent St, Winchester, VA 22601. 9AM-5PM. **540-667-5770**. 🤚🖳

26th District Court *Misdemeanor, Civil Actions up to $15,000* 5 N Kent St, Winchester, VA 22601. 8AM-4PM. **540-722-7208**, Fax: 540-722-1063. 🤚🖳

Giles County

27th Circuit Court *Felony, Civil Actions Over $15,000, Probate* 501 Wenonah Ave PO Box 502, Pearisburg, VA 24134. 9AM-5PM. **540-921-1722**, Fax: 540-921-3825. 🤚

27th General District Court *Misdemeanor, Civil Actions Under $15,000, Eviction, Small Claims* 120 N Main St, #1, Pearisburg, VA 24134. 8:30AM-4:30PM. **540-921-3533**, Fax: 540-921-3752. Fax✉🖳🤚

Gloucester County

9th Circuit Court *Felony, Civil Over $15,000, Probate* www.co.gloucester.va.us PO Box 2118, Gloucester, VA 23061-0570. 8AM-4:30PM. **804-693-2502**, Fax: 804-693-2186. 🖳🤚

9th General District Court *Misdemeanor, Civil Actions Under $15,000, Eviction, Small Claims* PO Box 873, Gloucester, VA 23061. 8:30AM-4:30PM. **804-693-4860**, Fax: 804-693-6669. Fax✉🖳🤚

Goochland County

16th Circuit Court *Felony, Civil Actions Over $15,000, Probate* PO Box 196, Goochland, VA 23063. 8:30AM-4:15 PM. **804-556-5353**. 🖳🤚

General District Court *Misdemeanor, Civil Actions Under $15,000, Eviction, Small Claims* PO Box 47, Goochland, VA 23063. 8:30AM-4:30PM. **804-556-5309**. 🖳🤚

Grayson County

27th Circuit Court *Felony, Civil Actions Over $15,000, Probate* PO Box 130, Independence, VA 24348. 8AM-5PM. **276-773-2231**, Fax: 276-773-3338. ✉🖳🤚

27th General District Court *Misdemeanor, Civil Actions Under $15,000, Eviction, Small Claims* PO Box 280, Independence, VA 24348. 8AM-4:30PM. **276-773-2011**. ✉🖳🤚

Greene County

16th Circuit Court *Felony, Civil Actions Over $15,000, Probate* PO Box 386, Stanardsville, VA 22973. 8:15AM-4:30PM. **434-985-5208**, Fax: 434-985-6723. ✉🤚

16th General District Court *Misdemeanor, Civil Actions Under $15,000, Eviction, Small Claims* Greene County Courthouse (PO Box 245), Stanardsville, VA 22973. 8:30AM-4PM. **434-985-5224**, Fax: 434-985-1448. 🤚

Greensville County

6th Circuit Court *Felony, Civil Actions Over $15,000, Probate* PO Box 631, Emporia, VA 23847. 9AM-5PM. **434-348-4215**. 🖳🤚

Greenville/Emporia Combined Court *Misdemeanor, Civil Actions Under $15,000, Eviction, Small Claims* 315 S Main, Emporia, VA 23847. 8:30AM-4:30PM. **434-634-5460**, Fax: 434-634-0049. 🖳🤚

Halifax County

10th Circuit Court *Felony, Civil Actions Over $15,000, Probate* PO Box 729, Halifax, VA 24558. 8:30AM-4:30PM. **434-476-6211**, Fax: 434-476-2890. ✉🖳🤚

10th General District Court *Misdemeanor, Civil Actions Under $15,000, Eviction, Small Claims* Halifax County Courthouse, PO Box 458, Halifax, VA 24558. 8:30AM-4:30PM. **434-476-3385**, Fax: 434-476-3387. **Fax**✉🖥🤚

Hanover County

15th Circuit Court *Felony, Civil Actions Over $15,000, Probate* 7507 Library Dr PO Box 39, Hanover, VA 23069. 8:30AM-4:30PM. **804-365-6151**, Fax: 804-365-6278. Civil phone: 804-365-6143, crim: 804-365-6843, Probate: 804-365-6478. 🖥🤚

15th General District Court *Misd., Civil Actions Under $15,000, Eviction, Small Claims* Hanover County Courthouse, PO Box 176, Hanover, VA 23069. 8AM-4PM. **804-365-6191**, Fax: 804-365-6290; 804-365-6436 (Civil Fax). Civil phone: 804-365-6457. ✉🖥🤚

Henrico County

14th Circuit Court *Felony, Civil Over $15,000, Probate* www.co.henrico.va.us/clerk/ PO Box 27032, Richmond, VA 23273-7032. 8AM-4:30PM. **804-501-4202**, Civil: 804-501-5422, crim: 804-501-4758, Probate: 804-501-4763. Access records-✉🤚🖥

14th General District Court *Misdemeanor, Civil Actions Under $15,000, Eviction, Small Claims* PO Box 27032, Richmond, VA 23273. 8AM-4PM, Fax: 804-501-4141. Civil phone: 804-501-4727, crim: 804-501-4723. 🖥🤚✉

Henry County

21st Circuit Court *Felony, Civil Over $15,000, Probate* www.courts.state.va.us 3160 Kings Mountain Rd, #B, Martinsville, VA 24112. 9AM-5PM, except Tues 9AM-2PM. **276-634-4880** or 276-634-4884 (Law), Civil: 276-634-4886 (Chancery), crim: 276-634-4889 or 276-634-4885, Probate: 276-634-4883. 🖥🤚

21st General District Court *Misdemeanor, Civil Actions Under $15,000, Eviction, Small Claims* www.courts.state.va.us 3160 King's Mountain Rd #A, Martinsville, VA 24112. 9AM-5PM. **276-634-4815**, Fax: 276-634-4825. 🖥🤚

Highland County

25th Circuit Court *Felony, Civil Actions Over $15,000, Probate* PO Box 190, Monterey, VA 24465. 8:45AM-4:30PM.

540-468-2447, Fax: 540-468-3447. ✉🖥🤚

25th General District Court *Misdemeanor, Civil Actions Under $15,000, Eviction, Small Claims* Highland County Courthouse PO Box 88, Monterey, VA 24465. 8:30AM-5:00PM. **540-468-2445**, Fax: 540-468-3449. **Fax**✉🖥🤚

Isle of Wight County

5th Circuit Court *Felony, Civil Actions Over $15,000, Probate* 17122 Monument Circle PO Box 110, Isle of Wight, VA 23397. 9AM-5PM. **757-365-6233**. Clerk phone is 757-365-6233. 🖥🤚

5th General District Court *Misd., Civil Actions Under $15,000, Eviction, Small Claims* Isle of Wight Courthouse PO Box 122, Isle of Wight, VA 23397. 8AM-4PM. **757-365-6243**, Fax: 757-365-6246. Clerk: 757-365-6244. 🖥🤚

James City County

Williamsburg-James City Circuit Court *Felony, Civil Actions Over $15,000, Probate* 5201 Monticello Ave #6, Williamsburg, VA 23188-8218. 8:30AM-4:30PM. **757-564-2242**, Fax: 757-564-2329. ✉🖥🤚

9th General District Court *Misd., Civil Actions Under $15,000, Eviction, Small Claims* James City County Courthouse 5201 Monticello Ave, #2, Williamsburg, VA 23188-8218. 7:30AM-4PM. **757-564-2400**, Fax: 757-564-2410. **Fax**✉🤚

King and Queen County

9th Circuit Court *Felony, Civil Actions Over $15,000, Probate* PO Box 67 234 Allen's Circle, King & Queen Court House, VA 23085. 9AM-5PM. **804-785-5984**, Fax: 804-785-5698. 🖥🤚

King & Queen General District Court *Misd., Civil Under $15,000, Eviction* www.kingandqueenco.net/html/Govt/gendist.html PO Box 86, King & Queen Courthouse, VA 23085-0086. 8:30AM-4:30PM. **804-785-5982**, Fax: 804-785-5694. **Fax**✉🖥🤚

King George County

15th Circuit Court *Felony, Civil Actions Over $15,000, Probate* 9483 Kings Highway, #3, King George, VA 22485. 8:30AM-4:30PM. **540-775-3322**. ✉🤚

15th Judicial District King George Combined Court *Misdemeanor, Civil*

Actions Under $15,000, Eviction, Small Claims County Courthouse PO Box 279, King George, VA 22485. 8AM-4:00PM. **540-775-3573**. ✉🤚

King William County

9th Circuit Court *Felony, Civil Actions Over $15,000, Probate* 227 Courthouse Ln PO Box 216, King William, VA 23086. 8:30AM-4:30PM. **804-769-4936**. ✉🤚🖥

King William General District Court *Misdemeanor, Civil Actions Under $15,000, Eviction, Small Claims* PO Box 5, King William, VA 23086. 8:30AM-4:30PM. **804-769-4948**, Fax: 804-769-4971. **Fax**✉🖥🤚

Lancaster County

15th Circuit Court *Felony, Civil Actions Over $15,000, Probate* Courthouse Bldg PO Box 99, Lancaster, VA 22503. 8:30-4:30PM. **804-462-5611**. ✉🖥🤚

15th General District Court *Misdemeanor, Civil Actions Under $15,000, Eviction, Small Claims* PO 129, Lancaster, VA 22503. 8:AM-12:00, 1-4:30PM. **804-462-0012**. ✉🖥🤚

Lee County

30th Circuit Court *Felony, Civil Actions Over $15,000, Probate* PO Box 326, Jonesville, VA 24263. 8:30AM-5PM M-F; 9AM-N Sat. **276-346-7763**, Fax: 276-346-3440. ☎**Fax**✉🖥🤚

30th General District Court *Misd., Civil Actions Under $15,000, Eviction, Small Claims* Lee County Courthouse, PO Box 306, Jonesville, VA 24263. 8AM-4:30PM. **276-346-7729**, Fax: 276-346-7701. ✉🖥🤚**Fax**

Loudoun County

20th Circuit Court *Felony, Civil Over $15,000, Probate* www.loudoun.gov/clerk/ 18 E Market St, Leesburg, VA 20178. 8:30AM-4:30PM. **703-777-0270**, Fax: 703-777-0376 Prob:703-777-0272. 🖥🤚

20th General District Court *Misd., Civil Actions Under $15,000, Eviction* 18 E Market St, Leesburg, VA 20176. 8AM-4PM. **703-777-0312**, Fax: 703-777-0311. ✉**Fax**🖥🤚

Louisa County

16th Circuit Court *Felony, Civil Actions Over $15,000, Probate* Box 37, Louisa,

VA 23093. 8:30AM-5PM. **540-967-5312**, Fax: 540-967-2705. 💻✋

16th General District Court *Misd., Civil Actions Under $15,000, Eviction, Small Claims* PO Box 452, Louisa, VA 23093. 8:30AM-4:30PM. **540-967-5330**, Fax: 540-967-2369. 💻✋

Lunenburg County

10th Circuit Court *Felony, Civil Actions Over $15,000, Probate* 11435 Courthouse Rd, Lunenburg, VA 23952. 8:30AM-4:30PM. **434-696-2230**, Fax: 434-696-3931. I✋✉

10th General District Court *Misdemeanor, Civil Actions Under $15,000, Eviction, Small Claims* 11413 Courthouse Rd, Lunenburg, VA 23952. 8:30AM-4:30PM. **434-696-5508**, Fax: 434-696-3665. Access records-✉💻✋

Madison County

16th Circuit Court *Felony, Civil Actions Over $15,000, Probate* 100 Court Sq,1 Main St (PO Box 220), Madison, VA 22727. 8:30AM-4:30PM. **540-948-6888**, Fax: 540-948-3759. ✉💻✋

16th General District Court *Misd., Civil Actions Under $15,000, Eviction, Small Claims* Madison County Courthouse PO Box 470, Madison, VA 22727. 8:30AM-4:30PM. **540-948-4657**, Fax: 540-948-5649. ☎Fax✉💻✋

Mathews County

9th Circuit Court *Felony, Civil Actions Over $15,000, Probate* www.courts.state.va.us/courts/circuit/Mathews/home.html PO Box 463, Mathews, VA 23109. 8AM-4PM. **804-725-2550**. 💻✋

9th General District Court *Misdemeanor, Civil Actions Under $15,000, Eviction, Small Claims* PO Box 169, Saluda, VA 23149. 8:30AM-4:30PM. **804-758-4312**. ✉💻✋

Mecklenburg County

10th Circuit Court *Felony, Civil Actions Over $15,000, Probate* PO Box 530, Boydton, VA 23917. 8:30AM-4:30PM. **434-738-6191**, Fax: 434-738-6861. 💻✋

10th General District Court *Misd., Civil Actions Under $15,000, Eviction, Small Claims* 1294 Jefferson St (PO Box 306), Boydton, VA 23917. 8:30AM-4:30PM.

434-738-6191 X223, Fax: 434-738-0761. Fax✉💻✋

Middlesex County

9th Circuit Court *Felony, Civil Actions Over $15,000, Probate* PO Box 158, Saluda, VA 23149. 8:30AM-4:30PM. **804-758-5317**, Fax: 804-758-0792. ✋

9th General District Court *Misd., Civil Actions Under $15,000, Eviction, Small Claims* PO Box 169, Saluda, VA 23149. 8:30-4:30PM. **804-758-4312**. ✉💻✋

Montgomery County

27th Circuit Court *Felony, Civil Actions Over $15,000, Probate* PO Box 6309, Christiansburg, VA 24068. 8:30AM-4:30PM. **540-382-5760**, Fax: 540-382-6937. 💻✋

27th General District Court *Misdemeanor, Civil Actions Under $15,000, Eviction, Small Claims* Montgomery County Courthouse 1 E Main St, #201, Christiansburg, VA 24073. 8:30AM-4:30PM. **540-382-5735**, Fax: 540-382-6988. Civil phone: 540-394-2085, crim: 540-394-2086. ✋

Nelson County

24th Circuit Court *Felony, Civil Actions Over $15,000, Probate* PO Box 10, Lovingston, VA 22949. 8AM-5PM. **434-263-7020**, Fax: 434-263-7027. 💻✋

24th General District Court *Misdemeanor, Civil Actions Under $15,000, Eviction, Small Claims* Nelson County Courthouse 84 Courthouse Sq, PO Box 514, Lovingston, VA 22949. 8AM-4:30PM. **434-263-7040**, Fax: 434-263-7033. Fax✉💻✋

New Kent County

9th Circuit Court *Felony, Civil Actions Over $15,000, Probate* PO Box 98 12001 Court House Circle, New Kent, VA 23124. 8:30AM-4:30PM. **804-966-9520**, Fax: 804-966-9528. 💻✋

9th General District Court *Misd., Civil Actions Under $15,000, Eviction, Small Claims* PO Box 127, New Kent, VA 23124. 8:30AM-4:30PM. **804-966-9530**, Fax: 804-966-9535. ✉💻✋

Northampton County

2nd Circuit Court *Felony, Civil Actions Over $15,000, Probate* PO Box 36 (16404 Courthouse Rd), Eastville, VA

23347-0036. 9AM-4:30PM. **757-678-0465**, Fax: 757-678-5410. Oldest continuous records in the USA. ☎Fax✉💻✋

Northampton General District Court *Misdemeanor, Civil Actions Under $15,000, Eviction, Small Claims* PO Box 1289, Eastville, VA 23347. 8:30AM-4:30PM. **757-678-0466**. ✉💻✋

Northumberland County

15th Circuit Court *Felony, Civil Actions Over $15,000, Probate* PO Box 217, Heathsville, VA 22473. 8:30AM-4:45PM. **804-580-3700**, Fax: 804-580-2261. ✉💻✋

15th General District Court *Misdemeanor, Civil Actions Under $15,000, Eviction, Small Claims* Northumberland Courthouse, PO Box 114, Heathsville, VA 22473. 8AM-4:30PM. **804-580-4323**, Fax: 804-580-6702. 💻✋

Nottoway County

11th Circuit Court *Felony, Civil Actions Over $15,000, Probate* Courthouse, PO Box 25, Nottoway, VA 23955. 8:30AM-4:30PM. **434-645-9043**, Fax: 434-645-2201. 💻✋

11th General District Court *Misd., Civil Actions Under $15,000, Eviction, Small Claims* PO Box 25, Nottoway, VA 23955. 8AM-4:15PM. **434-645-9312**, Fax: 434-645-8584. ✉💻✋

Orange County

16th Circuit Court *Felony, Civil Actions Over $15,000, Probate* PO Box 230, Orange, VA 22960. 8:30AM-4:30PM. **540-672-4030**, Fax: 540-672-2939. ☎Fax✉💻✋

16th General District Court *Misdemeanor, Civil Actions Under $15,000, Eviction, Small Claims* Orange County Courthouse, PO Box 821, Orange, VA 22960. 8:30AM-4:30PM. **540-672-3150**, Fax: 540-672-9438. ✉💻✋

Page County

26th Circuit Court *Felony, Civil Actions Over $15,000, Probate* 116 S Court St, #A, Luray, VA 22835. 9AM-5PM. **540-743-4064**, Fax: 540-743-2338. 💻✋

26th General District Court *Misdemeanor, Civil Actions Under $15,000, Eviction, Small Claims* 116 S

Court St, Luray, VA 22835. 8AM-4:30PM. **540-743-5705**. ✉🖥✋

Patrick County

21st Circuit Court *Felony, Civil Actions Over $15,000, Probate* PO Box 148, Stuart, VA 24171. 9AM-5PM. **276-694-7213**. 🖥✋

21st General District Court *Misd., Civil Actions Under $15,000, Eviction, Small Claims* PO Box 149, Stuart, VA 24171. 8:30AM-5PM. **276-694-7258**, Fax: 276-694-5614. ✉🖥✋

Pittsylvania County

22nd Circuit Court *Felony, Civil Actions Over $15,000, Probate* PO Drawer 31, Chatham, VA 24531. 8:30AM-5PM. **434-432-7887**, Fax: 434-432-7913. 🖥✋

22nd General District Court *Misdemeanor, Civil Actions Under $15,000, Eviction, Small Claims* www.courts.state.va.us/courts/gd/Pittsylvania/home.html Pittsylvania Courthouse Annex 2nd Fl PO Box 695, Chatham, VA 24531. 8:30AM-4:30PM. **434-432-7879**, Fax: 434-432-7915. Access records-🖥✋

Powhatan County

11th Circuit Court *Felony, Civil Actions Over $15,000, Probate* PO Box 37, Powhatan, VA 23139-0037. 8:30AM-5PM. **804-598-5660**, Fax: 804-598-5608. ✋🖥

11th Judicial District Court *Misdemeanor, Civil Actions Under $15,000, Eviction, Small Claims* Courthouse, 3880 D Old Buckingham Rd, Powhatan, VA 23139. 8:30AM-5PM. **804-598-5665**, Fax: 804-598-5608. ☎Fax✉🖥✋

Prince Edward County

Circuit Court *Felony, Civil Actions Over $15,000, Probate* PO Box 304 Court House, 111 South St, Farmville, VA 23901-0304. 8:30AM-4:30PM. **434-392-5145**. ✋🖥

General District Court *Misdemeanor, Civil Actions Under $15,000, Eviction, Small Claims* PO Box 41, Farmville, VA 23901-0041. 8:30AM-4:30PM. **434-392-4024**, Fax: 434-392-3800. ✉🖥✋

Prince George County

Circuit Court *Felony, Civil Actions Over $15,000, Probate* PO Box 98, Prince George, VA 23875. 8:30AM-5PM. **804-733-2640**, Fax: 804-861-5721. 🖥✋

6th General District Court *Misdemeanor, Civil Actions Under $15,000, Eviction, Small Claims* P.C. Courthouse PO Box 187, Prince George, VA 23875. 8:30AM-4:30PM. **804-733-2783**. 🖥✋

Prince William County

31st Circuit Court *Felony, Civil Over $15,000, Probate* www.pwcgov.org/ccourt 9311 Lee Ave, Manassas, VA 20110. 8:30AM-5PM. **703-792-6015**, Fax: 703-792-4721. Civil phone: 703-792-6021, crim: 703-792-6031, Probate: 703-792-6085. ✉✋

31st General District Court *Misdemeanor, Civil Actions Under $15,000, Eviction, Small Claims* www.courts.state.va.us/courts/gd/Prince_William/home.html 9311 Lee Ave, Manassas, VA 20110. 8AM-4PM. Fax: 703-792-6121. Civil phone: 703-792-6149, crim: 703-792-6141. ✉**Fax**🖥✋

Pulaski County

27th Circuit Court *Felony, Civil Over $15,000, Probate* www.pulaskicircuitcourt.com 45 3rd St NW, #101, Pulaski, VA 24301. 8:30AM-4:30PM. **540-980-7825**, Fax: 540-980-7835. Access records-🖥✋

27th General District Court *Misdemeanor, Civil Actions Under $15,000, Eviction, Small Claims* 45 3rd St NW, #102, Pulaski, VA 24301. 8:30AM-4:30PM. **540-980-7470**, Fax: 540-980-7792. 🖥✋

Rappahannock County

20th Circuit Court *Felony, Civil Actions Over $15,000, Probate* 238 Gay St (PO Box 517), Washington, VA 22747. 8:30-4:30PM. **540-675-5350**. ✉🖥✋

20th Combined District Court *Misdemeanor, Civil Actions Under $15,000, Eviction, Small Claims* PO Box 206, Washington, VA 22747. 8:30AM-4:30PM. **540-675-5356**. ✉🖥✋

Richmond County

15th Circuit Court *Felony, Civil Actions Over $15,000, Probate* 101 Court Cir, PO Box 1000, Warsaw, VA 22572. 9AM-5PM. **804-333-3781**, Fax: 804-333-5396. ✉✋🖥

15th Judicial District Court *Misd., Civil Actions Under $15,000, Eviction, Small Claims* Richmond County Courthouse, PO Box 1000, Warsaw, VA 22572. 8AM-4:30PM. **804-333-4616**, Fax: 804-333-3741. ✉🖥✋

Roanoke County

23rd Circuit Court *Felony, Civil Over $15,000, Probate* www.co.roanoke.va.us PO Box 1126, Salem, VA 24153-1126. 8:30AM-4:30PM. **540-387-6260**. 🖥✋

23rd General District Court *Misdemeanor, Civil Actions Under $15,000, Eviction, Small Claims* www.co.roanoke.va.us PO Box 997, Salem, VA 24153. 8:15AM-4:15PM. **540-387-6168**, Fax: 540-387-6066. ✉🖥✋

Rockbridge County

25th Circuit Court *Felony, Civil Actions Over $15,000, Probate* Courthouse Sq, 2 S Main St, Lexington, VA 24450. 8:30AM-4:30PM. **540-463-2232**, Fax: 540-463-3850. 🖥✋

District Court *Misdemeanor, Civil Actions Under $15,000, Eviction, Small Claims* 150 S Main St, Lexington, VA 24450. 8:30AM-4:30PM. **540-463-3631**, Fax: 540-463-4213. Lexington-Rockbridge is a combined district court. ✉🖥✋

Rockingham County

26th Circuit Court *Felony, Civil Actions Over $15,000, Probate* Courthouse, Court Sq, Harrisonburg, VA 22801. 9AM-5PM. Fax: 540-564-3127. Civil phone: 540-564-3114, crim: 540-564-3118. 🖥✋

26th General District Court *Misdemeanor, Civil Actions Under $15,000, Eviction, Small Claims* 53 Court Sq, Harrisonburg, VA 22801. 8AM-4PM. Fax: 540-564-3096. Civil phone: 540-564-3135, crim: 540-564-3130. ☎✉🖥✋

Russell County

29th Circuit Court *Felony, Civil Actions Over $15,000, Probate* PO Box 435, Lebanon, VA 24266. 8AM-5PM. **276-889-8023**, Fax: 276-889-8003. 🖥✋

29th General District Court *Misd., Civil Actions Under $15,000, Eviction, Small Claims* Russell County Courthouse PO Box 65, Lebanon, VA 24266. 8:30AM-4:30PM. **276-889-8051**, Fax: 276-889-8091. ☎Fax✉🖥✋

Scott County

Circuit Court *Felony, Civil Actions Over $15,000, Probate* 104 E Jackson St, #2, Gate City, VA 24251. 8:30AM-5PM. **276-386-3801**. ⊠💻✋

30th General District Court *Misd., Civil Actions Under $15,000, Eviction, Small Claims* 104 E Jackson St, #9, Gate City, VA 24251. 8:15AM-4:45PM. **276-386-7341**. ⊠💻✋

Shenandoah County

26th Circuit Court *Felony, Civil Actions Over $15,000, Probate* 112 S Main St, PO Box 406, Woodstock, VA 22664. 9AM-5PM. **540-459-6150**, Fax: 540-459-6155. 💻✋

26th General District Court *Misdemeanor, Civil Actions Under $15,000, Eviction, Small Claims* 114 W Court St, Woodstock, VA 22664. 8:30AM-4:30PM. **540-459-6130**, Fax: 540-459-7279. Access records-💻⊠✋

Smyth County

28th Circuit Court *Felony, Civil Actions Over $15,000, Probate* 109 W Main St, #144, Marion, VA 24354-2510. 9AM-5PM. **276-782-4044**, Fax: 276-782-4045. ⊠Fax💻✋

28th General District Court *Misd., Civil Actions Under $15,000, Eviction, Small Claims* Smythe County Courthouse, Rm 231 109 W Main St, Marion, VA 24354. 8:30AM-4:30PM. **276-782-4047**, Fax: 276-782-4048. ☎⊠💻✋

Southampton County

5th Circuit Court *Felony, Civil Actions Over $15,000, Probate* PO Box 190, Courtland, VA 23837. 8:30AM-5PM. **757-653-2200**. Access records-⊠💻✋

5th General District Court *Misdemeanor, Civil Actions Under $15,000, Eviction, Small Claims* PO Box 347, Courtland, VA 23837. 8:30AM-4:30PM. **757-653-2673**. ⊠💻✋

Spotsylvania County

15th Circuit Court *Felony, Civil Actions Over $15,000, Probate* PO Box 96 9113 Courthouse Rd, Spotsylvania, VA 22553. 8AM-4:30PM. **540-582-7090**, Fax: 540-582-2169. 💻✋

15th General District Court *Misd., Civil Actions Under $15,000, Eviction, Small Claims* Judicial Center PO Box 339, Spotsylvania, VA 22553. 8AM-4PM. **540-582-7110**. ⊠💻✋

Stafford County

15th Circuit Court *Felony, Civil Over $15,000, Probate* www.co.stafford.va.us/courts/ PO Box 69, Stafford, VA 22554. 8AM-4PM. **540-658-8750**. ⊠💻✋

15th General District Court *Misd., Civil Actions Under $15,000, Eviction, Small Claims* 1300 Courthouse Rd PO Box 940, Stafford, VA 22555. 8:AM-4PM. **540-658-8763**, Fax: 540-658-4834. Civil phone: 540-658-4642, crim: 540-658-8935. Fax⊠💻✋

Surry County

6th Circuit Court *Felony, Civil Actions Over $15,000, Probate* 28 Colonial Trail E PO Box 203, Surry, VA 23883. 9AM-5PM. **757-294-3161**, Fax: 757-294-0471. ✋💻

6th General District Court *Misd., Civil Actions Under $15,000, Eviction, Small Claims* Hwy 10 and School St, PO Box 332, Surry, VA 23883. 8:30AM-4:30PM. **757-294-5201**, Fax: 757-294-0312. Access records-💻✋

Sussex County

6th Circuit Court *Felony, Civil Actions Over $15,000, Probate* PO Box 1337, Sussex, VA 23884. 9AM-5PM. **434-246-5511 X3276**, Fax: 434-246-2203. ⊠💻✋

6th Judicial District Court *Misd., Civil Actions Under $15,000, Eviction, Small Claims* Sussex Cnty Courthouse, 15098 Courthouse Rd, Rte 735 PO Box 1315, Sussex, VA 23884. 8:30AM-4:30PM. **434-246-5511**, Fax: 434-246-6604. Civil phone: x3240, crim: x3273. 💻✋

Tazewell County

29th Circuit Court *Felony, Civil Actions Over $15,000, Probate* PO Box 968, Tazewell, VA 24651-0968. 8AM-4:30PM. **276-988-1222**, Fax: 276-988-7501. ⊠💻✋

29th General District Court *Misd., Civil Actions Under $15,000, Eviction, Small Claims* PO Box 566, Tazewell, VA 24651. 8:30AM-4:30PM. **276-988-9057**, Fax: 276-988-6202. ⊠Fax💻✋

Warren County

Circuit Court *Felony, Civil, Probate* www.courts.state.va.us/courts/circuit/warren/home.html 1 E Main St, Front Royal, VA 22630. 9AM-5PM. **540-635-2435**, Fax: 540-636-3274. ☎Fax⊠💻✋

26th General District Court *Misdemeanor, Civil Actions Under $15,000, Eviction, Small Claims* 1 E Main St, Front Royal, VA 22630. 8:15AM-4:15PM. **540-635-2335**, Fax: 540-636-8233. ⊠Fax💻✋

Washington County

Circuit Court *Felony, Civil Actions Over $15,000, Probate* PO Box 289, Abingdon, VA 24212-0289. 7:30AM-5PM; Recording: 8:30AM-4PM. **276-676-6224/6226**, Fax: 276-676-6218. 💻✋

28th General District Court *Misd., Civil Actions Under $15,000, Eviction, Small Claims* 191 E Main St, Abingdon, VA 24210. 8:30AM-4:30PM. **276-676-6281**, Fax: 276-676-3136. ⊠💻✋

Westmoreland County

15th Circuit Court *Felony, Civil Actions Over $15,000, Probate* PO Box 307, Montross, VA 22520. 9AM-5PM. **804-493-0108**, Fax: 804-493-0393. ✋

15th General District Court *Misd., Civil Actions Under $15,000, Small Claims* PO Box 688, Montross, VA 22520. 8AM-4:30PM. **804-493-0105**. ⊠💻✋

Wise County

30th Circuit Court *Felony, Civil Over $15,000, Probate* www.wisecircuitcourt.com PO Box 1248, Wise, VA 24293-1248. 8:30AM-5PM. **276-328-6111**, Fax: 276-328-0039. ☎Fax⊠💻✋

30th General District Court *Misd., Civil Under $15,000, Eviction, Small Claims* Wise County Courthouse, PO Box 829, Wise, VA 24293. 8AM-4PM. **276-328-3426**, Fax: 276-328-4576. ☎⊠💻✋

Wythe County

27th Circuit Court *Felony, Civil Actions Over $15,000, Probate* 225 S 4th St, Rm 105, Wytheville, VA 24382. 8:30AM-5PM. **276-223-6050**, Fax: 276-223-6057. ✋💻

Wythe General District Court *Misdemeanor, Civil Actions Under $15,000, Eviction, Small Claims* 245 S

Key: Symbols refer to criminal records access unless otherwise noted. phone-☎ mail-⊠ fax-Fax in person-✋ online-💻 email-**Email**

4th St, #205, Wytheville, VA 24382-2595. 8AM-4:30PM. **276-223-6075**, Fax: 276-223-6087. 🖥🖐

York County

9th Circuit Court *Felony, Civil Over $15,000, Probate* www.yorkcounty.gov/circuitcourt/ PO Box 371, Yorktown, VA 23690. 9AM-5PM. **757-890-3350**, Fax: 757-890-3364. Civil phone: 757-890-4105, crim: 757-890-4104, Probate: 757-890-4106. Also includes City of Poquoson. ✉🖥🖐

9th Judicial District Court *Misdemeanor, Civil Actions Under $15,000, Eviction, Small Claims* www.yorkcounty.gov/districtcourt York County GDC PO Box 316, Yorktown, VA 23690-0316. 8:30AM-4:30PM. **757-890-3450**, Fax: 757-890-3459. **Fax**✉🖥🖐

Virginia Cities
Alexandria City

18th Circuit Court *Felony, Civil Over $15,000, Probate* http://ci.alexandria.va.us/courts/courts_index.html 520 King St, #307, Alexandria, VA 22314. 9AM-5PM. Civil: 703-838-4044, crim: 703-838-4047, Probate: 703-838-4055. 🖐

18th District Court *Misdemeanor, Civil Actions Under $15,000, Eviction, Small Claims* 520 King St #201, Alexandria, VA 22314. 8AM-4PM. 703-838-4041 (traffic), Civil: 703-838-4021, Crim: 703-838-4030. Mail can go to PO Box 20206, Zip is 22320. 🖥🖐

Bristol City

28th Circuit Court *Felony, Civil Actions Over $15,000, Probate* 497 Cumberland St, Bristol, VA 24201. 9AM-5PM. **276-645-7321**, Fax: 276-821-6097. 🖥🖐

28th General District Court *Misd., Civil Actions Under $15,000, Eviction, Small Claims* 497 Cumberland St, Bristol, VA 24201. 8:30AM-4PM. **276-645-7341**, Fax: 276-645-7342. ✉**Fax**🖥🖐

Buena Vista City

25th Circuit & District Court *Felony, Misdemeanor, Civil, Eviction, Probate* 2039 Sycamore Ave, Buena Vista, VA 24416. 8:30AM-5PM. **540-261-8627 X626/627**, Fax: 540-261-8625. ✉🖥🖐

Charlottesville City

16th Circuit Court *Felony, Civil Actions Over $15,000, Probate* 315 E High St, Charlottesville, VA 22902. 8:30AM-4:30PM. **434-295-3182**. 🖥🖐

Charlottesville General District Court *Misdemeanor, Civil Actions Under $15,000, Eviction, Small Claims* 606 E Market St, PO Box 2677, Charlottesville, VA 22902. 8:30AM-4:30PM. **434-970-3385**, Fax: 434-970-3387. Civil phone: 434-970-3392, crim: 434-970-3388. ✉🖥🖐

Chesapeake City

1st Circuit Court *Felony, Civil Actions Over $15,000, Probate* 307 Albemarle Dr, #300A, Chesapeake, VA 23322-5579. 8:30AM-4PM. **757-382-3000**, Fax: 757-382-3035. ✉**Fax**🖥🖐

1st General District Court *Misdemeanor, Civil Actions Under $15,000, Eviction, Small Claims* 307 Albemarle Dr, #100, Chesapeake, VA 23322. 8AM-4PM. Fax: 757-382-3171. Civil phone: 757-382-3143, crim: 757-382-3134. Indicate division (civil, criminal or traffic) in address. ✉🖥🖐

Colonial Heights City

12th Circuit Court *Felony, Civil Actions Over $15,000, Probate* 401 Temple Ave, PO Box 3401, Colonial Heights, VA 23834. 8:30AM-5PM. **804-520-9364**. ✉🖥🖐

12th General District Court *Misd., Civil Actions Under $15,000, Eviction, Small Claims* 401 Temple Ave PO Box 279, Colonial Heights, VA 23834. 8AM-4PM. **804-520-9346 (Dial 0)**, Fax: 804-520-9370. ✉**Fax**🖥🖐

Danville City

22nd Circuit Court *Felony, Civil Actions Over $15,000, Probate* www.danville-va.gov/home.asp PO Box 3300 (401 Patton St), Danville, VA 24543. 9AM-4:30PM. **434-799-5168**, Fax: 434-799-6502. 🖥🖐

22nd General District Court *Misd., Civil Actions Under $15,000, Eviction, Small Claims* PO Box 3300, Danville, VA 24543. 8:30AM-4:30PM. **434-799-5179**, Fax: 434-797-8814. ✉🖥🖐

Emporia City

6th General District Court *Misd., Civil Actions Under $15,000, Eviction, Small Claims* 315 S Main, Emporia, VA 23847. 8:30AM-4:30PM. **434-634-5400**. 🖥🖐

Fairfax City

19th General District Court *Misdemeanor, Traffic* www.ci.fairfax.va.us/Services/Courts/Courts.htm 10455 Armstrong St, #304, Fairfax, VA 22030. 8:30AM-4:30PM. **703-385-7866**, Fax: 703-352-3195. Find Circuit Court cases and General District civil cases for this city in the Fairfax County listing ✉🖐

Falls Church City

17th District Courts Combined *Misdemeanor, Civil Actions Under $15,000, Eviction, Small Claims* www.ci.falls-church.va.us Falls Church District 300 Park Ave, Falls Church, VA 22046-3305. 8AM-4PM. **703-248-5096 (GDC)**, Fax: 703-241-1407. Civil phone: 703-248-5098. Small claims phone is 703-248-5157; juvenile and domestic relations is 703-248-5099. **Fax**🖥🖐

Franklin-City

5th Judicial General District Combined *Misdemeanor, Civil Under $15,000, Eviction, Traffic* www.courts.state.va.us/courts/combined/Franklin_City/home.html 1020 Pretlow St, Franklin, VA 23851. 8AM-4PM. **757-562-8550**, Fax: 757-562-8561. Southampton County serves as the Circuit Court for the City of Franklin. ✉🖐

Fredericksburg City

15th Circuit Court *Felony, Civil Actions Over $15,000, Probate* 815 Princess Anne St, PO Box 359, Fredericksburg, VA 22404-0359. 8AM-4PM. **540-372-1066**. 🖥🖐

15th General District Court *Misdemeanor, Civil Actions Under $15,000, Eviction, Small Claims* PO Box 180, Fredericksburg, VA 22404. 8AM-4PM. **540-372-1044**, Civil: 540-372-1044, crim: 540-372-1043. ✉🖥🖐

Galax City

27th General District Court *Misdemeanor, Civil Actions Under $15,000, Eviction, Small Claims* 353 N Main St, PO Box 214, Galax, VA 24333-0214. 8AM-4:30PM. **276-236-8731**, Fax: 276-236-2754. Circuit Court jurisdiction for this city can be in Carroll County or Grayson County depending on side of the city the offense occurred. ✉**Fax**🖥🖐

Hampton City

8th Circuit Court *Felony, Civil Actions Over $15,000, Probate* 101 King's Way, PO Box 40, Hampton, VA 23669-0040. 8:30-4PM. **757-727-6105.** ✉️🖥️👆🖥️

8th General District Court *Misd., Civil Actions Under $15,000, Eviction, Small Claims* Courthouse, PO Box 70, Hampton, VA 23669-0070. 8AM-4PM. Civil: 757-727-6480, crim: 757-727-6260. 🖥️👆

Hopewell City

6th Circuit Court *Felony, Civil Actions Over $15,000, Probate* 100 E Broadway, PO Box 310 2nd Fl, Rm 251, Hopewell, VA 23860. 8:30AM-4PM. **804-541-2239,** Fax: 804-541-2438. Access records-🖥️👆

Hopewell District Court *Misd., Civil Actions Under $15,000, Eviction, Small Claims* 100 E Broadway, Hopewell, VA 23860. 8:30AM-4:30PM. **804-541-2257,** Fax: 804-541-2364. ✉️🖥️👆

Lynchburg City

24th Circuit Court *Felony, Civil Actions Over $15,000, Probate* 900 Court St PO Box 4, Lynchburg, VA 24505-0004. 8:15AM-4:45PM. **434-847-1590,** Fax: 434-847-1864. 🖥️👆

24th General District Court - Civil Division *Civil Actions Under $15,000, Eviction, Small Claims* 905 Court St, Lynchburg, VA 24504. 8AM-4PM. Fax: 434-847-1779. Civil phone: 434-455-2640, crim: 434-455-2630. Access civil records-✉️🖥️👆

24th General District Court - Criminal *Misdemeanor* 905 Court St, Lynchburg, VA 24504. 8AM-4PM. Fax: 434-847-1779. Phone: 434-455-2630. 🖥️👆

Martinsville City

21st Circuit Court *Felony, Civil Over $15,000, Probate* www.ci.martinsville.va.us/circuitclerk/ PO Box 1206, Martinsville, VA 24114-1206. 9AM-5PM. **276-656-5106,** Fax: 276-403-5232. 🖥️👆✉️**Fax**

21st General District Court *Misdemeanor, Civil Actions Under $15,000, Eviction, Small Claims* www.courts.state.va.us PO Box 1402, Martinsville, VA 24112. 9AM-5PM. **276-656-5125,** Fax: 276-403-5114. 🖥️👆

Newport News City

7th Circuit Court *Felony, Civil Actions Over $15,000, Probate* 2500 Washington Ave, Newport News, VA 23607. 8AM-4:45PM. **757-926-8561,** Fax: 757-926-8531. 🖥️👆

7th General District Court *Misdemeanor, Civil Actions Under $15,000, Eviction, Small Claims* 2500 Washington Ave, Newport News, VA 23607. 7:30AM-4PM. Fax: 757-926-8496. Civil phone: 757-926-3520, crim: 757-926-8811. ☎️**Fax**✉️🖥️👆

Norfolk City

4th Circuit Court *Felony, Civil Over $15,000, Probate* 100 St Paul's Blvd, Norfolk, VA 23510. 8:45AM-4:45PM. **757-664-4380,** Fax: 757-664-4581. Civil phone: 757-664-4387, crim: 757-664-4384, Probate: 757-664-4385. 🖥️👆

4th General District Court *Misdemeanor, Civil Actions Under $15,000, Eviction, Small Claims* 811 E City Hall Ave, Norfolk, VA 23510. 8AM-4PM. **757-664-4910,** Civil: 757-664-4913/4, crim: 757-664-4915/6. ✉️🖥️👆

Petersburg City

11th Circuit Court *Felony, Civil Actions Over $15,000, Probate* 7 Courthouse Ave, Petersburg, VA 23803. 8AM-4PM. **804-733-2367,** Fax: 804-732-5548. 🖥️👆

11th Judicial District Court *Misdemeanor, Civil Actions Under $15,000, Eviction, Small Claims* 35 E Tabb St, Petersburg, VA 23803. 8AM-4PM. **804-733-2374,** Fax: 804-733-2375 (Attn: Civil or Crimnal). Civil phone: X4153, crim: X4152. **Fax**✉️🖥️👆

Portsmouth City

Circuit Court *Felony, Civil Actions Over $15,000, Probate* PO Drawer 1217, Portsmouth, VA 23705. 8:30AM-5:30PM. **757-393-8671,** Fax: 757-399-4826. ✉️🖥️👆

General District Court *Misdemeanor, Civil Actions Under $15,000, Eviction, Small Claims* PO Box 129, Portsmouth, VA 23705. 8:30AM-4:30PM. Fax: 757-393-8634. Civil phone: 757-393-8624, crim: 757-393-8681. Traffic Division: 757-393-8506. ✉️**Fax**🖥️👆

Radford City

27th Circuit Court *Felony, Civil Actions Over $15,000, Probate* 619 2nd St, Radford, VA 24141. 8AM-5PM (no machine receipts after 4:30PM). **540-731-3610,** Fax: 540-731-3612. **Fax**✉️🖥️👆

27th General District Court *Misd., Civil Actions Under $15,000, Eviction, Small Claims* 619 2nd St, Radford, VA 24141. 8:30AM-4:30PM. **540-731-3609,** Fax: 540-731-3692. **Fax**✉️🖥️👆

Richmond City

13th Circuit Court - Division I *Felony, Civil Actions Over $15,000, Probate* www.courts.state.va.us/courts/circuit/Richmond/home.html John Marshall Courts Bldg 400 N 9th St, Richmond, VA 23219. 8:45AM-4:45PM. **804-646-6505,** Civil: 804-646-6536, crim: 804-646-6553. Also search for felony records at the Manchester Courthouse location, 10th & Hull St. ✉️🖥️👆

13th General District Court - Civil *Civil Under $15,000, Eviction, Small Claims* 400 N 9th St, Rm 203, Richmond, VA 23219. 8AM-4PM. **804-646-6461.** Access civil records-☎️✉️🖥️👆

13th General District Court - Division II *Misdemeanor, Traffic* 905 Decatur St, Richmond, VA 23224. 8AM-4PM. **804-646-8990,** Fax: 804-646-0387. ✉️🖥️👆

Richmond City - Manchester County

13th Circuit Court *Felony* www.vipnet.org/vipnet/clerks/richmondmanchester.html Manchester Courthouse, 10th and Hull St, Richmond, VA 23224-4070. 8:45AM-4:45PM. **804-646-8470,** Fax: 804-646-8122. Also search for felony records at the John Marshall Courthouse (Division I) location. ✉️🖥️👆

Roanoke City

23rd Circuit Court *Felony, Civil Over $15,000, Probate* www.co.roanoke.va.us PO Box 2610, Roanoke, VA 24010-2610. 8:15AM-4:45PM. Civil: 540-853-6702, crim: 540-853-6723. ✉️🖥️👆

General District Court *Misd., Civil Under $15,000, Eviction, Small Claims* 315 W Church Ave, 2nd Fl, Roanoke, VA 24016-5007. 8AM-4PM. Civil: 540-853-2364, crim: 540-853-2361. 🖥️👆

Key: Symbols refer to criminal records access unless otherwise noted. phone-☎️ mail-✉️ fax-**Fax** in person-👆 online-🖥️ email-**Email**

Salem City

23rd Circuit Court *Felony, Civil Actions Over $15,000, Probate* 2 E Calhoun St, PO Box 891, Salem, VA 24153. 8:30-5. **540-375-3067**, Fax: 540-375-4039. 💻 🖐

23rd General District Court *Misd., Civil Actions Under $15,000, Eviction, Small Claims* 2 E Calhoun St, Salem, VA 24153. 8AM-4PM. **540-375-3044**, Fax: 540-375-4024. 💻 🖐

Staunton City

25th Circuit Court *Felony, Civil Actions Over $15,000, Probate* PO Box 1286, Staunton, VA 24402-1286. 8:30AM-5PM. **540-332-3874**, Fax: 540-332-3970. 💻 🖐

Staunton General District Court *Misdemeanor, Civil Actions Under $15,000, Eviction, Small Claims* 113 E Beverly St, Staunton, VA 24401-4390. 8:30AM-4:30PM. **540-332-3878**, Fax: 540-332-3985. Access records-✉ 💻 🖐

Suffolk City

Suffolk Circuit Court *Felony, Civil Actions Over $15,000, Probate* PO Box 1604, Suffolk, VA 23439-1604. 8:30-5. **757-923-2251**, Fax: 757-934-3490. 💻 🖐

5th General District Court *Misd., Civil up to $15,000, Eviction, Small Claims* 150 N Main St, PO Box 1648, Suffolk, VA 23434. 8AM-4PM. **757-923-2281**, Fax: 757-925-1790. 💻 ✉ 🖐

Virginia Beach City

2nd Circuit Court *Felony, Civil Over $15,000, Probate* www.vbgov.com/courts/ 2425 Nimmo Pky, Virginia Beach, VA 23456-9017. 8:30AM-5PM. **757-427-4181**, Fax: 757-426-5686. 💻 🖐

2nd General District Court *Misd., Civil Actions Under $15,000, Eviction, Small Claims* www.vbgov.com 2425 Nimmo Pky Judicial Center, Virginia Beach, VA 23456-9057. 8:30AM-4PM. **757-427-8531**, Fax: 757-426-5672. Civil phone: 757-427-4277, crim: 757-427-4707. Access records-✉ 💻 🖐

Waynesboro City

25th Circuit Court *Felony, Civil Actions Over $15,000, Probate* 250 S Wayne Ave, PO Box 910, Waynesboro, VA 22980. 8:30AM-5PM. **540-942-6616**, Fax: 540-942-6774. Access records-💻 🖐

25th General District Court - Waynesboro *Misdemeanor, Civil Actions Under $15,000, Eviction, Small Claims* 250 S Wayne PO Box 1028, Waynesboro, VA 22980. 8:30AM-4:30PM. **540-942-6636**, Fax: 540-942-6666. ✉**Fax**💻 🖐

Winchester City

26th Circuit Court *Felony, Civil Over $15,000, Probate* www.winfredclerk.com 5 N Kent St, Winchester, VA 22601. 9AM-5PM. **540-667-5770**, Fax: 540-667-6638. The Winchester Court and the Frederick County Court Clerks are housed in the same office, sharing microfilming and deed indexing systems. ✉ 💻 🖐

26th General District Court *Misd., Civil Actions Under $15,000, Eviction, Small Claims* 5 N Kent St PO Box 526, Winchester, VA 22604. 8AM-4PM. **540-722-7208**, Fax: 540-722-1063. 💻 🖐

Washington

State Court Administration (All Superior & District Courts): Court Administrator, Temple of Justice, PO Box 41174, Olympia, WA, 985041174; 360-357-2121, Fax: 360-357-2127. www.courts.wa.gov

Court Structure: District Courts retain civil records for ten years from date of final disposition, then the records are destroyed. District Courts retain criminal records forever.

Washington has a mandatory arbitration requirement for civil disputes for $35,000 or less. However, either party may request a trial in Superior Court if dissatisfied with the arbitrator's decision. The small claims court maximum was raised to $4,000 in 2002.

Online Access: Appellate, Superior, and District Court records are available online. The Superior Court Management Information System (SCOMIS), the Appellate Records System (ACORDS) and the District/Municipal Court Information System (DISCIS) are on the Judicial Information System's JIS-Link. Case records available through JIS-Link from 1977 include criminal, civil, domestic, probate, and judgments. JIS-Link is generally available 24-hours daily. Minimum browser requirement is Internet Explorer 5.5 or Netscape 6.0. There is a one-time installation fee of $100.00 per site, then $.065 charge per transaction. For information or a registration packet, contact: JISLink Coordinator, Administrative Office of the Courts, 1206 S Quince St., PO Box 41170, Olympia WA 98504-1170, 360-357-3365 or visit www.courts.wa.gov/jislink.

Supreme Court and Appellate opinions can be found at www.courts.wa.gov/appellate_trial_courts.

Additional Information: An SASE is required in most courts that respond to written search requests.

Adams County

Superior Court *Felony, Civil, Eviction, Probate* 210 W Broadway (PO Box 187), Ritzville, WA 99169-0187. 8:30AM-N, 1-4:30PM. **509-659-3257**, Fax: 509-659-0118. ☎**Fax**✉ 💻 🖐

Ritzville District Court *Misdemeanor, Civil Actions Under $50,000, Small Claims* 210 W Broadway, Ritzville, WA 99169. 8:30AM-4:30PM. **509-659-1002**, Fax: 509-659-0118. **Fax**✉ 💻 🖐

Othello District Court *Misdemeanor, Civil Actions Under $50,000, Small Claims* 165 N 1st, Othello, WA 99344. 8:30AM-4:30PM. **509-488-3935**, Fax: 509-488-3480. ☎**Fax**✉ 💻 🖐

Asotin County

Superior Court *Felony, Civil, Eviction, Probate* PO Box 159, Asotin, WA 99402-

---

Key: Symbols refer to criminal records access unless otherwise noted. phone-☎ mail-✉ fax-**Fax** in person-🖐 online-💻 email-**Email**

0159. 8AM-5PM. **509-243-2081**, Fax: 509-243-4978. ☎**Fax**✉🖥✋

District Court *Misdemeanor, Civil Actions Under $50,000, Small Claims* PO Box 429, Asotin, WA 99402-0429. 8AM-5PM. **509-243-2027**, Fax: 509-243-2091. **Fax**✉🖥✋

Benton County

Superior Court *Felony, Civil, Probate* 7320 W Quinault, Kennewick, WA 99336-7690. 8AM-N, 1-4PM. **509-735-8388**. ✉✋

District Court *Misdemeanor, Civil Actions Under $50,000, Small Claims* 7122 W Okanogan Pl, Box E, Kennewick, WA 99336. 8AM-N, 1-4PM. **509-735-8476; 786-5602**, Fax: 509-736-3069. ✉**Fax**✋

Chelan County

Superior Court *Felony, Civil, Eviction, Probate, Domestic* www.co.chelan.wa.us 350 Orondo (PO Box 3025), Wenatchee, WA 98807-3025. 9-5PM. **509-667-6380**, Fax: 509-667-6611. ☎**Fax**✉🖥✋

Chelan County District Court *Misdemeanor, Civil Under $50,000, Small Claims* www.co.chelan.wa.us/dc/dc1.htm PO Box 2182 350 Orondo, Courthouse 4th Fl, Wenatchee, WA 98807. 8:30AM-4:30PM. **509-667-6600**, Fax: 509-667-6456. **Fax**✉🖥✋

Clallam County

Superior Court *Felony, Civil, Eviction, Probate* www.clallam.net/scourt/ 223 E 4th St, #9, Port Angeles, WA 98362-3098. 8:30AM-4:30PM. **360-417-2508**. Probate: 306-417-2507. ☎✉🖥✋

District Court II *Misdemeanor, Civil Actions Under $50,000, Small Claims* www.clallam.net/Courts/html/court_district_2.htm 502 E Division St, Forks, WA 98331. 8:30AM-4:30PM. **360-374-6383**, Fax: 360-374-2100. Clallam County District Court II serves the West End of Clallam County including Forks, Neah Bay, Clallam Bay, Sekiu and LaPush. ✉🖥✋

District Court 1 *Misdemeanor, Civil Actions Under $50,000, Small Claims* www.clallam.net/Departments/html/dept_dc1.htm 223 E 4th St, Port Angeles, WA 98362. 8:30AM-4:30PM. **360-417-2560**, Fax: 360-417-2403. District 1 Court also

has jurisdiction on Civil Anti-Harassment Petitions and Orders. ✉**Fax**🖥✋

Clark County

Superior Court *Felony, Civil, Eviction, Probate* www.clark.wa.gov/courts/superior/index.html PO Box 5000 (1200 Franklin St.) Attention-County Clerk, Vancouver, WA 98666. 8AM-4:30PM. **360-397-2049 Court Admin.**, Fax: 360-397-6099. Civil phone: 360-397-2292, crim: 360-397-2292. ☎✉🖥✋**Email**

District Court *Misdemeanor, Civil Actions Under $50,000, Small Claims* www.clark.wa.gov/courts/district/index.html PO Box 9806 1200 Franklin St, Vancouver, WA 98666-8806. 8AM-5PM. Fax: 360-397-6044. Civil phone: 360-397-2424, crim: 360-397-2424. **Fax**✉🖥✋

Columbia County

Superior Court *Felony, Civil, Eviction, Probate* 341 E Main St, Dayton, WA 99328. 8:30AM-N, 1-4:30. **509-382-4321**, Fax: 509-382-4830. ☎**Fax**✉🖥✋

District Court *Misdemeanor, Civil Actions Under $50,000, Small Claims* 341 E Main St, Dayton, WA 99328-1361. 8:30AM-4:30PM. **509-382-4812**, Fax: 509-382-4830. Access records-✉🖥✋

Cowlitz County

Superior Court *Felony, Civil, Eviction, Probate* www.co.cowlitz.wa.us/clerk/ 312 SW 1st Ave Attn: County Clerk, Kelso, WA 98626-1724. 8:30-4:30PM. **360-577-3016**, Fax: 360-577-2323. Criminal phone: 360-577-3017. ☎**Fax**✉🖥✋

District Court *Misdemeanor, Civil Actions Under $50,000, Small Claims* www.co.cowlitz.wa.us 312 SW 1st Ave, Kelso, WA 98626-1724. 8:30AM-5PM. **360-577-3073**. ✉**Fax**🖥✋

Douglas County

Superior Court *Felony, Civil, Eviction, Probate* www.douglascountywa.net/ PO Box 516, Waterville, WA 98858-0516. 8AM-5PM. **509-745-9063**, Fax: 509-745-8027. Clerk is reached at 509-745-8529. ☎**Fax**✉🖥✋

District Court - East Wenatchee *Misdemeanor, Civil Under $50,000, Small Claims* www.douglascountywa.net/departments/district_court/index.html 110 3rd St NE, East Wenatchee, WA 98802. 8:30AM-4:30PM. **509-884-3536**, Fax:

509-884-5973. If record not found in this court, request forwarded to Bridgeport Branch (North) County District Court. **Fax**✉🖥✋

District Court - Bridgeport *Misd., Small Claims* www.douglascountywa.net/departments/district_court/ 1206 Columbia Ave (PO Box 730), Bridgeport, WA 98813-0730. 8:30AM-4:30PM. **509-686-2034**, Fax: 509-686-4671. This is a rural branch. If record not found in this court, request forwarded to East Wenatchee court (main court). **Fax**✉🖥✋

Ferry County

Superior Court *Felony, Civil, Probate* 350 E Delaware, #4, Republic, WA 99166. 8AM-4PM. **509-775-5245**. ☎✉🖥✋

District Court *Misdemeanor, Civil Actions Under $50,000, Small Claims* 350 E Delaware Ave, #6, Republic, WA 99166-9747. 8AM-4PM. **509-775-5244**, Fax: 509-775-5221. ✉**Fax**🖥✋

Franklin County

Superior Court *Felony, Civil, Eviction, Probate* www.co.franklin.wa.us 1016 N 4th Ave, Pasco, WA 99301. 8:30AM-5PM. **509-545-3525**, Fax: 509-545-2243. ✉🖥✋

District Court *Misdemeanor, Civil Actions Under $50,000, Small Claims* 1016 N 4th St, Pasco, WA 99301. 8:30AM-5PM. **509-545-3593**, Fax: 509-545-3588. ✉🖥✋**Fax**

Garfield County

Superior Court *Felony, Civil, Eviction, Probate* PO Box 915, Pomeroy, WA 99347-0915. 8:30AM-N, 1-5PM. **509-843-3731**, Fax: 509-843-1224. **Fax**✉🖥✋**Email**

District Court *Misdemeanor, Civil Actions Under $50,000, Small Claims* PO Box 817, Pomeroy, WA 99347-0817. 8:30AM-5PM. **509-843-1002**, Fax: 509-843-3815. Access records-✉🖥✋fax.

Grant County

Superior Court *Felony, Civil, Eviction, Probate* PO Box 37, Ephrata, WA 98823-0037. 8AM-4:30PM. **509-754-2011 X430**, Fax: 509-754-6568. ☎✉🖥✋

District Court *Misdemeanor, Civil Actions Under $50,000, Small Claims* www.co.grant.wa.us/ PO Box 37, Ephrata,

WA 98823-0037. 8AM-5PM. **509-754-2011 X628**, Fax: 509-754-6099. ✉️💻✋

Grays Harbor County

Superior Court *Felony, Civil, Eviction, Probate* 102 W Broadway, Rm 203, Montesano, WA 98563-3606. 8AM-5PM. **360-249-3842**, Fax: 360-249-6381. ☎**Fax**✉️💻✋

District Court No 2 *Civil Actions Under $50,000, Small Claims* www.co.grays-harbor.wa.us PO Box 142, Aberdeen, WA 98520-0035. 8AM-N, 1-5PM. **360-532-7061**, Fax: 360-532-7704. Access civil records-☎**Fax**✉️💻✋

District Court No 1 *Misdemeanor* www.co.grays-harbor.wa.us/info/judicial/ 102 W Broadway, Rm 202, Montesano, WA 98563. 8AM-N, 1-5PM. **360-249-3441**, Fax: 360-249-6382. All civil filings and hearings are held in the District Court Dept 2 in Aberdeen. ☎**Fax**✉️💻✋

Island County

Superior Court *Felony, Civil, Eviction, Probate* PO Box 5000, Coupeville, WA 98239-5000. 8AM-4:30PM. **360-679-7359**. ☎✉️💻✋

District Court *Misdemeanor, Civil Actions Under $50,000, Small Claims* 800 S 8th Ave, Oak Harbor, WA 98277. 8AM-4:30PM. **360-675-5988**, Fax: 360-675-8231. Records requests are done as time permits. Access records-**Fax**✉️💻✋

Jefferson County

Superior Court *Felony, Civil, Eviction, Probate* PO Box 1220, Port Townsend, WA 98368-0920. 9AM-5PM. **360-385-9125**. ☎✉️💻✋

District Court *Misdemeanor, Civil Actions Under $50,000, Small Claims* www.co.jefferson.wa.us PO Box 1220, Port Townsend, WA 98368-0920. 8AM-5PM. **360-385-9135**, Fax: 360-385-9367. ☎**Fax**✉️💻✋

King County

Superior Court *Felony, Civil, Eviction, Probate* www.metrokc.gov/kcscc 516 3rd Ave, E-609 Courthouse, Seattle, WA 98104-2386. 8:30AM-4:30AM. **206-296-9300, 800-325-6165 in state**. ✉️💻✋

District Court East Division - Redmond *Misd., Civil Actions Under $50,000, Small Claims* www.metrokc.gov/kcdc 8601 160th Ave NE, Redmond, WA 98052-

3548. 8:30AM-4:30PM. **206-296-3667; 800-325-6165 x59200; 206-205-9200**. Formerly known as the Northeast Division. Civil Filing Area: Redmond, Kirkland, Woodinville, Bothell, Duvall, Carnation, Juanita. ✉️💻✋

District Court Shoreline Division *Misd., Civil Under $50,000, Small Claims* www.metrokc.gov/kcdc 18050 Meridian Ave N, Shoreline, WA 98133-4642. 8:30AM-4:30PM. **800-325-6165 +59200; 206-205-9200**, Fax: 206-296-0594. Civil Filing Area: Shoreline, Kenmore, Lake Forest Park. ☎**Fax**✉️💻✋

District Court West Division - Seattle *Misd., Civil Actions Under $50,000, Small Claims* www.metrokc.gov/kcdc 516 3rd Ave, #E-327, Courthouse, Seattle, WA 98104-3273. 8:30AM-4:30PM. **800-325-6165 +59200; 206-205-9200**, Civil: 206-296-3550, crim: 206-296-3565 (crim. traf.). Formerly known as Seattle Div.. Civil Filing Area: Seattle. ✉️💻✋

District Court East Division - Issaquah *Misdemeanor, Civil Under $50,000, Small Claims* www.metrokc.gov/kcdc 5415 220th Ave SW, Issaquah, WA 98029-6839. 8:30AM-4:30PM. **206-205-9200**, Fax: 206-296-0591. Civil phone: 206-205-1747. Formerly known as the Issaquah Division. Civil Filing Area: Issaquah, Sammamish, High Point, Preston, Fall City, Snoqualmie, North Bend, Cedar Falls, Tokul, Alpental. ✉️💻✋

District Court East Division - Bellevue *Misd., Civil Actions Under $50,000, Small Claims* www.metrokc.gov/kcdc 585 112th Ave SE, Bellevue, WA 98004. 8:30AM-4:30PM. **206-296-3650; 800-325-6165 +59200; 206-205-9200**, Fax: 206-296-0589. Formerly known as the Bellevue Division. Civil Filing Area: Bellevue, Eastgate, Factoria, Mercer Island, Clyde Hill, Beaux Arts, Newcastle. ☎✉️💻✋

District Court South Division - Kent *Misd., Civil Actions Under $50,000, Small Claims* www.metrokc.gov/kcdc 1210 S Central, Kent, WA 98032-7426. 8:30AM-4:30PM. **206-205-9200; 800-325-6165 +59200; 206-205-9200**. Formerly known as Aukeen Division. Civil Filing Area: Enumclaw, Auburn, Black Diamond, Maple Valley, Covington, Algona, Pacific, Ravensdale, Hobart, Federal Way. ✉️💻✋

District Court South Division - Burien *Misd., Civil Actions Under $50,000, Small Claims* www.metrokc.gov/kcdc King

County District Court 601 SW 149th St, Burien, WA 98166-1935. 8:30AM-4:30PM. **800-325-6165 +59200; 206-205-9200**. Formerly located in Vashon. Formerly Southwest Division. All civil cases filed at South Division in Kent. ✉️💻✋

Kitsap County

Superior Court *Felony, Civil, Eviction, Probate* www.kitsapgov.com/sc/ 614 Division St, MS34, Port Orchard, WA 98366-4699. 8AM-4:30PM. **360-337-7164**, Fax: 360-337-4927. ✉️💻✋

District Court North *Misdemeanor, Civil Actions Under $50,000, Small Claims* 614 Division St, MS-25, Port Orchard, WA 98366. 8:30AM-12:15PM; 1:15-4:30PM. **360-337-7109**, Fax: 360-337-4865. The court physical address is 19050 Jensen Way NE, Poulsbo, WA. ✉️💻✋phone(1 only).

District Court *Misdemeanor, Civil Actions Under $50,000, Small Claims* www.kitsapgov.com/dc/ 614 Division St, MS 25, Port Orchard, WA 98366-4614. 8AM-12:15PM, 1:15-4:30. **360-337-7109**, Fax: 360-337-4865. ☎**Fax**✉️💻✋

Kittitas County

Superior Court *Felony, Misdemeanor, Civil, Eviction, Probate* 205 W 5th, Rm 210, Ellensburg, WA 98926. 9AM-N, 1-5PM. **509-962-7531**, Fax: 509-962-7667. ☎**Fax**✉️💻✋

District Court Upper Kittitas *Misdemeanor, Civil Actions Under $50,000, Small Claims* 700 E 1st, Cle Elum, WA 98922. 7AM-5PM. **509-674-5533**, Fax: 509-674-4209. ✉️💻✋

District Court Lower Kittitas *Misdemeanor, Civil Actions Under $50,000, Small Claims* 205 W 5th, Rm 180, Ellensburg, WA 98926. 9AM-5PM. **509-962-7511**. ✉️💻✋

Klickitat County

Superior Court *Felony, Civil, Eviction, Probate* Superior Court Clerk 205 S Columbus, MS CH-O3, Goldendale, WA 98620. 9AM-5PM. **509-773-5744**. ☎☎✉️💻✋

East District Court *Misd., Civil Actions Under $50,000, Small Claims* 205 S Columbus, MS-CH11, Goldendale, WA 98620-9290. 8AM-12, 1-5. **509-773-4670**, Fax: 509-773-4653. ☎✉️**Fax**💻✋

Key: Symbols refer to criminal records access unless otherwise noted. phone-☎ mail-✉️ fax-Fax in person-✋ online-💻 email-Email

West District Court *Misdemeanor, Civil Actions Under $50,000, Small Claims* PO Box 435, White Salmon, WA 98672-0435. 8AM-5PM. **509-493-1190**, Fax: 509-493-4469. ✉☝

Lewis County

Superior Court *Felony, Misd., Civil, Eviction, Probate* www.co.lewis.wa.us/clerk/clerk.htm 360 NW North St MS:CLK 01, Chehalis, WA 98532-1900. 8AM-5PM. **360-740-2704**, Fax: 360-748-1639. Civil phone: 360-740-2776, crim: 360-740-1395, Probate: 360-740-1177. ☎✉💻☝

District Court *Misdemeanor, Civil Actions Under $50,000, Small Claims* PO Box 336, Chehalis, WA 98532-0336. 8AM-5PM. **360-740-1203**, Fax: 360-740-2779. **Fax**✉💻☝

Lincoln County

Superior Court *Felony, Misd., Civil, Eviction, Probate* Box 68, Davenport, WA 99122-0396. 8AM-5PM. **509-725-1401**, Fax: 509-725-1150. ✉💻☎

District Court *Misdemeanor, Civil Actions Under $35,000, Small Claims* PO Box 329, Davenport, WA 99122-0329. 8AM-5PM. **509-725-2281**, Fax: 509-725-6481. Limited time for searches. ✉**Fax**💻☎

Mason County

Superior Court *Felony, Civil, Eviction, Probate* www.co.mason.wa.us/Clerk/ PO Box 340, Shelton, WA 98584. 8:30AM-5PM. **360-427-9670 X346**. ☎✉💻☝

District Court *Misdemeanor, Civil Actions Under $50,000, Small Claims* PO Box "O", Shelton, WA 98584-0090. 8:30AM-5PM. **360-427-9670 X339**, Fax: 360-427-7776. ✉☝

Okanogan County

Superior Court *Felony, Misdemeanor, Civil, Eviction, Probate* PO Box 72, Okanogan, WA 98840. 8:30AM-5:00PM. **509-422-7275**, Fax: 509-422-7277. ☎**Fax**✉💻☝

District Court *Misdemeanor, Civil Actions Under $50,000, Small Claims* PO Box 980, Okanogan, WA 98840-0980. 8AM-5PM. **509-422-7170**, Fax: 509-422-7174. ☎**Fax**✉☝

Pacific County

Superior Court *Felony, Civil, Eviction, Probate* PO Box 67, South Bend, WA 98586. 8:30AM-4:30PM. **360-875-9320**, Fax: 360-875-9321. ✉💻☝

District Court North *Misdemeanor, Civil Actions Under $50,000, Small Claims* Box 134, South Bend, WA 98586-0134. 9AM-5PM. **360-875-9354**, Fax: 360-875-9351. Phone,✉☝

District Court South *Misdemeanor, Civil Actions Under $50,000, Small Claims* PO Box 794, Ilwaco, WA 98624. 7:30AM-4:30PM. **360-642-9417**, Fax: 360-642-9416. **Fax**✉💻☝

Pend Oreille County

Superior Court *Felony, Civil, Eviction, Probate* 229 S Garden Ave (PO Box 5020), Newport, WA 99156-5020. 8AM-4:30PM. **509-447-2435**, Fax: 509-447-2734. ☎✉☝

District Court *Misdemeanor, Civil Actions Under $50,000, Small Claims* PO Box 5030 229 S Garden Ave, Newport, WA 99156-5030. 8AM-4:30PM. **509-447-4110**, Fax: 509-447-5724. Civil phone: 800-359-1506. **Fax**✉💻☝

Pierce County

Superior Court *Felony, Civil, Eviction, Probate* www.co.pierce.wa.us/abtus/ourorg/supct/abtussup.htm 930 Tacoma Ave S, Rm 110, Tacoma, WA 98402. 8:30AM-4:30PM. **253-798-7455**, Fax: 253-798-3428. ✉💻☝

District Court - Criminal *Misdemeanor* www.co.pierce.wa.us/pc/abtus/ourorg/distct/abtusd1.htm 930 Tacoma Ave S, Rm 601, Tacoma, WA 98402-2175. 8:30AM-4:30PM. **253-798-7457**, Fax: 253-798-6166. District Court #3 in Eatonville was closed 01/13/03, all misdemeanor were transferred to this court. ✉**Fax**☝

District Court - Civil Infractions Division *Civil Under $50,000, Small Claims, Traffic* www.co.pierce.wa.us/abtus/ourorg/distct/abtusd1.htm 1902 96th St S, Tacoma, WA 98444. 8:30AM-4:30PM M-Th. **253-798-7474**, Fax: 253-798-6310. District Court #3 in Eatonville, #2 in Gig Harbor, and #4 in Buckley were closed 01/13/03, all civil records were transferred to this court. Access civil records-☎✉💻☝

San Juan County

Superior Court *Felony, Misd., Civil, Eviction, Probate* www.co.san-juan.wa.us/ 350 Court St, #7, Friday Harbor, WA 98250. 8-5PM. **360-378-2163**, Fax: 360-378-3967. ☎**Fax**✉💻☝

District Court *Misdemeanor, Civil Actions Under $50,000, Small Claims* PO Box 127, Friday Harbor, WA 98250-0127. 8:30AM-4:30PM. **360-378-4017**, Fax: 360-378-4099. ✉☝ **Fax**

Skagit County

Superior Court *Felony, Civil, Eviction, Probate* 205 W Kincaid St, #103, Mount Vernon, WA 98273. 8:30AM-4:30PM. **360-336-9440**. Access records-✉💻☝

District Court *Misdemeanor, Civil Actions Under $50,000, Small Claims* PO Box 340, Mount Vernon, WA 98273-0340. 8:30AM-4:30PM. **360-336-9319**, Fax: 360-336-9318. **Fax**✉💻☝

Skamania County

Superior Court *Felony, Civil, Eviction, Probate* PO Box 790, Stevenson, WA 98648. 8:30AM-5PM. **509-427-9431**, Fax: 509-427-7386. ☎✉💻☝

District Court *Misdemeanor, Civil Actions Under $50,000, Small Claims* PO Box 790, Stevenson, WA 98648. 8:30AM-5PM. **509-427-9430**, Fax: 509-427-7386. ☎**Fax**✉💻☝

Snohomish County

www.co.snohomish.wa.us

Superior Court *Felony, Civil Actions, Eviction, Probate* 3000 Rockefeller MS 605, Everett, WA 98201. 8:30AM-5PM. **425-388-3466**. ☎✉💻☝

Evergreen Division District Court *Misdemeanor, Civil Actions Under $50,000, Small Claims* 14414 179th Ave SE PO Box 625, Monroe, WA 98272-0625. 8:30AM-5PM. **360-805-6776**, Fax: 360-805-6755. ✉☝

Cascade Division District Court *Misd., Civil Actions Under $50,000, Small Claims* 415 E Burke St, Arlington, WA 98223. 8:30AM-5PM. **360-435-7700**, Fax: 360-435-0873. ✉💻☝

Everett Division District Court *Misd., Civil Actions Under $50,000, Small Claims* 3000 Rockefeller Ave, MS 508, Everett, WA 98201. 8:30AM-5PM. **425-**

388-3331, Fax: 425-388-3565. Civil phone: 425-388-3595. **Fax** ⬚ 🖥 ✋

South Div. District Court *Misd., Civil Under $50,000, Small Claims* 20520 68th Ave W, Lynnwood, WA 98036-7406. 8:30AM-4:30PM. **425-774-8803**, Fax: 425-744-6820. Access records-⬚ 🖥 ✋

Spokane County

Superior Court *Felony, Civil, Eviction, Probate* www.spokanecounty.org/clerk/ 1116 W Broadway, Spokane, WA 99260. 8:30-5PM. **509-477-2211**. ☎ ⬚ 🖥 ✋

District Court *Misdemeanor, Civil Actions Under $50,000, Small Claims* www.spokanecounty.org/districtcourt 1100 Mallon W, Spokane, WA 99260. 8:30-5PM. **509-477-4770**. ☎ ⬚ 🖥 ✋

Stevens County

Superior Court *Felony, Civil, Eviction, Probate* 215 S Oak, Rm 206, Colville, WA 99114. 8AM-N, 1-4:30PM. **509-684-7575**. ⬚ 🖥 ✋

District Court *Misdemeanor, Civil Actions Under $50,000, Small Claims* www.co.stevens.wa.us/distcourt/departments .htm 215 S Oak, Rm 213, Colville, WA 99114. 8AM-N, 1-4:30PM. **509-684-5249**, Fax: 509-684-7571. ⬚ 🖥 ✋

Thurston County

Superior Court *Felony, Misd., Civil, Eviction, Probate* www.co.thurston.wa.u s/clerk Thurston County Clerk 2000 Lakeridge Dr SW, Bldg 2, Olympia, WA 98502. 8AM-5PM. **360-786-5430**. ☎ ⬚ ✋ e⬚

District Court *Misd., Civil Actions Under $50,000, Small Claims* www.co.thurst on.wa.us/distcrt 2000 Lakeridge Dr SW, Bldg 3, Olympia, WA 98502. 8:30AM-4PM. **360-786-5450**, Fax: 360-754-3359. Daily court calendars are at www.co.thurston.wa.us/distcrt/courtcalen dars.htm. ☎ Fax ⬚ 🖥 ✋

Wahkiakum County

Superior Court *Felony, Misdemeanor, Civil, Eviction, Probate* PO Box 116, Cathlamet, WA 98612. 8AM-4PM. **360-795-3558**, Fax: 360-795-8813. ⬚ 🖥 ✋

District Court *Misdemeanor, Civil Actions Under $50,000, Small Claims* PO Box 144, Cathlamet, WA 98612. 8AM-4PM. **360-795-3461**, Fax: 360-795-6506. ☎ Fax ⬚ 🖥 ✋

Walla Walla County

Superior Court *Felony, Civil, Eviction, Probate* PO Box 836, Walla Walla, WA 99362. 9AM-4PM. **509-527-3221**, Fax: 509-527-3214. ☎ ⬚ 🖥 ✋

District Court *Misdemeanor, Civil Actions Under $50,000, Small Claims* 317 W Rose St, Walla Walla, WA 99362. 9AM-4PM. **509-527-3236**. ⬚ 🖥 ✋

Whatcom County

Superior Court *Felony, Civil, Eviction, Probate* PO Box 1144, Bellingham, WA 98227. 8:30-4:30PM. **360-676-6777**, x50014 for criminal; x50018 for civil. Fax: 360-676-6693. ☎ Fax ⬚ 🖥 ✋

District Court *Misdemeanor, Civil Actions Under $50,000, Small Claims* www.co.whatcom.wa.us 311 Grand Ave, #401, Bellingham, WA 98225. 8AM-4:30PM. **360-676-6770**, Fax: 360-738-2452. ⬚ 🖥 ✋

Whitman County

Superior Court *Felony, Civil, Eviction, Probate* Whitman County Clerk PO Box 390, Colfax, WA 99111. 9AM-5PM. **509-397-6240**, Fax: 509-397-3546. ☎ Fax ⬚ 🖥 ✋

District Court *Misdemeanor, Civil Actions Under $50,000, Small Claims* 325 SE Paradise St, Pullman, WA 99163. 8AM-5PM. **509-332-2065**, Fax: 509-338-3318. Fax ⬚ 🖥 ✋

District Court *Misdemeanor, Civil Actions Under $50,000, Small Claims* 400 N Main St PO Box 230, Colfax, WA 99111. 8AM-5PM; Public Hours: 8:30AM-4:30PM. **509-397-6260**, Fax: 509-397-5584. ☎ Fax ⬚ 🖥 ✋

Yakima County

Superior Court *Felony, Civil, Probate* www.pan.co.yakima.wa.us/clerk 128 N 2nd St, Rm 314, Yakima, WA 98901. 8:30-4:30PM. **509-574-1430**. ☎ ⬚ ✋

District Court *Misdemeanor, Civil Actions Under $50,000, Small Claims* www.co.yakima.wa.us/courts 128 N 2nd St, Rm 217, Yakima, WA 98901-2631. 8:30AM-4:30PM. **509-574-1800**, Fax: 509-574-1831. ☎ Fax ⬚ 🖥 ✋

West Virginia

State Court Administration: Administrative Office, Supreme Court of Appeals, 1900 Kanawha Blvd, 1 E 100 State Capitol, Charleston, WV, 25305; 304-558-0145, Fax: 304-558-1212. www.state.wv.us/wvsca

Court Structure: The 55 Circuit Courts are the courts of general jurisdiction. Probate is handled by the Circuit Court. Records are held at the County Commissioner's Office.

Family Courts were created by constitutional amendment and were formed as of 01/01/02. Family Courts hear cases involving such matters as divorce, annulment, separate maintenance, family support, paternity, child custody, and visitation. Family court judges also conduct final hearings in domestic violence cases.

Online Access: The state is working towards a statewide system that will allow access to public records, but one is not yet available. Search opinions from the Supreme Court at http://www.state.wv.us/wvsca/opinions.htm. There is a commercial system available only to law firms and government agencies that gives access to case information from six Circuit Courts and all of the Magistrate Courts. Visit http://www.swcg-inc.com/swcg/index.html for details.

Additional Information: There is a statewide requirement that search turnaround times not exceed five business days. However, most courts do far better than that limit. Release of public information is governed by WV Code Sec.29B-1-1 et seq.

Barbour County

Circuit Court *Felony, Civil Actions Over $5,000, Probate* 8 N Main St, Philippi, WV 26416. 8:30AM-4:30PM. **304-457-3454**, Fax: 304-457-2790. Probate is handled by the County Clerk at this address. ☎ ✉ ✋

Magistrate Court *Misdemeanor, Civil Actions Under $5,000, Eviction, Small Claims* PO Box 541, Philippi, WV 26416. 8:30AM-4:30PM. **304-457-3676**, Fax: 304-457-4999. ✋ ✉

Berkeley County

Circuit Court *Felony, Civil Actions Over $5,000, Probate* 110 W King St, Martinsburg, WV 25401-3210. 9AM-5PM. **304-264-1918**, Probate: 304-264-1940. Probate is handled by Fiduciary Records Clerk, 100 W King St, Rm 2, Martinsburg, WV 25401. ✋

Magistrate Court *Misdemeanor, Civil Actions Under $5,000, Eviction, Small Claims* 120 W John St, Martinsburg, WV 25401. 9AM-4PM. **304-264-1956**, Fax: 304-263-9154. ✋

Boone County

Circuit Court *Felony, Civil Actions Over $5,000, Probate* 200 State St, Madison, WV 25130. 8AM-4PM. **304-369-3925**, Fax: 304-369-7326 Probate: 304-369-7337. Probate is handled by County Clerk, 200 State St, Madison, WV 25130. ☎ Fax ✉ ✋

Magistrate Court *Misdemeanor, Civil Actions Under $5,000, Eviction, Small Claims* 200 State St., Madison, WV 25130. 8AM-4PM. **304-369-7364**, Fax: 304-369-1932. ✋

Braxton County

Circuit Court *Felony, Civil Actions Over $5,000, Probate* 300 Main St, Sutton, WV 26601. 8AM-4PM. **304-765-2837**, Fax: 304-765-2947 Probate: 304-765-2833. ☎ Fax ✉ ✋

Magistrate Court *Misdemeanor, Civil Actions Under $5,000, Eviction, Small Claims* 307 Main St, Sutton, WV 26601. 8:30AM-4:30PM. **304-765-5678**, Fax: 304-765-3756. ✋

Brooke County

Circuit Court *Felony, Civil Actions Over $5,000, Probate* Brooke County Courthouse PO Box 474, Wellsburg, WV 26070. 9AM-5PM. **304-737-3662**, Fax: 304-737-0352 Probate: 304-737-3661. Probate is handled by County Clerk, 632 Main St, Courthouse, Wellsburg, WV 26070. ✉ ✋

Magistrate Court *Misdemeanor, Civil Actions Under $5,000, Eviction, Small Claims* 632 Main St, Wellsburg, WV 26070. 9AM-4PM. **304-737-1321**, Fax: 304-737-1509. ✋

Cabell County

Circuit Court *Felony, Civil Actions Over $5,000, Probate* PO Box 0545, Huntington, WV 25710-0545. 8:30AM-4:30PM. **304-526-8622**, Fax: 304-526-8699. ✋ ✉

Magistrate Court *Misdemeanor, Civil Actions Under $5,000, Eviction, Small Claims* 750 5th Ave, Basement Rm B 113 Courthouse, Huntington, WV 25701. 8:30AM-4:30PM. **304-526-8642**, Fax: 304-526-8646. ✋

Calhoun County

Circuit Court *Felony, Civil Actions Over $5,000, Probate* PO Box 266, Grantsville, WV 26147. 8:30AM-4PM. **304-354-6910**, Fax: 304-354-6910. ☎ Fax ✉ ✋

Magistrate Court *Misdemeanor, Civil Actions Under $5,000, Eviction, Small Claims* PO Box 186, Grantsville, WV 26147. 8:30AM-12:00, 1-4PM. **304-354-6698**, Fax: 304-354-6698. Civil phone: 304-354-6844. Access records- ✋ ✉ ☎

Clay County

Circuit Court *Felony, Civil Actions Over $5,000, Probate* PO Box 129, Clay, WV 25043. 8AM-4PM. **304-587-4256**, Fax: 304-587-4346. ☎ Fax ✉ ✋

Magistrate Court *Misdemeanor, Civil Actions Under $5,000, Eviction, Small Claims* PO Box 393, Clay, WV 25043. 8:30AM-4:30PM. **304-587-2131**, Fax: 304-587-2727. ✋ ✉

Doddridge County

Circuit Court *Felony, Civil Actions Over $5,000, Probate* 118 E. Court St, West

Union, WV 26456. 8:30AM-4PM. **304-873-2331**. Access records- ☎ ✉ Fax ✋

Magistrate Court *Misdemeanor, Civil Actions Under $5,000, Eviction, Small Claims* PO Box 207, West Union, WV 26456. 8AM-4PM. **304-873-2694**, Fax: 304-873-2643. Access records- ✋ ✉ Fax

Fayette County

Circuit Court *Felony, Civil Actions Over $5,000, Probate* 100 Court St, Fayetteville, WV 25840. 8AM-4PM. Civil: 304-574-4249, crim: 304-574-4303/4250, Probate: 304-574-4226. Probate is handled by County Clerk, PO Box 569, Fayetteville, WV 25840. ✉ ✋

Magistrate Court *Misdemeanor, Civil Actions Under $5,000, Eviction, Small Claims* 100 Church St, Fayetteville, WV 25840. 8AM-4PM. **304-574-4279**, Fax: 304-574-2458. ✋

Gilmer County

Circuit Court *Felony, Civil Actions Over $5,000, Probate* Gilmer County Courthouse 10 Howard St, Glenville, WV 26351. 8AM-4PM. **304-462-7241**, Fax: 304-462-7038. ☎ ✉ Fax ✋

Magistrate Court *Misdemeanor, Civil Actions Under $5,000, Eviction, Small Claims* Courthouse Annex, Glenville, WV 26351. 8:30AM-4PM. **304-462-7812**, Fax: 304-462-8582. Access records- ✋ ✉

Grant County

Circuit Court *Felony, Civil Actions Over $5,000, Probate* 5 Highland Ave, Petersburg, WV 26847. 8:30AM-4:30PM. **304-257-4545**, Fax: 304-257-2593 (Attn: Circuit Court). Access records- Fax ✉ ✋

Magistrate Court *Misdemeanor, Civil Under $5,000, Eviction, Small Claims* 5 Highland Ave (PO Box 216), Petersburg, WV 26847. 8:30AM-4:30PM. **304-257-4637/1289**, Fax 304-257-9501. Fax ✉ ✋

Greenbrier County

Circuit Court *Felony, Civil Actions Over $5,000, Probate* PO Drawer 751, Lewisburg, WV 24901. 8:30AM-4:30PM. **304-647-6626**, Fax: 304-647-6666. ✉ ✋

Key: Symbols refer to criminal records access unless otherwise noted. phone- ☎ mail- ✉ fax- Fax in person- ✋ online- 💻 email- Email

Magistrate Court *Misdemeanor, Civil Actions Under $5,000, Eviction, Small Claims* 200 N Court St, Lewisburg, WV 24901. 8:30AM-4:30PM. **304-647-6632**, Fax: 304-647-6668. ✉✍

Hampshire County

Circuit Court *Felony, Civil Actions Over $5,000, Probate* PO Box 343, Romney, WV 26757. 9AM-4PM M-Th, 9AM-8PM Friday. **304-822-5022**, Probate: 304-822-5112. Probate handled by County Clerk, PO Box 806, Romney, WV 26757. **Fax**✉✍

Magistrate Court *Misdemeanor, Civil Actions Under $5,000, Eviction, Small Claims* 239 W Birch Ln, PO Box 881, Romney, WV 26757. 8:00AM-4PM. **304-822-4311**, Fax: 304-822-3981. ✉**Fax**✍

Hancock County

Circuit Court *Felony, Civil Actions Over $5,000, Probate* PO Box 428, New Cumberland, WV 26047. 8:30AM-4:30PM. **304-564-3311**, Fax: 304-564-5014. Probate address is PO Box 367. **Fax**✉✍🖥

Magistrate Court *Misdemeanor, Civil Actions Under $5,000, Eviction, Small Claims* 106 Court St, New Cumberland, WV 26047. 8:30-4:30PM. **304-564-3355**, Fax: 304-564-3852. ✍✉

Hardy County

Circuit Court *Felony, Civil Actions Over $5,000, Probate* 204 Washington St, Rm 237, Moorefield, WV 26836. 9AM-4PM. **304-538-7869**, Fax: 304-538-6197. ✍

Magistrate Court *Misdemeanor, Civil Actions Under $5,000, Eviction, Small Claims* 204 Washington St, Moorefield, WV 26836. 9AM-4PM. **304-538-6836**, Fax: 304-538-2072. **Fax**✉✍

Harrison County

Circuit Court *Felony, Civil Actions Over $5,000, Probate* 301 W. Main, #301, Clarksburg, WV 26301-2967. 8:30AM-4:30PM. **304-624-8640**, Fax: 304-624-8710 Probate: 304-624-8673. Probate is handled by County Clerk, 301 W Main St, Courthouse, Clarksburg, WV 26301. ✍

Magistrate Court *Misdemeanor, Civil Actions Under $5,000, Eviction, Small Claims* 306 Washington Ave, Rm 222, Clarksburg, WV 26301. 8AM-4PM. **304-624-8645**, Fax: 304-624-8740. ✍✉

Jackson County

Circuit Court *Felony, Civil Actions Over $5,000, Probate* PO Box 427, Ripley, WV 25271. 9AM-4PM M-F, 9AM-N Sat. **304-373-2214**, Fax: 304-372-6237. ☎✉✍

Magistrate Court *Misdemeanor, Civil Under $5,000, Eviction, Small Claims* PO Box 368, Ripley, WV 25271. 9AM-4PM. **304-373-2313**, Fax: 304-372-7155. ✍

Jefferson County

Circuit Court *Felony, Civil Actions Over $5,000* PO Box 1234, Charles Town, WV 25414. 9AM-5PM. **304-728-3231**, Fax: 304-728-3398. ✍

Magistrate Court *Misdemeanor, Civil Actions Under $5,000, Eviction, Small Claims* PO Box 607, Charles Town, WV 25414. 7:30AM-4:30PM. **304-728-3233**, Fax: 304-728-3235. ✍

Kanawha County

Circuit Court *Felony, Civil Actions Over $5,000, Probate* PO Box 2351, Charleston, WV 25328. 8AM-5PM. **304-357-0440**, Fax: 304-357-0473 Probate: 304-357-0130. Probate is handled by County Clerk, 409 Virginia St E, Charleston, WV 25301. ✍🖥

Magistrate Court *Misdemeanor, Civil Actions Under $5,000, Eviction, Small Claims* 111 Court St, Charleston, WV 25333. 8:30AM-5PM. **304-357-0400**, Fax: 304-357-0205. ✍✉ **Fax**

Lewis County

Circuit Court *Felony, Civil Actions Over $5,000, Probate* PO Box 69, Weston, WV 26452. 8:30AM-4:30PM. **304-269-8210**, Fax: 304-269-8249. ☎**Fax**✉✍

Magistrate Court *Misdemeanor, Civil Actions Under $5,000, Eviction, Small Claims* 111 Court St, PO Box 260, Weston, WV 26452. 8:30AM-N, 1-4:30PM. **304-269-8230**, Fax: 304-269-8239. ✍✉fax.

Lincoln County

Circuit Court *Felony, Civil Actions Over $5,000, Probate* PO Box 338, Hamlin, WV 25523. 9AM-4:30PM. **304-824-7887 x239**, Fax: 304-824-7909 Probate: x233. Probate mailing address is PO Box 497; direct probate requests to the county clerk at x233. ☎✉✍

Magistrate Court *Misdemeanor, Civil Actions Under $5,000, Eviction, Small Claims* PO Box 573, Hamlin, WV 25523. 9AM-4PM. **304-824-5001 x235**, Fax: 304-824-5280. Searches performed by court only on second and fourth Thursday of month. ✍✉

Logan County

Circuit Court *Felony, Civil Actions Over $5,000, Probate* Logan County Courthouse, Rm 311, Logan, WV 25601. 8:30AM-4:30PM. **304-792-8550**, Fax: 304-792-8555. Access records-✉**Fax**✍

Logan Magistrate Court *Misdemeanor, Civil Actions Under $5,000, Eviction, Small Claims* Logan County Courthouse 300 Stratton St, Logan, WV 25601. 8:30AM-N; 1-4:30PM. **304-792-8651**, Fax: 304-752-0790. ✍✉

McDowell County

Circuit Court *Felony, Civil Actions Over $5,000, Probate* PO Box 400, Welch, WV 24801. 9AM-5PM. **304-436-8535**, Probate: 304-436-8544. Probate is handled by County Clerk, 90 Wyoming St, #109, Welch, WV 24801. ✉✍

Magistrate Court *Misdemeanor, Civil Actions Under $5,000, Eviction, Small Claims* PO Box 447, Welch, WV 24801. 9AM-5PM. **304-436-8588**, Fax: 304-436-8575. ✉**Fax**✍

Marion County

Circuit Court *Felony, Civil Actions Over $3,000* PO Box 1269, Fairmont, WV 26554. 8:30AM-4:30PM. **304-367-5360**, Fax: 304-367-5374. ✍✉**Fax**☎

Magistrate Court *Misdemeanor, Civil Actions Under $5,000, Eviction, Small Claims* 200 Jackson St, Fairmont, WV 26554. 8:30AM-4:30PM M-T-W-F; 8:30AM-7PM Th. **304-367-5330**, Fax: 304-367-5336. No record checks performed between 11:30AM and 1:30PM. ✍✉

Marshall County

Circuit Court *Felony, Civil Actions Over $5,000* Marshall County Courthouse, 7th St, Moundsville, WV 26041. 8:30AM-4:30PM M-Th; 8:30AM-5:30PM F. **304-845-2130**, Fax: 304-845-3948. **Fax**✉✍

Mason County

Circuit Court *Felony, Civil Actions Over $5,000, Probate* Mason County Courthouse, Point Pleasant, WV 25550.

8:30AM-4:30PM. **304-675-4400**, Fax: 304-675-7419. ✋

Magistrate Court *Misdemeanor, Civil Actions Under $5,000, Eviction, Small Claims* 200 6th St, Point Pleasant, WV 25550. 8:30AM-4:30PM. **304-675-6840**, Fax: 304-675-5949. ✋✉

Mercer County

Circuit Court *Felony, Civil Actions Over $5,000* 1501 W Main St, Princeton, WV 24740. 8:30AM-4:30PM. **304-487-8323**, Fax: 304-425-8351. Criminal phone: 304-487-8410 / 304-487-8372, Probate: 304-487-8336. Probate court is a separate office at the same address. ☎Fax✉✋

Magistrate Court *Misdemeanor, Civil Actions Under $5,000, Eviction, Small Claims* 1519 N Walker St, Princeton, WV 24740. 8:30AM-4:30PM. **304-431-7115**. ✋✉fax.

Mineral County

Circuit Court *Felony, Civil Actions Over $5,000, Probate* 150 Armstrong St, Keyser, WV 26726. 8:30AM-5PM. **304-788-1562**, Fax: 304-788-4109. Probate court is a separate office at the same address, 2nd Fl, 304-788-3924. **Fax**✉✋💻

Magistrate Court *Misdemeanor, Civil Actions Under $5,000, Eviction, Small Claims* 105 West St, Keyser, WV 26726. 8:30AM-4:30PM. **304-788-2625**, Fax: 304-788-9835. ✉✋

Mingo County

Circuit Court *Felony, Civil Actions Over $5,000, Probate* PO Box 435, Williamson, WV 25661. 8:30AM-4:30PM. **304-235-0320**, Fax: 304-235-0320 Probate: 304-235-0330. Probate is handled by County Clerk, 75 E 2nd Ave, Williamson, WV 25661. ✉✋

Magistrate Court *Misdemeanor, Civil Actions Under $5,000, Eviction, Small Claims* PO Box 986, Williamson, WV 25661. 8:30AM-4:30PM. **304-235-2445**, Fax: 304-235-3179. ☎✉**Fax**✋

Monongalia County

Circuit Court *Felony, Civil Actions Over $5,000, Probate* County Courthouse, 243 High St, Rm 110, Morgantown, WV 26505. 9AM-7PM M; 9AM-5PM T-F. **304-291-7240**, Fax: 304-291-7273 Probate: 304-291-7236. Estates/Probate is

handled by County Clerk, 243 High St, Rm 123, Morgantown, WV 26505. ✉✋

Magistrate Court *Misdemeanor, Civil Actions Under $5,000, Eviction, Small Claims* 265 Spruce St, Morgantown, WV 26505. 8AM-7PM. **304-291-7296**, Fax: 304-284-7313. ✉**Fax**✋

Monroe County

Circuit Court *Felony, Civil Actions Over $5,000, Probate* PO Box 350, Union, WV 24983-0350. 8AM-4PM. **304-772-3017**, Fax: 304-772-4497 Probate: 304-772-3096. ☎✉✋

Magistrate Court *Misdemeanor, Civil Actions Under $5,000, Eviction, Small Claims* PO Box 4, Union, WV 24983. 8:30AM-4:30PM. **304-772-3321/3176**, Fax: 304-772-4357. ✉✋fax.

Morgan County

Circuit Court *Felony, Civil Actions Over $5,000, Probate* 77 Fairfax St, #2F, Berkeley Springs, WV 25411-1501. 9AM-5PM Monday - Friday. **304-258-8554**, Fax: 304-258-7319. Probate is located at the same address in #1A; telephone is 304-258-8547 ✋

Magistrate Court *Misdemeanor, Civil Actions Under $5,000, Eviction, Small Claims* 111 Fairfax St, Berkeley Springs, WV 25411. 9AM-4:30PM. **304-258-8631**, Fax: 304-258-8639. ✋

Nicholas County

Circuit Court *Felony, Civil Actions Over $5,000, Probate* 700 Main St, Summersville, WV 26651. 8:30AM-4:30PM. **304-872-7810**, Probate: 304-872-7820. Probate is handled by County Clerk, 700 Main St, #2, Summersville, WV 26651. ✉✋

Magistrate Court *Misdemeanor, Civil Actions Under $5,000, Eviction, Small Claims* 511 Church St, #206, 2nd Fl, Summersville, WV 26651. 8:30AM-4:30PM. **304-872-7829**, Fax: 304-872-7888. ✉✋

Ohio County

Circuit Court *Felony, Civil Actions Over $5,000, Probate* 1500 Chapline St City & County Bldg, Rm 403, Wheeling, WV 26003. 8:30AM-5PM. **304-234-3613**, Fax: 304-232-0550. **Fax**✉✋💻

Magistrate Court *Misdemeanor, Civil Actions Under $5,000, Eviction, Small*

Claims Courthouse Annex, 26 15th St, Wheeling, WV 26003. 8:30AM-4:30PM. **304-234-3709**, Fax: 304-234-3898. ✋**Fax**✉

Pendleton County

Circuit Court *Felony, Civil Actions Over $5,000, Probate* PO Box 846, Franklin, WV 26807. 8:30AM-4PM. **304-358-7067**, Fax: 304-358-2152. ☎**Fax**✉✋

Magistrate Court *Misdemeanor, Civil Actions Under $5,000, Eviction, Small Claims* PO Box 637, Franklin, WV 26807. 8:30AM-4PM. **304-358-2343**, Fax: 304-358-3870. ✋✉

Pleasants County

Circuit Court *Felony, Civil Actions Over $5,000, Probate* 301 Court Ln, Rm 201, St. Mary's, WV 26170. 8:30AM-4:30PM. **304-684-3513**, Fax: 304-684-3514 Probate: 304-684-3542. Probate is handled by County Clerk, 301 Court Lane, Rm 101, St Mary's, WV 26170. ✋

Magistrate Court *Misdemeanor, Civil Actions Under $5,000, Eviction, Small Claims* 301 Court Ln, Rm B-6, St Mary's, WV 26170. 8:30AM-4:30PM. **304-684-7197**, Fax: 304-684-3882. ☎✉**Fax**✋

Pocahontas County

Circuit Court *Felony, Civil Actions Over $5,000, Probate* 900-D 10th Ave, Marlinton, WV 24954. 9AM-4:30PM. **304-799-4604**, Fax: 304-799-6809. ☎☎✉✋

Magistrate Court *Misdemeanor, Civil Actions Under $5,000, Eviction, Small Claims* 900 10th Ave, Marlinton, WV 24954. 9AM-4:30PM. **304-799-6603**, Fax: 304-799-6331. ✋

Preston County

Circuit Court *Felony, Misdemeanor, Civil Actions Over $5,000, Probate* 101 W Main St, Rm 301, Kingwood, WV 26537. 9AM-5PM M-Th, 9AM-7PM Fri. **304-329-0047**, Fax: 304-329-1417 Probate: 304-329-0070. Probate is handled by County Clerk, 101 W Main St, Rm 201, Kingwood, WV 26537. ☎**Fax**✉✋

Magistrate Court *Misdemeanor, Civil Actions Over $5,000, Eviction, Small Claims* 328 Tunnelton St, Kingwood, WV 26537. 8:30AM-4:30PM. **304-329-2764**, Fax: 304-329-0855. ✋✉

Putnam County

Circuit Court *Felony, Civil Actions Over $5,000, Probate* Putnam County Judicial Bldg 3389 Winfield Rd, Winfield, WV 25213. 8:30AM-4:30PM M F. **304-586-0203**, Fax: 304-586-0221. ✋🖥

Magistrate Court *Misdemeanor, Civil Actions Under $5,000, Eviction, Small Claims* 3389 Winfield Rd, Winfield, WV 25213. 8:30AM-4:30PM. **304-586-0234**, Fax: 304-586-0234. ✋✉

Raleigh County

Circuit Court *Felony, Civil Actions Over $5,000, Probate* 215 Main St, Beckley, WV 25801. 8:30AM-4:30PM. **304-255-9135**, Fax: 304-255-9353 Probate: 304-255-9123. Probate is handled by County Clerk, 215 Main St, Courthouse, Beckley, WV 25801. ☎✉✋

Magistrate Court *Misdemeanor, Civil Actions Under $5,000, Eviction, Small Claims* 115 W Prince St, #A, Beckley, WV 25801. 8AM-4PM. **304-255-9197**, Fax: 304-255-9354. ✋

Randolph County

Circuit Court *Felony, Civil Actions Over $5,000, Probate* Courthouse 2 Randolph Ave, Elkins, WV 26241. 8AM-4:30PM. **304-636-2765**, Fax: 304-637-3700. ✋

Magistrate Court *Misdemeanor, Civil Actions Under $5,000, Eviction, Small Claims* #11 Randolph Ave, Elkins, WV 26241. 8AM-4:30PM. **304-636-5885**, Fax: 304-636-2510. ✋✉

Ritchie County

Circuit Court *Felony, Civil Actions Over $5,000, Probate* 115 E. Main St, Harrisville, WV 26362. 8AM-4PM. **304-643-2164 x229**, Probate: 304-643-2164 x229. Probate office is located at the same address, but in county clerks office. ☎✉✋

Magistrate Court *Misdemeanor, Civil Actions Under $5,000, Eviction, Small Claims* 319 E. Main St, Harrisville, WV 26362. 8AM-4PM. **304-643-4409**, Fax: 304-643-2098. ✋✉

Roane County

Circuit Court *Felony, Civil Actions Over $5,000, Probate* PO Box 122, Spencer, WV 25276. 8:30AM-N, 1-4PM M-F; 9AM-N Sat. **304-927-2750**, Fax: 304-927-2164. ☎Fax✉✋

Magistrate Court *Misdemeanor, Civil Actions Under $5,000, Eviction, Small Claims* 201 Main St, Spencer, WV 25276. 9AM-4PM. **304-927-4750**, Fax: 304-927-2754. Record requests can be directed to 304-746-2180. ✋

Summers County

Circuit Court *Felony, Civil Actions Over $5,000, Probate* PO Box 1058, Hinton, WV 25951. 8:30AM-4:30PM. **304-466-7103**, Fax: 304-466-7124 (Attn:Circuit Court). ☎Fax✉✋

Magistrate Court *Misdemeanor, Civil Actions Under $5,000, Eviction, Small Claims* PO Box 1059, Hinton, WV 25951. 9:00AM-4:00PM. **304-466-7108**, Fax: 304-466-4912. ☎Fax✉✋

Taylor County

Circuit Court *Felony, Civil Actions Over $5,000, Probate* 214 W Main St, Rm 104, Grafton, WV 26354. 8:30AM-N, 1-4:30PM. **304-265-2480**. ☎✉✋

Magistrate Court *Misdemeanor, Civil Actions Under $5,000, Eviction, Small Claims* 214 W Main St, Grafton, WV 26354. 8:30AM-4:30PM. **304-265-1322**, Fax: 304-265-5708. Access records-✋✉

Tucker County

Circuit Court *Felony, Civil Actions Over $5,000* 215 1st St, #2, Parsons, WV 26287. 8AM-4PM. **304-478-2606**, Fax: 304-478-4464. ✉✋

Magistrate Court *Misd., Civil Under $5000, eviction, small claims* 201 Walnut St, Parsons, WV 26287. 8:30-4:00. **304-478-2665**, Fax: 304-478-4836. ✋

Tyler County

Circuit Court *Felony, Civil Actions Over $5,000* PO Box 8, Middlebourne, WV 26149. 8AM-4PM. **304-758-4811**, Fax: 304-758-4008. ☎✉Fax✋

Magistrate Court *Misdemeanor, Civil Actions Under $5,000, Eviction, Small Claims* PO Box 127, Middlebourne, WV 26149. 9AM-4PM. **304-758-2137**. ✋✉

Upshur County

Circuit Court *Felony, Civil Actions Over $5,000, Probate* 38 W. Main St, Rm 304, Buckhannon, WV 26201. 8AM-4:30PM. **304-472-2370**, Fax: 304-472-2168 Probate: 304-472-1068. Probate is handled by County Clerk, 40 W Main, Courthouse, Rm 101, Buckhannon, WV 26201. Fax✉✋

Magistrate Court *Misdemeanor, Civil Actions Under $5,000, Eviction, Small Claims* 38 W Main, Rm 204 Courthouse Annex, Buckhannon, WV 26201. 8AM-4PM. **304-472-2053**. ✉✋

Wayne County

Circuit Court *Felony, Civil Actions Over $5,000, Probate* PO Box 38, Wayne, WV 25570. 8AM-4PM M,T,W,F; 8AM-8PM Th. **304-272-6360**, Probate: 304-272-4372. Probate is handled by County Clerk, PO Box 248, Wayne, WV 25570. ✋

Magistrate Court *Felony, Misd., Civil Under $5,000, Eviction, Small Claims* PO Box 667, Wayne, WV 25570. 8AM-4PM. **304-272-5648/6388**. ☎Fax✉✋

Webster County

Circuit Court *Felony, Civil Actions Over $5,000, Probate* 2 Court Square, Rm G-4, Webster Springs, WV 26288. 8:30AM-4PM. **304-847-2421**, Fax: 304-847-2062. ☎Fax✉✋

Magistrate Court *Misdemeanor, Civil Actions Under $5,000, Eviction, Small Claims* 2 Court Square, Rm B-1, Webster Springs, WV 26288. 8:30AM-4PM. **304-847-2613**, Fax: 304-847-7747. ✉✋

Wetzel County

Circuit Court *Felony, Civil Actions Over $5,000* PO Box 263, New Martinsville, WV 26155. 9AM-4:30PM. **304-455-8219**, Fax: 304-455-1069. ✋

Magistrate Court *Misdemeanor, Civil Under $5,000, Eviction, Small Claims* PO Box 147, New Martinsville, WV 26155. 8:30-4:30PM. **304-455-5040\5171\2450**, Fax: 304-455-2859. ✉Fax✋

Wirt County

Circuit Court *Felony, Civil Actions Over $5,000, Probate* PO Box 465, Elizabeth, WV 26143. 8:30AM-4PM. **304-275-6597**, Fax: 304-275-3230 Probate: 304-275-4271. Probate records located at the county clerk's office. ☎Fax✉✋

Magistrate Court *Misdemeanor, Civil Actions Under $5,000, Eviction, Small Claims* PO Box 249, Elizabeth, WV 26143. 8:30AM-4PM. **304-275-3641**, Fax: 304-275-4882. Access records-☎✋

Key: Symbols refer to criminal records access unless otherwise noted.   phone-☎   mail-✉   fax-**Fax**   in person-✋   online-🖥   email-**Email**

Wood County

Circuit Court *Felony, Civil Actions Over $5,000, Probate* Wood County Judicial, #2 Government Sq, Parkersburg, WV 26101-5353. 8:30AM-4:30PM. **304-424-1700**, Fax: 304-424-1804 Probate: 304-424-1850. Probate is handled by County Clerk, PO Box 1474, Parkersburg, WV 26102. ✉✋

Magistrate Court *Misd., Civil Actions Under $5,000, Eviction, Small Claims* 208 Avery St, Parkersburg, WV 26101. 8:30AM-4:30PM. **304-422-3444**. ✋✉

Wyoming County

Circuit Court *Felony, Civil Actions Over $5,000* PO Box 190, Pineville, WV 24874. 9AM-4PM. **304-732-8000 X238**, Fax: 304-732-7262. ☎✉✋

Magistrate Court *Misd., Civil Actions Under $5,000, Eviction, Small Claims* PO Box 598, Pineville, WV 24874. 9AM-4PM M-Th, 9AM-6PM Fri. **304-732-8000 X218**, Fax: 304-732-7247. ✉✋

Wisconsin

State Court Administration (Circuit Courts: Director of State Courts), Supreme Court, PO Box 1688, Madison, WI, 53701; 608-266-6828, Fax: 608-267-0980. http://wicourts.gov

Court Structure: The Circuit Court is the court of general jurisdiction. The Register in Probate maintains guardianship and mental health records, most of which are sealed but may be opened for cause with a court order. In some counties, the Register also maintains termination and adoption records, but practices vary widely across the state.

Most Registers in Probate are putting pre-1950 records on microfilm and destroying the hard copies. This is done as "time and workloads permit," so microfilm archiving is not uniform across the state.

The small claims limit was raised to $5000 in mid-1995.

Probate Courts: Probate filing is a function of the Circuit Court; however, each county has a Register in Probate who maintains and manages the probate records. Probate records are available online at http://wcca.wicourts.gov/index.xsl for all counties.

Online Access: Wisconsin Circuit Court Access (WCCA) allows users to view circuit court case information at http://wcca.wicourts.gov which is the Wisconsin court system website. Data is available from all counties. Portage County offers only probate records online.Searches can be conducted statewide or county by county. WCCA provides detailed information about circuit cases and for civil cases, the program displays judgment and judgment party information. WCCA also offers the ability to generate reports. In addition, public access terminals are available at each court. Due to statutory requirements, WCCA users will not be able to view restricted cases. Appellate and Supreme Courts opinions are available from http://old.wicourts.gov/wscca/.

Additional Information: The statutory fee schedule for the Circuit Courts is as follows: Search Fee - $5.00 per name; Copy Fee - $1.25 per page; Certification Fee - $5.00. In about half the Circuit Courts, no search fee is charged if the case number is provided. There is normally no search fee charged for in-person searches.

The fee schedule for probate is as follows: Search Fee - $4.00 per name; Certification Fee - $3.00 per document plus copy fee; Copy Fee - $1.00 per page.

Adams County

Circuit Court *Felony, Misdemeanor, Civil, Eviction, Small Claims* PO Box 220, Friendship, WI 53934. 8AM-4:30PM. **608-339-4208**, Fax: 608-339-4503. ☎✉🖥✋

Register in Probate PO Box 200, Friendship, WI 53934. 8AM-4:30PM. **608-339-4213**, Fax: 608-339-4503. 🖥

Ashland County

Circuit Court *Felony, Misdemeanor, Civil, Eviction, Small Claims* Courthouse 201 W Main St, Rm 307, Ashland, WI 54806. 8AM-N, 1-4PM. **715-682-7016**, Fax: 715-682-7919. Fax✉🖥✋

Register in Probate Courthouse, Rm 203 201 W Main, Ashland, WI 54806. 8AM-N, 1-4PM. **715-682-7009**, Fax: 715-682-7919. 🖥

Barron County

Circuit Court *Felony, Misdemeanor, Civil, Eviction, Small Claims* Barron County Courthouse 330 E LaSalle Ave, Rm 208, Barron, WI 54812. 8AM-4:30PM. **715-537-6265**, Fax: 715-537-6269. Civil phone: 715-537-6271, crim: 715-537-6268. 🖥✋

Register in Probate Barron Justice Ctr 1420 State Hwy 25 N, Barron, WI 54812. 8AM-4:30PM. **715-537-6261**, Fax: 715-537-6269. 🖥

Bayfield County

Circuit Court *Felony, Misdemeanor, Civil, Eviction, Small Claims* 117 E 5th, Washburn, WI 54891. 8AM-4PM. **715-373-6108**, Fax: 715-373-6153 ✉🖥✋

Register in Probate 117 E 5th PO Box 536, Washburn, WI 54891. 8AM-4PM. **715-373-6155**, Fax: 715-373-6153. 🖥

Brown County

Circuit Court *Felony, Misdemeanor, Civil, Eviction, Small Claims* PO Box 23600, Green Bay, WI 54305-3600. 8AM-4:30PM. **920-448-4161**, Fax: 920-448-4156 ✉🖥✋

Register in Probate PO Box 23600, Green Bay, WI 54305-3600. 8-4:30. **920-448-4275**, Fax: 920-448-6208. 💻

Buffalo County

Circuit Court *Felony, Misdemeanor, Civil, Eviction, Small Claims* 407 S 2nd, PO Box 68, Alma, WI 54610. 8AM-4:30PM. **608-685-6212**, Fax: 608-685-6211. ☎Fax✉💻🖐

Register in Probate 407 S 2nd PO Box 68, Alma, WI 54610. 8AM-4:30PM. **608-685-6202**, Fax: 608-685-6211. 💻

Burnett County

Circuit Court *Felony, Misdemeanor, Civil, Eviction, Small Claims* 7410 County Road K, #115, Siren, WI 54872. 8:30-4:30PM. **715-349-2147**. ✉💻🖐

Probate 7410 County Road K #110, Siren, WI 54872. 8:30AM-4:30PM. **715-349-2177 x0301**, Fax: 715-349-7659. 💻

Calumet County

Circuit Court *Felony, Misd., Civil, Eviction, Small Claims* 206 Court St, Chilton, WI 53014. 8AM-4:30PM. **920-849-1414**, Fax: 920-849-1483. ✉💻🖐

Register in Probate 206 Court St, Chilton, WI 53014-1198. 8AM-N, 1-4:30PM. **920-849-1455**, Fax: 920-849-1483. 💻

Chippewa County

Circuit Court *Felony, Misdemeanor, Civil, Eviction, Small Claims* 711 N Bridge St, Chippewa Falls, WI 54729-1879. 8AM-4:30PM. **715-726-7758**, Fax: 715-726-7786. ✉Fax💻🖐

Register in Probate 711 N Bridge St, Chippewa Falls, WI 54729. 8AM-4:30PM. **715-726-7737**, Fax: 715-738-2626. 💻

Clark County

Circuit Court *Felony, Misdemeanor, Civil, Eviction, Small Claims* 517 Court St, Neillsville, WI 54456-1971. 8AM-4:30PM. **715-743-5181**, Fax: 715-743-5120. ✉💻🖐

Register in Probate 517 Court St, Rm 403, Neillsville, WI 54456. 8AM-4:30PM. **715-743-5172**, Fax: 715-743-5120. 💻

Columbia County

Circuit Court *Felony, Misdemeanor, Civil, Eviction, Small Claims* PO Box 587, Portage, WI 53901. 8AM-4:30PM. **608-742-9642**, Fax: 608-742-9601. Civil phone: 608-742-9624, crim: 608-742-9643, ✉💻🖐

Register in Probate 400 DeWitt PO Box 587, Portage, WI 53901. 8AM-4:30PM. **608-742-9636, 742-9637**, Fax: 608-742-9601. 💻

Crawford County

Circuit Court *Felony, Misd., Civil, Eviction, Small Claims* 220 N Beaumont Rd, Prairie Du Chien, WI 53821. 8AM-4:30PM. **608-326-0211**, Civil: 608-326-0208, crim: 608-326-010. ✉💻🖐

Register in Probate 220 N Beaumont Rd, Prairie Du Chien, WI 53821. 8AM-4:30PM. **608-326-0206**, Fax: 608-326-0288. 💻

Dane County

Circuit Court *Felony, Misdemeanor, Civil, Eviction, Small Claims* www.co.dane.wi.us/clrkcort/clrkhome.htm 210 Martin Luther King Jr Blvd, Rm GR10, Madison, WI 53703. 7:45AM-4:30PM. **608-266-4311**, Fax: 608-267-8859 Fax✉💻🖐

Register in Probate 210 Martin Luther King Jr Blvd, Rm 305, Madison, WI 53703-3344. 7:45AM-4:30PM. **608-266-4331**. 💻

Dodge County

Circuit Court *Felony, Misdemeanor, Civil, Eviction, Small Claims* 210 W Center St, Juneau, WI 53039. 8AM-4:30PM. **920-386-3820**, Fax: 920-386-3587. ✉💻🖐

Register in Probate 210 W Center St, Juneau, WI 53039-1091. 8AM-4:30PM. **920-386-3550**, Fax: 920-386-3933. 💻

Door County

Circuit Court *Felony, Misdemeanor, Civil, Eviction, Small Claims* PO Box 670, Sturgeon Bay, WI 54235. 8AM-4:30PM. **920-746-2205**, Fax: 920-746-2520. ✉💻🖐

Register in Probate PO Box 670 421 Nebraska St, Rm C375, Sturgeon Bay, WI 54235-2470. 8AM-4:30PM. **920-746-2482**, Fax: 920-746-2470. 💻

Douglas County

Circuit Court *Felony, Misd., Civil, Eviction, Small Claims* 1313 Belknap, Superior, WI 54880. 8AM-4:30PM. Fax: 715-395-1421. Civil phone: 715-395-1237, crim: 715-395-1240. ✉💻🖐

Register in Probate 1313 Belknap, Superior, WI 54880. 8AM-4:30PM. **715-395-1229**, Fax: 715-395-1421. 💻

Dunn County

Circuit Court *Felony, Misdemeanor, Civil, Eviction, Small Claims* Stokke Parkway, #1500, Menomonie, WI 54751. 8AM-4:30PM. **715-232-2611**. ✉💻🖐

Register in Probate 615 Stokke Pky, #1300, Menomonie, WI 54751. 8AM-4:30PM. **715-232-6782**, Fax: 715-232-6787. 💻

Eau Claire County

Circuit Court *Felony, Misd., Civil, Eviction, Small Claims* 721 Oxford Ave, Eau Claire, WI 54703. 8AM-5PM. **715-839-4816**, Fax: 715-839-4817. ✉💻🖐

Register in Probate 721 Oxford Ave, Rm 2201, Eau Claire, WI 54703. 8AM-5PM. **715-839-4823**. 💻

Florence County

Circuit Court *Felony, Misd., Civil, Eviction, Small Claims* PO Box 410, Florence, WI 54121. 8:30AM-4PM. **715-528-3205**, Fax: 715-528-5470. ✉💻🖐

Register in Probate PO Box 410, Florence, WI 54121. 8:30AM-N, 1-4PM. **715-528-3205**, Fax: 715-528-5470. 💻

Fond du Lac County

Circuit Court *Felony, Misdemeanor, Civil, Eviction, Small Claims* 160 S Macy, Fond du Lac, WI 54936-1355. 8AM-4:30PM. **920-929-3040**, Fax: 920-929-3933. ✉💻🖐

Register in Probate PO Box 1576, Fond du Lac, WI 54936-1576. 8AM-4:30PM. **920-929-3084**, Fax: 920-929-7058. 💻

Forest County

Circuit Court *Felony, Misdemeanor, Civil, Eviction, Small Claims* 200 E Madison St, Crandon, WI 54520. 8:30AM-4:30PM. **715-478-3323**, Fax: 715-478-3211. Access records-✉💻🖐

Register in Probate 200 E Madison St, Crandon, WI 54520. 8:30AM-12:00,1-

4:30PM. **715-478-2418**, Fax: 715-478-2430. 💻

Grant County

Circuit Court *Felony, Misdemeanor, Civil, Eviction, Small Claims* PO Box 110, Lancaster, WI 53813. 8AM-4:30PM. **608-723-2752**, Fax: 608-723-7370. ☎✉**Fax**💻✋

Register in Probate 130 W Maple St, Rm A360, Lancaster, WI 53813. 8AM-4:30PM. **608-723-2697**, Fax: 608-723-7370. 💻

Green County

Circuit Court *Felony, Misdemeanor, Civil, Eviction, Small Claims* www.co.green.wi.gov/ 1016 16th Ave, Monroe, WI 53566. 8AM-4:30PM. **608-328-9433**, Fax: 608-328-9459. ✉💻✋

Register in Probate 1016 16th Ave, Monroe, WI 53566. 8AM-12, 1PM-4:30PM. **608-328-9567**, Fax: 608-328-9459. 💻

Green Lake County

Circuit Court *Felony, Misdemeanor, Civil, Eviction, Small Claims* 492 Hill St, PO Box 3188, Green Lake, WI 54941. 8AM-4:30PM. **920-294-4142**, Fax: 920-294-4150. ✉💻✋

Register in Probate 492 Hill St, PO Box 3188, Green Lake, WI 54941. 8AM-4:30PM. **920-294-4044**. 💻

Iowa County

Circuit Court *Felony, Misdemeanor, Civil, Eviction, Small Claims* 222 N Iowa St, Dodgeville, WI 53533. 8:30AM-4:30PM. **608-935-0395**, Fax: 608-935-0386. ✉💻✋

Register in Probate 222 N Iowa St, Dodgeville, WI 53533. 8:30AM-N, 12:30-4:30PM. **608-935-0347**, Fax: 608-935-0386. 💻

Iron County

Circuit Court *Felony, Misdemeanor, Civil, Eviction, Small Claims* 300 Taconite St, #207, Hurley, WI 54534. 8AM-4PM. **715-561-4084**, Fax: 715-561-4054. ✉💻✋

Register in Probate 300 Taconite St, #207, Hurley, WI 54534. 8AM-4PM. **715-561-3434**, Fax: 715-561-4054. 💻

Jackson County

www.co.jackson.wi.us

Circuit Court *Felony, Misdemeanor, Civil, Eviction, Small Claims* 307 Main St, Black River Falls, WI 54615. 8AM-4:30PM. **715-284-0208**, Fax: 715-284-0270. ✉💻✋

Register in Probate 307 Main St, Black River Falls, WI 54615. 8AM-4:30PM. **715-284-0213**, Fax: 715-284-0277. 💻

Jefferson County

Circuit Court *Felony, Misd., Civil, Eviction, Small Claims* 320 S Main St, Jefferson, WI 53549. 8AM-4:30PM. **920-674-7150**, Fax: 920-674-7425. ✉💻✋

Register in Probate 320 S Main St, Jefferson, WI 53549. 8AM-4:30PM. **920-674-7245**, Fax: 920-675-0134. 💻

Juneau County

Circuit Court *Felony, Misdemeanor, Civil, Eviction, Small Claims* www.wcca.wicourts.gov 200 Oak St Juneau County Justice Ctr, Mauston, WI 53948. 8AM-4:30PM. **608-847-9356**, Fax: 608-847-9360. ✉💻**Fax**✋

Register in Probate 200 Oak St, Rm 2300, Mauston, WI 53948. 8AM-4:30PM. **608-847-9346**, Fax: 608-847-9349. 💻

Kenosha County

Circuit Court *Felony, Misdemeanor, Civil, Eviction, Small Claims* 912 56th St, Kenosha, WI 53140. 8AM-5PM. **262-653-2664**, Fax: 262-653-2435. ✉💻✋fax.

Register in Probate Courthouse, Rm 304, 912 56th St, Kenosha, WI 53140. 8-5PM. **262-653-2675**, Fax: 262-653-2673. 💻

Kewaunee County

Circuit Court *Felony, Misdemeanor, Civil, Eviction, Small Claims* 613 Dodge St, Kewaunee, WI 54216. 8AM-4:30PM. **920-388-7144**, Fax: 920-388-3139. ☎✉💻✋

Register in Probate 613 Dodge St, Kewaunee, WI 54216. 8AM-4:30PM. **920-388-7143**, Fax: 920-388-3139. 💻

La Crosse County

Circuit Court *Felony, Misdemeanor, Civil, Eviction, Small Claims* 333 Vine St, La Crosse, WI 54601. 8:30AM-5PM.

608-785-9590/9573, Fax: 608-789-7821. ☎✉💻✋

Register in Probate 333 Vine St, Rm 1201, La Crosse, WI 54601. 8:30AM-5PM. **608-785-9882**. 💻

Lafayette County

Circuit Court *Felony, Misdemeanor, Civil, Eviction, Small Claims* 626 Main St, Darlington, WI 53530. 8AM-4:30PM. **608-776-4832**. Access records-✉💻✋

Register in Probate 626 Main St, Rm 302, Darlington, WI 53530. 8AM-4:30PM. **608-776-4811**. 💻

Langlade County

Circuit Court *Felony, Misdemeanor, Civil, Eviction, Small Claims* 800 Clermont St, Antigo, WI 54409. 8:30AM-4:30PM. **715-627-6215**. ✉💻✋

Register in Probate 800 Clermont St, Antigo, WI 54409. 8:30AM-4:30PM. **715-627-6213**, Fax: 715-627-6329. 💻

Lincoln County

Circuit Court *Felony, Misdemeanor, Civil, Eviction, Small Claims* 1110 E Main St, Merrill, WI 54452. 8AM-4:30PM. **715-536-0319**, Fax: 715-536-0361. ✉💻✋

Register in Probate 1110 E Main St, Merrill, WI 54452. 8:15AM-N, 1-4:30PM. **715-536-0342; 536-0378**, Fax: 715-539-2762. 💻

Manitowoc County

Circuit Court *Felony, Misdemeanor, Civil, Eviction, Small Claims* PO Box 2000, Manitowoc, WI 54221-2000. 8:30AM-5PM M; 8:30AM-4:30PM T-F. **920-683-4030**. ☎✉💻✋

Register in Probate 1010 S 8th St, Rm 116, Manitowoc, WI 54220. 8:30AM-4:30PM T-F; 8:30AM-5PM M. **920-683-4016**, Fax: 920-683-5182. 💻

Marathon County

Circuit Court *Felony, Misdemeanor, Civil, Eviction, Small Claims* 500 Forest St, Wausau, WI 54403. 8AM-5PM (Summer hours 8AM-4:30PM Memorial-Labor Day). **715-261-1300**, Fax: 715-261-1319 Civ; 261-1280 Crim. Civil phone: 715-261-1300. Small claims phone is 261-1310; Traffic, 261-1270. Fax for criminal: 715-261-1279. ✉💻✋

Key: Symbols refer to criminal records access unless otherwise noted. phone-☎ mail-✉ fax-**Fax** in person-✋ online-💻 email-**Email**

Register in Probate 500 Forest St, Wausau, WI 54403. 8AM-5PM. **715-261-1260**, Fax: 715-261-1269. 💻

Marinette County

Circuit Court *Felony, Misd., Civil, Eviction, Small Claims* 1926 Hall Ave, Marinette, WI 54143-1717. 8:30AM-4:30PM. **715-732-7450**. ✉️💻👋

Register in Probate 1926 Hall Ave, Marinette, WI 54143-1717. 8:30AM-4:30PM. **715-732-7475**, Fax: 715-732-7561. 💻

Marquette County

Circuit Court *Felony, Misdemeanor, Civil, Eviction, Small Claims* PO Box 187, Montello, WI 53949. 8AM-N, 12:30-4:30PM. **608-297-9102**, Fax: 608-297-9188. ✉️💻👋

Register in Probate 77 W Park St PO Box 749, Montello, WI 53949. 8AM-4:30PM. **608-297-9105**, Fax: 608-297-9188. 💻

Menominee County

Circuit Court *Felony, Misd., Civil, Eviction, Small Claims* PO Box 279, Keshena, WI 54135. 8-4:30PM. **715-799-3313**, Fax: 715-799-1322. ✉️💻👋fax.

Register in Probate 311 N Main St, Rm 203, Shawano, WI 54166. 8AM-4:30PM. **715-526-8631**, Fax: 715-526-8622. Tribal probate records only in Keshena (Menominee Tribal Court); Non-tribal records are in Shawano County. 💻

Milwaukee County

Circuit Court - Civil *Civil, Eviction, Small Claims* http://204.194.250.11/ 901 N 9th St, Rm G-9, Milwaukee, WI 53233. 8AM-5PM. **414-278-4128**, Fax: 414-223-1256. Access civil records-✉️💻👋

Circuit Court - Criminal Division *Felony, Misd.* http://204.194.250.11 821 W State St, Milwaukee, WI 53233. 8AM-5PM. **414-278-4121, 2784599**, Fax: 414-223-1262. **Fax**✉️💻👋

Register in Probate 901 N 9th St, Rm 207, Milwaukee, WI 53233. 8AM-4:30PM. **414-278-4444**, Fax: 414-223-1814. 💻

Monroe County

Circuit Court *Felony, Misdemeanor, Civil, Eviction, Small Claims* 112 S Court St, #203, Sparta, WI 54656-1764. 8AM-4:30PM. **608-269-8745**. **Fax**✉️💻👋

Register in Probate 112 S Court, Rm 301, Sparta, WI 54656-1765. 8AM-N. **608-269-8701**, Fax: 608-269-8950. 💻

Oconto County

Circuit Court *Felony, Misdemeanor, Civil,, Small Claims* 301 Washington St, Oconto, WI 54153. 8AM-4PM. **920-834-6855**, Fax: 920-834-6867. ✉️💻👋

Register in Probate 301 Washington St, Oconto, WI 54153. 8AM-4PM. **920-834-6839**, Fax: 920-834-6867. 💻

Oneida County

Circuit Court *Felony, Misdemeanor, Civil, Eviction, Small Claims* PO Box 400, Rhinelander, WI 54501. 8AM-4:30PM. **715-369-6120**. ✉️💻👋

Register in Probate PO Box 400, Rhinelander, WI 54501. 8AM-12, 1-4:30PM. **715-369-6159**. 💻

Outagamie County

Circuit Court *Felony, Misdemeanor, Civil, Eviction, Small Claims* 320 S Walnut St, Appleton, WI 54911. 8:00AM-4:30PM. **920-832-5130**, Fax: 920-832-5115. Civil phone: 920-832-5136. Small claims and eviction records at 920-832-5135. ✉️👋

Register in Probate 320 S Walnut St, Appleton, WI 54911. 8:30AM-N, 1-5PM. **920-832-5601**, Fax: 920-832-5115. 💻

Ozaukee County

Circuit Court *Felony, Misdemeanor, Civil, Eviction, Small Claims* www.co.ozaukee.wi.us/ClerkCourts/default.htm 1201 S Spring St, Port Washington, WI 53074. 8:30AM-5PM. **262-284-8409**, Fax: 262-284-8491. ✉️💻👋

Register in Probate PO Box 994, Port Washington, WI 53074. 8:30AM-5PM. **262-284-8370/8409** Fax 262-284-8491 💻

Pepin County

Circuit Court *Felony, Misdemeanor, Civil, Eviction, Small Claims* PO Box 39, Durand, WI 54736. 8:30AM-N, 12:30-4:30PM. **715-672-8861**, Fax: 715-672-8521. ✉️💻👋

Register in Probate PO Box 39, Durand, WI 54736. 8:30AM-N, 1-4:30PM. **715-**672-8859/715-672-8868, Fax: 715-672-8521. 💻

Pierce County

Circuit Court *Felony, Misdemeanor, Civil, Eviction, Small Claims* PO Box 129, Ellsworth, WI 54011. 8AM-5PM. **715-273-3531**. ✉️💻👋

Register in Probate PO Box 97, Ellsworth, WI 54011. 8AM-5PM. **715-273-3531 x6460**, Fax: 715-273-6794. 💻

Polk County

Circuit Court *Felony, Misdemeanor, Civil, Eviction, Small Claims* PO Box 549, (100 Polk Plaza), Balsam Lake, WI 54810. 8:30AM-4:30PM. **715-485-9299**, Fax: 715-485-9262. ✉️💻👋

Register in Probate 1005 W Main, #500, Balsam Lake, WI 54810. 8:30AM-4:30PM. **715-485-9238**, Fax: 715-485-9275. 💻

Portage County

Circuit Court (Branches 1, 2 & 3) *Felony, Misdemeanor, Civil, Eviction, Small Claims* 1516 Church St, Stevens Point, WI 54481. 7:30AM-4:30PM. **715-346-1364**, Fax: 715-346-1236. ✉️👋💻

Register in Probate 1516 Church St, Stevens Point, WI 54481. 7:30AM-4:30PM. **715-346-1362**, Fax: 715-346-1486. 💻

Price County

Circuit Court *Felony, Misdemeanor, Civil, Eviction, Small Claims* Courthouse 126 Cherry St, Phillips, WI 54555. 8AM-N, 1-4:30PM. **715-339-2353**, Fax: 715-339-3079. ✉️💻👋

Register in Probate Courthouse, 126 Cherry St, Rm209, Phillips, WI 54555. 8AM-4:30PM. **715-339-3078**, Fax: 715-339-3079. 💻

Racine County

Circuit Court *Felony, Misdemeanor, Civil, Eviction, Small Claims, Probate* 730 Wisconsin Ave, Racine, WI 53403. 8AM-5PM. **262-636-3333**, Fax: 262-636-3341. ✉️💻👋

Register in Probate 730 Wisconsin Ave, Racine, WI 53403. 8AM-5PM. **262-636-3137**, Fax: 262-636-3870. 💻

Richland County

Circuit Court *Felony, Misdemeanor, Civil, Eviction, Small Claims* PO Box

655, Richland Center, WI 53581. 8:30-4:30PM. **608-647-3956**. ✉️💻🖐️

Register in Probate PO Box 427, Richland Center, WI 53581. 8:30AM-N, 1-4:30PM. **608-647-2626**, Fax: 608-647-6134. 💻

Rock County
Circuit Court - South *Felony, Misdemeanor, Civil, Eviction, Small Claims* Janesville Courthouse 51 S Main St, Janesville, WI 53545. 8AM-5PM. **608-743-2200**, Fax: 608-743-2223. ✉️💻🖐️

Circuit Court *Felony, Misdemeanor, Civil, Eviction, Small Claims* 51 S Main, Janesville, WI 53545. 8AM-5PM. **608-743-2200**, Fax: 608-743-2223. ✉️💻🖐️

Register in Probate 51 S Main, Janesville, WI 53545. 8AM-5PM. **608-757-5635**, Fax: 608-757-5769. 💻

Rusk County
Circuit Court *Felony, Misdemeanor, Civil, Small Claims* 311 Miner Ave E, #L350, Ladysmith, WI 54848. 8AM-4:30PM. **715-532-2108**. ✉️💻🖐️💻

Register in Probate 311 E Miner Ave, Ladysmith, WI 54848. 8AM-4:30PM. **715-532-2147**, Fax: 715-532-2266. 💻

St. Croix County
Circuit Court *Felony, Misdemeanor, Civil, Eviction, Small Claims* 1101 Carmichael Rd, Hudson, WI 54016. 8AM-5PM. **715-386-4630**. ✉️💻🖐️

Register in Probate 1101 Carmichael Rd, Rm 2242, Hudson, WI 54016. 8AM-5PM. **715-386-4618**, Fax: 715-381-4318. 💻

Sauk County
Circuit Court *Felony, Misdemeanor, Civil, Eviction, Small Claims* 515 Oak St, Baraboo, WI 53913. 8AM-4:30PM. **608-355-3287**, Fax: 608-355-3514. Fax✉️💻🖐️

Register in Probate 515 Oak St, Baraboo, WI 53913. 8AM-4:30PM. **608-355-3226**, Fax: 608-355-3480. 💻

Sawyer County
Circuit Court *Felony, Misdemeanor, Civil, Eviction, Small Claims* PO Box 508, Hayward, WI 54843. 8AM-4PM. **715-634-4887**, Fax: 715-638-3297. ✉️💻🖐️

Register in Probate PO Box 447, Hayward, WI 54843. 8AM-4PM. **715-634-7519**, Fax: 715-638-3297. 💻

Shawano County
Circuit Court *Felony, Misdemeanor, Civil, Eviction, Small Claims* www.co.shawano.wi.us/ 311 N Main, Rm 206, Shawano, WI 54166. 8AM-4:30PM. **715-526-9347**, Fax: 715-526-4915. Fax✉️💻🖐️

Register in Probate 311 N Main, Rm 203, Shawano, WI 54166. 8AM-4:30PM. **715-526-8631**, Fax: 715-526-8622. 💻

Sheboygan County
Circuit Court *Felony, Misdemeanor, Civil, Eviction, Small Claims* www.co.sheboygan.wi.us/html/d_crtclrk.html 615 N 6th St, Sheboygan, WI 53081. 8AM-5PM. **920-459-3068**, Fax: 920-459-3921. ✉️💻🖐️

Register in Probate 615 N 6th St, Sheboygan, WI 53081. 8AM-5PM. **920-459-3050, 459-3202, 459-3051**, Fax: 920-459-0541. 💻

Taylor County
Circuit Court *Felony, Misdemeanor, Civil, Eviction, Small Claims* 224 S 2nd St, Medford, WI 54451-1811. 8:30AM-4:30PM. **715-748-1425**, Fax: 715-748-2465. ✉️💻🖐️

Register in Probate 224 S 2nd, Medford, WI 54451. 8:30AM-4:30PM. **715-748-1435**, Fax: 715-748-1524. 💻

Trempealeau County
Circuit Court *Felony, Misdemeanor, Civil, Eviction, Small Claims* 36245 Main St, Whitehall, WI 54773. 8AM-4:30PM. **715-538-2311**. Fax✉️💻🖐️

Register in Probate 36245 Main St PO Box 67, Whitehall, WI 54773. 8AM-4:30PM. **715-538-2311 X238**, Fax: 715-538-4123. 💻

Vernon County
Circuit Court *Felony, Misdemeanor, Civil, Eviction, Small Claims* PO Box 426, Viroqua, WI 54665. 8:30AM-4:30PM. **608-637-5340**, Fax: 608-637-5554. ☎️Fax✉️💻🖐️

Register in Probate PO Box 448, Viroqua, WI 54665. 8:30AM-4:30PM. **608-637-5347**, Fax: 608-637-5554. 💻

Vilas County
Circuit Court *Felony, Misd., Civil, Eviction, Small Claims* 330 Court St, Eagle River, WI 54521. 8AM-4PM. **715-479-3632**, Fax: 715-479-3740. ✉️💻🖐️

Register in Probate 330 Court St, Eagle River, WI 54521. 8AM-4PM. **715-479-3642**, Fax: 715-479-3740. 💻

Walworth County
www.co.walworth.wi.us
Circuit Court *Felony, Misdemeanor, Civil, Eviction, Small Claims* PO Box 1001, Elkhorn, WI 53121-1001. 8AM-5PM. **262-741-4224**, Fax: 262-741-4379. ✉️🖐️💻

Register in Probate PO Box 1001, Elkhorn, WI 53121. 8AM-5PM. **262-741-4256**, Fax: 262-741-4182. 💻

Washburn County
Circuit Court *Felony, Misdemeanor, Civil, Eviction, Small Claims* PO Box 339, Shell Lake, WI 54871. 8AM-4:30PM. **715-468-4677**, Fax: 715-468-4678. ✉️💻🖐️

Register in Probate PO Box 316, Shell Lake, WI 54871. 8AM-4:30PM. **715-468-4688**, Fax: 715-468-4678. 💻

Washington County
www.co.washington.wi.us
Circuit Court *Felony, Misdemeanor, Civil, Eviction, Small Claims* PO Box 1986, West Bend, WI 53095-7986. 8AM-4:30PM. **262-335-4341**, Fax: 262-335-4776. ✉️Fax💻🖐️

Register in Probate PO Box 82, West Bend, WI 53095-0082. 8AM-4:30PM. **262-335-4334**, Fax: 262-306-2224. 💻

Waukesha County
Circuit Court *Felony, Misdemeanor, Civil, Eviction, Small Claims* circuitcourts.waukeshacounty.gov 515 W Moreland Blvd, Waukesha, WI 53188. 8AM-4:30PM. Civil: 262-548-7525, crim: 262-548-7484. Access records-✉️💻🖐️

Register in Probate 515 W Moreland, Rm 380, Waukesha, WI 53188. 8AM-4:30PM. **262-548-7468**. 💻

Waupaca County
Circuit Court *Felony, Misd., Civil, Eviction, Small Claims* 811 Harding St,

---

Key: Symbols refer to criminal records access unless otherwise noted. phone-☎️ mail-✉️ fax-**Fax** in person-🖐️ online-💻 email-**Email**

Waupaca, WI 54981. 8AM-4PM. **715-258-6460**, Fax: 715-258-6497. ✉️🖥️✋

Register in Probate 811 Harding St, Waupaca, WI 54981. 8AM-4PM. **715-258-6429**, Fax: 715-258-6440 Probate Deputy Registr.: 715-258-6431 🖥️

Waushara County

Circuit Court *Felony, Misdemeanor, Civil, Eviction, Small Claims* PO Box 507, Wautoma, WI 54982. 8AM-4:30PM. **920-787-0441**, Fax: 920-787-0481 ✉️**Fax**🖥️✋

Register in Probate PO Box 508, Wautoma, WI 54982. 8AM-4:30PM. **920-787-0448**, Fax: 920-787-0481. 🖥️

Winnebago County

Circuit Court *Felony, Misdemeanor, Civil, Eviction, Small Claims* PO Box 2808, Oshkosh, WI 54903-2808. 8AM-4:30PM. **920-236-4848**, Fax: 920-424-7780. Civil phone: 920-236-4848, crim: 920-236-4855. ✉️**Fax**🖥️✋

Register in Probate PO Box 2808, Oshkosh, WI 54903-2808. 8AM-N, 1-4:30. **920-236-4833**, Fax: 920-424-7536.

Wood County

Circuit Court *Felony, Misdemeanor, Civil, Eviction, Small Claims* 400 Market St, PO Box 8095, Wisconsin Rapids, WI 54494-958095. 8AM-4:30PM. **715-421-8490**. ✉️🖥️✋

Register in Probate Wood County Courthouse PO Box 8095, Wisconsin Rapids, WI 54495-8095. 8AM-4:30PM. **715-421-8520, 421-8523**, Fax: 715-421-8896. 🖥️

Wyoming

State Court Administration: Court Administrator, 2301 Capitol Av, Supreme Court Bldg, Cheyenne, WY, 82002; 307-777-7583, Fax: 307-777-3447. www.courts.state.wy.us

Court Structure: Each county has a District Court ("higher" jurisdiction) and a Circuit. Prior to 2003, for their "lower" jurisdiction court some counties had Circuit Courts and others had Justice Courts. Effective January 1, 2003 all Justice Courts became Circuit Courts and follow Circuit Court rules.Circuit Courts handle civil claims up to $7,000 while Justice Courts handle civil claims up to $3,000. The District Courts take cases over the applicable limit in each county. Three counties have two Circuit Courts each: Fremont, Park, and Sweetwater. Cases may be filed in either of the two court offices in those counties, and records requests are referred between the two courts. Municipal courts operate in all incorporated cities and towns. Their jurisdiction covers all ordinance violations, and it has no civil jurisdiction. The municipal court judge may assess penalties of up to $750 and/or six months in jail.

Probate is handled by the District Court.

Online Access: Wyoming's statewide case management system is for internal use only. Planning is underway for a new case management system that will ultimately allow public access.

Albany County

2nd Judicial District Court *Felony, Civil Actions Over $7,000, Probate* County Courthouse, 525 Grand, Rm 305, Laramie, WY 82070. 9AM-5PM. **307-721-2508**. ✉️✋

Albany Circuit Court *Misdemeanor, Civil Actions Under $7,000, Eviction, Small Claims* County Courthouse, 525 Grand, Rm 105, Laramie, WY 82070. 8AM-5PM. **307-742-5747**, Fax: 307-742-5610. ✉️✋fax.

Big Horn County

5th Judicial District Court *Felony, Civil Actions Over $7,000, Probate* PO Box 670, Basin, WY 82410. 8AM-N, 1-5PM. **307-568-2381**, Fax: 307-568-2791. **Fax**✉️✋

Lovell Circuit Court *Misdemeanor, Civil Actions Under $7,000, Small Claims* PO Box 595, Lovell, WY 82431. 8AM-5PM.

307-548-7601, Fax: 307-548-9691. Note that misdemanor records from the Basin Circuit Court and this Lovell Court are not combined. **Fax**✉️✋

Basin Circuit Court *Misdemeanor, Civil Actions Under $7,000, Small Claims* PO Box 749, Basin, WY 82410. 8AM-5PM. **307-568-2367**, Fax: 307-568-2554. Note that misdemanor records from this Basin Court and the Lovell Court are not combined. **Fax**✉️✋

Campbell County

6th Judicial District Court *Felony, Civil Actions Over $7,000, Probate* PO Box 817 500 S Gillette, Gillette, WY 82717. 8AM-5PM. **307-682-3424**, Fax: 307-687-6209. **Fax**✉️✋

Campbell Circuit Court *Misdemeanor, Civil Actions Under $7,000, Eviction, Small Claims* 500 S Gillette Ave, #301,

Gillette, WY 82716. 8AM-5PM. **307-682-2190**, Fax: 307-687-6214. ✉️✋

Carbon County

Carbon County District Court *Felony, Civil Actions Over $7,000, Probate* Clerk of District Court PO Box 67, Rawlins, WY 82301. 8AM-5PM. **307-328-2628**, Fax: 307-328-2629. ☎**Fax**✉️✋

Carbon Circuit Court *Misdemeanor, Civil Actions Under $7,000, Eviction, Small Claims* Attn: Chief Clerk, Courthouse Bldg 415 W Pine St, Rawlins, WY 82301. 8AM-5PM. **307-324-6655**, Fax: 307-324-9465. ✉️**Fax**✋

Converse County

8th Judicial District Court *Felony, Civil Actions Over $7,000, Probate* Box 189, Douglas, WY 82633. 8AM-5PM. **307-358-3165**, Fax: 307-358-9783. ☎**Fax**✉️✋

Converse Circuit Court *Misdemeanor, Civil Actions Under $7,000, Eviction, Small Claims* 107 N 5th St, #231 PO Box 45, Douglas, WY 82633. 8AM-5PM. **307-358-2196**, Fax: 307-358-2501. ✉ ✋

Crook County

6th Judicial District Court *Felony, Civil Actions Over $7,000, Probate, High Misdemeanor pre-7/1/02* Box 904, Sundance, WY 82729. 8AM-5PM. **307-283-2523**, Fax: 307-283-2996. High misdemanor cases are no longer heard by this court effective 7/1/02; High misdemeanor records prior to that date can be found here. ✉ ✋

Circuit Court *Misdemeanor, Civil Actions Under $7,000, Small Claims* PO Box 650, Sundance, WY 82729. 8AM-5PM. **307-283-2929**, Fax: 307-283-2931. This former Justice Court became a Circuit Court on 7/1/2002. ✉Fax✋

Fremont County

9th Judicial District Court *Felony, Civil Actions Over $7,000, Probate* PO Box 370, Lander, WY 82520. 8AM-N, 1-5PM. **307-332-1134**, Fax: 307-332-1143. ☎Fax✉ ✋

Riverton Circuit Court *Misdemeanor, Civil Under $7,000, Eviction, Small Claims* www.courts.state.wy.us/Brochure_files/ccriv.htm 818 S Federal Blvd, Riverton, WY 82501. 8AM-5PM. **307-856-7259**, Fax: 307-857-3635. ✉ ✋

Lander Circuit Court *Misdemeanor, Civil Actions Under $7,000, Eviction, Small Claims* 450 N 2nd, Rm 230, Lander, WY 82520. 8AM-5PM. **307-332-3239**, Fax: 307-332-1152. This is the main Circuit Court for Fremont County. ☎Fax✉ ✋

Dubois Circuit Court *Misdemeanor, Civil Actions Under $7,000, Eviction, Small Claims* Box 952, Dubois, WY 82513. 8AM-2:00PM. **307-455-2920**, Fax: 307-455-2132. This is a satellite of the Lander Court. ✉ ✋

Goshen County

8th Judicial District Court *Felony, Civil Actions Over $7,000, Probate* Clerk of District Court, PO Box 818, Torrington, WY 82240. 7:30AM-4PM. **307-532-2155**, Fax: 307-532-8608. ✉ ✋

Goshen Circuit Court *Misdemeanor, Civil Actions Under $7,000, Eviction,* Small Claims Drawer BB, Torrington, WY 82240. 7AM-4PM. **307-532-2938**, Fax: 307-532-5101. Civil phone: X251, crim: X250. ✉ ✋

Hot Springs County

5th Judicial District Court *Felony, Civil Actions Over $7,000, Probate* 415 Arapahoe St, Thermopolis, WY 82443. 8AM-5PM. **307-864-3323**, Fax: 307-864-3210. ✉ ✋

Hot Springs Circuit Court *Misdemeanor, Civil Actions Under $7,000, Small Claims* 417 Arapahoe St, Thermopolis, WY 82443. 8AM-5PM. **307-864-5161**, Fax: 307-864-2067. ✉ ✋

Johnson County

4th Judicial District Court *Felony, Civil Actions Over $7,000, Probate* 76 N Main, Buffalo, WY 82834. 8AM-5PM. **307-684-7271**, Fax: 307-684-5146. Fax✉ ✋

Circuit Court *Misdemeanor, Civil Actions Under $7,000, Small Claims* 76 N Main St, Buffalo, WY 82834-1847. 8AM-5PM. **307-684-5720**, Fax: 307-684-5146. This was formally a Justice Court, it became a Circuit Courts on 1/03. ✉Fax✋

Laramie County

1st Judicial District Court *Felony, Misdemeanor, Civil Over $7,000, Probate* http://webgate.co.laramie.wy.us/dc/dc.html 309 W 20th St, #3205 PO Box 787, Cheyenne, WY 82003. 8AM-5PM. **307-633-4270**, Fax: 307-633-4277. Fax✉ ✋

Laramie County Circuit Court *Misdemeanor, Civil Actions Under $7,000, Eviction, Small Claims* 309 W 20th St, Rm 2300, Cheyenne, WY 82001. 8AM-5PM. **307-633-4298**, Fax: 307-633-4392. Fax✉ ✋

Lincoln County

3rd Judicial District Court *Felony, Civil Actions Over $7,000, Probate* PO Drawer 510, Kemmerer, WY 83101. 8AM-5PM. **307-877-9056**, Fax: 307-877-6263. Fax✉ ✋

Lincoln Circuit Court *Misdemeanor, Civil Actions Under $7,000, Eviction, Small Claims* PO Box 949, Kemmerer, WY 83101. 8AM-5PM. **307-877-4431**, Fax: 307-877-4936. Access records-✉ ✋

Natrona County

7th Judicial District Court *Felony, Civil Actions Over $7,000, Probate* Clerk of District Court, PO Box 2510, Casper, WY 82602. 8AM-5PM. **307-235-9243**, Fax: 307-235-9493. ☎Fax✉

Natrona Circuit Court *Misdemeanor, Civil Actions Under $7,000, Eviction, Small Claims* PO Box 1339, Casper, WY 82602. 8AM-5PM. **307-235-9266**, Fax: 307-235-9331. Fax✉ ✋

Niobrara County

8th Judicial District Court *Felony, Civil Actions Over $7,000, Probate* Clerk of District Court PO Box 1318, Lusk, WY 82225. 8AM-N, 1-4PM. **307-334-2736**, Fax: 307-334-2703. ✉ ✋

Circuit Court *Misdemeanor, Civil Actions Under $7,000, Small Claims* PO Box 209, Lusk, WY 82225. 9AM-N, 1-5PM. **307-334-3845**, Fax: 307-334-3846. This was a Justice Court until 01/03. Fax✉ ✋

Park County

5th Judicial District Court *Felony, Civil Actions Over $7,000, Probate* www.wtp.net/parkco/districtcourt.htm Clerk of District Court, PO Box 1960, Cody, WY 82414. 8AM-5PM. **307-527-8690**, Fax: 307-527-8687. ☎Fax✉ ✋

Powell Circuit Court *Misdemeanor, Civil Actions Under $7,000, Eviction, Small Claims* 109 W 14th, Powell, WY 82435. 8AM-N, 1-5PM. **307-754-8890**, Fax: 307-754-8896. Powell court misdemeanor records are also available at the main Circuit Court in Cody. ✉ ✋

Cody Circuit Court *Misdemeanor, Civil Actions Under $7,000, Eviction, Small Claims* 1002 Sheridan Ave., Cody, WY 82414. 8AM-5PM. **307-527-8590**, Fax: 307-527-8596. On January 2, 1995 this court changed status from a Justice Court to a Circuit Court. They also have records for the Powell Circuit Court Branch. ✉ ✋

Platte County

8th Judicial District Court *Felony, Civil Actions Over $7,000, Probate* PO Box 158, Wheatland, WY 82201. 8AM-5PM. **307-322-3857**, Fax: 307-322-5402. ✉Fax✋

Circuit Court *Misdemeanor, Civil Actions Under $3,000, Small Claims* PO Box 306, Wheatland, WY 82201. 8AM-5PM. **307-322-3441**, Fax: 307-322-1371. This former Justice Court became a Circuit Court as of 01/03. ☎☒Fax🖐

Sheridan County

4th Judicial District Court *Felony, Civil Actions Over $7,000, Probate* 224 S. Main, #B-11, Sheridan, WY 82801. 8AM-5PM. **307-674-2960**, Fax: 307-674-2589. ☎☒Fax🖐

Circuit Court *Misdemeanor, Civil Actions Under $7,000, Eviction, Small Claims* 224 S Main, #B-7, Sheridan, WY 82801. 8AM-5PM. **307-674-2940**, Fax: 307-674-2944. ☒🖐

Sublette County

9th Judicial District Court *Felony, Civil Actions Over $7,000, Probate* PO Box 764, Pinedale, WY 82941-0764. 8AM-5PM. **307-367-4376**, Fax: 307-367-6474. ☒🖐

Sublette Circuit Court *Misdemeanor, Civil Actions Under $7,000, Eviction, Small Claims* PO Box 1796, Pinedale, WY 82941. 8AM-5PM. **307-367-2556**, Fax: 307-367-2658. ☒🖐

Sweetwater County

3rd Judicial District Court *Felony, Civil Actions Over $7,000, Probate* PO Box 430, Green River, WY 82935. 9AM-5PM. **307-872-6440**, Fax: 307-872-6439. ☎Fax☒🖐

Sweetwater Circuit Court *Misdemeanor, Civil Actions Under $7,000, Eviction, Small Claims* PO Box 2028, Rock Springs, WY 82902. 8AM-5PM. **307-352-6817**, Fax: 307-352-6758. Fax☒🖐

Green River Circuit Court *Misd., Civil Under $7,000, Eviction, Small Claims* PO Drawer 1720, Green River, WY 82935. 8AM-5PM. **307-872-6460**, Fax: 307-872-6375. ☒🖐

Teton County

9th Judicial District Court *Felony, Civil Actions Over $7,000, Probate* PO Box 4460, Jackson, WY 83001. 8AM-5PM. **307-733-2533**, Fax: 307-734-1562. ☎Fax☒🖐

Circuit Court *Misdemeanor, Civil Actions Under $7,000, Small Claims under $3,000.* PO Box 2906 (180 S King St), Jackson, WY 83001. 8AM-5PM. **307-733-7713**, Fax: 307-733-8694. This was a Justice Court until 2003. ☒🖐

Uinta County

www.uintacounty.com

3rd Judicial District Court *Felony, Civil Actions Over $7,000, Probate* PO Drawer 1906 Attn: Clerk of District Court, Evanston, WY 82931. 8AM-5PM. **307-783-0456**, Fax: 307-783-0400. ☎Fax☒🖐

Uinta Circuit Court *Misdemeanor, Civil Actions Under $7,000, Eviction, Small Claims* 225 9th St, 2nd Fl, Evanston, WY 82931. 8AM-5PM. **307-789-2471**, Fax: 307-789-5062. ☒🖐

Washakie County

5th Judicial District Court *Felony, Civil Actions Over $7,000, Probate* PO Box 862, Worland, WY 82401. 8AM-5PM. **307-347-4821**, Fax: 307-347-4325. ☎Fax☒🖐

Justice Court *Misdemeanor, Civil Actions Under $7,000, Small Claims* courts.state.wy.us. PO Box 927, Worland, WY 82401. 8AM-5PM. **307-347-2702**, Fax: 307-347-8459. This was a Justice Court until 01/03. ☒Fax🖐

Weston County

6th Judicial District Court *Felony, Civil Actions Over $7,000, Probate* 1 W Main, Newcastle, WY 82701. 8AM-5PM. **307-746-4778**, Fax: 307-746-4778. ☎Fax☒🖐

CircuitCourt *Misdemeanor, Civil Actions Under $7,000, Small Claims* 6 W Warwick, Newcastle, WY 82701. 8AM-5PM. **307-746-3547**, Fax: 307-746-3558. This was a Justice Court until 01/03. Fax☒🖐

Chapter 7

Federal Courts

Federal Court Structure

The Federal Court system includes three levels of courts, plus some special courts, described as follows—

Supreme Court of the United States

The Supreme Court of the United States is the court of last resort in the United States. It is located in Washington, DC, where it hears appeals from the United States Courts of Appeals and from the highest courts of each state.

United States Court of Appeals

The **United States Court of Appeals** consists of thirteen appellate courts that hear appeals of verdicts from the courts of general jurisdiction. They are designated as follows:

The **Federal Circuit Court of Appeals** hears appeals from the U.S. Claims Court and the U.S. Court of International Trade. It is located in Washington, DC.

The **District of Columbia Circuit Court of Appeals** hears appeals from the district courts in Washington, DC as well as from the Tax Court.

Eleven geographic **Courts of Appeals** — each of these appeal courts covers a designated number of states and territories. The chart to follow lists the circuit numbers (1 through 11) and location of the Court of Appeals for each state.

United States District Courts

The United States District Courts are the courts of general jurisdiction, or trial courts, and are subdivided into two categories—

The **District Courts** are courts of general jurisdiction, or trial courts, for federal matters, excluding bankruptcy. Essentially, this means they hear cases involving federal law and cases where there is diversity of citizenship. Both civil and criminal cases come before these courts.

The **Bankruptcy Courts** generally follow the same geographic boundaries as the U.S. District Courts. There is at least one bankruptcy court for each state; within a state there may be one or more judicial districts and within a judicial district there may be more than one location (division) where the courts hear cases. While civil lawsuits may be filed in either state or federal courts depending upon the applicable law, all bankruptcy actions are filed with the U.S. Bankruptcy Courts.

Special Courts/Separate Courts

The Special Courts/Separate Courts have been created to hear cases or appeals for certain areas of litigation demanding special expertise. Examples include the U.S. Tax Court, the Court of International Trade and the U.S. Claims Court.

How Federal Trial Courts are Organized

At the federal level, all cases involve federal or U.S. constitutional law or interstate commerce. The task of locating the right court is seemingly simplified by the nature of the federal system—

- All court locations are based upon the plaintiff's county of domicile.
- All civil and criminal cases go to the U.S. District Courts.
- All bankruptcy cases go to the U.S. Bankruptcy Courts.

However, a plaintiff or defendant may have cases in any of the 500 court locations, so it is really not all that simple to find them.

There is at least one District Court and one Bankruptcy Court in each state. In many states there is more than one court, often divided further into judicial districts — e.g., the State of New York consists of four judicial districts: the Northern, Southern, Eastern and Western. Further, many judicial districts contain more than one court location (usually called a division).

The Bankruptcy Courts generally use the same hearing locations as the District Courts. If court locations differ, the usual variance is to have fewer Bankruptcy Court locations.

Case Numbering

When a case is filed with a federal court, a case number is assigned. This is the primary indexing method. Therefore, in searching for case records, you will need to know or find the applicable case number. If you have the number in good form already, your search should be fast and reasonably inexpensive.

You should be aware that case numbering procedures are not consistent throughout the Federal Court system: one judicial district may assign numbers by district while another may assign numbers by location (division) within the judicial district or by judge. Remember that case numbers appearing in legal text citations may not be adequate for searching unless they appear in the proper form for the particular court.

All the basic civil case information that is entered onto docket sheets, and into computerized systems like PACER (see below), starts with standard form JS-44, the Civil Cover Sheet, or the equivalent.

Docket Sheet

As in the state court system, information from cover sheets, and from documents filed as a case goes forward, is recorded on the docket sheet, which then contains the case history from initial filing to its current status. While docket sheets differ somewhat in format, the basic information contained on a docket sheet is consistent from court to court. As noted earlier in the state court section, all docket sheets contain:

- Name of court, including location (division) and the judge assigned;
- Case number and case name;
- Names of all plaintiffs and defendants/debtors;
- Names and addresses of attorneys for the plaintiff or debtor;
- Nature and cause (e.g., U.S. civil statute) of action;
- Listing of documents filed in the case, including docket entry number, the date and a short description (e.g., 12-2-92, #1, Complaint).

Assignment of Cases and Computerization

Traditionally, cases were assigned within a district by county. Although this is still true in most states, the introduction of computer systems to track dockets has led to a more flexible approach to case assignment, as is the case in Minnesota and Connecticut. Rather than blindly assigning all cases from a county to one judge, their districts are using random numbers and other logical methods to balance caseloads among their judges.

This trend may appear to confuse the case search process. Actually, the only problem the searcher may face is to figure out where the case records themselves are located. Finding cases has become significantly easier with the wide availability of PACER from remote access and onsite terminals in each court location with the same district-wide information base.

Computerized Indexes are Available

Computerized courts generally index each case record by the names of some or all the parties to the case — the plaintiffs and defendants (debtors and creditors in Bankruptcy Court) as well as by case number. Therefore, when you search by name you will first receive a listing of all cases in which the name appears, both as plaintiff and defendant.

Electronic Access to Federal Courts

One development that continues to change the fundamental nature of Federal Courts case record access is, of course, computerization. Now, every Federal Court in the United States has converted to a computerized index.

Numerous programs have been developed for electronic access to Federal Court records. In recent years the Administrative Office of the United States Courts in Washington, DC has developed three innovative public access programs: VCIS, PACER, and the Case Management/ Electronic Case Files (CM/ECF) project. The most useful program for online searching is PACER.

PACER

PACER, the acronym for **P**ublic **A**ccess to **E**lectronic **C**ourt **R**ecords, provides docket information online for open cases at all U.S. Bankruptcy courts and most U.S. District courts. Access is via either a commercial dial-up system (user fee of $.60 a minute) or through the Internet (user fee is $.07 per page). Cases for the U.S. Court of Federal Claims are also available.

Each court controls its own computer system and case information database; therefore, there are some variations among jurisdictions as to the information offered.

Sign-up and technical support is handled at the PACER Service Center in San Antonio, Texas (800) 676-6856. You can sign up for all or multiple districts at once. In many judicial districts, when you sign up for PACER access, you will receive a PACER Primer that has been customized for each district. The primer contains a summary of how to access PACER, how to select cases, how to read case numbers and docket sheets, some searching tips, who to call for problem resolution, and district specific program variations.

A continuing problem with PACER is that each court determines when records will be purged and how records will be indexed, leaving you to guess how a name is spelled or abbreviated and how much information about closed cases your search will uncover. A PACER search for anything but open cases cannot take the place of a full seven-year search of the federal court records available by written request from the court itself or through a local document retrieval company. Many districts report that they have closed records back a number of years, but at the same time indicate they purge docket items every six months.

Another problem is the lack of identifiers. Many federal courts are now cloaking the DOB on records available to the public. Thus, if a record searcher has a common name and gets one or more hits, each individual case file may need to be reviewed to determine if the case belongs to the subject in mind.

Before Accessing PACER, Search the "National" U.S. Party/Case Index

It is no longer necessary to call each court in every state and district to determine where a debtor has filed bankruptcy, or if someone is a defendant in federal litigation. National and regional searches of district and bankruptcy filings can be made with one call (via modem) to the U.S. Party/Case Index.

The U.S. Party/Case Index is a national index for U.S. district, bankruptcy, and appellate courts. This index allows searches to determine whether or not a party is involved in federal litigation almost anywhere in the nation.

The U.S. Party/Case Index provides the capability to perform national or regional searches on party name and Social Security Number in the bankruptcy index, party name and nature of suit in the civil index, and party name in the criminal and appellate indices.

The search will provide a list of case numbers, filing locations and filing dates for those cases matching the search criteria. If you need more information about the case, you must obtain it from the court directly or through that court's individual PACER system.

You may access the U.S. Party/Case Index by dialup connection or via the Internet. The Internet site for the U.S. Party/Case Index is http://pacer.uspci.uscourts.gov. The toll-free dial-up number for the U.S.

Party/Case Index is 800-974-8896. For more information, call the PACER service center at 800-676-6856. If you have comments, suggestions or questions, please send email to the PACER Service Center at pacer@psc.uscourts.gov.

In accordance with Judicial Conference policy, most courts charge a $.60 per minute access fee for the traditional dial-up service, or $.07 per page for Internet service.

RACER

RACER stands for **R**emote **A**ccess to **C**ourt **E**lectronic **R**ecords. Accessed through the Internet, RACER offers access to the same records as PACER. At present, searching RACER is free in a few courts. Normally the fee structure is $.07 per page.

Miscellaneous Online Systems

Some courts have developed their own online systems. In addition to RACER, Idaho's Bankruptcy and District Courts have other searching options available on their website. Likewise, the Southern District Court of New York offers CourtWeb, which provides information to the public on selected recent rulings of those judges who have elected to make information available in electronic form.

Case Management/Electronic Case Files (CM/ECF)

Electronic Case Files (ECF) is a prototype system for the filing of cases electronically. This service, initially introduced in January 1996, enables participating attorneys and litigants to electronically submit pleadings and corresponding docket entries to the court via the Internet, thereby eliminating substantial paper handling and processing time. ECF permits any interested parties to instantaneously access the entire official case docket and documents on the Internet of selective civil and bankruptcy cases within these jurisdictions.

The federal judiciary's Case Management/Electronic Case Files (CM/ECF) project is designed to replace the aging electronic docketing and case management systems in more than 200 bankruptcy, district, and appellate courts by the end of 2005. CM/ECF will provide the capability for courts to have case file documents in electronic format and to accept filings over the Internet. About two-thirds of all federal courts are currently operational as we go to press, and the remaining courts are in the process of implementing CM/ECF.

It is important to note that when you search ECF, you are ONLY searching cases that have been filed electronically. A case may not have been filed electronically through CM-ECF, so you must still conduct a search using PACER if you want to know if a case exists.

One important feature of this system is their National Locator, known as the United States Party Index. This is a name search, used to locate the specific court where records are available.

For further information about CM/ECF visit http://pacer.psc.uscourts.gov/cmecf/index.html.

VCIS

Another access system is VCIS (Voice Case Information System). At one time nearly all of the U.S. Bankruptcy Court judicial districts provided VCIS as a means of accessing information regarding open bankruptcy cases. Access was by touch-tone telephone. VCIS is gradually being phased out and now only a few dozen courts allow VCIS dialup. Still, there is no charge. Individual names are entered last name first with as much of the first name as you wish to include. For example, Carl R. Ernst could be entered as ERNSTC or ERNSTCARL. Do not enter the middle initial. Business names are entered as they are written, without blanks.

VCIS, like the RACER System, is being replaced by newer technology.

Federal Courts Searching Hints

- Since this publication includes the counties of jurisdiction for each court, the list of counties in each Court profile is a good starting point for determining where case records may or may not be found.

- Before performing a general PACER search to determine whether cases exist under a particular plaintiff, debtor, or defendant name, first be certain to review that Court's profile, which indicates the various methods of records access there.

- Experience shows that court personnel are typically not aware of — nor concerned about — the types of searches performed by readers of this publication. Court personnel often focus on only open cases, whereas a searcher may want to know as much about closed cases as open ones. Thus, court personnel are sometimes fuzzy in answering questions about how far back case records go on PACER, and whether closed cases have been purged. If you are looking for cases older than a year or two, there is no substitute for a real, onsite search performed by the court itself or by a local search expert (if that court allows full access to its indexes). You may search online for a search expert – a professional document retriever who is a member of the Public Record Retriever Network (PRRN) – at www.brbpub.com/PRRN/search.asp.

- Also, when communicating to a court, searchers need to be sure that the court's case index includes all cases open and closed for that particular period. Be aware that some courts purge older, closed cases after a period of time, making a PACER search incomplete. Purge times vary from court to court and state to state.

- Some courts may be more willing than others to give out information by telephone. This is because a court may or may not have converted from the old card index system to fully computerized indexes that are easily accessible while on the phone.

- If available, VCIS should only be used to locate information about open cases. Do not attempt to use VCIS as a substitute for a PACER search.

Federal Records Centers and the National Archives

After a federal case is closed, the documents are held by Federal Courts themselves for a number of years, then stored at a designated Federal Records Center (FRC). After 20 to 30 years, the records are then transferred from the FRC to the regional archives offices of the National Archives and Records Administration (NARA). The length of time between a case being closed and its being moved to an FRC varies widely by district. Each court has its own transfer cycle and determines access procedures to its case records even after they have been sent to the FRC.

When case records are sent to an FRC, the boxes of records are assigned accession, location, and box numbers. These numbers, which are called **case locator information**, must be obtained from the originating court and are necessary to retrieve documents from the FRC. Some courts will provide case locator information over the telephone, but other courts require a written request. This information is now available on PACER in certain judicial districts.

The Federal Records Center for each state is listed below. Also included is the location of the Federal Appeals Court and the Circuit Number.

State	Circuit	Appeals Court	Federal Records Center
Alaska	9	San Francisco, CA	Anchorage (Some records are in temporary storage in Seattle)
Alabama	11	Atlanta, GA	Atlanta
Arkansas	8	St. Louis, MO	Fort Worth
Arizona	9	San Francisco, CA	Los Angeles
California	9	San Francisco, CA	Los Angeles (Central & Southern CA) San Francisco (Eastern & Northern CA)
Colorado	10	Denver, CO	Denver
Connecticut	2	New York, NY	Boston
DC		Washington, DC	Washington, DC
Delaware	3	Philadelphia, PA	Philadelphia
Florida	11	Atlanta, GA	Atlanta
Georgia	11	Atlanta, GA	Atlanta
Guam	9	San Francisco, CA	San Francisco
Hawaii	9	San Francisco, CA	San Francisco
Iowa	8	St. Louis, MO	Kansas City, MO
Idaho	9	San Francisco, CA	Seattle
Illinois	7	Chicago, IL	Chicago
Indiana	7	Chicago, IL	Chicago
Kansas	10	Denver, CO	Kansas City, MO
Kentucky	6	Cincinnati, OH	Atlanta
Louisiana	5	New Orleans, LA	Fort Worth
Massachusetts	1	Boston, MA	Boston
Maryland	4	Richmond, VA	Philadelphia
Maine	1	Boston, MA	Boston
Michigan	6	Cincinnati, OH	Chicago
Minnesota	8	St. Louis, MO	Chicago
Missouri	8	St. Louis, MO	Kansas City, MO

State	Circuit	Appeals Court	Federal Records Center
Mississippi	5	New Orleans, LA	Atlanta
Montana	9	San Francisco, CA	Denver
North Carolina	4	Richmond, VA	Atlanta
North Dakota	8	St. Louis, MO	Denver
Nebraska	8	St. Louis, MO	Kansas City, MO
New Hampshire	1	Boston, MA	Boston
New Jersey	3	Philadelphia, PA	New York
New Mexico	10	Denver, CO	Denver
Nevada	9	San Francisco, CA	Los Angeles (Clark County, NV) San Francisco (Other NV counties)
New York	2	New York, NY	New York
Ohio	6	Cincinnati, OH	Chicago (The Dayton Records Center also has some bankruptcy records)
Oklahoma	10	Denver, CO	Fort Worth
Oregon	9	San Francisco, CA	Seattle
Pennsylvania	3	Philadelphia, PA	Philadelphia
Puerto Rico	1	Boston, MA	New York
Rhode Island	1	Boston, MA	Boston
South Carolina	4	Richmond, VA	Atlanta
South Dakota	8	St. Louis, MO	Denver
Tennessee	6	Cincinnati, OH	Atlanta
Texas	5	New Orleans, LA	Fort Worth
Utah	10	Denver, CO	Denver
Virginia	4	Richmond, VA	Philadelphia
Virgin Islands	3	Philadelphia, PA	New York
Vermont	2	New York, NY	Boston
Washington	9	San Francisco, CA	Seattle
Wisconsin	7	Chicago, IL	Chicago
West Virginia	4	Richmond, VA	Philadelphia
Wyoming	10	Denver, CO	Denver

Notes to the Chart:

- According to some odd logic, the following Federal Records Centers are not located in the city named above, but are actually somewhere else. Below are the exceptions:

  Atlanta—in East Point, GA;
  Boston—in Waltham, MA;
  Los Angeles—in Laguna Niguel, CA;

  New York—in Bayonne, NJ;
  San Francisco—in San Bruno, CA.

The universal PACER sign-up number is 800-676-6856. Find PACER and Party/Case Index at http://pacer.psc.uscourts.gov.

All court addresses are "MAILING ADDRESSES." The physical address may be different. See the court's website.

Alabama

U.S. District Court

Middle District of Alabama

www.almd.uscourts.gov Pacer is online-http://pacer.almd.uscourts.gov.
Dothan Division c/o Montgomery Division, PO Box 711, Montgomery, AL 36101. 334-223-7308. Counties: Coffee, Dale, Geneva, Henry, Houston. ✉ Pacer
Montgomery Division Records Search, PO Box 711, Montgomery, AL 36101-0711. 334-223-7308. Counties: Autauga, Barbour, Bullock, Butler, Chilton, Coosa, Covington, Crenshaw, Elmore, Lowndes, Montgomery, Pike. ✉ Pacer
Opelika Division c/o Montgomery Division, PO Box 711, Montgomery, AL 36101. 334-223-7308. Counties: Chambers, Lee, Macon, Randolph, Russell, Tallapoosa. ✉ Pacer

Northern District of Alabama

www.alnd.uscourts.gov Pacer is online at http://pacer.alnd.uscourts.gov.
Birmingham Division Room 104, US Courthouse, 1729 5th Ave N, Birmingham, AL 35203. 205-278-1700. Counties: Bibb, Blount, Calhoun, Clay, Cleburne, Greene, Jefferson, Pickens, Shelby, Sumter, Talladega, Tuscaloosa. ✉ ☎ Pacer
Florence Division PO Box 776, Florence, AL 35630. 205-760-5815, Fax: 205-760-5727. Colbert, Franklin, Lauderdale. ✉ ☎ Pacer
Gadsden Division c/o Birmingham Division, Room 140, US Courthouse, 1729 5th Ave N, Birmingham, AL 35203. 205-278-1700. Counties: Cherokee, De Kalb, Etowah, Marshall, St. Clair. ✉ Pacer
Huntsville Division Clerk's Office, US Post Office & Courthouse #302, 101 Holmes Ave NE, Huntsville, AL 35801. 205-534-6495. Counties: Cullman, Jackson, Lawrence, Limestone, Madison, Morgan. ✉ ☎ Pacer
Jasper Division c/o Birmingham Div., Room 140, US Courthouse, 1729 5th Ave N, Birmingham, AL 35203. 205-278-1700. Counties: Fayette, Lamar, Marion, Walker, Winston. ✉ Pacer

Southern District of Alabama

www.als.uscourts.gov Pacer is online at http://pacer.alsd.uscourts.gov. CM-ECF: https://ecf.almd.uscourts.gov.
Mobile Division Clerk, 113 St Joseph St, Mobile, AL 36602. Phone: 251-690-2371, Fax: 251-694-4297. Baldwin, Choctaw, Clarke, Conecuh, Escambia, Mobile, Monroe, Washington. ✉ ☎ Pacer
Selma Division c/o Mobile Division, 113 St Joseph St, Mobile, AL 36602. Phone: 251-690-2371, Fax: 251-694-4297. Counties: Dallas, Hale, Marengo, Perry, Wilcox. ✉ Pacer

Bankruptcy Court

Middle District of Alabama

www.almb.uscourts.gov Pacer is online at http://pacer.almb.uscourts.gov. CM-ECF: https://ecf.almb.uscourts.gov.
Montgomery Division PO Box 1248, Montgomery, AL 36102-1248. Phone: 334-954-3800, Fax: 334-954-3819. Counties: Autauga, Barbour, Bullock, Butler, Chambers, Chilton, Coffee, Coosa, Covington, Crenshaw, Dale, Elmore, Geneva, Henry, Houston, Lee, Lowndes, Macon, Montgomery, Pike, Randolph, Russell, Tallapoosa. ✉ ☎ Pacer

Northern District of Alabama

www.alnb.uscourts.gov Pacer is online at http://pacer.alnb.uscourts.gov. CM-ECF: https://ecf.alnb.uscourts.gov.

Anniston Division PO Box 2008, Anniston, AL36202-2008. Phone: 256-741-1500, Fax: 256-741-1503. Counties: Calhoun, Cherokee, Clay, Cleburne, De Kalb, Etowah, Marshall, St. Clair, Talladega. ✉ ☎ Pacer
Birmingham Division Room 120, 1800 5th Ave N, Birmingham, AL 35203. Phone: 205-714-4000, Fax: 205-714-3913. Counties: Blount, Jefferson, Shelby. ✉ ☎ Pacer
Decatur Division PO Box 2748, Decatur, AL 35602. Phone: 256-584-7900, Fax: 256-584-7977. Counties: Colbert, Cullman, Franklin, Jackson, Lauderdale, Lawrence, Limestone, Madison, Morgan. The part of Winston County North of Double Springs is handled by this division. ✉ ☎ Pacer
Tuscaloosa Division PO Box 3226, Tuscaloosa, AL 35403. Phone: 205-752-0426, Records Rm: 205-752-0426, Fax: 205-752-6468. Counties: Bibb, Fayette, Greene, Lamar, Marion, Pickens, Sumter, Tuscaloosa, Walker, Winston. The part of Winston County North of Double Springs is handled by Decatur Div. ✉ ☎ Pacer

Southern District of Alabama

www.alsb.uscourts.gov Court uses new CM/ECF system for PACER. CM-ECF: https://ecf.alsb.uscourts.gov.
Mobile Division Clerk, 201 St. Louis St, Mobile, AL 36602. Phone: 251-441-5391, Fax: 251-441-6286. Counties: Baldwin, Choctaw, Clarke, Conecuh, Dallas, Escambia, Hale, Marengo, Mobile, Monroe, Perry, Washington, Wilcox. ✉ ☎ Pacer

Alaska

U.S. District Court

www.akd.uscourts.gov
Anchorage Division Room 229, 222 W 7th Ave, Anchorage, AK 99513-7564. Phone: 907-677-6100, 866-243-3814. Jurisdiction: Aleutian Islands-East, Aleutian Islands-West, Anchorage Borough, Bristol Bay Borough, Dillingham, Kenai Peninsula Borough, Kodiak Island Borough, Lake and Peninsula, Matanuska-Susitna Borough, Valdez-Cordova. ✉ ☎ Pacer
Fairbanks Division Room 332, 101 12th Ave, Fairbanks, AK 99701. Phone: 907-451-5791, 866-243-3813. Jurisdiction: Bethel, Denali, Fairbanks North Star Borough, North Slope Borough, Northwest Arctic Borough, Southeast

Fairbanks, Wade Hampton, Yukon-Koyukuk. ✉ ☎ Pacer
Juneau Division PO Box 020349, 709 W. 9th Ave., Rm 979, Juneau, AK 99802-0349. Phone: 907-586-7458, 866-243-3812. Jurisdiction: Haines Borough, Juneau Borough, Prince of Wales-Outer Ketchikan, Sitka Borough, Skagway-Hoonah-Angoon, Wrangell-Petersburg. ✉ ☎ Pacer
Ketchikan Division 648 Mission St, Room 507, Ketchikan, AK 99901. 907-247-7576. Jurisdiction: Ketchikan Gateway Borough. ✉ ☎ Pacer
Nome Division PO Box 130, Nome, AK 99762. Phone: 907-443-5216, Fax: 907-443-2192. Jurisdiction: Nome. ✉ Fax ☎ Pacer

Bankruptcy Court

http://www2.akb.uscourts.gov/mainpage.htm Pacer is now online at http://pacer.akb.uscourts.gov. CM-ECF: https://ecf.akb.uscourts.gov.
Anchorage Division Historic Courthouse, Suite 138, 605 W 4th Ave, Anchorage, AK 99501-2296. Phone: 907-271-2655. Jurisdiction: All boroughs/districts in Alaska. ✉ Pacer

Arizona

U.S. District Court

District of Arizona

www.azd.uscourts.gov Pacer is online at http://pacer.azd.uscourts.gov.
Phoenix Division Sandra Day O'Connor U.S. Courthouse, #130, 401 W. Washington Street, SPC 1, Phoenix, AZ 85025-2118. Phone: 602-322-7200, Records Rm: 602-322-7205. Counties: Gila, La Paz, Maricopa, Pinal, Yuma. Some Yuma cases handled by San Diego Division of the Southern District of California. ✉ Pacer
Prescott Division 101 W Goodwin St, US Post Office Bldg, Prescott, AZ 86303. Phone: 928-445-6598. Counties: Apache, Coconino, Mohave, Navajo, Yavapai. ✉ Pacer

Tucson Division US Court House, 405 W. Congress Ste 1500, Tucson, AZ 85701-5010. Phone: 520-205-4200, Fax: 520-205-4209. Counties: Cochise, Graham, Greelee, Pima, Santa Cruz. The Globe Division was closed effective January 1994, and all case records for that division are now found here. ✉☎Pacer

Bankruptcy Court

District of Arizona

www.azb.uscourts.gov Pacer is online at http://pacer.azb.uscourts.gov. Searching of electronically filed cases requires registration and password with the court. CM-ECF: https://ecf.azb.uscourts.gov.
Phoenix Division PO Box 34151, (2929 N Central, 9th Fl), Phoenix, AZ 85067-

4151. Phone: 602-640-5800. Counties: Apache, Coconino, Maricopa, Navajo, Yavapai. ✉ ☎ Pacer
Tucson Division Suite 8112, 110 S Church Ave, Tucson, AZ 85701-1608. Phone: 520-620-7500. Counties: Cochise, Gila, Graham, Greenlee, Pima, Pinal, Santa Cruz. ✉ ☎ Pacer
Yuma Division PO Box 13011, Yuma, AZ 85366. Phone: 928-783-2288. Counties: La Paz, Mohave, Yuma. ✉ ☎ Pacer

Arkansas

U.S. District Court

Eastern District of Arkansas

www.are.uscourts.gov
Batesville Division c/o Little Rock Division, PO Box 869, Little Rock, AR 72201-3325. Phone: 501-604-5351. Counties: Cleburne, Fulton, Independence, Izard, Jackson, Sharp, Stone. ⊠ ☎ Pacer

Helena Division c/o Little Rock Division, 600 W Capital Rm 402, Little Rock, AR 72201-3325. Phone: 501-604-5351. Counties: Cross, Lee, Monroe, Phillips, St. Francis, Woodruff. ⊠ ☎ Pacer

Jonesboro Division PO Box 7080, Jonesboro, AR 72403. Phone: 870-972-4610, Fax: 870-972-4612. Counties: Clay, Craighead, Crittenden, Greene, Lawrence, Mississippi, Poinsett, Randolph.
⊠ Fax ☎ Pacer

Little Rock Division Room 402, 600 W Capitol, Little Rock, AR 72201. Phone: 501-604-5351. Counties: Conway, Faulkner, Lonoke, Perry, Pope, Prairie, Pulaski, Saline, Van Buren, White, Yell.
⊠ ☎ Pacer

Pine Bluff Division PO Box 8307, Pine Bluff, AR 71611-8307. Phone: 870-536-1190, Fax: 870-536-6330. Counties: Arkansas, Chicot, Cleveland, Dallas,

Desha, Drew, Grant, Jefferson, Lincoln. ⊠ ☎ Pacer

Western District of Arkansas

www.arwd.uscourts.gov Pacer is online at http://pacer.arwd.uscourts.gov.
El Dorado Division PO Box 1566, El Dorado, AR 71731. Phone: 870-862-1202. Ashley, Bradley, Calhoun, Columbia, Ouachita, Union. ⊠ Fax ☎ Pacer

Fayetteville Division PO Box 6420, Fayetteville, AR 72702. Phone: 479-521-6980, Fax: 479-575-0774. Benton, Madison, Washington. ⊠ Fax ☎ Pacer

Fort Smith Division PO Box 1547, Fort Smith, AR 72902. Phone: 479-783-6833, Fax: 479-783-6308. Counties: Crawford, Franklin, Johnson, Logan, Polk, Scott, Sebastian. ⊠ ☎ Pacer

Hot Springs Division PO Drawer6486, Hot Springs, AR 71902. Phone: 501-623-6411. Counties: Clark, Garland, Hot Springs, Montgomery, Pike.⊠ ☎Pacer

Texarkana Division PO Box 2746, Texarkana, AR 75504-2746. Phone: 870-773-3381. Counties: Hempstead, Howard, Lafayette, Little River, Miller, Nevada, Sevier. ⊠ ☎ Pacer

Bankruptcy Court

Eastern District of Arkansas

www.areb.uscourts.gov Court uses new CM/ECF system for PACER. CM-ECF: https://ecf.areb.uscourts.gov.
Little Rock Division PO Drawer 3777, Little Rock, AR 72203. Phone: 501-918-5500, Fax: 501-918-5520. Counties: Same counties as included in Eastern District of Arkansas, plus the counties included in the Western District divisions of El Dorado, Hot Springs and Texarkana. All bankruptcy cases in Arkansas prior to mid-1993 were heard here. ⊠ ☎ Pacer

Western District of Arkansas

www.arb.uscourts.gov Court uses new CM/ECF system for PACER. CM-ECF: https://ecf.arwb.uscourts.gov.
Fayetteville Division: Mail address: PO Box 3097, Fayetteville, AR 72702-3097. Phone: 479-582-9800, Fax: 479-582-9825. Counties: Same counties as included in the US District District Court - Western District of Arkansas except that counties included in the divisions of El Dorado and Texarkana are heard in Little Rock. ⊠ ☎ Pacer

California

U.S. District Court

Central District of California

www.cacd.uscourts.gov Pacer is online at http://pacer.cacd.uscourts.gov. CM-ECF: https://ecf.cacd.uscourts.gov.
Los Angeles (Western) Division US Courthouse, Attn: Correspondence, 312 N Spring St, Room G-8, Los Angeles, CA 90012. Phone: 213-894-5261. Counties: Los Angeles, San Luis Obispo, Santa Barbara, Ventura. ⊠ Fax Pacer

Riverside (Eastern) Division US District Court, PO Box 13000, Riverside, CA

92502 Phone: 951-328-4450. Counties: Riverside, San Bernardino. ⊠ Pacer
Santa Ana (Southern) Division 411 W 4th St Rm 1053, Santa Ana, CA 92701-4516. Phone: 714-338-4750. Counties: Orange. ⊠ ☎ Pacer

Eastern District of California

www.caed.uscourts.gov Pacer is online at http://pacer.caed.uscourts.gov.
Fresno Division US Courthouse, Room 5000, 1130 "O" St, Fresno, CA 93721-2201. Phone: 559-498-7483, Records Rm: 559-498-7372. Fresno, Inyo, Kern, Kings,

Madera, Mariposa, Merced, Stanislaus, Tulare, Tuolumne. ⊠☎Pacer
Sacramento Division 501 I St, Sacramento, CA 95814. Phone: 916-930-4000, Records Rm: 916-498-5415, Fax: 916-930-4015. Counties: Alpine, Amador, Butte, Calaveras, Colusa, El Dorado, Glenn, Lassen, Modoc, Mono, Nevada, Placer, Plumas, Sacramento, San Joaquin, Shasta, Sierra, Siskiyou, Solano, Sutter, Tehama, Trinity, Yolo, Yuba. ⊠☎Pacer

Northern District of California

www.cand.uscourts.gov Pacer is online at http://pacer.cand.uscourts.gov. ECF cases data back to 4/2001. CM-ECF: https://ecf.cand.uscourts.gov.
Oakland Division 1301 Clay St, Ste 400S, Oakland, CA 94612-5212. Phone: 510-637-3530. Counties: Alameda, Contra Costa (Note: Cases may be filed here or at San Francisco Div.; records available electronically at either; the 1st number of the case # indicates the file location: 3=SF, 4=Oak., 5=SJ. ✉☎Pacer
San Francisco Division 450 Golden Gate Ave, 16th Fl, San Francisco, CA 94102. Phone: 415-522-2000. Counties: Del Norte, Humboldt, Lake, Marin, Mendocino, Napa, San Francisco, San Mateo, Sonoma (Note: Cases may be filed here or at Oakland Div; records available electronically at either; the 1st number of the case # indicates the file location: 3=SF, 4=Oak., 5=SJ. ✉ ☎ Pacer
San Jose Division Room 2112, 280 S 1st St, San Jose, CA 95113. Phone: 408-535-5364. Counties: Monterey, San Benito, Santa Clara, Santa Cruz. ✉ ☎ Pacer

Southern District of California

www.casd.uscourts.gov Pacer is online at http://pacer.casd.uscourts.gov.
San Diego Division Clerk of Court, Room 4290, 880 Front St, San Diego, CA 92101-8900. Phone: 619-557-5600, Records Rm: 619-557-7362, Fax: 619-557-6684. Counties: Imperial, San Diego. Court also handles some cases from Yuma County, AZ. ✉ Pacer

Bankruptcy Court

Central District of California

www.cacb.uscourts.gov Pacer is online at https://pacer.login.uscourts.gov/cgi-bin/login.pl?court_id=CACBLA.
Los Angeles Division 255 E Temple St, Roybal Bldg, #945, Los Angeles, CA 90012. Phone: 213-894-3118, Records

Rm: 213-894-7205, Fax: 213-894-1261. Counties: Los Angeles (cases filed in certain northern Los Angeles County ZIP Codes may be shared with the San Fernando Valley Div.). ✉ Fax Pacer
Riverside (East) Division 3420 12th St #125, Riverside, CA 92501-3819. 951-774-1000. Counties: Riverside, San Bernardino. ✉ ☎ Pacer
San Fernando Valley Division 21041 Burbank Blvd, Woodland Hills, CA 91367. Phone: 818-587-2900. Counties: Los Angeles, Ventura (cases filed in certain northern Los Angeles County ZIP Codes are shared with the Los Angeles Division, and cases filed in certain eastern Ventura County ZIP Codes are shared with Ventura Div.). ✉ Fax ☎ Pacer
Santa Ana Division Ronald Reagan Federal Bldg & US Courthouse, 411 W 4th St #2030, Santa Ana, CA 92701-4593. Phone: 714-836-5300. Counties: Orange. ✉ ☎ Pacer
Santa Barbara (Northern) Division 1415 State St, Santa Barbara, CA 93101. Phone: 805-884-4800. Counties: San Luis Obispo, Santa Barbara, Ventura. Certain Ventura County ZIP Codes are assigned to the new office in San Fernando Valley. ✉ Pacer

Eastern District of California

www.caeb.uscourts.gov Pacer is online at http://pacer.caeb.uscourts.gov/pacerhome.html.
Fresno Division Room 2656, 1130 O Street, Fresno, CA 93721. Phone: 559-498-7217. Counties: Fresno, Inyo, Kern, Kings, Madera, Mariposa, Merced, Tulare. Three Kern ZIP Codes, 93243 and 93523-24, are handled by San Fernando Valley in the Central District. ✉ ☎ Pacer
Modesto Division PO Box 5276, Modesto, CA 95352. Phone: 209-521-5160. Counties: Calaveras, San Joaquin, Stanislaus, Tuolumne. The following ZIP Codes in San Joaquin County are handled by the Sacramento Division: 95220,

95227, 95234, 95237, 95240-95242, 95253, 95258, and 95686. Mariposa and Merced counties were transferred to the Fresno Division as of January 1, 1995. ✉ ☎ Pacer
Sacramento Division US Courthouse, 501 I St, Rm 3-200, Sacramento, CA 95814. Phone: 916-930-4400. Counties: Alpine, Amador, Butte, Colusa, El Dorado, Glenn, Lassen, Modoc, Mono, Nevada, Placer, Plumas, Sacramento, Shasta, Sierra, Siskiyou, Solano, Sutter, Tehama, Trinity, Yolo, Yuba. This court also handles the following ZIP Codes in San Joaquin County: 95220, 95227, 95234, 95237, 95240-95242, 95253, 95258 and 95686. ✉ ☎ Pacer

Northern District of California

www.canb.uscourts.gov Pacer is online at http://pacer.canb.uscourts.gov. CM-ECF: https://ecf.canb.uscourts.gov.
Oakland Division PO Box 2070, Oakland, CA 94604. Phone: 510-879-3600. Alameda, Contra Costa. ✉ Pacer
San Francisco Division PO Box 7341, San Francisco, CA 94120-7341. 415-268-2300. Counties: San Francisco, San Mateo. ✉ ☎ Pacer
San Jose Division Room 3035, 3rd Fl, 280 S 1st St, San Jose, CA 95113-3099. Phone: 408-535-5118. Counties: Monterey, San Benito, Santa Clara, Santa Cruz. ✉ ☎ Pacer
Santa Rosa Division 99 South E St, Santa Rosa, CA 95404. Phone: 369-525-8539, Fax: 369-579-0374. Counties: Del Norte, Humboldt, Lake, Marin, Mendocino, Napa, Sonoma. ✉ ☎ Pacer

Southern District of California

www.casb.uscourts.gov Pacer is online at http://pacer.casb.uscourts.gov. CM-ECF: http://ecf.casb.uscourts.gov.
San Diego Division Office of the Clerk, US Courthouse, 325 West "F" St., San Diego, CA 92101. Phone: 619-557-5620. Counties: Imperial, San Diego. ✉ Fax ☎ Pacer

Colorado

U.S. District Court

www.co.uscourts.gov Pacer is online at http://pacer.cod.uscourts.gov Mail: US Courthouse, 901 19th Street, Denver, CO 80294-3589. Phone: 303-844-3433. Counties: All counties. ✉ ☎ Pacer

Bankruptcy Court

www.cob.uscourts.gov/bindex.htm Pacer is online at http://pacer.cob.uscourts.gov. CM-ECF: https://ecf.cob.uscourts.gov US Custom House, Room 114, 721 19th St, Denver, CO 80202-2508. Phone: 303-844-4045, Records Rm: 303-844-0235. Counties: All counties. ✉ ☎ Pacer

Connecticut

U.S. District Court

www.ctd.uscourts.gov Pacer is online at http://pacer.ctd.uscourts.gov. CM-ECF: https://ecf.ctd.uscourts.gov.
Bridgeport Division Office of the clerk, Room 400, 915 Lafayette Blvd, Bridgeport, CT 06604. Phone: 203-579-5861. Counties: Fairfield (prior to 1993). Since 1993, cases from any county may be assigned to any of the divisions in the district. ✉ ☎ Pacer
Hartford Division 450 Main St, Hartford, CT 06103. Phone: 860-240-3200. Counties: Hartford, Tolland, Windham (prior to 1993). Since 1993, cases from

any county may be assigned to any of the divisions in the district. ✉ ☎ Pacer
New Haven Division 141 Church St, New Haven, CT 06510. Phone: 203-773-2140. Counties: Litchfield, Middlesex, New Haven, New London (prior to 1993). Since 1993, cases from any county may be assigned to any of the divisions in the district. ✉ ☎ Pacer

Bankruptcy Court

www.ctb.uscourts.gov Pacer is online at http://pacer.ctb.uscourts.gov. CM-ECF: https://ecf.ctb.uscourts.gov/.

Bridgeport Division 915 Lafayette Blvd, Bridgeport, CT 06604. Phone: 203-579-5808, Records Rm: 203-579-5808. Counties: Fairfield. ✉ Pacer
Hartford Division 450 Main St, Hartford, CT 06103. Phone: 860-240-3675. Counties: Hartford, Litchfield, Middlesex, Tolland, Windham. ✉ ☎ Pacer
New Haven Division The Connecticut Financial Center, 157 Church St, 18th Floor, New Haven, CT 06510. Phone: 203-773-2009. Counties: New Haven, New London. ✉ ☎ Pacer

Delaware

U.S. District Court

www.ded.uscourts.gov Pacer is online at http://pacer.ded.uscourts.gov US Courthouse, Lock Box 18, 844 N King St, Wilmington, DE 19801. Phone: 302-573-6170, Records Rm: 302-573-6158. Counties: All. ✉ ☎ Pacer

Bankruptcy Court

www.deb.uscourts.gov (online search free) Uses new CM/ecf system for Pacer. CM-ECF: https://ecf.deb.uscourts.gov 824 North Market St, 3rd Floor, Marine Midland Plaza, Wilmington, DE 19801. Phone: 888-667-5530. ✉ ☎ Pacer

District of Columbia

U.S. District Court

www.dcd.uscourts.gov Pacer is at http://pacer.dcd.uscourts.gov CM-ECF: https://ecf.dcd.uscourts.gov.
Washington DC Division US Courthouse, Clerk's Office, Room 1225, 333 Constitution Ave NW, Washington, DC 20001. Phone: 202-727-2947, Records Rm: 202-354-3000, Fax: 202-354-3524. Counties: District of Columbia. ✉ ☎ Pacer

Bankruptcy Court

www.dcb.uscourts.gov Pacer is at http://pacer.dcb.uscourts.gov CM-ECF: https://ecf.dcb.uscourts.gov
Washington DC Division E Barrett Prettyman Courthouse, Room 4400, 333 Constitution Ave NW, Washington, DC 20001. Phone: 202-565-2500. ✉ Pacer

Florida

U.S. District Court

Middle District of Florida

www.flmd.uscourts.gov Pacer is online at http://pacer.flmd.uscourts.gov. CM-ECF: https://ecf.flmd.uscourts.gov.
Fort Myers Division 2110 First St, Room 2-194, Fort Myers, FL 33901. Phone: 239-461-2000. Counties: Charlotte, Collier, De Soto, Glades, Hendry, Lee. ✉ ☎ Pacer
Jacksonville Division PO Box 53558, Jacksonville, FL 32201. Phone: 904-549-1900. Counties: Baker, Bradford, Clay, Columbia, Duval, Flagler, Hamilton, Nassau, Putnam, St. Johns, Suwannee, Union. ✉ Pacer
Ocala Division US Court House, 207 NW Second St., Ocala, FL 34475. Phone: 352-369-4860. Counties: Citrus, Lake, Marion, Sumter. ✉ Pacer
Orlando Division Room 218, 80 North Hughey Ave, Orlando, FL 32801. Phone: 407-835-4200. Brevard, Orange, Osceola, Seminole, Volusia. ✉ ☎ Pacer
Tampa Division Office of the clerk, 801 N Florida Ave #223, Tampa, FL 33602-4500. Phone: 813-301-5400. Counties: Hardee, Hernando, Hillsborough, Manatee, Pasco, Pinellas, Polk, Sarasota. ✉ ☎ Pacer

Northern District of Florida

www.flnd.uscourts.gov Pacer is online at http://pacer.flnd.uscourts.gov. CM-ECF: https://ecf.flnd.uscourts.gov.
Gainesville Division 401 SE First Ave, Room 243, Gainesville, FL 32601. Phone:

352-380-2400, Fax: 352-380-2424. Counties: Alachua, Dixie, Gilchrist, Lafayette, Levy. Records for cases prior to July 1996 are maintained at the Tallahassee Division. ✉ ☎ Pacer
Panama City Division 30 W. Government St., Panama City, FL 32401. Phone: 850-769-4556, Fax: 850-769-7528. Counties: Bay, Calhoun, Gulf, Holmes, Jackson, Washington. ✉ Pacer
Pensacola Division US Courthouse, 1 N Palafox St, #226, Pensacola, FL 32502. Phone: 850-435-8440, Fax: 850-433-5972. Counties: Escambia, Okaloosa, Santa Rosa, Walton. ✉ ☎ Pacer
Tallahassee Division Suite 122, 111 North Adams St., Tallahassee, FL 32301. Phone: 850-521-3501, Fax: 850-521-3656. Counties: Franklin, Gadsden, Jefferson, Leon, Liberty, Madison, Taylor, Wakulla. ✉ ☎ Pacer

Southern District of Florida

www.flsd.uscourts.gov Pacer is online at http://pacer.flsd.uscourts.gov.
Fort Lauderdale Division 299 E Broward Blvd, Fort Lauderdale, FL 33301. Phone: 954-769-5400. Counties: Broward. ✉ Pacer
Fort Pierce Division U S Court House, 300 South Sixth Street, Miami, FL 33128. Phone: 772-595-9691. Counties: Highlands, Indian River, Martin, Okeechobee, St. Lucie. ✉ ☎ Pacer
Key West Division 301 Simonton St., Key West, FL 33040. Phone: 305-295-8100. Counties: Monroe. ✉ Pacer

Miami Division Room 150, 301 N Miami Ave, Miami, FL 33128 Phone: 305-523-5100. County Miami-Dade. ✉ ☎ Pacer
West Palm Beach Division Room 402, 701 Clematis St, West Palm Beach, FL 33401. Phone: 561-803-3400. Counties: Palm Beach. ✉ ☎ Pacer

Bankruptcy Court

Middle District of Florida

www.flmb.uscourts.gov Pacer is online at http://pacer.flmb.uscourts.gov. CM-ECF: https://ecf.flmb.uscourts.gov.
Jacksonville Division PO Box 559, Jacksonville, FL 32201. Phone: 904-301-6490. Counties: Baker, Bradford, Citrus, Clay, Columbia, Duval, Flagler, Hamilton, Marion, Nassau, Putnam, St. Johns, Sumter, Suwannee, Union, Volusia. ✉ ☎ Pacer
Orlando Division Suite 950, 135 W Central Blvd, Orlando, FL 32801. Phone: 407-648-6365. Counties: Brevard, Lake, Orange, Osceola, Seminole. ✉ ☎ Pacer
Tampa Division 801 N Florida Ave #727, Tampa, FL 33602. Phone: 813-301-5065. Counties: Charlotte, Collier, De Soto, Glades, Hardee, Hendry, Hernando, Hillsborough, Lee, Manatee, Pasco, Pinellas, Polk, Sarasota. ✉ Pacer

Northern District of Florida

www.flnb.uscourts.gov/ Pacer is online at http://pacer.flnb.uscourts.gov. CM-ECF: https://ecf.flnb.uscourts.gov/.
Pensacola Division Suite 700, 220 W Garden St, Pensacola, FL 32502. Phone:

850-435-8475. Counties: Escambia, Okaloosa, Santa Rosa, Walton. ✉ Pacer
Tallahassee Division Room 3120, 227 N Bronough St, Tallahassee, FL 32301-1378. Phone: 850-942-8933. Counties: Alachua, Bay, Calhoun, Dixie, Franklin, Gadsden, Gilchrist, Gulf, Holmes, Jackson, Jefferson, Lafayette, Leon, Levy, Liberty, Madison, Taylor, Wakulla, Washington. ✉ Pacer

Southern District of Florida
www.flsb.uscourts.gov Pacer is online at http://pacer.flsb.uscourts.gov.
Miami Division Room 1517, 51 SW 1st Ave, Miami, FL 33130. Phone: 305-536-5216. Counties: Broward, Dade, Highlands, Indian River, Martin, Miami-Dade, Monroe, Okeechobee, Palm Beach, St. Lucie. Cases may also be assigned to Fort Lauderdale or to West Palm Beach. ✉ Pacer

Georgia

U.S. District Court
Middle District of Georgia
www.gamd.uscourts.gov Pacer is online at http://pacer.gamd.uscourts.gov.
Albany/Americus Division PO Box 1906, Albany, GA 31702. Phone: 229-430-8432, Fax: 229-430-8538. Counties: Baker, Ben Hill, Calhoun, Crisp, Dougherty, Early, Lee, Miller, Mitchell, Schley, Sumter, Terrell, Turner, Webster, Worth. Ben Hill and Crisp were transfered from the Macon 10/1/1997. ✉ ☎ Pacer
Athens Division PO Box 1106, Athens, GA 30603. Phone: 706-227-1094, Fax: 706-546-2190. Counties: Clarke, Elbert, Franklin, Greene, Hart, Madison, Morgan, Oconee, Oglethorpe, Walton. Closed cases before 4/1997 are located in the Macon Division. ✉ Pacer
Columbus Division PO Box 124, Columbus, GA 31902. Phone: 706-649-7816. Chattahoochee, Clay, Harris, Marion, Muscogee, Quitman, Randolph, Stewart, Talbot, Taylor. ✉ Pacer
Macon Division PO Box 128, Macon, GA 31202-0128. Phone: 912-752-3497, Fax: 912-752-3496. Counties: Baldwin, Ben Hill, Bibb, Bleckley, Butts, Crawford, Crisp, Dooly, Hancock, Houston, Jasper, Jones, Lamar, Macon, Monroe, Peach, Pulaski, Putnam, Twiggs, Upson, Washington, Wilcox, Wilkinson. Athens Div. cases closed before 4/1997 are also located here. ✉ Fax ☎ Pacer
Thomasville Division c/o Valdosta Div., PO Box 68, Valdosta, GA 31601. Phone: 912-226-3651. Counties: Brooks, Colquitt, Decatur, Grady, Seminole, Thomas. ✉ Pacer
Valdosta Division PO Box 68, Valdosta, GA 31603. Phone: 912-242-3616, Fax: 912-244-9547. Counties: Berrien, Clinch, Cook, Echols, Irwin, Lanier, Lowndes, Tift. ✉ ☎ Pacer

Northern District of Georgia
www.gand.uscourts.gov Pacer is online at http://pacer.gand.uscourts.gov. CM-ECF: https://ecf.gand.uscourts.gov.
Atlanta Division 2211 US Courthouse, 75 Spring St SW, Atlanta, GA 30303-3361. Phone: 404-215-1660. Counties: Cherokee, Clayton, Cobb, De Kalb, Douglas, Fulton, Gwinnett, Henry, Newton, Rockdale. ✉ ☎ Pacer
Gainesville Division Federal Bldg, Room 201, 121 Spring St SE, Gainesville, GA 30501. Phone: 678-450-2760. Counties: Banks, Barrow, Dawson, Fannin, Forsyth, Gilmer, Habersham, Hall, Jackson, Lumpkin, Pickens, Rabun, Stephens, Towns, Union, White. ✉ Pacer
Newnan Division PO Box 939, Newnan, GA 30264. Phone: 678-423-3060. Counties: Carroll, Coweta, Fayette, Haralson, Heard, Meriwether, Pike, Spalding, Troup. ✉ ☎ Pacer
Rome Division PO Box 1186, Rome, GA 30162-1186. Phone: 706-291-5629. Counties: Bartow, Catoosa, Chattooga, Dade, Floyd, Gordon, Murray, Paulding, Polk, Walker, Whitfield. ✉ ☎ Pacer

Southern District of Georgia
www.gasd.uscourts.gov Pacer is online at http://pacer.gasd.uscourts.gov.
Augusta Division PO Box 1130, Augusta, GA 30903. Phone: 706-849-4400. Counties: Burke, Columbia, Dodge, Glascock, Jefferson, Johnson, Laurens, Lincoln, McDuffie, Montgomery, Richmond, Taliaferro, Telfair, Treutlen, Warren, Wheeler, Wilkes. ✉ ☎ Pacer
Brunswick Division PO Box 1636, Brunswick, GA 31521. Phone: 912-280-1330. Counties: Appling, Camden, Glynn, Jeff Davis, Long, McIntosh, Wayne. ✉ ☎ Pacer
Savannah Division PO Box 8286, Savannah, GA 31412. Phone: 912-650-4020, Fax: 912-650-4030. Counties: Atkinson, Bacon, Bulloch, Brantley, Bryan, Candler, Charlton, Chatham, Coffee, Effingham, Emanuel, Evans, Jenkins, Liberty, Pierce, Screven, Tattnall, Toombs, Ware. ✉ Pacer

Bankruptcy Court
Middle District of Georgia
www.gamb.uscourts.gov Pacer is online at http://pacer.gamb.uscourts.gov.
Columbus Division. PO Box 2147, Columbus, GA 31902. Phone: 706-649-7837, Fax: 706-649-7845. Counties: Berrien, Brooks, Chattahoochee, Clay, Clinch, Colquitt, Cook, Decatur, Echols, Grady, Harris, Irwin, Lanier, Lowndes, Marion, Muscogee, Quitman, Randolph, Seminole, Stewart, Talbot, Taylor, Thomas, Tift This court has records for the Thomasville and Valdosta branches, also Chapter 11 & 12 records for the Albany branch. ✉ ☎ Pacer
Macon Division PO Box 1957, Macon, GA 31201. Phone: 478-752-3506, Fax: 478-752-8157. Counties: Baldwin, Baker, Ben Hill, Bibb, Bleckley, Butts, Calhoun, Clarke, Crawford, Crisp, Dooly, Dougherty, Early, Elbert, Franklin, Greene, Hancock, Hart, Houston, Jasper, Jones, Lamar, Lee, Macon, Madison, Miller, Mitchell, Monroe, Morgan, Oconee, Oglethorpe, Peach, Pulaski, Putnam, Schley, Sumter, Terrell, Turner, Twiggs, Upson, Walton, Washington, Webster, Wilcox, Wilkinson, Worth This court has records for the Athens branch as

well as Chapter 7 & 13 records from the Albany branch. ☒ ☎ Pacer

Northern District of Georgia

www.ganb.uscourts.gov Court uses new CM/ECF system for PACER. CM-ECF: http://ecf.ganb.uscourts.gov.
Atlanta Division 1340 US Courthouse, 75 Spring St SW, Atlanta, GA 30303-3361. Phone: 404-215-1000. Counties: Cherokee, Clayton, Cobb, DeKalb, Douglas, Fulton, Gwinnett, Henry, Newton, Rockdale.☒ Fax Pacer
Gainesville Division 121 Spring St SE, Room 120, Gainesville, GA 30501. Phone: 678-450-2700. Counties: Banks, Barrow, Dawson, Fannin, Forsyth, Gilmer, Habersham, Hall, Jackson,

Lumpkin, Pickens, Rabun, Stephens, Towns, Union, White. ☒ ☎ Pacer
Newnan Division. Clerk, PO Box 2328, Newnan, GA 30264. Phone: 678-423-3000. Counties: Carroll, Coweta, Fayette, Haralson, Heard, Meriwether, Pike, Spalding, Troup. ☒ ☎ Pacer
Rome Division Clerk, 600 E 1st St, Room 339, Rome, GA 30161-3187. Phone: 706-291-5639. Bartow, Catoosa, Chattooga, Dade, Floyd, Gordon, Murray, Paulding, Polk, Walker, Whitfield. ☒ Pacer

Southern District of Georgia

www.gas.uscourts.gov Pacer is online at http://pacer.gasb.uscourts.gov.
Augusta Division PO Box 1487, Augusta, GA 30903. Phone: 706-724-

2421. Counties: Bulloch, Burke, Candler, Columbia, Dodge, Emanuel, Evans, Glascock, Jefferson, Jenkins, Johnson, Laurens, Lincoln, McDuffie, Montgomery, Richmond, Screven, Taliaferro, Tattnall, Telfair, Toombs, Treutlen, Warren, Wheeler, Wilkes. ☒ ☎ Pacer
Savannah Division. PO Box 8347, Savannah, GA 31412. Phone: 912-650-4100, Records Rm: 912-650-4107. Counties: Appling, Atkinson, Bacon, Brantley, Bryan, Camden, Charlton, Chatham, Coffee, Effingham, Glynn, Jeff Davis, Liberty, Long, McIntosh, Pierce, Ware, Wayne. ☒ ☎ Pacer

Hawaii

U.S. District Court

www.hid.uscourts.gov Pacer is at http://pacer.hid.uscourts.gov.
Honolulu Division 300 Ala Moana Blvd, Rm C-338, Honolulu, HI 96850. Phone: 808-541-1300, Fax: 808-541-1303. Counties: All. ☒ Pacer

Bankruptcy Court

www.hib.uscourts.gov PACER now on new ECF system at https://ecf.hib.uscourts.gov. No need to access old webRACER system. CM-ECF: https://ecf.hib.uscourts.gov.
Honolulu Division 1132 Bishop St, Suite 250-L, Honolulu, HI 96813. Phone: 808-522-8100, Fax: 800-522-8120. ☒ ☎ Pacer

Idaho

U.S. District Court

www.id.uscourts.gov
Boise Division MSC 039, Federal Bldg, 550 W Fort St, Room 400, Boise, ID 83724. Phone: 208-334-1361 1-800-448-6172, Fax: 208-334-9362. Counties: Ada, Adams, Blaine, Boise, Camas, Canyon, Cassia, Elmore, Gem, Gooding, Jerome, Lincoln, Minidoka, Owyhee, Payette, Twin Falls, Valley, Washington. ☒ Fax ☎ Pacer
Coeur d' Alene Division c/o Boise Division, MSD 039, Federal Bldg, 550 W Fort St, Room 400, Boise, ID 83724. Phone: 208-334-1361, Fax: 208-334-9386. Counties: Benewah, Bonner, Boundary, Kootenai, Shoshone.☒ Pacer
Moscow Division c/o Boise Division, PO Box 039, Federal Bldg, 550 W Fort St, Boise, ID 83724. Phone: 208-334-1074,

Fax: 208-883-1576. Counties: Clearwater, Latah, Lewis, Nez Perce. ☒ Pacer
Pocatello Division c/o Boise Division, 801 E Sherman, Pocatello, ID 83201. Phone: 208-334-1074 1-800-448-6172. Counties: Bannock, Bear Lake, Bingham, Bonneville, Butte, Caribou, Clark, Custer, Franklin, Fremont, Idaho, Jefferson, Lemhi, Madison, Oneida, Power, Teton. ☒ Pacer

Bankruptcy Court

www.id.uscourts.gov No PACER online.
Boise Division MSC 042, US Courthouse, 550 W Fort St, Room 400, Boise, ID 83724. Phone: 208-334-1074, Fax: 208-334-9362. Counties: Ada, Adams, Blaine, Boise, Camas, Canyon, Cassia, Elmore, Gem, Gooding, Jerome, Lincoln,

Minidoka, Owyhee, Payette, Twin Falls, Valley, Washington. ☒ Fax ☎ Pacer
Coeur d' Alene Division 205 N 4th St, 2nd Floor, Coeur d'Alene, ID 83814. Phone: 208-664-4925, Fax: 208-765-0270. Benewah, Bonner, Boundary, Kootenai, Shoshone. ☒ Fax ☎ Pacer
Moscow Division 220 E 5th St, Moscow, ID 83843. 208-882-7612, Fax: 208-883-1576. Counties: Clearwater, Idaho, Latah, Lewis, Nez Perce. ☒ ☎ Pacer
Pocatello Division 801 E Sherman, Pocatello, ID 83201. Phone: 208-478-4123, Fax: 208-478-4106. Counties: Bannock, Bear Lake, Bingham, Bonneville, Butte, Caribou, Clark, Custer, Franklin, Fremont, Jefferson, Lemhi, Madison, Oneida, Power, Teton. ☒ Fax ☎ Pacer

Illinois

U.S. District Court

Central District of Illinois

www.ilcd.uscourts.gov Pacer is online at http://pacer.ilcd.uscourts.gov. CM-ECF: https://ecf.ilcd.uscourts.gov.
Danville/Urbana Division 201 S Vine, Room 218, Urbana, IL 61802. Phone: 217-373-5830, Fax: 217-373-5834. Counties: Champaign, Coles, Douglas, Edgar, Ford, Iroquois, Kankakee, Macon, Moultrie, Piatt, Vermilion. ✉ ☎ Pacer
Peoria Division US District Clerk's Office, 309 Federal Bldg, 100 NE Monroe St, Peoria, IL 61602. Phone: 309-671-7117, Fax: 309-671-0780. Counties: Bureau, Fulton, Hancock, Knox, Livingston, McDonough, McLean, Marshall, Peoria, Putnam, Stark, Tazewell, Woodford. ✉ Pacer
Rock Island Division US District Clerk's Office, Room 40, US Court House, 211 19th St, Rock Island, IL 61201. Phone: 309-793-5778, Fax: 309-793-5878. Counties: Henderson, Henry, Mercer, Rock Island, Warren.
✉ ☎ Pacer
Springfield Division Clerk, 151 US Courthouse, 600 E Monroe, Springfield, IL 62701. Phone: 217-492-4020, Fax: 217-492-4028. Counties: Adams, Brown, Cass, Christian, De Witt, Greene, Logan, Macoupin, Mason, Menard, Montgomery, Morgan, Pike, Sangamon, Schuyler, Scott, Shelby. ✉ Pacer

Northern District of Illinois

www.ilnd.uscourts.gov Pacer is online at http://pacer.ilnd.uscourts.gov. Document images available in RACER section.
Chicago (Eastern) Division 20th Floor, 219 S Dearborn St, Chicago, IL 60604. Phone: 312-435-5698, Records Rm: 312-435-5863, Fax: 312-554-8512. Counties: Cook, Du Page, Grundy, Kane, Kendall, Lake, La Salle, Will. ✉ Pacer
Rockford Division Room 211, 211 S Court St, Rockford, IL 61101. Phone: 815-987-4355, Fax: 815-987-4291.

Counties: Boone, Carroll, De Kalb, Jo Daviess, Lee, McHenry, Ogle, Stephenson, Whiteside, Winnebago.
✉ Pacer

Southern District of Illinois

www.ilsd.uscourts.gov Pacer is online at http://pacer.ilsd.uscourts.gov. CM-ECF: https://ecf.ilsd.uscourts.gov.
Benton Division 301 W Main St, Benton, IL 62812. Phone: 618-439-7760. Counties: Alexander, Clark, Clay, Crawford, Cumberland, Edwards, Effingham, Franklin, Gallatin, Hamilton, Hardin, Jackson, Jasper, Jefferson, Johnson, Lawrence, Massac, Perry, Pope, Pulaski, Richland, Saline, Union, Wabash, Wayne, White, Williamson. Cases may also be allocated to the Benton Division.
✉ ☎ Pacer
East St Louis Division PO Box 249, East St Louis, IL 62202. Phone: 618-482-9371, Records Rm: 618-482-9371. Counties: Bond, Calhoun, Clinton, Fayette, Jersey, Madison, Marion, Monroe, Randolph, St. Clair. Cases for these counties may also be allocated to Benton Div. ✉ ☎ Pacer

Bankruptcy Court

Central District of Illinois

www.ilcb.uscourts.gov Pacer is online at http://pacer.ilcb.uscourts.gov. CM-ECF: https://ecf.ilcb.uscourts.gov.
Danville Division 201 N Vermilion #130, Danville, IL 61832-4733. Phone: 217-431-4820, Fax: 217-431-2694. Counties: Champaign, Coles, Douglas, Edgar, Ford, Iroquois, Kankakee, Livingston, Moultrie, Piatt, Vermilion. ✉ ☎ Pacer
Peoria Division Room 216, 100 NE Monroe St, Peoria, IL 61602. Phone: 309-671-7035, Fax: 309-671-7076. Counties: Bureau, Fulton, Hancock, Henderson, Henry, Knox, Marshall, McDonough, Mercer, Peoria, Putnam, Rock Island, Stark, Tazewell, Warren, Woodford.
✉ Pacer

Springfield Division 226 US Courthouse, Springfield, IL 62701. Phone: 217-492-4551, Fax: 217-492-4556. Counties: Adams, Brown, Cass, Christian, De Witt, Greene, Logan, Macon, Macoupin, Mason, McLean, Menard, Montgomery, Morgan, Pike, Sangamon, Schuyler, Scott, Shelby. ✉ Fax Pacer

Northern District of Illinois

www.ilnb.uscourts.gov Access to PACER/RACER is at the website. CM-ECF: https://ecf.ilnb.uscourts.gov.
Chicago (Eastern) Division 219 S Dearborn St, Chicago, IL 60604-1802. Phone: 312-435-5694, Records Rm: 312-435-5862, Fax: 312-408-7750. Counties: Cook, Du Page, Grundy, Kane, Kendall, La Salle, Lake, Will. ✉ Pacer
Rockford Division Room 110, 211 S Court St, Rockford, IL 61101. Phone: 815-987-4350, Fax: 815-987-4205. Counties: Boone, Carroll, De Kalb, Jo Daviess, Lee, McHenry, Ogle, Stephenson, Whiteside, Winnebago.
✉ ☎ Pacer

Southern District of Illinois

www.ilsb.uscourts.gov Pacer is online at http://pacer.ilsb.uscourts.gov. CM-ECF: https://ecf.ilsb.uscourts.gov.
Benton Division 301 W Main, Benton, IL 62812. Phone: 618-435-2200. Counties: Alexander, Edwards, Franklin, Gallatin, Hamilton, Hardin, Jackson, Jefferson, Johnson, Massac, Perry, Pope, Pulaski, Randolph, Saline, Union, Wabash, Washington, Wayne, White, Williamson.
✉ Pacer
East St Louis Division PO Box 309, East St Louis, IL 62202-0309. Phone: 618-482-9400. Counties: Bond, Calhoun, Clark, Clay, Clinton, Crawford, Cumberland, Effingham, Fayette, Jasper, Jersey, Lawrence, Madison, Marion, Monroe, Richland, St. Clair.
✉ ☎ Pacer

Indiana

U.S. District Court

Northern District of Indiana

www.innd.uscourts.gov Pacer is online at http://pacer.innd.uscourts.gov. CM-ECF: https://ecf.innd.uscourts.gov/cgi-bin/login.pl.
Fort Wayne Division Room 1108, Federal Bldg, 1300 S Harrison St, Fort Wayne, IN 46802. Phone: 260-424-7360. Counties: Adams, Allen, Blackford, DeKalb, Grant, Huntington, Jay, Lagrange, Noble, Steuben, Wells, Whitley. ✉ ☎ Pacer
Hammond Division Room 101, 507 State St, Hammond, IN 46320. Phone: 219-937-5235. Counties: Lake, Porter. ✉ ☎ Pacer
Lafayette Division PO Box 1498, Lafayette, IN 47902. Phone: 765-420-6250. Counties: Benton, Carroll, Jasper, Newton, Tippecanoe, Warren, White. ✉ Fax ☎ Pacer
South Bend Division Room 102, 204 S Main, South Bend, IN 46601. Phone: 574-246-8000, Fax: 574-246-8002. Counties: Cass, Elkhart, Fulton, Kosciusko, La Porte, Marshall, Miami, Pulaski, St. Joseph, Starke, Wabash. ✉ ☎ Pacer

Southern District of Indiana

www.insd.uscourts.gov online search free CM-ECF: https://ecf.insd.uscourts.gov.
Evansville Division 304 Federal Bldg, 101 NW Martin Luther King Blvd, Evansville, IN 47708. Phone: 812-434-6410, Records Rm: 812-465-6427, Fax: 812-434-6418. Counties: Daviess, Dubois, Gibson, Martin, Perry, Pike, Posey, Spencer, Vanderburgh, Warrick. ✉ Pacer
Indianapolis Division Clerk, Room 105, 46 E Ohio St, Indianapolis, IN 46204. Phone: 317-229-3700, Fax: 317-229-3959. Counties: Bartholomew, Boone, Brown, Clinton, Decatur, Delaware,

Fayette, Fountain, Franklin, Hamilton, Hancock, Hendricks, Henry, Howard, Johnson, Madison, Marion, Monroe, Montgomery, Morgan, Randolph, Rush, Shelby, Tipton, Union, Wayne. ✉ ☎ Pacer
New Albany Division Room 210, 121 W Spring St, New Albany, IN 47150. Phone: 812-542-4510, Fax: 812-542-4515. Counties: Clark, Crawford, Dearborn, Floyd, Harrison, Jackson, Jefferson, Jennings, Lawrence, Ohio, Orange, Ripley, Scott, Switzerland, Washington. ✉ Pacer
Terre Haute Division 210 Federal Bldg, Terre Haute, IN 47808. Phone: 812-234-9484, Fax: 812-238-1831. Counties: Clay, Greene, Knox, Owen, Parke, Putnam, Sullivan, Vermillion, Vigo. ✉ ☎ Pacer

Bankruptcy Court

Northern District of Indiana

www.innb.uscourts.gov Pacer is online at http://pacer.innb.uscourts.gov. CM-ECF: https://ecf.innb.uscourts.gov.
Fort Wayne Division PO Box 2547, Fort Wayne, IN 46801-2547. Phone: 260-420-5100. Counties: Adams, Allen, Blackford, DeKalb, Grant, Huntington, Jay, Lagrange, Noble, Steuben, Wells, Whitley. ✉ ☎ Pacer
Hammond at Gary Division US Bankruptcy Court, Northern District of Indiana, 5400 Federal Plaza, Hammond, Indiana 46320. Phone: 219-852-3480, Fax: 219-881-3307. Counties: Lake, Porter. ✉ ☎ Pacer
Hammond at Lafayette Division c/o Fort Wayne Division, PO Box 2547, Fort Wayne, IN 46801-2547. Phone: 260-420-5100. Counties: Benton, Carroll, Jasper, Newton, Tippecanoe, Warren, White. ✉ Pacer

South Bend Division. PO Box 7003, South Bend, IN 46634-7003. Phone: 574-968-2100, Fax: 574-968-2205. Counties: Cass, Elkhart, Fulton, Kosciusko, La Porte, Marshall, Miami, Pulaski, St. Joseph, Starke, Wabash. ✉ ☎ Pacer

Southern District of Indiana

www.insb.uscourts.gov PACER is now available at www.insb.uscourts.gov.
Evansville Division 352 Federal Building, 101 NW Martin Luther King Blvd, Evansville, IN 47708. Phone: 812-434-6470, Fax: 812-434-6471. Counties: Daviess, Dubois, Gibson, Martin, Perry, Pike, Posey, Spencer, Vanderburgh, Warrick. ✉ ☎ Pacer
Indianapolis Division US Courthouse, Rm 116, 46 E Ohio St, Indianapolis, IN 46204. Phone: 317-229-3800, Fax: 317-229-3801. Counties: Bartholomew, Boone, Brown, Clinton, Decatur, Delaware, Fayette, Fountain, Franklin, Hamilton, Hancock, Hendricks, Henry, Howard, Johnson, Madison, Marion, Monroe, Montgomery, Morgan, Randolph, Rush, Shelby, Tipton, Union, Wayne. ✉ ☎ Pacer
New Albany Division US Courthouse, Rm 110, 121 W Spring St, New Albany, IN 47150. Phone: 812-452-4540, Fax: 812-542-4541. Counties: Clark, Crawford, Dearborn, Floyd, Harrison, Jackson, Jefferson, Jennings, Lawrence, Ohio, Orange, Ripley, Scott, Switzerland, Washington. ✉ ☎ Pacer
Terre Haute Division Federal Bldg Rm 207, 30 N 7th St, Terre Haute, IN 47808. Phone: 812-238-1550, Fax: 812-238-1831. Counties: Clay, Greene, Knox, Owen, Parke, Putnam, Sullivan, Vermillion, Vigo. ✉ ☎ Pacer

Iowa

U.S. District Court

Northern District of Iowa

www.iand.uscourts.gov Pacer is online at http://pacer.iand.uscourts.gov. CM-ECF: https://ecf.iand.uscourts.gov.
Cedar Rapids (Eastern) Division Court Clerk, PO Box 74710, Cedar Rapids, IA 52407-4710. Phone: 319-286-2300. Counties: Allamakee, Benton, Black Hawk, Bremer, Buchanan, Cedar, Chickasaw, Clayton, Delaware, Dubuque, Fayette, Floyd, Grundy, Hardin, Howard, Iowa, Jackson, Jones, Linn, Mitchell, Tama, Winneshiek. Court also has records for Dubuque Branch. ☒ ☎ Pacer
Sioux City (Western) Division Room 301, Federal Bldg, 320 6th St, Sioux City, IA 51101. Phone: 712-233-3900. Counties: Buena Vista, Butler, Calhoun, Carroll, Cerro Gordo, Cherokee, Clay, Crawford, Dickinson, Emmet, Franklin, Hamilton, Hancock, Humboldt, Ida, Kossuth, Lyon, Monona, O'Brien, Osceola, Palo Alto, Plymouth, Pocahontas, Sac, Sioux, Webster, Winnebago, Woodbury, Worth, Wright Court has records for the Ft. Dodge, Independence, and Mason City Divisions. Court is held occasionally in Ft. Dodge, but records are in Sioux City. ☒ ☎ Pacer

Southern District of Iowa

www.iasd.uscourts.gov Pacer is online at http://pacer.iasd.uscourts.gov.
Council Bluffs (Western) Division. PO Box 307, Council Bluffs, IA 51502. Phone: 712-328-0283, Fax: 712-328-

1241. Counties: Audubon, Cass, Fremont, Harrison, Mills, Montgomery, Page, Pottawattamie, Shelby. ☒ ☎ Pacer
Davenport (Eastern) Division PO Box 256, Davenport, IA 52805. Phone: 563-322-3223, Fax: 563-322-2962. Counties: Henry, Johnson, Lee, Louisa, Muscatine, Scott, Van Buren, Washington. ☒ Fax ☎ Pacer
Des Moines (Central) Division PO Box 9344, Des Moines, IA 50306-9344. Phone: 515-284-6248, Fax: 515-284-6418. Counties: Adair, Adams, Appanoose, Boone, Clarke, Clinton, Dallas, Davis, Decatur, Des Moines, Greene, Guthrie, Jasper, Jefferson, Keokuk, Lucas, Madison, Mahaska, Marion, Marshall, Monroe, Polk, Poweshiek, Ringgold, Story, Taylor, Union, Wapello, Warren, Wayne. ☒ Fax Pacer

Bankruptcy Court

Northern District of Iowa

www.ianb.uscourts.gov Pacer is online at http://pacer.iasnb.uscourts.gov. CM-ECF: https://ecf.ianb.uscourts.gov.
Cedar Rapids (Eastern) Division PO Box 74890, Cedar Rapids, IA 52407. Phone: 319-286-2200, Fax: 319-286-2280. Counties: Allamakee, Benton, Black Hawk, Bremer, Buchanan, Cedar, Chickasaw, Clayton, Delaware, Dubuque, Fayette, Floyd, Grundy, Howard, Iowa, Jackson, Jones, Linn, Mitchell, Tama, Winneshiek. Also has electronic records

of cases from the Sioux City Division. ☒ ☎ Pacer
Souix City (Western) Division PO Box 3857, Souix City, IA 51102. Phone: 712-233-3939, Fax: 712-233-3942. Counties: Buena Vista, Calhoun, Carroll, Cerro Gordo, Cherokee, Clay, Crawford, Dickinson, Emmet, Floyd, Franklin, Hamilton, Hancock, Hardin,Humboldt, Ida, Kossuth, Lyon, Mitchell, Monona, O'Brien, Osceola, Palo Alto, Plymouth, Pocahontas, Sac, Sioux, Webster, Winnebago, Woodbury, Worth, Wright. Case records also available electronically at Cedar Rapids Division. ☒ ☎ Pacer

Southern District of Iowa

www.iasb.uscourts.gov New CM/ECF online system access only. CM-ECF: https://ecf.iasb.uscourts.gov.
Des Moines Division PO Box 9264, Des Moines, IA 50306-9264. Phone: 515-284-6230, Fax: 515-284-6404. Counties: Adair, Adams, Appanoose, Audubon, Boone, Cass, Clarke, Clinton, Dallas, Davis, Decatur, Des Moines, Fremont, Greene, Guthrie, Harrison, Henry, Jasper, Jefferson, Johnson, Keokuk, Lee, Louisa, Lucas, Madison, Mahaska, Marion, Marshall, Mills, Monroe, Montgomery, Muscatine, Page, Polk, Pottawattamie, Poweshiek, Ringgold, Scott, Shelby, Story, Taylor, Union, Van Buren, Wapello, Warren, Washington, Wayne. ☒ ☎ Pacer

Kansas

U.S. District Court

www.ksd.uscourts.gov Pacer is online at http://pacer.ksd.uscourts.gov. CM-ECF: https://ecf.ksd.uscourts.gov.
Kansas City Division Clerk, 500 State Ave, Kansas City, KS 66101. Phone: 913-551-6719. Counties: Atchison, Bourbon, Brown, Cherokee, Crawford, Doniphan, Johnson, Labette, Leavenworth, Linn,

Marshall, Miami, Nemaha, Wyandotte. ☒ Pacer
Topeka Division Clerk, US District Court, Room 490, 444 SE Quincy, Topeka, KS 66683. Phone: 785-295-2610. Counties: Allen, Anderson, Chase, Clay, Cloud, Coffey, Dickinson, Douglas, Franklin, Geary, Jackson, Jewell, Lincoln, Lyon, Marion, Mitchell, Morris, Neosho, Osage, Ottawa, Pottawatomie, Republic,

Riley, Saline, Shawnee, Wabaunsee, Washington, Wilson, Woodson. ☒ ☎ Pacer
Wichita Division 204 US Courthouse, 401 N Market, Wichita, KS 67202-2096. Phone: 316-269-6491. Counties: All counties in Kansas. Cases may be heard from counties in the other division. ☒ ☎ Pacer

Bankruptcy Court

www.ksb.uscourts.gov Pacer is online at http://pacer.ksb.uscourts.gov. CM-ECF: https://ecf.ksb.uscourts.gov

Kansas City Division 500 State Ave, Room 161, Kansas City, KS 66101. Phone: 913-551-6732, Fax: 913-551-6715. Counties: Atchison, Bourbon, Brown, Cherokee, Comanche, Crawford, Doniphan, Johnson, Labette, Leavenworth, Linn, Marshall, Miami, Nemaha, Wyandotte. ✉ ☎ Pacer

Topeka Division 240 US Courthouse, 444 SE Quincy, Topeka, KS 66683. Phone: 785-295-2750, Fax: 785-295-2964. Counties: Allen, Anderson, Chase, Clay, Cloud, Coffey, Dickinson, Douglas, Franklin, Geary, Jackson, Jewell, Lincoln, Lyon, Marion, Mitchell, Morris, Neosho, Osage, Ottawa, Pottawatomie, Republic, Riley, Saline, Shawnee, Wabaunsee, Washington, Wilson, Woodson. ✉ ☎ Pacer

Wichita Division 167 US Courthouse, 401 N Market, Wichita, KS 67202. Phone: 316-269-6486, Fax: 316-269-6181. Counties: Barber, Barton, Butler, Chautauqua, Cheyenne, Clark, Comanche,

Cowley, Decatur, Edwards, Elk, Ellis, Ellsworth, Finney, Ford, Gove, Graham, Grant, Gray, Greeley, Greenwood, Hamilton, Harper, Harvey, Haskell, Hodgeman, Jefferson, Kearny, Kingman, Kiowa, Lane, Logan, Mcpherson, Meade, Montgomery, Morton, Ness, Norton, Osborne, Pawnee, Phillips, Pratt, Rawlins, Reno, Rice, Rooks, Rush, Russell, Scott, Sedgwick, Seward, Sheridan, Smith, Stafford, Stanton, Stevens, Sumner, Thomas, Trego, Wallace, Wichita. ✉ ☎ Pacer

Kentucky

U.S. District Court

Eastern District of Kentucky

www.kyed.uscourts.gov Pacer is online at http://pacer.kyed.uscourts.gov. CM-ECF: https://ecf.kyed.uscourts.gov/cgi-bin/login.pl.
Ashland Division Suite 336, 1405 Greenup Ave, Ashland, KY 41101. Phone: 606-329-8652. Counties: Boyd, Carter, Elliott, Greenup, Lawrence, Lewis, Morgan, Rowan. ✉ ☎ Pacer
Covington Division Clerk, PO Box 1073, Covington, KY 41012. Phone: 859-392-7925. Counties: Boone, Bracken, Campbell, Gallatin, Grant, Kenton, Mason, Pendleton, Robertson. ✉ Pacer
Frankfort Division Room 313, 330 W Broadway, Frankfort, KY 40601. Phone: 502-223-5225. Counties: Anderson, Carroll, Franklin, Henry, Owen, Shelby, Trimble. ✉ ☎ Pacer
Lexington Division PO Box 3074, Lexington, KY 40588. Phone: 859-233-2503. Counties: Bath, Bourbon, Boyle, Clark, Estill, Fayette, Fleming, Garrard, Harrison, Jessamine, Lee, Lincoln, Madison, Menifee, Mercer, Montgomery, Nicholas, Powell, Scott, Wolfe, Woodford. Lee and Wolfe counties were part of the Pikeville Division before '93. Perry became part of Pikeville after 1992. ✉ ☎ Pacer
London Division PO Box 5121, London, KY 40745-5121. Phone: 606-877-7910. Counties: Bell, Clay, Harlan, Jackson, Knox, Laurel, Leslie, McCreary, Owsley,

Pulaski, Rockcastle, Wayne, Whitley. ✉ ☎ Pacer
Pikeville Division Office of the clerk, 203 Federal Bldg, 110 Main St, Pikeville, KY 41501. Phone: 606-437-6160. Counties: Breathitt, Floyd, Johnson, Knott, Letcher, Magoffin, Martin, Perry, Pike. Lee and Wolfe Counties were part of this division until 10/31/92, when they were moved to the Lexington Division. ✉ ☎ Pacer

Western District of Kentucky

www.kywd.uscourts.gov Court converted online WebPACER service to PACER. CM-ECF: www.kywd.uscourts.gov/CMECFWelcome.php.
Bowling Green Division US District Court, 241 E Main St, Room 120, Bowling Green, KY 42101-2175. Phone: 270-389-2500, Fax: 270-393-2519. Counties: Adair, Allen, Barren, Butler, Casey, Clinton, Cumberland, Edmonson, Green, Hart, Logan, Metcalfe, Monroe, Russell, Simpson, Taylor, Todd, Warren. ✉ ☎ Pacer
Louisville Division. Clerk, US District Court, 601 Broadway, Rm106, Louisville, KY 40202. Phone: 502-625-3500, Fax: 502-625-3880. Counties: Breckinridge, Bullitt, Hardin, Jefferson, Larue, Marion, Meade, Nelson, Oldham, Spencer, Washington. ✉ Pacer
Owensboro Division Federal Bldg, Room 126, 423 Frederica St, Owensboro, KY 42301. Phone: 270-689-4400, Fax: 207-689-4419. Counties: Daviess, Grayson, Hancock, Henderson, Hopkins, McLean,

Muhlenberg, Ohio, Union, Webster. ✉ ☎ Pacer
Paducah Division 501 Broadway, Ste127, Paducah, KY 42001. Phone: 270-415-6400, Fax: 270-415-6419. Counties: Ballard, Caldwell, Calloway, Carlisle, Christian, Crittenden, Fulton, Graves, Hickman, Livingston, Lyon, McCracken, Marshall, Trigg. ✉ ☎ Pacer

Bankruptcy Court

Eastern District of Kentucky

www.kyeb.uscourts.gov Pacer is online at http://pacer.kyeb.uscourts.gov. CM-ECF: https://ecf.kyeb.uscourts.gov.
Lexington Division PO Box 1111, Lexington, KY 40589-1111. Phone: 859-233-2608. Counties: Anderson, Bath, Bell, Boone, Bourbon, Boyd, Boyle, Bracken, Breathitt, Campbell, Carroll, Carter, Clark, Clay, Elliott, Estill, Fayette, Fleming, Floyd, Franklin, Gallatin, Garrard, Grant, Greenup, Harlan, Harrison, Henry, Jackson, Jessamine, Johnson, Kenton, Knott, Knox, Laurel, Lawrence, Lee, Leslie, Letcher, Lewis, Lincoln, Madison, Magoffin, Martin, Mason, McCreary, Menifee, Mercer, Montgomery, Morgan, Nicholas, Owen, Owsley, Pendleton, Perry, Pike, Powell, Pulaski, Robertson, Rockcastle, Rowan, Scott, Shelby, Trimble, Wayne, Whitley, Wolfe, Woodford. ✉ ☎ Pacer

Western District of Kentucky

www.kywb.uscourts.gov Pacer is online at http://pacer.kywb.uscourts.gov. CM-ECF: https://ecf.kywb.uscourts.gov.
Louisville Division 546 US Courthouse, 601 W Broadway, Louisville, KY 40202. Phone: 502-627-5800. Counties: Adair, Allen, Ballard, Barren, Breckinridge,

Bullitt, Butler, Caldwell, Calloway, Carlisle, Casey, Christian, Clinton, Crittenden, Cumberland, Daviess, Edmonson, Fulton, Graves, Grayson, Green, Hancock, Hardin, Hart, Henderson, Hickman, Hopkins, Jefferson, Larue, Livingston, Logan, Lyon, Marion, Marshall, McCracken, McLean, Meade,

Metcalfe, Monroe, Muhlenberg, Nelson, Ohio, Oldham, Russell, Simpson, Spencer, Taylor, Todd, Trigg, Union, Warren, Washington, Webster. ✉ ☎ Pacer

Louisiana

U.S. District Court

Eastern District of Louisiana

www.laed.uscourts.gov Pacer is online at http://pacer.laed.uscourts.gov.
New Orleans Division Clerk, 500 Poydras St, New Orleans, LA 70130. Phone: 504-589-7650, Fax: 504-589-7189. Parishes: Assumption , Jefferson Parish, Lafourche Parish, Orleans Parish, Plaquemines Parish, St. Bernard Parish, St. Charles Parish, St. James Parish, St. John the Baptist Parish, St. Tammany Parish, Tangipahoa Parish, Terrebonne Parish, Washington Parish. ✉ Pacer

Middle District of Louisiana

www.lamd.uscourts.gov Pacer is online at http://pacer.lamd.uscourts.gov.
Baton Rouge Division PO Box 2630, Baton Rouge, LA 70821-2630. Phone: 225-389-3500, Fax: 225-389-3501. Parishes: Ascension Parish, East Baton Rouge Parish, East Feliciana Parish, Iberville Parish, Livingston Parish, Pointe Coupee Parish, St. Helena Parish, West Baton Rouge Parish, West Feliciana Parish. ✉ ☎ Pacer

Western District of Louisiana

www.lawd.uscourts.gov Pacer is online at https://pacer.lawd.uscourts.gov. CM-ECF: https://ecf.lawd.uscourts.gov.
Alexandria Division PO Box 1269, Alexandria, LA 71309. Phone: 318-473-7415, Records Rm: 318-676-4273, Fax: 318-473-7345. Parishes: Avoyelles Parish, Catahoula Parish, Concordia Parish, Grant Parish, La Salle Parish, Natchitoches Parish, Rapides Parish, Winn Parish. ✉ ☎ Pacer
Lafayette Division Room 113, Federal Bldg, 705 Jefferson St, Lafayette, LA 70501. Phone: 337-593-5000. Parishes: Acadia Parish, Evangeline Parish, Iberia

Parish, Lafayette Parish, St. Landry Parish, St. Martin Parish, St. Mary Parish, Vermilion Parish. ✉ ☎ Pacer
Lake Charles Division 611 Broad St, Suite 188, Lake Charles, LA 70601. Phone: 337-437-3870. Parishes: Allen Parish, Beauregard Parish, Calcasieu Parish, Cameron Parish, Jefferson Davis Parish, Vernon Parish. ✉ ☎ Pacer
Monroe Division PO Drawer 3087, Monroe, LA 71210. Phone: 318-322-6740. Parishes: Caldwell Parish, East Carroll Parish, Franklin Parish, Jackson Parish, Lincoln Parish, Madison Parish, Morehouse Parish, Ouachita Parish, Richland Parish, Tensas Parish, Union Parish, West Carroll Parish. ✉ ☎ Pacer
Shreveport Division US Courthouse, Suite 1167, 300 Fannin St, Shreveport, LA 71101-3083. Phone: 318-676-4273. Parishes: Bienville Parish, Bossier Parish, Caddo Parish, Claiborne Parish, De Soto Parish, Red River Parish, Sabine Parish, Webster Parish. ✉ ☎ Pacer

Bankruptcy Court

Eastern District of Louisiana

www.laeb.uscourts.gov Pacer is online at http://pacer.laeb.uscourts.gov. CM-ECF: https://ecf.laeb.uscourts.gov.
New Orleans Division Clerk, 500 Poydras St, New Orleans, LA 70130. Phone: 504-589-7878. Parishes: Assumption Parish, Jefferson Parish, Lafourche Parish, Orleans Parish, Plaquemines Parish, St. Bernard Parish, St. Charles Parish, St. James Parish, St. John the Baptist Parish, St. Tammany Parish, Tangipahoa Parish, Terrebonne Parish, Washington Parish. ✉ ☎ Pacer

Middle District of Louisiana

www.lamb.uscourts.gov Pacer is online at http://pacer.lamb.uscourts.gov. CM-ECF: https://ecf.lamb.uscourts.gov.
Baton Rouge Division Room 119, 707 Florida St, Baton Rouge, LA 70801. Phone: 225-389-0211. Parishes: Ascension Parish, East Baton Rouge Parish, East Feliciana Parish, Iberville Parish, Livingston Parish, Pointe Coupee Parish, St. Helena Parish, West Baton Rouge Parish, West Feliciana Parish. ✉ ☎ Pacer

Western District of Louisiana

www.lawb.uscourts.gov Pacer is online at http://pacer.lawb.uscourts.gov. CM-ECF: https://ecf.lawb.uscourts.gov.
Alexandria Division 300 Jackson St, Suite 116, Alexandria, LA 71301-8357. 318-445-1890. Parishes: Avoyelles Parish, Catahoula Parish, Concordia Parish, Grant Parish, La Salle Parish, Natchitoches Parish, Rapides Parish, Vernon Parish, Winn Parish. ✉ ☎ Pacer
Lafayette-Opelousas Division PO Box J, Opelousas, LA 70571-1909. Phone: 318-948-3451, Fax: 318-948-4426. Parishes: Acadia Parish, Evangeline Parish, Iberia Parish, Lafayette Parish, St. Landry Parish, St. Martin Parish, St. Mary Parish, Vermilion Parish. ✉ ☎ Pacer
Lake Charles Division c/o Lafayette-Opelousas Division, PO Box J, Opelousas, LA 70571-1909. Phone: 318-948-3451. Parishes: Allen Parish, Beauregard Parish, Calcasieu Parish, Cameron Parish, Jefferson Davis Parish. ✉ Pacer
Monroe Division. c/o Shreveport Division, Suite 2201, 300 Fannin St, Shreveport, LA 71101. Phone: 318-676-4267. Parishes: Caldwell Parish, East Carroll Parish, Franklin Parish, Jackson

Parish, Lincoln Parish, Madison Parish, Morehouse Parish, Ouachita Parish, Richland Parish, Tensas Parish, Union Parish, West Carroll Parish. ✉ Pacer

Shreveport Division Suite 2201, 300 Fannin St, Shreveport, LA 71101-3089. Phone: 318-676-4267. Parishes: Bienville Parish, Bossier Parish, Caddo Parish,

Claiborne Parish, De Soto Parish, Red River Parish, Sabine Parish, Webster Parish. ✉ Pacer

Maine

U.S. District Court

www.med.uscourts.gov Pacer is online at https://pacer.med.uscourts.gov. CM-ECF: https://ecf.med.uscourts.gov.
Bangor Division Court Clerk, PO Box 1007, Bangor, ME 04402-1007. Phone: 207-945-0575, Fax: 207-945-0362. Counties: Aroostook, Franklin, Hancock, Kennebec, Penobscot, Piscataquis, Somerset, Waldo, Washington. ✉ ☎ Pacer

Portland Division Court Clerk, 156 Federal St, Portland, ME 04101. Phone: 207-780-3356, Fax: 207-780-3772. Counties: Androscoggin, Cumberland, Knox, Lincoln, Oxford, Sagadahoc, York. ✉ ☎ Pacer

Bankruptcy Court

www.meb.uscourts.gov Pacer is online at http://pacer.meb.uscourts.gov. CM-ECF: https://ecf.meb.uscourts.gov.

Bangor Division PO Box 1109, Bangor, ME 04402-1109. Phone: 207-945-0348, Fax: 207-945-0304. Counties: Aroostook, Franklin, Hancock, Kennebec, Knox, Lincoln, Penobscot, Piscataquis, Somerset, Waldo, Washington. ✉ Pacer
Portland Division. 537 Congress St, Portland, ME 04101. Phone: 207-780-3482, Fax: 207-780-3679. Counties: Androscoggin, Cumberland, Oxford, Sagadahoc, York. ✉ ☎ Pacer

Maryland

U.S. District Court

Northern District of Maryland

www.mdd.uscourts.gov Pacer is online at http://pacer.mdd.uscourts.gov. CM-ECF: https://ecf.mdd.uscourts.gov.
Baltimore Division Clerk, 4th Floor, Room 4415, 101 W Lombard St, Baltimore, MD 21201. Phone: 410-962-2600. Counties: Allegany, Anne Arundel, Baltimore, City of Baltimore, Caroline, Carroll, Cecil, Dorchester, Frederick, Garrett, Harford, Howard, Kent, Queen Anne's, Somerset, Talbot, Washington, Wicomico, Worcester. ✉ ☎ Pacer

Southern District of Maryland

www.mdd.uscourts.gov Pacer is online at http://pacer.mdd.uscourts.gov. CM-ECF: https://ecf.mdd.uscourts.gov.
Greenbelt Division Clerk, Room 240, 6500 Cherrywood Lane, Greenbelt, MD 20770. Phone: 301-344-0660. Counties: Calvert, Charles, Montgomery, Prince George's, St. Mary's. ✉ Fax ☎ Pacer

Bankruptcy Court

Northern District of Maryland

www.mdb.uscourts.gov Pacer is online at http://pacer.mdb.uscourts.gov. CM-ECF: https://ecf.mdb.uscourts.gov.

Baltimore Division US Courthouse, 101 W Lombard St, Ste 8303, Baltimore, MD 21201. Phone: 410-962-2688. Counties: Anne Arundel, Baltimore, City of Baltimore, Caroline, Carroll, Cecil, Dorchester, Harford, Howard, Kent, Queen Anne's, Somerset, Talbot, Wicomico, Worcester. ✉ ☎ Pacer

Southern District of Maryland

www.mdb.uscourts.gov Pacer is online at http://pacer.mdb.uscourts.gov. CM-ECF: https://ecf.mdb.uscourts.gov.
Greenbelt Division 6500 Cherrywood Ln, #300, Greenbelt, MD 20770. Phone: 301-344-8018. Counties: Allegany, Calvert, Charles, Frederick, Garrett, Montgomery, Prince George's, St. Mary's, Washington. ✉ ☎ Pacer

Massachusetts

U.S. District Court

District of Massachusetts

www.mad.uscourts.gov Pacer is online at http://pacer.mad.uscourts.gov. CM-ECF: https://ecf.mad.uscourts.gov.
Boston Division US Courthouse, 1 Courthouse Way Ste 2300, Boston, MA 02210. Phone: 617-748-9152, Records Rm: 617-748-9086, Fax: 617-748-9096. Counties: Barnstable, Bristol, Dukes, Essex, Middlesex, Nantucket, Norfolk, Plymouth, Suffolk. ✉ Pacer
Springfield Division 1550 Main St, Springfield, MA 01103. Phone: 413-785-0015, Fax: 413-785-0204. Counties: Berkshire, Franklin, Hampden, Hampshire. ✉ Fax ☎ Pacer

Worcester Division 595 Main St., Room 502, Worcester, MA 01608. Phone: 508-929-9900. Counties: Worcester. ✉ Fax ☎ Pacer

Bankruptcy Court

District of Massachusetts

www.mab.uscourts.gov Pacer is online at http://pacer.mab.uscourts.gov. CM-ECF: https://ecf.mab.uscourts.gov.
Boston Division Room 1101, 10 Causeway, Boston, MA 02222-1074. Phone: 617-565-8950, Fax: 617-565-6651. Counties: Barnstable, Bristol, Dukes, Essex (except towns assigned to Worcester Division), Nantucket, Norfolk (except towns assigned to Worcester Division), Plymouth, Suffolk, and the

following towns in Middlesex: Arlington, Belmont, Burlington, Everett, Lexington, Malden, Medford, Melrose, Newton, North Reading, Reading, Stoneham, Wakefield, Waltham, Watertown, Wilmington, Winchester and Woburn. ✉ Fax ☎ Pacer
Worcester Division. 595 Main St, Room 211, Worcester, MA 01608. Phone: 508-770-8900, Fax: 508-793-0189. Counties: Berkshire, Franklin, Hampden, Hampshire, Middlesex (except the towns assigned to the Boston Division), Worcester and the following towns: in Essex-Andover, Haverhill, Lawrence, Methuen and North Andover; in Norfolk-Bellingham, Franklin, Medway, Millis and Norfolk. ✉ ☎ Pacer

---

Michigan

U.S. District Court

Eastern District of Michigan

www.mied.uscourts.gov Pacer is online at http://pacer.mied.uscourts.gov. CM-ECF: https://ecf.mied.uscourts.gov.
Ann Arbor Division PO Box 8199, Ann Arbor, MI 48107. Phone: 734-741-2380, Fax: 734-741-2065. Counties: Jackson, Lenawee, Monroe, Oakland, Washtenaw, Wayne. Civil cases in these counties are assigned randomly to the Detroit, Flint or Port Huron Divisions. Case files are maintained where the case is assigned. ✉ ☎ Pacer

Bay City Division 1000 Washington Ave Rm 304, PO Box 913, Bay City, MI 48707. Phone: 989-894-8800, Fax: 989-894-8804. Counties: Alcona, Alpena, Arenac, Bay, Cheboygan, Clare, Crawford, Gladwin, Gratiot, Huron, Iosco, Isabella, Midland, Montmorency, Ogemaw, Oscoda, Otsego, Presque Isle, Roscommon, Saginaw, Tuscola. ✉ ☎ Pacer
Detroit Division 231 W Lafayette Blvd, Detroit, MI 48226. Phone: 313-234-5005,

Records Rm: 313-234-5010, Fax: 313-234-5393. Counties: Macomb, St. Clair, Sanilac. Civil cases for these counties are assigned randomly among the Flint, Ann Arbor and Detroit divisions. Port Huron cases may also be assigned here. Case files are kept where case is assigned. ✉ Fax ☎ Pacer
Flint Division Clerk, Federal Bldg, Room 140, 600 Church St, Flint, MI 48502. Phone: 810-341-7840. Counties: Genesee, Lapeer, Livingston, Shiawassee. This office handles all criminal cases for these counties. Civil cases are assigned randomly among the Detroit, Ann Arbor and Flint divisions. ✉ ☎ Pacer

Western District of Michigan

www.miwd.uscourts.gov Pacer is online at http://pacer.miwd.uscourts.gov. CM-ECF: https://ecf.miwd.uscourts.gov.
Grand Rapids Division PO Box 3310, Grand Rapids, MI 49501. Phone: 616-456-2381. Counties: Antrim, Barry, Benzie, Charlevoix, Emmet, Grand Traverse, Ionia, Kalkaska, Kent, Lake, Leelanau, Manistee, Mason, Mecosta, Missaukee, Montcalm, Muskegon, Newaygo, Oceana, Osceola, Ottawa,

Wexford. The Lansing and Kalamazoo Divisions also handle cases from these counties. ✉ ☎ Pacer
Kalamazoo Division 410 W Michigan, Rm B-35, Kalamazoo, MI 49007. Phone: 269-337-5706. Counties: Allegan, Berrien, Calhoun, Cass, Kalamazoo, St. Joseph, Van Buren. Also handle cases from the counties in the Grand Rapids Division. ✉ ☎ Pacer
Lansing Division 113 Federal Building, 315 W Allegan, Rm 101, Lansing, MI 48933. Phone: 517-377-1559. Counties: Branch, Clinton, Eaton, Hillsdale, Ingham. Also handle cases from the counties in the Grand Rapids Division. ✉ ☎ Pacer
Marquette-Northern Division PO Box 698, Marquette, MI 49855. Phone: 906-226-2117, Fax: 906-226-6735. Counties: Alger, Baraga, Chippewa, Delta, Dickinson, Gogebic, Houghton, Iron, Keweenaw, Luce, Mackinac, Marquette, Menominee, Ontonagon, Schoolcraft. ✉ ☎ Pacer

---

Key: Federal Courts Record Access: phone-☎ mail-✉ fax-**Fax** online PACER- Pacer email-**Email**

Bankruptcy Court

Eastern District of Michigan

www.mieb.uscourts.gov Pacer is online at http://pacer.mieb.uscourts.gov.
Bay City Division PO Box 911, Bay City, MI 48707. Phone: 989-894-8840. Counties: Alcona, Alpena, Arenac, Bay, Cheboygan, Clare, Crawford, Gladwin, Gratiot, Huron, Iosco, Isabella, Midland, Montmorency, Ogemaw, Oscoda, Otsego, Presque Isle, Roscommon, Saginaw, Tuscola. ✉ ☎ Pacer
Detroit Division Clerk, 21st Floor, 211 W Fort St, Detroit, MI 48226. Phone: 313-234-0065, Records Rm: 313-234-0051. Counties: Jackson, Lenawee, Macomb, Monroe, Oakland, Sanilac, St. Clair, Washtenaw, Wayne. ✉ ☎ Pacer

Flint Division 226 W 2nd St, Flint, MI 48502. Phone: 810-235-4126. Counties: Genesee, Lapeer, Livingston, Shiawassee. ✉ ☎ Pacer

Western District of Michigan

www.miwb.uscourts.gov Pacer is online at http://pacer.miwb.uscourts.gov. CM-ECF: https://ecf.miwb.uscourts.gov.
Grand Rapids Division PO Box 3310, Grand Rapids, MI 49501. Phone: 616-456-2693, Fax: 616-456-2919. Counties: Allegan, Antrim, Barry, Benzie, Berrien, Branch, Calhoun, Cass, Charlevoix, Clinton, Eaton, Emmet, Grand Traverse, Hillsdale, Ingham, Ionia, Kalamazoo, Kalkaska, Kent, Lake, Leelanau, Manistee, Mason, Mecosta, Missaukee, Montcalm, Muskegon, Newaygo, Oceana, Osceola, Ottawa, St. Joseph, Van Buren,

Wexford Marquette cases are also available electronically on the Grand Rapids Division public access terminal. ✉ Fax ☎ Pacer
Marquette Division PO Box 909, Marquette, MI 49855. Phone: 906-226-2117, Fax: 906-226-7388. Counties: Alger, Baraga, Chippewa, Delta, Dickinson, Gogebic, Houghton, Iron, Keweenaw, Luce, Mackinac, Marquette, Menominee, Ontonagon, Schoolcraft Marquette cases are also available electronically on the Grand Rapids Division public access terminal, but Grand Rapids cases are not available on Marquette's public access computer as yet. ✉ Fax ☎ Pacer

Minnesota

U.S. District Court

District of Minnesota

www.mnd.uscourts.gov Pacer is online at http://pacer.mnd.uscourts.gov. CM-ECF: https://ecf.mnd.uscourts.gov/cgi-bin/login.pl.
Duluth Division Clerk's Office, 417 Federal Bldg, 515 W. 1st St., Duluth, MN 55802-1397. Phone: 218-529-3500, Fax: 218-529-3505. Counties: Aitkin, Becker*, Beltrami*, Benton, Big Stone*, Carlton, Cass, Clay*, Clearwater*, Cook, Crow Wing, Douglas*, Grant*, Hubbard*, Itasca, Kanabec, Kittson*, Koochiching, Lake, Lake of the Woods*, Mahnomen*, Marshall*, Mille Lacs, Morrison, Norman*, Otter Tail,* Pennington*, Pine, Polk*, Pope*, Red Lake*, Roseau*, Stearns*, Stevens*, St. Louis, Todd*, Traverse*, Wadena*, Wilkin*. From March 1, 1995, to 1998, cases from the counties marked with an asterisk (*) were heard here. Before and after that period, cases were and are allocated between St. Paul and Minneapolis. ✉ ☎ Pacer
Minneapolis Division Court Clerk, Room 202, 300 S 4th St, Minneapolis, MN 55415. Phone: 612-664-5000, Fax: 612-664-5033. Counties: All counties not covered by the Duluth Division. Cases are allocated between Minneapolis and St Paul. ✉ ☎ Pacer

St Paul Division 700 Federal Bldg, 316 N Robert, St Paul, MN 55101. Phone: 651-848-1100, Fax: 651-848-1109. Counties: All counties not covered by the Duluth Division. Cases are allocated between Minneapolis and St Paul. ✉ Fax ☎ Pacer

Bankruptcy Court

District of Minnesota

www.mnb.uscourts.gov (online search free) PACER online is not available.
Duluth Division 416 US Courthouse, 515 W 1st St, Duluth, MN 55802. Phone: 218-529-3600. Counties: Aitkin, Benton, Carlton, Cass, Cook, Crow Wing, Itasca, Kanabec, Koochiching, Lake, Mille Lacs, Morrison, Pine, St. Louis. A petition commencing Chapter 11 or 12 proceedings may initially be filed in any of the four divisons, but may be assigned to another division. ✉ ☎ Pacer
Fergus Falls Division 204 US Courthouse, 118 S Mill St, Fergus Falls, MN 56537. Phone: 218-739-4671. Counties: Becker, Beltrami, Big Stone, Clay, Clearwater, Douglas, Grant, Hubbard, Kittson, Lake of the Woods, Mahnomen, Marshall, Norman, Otter Tail, Pennington, Polk, Pope, Red Lake, Roseau, Stearns, Stevens, Todd, Traverse, Wadena, Wilkin. A petition commencing

Chapter 11 or 12 proceedings may be filed initially in any of the four divisions, but may then be assigned to another division. ✉ ☎ Pacer
Minneapolis Division 301 US Courthouse, 300 S 4th St, Minneapolis, MN 55415. Phone: 612-664-5200, Records Rm: 612-664-5209. Counties: Anoka, Carver, Chippewa, Hennepin, Isanti, Kandiyohi, McLeod, Meeker, Renville, Sherburne, Swift, Wright. Initial petitions for Chapter 11 or 12 may be filed initially at any of the four divisions, but may be assigned to a judge in another division. ✉ ☎ Pacer
St Paul Division 200 US Courthouse, 316 N Robert St, St Paul, MN 55101. Phone: 651-848-1000. Counties: Blue Earth, Brown, Chisago, Cottonwood, Dakota, Dodge, Faribault, Fillmore, Freeborn, Goodhue, Houston, Jackson, Lac qui Parle, Le Sueur, Lincoln, Lyon, Martin, Mower, Murray, Nicollet, Nobles, Olmsted, Pipestone, Ramsey, Redwood, Rice, Rock, Scott, Sibley, Steele, Wabasha, Waseca, Washington, Watonwan, Winona, Yellow Medicine. Cases from Benton, Kanabec, Mille Lacs, Morrison and Pine may also be heard here. A petition commencing Chapter 11 or 12 proceedings may be filed initially with any of the four divisions, but may then be assigned to another division. ✉ ☎ Pacer

Mississippi

U.S. District Court

Northern District of Mississippi

www.msnd.uscourts.gov Pacer is online at http://pacer.msnd.uscourts.gov.
Aberdeen-Eastern Division PO Box 704, Aberdeen, MS 39730. Phone: 662-369-4952. Counties: Alcorn, Attala, Chickasaw, Choctaw, Clay, Itawamba, Lee, Lowndes, Monroe, Oktibbeha, Prentiss, Tishomingo, Winston.✉ Pacer
Clarksdale/Delta Division c/o Oxford-Northern Division, PO Box 727, Oxford, MS 38655. Phone: 662-234-1971, Records Rm: 662-234-1351. Counties: Bolivar, Coahoma, De Soto, Panola, Quitman, Tallahatchie, Tate, Tunica. ✉ Pacer
Greenville Division. PO Box 190, Greenville, MS 38702-0190. Phone: 662-335-1651, Fax: 662-332-4292. Counties: Carroll, Humphreys, Leflore, Sunflower, Washington. ✉ ☎ Pacer
Oxford-Northern Division PO Box 727, Oxford, MS 38655. Phone: 662-234-1971, Records Rm: 662-234-1351. Counties: Benton, Calhoun, Grenada, Lafayette, Marshall, Montgomery, Pontotoc, Tippah, Union, Webster, Yalobusha. ✉ Pacer

Southern District of Mississippi

www.mssd.uscourts.gov Pacer is online at http://pacer.mssd.uscourts.gov.
Biloxi-Southern Division Room 243, 725 Dr. Martin Luther King Jr. Blvd, Biloxi, MS 39530. Phone: 228-432-8623, Fax: 601-436-9632. Counties: George,
Hancock, Harrison, Jackson, Pearl River, Stone. ✉ Pacer
Eastern Division c/o Jackson Division, Suite 316, 245 E Capitol St, Jackson, MS 39201. Phone: 601-965-4439. Clarke, Jasper, Kemper, Lauderdale, Neshoba, Newton, Noxubee, Wayne. ✉ Pacer
Hattiesburg Division Suite 200, 701 Main St, Hattiesburg, MS 39401. Phone: 601-583-2433. Counties: Covington, Forrest, Greene, Jefferson Davis, Jones, Lamar, Lawrence, Marion, Perry, Walthall. ✉ ☎ Pacer
Jackson Division Suite 316, 245 E Capitol St, Jackson, MS 39201. Phone: 601-965-4439. Counties: Amite, Copiah, Franklin, Hinds, Holmes, Leake, Lincoln, Madison, Pike, Rankin, Scott, Simpson, Smith. ✉ Pacer
Weatern Division c/o Jackson Division, Suite 316, 245 E Capitol St, Jackson, MS 39201. Phone: 601-965-4439. Counties: Adams, Claiborne, Issaquena, Jefferson, Sharkey, Warren, Wilkinson, Yazoo. ✉ Pacer

Bankruptcy Court

Northern District of Mississippi

www.msnb.uscourts.gov Pacer is online at http://pacer.msnb.uscourts.gov. CM-ECF: https://ecf.msnb.uscourts.gov.
Aberdeen Division PO Drawer 867, Aberdeen, MS 39730-0867. Phone: 662-369-2596, Records Rm: 662-369-2596. Counties: Alcorn, Attala, Benton, Bolivar, Calhoun, Carroll, Chickasaw, Choctaw,
Clay, Coahoma, De Soto, Grenada, Humphreys, Itawamba, Lafayette, Lee, Leflore, Lowndes, Marshall, Monroe, Montgomery, Oktibbeha, Panola, Pontotoc, Prentiss, Quitman, Sunflower, Tallahatchie, Tate, Tippah, Tishomingo, Tunica, Union, Washington, Webster, Winston, Yalobusha. ✉ ☎ Pacer

Southern District of Mississippi

www.mssb.uscourts.gov Pacer is online at https://pacer.login.uscourts.gov/cgi-bin/login.pl?court_id=mssbk.
Biloxi Division Room 117, 725 Dr. Martin Luther King Jr. Blvd, Biloxi, MS 39530. Phone: 228-432-5542. Counties: Clarke, Covington, Forrest, George, Greene, Hancock, Harrison, Jackson, Jasper, Jefferson Davis, Jones, Kemper, Lamar, Lauderdale, Lawrence, Marion, Neshoba, Newton, Noxubee, Pearl River, Perry, Stone, Walthall, Wayne. ✉ Pacer
Jackson Division PO Box 2448, Jackson, MS 39225-2448. Phone: 601-965-5301. Counties: Adams, Amite, Claiborne, Copiah, Franklin, Hinds, Holmes, Issaquena, Jefferson, Leake, Lincoln, Madison, Pike, Rankin, Scott, Sharkey, Simpson, Smith, Warren, Wilkinson, Yazoo. ✉ Pacer

Missouri

U.S. District Court

Eastern District of Missouri

www.moed.uscourts.gov Pacer is online at http://pacer.moed.uscourts.gov. CM-ECF: https://ecf.moed.uscourts.gov.
Cape Girardeau Division 339 Broadway, Room 240, Cape Girardeau, MO 63701. Phone: 573-335-8538, Fax: 573-335-0379. Counties: Bollinger,
Butler, Cape Girardeau, Carter, Dunklin, Madison, Mississippi, New Madrid, Pemiscot, Perry, Reynolds, Ripley, Scott, Shannon, Stoddard, Wayne. ✉ ☎ Pacer
St Louis Division 111 S. 10th St, Ste 3.300, St Louis, MO 63102. Phone: 314-244-7900, Fax: 314-244-7909. Counties: Adair, Audrain, Chariton, Clark, Crawford, Dent, Franklin, Gasconade,
Iron, Jefferson, Knox, Lewis, Lincoln, Linn, Macon, Maries, Marion, Monroe, Montgomery, Phelps, Pike, Ralls, Randolph, Schuyler, Scotland, Shelby, St. Charles, St. Francois, St. Louis, St. Louis City, Ste. Genevieve, Warren, Washington, This court also holds records for the Hannibal Division. ✉ ☎ Pacer

Western District of Missouri

www.mow.uscourts.gov Pacer is online at http://pacer.mowd.uscourts.gov. CM-ECF: https://ecf.mowd.uscourts.gov.
Jefferson City-Central Division 131 W High St, Jefferson City, MO 65101. Phone: 573-636-4015, Fax: 573-636-3456. Counties: Benton, Boone, Callaway, Camden, Cole, Cooper, Hickory, Howard, Miller, Moniteau, Morgan, Osage, Pettis. ✉ ☎ Pacer
Joplin-Southwestern Division c/o Kansas City Division, Charles Evans Whitttaker Courthouse, 400 E 9th St, Kansas City, MO 64106. Phone: 816-512-5000, Fax: 816-512-5078. Counties: Barry, Barton, Jasper, Lawrence, McDonald, Newton, Stone, Vernon. ✉ Pacer
Kansas City-Western Division Clerk of Court, 201 US Courthouse, Rm 1056, 400 E 9th St, Kansas City, MO 64106. Phone: 816-512-5000, Fax: 816-512-5078. Counties: Bates, Carroll, Cass, Clay, Henry, Jackson, Johnson, Lafayette, Ray, St. Clair, Saline. ✉ Fax ☎ Pacer
Springfield-Southern Division 222 N John Q Hammons Pkwy, Suite 1400, Springfield, MO 65806. Phone: 417-865-3869, Fax: 417-865-7719. Counties: Cedar, Christian, Dade, Dallas, Douglas,

Greene, Howell, Laclede, Oregon, Ozark, Polk, Pulaski, Taney, Texas, Webster, Wright. ✉ ☎ Pacer
St Joseph Division PO Box 387, 201 S 8th St, St Joseph, MO 64501. Phone: , Fax: 816-279-0177. Counties: Andrew, Atchison, Buchanan, Caldwell, Clinton, Daviess, De Kalb, Gentry, Grundy, Harrison, Holt, Livingston, Mercer, Nodaway, Platte, Putnam, Sullivan, Worth. ✉ ☎ Pacer

Bankruptcy Court

Eastern District of Missouri

www.moeb.uscourts.gov Pacer is online at http://pacer.moeb.uscourts.gov. CM-ECF: https://ecf.moeb.uscourts.gov.
St Louis Division 4th Floor, 111 S. 10th St, St Louis, MO 63102-2734. Phone: 314-244-4500, Fax: 314-244-4990. Counties: Adair, Audrain, Bollinger, Butler, Cape Girardeau, Carter, Chariton, Clark, Crawford, Dent, Dunklin, Franklin, Gasconade, Iron, Jefferson, Knox, Lewis, Lincoln, Linn, Macon, Madison, Maries, Marion, Mississippi, Monroe, Montgomery, New Madrid, Pemiscot, Perry, Phelps, Pike, Ralls, Randolph,

Reynolds, Ripley, Schuyler, Scotland, Scott, Shannon, Shelby, St. Charles, St. Francois, St. Louis, St.Louis City, Ste. Genevieve, Stoddard, Warren, Washington, Wayne. ✉ ☎ Pacer

Western District of Missouri

www.mow.uscourt.gov Pacer is online at http://pacer.mowb.uscourts.gov/bc/index.html. Ecf: https://ecf.mowb.uscourts.gov.
Kansas City-Western Division Room 1510, 400 E 9th st, Kansas City, MO 64106. Phone: 816-512-1800. Counties: Andrew, Atchison, Barry, Barton, Bates, Benton, Boone, Buchanan, Caldwell, Callaway, Camden, Carroll, Cass, Cedar, Christian, Clay, Clinton, Cole, Cooper, Dade, Dallas, Daviess, De Kalb, Douglas, Gentry, Greene, Grundy, Harrison, Henry, Hickory, Holt, Howard, Howell, Jackson, Jasper, Johnson, Laclede, Lafayette, Lawrence, Livingston, McDonald, Mercer, Miller, Moniteau, Morgan, Newton, Nodaway, Oregon, Osage, Ozark, Pettis, Platte, Polk, Pulaski, Putnam, Ray, Saline, St. Clair, Stone, Sullivan, Taney, Texas, Vernon, Webster, Worth, Wright. ✉ Pacer

Montana

U.S. District Court

District of Montana

www.mtd.uscourts.gov Pacer is online at http://pacer.mtd.uscourts.gov.
Billings Division Clerk, Room 5405, Federal Bldg, 316 N 26th St, Billings, MT 59101. Phone: 406-247-7000, Fax: 406-247-7008. Counties: Big Horn, Carbon, Carter, Custer, Daniels, Dawson, Fallon, Garfield, Golden Valley, McCone, Musselshell, Park, Petroleum, Powder River, Prairie, Richland, Rosebud, Sheridan, Stillwater, Sweet Grass, Treasure, Wheatland, Wibaux, Yellowstone, Yellowstone National Park. ✉ Fax ☎ Pacer
Butte Division U.S. District Court, 400 North Main, Butte, MT 59701. Phone:

406-782-0432, Fax: 406-782-0537. Counties: Beaverhead, Deer Lodge, Gallatin, Madison, Silver Bow. ✉ Fax Pacer
Great Falls Division Clerk, PO Box 2186, Great Falls, MT 59403. Phone: 406-727-1922, Fax: 406-727-7648. Counties: Blaine, Cascade, Chouteau, Daniels, Fergus, Glacier, Hill, Judith Basin, Liberty, Phillips, Pondera, Roosevelt, Sheridan, Teton, Toole, Valley. ✉ ☎ Pacer
Helena Division Paul G. Hatfield Courthouse, 901 Front Street, Helena, MT 59626. Phone: 406-441-1355, Fax: 406-441-1357. Counties: Broadwater, Jefferson, Lewis and Clark, Meagher, Powell. ✉ ☎ Pacer
Missoula Division Russell Smith Courthouse, 201 E Broadway, Missoula,

MT 59801. Phone: 406-542-7260, Fax: 406-542-7272. Counties: Flathead, Granite, Lake, Lincoln, Mineral, Missoula, Ravalli, Sanders. ✉ ☎ Pacer

Bankruptcy Court

District of Montana

www.mtb.uscourts.gov Pacer is online at http://pacer.mtb.uscourts.gov. CM-ECF: https://ecf.mtb.uscourts.gov.
Butte Division PO Box 689, Butte, MT 59703. Phone: 406-782-3354, Fax: 406-782-0537. Counties: All. ✉ Fax ☎ Pacer

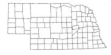

Nebraska

U.S. District Court

District of Nebraska

www.ned.uscourts.gov Pacer is online at http://pacer.ned.uscourts.gov. CM-ECF: https://ecf.ned.uscourts.gov.
Lincoln Division PO Box 83468, Lincoln, NE 68501. Phone: 402-437-5225, Fax: 402-437-5651. Counties: Nebraska cases may be filed in any of the three courts at the option of the attorney, except that filings in the North Platte Division must be during trial session. **Pacer**
North Platte Division c/o Lincoln Division, PO Box 83468, Lincoln, NE 68501. Phone: 402-437-5225, Fax: 402-437-5651. Counties: Nebraska cases may be filed in any of the three courts at the option of the attorney, except that filings in the North Platte Division must be during trial session. Some case records may be in the Omaha Division as well as the Lincoln Division. Pacer
Omaha Division 111 S 18th Plaza, Ste 1152, Omaha, NE 68102. Phone: 402-661-7350, Fax: 402-661-7387. Counties: Nebraska cases may be filed in any of the three courts at the option of the attorney, except that filings in the North Platte Division must be during trial session. Pacer

Bankruptcy Court

District of Nebraska

www.neb.uscourts.gov Pacer is online at http://pacer.neb.uscourts.gov. CM-ECF: https://ecf.neb.uscourts.gov.
Lincoln Division 460 Federal Bldg, 100 Centennial Mall N, Lincoln, NE 68508. Phone: 402-437-5100, Fax: 402-437-5454. Counties: Adams, Antelope, Boone, Boyd, Buffalo, Butler, Cass, Clay, Colfax, Fillmore, Franklin, Gage, Greeley, Hall, Hamilton, Harlan, Holt, Howard, Jefferson, Johnson, Kearney, Lancaster, Madison, Merrick, Nance, Nemaha, Nuckolls, Otoe, Pawnee, Phelps, Platte, Polk, Richardson, Saline, Saunders, Seward, Sherman, Thayer, Webster, Wheeler, York. Cases from the North Platte Division may also be assigned here. Pacer
North Platte Division c/o Omaha Division, 111 S 18th Plaza, Ste 1125, Omaha, NE 68102. Phone: 402-661-7444, Fax: 402-661-7492. Counties: Arthur, Banner, Blaine, Box Butte, Brown, Chase, Cherry, Cheyenne, Custer, Dawes, Dawson, Deuel, Dundy, Frontier, Furnas, Garden, Garfield, Gosper, Grant, Hayes, Hitchcock, Hooker, Keith, Keya Paha, Kimball, Lincoln, Logan, Loup, McPherson, Morrill, Perkins, Red Willow, Rock, Scotts Bluff, Sheridan, Sioux, Thomas, Valley. Cases may be randomly allocated to Omaha or Lincoln. Pacer
Omaha Division 111 S. 18th Plaza, Ste 1125, Omaha, NE 68102. Phone: 402-661-7444, Fax: 402-661-7441. Counties: Burt, Cedar, Cuming, Dakota, Dixon, Dodge, Douglas, Knox, Pierce, Sarpy, Stanton, Thurston, Washington, Wayne. Pacer

Nevada

U.S. District Court

District of Nevada

www.nvd.uscourts.gov Pacer is online at https://pacer.psc.uscourts.gov/cgi-bin/login/login.pl?court_id=nvdc.
Las Vegas Division Room 4425, 300 Las Vegas Blvd S, Las Vegas, NV 89101. Phone: 702-464-5400. Counties: Clark, Esmeralda, Lincoln, Nye. Pacer
Reno Division Room 301, 400 S Virginia St, Reno, NV 89501. Phone: 775-686-5800, Records Rm: 775-686-5909, Fax: 702-686-5851. Counties: Carson City, Churchill, Douglas, Elko, Eureka, Humboldt, Lander, Lyon, Mineral, Pershing, Storey, Washoe, White Pine. Fax Pacer

Bankruptcy Court

District of Nevada

www.nvb.uscourts.gov Pacer is online at http://pacer.nvb.uscourts.gov. This also contains all the former RACER records. CM-ECF: https://ecf.nvb.uscourts.gov.
Las Vegas Division 8th Floor, Suite 8112, Lloyd D. George Federal Bldg, 333 Las Vegas Boulevard South, Las Vegas, NV 89101. Phone: 702-388-6257. Counties: Clark, Esmeralda, Lincoln, Nye. Pacer
Reno Division Room 1109, 300 Booth St, Reno, NV 89509. Phone: 775-784-5559. Counties: Carson City, Churchill, Douglas, Elko, Eureka, Humboldt, Lander, Lyon, Mineral, Pershing, Storey, Washoe, White Pine. Pacer

New Hampshire

U.S. District Court

www.nhd.uscourts.gov   Pacer is online at http://pacer.nhd.uscourts.gov. CM-ECF: https://ecf.nhd.uscourts.gov.
Concord Division Warren B Rudman Courthouse, 55 Pleasant St, #110, Concord, NH 03301. Phone: 603-225-1423. Counties: Belknap, Carroll, Cheshire, Coos, Grafton, Hillsborough, Merrimack, Rockingham, Strafford, Sullivan. ✉ ☎ Pacer

Bankruptcy Court

www.nhb.uscourts.gov Pacer is online at http://pacer.nhb.uscourts.gov. CM-ECF: https://ecf.nhb.uscourts.gov.
Manchester Division Room 404, 275 Chestnut St, Manchester, NH 03101. Phone: 603-222-2600, Records Rm: 603-666-7626, Fax: 603-666-7408. Counties: Belknap, Carroll, Cheshire, Coos, Grafton, Hillsborough, Merrimack, Rockingham, Strafford, Sullivan. ✉ ☎ Pacer

New Jersey

U.S. District Court

http://pacer.njd.uscourts.gov   Pacer is online at http://pacer.njd.uscourts.gov. CM-ECF: https://ecf.njd.uscourts.gov.
Camden Division Clerk, PO Box 2797, Camden, NJ 08101. Phone: 856-757-5021, Fax: 856-757-5370. Counties: Atlantic, Burlington, Camden, Cape May, Cumberland, Gloucester, Salem. ✉ ☎ Pacer
Newark Division ML King, Jr Federal Bldg. & US Courthouse, 50 Walnut St, Room 4015, Newark, NJ 07101. Phone: 973-645-3730, Records Rm: 973-645-4565. Counties: Bergen, Essex, Hudson, Middlesex, Monmouth, Morris, Passaic, Sussex, Union. Monmouth County was transferred from Trenton Division in late 1997; closed cases remain in Trenton. ✉ ☎ Pacer
Trenton Division Clerk, US District Court, Room 2020, 402 E State St, Trenton, NJ 08608. Phone: 609-989-2065. Counties: Hunterdon, Mercer, Ocean, Somerset, Warren. Monmouth County transferred to Newark & Camden Division in late 1997; closed Monmouth cases remain in Trenton. ✉ ☎ Pacer

Bankruptcy Court

www.njb.uscourts.gov   Pacer is online at http://pacer.njb.uscourts.gov. CM-ECF: https://ecf.njb.uscourts.gov.
Camden Division PO Box 2067, Camden, NJ 08101. Phone: 856-757-5485. Atlantic, Burlington (partial), Camden, Cape May, Cumberland, Gloucester, Salem. ✉ ☎ Pacer
Newark Division PO Box 1352, Newark, NJ 07101-1352. Phone: 973-645-4764. Counties: Bergen, Essex, Hudson, Morris, Passaic, Sussex. Also Elizabeth, Springfield and Hillside townships in Union County. ✉ Pacer
Trenton Division Clerk of Court, 402 E State St, 1st Fl, Trenton, NJ 08608. Phone: 609-989-2129. Counties: Burlington (partial), Hunterdon, Mercer, Middlesex, Monmouth, Ocean, Somerset, Warren, Union except towns of Elizabeth, Hillside and Springfield. ✉ Pacer

New Mexico

U.S. District Court

www.nmcourt.fed.us/dcdocs (register for free online searching) This utilizes ACE (Advanced Court Engin.), and not the US Courts standard CM/ECF system. www.nmcourt.fed.us/dcdocs (Click on Electronic Filing) 333 Lomas Blvd NW #270, Albuquerque, NM 87102-2274. Phone: 505-348-2000, Records Rm: 505-348-2020, Fax: 505-348-2028. Counties: All counties in New Mexico. Cases may be assigned to any of its three divisions - Santa Fe (505-988-6481), Las Cruces (505-528-1400), and Roswell (505-625-2388). Santa Fe and Las Cruces have searchable records; Roswell does not. ✉ ☎ Pacer

Bankruptcy Court

www.nmcourt.fed.us/bkdocs   Pacer is online at http://pacer.nmb.uscourts.gov PO Box 546, Albuquerque, NM 87103-0546. Phone: 505-348-2500, Fax: 505-348-2473. Counties: All counties in New Mexico. Judges do travel to Los Cruces and Roswell, however, bankruptcy records are not searchable at those courthouses. ✉ Fax ☎ Pacer

Key: Federal Courts Record Access: phone-☎   mail-✉   fax-**Fax**   online PACER- **Pacer**   email-**Email**

New York

U.S. District Court

Eastern District of New York

www.nyed.uscourts.gov Pacer is online at http://pacer.nyed.uscourts.gov. This PACER system includes electronic records from Suffolk and Nassau Counties, Long Island. CM-ECF: https://ecf.nyed.uscourts.gov.
Brooklyn Division Brooklyn Courthouse, 225 Cadman Plaza E, Room 130, Brooklyn, NY 11201. Phone: 718-260-2600, Records Rm: 718-260-2285. Counties: Kings, Queens, Richmond. Cases from Nassau and Suffolk may also be filed here (but paper records and cases are heard in Central Islip Div.), but all records are available electronically trhough PACER from this Brooklyn Division. ✉ Pacer
Central Islip Division 100 Federal Plaza, Central Islip, NY 17722-4438. Phone: 613-712-6000. Counties: Nassau, Suffolk. Cases from these counties may be filed in Brooklyn Div, but heard in Central Islip. Central Islip cases can be found on Brooklyn's PACER system.
✉ Fax ☎ Pacer

Northern District of New York

www.nynd.uscourts.gov Pacer is online at http://pacer.nynd.uscourts.gov. CM-ECF: https://ecf.nynd.uscourts.gov.
Albany Division 445 Broadway, Room 509, James T Foley Courthouse, Albany, NY 12207-2924. Phone: 518-257-1800. Counties: Albany, Clinton, Columbia, Essex, Greene, Rensselaer, Saratoga, Schenectady, Schoharie, Ulster, Warren, Washington. ✉ Pacer
Binghamton Division 15 Henry St, Binghamton, NY 13902. Phone: 607-773-2893. Counties: Broome, Chenango, Delaware, Franklin, Jefferson, Lewis, Otsego, St. Lawrence, Tioga This court provides the judges for the Watertown Division. ✉ Pacer
Syracuse Division PO Box 7367, Syracuse, NY 13261-7367. Phone: 315-234-8500. Counties: Cayuga, Cortland, Fulton, Hamilton, Herkimer, Madison, Montgomery, Onondaga, Oswego, Tompkins. ✉ Pacer

Utica Division Alexander Pirnie Bldg, 10 Broad St, Utica, NY 13501. Phone: 315-793-8151. Counties: Oneida. ✉ ☎ Pacer

Southern District of New York

www.nysd.uscourts.gov The old system replaced by new CM/ECF system. CM-ECF: https://ecf.nysd.uscourts.gov.
New York City Division 500 Pearl St, New York, NY 10007. Phone: 212-805-0136, Records Rm: Open Recs: 212-805-0710; Closed recs: 212-805-0715. Counties: Bronx, New York. A 2nd courthouse at 40 Centre St is an Appelate Division with some District Cases heard there; search both at Pearl St location. Some cases from the counties in the White Plains Div. are also assigned to this New York Division. ✉ Pacer
White Plains Division US Courthouse, 300 Quarropas St, White Plains, NY 10601. Phone: 914-390-4100. Counties: Dutchess, Orange, Putnam, Rockland, Sullivan, Westchester. Some cases may be assigned to New York Div.. ✉ Pacer

Western District of New York

www.nywd.uscourts.gov Pacer is online at http://pacer.nywd.uscourts.gov. CM-ECF: https://ecf.nywd.uscourts.gov.
Buffalo Division Room 304, 68 Court St, Buffalo, NY 14202. Phone: 716-551-4211, Fax: 716-551-4850. Counties: Allegany, Cattaraugus, Chautauqua, Erie, Genesee, Niagara, Orleans, Wyoming. Prior to 1982, this division included what is now the Rochester Div. ✉ Pacer
Rochester Division. Room 2120, 100 State St, Rochester, NY 14614. Phone: 585-263-6263, Fax: 585-263-3178. Counties: Chemung, Livingston, Monroe, Ontario, Schuyler, Seneca, Steuben, Wayne, Yates. ✉ Fax ☎ Pacer

Bankruptcy Court

Eastern District of New York

www.nyeb.uscourts.gov Pacer is online at http://pacer.nyeb.uscourts.gov. CM-ECF: https://ecf.nyeb.uscourts.gov.
Brooklyn Division 75 Clinton St, Brooklyn, NY 11201. Phone: 718-330-2188. Counties: Kings, Queens, Richmond. Kings and Queens County

Chapter 11 cases may also be assigned to Westbury. Other Queens County cases may be assigned to Westbury Division. Nassau County Chapter 11 cases may be assigned here. ✉ ☎ Pacer
Central Islip Division Long Island Federal Courthouse, 290 Federal Plaza, 2nd Fl, Central Islip, NY 11722. Phone: 631-712-6200. Counties: Suffolk, Nassau. ✉ ☎ Pacer

Northern District of New York

www.nynb.uscourts.gov Pacer is online at http://pacer.nynb.uscourts.gov. CM-ECF: https://ecf.nynb.uscourts.gov.
Albany Division James T Foley Courthouse, 445 Broadway #330, Albany, NY 12207. Phone: 518-257-1661. Counties: Albany, Clinton, Essex, Franklin, Fulton, Jefferson, Montgomery, Rensselaer, Saratoga, Schenectady, Schoharie, St. Lawrence, Warren, Washington. ✉ ☎ Pacer
Utica Division. Room 230, 10 Broad St, Utica, NY 13501. Phone: 315-793-8101, Fax: 315-793-8128. Counties: Broome, Cayuga, Chenango, Cortland, Delaware, Hamilton, Herkimer, Lewis, Madison, Oneida, Onondaga, Otsego, Oswego, Tioga, Tompkins. ✉ ☎ Pacer

Southern District of New York

www.nysb.uscourts.gov Pacer online https://ecf.nysb.uscourts.gov/cgi-bin/login.pl CM-ECF: http://ecf.nysb.uscourts.gov.
New York Division. Room 534, 1 Bowling Green, New York, NY 10004-1408. Phone: 212-668-2870. Counties: Bronx, New York. ✉ ☎ Pacer
Poughkeepsie Division 176 Church St, Poughkeepsie, NY 12601. Phone: 845-452-4200, Fax: 845-452-8375. Counties: Columbia, Dutchess, Greene, Orange, Putnam, Sullivan, Ulster. ✉ ☎ Pacer
White Plains Division 300 Quarropas St, White Plains, NY 10601. Phone: 914-390-4060. Counties: Rockland, Westchester. ✉ ☎ Pacer

Western District of New York

www.nywb.uscourts.gov Pacer is online at http://pacer.nywb.uscourts.gov. CM-ECF: https://ecf.nywb.uscourts.gov.

Buffalo Division Olympic Towers, 300 Pearl St #250, Buffalo, NY 14202-2501. Phone: 716-551-4130. Allegany, Cattaraugus, Chautauqua, Erie, Genesee, Niagara, Orleans, Wyoming. ✉ ☎ Pacer
Rochester Division Room 1220, 100 State St, Rochester, NY 14614. Phone: 585-263-3148. Counties: Chemung, Livingston, Monroe, Ontario, Schuyler, Seneca, Steuben, Wayne, Yates. ✉ ☎ Pacer

North Carolina

U.S. District Court

Eastern Dist. of North Carolina

www.nced.uscourts.gov The RACER system is now administered by PACER, see www.nced.uscourts.gov/Racer.htm.
Eastern Division Room 209, 201 S Evans St, Greenville, NC 27858-1137. Phone: 252-830-6009, Fax: 252-830-2793. Counties: Beaufort, Carteret, Craven, Edgecombe, Greene, Halifax, Hyde, Jones, Lenoir, Martin, Pamlico, Pitt. ✉ ☎ Pacer
Northern Division c/o Raleigh Division, PO Box 25670, Raleigh, NC 27611. Phone: 919-856-4370. Counties: Bertie, Camden, Chowan, Currituck, Dare, Gates, Hertford, Northampton, Pasquotank, Perquimans, Tyrrell, Washington. ✉ Pacer
Southern Division Alton Lennon Fed. Bldg., '2 Princess Street, Wilmington, NC 28401. Phone: 910-815-4663, Fax: 910-815-4518. Counties: Bladen, Brunswick, Columbus, Duplin, New Hanover, Onslow, Pender, Robeson, Sampson. ✉ ☎ Pacer
Western Division Clerk's Office, PO Box 25670, Raleigh, NC 27611. Phone: 919-645-1700, Fax: 919-645-1750. Counties: Cumberland, Franklin, Granville, Harnett, Johnston, Nash, Vance, Wake, Warren, Wayne, Wilson. ✉ ☎ Pacer

Middle Dist. of North Carolina

www.ncmd.uscourts.gov Pacer is online at http://pacer.ncmd.uscourts.gov.
Greensboro Division Clerk's Office, PO Box 2708, Greensboro, NC 27402. Phone: 336-332-6000. Counties: Alamance, Cabarrus, Caswell, Chatham, Davidson, Davie, Durham, Forsyth, Guilford, Hoke, Lee, Montgomery, Moore, Orange, Person, Randolph, Richmond, Rockingham, Rowan, Scotland, Stanly, Stokes, Surry, Yadkin. ✉ Pacer

Western Dist. of North Carolina

www.ncwd.uscourts.gov WebPACER at www.ncwd.uscourts.gov/index.html.
Asheville Division Clerk of the Court, Room 309, US Courthouse Bldg, 100 Otis St, Asheville, NC 28801-2611. Phone: 828-771-7200, Fax: 828-271-4343. Counties: Avery, Buncombe, Haywood, Henderson, Madison, Mitchell, Transylvania, Yancey. ✉ ☎ Pacer
Bryson City Division c/o Asheville Division, Clerk of the Court, Room 309, US Courthouse, 100 Otis St, Asheville, NC 28801-2611. Phone: 828-771-7200. Counties: Cherokee, Clay, Graham, Jackson, Macon, Swain. ✉ Pacer
Charlotte Division Clerk, Room 210, 401 W Trade St, Charlotte, NC 28202. Phone: 704-350-7400. Counties: Anson, Gaston, Mecklenburg, Union. ✉ Pacer
Shelby Division c/o Asheville Division, Clerk of the Court, Room 309, US Courthouse, 100 Otis St, Asheville, NC 28801-2611. Phone: 828-771-7200. Counties: Burke, Cleveland, McDowell, Polk, Rutherford. ✉ Pacer
Statesville Division PO Box 466, Statesville, NC 28687. Phone: 704-883-1000. Counties: Alexander, Alleghany, Ashe, Caldwell, Catawba, Iredell, Lincoln, Watauga, Wilkes. ✉ ☎ Pacer

Bankruptcy Court

Eastern Dist. of North Carolina

www.nceb.uscourts.gov (online search free) Court uses new CM/ECF system for PACER. For information on their electronic noticing and filing system, visit www.nceb.uscourts.gov/efiling.htm. CM-ECF: https://ecf.nceb.uscourts.gov.
Raleigh Division PO Box 1441, Raleigh, NC 27602. Phone: 919-856-4752. Franklin, Granville, Harnett, Johnston, Vance, Wake, Warren. ✉ Pacer
Wilson Division PO Drawer 2807, Wilson, NC 27894-2807. Phone: 252-237-0248. Counties: Beaufort, Bertie, Bladen,

Brunswick, Camden, Carteret, Chowan, Columbus, Craven, Cumberland, Currituck, Dare, Duplin, Edgecombe, Gates, Greene, Halifax, Hertford, Hyde, Jones, Lenoir, Martin, Nash, New Hanover, Northampton, Onslow, Pamlico, Pasquotank, Pender, Perquimans, Pitt, Robeson, Sampson, Tyrrell, Washington, Wayne, Wilson. ✉ Pacer

Middle Dist. of North Carolina

www.ncmb.uscourts.gov Pacer is online at http://pacer.ncmb.uscourts.gov. ECF images go back to 1999. CM-ECF: https://ecf.ncmb.uscourts.gov.
Greensboro Division PO Box 26100, Greensboro, NC 27420-6100. Phone: 336-333-5647. Counties: Alamance, Cabarrus, Caswell, Chatham, Davidson, Davie, Durham, Guilford, Hoke, Lee, Montgomery, Moore, Orange, Person, Randolph, Richmond, Rockingham, Rowan, Scotland, Stanly. ✉ ☎ Pacer
Winston-Salem Division. 226 S Liberty St, Winston-Salem, NC 27101. Phone: 336-631-5340. Counties: Forsyth, Stokes, Surry, Yadkin. ✉ ☎ Pacer

Western Dist. of North Carolina

www.ncwb.uscourts.gov Court uses new CM/ECF system for PACER. CM-ECF: https://ecf.ncwb.uscourts.gov.
Charlotte Division P.O. Box 34189, Charlotte, NC 28234-4189. Phone: 704-350-7500. Counties: Alexander, Alleghany, Anson, Ashe, Avery, Buncombe, Burke, Caldwell, Catawba, Cherokee, Clay, Cleveland, Gaston, Graham, Haywood, Henderson, Iredell, Jackson, Lincoln, Macon, Madison, McDowell, Mecklenburg, Mitchell, Polk, Rutherford, Swain, Transylvania, Union, Watauga, Wilkes, Yancey. There are five offices within this division; records for all may be searched here or at Asheville: 100 Otis St #112, Asheville, NC 28801, 828-771-7300. ✉ ☎ Pacer

---

Key: Federal Courts Record Access: phone-☎ mail-✉ fax-**Fax** online PACER- Pacer email-**Email**

North Dakota

U.S. District Court

District of North Dakota

www.ndd.uscourts.gov Pacer is online at http://pacer.ndd.uscourts.gov.
Bismarck-Southwestern Division PO Box 1193, Bismarck, ND 58502. Phone: 701-530-2300, Fax: 701-530-2312. Counties: Adams, Billings, Bowman, Burleigh, Dunn, Emmons, Golden Valley, Grant, Hettinger, Kidder, Logan, McIntosh, McLean, Mercer, Morton, Oliver, Sioux, Slope, Stark. ✉ ☎Pacer
Fargo-Southeastern Division PO Box 870, Fargo, ND 58107. Phone: 701-297-7000, Fax: 701-297-7005. Counties: Barnes, Cass, Dickey, Eddy, Foster,

Griggs, La Moure, Ransom, Richland, Sargent, Steele, Stutsman. Rolette County cases prior to 1995 may be located here. ✉ Fax ☎ Pacer
Grand Forks-Northeastern Division c/o Fargo-Southeastern Division, 102 N 4th St, Grand Forks, ND 58201. Phone: 701-772-0511, Fax: 701-746-7544. Counties: Benson, Cavalier, Grand Forks, Nelson, Pembina, Ramsey, Towner, Traill, Walsh. ✉ Pacer
Minot-Northwestern Division c/o Bismarck Division, PO Box 1193, Bismarck, ND 58502. Phone: 701-839-6251, Fax: 701-838-3276. Counties: Bottineau, Burke, Divide, McHenry, McKenzie, Mountrail, Pierce, Renville,

Rolette, Sheridan, Ward, Wells, Williams. Case records from Rolette County prior to 1995 may be located in Fargo-Southeastern Division. ✉ Pacer

Bankruptcy Court

www.ndb.uscourts.gov Pacer is online at http://pacer.okwd.uscourts.gov. CM-ECF: https://ecf.ndb.uscourts.gov.
Fargo Division 655 1st Ave N. #210, Fargo, ND 58102-4932. Phone: 701-297-7100, Fax: 701-297-7104. Counties: All counties in North Dakota. ✉ ☎ Pacer

Ohio

U.S. District Court

Northern District of Ohio

www.ohnd.uscourts.gov Pacer is online at http://pacer.ohnd.uscourts.gov. PACER may be phased out. CM-ECF: http://ecf.ohnd.uscourts.gov.
Akron Division 568 US Courthouse, 2 S Main St, Akron, OH 44308. Phone: 330-375-5705. Counties: Carroll, Holmes, Portage, Stark, Summit, Tuscarawas, Wayne. Cases filed prior to 1995 for Youngstown Division counties may be located here. ✉ ☎ Pacer
Cleveland Division 801 West Superior Ave, Cleveland, OH 44114-1830. Phone: 216-357-7000. Counties: Ashland, Ashtabula, Crawford, Cuyahoga, Geauga, Lake, Lorain, Medina, Richland. Cases prior to July 1995 for the counties of Ashland, Crawford, Medina and Richland are located in the Akron Division. Cases filed prior to 1995 from the counties in the Youngstown Division may be located here. ✉ ☎ Pacer
Toledo Division 114 US Courthouse, 1716 Spielbusch, Toledo, OH 43624. Phone: 419-259-6412. Counties: Allen, Auglaize, Defiance, Erie, Fulton, Hancock, Hardin, Henry, Huron, Lucas, Marion, Mercer, Ottawa, Paulding,

Putnam, Sandusky, Seneca, Van Wert, Williams, Wood, Wyandot. ✉ ☎Pacer
Youngstown Division 337 Federal Bldg, 125 Market St, Youngstown, OH 44503-1780. Phone: 330-746-1906, Fax: 330-746-2027. Counties: Columbiana, Mahoning, Trumbull. This division was re-activated in the middle of 1995. Older cases will be found in Akron or Cleveland. ✉ Fax ☎ Pacer

Southern District of Ohio

www.ohsd.uscourts.gov Pacer is online at http://pacer.ohsd.uscourts.gov. CM-ECF: https://ecf.ohsd.uscourts.gov.
Cincinnati Division Clerk, US District Court, Potter Stewart Courthouse Rm 324, 100 E 5th St, Cincinnati, OH 45202. Phone: 513-564-7500, Fax: 513-564-7505. Counties: Adams, Brown, Butler, Clermont, Clinton, Hamilton, Highland, Lawrence, Scioto, Warren.✉ ☎ Pacer
Columbus Division Office of the clerk, Room 260, 85 Marconi Blvd, Columbus, OH 43215. Phone: 614-719-3000, Fax: 614-469-5953. Counties: Athens, Belmont, Coshocton, Delaware, Fairfield, Fayette, Franklin, Gallia, Guernsey, Harrison, Hocking, Jackson, Jefferson, Knox, Licking, Logan, Madison, Meigs, Monroe, Morgan, Morrow, Muskingum,

Noble, Perry, Pickaway, Pike, Ross, Union, Vinton, Washington. ✉☎Pacer
Dayton Division Federal Bldg, 200 W 2nd, Room 712, Dayton, OH 45402. Phone: 937-512-1400. Counties: Champaign, Clark, Darke, Greene, Miami, Montgomery, Preble, Shelby.
✉ ☎ Pacer

Bankruptcy Court

Northern District of Ohio

www.ohnb.uscourts.gov Pacer is online at http://pacer.ohnb.uscourts.gov. CM-ECF: https://ecf.ohnb.uscourts.gov.
Akron Division 455 US Courthouse, 2 S Main, Akron, OH 44308. Phone: 330-375-5840. Counties: Medina, Portage, Summit. ✉ Pacer
Canton Division Frank T Bow Federal Bldg, 201 Cleveland Ave SW, Canton, OH 44702. Phone: 330-489-4426, Fax: 330-489-4434. Counties: Ashland, Carroll, Crawford, Holmes, Richland, Stark, Tuscarawas, Wayne. ✉Fax Pacer
Cleveland Division Key Tower, Room 3001, 127 Public Square, Cleveland, OH 44114. Phone: 216-522-4373. Counties: Cuyahoga, Geauga, Lake, Lorain.✉ Pac

Key: Federal Courts Record Access: phone-☎ mail-✉ fax-Fax online PACER- Pacer email-Email

Toledo Division Room 411, 1716 Spielbusch Ave, Toledo, OH 43624. Phone: 419-259-6440. Counties: Allen, Auglaize, Defiance, Erie, Fulton, Hancock, Hardin, Henry, Huron, Lucas, Marion, Mercer, Ottawa, Paulding, Putnam, Sandusky, Seneca, Van Wert, Williams, Wood, Wyandot. ✉ Pacer

Youngstown Division US Courthouse, 10 East Commerce Street, Youngstown, OH 44501. Phone: 330-746-7027. Counties: Ashtabula, Columbiana, Mahoning, Trumbull. ✉ Pacer

Southern District of Ohio

www.ohsb.uscourts.gov Pacer is online at http://pacer.ohsb.uscourts.gov. CM-ECF: https://ecf.ohsb.uscourts.gov.

Cincinnati Division. Atrium Two, Suite 800, 221 E Fourth St, Cincinnati, OH 45202. Phone: 513-684-2572. Counties: Adams, Brown, Clermont, Hamilton, Highland, Lawrence, Scioto and a part of Butler. ✉ ☎ Pacer

Columbus Division 170 N High St, Columbus, OH 43215. Phone: 614-469-6638. Counties: Athens, Belmont, Coshocton, Delaware, Fairfield, Fayette, Franklin, Gallia, Guernsey, Harrison,

Hocking, Jackson, Jefferson, Knox, Licking, Logan, Madison, Meigs, Monroe, Morgan, Morrow, Muskingum, Noble, Perry, Pickaway, Pike, Ross, Union, Vinton, Washington. ✉ Pacer

Dayton Division 120 W 3rd St, Dayton, OH 45402. Phone: 937-225-2516. Counties: Butler, Champaign, Clark, Clinton, Darke, Greene, Miami, Montgomery, Preble, Shelby, Warren; parts of Butler County are handled by Cincinnati Division. ✉ ☎ Pacer

Oklahoma

U.S. District Court

Eastern District of Oklahoma

www.oked.uscourts.gov Pacer is online at http://pacer.oked.uscourts.gov.

Muskogee Division Clerk, PO Box 607, Muskogee, OK 74401. Phone: 918-684-7920, Fax: 918-684-7902. Counties: Adair, Atoka, Bryan, Carter, Cherokee, Choctaw, Coal, Haskell, Hughes, Johnston, Latimer, Le Flore, Love, McCurtain, McIntosh, Marshall, Murray, Muskogee, Okfuskee, Pittsburg, Pontotoc, Pushmataha, Seminole, Sequoyah, Wagoner. ✉ ☎ Pacer

Northern District of Oklahoma

www.oknd.uscourts.gov Pacer is online at http://pacer.oknd.uscourts.gov.

Tulsa Division 411 US Courthouse, 333 W 4th St, Tulsa, OK 74103. Phone: 918-699-4700, Fax: 918-699-4756. Counties: Craig, Creek, Delaware, Mayes, Nowata, Okmulgee, Osage, Ottawa, Pawnee, Rogers, Tulsa, Washington. ✉ ☎ Pacer

Western District of Oklahoma

www.okwd.uscourts.gov Pacer online at http://pacer.okwd.uscourts.gov. Document images available on the RACER system. CM-ECF: https://ecf.okwd.uscourts.gov.

Oklahoma City Division Clerk, Room 1210, 200 NW 4th St, Oklahoma City, OK 73102. Phone: 405-609-5000, Fax: 405-609-5099. Counties: Alfalfa, Beaver, Beckham, Blaine, Caddo, Canadian, Cimarron, Cleveland, Comanche, Cotton, Custer, Dewey, Ellis, Garfield, Garvin, Grady, Grant, Greer, Harmon, Harper, Jackson, Jefferson, Kay, Kingfisher, Kiowa, Lincoln, Logan, McClain, Major, Noble, Oklahoma, Payne, Pottawatomie, Roger Mills, Stephens, Texas, Tillman, Washita, Woods, Woodward. ✉ ☎ Pacer

Bankruptcy Court

Eastern District of Oklahoma

www.okeb.uscourts.gov Pacer is online at http://pacer.okeb.uscourts.gov. CM-ECF: https://ecf.okeb.uscourts.gov.

Okmulgee Division PO Box 1347, Okmulgee, OK 74447. Phone: 918-758-0126, Fax: 918-756-9248. Counties: Adair, Atoka, Bryan, Carter, Cherokee, Choctaw, Coal, Haskell, Hughes, Johnston, Latimer, Le Flore, Love, Marshall, McCurtain, McIntosh, Murray, Muskogee, Okfuskee, Okmulgee, Pittsburg, Pontotoc, Pushmataha, Seminole, Sequoyah, Wagoner. ✉ Fax ☎ Pacer

Northern District of Oklahoma

www.oknb.uscourts.gov Pacer online at https://pacer.login.uscourts.gov/cgi-bin/login.pl?court_id=OKNBK. CM-ECF: https://ecf.oknb.uscourts.gov.

Tulsa Division. 224 S. Boulder Ave, Tulsa, OK 74103. Phone: 918-699-4000, Fax: 918-699-4051. Counties: Craig, Creek, Delaware, Mayes, Nowata, Osage, Ottawa, Pawnee, Rogers, Tulsa, Washington. ✉ Fax ☎ Pacer

Western District of Oklahoma

www.okwb.uscourts.gov No PACER access for this court; free searching is available, see website.

Oklahoma City Division 1st Floor, Old Post Office Bldg, 215 Dean A McGee Ave, Oklahoma City, OK 73102. Phone: 405-609-5700, Fax: 405-609-5752. Counties: Alfalfa, Beaver, Beckham, Blaine, Caddo, Canadian, Cimarron, Cleveland, Comanche, Cotton, Custer, Dewey, Ellis, Garfield, Garvin, Grady, Grant, Greer, Harmon, Harper, Jackson, Jefferson, Kay, Kingfisher, Kiowa, Lincoln, Logan, Major, McClain, Noble, Oklahoma, Payne, Pottawatomie, Roger Mills, Stephens, Texas, Tillman, Washita, Woods, Woodward. ✉ Pacer

Oregon

U.S. District Court

www.ord.uscourts.gov Pacer is online at http://pacer.ord.uscourts.gov. CM-ECF: https://ecf.ord.uscourts.gov.

Eugene Division 100 Federal Bldg, 211 E 7th Ave, Eugene, OR 97401. Phone: 541-465-6423, Fax: 541-465-6344. Counties: Benton, Coos, Deschutes, Douglas, Lane, Lincoln, Linn, Marion. ⊠ ☎ Pacer

Medford Division 201 James A Redden US Courthouse, 310 W 6th St, Medford, OR 97501. Phone: 541-776-3926, Fax: 541-776-3925. Counties: Curry, Jackson, Josephine, Klamath, Lake. Court set up in April 1994; Cases prior to that time were tried in Eugene. ⊠ Fax ☎ Pacer

Portland Division Clerk, 740 US Courthouse, 1000 SW 3rd Ave, Portland, OR 97204-2902. Phone: 503-326-8000, Records Rm: 503-326-8020, Fax: 503-326-8010. Counties: Baker, Clackamas, Clatsop, Columbia, Crook, Gilliam, Grant, Harney, Hood River, Jefferson, Malheur, Morrow, Multnomah, Polk, Sherman, Tillamook, Umatilla, Union, Wallowa, Wasco, Washinton, Wheeler, Yamhill. ⊠ Fax ☎ Pacer

Bankruptcy Court

www.orb.uscourts.gov Pacer is online at http://pacer.orb.uscourts.gov. CM-ECF: https://ecf.orb.uscourts.gov.

Eugene Division PO Box 1335, Eugene, OR 97440. Phone: 541-465-6448. Counties: Benton, Coos, Curry, Deschutes, Douglas, Jackson, Josephine, Klamath, Lake, Lane, Lincoln, Linn, Marion. ⊠ ☎ Pacer

Portland Division 1001 SW 5th Ave, #700, Portland, OR 97204. Phone: 503-326-2231. Counties: Baker, Clackamas, Clatsop, Columbia, Crook, Gilliam, Grant, Harney, Hood River, Jefferson, Malheur, Morrow, Multnomah, Polk, Sherman, Tillamook, Umatilla, Union, Wallowa, Wasco, Washington, Wheeler, Yamhill. ⊠ ☎ Pacer

Pennsylvania

U.S. District Court

Eastern Dist. of Pennsylvania

www.paed.uscourts.gov (online search free at website) Pacer is online at http://pacer.paed.uscourts.gov. CM-ECF: https://ecf.paed.uscourts.gov.

Allentown/Reading Division c/o Philadelphia Division, Room 2609, US Courthouse, 601 Market St, Philadelphia, PA 19106-1797. Phone: 215-597-7704, Records Rm: 215-597-7721, Fax: 215-597-6390. Counties: Berks, Lancaster, Lehigh, Northampton, Schuylkill⊠Pacer

Philadelphia Division Room 2609, US Courthouse, 601 Market St, Philadelphia, PA 19106-1797. Phone: 215-597-7704, Records Rm: 215-597-7721, Fax: 215-597-6390. Counties: Bucks, Chester, Delaware, Montgomery, Philadelphia. ⊠ Fax ☎ Pacer

Middle District of Pennsylvania

www.pamd.uscourts.gov Pacer is online at http://pacer.pamd.uscourts.gov. CM-ECF: https://ecf.pamd.uscourts.gov/cgi-bin/login.pl.

Harrisburg Division PO Box 983, Harrisburg, PA 17108-0983. Phone: 717-221-3920, Records Rm: 717-221-3924, Fax: 717-221-3959. Counties: Adams,

Cumberland, Dauphin, Franklin, Fulton, Huntingdon, Juniata, Lebanon, Mifflin, York. ⊠ Fax Pacer

Scranton Division Clerk's Office, William J Nealon Fedearl Bldg & US Courthouse, PO Box 1148, Scranton, PA 18501. Phone: 570-207-5680, Fax: 717-207-5689. Counties: Bradford, Carbon, Lackawanna, Luzerne, Monroe, Pike, Susquehanna, Wayne, Wyoming.

⊠ Fax ☎ Pacer

Williamsport Division PO Box 608, Williamsport, PA 17703. Phone: 570-323-6380, Fax: 717-323-0636. Counties: Cameron, Centre, Clinton, Columbia, Lycoming, Montour, Northumberland, Perry, Potter, Snyder, Sullivan, Tioga, Union.⊠Fax ☎ Pacer

Western Dist. of Pennsylvania

www.pawd.uscourts.gov Pacer is online at http://pacer.pawd.uscourts.gov.

Erie Division. PO Box 1820, Erie, PA 16507. Phone: 814-453-4829. Counties: Crawford, Elk, Erie, Forest, McKean, Venango, Warren. ⊠ ☎ Pacer

Johnstown Division Penn Traffic Bldg, Room 208, 319 Washington St, Johnstown, PA 15901. Phone: 814-533-4504, Fax: 814-533-4519. Counties:

Bedford, Blair, Cambria, Clearfield, Somerset. ⊠ ☎ Pacer

Pittsburgh Division US Post Office & Courthouse, Room 829, 7th Ave & Grant St, Pittsburgh, PA 15219. Phone: 412-208-7500, Records Rm: 412-208-7507. Counties: Allegheny, Armstrong, Beaver, Butler, Clarion, Fayette, Greene, Indiana, Jefferson, Lawrence, Mercer, Washington, Westmoreland. ⊠ ☎ Pacer

Bankruptcy Court

Eastern Dist. of Pennsylvania

www.paeb.uscourts.gov Pacer is online at http://pacer.paeb.uscourts.gov. CM-ECF: https://ecf.paeb.uscourts.gov.

Philadelphia Division 4th Floor, 900 Market St, Philadelphia, PA 19107. Phone: 215-408-2800. Counties: Bucks, Chester, Delaware, Montgomery, Philadelphia. ⊠ Pacer

Reading Division The Madison, 400 Washington St, Reading, PA 19601. Phone: 610-320-5255. Counties: Berks, Lancaster, Lehigh, Northampton, Schuylkill. ⊠ ☎ Pacer

Middle District of Pennsylvania

www.pamb.uscourts.gov/ Pacer is online at http://pacer.pamb.uscourts.gov. CM-ECF: https://ecf.pamb.uscourts.gov.
Harrisburg Division PO Box 908, Harrisburg, PA 17108. Phone: 717-901-2800, Fax: 717-901-2822. Counties: Adams, Centre, Cumberland, Dauphin, Franklin, Fulton, Huntingdon, Juniata, Lebanon, Mifflin, Montour, Northumberland, Perry, Schuylkill, Snyder, Union, York. ⊠ ☎ Pacer
Wilkes-Barre Division Clerk's Office, Max Rosen US Courthouse, 197 S Main St, Wilkes-Barre, PA 18701. Phone: 570-

826-6450, Fax: 570-826-6694. Counties: Bradford, Cameron, Carbon, Clinton, Columbia, Lackawanna, Luzerne, Lycoming, Monroe, Pike, Potter, Schuylkill, Sullivan, Susquehanna, Tioga, Wayne, Wyoming. ⊠ ☎ Pacer

Western Dist. of Pennsylvania

www.pawb.uscourts.gov Pacer is online at http://pacer.pawb.uscourts.gov. CM-ECF: https://ecf.pawb.uscourts.gov.
Erie Division 717 State St, #501, Erie, PA 16501. Phone: 814-453-7580, Fax: 814-453-3795. Clarion, Crawford, Elk,

Erie, Forest, Jefferson, McKean, Mercer, Venango, Warren. ⊠ Pacer
Pittsburgh Division 600 Grant St #5414, Pittsburgh, PA 15219-2801. Phone: 412-644-2700. Counties: Allegheny, Armstrong, Beaver, Bedford, Blair, Butler, Cambria, Clearfield, Fayette, Greene, Indiana, Lawrence, Somerset, Washington, Westmoreland. ⊠ Pacer

Rhode Island

U.S. District Court

www.rid.uscourts.gov Pacer is at http://pacer.rid.uscourts.gov. Mail address: Clerk's Office, One Exchange Terrace, Federal Bldg, Providence, RI 02903. Phone: 401-752-7200, Fax: 401-752-7247. Counties: All counties. ⊠ ☎ Pacer

Bankruptcy Court

www.rib.uscourts.gov Pacer is at http://pacer.rib.uscourts.gov. CM-ECF: https://ecf.rib.uscourts.gov. Mail address: 6th Floor, 380 Westminster St, Providence, RI 02903. Phone: 401-528-4477, Fax: 401-528-4470. Counties: All. ⊠ Fax ☎ Pacer

South Carolina

U.S. District Court

District of South Carolina

www.scd.uscourts.gov Pacer is online at http://pacer.scd.uscourts.gov.
Anderson Division c/o Greenville Division, PO Box 10768, Greenville, SC 29603. Phone: 864-241-2700. Counties: Anderson, Oconee, Pickens. ⊠ Pacer
Beaufort Division c/o Charleston Division, PO Box 835, Charleston, SC 29402. Phone: 843-579-1401, Fax: 803-579-1402. Counties: Beaufort, Hampton, Jasper. ⊠ Pacer
Charleston Division PO Box 835, Charleston, SC 29402. Phone: 843-579-1401, Fax: 803-579-1402. Berkeley, Charleston, Clarendon, Colleton, Dorchester, Georgetown. ⊠ ☎ Pacer

Columbia Division 1845 Assembly St, Columbia, SC 29201. Phone: 803-765-5816. Counties: Kershaw, Lee, Lexington, Richland, Sumter. ⊠ Fax Pacer
Florence Division PO Box 2317, Florence, SC 29503. Phone: 843-676-3820, Fax: 843-676-3831. Counties: Chesterfield, Darlington, Dillon, Florence, Horry, Marion, Marlboro, Williamsburg. ⊠ Fax Pacer
Greenville Division. PO Box 10768, Greenville, SC 29603. Phone: 864-241-2700, Fax: 864-241-2711. Counties: Greenville, Laurens. ⊠ ☎ Pacer
Greenwood Division c/o Greenville Division, PO Box 10768, Greenville, SC 29603. Phone: 864-241-2700, Fax: 864-241-2711. Counties: Abbeville, Aiken, Allendale, Bamberg, Barnwell, Calhoun, Edgefield, Fairfield, Greenwood,

Lancaster, McCormick, Newberry, Orangeburg, Saluda. ⊠ Pacer
Spartanburg Division c/o Greenville Division, PO Box 10768, Greenville, SC 29603. Phone: 864-241-2700, Fax: 864-241-2711. Counties: Cherokee, Chester, Spartanburg, Union, York. ⊠ Pacer

Bankruptcy Court

District of South Carolina

www.scb.uscourts.gov Pacer is online at http://pacer.scb.uscourts.gov. CM-ECF: https://ecf.scb.uscourts.gov.
Columbia Division PO Box 1448, Columbia, SC 29202. Phone: 803-765-5436. Counties: All counties in South Carolina. ⊠ Pacer

---

Key: Federal Courts Record Access: phone-☎ mail-⊠ fax-**Fax** online PACER- Pacer email-**Email**

South Dakota

U.S. District Court

www.sdd.uscourts.gov Pacer is online at
http://pacer.sdd.uscourts.gov. Court does
not allow electronic access to criminal
cases. Civil only.

Aberdeen Division c/o Pierre Division,
Federal Bldg & Courthouse, 225 S Pierre
St, Room 405, Pierre, SD 57501. Phone:
605-224-5849, Fax: 605-224-0806.
Counties: Brown, Campbell, Clark,
Codington, Corson, Day, Deuel,
Edmunds, Grant, Hamlin, McPherson,
Marshall, Roberts, Spink, Walworth.
Judge Battey's closed case records are
located at Rapid City Div. ✉ Pacer

Pierre Division Federal Bldg &
Courthouse, Room 405, 225 S Pierre St,
Pierre, SD 57501. Phone: 605-224-5849,
Fax: 605-224-0806. Counties: Buffalo,
Dewey, Faulk, Gregory, Haakon, Hand,
Hughes, Hyde, Jackson, Jerauld, Jones,
Lyman, Mellette, Potter, Stanley, Sully,
Todd, Tripp, Ziebach. ✉ Fax ☎ Pacer

Rapid City Division Clerk's Office,
Room 302, 515 9th St, Rapid City, SD
57701. Phone: 605-343-3744, Fax: 605-
343-4367. Counties: Bennett, Butte,
Custer, Fall River, Harding, Lawrence,
Meade, Pennington, Perkins, Shannon.
Judge Battey's closed cases are located
here. ✉ ☎ Pacer

Sioux Falls Division P.O. Box 5060,
Sioux Falls, SD 57117-5060. Phone: 605-
330-4447, Fax: 605-330-4312. Counties:
Aurora, Beadle, Bon Homme, Brookings,
Brule, Charles Mix, Clay, Davison,
Douglas, Hanson, Hutchinson, Kingsbury,
Lake, Lincoln, McCook, Miner,
Minnehaha, Moody, Sanborn, Turner,
Union, Yankton. ✉ Fax ☎ Pacer

Bankruptcy Court

www.sdb.uscourts.gov Pacer is online at
http://pacer.sdb.uscourts.gov. CM-ECF:
https://ecf.sdb.uscourts.gov.
Pierre Division Clerk, Room 203,
Federal Bldg, 225 S Pierre St, Pierre, SD
57501. Phone: 605-224-0560, Fax: 605-

224-9020. Counties: Bennett, Brown,
Buffalo, Butte, Campbell, Clark,
Codington, Corson, Custer, Day, Deuel,
Dewey, Edmunds, Fall River, Faulk,
Grant, Gregory, Haakon, Hamlin, Hand,
Harding, Hughes, Hyde, Jackson, Jerauld,
Jones, Lawrence, Lyman, Marshall,
McPherson, Meade, Mellette, Pennington,
Perkins, Potter, Roberts, Shannon, Spink,
Stanley, Sully, Todd, Tripp, Walworth,
Ziebach. ✉ Fax ☎ Pacer

Sioux Falls Division PO Box 5060, Sioux
Falls, SD 57117-5060. Phone: 605-330-
4544, Fax: 605-330-4560. Counties:
Aurora, Beadle, Bon Homme, Brookings,
Brule, Charles Mix, Clay, Davison,
Douglas, Hanson, Hutchinson, Kingsbury,
Lake, Lincoln, McCook, Miner,
Minnehaha, Moody, Sanborn, Turner,
Union, Yankton. ✉ Fax ☎ Pacer

Tennessee

U.S. District Court

Eastern District of Tennessee

www.tned.uscourts.gov Pacer is online at
http://pacer.tned.uscourts.gov. CM-ECF:
https://ecf.tned.uscourts.gov.
Chattanooga Division. Clerk's Office,
PO Box 591, Chattanooga, TN 37401.
Phone: 423-752-5200, Fax: 423-752-
5205. Counties: Bledsoe, Bradley,
Hamilton, McMinn, Marion, Meigs, Polk,
Rhea, Sequatchie. ✉ ☎ Pacer

Greeneville Division US District Court,
220 West Depot Street, Ste 200,
Greenville, TN 37743. Phone: 423-639-
3105, Fax: 423-639-7134. Counties:
Carter, Cocke, Greene, Hamblen,
Hancock, Hawkins, Johnson, Sullivan,
Unicoi, Washington. ✉ ☎ Pacer

Knoxville Division Clerk's Office, 800
Market St Ste 130, Knoxville, TN 37902.
Phone: 865-545-4228, Fax: 865-545-

4247. Counties: Anderson, Blount,
Campbell, Claiborne, Grainger, Jefferson,
Knox, Loudon, Monroe, Morgan, Roane,
Scott, Sevier, Union. ✉ ☎ Pacer
Winchester Division PO Box 459,
Winchester, TN 37398. Phone: 931-967-
1444, Fax: 931-967-9693. Bedford,
Coffee, Franklin, Grundy, Lincoln,
Moore, Van Buren, Warren. ✉ ☎ Pacer

Middle District of Tennessee

www.tnmd.uscourts.gov Pacer is online
at http://pacer.tnmd.uscourts.gov.
Columbia Division c/o Nashville
Division, 800 US Courthouse, 801
Broadway, Nashville, TN 37203. Phone:
615-736-5498. Counties: Giles, Hickman,
Lawrence, Lewis, Marshall, Maury,
Wayne. ✉ Pacer
Cookeville Division c/o Nashville
Division, 800 US Courthouse, 801
Broadway, Nashville, TN 37203. Phone:

615-736-5498, Fax: 615-736-7488. Clay,
Cumberland, De Kalb, Fentress, Jackson,
Macon, Overton, Pickett, Putnam, Smith,
White. ✉ ☎ Pacer
Nashville Division 800 US Courthouse,
801 Broadway, Nashville, TN 37203.
Phone: 615-736-5498, Records Rm: 615-
736-5498, Fax: 615-736-7488. Counties:
Cannon, Cheatham, Davidson, Dickson,
Houston, Humphreys, Montgomery,
Robertson, Rutherford, Stewart, Sumner,
Trousdale, Williamson, Wilson.
✉ Fax ☎ Pacer

Western District of Tennessee

www.tnwd.uscourts.gov Pacer online at
http://pacer.tnwd.uscourts.gov. CM-ECF:
https://ecf.tnwd.uscourts.gov.
Jackson Division Rm 26, US Courthouse
262, 111 S Highland, Jackson, TN 38301.
Phone: 731-421-9200, Fax: 731-421-
9210. Counties: Benton, Carroll, Chester,

Crockett, Decatur, Gibson, Hardeman, Hardin, Haywood, Henderson, Henry, Lake, McNairy, Madison, Obion, Perry, Weakley. ✉ ☎ Pacer

Memphis Division Federal Bldg, Room 242, 167 N Main, Memphis, TN 38103. Phone: 901-495-1200, Records Rm: 901-495-1206, Fax: 901-495-1250. Counties: Dyer, Fayette, Lauderdale, Shelby, Tipton. ✉ Fax ☎ Pacer

Bankruptcy Court

Eastern District of Tennessee

www.tneb.uscourts.gov Pacer is online at http://pacer.tneb.uscourts.gov.
Northern Division 800 Market St #330, Howard H Baker Jr US Courthouse, Knoxville, TN 37902. Phone: 865-545-4279. Counties: Anderson, Blount, Campbell, Carter, Claiborne, Cocke, Grainger, Greene, Hamblen, Hancock, Hawkins, Jefferson, Johnson, Knox, Loudon, Monroe, Morgan, Roane, Scott,

Sevier, Sullivan, Unicoi, Union, Washington. ✉ ☎ Pacer
Southern Division Historic US Courthouse, 31 E 11th St, Chattanooga, TN 37402. Phone: 423-752-5163. Counties: Bedford, Bledsoe, Bradley, Coffee, Franklin, Grundy, Hamilton, Lincoln, Marion, McMinn, Meigs, Moore, Polk, Rhea, Sequatchie, Van Buren, Warren. ✉ ☎ Pacer

Middle District of Tennessee

www.tnmb.uscourts.gov Pacer is online at http://pacer.tnmb.uscourts.gov. Search without paying registration fee- request an exemption by downloading a registration form- http://pacer.psc.uscourts.gov/faxform.html. Fax form to 210-301-6441.
Nashville Division PO Box 24890, Nashville, TN 37202-4890. Phone: 615-736-5584. Counties: Cannon, Cheatham, Clay, Cumberland, Davidson, De Kalb, Dickson, Fentress, Giles, Hickman, Houston, Humphreys, Jackson, Lawrence, Lewis, Macon, Marshall, Maury,

Montgomery, Overton, Pickett, Putnam, Robertson, Rutherford, Smith, Stewart, Sumner, Trousdale, Wayne, White, Williamson, Wilson. ✉ ☎ Pacer

Western District of Tennessee

www.tnwb.uscourts.gov Pacer online at http://pacer.tnwb.uscourts.gov. CM-ECF: https://ecf.tnwb.uscourts.gov.
Eastern Division Room 107, 111 S Highland Ave, Jackson, TN 38301. Phone: 731-421-9300. Benton, Carroll, Chester, Crockett, Decatur, Gibson, Hardeman, Hardin, Haywood, Henderson, Henry, Lake, Madison, McNairy, Obion, Perry, Weakley. ✉ ☎ Pacer
Western Division Suite 413, 200 Jefferson Ave, Memphis, TN 38103. Phone: 901-328-3500, Records Rm: 901-544-4429, Fax: 901-328-3500. Counties: Dyer, Fayette, Lauderdale, Shelby, Tipton. ✉ ☎ Pacer

Texas

U.S. District Court

Eastern District of Texas

www.txed.uscourts.gov Pacer is online at http://pacer.txed.uscourts.gov. Document images available on the RACER system. CM-ECF: https://ecf.txed.uscourts.gov.
Beaumont Division PO Box 3507, Beaumont, TX 77704. Phone: 409-654-7000. Counties: Delta*, Fannin*, Hardin, Hopkins*, Jasper, Jefferson, Lamar*, Liberty, Newton, Orange, Red River. Counties marked with an asterisk are Paris Division, whose case records are maintained here. ✉ ☎ Pacer
Lufkin Division 104 N. Third St., Lufkin, TX 75901. Phone: 936-632-2739. Angelina, Houston, Nacogdoches, Polk, Sabine, San Augustine, Shelby, Trinity, Tyler. ✉ ☎ Pacer
Marshall Division PO Box 1499, Marshall, TX 75671-1499. Phone: 903-935-2912, Fax: 903-938-2651. Counties: Camp, Cass, Harrison, Marion, Morris, Upshur. ✉ ☎ Pacer
Sherman Division. 101 E Pecan St Rm112, Sherman, TX 75090. Phone: 903-

892-2921. Counties: Collin, Cooke, Denton, Grayson. ✉ ☎ Pacer
Texarkana Division Clerk's Office, 500 State Line Ave, Room 301, Texarkana, TX 75501. Phone: 903-794-8561, Fax: 903-794-0600. Counties: Bowie, Franklin, Titus. ✉ ☎ Pacer
Tyler Division Clerk, Room 106, 211 W Ferguson, Tyler, TX 75702. Phone: 903-590-1000. Counties: Anderson, Cherokee, Gregg, Henderson, Panola, Rains, Rusk, Smith, Van Zandt, Wood. ✉ ☎ Pacer

Northern District of Texas

www.txnd.uscourts.gov Pacer is online at http://pacer.txnd.uscourts.gov. CM-ECF: https://ecf.txnd.uscourts.gov.
Abilene Division PO Box 1218, Abilene, TX 79604. Phone: 915-677-6311. Counties: Callahan, Eastland, Fisher, Haskell, Howard, Jones, Mitchell, Nolan, Shackelford, Stephens, Stonewall, Taylor, Throckmorton. ✉ ☎ Pacer
Amarillo Division 205 E 5th St, Amarillo, TX 79101. Phone: 806-324-2352. Counties: Armstrong, Briscoe, Carson, Castro, Childress, Collingsworth, Dallam, Deaf Smith, Donley, Gray, Hall,

Hansford, Hartley, Hemphill, Hutchinson, Lipscomb, Moore, Ochiltree, Oldham, Parmer, Potter, Randall, Roberts, Sherman, Swisher, Wheeler. ✉ ☎ Pacer
Dallas Division Room 1452, 1100 Commerce St, Dallas, TX 75242. Phone: 214-753-2200, Records Rm: 214-753-2196. Counties: Dallas, Ellis, Hunt, Johnson, Kaufman, Navarro, Rockwall. ✉ ☎ Pacer
Fort Worth Division Clerk's Office, 501 W Tenth St, Room 310, Fort Worth, TX 76102. Phone: 817-978-3132. Counties: Comanche, Erath, Hood, Jack, Palo Pinto, Parker, Tarrant, Wise. ✉ ☎ Pacer
Lubbock Division Clerk, Room 209, 1205 Texas Ave, Lubbock, TX 79401. Phone: 806-472-7624. Bailey, Borden, Cochran, Crosby, Dawson, Dickens, Floyd, Gaines, Garza, Hale, Hockley, Kent, Lamb, Lubbock, Lynn, Motley, Scurry, Terry, Yoakum. ✉ ☎ Pacer
San Angelo Division Clerk's Office, Room 202, 33 E Twohig, San Angelo, TX 76903. Phone: 325-655-4506, Fax: 325-658-6826. Counties: Brown, Coke, Coleman, Concho, Crockett, Glasscock, Irion, Menard, Mills, Reagan, Runnels,

Schleicher, Sterling, Sutton, Tom Green. ✉ Fax ☎ Pacer

Wichita Falls Division PO Box 1234, Wichita Falls, TX 76307. Phone: 940-767-1902, Fax: 940-767-2526. Counties: Archer, Baylor, Clay, Cottle, Foard, Hardeman, King, Knox, Montague, Wichita, Wilbarger, Young. ✉ Fax ☎ Pacer

Southern District of Texas

www.txsd.uscourts.gov Pacer is online at http://pacer.txs.uscourts.gov.

Brownsville Division 600 E Harrison St Rm 101, Brownsville, TX 78520-7114. Phone: 956-548-2500, Fax: 956-548-2598. Cameron, Willacy. ✉ ☎ Pacer

Corpus Christi Division Clerk's Office, 1133 N. Shoreline Blvd., #208, Corpus Christi, TX 78401. Phone: 361-888-3142. Counties: Aransas, Bee, Brooks, Duval, Jim Wells, Kenedy, Kleberg, Live Oak, Nueces, San Patricio. ✉ Pacer

Galveston Division Clerk's Office, PO Box 2300, Galveston, TX 77553. Phone: 409-766-3530. Brazoria, Chambers, Galveston, Matagorda. ✉ ☎ Pacer

Houston Division PO Box 61010, Houston, TX 77208. Phone: 713-250-5500, Records Rm: 713-250-5543. Counties: Austin, Brazos, Colorado, Fayette, Fort Bend, Grimes, Harris, Madison, Montgomery, San Jacinto, Walker, Waller, Wharton. ✉ Pacer

Laredo Division PO Box 597, Laredo, TX 78042-0597. Phone: 956-723-3542, Fax: 956-726-2289. Jim Hogg, La Salle, McMullen, Webb, Zapata. ✉ Pacer

McAllen Division. Suite 1011, 1701 W Business Hwy 83, McAllen, TX 78501. Phone: 956-618-8065. Counties: Hidalgo, Starr. ✉ ☎ Pacer

Victoria Division. Clerk US District Court, PO Box 1638, Victoria, TX 77902. Phone: 361-788-5000. Counties: Calhoun, De Witt, Goliad, Jackson, Lavaca, Refugio, Victoria. ✉ ☎ Pacer

Western District of Texas

www.txwd.uscourts.gov Pacer is online at http://pacer.txwd.uscourts.gov.

Austin Division Room 130, 200 W 8th St, Austin, TX 78701. Phone: 512-916-5896. Counties: Bastrop, Blanco, Burleson, Burnet, Caldwell, Gillespie, Hays, Kimble, Lampasas, Lee, Llano, McCulloch, Mason, San Saba, Travis, Washington, Williamson. ✉ ☎ Pacer

Del Rio Division Room L100, 111 E Broadway, Del Rio, TX 78840. Phone: 830-703-2054. Counties: Edwards, Kinney, Maverick, Terrell, Uvalde, Val Verde, Zavala. ✉ ☎ Pacer

El Paso Division US District Clerk's Office, Room 350, 511 E San Antonio, El Paso, TX 79901. 915-534-6725. County: El Paso. ✉ ☎ Pacer

Midland Division Clerk, US District Court, 200 E Wall St, Rm 107, Midland, TX 79701. Phone: 432-686-4001. Counties: Andrews, Crane, Ector, Martin, Midland, Upton. ✉ ☎ Pacer

Pecos Division US Courthouse, 410 S Cedar St, Pecos, TX 79772. Phone: 432-445-4228. Counties: Brewster, Culberson, Hudspeth, Jeff Davis, Loving, Pecos, Presidio, Reeves, Ward, Winkler ✉ Pacer

San Antonio Division US Clerk's Office, 655 E Durango Blvd, Suite G-65, San Antonio, TX 78206. Phone: 210-472-6550. Counties: Atascosa, Bandera, Bexar, Comal, Dimmit, Frio, Gonzales, Guadalupe, Karnes, Kendall, Kerr, Medina, Real, Wilson. ✉ ☎ Pacer

Waco Division Clerk, Room 303, 800 Franklin, Waco, TX 76701. Phone: 254-750-1501. Counties: Bell, Bosque, Coryell, Falls, Freestone, Hamilton, Hill, Leon, Limestone, McLennan, Milam, Robertson, Somervell. ✉ ☎ Pacer

Bankruptcy Court

Eastern District of Texas

www.txeb.uscourts.gov Pacer is online at http://pacer.txeb.uscourts.gov. CM-ECF: https://ecf.txeb.uscourts.gov.

Beaumont Division Suite 100, 300 Willow, Beaumont, TX 77701. Phone: 409-839-2617. Counties: Angelina, Hardin, Houston, Jasper, Jefferson, Liberty, Nacogdoches, Newton, Orange, Polk, Sabine, San Augustine, Shelby, Trinity, Tyler. ✉ ☎ Pacer

Marshall Division. c/o Tyler Division, 200 E Ferguson, Tyler, TX 75702. Phone: 903-590-1212, Fax: 903-590-1226. Counties: Camp, Cass, Harrison, Marion, Morris, Upshur. ✉ Pacer

Plano Division Suite 300B, 660 N Central Expressway, Plano, TX 75074. Phone: 972-509-1240, Fax: 972-509-1245. Counties: Collin, Cooke, Delta, Denton, Fannin, Grayson, Hopkins, Lamar, Red River. ✉ ☎ Pacer

Texarkana Division c/o Plano Division, Suite 300B, 660 N Central Expressway,

Plano, TX 75074. Phone: 972-509-1240, Fax: 972-509-1245. Counties: Bowie, Franklin, Titus. ✉ Pacer

Tyler Division. 200 E Ferguson, 2nd Floor, Tyler, TX 75702. Phone: 903-590-1212, Fax: 903-590-1226. Counties: Anderson, Cherokee, Gregg, Henderson, Panola, Rains, Rusk, Smith, Van Zandt, Wood. ✉ ☎ Pacer

Northern District of Texas

www.txnb.uscourts.gov Pacer is online at https://pacer.txnb.uscourts.gov. CM-ECF: https://ecf.txnb.uscourts.gov.

Amarillo Division PO Box 15960, Amarillo, TX 79105. Phone: 806-324-2302. Counties: Armstrong, Briscoe, Carson, Castro, Childress, Collingsworth, Dallam, Deaf Smith, Donley, Gray, Hall, Hansford, Hartley, Hemphill, Hutchinson, Lipscomb, Moore, Ochiltree, Oldham, Parmer, Potter, Randall, Roberts, Sherman, Swisher, Wheeler. ✉ ☎ Pacer

Dallas Division 1100 Commerce St, Suite 12A24, Dallas, TX 75242-1496. Phone: 214-753-2000, Records Rm: 214-753-2080. Counties: Dallas, Ellis, Hunt, Johnson, Kaufman, Navarro, Rockwall. ✉ ☎ Pacer

Fort Worth Division 501 W 10th, Suite 147, Fort Worth, TX 76102. Phone: 817-333-6000, Fax: 817-333-6001. Counties: Comanche, Erath, Hood, Jack, Palo Pinto, Parker, Tarrant, Wise. ✉ ☎ Pacer

Lubbock Division 306 Federal Bldg, 1205 Texas Ave, Lubbock, TX 79401-4002. Phone: 806-472-5000. Counties: Bailey, Borden, Brown, Callahan, Cochran, Cooke, Coleman, Concho, Crockett, Crosby, Dawson, Dickens, Eastland, Fisher, Floyd, Gaines, Garza, Glasscock, Hale, Haskell, Hockley, Howard, Irion, Jones, Kent, Lamb, Lubbock, Lynn, Menard, Mills, Mitchell, Motley, Nolan, Reagan, Runnels, Schleicher, Scurry, Shackelford, Stephens, Sterling, Stonewall, Sutton, Taylor, Terry, Throckmorton, Tom Green, Yoakum. ✉ ☎ Pacer

Wichita Falls Division c/o Dallas Division, Suite 12A24, 1100 Commerce St, Dallas, TX 75242-1496. Phone: 214-753-2000, Records Rm: 214-767-0814. Counties: Archer, Baylor, Clay, Cottle, Foard, Hardeman, King, Knox, Montague, Wichita, Wilbarger, Young. ✉ Pacer

Southern District of Texas

www.txsd.uscourts.gov Pacer is online at http://pacer.txs.uscourts.gov. CM-ECF: https://ecf.txsb.uscourts.gov.
Corpus Christi Division 1133 N. Shoreline Blvd. - 3rd Fl., Corpus Christi, TX 78401. Phone: 361-888-3484. Counties: Aransas, Bee, Brooks, Calhoun, Cameron, Duval, Goliad, Hidalgo, Jackson, Jim Wells, Kenedy, Kleberg, Lavaca, Live Oak, Nueces, Refugio, San Patricio, Starr, Victoria, Willacy. Files from Brownsville, Corpus Christi, and McAllen maintained here. ✉ Pacer
Houston Division Room 1217, 515 Rusk Ave, Houston, TX 77002. Phone: 713-250-5500. Counties: Austin, Brazoria, Brazos, Chambers, Colorado, De Witt, Fayette, Fort Bend, Galveston, Grimes, Harris, Jim Hogg*, La Salle*, Madison, Matagorda, McMullen*, Montgomery, San Jacinto, Walker, Waller, Wharton,

Webb* Zapata*. Open case records for the counties marked with an asterisk are being moved to the Laredo Div. ✉ ☎ Pacer

Western District of Texas

www.txwb.uscourts.gov Pacer is online at http://pacer.txwb.uscourts.gov. CM-ECF: http://ecf.txwb.uscourts.gov.
Austin Division Homer Thornberry Judicial Bldg, 903 San Antonio, Room 322, Austin, TX 78701. Phone: 512-916-5237. Counties: Bastrop, Blanco, Burleson, Burnet, Caldwell, Gillespie, Hays, Kimble, Lampasas, Lee, Llano, Mason, McCulloch, San Saba, Travis, Washington, Williamson. ✉ ☎ Pacer
El Paso Division PO Box 971040, El Paso, TX 79925. Phone: 915-779-7362, Fax: 915-779-5693. Counties: El Paso. ✉ ☎ Pacer
Midland/Odessa Division US Post Office Annex, Room P-163, 100 E Wall St,

Midland, TX 79701. Phone: 432-683-1650. Counties: Andrews, Brewster, Crane, Culberson, Ector, Hudspeth, Jeff Davis, Loving, Martin, Midland, Pecos, Presidio, Reeves, Upton, Ward, Winkler. ✉ ☎ Pacer
San Antonio Division PO Box 1439, San Antonio, TX 78295. Phone: 210-472-6720, Fax: 210-472-5916. Counties: Atascosa, Bandera, Bexar, Comal, Dimmit, Edwards, Frio, Gonzales, Guadalupe, Karnes, Kendall, Kerr, Kinney, Maverick, Medina, Real, Terrell, Uvalde, Val Verde, Wilson, Zavala. ✉ ☎ Pacer
Waco Division St. Charles Place, Ste. 20, 600 Austin Ave, Waco, TX 76701. Phone: 254-754-1481, Fax: 254-754-8385. Counties: Bell, Bosque, Coryell, Falls, Freestone, Hamilton, Hill, Leon, Limestone, McLennan, Milam, Robertson, Somervell. ✉ ☎ Pacer

Utah

U.S. District Court

www.utd.uscourts.gov Pacer is at http://pacer.utd.uscourts.gov Clerk's Office, Room 150, 350 S Main St, Salt Lake City, UT 84101-2180. Phone: 801-524-6100, Fax: 801-526-1175. Counties: All counties in Utah. Although all cases are heard here, the district is divided into Northern and Central Divisions. The Northern Division includes the counties of Box Elder, Cache, Rich, Davis, Morgan and Weber, and the Central Division includes all other counties. ✉ ☎ Pacer

Bankruptcy Court

www.utb.uscourts.gov Pacer at http://pacer.utb.uscourts.gov. Recent case filings reports are free. CM-ECF: https://ecf.utb.uscourts.gov Clerk of Court, Frank E Moss Courthouse, 350 S Main St, Room 301, Salt Lake City, UT 84101. Phone: 801-524-6687, Fax: 801-524-4409. Counties: All counties in Utah. Although all cases are handled here, the court divides itself into two divisions. The Northern Division includes the counties of Box Elder, Cache, Rich, Davis, Morgan and Weber, and the Central Division includes the remaining counties. Court is held once per week in Ogden for Northern cases. ✉ Fax ☎ Pacer

Vermont

U.S. District Court

www.vtd.uscourts.gov Login to PACER at https://pacer.login.uscourts.gov/cgi-bin/login.pl?court_id=r_vtdc. Brattleboro is a hearing location only, not listed here.
Burlington Division Clerk's Office, PO Box 945, Burlington, VT 05402-0945. Phone: 802-951-6301. Counties: Caledonia, Chittenden, Essex, Franklin, Grand Isle, Lamoille, Orleans,

Washington. However, cases from all counties are assigned randomly to either Burlington or Brattleboro. ✉ ☎ Pacer
Rutland Division PO Box 607, Rutland, VT 05702-0607. Phone: 802-773-0245. Counties: Addison, Bennington, Orange, Rutland, Windsor, Windham. However, cases from all counties in the state are randomly assigned to either Burlington or Brattleboro. Rutland is a hearing location only, not listed here. ✉ ☎ Pacer

Bankruptcy Court

www.vtb.uscourts.gov Pacer is online at http://pacer.vtb.uscourts.gov. CM-ECF: https://ecf.vtb.uscourts.gov.
Rutland Division PO Box 6648, Rutland, VT 05702-6648. Phone: 802-776-2000, Fax: 802-776-2020. Counties: All counties. ✉ Fax Pacer

---

Key: Federal Courts Record Access: phone-☎ mail-✉ fax-**Fax** online PACER- **Pacer** email-**Email**

Virginia

U.S. District Court

Eastern District of Virginia

www.vaed.uscourts.gov Pacer is online at http://pacer.vaed.uscourts.gov.
Alexandria Division 401 Courthouse Square, Alexandria, VA 22314. Phone: 703-299-2100, Records Rm: 703-299-2128. Counties: Arlington, Fairfax, Fauquier, Loudoun, Prince William, Stafford, City of Alexandria, City of Fairfax, City of Falls Church, City of Manassas, City of Manassas Park. ✉ ☎ Pacer
Newport News Division Clerk's Office, PO Box 494, Newport News, VA 23607. Phone: 757-247-0784. Counties: Gloucester, James City, Mathews, York, City of Hampton, City of Newport News, City of Poquoson, City of Williamsburg. ✉ ☎ Pacer
Norfolk Division US Courthouse, Room 193, 600 Granby St, Norfolk, VA 23510. Phone: 757-222-7204. Counties: Accomack, City of Chesapeake, City of Franklin, Isle of Wight, City of Norfolk, Northampton, City of Portsmouth, City of Suffolk, Southampton, City of Virginia Beach. ✉ Pacer
Richmond Division Lewis F Powell, Jr Courthouse Bldg, 1000 E Main St, Room 305, Richmond, VA 23219-3525. Phone: 804-916-2200. Counties: Amelia, Brunswick, Caroline, Charles City, Chesterfield, Dinwiddie, Essex, Goochland, Greensville, Hanover, Henrico, King and Queen, King George, King William, Lancaster, Lunenburg, Mecklenburg, Middlesex, New Kent, Northumberland, Nottoway, Powhatan, Prince Edward, Prince George, Richmond, City of Richmond, Spotsylvania, Surry, Sussex, Westmoreland, Cities: Colonial Heights, Emporia, Fredericksburg, Hopewell, Petersburg. ✉ ☎ Pacer

Western District of Virginia

www.vawd.uscourts.gov Pacer is online at http://pacer.vawd.uscourts.gov. CM-ECF: https://ecf.vawd.uscourts.gov.
Abingdon Division Clerk's Office, PO Box 398, Abingdon, VA 24212. Phone: 276-628-5116, Fax: 276-628-1028. Counties: Buchanan, City of Bristol,

Russell, Smyth, Tazewell, Washington. ✉ Fax ☎ Pacer
Big Stone Gap Division PO Box 490, Big Stone Gap, VA 24219. Phone: 276-523-3557, Fax: 276-523-6214. Counties: Dickenson, Lee, Scott, Wise, City of Norton. ✉ ☎ Pacer
Charlottesville Division Clerk, Room 304, 255 W Main St, Charlottesville, VA 22902. Phone: 434-296-9284. Counties: Albemarle, Culpeper, Fluvanna, Greene, Louisa, Madison, Nelson, Orange, Rappahannock, City of Charlottesville. ✉ Pacer
Danville Division PO Box 1400, Danville, VA 24543-0053. Phone: 434-793-7147, Fax: 434-793-0284. Counties: Charlotte, Halifax, Henry, Patrick, Pittsylvania, Cities:Danville, Martinsville, South Boston. ✉ ☎ Pacer
Harrisonburg Division. Mail: Clerk, PO Box 1207, Harrisonburg, VA 22803. Phone: 540-434-3181. Counties: Augusta, Bath, Clarke, Frederick, Highland, Page, Rockingham, Shenandoah, Warren, Cities: Harrisonburg, Staunton, Waynesboro, Winchester. ✉ ☎ Pacer
Lynchburg Division Clerk, PO Box 744, Lynchburg, VA 24505. Phone: 434-847-5722. Amherst, Appomattox, Bedford, Buckingham, Campbell, Cumberland, Rockbridge, Cities: Bedford, Buena Vista, Lexington, Lynchburg. ✉ ☎ Pacer
Roanoke Division Clerk, PO Box 1234, Roanoke, VA 24006. Phone: 540-857-5100, Fax: 540-857-5110. Counties: Alleghany, Bland, Botetourt, Carroll, Craig, Floyd, Franklin, Giles, Grayson, Montgomery, Pulaski, Roanoke, Wythe, City of Covington, City of Clifton Forge, City of Galax, City of Radford, City of Roanoke, City of Salem. ✉ ☎ Pacer

Bankruptcy Court

Eastern District of Virginia

www.vaeb.uscourts.gov PACER access is online at the CM/ECF website. This replaces the free NIBS system. CM-ECF: http://ecf.vaeb.uscourts.gov.
Alexandria Division PO Box 19247, Alexandria, VA 22320-0247. Phone: 703-258-1200. Counties: City of Alexandria,

Arlington, Fairfax, City of Fairfax, City of Falls Church, Fauquier, Loudoun, City of Manassas, City of Manassas Park, Prince William, Stafford. ✉ Pacer
Newport News Division Norfolk Bankruptcy Court, PO Box 1938, Norfolk, VA 23501-1938. Phone: 757-222-7500. Counties: Newport News City. Records are at the Norfolk Court. ✉ ☎ Pacer
Norfolk Division PO Box 1938, Norfolk, VA 23501-1938. Phone: 757-222-7500. Counties: Accomack, City of Cape Charles, City of Chesapeake, City of Franklin, Gloucester, City of Hampton, Isle of Wight, James City, Matthews, City of Norfolk, Northampton, City of Poquoson, City of Portsmouth, Southampton, City of Suffolk, City of Virginia Beach, City of Williamsburg, York. ✉ ☎ Pacer
Richmond Division Office of the clerk, 1100 E Main St, Room 310, Richmond, VA 23219-3515. Phone: 804-916-2400. Counties: Amelia, Brunswick, Caroline, Charles City, Chesterfield, City of Colonial Heights, Dinwiddie, City of Emporia, Essex, City of Fredericksburg, Goochland, Greensville, Hanover, Henrico, City of Hopewell, King and Queen, King George, King William, Lancaster, Lunenburg, Mecklenburg, Middlesex, New Kent, Northumberland, Nottoway, City of Petersburg, Powhatan, Prince Edward, Prince George, Richmond, City of Richmond, Spotsylvania, Surry, Sussex, Westmoreland. ✉ ☎ Pacer

Western District of Virginia

www.vawb.uscourts.gov Pacer is online at https://pacer.vawb.uscourts.gov.
Harrisonburg Division PO Box 1407, Harrisonburg, VA 22803. Phone: 540-434-8327, Fax: 540-434-9715. Counties: Alleghany, Augusta, Bath, City of Buena Vista, Clarke, City of Clifton Forge, City of Covington, Frederick, City of Harrisonburg, Highland, City of Lexington, Page, Rappahannock, Rockbridge, Rockingham, Shenandoah, Warren. Cities: Staunton, Waynesboro, Winchester. ✉ ☎ Pacer
Lynchburg Division PO Box 6400, Lynchburg, VA 24505. Phone: 434-845-0317. Counties: Albemarle, Amherst,

Appomattox, Bedford, City of Bedford, Buckingham, Campbell, Charlotte, City of Charlottesville, Culpeper, Cumberland, City of Danville, Fluvanna, Greene, Halifax, Henry, Louisa, City of Lynchburg, Madison, City of Martinsville,

Nelson, Orange, Patrick, Pittsylvania, City of South Boston. ✉ ☎ Pacer
Roanoke Division PO Box 2390, Roanoke, VA 24010. Phone: 540-857-2391, Fax: 540-857-2873. Counties: Bland, Botetourt, City of Bristol, Buchanan, Carroll, Craig, Dickenson,

Floyd, Franklin, City of Galax, Giles, Grayson, Lee, Montgomery, City of Norton, Pulaski, City of Radford, Roanoke, City of Roanoke, Russell, City of Salem, Scott, Smyth, Tazewell, Washington, Wise, Wythe. ✉ Pacer

Washington

U.S. District Court

Eastern District of Washington

www.waed.uscourts.gov Pacer is online at http://pacer.waed.uscourts.gov.
Spokane Division PO Box 1493, Spokane, WA 99210-1493. Phone: 509-353-2150. Counties: Adams, Asotin, Benton, Chelan, Columbia, Douglas, Ferry, Franklin, Garfield, Grant, Lincoln, Okanogan, Pend Oreille, Spokane, Stevens, Walla Walla, Whitman. Also, some cases from Kittitas, Klickitat and Yakima are heard here. ✉ Pacer
Yakima Division PO Box 2706, Yakima, WA 98907. Phone: 509-575-5838. Counties: Kittitas, Klickitat, Yakima. Cases assigned primarily to Judge McDonald are here. Some cases from Kittitas, Klickitat and Yakima are heard in Spokane. ✉ ☎ Pacer

Western District of Washington

www.wawd.uscourts.gov Pacer is online at http://pacer.wawd.uscourts.gov. CM-ECF: https://ecf.wawd.uscourts.gov.

Seattle Division Clerk of Court, 215 US Courthouse, 1010 5th Ave, Seattle, WA 98104. Phone: 206-553-5598, Records Rm: 206-553-5598. Counties: Island, King, San Juan, Skagit, Snohomish, Whatcom. ✉ ☎ Pacer
Tacoma Division Clerk's Office, Room 3100, 1717 Pacific Ave, Tacoma, WA 98402-3200. Phone: 253-593-6313. Counties: Clallam, Clark, Cowlitz, Grays Harbor, Jefferson, Kitsap, Lewis, Mason, Pacific, Pierce, Skamania, Thurston, Wahkiakum. ✉ ☎ Pacer

Bankruptcy Court

Eastern District of Washington

www.waeb.uscourts.gov Pacer is online at http://pacer.waeb.uscourts.gov CM-ECF: https://ecf.waeb.uscourts.gov.
Spokane Division PO Box 2164, Spokane, WA 99210-2164. Phone: 509-353-2404. Counties: Adams, Asotin, Benton, Chelan, Columbia, Douglas, Ferry, Franklin, Garfield, Grant, Kittitas, Klickitat, Lincoln, Okanogan, Pend

Oreille, Spokane, Stevens, Walla Walla, Whitman, Yakima. ✉ ☎ Pacer

Western District of Washington

www.wawb.uscourts.gov Pacer is online at http://pacer.wawb.uscourts.gov. CM-ECF: https://ecf.wawb.uscourts.gov.
Seattle Division Clerk of Court, 315 Park Place Bldg, 1200 6th Ave, Seattle, WA 98101. Phone: 206-553-7545, Fax: 206-553-0131. Counties: Clallam, Island, Jefferson, King, Kitsap, San Juan, Skagit, Snohomish, Whatcom. ✉ Fax Pacer
Tacoma Division Suite 2100, 1717 Pacific Ave, Tacoma, WA 98402-3233. Phone: 253-593-6310. Counties: Clark, Cowlitz, Grays Harbor, Lewis, Mason, Pacific, Pierce, Skamania, Thurston, Wahkiakum. ✉ Pacer

West Virginia

U.S. District Court

Northern Dist. of West Virginia

www.wvnd.uscourts.gov Pacer is online at http://pacer.wvnd.uscourts.gov.
Clarksburg Division PO Box 2857, Clarksburg, WV 26302 Phone: 304-622-8513, Fax: 304-623-4551. Braxton, Calhoun, Doddridge, Gilmer, Harrison, Lewis, Marion, Monongalia, Pleasants, Ritchie, Taylor, Tyler. ✉ ☎ Pacer

Elkins Division. PO Box 1518, Elkins, WV 26241. Phone: 304-636-1445, Fax: 304-636-5746. Counties: Barbour, Grant, Hardy, Mineral, Pendleton, Pocahontas, Preston, Randolph, Tucker, Upshur, Webster. ✉ Fax ☎ Pacer
Martinsburg Division. Room 207, 217 W King St, Martinsburg, WV 25401. Phone: 304-267-8225, Fax: 304-264-0434. Counties: Berkeley, Hampshire, Jefferson, Morgan. ✉ ☎ Pacer

Wheeling Division Clerk, PO Box 471, Wheeling, WV 26003. Phone: 304-232-0011, Fax: 304-233-2185. Counties: Brooke, Hancock, Marshall, Ohio, Wetzel. ✉ ☎ Pacer

Southern Dist. of West Virginia

www.wvsd.uscourts.gov Pacer online at http://pacer.wvsd.uscourts.gov. CM-ECF: https://ecf.wvsd.uscourts.gov/cgi-bin/login.pl.

Key: Federal Courts Record Access: phone-☎ mail-✉ fax-**Fax** online PACER- Pacer email-**Email**

Beckley Division PO Drawer 5009, Beckley, WV 25801. Phone: 304-253-7481, Fax: 304-253-3252. Counties: Fayette, Greenbrier, Raleigh, Sumners, Wyoming. ⌧ Fax ☎ Pacer

Bluefield Division Clerk's Office, PO Box 4128, Bluefield, WV 24701. Phone: 304-327-9798. Counties: McDowell, Mercer, Monroe. ⌧ Fax ☎ Pacer

Charleston Division PO Box 3924, Charleston, WV 25339. Phone: 304-347-3000. Counties: Boone, Clay, Jackson, Kanawha, Lincoln, Logan, Mingo, Nicholas, Putnam, Roane⌧Fax☎Pacer

Huntington Division Clerk of Court, PO Box 1570, Huntington, WV 25716. Phone: 304-529-5588, Fax: 304-529-5131. Counties: Cabell, Mason, Wayne. ⌧ Fax ☎ Pacer

Parkersburg Division Clerk of Court, PO Box 1526, Parkersburg, WV 26102. Phone: 304-420-6490, Fax 304-420-6363. Counties: Wirt, Wood. ⌧Fax☎Pacer

Bankruptcy Court

Northern Dist. of West Virginia

www.wvnb.uscourts.gov Pacer is online at http://pacer.wvnb.uscourts.gov. CM-ECF: https://ecf.wvnb.uscourts.gov.

Wheeling Division PO Box 70, Wheeling, WV 26003. Phone: 304-233-1655. Counties: Barbour, Berkeley, Braxton, Brooke, Calhoun, Doddridge, Gilmer, Grant, Hampshire, Hancock, Hardy, Harrison, Jefferson, Lewis, Marion, Marshall, Mineral, Monongalia, Morgan, Ohio, Pendleton, Pleasants,

Pocahontas, Preston, Randolph, Ritchie, Taylor, Tucker, Tyler, Upshur, Webster, Wetzel. ⌧ ☎ Pacer

Southern Dist. of West Virginia

www.wvsd.uscourts.gov/bankruptcy/index.htm Pacer is online at http://pacer.wvsb.uscourts.gov. CM-ECF: https://ecf.wvsb.uscourts.gov.

Charleston Division PO Box 3924, Charleston, WV 25339. Phone: 304-347-3000. Boone, Cabell, Clay, Fayette, Greenbrier, Jackson, Kanawha, Lincoln, Logan, Mason, McDowell, Mercer, Mingo, Monroe, Nicholas, Putnam, Raleigh, Roane, Summers, Wayne, Wirt, Wood, Wyoming. ⌧ ☎ Pacer

Wisconsin

U.S. District Court

Eastern District of Wisconsin

www.wied.uscourts.gov Pacer is online at http://pacer.wied.uscourts.gov. CM-ECF: https://ecf.wied.uscourts.gov/cgi-bin/login.pl.

Milwaukee Division Clerk's Office, Room 362, 517 E Wisconsin Ave, Milwaukee, WI 53202. Phone: 414-297-3372. Counties: Brown, Calumet, Dodge, Door, Florence, Fond du Lac, Green Lake, Kenosha, Kewaunee, Langlade, Manitowoc, Marinette, Marquette, Menominee, Milwaukee, Oconto, Outagamie, Ozaukee, Racine, Shawano, Sheboygan, Walworth, Washington, Waukesha, Waupaca, Waushara, Winnebago. ⌧ ☎ Pacer

Western District of Wisconsin

www.wiw.uscourts.gov Pacer is online at http://pacer.wiwd.uscourts.gov.

Madison Division PO Box 432, Madison, WI 53701. Phone: 608-264-5156. Counties: Adams, Ashland, Barron, Bayfield, Buffalo, Burnett, Chippewa,

Clark, Columbia, Crawford, Dane, Douglas, Dunn, Eau Claire, Grant, Green, Iowa, Iron, Jackson, Jefferson, Juneau, La Crosse, Lafayette, Lincoln, Marathon, Monroe, Oneida, Pepin, Pierce, Polk, Portage, Price, Richland, Rock, Rusk, Sauk, Sawyer, St. Croix, Taylor, Trempealeau, Vernon, Vilas, Washburn, Wood. ⌧ ☎ Pacer

Bankruptcy Court

Eastern District of Wisconsin

www.wieb.uscourts.gov Pacer is online at http://pacer.wieb.uscourts.gov. CM-ECF: https://ecf.wieb.uscourts.gov.

Milwaukee Division Room 126, 517 E Wisconsin Ave, Milwaukee, WI 53202. Phone: 414-297-3291, Records Rm: 414-297-4111. Counties: Brown, Calumet, Dodge, Door, Florence, Fond du Lac, Forest, Green Lake, Kenosha, Kewaunee, Langlade, Manitowoc, Marinette, Marquette, Menominee, Milwaukee, Oconto, Outagamie, Ozaukee, Racine, Shawano, Sheboygan, Walworth,

Washington, Waukesha, Waupaca, Waushara, Winnebago. ⌧ Pacer

Western District of Wisconsin

www.wiw.uscourts.gov/bankruptcy WebPACER available at http://pacer.wiwb.uscourts.gov/js_index.html. CM-ECF: https://ecf.wiwb.uscourts.gov.

Eau Claire Division PO Box 5009, Eau Claire, WI 54702-5009. Phone: 715-839-2980, Fax: 715-839-2996. Counties: Ashland, Barron, Bayfield, Buffalo, Burnett, Chippewa, Clark, Douglas, Dunn, Eau Claire, Iron, Jackson, Juneau, La Crosse, Lincoln, Marathon, Monroe, Oneida, Pepin, Pierce, Polk, Portage, Price, Rusk, Sawyer, St. Croix, Taylor, Trempealeau, Vernon, Vilas, Washburn, Wood. Division has satellite offices in LaCrosse and Wausau. ⌧ ☎ Pacer

Madison Division PO Box 548, Madison, WI 53701. Phone: 608-264-5178. Adams, Columbia, Crawford, Dane, Grant, Green, Iowa, Jefferson, Lafayette, Richland, Rock, Sauk.⌧ Fax ☎ Pacer

Wyoming

U.S. District Court

www.ck10.uscourts.gov/wyoming/district/index.html Pacer is online at http://pacer.wyd.uscourts.gov. CM-ECF: https://ecf.wyd.uscourts.gov. Address: 2120 Capitol Ave, Room 2141, Cheyenne, WY 82001. Phone: 307-433-2120. Counties: All. Some criminal records are held in Casper, but all are available electronically here. ✉ Pacer

Bankruptcy Court

www.wyb.uscourts.gov Pacer at http://pacer.wyb.uscourts.gov. CM-ECF: https://ecf.wyb.uscourts.gov. Address: 2120 Capitol Ave, #6004, Cheyenne, WY 82001. Phone: 307-772-2191. Counties: All. The Casper Bankruptcy Court records are located here. ✉ Pacer

Chapter 8

Other Federal Records

EDGAR

EDGAR – the **E**lectronic **D**ata **G**athering **A**nalysis and **R**etrieval system – was established by the United States Securities and Exchange Commission (SEC) to allow companies to make required filing to the SEC by direct transmission. As of May 6, 1996, all public domestic companies are required to make their filings on EDGAR, except for filings made to the Commission's regional offices and those filings made on paper due to a hardship exemption.

EDGAR is an extensive repository of U.S. corporation information and it is available online.

What Information is Available on EDGAR?

Companies must file the following reports with the SEC:

- 10-K – an annual financial report that includes audited year-end financial statements.
- 10-Q – a quarterly report, unaudited.
- 8K – a report detailing significant or unscheduled corporate changes or events.
- Securities offerings, trading registrations, and the final prospectus.

The list above is not conclusive. There are other miscellaneous reports filed, including those dealing with security holdings by institutions and insiders.

How to Access EDGAR Online

EDGAR is searchable online at www.sec.gov/info/edgar.shtml. Also, a number of private vendors offer access to EDGAR records. LexisNexis acts as the data wholesaler or distributor on behalf of the government. LexisNexis sells data to information retailers, including its own Nexis service.

Aviation Records

The Federal Aviation Association (FAA) is the U.S. government agency with the responsibility for all matters related to the safety of civil aviation. Among its functions, the FAA provides the system that registers aircraft and the documents showing title or interest in aircraft. The FAA website, at www.faa.gov, is the ultimate source of aviation records, airports and facilities, safety regulations, and related civil research and engineering.

The Aircraft Owners and Pilots Association is the largest organization of its kind. Their website is www.aopa.org and is an excellent source of information regarding the aviation industry.

Another excellent source of aircraft information is Jane's World Airlines at www.janes.com.

Military Records

This topic is so broad that there is a book written about it, *The Armed Forces Locator Directory* from MIE Publishing (800-937-2133). The book, now in its 8th edition, covers every conceivable topic regarding military records. Their website www.militaryusa.com offers free access to some useful databases.

The Privacy Act of 1974 (5 U.S.C. 552a) and Department of Defense directives require a written request, signed and dated, to access military personnel records. For further details, visit the NPRC site at www.nara.gov/regional/mpr.html.

Military Internet Sources

There are a number of great internet sites that provide valuable information on obtaining military and military personnel records. The National Personnel Records Center (NPRC), maintained by the National Archives & Records Administration, is on the Internet at www.nara.gov/regional/mpr.html. The NPRC site is full of useful information and links. Other excellent sites include:

www.army.mil	The official site of the U.S. Army
www.af.mil	The official site of the U.S. Air Force
www.navy.mil	The official site of the U.S. Navy
www.usmc.mil	The official site of the U.S. Marine Corps
www.arng.army.mil	The official site of the Army National Guard
www.ang.af.mil	The official site of the Air National Guard
www.uscg.mil/USCG.shtm	The official site of the U.S. Coast Guard

Best U.S. Government Gateways

> The remainder of this Chapter is written and contributed by online pioneer and award winning journalist **Alan M. Schlein**, author of *Find It Online!* We sincerely thank Alan for permitting the use of his material in this book. Alan can be reached at www.deadlineonline.com.

In the U.S., almost every federal government agency is online. There are almost 5000 government websites from more than forty-two U.S. departments and agencies. There is a nationwide network of depository libraries, including the enormous resources of the National Archives (www.nara.gov), the twelve presidential libraries, and four national libraries – the Library of Congress, the National Agricultural Library, the National Library of Education, and the National Library of Medicine.

in order to find the starting point for your research – because there are so many government websites – you may need to turn to specialized, purpose-built websites called *government gateways* that organize and link government sites. Some gateways are simply collections of links. Others provide access to bulletin boards of specific government agencies so that you find and contact employees with specific knowledge. The use of human guides is becoming increasingly important in light of the growing number of reports and publications that are no longer printed but simply posted online.

Best Government Gateways (listed alphabetically)

Documents Center   www.lib.umich.edu/govdocs/index.html

Documents Center is a clearinghouse for local, state, federal, foreign, and international government information. It is one of the more comprehensive online searching aids for all kinds of government information on the Internet.

Federal Web Locators   www.infoctr.edu/fwl/

This web locator is really two sites in one: a federal government website (www.infoctr.edu/fwl) and a separate site that tracks federal courts (www.infoctr.edu/fwl/fedweb.juris.htm). Both are browsable by category or keyword. They provide links to thousands of government agencies and departments.

FedLaw   www.thecre.com/fedlaw/default.htm

Containing 1,600+ links to law-related information, FedLaw is an extremely broad resource for federal legal and regulatory research. It has very good topical and title indices that group web links into hundreds of subjects. The site is operated by the General Services Administration (GSA).

Fedstats   www.fedstats.gov

A collection of statistical sites from the federal government and a good central clearinghouse for other federal statistics sites.

FedWorld Information Network   www.fedworld.gov

FedWorld helps you search over thirty million U.S. government pages. It is a massive collection of 15,000 files and databases of government sites, including bulletin boards that can help you identify government employees with expertise in a broad range of subjects.

FirstGov   www.firstgov.gov

Responding to the need for a central clearinghouse of U.S. federal government sites, the U.S. government developed FirstGov and linked every federal agency to its site as well as every state government. It has an easy-to-use search tool, allowing you to specify if you want federal or state agencies and to easily locate business regulations and vital records. It also lets you look for federal government phone numbers and email addresses. Also, check out the FAQs of the U.S. government for questions and answers about the U.S. government (www.faq.gov).

Google's Uncle Sam   www.google.com/unclesam

Google's Uncle Sam site is a search engine geared to looking at U.S. government sites. It is an easy-to-use tool if you know what you are looking for.

Healthfinder   www.healthfinder.gov

This is a great starting point for health-related government information.

InfoMine: Scholarly Internet Resource Collections   http://infomine.ucr.edu

InfoMine provides collections of scholarly Internet resources. InfoMine's Government Information section is easily searchable by subject. Its detailed headings and its resource listings are very specific. Since it is run by a university, some of its references are limited to student use only.

SearchGov.com `www.searchgov.com`

A private company that has an effective search for U.S. government sites.

Speech & Transcript Center `www.freepint.com/gary/speech.htm`

This site links directly to websites containing transcripts of speeches. A large section is devoted to U.S. and international government speech transcripts, including Congressional hearings, expert testimony, and transcripts.

U.S. Federal Government Agencies Directory `www.lib.lsu.edu/gov/fedgov.html`

This directory of federal agencies links to hundreds of federal government internet sites. It is divided by branch and agency and is very thorough.

U.S. Government Information `www.libraries.colorado.edu/ps/gov/us/federal.htm`

A good starting point. Very valuable.

Best U.S. Federal Government Websites

U.S. tax dollars are put to good and visible use here. A few of the government's web pages are rated as excellent. A few of the top government sites – the Census and the Securities and Exchange Commission – are models of content and presentation. They are very deep, very thorough, and easy to use. Not all agencies maintain such detailed and relevant resources.

Following are the crown jewels of the government's collection, in ranked order:

U.S. Census Bureau `www.census.gov`

Without question, this is the U.S. government's top site. It is saturated with information and census publications – at times overwhelmingly so – but worth every minute of your time. A few hours spent here is a worthwhile investment for almost anyone seeking to background a community, learn about business, or find any kind of demographic information. You can search several ways: alphabetically by subject, by word, by location, and by geographic map. The only problem is the sheer volume of data.

The Thematic Mapping System allows users to extract data from Census CD-ROMs and display them in maps by state or county. You can create maps on all kinds of subjects – for examples, tracking violent crime or comparing farm income.

The census website also features the Statistical Abstract of the U.S. with a searchable index at www.census.gov/statab/www/stateabs.html.

Additional census resources include:

1990 U.S. Census LOOKUP `http://venus.census.gov/cdrom/lookup/`

State and County QuickFacts `http://quickfacts.census.gov/qfd/`

Census FactFinder `http://factfinder.census.gov`

Census Industry Statistics `www.census.gov/main/www/industries.html`

The University of Virginia's Fisher Library's historical census data browser goes all the way back to 1790. It can be found at http://fisher.lib.virginia.edu/collections/stats/histcensus/.

U.S. Securities and Exchange Commission (SEC)   `www.sec.gov`
The SEC site is a must-stop place for information shopping on U.S. companies. Its EDGAR database search site (www.sec.gov/edaux/searches.htm) is easy to use and provides access to documents that companies and corporations are required to file under regulatory laws. The SEC site is a great starting point for information about specific companies and industry trends.

Library of Congress (LOC)   `www.loc.gov`
This site is an extraordinary collection of documents. Thomas, the Library's Congressional online center site (http://thomas.loc.gov/home) provides an exhaustive collection of congressional documents, including bill summaries, voting records, and the full Congressional Record, which is the official record of Congressional action. This LOC site also links to many international, federal, state, and local government sites. You can also access the library's more than five million records online, some versions in full-text and some in abstract form. The Library of Congress also has a terrific collection of international data on its website at www.loc.gov/rr/international/portals.html.

Superintendent of Documents Home Page (GPO)   `www.access.gpo.gov/su_docs`
The GPO is the federal government's primary information printer and distributor. Luckily, the GPO site is well-constructed and easy to use. For example, it has the full text of the Federal Register, which lists all federal regulations and proposals, and full-text access to the Congressional Record. The GPO also produces an online version of the Congressional Directory, providing details on every congressional district, profiles of members, staff profiles, maps of every district and historical documents about Congress. If you need some help finding things, use the topic-specific finder at this site.

National Technical Information Service (NTIS)   `www.ntis.gov`
The best place to find federal reports related to technology and science, NTIS is the nation's clearinghouse for unclassified technical reports of government-sponsored research. NTIS collects, indexes, abstracts, and sells research in science, technology, behavioral, and social science data.

IGnet   `www.ignet.gov`
Collection of reports and information from the Inspector Generals of about sixty federal agency departments. They find waste and abuse within government agencies.

General Accounting Office GAO Reports   `www.gao.gov/decisions/decision.htm`
The Comptroller General Opinions from the last sixty days are posted on this GAO website. These reports and opinions are excellent references. For historical opinions back to 1996, go online to www.access.gpo.gov/su_docs/aces/aces170.shtml.

White House   `www.whitehouse.gov`
Check the economic statistics page at www.whitehouse.gov/fsbr/es_br.html and the transcript of every official action the U.S. President takes at www.whitehouse.gov/news.

DefenseLINK – U.S. Department of Defense (DOD)   `www.defenselink.mil`
This is the brand-name site for Pentagon-related information including U.S. troop deployments worldwide. To the Pentagon's credit, they have made this a very easy site to use.

Defense Technical Information Center (DTIC) `www.dtic.mil`

The DTIC site is loaded with links and defense information – everything from contractors to weapon systems. It is the best place to start for defense information. Find a list of all military-related contracts, including beneficiary communities and the kinds of contracts awarded.

Bureau of Transportation Statistics `www.bts.gov`

Here is the U.S. Department of Transportation's enormous collection of information about every facet of transportation, including the Transportation Statistics Annual Report. Holds financial data for airlines and searchable databases containing information about fatal accidents and on-time statistics for airlines.

National Archives and Records Administration `www.nara.gov`

In addition to its world-class database of historical documents, its Archives Research Center Online has great collections of family history/genealogy research and veterans' service records.

FedWorld.gov `www.fedworld.gov`

This thorough government clearinghouse site, run by the Commerce Department's National Technical Information Service, offers access to FirstGov and allows you to search government publications, U.S. Supreme Court decisions, and helps you find government jobs.

Federal Consumer Information Center Nat. Contact Center `www.info.gov`

While this is largely a telephone service that gets more than a million calls a year, this website tries to provide a way through the maze of federal agencies. It includes a clearinghouse of phone numbers for all federal agencies, state, and local government sites.

SciTechResources.gov `www.scitechresources.gov`

This is a tremendous directory of about 700 science and technology resources on U.S. government sites from the U.S. Department of Commerce, National Technical Information Service.

Department of Homeland Security `www.whitehouse.gov/homeland/`

While the U.S. Government has made the Department of Homeland Security a separate agency, it maintains the website under the White House's auspices. It has good information, but is more about public relations for the current president and his staff than it is about information. Find useful information about the current threat level and information about what U.S. state and local governments are doing on homeland security.

Bureau of National Affairs, The `www.bna.com`

An expensive but useful group of topic-focused newsletters providing details on U.S. government action at different federal agencies. Titles include the *Daily Labor Report, Bankruptcy Law Daily*, and the *Biotech Watch*. This private company has hundreds of newsletters you will not find elsewhere.

* * *